☆ **HOW THE NORTH WON** ☆

Illustrations by
Jerry A. Vanderlinde

HOW THE NORTH WON

A Military History of the Civil War

HERMAN HATTAWAY

and

ARCHER JONES

UNIVERSITY OF ILLINOIS PRESS

Urbana   Chicago   London

LIBRARY OF CONGRESS CATALOGING IN PUBLICATION DATA

Hattaway, Herman.
    How the North won.

    Bibliography: p. 733
    Includes index.
    1. United States—History—Civil War, 1861–1865—
Campaigns and battles.   I. Jones, Archer, 1926–   II.
Title.
U727.H37   973.7′3   81-16332
ISBN 0-252-00918-5   AACR2

To T. Harry Williams

☆ CONTENTS ☆

☆ INTRODUCTION ☆

WE BELIEVE this book offers something to a number of different groups of readers. To those unacquainted with military history, it provides an elementary, instructive, and readable military account of the American Civil War. The basic concepts of war, its conduct, management, and support, are thoroughly explained and explicitly applied throughout in order to make clear what many authors often incorrectly take for granted that readers already know. Further, an appended introduction to the study of military operations treats much of that which the text assumes. For the reader beginning* to pursue a special interest, we believe that the focus on high command and the frequent use of the comparative approach will put campaigns in a coherent perspective and thus provide an ample introduction to reading in more specialized areas. For those with a matured interest, we believe we offer some new insights that will provoke discussion.

We have tried to tell the military history of the war from the viewpoint of the higher commanders on both sides. We therefore emphasize strategy and logistics rather than tactics; maps and diagrams have saved us many words and allowed us to avoid minutely extensive accounts of individual battles. Though we used many original sources, we did not attempt to build a new and complete story of the war from the bottom up; neither did we try to synthesize all of the recent nonmilitary scholarship. Rather, we stressed the influence of purely military factors, advanced some new interpretations about the nature of the war, and tried to delineate how the North won.

Strategy, management, and execution weigh more than superior numbers and resources in dictating the outcome of wars, and the Civil War is no exception. The weaker side can win; the South almost did. The turning points of the war were not Gettysburg, Vicksburg, and Chattanooga; better cases can be made for the fall of forts Henry and Donelson and Sherman's march to the sea. But we denigrate turning points and immediate surface accomplishments, emphasizing instead fundamentals such as logistics, which underlay the strategies of both Grant and Lee. In its stress upon the importance of guerrillas and raids, this book takes advantage of knowledge gained from the recent war in Vietnam; our country's experience with this kind of struggle makes its importance more comprehensible. Yet more basically, this book takes the lessons of World War I as an essential element in its thesis, because it was in that war that the power of the defense reached its apogee. Like World War I, the American Civil War was fought before the tank and aeroplane had partially overcome the intrinsic superiority of infantry on the

*We suggest that readers who are relatively unfamiliar with the study of military operations should begin with our Appendix A.

defense. The Civil War also shares with World War I and the Vietnam War the important place occupied by the nationalism of the combatants and their perceptions of the importance of the goals sought. Ultimately the North's allegiance to its cause was adequate to the needs of achieving victory; that of the South was not.

Further, an important key to northern success lay not in specific battles so much as in the North's development of superior managerial systems among both soldiers and civilians. This involved the rise of businessmen to prominent roles in war, superior military staff organization, and coordination, sometimes fortuitous, on both formal and informal levels which outperformed southern counterparts.

With regard to the war's general direction, we offer some new theories about command organization and the roles of Lincoln and Grant, and we propose modifications in several other presently standard interpretations. Though we present these new explanations with great emphasis, we expect our fellow specialists to view them as hypotheses to be tested. Some of them, the interpretation of Grant, for example, are based upon considerable primary investigations and are advanced with a good deal of solid underpinning. Others, though suggested by our selective—and we hope discriminating—examination of the sources, are offered more as questions than answers.

Because of our approach, we have based much of the work upon secondary materials, documenting only quotations, except when necessary to show the origin of a new tack. We have tried to use often the words of the participants to give a better insight into their outlook and some flavor of the time. We took particular pains to allow the participants themselves to enunciate the military fundamentals upon which, we believe, they consciously based their actions.

We dedicate our work to T. Harry Williams and we feel grateful that before his death in 1979 he learned that we were going to do so. He gave to both of us frequent and ongoing help over many years, as well as friendship, personal guidance, criticism, and exemplary inspiration. As will be obvious to knowledgeable students, we have to come to disagree with his interpretations. Still, his works are, we feel, the most meritorious examples of that collection of ideas with which we now wish to take issue; he was often wrong for the right reasons. As Marx felt he had found Hegel standing on his head and turned him rightside up, we think we have done the same thing to Williams. Our work stands in a reciprocative relationship to his. But while we strive to revise, at the same time we honestly mean to honor and revere him, and we humbly acknowledge that we continue in the same tradition of Civil War military history that he did much to establish, beginning with his influential *Lincoln and His Generals* in 1952. We also have tried to produce—so far as we could—as he always did, a vivid, lucid history with high readability and appeal, and in doing so have gained an even more acute appreciation of his great abilities.

It will be obvious, throughout the narrative portions of this work, the degree to which the authors have relied on those who have written particularly readable Civil War books. We are especially indebted to the works of Bruce Catton, Shelby Foote, Robert S. Henry, and Stanley F. Horn, who so well exemplify the principle that fine historical writing is fun to read.

The authors gratefully acknowledge permissions to quote from the following works: Douglas Southall Freeman, *R. E. Lee* (Charles Scribner's Sons, 1934–35); R. Ernest Dupuy, *Men of West Point: The First 150 Years of the United States Military Academy* (William Sloane, 1951); J. D. Hittle, *Jomini and His Summary of the Art of War* (Military Service Publishing, 1947); Richard D. Goff, *Confederate Supply* (Duke University Press, 1969); Robert S. Henry, *The Story of the Confederacy* (Bobbs-Merrill, 1936); Norman Dixon, *On the Psychology of Military Incompetence* (Basic Books, 1976); C. V. Wedgwood, *The Thirty Years War* (Doubleday, 1938); Virgil C. Jones, *Ranger Mosby* (University of North Carolina Press, 1944); William Hanchett, *Irish Charles G. Halpine in Civil War America* (Syracuse University Press, 1970); T. Harry Williams, *Lincoln and the Radicals* (University of Wisconsin Press, 1965); Michael C. C. Adams, *Our Masters the Rebels: A Speculation on Union Military Failure in the East, 1861–1865* (Harvard University Press, 1978); Grady McWhiney, *Braxton Bragg and Confederate Defeat* (Columbia University Press, 1969); Jay Monaghan, *Civil War on the Western Border: 1854–1865* (Little, Brown, 1955); T. Harry Williams, *Americans at War* (Louisiana State University Press, 1960); T. L. Connelly, *Autumn of Glory* (Louisiana State University Press, 1971); William M. Lamers, *Edge of Glory, A Biography of General William S. Rosecrans, U.S.A.* (Harcourt Brace Jovanovich, 1961); Russell F. Weigley, *Quartermaster General of the Union Army* (Columbia University Press, 1959); John Gibbon, *Personal Recollections of the Civil War* (G. P. Putnam's Sons, 1928); Emory M. Thomas, *The Confederacy as a Revolutionary Experience* (Prentice-Hall, 1971); Arthur N. Strahler, *Introduction to Physical Geography* (John Wiley & Sons, 1965); Stanley F. Horn, *The Army of Tennessee* (University of Oklahoma Press, 1941); Benjamin P. Thomas, *Abraham Lincoln* (Random House, 1952); Shelby Foote, *The Civil War: A Narrative* (Random House, 1958–74); T. Harry Williams, *Lincoln and His Generals* (Random House, 1952); Benjamin P. Thomas and Harold M. Hyman, *Stanton, The Life and Times of Lincoln's Secretary of War* (Random House, 1962); Arthur N. Strahler, *The Earth Sciences* (Harper & Row, 1971); Edward G. Longacre, *The Man Behind the Guns: A Biography of General Henry J. Hunt, Commander of Artillery, Army of the Potomac* (A. S. Barnes, 1977); Bruce Catton, *Mr. Lincoln's Army* (Doubleday, 1962); Bruce Catton, *Never Call Retreat* (Doubleday, 1965); Bruce Catton, *A Stillness at Appomattox* (Doubleday, 1953); E. B. Long, *The Civil War, Day by Day: An Almanac, 1861–1865* (Doubleday, 1971); William C. Davis, *The Battle of New Market* (Doubleday, 1975); Thomas F. Thiele, "The Evolution of Cavalry in the American Civil War, 1861–1863" (Ph.D. dissertation, University of Michigan, 1951); T. Harry Williams, "The Attack upon West Point during the Civil War," *Mississippi Valley Historical Review* (Mar., 1939); F. N. Maude,

"Strategy," *Encyclopaedia Britannica* (1926); Stephen B. Oates, *With Malice Toward None: The Life of Abraham Lincoln* (Harper & Row, 1977).

We are indebted to John W. Aljets for his help in formulating some of the approaches to operations, to Catherine Heiraas for her superb typing and ability to detect errors, to Joanne L. Jones for her editing and help with our writing, and to Margaret T. Hattaway for her warm support, sound advice, and yeoman labors. Among many other persons who have contributed significantly to this work, and to whom we now express our keen appreciation are: James B. Agnew, Richard Beringer, D. K. Cliff, Todd Conklin, Terrence Durrill, C. F. Eisele, Kenneth Fine, Robert Gordon, R. R. Hare, Warren W. Hassler, Jr., Edward L. Henson, Doris Hertsgaard, Andrew Keogh, Raimondo Luraghi, Bruce Nelson, George T. Ness, Jr., Patrick A. Peebles, Jerry Phillips, Robert C. Powell, Evelyn Randolph, John Y. Simon, Richard Sommers, Harry Stafford, Linda W. Thornton, John Tuttle, Susanne Tyler, Richard Vollmer, Terry Wiebenga, and Tommy R. Young.

☆ **HOW THE NORTH WON** ☆

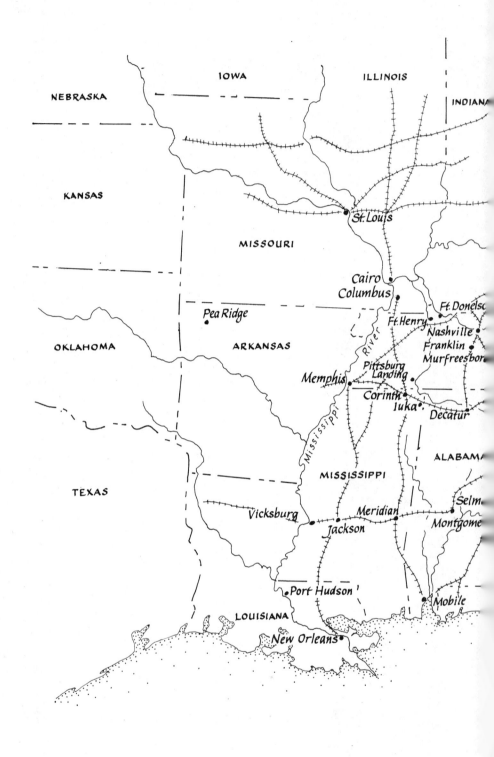

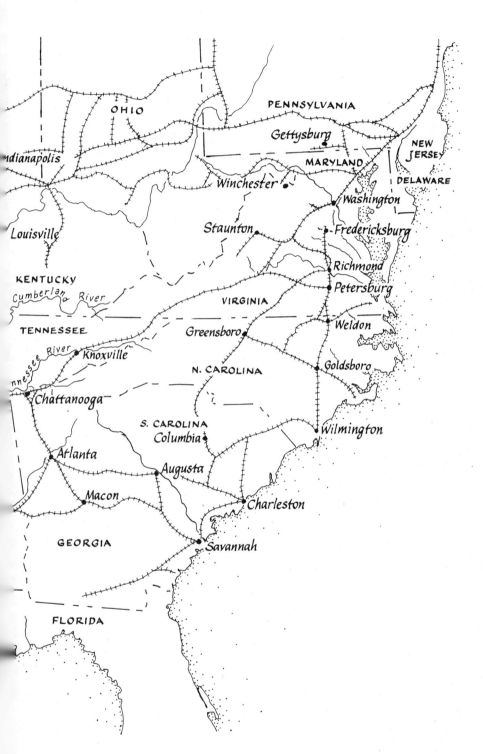

The Civil War Area of Operations

I ☆ CIVIL AND MILITARY LEADERS

Abraham Lincoln

A CIVIL WAR became the only way two regions of the United States could resolve their long-festering differences. The secession of eleven southern states from the Union represented a singular failure of the American political process, a process normally characterized by compromise. Bullets replaced ballots, debate eroded away to be replaced by cold separation, and compromise degenerated into violence.

More than mere secession of several states was required for war to break out. After their secession, the North made the decision to fight to force the seceded states back into a union from which they had withdrawn and in which they did not wish to remain; the South, faced with the necessity of fighting to continue what might still have been recanted as rashness, had to be willing to respond no less violently.

The necessary resolve on both sides had been developing for many years. Innumerable factors—economic, political, and social—played upon and intensified the breach between the North and the South. One difference, the anachronistic lingering of human slavery in the South and arguments over the future growth of that institution, became the insoluble problem. Though abolitionists in the North fiercely attacked slavery, many northerners disparaged these northern critics and were content to leave the issue alone. Most northerners agreed, however, that slavery should not be allowed to expand into the new territories being opened by westward expansion.

At the same time most southerners had come to defend the institution as a positive good and increasingly insisted that they had a right to expand it into the newly settled regions. By 1860 the expansion of slavery had become a fairly clear-cut sectional issue which had helped to disrupt the historic two-party system by destroying the Whigs and dividing the Democrats. The Republican party, born in 1854, promised to stand resolutely and block any further expansion of slavery. Six years after its birth, that party captured the presidency, precipitating the secession first of South Carolina then, within a month and a half, of six more deep-South states.

At his inauguration on March 4, 1861, Abraham Lincoln became President of a North fairly well united in opposition to the expansion of slavery, already

made a dead issue by secession. Little else united the North. Some northerners wanted a war to free the slaves; many wanted a war, if necessary, to
restore the Union; but there were also many who not only opposed a war
against slavery but wished to let the slave states go in peace. Lincoln would
lead a divided northern nation.

The seceded states seemed united in their determination to maintain their
independence. During the crisis between Lincoln's election and inauguration,
the seceded states formed a joint government, the Confederate States of
America, and seized federal property, forts, and arsenals within their borders.
No casualties resulted. Indeed the process produced little fanfare and sometimes the seizures occurred with enemy cooperation, as in Texas where U.S.
brevet Major General David Twiggs surrendered his entire command without
a struggle. Only three installations held out, Fort Taylor at Key West, Fort
Pickens outside Pensacola, and Fort Sumter in Charleston Harbor. The two
Florida forts remained in Union hands, but the third became the locale of the
opening scene of the Civil War.

Until the formation of the Confederate government on February 4, 1861,
South Carolina functioned as a separate nation. During that time, and briefly
thereafter, it maintained its own army. State troops, cadets from the state's
military college, the Citadel, and numerous other volunteers provided an
increasing pressure upon the "foreign troops" which South Carolina demanded be evacuated. Even after January 9, 1861, when cadets with artillery
drove away the merchant vessel *Star of the West*, loaded with reinforcements
and supplies for Fort Sumter, the southerners allowed for a time a daily mail
and fresh beef and vegetables to go from the city to the federal garrison. But
an impasse gradually developed as the Federals steadfastly refused to leave,
and, during the first week in April, the Confederates cut off all supplies to
the fort.

The war, then at the very verge of eruption, had long been brewing.
Certainly Lincoln's election was only a final straw; yet his capture of the
presidency did precipitate disunion. Much in Lincoln's background indicates
both why the South considered him so unacceptable and what kind of war
leader he would prove to be. The son of a frontier farm family, Lincoln was
born in Kentucky, February 12, 1809. Popular mythology has both over-
drawn and distorted his poverty; no doubt Lincoln himself fed the image for
political advantage in adulthood. The Lincolns owned land, fared reasonably
well, and moved successively to Indiana and eventually to Illinois. Of course
Lincoln was not born into wealth, but neither was he destitute. In his youth,
typical of then-contemporary American middle-class frontiersmen, he experienced hard work, and it left him with a tough, strong body and good
physical health. Likewise his mind resembled his body, powerful but slow
moving and rustic, always characteristic of his ways and manner.

He tended at times to display manic-depressive behavior. As a young man,
a strange and severe melancholy periodically afflicted him, and it became

more pronounced as he grew older. He suffered deep depression, which created intermittent mental tensions; and these he sometimes masked with exuberant though perhaps strained humor. Yet this humor appealed to many persons, and by 1863 at least several editions of Lincoln joke books had been printed.

His humor was most representative of a man who always remained a son of the American frontier, roughhewn and self-reliant. However deep his thoughts might be, and he had a remarkable mental and literary capability, he retained a tempering of simplicity and forthrightness. As one wrestler pitting himself singly against the prowess and might of another, as a "rail splitter" working alone, Lincoln viewed matters in simple, direct terms.

Lincoln's only firsthand experience with military service, the Black Hawk War in 1832, left an indelible impression on the twenty-three-year old. Disgruntled Sauk and Fox Indians under Chief Black Hawk, 500 warriors and 1,500 women and children, moved into northern Illinois to grow corn, because they felt that the lands west of the Mississippi River into which they had been pushed were insufficiently fertile. To counter them, regular U.S. troops began moving from Jefferson Barracks, Missouri, and from the east coast. In the meantime the Illinois militia, swollen with volunteers, sallied out to engage the Indians. The citizen-soldiers forced several minor skirmishes before being replaced by the arriving regulars, who proceeded on August 3 to massacre the Indians at Bad Axe, Wisconsin. The wanton annihilation killed all but 150 of the Indians, most of whom were forced into the Mississippi River at bayonet point and then shot as they struggled in the water.

Lincoln joined and rejoined the militia three times, serving a total of eighty days. Still he experienced no combat action at all, though he did help bury five soldiers whom the Indians had scalped. During his first tour his company elected him its captain, an honor that he regarded, even after gaining nomination to the presidency, as the most satisfying of his life. After the expiration of his initial thirty-day muster, he so passionately wanted to remain in service that he accepted duty thereafter as a private.

One episode illustrates both Lincoln's ingenuity and his simple, direct approach to problems. "Leading his company across a field one morning, twenty abreast, he saw ahead a narrow gate through which his men must pass. But he could not remember the command to 'turn the company endwise,' and, as a desperate expedient, at the last moment he wheeled suddenly to face his men and shouted: 'Halt. This company will break ranks and reform immediately on the other side of that gate.' The movement was successfully executed."[1]

After spending the last days of his enlistment in a futile search for Chief Black Hawk and his warriors in the swamps of southern Wisconsin, Lincoln mustered out on July 10. In later years he made light of his military experience, which he admitted had been highlighted by his being twice under arrest. But that he mentioned it so often betrays that he remembered it well, and his law partner, William H. Herndon, believed him rather proud of it.

Most of Lincoln's other education resembled his military service, a combination of practical experience and self-teaching. Despite his lack of formal schooling, he enjoyed, as a young man, numerous consultations with Mentor Graham, a schoolmaster who helped direct Lincoln's voracious reading and doubtless discussed much of it with him. Lincoln read and mastered Euclid, the Bible, Shakespeare, classical history, and Blackstone's commentaries on the law.

In spite of the classical flavor of his early studies, Lincoln's interests remained quite circumscribed. Herndon possessed an eclectic mental appetite, read quite a lot, and tried to interest Lincoln in good books to no avail. Lincoln read and pondered upon only that in which he perceived a specific utility. More a man of thought, slow, methodical, and deep, he tried always to find the "nub" of a question, stripped of irrelevancies. He became almost unbeatable in arguments involving simple right and justice.

He became a very successful frontier lawyer and built a lucrative practice handling a wide variety of cases. By the time of his marriage in 1842, his income amounted to twelve or fifteen hundred dollars a year, a handsome sum indeed in those days when a governor's salary was $1,200 annually and a circuit judge's but $750. During the 1850s, particularly, he acquired the legal business of many large corporations—railroads, "banks, insurance companies, gas companies, large mercantile and manufacturing concerns. He was retained in a number of patent cases."[2]

Beginning to dabble in politics early in his professional life, Lincoln discovered his real passion. He relished power and the management of people. He loved and thoroughly learned the techniques of appeal, persuasion, compromise, and maneuver. And he carefully plotted his political career. As his partner Herndon wrote: "That man who thinks that Lincoln sat calmly down and gathered his robes about him, waiting for the people to call him, has a very erroneous knowledge of Lincoln. He was always calculating, and always planning ahead. His ambition was a little engine that knew no rest." His ideology quite naturally brought him into the Whig Party and in it he held a number of positions on the local and state level, eventually rising to become the leading Whig in Illinois.[3]

Lincoln won a seat in the Thirtieth U.S. Congress, which sat from December 1847 to early 1849. There he consistently expressed typical Whig sentiments. His most notable experience was his introduction of a series of "spot resolutions" calculated to embarrass the Democratic President, James K. Polk, by forcing him to admit that Mexico and not the United States had jurisdiction over the "spot" where the first blood was shed in the episodes that began the war between the two countries. In Washington during the Mexican War he observed how President Polk kept the strategy of the war firmly in his own hands, even debating strategy during sessions of the Cabinet. Lincoln also observed how political benefits so often resulted from military appointments. He noted that Senator Thomas Hart Benton of Missouri desired the command of the expedition to Mexico City. This position ultimately went to Winfield Scott, a professional soldier who later won nomination for the presidency, as did Zachary Taylor, the other major commander in the war.

The 1858 senatorial election in Illinois, where he lost to the incumbent, Stephen A. Douglas, marks Lincoln's only other major political involvement before the 1860 presidential contest. Their debates attracted national attention because Douglas ranked among the leading Democrats in the nation, was a presidential contender, and was the foremost proponent of popular sovereignty—a plan to let the people of the western territories decide for themselves if slavery should or should not be allowed to expand into these new regions. Lincoln cleverly maneuvered Douglas into taking a position that made his advocacy of this policy badly damaging to national Democratic party unity.

Lincoln himself supported an antislavery policy, having made his first public avowal of dislike for the institution at the age of twenty-eight. But he felt no sense of urgency to eliminate slavery, believing that it would die out eventually if the Union could prevent it from spreading into any additional areas. He believed slavery wrong and considered it very important that the institution be recognized as wrong and thus eliminated.

"The Great Nationalist" might be a better sobriquet for Lincoln than "The Great Emancipator," the nickname he earned because of his association with the ultimate destruction of slavery. He shared the belief that the American Union was sacred, something that should be preserved at any cost, for it enabled mankind to attain a degree of freedom not possible anywhere else. He hoped that the United States's example might eventually spread over the entire world. Like most American Caucasians of his time, Lincoln believed the darker races inferior, but he never defined exactly in what way. Although he viewed slavery as wrong, he harbored some conception that Negroes perhaps should not in every way be as free as Caucasians. Assuming that the white and black races could not live together as equals, he favored colonization, hoping that the blacks would voluntarily participate. During the Civil War he changed his views about the compatibility of the two races, perhaps because he observed blacks in ways that he had not in earlier years.

The image of "humble Mr. Lincoln" is a false one. Confident and keenly aware of his abilities, Lincoln saw an advantage in appearing to be humble, using humility, just as he did his humor and his remarkable literary capacities, as a potent political instrument. He could easily parry hostile thrusts and at the same time illustrate points in a pleasing or amusing manner. He could use people even when they were not his sympathetic admirers, but this proved more true in civilian and political instances than in high-level military matters.

Lincoln's work in law and politics dealt with issues, with adversary relationships, and with scoring either legal or debating points against opponents. His background consisted of bargaining and of shifting political alliances, but he totally lacked any experience of bureaucratic hierarchy or of the structured, purposeful, and collaborative relationships of the administrative world of either business organizations or the state of federal governments. His world had been completely different from that of the administrator or professional soldier. Yet this very lack of experience left him ample room for learning and growth. The war would demonstrate his capacity to profit from his presidential experience and to develop his latent administrative ability.

In a sense, having command over professional soldiers, all of whom possessed varying degrees of relevant experience, aided in Lincoln's process of growth. In addition, the army officer belonged to one of the best-educated groups of professionals in the country. Not only did West Point provide a specialized college education in an era when the high school graduate was a rarity, but just prior to the Civil War the academy lengthened the course from four to five years. This preparation markedly contrasted with that for Lincoln's own profession, which remained still a rather brief and casual "reading" of law that demanded no formal educational background. Curiously, in a virtually unarmed republic where lawyers dominated politics, the standard for admission to the bar stood far lower that in Europe, while the standard of preparation for military leadership demanded much higher qualifications. This difference in background between Lincoln and his generals could be either a source of friction or a source of strength to Lincoln, by providing him with well-prepared subordinates from whom he could learn. Events of the war would prove that Lincoln made the most of any situation, including this one.

A number of interesting comparisons appear in the lives of Abraham Lincoln and his adversary, the President of the Confederacy, Jefferson Davis. Davis was also born in Kentucky, scarcely one hundred miles from Lincoln's birthplace, on June 3, 1808, and his family resembled Lincoln's in economic and social circumstances. Both were middle class. Where the Lincoln family moved north to seek fresh opportunities, the Davis family moved south toward the newly booming cotton culture and there acquired a fairly substantial fortune.

Davis was something of a late bloomer; nothing in his first thirty-two years indicated his future promise. He did acquire one of the best formal educations then available in the United States, graduating both from Transylvania University in Kentucky and from West Point. Unlike the austere person mythology often depicts, Davis was a fun-loving, frolicking lad who wrote to his older brother pleading for spending money, and who got into occasional trouble over visiting taverns and imbibing alcoholic drinks.

An incident that occurred while he was a cadet illustrates a theme that ran through Davis's entire military career. An affair at the notorious Benny Haven's "public house," and a subsequent eggnog party in the barracks, brought Davis's arrest and a trial by court-martial. Probably he followed a typical cadet practice of drinking with his back to fellow tipplers, so that, if called upon to testify in the matter, they could honestly say that no one had "seen" Cadet So-and-So drinking. Nevertheless, the court found Davis guilty and sentenced him to dismissal, but then recommended remission of the punishment in consideration of his past exemplary conduct. In this and in later episodes, Davis made friends, formed several lifelong acquaintances, performed as a good but not a consistently outstanding soldier, and occasionally encountered difficulties. He was court-martialed and acquitted again in 1835 on charges of disrespect and insubordination. His friend and fellow officer, Lieutenant Lucius B. Northrop, testifying in Davis's behalf, declared, His manner has "been strictly and rigidly military" but "too rigid in the minutiae of the Service. . . . I was struck with his attention to . . . duties."[4]

Tradition holds that Davis feuded with his first father-in-law, Zachary Taylor, because the latter preferred that his daughter not marry a soldier. The enmity was short-lived if it existed at all, for, although the Zachary Taylors could not attend the wedding, the large number of other Taylor relatives in attendance clearly indicated family approval. Yet, for whatever combination of reasons, Davis had decided to leave the army before taking a wife, "my individual interests interfering with my duties," he wrote shortly before the wedding.

Malaria struck both newlyweds, causing his wife's tragic death. In touring Cuba Davis attempted to recover his own health and to ease the pain of losing her after only three months of marriage. During the next several years he spent much time at his brother Joseph's home and became a small-scale planter. By 1840 he owned forty slaves, with twenty-nine engaged in agriculture. He never fully regained perfect health, the most serious residual malady being eye trouble. Beginning possibly with a congenital defect, the eye was aggravated after Davis's malaria in 1835, and he suffered recurrent attacks thereafter. In youth Davis showed only the dimmest glimmers of his later consuming interest and ability in politics. In 1839 he wrote, "You will perceive that when I wrote of Politics I am out of my element and naturally slip back to seeding and ploughing."[5]

But Davis turned intently to both politics and military service in the next two decades. He raised a regiment of volunteers and served as its colonel during the Mexican War. He saw considerable action under his former father-in-law, Zachary Taylor, and attained renown by leading a countercharge at Buena Vista where, employing an unorthodox formation, he turned the tide of battle in the nick of time. Many students have ridiculed him for this and have cited the formation as a prime example of his allegedly unrealistic attitudes toward warfare. Returning to Mississippi, Davis met defeat in a gubernatorial race, but soon became a U.S. senator, serving on the military affairs committee. He held the Senate seat until the Civil War except for four years' service as secretary of war in President Franklin Pierce's Cabinet.

As the nation's top civilian administrator in the War Department, Davis performed in an exemplary manner. He brought about some notable improvements in the American army, although some of his innovative experiments did not succeed. The most celebrated of these, his attempt to use camels in arid or semi-desert areas of the United States, could have worked; but the disgruntled military professionals stymied the plan by letting most of the beasts escape. However, the episode reveals Davis's striking degree of mental flexibility and ingenuity.

Although intelligent, industrious, and a reasonably good judge of men, Davis did make several bad decisions. His intense loyalty to old friends sometimes blinded him to their flaws. He preferred associating with people who agreed with him, and encountered difficulty working with people who did not. A meticulous thinker, Davis valued give-and-take discussions of difficult problems, but lacked sufficient diplomacy to avoid occasionally offending a potentially useful ally. People tended either to like him very much or to assess him harshly indeed. General Winfield Scott, whom Davis once called to account for overcharging mileage expenses, delivered an amusing judgment: "He is not a cheap Judas. I do not think he would have sold the Saviour for thirty shillings. But for the successorship to Pontius Pilate he would have betrayed Christ and the Apostles and the whole Christian church." Sam Houston of Texas, also reacting to Davis's crisp business manner, declared him "ambitious as Lucifer and cold as a lizard."[6]

By the time of the Civil War, Davis had grown into a leader and administrator of considerable experience and ability, with lofty principles and boundless courage. A warmhearted human being, he became a devoted husband and father, having remarried in 1845. He possessed great kindliness, patience, and charm, a southern gentleman in every respect. He espoused devout Episcopalianism. He loved books and the contemplative life, believed with conviction in state sovereignty and the right of secession, exhibited a certain paternalistic sympathy for the Negro, but also embraced the firm conviction that control of race relations belonged in southern hands. When John C. Calhoun died, Davis inherited the position of leading ideological spokesman of the South in the Senate. During the 1850s, Davis consistently expressed the dominant sentiment of his region that slavery must be allowed to expand, unfettered, into any territory where slaveholders might wish to take it. By 1859 that idea not only predominated in the South but had been sanctioned as mandatory by the Supreme Court via the Dred Scott decision. The Republican party countered, damning the decision as not legal but political, handed down by a biased Democratic-controlled court, and it declared firm an intent to overturn the decision should it ever gain control of the government. This helped make Lincoln's election to the presidency a logical reason for southern secession.

☆   ☆

Though both were politicians, Davis and Lincoln differed as much in background and personal style as they did in political convictions. The essential contrast in their backgrounds was not that one was a planter and the other a lawyer. Davis had been well educated as a military professional and had used and developed this expertise as a lieutenant in the regular army, as a battle-tested regimental commander in the Mexican War, and as secretary of war and chairman of the military affairs committee of the U.S. Senate. Davis's breadth of background probably better qualified him for high army command than any man in the United States. In contrast, Lincoln lacked not only military education and experience, but also any administrative accomplishments at all. He further lacked Davis's initial understanding of and affinity for the professionals who would inevitably supply the leadership for the armies. Yet some of Davis's background would also be a handicap. He served in the War Department during peace. The departmental structure put everything into the hands of the secretary. The competent and knowledgeable Davis used this power so fully that Winfield Scott, the bypassed general in chief, actually left Washington in disgust. The able and energetic Davis found it easy to manage a peacetime army of some 15,000 men, but that organization would not suffice for 250,000 men fighting a multifront war. Davis would, during the war, have trouble changing from the organization which he had mastered, one familiar but inadequate, to a structure capable of coping with a vast and integrated war effort. Lincoln encountered no such difficulty.

In 1861 Lincoln had no war machine to which he could turn to suppress the rebellion which Davis was leading. On the eve of the war, the regular army contained only 1,105 officers and 15,259 enlisted men, the majority of whom were foreign-born (some 700 were sick or on detached duty). The ten regiments of infantry, four of artillery, two of cavalry, two of dragoons, and one of mounted riflemen were scattered widely. Of 197 extant companies, 179 occupied 79 isolated posts in the western territories and the remaining 18 manned 10 garrisons east of the Mississippi River, mostly along the Canadian border and on the Atlantic coast.

Yet this minute force would provide the leadership cadre upon which were built two powerful armies, eventually fully equal to the armies of the great military nations of Europe. The process began on March 6, 1861, when Davis created the Confederate army by calling for 100,000 volunteers to serve for twelve months. Only five days before, Davis had named the first brigadier general in the Provisional Army of the Confederate States, a Louisianan and former United States major of engineers and superintendent of West Point, Pierre Gustave Toutant Beauregard. He was among the 296 officers who were allowed to resign or were dismissed from the federal army. Including Beauregard, 239 of these 296 joined the Confederate military forces before the end of 1861. Another thirty-one joined after 1861. Twenty-six took no known part in the war, for any of several reasons: superannuation, ill health, death, or precluding occupation. The others of the prewar active officer corps—809—remained with the Union. At least twenty-six enlisted men managed to get out of United States service in order to go South.

West Point graduates on the active list numbered 824; of these, 184 became Confederate officers. Of the approximately 900 military academy graduates then in civilian life, 114 returned to the Union army and ninety-nine others acquired southern commissions. Thus the North enjoyed the services of 754 West Pointers while the South had but 283; the North possessed two-and-two-thirds times as many West Point-trained personnel.

Almost all of the officers from the Deep South went with the Confederacy, but numerous individuals from the Upper South remained loyal to the Union. Of the 184 officers from non-seceding slave states 128 remained in blue, seven took no part, and forty-nine went South; of the 286 Confederate-state natives among the pre-1861 officers in the U.S. Army, 80 stayed loyal, fourteen took no part, and 192 joined the Confederacy. Twenty-six natives of northern non-slave states went South, sixteen of those being West Pointers.[7]

The Confederacy initially patterned its military system exactly after that of the Union. Since its earliest days, the United States maintained two separate military forces: one, an active, regular organization of professionals; the other, the militia, a volunteer, civilian force to be swelled in size commensurate with any emergency. The United States kept its regular army intact for the duration of the war. Many critics believed that the army should have used the regulars as a cadre for the volunteers, but this was not done for several reasons. Lincoln did not foresee a long war, the regulars seemed needed on the frontier, and it appeared politically expedient to appoint high-ranking officers from the volunteers. Additionally, many of the old-line regiments possessed proud histories and honors dating back to the War of 1812. Had they been broken up and their members widely dispersed, morale would have suffered. Meanwhile, the Confederate regular army never got beyond the blueprint stage, save for the appointment of six full generals.

Historic laxness in organization, training, and supply had produced militia units of limited potency. In many respects the militia amounted to nothing but a political spoils system, with generals and colonels appointed to reconcile factional interests, build party power, and pay debts. Political oratory, a barrel of whiskey, and very little military training often distinguished the militia muster.

The Union used a departmental system of regional responsibility, created by Secretary of War Calhoun and modified by Davis when he had held the office. In each department a senior colonel or general officer by brevet commanded whatever officers and men were stationed therein. This usually meant about twenty-five widely scattered companies of about eighty men each. Regiments existed on paper, but rarely ever did an entire regiment find itself stationed at any one post. There existed almost no command staff at all.

Since neither regular nor militia organization provided a suitable base, the belligerents built their armies from scratch. Both the Union volunteer forces and the Confederacy's provisional army were modeled on the regular army and relied for leadership on a mixture of regular and militia officers, Mexican War veterans, men of political significance, and assorted prominent citizens. Initially, state and individual initiative played a large role in the formation of regiments, the basic unit of the armies. The volunteer infantry regiment comprised ten companies with no battalion organization intervening between the colonel and the ten captains and their companies, each numbering between fifty and one hundred men. Usually four to six regiments, grouped together, formed a brigade under a brigadier general. The next higher unit, the division, commanded by a major general, was quite unstandardized as was the next larger unit, the corps.

The armies, alike in their personnel and their organization, resembled each other in their doctrine, because West Point graduates filled the highest commands on both sides. Modeled on the Ecole Polytechnique in France, the West Point curriculum emphasized engineering. It provided an excellent technical education, the best graduates being selected for service in the engineers. Its military education instilled a good understanding of weapons and of army routine, making the graduates adept at map reading, drill, and small-unit tactics. The regular army service which followed provided West Pointers with a knowledge of troop leading, logistics, and small-unit staff duties. Beyond the experience of wars with the Indians, regular army service could add little else because the army was so minute and no portion of that scattered force ever concentrated for maneuvers.

In addition, though the army gave its officers an excellent start at West Point, thereafter it neglected their education. Whereas the present-day U.S. Army requires of senior officers three years of advanced military schooling as well as service on higher staffs, the antebellum army offered nothing but a continuing round of small-unit duty or construction assignments. There were no advanced courses for the different branches, no Command and General Staff College, nor any War College. Yet three major influences did exist and did shape the West Point graduate. In some respects these forces built upon that excellent educational foundation and supplied the place of the advanced schooling and diversified experience of today's officers, notably: the teachings of West Point's tactical instructor, Dennis Hart Mahan; the books available to and read by many career officers; and the experience of the Mexican War.

At West Point all cadets studied tactics under the charismatic Mahan, professor of engineering and the art of war from 1830 to 1871. He himself had received his education at West Point and later by extensive foreign study, particularly in France, and his teachings stressed the value of field fortifications and the importance of celerity in military operations. Mahan impressed on the cadets the importance of intrenching, an emphasis which correlated well with the engineering orientation of the curriculum. His inculcation that the "spade, implementing the terrain, went hand in hand with rifle and bayonet," certainly found receptive ears among a student body so unstintingly dedicated to the study of military engineering.[8]

Though the significance Mahan attached to field intrenchments stood at variance with the prevailing Napoleonic tactical legacy, Mahan's teachings would prove to be the right doctrine for a battlefield dominated by the muzzle-loading rifle. Introduced after the Mexican War, the rifle had considerably greater range and accuracy than the smoothbore musket. Rifles revolutionized tactics by neutralizing the cavalry charge on the battlefield and by placing a premium upon cover for the infantry. Combined with the intrenchments advocated by Mahan, the new weapon immensely augmented the power of the defense.

West Point contributed little on strategy to its graduate, for the curriculum contained only a few classroom hours on that subject. Until 1832, the cadets had to rely on a one-hundred-page selection drawn from the *Traité des Grandes opérations Militaire* of Baron Antoine Henri Jomini (1779–1869). A Swiss who had served in the French army under Napoleon, Jomini ranked then as the world's foremost military authority and principal interpreter of Napoleon. Primarily interested in strategy, he sought to systematize Napoleon's method through the concept of lines of operations, Napoleon's way of concentrating a superior force against an inferior force of the enemy. To achieve success, according to Jomini, an army must operate on interior lines, which would permit concentration against an opponent on an exterior line. All forces in the diagram are of approximately equal combat strength. With forces A and B on interior lines and forces X and Y on exterior lines, the bulk of forces A and B can concentrate first against X and then against Y, X and Y, on exterior lines, being powerless to concentrate.

Even this simple lesson, the thrust of the text selection from Jomini, may well have made no impression, so brief was the curriculum's attention to the subject of strategy. Nevertheless, the West Point curriculum made the graduates aware of military history and strategy, which the professionally well motivated and the intellectually inclined could and did pursue on their own. Mahan's influential teaching would have helped the students appreciate military history, for it was important in his approach, Mahan being the founder of the academy's Napoleon Club.[9]

So the West Point graduate, through necessity, would learn his strategy by individual study, especially by reading military history. During the war there were references to what must have been familiar books of principles, as when Union General in Chief Henry Wager Halleck called an officer's attention to Napoleon's *Maxims*. The general replied: "I have kept Napoleon's Maxims in view (you called my attention to those Maxims) in coming to my conclusions." Early in the war General William T. Sherman reminded his officers that they "must now study their books" and recommended the works of Jomini and Mahan. Some leaders alluded to campaigns, as when Confederate General Ambrose P. Hill called to the attention of the secretary of war that the Confederates were "committing the mistake of the Austrians in Napoleon's first Italian campaign." Diversified reading is also suggested by one of Grant's staff officers, who compared the camp life of a Union general with "a fine string of horses and a pack of greyhounds" to the sumptuous style of Marshal Soubise, an inept opponent of Frederick the Great.[10]

The writings on the art of war by two West Pointers, Beauregard and Halleck, who both held important Civil War positions, provide a systematic treatment of some of the results of individual study. Because Beauregard spoke French, his native tongue, and Halleck had taught French at West Point and had traveled for a half year in Europe, each encountered approximately equal opportunities for studying military science, often available only in French. Graduating from West Point within one year of each other, Beauregard and Halleck ranked second and third in their classes respectively. Both held commissions in the engineers.

Halleck's *Elements of Military Art and Science* relied heavily upon another of Jomini's works, his *Précis* of the art of war. The kind of influence the latter book exerted can be best appreciated by Halleck's injunction that the "first and most important rule in offensive war is, to keep your forces as much concentrated as possible." He went on to point out that this "will not only prevent misfortune, but secure victory—since, by its necessary operation, you possess the power of throwing your whole force upon any exposed point of your enemy's position." The means of thus concentrating against weakness were "interior lines of operations," which "have almost invariably led to success." He concluded, "There may, however, be cases where it will be preferable to direct our forces on the enemy's flank."

Halleck's bibliography on strategy was historical, including Napier's *Peninsular War*, and theoretical, citing the classics of Guibert and Clausewitz. It gave prominence to the *Mémoirs de Napoléon*, which contained "all the general principles of military art and science. No military man should fail to study them thoroughly." Unlike Jomini and most of his other authorities, Halleck, true to his engineering background and the West Point teachings of Mahan, stressed the value of fortifications. Himself the author of a work on fortifications, the young Halleck summoned to his aid an eminent proponent, the Archduke Charles, also an exponent of fortifications, who advocated an extremely cautious approach to strategy. This distinguished adversary of Napoleon promulgated the doctrine, for example, that the primary purpose of a reserve force in battle was to cover the army's retreat, if defeated.[11]

Beauregard reached substantially the same conclusions in his *Principles and Maxims of the Art of War*, a briefer book with a less eclectic bibliography, published as a guide for his officers during the war. He began by giving his version of Jomini's principles:

> The whole science of war may be briefly defined as the art of placing in the right position, at the right time, a mass of troops greater than your enemy can there oppose to you.
>
> PRINCIPLE NO 1: *To place masses of your army in contact with fractions of your enemy.*
>
> PRINCIPLE NO 2. *To operate as much as possible on the communications of your enemy without exposing your own.*
>
> PRINCIPLE NO 3: *To operate always on interior lines (or shorter ones in point of time).*

Thus he stressed the same themes as Halleck but, in Principle No. 2, gave much more emphasis to what was called the turning movement, in which the whole army or a part of it moves around the flank of the opposing force. Depending upon circumstances, a successful turning movement would enable an army to attack the enemy's rear, compel the enemy to withdraw, or force him to attack to recover his communications.

After the enunciation of these principles, Beauregard modeled the remainder of his small book on Napoleon's *Maxims*, encompassing thirty-four maxims. The substance as well as the form was Napoleonic, some of the maxims being quoted verbatim. For principles of selection, Beauregard chose those rules he deemed valid for 1863 and relevant to the duties officers encountered in his department. As in the case of Halleck, Beauregard's writings exhibited the influence of Mahan and the West Point curriculum with its emphasis on fortifications. The thoughts occasionally went beyond Napoleon, as in "Maxim 18—*A position cannot be too strong; lose no opportunity of strengthening it by means of field fortifications.*"[12]

Thus Halleck and Beauregard agreed on certain fundamentals. From their reading and training they had derived what today would be called doctrine. In strategy they emphasized interior lines of operations and advocated the turning movement rather than the frontal battle. The Mexican War would provide a chance to see these ideas applied. The war also would supply, to a degree, the army's want of higher military education and opportunities to exercise higher units. Some, such as Robert E. Lee at Cerro Gordo (April 9–18, 1847), played key operational roles. Later William T. Sherman spoke of the value of this "schooling with large masses of troops in the field."[13]

Participation in the war would be the only common learning experience for many of the most important Civil War military leaders who had not dedicated themselves to historical study or who had derived no doctrine from their study. The scale of operations and the small size of the United States armies permitted even company-grade officers to get a perspective on operations, enabling them to appreciate the grand tactics of the battles.

The Mexican War battles contained one recurring aspect: the turning movement, in which a detached force moved around the flank of the opposing body of troops. This maneuver played a key role in the battles of Monterey (September 19–20, 1846) and Cerro Gordo and characterized the operations around Mexico City.[14]

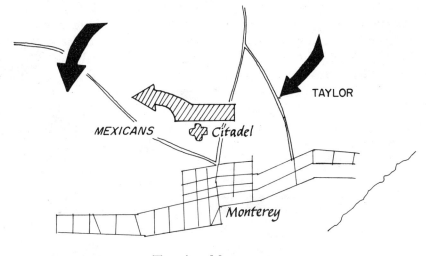

Turning Movement

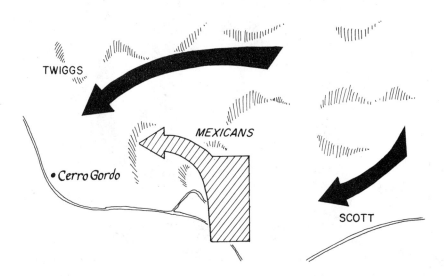

Turning Movement

Even the grand strategy of the war included a turning movement. When the barren nature of the country between the Rio Grande River and Mexico City made Major General Zachary Taylor conclude that a move directly on the city was impossible, an amphibious expedition under Major General Winfield Scott turned General Santa Anna's position by a landing at Vera Cruz

and a march inland to capture Mexico City. In a brilliant campaign, Scott
daringly abandoned his communications, overcame a powerful Mexican army,
and managed to subsist his own army on the country, despite formidable
guerrilla attacks.

In a new edition of his book, Halleck emphasized that the "manner in
which Scott handled his troops on his line of march to the capital, proved
him to be one of the best generals of the age. At Cerro Gordo he so completely
turned Santa Anna's left as to cut off his line of retreat, and nearly destroyed
his army, the general himself barely escaping capture." Scott's movement to
Vera Cruz, which Halleck labeled "truly strategic," had separated the U.S.
forces, and Santa Anna exploited his interior lines by attacking Taylor at
Buena Vista before Scott could menace Mexico City. Though outnumbered

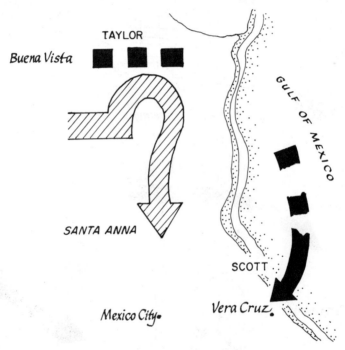

Santa Anna's Interior Lines

nearly three to one, Taylor successfully defended against the Mexican attack
at the battle of Buena Vista. Santa Anna then turned south to make what
proved an unsuccessful resistance against Scott, who was commanding the
principal U.S. troops. As Halleck, disapproving of Taylor's line of operations, pointed out, "Santa Anna, from his central position fought, with the
same troops, the battles of Buena Vista and Cerro Gordo."[15]

Beauregard greatly admired Scott and thought him "the best general of the
day," but added, "still he has not been faultless." In his reminiscences of the
war, Beauregard wrote that if the Mexicans had been more formidable oppo-

nents, Scott would have been forced to observe more closely "the true principles of the art of war, on the one or two occasions he departed from them and which does not happen with impunity in a well conducted war." Turning movements made Beauregard apprehensive because they divided the army, "for the enemy occupying a central position to our lines of operations," he observed, "might then concentrate all his means" against one or the other parts. Beauregard would be one of the few important Civil War generals who would not typically employ the turning movement.

The Civil War reflects many instances of the influence of the Mexican War. For example, Grant, then an admirer of Taylor, criticized Scott's approach to Mexico City, "wondering" whether there was "not some other route by which the city could be captured, without meeting such formidable obstructions, and at such great loss." He believed that "the army could have reached the northwest" defenses of "the city at their weakest and most undefensible, as well as approachable points." As the title of one general history of the Mexican War, *Rehearsal for Conflict*, denotes, the Mexican War was in a real sense a dress rehearsal for the Civil War leadership.[16]

A few years later, the Crimean War accentuated the importance of sea power, so striking in making possible Scott's great turning movement, when a seaborne Anglo-French army attacked the Crimean peninsula and besieged the Russian port of Sebastopol. The siege itself doubtless also struck a responsive chord in an army educated as engineers and taught by Dennis Hart Mahan. A member of the U.S. Army delegation sent to observe, George B. McClellan, himself a young West Point veteran of the Mexican War, fully chronicled these operations, together with a report on the latest military developments.[17]

The Presidents and their soldiers had at their disposal an unequal distribution of resources. The 1860 census numbered the U.S. population at 31,443,321 persons. The eleven states that seceded encompassed 9,103,332 of this number: 5,449,462 whites, 3,521,110 slaves, and 132,760 free Negroes. Some whites residing in the states that remained in the Union, approximately 600,000, also cast their sympathies and efforts in behalf of the South, to bring the white population in support of the Confederacy to about 6 million. The North's population therefore stood at 22,339,989 less the 600,000 estimated southern sympathizers, or an effective 21,739,989. From the southern totals should be subtracted West Virginia and areas such as East Tennessee, which contributed substantial support to the Union. That blacks did not serve in the Confederacy's army did not significantly handicap the South; it simply meant that whites performed a disproportionate share of Confederate combat service, while more blacks performed fatigue labors. Nearly 100,000 southern blacks did serve in the Union army. The approximate ratio of manpower resources was about five to two in favor of the North.

And by almost any material measure, the North enjoyed greater riches. At the outset, the north had 110,000 manufacturing establishments employing 1,300,000 industrial workers; the South contained 18,000 establishments with 110,000 workers. The northern rail net comprised 21,973 miles of railroad, but the South, with only 9,283 miles, had less than half of the North's mileage. The South built only 4 percent of all the locomotives produced in the United States during 1860 and only 3 percent of the firearms. The North's nearly 800,000 draft animals contrasted with only 300,000 in the South, a logistical advantage of great importance. The North had a Navy of 90 ships and 9,000 sailors, while the South began with just the few U.S. revenue cutters or small ships which the states possessed or had been able to seize in the secession actions. Even the North's crops, produced with the aid of almost all of the nation's labor-saving machines, amounted to more annual worth than those of the predominately agricultural South.

Yet some significant factors did favor the South. East of the Mississippi it had a good military railway net which would offer opportunities for possible interior lines of operations, and its 3,500-mile coastline embraced 189 harbors and navigable river mouths. The Confederacy also possessed an open-land border across the Rio Grande River from Texas into Mexico. The Union proved unable to close off completely the South's access to the outside world.

More significant, the Confederacy's size made it a formidable military obstacle. Its three-quarters of a million square miles of territory exceeded the land area of the present-day United Kingdom, West Germany, France, Italy, and Spain combined. Confederate Secretary of War George W. Randolph realized that the conquest of such an immense land area was truly a daunting prospect when, at the beginning of the war, he wrote, "They may overrun our frontier States and plunder our coast but, as for conquering us, the thing is an impossibility. There is no instance in history of a people as numerous as we are inhabiting a country so extensive as ours being subjected if true to themselves."[18]

Recent military developments also favored the Confederacy. In the Mexican War, Santa Anna's essentially frontal attack at the Battle of Buena Vista failed decisively in spite of a numerical superiority of nearly three to one. The officers on both sides realized this preponderance which the defense showed even before the introduction of the rifle. Not only could armies effectively defend themselves from frontal attacks but even the turning movement would prove ineffective in trapping or attacking an opponent from the rear; the armies were just too maneuverable. Good subdivision into divisions, brigades, and regiments enabled armies to face about so readily that literally battles took place in which troops stood almost back-to-back fighting in two directions simultaneously. Nor could the Union count on superior armaments. Imports, captures, and an aggressive domestic manufacturing program enabled the Confederate forces essentially to have parity in the quality and quantity of weapons.

These military developments, coupled with the natural advantage of the defense and the leadership's belief in intrenching, rendered the battle of annihilation a thing of the past. Cannae, where Hannibal destroyed the Roman army, and Hastings, where Duke William destroyed Harold's army, are celebrated examples of annihilation. Though much of the public tended to think in terms of these famous and decisive battles, the soldiers in the mid-nineteenth century knew them to be no longer possible. The North needed some other strategy, and the only likely one was to exhaust the rebels by occupying territory and gradually depriving them of the resources and recruits for maintaining their armies.

This would be a difficult task. Americans in the post-Vietnam era surely must realize that no side automatically wins merely because it has the most people and the most materiel. Numbers and resources, while important, do not dictate the outcome of wars. Utilization, execution, and the will to win determine victory. The quality of the management of available resources and the quality of the strategy and its direction profoundly influence these factors. If one side has fewer resources than the other, it may win if it decides more wisely and manages more effectively.

In another special way the South might have altered its situation and even become the materielly richer side. The possibility of foreign recognition, and perhaps direct aid as well, could have provided a crucially significant tipping of the scales. Both presidents realized early the singular importance of this possibility. One of Davis's first acts was to dispatch three commissioners to Britain in an attempt to negotiate recognition. Lincoln meanwhile named Charles Francis Adams as minister to Britain and William L. Dayton minister to France, both sage and skillful diplomats, although he otherwise made, for political reasons, a number of haphazard appointments of men with marginal capabilities.

As Lincoln and Davis left their homes on the same day, February 11, 1861, to make journeys to their respective capitals, they each enjoyed exactly the same amount of time to make whatever preparations they might elect. Sixty days elapsed between their departures and the firing at Fort Sumter. Regardless of rhetoric or inmost hopes, doubtless both men realized consciously the probability of war. Lincoln specified firmly in his inaugural on March 4 that the seceded states must return to the Union; Davis, meanwhile, said at his installation on February 16 that "the time for compromise has now passed, and the South is determined to maintain her position, and make all who oppose her smell Southern powder and feel Southern steel."[19]

In selecting his Cabinet, Davis chose, for the most part, highly qualified men. The Provisional Congress of the Confederacy authorized him to make contracts in order to buy and manufacture materiel of war and officially established an army and a navy. In March, 1861, the southern Congress authorized issuance of treasury notes up to a million dollars and expressed thanks to Louisiana for turning over $536,000 taken from the former U.S. Mint in New Orleans. On February 22, just as had northerners, southerners celebrated Washington's birthday, manifesting a feeling of ongoing political heritage. Charlestonians honored the day with parades of military companies. Meanwhile Davis named three commissioners to Washington to attempt negotiations with the Federals, while at the same time extensive Confederate works gradually appeared at various points around Charleston Harbor, and troops trained and drilled.

Since Lincoln took over an existing government already equipped with military and naval forces and systems of finance and procurement, his initial preparations could quite naturally be less elemental than those of Davis. Lincoln listened to politicians pleading for favors and to statesmen and border-state men pleading for conciliation or compromise. He ordered troops to Washington, ostensibly for preserving the peace, but also to guard the capital against possible military attack and to quell the feared rioting or even assassination attempts. Lincoln used the well-selected Cabinet, representing the various factions of the Republican party and diverse opinions on the issues of the day, as a debating forum as well as his principal operations staff. The commander of the garrison at Sumter, Major Robert Anderson, maintained daily telegraphic communication with his government until the Confederate commander, Brigadier General Beauregard, ordered the channels closed on April 7. The major said that the government probably could not throw reinforcements into Fort Sumter before the limited supplies ran out, and that it would take at least 20,000 men to do the job. The President conferred with the general in chief, Winfield Scott, who concurred with Major Anderson. Lincoln continued Cabinet conferences and negotiations with Unionists in Virginia, with whom he hoped to reach satisfactory arrangements that would keep their state firmly with the Federals. His efforts would be doomed by the bombardment of Fort Sumter.

1. Benjamin P. Thomas, *Abraham Lincoln* (New York, 1952), 31–32.

2. *Ibid.*, 157–58.

3. *Ibid.*, 153.

4. Proceedings of a General Court Martial— Third Day Trial of Jefferson Davis, Feb. 14, 1835, eds. Haskell M. Monroe and James T. McIntosh, in *The Papers of Jefferson Davis*, I (Baton Rouge, 1971), 372.

5. Matthew Arbuckle to Roger Jones, May 12, 1835, Enclosure 1, *The Papers of Jefferson Davis*, I, 402; Davis to George W. Jones, Feb. 9, 1839, *ibid.*, 455.

6. Shelby Foote, *The Civil War: A Narrative*, 3 vols. (New York, 1958–74), I, 13.

7. The numbers stated in these paragraphs are drawn from the following sources: E. B. Long, *Civil War, Day by Day* (New York, 1971) 706–9; Ezra J. Warner, *Generals in Gray* (Baton Rouge, 1959), xiv–xxvi; and Maurice Matloff, ed., *American Military History* (Washington, 1969), 188ff. The data therein are not complete nor do they always agree. We have interpolated, and have been aided by the excellent research of George T. Ness, Jr., author of the unpublished book-length manuscript "The Army on the Eve

of the Civil War." Ness to Hattaway, Apr. 19, 24, and 28, 1981, in possession of Hattaway.

8. R. Ernest Dupuy, *Men of West Point: The First 150 Years of the United States Military Academy* (New York, 1951), 12–24. See also: James L. Morrison, Jr., "Educating the Civil War Generals: West Point, 1833–1861," *Military Affairs* (Oct. 1974), 108–11; Edward Hagerman, "From Jomini to Dennis Hart Mahan: The Evolution of Trench Warfare and the American Civil War," *Civil War History* (Sept. 1967), 197–220 and "The Evolution of Trench Warfare in the Civil War," Ph.D. dissertation, Duke University, 1965; and Thomas F. Griess, "Dennis Hart Mahan: West Point Professor and Advocate of Professionalism, 1830–1871," Ph.D. dissertation, Duke University, 1969. Brigadier General Griess and Professor Hagerman make clear that Mahan taught the primacy of defense aided by field fortifications. This doctrine differed from the prevailing stress on the offensive engendered by the Napoleonic wars. The Civil War demonstrated the correctness of Mahan's thesis and that his pupils learned his lesson well.

Perry D. Jamieson in his "The Development of Civil War Tactics" reviews the standard Napoleonic era tactics taught in the U.S. Army and their modification in the 1850s to take into account the increase in firepower brought about by the substitution of the rifle for the musket. The attack was to be accelerated because of the rifle's greater range and accuracy. He stresses the attention given to the problem of the enhanced power of the defense, quoting the conclusion from one manual: "A *cool, well-directed* fire from a body of men armed with the new rifle or rifle musket is sufficient to stop the advance of almost any kind of troops."

But, to some degree, Jamieson draws the opposite conclusion from his sources, believing that the bulk of regular officers entered the war with a faith in the frontal attack derived from the Army's Mexican War experience. Certainly there were many believers in frontal attacks and many such during the war, but we believe that the dominant culture in both Union and Confederate armies was a faith in the defense aided by field fortifications and a belief that the offensive must rely on the turning movement. Beauregard, Bragg, and, initially, Rosecrans were notable exceptions to this generalization and Lee, not a pupil of Mahan, was among those who were slow to adopt intrenchments.

Perry D. Jamieson, "The Development of Civil War Tactics," Ph.D. dissertation, Wayne State University, 1979, 51 and *passim*. See,

however: Edward Hagerman, "The Tactical Thought of R. E. Lee and the Origins of Trench Warfare in the American Civil War, 1861–62," *The Historian* (November, 1975), 21–38.

9. Thomas Lawrence Connelly and Archer Jones, *The Politics of Command: Factions and Ideas in Confederate Strategy* (Baton Rouge, 1973), xii–xiii, 3–30.

The interior lines concept and its elaboration were the essence of much that was new which Jomini had to say. Its simplicity led Colonel F. N. Maude, the British military expert, to write in 1910: "These ideas are, after all, elementary and readily grasped even by the average intellect, though many volumes have been devoted to proving them, and yet they are all that Jomini and his followers have to offer us— a fact that both explains and justifies the contempt with which military study was so long regarded by practical soldiers in England" (F. N. Maude, "Strategy," 986–97; *The Encyclopaedia Britannica*, 11th ed., [London and N.Y., 1926], XXV, 992).

In addition to interior lines Jomini stressed concentration against the enemy's weakness and advocated turning movements through which the army on the offensive would place itself on the enemy's communications. In that these ideas had a major place in the thinking of the higher commanders on both sides, all may be said to have been conscious or unconscious disciples of Jomini's strategy. But, as Napoleon also advocated these concepts and was their leading practitioner, Napoleon could equally well have been the mentor of Civil War military leaders.

If Jomini did, as he claimed, teach Napoleon's way of war, the question for historians would be merely to determine if generals were influenced and whether by Jomini, by a study of Napoleon's campaigns, or by a combination. But whether the influence was that of Jomini or Napoleon would not be very material to this work as long as their impact was the same. In recent times, however, scholars in the United States have distinguished between the ideas of Napoleon and Jomini and think that Jomini's influence was predominant with generals on both sides. Seeing his teaching as antithetical to that of Napoleon, they believe that, in studying the campaigns of Frederick the Great and using them to illustrate his Napoleonic principles, Jomini had imbibed and taught the ideas of war characteristic of the eighteenth century, when war was more circumspect and less decisive than in Napoleon's day. Since none of Jomini's works were translated into English until 1854, his influence must have been limited and, in view of the slight attention to strategy at West Point, it is not surprising that the index to *The War of the Rebellion: A Compilation of the Official Records of the Union and Confederate Armies* contains only two references to Jomini, one of these by Union Secretary of War Cameron citing his biography of Napoleon. The exposure to Jomini was too limited for him to have had any universal impact, much less "that many a Civil War general went into battle with a sword in one hand and a Jomini's *Summary of the Art of War* in the other." It also seems unlikely that his influence, unless misunderstood, could have been so much the opposite of the principles of Napoleonic warfare which he claimed to be seeking to teach (J. D. Hittle, *Jomini and His Summary of the Art of War* [Harrisburg, Pa., 1947], 2).

For this controversy, see also: T. Harry Williams, "The Return of Jomini: Some Thoughts on Recent Civil War Writing," *Military Affairs*, XXXIX (Dec., 1975), 204–6; Joseph L. Harsh, "Battlesword and Rapier: Clausewitz, Jomini, and the American Civil War," *ibid.*, XXXVIII (Dec., 1974), 133–38; and Archer Jones, "Jomini and the Strategy of the American Civil War, A Reinterpretation," *ibid.*, XXXIV (Dec., 1970), 127–31. For a recent treatment of Jomini not elsewhere cited, see: Michael Howard, "Jomini and the Classical Tradition in Military Thought," *The Theory and Practice of War*, ed. Michael Howard (Bloomington, London, 1965), 3–20. Also of value are: John I. Alger, *Antoine-Henri Jomini: A Bibliographical Survey* (West Point, New York, 1975), and John R. Elting, "Jomini: Disciple of Napoleon?" *Military Affairs*, XXVIII (Spring, 1964), 17–26.

If Jomini were influential, it seems to us too difficult to make him into a critic of Napoleon and, presumably, an exponent of Leopold von Daun's geographically-oriented Austrian school, when Jomini was so merciless in his criticism of Duan's safety-first strategy. Much of the thesis for Jomini's preference for Austrian strategy rests upon Jomini's analysis of what he called national wars. These were wars in which the invading army was faced by a united people, "or a great majority of them, filled with a noble ardor and determined to sustain their independence."

The people in arms as guerrillas could, Jomini explained, be effectively aided by the terrain. In mountainous countries "the people are always most formidable; next to these are countries covered with extensive forests." Guerrillas were particularly powerful when "supported by a considerable nucleus of disciplined troops. The invader has only an army: his adversaries have an army, and a people wholly or almost wholly in arms, and making means of resistance out of every thing, each individual of whom conspires against the common enemy; even the noncombatants have an interest in his ruin and accelerate it by every means in their power. He holds scarcely any ground but that upon which he encamps; outside the limits of his camp everything is hostile and multiplies a thousandfold the difficulties he meets at every step.

"These obstacles become almost insurmountable when the country is difficult. Each armed inhabitant knows the smallest paths and their connections; he finds everywhere a relative or friend who aids him; the commanders also know the country, and, learning immediately the slightest movement on the part of the invader, can adopt the best measures to defeat his projects; while the latter, without information of their movements, and not in a condition to send out detachments to gain it, having no resource but in his bayonets, and certain safety only in the concentration of his columns, is like a blind man: his combinations are failures; and when, after the most carefully-concerted movements and the most rapid and fatiguing marches, he thinks he is about to accomplish his aim and deal a terrible blow, he finds no signs of the enemy but his campfires: so that while, like Don Quixote, he is attacking windmills, his adversary is on his line of communications, destroys the detachments left to guard it, surprises his convoys, his depots, and carries on a war so disastrous for the invader that he must inevitably yield after a time."

Having faced this kind of war when he had served with the French armies in Spain, Jomini fully realized the difficulties of fighting such a resistance. "No army, however disciplined, can contend successfully against such a system applied to a great nation, unless it be strong enough to hold all the essential points of the country, cover its communications, and at the same time furnish an active force sufficient to beat the enemy wherever he may present himself. If this enemy has a regular army of respectable size to be a nucleus around which to rally the people, what force will be sufficient to be superior everywhere, and to assure the safety of the long lines of communication against numerous bodies?"

His prescription for the conduct of such a war, more political than military, was to make a display "of a mass of troops proportioned to the obstacles and resistance likely to be encountered, calm the popular passions in every possible way, exhaust them by time and patience, display courtesy, gentleness, and severity united, and, particularly, deal justly."

"The immense obstacles encountered by an invading force in these wars have," Jomini commented, "led some speculative persons to hope that there should never be any other kind, since then wars would become more rare, and, conquest being also more difficult, would be less a temptation to ambitious leaders." But, Jomini pointed out, this kind of defense had serious drawbacks, for it would provoke, "by way of reprisals, murder, pillage, and incendiarism throughout the country." The cost of such a war was thus very high to both combatants, the invaded suffering severe reprisals from the invaders whom they ambushed in guerrilla war. Jomini clearly believed that, because of its cost, such an escalation of effort by the defenders should only be a last resort. He asked: "But is there no means of repelling such an invasion without bringing about an uprising of the whole population and a war of extermination?"

Instead of meeting the invader with a war of extermination, Jomini advocated the augmentation of the regular army by national reserves, or militia, which would take the field with the regulars and which, uniformed and called "by their governments into service, would regulate the part the people should take in the war, and place just limits to its barbarities." He believed that such a national defense would be adequate and would make it unnecessary for the defenders to resort to guerrilla warfare and so not have to suffer the inevitable reprisals of "murder, pillage, and incendiarism."

Jomini then summed up his brief discussion by asserting that, "without being a utopian philanthropist, or a condottieri, a person may desire that wars of extermination may be banished from the code of nations, and that the defenses of nations by disciplined militia, with the aid of good political alliances, may be sufficient to insure their independence.

"As a soldier, preferring loyal and chivalrous warfare to organized assassination, if it be necessary to make a choice, I acknowledge that my prejudices are in favor of the good old times when the French and English Guards courteously invited each other to fire first,—as at Fontenoy,—preferring them to the frightful epoch when priests, women, and children throughout Spain plotted the murder of isolated soldiers."

This last paragraph has been cited in support of the thesis that Jomini was an advocate of pre-Napoleonic war. But clearly Jomini is not contrasting two systems of operations but rather what has in recent times been called conventional and unconventional war. Obviously he is not anti-Napoleon, for it was against the armies of Napoleon that the Spanish waged the guerrilla warfare which Jomini witnessed in Spain. It is likely that Napoleon also shared his distaste for that kind of war, for the emperor once said that it was the Spanish ulcer which ruined him. Certainly also, as an eighteenth-century man and a humanitarian, Jomini felt abhorence for the barbarities of a war of extermination. Most significant, however, was that he perceived the degree to which the key to such operations was political rather than military and that guerrilla warfare was not the kind of war he understood and was outside of his specialty of operational analysis. For one kind of civil war, for example, he remarked: "To give maxims in such wars would be absurd." A political, not a military, solution was required (Baron de Jomini, *The Art of War*, G. H. Mendell and W. P. Craighill, translators [Philadelphia, 1862], 29–35).

Thus Jomini's difficulty in dealing with guerrilla war was that he was an historian of conventional military operations, the *grandes opérations* of his first book. A concept such as lines of operations and interior lines is an historical interpretation, one which seeks to describe and explain the causes of the outcome of military campaigns. Jomini used these just as political historians use economic or status motivations to explain political events. Jomini went beyond historical explanation to say that his interpretations provide a guide to the conduct of operations in the future, and, in an effort to be the Newton of the art of war, elevated his interpretations to principles. His proof of the validity of his operational principles was to show that they have worked for every major European campaign from the War of the Spanish Succession through those of Napoleon. An interpreter rather than a researcher, Jomini published a history of the operations in the Seven Years War in Germany and of the campaigns of the French Revolution and Napoleon.

Though he believed that his interpretations or principles applied equally to all wars he studied, he insisted that Napoleon's campaigns best exemplified them and that Napoleon's success was due to the genius with which he applied the principles which Jomini had uncovered. Jomini did discern an important difference between "the old system of wars of position" and what he termed the "modern system of marches." Napoleon's turning movements in the Marengo, Ulm, and Jena campaigns best exemplified the new "science of marches in the great operations of strategy." He did wonder if Napoleon's feats could be duplicated by others and asked whether this "system of Napoleon is adapted to all capacities, epochs, and armies" or if "the adventurous character of this great man, his personal situation, and the tone of the French mind, all concurred in urging him to undertakings which no other person, whether born upon a throne, or a general under the orders of his government, would ever dare to adopt. This is probably true; but between the extremes of very distant invasions and wars of position, there is a proper mean and, without imitating his impetuous audacity, we may pursue the line he has marked out. It is probable that the old system of wars of position will for a long time be proscribed, or that, if adopted, it will be much modified and improved" (Jomini, *Art of War*, 70–71, 135–39, 175–77).

In his final work, the *Summary of the Art of War*, Jomini reversed his usual procedure and built upon his generalizations, only referring to the campaigns to illustrate the principles which were derived from their study. There is actually little historical narrative in the work, because the reader is presumed to have a detailed knowledge of the campaigns. This limited the utility of the book for a text, and it was followed by similar works such as P. L. MacDougall, *The Theory of War* and Sir Edward Hamley, *The Operations of War*. These books were modeled on Jomini's but include narratives of campaigns which illustrated the principles. This approach to military study continued until the end of the century, when it began to be eclipsed by the romantic resurgence, the stress upon moral factors in combat, and the cult of the offensive. Representative of this change in the military climate is F. N. Maude's criticism of Jomini's complex development of the concept of the turning movement through the theory of the base, an approach based on the ideas of the eighteenth-century geometrical theorist, Bulow. Maude felt that "the days of eighteenth century tricks and stratagems are past and done with. . . . The essence of successful leadership in the future will be . . . a rapid and sustained advance which will overrun all opposition by its very momentum." Colonel Maude, one of the pre-World War I exponents of the offensive, stressed "that bloodshed was a usual consequence of the armed collision of combatants," and "in the words of Clausewitz, 'One should teach the soldier how to die, not how to avoid dying.' " World War I proved the correctness of his belief about bloodshed, if not of the offensive (F. N. Maude, *The*

Evolution of Modern Strategy [London, 1905], 126, 134, and *passim*).

10. H. W. Halleck to E. D. Keyes, Apr. 11, 1863, *The War of the Rebellion: A Compilation of the Official Records of the Union and Confederate Armies* (Washington, 1880–1901), series 1, vol. XVIII, 595 (cited hereafter as *Official Records* and abbreviated *O.R.* All references will be to series 1 unless otherwise noted.); Keyes to Halleck, Apr. 14, 1863, *ibid.*, 609; W. T. Sherman, General Orders, July 24, 1862, *ibid.*, XVII, pt. 2, 119; A. P. Hill to G. W. Randolph, Apr. 24, 1862, *ibid.*, XI, pt. 2, 461; James Harrison Wilson, *Under the Old Flag*, 2 vols. (New York and London, 1912), I, 251–52. The reference to Jomini by Sherman is the other reference to Jomini found in the *Official Records* and mentioned in note 9.

11. H. Wager Halleck, *Elements of Military Art and Science; or Course of Instruction in Strategy, Fortifications, Tactics of Battles, etc., Embracing the Duties of Staff, Infantry, Cavalry, and Engineers* (New York, 1846), 40, 54, 59–60; Rudolph von Caemmerer, *The Development of Strategical Science in the Nineteenth Century*, trans. Karl von Donat (London, 1905), 60. For a different view of Halleck, see Connelly and Jones, *Politics of Command*, 26–29.

12. G. T. Beauregard, *Principles and Maxims of the Art of War—Outpost Service; general instructions for battles; Reviews* (Charleston, 1863), 3–4, 7, *passim*. This is reprinted in G. T. Beauregard, *A Commentary on the Campaign and Battle of Manassas . . .* (New York, 1891). There is a "third edition," published in New Orleans in 1890. See also Conrad H. Lanza, *Napoleon and Modern War* (Harrisburg, Pa., 1943), maxim xiii and *passim*. Beauregard also plagiarized part of his principles from a British interpreter of Jomini, P. L. MacDougall, *The Theory of War*, second ed. (London, 1958), 51–52. For the role of Jomini and MacDougall in the development of the modern principles of war, see John I. Alger, "Thought, Theory and the Military Mind," paper presented at the Northern Great Plains History Conference, Oct. 27, 1978.

13. William T. Sherman to John Sherman, May 24, 1862, *The Sherman Letters; Correspondence Between General and Senator Sherman, 1837 to 1891*, ed. Rachel Sherman Thorndike (New York, 1894), 122.

14. Technically most of the Mexican War turning movements were enveloping movements, aimed at attacking the flank or rear of the enemy in his present position. The turning movement, on the other hand, avoids the enemy

in his present position and, by threatening something vital in his rear, aims to force the enemy from his position, compelling him either to withdraw or fight at a disadvantage. For simplicity and because most of the movements referred to later will be turning movements, no distinction will be made between the two in this work. Civil War soldiers tended to ignore the distinction and use the term "turning movement" for envelopments as well.

15. H. Wager Halleck, *Elements of Military Art and Science* (New York, 1862), 415, 410.

16. T. Harry Williams, *With Beauregard in Mexico: The Mexican War Reminiscences of P. G. T. Beauregard* (Baton Rouge, 1956), 104, 36; Grady McWhiney, *Southerners and Other Americans* (New York, 1973), 61–71; U. S. Grant to unknown addresses, Aug. 22, Sept. 12, 1847, *The Papers of Ulysses S. Grant*, ed. John Y. Simon (Carbon-

dale and Edwardsville, Ill. 1967–   ), I, 144, 145.

17. George B. McClellan, *The Armies of Europe: comprising descriptions in detail of the military systems of England, France, Russia, Prussia, Austria, Sardinia, Adapting their Advantages to all arms of the United States Service: and embodying the Report of Observations in Europe during the Crimean War, as military commissioner from the United States government, in 1855–56* (Philadelphia, 1861). The report on the Crimean War is found on pp. 9–35. His description of the siege and the fortifications is on pp. 20–33.

18. George W. Randolph to Molly Randolph, Oct. 10, 1861, Edgehill-Randolph Papers, Alderman Library, University of Virginia, Charlottesville.

19. Long, *The Civil War, Day by Day*, 37.

2 ☆ THE CIVIL WAR STAGE

Jefferson Davis

I DO NOT PRETEND TO GO TO SLEEP," Mary B. Chesnut wrote in her diary on April 12, 1861. "How can I?" She asked, as she and other citizens of Charleston, South Carolina, awaited sounds of the first Confederate artillery bombardment upon the federal garrison of eighty-five soldiers and forty-three civilians holding nearby Fort Sumter. "The women were wild," she noted. The long impasse was about to end; this Rubicon about to be crossed heralded civil war between North and South. Even as Mrs. Chesnut wrote, her husband tossed uncomfortably in a small boat with other military aides on the mission that ended with the eruption of fire from batteries of artillery.[1]

All the preliminary activities by subalterns notwithstanding, the decision to commence fire resulted from the interaction of the thought processes of two men: Abraham Lincoln and Jefferson Davis. Every other actor and scene in the drama followed from their direction.

Lincoln considered revocation of secession a *sine qua non*; Davis was obviously committed to the South's assertion of nationhood. Beyond that, southerners conceived it to be absolutely essential that their country have integrity and the visible trappings of legitimate and even stable existence. Southerners lacked the patient dedication typically manifested by other nation-builders of modern times; the quality did not reside in Davis, just as it was not characteristic of southerners, to reason that they might achieve their goal without taking Fort Sumter. Obviously the South could have done without that one miserable island stronghold, but it would not then have enjoyed free use of the valuable Charleston Harbor and, worse, the country would have to sustain a lesser symbolic status. Lincoln did not expect under any circumstances to allow the southern goal to be achieved, and his rhetoric and actions rendered that obvious to Davis.

The Confederate capture of Fort Sumter required them to fire upon it, because Lincoln forced the issue to that point. The accident of physical circumstance, which made Sumter hard to reach, combined with the loyal resolution of the garrison commander, Major Robert Anderson, permitted the episode. If the confrontation had not occurred at Fort Sumter, it would have occurred somewhere else, most likely at Fort Pickens. After a brief bombardment, Major Anderson surrendered to the Confederate commander, Beauregard. Ironically, Beauregard had studied under Anderson and considered him his favorite teacher at West Point.[2]

Lincoln's decision to use force to drive the seceded states back into the Union and his call for new volunteer soldiers precipitated a second departing wave of four additional states, but it also provided the catalyst that rallied northern war support. In the months that followed, the two sides steadily groped toward military preparedness. The process began two days after Sumter fell, when Lincoln issued a proclamation declaring the existence of an insurrection in the then seven Confederate states, called out 75,000 militia for three months service, and scheduled a special session of Congress to convene on July 4, more than six weeks away. On April 29 Jefferson Davis sent a lengthy message to his Congress, meticulously detailing the history of the establishment of the southern government and terming Lincoln's proclamation a presidential declaration of war, which it was.

The strongly pro-Union northern states immediately wired their acceptance of the call for troops, but the border states balked. Virginia seceded on April 17 and promptly raised forces to protect her borders from federal encroachment. North Carolina state troops seized Fort Caswell and Fort Johnston. Jefferson Davis invited applications for letters of marque, thus giving Confederate sanction for privateering on the high seas. Meetings of patriotic groups stirred attention in both the North and the South, but primary efforts everywhere concentrated upon mustering and organizing militia. Intensely worried about defending Washington, Abraham Lincoln conferred with his general-in-chief, brevet Lieutenant General Winfield Scott. Scott held the highest rank in the army and the second highest ever attained to that time. The only previous American lieutenant general had been George Washington. Scott was a permanent major general. Because brevet denoted essentially an honorary promotion to a higher rank and carried neither pay nor, usually, command assignment, Scott's brevet rank approached but did not equal that of the revered Washington.

"Old Fuss and Feathers," as Scott's men irreverently but affectionately called him because of his rigorous adherence to regulations and attention to detail and discipline, cut an imposing figure. Ulysses S. Grant, later recalling his cadet days, remembered that, "with his commanding figure, his quite colossal size and showy uniform, I thought him the finest specimen of manhood my eyes had ever beheld, and the most to be envied." But the general in chief, aged seventy-five at the beginning of the war, was, as he said, "one year older than the constitution." To his imposing physical appearance, a robust 6′5″, time had added girth, and now the crusty and grizzled general in chief weighed 350 pounds. Gout, dropsy, and vertigo added to the infirmities of age and obesity. The vain and always gorgeously uniformed hero could take no more than a few steps at a time and could mount a horse only by being hoisted up with a winch. But, though prone to doze in meetings, the general in chief still enjoyed powerful mental faculties.[3]

As a young man during the War of 1812, he emerged as a perspicacious and competent officer. He became general in chief in 1841 both because he deserved it and because he outlived or outlasted his rivals. As the architect of victory in the Mexican War, he owed much of his success to the brilliant young staff officers, particularly the West Point-trained engineers with whom he had surrounded himself.

Even though Scott had spent more than half a century in the U.S. regular army, he lived originally in Virginia and he retained some identity as a southerner. Many northerners, especially radical Republicans, believed that for nearly twenty years before the Civil War Scott had molded the army into a southern clique; southerners allegedly advanced more rapidly, while northerners grew frustrated and left the service for positions in civilian life where advancement might come more swiftly.

None of this was quite true. To be sure, many northerners did grow frustrated in the antebellum army and left it for more lucrative employment. In the process they gained an opportunity at an earlier age to manage larger organizations and groups of men than they would have if they had waited for slow advancement in the regular army. Scott betrayed bias not for southerners but for West Point men. During the Mexican War, he assembled an able staff which he lovingly called his "little cabinet," perhaps reflecting his ambition to become President. The chief of engineers, Joseph G. Totten, hailed from New Haven, Connecticut; the inspector general, Ethan Allen Hitchcock, came from Vergennes, Vermont. Another engineer, Robert E. Lee, and the assistant adjutant general, Henry Lee Scott, were southerners. All graduated high in their West Point classes and demonstrated noticeable mental acuity therafter.

The officers assigned to Scott also represented various sections. He thought highly of northerners William J. Worth, Zebulon B. Tower, Robert Patterson, and George G. Meade. Scott also praised southerners Joseph E. Johnston and Pierre G. T. Beauregard, but he rated lowest David E. Twiggs of Georgia and Gideon J. Pillow of Tennessee. Interestingly, although Scott clashed with them in political outlooks as well, neither Twiggs nor Pillow were West Pointers.

On April 18, 1861, five companies of Pennsylvanians reached Washington, the vanguard of troops to defend the capital. On the same day Scott held a conference with another Virginian, his former engineer staff officer brevet Colonel Robert E. Lee, and offered him command of the Union army. In a way this was remarkable since some twenty officers outranked the Virginian. His recognized ability and recommendations by Scott, Secretary of War Simon Cameron, and the elder statesman, former editor of the *Congressional Globe*, Francis P. Blair, Sr., made Lee acceptable to Lincoln. But Lee declined, resigned his commission two days later, and within a week became major general in command of all of Virginia's military forces.

Robert E. Lee, born in 1807 to the famed Revolutionary War cavalry leader Henry ("Light Horse Harry") Lee, graduated second in the West Point class of 1829. His friend Charles Mason, who graduated first, did not pursue a career in the army, opting instead to become a teacher, lawyer, editor, and eminent civil servant. In 1831 Lee married Mary Custis, a relative of George Washington, and they eventually had seven children. All three of their sons served in the Confederate Army, two as major generals and one as a captain. Lee's U.S. Army duty primarily involved engineering projects, notably controlling the shifting sand bars of the Mississippi River near St. Louis and making coastal improvements in New York and Baltimore. Joining Scott's Mexican War staff on the recommendation of the chief engineer, Totten, Lee received three brevet promotions, emerging from the war a warm, personal friend and protégé of Scott. After a three-year tour as superintendent of West Point, in 1855 he accepted the lieutenant colonelcy of the newly organized Second Cavalry Regiment. In 1859, while on leave in Virginia, he drew the duty of conducting a detachment of marines to Harper's Ferry against the insurgent John Brown.

With Lee unavailable for the overall field command offered him by Scott, the Union continued with its departmental structure, modifying it with additional subdivisions as conditions seemed to warrant. Lincoln retained Scott and displayed much interest in military operations, introducing himself to the subject through reading Halleck's *Elements of Military Art and Science*. The President hardly could have avoided involvement, even had he wished, for he bore the constitutional responsibility for the appointment of general officers.

As the war began, the U.S. Army rolls included virtually no general officers fit for field duty. The swelling size of both armies forced Lincoln and Davis to elevate numerous individuals to that lofty martial status. In 1861 alone Lincoln named 126 generals and Davis commissioned eighty-nine. Often it is incorrectly stated that Lincoln made far more political appointments than Davis. Actually professional soldiers accounted for 65 percent of the generals Lincoln named in 1861, but only 50 percent of those chosen by Davis. The others, forty-four Union and forty-five Confederate generals, gained appointment for other reasons, often political.

Lincoln could select almost two-thirds of his general officers from among the ranks of the regulars because, contrary to the traditional supposition, he had three times as many as Davis from whom to choose. Yet Lincoln, without Davis's regular military background, must have been sorely tempted to give less recognition to military professionalism. His nation suffered from far more division than Davis's and the appointment of general officers constituted a valuable resource for the use of patronage in enlisting support for the war among the various political, ethnic, and other interest groups. With politics then so intimately involved in American life, and military glory then so sure a path to political preferment, both sides inevitably continued the institution of the political general.

In appointing generals Lincoln sought a broad base of support for the war, drawing appointees from the hard-core abolitionists, the high tariff advocates, the War Democrats, and the foreign-language immigrant groups. In 1861 he made generals of two Dutchmen, two Germans, a Hungarian, an Irishman, and a Pole. He named Democrat John A. McClernand a brigadier general simply to help hold southern Illinois to the Union. Yet, Lincoln also recognized the professional expertise of the regulars and appointed, proportionately, half again more career soldiers than did Davis, handicapped as Davis was by a far smaller number from whom to choose.

Quite importantly, however, most of the nonprofessionals on either side did possess significant military education and/or experience. In 1861 the North named sixteen generals with no military background at all and the South but seven. Lincoln made forty-four political appointments in 1861, seven of them West Pointers and one a graduate of the military academy in Karlsruhe, Germany. Davis chose forty-five political generals in 1861, including twenty graduates of West Point and three of the Virginia Military Institute. Among the others, eleven for the North and thirteen for the South had seen service in the Mexican War. One of Lincoln's generals had had twenty years of naval duty and one of Davis's, like himself, had served as U.S. secretary of war. Statistically, therefore, the South's nonprofessional generals as a group held *slightly* better qualifications than the North's: 12.7 percent of the Union's 1861 generals and 7.9 percent of the South's possessed no military credentials.

Two other factors stand out when comparing the North's and South's 1861 generals as groups. Sixteen of the North's professionals and seventeen of its nonprofessionals, 26 percent of the total, had significant prior experience in some aspect of business; twenty-five of the South's, or 28 percent, shared this quality, although seven of them were planters, work which did not necessarily compare with business in providing similar levels of managerial experience. This business expertise and managerial background among these first general officers had a great impact on the war. The other interesting factor is age. The average age of the Union generals appointed in 1861 was 38; the southerners averaged 47. This suggests that the initial southern commanders could be expected to be less physically robust and less flexible or innovative, but somewhat more seasoned and mature in judgment.

Both Presidents found an immediate command problem: deciding just whom among the general officers they should entrust with the critical field assignments. The answers were not obvious. Chance often entered and, to an extent, both Presidents followed lines of least resistance, allowing pragmatism to prevail where possible. Lincoln acted perhaps less selectively and cautiously than did Davis. People went in to ask Lincoln for appointments and their surface qualifications often prompted him to oblige.

Major Irvin McDowell provides a characteristic example. An assistant adjutant general in the regular army, in January, 1861, he assumed command over several hundred militia volunteers who garrisoned the Capitol each night. A protégé of Lincoln's secretary of the treasury, Salmon P. Chase, McDowell slipped by default into a commission as a brigadier general and command of the Department of Northeastern Virginia. Lincoln could have chosen a better-qualified man. Although McDowell was an 1834 graduate of West Point with further education in France, he had in twenty-three-years' service never commanded a unit of any size. His fellow Ohioan and West Point friend, the more experienced William T. Sherman, refused a similar appointment, and, preferring to work up to such a rank, accepted instead a colonelcy. Because he had been in California during the Mexican War, Sherman had missed the big actions and therefore felt yet unready for higher command. The two men met as McDowell walked down the steps of the White House wearing new stars on his shoulder straps.

"Hello, Sherman," McDowell said. "What did you ask for?"

"A colonelcy."

"What? You should have asked for a brigadier general's rank. You're just as fit for it as I am."

"I know it," Sherman retorted.[4]

Another federal area command, destined to be crucial, went to the experienced but superannuated Robert Patterson. Although he had served as a sometime militiaman and as an officer in both the War of 1812 and the Mexican War, Patterson had far more civilian experience than military. His career had embraced the grocery business, politics, and numerous industrial endeavors, in which he acquired interests in sugar and cotton plantations and eventually owned some thirty cotton mills in Pennsylvania. In addition he wrote well and kept a notable diary, published some years after his death. But, at age sixty-nine, he hardly measured up to the duty that now befell him, command of a substantial body of troops in the Shenandoah Valley.

The other initial important Union field commands went to Major General Benjamin F. Butler, a gifted politician with a militia background; Major General George B. McClellan, a professional who had left the service to become vice president of the Illinois Central Railroad; Brigadier General George Cadwallader, a Mexican War veteran; and Colonel Joseph K. F. Mansfield, a senior regular officer. Initially Butler headed the Department of Annapolis, later expanded to include all of critical Maryland, and eventually transferred to command Fort Monroe, the vital federal base in Virginia at Hampton Roads. Cadwallader replaced him in Maryland. Mansfield took charge of Washington's defenses. Young McClellan, only thirty-four-years old at this time and destined to be one of the Civil War's principal figures, oversaw the Department of the Ohio, comprising Ohio, Indiana, and Illinois.

He established headquarters in Cincinatti, which, with Kentucky still in the Union, certainly did not constitute a danger spot threatened by Confederate invasion.

On the southern side, Robert E. Lee initially headed only the Virginia state military establishment, and, when Virginia joined the Confederacy, he was eclipsed and temporarily not utilized. Meanwhile Colonel Thomas Jonathan Jackson, a mathematics professor at the Virginia Military Institute, took charge of Virginia troops around Harper's Ferry, where the Shenandoah River joined the Potomac. An important rail junction, Harper's Ferry also was the site of a former federal arsenal which John Brown had tried to capture two years earlier. Major General Joseph E. Johnston, former quartermaster general of the Union army, took command of the Virginia forces gathering in and around Richmond. Johnston eventually relieved Jackson and, as a full general in the Confederate army, took charge of the South's troops in the Shenandoah Valley, while the Confederacy's hero of Fort Sumter, Brigadier General Beauregard, transferred north to command "the Alexandria Line," which embraced all of the other southern troops in northern Virginia. Except for Professor Jackson, all of these men held regular army commissions at the outbreak of the war. All four had graduated from West Point and served in the Mexican War.

To protect western Virginia from intrusion from the north or west, the Confederacy sent Brigadier General Henry A. Wise, a former governor of Virginia, to take command of troops in the Kanawha Valley. Soon Brigadier General Robert S. Garnett, a professional with long experience, also arrived to relieve Colonel George A. Porterfield after that militiaman and Mexican War veteran had failed in an early small engagement. Far to the west, Brigadier General Henry Hopkins Sibley, ordered into Texas, assumed command of southern efforts to expel Union forces from New Mexico Territory, then claimed by the Confederacy. Even before secession, irregular forces had been gathering, posing as a buffalo hunt, but really aiming eventually to seize as much of the region as they could for the South. In the Indian country, the Confederacy's agent, Brigadier General Albert Pike, signed treaties with the Creek, Choctaw, and Chickasaw nations. Eventually the colorful and multi-talented, though militarily inept, Pike concluded nine such treaties.

During this formative period the Confederacy managed to add to its meagre Navy. Although only half the 600 southern naval officers resigned their U.S. commissions, there was an adequate number of Confederate naval officers, even though many of them took appointments in the army. They found that service attractive because they expected the war to be short, decided in a land engagement, and army promotions quicker than nautical ones. But Confederate Secretary of the Navy Stephen R. Mallory secured fully enough officers from the remaining veterans, having an excellent cadre in each rank.

Mallory, a senator from Florida before the Civil War and chairman of the naval affairs committee, managed remarkably with his limited resources. A man of unusual ability and force and long interested in shipbuilding and modernization, he realized far earlier than his northern counterpart, Gideon Welles, that the Civil War marked an era of naval transition. As long as fifty years before, no less than five great revolutions had begun affecting sea warfare: the use of steam, shell guns, the screw propeller, rifled ordnance, and armor. The Confederacy employed these creative innovations whenever its resources allowed, and also otherwise experimented, notably with mines, then called torpedoes, and submarines.

Mallory's innovative sea service early made some significant additions to the inventory of ships. On April 17 near Indianola, Texas, southerners captured the *Star of the West*, the ship involved in the abortive January incident to supply Fort Sumter. When the Union abandoned its Norfolk naval yards, the gleeful Confederates immediately moved in to raise and refloat four scuttled ships, including the U.S.S. *Merrimack*, renamed the C.S.S. *Virginia*, and to seize the ancient frigate *United States*. Equally if not more important to the South were the dry dock, the shops, and many of the one thousand restorable old guns found there. Early in May the Confederate Navy sent James D. Bullock to Britain to purchase ships and arms, a mission he ably carried out. On May 10 President Davis signed an act of Congress calling for purchase abroad of six warships, arms, and stores. But the naval event of the most importance to the South in 1861 occurred on June 30 when, below New Orleans, the C.S.S. *Sumter* under Captain Raphael Semmes ran the blockade and began a spectacular career as a commerce raider.

The Confederacy began to give some indication that it realized the magnitude of the struggle ahead. Southern women formed associations to make articles for hospital use. The army seized additional U.S. ordnance stores, and the Phoenix Iron Works at Gretna, Louisiana, began casting guns for the Confederate Navy, just as President Davis signed two important bills. One authorized him to accept into volunteer service such forces as he might deem expedient for the war's duration. The other sanctioned a loan of $50,000,000 and the issuance of treasury notes.

To the North, the federal Navy Department worked in haste to remedy its unreadiness. So many of its ninety vessels were in dire need of major repairs that only forty-two were in commission. Of these a mere six were available in northern ports, four were anchored at Pensacola, and one plied the Great Lakes, while all the rest sailed farflung over the globe from the Mediterranean to the East Indies. With no transoceanic cable yet in existence, one ship had to go after another to deliver word ordering its return. Essentially a deepwater navy quite ill-suited for the inland and coastal work ahead in the Civil War, one by one its ships commenced duty on blockading stations at major ports, as officials proceeded with dizzying speed to buy, build, and equip new vessels. By July 4, 1861, the secretary proudly reported eighty-two ships in commission, with the number increasing rapidly.

Meanwhile Abraham Lincoln continued conferences, reviewed troops, and, while he awaited the states' responses to his calls for militia, fretted plaintively, "Why don't they come! Why don't they come!" Though more U.S. troops surrendered, at Saluria, Texas, on April 25, not all news was bad. At St. Louis, Captain James H. Stokes, told to get arms for Illinois troops from the federal arsenal, secretly conducted a steamer from Alton and late at night landed at the St. Louis arsenal wharf. He and his men removed 10,000 muskets and other arms from under the noses of the secessionist elements in St. Louis and returned safely to Alton. Finally in Washington troops began arriving to relieve the tension and quell fear that the capital might fall easily. "Bayonets now replace buncombe," proclaimed the pompous spokesman of the Sixth Massachusetts Regiment. Wealthy citizens contributed money and, as an example, the firearms inventor, Samuel Colt, raised a regiment and provided the soldiers with his new revolving breech-loading rifles. Others responded admirably, and by early May citizens of the North already had contributed $23,277,000 to the war effort. In July President Lincoln approved a congressional authorization of a $250,000,000 loan.[5]

In other ways, too, the North was becoming more deeply committed to the war between the sections. Postmaster General Montgomery Blair ruled that postal ties with the southern states would end on May 31. A potentially more significant event occurred on May 23 when Major General Butler at Fort Monroe received the first three Negro slaves who fled into his lines and refused to give them up when southerners demanded their return, proclaiming them "contraband" of war. The whole issue of what to do about slaves within federal lines generated a great deal of correspondence and debate. Lincoln soon decided that refugees should be cared for and given work in federal military installations, only a step from the later measure of putting the able-bodied "contrabands" into uniforms.

The summer days of the early weeks of the war hummed actively with enlistment, drilling, equipping, distribution of troops, and all that goes into mobilizing for war. Presidents Lincoln and Davis lent moral support by often visiting camps, writing encouraging letters to governors, and carrying out morale-raising activities. The organization of nurses for the armies greatly affected morale. In the North Dorothea Dix, the social reformer, received sanction to establish hospitals and to supervise care for the sick and wounded. The North also created the U.S. Sanitary Commission, which eventually rendered quintessential service to the health and comfort of the federal soldiers.

In late June Lincoln showed his interest in weapons by watching experiments with rifled cannon and the "Coffee Mill," an early rapid-firing weapon, while Davis, who already knew a great deal about technical military matters, remained more reserved and businesslike. Like Lincoln, Davis was near the scene of active military operations. With the secession of Virginia and the movement of the southern capital to Richmond, the focus of the struggle shifted from Charleston to the land frontiers. Both sides made troop concentrations and deployments designed to defend their capital cities and possibly to attack the other's. For an overall plan, the South had merely to counteract anything the Union might do and thus could win by doing nothing, unless the Federals invaded.

Lieutenant General Scott focused his powerful intellect and vast experience on the North's infinitely complex strategic problem. He conceived "a powerful movement down the Mississippi" by a naval flotilla supported on land by 80,000 men in two "unequal columns," to begin in the late fall when the rivers rose. The smaller of the two columns would proceed by water, "the other column to proceed as nearly abreast as practicable by land—of course without the benefit of rail transportation—and receiving at certain points on the river its heavier articles of consumption from the freight boats of the first column. By this means the wagon train of the land" force could "be much diminished" but would still "constitute a great impediment to the movement." The two forces together would be able to "turn and capture" all of the rebel fortifications on the river. The general in chief feared, he stated, that "the impatience of our patriotic and loyal Union friends" would be too great for them to wait for the four and a half months of instruction for volunteers, for the rise of rivers, and for "the return of frosts to kill the malignant fevers below Memphis."

Designed to "clear out and keep open this great line of communication in connection with the strict blockade of the seaboard," the strategy thus aimed "to envelop the insurgent states and bring them to terms with less bloodshed than any other plan." Should this Mississippi River strategy fail, General Scott foresaw the necessity of conquering "the seceding states by invading armies. No doubt this might be done in two or three years . . . with 300,000 disciplined men, estimating a third for garrisons, and the loss of yet a greater number by skirmishes, sieges, battles and Southern fevers."

Except for underestimating by one-half the number of men and the time needed, the old general had provided a fairly accurate forecast of most of the difficulties encountered in the war and of most of the elements of the strategy ultimately used. Scott's proposal for a blockade and an advance down the Mississippi soon became known, initially among its ridiculing critics and then generally, as the "anaconda plan," aptly named after the serpent which squeezes its prey. At a special federal Cabinet meeting on June 29, with the leading generals in attendance to discuss future action, Scott urged implementing his proposal, while Brigadier General Irvin McDowell outlined his scheme for attacking the Confederates at Manassas. Fearing that the impatient public might lose enthusiasm with Scott's plan, as the lieutenant general himself predicted, the generals agreed that they should attend to the enemy in Virginia first.[6]

Though planning and preparations dominated the scene, minor actions which attracted a disproportionate share of public attention marked the early months of war. On April 19 shots rang out in turbulent Baltimore, killing at least four soldiers and nine civilians. On May 10 occurred the "battle" of St. Louis, where nearly thirty people died in a series of disjointed military and mob maneuvers which had the important result of stymying Confederate efforts to snatch eastern Missouri. Four days later, back in Virginia, Thomas J. Jackson captured a large number of coal trains at Harper's Ferry. The Federals had abandoned that crucial rail junction located at the confluence of the Potomac and the Shenandoah rivers, having burned the government armory there before they left. Nevertheless, the Confederates recovered much of the machinery intact. For several weeks, in order not to alienate the people of Maryland, the southerners had allowed the Baltimore & Ohio Railroad to continue moving through on the main line between Washington and the West. But in mid-May Jackson pulled his coup, sending many of the locomotives to Winchester and Strasburg, Virginia.

The first federal advance into Virginia began on May 24. As stealthily as the partially trained troops could move, they crossed the Potomac River and occupied Alexandria, encountering only minimal resistance. The federal troops captured one captain of militia and thirty-five of his comrades, who made a futile attempt to halt the three invading regiments. The Union thus secured an important foothold on Virginia soil.

The Federals lost their first officer in the war during this operation, the hyperactive and somewhat silly commander of the New York Fire Zouaves, Colonel Elmer Ellsworth. Accompanied by a few companions, near the center of Alexandria he saw a secession flag flying from a hotel, the Marshall House. Ellsworth rushed in to tear down the banner and received a fatal shotgun blast to the belly from the irate hotel proprietor, James Jackson. Both sides obtained martyrs when a federal private completed the tragic melodrama by killing Jackson. Poems, songs, and graphic drawings dramatizing the incident circulated widely. Washington plunged into a spasm of grief as Ellsworth's body lay in state at the White House, while the southern press proclaimed that poor "Jackson perished amid the pack of wolves."

Minor skirmishes erupted nearby at Arlington Mills and Fairfax Court House, Virginia, where federal cavalry entered and promptly withdrew. Due to the newness of the war, these insignificant affairs attracted more attention than they deserved. The first serious land engagement occurred in northwestern Virginia. There McClellan commanding troops in Ohio that had enlisted for only three months, and blocked on the south by neutral Kentucky, early assumed the offensive across the Ohio River into Virginia. Originally, McClellan had proposed to General Scott that he march from Ohio through western Virginia "to Richmond. In spite of difficulties in crossing the mountains," but moving "with the utmost promptness," McClellan felt that his advance "could not fail to relieve Washington as well as secure the destruction of the Southern Army, if aided by a decided advance on the eastern line."

After pointing out that McClellan's three-months troops would be discharged before they reached Richmond, General in Chief Scott disposed of the young general's plan by pointing out that McClellan had ignored logistics, an unforgivable omission for an experienced soldier turned railroad executive! McClellan's plan, Scott wrote, avoided the use of "water transportation by the Ohio and Mississippi in favor of long, tedious and breakdown (of men, horses, and wagons) marches." Scott added that "the transportation of men and all supplies by water is about a fifth of the land cost, besides the immense saving in time." He explained his anaconda plan to McClellan, who, apparently chastened, said he wished to "justify the good opinion" of the old soldier and show that Scott could "not only command armies himself, but teach others to do so." McClellan wrote Scott: I hope to be "no unworthy disciple of your school."[7]

Nevertheless, McClellan persisted with a less ambitious offensive into Virginia, which resulted in a battle at Philippi, Virginia. He perceived the area as especially important to Confederate integrity, since the western Virginia populace was pro-Union, eventually breaking away to become the new state of West Virginia. The area was of strategic importance to the Federals, who were concerned to keep open the Baltimore & Ohio Railroad line which ran through the northern part of the region.

On May 26, from his headquarters at Cincinnati, Major General McClellan ordered 3,000 troops into western Virginia. The main drive pushed toward the town of Grafton on the Baltimore & Ohio, which the Federals occupied on May 30 with a 1,600-man force under Colonel Benjamin F. Kelley. The other 1,400 men, under Colonel Ebenezer Dumont, took Webster several miles to the west. On June 2 the two columns departed by train from Grafton and Webster, expecting to converge at Philippi, Kelley from the south and Dumont from the north, to catch in a pincers the 800 southern recruits there under Confederate Colonel George A. Porterfield. Philippi is on the Tygard's Valley River in the hills of the Allegheny Plateau, something more than 200 miles west of Washington and 120 miles south of Pittsburgh, a curious stronghold of Confederate sentiment surrounded by a sea of Unionists.

The Federals planned their coordinated attack to begin on June 3 with a pistol-shot signal at dawn. In the cold rain which fell just before daylight, the undisciplined Confederate pickets retired to shelter, abandoning their duty to provide security. But a secessionist sympathizer, Mrs. Thomas Humphreys, saw Union troops dragging two cannon to the crest of Talbott Hill near her home and sent her young son on horseback to warn Porterfield. A Union outpost captured the boy while still in Mrs. Humphreys's view. She fired her pistol at the blue-clad soldiers and, although she mised, her shot set the attack prematurely in motion.

The Federals opened up with cannon, awakening the sleeping Confederates who exchanged a few shots with the advancing Federals. Then the southerners broke and began running to the south with such speed that cynical critics later dubbed the battle the "Races at Philippi." The recruits abandoned not only almost all of their equipment, but in some cases even their trousers. Dumont's troops stormed into the town, while Kelley's, arriving late, found themselves in the wrong position to block the escaping southerners. Kelley himself chased some of the retreating Confederates and became the only Union casualty, receiving a shot in the chest.

Only two Confederates sustained wounds, James E. Hanger and Fauntleroy Daingerfield, a VMI cadet. Both suffered injuries which led to amputation, the first such operations of the war. Daingerfield managed to get away with his comrades, but tragically the Confederate surgeon lost his medical kit in the retreat and had to remove the young man's leg with a butcher knife and a carpenter's saw. Hanger, with the better luck to be captured, was operated on by a Union surgeon, and, while recuperating at Philippi, improvised an artificial limb from barrel staves. It proved to be so good a piece of work that after his exchange Virginia officials commissioned him to manufacture artificial limbs for Confederate soldiers. It marked the beginning of an international artificial-limb business which still remains in operation.

Otherwise this small and relatively bloodless non-battle achieved significance for beginning a never-reversed Confederate retrograde in western Virginia and for simultaneously catapulting McClellan into national prominence. The following weeks did not disappoint news-hungry northerners in their thirst for more. The Federals continued their advance, with skirmishes on June 26 at Frankfort and on Patterson's Creek, and for several days in early July at Bellington and Laurel Hill with a full-day fight at Glenville. McClellan concentrated three brigades at Buckhannon and one at Philippi to move against the smaller forces now under Brigadier General Robert S. Garnett, who replaced Porterfield. The Confederates desperately tried to hold passes at Rich Mountain and Laurel Mountain and another hot fight ensued.

On July 10 four regiments of McClellan's men under the talented West Pointer, Brigadier General William S. Rosecrans, pressed doggedly forward at Rich Mountain. The next day Rosecrans's 2,000 men attacked the 1,300 Confederates under Lieutenant Colonel John Pegram. Marching over rough terrain, Rosecrans brilliantly turned Pegram's left, using an unguarded mountain path to get behind him and cut off his withdrawal to Beverly. On July 13 Pegram surrendered his 555 remaining men, while an undetermined number of his original 1,300 troops escaped. Rosecrans lost only twelve killed and forty-nine wounded and brought himself to the favorable attention of the public and his government.

Meanwhile Garnett, with the 4,000 remaining Confederates in western Virginia, retreated into the Cheat River Valley. Some Federals pursued, but for the most part McClellan's men systematically occupied nearby towns. On July 13 at Carrick's Ford the southerners met another defeat, losing an estimated twenty killed and some fifty wounded. In mid-July troops under Brigadier General Henry A. Wise blocked a further federal advance up the

Kanawha River Valley, an ephemeral achievement. In spite of a new Confederate commander, Robert E. Lee, Rosecrans's successful follow-up campaign in the Kanawha Valley permanently ended the last Confederate hopes for retaining western Virginia.

In another border area, Missouri, the Union also attained an even more important success. Under the skillful political leadership of Frank Blair, influential brother of Lincoln's Postmaster General, Unionists in Missouri organized, with Captain Nathaniel Lyon of the regular army supplying capable and energetic military direction. After being driven away from St. Louis, the secessionists under Governor Claiborne Jackson evacuated the capital, Jefferson City. On June 17 Lyon moved 1,700 men by boat up the Missouri River, landed below Boonville, the temporary Confederate state capital, advanced on the town, and captured the place, each side sustaining only light casualties. This serious secessionist loss helped the Union to retain control on the Missouri River and severely hindered Confederate efforts to secure the prosouthern part of Missouri north of the river.

While Lyon and McClellan were on the offensive, action flared in southeastern Virginia on June 10 when a strong federal force of seven regiments from Fort Monroe blundered through the night to attack Confederate positions at Big or Great Bethel, also known as Bethel Church. After an hour's hesitant and confused attack the Union troops retired, having engaged something over 2,500 men and lost eighteen killed, fifty-three wounded, and five missing. The Confederates engaged 1,200 with only one killed and seven wounded. Elated and encouraged by the engagement, southerners displayed trophies of the fight in Richmond store windows. Major George W. Randolph, commanding a Confederate artillery battalion, received much praise from his superiors, who marked him for advancement.

Near Washington, relative quiet prevailed in spite of the wording of a florid proclamation from Brigadier General Beauregard: "A reckless and unprincipled tyrant has invaded your soil," Beauregard announced; "Abraham Lincoln, regardless of all moral, legal, and constitutional restraints, has thrown his abolition hosts among you, . . . murdering and imprisoning your citizens, confiscating and destroying your property, and committing other acts of violence and outrage too shocking and revolting to humanity to be enumerated."[8]

Yet it was here in northern Virginia that the desire for decisive action ripened into a major offensive and a big battle at Bull Run. The first move in this campaign occurred when the Confederates under Joseph E. Johnston evacuated Harper's Ferry, falling back in the Shenandoah Valley to Bunker Hill, north of Winchester. Johnston feared that Patterson, north of him in the Valley, and McClellan, in western Virginia, might move their troops to catch his in a pincers. Patterson in turn cautiously began to feel his way forward.

The two aged warriors, Robert Patterson and Winfield Scott, argued over operations until finally on a bright summer day Patterson moved. The federal plan envisioned Patterson's marching deeper into the Shenandoah Valley to hold Johnston's troops there while the main Union army carried out a major attack toward Manassas. Meanwhile the Confederate leaders, equally aware of the interrelationship of the two lines of operations, conceived a comparable idea—to hold Patterson in the Valley and, at the critical moment, to shift Johnston's men eastward to join Beauregard's force for a quick offensive. Patterson pushed haltingly onward, engaging in small skirmishes, while Johnston fell back toward Winchester, never revealing what he might do and keeping his foe constantly on the alert for a counterattack. "Granny" Patterson, as his troops surreptitiously called him, said he would assault Johnston's emplacements if occasion presented itself, but gingerly he elected not to seek such an occasion. Meanwhile to the east, as a preliminary, federal troops carried out a land reconnaissance from Alexandria.

Of course Beauregard expected the impending Union advance. With all the preliminaries, how could he not? "Forward to Richmond! Forward to Richmond—the Rebel Congress must not be allowed to meet there on the 20th of July! By that date the place must be held by the national army!" For nearly a month the New York *Tribune* and other papers so cried. Earlier, Beauregard's chief of staff, Colonel Thomas Jordan, established a spy apparatus in Washington. He asked Mrs. Rose Greenhow, prominent capital society dowager and southern sympathizer, to send him information of important federal movements. She dispatched her first message early in July; a beautiful girl named Bettie Duvall, disguised as a country girl riding in a farm wagon to Virginia, carried it from Washington. Mrs. Greenhow predicted McDowell's advance on the sixteenth of July. Since, as T. Harry Williams put it, "at this time volunteer girl spies . . . were bursting into Beauregard's lines at every turn, all bearing news that the Yankees were coming," another messenger departed to confirm Mrs. Greenhow's intelligence. True enough, McDowell would leave Washington the night of the sixteenth. Beauregard received further assurance of her veracity when he read the same thing in the Washington newspapers the next day![9]

Advancing at the appointed hour, McDowell's army moved slowly and carefully from Fairfax Court House, taking a day and a half to cover the few miles to Centreville, where he established an advanced base of operations. Though neither side believed that their untrained troops were ready for a major battle, McDowell and Scott, in launching the offensive, bowed to public impatience and pressure from Lincoln. The northern President thought that superior Union numbers made it possible to win a decisive victory in the field at this early date. He believed that such a victory would produce general southern discouragement, possibly causing abandonment of the war.

This First Bull Run campaign contained many elements which would prove representative of the Civil War just beginning. Outside Washington, both the 30,000-man Union army of Brigadier General McDowell and the 20,000-man Confederate army, under Brigadier General Beauregard, were in touch with the same railroad. To the west, in the Shenandoah Valley, the 14,000-strong Union army of Major General Patterson drew its supplies from a spur of the Baltimore & Ohio Railroad. The opposing Confederate force, numbering 11,000 under General Joseph E. Johnston, stood only twenty miles from the railroad in his rear. Over that short distance wagons could easily bring the few supplies needed by such a small army, situated during early summer in the rich farming country of the valley of the Shenandoah River.

The Confederate pair of lines of operations were interior in relation to the Union pair because the two Confederate armies enjoyed somewhat better-connecting rail communication. Patterson and McDowell, linked only by the Baltimore & Ohio Railroad, could only reinforce each other by rail via the circuitous route through Baltimore. A short march by Johnston would bring his forces to the Manassas Gap Railroad, which ran directly to Beauregard's army.

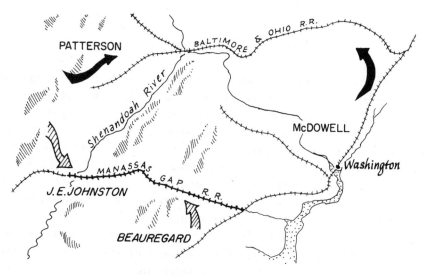

Confederate Interior Lines

Apprehensive about the possibility of the rapid union of Johnston's and Beauregard's troops, McDowell felt that he "could not undertake to meet all their forces together." The wisdom of the plan for McDowell's advance thus depended on whether "General J. E. Johnston is kept engaged by Major-General Patterson." Should Patterson fail to keep Johnston in the Valley, General Scott had assured McDowell that, "If Johnston joins Beauregard, he shall have Patterson on his heels." Patterson's performance would disappoint Scott.[10]

In his advance against Beauregard, McDowell did not intend to pit his army frontally against the Confederates, for his plan, approved by Scott, held true to the doctrine of the turning movement. McDowell proposed to send two of his five divisions to his right on a wide march to turn the Confederate left. Also planning to attack, Beauregard, apparently reflecting his apprehension that a turning movement conferred on the enemy the advantage of the central position, planned merely to advance his strengthened right wing directly against the Union left.

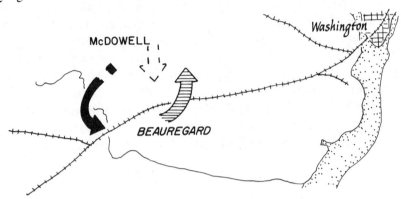

Planned Union Turning Movement

Beauregard and McDowell, both recently majors in the regular army, now had been elevated to the command of armies larger than those previously led by any American save George Washington, and McDowell's surpassed in size any under Washington. The two generals possessed a good theoretical understanding of the conduct of operations, but their lack of any experience in sizable command meant almost inevitably that they would perform ineptly. The subordinates on each side stood in an almost equally difficult situation. Even far more seasoned officers would have encountered insuperable obstacles with the raw troops composing the armies.

Also the primitive nature of the staff organization in the American army on the eve of the Civil War caused bungling and confusion. The modern staff basically constitutes the commander's management team, analyzing the situation, recommending action, and supervising personnel, intelligence, operations, and logistics. At the outbreak of the Civil War the U.S. army lagged far behind Prussia and France in conceptualizing and developing the staff. This weakness, particularly acute in the operations and intelligence area, naturally resulted in a serious lack of seasoned people to occupy staff positions. Officers drawn from civilian life possessed an even dimmer understanding of the functions of the staff and the difficulties of coordinating operations and logistics than did their regular-army-trained counterparts.

On the first night of McDowell's advance, an English journalist, William Howard Russell, encountered McDowell himself searching for two batteries of late-arriving artillery, and later penned: "I was surprised to find the General engaged on such duty, and took leave to say so. 'Well, it is quite true, Mr. Russell; but I am obliged to look after them myself, as I have so small a staff, and they are all engaged out with my headquarters.' " Russell contrasted this situation with that in the still-primitive British army where, he added, "the worst-served English general has always a young fellow or two about him who can fly across the country, draw a rough sketch map, ride like a foxhunter, and find something out about the enemy and their position, understand and convey orders, and obey them. I look about for these types in vain."[11]

The subordinate officers and enlisted men of both armies had come straight from civilian life, most with very rudimentary and all-too-brief training. Yet all of the disadvantages were mutual and each could expect his opponent to fight with a degree of incompetence equal to his own. Since both sides committed themselves to the offensive, the only initial advantage for either was the Union numerical superiority of three to two. This superiority disappeared when the Confederates not only made but successfully executed the proper decision. Aware on July 16 of McDowell's advance, Beauregard called for additional troops, and President Davis ordered both Brigadier General Theophilus H. Holmes from Aquia and Johnston from the Valley to reinforce Beauregard. Since the telegraph provided prompt communication, the unopposed Holmes joined Beauregard by July 19, and Johnston, sending cavalry under J. E. B. Stuart to distract and deceive Patterson, marched to the railroad and joined Beauregard with most of his army by July 20, the day before McDowell's attack.

The Confederates thus successfully employed their interior lines, while the Union plan to thwart this failed. On the 18th, even as Johnston moved eastward, Scott told Patterson: I have "been expecting you to beat the enemy. If not, to hear you had felt him strongly, or, at least, had occupied him by threats and demonstrations. . . . Has he not stolen a march and sent reinforcements toward Manassas Junction?" After first reporting Johnston's being reinforced, Patterson wired that Johnston was indeed moving east but that Patterson's army was withdrawing to the north bank of the Potomac. Two days after McDowell's defeat and the day after Scott had relieved him, Patterson wired Scott that he was moving toward McDowell "with all available force." Not only had Patterson not "engaged" or "occupied" Johnston, he had not even been "on his heels." His force would have been several days late and on the wrong side of the river.[12]

Meanwhile just before the battle McDowell's assemblage took on some curious additions. He invited newspaper correspondents to accompany the army and suggested to them "they should wear a white uniform, to indicate the purity of their character." Large numbers of other citizens and assorted dignitaries also helped themselves to what they considered an open invitation. Russell, the English journalist, perhaps prepared typically: "I swallowed a cup of tea and a morsel of bread, put the remainder of the tea into a bottle, got a flask of light Bordeaux, a bottle of water, a paper of sandwiches, and having replenished my small flask with brandy, stowed them all away in the bottom of the gig." War still struck many people as something of a picnic.

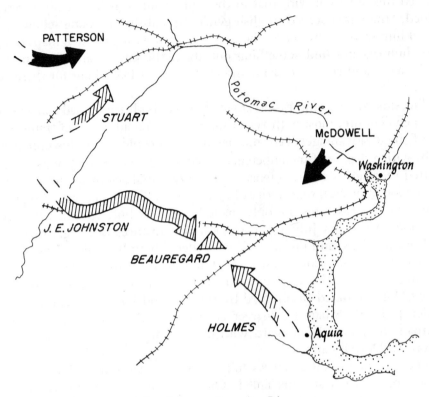

Confederate Interior Lines

But unexpected troubles commenced, at least for the soldiers, when Mc-Dowell "found the country on his left densely wooded and difficult. It [was] as new to him as it was to Braddock." Nevertheless McDowell did get his units into assault position on time.[13]

Poor staff work resulted in the delay of Beauregard's planned attack on his right; it had not begun when the well-conceived Union turning movement threw the southerners on the defensive. The Confederates, now commanded by Johnston, the senior officer, used Johnston's newly arrived troops, together with some of Beauregard's men and Kirby Smith's brigade, which arrived during the battle, to stop the Union attack. Moved from right to left as the battle developed, these Confederate troops resisted the Union turning movement by forming at right angles to the original Confederate line. Even the green men under green officers showed the ability to march in column on the battlefield, deploy promptly if raggedly, use their smoothbores and rifles to stop the assault, and ultimately outflank the attackers, precipitating a Union withdrawal.

Some Union units broke as rumors spread that the southerners were preparing to unleash the "Black Horse Cavalry." Fear of the unknown paled the volunteers of three months' service. Some real cavalry did make a few rallies,

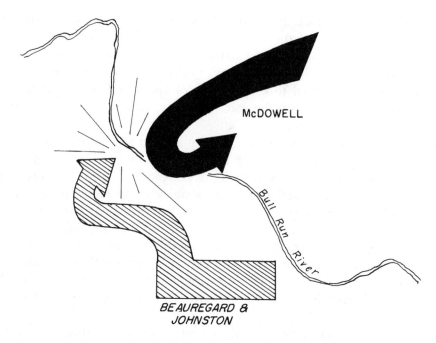

Union Turning Movement Outflanked

but the Confederates had only small numbers of mounted men. Despite an insignificant combat role, their psychological impact was potent. "I talked with those on all sides of me," Russell wrote. "Some uttered prodigious nonsense, describing batteries tier over tier, and ambuscades, and blood running knee deep." Probably the crowd of civilians panicked more than did the soldiers. "Once more the dreaded cry," as thousands began to stampede, "The cavalry! cavalry are coming!"[14]

One Ohio congressman, out for the expected festivities, described the spectacle that followed: "There was never anything like it for causeless, sheer, absolute, absurd cowardice, or rather panic, on this miserable earth before. Off they went, . . . anywhere, everywhere, to escape. . . . The further they ran the more frightened they grew. . . . To enable them better to run, they threw away their blankets, knapsacks, canteens, and finally muskets, cartridge-boxes, and everything else . . . a cruel, crazy, mad, hopeless panic possessed them." But this particular observer saw only a small portion of the total federal army, much of the remainder withdrawing in fairly commendable order.[15]

Save for the spectators, the campaign and Battle of First Bull Run were representative of many later operations. The Confederates, directed from Richmond, used the telegraph and the railroad to exploit interior lines and so effect a rapid concentration. In the battle itself both sides planned to attack the other with their right. In spite of achieving surprise, McDowell's well-conceived turning movement failed due to the defensive power possessed by nineteenth-century armies. Even though neither side was fully armed with rifles, the effectiveness of the infantry's weapons meant that there was no danger that a cavalry charge might actually overwhelm the infantry. Thus it proved unnecessary, as in earlier times, to deploy into a continuous front, heretofore always essential to keep cavalry or enemy infantry from getting through gaps in the line into the rear. The new, long-range firepower now covered the gaps in the line.

Since this firepower rendered a carefully aligned formation unnecessary, McDowell could move his turning force rapidly by road and engage the Confederate army before it could avoid, or be ready for, him. As soon as his men reached the scene of action, they went quickly into a loose linear formation and advanced, relying on their rifles rather than their bayonets. This would not have been as easy in the days before the rifle and before the creation of such maneuverable and easily controlled units as regiments, brigades, and divisions. In earlier times McDowell's men would have stopped at a distance, formed their line with great care, and advanced slowly across the fields, keeping their lines dressed so as to avoid the previously vulnerable gaps.

Yet this new power of more rapid movement and deployment which permitted McDowell to catch his opponent and force an engagement at an expected enemy disadvantage also enabled the Confederates to counter it. They could not avoid the battle but they too could move men speedily by road to the threatened point and also quickly deploy them into rough defensive lines with strong firepower. The defensive power of even green troops equipped with rifles permitted them to make a successful stand. One critical moment occurred when many Confederates did fall back, and only Colonel Thomas J. Jackson's Virginia brigade and Colonel Wade Hampton's South Carolina legion remained in line, waiting for the concluding onslaught. Here Brigadier General Barnard E. Bee made his final though quite dramatic contribution to the war. With all his field officers down, he personally rallied his brigade, shouting to them: "Look! There is Jackson standing like a stone wall! Rally behind the Virginians." He thus gave one of the Confederacy's most popular battle captains an immortal nickname, as well as providing the needed reformation of the troop lines. Bee paid a high price, for he took a fatal bullet in the abdomen.[16]

Whereas a century before, such an attack against flank and rear would have meant a Confederate disaster, the flexible formations and maneuverability which made McDowell's movement possible and compelled an engagement also enabled the Confederates to change their front, deploy, and successfully stop the attack. Equally significant was the condition of the defeated army; though momentarily in panic with many men fleeing precipitously with the spectators, it actually sustained only a little hurt by its defeat, withdrawing easily to the defenses of Washington. In retreat the Union army also demonstrated its mobility, covering in one night more distance than it had managed to cover in three days of southward marching the week before. No doubt many Union soldiers grew red-faced over the humorist Bill Arp's comment that "the Yankees remarked at Bull Run, 'these are the times that try men's soles.' " The victorious army, almost equally disorganized, could not immediately pursue. Though green troops led by amateurs showed that they panicked and disorganized easily, they also demonstrated their more enduring quality, great resistance to ultimate damage.[17]

The conventional idea that it is the proper and attainable objective for one army to annihilate the other in the open field has been attributed to the German military theoretician, Clausewitz, and became popular in the late nineteenth century. Though Clausewitz had not been translated into English at the time of the Civil War, his inspiration was not needed, for, in 216 B.C., Hannibal destroyed the Roman army at Cannae, making a battle of annihilation a military ideal ever since. But the annihilation of an army in the open field was an ideal rarely achieved in modern times. Even the flintlock musket and the bayonet of the late seventeenth century made infantry very strong defensively. The era of the French Revolution and Napoleon yielded armies with greatly improved maneuverability. Able to deploy quickly from march to battle formation and subdivided into corps and divisions, the armies of that period grew more able to execute, but also less vulnerable to, attacks against flanks or rear. These developments continued in the nineteenth century. Then not only did rifle fire drive cavalry from the battlefield, but infantry, which in the Civil War soon learned to protect itself with intrenchments, proved almost impregnable to frontal attack by other infantry, much less by cavalry. With the maneuverability and articulation enhanced by the organization of companies, regiments, brigades, divisions, and army corps, the mid-nineteenth-century, rifle-equipped army stood almost invulnerable to annihilation.

West Point had prepared these Civil War officers for this result of technological and tactical change. The teachings of Dennis Hart Mahan and the predilection ingrained by their engineering educations trained them to value field fortifications, now so much more important with the advent of the new firepower. In this respect they surged ahead of their European counterparts who, in stressing mobility, neglected the importance of field fortifications. Though their Mexican military experience occurred in a war without rifles, most Civil War officers seemed to understand the immense power of the defense. Perhaps their scientific educations predisposed them to appreciate the influence of technological change, as well as to understand that their classmates on the other side knew how to lay out and fortify defensive positions.

In understanding the power of the defense, American officers in this war proved far more perceptive than later high commands in Europe. In spite of the development of the machine gun and quick-firing artillery with improved shrapnel, European soldiers a half century later in World War I would have

great difficulty in understanding the by-then quite obvious and almost impregnable power of the defense. But most Union and Confederate leaders
already appreciated the real but less apparent tactical stalemate of their time,
and, realizing that there could be no big battles like Cannae, fashioned their
tactics and strategy accordingly.[18]

Why did the Confederates not pursue their vanquished foes to Washington
after the southern success at First Bull Run? Jefferson Davis arrived personally on the field and at about 11 P.M. on the night following the battle finally
got around to asking about such plans. "None have been made at all," was
the reply. Stonewall Jackson begged Davis to give him 10,000 fresh men,
adding "and I will be in Washington City tomorrow morning," but probably
more in delirium than seriousness. There were not 10,000 fresh men to be
found, and Jackson was suffering from a painful wound in the hand, which
one surgeon insisted required amputation of a finger. The careful and tender
care of Jackson's personal physician, Dr. Hunter Holmes McGuire, saved the
finger and prevented serious permanent impairment.[19]

Jackson, incidentally, waved his hand high in the air quite often—little
wonder that it attracted a bullet! Many persons thought that the stern, pious
Presbyterian assumed such posture to pray, while others maintained that he
used gestures to direct and control his men. He himself allowed that it was
due to his strange biological beliefs, that his body was "out of balance." He
raised one arm so the blood would flow down into his body and establish an
equilibrium. A modern physician attributes this habit and the other maladies
that Jackson complained of—incessant dyspepsia and inability to sit comfort-
ably except in a bolt upright position as Jackson thought with "his organs
held naturally one atop another"—most likely to a diaphragmatic hernia.[20]

General Johnston concluded, Beauregard and even Davis concurring, that
the battle had too disorganized the Confederate army to mount a rapid pursuit
in the gloom and rain which swept the area that night. The southerners'
solitary fresh brigade had moved to check on reports that a "strong unknown
force" seemed to be approaching from the extreme right. This menace turned
out to be merely the Confederate brigade under Brigadier General David R.
"Neighbor" Jones which had, in the confusion caused by incomplete orders,
crossed and recrossed Bull Run all day.

Much speculation exists among historians as to whether or not the Confederates could have captured Washington. Careful analysis of military realities—available Union reserves, gunboats on the Potomac River, and indeed
the unfordable river itself, as well as the condition of both the forces that
fought—indicates that they could not have done so. Yet the viewpoint expressed in 1954 by the distinguished and discerning historian, Clement Eaton, that "it seems from the vantage point of today that the bold course of
attempting to capture Washington should have been adopted" actually may be

timelessly correct. B. Franklin Cooling, another careful scholar, after probing the matter, more recently observed that "the Confederates did not actually have to march into Washington. They could have pushed McDowell's rear guard back against the Potomac, perhaps across the river, and simply occupied the heights of Arlington." Though hardly a pursuit nor posing any threat to Washington, such a move could have effected a siege and, "with well entrenched artillery and infantry, . . . held the Federal capital hostage with irreparable harm to the political, if not the military, efficacy of the Lincoln administration." An unimaginative Confederate decision saved the Federals from this.[21]

Otherwise the stalemate in Virginia, which First Bull Run confirmed, or at least established, continued until the spring of 1862, while both sides prepared their eastern armies for the renewal of active operations. Meanwhile dramatic success would reward Union efforts in the bigger spaces and more promising topography of the West.

1. Mary Boykin Chesnut, *A Diary from Dixie*, ed. Ben Ames Williams (Boston, 1949), 36.

2. McWhiney, *Southerners and Other Americans*, 72–82.

3. U.S. Grant, *Personal Memoirs of U.S. Grant*, ed. E. B. Long (Cleveland and New York, 1952), 17.

4. W. T. Sherman to John Sherman, May 24, 1861, *The Sherman Letters*, 122; Foote, *The Civil War*, I, 59.

5. Benjamin F. Cooling, *Symbol, Sword, and Shield: Defending Washington During the Civil War* (Hamden, Conn., 1975), 37.

6. Winfield Scott to George B. McClellan, May 3, 21, 1861, *O.R.*, LI, pt. 1, 369–70, 387; Scott to William H. Seward, Mar. 3, 1861, in Charles Winslow Elliott, *Winfield Scott: The Soldier and the Man* (New York, 1937), 698.

7. George B. McClellan to Scott, Apr. 27, 1861, *O.R.*, LI, pt. 1, 338–39; Scott's endorsement, May 2, 1861, *ibid*; McClellan to Scott, May 9, 1861, *ibid.*, 373.

8. Long, *Civil War, Day by Day*, 83.

9. *Ibid.*, 95; T. Harry Williams, *Beauregard*, 76–77.

10. Elliott, *Winfield Scott*, 728; Irvin McDowell to E. D. Townsend, June 24, *ca.* 24, 1861, *O.R.*, II, pt. 2, 718, 722.

11. William Howard Russell, *My Diary North and South*, originally published 1954, ed. Fletcher Pratt (Gloucester, Mass., 1969), 207–9.

12. Winfield Scott to Robert Patterson, July 18, 1861, *O.R.*, II, 168; Patterson to Townsend, July 19, 20, 23, 1863, *ibid.*, 171–72; Scott to N. P. Banks, July 22, 1861, *ibid.*, 172.

13. Russell, *Diary*, 208, 212, 217.

14. *Ibid.*, 226, 229.

15. J. G. Randall, *The Civil War and Reconstruction* (Boston, 1937), 275–76.

16. Lenoir Chambers, *Stonewall Jackson*, 2 vols. (New York, 1959), I, 377. See also: Douglas Southall Freeman, *Lee's Lieutenants*, 3 vols. (New York, 1942–44), I, 733–34.

17. Charles H. Smith, *Bill Arp: From the Uncivil War to Date* (Atlanta, 1903), 79.

18. John K. Mahan, "Civil War Infantry Assault Tactics," *Military Affairs* (Summer, 1961), 57–67.

19. Chambers, *Jackson*, I, 388–90.

20. Burke Davis, *Our Incredible Civil War* (New York, 1960), 78–79.

21. Clement Eaton, *A History of the Southern Confederacy* (New York, 1954), 153, our italics; Cooling, *Symbol, Sword, and Shield*, 60.

3 ☆ THE EMERGENCE OF HALLECK

Henry Wager Halleck

DO YOU KNOW, in this country, if you can get enough people to start a rumor about any man, he would be ruined?" So commented a federal general to the journalist William Howard Russell three days after the fight at Bull Run. "There are thousands of people," the general continued, "who this moment believe that McDowell, who never tasted anything stronger than a watermelon in all his life, was helplessly drunk at Bull's Run." President Lincoln may not have believed the rumor, but he surely wanted a replacement and, as soon as he ascertained the disaster beyond doubt, he telegraphed Major General George B. McClellan to come and take charge of the army.[1]

Lincoln further proceeded with a number of drastic steps. In one of the war's stranger ironies, he named McDowell to head a corps in McClellan's army, without consulting the new general. (McDowell later encountered difficulty in the field, particularly in August, 1862, at Second Bull Run, but nevertheless he stayed in the army. At the end of the Civil War, he commanded the Department of the Pacific. Then by the relentless process of peacetime seniority promotion, he achieved the rank of a regular army major general in 1872 and remained in service until retired in 1882.)

Much attention immediately focused upon Lincoln's new principal field commander, George Brinton McClellan. Rapid success characterized the early career of the thirty-four-year-old "Young Napoleon." Born in Philadelphia of well-to-do upper-middle-class parents, he graduated from the University of Pennsylvania preparatory school at fifteen and entered West Point two years before the regulation age. He finished second in the class of 1846, in time to serve during the Mexican War under Winfield Scott and with Robert E. Lee, Beauregard, and Ulysses S. Grant. Showing high promise, McClellan gained two brevet promotions. Later, when Secretary of War Jefferson Davis sent him and two other officers to Europe and to the Crimean War as observers, McClellan toured military posts, fortifications, and hospitals, and wrote an able report which added to his blossoming reputation. He also returned with plans for a new saddle, which the American army adopted as standard in 1856. The "McClellan saddle" must have been more his original creation than anything he had observed, for Russell wrote that it "is adapted to a man who cannot ride: if a squadron so mounted were to attempt a fence or ditch, half of them would be ruptured or spilled. The seat is a marvel to any European."[2]

Despite McClellan's varied duties and many accomplishments, he actually had done little to merit the high esteem and confidence he enjoyed. For three years he instructed at West Point, while adapting to American usage a French treatise on bayonet exercises. His various engineering tasks included exploring the sources of the Red River and surveying for possible transcontinental railroad routes. In 1856 he resigned his commission, having risen only to captain, to seek civilian employment. By the outbreak of the Civil War he had become president of the Ohio & Mississippi Railroad. Even Russell overestimated McClellan's combat experience, crediting him with "some skirmishes with bands of Confederates in western Virginia." When these took place, McClellan had been in Cincinnati.[3]

Winfield Scott would have preferred Henry Wager Halleck to McClellan. But "the cabinet, including the President," Scott wrote McClellan, has been "charmed with your activity, valor, and consequent success" in western Virginia. The opinion of the professionals well supported the choice; William T. Sherman thought him "a naturally superior man," who "had the finest opportunities in Mexico and Europe. Even his juniors admit his qualifications."

The elderly Scott and the young Napoleon, the two most important generals in the army at that time, quarreled, and relations between them grew increasingly abrasive. Finally Scott bowed to the inevitable and requested retirement effective November 1, 1861. Because Halleck's presence in Washington would give Scott "increased confidence in the safety of the Union," Scott hoped for his appointment as general in chief. But the same day that Scott retired, McClellan assumed that high post. "The sight of this morning was a lesson to me which I hope not soon to forget," McClellan wrote to his wife in describing Scott's departure on a train for New York. "It was a feeble old man scarce able to walk; hardly anyone there to see him off but his successor. Should I ever become vainglorious and ambitious, remind me of that spectacle."[4]

McClellan also retained command of the Army of the Potomac, really an impossible dual assignment. Nevertheless, Lincoln deemed McClellan ready for supreme command, the young man having already expressed broad strategic views to the president. McClellan's proposals exhibited Scott's influence, for, in addition to completing the conquest of Missouri, he advised "that a strong movement be made on the Mississippi." His ideas also showed the influence of Scott's lesson in logistics, for the movements of his own army were to "be so directed that water transportation can be availed of from point to point by means of the ocean and the rivers emptying into it." The influence of the Mexican War and of his Crimean War experience also emerged in his reliance upon "a strong naval force" to protect the seaborne communications of his projected offensive down the Atlantic coast, a movement intended to be coordinated with that down the Mississippi.

"It cannot be ignored," the former railroad executive further emphasized, "that the construction of railroads has introduced a new and very important element into war, by the great facilities thus given for concentrating at particular positions large masses of troops from remote sections, and by creating new strategic points and lines of operations." To cut an extremely important rebel railroad he recommended, as soon as Kentucky should be "cordially united with us," a movement "into Eastern Tennessee, for the purpose of assisting the Union men of that region and of seizing the railroads leading from Memphis to the East." Railroads, as well as water transportation, offered valuable routes of advance.

Though a proposed thrust from Kansas to western Texas revealed him not yet divested of all of his logistical naiveté, McClellan realistically assessed the situation, especially in his insisting on the necessity of very large forces "to crush a population sufficiently numerous, intelligent, and warlike to constitute a nation." Military reasons also made huge armies necessary because, as he said, "every mile we advance carries us farther from our base of operations and renders detachments necessary to cover our communications, while the enemy will be constantly concentrating as he falls back."[5]

But the new general in chief prescribed no immediate offensives, even though the fall season of dry weather brought an ideal campaigning time in the South. The steadily growing volunteer armies still mainly devoted most of their time to preparation, although already in the fiercely divided border state of Missouri action had preceded preparation. On August 10 a small federal army, 5,400 men under Brigadier General Nathaniel Lyon, attacked a much larger force, 11,000 Confederate effectives, near Springfield, Missouri. Some observers called this Battle of Wilson's Creek, between four and five hours of ferocious struggle, "the hardest ever on the American continent." One officer later termed it "one of the stubbornest and bloodiest battles of the war," and another thought it "the severest battle since Waterloo." The Confederates lost about 1,200 men and the Federals 1,300. Although the defenders killed Lyon and defeated his army in its attempt to charge them, Lyon still inflicted enough damage to force the Confederates to halt rather than move farther into Missouri as they had planned. The ultimate result kept Missouri technically in the Union; the southerners failed to move adequate numbers of troops into the state at this critical moment. Even so, the Confederates retained domination in the southwestern section, and continued a serious threat to Union control.[6]

Earlier, when Lincoln had sought nominations for brigadier general from political leaders in each state, Elihu B. Washburne, an influential congressman from Illinois, had nominated an obscure colonel named Ulysses S. Grant. Lincoln's decision to hazard a brigadier general's commission on Grant began bearing fruit immediately. On November 7, acting under Fremont's orders, Grant, with over 3,000 troops, steamed down the Mississippi River from Cairo, Illinois, with an escort of two makeshift, timberclad gunboats, the *Tyler* and the *Lexington*, hastily converted from river transports. Grant landed from the flotilla on the Missouri shore just north of the hamlet of Belmont, opposite the bluffs at Columbus, Kentucky, a key Confederate stronghold defended by heavy guns and a huge garrison. Grant's men advanced to Belmont and captured it, but retreated when Confederate Major General Leonidas Polk sent troops on boats from Columbus to counter them. Though only a large raid and reconnaissance, the battle produced high casualties: 607 Unionists and 641 of the 5,000 secessionists in action. Grant accomplished little, for he already knew what he could have learned, the great strength of Columbus; but the battle delighted Lincoln, who desperately desired action—any action. It also gave Grant and his men valuable experience.

Afterwards, officers from both sides participated in a series of meetings to decide various procedures, especially prisoner exchange. Light and friendly moods prevailed. At one of them, Confederate Brigadier General Benjamin F. Cheatham and Grant had a lively discussion of horse racing, which interested both of them. Cheatham playfully suggested that they go ashore and have a horse race to decide the war. Grant said that he wished they could, although of course he declined. One wonders how Lincoln might have reacted for, back in 1832, he had wrestled and lost to the captain of a rival militia company the right to decide which unit should be entitled to a choice campground.[7]

Grant had obtained his Cairo command in the first place by showing that he would fight, but no one sensed his real worth. Thirty-nine years old at the beginning of the war, he had resigned his captaincy in the U.S. Army in 1854 under something of a cloud. Grant had yet to stand out, for his career never surpassed the modest future forecast by his graduating from West Point in 1843 only twenty-first in a class of thirty-nine. His performance had not distinguished him, although he had exhibited competence and courage in his conduct on the march to Mexico City. A commendation, typical of those he won, and faint praise indeed, came from his regimental commander, who wrote that "lieutenant Grant . . . was usefully employed in his appropriate duties." At one point Grant managed to "capture" a group of Mexicans who already had surrendered to someone else.

Peacetime service thereafter and the routine duties of a quartermaster depressed Grant terribly. Inactivity and separation from his wife made duty on frontier posts more unbearable, and he resorted to heavy drinking. Increasingly disenchanted, he resigned. The desire to escape trial for charges of misconduct probably precipitated his resignation, even though, clearly innocent, he certainly could have won the case. When out of the army, he tried several jobs: farming, land speculation, shopkeeping—all unsuccessful ventures. "Forty Years of Failure" is what one biographer aptly titled an introductory chapter on Grant through 1861. Absolutely no one envisioned Grant as the ultramasculine, whiskered warrior that his image later suggested. Indeed, in youth he had the face of a girl and a high, soft voice.

Grant even encountered trouble getting a Civil War commission at all, for his old army acquaintance McClellan was too busy to talk to him, and his West Point comrade Nathaniel Lyon turned him down. Richard Yates, governor of Illinois, finally gave him command of a regiment. The riotous volunteer outfit, soon known as "Governor Yates' Hellions," scourged central Illinois with their drinking, fighting, and robbing of chicken roosts, until Grant rapidly turned them into a disciplined and effective force by his strict rule. Congressman Washburne, in whose district Grant resided, led the successful effort to secure Grant's reward, one of the four brigadierships allocated to the state. Grant then took over the Cairo naval base and army district, a part of Major General Halleck's command.[8]

The forty-six-year-old Halleck, one of the Civil War's key figures, had already demonstrated brilliant potential. At the age of sixteen he ran away from home to escape the drudgery of farmwork, attended Fairfield Academy, won election to Phi Beta Kappa at Union College, and compiled an outstanding record at West Point, graduating in 1839. He taught French at the Military Academy and then went to France to inspect harbors. Upon his return, Halleck wrote a *Report on the Means of National Defense*, a congressional publication which brought him an invitation to deliver a lecture series that soon appeared in print as his famous book, *Elements of Military Art and Science*. He well merited his nickname "Old Brains." Having already published a two-hundred-page book on the uses of asphalt, he earned appropriate recognition from his scholarly attainments: an A.M. from Union College in 1843, and in 1848 the offer of a professorship of engineering from Harvard. Halleck continued his scholarly interests throughout his life, publishing a compilation and translation of Spanish and Mexican mining law in 1859. His nine-hundred-page work on international law, published in 1861 and revised by others after his death, remained in print into the twentieth century.

Halleck's Mexican War assignment took him to California on a seven-month sea voyage with several fellow officers including William T. Sherman. His army duties involved practically no combat but included serving as secretary of state in California, chief of staff, and lieutenant governor of the Mexican city of Mazatlan, as well as a number of engineering assignments. Having already studied law, he resigned his commission in 1854 to become a highly successful lawyer and businessman, quickly amassing a substantial fortune, owning two railroads and a large quicksilver mine. He helped write the California constitution and by 1861 had become president of a railroad running from San Francisco to San Jose and a major general in the California militia. In August 1861 he accepted appointment as a major general in the regular army. People quite reasonably expected great things of him.

Strangely, considering his capabilities, many persons either disliked or felt uncomfortable about Halleck, because he lacked charisma and had an occasionally abrasive personality. His physique also belied his reputation, for, unlike the handsome McClellan, nothing of the classic soldierly image appeared in this paunchy, balding general. One observer commented disparagingly on his "flabby cheeks . . . slack-twisted figure and . . . slow and deliberate movements." His biographer says, "given to violent hating, and never cultivating close friendships, he inspired neither love, confidence, nor respect." A reporter summarized the opinion of unappreciative contemporaries, describing Halleck as a "cold, calculating owl," brooding, "in the shadows." Others noticed that when he spoke, his words were "few, pithy, and to the point." His mannerisms sometimes intimidated associates, especially the less efficient, who noted his "habit of looking at people with eyes wide open, staring, dull, fishy" and his stare which could "make all rogues tremble, and even honest men look about them to be sure they had not been up to some mischief."[9]

Halleck's department stretched westward from the Cumberland River and included that part of the still-disturbed and divided state of Missouri then held by Union arms. His predecessor, John C. Fremont, had seemed upon appointment to embody all of the virtues needed by a Civil War general: he had political availability and military expertise. As a regular army officer, Fremont gained such fame in the Mexican War and in exploring the West that he had been the first Republican nominee for president in 1856. Though his political credentials remained strong, he proved a disastrous failure as a military executive. His buoyant, even giddy, temperament was ill adapted for management, and, magnifying difficulties, he had surrounded himself with incompetents and built a complex and ineffective administration in Missouri. After this emphatic failure, Lincoln felt compelled to replace him with the prestigious Halleck.

Halleck initially faced the task of bringing order out of "chaos" in finance, supply, and organization, all left behind by Fremont. Under Halleck's new regime "fraudulent contracts were annulled; useless stipendiaries were dismissed; a colossal staff hierarchy, with more titles than brains, was disbanded; . . . the construction of fantastic fortifications was suspended; and in a few weeks order reigned in Missouri." Halleck then set to work to implement the directive of the new general in chief, McClellan, to consolidate the Union hold on Missouri and concentrate "the mass of the troops on or near the Mississippi" in preparation for future offensive operations.[10]

☆ ☆

Brigadier General Don Carlos Buell commanded the other major western department, centered in Unionist Kentucky east of the Cumberland. A respected and competent regular officer, the austere, methodical, and painfully conscientious Buell possessed the character and ability to make hard decisions. This led his superiors to expect him to become a good commander, but he lacked brilliance. Ordinary abilities, coupled with his systematic care for details and thoroughness, rendered him more suited to be a staff officer, which he had been for thirteen years before the war, in the adjutant general's department. Buell had a force half the size of Halleck's, and his instructions from the general in chief forecast serious military difficulties. McClellan wrote: "The military problem would be a simple one could it be entirely separated from political influences. Such is not the case. Were the population among which you are to operate wholly or generally hostile, it is probable that Nashville should be your first and principal objective point. It so happens that a large majority of the inhabitants of Eastern Tennessee are in favor of the Union."

McClellan thus exhibited his own as well as Lincoln's desire to integrate political and military strategy, which led him, in this case, to ignore the absence of water or rail communications directly from Kentucky to East Tennessee. The general in chief directed Buell: "Throw the mass of your forces by rapid marches . . . on Knoxville, in order to occupy the railroad at that point, and thus enable the loyal citizens of Eastern Tennessee to rise, while you at the same time cut off the rail-communication between Eastern Virginia and the Mississippi." This concern to break the East Tennessee and Virginia Railroad responded to McClellan's desire to prevent the rebels from countering his projected Virginia advance by shifting troops eastward over that railroad.

McClellan's instructions not only reflected his and Scott's earlier strategic thinking but harmonized with the emerging military thought of his civilian commander in chief. The President obviously gave considerable thought to the strategy of the war. Bringing his mature intelligence to bear on an unfamiliar subject, Lincoln soon exhibited an increasingly sophisticated and comprehensive view of the military problems facing the Union. The realization that the executive mansion stood within "hearing of cannon-shot" of the rebel armies oppressed Lincoln, but his perception of the strategy of the war reached far beyond Virginia. Wishing not only to implement "the plan for making the blockade effective" as well as to send an expedition against the rebel coastline, he also aimed at the pacification of Missouri and the conquest of East Tennessee. As had McClellan, in earlier ideas and in instructions to Buell, the President emphasized East Tennessee because of his concern for its loyal population and because there, he realized, the Union could "seize and hold a point on the Railroad connecting Virginia and Tennessee."

This concern with the railroad reflects the theme of Lincoln's thought during the fall: lines of operations. Unencumbered by a concern for a particular army or theatre of operations, the President easily approached the military strategy of the war on his high level of generalization. Yet this concern doubtless emanated from the bitter experience of summer. Defeated at Bull Run by the rebel use of interior lines, Lincoln and the Union leadership would be obsessed with this problem throughout the war. In groping for a solution, Lincoln at first perceived the corresponding movement as the answer. The rebel army before Washington, he said, could "make a half circle around Southward, and move on Louisville; but," the President proposed, "when they do we will make a half circle around Northward, and meet them."

Lincoln's projected, but not implemented, fall campaign also illustrates his emerging understanding of strategy in terms of lines of operations. His plan envisioned a landing on the Atlantic coast and a rapid concentration of troops from Ohio and Kentucky for a move on East Tennessee. Forces at Washington and in Missouri, he reasoned, would be able then to "avail themselves of any advantages which the diversions may present." By December, 1861, in proposing a primitive turning movement for the Army of the Potomac, Lincoln began to mature the notion of simultaneous advances, already implicit in his fall campaign. If two forces advanced, one probably would get through, for he believed it unlikely that both could "be successfully resisted at the same time." Presumably the enemy would exploit their interior position by concentrating against one of the two advancing forces; but it, "if pressed too hardly, should fight back slowly into the entrenchments behind."

Thus Lincoln commenced to understand strategy and, with the help of Scott, McClellan, and his reading, perceived its essence in the same way as did the soldiers and the students of military history. Though his thinking was on a higher level of generalization than McClellan's, he and the general in chief remained in fundamental agreement. They agreed upon the need for an early advance, but none of their generals felt ready to move. Halleck, absorbed with administrative reform and with the conquest and pacification of Missouri, displayed scant regard for a move on the Mississippi. McClellan, himself, as commander of the Army of the Potomac, wished more time for training, and Don Carlos Buell considered instructions to advance almost a nuisance. The Kentucky commander declared: I do "not mean to be diverted more than is absolutely necessary from what I regard as of the first importance—the organization of my forces, now little better than a mob." Deciding to launch no immediate advance, Buell devoted himself methodically to training and organization and attempting to build up to an adequate level his army's field transportation.[11]

On the Confederate side, President Davis provided a superior departmental organization for the West, with a unified command under General Albert Sidney Johnston. This department stretched from the Appalachian Moun-

tains west to include forces in Arkansas soon placed under Major General
Earl Van Dorn. The handsome and flirtatious Van Dorn sported an enviable
reputation. A native of Mississippi and a graduate of West Point, he served
in the Mexican War with considerable distinction and later engaged in various
encounters against Indians in the West. While in command in Texas, he had
personally led the capture of three U.S. steamships, including the famous
Star of the West, which made him an instant hero in the South and a pirate in
the North. Stanley Horn found that "a fire-eating northern newspaper offered
a reward of $5,000 for his head—a great honor, since the same" paper prom-
ised only $3,000 for the head of General Beauregard.[12]

The commander of this huge department, General Albert Sidney Johnston,
fifty-eight-years old and the darling of Confederate luminaries who devoutly
believed that he could bring victory, possessed sound credentials. Educated
first at Transylvania University, Jefferson Davis's alma mater, Johnston then
graduated from West Point in 1826, two years ahead of Davis. He served
eight years in the army, saw action in the Black Hawk War, and in 1836
joined the Texas revolutionary army, soon rising to be senior brigadier general and chief commander. He held office as secretary of war in the Republic
of Texas from 1838 to 1840 and stayed in the military service after Texas
joined the Union. While colonel of the important U.S. Second Cavalry,
Johnston led the Utah expedition against the Mormons in 1858 and won a
brevet to brigadier general. From 1858 to 1860 he commanded the Department of Utah and eventually took over the Department of the Pacific.

In the early stages of secession he resigned to accept appointment as the
second-ranking full general in the Confederate Army, being its senior field
commander for he stood junior only to sixty-three-year-old Samuel Cooper,
the adjutant and inspector general. Davis, who stayed steadfastly loyal to his
dear friend Johnston even in difficult times, later said, "If Sidney Johnston is
not a general, we had better give up the war for we have no general."[13]

Sidney Johnston accepted a mission to defend a vast frontier vulnerable to
invasion by four major routes. Three of these routes, along the Mississippi,
Tennessee, and Cumberland rivers, were the most likely avenues of approach
because they offered the opportunity for excellent and secure communications
to invading forces. The fourth, along the Louisville and Nashville Railroad,
connected with rail lines leading to Chattanooga and the lower South. The
Confederates also necessarily guarded the frontiers in Missouri and eastern
Kentucky, even though these did not constitute major routes of invasion
because no large army could move without rail or water communications.
With wagon transportation so inefficient, even superior roads, then virtually
nonexistent in the United States, could not long support an army very far
from water or rail transportation.

After the war General William T. Sherman compared wagon and rail
transportation by estimating the wagons required to replace the single-track
railway that delivered 160 cars a day supplying his 100,000 men and 35,000

animals during his advance to Atlanta in 1864. "To have delivered regularly that amount of food and forage by ordinary wagons would have required thirty-six thousand eight hundred wagons of six mules each, allowing each wagon to have hauled two tons twenty miles each day, a simple impossibility in roads such as then existed in that region of the country." Even discounting the problem of how long any road might last when traversed regularly by 36,000 heavily laden wagons or how to feed their 220,800 mules, he concluded: "Therefore, I reiterate that the Atlanta campaign was an impossibility without these railroads; and only then, because we had the men and means to maintain and defend them, in addition to what were necessary to overcome the enemy."[14]

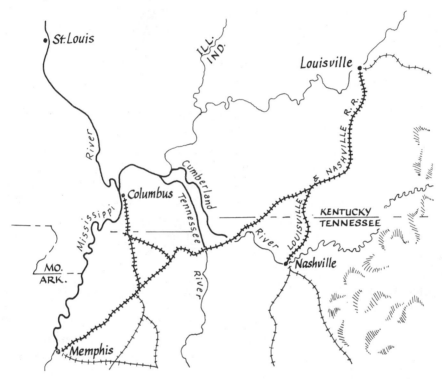

Johnston's Communications

Should the Confederates employ the excellent railroad connections in East Tennessee to base a strong defensive force there, by using these elementary logistical realities they would make it almost impossible for the Union to supply an army strong enough to defeat the defenders and occupy the region. The very railroad which made it an attractive objective rendered East Tennessee easy to defend. In Missouri the situation was reversed. The Union controlled the Missouri River and the railways radiating from St. Louis. South of these lay neither water nor rail communications for either army and both would have to live off the country. Nevertheless, the Confederates had placed strong forces in Arkansas and Missouri, despite their lack of promise as a route of invasion, not to resist invasion but to take advantage of sympathizers in Missouri to bring that state into the Confederacy. For a comparable reason, Union forces, also strong in Missouri, sought to complete northern control of the state.

Forts blocked each of the more promising river routes into the Confederacy, with guns commanding the waterways. At Columbus, Kentucky, by far the strongest of these fortified positions on the Mississippi, a powerful army complemented the formidable works. The Confederates posted troops strongly here because of both the commercial and historical importance of the Mississippi and Winfield Scott's well-advertised anaconda plan. About 12,000 men served in the garrison under the command of the Right Reverend/ Major General Leonidas Polk, Episcopal bishop as well as Confederate officer. Despite Polk's considerable fortifications and manpower, he remained very apprehensive because his position seemed such an obvious objective for the huge forces assembling under Halleck, headquartered up the river at St. Louis.

Polk's district also included the two defensive works which protected the line of the Tennessee and Cumberland rivers, Fort Henry on the former and Fort Donelson on the latter. In neither the strength of the forts nor in the size of their garrisons did these positions compare with the formidable position at Columbus. Furthermore, their construction lagged and both remained only partly complete at the end of 1861, the needed work on these neglected defenses proceeding very slowly. Polk assigned priority to the Mississippi defenses, overlooking these other important points in his district. Johnston, too, overlooked the forts in his intense concern with the approach to Nashville along the railroad from Louisville.

After his appointment as Confederate commander in the West, Johnston had the services of Brigadier General Simon Bolivar Buckner. Like many men, Buckner had experienced an agonizing choice in deciding between loyalty to the North or South. Despite all of the property he owned being in Kentucky and further North and that he had been offered a high rank in the U.S. Army, Buckner nevertheless opted for the Confederacy. Few men had been less selfishly motivated than he in siding with the South. After he chose the South, the press of the North vilified Buckner, and the courts later subjected him to unprecedented persecution: they confiscated his property and he lost a litigation for $62,000 to cover damages he did to the Louisville and Nashville Railroad while acting as a Confederate officer. Buckner demonstrated himself at least Beauregard's equal in rhetoric when he revealed his deep feelings in a proclamation to the people of Kentucky pressing them earnestly to secede, urging: "Join with me in expelling from our firesides the armies which an insane despotism sends amongst us to subjugate us to the iron rule of puritanical New England."[15]

On Johnston's order Buckner gathered every armed man he could find nearby, some 4,000, and moved with them from Nashville to Bowling Green. Eventually Major General William J. Hardee reinforced this position to a total of 25,000 men, blocking an invasion along the Louisville and Nashville Railroad. Brigadier General Felix K. Zollicoffer, a valiant, magnetic, and patriotic journalist and politician, otherwise quite unfit for command, took another 4,000 men to Cumberland Gap, a relatively secure position in the absence of any rail or water approach from Kentucky.

With these forces Johnston tried to hold the whole Tennessee-Kentucky border. His son wrote later in a bitter reminiscence that General Johnston "lacked nothing except men, munitions of war and the means of obtaining them." Many of the men had no arms save shotguns or fowling pieces. But General Johnston's rather substantial Confederate force, blessed with unity of command between the Appalachian Mountains and the Indian territory, enjoyed the advantage of interior lines of operations afforded by the excellent rail communications linking deployments in Kentucky and Tennessee. The Memphis and Ohio Railroad, running from Bowling Green, Kentucky, stretched past forts Henry and Donelson into West Tennessee, where it joined a railroad to Columbus. Offsetting these advantages, the Union possessed numerical superiority and good routes of advance, but a dual departmental structure hampered its conduct of operations. Whether or not the Confederates would derive benefits from their interior lines and single department would depend on the use made of the railroads by the department commander. The defense would be formidable if Sidney Johnston, the physically imposing and very experienced Confederate leader, lived up to his great reputation.[16]

Union dispositions east of the river corresponded to those of the Confederates. Buell located the bulk of his forces on the Louisville and Nashville Railroad north of Bowling Green with detachments in southeastern Kentucky, facing those of the distant Zollicoffer in Tennessee. Buell believed his army unprepared to move, but that mattered little, for he faced a three-horned dilemma. Urged by the general in chief to advance into East Tennessee, he knew that the only practical route for a truly powerful offensive ran over the railroad to Bowling Green and Nashville. Yet such an advance, relying on the railroad, was bound to be slow because the Confederates had "very much damaged it between the Green River and Bowling Green," leaving forty miles of difficult repair work.

A third route of advance offered the real choice. Buell became convinced that all the force that could "possibly be collected should be brought to bear on that front of which Columbus and Bowling Green" were "the flanks. The center, that is, the Cumberland and Tennessee where the railroad crosses them, is now the most vulnerable point." These rivers, he felt, constituted the "most important strategical point in the whole field of operations" because the possession of the Memphis and Ohio Railroad gave the Confederates interior lines, enabling them immediately to place "at least two-thirds of the whole" rebel force at "any one point that is threatened." If the Union could secure the rivers where the railroad crossed them, federal armies could defeat the rebels because of "access through the two rivers to the very center of their power." Yet this, the very desirable line of operations against forts Henry and Donelson, the enemy's "most vulnerable point," lay in Halleck's department and thus beyond Buell's reach. The Federals woefully lacked unity of command.[17]

So Buell pursued his organizing efforts and planned one campaign to turn the enemy position at Bowling Green and another into East Tennessee. He believed it essential that Halleck cooperate with his offensive by making a simultaneous demonstration on Columbus and sending riverborne expeditions up the Tennessee and Cumberland. After agreeing with Buell's plans for a strong move against Nashville and a weak one into East Tennessee, McClellan began efforts to secure Halleck's cooperation. Then, reversing himself when Lincoln stressed the importance of loyal East Tennessee citizens, the general in chief once again assigned primacy to the East Tennessee operation. "Simple feelings of humanity," he said, "dictated" the change: "We must preserve these noble fellows from harm." Furthermore, Tennessee politicians were "becoming frantic, and have President Lincoln's sympathy excited." Thus urging a thrust promptly into East Tennessee, he told Buell, "you have no idea of the political pressure brought to bear upon the Government for a forward movement."[18]

Yielding, Buell concentrated 14,000 men in southeastern Kentucky, giving the command to a capable regular officer, Brigadier General George H. Thomas. Here on January 19, 1862, Thomas's advance met the enemy, dug in on the north bank of the Cumberland River. Having advanced his 4,000 troops some seventy miles northwest of his original mountain position, the Confederate commander, Zollicoffer, had dug in near Beech Grove. Zollicoffer's immediate superior, Major General George B. Crittenden, a regular army veteran who had a brother and a cousin who were Union generals, had ordered that the Confederate force withdraw south of the river, but Zollicoffer delayed and Crittenden went out to take personal command. Upon arrival he discovered Thomas's advancing army of equal size, 4,000, and decided to defend the position. But then spurning the advantage of a static emplacement, he seized the initiative and sallied out in a driving rain to attack his attackers. At the height of the battle, Zollicoffer, brave to the point of rashness and conspicuous in a white rubber raincoat, rode far ahead of his troops and right up to the enemy. So nearsighted that he mistook a mounted federal officer for one of his own men, he rode up and proceeded to give him an order when the man fired at him point-blank and put a fatal bullet through his chest. The southerners soon withdrew, the first break in the Kentucky defense. Both sides sustained only slight losses; yet this small but significant battle demoralized Crittenden's force and presaged things to come in the West.

This Union victory, variously called Fishing Creek, Mill Springs, Somerset, Logan's Cross Roads, and Beech Grove, proved a potential source of embarrassment to Buell. Instead of opening the way for a winter advance to East Tennessee, Buell now faced a request from the victorious Thomas for his forces to move west to "cooperate with the main army against Bowling Green." Thomas cited supply difficulties as the reason, stating: "To procure forage it is necessary to send for it 15 miles, and the roads are so difficult that by the time the wagons reach here the teams have nearly consumed their loads."

This placed Buell in the position of explaining to McClellan why there could be no follow-up advance into East Tennessee. He maintained that over the 200-mile route to East Tennessee, food and forage for the wagon trains were "meager," and, "if they suffice for a trip or two," he added, "must by that time be entirely exhausted for any distance we can reach along both sides of the road." Because East Tennessee lay "almost entirely stripped of wheat by the enemy," it would, he reckoned, require "1,000 wagons constantly going to supply 10,000 men. We can judge the effect of that amount of hauling on the dirt roads of the country by the experience we have already had." To remedy this he had "five regiments now engaged in corduroying" part of the route, but it was too much work to be "undertaken on the whole route to East Tennessee."

Bad roads and no rail transport seemed like a lame excuse to Lincoln and those persons applying political pressure. With insight Buell remarked that people did not realize "armies with the appliances which are necessary to make them successful cannot move over dirt roads in the winter with quite as much facility as a man takes the cars at Washington and goes to Baltimore." Buell's problem afflicted both sides, for, at about the same time, Jefferson Davis remarked that the "public" had "no correct measure of military operations," and they, like the newspapers—"very reckless in their statements"—, measured the movements of an army "by the capacity of locomotion of an individual."[19]

As Buell was about to be crushed between the immovable object of intractable logistics and the irresistible force of a determined president pushed by an impatient public, the spectacular activity of his fellow department commander, Henry W. Halleck, rescued him.

Halleck's executive experience in California proved quite useful. His crisp, even tart, manner enabled him to dominate and yet to spur on subordinates despite his unprepossessing appearance and some eccentricities of manner. For example, his habit of scratching his elbows when in deep thought suggested to some observers that in these resided his vaunted brains. Invariably he began interviews with the question: "Have you any business with me?" When one officer replied, "I have a moment's," Halleck retorted, "Very well, Sir, a moment let it be." Halleck charted his own course since, except for directions to hold Missouri and prepare for future operations, he worked untrammeled by any instructions from the general in chief. Finding "complete chaos" in Missouri, the "troops unpaid; without clothing or arms," and the enemy "in possession of nearly one-half of the State," he immediately began redistributing his forces and concentrating those he deemed effective against the rebels in Missouri. His efforts broadly extended into finance, supply, and troop organization and elicited praise from even the enemy President: Jefferson Davis wryly announced that "the Federal forces are not hereafter, as heretofore, to be commanded by Pathfinders and holiday soldiers, but by men of military education and experience in war." Soon Halleck could report that the "machinery for the supply of the Army is rapidly getting into working order" and that he had good control over military operations in the state because the telegraph put him "in hourly communication with headquarters of divisions."[20]

General McClellan appreciated Halleck's problems and relieved him of the necessity of contributing troops to a projected expedition from Kansas to Texas. To the general in chief's request that he begin an offensive in Kentucky to aid Buell's planned advance, Halleck expressed sympathy but, in December, 1861, adamantly opposed the move. Halleck considered his force still only a "military rabble," destitute "of arms, organization and discipline." It is "madness to remove any of our troops" from Missouri, he said. Though "the 'On to Richmond' policy here," he added "will produce another Bull Run disaster," he promised McClellan that he would be ready to move in Tennessee by "the early part of February."[21]

Halleck's background prepared him well for the strategic as well as the logistical and administrative direction required of a department commander. After completing his *Elements of Military Art and Science*, he had steeped himself in Napoleon. During his Mexican War voyage to California via Cape Horn Halleck "undertook, partly as a military study and partly for the occupation of a mind not amused with trifles," the translation of Jomini's life of Napoleon. Though he completed the four-volume translation during the voyage, it was not published until 1864. On the basis of his profound knowledge of military history and theory and after "anxious inquiry and mature deliberation," Halleck arrived at an offensive strategy. His forces in southwest Missouri gradually pushed the rebels under Sterling Price out of the state. By early February, with this finished, the insurgents subdued elsewhere, and his troops armed, supplied, and at least partially trained, he planned to shift about 20,000 men from Missouri to the Kentucky line of operations.[22]

One night in late December or early January, Halleck sat talking with his chief of staff, George W. Cullum, and with his old friend from the Mexican

War, William T. Sherman. Sherman recalled that "General Halleck had a map on his table with a large pencil in his hand, and asked, 'where is the rebel line?' Cullum drew the pencil through Bowling Green, forts Donelson and Henry, and Columbus, Kentucky. 'That is their line,' said Halleck, 'Now where is the proper place to break it?' And either Cullum or I said, *'Naturally* the centre.' Halleck drew a line perpendicular to the other near its middle, and it coincided with the general course of the Tennessee River; and he said, 'That's the true line of operations.' "[23]

Like Buell Halleck correctly assessed his enemy's weakness on the Tennessee and Cumberland rivers and asserted that, though Columbus was "very strong," it could "be turned, paralyzed, and forced to surrender." This could be done by moving "up the Cumberland and Tennessee, making Nashville the first objective." Such an operation "would turn Columbus and force the abandonment of Bowling Green." With this his plan for early February, he hoped that the general in chief would send him large reinforcements to carry it out.[24]

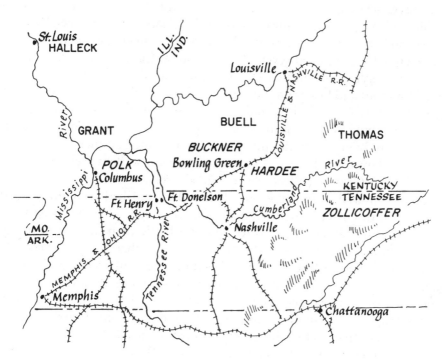

Situation Prior to the Henry-Donelson Campaign

Soon after Grant finished the demonstration, Halleck's offensive began prematurely, before he had completed his concentration at Paducah and Cairo and before he had secured additional troops or effected coordination with other departments. Halleck rushed into the offensive on the Tennessee immediately after he learned that Beauregard supposedly was coming from

Virginia to Kentucky with fifteen new southern regiments. Though the report later proved true only to the extent that Beauregard, himself, came, Halleck's offensive against forts Henry and Donelson thus began on January 30.[25]

Knowing the winter roads were in "horrible condition," Halleck planned to use the superior mobility conferred by water transportation. He laid plans to concentrate quickly, capture forts Henry and Donelson before the rebels could reinforce them, and break the Memphis and Ohio Railroad where it crossed the rivers, thus paralyzing Confederate mobility and depriving them of their interior lines. He instructed Grant to move by steamer up the river, land near Fort Henry, "and rapidly occupy the road to Dover and fully invest the place, so as to cut off the retreat of the garrison." Immediately after the Federals completed the investment, the railway bridges over the Tennessee and the Cumberland were to "be rendered impassable, but not destroyed," quickly before Beauregard arrived with the reinforcements.[26]

To support the water-borne move, Halleck had the full cooperation of a naval force, seven gunboats—four armored and three timberclad—under the capable leadership of Flag Officer Andrew H. Foote. The four metal-sheathed vessels had been constructed by the Eads shipbuilding company of St. Louis. Eads eventually completed seven of them, four at Carondelet, a suburb of St. Louis, and three at Mound City, a few miles up the Ohio from Cairo. All named for cities and towns on the Mississippi and Ohio rivers, the formidable 175-foot-long river craft drew only six feet of water and mounted thirteen guns. Their only major shortcoming, slowness, rendered them sometimes barely able to buck the swift currents. Two-and-one-half inches of iron protected their bows, machinery, and stern-mounted paddle wheels.[27]

In selecting Grant, Halleck chose a good executor for his enterprise and equipped him well; Grant not only believed in and had recommended the plan, he had discussed it with Halleck, and asserted: "There is no portion of our whole army better prepared to contest a battle than there is in my district." Commanding 15,000 men, "a larger force than General Scott ever commanded prior to [the] present difficulties," reinforced Grant's natural confidence. He promptly and energetically followed Halleck's orders to the letter. As soon as he landed, he sent half of his force to reach the rear of the fort, interrupt its communications, and entrap the 2,500-man garrison against the Tennessee River, which his seven gunboats controlled.[28]

Brigadier General Lloyd Tilghman, an 1836 West Point graduate whose only active duty had occurred during the Mexican War, commanded the Confederates. Understanding the peril presented by this threat to communications and believing his force far too small to attempt to stop or to drive Grant back, he withdrew his garrison before Grant's overwhelming force could entrap him. Even Tilghman's artillery chief thought Fort Henry "untenable," and that it "ought to be forthwith abandoned." Because of the rise in the river, it was, he observed, "surrounded by water, . . . cut off from the

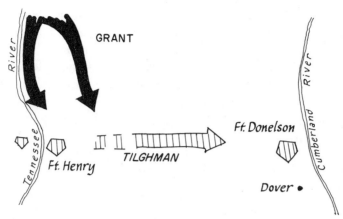

Tilghman's Withdrawal

support of the infantry, and . . . on the point of being submerged, [while]", he added, "our whole force [is] wholly inadequate to cope with that of the enemy, even if there had been no extraordinary rise in the river." Indeed, of the fort's nine riverside guns, only two, a rifled piece and a Columbiad, could damage the gunboats' armor. The only serious destruction that the Confederates managed to inflict upon the fleet resulted from one solid shot into the *Essex*. One of her boilers ruptured, killing several sailors and scalding the skipper, Commander William D. "Dirty Bill" Porter. The damaged ship quickly floated downriver and out of Confederate range. Later, when the crew told Porter of the white flag flying over Fort Henry, he struggled to raise himself on an elbow and called for three cheers. After only two he collapsed exhausted.[29]

Tilghman, after accompanying his fleeing men until he saw them well away, dramatically returned to share the fate of his remaining garrison of fifty-four men. He himself served as a gunner during the last artillery firing. The river meanwhile rose so high around the ill-situated fort that when a boat approached to receive the surrender, it floated right through the sally port. Over one-half of the fifty-nine hits Confederate artillery inflicted upon the Union gunboats during the entire attack landed on Commodore Foote's armored flagship *Cincinnati*. Later explaining why he did not concentrate more fire upon the three more vulnerable wooden vessels, Tilghman said he had hoped to get "the flag officer out of the way" and thus "disconcert the other boats."[30]

Grant promptly followed Halleck's instructions to break the Memphis and Ohio Railway bridge over the Tennessee and prepared to move his army swiftly eastward against Fort Donelson. Before and during the offensive Halleck remained apprehensive about what the enemy would do to exploit his interior lines, for an attack on "exterior lines against an enemy occupying a central position will fail, as it has always failed." He originally had objected that a force advancing on Columbus and another on Bowling Green would, because of the Confederate rail connections between them, "occupy precisely the same position in relation to each other and to the enemy as did the armies of McDowell and Patterson before the battle of Bull Run." Even with the Tennessee railway bridge cut and Fort Donelson about to fall, Halleck still feared that the secessionists at Bowling Green would use the railroad to reach Nashville, where the Cumberland River would afford them greater mobility. "An immense number of boats have been collected," he calculated, "and the whole Bowling Green force can come down in a day, attack Grant in the rear, and return to Nashville before Buell can get half way there."[31]

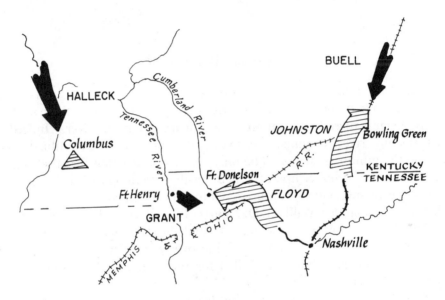

Confederate Interior Lines

Halleck's anxiety was ill founded. The southern leaders allowed themselves to lapse into a cordon defense with each of the separate detachments in the department committed to the defense of a particular point or locality. Instead of using the Cumberland River and the railroads to concentrate at a threatened point, each of the Confederate commanders thought only of his individual responsibilities. This state of mind infected the department commander, Albert Sidney Johnston, who not only had no plan for a coordinated defensive, but so focused his own attention on defending the Bowling Green line against Buell that he gave little consideration to the remainder of his department. A similar myopia afflicted the bishop/general, Polk, in whose district precariously nestled forts Henry and Donelson. Polk's fixation remained Columbus, and he determined not to weaken it.

Most significant, then, was the failure of the Confederate high command to perceive their separate detachments as part of a whole. Further, the forces west of the Mississippi, lacking rail connections with the remainder of the department, engaged in their own separate war.

On the other hand, the Union department commander used the rail net radiating south and west from St. Louis to concentrate his Missouri-based troops to bring large reinforcements rapidly to strengthen Grant's army. In shifting troops from Missouri to the Tennessee River, Halleck exploited that part of his transportation network which offered him interior lines, while the Confederates almost totally neglected their comparable advantages east of the Mississippi.

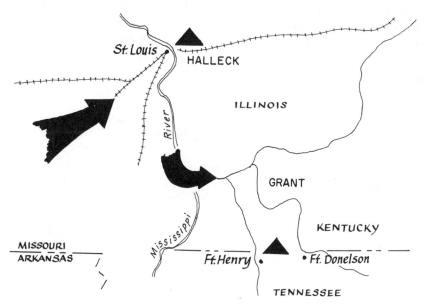

Halleck's Reinforcements

At his headquarters, with the army at Bowling Green, Johnston decided that, with the fall of Fort Henry, Fort Donelson would not be "long tenable," and "preparations should at once be made for the removal of this army to Nashville, in rear of the Cumberland River." In ordering most of the garrison at Columbus also to retreat, Johnston immediately and completely conceded Halleck's success in his aim of turning both of the department's principal Confederate positions.[32]

Yet while Johnston evacuated Bowling Green, he failed to concentrate at Nashville. Rather, the substantial forces previously deployed between Bowling Green and Fort Donelson ultimately concentrated at the fort. In this move, a curious one since he firmly believed that he only needed to keep the federal gunboats from passing the batteries at the fort, Johnston ironically sent thousands of infantry to Fort Donelson, a position vulnerable to entrapment against the river. The infantry could be of no use against gunboats.

Brigadier General John B. Floyd commanded the Donelson reinforcements, 12,000 men. A former governor of Virginia whose ignorance of military affairs had been little remedied by lackluster service as secretary of war in the late 1850s, Floyd proved indecisive and vacillating. He had not planned to move to Donelson, preferring instead to cover it by posting his forces to the south, on the flank of any army trying to invest the fort. Yet, when Johnston ordered him to Donelson, he adopted Johnson's view and concentrated his attention on the river.

Thus Johnston divided his army; he retreated with part of it to Nashville, while the other elements went to Fort Donelson to resist the passage of gunboats up the Cumberland. As Stanley Horn, one of the Army of Tennessee's distinguished historians, remarked scornfully, "Do history's pages record a similar picture of a commanding general marching leisurely off with a retreating column while nearby the great portion of the army girds for a life-and-death battle under inefficient and inexperienced underlings?"[33]

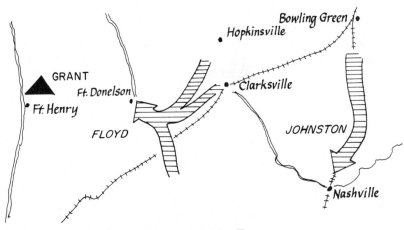

Johnston Divides Forces

Yet these half measures alarmed Halleck, who naturally believed Johnston likely to offer a more sensible and vigorous response. The Union general thought that the enemy would "attempt to regain his lost advantage" and strengthen Fort Donelson and counterattack at Fort Henry. Such a concentration threatened the flank of any Union advance, for, as Hallack explained, "The enemy would be certain to cut me off from my base." He calculated that the Confederates would take advantage of the Fort Donelson position because, in the military parlance of the day, it was a "flank position." In that position the Confederates threatened the communications of any Union advance south on the Tennessee while their own communications ran securely east and south along the Cumberland.[34]

Further, Halleck perceived greater danger from a counterattack because the federal forces were delayed. Grant originally expected to take Fort Donelson two days after the fall of Fort Henry, but he found himself slowed, "perfectly locked in by high water and bad roads and prevented from acting offensively." Snows followed by violent rain storms, he observed, "soaked the soft alluvial soil of the bottoms, until under the tread of the troops it speedily became reduced to the consistency of soft porridge of almost immeasurable depth, rendering marching very difficult for the infantry, and for the artillery almost impassable." Having initially expected a strong resistance and knowing that southern forces had left Bowling Green earlier, Halleck moved troops from as far away as southwest Missouri and asked Buell for a diversion. Every man he could "rake and scrape together from Missouri" concentrated in Tennessee, sent "without regard to the consequences of abandoning posts" in Missouri. If "the rebels rise," Halleck planned to "put them down afterwards." His appeals to Buell and McClellan secured a reinforcement of twelve regiments after he had, from his own resources, increased Grant's force from 15,000 to 23,000 men.[35]

Grant again proved himself a capable and energetic subordinate by making good use of Halleck's reinforcements, some of which came up the Tennessee, others up the Cumberland. A week after the fall of Fort Henry, Grant reached Donelson despite floods and bad roads. He outnumbered the Confederates under Floyd two to one.

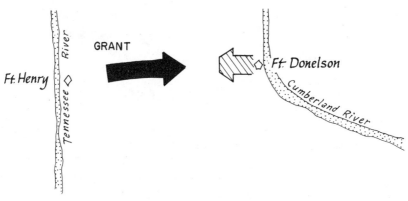

Grant's Flank Position

The inept Floyd elected to defend a position with a river at his back. The lack of a bridge rendered the Confederates susceptible to encirclement by the kind of energetic and competent opponent Grant proved to be. The Union general capitalized upon the situation by making an overland advance directly eastward from Fort Henry, thus putting himself on the flank of Floyd's line of communications. The Confederates, focusing their attention on their fort and its batteries, allowed Grant to reach them and make contact with the river both above and below the fort, cutting their communications and reestablishing his own direct link with the river system. Ironically, and inconsequentially in view of their predicament, the southern batteries drove back the gunboats, and the Confederates reported that they had won a victory. One Confederate regimental commander, Colonel Nathan Bedford Forrest, viewing the engagement purely as a spectator on the river bank, more perceptively assessed the situation. He turned to his deputy, Major D. C. Kelley, a former minister, and exclaimed, "Parson, for God's sake pray! Nothing but God Almighty can save that fort!"[36]

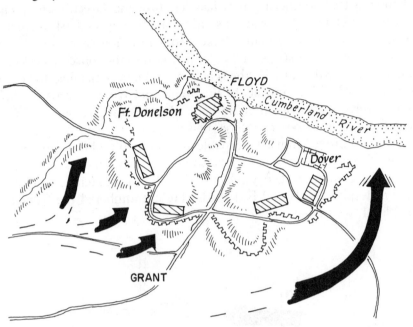

Floyd's Communications Cut

The Confederate higher commanders, at last dimly realizing their perilous situation, attempted to open a line of retreat almost as soon as the superior Union army formed its lines around them. Their delay and failure to meet Grant west of the fort deprived them of their previous advantage of standing on the tactical defensive. They now had to attack Grant in order to recover their lost communications, thus giving Grant the advantage of the tactical defensive. Nevertheless, concentrating most of the troops on the south flank, the secessionists succeeded in pushing back the Union army and opening a line of retreat to the south. Vacillating and inexperienced, Floyd failed to take advantage of this opportunity to extricate his army. Returning from a conference on a gunboat, Grant retained his composure, ordered a counterattack, again closed his lines around the fort, and soon obtained the garrison's surrender.

In the correspondence concerning surrender terms, Grant acquired another of many nicknames, and this time an immortal one. Floyd, fearing capture because he had once served as U.S. secretary of war, fled the fort and left the

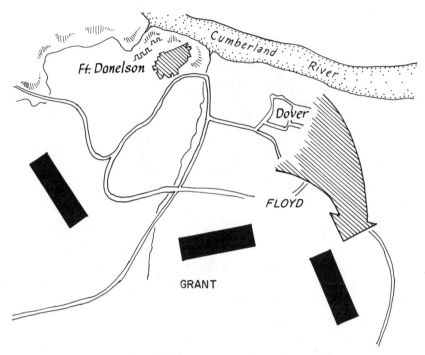

Floyd Reopens Communications

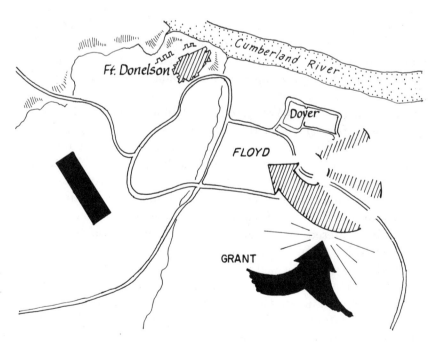

Grant's Counterattack

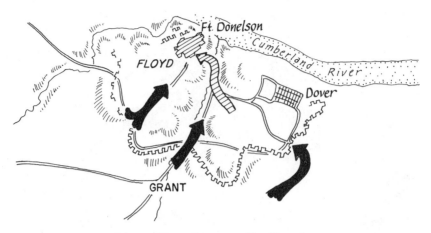

Grant Closes Lines on Ft. Donelson

negotiations to Brigadier General Buckner, who then proposed "the appointment of commissioners to agree upon terms of capitulation." Grant replied: "No terms except unconditional and immediate surrender can be accepted. I propose to move immediately upon your works." When news of these exchanges later spread around the country, northerners went wild with enthusiasm for "Unconditional Surrender" Grant. Only five feet one inch tall upon entering West Point, the grim little Illinoisan (christened Hiram Ulysses) previously had been called "Hug," coined from his real initials, or "Uncle Sam," because the beard he grew made him resemble the early versions of the cartooned American personification. Ironically, Major General Benjamin Butler the previous August, upon taking Fort Hatteras, North Carolina, had demanded "full capitulation. . . . No other terms admissible," but that episode and those words had not captured the popular imagination as did Grant's at Donelson.[37]

Tactically, the fighting at Fort Donelson demonstrated that by concentrating superior numbers at one part of a line, an attacker could push back an unintrenched enemy force. Grant's victory resulted from a sound maneuver, a successful execution of the one attempted at Fort Henry. The surrender of a major Confederate force, over one-fourth of Johnston's command, resulted from Grant's skillful exploitation of Floyd's blunder in holding a position with his communications running along his flank and with the river at his rear. The river offered an obstacle passable only by the slow process of ferrying, something Grant's energetic siege prevented.

Floyd had been sent to a bad position and faced a very difficult problem presented by Union naval superiority. If Federals could go up the river, they could immediately eliminate Confederate water traffic and not only destroy Floyd's communications, but break the Memphis and Ohio Railroad bridge not far behind him, a destruction which would have further fragmented Johnston's Confederate forces. Because the batteries of the fort blocked the river, Floyd committed his army to defending Fort Donelson, a position not only vulnerable but perilous. His troops, many of them just recovered from measles and suffering from frostbite, soon became exhausted because of their fighting and their many days of hard exposure.

The demoralized Confederate command surrendered without much effort to retreat, although Floyd and 3,000 or more troops, including his own Virginia brigade, did escape on the only available steamers. Colonel Forrest audaciously led his regiment through the backwaters with nearly every horse carrying double, an infantryman holding on behind each saddle. After escaping, Forrest personally investigated the numerous campfires which had been so important in convincing Floyd that enemy troops held all the nearby roads and found merely old campfires which had been started up again, mostly by wounded soldiers who dragged themselves up seeking warmth. Some Confederates also managed simply to walk through the enemy lines to safety. Even a brigadier general, Bushrod R. Johnson, who had not been reported or enrolled as a prisoner, took advantage of the situation and walked unchallenged through the federal lines.[38]

President Davis blamed Floyd specifically for the disaster and he never held another command; but much of the responsibility, even for the surrender, belonged to Sidney Johnston. Floyd faithfully followed Johnston's faulty gunboat-oriented instructions. Furthermore, Johnston committed a serious error in not sending a commander more capable than Floyd. In Major General William J. Hardee at Bowling Green, Johnston had available an experienced regular officer of solidly established reputation who might have had the good sense to deviate from instructions as conditions might warrant. Forty-six years of age, "Old Reliable" Hardee had graduated from West Point in 1838 and been in the Mexican War. Afterwards he served as commandant of cadets at the Military Academy and wrote the standard textbook, *Rifle and Light Infantry Tactics*, used in both armies by untrained company officers desperately trying to learn their new trade. Later, Hardee would have opportunities to show that he could live up to the promise of his already respectable career.

When Grant broke the railroad bridge over the Tennessee, Johnston lost some capability for bringing troops rapidly from the Mississippi for concentration at Donelson. Nevertheless, he could have taken advantage of the divided Union command and of Buell's quiescence on the Bowling Green line to move troops from Bowling Green by railroad and the Cumberland River. Halleck correctly believed that Johnston had little to fear from Buell, mired in the mud and stalled at broken railway bridges. Instead, Johnston withdrew on the Bowling Green line where no enemy advanced. He then compounded his blunders by sending an inadequate force under a more inadequate general to hold the critical position. Because of the efficiency and security of the Union lines of river communication and the great distance to which these rivers led into the Confederate rear, any failure to hold the lines of the Cumberland and the Tennessee would involve the loss of much of the rich and populous state of Tennessee. Johnston lost all of this and suffered disastrous defeat in the process, because sending Floyd with 12,000 men compromised between concentration and withdrawal.

The devastating failure of the compromise also forced evacuation of Nashville, a truly serious loss just in itself. With the exception of New Orleans, Nashville was the largest and most important city south of the Ohio River. Occupying a strategic position on the Cumberland River, Nashville had extensive rail connections, further enhanced by its giant arsenal, two powder mills and supply depot. A quickly constructed plant turned out 100,000 percussion caps per day. The Nashville Plow Works produced sabers, while other factories fashioned rifled guns using a precious machine made from plans obtained by a spy sent into a northern arsenal after the war had begun.[39]

With communications disrupted on the Tennessee and the Cumberland rivers, Johnston's command was separated into two halves, with Johnston himself retreating from Nashville southeastward along the railroad to north Alabama and Chattanooga. Johnston's retreat led him away from the Mississippi and the other half of his army. Buell, advancing along the rails from Louisville, occupied Nashville. Two Union forces, his and Grant's, stood between the two parts of Johnston's, the Middle Tennessee half under Johnston and the Mississippi River half under Beauregard who had just arrived and assumed jurisdiction over Polk and the West Tennessee forces.

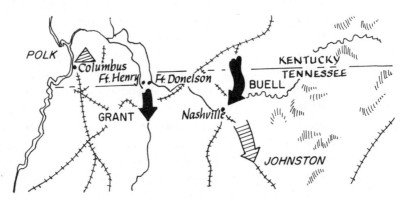

Union Interior Lines

"The brilliant results of the energetic action in the West fills the Nation with joy," the secretary of war wired Halleck. When news of the success spread around St. Louis, the city plunged into a frenzied celebration, and Halleck right along with it. He posted the news on an outside bulletin board and sat vigorously puffing a cigar while the crowd gathered. "Palmer," the well-to-do Halleck called out to a nearby clerk, "send up two dozen baskets of champagne, and open them here for the benefit of the crowd. . . . And I want you to give public notice that I shall suspect the loyalty of any male resident of St. Louis who can be found sober enough to walk or speak within the next half hour." After a bit more revelry, the satisfied Halleck returned to his habitual long hours of work and concentrated on future plans.[40]

On March 11, after making several requests, Halleck received enlarged and unified command in the West. His new Department of the Mississippi now stretched westward from a north-south line drawn through Knoxville, Tennessee. Further, recognizing the good work in the West, Lincoln also raised six men to the rank of major general, three of them upon Halleck's express recommendation: Grant, Buell, and John Pope, and other western generals, John McClernand, C. F. Smith, and Lew Wallace.

Halleck obviously excelled at what he was doing, for he was an extraordinarily able military manager whose business and administrative experience stood him in good stead as he brought order and efficiency to the St. Louis headquarters, organized and dispatched troops, and provided well-equipped, well-supplied fighting forces. But equally he was the historian in command, applying his study of military history and science to derive the strategy upon which he based his orders for the movement of substantial military forces over vast areas of the West. In using the telegraph to provide emphatic direction to the movements of a half dozen forces throughout his department, Halleck displayed an unallayed assurance that the conclusions from his study of history provided a certain guide for his confident decisions. His knowledge enabled him to excel in making war on the map. He intelligently concentrated his forces first in Missouri and then on the Tennessee and Cumberland rivers, the line of operations where the enemy was weakest and the fruits of success most promising. With Buell now placed under his command, Halleck would have a wider scope for the exercise of his talents, and the nation could look forward to more energetic action and brilliant results. Halleck's significant accomplishments in the West appeared still more impressive by comparison with the even more politically sensitive theatre in Virginia, where a Confederate army remained almost within cannon shot of the nation's capital.

1. Russell, *Diary*, 245.

2. *Ibid.*, 240.

3. *Ibid.*, 236.

4. Elliott, *Winfield Scott*, 733; Scott to Simon Cameron, Oct. 4, 1861, *O.R.*, LI, pt. 1, 492–93; Sherman to John Sherman, May 20, 1861, *The Sherman Letters*, 121; George B. McClellan, *McClellan's Own Story* (New York, 1887), 173.

5. McClellan to Lincoln, Aug. 4, 1861, *O.R.*, V, 6–8.

6. Stanley F. Horn, *The Army of Tennessee* (Indianapolis, 1941), 28; Edwin C. Bearss, *The Battle of Wilson's Creek* (Bozeman, Mont., 1975) 41–42, 44–47, 78–79, 97–98, 127–28, 134–37.

7. Horn, *Army of Tennessee*, 66; Harry Edward Pratt, *Lincoln, 1809–1839* (Springfield, Ill., 1941), 12; Thomas Lawrence Connelly, *Army of the Heartland* (Baton Rouge, 1967), 103–4.

8. Lloyd Lewis, *Captain Sam Grant* (Boston, 1950), 236; Bruce Catton, *U.S. Grant and the American Military Tradition* (New York, 1954), 43, 50; William B. Hesseltine, *Ulysses S. Grant, Politician* (New York, 1935), Chapter 1.

9. Stephen E. Ambrose, *Halleck: Lincoln's Chief*

of Staff (Baton Rouge, 1962), 9–10; George W. Cullum, "Biographical Sketch of Major-Gen. Henry W. Halleck," Sir Sherston Baker, *Halleck's International Law*, 3rd ed., 2 vols. (London, 1893), I, ix–xxi. The titles of Halleck's other prewar works were: *Bitumen: Its Varieties, Properties and Uses* (Washington, 1841), 200 pp; *Collection of Mining Laws of Spain and Mexico* (San Francisco, 1859), 650 pp; *International Law or Rules Regulating the Intercourse of States in Peace and War* (New York and San Francisco, 1861), 900 pp.

10. Cullum, "Halleck," xiii; McClellan to Halleck, Nov. 11, 1861, *O.R.*, V, 37–38.

11. McClellan to Buell, Nov. 7, 1861, Jan. 6, 13, 1862, *O.R.*, V, 36, VII, 531, 546; Lincoln to Oliver P. Morton, Sept. 29, 1861, *The Collected Works of Abraham Lincoln*, ed. Roy P. Basler, 8 vols., (New Brunswick, N.J., 1953), IV, 541–42; Lincoln to McClellan, Dec. 1, 1861, *ibid.*, V, 34–35; Lincoln Memoranda, July 23, 27, *ca.* Oct. 1, 1861, *ibid.*, IV, 457–58, 544–45; Buell to McClellan, Dec. 8, 1861, *O.R.*, VII, 483.

12. Horn, *Army of Tennessee*, 35.

13. *Ibid.*, 105; Connelly, *Army of the Heartland*, 60–61.

14. William T. Sherman, *Personal Memoirs of General W. T. Sherman*, 2 vols. (New York, 1890), II, 399. Though wagons, with the aid of good roads, could feed the soldiers of an army over a considerable distance, the animals could not be fed because they consumed five to ten times as much as men. The men could be fed only if fodder for the animals could be obtained along the route, for, even on good roads, carrying fodder reduced the practical radius of wagon supply to less than 100 miles. An army 100 miles from rail or water transportation would find its wagons unable to deliver as much as one ounce of cargo unless fodder could be supplied along the route.

An army far smaller than Sherman's could have received essentials by wagon because the animals of a smaller number of wagons could be fed along the route and a smaller number of wagons would not so quickly wear out the road. This would be true because a smaller army with less cavalry and fewer draft animals would not have to haul fodder, since its animals could live off the country. Even the infantry, if it were safe to disperse them, could live off the country also, especially if there were plenty of corn and potatoes which, unlike wheat, did not require milling and baking to be eaten.

This had been the time-honored method of supply when the army was small enough and the region in which it was operating was rich enough agriculturally. This could also be done by a large army, but very briefly. A large army not on the move would quickly exhaust local supplies. If the army could spread out over a large area, it could feed its men and animals for a much longer period, but it could only disperse enough if no enemy threatened it. When dispersed enough to feed, the army was quite vulnerable to defeat piecemeal. Thus such dispersal could be used only in winter quarters when the weather made campaigning impossible. Of course, even an army dispersed over the countryside would still need a supply line from which to draw munitions, replacement equipment, and provisions, such as coffee, not indigenous to the area.

For an army on the move the situation was different; it would come into untouched territory constantly reaching new sources of fodder and subsistence. For this reason raiders, because they were on the move and their occupation was temporary, would not require communications at all, whereas a permanent occupation would necessarily require open water or rail communication lines. Nevertheless an army which lived off the country could not both forage and fight. To forage it must disperse and keep moving but must concentrate and, often, wait to fight. A raiding army which lived off the country cannot, therefore, do more than raid for, lacking supplies, it cannot cope with a patient and persistent defender who possesses a line of communications. It must soon terminate its raid by withdrawal or by a successful attack against the enemy army in its chosen position. Greater population density usually implied greater agricultural production. Since, compared to Europe, the South was very thinly populated, Civil War armies had far greater logistical problems than armies of comparable size in Europe. The devotion of crop land to cotton and tobacco intensified this problem. See John G. Moore, "Mobility and Strategy in the Civil War," *Military Affairs* (Summer, 1960), 68–77.

15. Arndt M. Stickles, *Simon Bolivar Buckner* (Chapel Hill, N. C., 1940), 86; Horn, *Army of Tennessee*, 437n3: Connelly, *Army of the Heartland*, 53–54, 200.

16. William Preston Johnston, "Albert Sidney Johnston at Shiloh," *Battles and Leaders of the Civil War*, eds. R. U. Johnson and C. C. Buel, 4 vols. (New York, 1887–88), I, 542.

17. Buell to McClellan, Feb. 5, 1862, Dec. 29, 1861, Nov. 27, 1861, Dec. 10, 1861, *O.R.*, VII, 936–37, 520–21, 450–52, 487–88.

18. Buell to McClellan, Nov. 27, Dec. 3, 10, 1861, *O.R.*, VII, 450–54, 468, 487–88; McClellan to Buell, Nov. 29, Dec. 3, 29, 1861, Jan. 13, 1862, *ibid.*, 457–58, 468, 520, 547.

19. George H. Thomas to Buell, Jan. 23, 1863, *O.R.*, VII, 564; Buell to McClellan, Feb. 1, 15, 1863, *ibid.*, 931–33, 939; Davis to A. S. Johnston, Mar. 12, 1862, *ibid.*, 257.

20. Halleck to McClellan, Nov. 27, Dec. 6, 19, 1861, *O.R.*, VIII, 382, 408, 448–49; Ambrose, *Halleck*, 13–14.

21. McClellan to Halleck, Dec. 10, 1862, *O.R.*, VIII, 419; Halleck to McClellan, Dec. 6 (two communications), 26, 1861, *ibid.*, 408–10, 462–63.

22. Cullum, "Halleck," x; W. T. Sherman, *Personal Memoirs of General W. T. Sherman*, 2 vols. (New York, 1904), I, 206–7. All future references will be to the 1890 edition cited earlier.

23. Sherman, *Memoirs* (1890), I, 248.

24. Halleck to McClellan, Jan. 20, 1862, *O.R.*, VIII, 509–11; Halleck to Grant, Jan. 22, 1862, *ibid.*, VII, 561–62; Halleck to C. F. Smith, Jan. 24, 1862, *ibid.*, 930.

25. McClellan to Halleck, Jan. 29, 1862, *O.R.*, VII, 571; Halleck to Grant, Jan. 30, Feb. 6, 1862, *ibid.*, 121; Halleck to McClellan, Jan. 30, 1862, *ibid.*, 571–72; Halleck to Buell, Feb. 7, 1862, *ibid.*, 593.

26. Halleck to McClellan, Jan. 30, 1862, *O.R.*, VII, 571–72; Halleck to Buell, Jan. 30, Feb. 1, 1862, *ibid.*, 574, 576; Halleck to Lincoln, Jan. 6, 1862, *ibid.*, 532–33; Halleck to Grant, Jan. 30, Feb. 1, 1862, *ibid.*, 121–22, 577.

27. Bern Anderson, *By Sea and by River: The Naval History of the Civil War* (New York, 1962), 87.

28. Grant to Mary Grant, Jan. 23, 1862, *Papers of Grant*, IV, 96.

29. Report of Milton H. Haynes, Mar. 22, 1862, *O.R.*, VII, 145; Horn, *Army of Tennessee*,

82–83; Edwin C. Bearss, *The Fall of Fort Henry* (Dover, Tenn., 1963), 21–22.

30. Bearss, *The Fall of Fort Henry*, 22.

31. Halleck's written instructions did not include orders to advance against Donelson, but this was Halleck's intent, perhaps communicated orally on Grant's visit to St. Louis (Grant to J. C. Kelton, Feb. 6, 1862, *Papers of Grant*, IV, 155–57; Halleck to McClellan, Jan. 20, 30, *O.R.*, VIII, 509–11, *ibid.*, VII, 571–72; Halleck to Buell, Jan. 30, Feb. 2, 6, *ibid.*, 574, 568, 588); Halleck to Lincoln, Jan. 6, 1862, *ibid.*, 533; Halleck to McClellan, Feb. 10, 1862, *ibid.*, 599.

32. Beauregard Memorandum, Feb. 7, 1862, *O.R.*, VII, 861–62.

33. Horn, *Army of Tennessee*, 87.

34. Halleck to Buell, Feb. 7, 1862, *O.R.*, VII, 592; Halleck to McClellan, Feb. 8, 1862, *ibid.*, 594. See also Halleck to McClellan, Feb. 7, 10, *ibid.*, 591–92, 599.

35. Grant to George W. Cullum, Feb. 8, 1862, *Papers of Grant*, IV, 171; Bearss, *Fort Henry*, 28–29; Buell to Halleck, Feb. 3, 1862, *O.R.*, VII, 580; Halleck to Buell, Feb. 2, 5, 1862, *ibid.*, 579, 583; Halleck to Grant, Jan. 31, 1862, *ibid.*, 576; Halleck to McClellan, Feb. 7, 1862, *ibid.*, 591; Halleck to Buell, Feb. 7, 1862, *ibid.*, 593; Halleck to McClellan, Feb. 5, 1862, *ibid.*, 583–84; Buell to Halleck, Feb. 6, 1862, *ibid.*, 588; McClellan to Halleck, Feb. 6, 1862, *ibid.*, 587; Halleck to Buell, Feb. 7, 1862, *ibid.*, 593.

36. John Wyeth, *Life of Gen. Nathan Bedford Forrest* (New York, 1899), 47.

37. S. B. Buckner to Grant, Feb. 16, 1862, *O.R.*, VII, 160; Grant to Buckner, Feb. 16, 1862, *ibid.*, 161. Articles of Capitulation, Aug. 29, 1861, *Official Records of the Union and Confederate Navies in the War of the Rebellion*, 30 vols. (Washington, 1894–1922), VI, 120.

38. Horn, *Army of Tennessee*, 96, 44n22; Connelly, *Army of the Heartland*, 120–25.

39. Horn, *Army of Tennessee*, 75.

40. Edwin M. Stanton to Halleck, Feb. 21, 1862, *O.R.*, VII, 648; Ambrose, *Halleck*, 33.

4 ☆ LINCOLN AND McCLELLAN

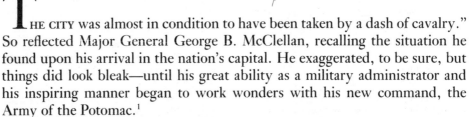

George B. McClellan

The CITY was almost in condition to have been taken by a dash of cavalry." So reflected Major General George B. McClellan, recalling the situation he found upon his arrival in the nation's capital. He exaggerated, to be sure, but things did look bleak—until his great ability as a military administrator and his inspiring manner began to work wonders with his new command, the Army of the Potomac.[1]

McClellan had an aura that drew men to him. Admirers said he was the only general who by merely riding up could induce enlisted men to leave their breakfasts and follow him. He stood five feet eight inches, and possessed tremendous shoulders and a chest that measured forty-five inches, a statistic which gave him immense pride. "Squarely-built, thick-throated, broad-chested," Russell thought, "with slightly-bowed legs" and "eyes deep and anxious-looking." The troops loved their charismatic general, the President confided in him and "Georged" him, the press fawned upon him, and people trusted him. "Just now," Russell believed, "that Americans must ride in his saddle, or in anything he likes."[2]

Lincoln and McClellan shared comparable ideas on the strategy to be pursued in the West, but they would disagree on the proper moves for McClellan's own army. Though absorbed with the problems, primarily political, of rallying and organizing the nation for a struggle to preserve the Union, the President wished to learn about military affairs. Lincoln proved an apt pupil and McClellan a poor teacher. But, while sometimes arrogant, McClellan not only disdained to confide in the civilian leaders, he patronized them. "I can't tell you," McClellan soon wrote to his wife, "how disgusted I am becoming with these wretched politicians."[3]

Though they definitely did not make a team, Lincoln learned fast in spite of McClellan's failure as a teacher. They also remained separated by McClellan's professional disgust with the chaotic volunteer armies, officered by rank amateurs often elected by their men. Although Lincoln asserted that the enemy shared the same predicament, he with the professionals felt impelled to wait until they could convert into trained soldiers the civilians who filled the army and issue them at least a minimum of essential accoutrements. In the fall of 1861, 11 percent of the regiments around Washington possessed no overcoats and 8 percent lacked even trousers—men frequently going on duty or on parade in their drawers alone! To the exasperation of Lincoln and the political leaders, the favorable fall season waned with only preparation and training, not campaigning.[4]

With a few exceptions, the remainder of 1861 passed quietly as each side concentrated on its mobilization. Like many officers trying to mold green troops into soldiers, Major General Butler at Fort Monroe, Virginia, grimly recognized the need to instill stiffer discipline and so banned the sale of intoxicating liquors to the troops. But the frolicsome fellows quickly found ways of evading the order. A problem emerged when pickets who left for guard duty began returning drunk. Puzzled officers could find no source for the liquor until one observant subaltern noticed that, when the men left, they carried their rifles at an unusually vertical angle. They were going out to their posts with the gun barrels full of liquid. The half-inch-diameter bore held nearly a pint! Butler tried to induce the men to give up alcoholic drink voluntarily and even struggled with abstinence himself, a sacrifice not only above and beyond the call of duty, but also beyond his ability. Other hiding places included hair oil bottles; gin drinkers no doubt substituted their potion for the more usual contents of rubbing alcohol bottles, if they used and could secure supplies of that new, clear antiseptic. At least the general's inspectors managed to find and eliminate some of the intoxicants. Nevertheless alcoholism emerged early as a major Civil War problem and remained for the duration.[5]

Smallpox, measles, or other epidemic diseases occasionally ravaged the ranks, somewhat less so among the slightly more urban northern troops than among southerners, but severely on both sides. Vaccination, like all still-primitive medical science and hygiene, depended largely upon the sophistication and enlightenment of any particular regiment's surgeon. Liquor, often the most available anesthesia, supplemented chloroform and together they provided relief from pain. Alcohol became the most important and typically obtainable supply item around the hospital tents. The escape and release that alcoholic drink offers for boredom, tension, or fear attracted many pilferers. McClellan found in good hard work, including drilling, target practice, and construction, a principal ally to deter disease as well as to decrease loitering around the tents.

The hard-training Federals received a blow to their pride on October 21, 1861, in the Battle of Ball's Bluff. The brave but tactically inept Colonel Edward D. Baker, senator from Oregon and friend of Lincoln, commanded the Union forces, who were engaged in "a slight demonstration" against the enemy. While pushing his troops into Virginia, Baker, with his brigade, was ambushed by Confederates commanded by Colonel Nathan G. "Shanks" Evans. Evans, who had rendered good service at Bull Run, had been the first to detect McDowell's turning movement. Here the victorious Confederates

lost only 155 men; the defeated Federals, 921, including their eminent colonel, and others who drowned in the Potomac as they tried to escape. The
defeat, militarily insignificant, embarrassed Lincoln politically, especially in
view of the public prominence of the senator/colonel who lost his life. This
tragic fiasco substituted poorly for an advance by the formidable army mater-
ializing on the banks of the Potomac. Yet significantly it caused McClellan
concern about his chain of command and convinced him of his army's unreadiness for an advance during the fine dry weather of the fall. He believed he
must delay any advance until the spring, after the mud of the winter rains
had dried.

Minor skirmishes continued almost everywhere. In the only significant
ground actions the Federals captured, on August 27–28, forts Hatteras and
Clark on the North Carolina coast. Then, on the same day that Grant assailed
Belmont, Missouri, November 7, 1861, the Navy seized Port Royal, South
Carolina, on the Atlantic coast between Savannah and Charleston. Besides
providing propaganda and morale value, these accomplishments, together
with the capture early in 1862 of several islands just off the Atlantic coast,
furnished bases for the blockading squadron and potential points of departure
for inland raiding parties. These first steps toward closing Confederate ports
by capture rather than blockade heralded implementation of a major feature
of Scott's anaconda plan.

Meanwhile, McClellan pondered the problem of taking the offensive with
the fine army he was building. Only a few miles from Washington stood Joe
Johnston's well-dug-in Confederates blocking the path to Richmond. When
two forces thus face each other, the military problem much resembles the
situation in checkers when each side possesses only one piece, a king. Since
each army, like each king in this game, offered essentially the same capabilities, neither adversary could obtain an advantage over the other if each maintained reasonable vigilance. Whatever the goal of the attackers—to assail the
enemy force, to acquire territory, or to capture a politically and logistically
important city like Richmond—the military problem remains the same. If
both the attacking and defending combatants desire a battle, then one will
occur, usually where and when the defending force chooses and with the
defender enjoying the advantage. If the defender does not care to fight, he
can retreat or intrench so that the attacker has no hope of success except by
employing superior numbers, if he has them, to threaten the defender's flanks
and force a retreat, a slow process.

The classic solution to this problem was the turning movement, by which
the attacking army, or a major part of it, passed around the flank of the
opposing force. Practiced by Napoleon, taught by Jomini, and frequently
applied by Scott and Taylor in Mexico, it provided the obvious answer to the
problem of the Union advance. A turning movement could be used to threaten
something vital in the enemy's rear, usually his communications, to force his
withdrawal. If the turning army could move with sufficient speed or

surprise, it could reach the adversary's rear before he could retreat, forcing the defender to attack in order to recover communications. Such a highly successful turning movement would confer on the turning force the quite significant advantage of a fight on the tactical defensive against an enemy without communications and forced to attack. This successful strategy of Napoleon led to his famous defensive victory at Marengo and to the capture of a part of an Austrian army in the Ulm campaign.

Such a turning movement would have a far greater chance of success if it were what may be termed a *penetration*, that is, an advance along a line of communications fully capable of supplying the attacking army. A penetration, which permits a long-term, essentially permanent occupation of territory, may be distinguished from a raid, which involves only transitory possession. A turning movement by a penetration offers obvious advantages over a raid, for the attacker would be able to supply himself while the defender, with his communications cut, could not. In this situation the defender must either attack or extricate himself by retreat over a roundabout route. On the other hand, if the attacker reaches the defender's communications by a raid, then neither of them would possess a line of communications and eventually the raiding attacker would have to leave the defender's communications. In this case the defender's situation would be determined by whether he had enough supplies on hand to afford to wait until a lack of supplies forced the attacker to leave. If the attacker could remain longer on the defender's communications than the defender could subsist from supplies on hand, the attacker would have created the same situation as if he had made a penetration. Even if the defender possessed ample supplies, he might feel impelled to attack to recover his communications because he was uncertain of the real situation, suffered from exaggerated apprehensions, was motivated by feelings of pique, conceived it necessary to regain lost prestige, or was compelled to act by public opinion. In these cases also the effect of a raid resembled exactly that of a penetration.

Such considerations entered into the thinking of McClellan and his staff as they discussed plans for the offensive. Yet he communicated little of this to his civilian superiors, for the vain McClellan had held an inflated opinion of himself from the beginning and, unfortunately, instead of instructing his civilian superiors and convincing them of his true capability, he continued to hold aloof. "I am becoming daily more disgusted with this administration—perfectly sick of it," he impatiently declared. "If I could with honor resign I would quit the whole concern to-morrow; but so long as I can be of any real use to the nation in its trouble I will make the sacrifice." He hated humoring the militarily uneducated political establishment: "Yesterday, after a long ride, I was obliged to attend a meeting of the cabinet at eight P.M., and was bored and annoyed. There are some of the greatest geese in the cabinet I have ever seen—enough to tax the patience of Job."[6]

McClellan was then quite insensitive to the need to interpret himself and military realities to politicians. Nothing better illustrates his arrogance than an occurrence in the fall of 1861 during one of Lincoln's frequent visits to his headquarters. Young John Hay, one of Lincoln's secretaries and later well known as Lincoln's biographer and McKinley's and Theodore Roosevelt's capable secretary of state, told the story. According to Hay the President and the secretary of state went to McClellan's house in the evening, and, finding him out, waited an hour for his return. On his return McClellan "came in and, without paying any particular attention to the porter who told him the President was waiting to see him, went up stairs, passing the door of the room where the President and Secretary of State were seated." After waiting a half hour for McClellan to come down to see them, the President and the secretary sent "a servant to tell the General they were there, and the answer cooly came that the General had gone to bed."

Lincoln put up with "this unparalleled insolence of epaulettes" not only because he was trying to learn about and keep abreast of military develop- ments but because of his concern with the rising popular dissatisfaction with the general. As the initial adulation of McClellan waned, he became increas- ingly vulnerable to the criticism of impatient public opinion. Much of this was voiced within Lincoln's own party by leaders often called radicals.[7]

Radical Republicans, vindictive in their attitude toward slaveholders, spoke for that segment of the population who desired to make abolition of slavery the objective of the war. Lincoln earned their hostility because, in appealing to conservatives, he stressed only the salvation of the Union as a war aim, avoiding any mention of slavery. With two former Democrats in his Cabinet, Lincoln was already striving to build a bipartisan or Union administration dedicated to the one principle upon which all could agree, saving the Union.

This made many radicals view Lincoln as a "well-meaning incompetent who lacked the 'inclination to put down this rebellion with the strong hand required.' " Feeling that the conservatives dominated Lincoln's administra- tion and the country, the radicals damned what they perceived as a "sickly policy of inoffensive war" and demanded action "suited to remorseless and revolutionary violence." One sarcastic radical reflected this in writing a friend in the army: "I infer your duties lie at some distance from the rebels. It is a pity to hurt those our Government treats so tenderly." The writer thus shared radical criticism of what they perceived as the "infernal hold-back proslavery" strategy pursued by "lukewarm, half secession officers in command who cannot bear to strike a blow lest it hurt their rebel friends or jeopardize the precious protectors of slavery." Believing in the special efficacy of generals with radical views, they "demanded 'generals with ideas' who on the battle- field would be 'almost irresistible because [they would be] swayed by the great invisible forces.' "[8]

McClellan's careful preparations and consequent delay exasperated the rad- icals and the significant segment of the public which shared their point of view. Nor did McClellan's military expertise or his West Point education and professional background impress them. Many radicals believed that the country had "advanced to a period when any gentleman, without any [particular] institution" such as West Point, could "make himself master of any science that he shall see fit to adopt," including, of course, military science. "The men who will eminently distinguish themselves in this war, who will come forward and show themselves capable of commanding great armies in the field, will be the men [the scope of] whose intellect has never been narrowed down to the rules of your military school." The attribute needed, said another, was "a stout heart," which would "do more to make a good general than all the lessons of West Point or the diagrams of Jomini."[9]

To the degree that the weakly developed ideas of professionalism might have restrained this concept of military appointment, First Bull Run virtually eliminated it for the radicals. The spectators at that battle included many radical leaders, and some played a role in trying to rally the troops after the defeat. Radical senators Wade of Ohio and Chandler of Michigan had "wheeled their carriage across a narrow road near Fairfax, completely blocking the passage. Then with Wade shouting 'Boys, we'll stop this damned runaway,' they placed themselves in the path" of the retreating troops, thus helping to rally McDowell's army. By December, 1861, the country's leading newspaper, Horace Greeley's New York *Tribune*, believed that "however imperfect the civil appreciation may be as to military science, common sense is an attribute which buttons and bullion do not alone confer; and common sense is quite as competent as tactical profundity to decide the questions of hastening or deferring operations against the rebels."[10]

The radical senators' experience at Bull Run and the panicky retreat of raw troops also reinforced the popular idea that war consisted of battles and military science consisted solely of leadership in combat. School history emphasized such major engagements as Cannae, Marathon, Hastings, Crécy, and Bunker Hill, to the almost total neglect of other aspects of military operations. The publication in 1851 in London and New York of Sir Edward Creasy's classic, *The Fifteen Decisive Battles of the World from Marathon to Waterloo*, exemplified this popular perception of war. This view emphasized courage and enthusiasm in combat and overlooked logistics and strategy.[11]

As early as October, 1861, radical leaders, dissatisfied with McClellan, had come to Lincoln "to worry the administration into a battle. The wild howl of the summer" which had led to the Bull Run offensive was, according to John Hay, beginning again. But Lincoln "stood up for McClellan's deliberateness. We then went over to the General's Headquarters," he said. McClellan told the President that one radical leader "preferred an unsuccessful battle to delay," believing that "a defeat could easily be repaired, by swarming recruits. McClellan answered that he would rather have a few recruits before a victory than a good many after a defeat. The President deprecated this new manifestation of senseless popular impatience but at the same time said it was a reality and should be taken into account. 'At the same time General, you must not fight till you are ready.' "[12]

Thus Lincoln succinctly summarized a problem which would always be a dominant theme in his conduct of the war. It had already appeared in the previous summer when the public demanded a movement "on to Richmond." The expert opinion of General Scott had advised against it and Lincoln was thus caught between the public on the one hand and professional advice on the other. Lincoln had sided with the civilians and had ordered the advance which culminated at the first Battle of Bull Run. Trapped between two fires at the beginning of his presidency, Lincoln remained in this difficult position throughout the war. It proved a hard, often insoluble task for him to strike a balance. His ability to understand the military reasoning while appreciating both the popular view and the strength, if not always the wisdom, of the radical desires made his task difficult. The fixation of both radical and popular attention on the Army of the Potomac did, however, make his task considerably easier in the West. Strategic decisions there would be under less popular and political constraint, whereas, to a marked degree, the less successful operations near the nation's capital often monopolized public concern.

Lincoln decided to support McClellan in his inaction during the good campaigning weather of the fall of 1861. This reflected his confidence in the general and, perhaps, that the Bull Run defeat had taught a lesson about impatience. In spite of his display of arrogance toward the President, McClellan had not initially held nearly so negative an opinion of Lincoln. Before the war, when he was vice president of the Illinois Central Railroad, McClellan remembered knowing Lincoln, then a counsel for the company. He wrote: "More than once I have been with him in out-of-the-way countryseats . . . and, in the lack of sleeping accommodations, have spent the night in front of a stove listening to the unceasing flow of anecdotes from his lips. . . . I could never quite make up my mind how many of them he had really heard before, and how many he invented on the spur of the moment . . . seldom refined, but . . . always to the point." Yet McClellan said Lincoln was "honest and means well," in the same condescending terms he viewed the general public. "What *do* you think I received as a present yesterday?" McClellan wrote his wife. "Some poor woman away up in New York sent me a half dozen pair of woolen socks. . . . Some infatuated individual sent me, a day or two ago, a 'McClellan Polka.' What in the world did he expect *me* to do with it? Not to whistle or dance it, I hope."[13]

For all his testy attitude, McClellan succeeded marvelously in building a large, well-trained army on the Potomac. Yet the victorious Confederate army under Joseph E. Johnston headquartered at Manassas, barely thirty miles from Washington, and the makeshift beginning of a rebel navy actually blockading the Potomac embarrassed both this powerful army and the Lincoln administration. Earlier in June, a small U.S. flotilla under Commander

James Ward tasted defeat trying to force open the river, Ward becoming the first naval officer killed in the war. By mid-October the southerners constructed river batteries along the Potomac below the Occoquan at Freestone Point, Cockpit Point, Shipping Point, and Evansport, all fortified with powerful earthworks and heavy ordnance. With the Potomac in essence closed to normal traffic, Washington became "the only city in the country really blockaded."[14]

To ensure Washington's safety the Federals built thirty-seven miles of encircling fortifications before the end of 1861. McClellan, who himself received much credit for creating the system, actually selected and entrusted most of the work to the "true father of the defenses," Major John G. Barnard, a quiet, middle-aged, and deaf, regular engineer officer.

Meanwhile strictly military camp life in McClellan's training installations hummed on quite busily. One unappreciative Confederate picket observed that "the enemy wasted numberless charges of powder and ball at target practice, . . . until their noise became annoying." But the training instilled precision, and discipline grew from the rigorous program as well as from a few exemplary executions for desertion and brandings or floggings for lesser transgressions.[15] In addition to training, the soldiers worked at preparing defensive positions for the army. This included felling trees on many miles of landscape. "The trees were cut about three feet from the ground, and all made to fall with their branches toward the enemy," recalled one soldier, and the "men took to it as a pastime." Soon, he continued, "the appearance of thousands of dead trees all lying in the same direction added greatly to the desolate looks of this war afflicted vicinity."[16]

McClellan visited the camps often, frequently accompanied by Lincoln and other officials. At least one such sortie proved embarrassing. One night, alert pickets of the Third New York Artillery stopped an unexpected carriage and sent the whole party therein under guard to Lieutenant Colonel Charles H. Steward, whom they found, quite commendably, in his tent engaged in diligent study of tactics. "Well, Colonel," he heard a testy voice snarl, "you've captured the administration." Indeed, there stood General McClellan, President Lincoln, and Secretary of State Seward.[17]

On November 20 the Army of the Potomac staged a grand review, awesome and indelible in impression. Larger than any military force ever mustered before on the American continent, it included ninety infantry regiments, twenty artillery batteries numbering 100 pieces of field artillery, and nine cavalry regiments—approximately 100,000 men. Now with all this force assembled and readied, Lincoln believed offensive action essential.[18]

McClellan had readied a plan based on the principle of the turning movement. Like Scott's movement to Vera Cruz, made possible by naval superiority, McClellan's plan was to take advantage of the excellent and firmly secure water communications available through the Chesapeake Bay and the Virginia rivers. He intended to use this water route to move to Urbanna and then turn Johnston's position, threatening both Confederate communications and the capital, which it was Johnston's mission to defend. Because McClellan would have good and secure water communications to the northeastern states, the movement would be a penetration rather than a raid. The turning movement could serve any of three purposes: getting in Johnston's rear and forcing him to fight at a disadvantage, on the offensive; acquiring the territory between Washington and Richmond; or providing an opportunity to capture Richmond by reaching it before Johnston could fall back to protect it. Because McClellan would be making a penetration he harbored no fear for the safety of Washington. If Johnston remained near Washington or even captured the city, his stay would be temporary because his communications would be cut, while McClellan's occupation of Richmond would be permanent unless Johnston's army, deprived of its supplies, could recapture it by attacking McClellan. The rapid growth in 1861 of the federal Navy was fundamental to the plan. With 42 commissioned ships in March, by July it numbered 82, and an impressive 264 by year's end.

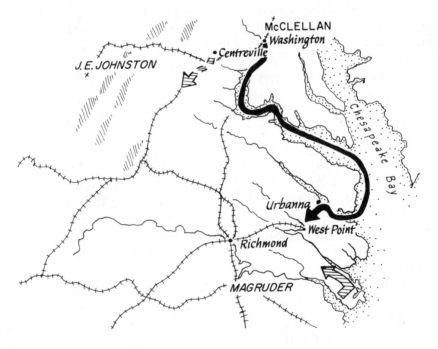

McClellan's Planned Turning Movement

McClellan's plan, evolved during the fall of 1861, closely resembled in principle the one Halleck and Grant used in the West, the turning movements against Fort Henry and Fort Donelson. At Fort Henry the enemy had retreated when their communications were threatened; at Fort Donelson their communications had been cut and they had attacked to recover them. After the victories at the forts, the Union successfully penetrated up the Tennessee and Cumberland rivers, turned the Confederates, and forced them to evacuate their main positions at Bowling Green and at Columbus on the Mississippi. Likewise McClellan's planned movement to Joe Johnston's rear would compel a retreat or would give the Union army the advantage of the tactical defensive. Johnston would have to attack McClellan's large army in an effort to relieve the threat to Confederate communications and capital.

McClellan's well-reasoned strategy offered great promise, but time soon ran out on him for his planning and preparation, for President Lincoln grew most impatient for an offensive. Lincoln's anxiety for an advance was all the greater because he had at last solved for himself the problem of campaigning on exterior lines. Rejecting concentrations corresponding to those of the enemy, Lincoln grasped that the answer lay in simultaneous advances. He explained: My "general idea of the war" is that "we have the greater numbers, and the enemy has the greater facility of concentrating forces upon the points of collision; that we must fail unless we can find some way of making our advantage an overmatch for his; and that this can be done by menacing him with superior forces at different points, at the same time; so that we can safely attack one, or both, if he makes no change, and if he weakens one to strengthen the other, forebear to attack the strengthened one, but seize, and hold the weakened one, gaining so much." To illustrate what would be a controlling idea in Union strategy, Lincoln cited the campaign of First Bull Run, when the Confederates used their interior lines to move troops from Winchester to Manassas. "Suppose," Lincoln wrote, when the Confederates at "Winchester ran away to re-enforce Manassas, we had foreborne to attack Manassas, but had seized and held Winchester. . . . In application of the general rule I am suggesting, every particular case will have its modifying circumstances, among which the most constantly present, and most difficult to meet, will be a perfect knowledge of the enemy's movements. This had its part in the Bull Run case." In this idea the President harmonized with his generals, both in understanding the war in terms of interior and exterior lines and in agreeing with McClellan's idea of simultaneous advances by Buell, Halleck, and himself.[19]

The President's knowledge of the proper strategy urged action, as did the adverse impact of military inactivity on every front, which affected national morale and political support for the war effort. Lincoln thought: "Delay is ruining us." In early January Lincoln found the word from General Halleck "exceedingly discouraging. As everywhere else, nothing can be done." The President ruefully admitted failure to compel either Halleck or Buell "to name the DAY when they can be ready to move." In the second week of January, with McClellan at home convalescing from typhoid fever, Lincoln assembled several Cabinet officers and generals, including McDowell, for discussions to be held at the White House. They considered but one topic: an advance by the Army of the Potomac.[20]

The President still remained ignorant of McClellan's now well-matured plan to move by water, for McClellan patronized the self-educated, small-town prairie lawyer. During one of Lincoln's frequent visits to McClellan's headquarters, the President made some suggestions about operations in Virginia. The general listened as if much enlightened, but, after the President's departure, remarked caustically of Lincoln, "Isn't he a rare bird." But now McClellan, realizing he must respond, rose from his sickbed to attend the conferences. Though he refused in the meeting to divulge more than the fact that he had formulated a definite plan and time for an advance, he at last acquainted Lincoln "in a general and casual way" with his intentions.[21]

This satisfied Lincoln for the day, but civilian patience was exhausted and the constant preparation and training undermined McClellan's credibility. The civilians little appreciated the serious problem which lack of discipline constituted, such as men exposing themselves—as they often did before seasoning—to provoke a shot from the enemy just for the fun of returning it. The civilians saw snowball fights, football games, and checker tournaments. They observed with amazement the Fortieth New York's "Mozart Drum Corps," its support for a theatrical association, and the "Sedgwick's Brigade Lyceum." These apparent frivolities and reports of champagne dinners further exasperated bellicose civilians and by midwinter McClellan's failure to take the offensive lost him the support of Edwin M. Stanton, the energetic new secretary of war.[22]

The forty-seven-year-old Stanton took over the war office from Simon Cameron on January 20, 1862. The unsatisfactory Cameron had received the secretaryship in the first place only as a political reward for swinging his powerful Pennsylvania machine in favor of Lincoln's nomination and election to the presidency. In office Cameron charted an independent course, repeatedly embarrassed Lincoln, and earned censure from the House of Representatives because of the numerous scandals and corruption emanating from army contracts and military appointments. Lincoln solved the festering problem by giving him a different post, minister to Russia. Congressman Thaddeus Stevens, who had feuded with Cameron for years, advised sending word to the Czar to secure his valuables at night. The Cabinet change proved highly successful, for Stanton brought into it tremendous drive and a high level of administrative competence.

Largely self-educated, Stanton had studied at Kenyon College in Gambier, Ohio, his native state, but failed to graduate because of financial difficulties. Later he became known as a competent lawyer, his energy, ability, and fidelity bringing him quick recognition and a comfortable income. His work as counsel for the state of Pennsylvania (1849–56) pushed him into the national spotlight and resulted in his retention for many important legal cases. . In 1858 he handled his most important litigation, combating fraudulent land claims allegedly deeded by Mexico to numerous individuals prior to the Mexican War, and saved the U.S. government perhaps $15,000,000. President Buchanan recognized his ability and rewarded him with appointment as attorney general late in 1860. Prior to that Stanton had taken little part in politics, holding only two minor offices.

Though loyally adhering to the Democratic party until his entrance into Lincoln's Republican Cabinet in 1862, Stanton heartily disapproved of slavery, but unquestionably accepted the controversial proslavery Dred Scott decision of the Supreme Court. Above all, however, a solid Unionist, he was required in Buchanan's Cabinet on the eve of the Civil War to work closely with radically inclined Republicans, a course which he perceived as his most effective way to help the country. In private life, during the early months of Lincoln's presidency, Stanton utterly distrusted the Cabinet and openly criticized what he termed "the imbecility of this administration." Indeed, he had reviled and criticized Lincoln since their first meeting four years previous. While working on a patent case in Cincinnati, Stanton and a group of big-city corporation lawyers had called in Lincoln as a consultant but rejected him upon seeing his rustic clothes and ball-handled, blue-cotton umbrella. "Where did that long-armed creature come from?" asked Stanton within Lincoln's hearing. Stanton later continued this cruel line in private conversation, variously terming Lincoln "a low, cunning clown," "that giraffe," and "the original gorilla," a term that initially amused General McClellan who picked it up and thereafter used it frequently. Ever since McClellan took command of the army, Stanton had cultivated the young general's friendship and became his confidential legal adviser. After Stanton entered the Cabinet, their warm association cooled as the radically inclined Stanton grew impatient with the general's slowness and apparent reluctance to act.[23]

Exactly how Lincoln came to select Stanton for the war office remains unclear. Stanton offered the political merit of continuing Pennsylvania's representation in the Cabinet and managed to be acceptable both to radicals and conservatives. Secretary of the Navy Gideon Welles firmly believed that Secretary of State William H. Seward secured the appointment, but Cameron claimed the credit. The appointment won praise in the press because Stanton enjoyed a high reputation for competence. At any rate, Lincoln certainly showed magnanimity by accepting so bitter a personal critic into his official family.

Stanton's physical appearance made him a darling among caricaturists, especially when difficult and not always popular decisions began causing praise to be tempered with disagreement and criticism. Thick-set and of medium height, he possessed a strong, heavy neck which supported a massive head thatched with long, black, curling hair. His large nose and eyes accentuated his wide and stern mouth. A luxuriant crop of coarse black whiskers concealed his jaws and chin. Altogether he was a rather fierce-looking man. Postmaster General Montgomery Blair disparingly called him the "black terrier," and indeed Stanton could be rude, dictatorial, abusive, outrageously blunt, and incomprehensibly devious. U. S. Grant said that Stanton "cared nothing for the feelings of others" and seemed to find it more pleasant "to disappoint than to gratify." But at least a few persons did find him occasionally charming: Mrs. Seward observed his cheery manner, a merry twinkle in his eye, and an air of hearty warmth; and Charles A. Dana, the newspaper editor who later became an assistant secretary of war, wrote: "Stanton had the loveliest smile I ever saw on a human face." But not many persons took such delight in this coldly efficient executive, and before very long the list of outraged Stanton-haters grew and included his former friend, General McClellan.[24]

The deteriorating relationship between the general and the secretary owed much to the secretary's contempt for military science and to McClellan's failure to comprehend the political importance of accomplishing something tangible in the East. Except for Ball's Bluff and the amphibious operations which secured bases on the Atlantic coast, no active military operations had occurred east of the mountains since Manassas. It was politically imperative that the North do something about the hostile army still at the gates of the nation's capital and the insubstantial, but nonetheless continuing and real, southern blockade of the Potomac River. Stanton's presence at the War Department would immediately increase this pressure to act, for the new secretary had just written one of his future assistants: As soon as I can "get the machinery of the office working, the rats cleared out, and the rat holes stopped we shall *move*. This army has to fight or run away; while men are striving nobly in the West, the champagne and oysters on the Potomac must be stopped."

Stanton's criticism transcended McClellan's failure to launch a campaign. The new secretary expressed some very emphatic ideas about the nature of war, and these did not include a respect for the Napoleonic tradition of the Union's "Young Napoleon." Notions of strategy, of "military combinations and organizing victory," caused Stanton "apprehension," because they had "commenced in infidel France with the Italian campaign and resulted in Waterloo." Writing after the fall of forts Henry and Donelson, Stanton explained: "Success on the battlefield" came from "the spirit of the Lord that moved out soldiers to rush into battle and filled the hearts of our enemies with dismay. . . . Patriotic spirit, with resolute courage in officers and men, is a military combination that never failed." Apparently without any appreciation for the strategy involved in the western campaigns, Stanton believed that the fall of forts Henry and Donelson taught: "Battles are to be won now and by us in the same and only manner they were ever won by any people, or in any age since Joshua, by boldly pursuing and striking the foe." The "true organization of victory and military combination to end this war was," he said, "declared in a few words by General Grant's message to General Buckner: '*I propose to move immediately on your works.*' "[25]

Such an impatient and bellicose new secretary of war undoubtedly had much to do with Lincoln's finally ordering, on January 27, 1862, simultaneous advances by all Union armies, to begin on Washington's birthday, February 22. He ordered McClellan's own army to thrust directly against Joe Johnston's intrenched Confederate army, southwest of Washington, directions which interdicted McClellan's proposed turning movement.

This order caused McClellan to abandon his secrecy and aloofness and write Stanton a twenty-two-page exposition on the merits of his proposed turning movement and of the principles and assumptions upon which it rested. Responding to the President's directive to drive Johnston beyond Manassas Junction, McClellan pointed out the difficulties of turning Johnston out of his "strong central position" protected by "a strong line of defense enabling him to remain on the defensive, with a small force on one flank, while he concentrates everything on the other." It was impractical to turn Johnston on the west because of the "long line of wagon communication" needed; turning the eastern flank would be difficult because the Confederates were posted in strength along a river, the Occoquan, which joined the more formidable Potomac.

McClellan more seriously objected to the President's plan and the secretary's ideas because, after a successful battle, the enemy "could fall back upon other positions," he said, "and fight us again and again" and in retreat "would destroy his railroad bridges and otherwise impede our progress" until reaching the "intrenchments of Richmond." Since the supply situation would then force the Army of the Potomac "to seek a shorter land route to Richmond" by the rivers southeast of the city, why, McClellan asked, "spend so much more time" getting to Richmond when he could "adopt the short line at once"?

McClellan argued: A landing at Urbanna "would probably cut off Magruder in the Peninsula, and enable us to occupy Richmond before it could be strongly re-enforced. Should we fail in that, we could, with the cooperation of the navy, cross the James and throw outselves in the rear of Richmond, thus forcing the enemy to come out and attack us," because "his position would be untenable with us on the southern bank of the river." Though McClellan stressed the strategic advantages of his proposal, the general gave equal emphasis to its tactical advantage. The threat to the rebel capital would force Johnston to try "entirely defeating us in battle, in which he must be the assailant," he added. The enemy would thus be forced "to abandon his prepared position" and either "beat us in a position selected by ourselves," he explained, or abandon Richmond, which would give "us the capital, the communications, the supplies of the rebels. Norfolk would fall, the waters of the Chesapeake would be ours, all Virginia would be in our power, and the enemy forced to abandon Tennessee and North Carolina." In his understanding of logistics and his desire to bring the "fleet into full play," McClellan had come a long way from his earlier plan to advance from the Ohio to Richmond over the bad roads of mountainous western Virginia.

McClellan sought to impress upon the secretary that the "history of every former war" had "conclusively shown the great advantages which are possessed by an army acting on the defensive and occupying strong positions." McClellan found that at the beginning of the war "but few civilians in our country, and indeed not all military men of rank," he added, "had a just appreciation of that fact." If "veteran troops frequently falter and are repulsed with loss," then "new levies . . . cannot be expected to advance without cover" against the "murderous fire" of intrenched defenders. He would solve this problem by turning the enemy, for "the effect of this movement" to the enemy's rear," he explained, "will be to reverse the advantages of position. They will have to seek us in our own works, as we sought them at Manassas."

The strength of the defense meant that offensive battles against an enemy with his back to his communications implied a victory which "produces no final results, & may require years of warfare & expenditure to follow up." Hence "a battle gained at Manassas will result merely in the possession of the field of combat—at best we can follow it up but slowly," said McClellan. Again stressing the futility of attacking an enemy army instead of trying to reach its rear, the general concluded by saying that when such a battle is won, "the question will at once arise—'What are we to do next?' "

McClellan had earlier warned the President that this was no "ordinary" war and that rather than having only to "conquer a peace and make a treaty on advantageous terms," it was "necessary to crush a population." In February McClellan stressed the entirely inadequate results even if a victory occurred near Washington. The results of a victory won with the enemy's rear to his own communications would, McClellan reiterated, "be confined to the possession of the field of battle, the evacuation of the line of the upper Potomac by the enemy, and the moral effect of the victory—important results it is true, but not decisive of the war; nor securing the destruction of the enemy's main army." For a decisive victory he planned to turn the Confederates and so force them to fight without an easy line of retreat over their own communications.[26]

McClellan had made a long and clear, if belated, exposition of the tactical and strategic realities as perceived by the professional soldiers. In his stress on the value of intrenchments and the power of the defense he adhered faithfully to the West Point teachings of Dennis Hart Mahan. In his proposed use of sea power and reliance on the turning movement, he was truly the disciple of Scott.

It is doubtful, however, that the subtleties of the strategic offensive coupled with the tactical defensive made any impression on the new secretary of war. The secretary was too fired with radical impatience and too firm a believer in "patriotic spirit," "resolute courage," and the efficacy of moving immediately upon enemy works. Events would prove, however, that President Lincoln better understood McClellan's belated exposition. Already mature in his understanding of the strategy of the war, Lincoln was moving rapidly to equal the soldiers' grasp of logistics and grand tactics. This comprehension would not, however, enable him to extricate himself from his difficult position.

The President's emerging grasp of the art of war would, however, confer on him and the country one inestimable advantage: it would make him a good judge of generals, their abilities, and their plans. In February, 1862, he used this developing ability to determine, on the whole correctly, that McClellan should move. Just as Lincoln could sense the validity of McClellan's tactical and strategic ideas, he knew intuitively that McClellan was proving to be a perfectionist and would never be satisfied with his own preparations. Political, if not military, necessity made an immediate movement of the army essential, even though it was not fully prepared.

If McClellan succeeded in making Lincoln understand the tactical problems of the offensive and the advantage of a turning movement to force the enemy to assume the tactical offensive, the President failed to make the general understand the importance of a victory. Lincoln sought a victory for its "moral effect," not really for its *moral* effect on the South, which McClellan had quite properly discounted, but rather for its *morale* effect on the Union, whose morale badly needed a success near its capital. Over six months after Bull Run the undefeated southern army still remained unmolested near the gates of Washington. McClellan, by his delay and his failure to confide earlier, exhausted a large amount of the reservoir of Lincoln's confidence with which he had begun, and lost much freedom of action.

Though McClellan integrated military and political factors as far as the Confederates and European powers were concerned, he proved unable to do so in relation to Lincoln's domestic political problems—an odd blindspot for a general so politically minded that he would run for President in 1864. Neither could McClellan grasp Lincoln's concern for the safety of Washington nor convince him that a southern raid could not threaten the national capital, even though the city was so elaborately fortified that its defenses compared with Wellington's famous defense line, which had stymied the French in Portugal.

If a Confederate concentration materialized that was strong enough to take Washington, the defense of Richmond necessarily would have been so weakened as to ensure its capture by McClellan's army. The fall of Richmond would cut the communications of the southern army holding Washington, while McClellan's communications by water still would be secure and functioning, thereby enabling him to draw supplies from many different northern Atlantic ports. The secessionists' capture of Washington would thus not only have been converted into a necessarily temporary occupation, a raid, but the Union army would have blocked the principal line of Confederate retreat. The southern army would then have been forced to retreat via the Shenandoah Valley, leaving eastern Virginia in Union hands. Lincoln apparently understood that any rebel occupation of Washington would be temporary, a "sack" of the city, but public opinion concerned him, making it necessary to protect the capital even from "danger or insult" or else the administration and the military leaders would lose their credibility with Congress and the people. In focusing upon purely military considerations, McClellan ignored this important problem of his civilian superiors. Perhaps also McClellan failed to convince Lincoln that he would act with enough energy to take Richmond if the rebels concentrated against Washington. Certainly McClellan serenely believed that Joe Johnston, his cautious friend of prewar years, would never risk trading the temporary capture of Washington for the permanent loss of Richmond, especially when it would leave the Union army in his rear.[27]

Though McClellan did not win his point in a formal way, he assumed that he could use his proposed turning movement and that conformity with the February 22 deadline was not required. McClellan later gained reinforcement for his arguments favoring a turning movement when Lincoln polled his division commanders. Doubtless his long and well-reasoned paper had made an impression on Lincoln, but this poll provided the occasion for the less-sophisticated Stanton to show that he remained unimpressed. When the results of the poll supported McClellan, the disappointed and exasperated Stanton remarked of the advocates of the turning movement: "We just saw ten generals afraid to fight." Compared to Stanton, Lincoln doubtless remained more amenable to McClellan's plans because a land advance was then stymied by roads which, having gone from bad to worse on account of unprecedented rains, were absolutely "impassable at present." McClellan and Lincoln also agreed on the timing of the advances. Both understood the necessity for simultaneous movements and McClellan had specified that his plan would be "carried into execution so nearly simultaneously with the final advance of Buell and Halleck that the columns will support each other." Nevertheless, in March, while Halleck and Buell moved south through Tennessee, Lincoln again felt it necessary to give McClellan a positive order to move, one with which McClellan finally complied.[28]

Basically Lincoln's clumsy intervention with his order to advance on Washington's birthday had succeeded. It caused McClellan to take the administration into his confidence and explain thoroughly his assumptions about the tactical and strategic nature of the war. Undoubtedly Lincoln learned much, something he obviously desired when he had so often visited McClellan's headquarters. After the order, however, Lincoln "stopped going to McClellan's and sent for the General to come to him." In his visits the general became "much more pleasant and social in manner than formerly." He seemed "to be anxious for the good opinion of everyone." But, though Lincoln had reluctantly agreed to McClellan's plans, the President felt constrained to intervene and insist upon crucial changes.[29]

Over McClellan's opposition, the President in early march reorganized the Union Army into four corps. Though militarily sound, such a change at this time and the particular corps commanders Lincoln appointed reflected radical political pressures and the President's own concern about McClellan's strategy. Soon after providing McClellan with corps commanders both radical Republican and lukewarm about the general's strategy, Lincoln relieved McClellan as general in chief, though retaining him in command of the Army of the Potomac. Through an unfortunate mix-up McClellan first learned of his removal by reading of it in the newspapers. Lincoln did not name a successor to McClellan as general in chief, the President himself taking direct control of military operations. He put the bulk of the trans-Appalachian forces under the successful Halleck and formed a command in the mountain areas for Halleck's predecessor in Missouri, John C. Fremont, a strong anti-slavery man very popular with the radicals. Lincoln probably had few illusions about Fremont, of whom one critic said he possessed "all of the qualities of genius except ability." In the East the President's arrangements evolved into several distinct commands in Virginia: the Shenandoah Valley—with poor old Patterson relieved and dismissed from service—now under former Massachusetts Governor Nathaniel P. Banks; Irvin McDowell's on the line between Washington and Richmond; McClellan's Army of the Potomac; and the command at Fort Monroe, now under the aged regular, Major General Wool. The federal multidepartmental organization in Virginia thus resulted from dissatisfaction with McClellan and lack of full confidence in his strategy.[30]

Concerned that the Confederate position at Manassas was too far forward and thus exposed to a turning movement, Joseph E. Johnston, with Davis's concurrence, began withdrawing from the vicinity of Washington in March and headed south toward Fredericksburg. Johnston wisely covered his communications and moved closer to Richmond than McClellan would be at Urbanna. He also removed the blockade from the Potomac, realizing its continuation was now unrealistic. McClellan immediately changed his Urbanna plan to one calling for an advance on Richmond via the York-James Peninsula and the line of water communications and operations along the York River. Meanwhile, much to Lincoln's relief, McClellan also at last took to the field, advancing ponderously southwestward to occupy the now-deserted Manassas.

With a pistol in his pocket, one from his personal collection of at least eleven handguns, and mounted upon his favorite steed, Kentuck, McClellan boldly sallied into the unknown enemy territory. Passing through Centreville, he noted there "quite a formidable series of works, which would have been somewhat uncomfortable for new troops to carry by storm." With no fighting, the Confederates had scurried away, taking with them all the provisions and equipment they could carry and burning the rest. Relieved from the necessity of any pitched battle, the Federals occupied the abandoned camps and studied the empty huts and deserted fortifications—some still mounted with fake wooden guns emplaced to conceal their withdrawal. The southern-

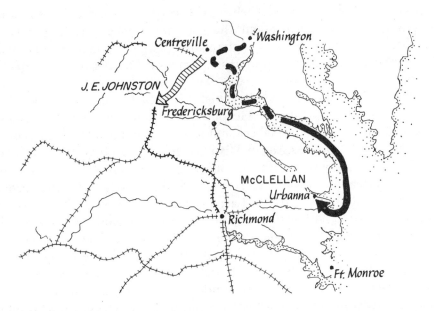

McClellan's Threatened Turning Movement and Johnston's Withdrawal

ers had not possessed nearly the powerful force that McClellan earlier believed. That happy discovery rendered the York-James Peninsula campaign even more viable, but exposed McClellan to much ridicule for apparently being stymied by wooden guns.[31]

Since Lincoln and Stanton continued to worry about the safety of the capital with McClellan away on the Peninsula, they insisted he leave a large garrison for Washington. The small distances and McClellan's communications, really quite short and secure, would allow McClellan to reach Richmond before Johnston possibly could use his interior lines to capture Washington and return in time to save Richmond. But the danger of an "insult" to the capital, much less a sack, made it imperative that Washington be completely secure. So to insure its safety, for which they intensely feared, Lincoln and Stanton had created the separate forces under Banks and McDowell.

Division of Union forces meant that there were two Union armies oriented on Richmond, inevitably operating on exterior lines. But this would not necessarily nullify McClellan's strategy if the Confederates would counterattack to protect their capital and McClellan was correct about the power of the defense. So McClellan's strategy still had a good chance of working. But in spite of his almost prescient grasp of military realities and his success in building the Army of the Potomac, the able McClellan had failed significantly because of his inability to work effectively with his indulgent President. The general seemed unable to grasp the political realities faced by an administration which sought to draw hostile elements into full support of the war for the Union. McClellan's perfectionism made him ignore political needs and the public's impatience until he had made his army as ready as he wished. Though he explained the power of the defense and the strategy of the turning movement, the sophistication of these belatedly explained ideas made them difficult for the President to grasp and beyond the ready understanding of most of the public and politicians.

In any case, soldiers faced a difficult task of interpreting military realities to the public. Not only did civilians not perceive that a muddy Washington's birthday was a bad time to advance, but their conception of war differed from that of the soldiers. Not grasping the constraints of logistics nor understanding the power of the defense, they saw warfare in terms of climactic battles. Further, lack of respect for the soldier's professionalism was aggravated by a suspicion of West Point and, by radicals, a positive distrust of generals not inspired by an antislavery fervor. A far more politically sensitive general than McClellan would have had great difficulty coping with these problems, and these were especially acute for the commanders of the army closest to the nation's capital and inevitably involved in its political struggles.

But McClellan had an opportunity, through military victory, to help the administration politically. McClellan's relief from his duties as general in chief enabled him to concentrate exclusively upon leading his Army of the Potomac. With no general in chief at all, at least for a time, Lincoln and Stanton readied a novel substitute. They succeeded, after several abortive attempts at persuasion, in bringing out of retirement Major General Ethan Allen Hitchcock to help advise and coordinate. Hitchcock, then sixty-four years of age, had retired after a distinguished army career of more than four decades to devote himself to philosophy, spiritualism, and mysticism. He now encountered a marvelous opportunity to fashion a lasting and invaluable contribution to the American military staff system, but he never clearly perceived his chance and eventually he abdicated.

But the new plans depended not so much on the man, Hitchcock or McClellan, as on the system, the creation of Stanton's great gifts as a manager. Stanton's innovation responded to his conviction that "to work an army of five hundred thousand with machinery adapted for peace establishment of twelve thousand" was "no easy task," making it necessary "to bring the War Department up to the standard of the times" by providing "time for thought, combination and conference." Stanton's contribution was not to be in strategy but in a business-like reform, which provided the managerial and operational requisites for fighting the big war in progress.[32]

1. Cooling, *Symbol, Sword, and Shield*, 63.

2. Russell, *Diary*, 240.

3. McClellan, *McClellan's Own Story*, 167.

4. George Worthington Adams, *Doctors in Blue: The Medical History of the Union Army in the Civil War* (New York, 1961), 186.

5. Robert Werlich, *"Beast" Butler* (Washington, 1962), 21; Cooling, *Symbol, Sword and Shield*, 85; William G. Rothstein, *American Physicians in the 19th Century* (Baltimore, 1972), 194–95.

6. J. G. Barnard to McClellan, Dec. 1, 1861, *O.R.*, V, 671–72; J. Shields to McClellan, Jan. 10, 1862, *ibid.*, 700–702; J. G. Barnard, *The Peninsular Campaign and its Antecedents* (New York, 1864), 51; McClellan, *Own Story*, 168–69.

7. *Lincoln and the Civil War in the Diaries and Letters of John Hay*, ed. Tyler Dennett (New York, 1939), 30–31. McClellan apparently behaved as he did because he had returned from a wedding reception and did not wish to see the President when he had had too much to drink (Warren W. Hassler, *George B. McClellan, Shield of the Union* [Baton Rouge, 1957], 41).

8. T. Harry Williams, *Lincoln and the Radicals* (Madison and Milwaukee, 1965), 10–17.

9. T. Harry Williams, "The Attack upon West Point during the Civil War," *Mississippi Valley Historical Review* (Mar. 1939), 502–3, 499, 500.

10. Williams, "Attack upon West Point," 492, 498; Williams, *Lincoln and the Radicals*, 30–31.

11. For Creasy's influence see: John Keegan, *The Face of Battle* (New York, 1976), 54–62.

12. *Lincoln and the Civil War*, 31.

13. McClellan, *Own Story*, 170, 176.

14. Cooling, *Symbol, Sword, and Shield*, 52–53, 76–77.

15. *Ibid.*, 66, 70, 84.

16. *Ibid.*, 87.

17. *Ibid.*, 88–89.

18. *Ibid.*, 89; Lincoln to McClellan, Dec. 1, 1861, Basler, *Collected Works*, I, 34–35.

19. Lincoln to Buell and Halleck, Jan. 13, 1862, Basler, *Collected Works*, V, 98–99; McClellan to Buell, Nov. 29, 1862, *O.R.*, V, 557–58; McClellan to Halleck, Dec. 10, 1862, *ibid.*, VIII, 419.

20. Lincoln to Buell, Jan. 7, 1862, Basler, *Collected Works*, V, 92; Lincoln's endorsement on Halleck to Lincoln, Jan. 6, 1862, *O.R.*, VII, 533; Lincoln to McClellan, Jan. 9, 1862, Basler, *Collected Works*, V, 94.

21. T. Harry Williams, *Lincoln and his Generals* (New York, 1952), 45; Hassler, *McClellan*, 49.

22. Cooling, *Symbol, Sword, and Shield*, 93, 96–98.

23. Bruce Catton, *The Coming Fury* (New York, 1961), 470; Foote, *The Civil War*, I, 28, 142, 245.

24. Grant, *Memoirs*, II, 536; Bruce Catton, *Terrible Swift Sword* (New York, 1963), 142.

25. Stanton to Charles A. Dana, Jan. 24, Feb. 1, Feb. ?, 1862, Charles A. Dana, *Recollections of the Civil War* (New York, 1898), 4–7.

26. G. B. McClellan to E. M. Stanton, Feb. 3, 1862, *O.R.*, V, 42–45, and Basler, *Collected Works*, V, 120–25 (reproduced here in part, including portions omitted in the *Official Records*); A. Lincoln to McClellan, Feb. 3, 1862, Basler, *Collected Works*, V, 118–19; President's Special War Order No. 1, Jan. 31, 1862, *ibid.*, 115; McClellan to Lincoln, Aug. 4, 1861, *ibid.*, 6–9; McClellan to W. Scott, Apr. 27, 1861, *ibid.*, LI, pt. 1, 338–39; Scott to Lincoln, May 2, 1861, *ibid.*, 339; Scott to McClellan, May 3, 1861, *ibid.*, 369–70; McClellan's report to L. Thomas, Aug. 4, 1863, *ibid.*, V, 54; J. Shields to McClellan, Jan. 10, 1862, *ibid.*, 700–702; J. G. Barnard to Jos. Totten, Dec. 10, 1861, *ibid.*, 683. For Field Marshal Count Helmuth von Moltke's comparable analysis of the tactical power of the defense and his similar reliance on turning movements in 1870, see Michael Howard, *The Franco-Prussian War* (New York, 1961), 7. For an interpretation of McClellan in the light of Mahan's influence, see: Edward Hagerman, "The Professionalization of George B. McClellan and Early Civil War Command: An Institutional Perspective," *Civil War History* (June, 1975), 113–35. For another view of McClellan's plan, see: Rowena Reed, *Combined Operations in the Civil War* (Annapolis, 1978), 33–40.

27. Lincoln to McClellan, Apr. 9, 1862; Lincoln, order constituting Army of Virginia, June 26, 1862, Basler, *Collected Works*, V, 184–85, 287.

28. Benjamin P. Thomas and Harold M. Hyman, *Stanton, The Life and Times of Lincoln's Secretary of War* (New York, 1962), 170–71; McClellan to Stanton, Feb. 3, 1862, Basler, *Collected Works*, V, 124–25.

29. Canby, *Lincoln and the Civil War*, 36, 38.

30. George Mayer, *The Republican Party, 1854–1966*, Second Edition (New York, 1967), 42.

31. McClellan, *Own Story*, 176, 179.

32. Stanton to Dana, Feb. 1, 1862, Dana, *Recollections*, 6.

5 ☆ HIGH COMMAND AND ORGANIZATION

Montgomery C. Meigs

"I ALREADY DISCOVER a great struggle among high officers for independent commands, the very thing I desire to avoid," wrote newly promoted Major General Ethan Allen Hitchcock. On March 7, 1862, he had received at St. Louis a telegraphic summons from Secretary of War Stanton for a personal conference in Washington. He boarded a train that same day and traveled directly to the secretary's office, arriving "covered with dust." Hitchcock recalled making "every effort to evade" but finally accepted a commission, not "to attain a command, but to be near the Secretary for any *contingency* aid I might render from my supposed past experiences in the army," he explained.

Hitchcock first reacted to the demand that he go to Washington with a violent nosebleed. He then suffered a second hemorrhage on the train, and a third upon arrival, each more violent than the one before. Stanton whisked the weak, queasy, and unhappy sixty-four-year-old soldier to the President and to "sundry other high functionaries of the government." Hitchcock confided: "I fear . . . I am out of place, considering my health and my habits of life for the past seven or eight years. . . . I am not strong enough for an active army life and the Secretary so understands the matter; and yet I fear he will ask too much of me." Hungry for aggressive and competent leaders and believing that Hitchcock's long military past rendered him extraordinarily capable, Lincoln and Stanton progressively offered Hitchcock a command in the West, where Halleck also sought his services, or with the Army of the Potomac, or with the Ordnance Department. Hitchcock disinterestedly parried all those possibilities, but yielded at last to accept a significant new staff job.[1]

This reluctant soldier, grandson of the famous Revolutionary War leader Ethan Allen, had graduated from West Point in 1817 and served in the U.S. Army until retirement in 1855. His writings and commentaries reveal him as a man of great intellectual appetite. His interests knew few bounds. "I have been a student all my life," he wrote in his diary; "I did not go to the military academy because I made a deliberate choice of a military profession. I went because being the grandson of Ethan Allen some friends thought it appropriate. If service can repay such an education, I served forty years. Is not that enough?"[2]

Hitchcock assumed a dual position as personal advisor to Stanton and as head of the War Board, an innovative and important creation of Stanton's. Formed soon after the secretary took office, this board, a sort of embryonic American version of a general staff, consisted of the heads of the various army bureaus. Stanton had established it in response to his expressed desire for an organization which could cope with the demands of a large-scale war. But, since Lincoln had not filled the post of general in chief, the War Board also would have to supply the President and the secretary with professional military advice on operational questions. Therefore, to have an experienced, even if reluctant, line officer as head of the board seemed particularly appropriate. Hitchcock helped Stanton, and at times effectively played the role of civil/military liaison; but for the role of embryo chief of staff he proved unable to innovate and lacked the drive to realize the full potential of the new organization. Actually only a scholarly hack, he could do a job in the properly prescribed manner but could not transcend. His thinking tended to be exact and absolute, his perceptions essentially static. Although a Biblical student of genuine merit, he developed little or no sense of history. He succeeded as Stanton's advisor but failed as a *de facto* chief of staff, because he could not conceptualize the job. But Hitchcock's failure did not defeat Stanton's effort to give the army a much better staff.

If few readers of military history possess a definite understanding of staffs and their historic significance in warfare, it is not surprising, for few books on military subjects treat the topic adequately. Nevertheless, the staff system demands attention by serious scholars. Simply stated, the staff of any unit consists of personnel especially assigned to assist its commander in the exercise of his responsibilities. The essential meaning of the term "staff" manifests some consistency in all armies throughout history, but their organization varies widely. All of them perform basic military-management functions: procuring information; preparing abstracts or elaborations of plans; translating decisions and plans into orders; causing directions to be transmitted to the troops; and coordinating, overseeing, and evaluating the execution of orders transmitted and carried out by the line organization. They also provide advice to their commander, keep him appropriately informed, and constantly generate and process data concerning contingencies. How efficiently they operate depends upon their constitution and their context. The staff officer does not command a unit nor exercise line authority, although he controls those who serve directly under him, and he sometimes communicates to the line units on behalf of the commander, conveying the weight of his word.

Typical types of staffs in modern history include general and special. These terms refer not to broad or narrow duties, but to their generic nature. General staff actually means general's staff, one that serves a general officer; however, that too causes confusion, for this type also functions at lower echelons serving a field grade commander, and sometimes is called a field staff. The concept becomes clearer when one realizes what particular staffs do. General staffs handle four or five departmentalized areas in the ongoing functions of a military unit and are so divided in the U.S. Army today: personnel (G-1), intelligence including security (G-2), operations and training (G-3), and logistics (G-4). These military-management functions are always essential and in the U.S. Army each exists as a separate staff section. In each an officer and his assistants direct their full efforts and attention to their one particular area, although sometimes smaller staff organizations combine the personnel and logistics sections and the intelligence and operations sections work together.

Special staffs, on the other hand, provide specialized services rather than deal with broad, functional areas. They include services such as ordnance, engineering, signal, medical, chemical, legal, finance, and chaplaincy. Most special staff officers serve as staff personnel themselves and also subordinately command their specialist troops, an exception to the rule that they do not command. Thus these officers command a unit composed of technical personnel, who perform some particular support service, such as signal, medical, chaplaincy, and so on. This unit is attached to a line unit in which the special staff officer serves as a subordinate specialist advisor to his commanding officer, who heads the line unit.

In the nineteenth-century United States, confusingly for students until they understand completely the discrepancy, the army used different terms. The words "general staff" constituted the official name for what actually amounted to special staffs. No real general staffs existed, but the embryonic, fragmented bodies that served as such were called personal staffs. This included anyone working in personnel (G-1), intelligence (G-2), operations (G-3), or logistics (G-4), and comprised, in addition, aides-de-camp, clerks, and body servants. Many students, including Douglas Southall Freeman, have used the archaic terminologies rather than attempt to translate them into consistent modern usage.[3]

Staffs evolved historically at the highest military echelons and gradually percolated to lower levels. An officer now fills the position of chief of staff on the more important staffs of most armies, especially those within units of division size or larger. He supervises the work of each general staff section, coordinates their activities, and serves as a link between them and the commander. The general staff sections in turn supervise the special staff sections such as ordnance, medical, and engineer. They function primarily to represent the commander in monitoring the line, or combat, units of the command and to ensure effective coordination of actions within their area of staff responsibility. The crucially important position of chief of staff developed somewhat haphazardly through time, just as did the staffs themselves. No one perceived precisely what was needed until the nineteenth century, when the importance of the staff was fully realized and general staffs began to be properly organized.[4]

The following diagram illustrates the most basic elements of the staff organization currently used in the U.S. Army.

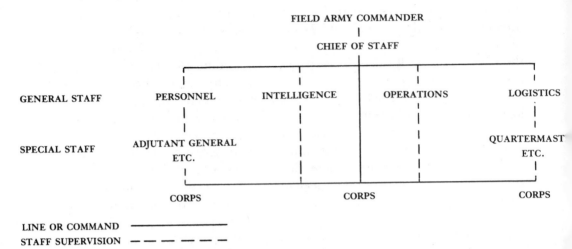

FIELD ARMY COMMANDER

CHIEF OF STAFF

| GENERAL STAFF | PERSONNEL | INTELLIGENCE | OPERATIONS | LOGISTICS |

| SPECIAL STAFF | ADJUTANT GENERAL ETC. | | | QUARTERMAST ETC. |

CORPS   CORPS   CORPS

LINE OR COMMAND
STAFF SUPERVISION

In the eighteenth and nineteenth centuries, France and Prussia boasted the world's most efficient and logically organized military staffs. The United States's staff concepts lagged far behind both of those models, being the products instead of an unsettled congressional attitude and imperfectly based upon British traditions. Despite the tremendous impact of the French upon the American military system, primarily because of France's military prestige and the French alliance during the Revolution, the British army staff actually furnished the pattern that George Washington and his lieutenants instituted. Washington himself was essentially the product of the British military system in both education and field experience.

The Americans developed a system that melded both special and general staffs, but one characterized more by the former's than by the latter's functions. Thus George Washington had an adjutant general, quartermaster general, commissary general of stores and provisions, paymaster general, commissary general of musters, and a chief of engineers. Later he acquired a wagonmaster, a commissary of artillery stores, a surgeon general, a judge advocate general, and a chaplaincy. Nevertheless, a budding general staff operation emerged, albeit provided almost singly by Major General Baron Frederick von Steuben, who had previously served on the staff of Frederick the Great and possessed almost twenty years of experience in the Prussian armies. Inspector General von Steuben knew what needed to be done and functioned as chief of staff in the areas of personnel, intelligence, operations, and supply, seeing to it that appropriate actions were taken during the Revolution. But he failed to instill his insight into the American tradition, for the Americans failed to comprehend the need for systematic implementation of a general staff in their very minute ongoing military establishment.

The staff system that existed in the U.S. Army at the outset of the Civil War, which the Confederate Army precisely duplicated, differed little from that of the American Revolutionary era. The few improvements that emerged during the intervening years came about by accident or perspicacious *ad hoc* employment of staff officers by particular leaders such as Winfield Scott. Basically the American staff concept remained primarily the performance of necessary special staff-housekeeping chores, vaguely coordinated by the commander himself with the help of his personal aides.

The national level had no general staff and, initially, little opportunity for coordination of the special staff. Legislation in 1813 organized only a loose bureau system. A step in the right direction, it brought the heads of vital departments within the army into offices at Washington, facilitating consultation with the secretary of war. At first the seniority system brought less-than-adequate men into positions as bureau heads, and one secretary begged Congress "for God's sake," "endeavor to rid the army of old women and blockheads" on the staff. An early reorganization removed some of the incompetents, but still the staff failed to develop and remained without coordination, each bureau head performing as an individual and offering advice only when specifically asked. The men who held posts as bureau heads, jealous of their authority and uncertain of their status, frequenty tried to assert independence from the general in chief, to take orders only from the President or the secretary of war, and sometimes even clashed with the secretary. Most importantly, they lacked coordination.[5]

Insofar as the organization of the headquarters of the army was influenced by any principle at all, it derived from ideas belatedly inspired by France, which separated command and administration. The bureau heads reported to the secretary of war rather than to the general in chief of the army, making a complete, formal separation between control of military operations and control of the necessary quartermaster, ordnance, and other logistical elements needed to support operations. The post of general in chief was not established in law and evolved by retaining on duty in Washington the senior general officer of the army. Without statutory authority, the general in chief struggled, usually in vain, to establish his control over the army and the bureau chiefs. He did manage to gain considerable control over the adjutant general.[6]

In theory the adjutant general's department functioned as a general staff, but in practice it confined its activities to personnel matters and to publishing orders. This system effectively ensured complete civilian control, for it reserved to the secretary the real power to control directly rather than by delegation and management. The subordinate headquarters, where orders to the quartermaster, ordnance, and other staff officers flowed downward from the corresponding staff officer at the higher headquarters, followed this concept. This system put so much authority in the hands of the secretary of war that it almost made the general in chief redundant. The feeling that the system emasculated them induced two very eminent generals in chief to move their headquarters away from Washington: Winfield Scott, before the Civil War, and William T. Sherman, after the war. The following diagram illustrates this organization:

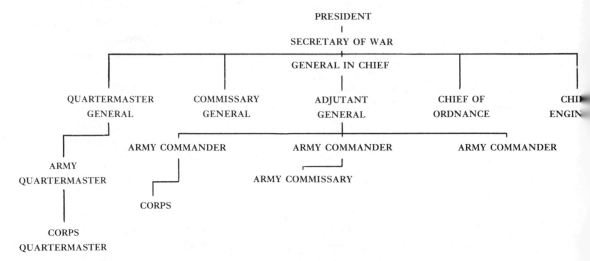

Before the Civil War, except during the brief Mexican War, no military units larger than a regiment actually existed. The necessarily small-unit army, scattered widely over a large territory, developed a staff system adequate only for its immediate and very modest needs. The regulations and laws authorized three kinds of staffs. In addition to the special staff at the national level, the heads of the various bureaus, there was a staff for each corps branch, infantry, artillery, etc., which administratively helped that corps perform its basic missions and at the same time helped to facilitate the well-being of the members of that particular corps by providing career management and guidance. Finally, each regimental headquarters had a staff, which in actual practice muddled general and special staff functions together.[7]

In 1861 each infantry regimental headquarters consisted of one colonel (the commander), one lieutenant colonel, one major, one adjutant (a personnel officer, usually a captain), one quartermaster, one surgeon, one assistant surgeon, and one chaplain. After the organizaiton of brigades, each of their headquarters included one brigadier general (in command), two aides-de-camp, one assistant adjutant general, one surgeon, one assistant quartermaster, and one commissary of supplies. Laws existed before the war that authorized a limited number of aides for any general officer: full generals and lieutenant generals—although no one then held these high ranks—could have four aides with the rank of lieutenant colonel; major generals, two majors as aides; and brigadier generals, one captain. In both the Union and Confederacy, general officers ignored these limitations and assembled aides in whatever numbers they desired as long as they could secure approval by their War Departments. Thus the staff of each Civil War field army varied somewhat

from that of all of the others. Furthermore, in opposition to the real requirement for more adequate staffs, many persons in both armies consistently and
staunchly resisted large staffs because they fretted about personal aggrandize-
ment by particular generals or possibly even military dictatorship. In the face
of sustained active operations, the utter inadequacy of staffs early became
obvious; but rather than rejuvenate and strengthen the von Steuben example
or implement the excellent example offered within the Prussian army, the
two armies only slightly increased the number of officers allowed in the
various departments. The size and complexity of the war further aggravated
the situation at the national level.

Strangely, little excuse existed for the American failure to copy France or
to emulate the better Prussian model more faithfully; the Crimean War commission, for which McClellan reported, had actually toured Europe also,
including Prussia. Unfortunately its technically educated members concentrated upon the material aspects of war, rather than upon organizational
concepts. One scholar condemned them for spending too much time "analyzing the methods of hanging hammocks aboard ship," and implied that they
might otherwise have noticed and understood the Prussian staff system, perhaps the most important new military development then on the European
continent. Still, to McClellan's credit, whatever his and the other commission
members' shortcomings, he appointed his father-in-law Colonel Randolph B.
Marcy chief of staff in the Army of the Potomac, making him the first officer
in American military history officially to hold the chief of staff title. In truth
the job had not previously existed though in practice the senior officer on any
staff had taken the title honorifically while still continuing in his other functions. Both North and South groped toward better staff arrangements
throughout the Civil War, but most of the few improvements were developed
and instituted only at army headquarters and did not survive the war.[8]

The Confederacy adopted the military practices of the United States but
appointed no general in chief, probably because Davis, as secretary of war,
had engaged in a struggle to assert his authority against Winfield Scott, the
general in chief. Instead of appointing a general in chief, Davis strengthened
the post of adjutant general, making the incumbent the senior full general in
the Confederate Army. For this position President Davis chose his ally in his
struggle with Scott, the sixty-three-year-old Samuel Cooper, who for the
previous nine years had been adjutant general of the U.S. Army. But just as
with Hitchcock in the North, General Cooper did not adequately handle his
enlarged responsibilities. If a strengthened adjutant general was meant to fill
the partially redundant role of a general in chief, Cooper made no effort so to
construe his authority, stressing instead the efficient dispatch of paperwork.
Thus, though Davis innovated by dropping the position of general in chief
and strengthening the adjutant general, fundamentally he at first continued

essentials of the peacetime structure, which he learned from his service as secretary of war.[9]

With some assistance from Adjutant General Cooper, President Davis and his successive secretaries of war together performed the duties of commander in chief. The structure mandated by law thrust these duties upon them because, whether or not there was a general in chief, only the secretary and the President controlled both logistics and the armies in the field. The able and experienced Davis was quite competent to fill these duties, but too much of a burden thus fell on the President. He wanted and needed a capable war secretary to complement his efforts. Many previous students have incorrectly asserted that Davis frustrated any successful operation of the War Office by continually meddling in the war secretary's province. In addition to a good administrator, Davis wished for a man who could engage in give-and-take discussions of strategy, collaborate in exercising command functions, and serve as a source of mutual intellectual stimulation in reaching the best decisions. Characteristically, he rarely interfered in the business transactions of the War Department.

The Confederacy's first secretary of war, Leroy Pope Walker of Alabama, like Simon Cameron in the North, attained his appointment entirely through political considerations. Perhaps Davis otherwise would have chosen Braxton Bragg of Louisiana for the secretaryship, but both the powerful Walker and his political friends actively promoted the Alabaman. Davis obliged, wanting to please the people of that state, and particularly since he already had in the Cabinet a Louisianian, Judah P. Benjamin. The forty-four-year-old Walker possessed impressive educational credentials, having been taught by private tutors and having attended the universities of Alabama and Virginia. An eminent lawyer and immensely popular in his home state, he had previously held many state offices; but he had no military experience whatever nor, as it turned out, any military aptitude. His commission as brigadier general in the Alabama militia was merely honorific, and he lacked administrative experience. Quite successful in his civilian endeavors, he proved only modestly effective as a high-level military administrator.

In addition to his inability to cope adequately with the tremendous amount of day-to-day detail inherent in the job, the tobacco-addicted, profusely spitting Walker operated with the initial handicap of believing at first that there would not be any war at all. When he had canvassed his state urging secession, he declared his faith that he would be able to wipe up with his pocket handkerchief all the blood shed as a result of the South's withdrawal from the Union. Despite the new secretary's energy, this attitude inevitably weakened his early effort at military establishment and diminished his sense of urgency. Nevertheless, and much to his credit considering this outlook, he performed adequately when the real situation became obvious.

At first Walker requested the states to equip a definite number of troops and transport them to a given point; but, pragmatically, he later demanded that each state drill, equip, and hold troops in readiness. Immense problems arose immediately. Many units offered for service had a full complement of officers but only a skeleton force of men in the ranks. Walker refused to accept any but complete units. The War Department became deluged with offers to raise companies in exchange for officers' commissions; but the department declined all on the grounds that most of the offers reflected little more than wistful visions, even though some few might be based on a real ability to recruit. Huge numbers of unarmed troops mustered for duty, but Walker sagely accepted men without equipment only if they would enlist for the war's duration and limited acceptance of twelve-month voluntary terms exclusively to already-armed personnel.

Arms, and not men, posed the real problem for the South early in the war. In the summer of 1861 the immediate lack of weapons compelled Walker to abandon the possibility of enlisting 200,000 available recruits. The states possessed stockpiles of needed materiel, but War Department attempts to tap these resources met with little success. Government purchasing agents departed to foreign countries, and the administration encouraged new domestic manufactures of arms. In July, 1861, the government let contracts for 61,200 stands of small arms, and large advance orders began spurring development of a Confederate munitions industry.

Walker's principal shortcoming lay in his limited capacity to administer a large and complex operation and his inability to react to other people with sufficient diplomacy. Many persons chafed at the cold and impersonal way he handled their various special requests, and a widespread feeling grew that he was dim-witted. A famous diarist relates one incident when Davis's nephew plaintively declared, "Would Heaven only send us a Napoleon!" and someone replied, "Not one bit of use. If Heaven did, Walker would not give him a commission." Walker did work industriously, although he misdirected much of his effort, and eventually his health broke under the strain. Illnesses forced his absence from duty on several occasions. Intermittently indecisive, he failed to function well as a collaborator with Davis in formulating strategy. When Walker made a speech which many persons interpreted to mean that the Confederacy might soon invade and seize a part of the North, Davis at last concluded gently to force him out of the Cabinet. Walker really desired to enter the Confederate Senate, but he failed to secure election; he resigned after serving for several months with little satisfaction as brigadier general of Alabama troops. Later, in April, 1864, he accepted a colonelcy as presiding judge of a military court in north Alabama.[10]

In late August, 1861, a brilliant and urbane lawyer and former U. S. senator, Judah P. Benjamin, replaced Walker, moving up from attorney general, a post for which he was vastly overqualified and hence poorly employed. Benjamin introduced more systematic procedures, coordinated and managed more effectively, supervised energetically, and successfully delegated authority. At the outset he enjoyed great popularity as war secretary.

He assumed the post at a critical time. Walker had organized and created the army and oversaw its initial supply; now war materiel was still scarce, while complacency, resulting from the southern success at Manassas, impeded further progress. In his first report to the President, Benjamin astutely analyzed the error of enlisting any more twelve-month troops: a recruit spent the first few months mustering and in basic training camps, winter brought another period of lessened activity, and probably the average time of active usefulness of a twelve-month volunteer amounted to scarcely more than ninety days. Benjamin urged a policy of encouraging re-enlistment by granting moderate furloughs and liberal bounties, and Congress responded favorably by voting a fifty-dollar bounty and sixty days of leave to twelve-month men who extended for three years.

The state governments, however, began increasing their own independent armies, tightly holding arms and ammunition within their borders, and allowing short-term volunteering for the state forces. Many units whose terms expired simply transferred from national to state service. Yet by February, 1862, the Confederate Army strength stood at an imposing 435 regiments, about two-thirds of the troops being twelve-month men, though Benjamin believed that four-fifths of the short termers would re-enlist for the duration with the offer of sufficient bounties and furloughs. In spite of so many twelve-month enlistments, a very shaky foundation, the force was imposing and clearly represented tremendous progress in creating a powerful Confederate war machine. Nevertheless, just before his departure as war secretary in March, 1862, Benjamin submitted an estimate to Congress that the Confederacy needed much more: 350,000 men, 500,000 arms, 1,000 artillery pieces, 2,000 tons of powder, and $200,000,000 in military appropriations.

Though less than had his predecessor, Benjamin encountered vexing personality clashes. After only a few days in office, a feud began with General Joseph E. Johnston, who accused the secretary of interfering and in turn refused to cooperate or to submit certain required reports. Johnston appealed to Davis and found scant satisfaction in the President's supportive attitude toward the secretary. This tiff also added a little more tension to the festering and long-strained relations between Davis and this important commander. Others, including the popular generals, Stonewall Jackson and Beauregard, also eventually fell out with Benjamin for one reason or another. As the secretary's effectiveness thus lessened, even men in the ranks came to regard him as the embodiment of all they viewed as wrong with the administration. Halleck's successful operations in Tennessee particularly intensified Benjamin's unpopularity, already mushrooming. It seemed that Benjamin had brought in a frustrating and unprofitable policy of defensive warfare.

As a climax, the secretary took the full brunt of public outrage for the disaster at Roanoke Island, North Carolina. Slightly more than 2,500 ill-organized and ill-equipped Confederates had defended that island between Pamlico and Albermarle sounds. The federal operation developed in the fall of 1861 as the brainchild of the young Brigadier General Ambrose E. Burnside, a genial West Pointer then busy but bored training raw recruits for McClellan's Army of the Potomac. McClellan liked the proposal and soon Burnside found himself at Annapolis preparing troops and vessels for his venture. By December he had 15,000 men and an adequate but motley fleet of eighty vessels, including sailboats, passenger steamers, converted barges, ferry boats, and tugs. The "Burnside Expedition," as it was popularly known, sailed on January 9, 1862, for rendezvous with its supply ships at Fort Monroe, Virginia, and put to sea on the night of the 11th. At Hatteras Inlet twenty warships from the North Atlantic Blockading Squadron of the competent Louis M. Goldsborough augmented the flotilla. On January 13 they reached the mouth of Hatteras Inlet but required nearly two weeks of work coaxing their way through the too-shallow channel. By February 4 the whole force lay at anchor in Pamlico Sound. To be sure, the Confederates knew about the impending invasion under Burnside, but they did not know exactly where he planned to land.

The Confederate occupation of Roanoke Island had begun in August, 1861, after Union forces seized Fort Hatteras and Fort Clark. The island lay within jurisdiction of the department commanded by a former regular army officer, Confederate Major General Benjamin Huger, but Huger did not want responsibility for it and momentarily had it excluded from his assigned area which he commanded from Norfolk, Virginia. Later, Secretary Benjamin ordered him to resume its supervision. When Burnside left Annapolis, the South had posted approximately 1,500 North Carolina state troops on Roanoke Island under Colonel Henry M. Shaw and a "mosquito" fleet under Captain William F. Lynch of the Navy. This fleet consisted of two side-wheel steamers, six tiny gunboats, and a floating artillery battery. Benjamin bolstered the force by sending the brigade-size legion raised and commanded by the politically powerful but militarily inept Brigadier General Henry A. Wise, a former governor of Virginia. Already a succession of ill-conceived attempts to fortify the place had produced results little more than ludicrous.

Wise at least possessed sufficient perspicacity to perceive the seriousness of his situation and decided to try to help by doing what he did best, politicking, in Norfolk with Huger and in Richmond with governmental officials, seeking more troops, supplies, and equipment. Huger and Benjamin responded with expressions of concern but, themselves forced to oversee many threatened points with strained resources, provided no added support. Upon returning to his headquarters, Wise became severely ill with pleurisy. Between spasms he sent a few instructions to Shaw but essentially gave his subordinate a free hand in directing the defending troops, which included the general's son, Captain O. Jennings Wise.

On February 7, the day Fort Henry fell, Burnside's Expedition steamed up Pamlico Sound, blessed with fairly accurate maps and charts and good advice about landing sites from a black refugee. Making first contact at about 11:30.

in the morning, Union warships managed to sink one southern gunboat and disable another before the southern naval force broke off the engagement to replenish ammunition. At about 3:30 P.M. federal troops met no resistance as they began debarking on the sandy beach of Ashby's Harbor near the center of the island. They used a clever and revolutionary scheme to get the landing craft ashore, with every brigade assigned one light-draft steamer which towed twenty surfboats in tandem, each filled with soldiers. The steamers chugged rapidly toward a preselected landing point, and, when they attained sufficient speed to carry the surfboats to the shore by momentum, cast off the towlines. Ten thousand men reached shore before midnight.

Confederate Colonel Shaw chose to make a stand in the swamps which bordered a low hill. Bringing up three pieces of artillery and placing them in a hastily constructed redoubt, he then discovered that no one in his entire command knew how to fire the pieces. A frantic plea for help went to the wretchedly sick General Wise, who sent a captain over from Nags Head to give lessons—which he was still conducting when the Union advance began at 7 A.M. The fight finished at noon. When the Confederates had exhausted their ammunition at the redoubt and their right flank crumbled, nearly 2,500 men surrendered. O. Jennings Wise lay among the twenty-four southern dead; Union casualties numbered 264.

At the same time that McClellan was moving in Virginia and Halleck and Buell were advancing in Tennessee, Burnside exploited his victory by pressing on to capture New Bern on March 14. He encountered some occasional sharp resistance and suffered 470 casualties, but he secured an important base and captured significant quantities of cotton and supplies. Simultaneously the Union Navy swept the nearby coast line, captured Elizabeth City, North Carolina, sank or burned four Confederate gunboats, captured another, drove two more up the Dismal Swamp Canal, and obstructed that waterway which connects Elizabeth City with Norfolk. Burnside's fruitful ventures gained him a promotion to major general.

Meanwhile Wise grieved for his son and prepared a blistering report. A Confederate congressional investigating committee soon looked into the "causes and circumstances of the capitulation of Roanoke Island." It received 142 pages of venomous invective from Wise. The committee concurred with Wise's indictment and placed full blame upon Huger and Benjamin. The public and press focused their ire upon Benjamin and by the end of March, 1862, he probably was the most hated man in the Confederacy. Davis, however, correctly perceived Benjamin's immense ability, and adversity only strengthened their growing friendship. They decided it was wiser to bear odium in silence than to defend Benjamin's failure to send more men and munitions to Roanoke Island. To do so would reveal to the enemy and the world the Confederacy's critical weakness when threatened on so many fronts. The President made every effort to preserve Benjamin in office as secretary of war. When that became clearly impossible, a face-saving compromise evolved whereby

Benjamin left the War Office and moved up to be secretary of state, a post then vacant and a position where Davis could continue to have Benjamin's advice and assistance.

Thus Davis had to seek his third secretary of war, but not because the previous incumbents failed to fill their roles appropriately nor because Davis interfered in the war office by trying to run it himself. With Benjamin, even more than with Walker, the President controlled military planning and strategy, though Davis and the secretary worked out such plans together. Otherwise the secretary continued to enjoy virtually a free hand in the business of managing the department. Save for his inability to handle the hypersensitive generals and his loss of public esteem, Benjamin had served as a very good secretary of war.

Davis then appointed Brigadier General George Wythe Randolph as Confederate secretary of war. Though not a West Pointer, he was, unlike his two predecessors, a soldier. Earlier, at the age of thirteen, he had been appointed a midshipman in the Navy, and had served for six years, mostly at sea. He eventually became a well-to-do Richmond lawyer and strong secessionist. Continuing his military interests and well read in military history and policy, he had introduced into Virginia a manpower procurement system obviously inspired by that of Prussia. As a major serving as a chief of artillery, he performed in an outstanding manner at the Battle of Big Bethel, a feat which brought him advancement and recognition. It was perhaps fitting that a prominent position in the Cabinet should go to this urbane, cultured, and competent Virginian, for, as a grandson of Thomas Jefferson, he reinforced the Confederates' perception of themselves as engaged in a second American Revolution. Randolph brought to the War Department recent field experience, firsthand knowledge of how the military systems functioned, and a great sense of urgency concerning manpower needs.

During the transition period, Benjamin helped the President to formulate a critically important and unprecedented conscription act, and Randolph thereafter completed the bill and put it into effective operation. This vital measure provided needed recruits for the southern ranks. More significantly, just as the 1862 Union spring campaigns began, the law, at Randolph's insistence, retained in the Confederate Army all of the numerous one-year volunteers whose terms neared expiration. Thus he solved the one-year enlistment problem which Benjamin had sought to resolve by bounties and furloughs.

The problem of short-term enlistments had originated in February, 1861, when, in spite of Davis's request for three-year enlistment terms, Congress had authorized only twelve-month duty periods for regular volunteers and a scanty six months for militia. Worse, the states then jealously demanded ultimate control of the militia *and* of the manpower input to the national forces. In May, 1861, Congress had passed a new bill which weakened the state control over the army personnel and also authorized a ten-dollar bounty for recruits, primarily to pay for their transportation to basic-training camps.

After the first Battle of Bull Run the Confederate Congress approved raising a 400,000-man army for a term of one to three years, but they could not
muster nearly that number. Flocks of volunteers came during the rush of
enthusiasm after early victory, but most of them preferred shorter terms of
commitment. In an effort to mitigate this evil, Secretary Walker had turned
away volunteers unless they accepted a three-year tour, except in the rare
cases where whole units appeared already armed. Yet by the end of 1861 one-
half of the troops were twelve-month volunteers. Continuing to rely on the
volunteer principle, Benjamin instigated inducements for three-year re-enlist-
ments, approved by Congress on December 11, containing a provision which
caused chaos within the officer corps. The army gave re-enlisted units permission to elect new officers if they wished, and sometimes very poor choices
resulted. Both the military establishment and the press at last began to favor
instituting a draft. In March one estimate indicated that the terms of 148
regiments would expire within thirty days.

Odds dictated that the South had no reasonable chance to keep up with the
northern rate of volunteering; according to the 1860 census, white males in
the Confederacy of military age, between fifteen and forty, totaled 1,140,000
while those in the North numbered 4,010,000. On January 23, 1862, Congress had granted Davis's request for power to call on the states for men.
Though this produced some beneficial results, it still failed to fill needs adequately and failed to solve the problem of the impending discharge of the
one-year men. Congress, at last ready to act, approved Randolph's drastic
recommendation. On March 29, 1862, after a few states already had enacted
conscription laws and after careful and sometimes heated deliberation, Congress passed a draft law, forcefully retaining volunteers and making every
able white male between eighteen and thirty-five years of age liable to call.
Some members of the Congress thought the law unconstitutional, but eventually the majority realized it was a necessity.

Only five days after the law passed, Congress enacted the first Exemption
Act. This vexing proviso excluded from the draft Confederate and state governmental officials, mail carriers, ferrymen, woolen and cotton laborers, railroad employees, newspaper printers, one apothecary per establishment,
ministers, college professors, teachers of more than twenty pupils, all who
worked in institutions for the deaf, dumb, or blind, and hospital nurses or
attendants. Many of the persons opposed to the draft used these provisions in
their resistance efforts. Governors who opposed conscription abruptly and
vastly increased the number of "state officials," while some judges issued
writs of habeas corpus to retrieve unwilling soldiers from the army. New
schools sprang up and "teachers" scrambled to obtain the needed twenty
pupils by offering free tuition; some dodgers proclaimed their allegiance to a
foreign country; and many lawyers made lucrative livings helping to legalize
clients' exemptions. Clearly the flush of martial enthusiasm at the war's start
had lost much of its charm by early 1862.

Some months later, on October 11, 1862, a second Exemption Act passed. This increased the number of persons excused from the draft by including one editor per newspaper, shoemakers, blacksmiths, saltworkers, tanners, millers, wheelwrights, industrial workers, and all persons making munitions and war materials. Agricultural exclusions included one person per five hundred cattle or two hundred and fifty mules and one overseer for every twenty slaves. The act also included for the first time in American history provisions for people who opposed war upon religious grounds. Friends, Dunkards, Nazarenes, and Mennonites could avoid service if they provided someone to take their place or paid $500 to the government.

A very damaging proviso in the draft law allowed any man called, not just religious objectors, to offer a substitute in his stead. Substitute brokers began to multiply, some charging exorbitant fees but openly advertising their services. The rates eventually ranged from $100 to $5,000. Many of the standings, the dregs of southern society or older and economically depressed individuals, made poor soldiers or soon deserted. Quite a number of them apparently made a business of pocketing the money they got for enlisting and deserting to repeat the process over and over again. Some commanders refused to accept these replacements into their ranks. Congress finally abolished the substitute system on December 28, 1863, but not before it had caused much discord.

The draft procedures changed several times during the life of the Confederacy. A Bureau of Conscription, eventually set up under the direction of Colonel, later Brigaider General, John S. Preston, used state officials where practicable; but gradually its own bureaucratic structure increased and by 1864 it had 2,813 employees. Preston, who had been born in 1809 and excellently educated at Hampden-Sydney College, the University of Virginia, and the Harvard Law School, showed considerable ability, as reflected in his amassed fortune derived from operation of a large sugar plantation in Louisiana before the war. He was also well connected throughout the Confederacy with relatives in Kentucky and such prominent Virginia cousins as Joseph E. Johnston, John B. Floyd, and Confederate Senator William Ballard Preston. During the war he held various staff assignments but found his real forte in April, 1862, with assignment to command a conscript camp at Columbia, South Carolina. Although he claimed to dislike the task, he carried out his duties so effectively that in July, 1863, the secretary of war urged upon him the job as head of the Bureau of Conscription in Richmond. Preston personally made a splendid record, acting with vigor, initiative, and independence; but the efficiency of the bureau varied greatly from one geographic region to another, depending on the quality of the men operating in that area. Many bureau officials had been previously weeded out of the army for one reason or another. Originally the army used drafted men to fill skeleton companies from their home states, whereas volunteers could even choose their own company. These impractically liberal provisions could not be long continued.

In September, 1862, the Congress expanded the draft age upwards to forty-five, but required the President to *ask* the various governors for the older men if they were truly needed; only if the governors refused could the army take these older men by the draft. By February, 1864, the age span of liability widened again, to include men from seventeen to fifty.

Throughout the war, a number of recruits nearly equal to those generated by the draft volunteered in order to escape the stigma of being conscripts, though it may seem strange that men who resisted all the many other pressures to enlist should be induced finally by the prospect of such a nebulous dishonor. Yet an individual certainly had to be thick-skinned to cope with such potent efforts that young *women* all over the South exerted, when, for example, the "girls of Selma, Alabama . . . put on a 'pout and sulk' campaign to stimulate volunteering. One . . . announced that she would not keep company with a civilian. Another stated that she would become an old maid rather than marry a slacker. A third broke her engagement to a suitor who was slow to enlist and sent him a skirt and a petticoat with the message: 'Wear these or volunteer.' " Indeed about 78.9 percent of the estimated 7,500,000 individuals who comprised the Confederacy's ultimate total number of military men did volunteer freely. The draft produced 81,993 conscripts, 10.9 percent of the total manpower, and it directly influenced another 76,206 volunteers, 10.2 percent.[11]

Likewise in the North, early in the war huge numbers of willing volunteers rallied to the flag. In 1861 so many responded to Lincoln's calls that recruiting stations closed. But, as happened in the South, late 1861 and early 1862 brought lessened appeal for the great campaign to save the Union. The meagre musters, following new calls for volunteers, became increasingly alarming. Yet the United States avoided resorting to the draft for more than another year. Though its armies outnumbered those of the Confederacy by two to one, the North possessed manpower resources two-and-a-half times as great, and, of course, even greater manufacturing resources for equipping them. The North's war effort was not, proportionately, as great as the South's.

The North found a stopgap measure in 1862 when Congress passed a new Militia Act, designed to force the northern states to fill their quotas of volunteers. The President received the power to enroll the necessary men if the states failed to do so themselves, and he could authorize generous bounty payments as bonuses for enlistment. Two calls occurred under this Militia Act; the first was filled a month late and the second failed to produce the total number of men needed, because widespread evasion and resistance resulted in violence in five states. The authorities arrested as many as 13,000 persons and tried by court-martial men called who refused to serve. Nevertheless the

Union limped along without a national conscription for the time being, while the South began reaping beneficial results from its draft almost at once. During April, May, and June, 1862, healthy musters filled the Confederate training camps and bolstered the ranks for the early summer campaigns.

Davis introduced other military changes in March of 1862 besides a new secretary of war and an effective new manpower system. The organization of the command system contained a flaw and Davis dimly perceived it. The system, adopted from that of the United States, was oriented toward peacetime needs. Even with a competent war secretary and a somewhat strengthened adjutant general's office, the existing system obviously required the President to do too much. Davis called General Robert E. Lee from obscure coastal defense duty in South Carolina, to which he had been relegated late in 1861 after his lackluster western Virginia performance. Davis now assigned him to "the seat of the government . . . under the direction of the President" in charge of "the conduct of military operations in the armies of the Confederacy."[12]

In making the appointment Davis used the same words adopted by Congress in legislation to create the post of commanding general who would, "under the direction of the President," have "control of military operations, the movement and discipline of the troops, and the distribution of supplies among the armies of the Confederate states." Davis had vetoed the law because of defects in its wording, but, as he did "fully approve" of the law, he promptly implemented its purpose by executive action. Professor Dennis Hart Mahan of West Point had suggested the same powerful chief of staff for the Union.[13]

Davis chose Lee because he retained complete confidence in his ability. Though Davis had apparently long planned to have Lee stationed in Richmond, significantly he called Lee to the capital on March 3, only a little over two weeks after the fall of Fort Donelson. He appointed Lee ten days later. The disasters in the West evidently showed Davis that during wartime the War Department must be an operational as well as an administrative headquarters. It must have a command system adequate to control the movement of armies along the Confederacy's vast military frontier. The position given Lee significantly departed from the prewar United States organization, and also Confederate practice, for it gave to Lee not only the historic powers of the ineffectual general in chief but also the President's power over the staff departments. Lee, unlike the old U.S. generals in chief, gained ample power to control both logistics and operations. His powers resembled those of the present-day chief of staff of the U.S. Army.[14]

In the same month, March, 1862, the exigencies of the war had brought about fundamental organizational reform in both Washington and Richmond. Just as Lincoln and Stanton were dispensing with the general in chief and inaugurating the War Board headed by Hitchcock, Davis was making a dif-

ferent innovation but one comparable in purpose. Both presidents aimed at
strengthening the command system and both sought to achieve the same goal,
providing increased coordination, especially over the staff departments.

Many observers failed to appreciate Davis's revolutionary step toward mod-
ernity: the *Charleston Mercury* said, for example, that Davis was reducing Lee
"from a commanding general to an orderly sergeant." Lee himself allowed: "I
cannot see either advantage or pleasure in my duties," and his great biographer, Douglas S. Freeman, called it "an impossible assignment." Though
Freeman never managed to perceive fully the real significance of the experiment, he did admit that "there were few, if any," periods of Lee's service
"during which he contributed more to sustain the Confederate cause."[15]

The Congress enacted a law which provided Lee with a staff of one colonel
and four majors plus up to four clerks. For the top assignment, Lee brought
in Major Armistead L. Long, promoting him immediately two grades to full
colonel. The thirty-seven-year-old Long had graduated frow West Point in
1850 and served in the U. S. Army artillery for nearly eleven years. Lee
inherited him as a staff officer from Brigadier General William "Old Blizzards" Loring in western Virginia where Long impressed Lee immensely with
his efficient military bearing and performance. Lee took Long with him to
South Carolina, and their friendship grew into an intimate companionship
after they fled together from a great fire at the Mills House in Charleston
where they had taken rooms, each of them escaping the conflagration clasping
a baby in his arms.

The majors included T. M. R. Talcott, an able engineer and son of an old
Lee friend; Charles Marshall, a Baltimore lawyer who proved excellent in
drafting papers; T. A. Washington, who had nearly a decade of pre-Civil
War service in the U. S. Army infantry; and Charles Venable, a man of
superior intellect. Major Venable had entered Hampden-Sydney College at
the age of twelve, graduated at fifteen in 1842, served as a mathematics tutor,
studied mathematics and astronomy in Berlin and Bonn, and held professor-
ships at the universities of Virginia and Georgia. Washington left the staff
late in April, making room for Major Walter H. Taylor, whom Lee had
retained as an aide, at the rank of captain, through the western Virginia and
South Carolina episodes, and who proved most capable in performing personnel (G-1) duties. The twenty-four-year-old Taylor had been three years a
cadet at the Virginia Military Institute, had worked several years as a railroad
auditor, and had extensive as well as highly successful banking experience.
His uncle by marriage, Lee's first cousin, had secured Taylor's initial appointment; but above-average intelligence, a powerful memory, and a high sense
of organization convinced Lee of Taylor's immense value and Lee retained
him as an important staff officer for the entire war.[16]

This staff did not divide into separate sections, G-1 through G-4, but
performed collectively as the operations staff of the Confederate high com-

mand. They issued orders in Lee's name to the staff departments and made requests of the secretary of war. There seems to have been no formal division of labor between Lee and Secretary of War Randolph, but Lee primarily supervised operations and Randolph devoted much of his time to coordinating logistics and to implementing the new conscription act, effectively allocating the flow of replacements it produced. Lee's "position was regarded by some as rather anomalous in character," Taylor, the young staff officer, recorded, "and yet there devolved upon the general a great deal of work that did not appear on the surface, and was a kind not to be generally appreciated. Exercising a constant supervision over the condition of affairs at each important point, thoroughly informed as to the resources and necessities of the several commanders of armies in the field, as well as of the dangers which respectively threatened them, he was enabled to give them wise counsel, to offer them valuable suggestions, and to respond to their demands for assistance and support to such extent as the limited resources of the Government would permit." Instead of going out in the secretary's name, operational orders henceforth emanated from Lee, the "General Commanding."[17]

Of course Davis did not abdicate his constitutional responsibilities as commander in chief; he simply created the modern post of chief of staff of the army. Nor did he abandon his lifelong interest in military affairs; but he and Lee made an admirable team. They had worked together the previous spring with Lee in charge of Virginia forces, and these two West Point veterans of the Mexican War understood warfare in the same way. Davis trusted Lee and Lee kept the President fully informed, sought counsel, made recommendations, and referred major operational decisions to the President.[18]

When Davis placed Lee in charge of military operations, the President delegated full powers over both operations and logistics. The relation between Lee and the secretary of war was not defined in law or in orders. There seemed to have been a workable, informal relationship between Lee and Randolph, two members of the Virginia establishment. That Lee was Randolph's senior in age, and in military rank, knowledge, and experience, may also have helped facilitate relations between the two, an arrangement in which in many ways the secretary was subordinate to the general. This relationship conformed to Davis's order, for Lee, in acting under the direction of the President, was the secretary's superior in operational matters.

In his reform, the northern war secretary, Stanton, had likewise attacked the same problem of securing unity of command by also going outside of the formal structure prescribed by law and tradition. The Union reorganization also concerned operations, primarily in the *implementation* of strategy otherwise selected. Even more important, the new organization, the War Board, facilitated logistics, and, as a body, recommended strategy. It did not function as a source of commands or operational directives as Lee's did. Under Stanton's plan these continued to come from the secretary, to whom the board reported.

Stanton himself had set the stage for improved logistical coordination by instituting cooperation and regulating relations between the government and both the railroads and telegraphs. In February, 1862, Stanton had brought together McClellan and Quartermaster General Montgomery C. Meigs. An engineer officer who quickly became an administrative expert, Meigs put his organizational ability and military knowledge fully at Stanton's disposal. Meigs soon spent perhaps half his time on tasks not clearly related to his formal office. Exemplifying their new functions, Stanton, McClellan, and Meigs met with a group of railroad operators to achieve a rate formula that prevented overcharges against the government. Stanton ordered standardization of track, pre-determined priorities for freight car use, and the uniform employment of signaling systems. The government's needs demanded priority over private interests, he pointed out, but he "infinitely preferred" that the companies regulate themselves in lieu of the Congress's taking them over. The railroad officials got the hint.[19]

The telegraph systems required more stringent measures, because military secrecy necessitated constant rather than intermittent control. Stanton appointed Edward S. Sanford, president of the American Telegraph Company, to the position of military supervisor of telegrams and demanded a rigid censorship. Peter H. Watson, one of the two new assistant secretaries Stanton had at the outset persuaded Congress to authorize for the War Department, screened out undesirable journalists, and required all newspapermen to work through him.

As Stanton strengthened the administration of the war effort, his two additional assistants brought the full complement to five. Stanton's initial assistant secretaries included only Watson, John Tucker, and one holdover, Thomas A. Scott. Watson, a Washington attorney, former Stanton associate, and close family friend, had almost as much driving energy as his chief. The stubby, fat, red-haired and whiskered Watson demonstrated keen business discernment. Further, he not only was the most prominent patent lawyer in the country but possessed an unexcelled familiarity with mechanical inventions. Stanton unreservedly relied upon him in ordnance matters and entrusted him with any number of confidential assignments. These included organizing and supervising the first national secret service, a secret police force called the National Detectives and headed by Colonel Lafayette C. Baker.

The second assistant secretary, John Tucker, had been general transportation agent of the War Department since May, 1861. He helped the previous war secretary, Cameron, organize the management of eastern rail and water transportation but came under criticism, particularly from rival political and railroad spoilsmen, who charged that he profited personally from questionable contracts. Stanton not only vouched personally for his honesty but asserted that no one else could do the job as well, and so the Senate confirmed his appointment; but thereafter Tucker maintained a rather low profile within the War Office. Stanton used him to supervise business dealings, to let contracts with private concerns, and to charter vessels.[20]

The third, Tom Scott, had served as superintendent and then vice president of the Pennsylvania Railroad. He had become deeply involved in efforts to sway public opinion and in controversial political battles in the railroad's behalf. Like Tucker, he came under political fire from Washington-based enemies. He, too, displayed managerial expertise of a broad caliber. With a military appointment at the rank of colonel, Scott had previously held two important positions of authority: at first he had been placed in "charge of the railways and telegraphs between Washington City and Annapolis," later expanded to "all Government railways and telegraphs or those appropriated for Government use," and then became the first assistant secretary of war in U.S. history. Even though he officially retired from the War Department in June, 1862, he continued for the remainder of the war to exercise an informal supervisory influence upon the two formal agencies, U.S. Military Telegraphs and U.S. Military Railroads. Stanton used Scott primarily as a trusted field observer and evaluator of remote conditions. In performing these duties, he proved extraordinarily capable and effective because of his personal charm, keen mind, discerning eye, and uncanny talent for perceiving defects and prescribing appropriate remedies.[21]

With this, and later a still larger staff, Stanton always aimed to secure "the aid of the highest business talent . . . this country can afford." He established an office pace of hard work and long days, his work habits obvious to all when he amazed applicants for interviews with the secretary by receiving appointments at previously unheard-of early hours. Stanton received guests one at a time, standing at his chest-high writing desk, which he used at the suggestion of concerned physicians who knew that he otherwise took no physical exercise. Often he worked far into the night. Realizing that he knew very little about war, he plunged himself into research on the administration of armies with the same gusto he previously applied to his legal practice.[22]

After establishing the War Board, the secretary then gathered together the heads of several bureaus of the army "to effect an *informal organization* for his own instruction, and in order [the more effectually] to bring to bear the whole power of the Government upon the operations of the present war." Unconsciously he began the creation of a general staff. The personnel of the War Board included several brigadier generals: Lorenzo Thomas, the adjutant general; Montogomery C. Meigs, the quartermaster general; James W. Ripley, the chief of ordnance; Joseph G. Totten, the chief engineer; and Colonel Joseph P. Taylor, commissary general. Major General Hitchcock did not join the board until its third meeting, and thereafter he served as its head, the *de facto* chief of staff, although he participated but little in its discussions.[23]

Lorenzo Thomas, a West Pointer, had, at age fifty-eight, served forty-three of his years in the army, mostly in routine personnel administration duties, except for service as quartermaster during the Seminole War (1836–37). Upon the resignation of Colonel Samuel Cooper as adjutant general of the army to accept the same position in the newly formed Confederacy, Thomas succeeded to the post and was promoted to brigadier general in August, 1861. Considerable laxity and inefficiency characterized his bureau, hopelessly inadequate in employees to handle its vastly increased workload.

Montgomery C. Meigs, but forty-six years old, had shown brilliant abilities as a student at the University of Pennsylvania and at West Point where he graduated fifth in the 1836 class. His career in the Engineer Corps of the army lived up to his early promise for he worked on many important projects, including supervision of the building of the wings and dome of the national Capitol and work on the Cabin John Bridge at Washington, unsurpassed for fifty years as the longest masonry arch in the world. In the critical days preceding the Civil War's actual outbreak, he and Lieutenant Colonel Erasmus D. Keyes, later one of McClellan's four corps commanders, drew up a secret plan for the relief of Fort Pickens, Florida, and in April, 1861, with naval Lieutenant, later Admiral, David D. Porter, carried it out. On May 14, 1861, Meigs accepted command of the Eleventh Infantry Regiment but, raised to brigadier general the next day, he became quartermaster general of the army. Congressman James G. Blaine glowingly testified concerning Meigs that he was "one of the ablest graduates of the Military Academy," who "was kept from the command of troops [only] by the inestimably important services he performed" in logistic management.[24]

James W. Ripley and the two other remaining War Board members were among the mere handful of Civil War officers born before 1800. Sixty-eight years old in 1862, Ripley was preceded by only 101 men at West Point where he graduated in 1814. He served eighteen years as an artillery officer in the field before he transferred to the staff in 1832. He directed the Kennebec Arsenal for ten years, superintended the Springfield Armory for twelve, and served as a chief of ordnance on the Pacific coast and as inspector of arsenals. When a friend observed after secession that his country needed him, Ripley replied colorfully, "It can have me and every drop of blood in me." Zealous, incorruptible, devoted to duty, and unendingly principled, as chief of ordnance he unfortunately showed a lack of imagination and opposed virtually every innovation suggested to the War Department, especially in fighting to the end the introduction of breech-loading weapons as standard equipment.

Even more venerable was the seventy-four-year-old Joseph G. Totten, a world figure in the development of seacoast fortifications and one of the leading military engineers in American history. In 1805 he had been the tenth graduate of West Point. His guardian-uncle held the first professorship of mathematics there. Outstanding in scholarship, industry, "gentlemanly deportment," and popularity, through his long career Totten set new standards for American engineers. So instrumental in the establishment of the third generation of U.S. seacoast fortifications that his name is synonomous with it, the Totten System, he devoted much of his professional life to the refinement of casemate details—the rooms of forts within which cannon are mounted. He perfected the size, shape, location, and protection of openings, making the personnel more secure and the guns able to swivel through wider arcs. Totten's accomplishments rendered American refinements far ahead of those in Europe at mid-nineteenth century. For more than two decades before the Civil War he held the posts of chief engineer of the army and inspector of the U.S. Military Academy. He served intermittently on the national Lighthouse Board from its first establishment and continuously as a regent of the Smithsonian Institution from its founding in 1846 until his death in 1864.[25]

The last War Board member, the sixty-six-year-old Colonel Joseph P. Taylor, through his kinships lent a touch of irony to the assembly: his brother Zachary served as twelfth President of the United States, but his nephew Richard became a lieutenant general in the Confederate Army, and his niece Sara Knox was the first wife of Jefferson Davis. Joseph Taylor began his military career as an enlisted man during the War of 1812, gained a battlefield promotion to second lieutenant, and remained in service for forty-five years, mostly in staff positions. Near the end of the Mexican War he became chief commissary of the army in the northern theater, and this led to his remaining in subsistence work thereafter. When the commissary general of the army, Colonel George Gibson, died in September, 1861, Taylor succeeded him.

Collectively the board became a body of such significance and importance that the famous military officer and scholar, Emory Upton, called it the "Second Aulic Council." The Hapsburg emperor, Maximilian I (1493–1519), established the Aulic Council and it endured long after. In military matters it facilitated control and coordination in operations, often prescribing the strategy of particular campaigns. The comparison did not altogether flatter the War Board, for the Aulic Council had often stood for over-centralized control. Later an authority on military administration, Upton incidentally was just beginning his career at the start of the Civil War, having graduated from West Point in 1861. He rose during the conflict to a brevet major generalcy and command of a division, but afterwards in peacetime reverted to captain. In 1867 he published *Infantry Tactics*, hailed as the greatest single advance in tactical instruction since the Revolution because for the first time it cited American experiences for examples and problem illustrations. He died in 1881 with his great work, *The Military Policy of the United States from 1775*, completed only through the middle of the Civil War. Nevertheless many officers read it in manuscript during the late nineteenth century and eventually it was published in 1907. Fact-filled, though polemical and highly critical, it probably ranks as the most influential book ever written by an American soldier.[26]

Though Upton failed adequately to appreciate the War Board, he correctly understood its sub rosa functioning. In bringing the bureau chiefs together in the War Board, Stanton unconsciously reinforced what very likely pre-existed as an informal organization within his department, alongside and in addition to the formal structure. But Stanton did far more than strengthen and give sanction and impetus to the existing or, at least incipient, informal organization, in which the bureau chiefs had collaborated informally. He gave it a new formal, but extralegal, charter. Charged not merely to work together to coordinate their own staff duties and help, advise, and regulate one another, the War Board members were to broaden their authority to cover operational concerns, normally only the province of the adjutant general and the general in chief. Again, Stanton probably exploited the natural inclinations of the bureau chiefs.[27]

Just as Davis created informally through Lee's appointment a modern chief of staff, Lincoln and Stanton, by a parallel route, attempted something analogous. Whereas Davis placed stress on the chief, Lincoln and Stanton placed it on the staff. Unlike Davis, the northerners brought the staff into control over operations, and their chief was only chief over the War Board. The Union President delegated nothing; but because of age, infirmity, and reluctance, Hitchcock, head of the War Board, would not function like Lee, even if Hitchcock had been endowed with that authority. Working toward the same goal, the War Board, based upon a collegial or commitee model, no doubt unconsciously followed the natural informal inclinations of the organization.

Stanton's unprecedented board in its formal meetings discussed topics that included: seacoast defense; ironclad vessels of various types; support for expeditions; ordnance; officer and enlisted personnel management matters; quartermaster functions; corps branch consolidation proposals; the Military Academy; army strength; staff appointments; and prisoner policies. The board also gave attention to operations for, when it held its first meeting, on March 13, 1862, five detached commands or expeditions were of particular concern. They were led by brigadier generals Thomas W. Sherman at Fernandina, Florida, John M. Brannan at Key West, and major generals John E. Wool at Fort Monroe, Benjamin F. Butler in the Gulf of Mexico, and Ambrose E. Burnside who would, on the 14th, complete his Roanoke Island success by capturing New Bern. All of these, Stanton thought, might require the kind of planning and coordination that the board could provide. But seacoast attack and defense and the impact of the new ironclad vessels that had made their first appearances in combat just days before demanded greatest immediate attention. As matters evolved, neither side gained a decisive advantage from the advent of ironclad war vessels; but their great initial clash presaged new phases of the war and set the stage for a grand Union triple-prolonged, simultaneous advance.[28]

☆   ☆   ☆

1. Foote, *The Civil War*, I, 266–67; Hitchcock to Mrs. Mann, Mar. 15, 1862, in Hitchcock Papers, Library of Congress.

2. W. A. Croffut, ed., *Fifty Years in Camp and Field: Diary of Major-General Ethan Allen Hitchcock, U.S.A.* (New York, 1909), 437.

3. Douglas Southall Freeman, *R. E. Lee*, 4 vols. (New York and London, 1934–35), I, Appendix I—4.

4. See J. D. Hittle, *The Military Staff, Its History and Development* (Harrisburg, Pa., 1952), 12 and *passim*.

5. Matloff, *American Military History*, 150.

6. T. Harry Williams, *Americans At War* (Baton Rouge, 1960), 3–43*ff*; Robert F. Stohlman, Jr., *The Powerless Position: The Commanding General of the Army of the United States, 1864–1903* (Manhattan, Kan., 1975), 1–21.

7. William P. Craighill, *The Army Officer's Pocket Companion; Principally Designed for Staff Officers in the Field* (New York, 1862), 257; H. L. Scott, *Military Dictionary: Comprising Technical Definitions; Information on Raising and Keeping Troops, Actual Service, Including Makeshifts and Improved Material; and Law, Government, Regulation and Administration Relating to Land Forces* (New York, 1861), 570.

8. Hittle, *The Military Staff*, 188.

9. June I. Gow, "Theory and Practice in Confederate Military Administration," *Military Affairs* (Oct., 1975), 119.

10. Chesnut, *Diary*, 85.

11. Bell Wiley, *Confederate Women* (Westport, Conn., 1975), 141–42; Wilfred B. Yearns, *The Confederate Congress* (Athens, 1960), 60–66; Eaton, *A History of the Southern Confederacy*, 88; Charles H. Wesley, *The Collapse of the Confederacy* (New York, 1968), 60–61; May S. Ringold, *The Role of the State Legislatures in the Confederacy* (Athens, 1966), 60; Albert B. Moore, *Conscription and Conflict in the Confederacy* (New York, 1924), 13–16; E. Merton Coulter, *The Confederate States of America, 1861–1865* (Baton Rouge, 1950), 314; Thomas L. Livermore, *Numbers and Losses in the Civil War in America, 1861–1865* (Boston and New York, 1901), *passim*; Lowell H. Harrison, "Conscription in the Confederacy," *Civil War Times—Illustrated*, IX (July, 1970), 10–18.

12. Freeman, *Lee*, II, 5.

13. An Act to create the office of commanding general of the armies of the Confederate States, *O.R.*, series 4, I, 997–98; Davis to speaker of the House of Representatives, Mar. 14, 1862, *ibid.*, 997; Griess, "Mahan," 334–35.

14. Davis to J. E. Johnston, Aug. 1, 1861, *O.R.*, V, 767.

15. Freeman, *Lee*, II, 6–7.

16. *O.R.*, XI, pt. 3, 419; XII, pt. 3, 891; LI, pt. 2, 554; Series 4, I, 997–98, 1021; A. L. Long, *Memoirs of Robert E. Lee* (New York, 1886), 143; Walter H. Taylor, *Four Years With General Lee*, (ed., with new introduction, index, and notes, by James I. Robertson, Jr. (New York, 1962), vi–vii, 37; Freeman, *Lee*, I, 640–41; II, 234–35.

17. Taylor, *Four Years With General Lee*, 38.

18. Representative of their collaborative relations are: Lee to Davis, June 5, 10, 1862, *The Wartime Papers of R. E. Lee*, eds. Clifford Dowdey and Louis H. Manarin (Boston, 1961), 183–84, 188. These communications occurred after Lee had also assumed command of the Army of Northern Virginia.

19. Thomas and Hyman, *Stanton*, 154.

20. *Ibid.*, 152–53.

21. *Ibid.*; *Guide to Federal Archives Relating to the Civil War* (Washington, 1962), 315–17; Samuel R. Kamm, *The Civil War Career of Thomas A. Scott* (Philadelphia, 1940), *passim*.

22. Stanton to Hannibal Hamlin, Jan. 27, 1862, Stanton Papers, Library of Congress; Thomas and Hyman, *Stanton*, 161.

23. Proceedings of the War Board, entry for Mar. 13, 1862, in Stanton Papers, Library of Congress. Italics supplied.

24. Charles Dudley Rhodes, "Montgomery C. Meigs," *Dictionary of American Biography*, ed. Dumas Malone, 20 vols. (New York, 1928–36), VI, 508.

25. Emanuel Raymond Lewis, *Seacoast Fortifications of the United States: An Introductory History* (Washington, 1970), 37–38, 43–45.

26. Emory Upton, *The Military Policy of the United States from 1775* (Washington, 1907), 291–94.

27. The various bureau chiefs undoubtedly already had many informal relationships which were not envisioned by the completely separate structure of the formal organization of the bureaus. Social psychologists call these relationships "informal organizations," and recent research has revealed that a multitude of such informal contacts abound in modern organiza-

tions. In every organization many groups exist to promote various ideas and interests. Veterans of army service are well aware of the strong but completely informal organization of supply sergeants through which shortages are covered and scarce items procured entirely outside of the channels of the formal supply system. Similar behavior exists, for example, in academic life, where groups of faculty and administrators often exercise an influence not obvious from their positions in the formal organization.

In creating the War Board Stanton con-sciously or unconsciously mobilized the natural tendencies of the organizaion to increase coordination among the bureaus and to provide a source of formal advice on operational questions.

For an excellent brief treatment of the informal organization and a bibliography, see Richard E. Beringer, *Historical Analysis, Contemporary Approaches to Clio's Craft* (New York, Santa Barbara, Chichester, Brisbane, Toronto, 1978), 153–57.

28. Proceedings of the War Board, Stanton Papers, Library of Congress.

6 ☆ UNION LOGISTICS AND STRATEGY

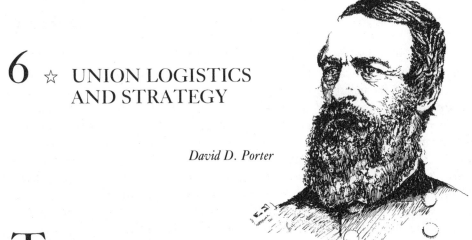

David D. Porter

THE OVERALL naval strategies of both the North and South revolved around attempts to establish, or to thwart, a blockade of the Confederate coastline. Lincoln wished to choke the South's commerce and to prevent her from obtaining significant supplies from abroad; and Davis countered by authorizing privateering and commerce raiding upon northern vessels, just as the United States had done years before when blockaded in its wars with Britain. The South proved more vulnerable than the Union for, despite its hundreds of bays, inlets, river mouths, and deltas, the Confederacy possessed only a handful of useful ports. For the northern blockade to produce effective results, only the ten seaports which possessed rail or water connections with the interior needed to be closed: Norfolk, Virginia; New Bern and Wilmington, North Carolina; Charleston, South Carolina; Savannah, Georgia; Jacksonville, Fernandina, and Pensacola, Florida; Mobile, Alabama; and New Orleans, Louisiana. Six of these ten had fallen by early 1862 and, save for Norfolk, the relatively shallow harbors of those remaining made them accessible only to ships of less than twenty feet draft. Federal seapower also could reach another vulnerability of southern commerce, its reliance on coastwise trade. Historically the South had depended less on its railroads for transportation to and from its cities on the ocean and the gulf and more upon coastal and river steamers and schooners. The existence of only three major shipyards—the navy yard at Norfolk, a naval repair yard at Pensacola, and private shipbuilding facilities at New Orleans—further handicapped the South.[1]

On April 20–21, 1861, the Federals burned or scuttled most of the ships at Norfolk, Virginia, and abandoned the important naval installation there near the mouth of the James River because they considered it indefensible against Confederate attack. Upon their occupation the southerners easily raised the sunken, screw-driven steam frigate *Merrimack*—named for the Merrimack River and not for Merrimac, Massachusetts, as is often presumed—and commenced refitting her as an ironclad warship.

Confederate Secretary of the Navy Stephen R. Mallory, formerly U.S. senator from Florida and chairman of the Senate Naval Affairs Committee, had astutely assessed the South's naval situation. He reasoned that with just one of the new ironclad vessels, recently designed in Europe and first employed by the French in the Crimean War, the Confederacy might find the answer to all its naval needs. The French-developed seagoing armored ship *Gloire* promised to render all wooden warships obsolete. If only the Confederacy could obtain one of that type without the Union's gaining a similar advantage at the same time, the scales might tip in the South's favor. Work on the *Merrimack* proceeded at a feverish pace, with the energies of almost the entire navy yard devoted to this one ship. Mallory allocated as many as fifteen hundred men to the job, often keeping them working on Sundays and through night shifts. But, typical of the South's constant transportation shortage, the railroad facilities between Richmond and Norfolk added to the construction problems. A shortage of flatcars caused some of the essential iron plate to sit on the banks of the James River awaiting shipment for a month or more at a time.

The strange appearance of the reconstructed ship led one War Department clerk to declare that "the government is constructing a monster at Norfolk." The Confederate engineers cut the *Merrimack's* hull down to the waterline and retopped it with a large superstructure sloping at 36 degrees, causing the vessel to look like a floating barn roof. From bow to stern she measured 262 feet and 9 inches. Two-inch-thick wrought-iron plates, hastily produced at Richmond's Tredegar Iron Works, crisscrossed over the two-foot thickness of solid pine and oak. These plates were heavily greased with tallow, in the naive hope that this would render them more likely to deflect enemy cannonballs. The armament included six 9-inch, smoothbore cannon, two 6.4-inch rifled and two 7-inch pivot-rifled guns, and, mounted just below the waterline, a four-foot-long, fifteen-hundred-pound, cast-iron ramming prow. With two 600-horsepower engines, the top-heavy and hard-to-maneuver vessel drew twenty-two feet of water and could produce a speed of but four knots. Worst of all, her designer had grossly miscalculated her displacement and she rode too high out of the water. In even the slightest swell the waves frequently exposed the hull below the plated eaves, where the armor was only one-inch thick—her Achilles' heel! The various defects rendered unrealistic any hope of ever taking her into the open sea.[2]

Recruiting the needed crew of about 350 proved most difficult. The navy easily located a sufficient complement of officers, but there were almost no common sailors with any seagoing experience available. Of the few southerners who did have such experience, almost all had already gone into the army. Indeed the navy at last recruited from the army many of the ironclad's seamen. Major General John Bankhead Magruder at Yorktown, for example, cooperated enthusiastically and his units produced eighty men with "sea legs." Other recruiting missions to commands located at Richmond and Petersburg slowly but surely mustered a crew.

Many persons were less than optimistic for the vessel. "Good-by Ramsay," a close friend said to her chief engineer, "I shall never see you again. She will prove your coffin." Captain Sidney Smith Lee, brother of General Robert E. Lee and executive officer of the yard, expressed equal gloom. Captain Lee asked the head constructor, "Mr. Porter, do you really think she will float?" But float she did and, completed on March 5, 1862, the navy renamed her C.S.S. *Virginia*. Many persons, including even some who served aboard her, would always call her by her former name. This strange ship, the Confederacy's great hope for destroying the Union blockade, sailed into Hampton Roads three days after completion.[3]

Alas for the South, the northerners also acquired an ironclad at precisely the same time. In a sense both the original American ironclads, the U.S.S. *Monitor* and the C.S.S. *Virginia*, owed their development to the same man, Swedish inventor John Ericsson, who had perfected the screw propeller, which allowed mounting steam engines below the waterline and eliminated the vulnerable paddle wheel. Ericsson's ideas found a good reception in the technologically progressive navy, and, happily for the Union, an extremely capable secretary, Gideon Welles, headed that efficient department. Called "Father Neptune" by Lincoln, the bewigged and white-bearded former Connecticut journalist had contracted with Ericsson himself to build a new type of ironclad for the Union, and she arrived in the nick of time. Ericsson's other ideas were not new: iron armor, the concept of a gun turret allowing the use of only two guns but themselves of extremely large caliber, light draft, steam power, and ventilation systems. What Ericsson did, which entitled him to historical fame, "was for the first time to incorporate all these features into one, superbly conceived vessel."[4]

Construction of the ship began at New York on October 25, 1861. Her boilers first produced steam on December 30, and she was launched on January 30, 1862, after only 101 working days, a remarkable achievement. A large crowd gathered at Greenpoint, Long Island, to cheer as the ship slipped into the water and received salutes from neighboring vessels. Built entirely of iron, and, like the *Virginia*, lacking in maneuverability, "Ericsson's Folly" drew ten and a half feet but required a crew of only fifty-eight men. The boat *did* float—despite negative predictions expressed by some of the best engineers in the navy and other experienced constructors. Not a seagoing vessel even with 320 horsepower, she offered a service speed of a mere six knots, and only the four-foot-high pilothouse and ingenious nine-foot-high revolving, armored gun turret showed above her low flat decks, which were almost constantly awash. Two eleven-inch smoothbore cannon were mounted in the power-operated turret, itself covered by eight layers of one-inch plates. She looked like her nicknames, "tin can on a shingle," or "Yankee cheese box on a raft." She went to sea for trials and an unknown destination on February 27, 1862.

Both ships represented early examples of a class of ship that came to be known as coast-defense vessels. By sacrificing speed and seaworthiness relatively small ships could incorporate heavy armor and powerful guns. The

Union eventually built sixty more "monitors" even though the original *Monitor* sank late in 1862 in a storm off Cape Hatteras. Much more cumbersome and hopelessly underpowered, the *Virginia* remained permanently in her first port until the rebels destroyed her to prevent the enemy from capturing her. Nevertheless the Confederacy entered into an ambitious ironclad building program: it began or planned perhaps another fifty of the warships of the *Virginia* casemate design and actually commissioned twenty-two.

Hampton Roads, the battle area where the ironclads first fought one another, is formed by the confluence of the James River flowing southeast from Richmond, the Nansemond running up from the southwest, and the Elizabeth River from the south. They form a corridor roughly eight miles long that empties into the Chesapeake Bay. On the north, Hampton Roads is bordered by "the Peninsula," that part of Virginia between the York and James rivers. At the easternmost corner of the Peninsula, upon Old Point Comfort, sat the Union-held Fort Monroe, the only major army installation in Virginia that did not fall to the Confederacy. In addition to this garrison, the Federals also had troops at Camp Hamilton, two miles east, and at Camp Butler in Newport News on the western corner of the Peninsula, near the mouth of the James. The Confederates meanwhile had artillery batteries and troops emplaced at the mouths of the Elizabeth and Nansemond rivers. Thus the Federals controlled the entire northern shore of Hampton Roads and the entrance to the James; the Confederates dominated the southern banks, the lower rivers, and thereby Norfolk.

As the time of the first conflict between iron-armored ships approached, the *Virginia* was being readied for a sortie into Hampton Roads and the *Monitor* was at sea, approaching Fort Monroe. Warned by a spy of the *Monitor's* approach, President Davis ordered martial law, first for the threatened cities of Norfolk and Portsmouth, and then in Richmond itself.

On March 8, 1862, at 1 P.M., the *Virginia* steamed down the Elizabeth River and attacked the wooden steamers of the Union blockading squadron. With astonishing ease she withstood heavy fire from the thirty-gun U.S.S. *Cumberland* and the fifty-gun U.S.S. *Congress*. The sloping, armored sides of the *Virginia's* superstructure proved invulnerable, even at close range, against the powerful broadsides. Soon the *Virginia* belched out "hot shot" and set the *Congress* afire. To produce this devastating effect, cannonballs were heated to red-hot temperature in the ship's furnaces and hauled up in iron buckets, to be placed in a gun muzzle by means of tongs which gripped "tugs," special holes in the ball. A water-soaked wad separated the glowing shot from the powder charge to prevent premature explosion. After the *Congress* sustained damage too heavy for her crew to remedy, the *Virginia* concentrated upon the *Cumberland* and began to run head on toward her, "like some devilish and superhuman monster, or the horrid creation of a nightmare," wrote one federal observer. The *Virginia* appeared to the *Cumberland*'s pilot to look "like a huge half-submerged crocodile." The federal ship fired bravely and her shots "struck and glanced off, having no more effect than peas from a pop-gun"; the Yankee seamen saw their projectiles "bounding upon her mailed sides like India-rubber, apparently making not the least impression." The ships crashed together and the *Virginia*'s ram opened a hole in the *Cumberland* wide enough to "drive in a horse and cart," thought one Confederate officer. It sank the game Union vessel, with the crew heroically sticking to the sinking *Cumberland* which went down with flags flying; but the action nearly cost the southern ship its life, too, as the *Virginia* almost failed to pull free. The collision did break off the ramming prow for, "like the wasp," wrote one of the *Virginia*'s officers, "we could sting but once, leaving the sting in the wound." Meanwhile the disabled *Congress* surrendered and three other federal frigates ran aground. *Virginia* crewmen, having boarded the *Congress* and taken off prisoners, insisted that the enemy officers reboard the *Congress* to retrieve their abandoned sidearms so that they could make the customary surrender. The southern seamen then set new fires to the *Congress*, which burned for many hours before the spectacular conflagration ended near midnight when the magazine exploded in a breathtaking finale. The *Virginia* had already withdrawn, expecting to return the next day to finish off the grounded *Minnesota*, which had been trapped by the receding tide, and then to destroy the *Roanoke* and the *St. Lawrence*.[5]

At dawn the next day, however, the Confederates spotted the *Monitor* lying between them and the *Minnesota*. "You can see surprise on a ship just the same as you can see it in a human being," declared one of the *Monitor*'s men, "and there was surprise all over the Merrimac." The crews of the two iron vessels watched intently until 9 A.M. when they commenced a two-hour duel. The *Monitor* outmaneuvered the *Virginia* but neither vessel could do serious damage to the other. Shot after shot ricocheted away. As the ships closed, one of the *Monitor*'s officers believed they actually touched at least five times. An engineer who had helped construct the Union vessel and now was aboard as an official observer for the Navy Department watched the gunners become quite agitated. They worriedly called his attention to the shot's hitting against the turret. "Did the shot come through?" he inquired. "No, sir, it didn't come through, but it made a big dent, just look a'there sir." "A big dent . . . of course it made a big dent—that is just what we expected, but what do you care about that so long as it keeps out the shot?" "Oh! It's all right then of course sir." The gunners then calmed down and went about their work with a snug feeling of safety.[6]

The battle waned as the Federals withdrew to resupply the turret with ammunition, renewing the engagement a half hour later. At one moment the *Virginia* ran aground, but she managed to pull free at the last moment before the *Monitor* could place a shot into a vulnerable spot. The *Virginia* eventually concentrated her fire on the *Monitor*'s pilothouse and at about noon managed to strike the sight hole, blinding the Union commanding officer and causing the vessel to disengage, thus ending the stalemated battle. The blinded officer eventually regained the sight of one eye and returned to duty after a long convalescence. Both sides claimed that they had won the great ironclad engagement, but that mattered not at all. Each contestant now possessed a form of the new iron ship and neither had gained the possibly overwhelming advantage that even temporary singular possession might have conferred. The *Minnesota* was saved, and the *Monitor* had at least demonstrated its ability to prevent the *Virginia* from seriously damaging the other federal vessels. In fact, the *Virginia* herself had been so severely damaged as to necessitate almost a month in dry dock for repairs. Her riddled smokestack "would have permitted a flock of crows to fly through it without inconvenience." Meanwhile the episodes at Hampton Roads sparked many agitated discussions, beginning with a Cabinet meeting.[7]

Secretary Stanton "was fearfully stampeded" by the appearance of the southern ironclad. If Jefferson Davis over-reacted to the *Monitor* by proclaiming martial law in Richmond, Stanton's initial response to the *Virginia* was one of panic. "He said they would capture our fleet, take Ft. Monroe, be in Washington before night." He sent nervous messages to the governors of states on the seaboard, proposing that they block the harbors. Lincoln was calmer, but a naval officer present shared Stanton's alarm when he suggested closing the mouth of the Potomac by sinking barges loaded with rocks. This was approved over the opposition of Secretary Welles, but, on his insistence, it was to be done at War Department expense. Since this move would also deny to the Union the use of the river, Lincoln ordered that the barges be readied but not sunk unless actually necessary. Lincoln later saw the never-used barges lining the river and remarked: "That is Stanton's navy, . . . as useless as the paps of a man to a sucking child. They may be of some show to amuse the child but they are good for nothing for service." More reasoned would be the subsequent deliberations of the War Board.[8]

"Fort Monroe," that important federal stronghold retained on the eastern tip of Virginia between the York and James rivers, "is as inaccessible to the *Merrimack* as if it were in the Moon," Chief Engineer Totten reassured the others. "I do not mean to say that they cannot take it," he continued, "but that *in the present state of affairs* they cannot do so." Adjutant General Thomas indicated that the fort, under Major General John E. Wool, a regular officer of vast experience, had a garrison which numbered 11,000 effectives. Secretary Stanton corrected him; it then stood at 15,000 men since an additional 4,000 troops had moved in after the ironclads engaged. General Totten next asserted that "it would be inexcusable for any officer not to hold the fort during a long siege" with as few as 1,000 men. What would the Confederates'

ironclad do? the secretary inquired. "She could stand off and throw shells," Totten admitted; "they would kill a few people but would not impair the inherent strength of the work at all." All the board members agreed that the size and land-connected situation of the fort, unlike the tiny island of Fort Sumter, rendered it very secure. Though enemy assaults might result in the occupation of nearby points, causing minor inconvenience to Fort Monroe, still more gun emplacements would soon defend even those points. "How, Mr. Commissary General, is Fortress Monroe supplied?" asked the secretary. "It is very well supplied," Taylor responded, but then admitted that he did not know for how long a period; "I think for about sixty days." The secretary instructed him to investigate and to take appropriate measures, the board agreeing that they should victual the place for six months or so in advance, and that they should install distilling equipment and permanent cisterns. They then spent considerable time discussing armaments, gun mounts, carriages, and ammunition supplies. "We have powder, and shot have been ordered," Ordnance Chief Ripley assured them, but then he revealed that more attention was needed, for "I do not know," he admitted, "how much powder is on hand."

The threat still posed by the *Virginia* caused Quartermaster General Meigs, and those whom he had swayed, more apprehension. "It is only a question of time," he counseled. "It may be two weeks or it may be a month. If she gets out, there is nothing in this country that can beat her. . . . It is a disgrace to the country that the Rebels, without resources, without means, have built a vessel with which we cannot cope." The board knew a great deal more about the *Monitor* than they did about the *Virginia* and the unknown produced fear in unrealistic proportions. They thought the *Virginia*'s speed nearly three times her actual rate and quailed at her numerous guns compared to the *Monitor*'s mere two and the massive power behind the iron prow. Meigs and others believed her untakable even if men got close enough to storm her decks, for "she is as high out of water as the ceilings of the rooms in the President's House." Meigs and his allies, thinking it tremendously important to bottle the *Virginia* in port and not to allow her to go to sea, urged the sinking of coal vessels "or anything else available in the channel." The quartermaster general asserted that "there is nothing in this country so valuable that it could not be well disposed of by being sunk in that channel," for he believed that "the *Monitor* will certainly be destroyed if the *Merrimack* comes out again." "But the question is," Secretary Stanton reminded them, "how do we do it?" Totten replied, "We are not sailors, Mr. Secretary." They all agreed, as Meigs voiced it, "that this task must be left to the Navy."

And thus the board finally reached a formal conclusion: to urge the navy to close the Elizabeth River mouth and to expedite the emplacement of more and larger guns, of both twelve and fifteen inch, near Fort Monroe. As matters evolved, however, the navy refused to try closing the channel, partly because of internal disagreements about the plan and partly because navy officials feared nearby Confederate land batteries. This forced the War Board to think in other terms.

As a stopgap against the *Virginia*, Stanton dispatched to Hampton Roads the 1700-ton side-wheel steamer *Vanderbilt*, which the millionaire shipowner Cornelius Vanderbilt literally gave to the government, selling it for $1.00. While this wooden steamer obviously offered only small hope at best of being able to contend against the *Virginia*, there was some method in the apparent madness. First Commodore Vanderbilt convincingly argued that the steamer might be effective if somehow she could ram the *Virginia*. More importantly, Vanderbilt further agreed to refit his first-class ship, the *Ocean Queen*, as an ironclad, and to lease her to the government at a mutually agreed fair price. The War Board discussed the matter thoroughly and concurred in the proposal.[9]

Turning their attention primarily to the procurement of more and better gunboats and ordnance, the War Board also ensured Fort Monroe's supply and conceived various improvements for the place, such as precautions against combustion of debris within the fort. Already, on March 20, 1862, Stanton had summoned Charles Ellet to a War Board meeting. Ellet, whom Stanton had met through his law practice, was the builder of the Wheeling Bridge and a railroad expert. During the Crimean War, both sides had used him for counsel. To Stanton he explained reassuringly that the *Virginia* need not be so feared for "in a fair fight, with artillery alone, I imagine that the *Monitor* will be a match." An exponent of ramming, he chuckled: "These naval officers have become sudden converts to the capability of steam rams," and perhaps now overestimated the *Virginia*'s threat. Nevertheless, he asserted, the *Monitor* would withstand any attack unless her "Achilles' heel should be struck" by a freak, lucky shot. They explored various possibilities whereby either ship might be destroyed, but, more importantly, they eventually commissioned Ellet to build a fleet of Union rams for use in the western waters.[10]

This was not the army's first involvement with river craft. In addition to the capture or destruction of various vessels that otherwise might aid the Confederacy, they already had underwritten the construction program which had provided the Eads gunboats used by the navy at forts Henry and Donelson. The more recent Ellet contracts proposed the building or converting of steamships into fast, unarmed ramming craft, depending entirely upon speed and surprise to sink Confederate vessels, even ironclads. Returning to his yards at Pittsburgh, he displayed electric energy in implementing his plan. He purchased nine of the fastest steamboats on the Ohio, reinforced their bows, and ran heavy, longitudinal timbers the length of their hulls to help absorb the shock of ramming. They carried only armor sufficient to protect the most vital machinery against gunfire. Stanton appointed him a colonel in the army, and Ellet in turn commissioned several of his relatives in what came to be known as the Ram Fleet. Although Ellet himself soon died of wounds sustained in clashes with the Confederate vessels, his Ram Fleet accompanied Union troops down the Ohio and the Mississippi rivers and eventually played a significant role in the capture of Memphis.

The fall of this city constituted a significant victory for the North and another severe loss to the Confederacy. The city was the terminus of four railroads, three routes to the east and south and one into Arkansas. The Union soon transformed it into an important federal army base, and turned a refurbished shipyard there into the principal repair center for the Union river squadron. The northerners even placed into their service three of the recovered Confederate gunboats. They renamed the smallest of them *General Pillow*, as a snide, satiric slap at the Confederate general who fled with Floyd from Fort Donelson to avoid capture. "The only objection to the name," Union naval Captain Charles H. Davis reported, "is that the little thing is sound in her hull, which can't be said of General Pillow. However, she resembles the general in another particular; she has a great capacity for blowing and making a noise altogether disproportionate to her dimensions."[11]

Although the army dabbled in nautical affairs, the Union naval successes sprang primarily from close cooperation between the two services and the effective administration of the navy. To a considerable degree, that new effectiveness resulted from the work of a Navy Board created by Secretary Welles in June, 1861. Initially he charged the board to study the conduct of the blockade and to devise ways and means for improving its efficiency. A professional naval officer and member of the talented Delaware manufacturing family, Captain Samuel F. DuPont, who had shown initiative earlier as commandant of the Philadelphia Navy Yard, headed it. Stanton chose the second member, Professor A. D. Bache, superintendent of the Coast Survey, for his specialized knowledge. The third member, Major John G. Barnard of the army engineers, and himself father of the Washington, D.C., defense system, provided effective liaison with the army. Commander Charles H. Davis, the board's secretary, would later command the Union squadron which took Memphis. Most significantly, this board provided the basis for a broad strategic naval plan. Later called the Board of Strategy to distinguish it from subsequent boards, its existence continued, with only occasional shiftings of personnel and alterations in the primary task at hand. The fall of 1861 saw the creation of another significant group, the Ironclad Board. Systematic policy formulation and coordination had come to the navy as well as to the army.

During the two months following the battle between the ironclads *Monitor* and *Virginia*, the southern vessel sailed into Hampton Roads several times as if to challenge combat, but the *Monitor* did not come out as long as the *Virginia* did not attack any Union ships. "They stood on the edge of the arena, each hesitating to advance, neither caring to retreat," one observer remarked.

"Each commander accurately surmised the intentions of his opponent, and just as correctly refused to take the bait." Perhaps most importantly, the northerners used that time to work busily on the construction of twenty-one more ironclads, a feat that the South could not begin to match. They built these low-freeboard, turreted vessels like the *Monitor* and armed some of them with potent fifteen-inch guns to give them power to damage other ironclad ships. They became primary elements in U.S. coastal operations, not only during the remainder of the Civil War, but for a long time thereafter. The *Monitor* types remained active into the 1920s the navy struck the last one from its list in 1937.[12]

The Union had to search somewhat more painstakingly for a satisfactory organization for land warfare than it did for the water-borne operations. Departmental organizations and the missions of various commands frequently fluctuated merely because no one could comprehend consistently the interrelationships of the various lines of operations. Changes began during the fall of 1861 in the wake of first Bull Run. When McClellan assumed command of the Army of the Potomac, a soldier of demonstrated competence, William S. Rosecrans, a West Pointer who had left the army for the oil business, replaced him in the Department of the Ohio. A former Democratic secretary of the treasury, John A. Dix of New York, took over in Maryland and proved to be a capable administrator. Ex-Governor Nathaniel P. Banks of Massachusetts replaced the unfortunate Patterson in the Shenandoah Valley. This was also a key political appointment, for the ambitious Banks had been the first Republican Speaker of the House of Representatives. The War Department would soon merge Banks's command into McClellan's Department of the Potomac. Another ambitious Massachusetts politician, the colorful and politically astute Benjamin F. Butler, headed the Department of Virginia, with headquarters at Fort Monroe. Later the aged but still competent regular, John E. Wool, replaced Butler, freeing Butler to prepare a special expedition which would eventually reach New Orleans. The Union also created a new department in the mountains of Virginia and western Virginia, termed the Mountain Department, under the politically attractive Major General Fremont, whose controversial activities in Missouri had prompted his removal. Though a former regular officer, Fremont had not attended West Point. This further ingratiated him with anti-professional, radical politicians who believed the West Point regular officers discriminated against him, because he lacked the "infant baptism" of attendance at the Military Academy.[13]

Interestingly, Fremont immediately stirred up more controversy, this time within the War Department, over the appointment of his staff. Hitchcock, head of the War Board, in a letter of advice to Stanton on the matter revealed his inflexibly conservative attitude. Fremont desired to appoint a colonel to be chief of staff within the department. Hitchcock pedantically declared that "the title . . . is nominal, . . . given by courtesy to the Senior officer of [a] staff. The organic law for the army does not recognize the title," nor the job for that matter, as Hitchcock apparently felt. Fremont also requested a topographical engineer for his staff; Hitchcock responded that there may already be some officers of that corps within Fremont's district who would "pass under his orders" and therefore need not be on his staff. Furthermore, Fremont apparently wished to assign qualified line officers to staff posts, either to do real general staff work or expand his retinue. Not perceiving, of course, a general staff as separate from a personal staff, Fremont requested twelve aides-de-camp, three of them colonels and none below captain. The incredulous Hitchcock retorted first that "colonels of cavalry and of artillery are not properly staff officers," and as to the number, "General Scott went through the Mexican War with but two . . . and both of them were lieutenants." Hitchcock thought that, though McClellan might have been justified in appointing a large number of aides because of the extraordinary size and inexperience of McClellan's command, this "was something new and hitherto unheard of in Armies," and not to be freely repeated.[14]

In the West Halleck took command of the Department of the Missouri. Still farther west, David Hunter, an elderly regular army paymaster who early had made a good impression on Lincoln, headed the Department of Kansas. East of the Mississippi, the Department of the Cumberland faced the Confederate forces in central Kentucky. Robert Anderson, the defender of Fort Sumter, was its first commander, but when nervous exhaustion forced his resignation in October, 1861, William T. Sherman, another West Pointer who had left the army, replaced him. After a career as banker, lawyer, college president, and street railway executive, the brilliant Sherman had returned to the army in time to fight at Bull Run. He did not bear up well under the responsibilities of his first command and was relieved. His insistence that hundreds of thousands of men would be required in the West alone enhanced his unfortunate reputation for instability. The careful and competent Don Carlos Buell had replaced Sherman who, after rest at home in Ohio, joined the department of his old friend Halleck. When Rosecrans left Ohio to take over forces in western Virginia, the leadership of this interior department passed to Brigadier General O. M. Mitchel, a West Point graduate, famed astronomer, and popular lecturer.

Coincident with all this consolidation and new delineations of area responsibilities, there occurred a Union reorganization. With the post of general in chief vacant, all generals with independent or departmental command thenceforth reported directly to the secretary of war. With the War Board functioning the secretary was well equipped to discharge these duties. McClellan thus gained freedom to concentrate on his field responsibilities, and the War Board, an embryo general staff led by Hitchcock, a potential chief, filled the gap created by the absence of a general in chief. At least to a partial degree, Hitchcock's cautious conservatism complemented Stanton's free willingness to make drastic changes. "My chief," Hitchcock once confided, is "full of prejudices, exceedingly violent, reckless of the rights and feelings of others, often acting like a wild man in the dark."[15]

Hitchcock counseled Stanton: "The Army is something like an organic (living) body; a whole in itself, and yet containing many subordinate organisms, no less *wholes* within their sphere. . . . It is exceedingly dangerous to make changes, unless called for by urgent necessity. . . . Touch the head of the Department and you shake the whole system. . . . Change the chief, and all is changed . . . a stranger whose want of knowledge (of the details of duty) makes him dependent upon the subordinates; who, at once, undergo a change of character. They take liberties; they neglect their duties, and the new chief has a herculean task before him, . . . but this requires time, and can only be undertaken with safety in a period of comparative quiet. . . . I would with all earnestness urge, that no [bureau chief] changes be made, unless there is reason to question the loyalty or fidelity of some one." The key proved to be not replacement of personnel but implementation of more efficient techniques, procedures, and methods. Hitchcock became "one of the major molders of Stanton's ideas," the secretary heeding much of the general's advice.[16]

Like the new department structure, the new Washington command organization offered advantages over the old. The War Board integrated both operations and logistics and drew on the administrative resources of all of the staff departments. It gave attention to many aspects of the spring offensives. The board took an important step when, in order to insure that the Ram Fleet had sufficient provisions while being fitted out and during its operations, it established a well-coordinated and greatly expanded supply system. "I propose to institute some new measures not hitherto applied to government contracts," Stanton declared. He requested that additional quartermaster personnel be made available to serve the fleet's needs at each city of any consequence along the Ohio River. "I like everything to be done systematically and in order," Stanton said. "I want a quartermaster at each of these places to make all contracts, to superintend all disbursements, to present and vouch for all accounts," and to see to the new fleet's ample and proper supply. Since the existing quartermaster personnel "have so much business as they can attend to," Stanton announced his readiness to appoint fifty additional men. Quartermaster General Meigs felt that men fit for such positions would be hard to find but the secretary responded: "Address a telegraphic dispatch to the Board of Trade in each city, asking them to appoint three of their most judicious members to act as an advisory committee . . . and that one of their number shall accept temporarily the post of quartermaster."[17]

This example well illustrates the myriad transitions and enlargements in all the Union services of supply. As quartermaster general, Meigs performed tasks monumental in the annals of military history. His successful management of northern resources made a major contribution to the eventual victory. The supply structure evolved from a skeleton force to one more vast by far than anything of which men in the old army ever dreamed. Naturally mistakes were made, and incompetence, deficiencies, and waste were present, but the abuses of the early months of the war soon disappeared, while more and more the Union soldier became the best-provided-for fighting man in all history. Fully equal to his prodigious job, "Meigs was a man of the new day, of the materialistic, mechanically and scientifically inclined America born in the second half of the century of industrialization, urbanization, and technological change."[18]

In procuring uniforms, shoes, tents, horses, mules, forage, and wagons, Meigs consumed at least one-half the output of all northern industry. Although he directed a huge and widely decentralized department, his own task remained largely supervisory. As a member of the War Board, through its formal and then later its informal existence, he gained an insight into needs and an influence over operations which significantly enhanced the effectiveness of his department and augmented its contribution.

Meigs successfully managed the establishment of new standards for American manufacturers. His efforts in exploiting the new machine-sewing of shoes merit recognition. Another significant improvement came with the introduction of the French shelter tent, a half-tent, carried on the back of each soldier, which was compatible with any other half to make one pup tent. Thus any two soldiers could, together, provide themselves with a tent, virtually eliminating both the large tents previously used and the wagons required for their transportation. Meigs also oversaw provision of the French mess equipment for field use.

Engaged in an enormous correspondence, he constantly strictured McClellan and other generals on the care of horses and equipment and intensely involved himself in an ongoing program to maintain materiel in serviceable condition. At times he lost his patience with careless procedures. Once he lamented, "We have over 125 regiments of cavalry and they [Union forces] have killed ten times as many horses for us as for the enemy." As the war progressed, Meigs became active in the outfitting of ambulance trains, the supervision of temporary barracks construction, coal purchases, and special refitting and resupplying of exhausted veteran forces. By the end of the war his annual departmental expenditures amounted to nearly a half billion dollars. And perhaps the most revolutionary aspect of its operation was the employment of many women workers, a landmark in American industry.[19]

Another agency, the Ordnance Department, handled the logistics pertinent to armament supply. Ripley's long and successful career in that field rendered him an able manager, but his staunch conservatism caused him persistently to resist innovation. Remaining consistently hostile to any new type of arms, he particularly resisted the large-scale use of breechloading rifles. Finally replaced in 1863, he nevertheless left a legacy of a smoothly functioning system of weapons and ammunition procurement and distribution. His subordinates performed effectively and the Union armies always possessed suf-

ficient armament; no delays or halts of northern military operations resulted
from a lack of ordnance. Ripley's successor, Brigadier General Alexander B.
Dyer, built upon the existing structure to create an even more effective system. Interested in technical innovation, he himself donated to the government
patent rights for a new artillery round he invented and encouraged greater
precision in all manufactures, more uniformity in arms, and better product
quality. After the Union cavalry achieved successes using breechloaders, Dyer
urged the rapid issue of these weapons to the infantry. Though he worked
for establishment of a government powder mill, many of the well-known
companies of the present day received their first large contracts from the
Ordnance Department—Dupont, Remington, and New Haven Arms among
them.

Still another staff bureau, the Commissary Department, provided for the
feeding of troops. Again, in all the previous history of warfare few nations
had faced such a tremendous task, but Commissary General Taylor's conscientious efforts created an impressive operation. Initially, responsibility for
providing food rested upon the individual states; so whenever a new organization formed, the state provided it with at least enough rations to reach its
first destination. This overly decentralized approach had drawbacks, for often
the states supplied their troops with too much food at one time. They waste-
fully threw much of it away and a considerable amount simply rotted.

The men in the field had to prepare their own individual meals, as there
were no special mess personnel. Even the men themselves received no training
in proper food preparation, though Taylor did order a book printed on cooking for the army. Unfortunately, not many of the volumes found their way
into soldiers' hands, and the book's effect remained slight. Sometimes individual companies might designate particular men as cooks and exempt them from
other fatigue duties, or occasionally a Negro contraband might be the cook.
Though some ovens were developed especially for field use, most of the men
preferred to cook over an open fire, using pots and pans hung over the flames
for either boiling or frying.

The standard foodstuffs very much resembled the typical fare the men ate
at home—primarily pork, beef, bread, and potatoes. The very enlightened
Commissary Department, realizing that "the health of the troops" required
it, issued fresh vegetables whenever possible. In lieu of potatoes, they provided a supply of beans, rice, peas, or hominy, and, when available, beets.
Sometimes they supplied onions, tomatoes, or cabbage. The men could obtain roasting ears of corn and peanuts locally in much of the South. Otherwise
the Union commissary stockpiled quantities of dessicated potatoes and dessicated mixed vegetables, which were primitive forms of "instant" dried foods
with the added advantage of long resistance to spoilage. The men loved coffee
and always had a good supply, so much that they often traded their surplus
for tobacco from the well-supplied rebels.[20]

The army continued to purchase most of the provisions at the local level, which, though providing ample supplies, allowed fraud and favoritism to flourish. Local depots generally retained too much control and independence, inevitably leading to speculation. Still, northern troops never encountered vexing hindrances in major operations because of any lack of provisions. Most significantly, while items sometimes did rot in warehouses, the North generally maintained adequate transportation and distribution with a minimum of delay or inefficiency. One of the real keys to this effective management lay in the relentless weeding out of inept workers, a procedure continued throughout the war. Not at all uncommon were sharp prods like this telegram that went to two railway agents at London, Tennessee: "McKeon and yourself appear to be incompetent to draw rations . . . and unless you do better in [the] future both of you will be discharged and competent men put in your places."[21]

The Union commissary structure also expanded itself sufficiently to provide for feeding the "contrabands," that is, the freed slaves whom the military personnel grouped into camps and cared for temporarily. Also, the Commissary Department detailed officers to "take possession of all the plantations heretofore occupied by rebels, and take charge of the inhabitants remaining thereon," to accomplish the continuing "cultivation of the lands."[22]

The North also benefited from activities of its recently formed Department of Agriculture. This agency lent its assistance both to the government and to farmers, providing information regarding the increase of livestock production, grain growing, and seed supply, as well as introducing even more widespread labor-saving implements than before. Even though the number of men involved in agricultural work decreased, northern farm production continued its consistent increase even as the war progressed. Most notably, hog production rose dramatically, as twenty-five new packing houses were constructed between 1861 and 1865, and the number of hogs slaughtered in Chicago alone increased from 270,000 per year at the start to 900,000 at the war's end.

Yet, with all this plenty, the North left many necessary improvements for a later generation. The Sanitary Commission reported to Taylor that even though the troops had essential rations, improper storage, preparation, and even usage wasted perhaps as much as half the amount supplied. Pointing to the dire need of special mess personnel, the Commission head declared that one trained cook would be worth ten doctors! Soldiers often engaged in playful fights, throwing food at one another as children throw balls; General Irvin McDowell said that his troops squandered enough food to feed a foreign army half the size of his. Proportionately, the Union army enjoyed twice the rations per man that Napoleon's army had a half-century earlier.

The War Board had come into existence at a critical and exciting moment in the evolution of Union strategy. Nashville and Columbus had just fallen, McClellan was starting for the Peninsula, and water-borne expeditions initiated earlier were beginning to meet success. By mid-March, 1862, Brigadier General Thomas W. Sherman succeeded in taking Fernandina, Florida, and used it as a base for his amphibious attempts to reduce Fort Pulaski and thus capture the important city of Savannah on the Georgia coast. The War Board first deemed mortars the only effective weapon that the expedition could use but later concluded: "The surest way . . . will be to treat the enemy as he treated us in Hampton Roads": build a ship especially for the need. As time passed and the fort but not the city fell, Chief Engineer Totten wryly observed: A compliment "should be paid to the officers and men who built these batteries on the Savannah. I do not believe that any but Yankees could have built them. By Yankees, of course, I mean Americans."[23]

In this episode the Union officials learned that their successes in taking various points on the Confederate coast had to be regarded as exceptional triumphs because guns ashore normally proved superior to guns afloat, an ageless naval rule of thumb. Since they could not reduce the well-defended shore installations from the sea, the Union had to assault the remaining Confederate ports from the land side. Thus, even though by taking Fort Pulaski on April 11, 1862, the Federals permanently closed Savannah as a Confederate port, the city itself withstood attack. Charleston, though not closed by seaborne attack, held out against the navy until evacuated, when William T. Sherman entered South Carolina in 1865.

Some of the early 1862 seaborne expeditions enjoyed good fortune and quick success, as, for example, Burnside's at Roanoke Island and New Bern. The board, however, expressed consternation over Burnside's long-term security; a railroad ran right to New Bern, which the board deemed a dangerous avenue by which the Confederates could concentrate rapidly against Burnside with no way to reinforce him in time. A voyage from Washington would take four days minimum, and, with Burnside's experience with the shallow water which delayed his landing, reinforcements might require as long as ten days. "I cannot but feel some apprehension," Totten declared. "Burnside is of an adventurous spirit [and] he has adventurous men with him." This very adventurousness, coupled with his positive accomplishments, marked Burnside as a man the Union would likely call upon later for more ambitious assignments.[24]

Meanwhile, Benjamin F. Butler's extended expedition, augmented by naval forces under David G. Farragut, eventually secured Ship Island off the coast of Mississippi and then pushed up the river to take New Orleans. This combined force significantly occupied the attention of the War Board. Before Butler completed this mission, the War Board fretted about the ironclads the Confederates were constructing in the Crescent City shipyards and began considering countermeasures should they need them. They followed Butler's periodic reports very carefully and at times nervously. Upon hearing that Butler had relieved one ship captain, thinking him derelict, Stanton blustered, "Why didn't he shoot him? When you write to Butler, tell him that the

Secretary of War thinks that he ought to punish the man, if he has the proper evidence."[25]

But Butler's ambitious venture succeeded brilliantly. The Union forces easily reoccupied Ship Island, which the Confederates had abandoned. By March 20 Butler arrived personally on the island to commence organization and preparation of his naval assault force, which would move simultaneously with Halleck's offensive on the Mississippi and Tennessee. Gunboats with huge, wide-mouthed mortars proceeded up the Mississippi River and on April 18 commenced shelling the two defending forts, named Jackson and St. Phillip. Farragut's fleet passed the strongholds on April 24, the "night the war was lost," as one exaggerating Louisiana scholar described it. The Union armada approached the city and, after negotiations for surrender, Butler moved in with his troops to commence official occupation on May 1.

As Butler's expedition pushed on to its successful conclusion, the Union war effort obviously was benefiting from an energetic and very combative new secretary of war and an incipient general staff organization to guide strategy and integrate logistics with operations. Nevertheless, Lincoln gave, if anything, more rather than less attention to the conduct of military operations. And he also, like Stanton, turned to the War Board for counsel. Whether or not Lincoln turned to the Board "frequently" as T. Harry Williams has asserted is moot; Lincoln *did* consult with the Board sometimes, for example, specifically on April 3 and 11, 1862, to talk out his worries about pressing military problems.[26]

Initially Lincoln approached his responsibilities as commander in chief very positively but quite amateurishly. As befitting a frontier lawyer with strong connections with the business community, Lincoln almost displayed an entrepreneurial tendency in his early view of military operations. These offensives included the proposed Lane expedition southward from Kansas. Of the last, Lincoln said: "It is my wish that the expedition commonly called the 'Lane Expedition' shall be as much as has been promised at the Adjutant General's Office, under the supervision of General McClellan, and not any more. I have not intended, and do not now intend, that it shall be a great exhausting affair, but a snug sober column of 10,000 or 15,000."[27]

Unlike the seaborne offensives against Confederate ports, such an operation as Lane's, moving without water or rail communications into a relatively unsettled country, would have required an enormous logistical effort for its support. In its original "snug sober" form it would have employed as much Union resources as Grant had at his disposal for his important offensive against Fort Henry. Fortunately for the Union, this overly large movement never materialized.

The multitude of offensives initially begun fitted well, however, with Lincoln's developing understanding of the North's military problem. Perceiving that the Confederates enjoyed interior lines of operations, Lincoln and Union generals constantly exaggerated the extent of the Confederate advantage and their willingness and ability to exploit it. After months of groping for a solution, Lincoln had, by January, 1862, perceived the best approach as *simultaneous* advances.

In part fortuitously, three seaborne expeditions were attacking the rebel coastline at the same time in the late winter of 1862. Lincoln desired that the major armies also advance simultaneously. Though the President and his general in chief, McClellan, agreed on the principle, McClellan had already delayed his movement for more thorough troop training and was waiting also until Halleck had finished the pacification of Missouri and could cooperate in a combined advance of his and Buell's army. The delay until the winter prevented any combined effort, because the fall dry spell in the South ended in December and the winter period of heavy rain, cool weather, and diminished sunlight converted the unsurfaced roads of the region into mud-filled canals. One of the roads in Halleck's area "was horrible, and new tracks had to be cut through the woods. It took an entire day for one brigade to move 3 miles." Yet in the West it would be only Halleck's projected movement up the Tennessee River which, when ready to begin, would, with its steamborne troops and supplies, be independent of the almost impassable state of the roads across the entire theatre of operations. Thus Lincoln faced the frustrating circumstance of three naval expeditions under way and the land forces unable to move simultaneously.[28]

Sophisticated as he was becoming in the elements of strategy, Lincoln, in his first winter of the war, had not yet fully understood basic logistics. Not only did he fail to perceive the problem of marching directly from Kentucky against East Tennessee, but he failed to understand how the winter climate had immobilized his armies and that McClellan had reason to delay until Halleck could reconcentrate troops from Missouri to the river lines. All of these factors underpinned Lincoln's all-embracing effort to implement his concept of simultaneous advances by ordering that Washington's birthday, February 22, "be the day for a general movement of the Land and Naval forces of the United States against the insurgent forces."[29]

The President obtained a forward movement, but of a single army only, and for reasons unrelated to his order. Halleck, untrammelled by bottomless roads, had jumped the gun in the West to attack before rebel reinforcements arrived from the East. He sent Grant up the Tennessee, forts Henry and Donelson fell before Washington's birthday, and the Union army forced the rebel line in the West into retreat from the Mississippi to the Appalachians. With Buell marching to follow up Halleck's success, Roanoke Island captured, and Sherman and Butler active, only McClellan's Army of the Potomac was not moving against the enemy. In this context, it is not difficult to understand Lincoln and Stanton's impatience with McClellan.

Deprived of his position as general in chief and pressured to move forward, McClellan began to implement his strategy for using the Chesapeake Bay and the Virginia rivers to turn the Confederate position in northern Virginia. His plan, however, had been deranged by two developments. The appearance of the *Virginia* caused momentary apprehensions for Union command of the sea, and Joe Johnston's withdrawal from advanced positions near Washington covered him against McClellan's planned movement to Urbanna.

Though McClellan would have to abandon his hope of reaching the rebel rear or interposing his army between Johnston's and Richmond, the basic concept of the campaign remained intact. By shifting his line of operations to the York-James Peninsula, he would circumvent the tactically strong defensive power of predominately rifle-armed infantry and, by a large-scale turning movement, combine the strategic offensive with the tactical defensive. Just as Halleck had turned the Confederate positions in the West at Columbus and Bowling Green, Kentucky, so too would McClellan also use Union naval superiority to turn the Confederate position in northern Virginia. On a much smaller scale, the Union general would also be duplicating Scott's turning of Mexican positions in northern Mexico by his advance against Mexico City, an advance in which McClellan had participated fifteen years earlier. Unlike Scott, McClellan would have excellent water communications, and naval superiority would also obviate any rebel resistance on the Peninsula and make unnecessary any frontal attacks on an intrenched enemy. Control of the rivers would permit McClellan to turn rebel defensive positions by moving troops toward their rear by water.

Having thus penetrated to the outskirts of Richmond without the necessity of assuming the tactical offensive, he could then begin a siege such as that unsuccessfully sustained seven years earlier by the Russian city of Sebastopol. Threatened with such an operation, the Union reasonably could expect the Confederates to attack in an effort to relieve their capital from this menace. Though he vastly over-estimated the Confederate forces and believed himself numerically inferior, McClellan felt his waterborne turning movement, with its excellent and secure water communications, naval support, and strong field and siege artillery, would nullify any numerical advantages the rebels might have.

President Lincoln ordered prompt movement, though reluctantly approving the plan of campaign because he feared for the security of Washington. Even though a strong rebel move against Washington would expose their own capital to permanent loss, doubtless Lincoln fretted about the gap that might well exist between the theory and the practice. Even the less unlikely event, a serious threat to or temporary loss of Washington, would produce disastrous domestic political repercussions and possibly serious diplomatic consequences. He therefore insisted on strong forces remaining near Washington to supplement its already formidable fortifications. Doubtless, too, he realized that this partially vitiated McClellan's turning movement and placed the Confederates on interior lines of operations between McClellan's army on the

Peninsula and the force covering Washington. On March 17, just over a month after the fall of Fort Donelson, McClellan began moving his force to the Peninsula.

Compared to McClellan's long delay and final ponderous movment, Halleck's continued energetic advance confirmed him as the Union's star, if somewhat precipitate, performer. Intent on exploiting Grant's success at forts Henry and Donelson, Halleck by his plans revealed a marked difference in strategic view between himself and his colleague, Don Carlos Buell, commanding in Kentucky and Tennessee east of the Cumberland. Before the fall of Donelson, as Halleck was "straining every nerve to increase" Grant's army for the attack on the fort, the strategic issue between Halleck and Buell had sharpened. Halleck then wished Buell to send the bulk of his forces by the rivers to reinforce Grant. Fearful that the rebels from Bowling Green or Columbus would concentrate against Grant's forces, Halleck stressed the need for a rapid forward movement, for he knew that it would take Buell's land-supplied advance almost two weeks merely to reach Bowling Green. Further, Halleck wanted to eliminate the rebel flank position at Fort Donelson, for from it the rebels could paralyze any operation going up the Tennessee River. In an effort to induce Buell to follow his ideas, Halleck offered him command of the joint expedition against Fort Donelson.

After thinking of dividing his force, Buell had decided to continue his direct advance on Nashville just as the Confederates evacuated Bowling Green. Halleck denounced Buell's route as likely to force too slow a pace, disparaged the "bad strategy" of exterior lines, and stressed that they could turn the rebel position at Nashville by concentrating all forces for a movement up the Tennessee River to Alabama. Though General in Chief McClellan sustained Buell, Lincoln shared Halleck's conviction about the importance of Fort Donelson and also felt the same apprehension as did Halleck that the rebels could employ their interior lines when he pointed out that the enemy force at "Columbus will not get at Grant but the the [sic] force from Bowling Green will. They hold the Railroad from Bowling Green to within a few miles of Donelson, with the bridge of Clarksburg [Clarksville] undisturbed." With a clear comprehension of the strategic possibilities, Lincoln pointed out that the Confederates could exploit this interior line to concentrate against Grant because, he said, "it is unsafe to rely that they will not dare expose Nashville to Buell. A small part of their force can retire slowly towards Nashville, breaking up the Railroad as they go, and keep Buell out of that city twenty days." Then, reflecting what would be the typical overestimate of Confederate capabilities, Lincoln added that in the meantime "Nashville will be abundantly defended by forces from all South and perhaps here at Manassas."[30]

The disputants in this strategic controversy never reached a full collision, because the prompt fall of Fort Donelson obviated it. The Confederates immediately evacuated Nashville, confirming Halleck's conviction that his river movements had turned that position. Nevertheless, this disagreement as to strategy persisted while the southerners fell back along diverging lines. Both Union generals continued unwilling to follow the other's strategy; Halleck and Buell pursued their own ideas with McClellan essentially approving the plans of each. Buell occupied Nashville, moved forward his troops, and began to consolidate his position in Middle Tennessee.

Meanwhile Halleck pushed vigorously forward on all fronts, ordering advances in Missouri and assembling a force under the energetic John Pope to turn Columbus from the Missouri side. Pope's movement against New Madrid and Island No. 10 would directly threaten Columbus's river communications and, by forcing its evacuation, both open the Mississippi and turn the Confederate positions in Missouri. At the same time, Halleck ordered Grant's forces forward to destroy the West Tennessee railway network, including the Memphis and Charleston railway at Corinth, Mississippi.[31]

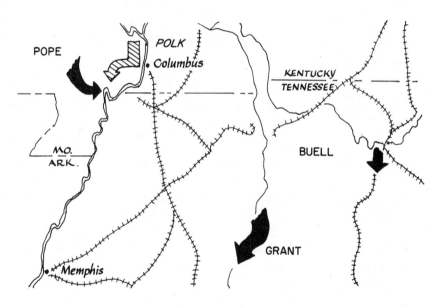

Confederates Turned

Soon Halleck reported that Columbus, "the boasted 'Gibralter of the West,' " had been evacuated, because "finding himself completely turned on both sides of the Mississippi, the enemy was obliged to evacuate or surrender." This success enabled Halleck immediately to order that the movement up the Tennessee be converted from a raid against railways into a penetration, directing the advance elements of Grant's army to establish themselves and remain at Savannah on the Tennessee. This was as far south as they had been able to reach, for they knew the rebels were assembling strong forces at

Corinth. Halleck planned to reinforce his Savannah force prior to another forward movement. This he proved able to do sooner than expected, for on March 6, 7, and 8, less than a week after the fall of Columbus, the Confederates under Earl Van Dorn had counterattacked in Arkansas. At the Battle of Pea Ridge, Union forces fought under the capable direction of Samuel R. Curtis, a West Point-trained political general who had served in the Mexican War. Curtis stymied Van Dorn's attempt to reproduce the Mexican War turning movements he had observed at Monterey and Cerro Gordo. The Union victory permitted Halleck further to reinforce Grant and concentrate at Savannah.[32]

Continued Union victories in the West meant the Confederates were beset in all major theatres, just what Lincoln had sought by his Washington's Birthday advance. Success in the field and Lincoln's emerging maturity as a strategist, reflected in his concept of simultaneous advances, matched the increasingly good management of Union logistics. Backed by an adequate national base in production and transportation, Union supply managers well provided for an army thirty times the peace establishment of 1861. Nothing exemplified this achievement nor contributed to it more than the fortunate appointment of the inexperienced but brilliant Meigs to the key position of quartermaster general.

The vigorous exploitation of Union naval superiority was in the competent hands of the professionally led navy, which protected Union communications and gradually tightened its blockade. The Confederates could make no real naval resistance on seas or rivers, though the *Virginia* created momentary alarm. But the navy, knowing that there was no real danger from the cumbersome Confederate ironclad, calmed civilian fears by being ready with the *Monitor*.

Thus Lincoln's simultaneous advances began at last because while Halleck's advance continued, McClellan could move to the Peninsula without fear for the security of his communications. Though the fall of Fort Donelson obviated the strategic dispute with Buell, the deliberate Buell planned to move away from Halleck, south and southeast from Nashville. Each general continued to perceive his line of operations as the best. Halleck persisted in wishing to exploit the river lines for deep turning penetrations and was anxious to keep moving rapidly, whereas Buell preferred an overland advance to consolidate the Union position in Middle Tennessee.

Lincoln had been "much pleased with the cautious vigor of General Buell," and counted on it "to guard, above all things, against any mishap by premature and unsupported movements." In spite of this implied criticism of the precipitate character of Halleck's operations, Lincoln at last conferred on him the western command he had sought. Much senior in rank to Buell, Halleck received command during the week following the fall of Columbus and the victory at Pea Ridge. This change, together with the removal of McClellan as general in chief, gave Halleck real control in the West and conferred upon the

Union the same unity of command long enjoyed by the Confederates. While Halleck coordinated his southward movements, Butler was preparing to attack New Orleans and McClellan was heading to the Peninsula. Lincoln at last realized his goal of simultaneous advances.[33]

With his new theatre commander's agreement, Buell left a substantial force to hold Middle Tennessee while moving with his strongest detachment overland to meet the troops at Savannah, Tennessee, now personally led by Grant. Planning to "concentrate everything possible against the enemy's center" near Corinth, Halleck felt it very important to have "an overwhelming force there," for he anticipated the "great battle of the war" on the Tennessee River with an enemy they could no longer turn. Though he knew about the rebel concentration at Corinth, he thought in terms of the offensive. Yet he warned Grant that the "instructions not to advance so as to bring on an engagement must be strictly obeyed." The general commanding at Savannah "must hold his position without exposing himself by detachments until we can strongly re-enforce him," he emphasized. "General Buell is moving in his direction" and more men were en route from Missouri. The Union army must "strike no blow until we are strong enough to admit of no doubt of the result."[34]

Halleck had based his strategy on a quick succession of turning movements, employing Union control of the waterways and the rapid advance made possible by this superior form of communication. It looked precipitate to Buell, McClellan, and perhaps Lincoln, but Grant, too, liked to advance as "rapidly as possible to save hard fighting. These terrible battles are very good things to read about for persons who lose no friends" he declared, "but I am decidedly in favor of having as little of it as possible. The way to avoid it is to push forward as vigorously as possible." It pleased him that Halleck was clearly of "the same way of thinking and with his clear head," he observed, "I think the congressional committee for investigating the Conduct of War will have nothing to enquire about in the West." Grant, of course, was referring to the famous Joint Committee on the Conduct of the War, first established under radical auspices in December, 1861, and whose investigations throughout the conflict caused great furor and criticism. Reflecting radical and popular ideas as to strategy and radical views about the selection of generals, the committee had a considerable impact upon strategy and upon the choice of army commanders. The members of the committee would hardly have concurred with Grant's expressed preference for turning movements and his hostility to battles.[35]

Although Halleck repeatedly had to urge Buell to move speedily to join Grant at Pittsburg Landing, the results of his strategy, his good management of resources, and the splendid execution by his subordinates pleased Halleck immensely. Halleck's forces in Missouri had driven the rebels from the state and advanced into Arkansas. He held all of West Tennessee and half of Middle Tennessee. Later, when Union gains had been somewhat augmented, he would proudly note: "We have reconquered and hold military possession of territory . . . as large as France or Austria, or the entire peninsula of Spain and Portugal, and twice as large as Great Britain, or Prussia, or Italy." The success exhilarated his whole command and inspired confidence in his leadership. Grant regarded Halleck as "one of the greatest men of the age" and Sherman viewed him as the "directing genius" of the events which had given the Union cause such "a tremendous lift" in the previous months.[36]

The effects of these successes were, for the Confederates, "the greatest single supply disaster of the war." They lost "the largest provision-raising areas of the Confederacy, . . . and large supply accumulations." These included "the iron-producing areas of the lower Tennessee Valley and a substantial part of the most valuable meat region of the Confederacy. One third of the hogs packed in 1861 for the use of the Confederate armies had come from areas now surrendered permanently to the Union. The daily diet of the Confederate soldiers in later campaigns amply demonstrated the magnitude of this loss." In the rich Middle Tennessee area, Nashville had been "a great administrative center for the Confederate supply system. Procurement and disribution for the armies in Tennessee, Kentucky, Arkansas, and Missouri were centered there, and the city held a substantial part of those reserves the Confederacy had been able to scrape together to face the 1862 campaigning year." The first of the Union's grand, concerted advances had thus commenced to make headway—but effective Confederate responses followed.[37]

1. Anderson, *By Sea and by River*, 15–16.

2. William C. Davis, *Duel Between the First Ironclads* (New York, 1975), 28.

3. *Ibid.*, 35.

4. *Ibid.*, 52.

5. *Ibid.*, 88–92, 100–101.

6. *Ibid.*, 120–22, 130.

7. *Ibid.*, 116, 141–42.

8. Thomas and Hyman, *Stanton*, 179–81.

9. Davis, *Ironclads*, 146; Proceedings of the War Board, entry for Mar. 26, 1862, Stanton Papers, Library of Congress.

10. Proceedings of the War Board, entry for Mar. 20, 1862, Stanton Papers, Library of Congress.

11. *O.R.*, *Navies*, XXIII, 210.

12. Davis, *Ironclads*, 149.

13. Williams, *Lincoln and the Radicals*, 39.

14. Hitchcock to Stanton, dated only 1862, Stanton Papers.

15. Thomas and Hyman, *Stanton*, 378.

16. Hitchcock to Stanton, Mar. 19, 1862, Stanton Papers; Thomas and Hyman, *Stanton*, 186, 191.

17. Proceedings of the War Board, entries for Mar. 14, 26, 1862, Stanton Papers.

18. Russell F. Weigley, *Quartermaster General of the Union Army* (New York, 1959), 7.

19. Allan Nevins, *The War for the Union*, 4 vols. (New York, 1959–71), II, 476.

20. Special Orders Number 207, supplementary, July 18, 1862; and John W. Barriger to J. C. Read, Apr. 5, 1864, both in Papers of the Commissary General of Subsistence, Military History Research Collection, Carlisle Barracks, Pennsylvania.

21. J. W. Barriger to C. F. Rix, Sept. 6, 1864, Papers of the Commissary General of Subsistence, Military History Research Collection.

22. Edwin M. Stanton to Brigadier General Rufus Saxton, Apr. 29, 1862; and Special Orders Number 13, Feb. 5, 1864, both in Papers of the Commissary General of Subsistence, Military History Research Collection.

23. Proceedings of the War Board, entries for Mar. 13 and 14, 1862, Stanton Papers.

24. Proceedings of the War Board, entries for Mar. 13, 14, 18, 1862, Stanton Papers.

25. Proceedings of the War Board, entry for Mar. 25, 1862, Stanton Papers.

26. Williams, *Lincoln and His Generals*, 75; Williams, *Americans at War*, 70.

27. Lincoln to Stanton, Jan. 31, 1862, Basler, *Collected Works*, V, 115–16.

28. McClellan to Buell, Nov. 25, Dec. 5, 1861, Jan. 6, Feb. 6, 1862, *O.R.*, VII, 458, 925, 531, 586; Buell to McClellan, Jan. 12, 20, Feb. 1, 1862, *ibid.*, 546, 76, 932; McClellan to Halleck, Dec. 10, 1861, *ibid.*, VIII, 419; Halleck to McClellan, Dec. 6, 26, 1861, Jan. 30, 1862, *ibid.*, 409–10, 462, 463, 571–72. The annual rainfall in Virginia and Tennessee averages 48 to 50 inches. It is light in the fall and uniformly heavy the remainder of the year. In spite of the relatively warm climate, the rainfall is so heavy that moisture loss only exceeds rainfall in the warm months of the year (Stephen Sargent Visher, *Climatic Atlas of the United States* [Cambridge, 1954], 117–23, 363–64; Joseph E. Williams, ed., *Prentice-Hall World Atlas* [Englewood Cliffs, N.J., 1960], 47).

Several variables govern this seasonal ground moisture pattern. When "soil has been saturated by prolonged rains and then drains until no more water moves downward under the force of gravity, the soil is said to be holding its *field capacity* of water." Moisture loss is governed by evaporation and transpiration, the drawing of water into the roots of plants from which it is carried "to the foliage and there exuded to the atmosphere." This evapotranspiration potential is the function of the region and the season.

"In late winter and early spring, melting of snow and soil ice releases much water, which infiltrates the surface, raising the moisture content to exceed the field capacity and causing the soil for a time to be completely saturated. Surplus water runs off to produce spring floods, whereas some percolates down through the intermediate belt to reach the ground water zone. The soil is in a soft state, easily yielding to a weak mud when churned up by wheels or hoofs.

"As April passes into May, air temperatures increase and new foliage appears. The resulting great increase in evapotranspiration causes a rapid decline in soil moisture throughout May and June to amounts far below the field capacity. Although an occasional rainstorm may temporarily cause a small increase in soil moisture, the summer months constitute a period of severe moisture deficit, for the losses by evapotranspiration normally continue to be heavy through midsummer.

"As autumn sets in, with lowering of air temperatures and the dropping of foliage, evapotranspiration is reduced, while rainfall replenishes soil moisture. Thus we see a sharp rise in the curve in late November and throughout December. Depending upon rainfall in the particular year, field capacity may be regained before soil moisture is frozen."

The following graph of a point in Ohio exhibits clearly this annual soil moisture cycle.

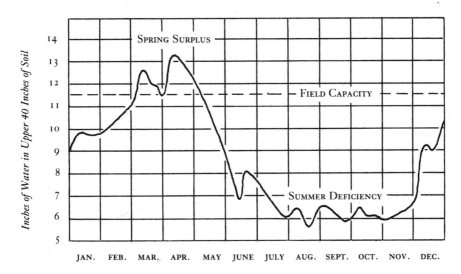

Thus it would appear that the marching potential of armies was inversely proportional to the soil moisture cycle. Marching potential in the southeastern United States is further reduced by the region's podsolic soils, which are characterized by the accumulation of clay in the subsoil. The clay gives rise to a high field moisture capacity and, consequently, adverse terrain conditions when the soil moisture is near field capacity.

Quotations are from Arthur N. Strahler, *The Earth Sciences*, 2nd ed. (New York, Evanston, and London, 1963, 1971), 589–91. The graph is after Arthur N. Strahler, *Introduction to Physical Geography*, 2nd ed. (New York, London, Sydney, Toronto, 1965), 142.

29. Lincoln, General War Order No. 1, Jan. 27, 1862, Basler, *Collected Works*, V, 111.

30. Halleck to David Hunter, Feb. 16, 1862, *O.R.*, LII, pt. 1, 212; Lincoln to Halleck, Feb. 16, 1862, Basler, *Collected Works*, V, 135; Halleck to McClellan, Feb. 7, 8, 10, 15, 17, 1862, *O.R.*, VII, 590–91, 594, 599, 617, 627–28; Halleck to Buell, Feb. 11, 13, 15, 1862, *ibid.*, 605, 609, 621–22; Buell to Halleck, Feb. 5, 12 (two communications), 15, 1862, *ibid.*, 936–37, 607–8, 621; Buell to McClellan, Feb. 12, 1862, *ibid.*, 938; McClellan to Halleck, Feb. 15, 1862, *ibid.*, 617–18.

31. Halleck to Frederick Steele, Mar. 1, 1862, *O.R.*, VIII, 578–80; Halleck to Buell, Feb. 28, Mar. 2, 1862, *ibid.*, VII, 671–76; Halleck to S. R. Curtis, Feb. 22, 28, 1862, *ibid.*, VIII, 563,

574; Halleck to McClellan, Feb. 28, 1862, *ibid.*, VII, 671–72; Halleck to John Pope, Feb. 25, 1862, *ibid.*, VIII, 566; Halleck to Grant, Mar. 1, 1862, *ibid.*, VII, 674.

32. Halleck to McClellan, Mar. 4, 1862, *O.R.*, VII, 683; Halleck to Grant, Mar. 5, 10, 1862, *ibid.*, X, pt. 2, 7, 27; Robert Hartje, *Van Dorn: The Life and Times of a Confederate General* (Nashville, 1967), 133.

33. Halleck to G. W. Cullum, Feb. 24, 1862, *O.R.*, VII, 661; Halleck to Buell, Mar. 4, 8, 1862, *ibid.*, VII, 682, X, pt. 2, 20; Halleck to McClellan, Mar. 10, 1862, *ibid.*, X, pt. 2, 24–25; Halleck to Thomas A. Scott, Mar. 6, 7, 1862, *ibid.*, 10, 16, Buell to Halleck, Mar. 14, 1862, *ibid.*, 273–38; E. M. Stanton to T. A. Scott, Mar. 8, 1862, *ibid.*, 20.

34. Halleck to Stanton, Mar. 23, 1862, *O.R.*, VIII, 634, X, pt. 2, 70; Halleck to Grant, Mar. 16, 20, 1862, *ibid.*, X, pt. 2, 41, 50–51; Halleck to S. R. Curtis, Apr. 5, 1862, *ibid.*, VIII, 661; Halleck to Buell, Mar. 16, 17, 26, 29, 1862, *ibid.*, X, pt. 2, 42, 43, 66, 77.

35. Grant to Julia Grant, Feb. 24, 1862, *Papers of Grant*, IV, 284.

36. Halleck, report to Stanton, Nov. 15, 1862, *O.R.*, series 3, III, 1042; Grant to Julia Grant, Mar. 1, 1862, *Papers of Grant*, IV, 306; Sherman to W. K. Strong, Mar. 24, 1862, *O.R.*, X, pt. 2, 65.

37. Richard D. Goff, *Confederate Supply* (Durham, 1969), 55–58.

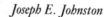

7 ☆ SIMULTANEOUS ADVANCES AND THE SOUTHERN RESPONSE

Joseph E. Johnston

FROM THE FIRST, Jefferson Davis functioned as Confederate commander in chief. But Davis, like Lincoln, necessarily remained disproportionately occupied with the events and threats occurring nearer to his capital. Both Secretary of War Randolph, a Richmond lawyer, and Virginian chief of staff Robert E. Lee reinforced Davis's propensity to give primary attention to eastern affairs.

Davis continually struggled with vexing personality problems among the Confederate military leadership. Joseph E. Johnston chafed at the "insult" of being the fourth-ranking officer, behind Samuel Cooper, Albert Sidney Johnston, and Robert E. Lee; and Beauregard waged what became practically a personal vendetta against both the commissary general and the secretary of war. The Creole also grew touchy about his status. After promotion to full general as a reward for his good work at Bull Run, he considered himself the equal of Johnston, each leading a separate army, or, at the very least, each heading a corps in a united army. It was not at all to his liking that a nearly exasperated war secretary finally told him: "You are second in command of the whole . . . and not first in command of half the army." Then, a few weeks later, when Johnston put Beauregard over a geographic district, while generals two or three grades below him in rank commanded the adjacent districts, he felt he had been markedly demeaned in status.[1]

Johnston's and Beauregard's grousings grew into disputes over reinforcements, supplies, strategy, and policy in general. In the touchiness of these two capable generals there was more than a little vanity, as evidenced by the rapid graying of Beauregard's hair during the war. The cares of high command did not, however, constitute the primary cause. This graying reportedly resulted from the blockade's interruption of his supply of imported hair dye. Johnston, equally sensitive as he had lost his hair during an illness, wore a hat, even at the dinner table.

The President worked with these two cantankerous generals, attempting, often with effusive rhetoric, to placate them so they would devote their full energies to their commands. Davis sought to soothe Beauregard's ruffled feelings by assuring him: "My appreciation of you as a soldier and my regard for you as a man cannot permit me willingly to wound your sensibility or to diminish your sphere of usefulness." In refusing Beauregard's request for a transfer, Davis reassured the general: The War Department desires that the "freest scope should be given for the exercise of your genius and gallantry in the further maintenance of the cause which amid the smoke and blaze of battle you have three times illustrated."[2]

Along with this fulsomely assuasive language, the President explained his own standard for the conduct of a general toward subordinates, one aspect of which Davis was taking pains to practice in his relations with Beauregard. Davis saw the general as "charged with the care, the direction, the preservation of the men," with "time to visit hospitals, to inquire into supplies, to supervise what others must execute, and the men [will] come to regard him, when habitually seen, as the friend of the individual." Trying both to be Beauregard's friend and to urge on him this model, Davis reminded Beauregard that it was drawn from their common experience. His general was "not an ideal, but a sketch of Taylor when general of the little army" in the Mexican War.[3]

As the war wore on, both Davis's time and his patience grew too short for such exercises in human relations as he had practiced with Beauregard. President Davis, himself, easily took offense and lacked Lincoln's broad sense of humor and great forbearance. Increasing criticism made the thin-skinned Confederate President more sensitive; and his nerves were frayed by overwork, bad health, and defeats.

Though the generals became less touchy and punctilious, a more fundamental defect in their behavior divided Johnston and Beauregard from their commander in chief. Both generals failed to confide fully in the President, making Davis anxious by not keeping him adequately informed. Though Beauregard later changed his habit, he did not do so before being relieved of field command. President Davis's greater respect for Johnston's ability meant that he longer retained in high command this not altogether satisfactory subordinate.

Otherwise progress came but slowly while Davis tried to induce some coordination and systematic management into diverse systems of railroad transportation, ranking of generals, organization of new troops, use of Negroes as laborers, acquisition or development of efficient staff officers, and selection of responses to federal operations. The South, more prone to individualism, less institutionalized, and a great deal behind the North in adoption of modern business and managerial techniques generally, could not match its adversary in effective organization.

The South's department system materialized haphazardly as each turn of events seemed to dictate. In October, 1861, Major General Mansfield Lovell superseded the too elderly Major General David E. Twiggs in Louisiana and Texas. Later that month an important change created the Department of Virginia, with Beauregard in command of the District of the Potomac, Major

General Theophilus H. Holmes, heading the adjacent Aquia District, and Major General Thomas J. "Stonewall" Jackson in charge of the Shenandoah Valley District. In November, Robert E. Lee went to the newly formed Department of South Carolina, Georgia, and East Florida, and later, in the spring, when Lee moved to Richmond to become chief of staff, the post devolved upon Major General John C. Pemberton, who received the command as senior officer. No specially demonstrated competence had marked him for command of this large department.

Jackson, particularly, proved himself a most excellent choice for his assignment. Energetic and filled with initiative, he campaigned as best his men could right through the winter. With a broad plan to break up the Baltimore and Ohio Railroad and destroy dams on the Chesapeake and Ohio Canal, in December he struck at one of the dams. Then on January 1, 1862, he moved northward from Winchester, Virginia, and two days later engaged in a skirmish at Bath. In the face of his threatening advance, the Federals evacuated the small town of Romney without a fight and Jackson settled into temporary winter quarters there.

While the other troops of the Department of Virginia remained in their winter cantonments, what later proved to be a significant command change took place. Beauregard revealed himself to be a restless agitator and persistent wirepuller. The lavish style at his headquarters included serving such delicacies as roast duck or juleps of dark cognac, made by his South Carolina aides in large buckets filled with ice and mint, to guests like Prince Jerome Bonaparte or the three beautiful Cary girls. These two sisters from Baltimore and their cousin from Alexandria, Virginia, had, upon his request, fashioned from their undergarments three copies of the Confederate battle flag he designed— and to one he extravagantly promised to plant the Confederate banner on the Washington Monument. When not so gaily entertaining at his headquarters, Beauregard maintained a constant correspondence with members of the Confederate Congress, who in turn advanced his often whimsical although dramatically stated strategic ideas from the floor, doubtless to the great annoyance of the President. For this reason, in late January Beauregard's orders sent him far from Richmond to become the deputy commander in Albert Sydney Johnston's vast western department. This very departure had precipitated Halleck's offensive against forts Henry and Donelson when Union intelligence reported, inaccurately, that Beauregard had with him a reinforcement of fifteen regiments.[4]

While Beauregard's transfer triggered the rapid and successful Union advance in the West, northerners drew inspiration and warm hope from Julia Ward Howe's "Battle Hymn of the Republic." This haunting and stirring war poem first appeared in the February, 1862, issue of the *Atlantic Monthly*. But southerners grimly realized that their shield against the "terrible swift sword" was being tested in the real world by the fall of forts Henry and Donelson. Both sides believed that God preferred their cause; the southerners more painfully perceived that God mostly helps those who do as much as they can for themselves. Davis wrote to Joseph E. Johnston that "events have cast on our arms and our hopes the gloomiest shadows, and at such a time we must show redoubled energy and resolution." Davis and his advisors planned to offer much more than courage and tenacity; they formulated two remarkable strategic concentrations: one immediately against Halleck in the West and another in the East against McClellan as the latter advanced.[5]

In the West, the response developed out of the threat posed by the separation of Albert Sidney Johnston's far-flung forces into two halves by Grant's successful penetration far up the Tennessee. Johnston yielded Nashville to Buell and retreated southeastward along the railroad which ran to Stevenson, Alabama, and Chattanooga. Thus, two Union forces, Grant's and Buell's, stood between the two parts of Johnston's Confederate army, the Middle Tennessee half and the Mississippi River half.

The Union armies possessed interior lines of operations and apparently enjoyed an opportunity, if they moved rapidly, to concentrate either against Beauregard or Johnston. The divided Union command prevented an immediate exploitation of this favorable circumstance and the concentration eventually took place toward Beauregard. Though the closer adversary was Johnston, it is doubtful, in view of the lack of field transportation in Grant's army and the bad state of the roads, that Johnston was truly vulnerable to being overtaken and attacked. Buell's subsequent slow march by road from Nashville to the Tennessee River illustrated the difficulties of springtime movement without rail or water communications. This same slow movement also showed the improbability of any overland advance catching either Beauregard or Johnston before they united. Though the Union occupied a geographically central position, the Confederates possessed the interior lines because they controlled the railroads, all of them then in working order. Only along the Tennessee River did the Union forces possess adequate mobility to exploit their interior position.

Nevertheless, the reuniting Confederate forces faced a deep penetration by Grant's army on the Tennessee River which, Grant felt, provided "such an inside track on the enemy that by following up our success we can go anywhere." Grant's army concentrated on the Tennessee above Savannah at Pittsburg Landing while Buell's was converging on the same "point so that the enemy," Halleck directed, "cannot get between us."[6]

Against this menace, the Confederates began to bring together their divided forces. In this race to concentrate first, the Confederates successfully united at Corinth, two weeks before Buell and Grant joined on the Tennessee. When they had nearly completed their concentration, Jefferson Davis wrote to Sidney Johnston: "I breathe easier in the assurance that you will be able to make a junction of your two armies." Beauregard and Johnston obviously shared this feeling of relief, and hardly needed Davis's advice to exploit their interior

Union Concentration

line by attacking "the division of the enemy moving from the Tennessee before it can make a junction with that advancing from Nashville."[7]

But the concentration at Corinth was not a mere combination of the forces of Beauregard and Johnston. The Confederate high command intended, under Beauregard's leadership, to concentrate almost all the departmental troops at Corinth, including Van Dorn's force in Arkansas. Furthermore, the fall of forts Henry and Donelson had precipitated a swift and drastic reaction by President Davis. Now he perceived how faulty his dispositions had been; he wrote: "I acknowledge the error of my attempt to defend all of the frontier, seaboard and inland." Planning on "abandoning the seaboard," he explained, "in order to defend the Tennessee line which is vital to our safety," Davis ordered reinforcements from New Orleans and the abandonment of Pensacola and Mobile. Major General Braxton Bragg, commanding at Pensacola and Mobile, agreed that Confederate "means and resources" were "too much scattered" and that "strategic points only should be held." But because of Mobile's importance as a port, Bragg declined to abandon the city, although he led 10,000 men, most of his command, to Corinth. He reported: All men not necessary for holding strategic points "should be concentrated for a heavy blow upon the enemy where we can best assail him," so that, "whilst the enemy would be weakened by dispersion," the united forces of the Confederates "could beat him in detail instead of the reverse."[8]

Under the leadership of Davis and Beauregard an almost Confederacy-wide movement of troops soon commenced. They even sought troops from Charleston, South Carolina, ultimately receiving one regiment. Van Dorn approached from Arkansas, Polk from Columbus, Kentucky, and Johnston himself moved first by road and then rail to Corinth. Meanwhile the 5,000 men ordered from New Orleans proceeded en route by river and rail and Bragg's men departed by rail from Mobile.[9]

These comprehensive Confederate strategic movements virtually embraced

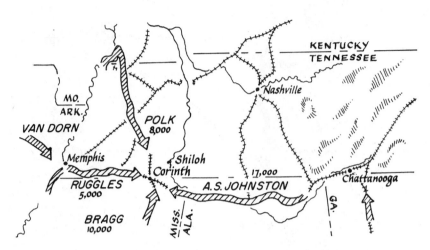

Confederate Concentration

forces from the length and breadth of the nation—from Kentucky to the Gulf
and from the Atlantic to Arkansas. These movements, made possible by the
telegraph and the railway, constituted an application on an unprecedented
scale of the principles of dispersion and concentration characteristic of Napoleonic operations. Thus Beauregard later explained, The railroad and the
telegraph permitted viewing the whole vast "theater of war as one subject of
which all points were but integral parts." The "great principles of war," said
Beauregard, remained the same as in "the time of Ceasar or Napoleon," but
their application had been but broadened and "intensified by the scientific
discoveries affecting transportation and the communication of intelligence."

Through a quirk in the impact of technological change, the railroad tended
to favor strategic maneuver by the defender. Though its logistic impact
strengthened the invader by immensely facilitating the supply of invading
armies, the railroad could confer a strategic advantage upon the defender: if
the defender destroyed the railroad as he retreated, he could deprive the
advancing army of the advantage of railways while at the same time he himself
could continue to enjoy their strategic use for defensive concentrations. Thus,
while the railroads lay wrecked in Union-occupied Middle and West Tennessee, trainloads of troops arrived at Corinth. Even with geographically exterior
lines of operation, possession of undestroyed railroads did, in effect, confer
the advantage of interior lines upon the defender. Most appropriately, therefore, Beauregard added to southern "defensive means" of "mountains and
rivers" the interrelated means of "railroads and telegraph, with the immense
advantage of interior lines."[10]

Meanwhile in the East, the Union pitted Lincoln, Stanton, and Hitchcock
with the War Board against Davis, Randolph, and Lee with his staff. In

northern Virginia federal forces included the garrison of well-fortified Washington, supplemented by McDowell's corps which Lincoln insisted on detaching from McClellan's army and retaining to help protect the politically sensitive capital city. A force under the then well-regarded militia general, Nathaniel P. Banks, had occupied the memorable arsenal site of Harper's Ferry on February 24. In March McClellan's powerful army began turning Johnston's by the water movement to the York-James Peninsula.

The widely dispersed Confederates held seven separate positions in the state. In the critical southeastern area, Major General Benjamin Huger, an inept, middle-aged ordnance officer, commanded 13,000 men at Norfolk. Nearby, on the Peninsula at Yorktown the flamboyant John Bankhead Magruder commanded 12,000 men. Joseph E. Johnston had positioned the main army of 37,000 men west of Fredericksburg, with 5,000 men under Stonewall Jackson opposing Banks in the Shenandoah Valley. Three other forces, totaling 6,000 men, manned observation points. Though dispersed along a long

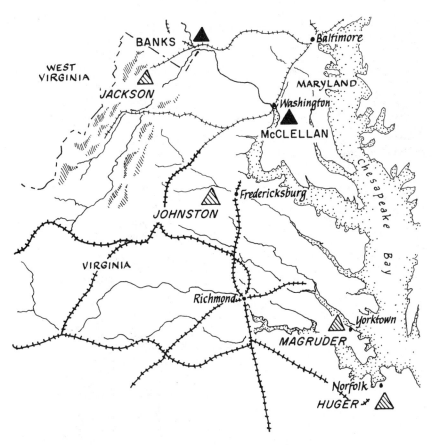

Confederate Communications

perimeter, the Confederate forces were fairly well interconnected by railroad and had good rail connections to the Confederate troops in North and South Carolina.

On March 24, 1862, the new chief of staff, Robert E. Lee, received word from Norfolk that more than twenty federal steamers had come down the Chesapeake Bay the previous evening. A telegram then arrived from Magruder at Yorktown; he believed the force confronting him had risen to 35,000. What did all this mean? Lee deduced three possibilities: (1) McClellan had detached troops to cooperate with Burnside in North Carolina; (2) a pincers move had begun toward Richmond, with McClellan coming from Manassas and the new troops near Norfolk moving up the Peninsula; (3) the reinforcements facing Magruder constituted the advance guard of McClellan's whole army preparing to thrust up the Peninsula. The third of these proved to be the real threat, but Lee could not know that and had to prepare for all of them. He devised a masterly plan, termed by his biographer "a most interest-

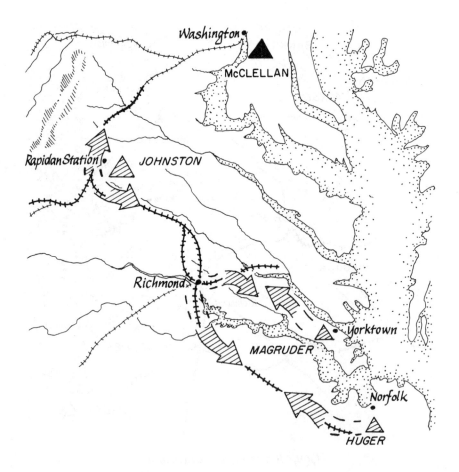

Confederate Provisional Reconcentration

ing example of provisional reconcentration to meet an undeveloped offensive." He would strengthen Confederate forces in North Carolina, either to contain Burnside or reinforce Virginia. Both Huger and Magruder should prepare to reinforce each other if either of their positions, Norfolk or the Peninsula, proved to be federal objectives. The ironclad *Virginia* could cover the mouth of the James River and prevent federal interference with Huger's or Magruder's troop movements. The few available reserves in and around Richmond would move to Yorktown to bolster Magruder, who received orders to hold the farthest possible line as long as he could and to make a new defensive stand if forced to retreat. In this, the Confederates aimed to gain time. And lastly, the greater part of Johnston's army would withdraw from the Rapidan and move quickly toward the lower Peninsula, but remain in readiness to return to its old position if the federal turning movement did not materialize. The railroad was fundamental to this plan.[11]

Magruder played the role of delayer magnificently. Something of an actor with a flair for the dramatic, with his ruses he created the impression that he possessed far more troops than he did. Once he sent a column on a march past a point in full view of the federal outposts. Hour after hour grayclad troops passed, but in reality only a few men moved in a large, continuous circle! McClellan decided he could take Yorktown only with a slow and methodical siege. By April 11 Magruder's actual strength more than doubled to 31,500.

Thereafter, as each day passed, it became more obvious that the main federal effort would come up the Peninsula. An informant's report confirmed "that General Hitchcock told him that McClellan had 120,000 men on the

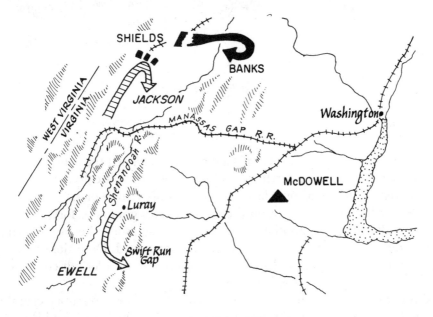

Valley Campaign

Peninsula" and was planning to advance to besiege Richmond. Thus Johnston could withdraw almost completely from the north, effectuating on interior lines of operations a major southern concentration for a big battle east of Richmond.[12]

On March 12, 1862, Jackson's troops moved southward up the Shenandoah Valley and close on their heels federal soldiers moved into Winchester, Virginia. The "Mighty Stonewall" then prepared to launch what became a major diversionary operation. Time slipped by as the Confederates worked zealously to achieve a more powerful concentration. Jackson's campaign began inauspiciously on March 23 when 3,500 of his men slashed into the strongly placed 9,000 Federals under the competent politician/soldier, James Shields, at Kernstown, Virginia. Despite the stark numerical disparity, the southerners fought well and inflicted 590 casualties, while losing 718 men, before retreating safely.

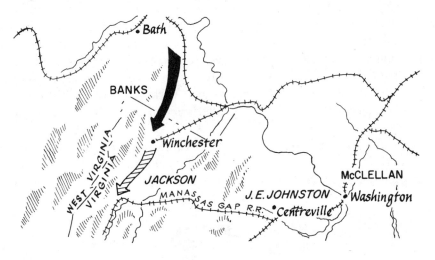

Valley Campaign

Meanwhile, far to the west, the Confederates claimed the southern portion of the vast New Mexico territory and organized it politically. A major fight for the region occurred on March 28 at Pigeon's Ranch in La Glorieta Pass near Santa Fe. In brisk fighting the Confederates gradually forced their enemy to fall back, but another federal column smashed the South's supply trains stationed toward the rear and the invasion ended. Desertions took a toll on the unsupplied ranks and soon the southern commander felt compelled to retreat southward along the Rio Grande.

While the Confederate dreams of a secure far-western territory crumbled, the Federals also continued to make headway along the Mississippi River. On

April 1, 1862, Yankee soldiers slipped onto Island No. 10 under cover of darkness and quickly brushed aside the rebel guards, spiked six guns, and returned safely, a prelude to the early fall of this fort which still blocked the river.

But east of the river the powerful southern response prepared to fall on the Union forces accumulated near Pittsburg Landing, Tennessee. Bragg and his troops from Mobile arrived, as did 5,000 men from New Orleans, the bulk of Polk's Mississippi River garrison, and Johnston with the old Bowling Green force. The still-missing, large, trans-Mississippi force under Earl Van Dorn created a far more serious deficiency than the delay of the single regiment from South Carolina. Diverted by his unsuccessful counteroffensive at Pea Ridge in northwestern Arkansas, Van Dorn, without rail communication, would not arrive until after the impending battle. The Confederate concentration, though impressive, would not produce numerical superiority. Nevertheless, Albert S. Johnston approved Beauregard's battle plan for a major blow to pit 40,335 effectives against Grant's 42,682 men, before Buell's 20,000 troops joined.

Informed by Halleck to be cautious and avoid battle until reinforced, Grant remained on the defensive. Though "of the opinion that the enemy are gathering strength at Corinth quite as rapidly as we are," Grant, though he had "scarcely the faintest idea of an attack," planned to "be prepared should such a thing take place." Grant's army, encamped for some time, did not organize into corps. His command consisted of six divisions: one each under Stephen A. Hurlbut, John A. McClernand, Benjamin M. Prentiss, William T. Sherman, W. H. L. Wallace, and Lew Wallace. Though only Sherman had graduated from West Point and had served as a regular army officer, all had had some type of prewar military experience. Sherman had command experience at Bull Run and McClernand and Lew Wallace had fought in the campaign against forts Henry and Donelson. All, including Sherman, were lawyers.[13]

The Confederate Army of the Mississippi (the same name then as Grant's army, and later changed to the Army of Tennessee) organized into four groups: one each under Leonidas Polk (four brigades), Braxton Bragg (six brigades), William J. Hardee (three brigades), and John C. Breckinridge (three brigades). Johnston's second in command, Beauregard, drew up a plan for them to march out of Corinth at noon on April 3 and make a frontal attack on the federal army on April 4. Beauregard's plan held true to his criticism of Scott's turning movements in Mexico which had necessitated dividing the attacking army. Instead of attempting to turn Grant in the Scott fashion Beauregard relied on a surprise frontal attack. With the river providing protection for the flanks of the Union army, the Confederates really had no choice.

But by nightfall on April 3 the gangly, untried army had barely left Corinth when it encamped for the night. Realizing the impossibility of an attack at the next dawn, Beauregard issued a verbal order postponing it for twenty-four hours. But again things went wrong during the march on April 4: the southerners moved slowly and sluggishly, their order of march grew badly fouled, and their projected battle array became disorganized. This meant that they started April 5 not with an attack but with a nearly all-day effort to deploy for battle. Moving in a dense fog, the army was not ready until 4:00 P.M., again too late to launch the operation that day.

Beauregard wanted to call the whole affair off and return to Corinth. "There is no chance for surprise," he lamented; "they will be entrenched to the eyes." Johnston conferred with Beauregard, Polk, Bragg, and Breckinridge. Not one of them sided with the Creole and they all felt certain that the absent Hardee wished to attack, too, for he usually spoiled for a fight. "Gentlemen, we shall attack at daylight tomorrow," Johnston pronounced; "I would fight them if they were a million." They would not be a million, but Buell's army *had* arrived at last, camping at Savannah, a few miles up the river from Grant's encampment. Halleck had completed his concentration in the nick of time.

Johnston, a big, well-built Texan who exuded both strength and gentleness, possessed an impressive collection of subordinates. Beauregard, the planner, stood at the top as a military scholar and a field captain. As a veteran of Bull Run, he alone had command experience in a major battle. But he had suffered bad health for several months, and before leaving Virginia he underwent a serious operation on his throat from which he had not fully recovered. He caught a cold in Bowling Green that forced him to bed for several days before the retreat from that point. Hostile legend contends that he spent the time before and during the Battle of Shiloh, until he succeeded Johnston in command, in a hospital wagon; he actually merely slept the night there because his personal baggage got lost during the hectic march from Corinth. Polk, the Episcopal bishop and West Point graduate, had excellent training, although little military experience. Not only had he seen no combat, apparently he had never read a single book on military science after he left West Point. Breckinridge, a former vice president of the United States, had no military training, but possessed great qualities as an organizer, administrator, and leader. Hardee nearly equaled Beauregard in scholarliness, training, and ability. The last, Bragg, one of the Confederacy's great hopes, enjoyed a high reputation made even keener by his political activities.

An 1837 West Point graduate, Bragg saw duty in the Seminole and Mexican wars. In Mexico he won three brevet promotions and served in the artillery at Buena Vista. After that battle his name became part of an American legend when word spread that Major General Zachary Taylor had crisply ordered "a little more grape, Captain Bragg." A stickler for dull detail at the expense of a harmless and more colorful story, Bragg always insisted that Taylor's actual order had been: "Captain, give them hell." Grant, who served with Bragg in the old army, spoke of him in his *Memoirs* as "a remarkably intelligent and well-informed man, professionally and otherwise." But a seeming flaw in Bragg's character made him a hairsplitter; he possessed an irascible temper and loved to argue. Grant wrote that "as a subordinate he was always on the lookout to catch his commanding officer infringing upon his prerogatives; as a post commander he was equally vigilant to detect the slightest neglect, even of the most trivial order." Grant related an illustrative, aprocryphal anecdote: "When stationed at a [small] post . . . [Bragg] was himself commanding one of the companies and at the same time acting as post quartermaster and commissary. . . . As commander of the company he made a requisition upon the quartermaster—himself. . . . As quartermaster he declined to fill the requisition. . . . As company commander he responded . . . urging . . . the quartermaster to fill it. As quartermaster he still persisted that he was right . . . [and] referred the whole matter to the commanding officer of the post, . . . [who] exclaimed: 'My God, Mr. Bragg, you have quarreled with every officer in the army, and now you are quarreling with yourself!'"[14]

Despite character flaws, Bragg possessed a propensity for arduous labors which, coupled with his undeniable intellect, impelled him into positions of grave trust and responsibility; he eventually became one of the Civil War's key figures. "Industry personified," one soldier noted, and another subordinate described Bragg as "untiring . . . methodical and systematic." Quite typical of the many favorable assessments that journalists made when Bragg enjoyed a good press, one reporter indicated that "General Bragg has the entire confidence of officers and men." He had one ultimate flaw, however: he never learned to pace himself and he overworked. This rendered him "abrupt and snappish," and it intensified his poor health; for years he had been afflicted with rheumatism, dyspepsia, nervousness, and severe migrane headaches. Throughout the war, he continued driving himself too severely, his responsibilities increased, and his chronic illnesses worsened. His health affected his disposition; one person described him as often "sour and petulant."[15]

This diverse group of leaders, professionally prepared but inexperienced and psychologically prone to occasional difficulty, attempted the execution of Beauregard's orders. The plan seemed beautiful on paper. Two roads ran from Corinth up to Pittsburg Landing. On the map they resembled a strung bow, with the two armies at the top and bottom tips. The southern route, through Monterey, was the string; the northern route, through Mickey's, was the bow. Bragg and Breckinridge traveled the string, Hardee and Polk the bow. The terrain proved difficult and the green troops moved sluggishly through densely thick brush and woods and over undulating ground. When they attacked, as Beauregard planned, with the corps strung out in single lines, Hardee in the lead and Bragg next with Polk and Breckinridge in the rear, control immediately evaporated and the corps became hopelessly intermingled.

Beauregard had decided on this unworkable arrangement because Hardee's

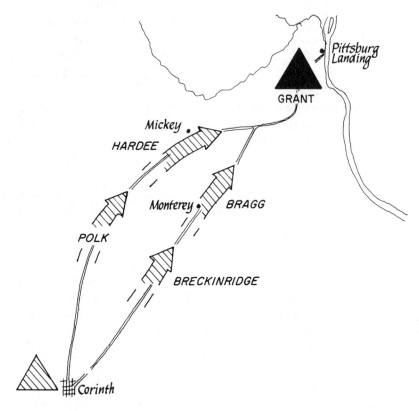

Confederate Advance on Shiloh

men were accustomed to marching together. Since Bragg admitted that his troops, fresh from garrison duty, were a "mob miscalled an army," it appeared that they would be more effective if following and supporting Hardee. Polk's and Breckinridge's slightly better-prepared men constituted the third wave.

Worse than the impending effects of this nightmarishly bad idea, the plan for a silent, surreptitious approach seemed to degenerate into nothing more than a joke. Within two miles of the federal outposts an entire Confederate regiment blazed away at a little five-point buck that ran the length of the column down a field adjoining the road. Many of the men began to tune up their yells, screaming like wild animals just for the sheer fun. At one point during the night Beauregard heard a drum rolling and sent orders to have it silenced at once; but the messenger returned to report that it could not be done—the drum was in the Union camp!

To be sure, the Federals knew there were Confederates in the vicinity, but nevertheless the bluecoats remained ignorant of the real situation. On April 5, Sherman reported to Grant that a patrol had clashed with some rebels the night before, but nothing indicated a general attack. With amazing good fortune the rebels caught the unintrenched federal army at breakfast, totally unready to fight what proved one of the biggest and hardest-fought battles of the war.

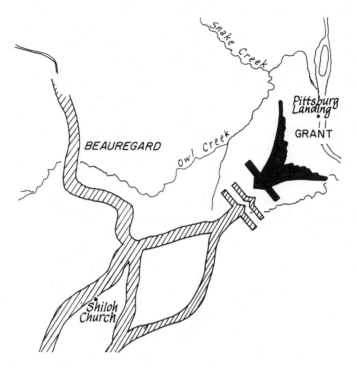

Frontal Assault

Just before launching the onslaught Johnston turned in his saddle and said to his staff, "Tonight we will water our horses in the Tennessee River!" First contact occurred at 5:00 A.M., Sunday, April 6. A federal combat patrol of three companies clashed with skirmishers of Hardee's corps. The engaged northerners received reinforcements, but by 8:00 A.M. the rebels had pushed them back. The full impact of the initial Confederate assault then slashed into Sherman's division. The whole Union force began abandoning its camps while excited Confederates swarmed into them. Gleefully, some of the hungry Confederates swarmed around the cooking pots and fires. Sam Houston, Jr., who scalded his arm while snatching a morsel of meat as he rushed through, later observed that if the attack did not totally surprise the Union army, then the army obviously possessed the most devoted cooks on record.[16]

Johnston rode through one of the captured camps and found a lieutenant and many of the men looting. The young officer proudly showed the general a fine brier pipe he had taken from a Yankee colonel's tent, but Johnston rebuked him. "None of that, Sir," he snapped, "we are not here for plunder." But then as Johnston saw he had hurt the subaltern's feelings, he leaned down from his horse to pick up a tin cup from a table, and said, "Let this be my share of the spoils today." He used it thereafter instead of a sword to direct the battle. He still grasped it tightly at mid-afternoon, as he died.

The main battle developed upon a parallelogram-shaped plateau, varying from five to three miles on a side, cross-hatched with a network of wagon trails running inland from the landing and footpaths connecting numerous forty- or fifty-acre farms. The landing itself lay between the mouths of two creeks that emptied into the Tennessee about five miles apart. Beyond the landing site, the distance between the creeks diminished. The essentially frontal assault succeeded reasonably well but proceeded more slowly than expected, making the fight last all day, again illustrating the resilience and relative defensive invulnerability of the very maneuverable, predominately rifle-armed troops. Though surprised, the blueclads fought well while falling back gradually, and subordinate commanders soon coordinated by the imperturbable Grant slowed the Confederate advance. Then, at a place called the Hornet's Nest, the Union division led by Brigadier General Benjamin M. Prentiss halted the rebel advance completely for several critical hours.

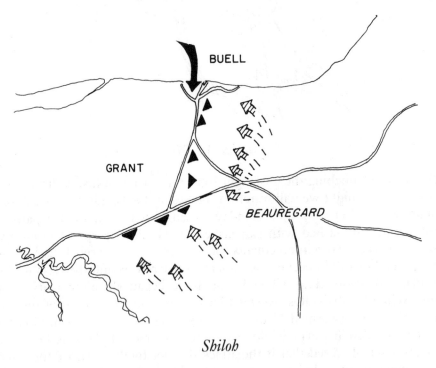

Shiloh

After eleven assaults, the Confederates massed sixty-two artillery pieces and finally, one hour before nightfall, blasted the last of Prentiss's men out of the Hornet's Nest. Johnston had bled to death earlier, the femoral artery in his leg severed by a stray projectile while his personal physician was away helping care for captured federal wounded. Johnston's loss dealt a severe blow to Confederate command resources, but Davis later exaggerated when, expressing a typical southern sentiment, he wrote that "the fortunes of a country hung by a single thread on the life that was yielded on the field of Shiloh." Beauregard immediately and very capably took charge, ordered the news about Johnston kept from the men, and continued the assault against the Hornet's Nest. But he did not try for the final push that day, having received an erroneous report asserting that Buell was too far away to reinforce Grant. Beauregard himself hoped, in vain, that additional Confederate forces under Van Dorn would arrive from Arkansas at any moment. The Confederates, exhausted and in frightful disarray, retired for the night. Beauregard and Bragg shared a tent occupied the night before by Sherman. And one battalion of Mississippi cavalry, far to the extreme flanks, did reach the Tennessee River and watered their horses therein as Johnston had promised.[17]

But time and the elements favored Grant's fortune. It rained mercilessly during the night and the tired troops on both sides enjoyed precious little sleep or rest. Union Brigadier General Lew Wallace arrived with a fresh division, as did Buell, who spent much of the night ferrying his 20,000 combat-ready men across the river while the federal gunboats maintained a continual, harassing fire into the Confederate camps. Some students erroneously conclude that the Confederates fell victim to Beauregard's ineptitude or sloth or to Grant's ability. They succumbed rather, as Stanley Horn put it, "to Grant's two stalwart allies—night and Buell."[18]

On the next day, April 7, a potent and now numerically quite superior Union army forced a reversal of the roles of the previous day, this time the Confederates fighting valiantly on the defensive. Beauregard held tenaciously, looking anxiously for Van Dorn's men. Around noon he thought he saw them. Through the trees, across a field, stood a body of men dressed in white coats firing into an oncoming line of Federals. Surely this was Van Dorn's advance guard; only those westerners would wear anything so outlandish. Actually they were the Orleans Guard battalion who had come into the battle wearing blue parade uniforms which naturally drew the fire of their fellow Confederates. At first the Orleanians simply returned the fire! When a staff officer frantically informed them that they were shooting at their own side, their colonel angrily replied, "I know it, Sir, but damn it we fire on anybody who fires on us!" Soon, however, they turned their coats inside out, showing the while silk linings, and continued the battle that way. When Beauregard realized finally that Van Dorn was not coming, he ordered a withdrawal and a regrouping in Corinth.[19]

North and South lost heavily in the Battle of Shiloh; the casualty lists appalled both sides. Confederate killed, wounded, and missing numbered 10,699; Union casualties amounted to 13,047. Northerners severely castigated Grant. Many critics called for his dismissal, but Lincoln stood by and defended him for, as he said, "I can't spare this man, he fights." Despite the essentially stalemated engagement, the North had turned the southern response to its western concentration into a strategic victory; the South had hoped to destroy Grant's force and thereafter to recapture western Tennessee, but Grant had now extinguished those hopes.

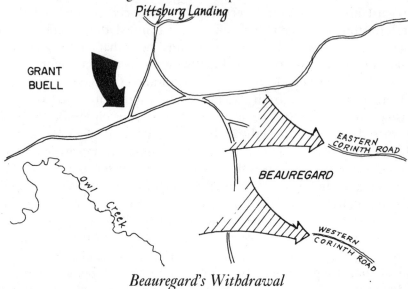

Beauregard's Withdrawal

Grant would not have responsibility for the further conduct of operations for, as he wrote his wife, "General Halleck is here and I am truly glad of it." Almost immediately after Shiloh, Major General Halleck arrived from St. Louis and assumed personal command of the now almost fully united armies of his vast department. Soon the remainder from the Mississippi area joined him, and with over 100,000 men he faced Beauregard's force of barely half that strength. Halleck appointed Grant second in command. If Halleck had as his purpose to have the collaboration of his most experienced subordinate, Grant found the result frustrating, since Halleck proved abler to manuever his huge army without Grant's active assistance. By-passing his second in command, the wary Halleck avoided dramatic turning movements and, using his superior numbers to threaten Beauregard's flanks, inched toward Corinth. By now an experienced army commander, the capable Beauregard protected himself well while seeking an opportunity to attack an exposed portion of the enemy force. But Halleck's army proved invulnerable for, true to his West Point training and the lesson of Shiloh, he intrenched at the end of every day's advance, a ponderous one in any case, further slowed by logistical problems.[20]

The Federals faced "a big job," according to Grant, "to get a large Army over country roads where it has been raining for the last five months." Not only were the roads "almost impassable," making it "very difficult to get up supplies for the army," but the presence of the rebels complicated the logistical task. "If we could go strung out along the road where there was not enemy it would be different. Here, however the front must be kept compact and we do well to approach a few miles everyday."[21]

Halleck could not then supply the huge federal force from the countryside, because the army remained well concentrated and immobilized by Beauregard's in its front, barring the way to their objective, the Memphis and Charleston Railroad at Corinth. Having left the Tennessee River and without a railroad running south, Halleck had to rely on wagon transportation. This meant that the men had to corduroy miles of roads in order to provide the dry, dependable, and durable surface needed to bring from a base on the Tennessee River the vast quantities of supplies demanded by the immense and fully concentrated army. Halleck's careful tactics, constant intrenching, and major road-building program held his progress to a snail's pace. The advance continued for nearly seven weeks, at the rate of less than one mile per day.[22]

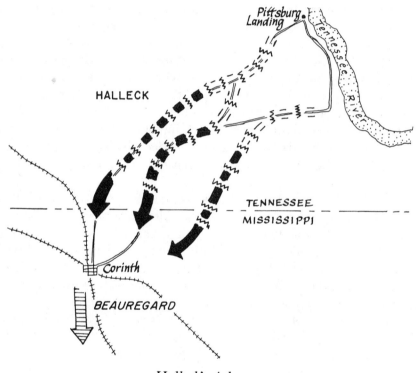

Halleck's Advance

To the east, on the Virginia Peninsula, McClellan's advance proved equally slow for somewhat different reasons. He would have an admirable supply route by water and the ability to turn the Confederates out of their defensive positions on the Peninsula if he could use the York River, but Confederate batteries blocked this waterway. The Confederates knew the vulnerability of Magruder's cross-Peninsula position. Lee had told him: Once the enemy fleet passes up the rivers, they could land troops "to intercept your retreat, and will have turned the line of your land defenses. You must take measures to guard against such a catastrophe, and be prepared . . . to delay the landing and advance of the enemy while you are withdrawing the body of your army behind the Chickahominy." As McClellan arranged to have troops ready "to make a strong attack upon West Point to turn" the "position of the enemy," Johnston anticipated that McClellan would "transport an army up that river and," he wrote Lee, "so compel me to fall back." He expected this as soon as McClellan attacked, for the Confederate batteries were vulnerable and their "guns will soon be dismounted and the river open to him."[23]

Magruder's defensive line, which Joe Johnston regarded as very badly designed and quite vulnerable, protected the batteries which closed the York River. Yet McClellan did not attack it, preparing rather to make a regular siege. Knowing the careful Union commander well from prewar days, Johnston thought that "no one but McClellan could have hesitated to attack."[24]

It has been suggested that McClellan's caution was not innate but induced by a belief "that Southern society was stronger in war." McClellan was representative of those northerners who had "what may by loosely termed" an "inferiority complex" which "handicapped the North in realizing its military potential." McClellan, aristocratic in outlook as were many other generals, was at a psychological disadvantage in fighting opponents who represented a supposedly martial and aristocratic society better adapted for war and which northern generals believed had begun preparation for war earlier than the North.[25]

McClellan's delay caused Lincoln anxiety, both military and political. The radical Republicans did not fail to note that McClellan was a Democrat; one of their number, Senator Ben Wade of Ohio, had already begun a series of demands for McClellan's removal. With whom could he replace him, the President asked irritably. "Anybody!" cried Wade. Lincoln shook his head; "anybody" might do for Wade, but *he* must have *somebody*. Now with the eyes of the whole country focused on military operations in Virginia, Lincoln felt it politically "indispensable" for McClellan to "strike a blow." The President was, he told the general, "powerless to help this. . . . The Country will not fail to note—is now noting—that the present hesitation to move upon an intrenched enemy, is but the story of Manassas repeated." The President concluded with an affirmation of his "purpose to sustain you," he assured McClellan, "so far as in my most anxious judgment I consistently can. *But you must act.*"[26]

McClellan's apparent inertia, timidity about attacking, and presumed preference for siege warfare aroused popular hostility toward the professional soldier. Particularly did it exacerbate the feeling against the Military Academy. Many "felt that the academy's curriculum definitely handicapped its graduates for the business of being successful generals. The theoretical, textbook presentation of military knowledge produced impractical, cautious officers, whose training" McClellan's inaction reflected. West Pointers "were• 'invariably men of all theory and no execution of results,' capable of constructing defensive bases, 'but for active offensive and successful results—never.' Another critic exclaimed, 'Their caution is educated until it is hardly distinguishable from cowardice.' "[27]

West Point was vulnerable, of course, because many of its graduates were fighting for the rebels. Secretary of War Cameron had dwelt upon the "extraordinary treachery" displayed by West Pointers and asked whether it "were not a result of 'a radical defect in the system of education itself.' "[28]

Many people felt strongly that the successful prosecution of the war did not require West Point-trained regulars. Horace Greeley's New York *Tribune* expressed this view well: "However imperfect the civil appreciation may be as to military science, common sense is an attribute which buttons and bullion do not alone confer; and common sense is quite as competent as tactical profundity to decide the question of hastening or deferring operations against the rebels." Long years of school were wasted because the "atmosphere, the fume of the bivouac" provided a better education than the textbooks of West Point.[29]

Impatience with the lack of quick victory, crystallized by McClellan's siegecraft, induced many critics to denounce professional military leadership. One disgusted radical insisted the regular army officers could never win the war. "Take off your engineering restraints; dismiss . . . from the Army every man who knows how to build a fortification, and let the men of the North, with their strong arms and indomitable spirit, move down upon the rebels, and I tell you they will grind them to powder in their power."[30]

Civilian critics confused McClellan's execution with the art of war which he sought to practice. They confused McClellan's practice with the tactical realism and sound strategy which he advocated and was falteringly executing. When his plans actually bore fruit, his manner of carrying them out and his unwillingness to follow up made success look like failure.

When Joe Johnson said that "no one but McClellan would have hesitated to attack," the Confederate general thus succinctly put his finger on the flaw in his friend's character which did so much to nullify Little Mac's great abilities. A good strategist, McClellan had an almost prescient grasp of the tactical realities. His organizational ability and his capacity to inspire the loyalty and affection of his troops well complemented these qualities. But as Johnston correctly realized, McClellan's excessive caution and tendency to exaggerate difficulties virtually nullified all of these outstanding attributes. These vexing traits apparently grew more intense as his relations with Lincoln deteriorated.

An exasperating example of Lincoln's "unjustified meddling" had appeared when the President issued on March 8, 1862, his General War Order No. 2 that reorganized McClellan's army into four corps, one each under the senior major generals, Irvin McDowell, Samuel P. Heintzelman, Erasmus D. Keyes, and Edwin V. "Bull Head" Sumner, so nicknamed because a musket ball was alleged to have once bounced off his head. In part this was a political move designed to vent some of the mounting criticism within Lincoln's party over the President's conduct of the war, for all of the new corps commanders were good Republicans. McClellan totally failed to appreciate the situation. Although the increasing size of the army justified it, McClellan probably acted partly out of spite when he later named two additional corps commanders, brigadier generals Fitz-John Porter and William Buell Franklin, able junior officers but both Democrats.

For McClellan the last straw occurred after he reached the Peninsula, when his army lost McDowell's powerful corps, retained by Lincoln to protect Washington. A council of generals earlier had established the number of troops to be left to protect Washington. General Hitchcock and Adjutant General Thomas studied the capital's defensive forces and had concluded "that the requirement of the President that this city shall be left entirely secure . . . has been fully complied with," but his reduction in McClellan's force, McClellan regarded as almost crippling to his chances of success. Further, he perceived this decision as inspired by his radical enemies and intended to cause his offensive to fail.[31]

To have plans questioned, his subordinates queried, his army reorganized against his will, and to read in the newspaper of his removal as general in chief would tend to demoralize anyone and induce a "safety first" propensity even in one not prone, as *was* McClellan, to such an attitude. The reduction of his army and his suspicion of political sabotage completed the destruction of McClellan's morale. Throughout his operations McClellan exhibited a disabling caution and a debilitating tendency to exaggerate his own difficulties and the enemy's strength and capabilities; he also showed a zeal to shift to the President all responsibility for failure.

In addition, Lincoln had strategic misgivings because the rebel army around Richmond stood between McClellan's on the Peninsula and McDowell's south of Washington. The President later cautioned McClellan "to prevent the main body of the enemy's forces from leaving Richmond and falling in overwhelming force upon General McDowell." So Lincoln, with his now firm grasp of the concept of lines of operation, saw how a turning movement, when carried out with less than the whole army, could readily confer upon the defender the advantage of interior lines of operations. Unless the attacker moved vigorously and retained the initiative, he very likely conferred that advantage upon his opponent. McClellan's cautious and deliberate movements were doing just this.

Of course, McClellan desired to move with virtually his entire army and so menace Richmond that the enemy would have no choice but to concentrate everything in its defense. But, from the imperative political necessity of being absolutely certain that the rebels gain no opportunity to "sack" Washington, Lincoln modified the plan, despite the clear realization that the Union armies faced the problem of operating on exterior lines.[32]

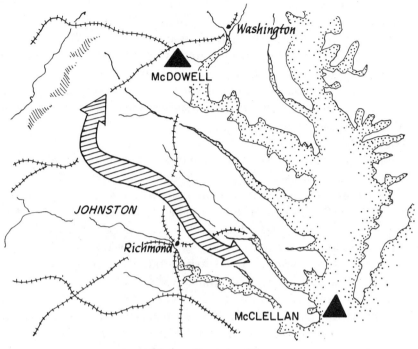

Union Exterior Lines

Yet, McClellan's plan gradually worked as designed. Johnston evacuated Yorktown on May 3, 1862, and, though he fought a delaying action at Williamsburg on the 5th, he continued to withdraw toward Richmond, because of the threat of McClellan's waterborne turning movement. Nevertheless just

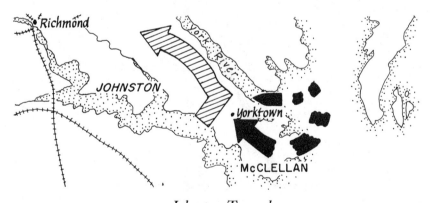

Johnston Turned

as his plan was working, McClellan began to lose his concept of the operation. Instead of perceiving that his menacing approach to the enemy capital would force the Confederates to counterattack, he began to conceive that it would be necessary for him to attack. At the same time he felt that in numbers his army was "undoubtedly considerably inferior to that of the rebels." Soon he envisioned the necessity to "attack in position, probably intrenched," he remarked, "a much larger force, perhaps double my numbers."[33]

His understanding of what he set out to do was sufficiently blurred so that, in reporting that "Richmond papers urge Johnston to attack," he commented: "I think he is too able for that." Though the Confederates were concentrating coastal troops at Richmond, their immediate response began with Jackson's important Valley campaign.[34]

In two weeks Jackson marched 170 miles, routed a total of 12,500 Federals, and occupied the attention of some 60,000 more. Always outnumbered seven to three, every time Jackson engaged he fought with odds of about four to three in his favor—because, moving rapidly on interior lines, he hit fractions of his enemy with the bulk of his own command. The Confederacy bolstered his strength to 17,000 to face McDowell's corps of 40,000, Banks's nearly 17,000, and Fremont's perhaps 12,000 men, plus any reserves that the Federals might choose to commit from Washington. Jackson enjoyed the great advantage that the northerners remained widely scattered on a perimeter within which his troops could maneuver to concentrate against first one and then another of the Union forces. Lincoln managed very well, personally maneuvering the scattered Union armies. Since neither Lincoln nor his advisors felt that Jackson's small force could truly threaten Washington, they chose an offensive response as they sought to exploit their overwhelming forces and exterior position to overwhelm his army. But Jackson's great abil-

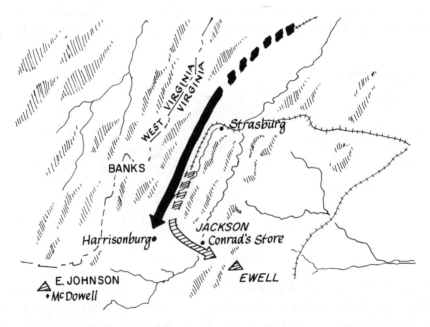

Jackson Moves to Flank Position

ity, celerity of movement, and successful series of small fights determined the
outcome.

Jackson's first exploitation of his central position culminated on May 8,
1862, near the town of McDowell, Virginia. Retreating South, he had stopped
Banks from advancing farther by taking up a "flank position" at Swift Run
Gap. In his flank position, the defensive analogue of the turning movement,
Jackson threatened Banks's communications should the Union commander
move deeper up the Valley. First planning on "threatening his flank and rear,"
expecting thus to "prevent his reaching Staunton," Jackson then called forward the division of the capable Major General Richard S. Ewell to the Swift
Run Gap position. He expected "to leave General Ewell here to threaten

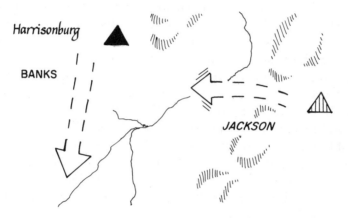

Threat of Flank Position

Banks' rear in the event of his advancing on Staunton," and move his own
army "rapidly on the force in front of General Edward Johnston." Moving
first southeast to mystify Banks as to his intentions, Jackson reached the
railroad after a ninety-two-mile march in four days. He headed west by train
and soon joined Brigadier General Edward Johnson's force near McDowell.

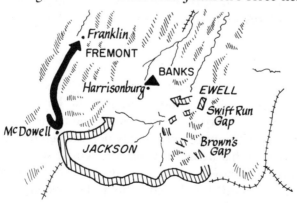

Jackson Exploits Interior Lines

Their forces, 9,000 men, united on their interior lines, withstood attack on May 8 by 6,000 Federals from Fremont's command. Repulsed, the Federals withdrew. After attempting a brief pursuit, Jackson halted on May 12, returned to the Shenandoah, and proceeded north.[35]

By May 9, as McClellan's Peninsula campaign made headway, the southerners felt compelled to evacuate Norfolk. This valuable military and naval supply depot, with vital stockpiles and machinery, constituted a severe loss. Most important, it left C.S.S. *Virginia* without a port, and the Confederates soon had to destroy the vessel to prevent her falling into federal hands. Until this movement *Virginia* had continued to exercise a powerful effect on McClellan's strategic thinking. She also exerted a disconcerting influence over the thinking of many Negroes in the area, for the seamen often walked out onto the fore and aft decks, which were covered by a few inches of water, and gave rise to a belief among the superstitious that "these men of the 'debble ship' could walk on water." But now, in order to render the vessel able to negotiate shallower waters up the James River, they had to remove much of her armor, and this resulted in her riding so high that she exposed two feet of her vulnerable hull. The rebels had no other choice left but reluctantly to destroy the vessel to prevent the Federals from easily sinking or capturing her. The sailors laboriously took her guns upriver to Drewry's Bluff, where some of them helped man the artillery emplacements that eventually proved impassable to the Union flotilla.[36]

Appreciating the necessity for the withdrawal from Norfolk, Davis wrote Johnston: "I have been much relieved by the successes which you have gained, and I hope for you the brilliant result which the drooping cause of our country now so imperatively claims." Nevertheless Davis wrote more apprehensively to Mrs. Davis, "If the withdrawal from the Peninsula and Norfolk had been done with due preparation and a desirable deliberation, I should be more sanguine of a successful defense of this city. . . . I know not what to expect when so many failures are to be remembered, yet will try to make a successful resistance."[37]

On May 15, 1862, Butler, occupying New Orleans, issued his notorious Order No. 28: "As the officers and soldiers of the United States have been subject to repeated insults from the women (calling themselves ladies) of New Orleans in return for the most scrupulous noninterference and courtesy on our part, it is ordered that hereafter when any female shall by word, gesture, or movement insult or show contempt for any officer or soldier of the United States she shall be regarded and held liable to be treated as a woman of the town plying her avocation." On the same day two other events of great significance occurred: in Liverpool, England, a British shipyard launched the

C.S.S. *Alabama*, destined for a smashingly successful career as a commerce raider and to be the most famous of all the Confederate vessels; and in Virginia a battle occurred at Drewry's Bluff. Five federal naval vessels, including the *Monitor*, moved up the James River and sailed to within eight miles of Richmond before being blocked and engaged in a four-hour artillery duel. The well-posted Confederate guns proved an unaided water approach to the rebel capital impracticable.[38]

During the next few days, while Halleck inched his way toward Corinth, Jackson succeeded in making a "happy diversion" for the Confederates, drawing public attention from both Halleck and McClellan. Jackson's men moved northward from Mount Solon, as the Federals maneuvered cautiously, trying to guess what Jackson would do next. Jackson divided his forces, his own troops going west of the Massanutten Mountain and those under Ewell to the east. Banks's main army covered the west side of the Valley; another small complement of Federals guarded the east at Front Royal.[39]

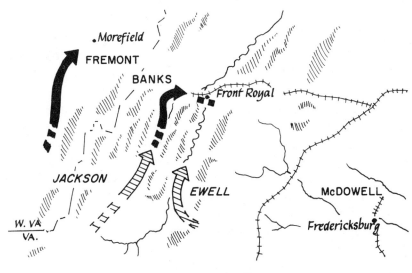

Jackson Divides Forces

Moving rapidly, Jackson executed a maneuver combining the intrinsic features of the turning movement and the concentration on a single line of operations. Crossing the Massanutten, Jackson joined Ewell, thereby concentrating the entire gray army against a miniscule federal force. On May 23 at Front Royal Jackson slammed into the body of about 1,000 men, easily defeated it, and captured many of the troops. The Unionists lost 904 killed, wounded, or captured; Jackson lost fewer than 50 men and took an estimated $300,000 worth of supplies. Banks soon acquired the dubiously distinctive nickname "Mr. Commissary" from the Confederates, because they so frequently captured supplies from his troops.

Having gobbled up this small detachment Jackson now proceeded to turn

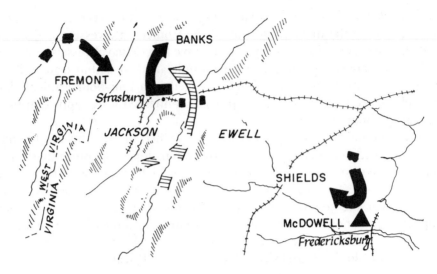

Concentration and Turning Movement

Banks's main force. Jackson lost a chance to get behind Banks by not pushing far enough or fast enough to catch the federal army, which made good its retreat to Winchester and there attempted to make a stand with its troops badly disorganized.

On Sunday, May 25, despite Jackson's stern religious scruples, another, much larger battle occurred at Winchester, where Stonewall's men hit most of the remainder of Banks's force. A federal soldier described it as "hell—or at least about as good an imitation as is often produced in the 'upper world.'" Trying to halt the federal retreat in its early stages, General Banks encountered the Third Wisconsin in flight and shouted, "Stop men! Don't you love your country?" One of the harried troopers looked back and replied, "Yes, by God, and I'm trying to get back to it just as fast as I can." The humorist Bill Arp reflected Jackson's dogged determination and fighting ability mingled with his religiosity when he commented: "I do not know whether Jackson is a Christian or not, but this I do know, if he decides to go to heaven, all hell won't be able to stop him."[40]

With the Confederate casualties at 400, Banks lost 2,019 and more supplies, munitions, and wagons. Falling back to Williamsport on the Potomac, the Union general left Jackson in possession of Winchester. But the Confederate position there remained perilous, even though defeat had weakened and disorganized Banks's battered army and the federal forces then concentrating at Harper's Ferry were not menacing. To the southwest Lincoln had ordered Fremont into the Shenandoah Valley, a move which heartened the opponents of West Point generalship, because they believed that a radical general like Fremont had "the earnest belief, the singlehearted, intense devotion to victory, the entire belief in justice which can cope with Stonewall Jackson." But Lincoln was relying neither on Fremont's radical fervor nor on his army alone. In the Valley Fremont was to meet fully half of McDowell's force, which Lincoln had ordered to march westward with all haste. Lincoln realized that both of these federal armies occupied a flank position with respect to Jackson's, now north of Winchester. Resolving to exploit this situation to take the offensive, Lincoln saw that, if these powerful forces could unite, they might "capture the enemy" or at least compel Jackson to attack them to retain his base in the southern Valley.[41]

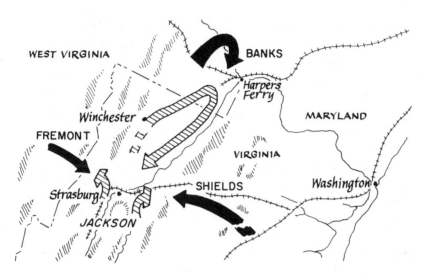

Federal Flank Position

The federal plan to entrap Jackson entailed one big weakness: McDowell's men had to move quite far over rough terrain, though Lincoln urged him on saying, It is "for you a question of legs. Put in all the speed you can." Furthermore, Fremont encountered delay, imposed by serious problems in feeding his men in the mountainous area west of the Valley. By May 30 Jackson knew the location of Fremont's and McDowell's forces and the purpose of their movements. So Jackson's "foot cavalry" began a hasty retreat back up the Valley, with the three Yankee commanders in separate pursuit. Escaping in the nick of time, Jackson passed through the federal pincers before they closed. Though Lincoln drove Jackson far from Washington, this was accomplished at the expense of arresting McDowell's advance and temporarily removing him as a menace to Richmond. These dramatic incidents in the Valley coincided with other events, as citizens in the North and South also awaited news from threatened Richmond and besieged Corinth.[42]

Inexperienced in field command, Halleck, in the words of his most battle-wise subordinate, Grant, "determined to make sure work," and moved "slowly but in a way to insure success." With Grant second in command,

Halleck organized the Federals into three groups under Buell, the capable George H. Thomas, and John Pope, whose force had been ordered to join Halleck after its capture of the Mississippi stronghold, Island No. 10. Feeling that the use of many troops elsewhere than on the Corinth line would "release our grasp on the enemy's throat," Halleck explained, "in order to pare his toenails," he also ordered eight regiments from Missouri. Thus, the Union, like the Confederacy, concentrated almost all its western forces before Corinth.

The army advanced systematically with Buell and Thomas pushing onward carefully. Acting on his own initiative, the energetic Pope thrust boldly forward, establishing an advanced base four miles from Corinth. Halleck sought to restrain Pope, thinking him "too far ahead; it is dangerous," he warned, "and effects no good." Beauregard, making the same assessment, shrewdly tried to cut Pope off from the main federal body, but several days of skirmishing produced no result. Meanwhile, Halleck continued his inexorable advance.[43]

The Confederate predicament, precarious from the start, worsened as the Corinth area bred pestilence, due mainly to a lack of pure water. Thousands of soldiers grew ill with typhoid fever, mumps, measles, and dysentery. Absolutely no space seemed free of wounded or sick men, with only inadequate medical attention available. Tetanus was common, erysipelas widespread, gangrene incredible, and botched amputations shockingly numerous—necessarily performed by "medical students or anyone claiming even the slightest knowledge of anatomy or medicine." Every day many men died.[44]

Aside from what Beauregard termed "the natural unhealthfulness of the place," he experienced serious supply difficulties, especially foodstuffs. Testily he telegraphed Richmond: "The false views of administration—to say the least—of Colonel Northrop will starve out his army unless I make other arrangements, which I have done." Beauregard had personally sent to Texas and Arkansas and had a large herd of cattle brought to Corinth just in time to save the army from real privation. Other important supplies, however, remained scant and of poor quality.[45]

"Colonel Northrop" was Lucius B. Northrop, chief of the Commissary Department of Richmond, and widely reputed to be incompetent. Despite this criticism he retained his post for most of the war, only because, many malcontents alleged, "he was an old crony of the President's." Northrop's friendship with Davis dated far back to their days as lieutenants in the U. S. Army, when Northrop testified in Davis's defense at a court-martial.[46] Certainly the army had more practical and less cantankerous men, but anyone would have faced similarly impossible circumstances. Northrop himself did rather well, all things considered, but his department, like the entire Confederate supply structure, woefully lacked administrative efficiency and adequate transportation capabilities.

Northrop did possess sound qualifications. Born in Charleston, South Carolina, in 1811, he had graduated from West Point in 1831 and served until 1839, when he went on indefinite sick leave (until 1861!) resulting from his accidentally shooting himself in the knee. He served briefly thereafter in the Subsistence Department in Washington but otherwise convalesced in Charleston, where he studied medicine. He then built up a lucrative practice in Charleston. Davis undoubtedly, and with sound reason, believed that his old friend not only knew what rations the average soldier might truly require, but that Northrop also understood the military problems one encountered in providing those needs. Northrop at once perceived the entire Confederacy as "a besieged fortress," with an invading enemy threatening constantly to "consume the bacon."[47]

Almost from the beginning, meat of any kind was a scarce and precious commodity for many soldiers and citizens within the Confederacy. Even as early as mid-1861 General Bragg out of necessity had ordered molasses substituted for some of his units' meat rations. "All the fresh meat *we* had," one doubtlessly lean veteran later recalled, "came in the hardtack, and I preferring my meat cooked, used to toast my hardtack before eating them." Siege conditions always and general scarcity sometimes reduced hungry southerners to eating mule meat, and occasionally even rats. Indeed food at times provided the impetus for Confederate gallantry in action: the colonel of a Louisiana regiment overheard a wounded soldier cry to his comrades, "Charge 'em boys! They have cheese in their haversacks!"[48]

The southern farmers theretofore had devoted most of their land to staple and cash crops such as cotton and tobacco. When staple-crop prices were high, the region had imported food. By 1862 the government, with cooperation from state administrations quite unfamiliar with such tasks, began to limit cash-crop production, and corn replaced cotton as the most favored harvest. But when large parts of the upper South fell to the Union onslaught, the Confederacy lost not only its traditional grain-growing regions, but also its principal meat-producing areas. Florida and Texas then became the chief sources of cattle and hogs, but the remoteness of these states placed a stunning strain upon an already overtaxed transportation network. The Commissary Department increasingly relied upon blockade running for meat supplies, although entrepreneur shippers balked at such bulky cargoes as sides of beef, preferring more profitable shipments of whiskey and frivolous luxury items.

Insuring a continuing supply of salt, not only a necessary diet item but also vital to field preservation of perishables and in meat-packing, remained constantly a critical matter that demanded attention. The army allocated each Confederate soldier one and one-half pounds of salt per month. Northrop

always managed, although with difficulty, to obtain enough salt for the needs
of the fighting forces, but the civilians suffered shortages. Under Northrop's
direction, an extensive bureaucracy of salt agents and commissioners made
some government salt available to the populace according to need. Salt even
became an item of exchange, substituting for currency, one sack (three bushels) being worth forty sides of bacon in Mississippi by October, 1862.

The Confederacy imported much salt and seized some from the enemy—
Jackson captured a considerable amount of it during his Valley Campaign.
But except for the vast dome at Avery Island, Louisiana, which the rebels
did not discover until 1862 and held for only eleven months, they obtained
their only domestic source by boiling down brine, either obtained from saline
springs, wells, or sea water. Northrop brought about the establishment of
government evaporating stations on the coast, but periodic Union naval raids
proved highly effective at destroying the equipment and usually restricted
such activity to unnavigable inland bays. One remarkable effort almost put
the government into the business of producing salt by solar evaporation in
specially devised basins near Lake Bisteneau, Louisiana. Lack of both local
interest and faith in the workability of the process, combined with the un-
timely death of the French geologist J. Raymond Thomassy, who had instigated it, caused its total abandonment. Every practicable spot on the Atlantic
and Gulf coasts was used sometime for salt-making, but the many bays and
inlets, comparative isolation, and abundant cheap fuel made Florida the most
important coastal state in producing salt.

The coastal operations notwithstanding, the principal government source
for brine, after the loss of the highly productive (two and a half million
bushels per year) and remarkably pure Kanawha Licks in western Virginia,
became the briny springs near Saltville, in the southwestern part of that state.
A Union raid there in January, 1862, inflicted only minor equipment damage
but induced the Confederacy to pay continuing attention to the area's defense.

Throughout the war both sides directed military and naval operations to
protect their own salt and to deprive the other of it. Save for temporary field
deprivations, however, the Union had no salt supply problem, its importation
and production facilities never being under serious attack. New York, Ohio,
and Pennsylvania alone produced 12,000,000 bushels annually.

The Confederacy's greatest problem in salt supply always remained transportation. The problem of moving the salt, especially from remote coastal
locations, caused great difficulty. The winter season or the floods of spring
brought almost, if not complete, cessation of the work. Roads became impassable so that they almost had to suspend salt-making from Christmas to
the first of May in Virginia, where, even if they could operate the works,
they could not ship the salt out.

Cold and wind at any salt-making location always vastly increased the
amount of fuel required to boil down any brine, again rendering much of the
year unprofitable for the activity. And brine sometimes proved unavailable,

or periodically lost sufficient salinity due to spring floods. Wood to fuel the evaporating fires became ever more difficult to obtain and, for example, had to be hauled to Saltville from cuttings thirty miles away. Little wonder that Lieutenant Colonel Frank Ruffin, one of Northrops's chief assistants, bleakly declared that the South "was completely exhausted of supplies," an overly pessimistic assessment.[49]

Several other factors hindered Northrop's efforts. At the war's outset he delegated responsibility in the various states to agents who purchased goods at inflated prices from food speculators. By March, 1863, the Impressment Act began regulating such procurements, but farmers constantly resisted its operation. And always poor transportation hampered logistics. In Virginia, huge rail traffic jams snarled the roads, as overloaded cars crawled at a snail's pace to the combat zones, often delaying meat shipments from twenty to thirty days. The southern ranks sometimes experienced forty-eight hours of marching and fighting without rations. Units could subsist off the countryside during periods of available harvest, but Union offensives frequently forced Confederate concentrations at unpropitious moments. Northrop never solved his manifold problems. His replacement late in the war, the able Isaac Monroe St. John, tried a new system with foodstuffs collected directly from farmers and moved to depots for immediate shipment, but, though it improved efficiency somewhat, it came too late to provide any substantial relief.

In other areas of supply, the Confederacy fared only slightly better than in subsistence. The Quartermaster Department, initially headed by Abraham C. Myers, who previously had directed the United States logistics during the Mexican War and at New Orleans thereafter, early encountered severe difficulties in procuring sufficient quantities of uniforms and shoes. More than once the southern troops considered their most fruitful means of supply to be plunder of the enemy. "In winter," one of the grayclad soldiers wrote, "the overcoat-bearing Federal was esteemed especially for his pelt."[50]

In August, 1863, Myers gave up his job to the very able Brigadier General Alexander R. Lawton, a West Pointer, experienced field commander, and prewar lawyer and railway executive. Lawton brought some improved administration, but nothing could change the recalcitrant attitudes of a balky populace and unwilling governors, such as Zebulon Vance of North Carolina. Vance quarreled with the government, especially over attempts to regulate blockade shipments, and threatened to burn the boats before complying with the demand for the reservation of one-half to one-third of the cargo space for military use. He also refused to allow the distillation of grain into whiskey in North Carolina, a violation of the state's laws, in order to provide the medical department with a desperately needed antiseptic and anesthesia substitute. In his most shocking action he ordered the stockpiling of some uniforms, shoes, and blankets for the future needs of the North Carolina troops while the main army marched barefoot in the snows of Virginia. Other state governments also similarly placed local defense above the Confederate military cause. While the federal government effectively coordinated the North's economic power and took new liberties with the U.S. Constitution, the southern citizenry often held stubbornly to the fundamental ideals of limited government, even if that should result in the new nation's failing to survive.

Otherwise, though it fell short of adequacy, the Confederate government's centralizing and coordinative impact upon logistical activities wrought a veritable revolution. As the Ordnance Chief, Brigadier General Josiah Gorgas, perceptively wrote in 1864, "In such a war as this—a war for national existence—the whole mass of the nation must be engaged. It must be divided into those who go into the field and fight, and those who stay at home and support." And, indeed, by the end of the war, the Confederate government "directly and indirectly managed broad segments of the southern economy and . . . the Richmond government raised a veritable army of bureaucrats to work the national will in every corner of the South." They established price control boards for specific areas. The government imposed price schedules and allocations of raw materials, channeling available sources into war production. A subsection of the Ordnance Bureau, the Niter and Mining Bureau, sought out and developed new sources of niter, metals, coal, and chemicals. It bought up mineral rights, explored caves, negotiated mining contracts, conducted patriotic scrap drives, and encouraged civilians at home to devise artificial niter beds. The Confederate supply agencies established and operated their own factories and shops under the direction of the ordnance, quartermaster, and medical bureaus; the government itself, employing both military and civilian labor working under bureau-officer management, produced clothing, wagons, laboratory items, arms and ammunition, harnesses, and shoes. Slaves erected fortifications, constructed and repaired railroads, and worked in managed agricultural production. A railroad authority maintained liaison with the various independent lines, and military officials occasionally stepped in boldly to control rail operations to the utter chagrin of the civilian managers and owners. The southern government even regulated trade across the enemy lines, buying cotton, tobacco, and other agricultural staples for shipment to points where it could be secured by civilians authorized to make the trips.[51]

Ordnance Chief Gorgas's efforts deserve singular mention. Under his capable direction the government established large arsenals at Richmond, Virginia; Fayetteville, North Carolina; Augusta and Macon, Georgia; Charleston and Columbia, South Carolina; and Selma, Alabama. These factories turned out rifled muskets, artillery, ammunition, and powder, while other installations produced chemicals or researched suitable substitutes, solving seemingly endless difficulties. In the arming of its troops, the Confederacy fared better than in any other logistical activity.

The ultimate and unsolvable supply problem within the Confederacy lay not in failing to try nor, for the most part, in lacking the resources with which to do that trying; it was in having too far to go in establishing managerial parity with the North, and in failing to achieve an adequate transportation capability. True enough, the South possessed too little in the way of technical capacity; but with similar disparities the Russians triumphed over the French, the Americans over the British, and the North Vietnamese over the Americans.[52]

Supply limitations, as so often was the case during the Civil War, played a prime role in forcing Beauregard's decision to evacuate Corinth, which he did on May 30, 1862, with great skill and efficiency. Pulling his army out of the siege, he headed south toward Tupelo, a much better-situated defensive position fifty miles deeper into the interior and one blessed with an abundance of fresh water. Late in the night Halleck's scouts reported great activity in the Confederate camp: from time to time the blare of bugles and the roll of drums could be heard and, as each train arrived, Beauregard's men let out wild cheers. Halleck concluded that the rebels were reinforcing at Corinth in order to attack him.

At the crack of dawn Halleck's men opened fire with their heavy guns toward the Confederate lines but, strangely, no fire returned. The puzzled Yankees could clearly see enemy gun muzzles and many Confederate caps peeking from behind trench lines. Finally the bluecoats spotted a white flag and smoke rising in the distance. Several citizens from Corinth approached the Union lines to report Beauregard's camp totally deserted. Investigations revealed the "gun muzzles" to be log ends painted black and the "becapped Rebel soldiers" merely scarecrows. The trains arriving with supposed reinforcements during the night actually had been empty ones, engaged in hauling personnel *out* of town. Beauregard had pulled a great hoax and withdrawn his army to let it refit to fight another day. He further compounded the Union problem of pursuit by removing all road signs, indispensable guides in an era of inadequate and inaccurate maps.

On the next morning, May 31, in Virginia, Johnston attacked two federal corps at Fair Oaks (or Seven Pines), a few scant miles east of Richmond. And in the Shenandoah Valley, Jackson hurried south in a heavy rainstorm to squeeze between converging federal columns under Fremont and McDowell. Some skirmishing erupted near Front Royal, but Jackson slipped safely away. Near Richmond, McClellan's ponderous but really effortless advance had reached the vicinity of the enemy capital because the Confederates had made no determined resistance on the Peninsula. The southerners had retreated, fearing the constant threat of a turning movement by water which the Federals, with their naval superiority and troops on transports, could execute at any time. When McClellan's army reached the outskirts of Richmond, it so menaced the capital that it compelled the Confederates to attack him, thus enabling him to fight Johnston's force with all of the tactical advantages of being on the defensive.

The Confederates felt constrained to attack, not only because they experienced the same pressure as did the Union to drive back a hostile army so close to their capital, but because they feared that McClellan, with his powerful artillery and superior numbers, could take the city by siege, even without surrounding it. Believing that McClellan would "depend for success on artillery and engineering," the Confederates were sure that they could "compete with him in neither." They believed that they were "engaged in a species of warfare" in which the foe overmatched them. It would be a contest "of artillery," "in which we cannot win," remarked Johnston. The kind of attack they envisioned by McClellan had occurred only seven years before in the Crimean War when an Anglo-French force took the heavily fortified Russian port of Sebastopol. The Confederate leaders could hardly escape the analogy, because none other than McClellan had served as an official U.S. observer at the siege of Sebastopol and had published a report of his observations there. A belief in what may be called the Sebastopol thesis meant that the Confederates thought that only an offensive could save the otherwise doomed capital.[53]

In the first Confederate attack, the still-inexperienced Johnston and his subordinates mismanaged a good plan, though McClellan's absence from the battlefield indicated that the Union army offered no coordinated resistance. Attempting no turning movement, the Confederates concentrated heavily against the intrenched Union troops south of the rain-swollen Chickahominy

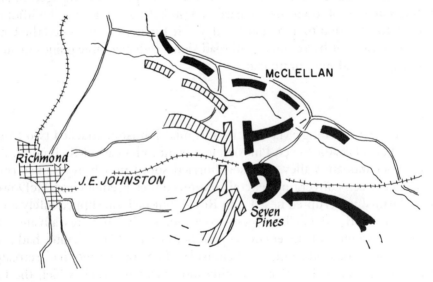

Stalemate at Seven Pines

River. The Confederates delivered a bungled attack against an almost haphazard defense. The results of the battle resembled Shiloh, demonstrating the resisting power of the contending armies. The Confederates, on the offensive, suffered about 6,000 casualties, whereas the Union casualties numbered about 5,000. In stopping the Confederate attack the Union army won the biggest battle yet fought in the East; but, as neither side retreated, the armies stood in the same position as before. The Confederates suffered a great loss, Johnston himself, who sustained a wound and had to be relieved.

The wounding of Johnston had, the President wrote Robert E. Lee, rendered "it necessary to interfere temporarily with the duties to which you were assigned in connection with the general service, but only so far as to make you available for command in the field of a particular army." Putting Lee into an active field command facilitated a more unified approach to the problem of preventing siege of the capital. With McClellan at the gates of Richmond and a battle in progress, this was a logically sensible move, since Lee already had been controlling all operations in Virginia except Johnston's army. "I prefer Lee to Johnston," McClellan declared when he received news of the enemy command change. "Lee," he said, "is too cautious and weak under grave responsibility. Personally brave and energetic to a fault, he yet is wanting in moral firmness when pressed by heavy responsibility, and is likely to be timid and irresolute in action." The President of course intended for Johnston to return to the army command eventually; but Johnston did not recover promptly as anticipated, and Lee continued in the field. In the Seven Days' campaign that ensued three and a half weeks later, Lee confirmed Davis's high estimate of his ability and the general never returned to his full-time duties in Richmond.[54]

Though the President intended for Lee to fill both positions, it proved impractical for Lee to continue his duties in Richmond while commanding an army. Nevertheless, Lee remained as Davis's advisor throughout the war. Thus, through a battle casualty, Davis lost his chief of staff and Lee's staff as well. As he appointed no replacement for a year and a half, operational duties again devolved personally upon Davis. Though the President, the secretary of war, and Adjutant and Inspector General Cooper constituted an effective team, they lacked important ingredients that had been present in the successful organization of the spring of 1862. The War Department personnel, reduced in size, could no longer perform the intelligence and operational work they had done before. Further, no more did an adequate staff provide the coordinative link between the field forces and the quartermaster, commissary, and ordnance departments. In Lee's brief service he had made these agencies immediately responsive to specific needs as they emerged. More important than the loss of a key position and skilled manpower at headquarters was the loss of Lee himself. Nothing replaced his knowledge, experience, and very high ability, and his rapport with the President was not enjoyed by Secretary of War Randolph. Without full confidence in the strategic judgment of Cooper or the secretary, Davis had too much on himself, and the President hardly had time to discharge all of these duties. He, General Cooper, and the secretaries of war concentrated their attention on operational problems to the detriment of logistics, which failed to receive the necessary supervision, co-

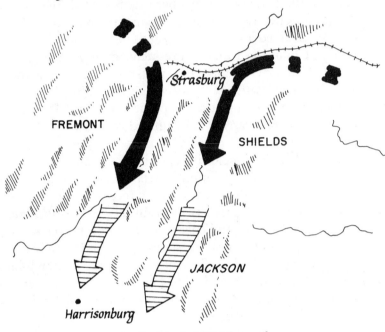

Jackson's Withdrawal

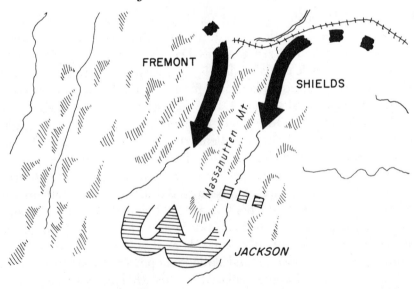

Jackson's Concentration

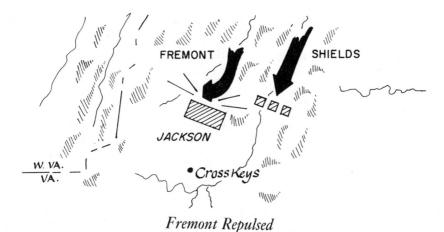

Fremont Repulsed

ordination, and executive vigor which they so pressingly required. Major problems awaited too long the high-level attention which they much needed.

While Lee assumed direct command of the troops around Richmond and Beauregard concentrated his forces around Tupelo, Mississippi, Jackson inflicted yet another defeat upon the Union in the Shenandoah Valley. Again the Massanutten Mountain aided him, for Fremont pursued him on the west side and Shields' portion of McDowell's forces pursued east of the mountain. Thus separated, the Union armies approached Jackson, who turned to meet his pursuers.

Planning to attack Fremont, Jackson concentrated when Fremont himself

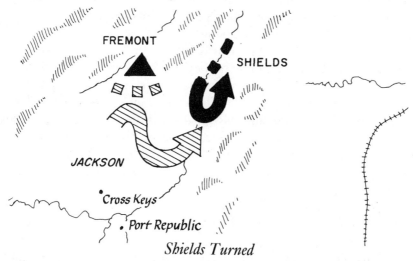

Shields Turned

attacked at Cross Keys on June 8. Repulsing Fremont's thrust, Jackson then concentrated in overwhelming force against the leading detachments of Shield's division. After a hard fought battle at Port Republic on June 9, Jackson successfully turned Shield's men out of their position and drove them back several miles. After so much marching and fighting since April, both sides finally grew content to be inactive. But Jackson had been effective in holding much of McDowell's corps away from Richmond.

Lee and Davis had agreed with Joe Johnston's gloomy estimate of their chances against McClellan's kind of warfare when Johnston said: "We can have no success while McClellan is allowed, as he is by our defensive, to choose his mode of warfare." Adhering also to the Sebastopol thesis, Lee believed McClellan would "take position from position, undercover of his heavy guns. . . . It will require 100,000 men to resist the regular siege of Richmond, which would only prolong not save it." Lee also initially believed McClellan was in an invulnerable position, for the Confederates could not "get at him without storming his works, which with our new troops," Lee remarked, "is extremely hazardous." The "experiment" of doing this at Fair Oaks had confirmed the judgment already expressed by McClellan and advocated by West Point Professor Dennis Hart Mahan, while Lee was superintendent and McClellan a member of the Napoleon Club.

They needed some "diversion" to avoid an attack doomed to failure by the defensive power of the intrenched Union troops. Lee and Davis momentarily considered reinforcing Jackson further in order to provide this diversion. They thought that Jackson, if stronger, might be able to cross the Potomac and divert federal troops from the threatening position on the Peninsula.

But the Confederates chose a more vigorous response. They felt impelled to do so first because time was running out; the weather "turned Union" in that a hot spell and a respite from recently heavy rains was rapidly drying the roads and thus facilitating McClellan's movements. Secondly the Confederates heard that McClellan was receiving reinforcements. Lastly they decided to attack because they were significantly influenced by reports from Confederate cavalry under Brigadier General James Ewell Brown "Jeb" Stuart, who had just returned from a daring reconnaissance ride all the way around the federal army. He reported that McClellan had an exposed right flank and furthermore that the Chickahominy River divided the enemy force, the smaller portion, about one-third of the whole, being on the northern side. So the Confederate leaders ambitiously decided to exploit their interior lines by concentrating the available 90,000 or so men against McClellan's approximately equal force.[55]

Planning first to reinforce Jackson with six regiments from Georgia and eight from Richmond, Lee and Davis intended for Jackson "to wipe out Fremont" before the Confederate general moved rapidly to Ashland, north of Richmond, to begin his role in the attack of McClellan. Though Fremont was not in fact harmed, Union troops in the Valley remained immobilized, adequately distracted by Jackson's previous activities. As in the Shiloh campaign, the Confederates employed the telegraph and the railroad to expolit their interior lines for a counterstroke. Reinforcements ordered to Richmond ar-

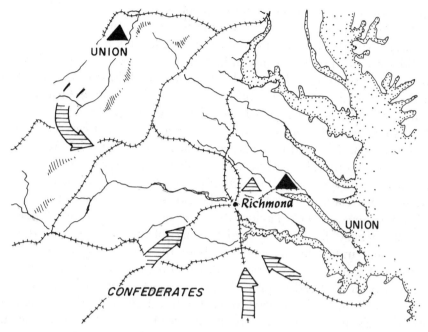

Exploitation of Railroads

rived from Georgia and the Carolinas and, at the last moment, Jackson moved stealthily by rail from the Valley. Lee organized his offensive force into four divisions, one each under Jackson, James Longstreet, Ambrose P. Hill, and Daniel Harvey Hill.[56]

   Unlike Shiloh, a frontal attack relying on surprise, or Seven Pines, an attempt to annihilate an isolated part of McClellan's army, Lee planned a turning movement to force McClellan to retreat. He ordered Jackson "to sweep down north of the Chickahominy, cut up McClellan's communications and rear," while Lee attacked McClellan in front. By pressing "forward toward the York River Railroad" and thus "threatening his communications" with the York River, Lee reasoned, "it was thought that the enemy would be

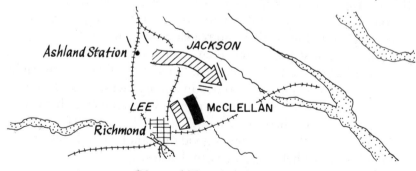

Planned Turning Movement

compelled to retreat or to give battle out of his entrenchments" in order to protect his communications. The turning force, Jackson's 18,000 men from the Valley, would advance in the rear of McClellan's north flank. But not only did Lee, inexperienced in conducting large-scale field operations, and his primitive staff bungle almost as badly as had Joe Johnston at Seven Pines, even the seasoned and usually brilliant Jackson likewise performed badly, arriving a day late. Cynical and caustic critics soon forgot Jackson's successful Valley campaign and recalled instead an earlier rumor that cast some disparagement upon how he had won his nickname at First Bull Run. According to this version, "Stonewall" had been a derisive term uttered by Bee in anger over Jackson's sluggishness. The actual comment had been, men now whispered about the camps, "There stands Jackson—like a damned stone wall!"[57]

Brigadier General Dick Taylor, the rebel leader and son of former U.S. President Zachary Taylor, observed that part of the problem was "the Confederate commanders knew no more about the topography of the country than they did about Central Africa." Although the northerners, lacking proper maps, had been "obliged to grope" their way up the Peninsula, they knew their own positions and managed to react with celerity each day to the movements of Lee's army, and so were always ready to fend off every assault. "Owing to our ignorance of the country and lack of reconnaissance of the successive battlefields," plaintively assessed Confederate Major General Daniel Harvey Hill, "throughout this campaign we attacked just when and where the enemy wished us to attack."[58]

In the absence of Jackson, the very well-conceived southern concentration and turning movement became a series of strong frontal attacks, the "Seven Days' Battles." Even after Fair Oaks, McClellan, himself, was still planning a "general attack," instead of awaiting the Confederate offensive which he had originally expected his movement to provoke. But Lee's attack came before McClellan had readied his own offensive.[59]

Originally optimistic about his defensive situation, the Union commander believed: "Assailed by double my numbers I should have no fear as to the result." But apprehensiveness grew when, coincident with the evacuation of Corinth, he wrote that an escaped slave had reported "that Beauregard arrived in Richmond day before yesterday with troops and amid great excitement." This rumor aggravated his earlier and realistic concern that the enemy might first concentrate against Banks and then against himself. By the day before Lee's offensive began, he had concluded: "Jackson will attack my right and rear. The rebel force is stated at 200,000 including Jackson and Beauregard." Fearful of defeat, he insisted: "The responsibility cannot be thrown on my shoulders; it must rest where it belongs." Later the same day, with spirits revived, he declared: "If I had another good division I could laugh at Jackson. . . . Nothing but overwhelming force can defeat us."[60]

When the battle began, his optimism continued as he reported: "I almost begin to think we are invincible." By the third day, however, his morale had collapsed. "I have lost this battle because my force was too small," he explained. Reflecting his demoralization and his apprehensions about a radical conspiracy against him, he insisted: The government "cannot hold me responsible for the result," because the govenment has "not sustained this army." He told the secretary of war: If I save my army, I will "owe no thanks to you or any other persons in Washington. You have done your best to sacrifice this army."[61]

McClellan's retreat and panicky telegrams caused the alarmed Lincoln to order reinforcements from the Carolinas, from Halleck in the West, and even to call out the militia as far away as Massachusetts. Lincoln, again exaggerating what the South could do with its interior lines, was convinced that Lee had received additional troops from Beauregard. Yet, while McClellan could only muster righteous indignation over Lincoln's refusal to send him "sufficient" troops, the President disarmed and charmed his own critics with humor: he likened McClellan's demands for more and more men to shoveling fleas across a barn lot; so few seemed to get there.[62]

In the series of widely dispersed clashes, the Confederates fought piecemeal, never precisely guessing where the enemy truly stood and never successfully bringing the mass of troops into engagement. "People find a small cable in the middle of the ocean, a thousand fathoms below the surface," later mused Dick Taylor, but "for two days we lost McClellan's great army in a few miles of woodland, and never had any definite knowledge of its movements."[63]

The southern effort during the "campaign will always," Douglas Freeman wrote, "remain a tragic monument to defective staff work." None of the battles began until late afternoon and no satisfactory liaison existed between Confederate units. Though Lee had assembled an admirable general staff for duty in Richmond, the same individuals proved unable adequately to transfer their talents to a field situation. In part this was because they themselves failed to perceive and appreciate the value and importance of staff work in the field. One, and quite probably several, of them longed constantly to grab a musket and rush personally into the front lines and at times actually did abandon their staff posts. In part they failed because they had an inadequate chief. Lee had been the chief of staff in Richmond, but now Colonel R. H. Chilton, a comrade of Lee's Texas days in the old army, but a misfit in his present position, served Lee as chief of staff.[64]

McClellan's staff outperformed Lee's in every particular. By no means, of course, does this indicate that McClellan suddenly had created an exemplary modern staff structure; in fact he apparently did not perceive any difference between general and special staff functions and in a rather hazy manner he conglomerated them in his army. The point is that his staff functioning surpassed that of the Confederates, if only because he had spent nearly a year developing the staff of his army and had recently tested it in battle at Fair Oaks.[65]

After some initial skirmishing the day before, the bloody struggles commenced on June 26, 1862, when two-thirds of Lee's army attacked the one-third of McClellan's force north of the Chickahominy. At Mechanicsville, Ellison's Mills, and on Beaver Dam Creek the southerners assaulted and, in bitter fighting, manged to take positions but failed seriously to harm the federal force, which fell back in good order. The next day the gray army hit the blue, now in new defensive positions at Gaines' Mill. After very hard and costly fighting, the Yankees abandoned their ground and slipped away south over the Chickahominy.

Jackson's unaccountable and uncharacteristic failure to appear on the first day made this initial effort against McClellan's right flank a frontal assault. He did not sweep down behind the Union right, for Jackson was not even in action until June 27. By the time he arrived the Union flank had withdrawn eastward and Jackson, too, made frontal assaults. On the second day they drove the heavily outnumbered Federals across the Chickahominy, exposed McClellan's communications, and turned his position.

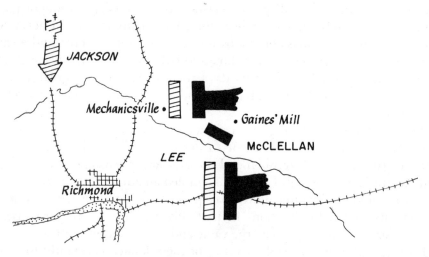

Frontal Assault

Despite his demoralization and efforts to shift responsibility, McClellan responded promptly and wisely to this situation. Instead of engaging in a futile effort to regain his lost communications with the York River, he simply shifted his base to the James River. He further chose to retreat south to the banks of the James, an additional decision not required by his change of base. He made this move in preference to standing firm or, as his subordinates suggested, to attacking Lee's weak right and trying to take Richmond.

This decision involved abandoning considerable supplies, and McClellan chose a strikingly extravagant means to destroy surplus ammunition not needed by his infantry in the overland march. "The din of combat was silenced to our ears," recalled an astonished Dick Taylor; "a train was heard approach-

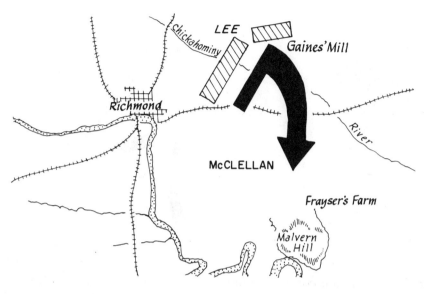

McClellan Retreats

ing. . . . Gathering speed, it came rushing on, and quickly emerged from the forest, two engines drawing a long string of carriages. Reaching the bridge, the engines exploded with terrific noise, followed in succession by explosions of the carriages, laden with ammunition. Shells burst in all directions, the river was lashed into foam, trees were torn for acres around, and several of my men were wounded." Otherwise the great waste merely emphasized the richness of the North and the comparative leanness of the South.[66]

McClellan's men left behind huge stockpiles of foodstuffs that the Confederates later gleefully and greedily foraged. The debris even included toothbrushes and delicacies such as chocolate mints and canned sardines. Though "bottles of champagne lay like quail in the grass," the Federals carried away or destroyed everything of significant military value, including medical supplies. To be sure, the retreat did entail a tremendous logistical endeavor: when McClellan ordered the change of base, the army had 25,000 tons of essential supplies to move by land, along with 25,000 horses and mules, 5,000 wagons, and 2,500 cattle.[67]

The Confederates pursued the retreating Union forces, fighting relatively small engagements at Garnett's and Golding's farms and, on June 29, big fights at Savage's Station and at Allen's farm. On the next day, June 30, another widespread episodic clash occurred at Frayser's farm and in the White Oak Swamp. Here Lee had tried vainly to achieve a double envelopment, but the gray army proved unready for a Cannae maneuver, the "bitterest disappointment Lee had ever sustained."[68]

Finally, on July 1, McClellan halted at Malvern Hill, ringed his high position with artillery, and made a stand. From this site McClellan's Signal Corps

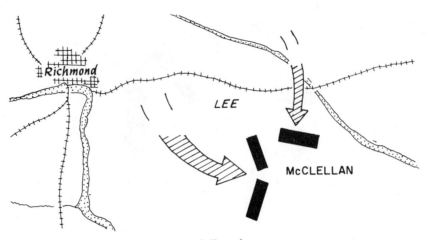

Attempted Envelopment

managed to maintain constant communication with the naval gunboats now in supporting distance from the James River. The signalmen directed the ship's gunfire and pinpointed with such accuracy that they completely routed several Confederate units along the river road. The ships' guns hurled huge elongated shells that the Confederates called "lamp posts," and their effect produced considerable panic. The Confederates suffered more difficulties because of obstructed roads, having only a few axes with which to clear the felled trees and brush, and from fuzzy leadership in places: for example, just as panic nearly swept through his green division, deaf old Theophilus Holmes stepped out of the house where he had his headquarters, cupped his hand to his ear, and blandly inquired, "I thought I heard firing?" Lee launched a frontal assault, one of the biggest and most vigorous of the war, only at last

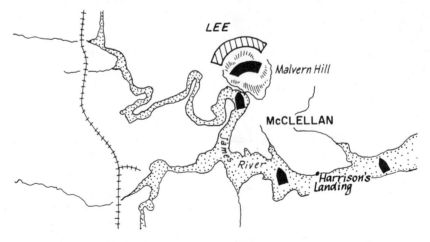

Frontal Assault

to fall back badly repulsed. "It was not war, it was murder," D. H. Hill later said.[69]

As it happened, throughout the campaign the southern division under A. P. Hill had managed to engage in much of the toughest fighting. Hill, a high-strung, intense fighter, relished the offensive. In combat he wore a red wool deer-hunter's shirt, his "battle shirt," he called it. Before the war Hill and McClellan had been rival suitors for the same girl, Ellen Marcy, but McClellan had gained the support of her father and ultimately won her hand. The troops learned the story and concluded that Hill had a fanatic, vindictive desire to kill McClellan's men. On at least one occasion, as Hill's grayclads swarmed forward sounding the shrill rebel yell, one of McClellan's defenders, who had just been through a similar trial the day before, shook his head fervently and groaned in disgust: "God's sake, Nelly—why didn't you marry him?"[70]

The series of battles concluded with the federal army arrayed in a defensive position at Harrison's Landing, its back to the river. If defeated in this position, McClellan, even with his ample river transportation, would have had difficulty escaping unscathed. Yet, after Malvern Hill, Lee found another attack "inexpedient." McClellan had "immediately begun to fortify his position, one which was of great natural strength, flanked on each side by a creek, and the approach to his front commanded by the guns of his ships in addition to those mounted in his entrenchments." In spite of the prospective fruits of success, Lee decided that the chances of failure and the high cost of success overbalanced these potential benefits.[71]

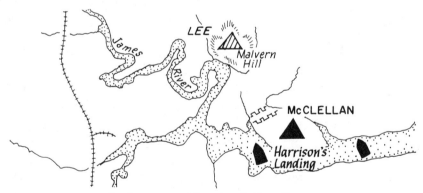

Stalemate at Harrison's Landing

These battles cost the Confederates just over 20,000 casualties compared to just below 16,000 for the Union, demonstrating again the tactical advantages of fighting on the defensive and, in this sense, again indicating the wisdom of the turning strategy which had worked so well in the West. By penetrating the enemy's rear and threatening something vital, his capital, McClellan compelled the rebels to attack him twice and thus combined the strategic offensive with the advantages of the tactical defensive. As a result of the well-conceived

if poorly executed attacks at Fair Oaks and the Seven Days' Battles, the
Confederates lost more than 26,000 men, nearly 30 percent of their available
force, whereas the federal losses of over 20,000 men amounted to only about
20 percent of their available men.

The Seven Days' Battles again displayed the relative invulnerability of the
armies engaged. On the only two occasions that Lee's men managed anything
resembling a breakthrough of the federal lines, Gaines' Mill on June 27 and
Frayser's farm on June 30, the breaches quickly closed. At Gaines' Mill
34,000 Union troops resisted for a whole day 57,000 Confederates led by
such talented commanders as Jackson and James Longstreet, and a part of the
defense crumbled momentarily only because of a bizarre mistake: federal
cavalry operating without orders charged between Union artillery and infantry, but the horses shied at the cannonading and ran wildly back into their
own lines. Some of the federal gunners concluded that the rebels were charging and scattered, while the Confederate infantry rushed forward to exploit
the situation. But after Gaines' Mill, McClellan drew back during the night
with relative ease. Then at Frayser's farm the rebels achieved a partial success
by the sheer weight of numbers, three to one in hand-to-hand combat, but
reserves quickly re-established the lines.[72]

Yet, in spite of attrition distinctly favorable to the Union, the Seven Days'
Battles were a Confederate victory, because victory is customarily determined
by who retreats from the battlefield. After his defeat at the battle of Malpla-
quet in 1709, the French commander, Marshal Villars, reported to Louis
XIV the far greater losses suffered by his opponent, Marlborough, pointing
out: "If God gives us another defeat like this, your Majesty's enemies will be
destroyed." With some exaggeration, McClellan could well have made the
same report. But McClellan faced relatively less powerful opponents and
lacked the ability, prestige, and long record of success of the famous eighteenth-century French marshal. More important, McClellan lacked the confidence of his civilian superiors, which had led King Louis XIV later to make
Villars the second man he elevated to the exalted rank of "Marshal General
of the Armies of the King."

Instead, McClellan campaigned without the confidence of Lincoln or Stanton, either before or after the battles, and, unlike the marshal, aggravated
their distrust by blaming them and by representing his situation as very
serious and as one requiring enormous reinforcements. Thus McClellan undermined what little faith his superiors still had in him, and his and their
attitudes prevented them from representing the Seven Days' Battles to the
public as anything other than a defeat. McClellan ultimately received orders
to withdraw from the Peninsula and send most of his men to join a unified
command, set up in northern Virginia under a sanguine and successful western general, John Pope.

Success in pushing the federal army back to thirty miles from Richmond
meant that not for the moment, at any rate, did the Confederate leaders need

to fear a Sebastopol-type siege whose withering fire of overwhelmingly superior artillery would inexorably demolish their defenses until the city fell or literally lay in uninhabitable ruins. Yet the immense losses made Lee wary of battles and confirmed for him the wisdom of his original intent, to force McClellan back by threatening his communications.

In the first eventful months of 1862, Union armies in the West and East had used their command of water routes of communication to turn their opponents and make significant advances. The Confederates had responded by using railroads to bring about two major offensive concentrations and carry out powerful attacks against the two main Union armies. But these resulted in frontal battles with heavy casualties on both sides and little real change in the strategic situation. McClellan had withdrawn a short distance and Grant and Halleck had only moved to take Corinth before stopping also. In this sense the Confederate offensives had succeeded, but, despite this achievement, manpower losses had been heavy and the logistic impact had "devastated the Confederate war effort." The seaborne expeditions, also part of the Union spring advance, seriously impeded southern overseas commerce. The Union "blockading squadrons, which could not concentrate off Wilmington, Charleston, and Mobile, raised the percentage of captures" from one in every eight blockade runners captured to one in four. In the East, McClellan's campaign imposed "severe supply losses. In moving to protect the Capital against McClellan," the Confederates "uncovered all of Virginia east of the Shenandoah Valley and north of the Rappahannock River and thus exposed large areas of Virginia's flour and beef belt to the enemy." But the disasters in the West "dwarfed the losses in Virginia." In addition to a reduction of provision-raising areas and population to which conscription could be applied, the fall of Corinth completed the destruction of "the nexus of the Confederate railroad network." "If communication with Mississippi had been rendered difficult, the loss of Memphis and New Orleans made communication with Texas little more than a theory."[73]

"There will be much unjust criticism" of the siege of Corinth, thought Grant, "but future effects will prove it a great victory." Though significant in depriving the rebels of control of the Memphis and Charleston railway, it was hardly spectacular as, instead of a battle to epitomize the success, Beauregard slipped quietly and deceptively away. Yet while McClellan remained immobile at Harrison's Landing, calling for reinforcements, Halleck, far from resting on his undramatic laurels at Corinth, planned new campaigns.[74]

☆   ☆   ☆

1. T. Harry Williams, *Beauregard, Napoleon in Gray* (Baton Rouge, 1955), 96–99, 101–4.

2. Davis to Beauregard, Oct. 17, 25, 1861, *O.R.*, V, 904, 920.

3. Davis to Beauregard, Oct. 17, 1861, *O.R.*, V, 903–4.

4. Williams, *Beauregard*, 92, 99.

5. Davis to J. E. Johnston, Feb. 19, 1862; Long, *Civil War, Day by Day*, 173.

6. Grant to Julia Grant, Mar. 11, 1862, *Papers of Grant*, IV, 348–49; Halleck to Buell, Mar. 16, 1862, *O.R.*, X, pt. 2, 42.

7. Davis to A. S. Johnston, Mar. 26, 1862, *O.R.*, X, pt. 2, 365.

8. Beauregard to Van Dorn, Feb. 21, 1862, *O.R.*, VII, 900–901; Beauregard, Confidential Circular, Feb. 21, 1862, *ibid.*, 899–900; Davis to Brooks, Mar. 15, 1862, *O.R.*, series 4, I, 998; Benjamin to Bragg, Feb. 18, 1862, *ibid.*, series 1, VI, 828; Bragg to Benjamin, Feb. 15, 1862, *ibid.*, 826; Bragg to Beauregard, Feb. 27, 1862, *ibid.*, 826. See also Bragg to Benjamin, Feb. 18, 1862, *ibid.*, 894.

9. Benjamin to R. E. Lee, Feb. 24, 1862, *ibid.*, VI, 398; Lee to Benjamin, Mar. 1, 1862, *ibid.*, 400.

10. G. T. Beauregard, "The First Battle of Bull Run," *Battles and Leaders of the Civil War*, eds. C. C. Buel and R. U. Johnson, 4 vols. (New York, 1887–88) I, 222–23.

11. Freeman, *R. E. Lee*, II, 8–16.

12. Robert Beverly to R. S. Ewell, Apr. 15, 1862, *O.R.*, XII, pt. 3, 849.

13. Grant to C. F. Smith, Mar. 23, 1862, *Papers of Grant*, IV, 411; Grant to Halleck, Apr. 5, 1862, *ibid.*, V, 13. See also Grant to McLean, Mar. 20, 1862, *ibid.*, IV, 396–97; Grant to Halleck, Mar. 21 (letter and telegram), 1862, *ibid.*, IV, 400, 401.

14. David Urquhart, "Bragg's Advance and Retreat," *Battles and Leaders*, III, 605; Grant, *Personal Memoirs*, 388.

15. Grady McWhiney, *Braxton Bragg and Confederate Defeat* (New York, 1969) I, 178–80.

16. Robert S. Henry, *The Story of the Confederacy*, rev. ed. (New York, 1936), 117.

17. *Ibid.*, 116.

18. Horn, *Army of Tennessee*, 136.

19. *Ibid.*, 140–41, 450*n28*; Connelly, *Army of the Heartland*, 167–75.

20. Grant to Julia Grant, Apr. 25, 1862, *Papers of Grant*, V, 72.

21. Grant to Julia Grant, May 4, Apr. 15, May 13, 1862, *Papers of Grant*, V, 110, 47, 117–18.

22. The long-haul price of railroad transportation at that time amounted to about three times the cost of that by river or ocean steamer. Wagon transportation rates were at least ten times those by rail or thirty times the rate by water. This understates the cost of wagon transportation somewhat, because it does not include amortizing the cost of building the road nor the cost of keeping it in repair.
In the reasonably well-developed market economy of the mid-nineteenth century, these prices probably reflect rather accurately the resources expended in these different forms of transportation. They serve, therefore, as a rough index of the relative efficiency of different means of transportation and of the resources which had been diverted from combat to logistics. Of course, the costs for the Union in corduroying the roads was in addition to the vast number of animals and wagons used and, further, the delay imposed by this inefficient form of transportation constituted a cost in another, non-resource dimension.
For transportation costs see George Rogers Taylor, *The Transportation Revolution* (New York, 1951), 134–37 and, also, Robert William Fogel, *Railroads and American Economic Growth* (Baltimore, 1964), 23, 38.

23. Lee to Magruder, Mar. 26, 1862, *Wartime Papers*, 137; McClellan to Lincoln, Apr. 18, 1862, *O.R.*, LI, pt. 1, 578; Johnston to Lee, Apr. 27, 1862, *ibid.*, XI, pt. 3, 496.

24. Johnston to Lee, Apr. 22, 1862, *O.R.*, XI, pt. 3, 455–56.

25. Michael C. C. Adams, *Our Masters the Rebels: A Speculation on Union Military Failure in the East, 1861–1865* (Cambridge, Mass., London, England, 1978), viii, 90–97 and *passim*.

26. Bruce Catton, *Mr. Lincoln's Army* (Garden City, New York, 1962), 200; Lincoln to McClellan, Apr. 9, 1862, Basler, *Collected Works*, V, 185.

27. Williams, "The Attack Upon West Point," 498–99.

28. *Ibid.*, 493.

29. *Ibid.*, 492, 498.

30. *Ibid.*, 502.

31. Thomas and Hitchcock to James Wadsworth, Apr. 2, 1862, *O.R.*, XI, pt. 3, 62.

32. Lincoln to McClellan, Apr. 9, 1862, Basler, *Collected Works*, V, 184–85; Stanton to McDowell, May 17, 1862, *O.R.*, XI, pt. 1, 27; Stanton to McClellan, May 18, 1862, *ibid.*, 27; McClellan to Seward, May 18, 1862, *ibid.*, pt. 3, 180.

33. McClellan to Stanton, May 5, 1862, *O.R.*, XI, pt. 1, 448–49; McClellan to Lincoln, May 14, 1862, *ibid.*, 26–27. See also: McClellan to Stanton, May 14, 1862, *ibid.*, pt. 3, 171.

34. Lee to John C. Pemberton, Apr. 20, 21, 1862, *Wartime Papers*, 150, *O.R.*, XI, pt. 3, 455; Lee to L. B. Northrop, Apr. 28, 1862, *ibid.*, XII, pt. 3, 871; Lee to J. E. Johnston, May 27, 1862, *ibid.*, XI, pt. 3, 552; W. Taylor to Pemberton, May 12, 1862, *ibid.*, 511–12; G. W. Randolph to B. Huger, May 3, 1862, *ibid.*, 490.

35. Jackson to Lee, Apr. 23, 29, 1862, *O.R.*, XII, pt. 3, 862–63, 872. For an excellent recent account see: Robert G. Tanner, *Stonewall in the Valley: Thomas J. "Stonewall" Jackson's Shenandoah Valley Campaign, Spring 1862* (Garden City, 1976).

36. Davis, *Duel Between the First Ironclads*, 150–57.

37. Davis to Johnston, May 11, 1862, *O.R.*, XI, pt. 3, 508; Long, *Civil War, Day by Day*, 211.

38. Mark Mayo Boatner, III, *The Civil War Dictionary* (New York, 1959), 945.

39. A. L. Long to R. S. Ewell, May 15, 1862, *O.R.*, XII, pt. 3, 891.

40. Long, *Civil War, Day by Day*, 216; James I. Robertson, Jr., "Stonewall in the Shenandoah: The Valley Campaign of 1862," *Civil War Times—Illustrated* (July, 1973), 26; Smith, *Bill Arp*, 41.

41. Adams, *Our Masters the Rebels*, 127; Stanton to John A. Andrew, May 27, 1862, *O.R.*, series 3, II, 85.

42. Lincoln to McDowell, May 28, 1862, Basler, *Collected Works*, V, 246.

43. Grant to Julia Grant, May 13, 16, 1862, *Papers of Grant*, V, 118, 123; Halleck to Pope, Apr. 15, 1862, *O.R.*, X, pt. 2, 107–8; Halleck to Buell, Apr. 26, 1862, *ibid.*, 128; Halleck to Ketchum, May 6, 1862, *ibid.*, XIII, 371; Curtis to Halleck, May 9, 1862, *ibid.*, 373; Halleck to T. A. Scott, May 9, 1862, *ibid.*, X, pt. 2, 177.

44. Horn, *Army of Tennessee*, 148–49; Connelly, *Army of the Heartland*, 175–80.

45. Horn, *Army of Tennessee*, 149; Connelly, *Army of the Heartland*, 129.

46. Proceedings of a General Court Martial—Third Day, Trial of Jefferson Davis, Feb. 14, 1835, *Davis Papers*, I, 371–72.

47. Goff, *Confederate Supply*, 248 and *passim*.

48. McWhiney, *Bragg*, I, 164n10; John Duncan, "A Historian in His Armchair; An Interview with Bell I. Wiley," *Civil War Times—Illustrated* (Apr. 1973), 240; Davis, *Our Incredible Civil War*, 76.

49. Ella Lonn, *Salt as a Factor in the Confederacy* (University, Ala., 1965), 14, 16, 19–20, 25, 30, 32–33, 45–46, 55, 67, 70, 72–75, 111–12, 119–22, 206, 223, 234n10, 235n1, 250n53.

50. Foote, *The Civil War*, II, 140.

51. Emory M. Thomas, *The Confederacy as a Revolutionary Experience* (Englewood Cliffs, N.J., 1971), especially chapters 3–5.

52. Winfred P. Minter, "Confederate Military Supply," in *Social Science* (June 1959), 163–71; Frank Vandiver, *Ploughshares Into Swords: Josiah Gorgas and Confederate Ordnance* (Austin, 1952), *passim*; Charles W. Ramsdell, "General Robert E. Lee's Horse Supply, 1862–1865," *American Historical Review* (July 1930), 759; Richard N. Current, "God and the Strongest Battalions," ed. David Donald, *Why the North Won the Civil War* (London and New York, 1960), 15; Northrup to Davis, Aug. 21, 1861, Dunbar Rowland, *Jefferson Davis, Constitutionalist*, 10 vols. (Jackson, Miss., 1923), V, 124–25; Coulter, *The Confederate States of America*, 241–43; Robert C. Black, III, *The Railroads of the Confederacy* (Chapel Hill, 1952), *passim*; Horace H. Cunningham, *Doctors in Gray, The Confederate Medical Service* (Baton Rouge, 1958), *passim*; Angus J. Johnston, *Virginia Railroads in the Civil War* (Chapel Hill, 1961), *passim*; William N. Still, *Iron Afloat: The Story of the Confederate Armorclads* (Nashville, 1971), *passim*; George E. Turner, *Victory Rode the Rails* (Indianapolis, 1953), *passim*; and Wesley, *The Collapse of the Confederacy*, *passim*.

53. Johnston to Lee, Apr. 29, 30, 1862, *O.R.*, XI, pt. 3, 473, 477; D. H. Hill to Randolph, June 10, 1862, *ibid.*, 587. Johnston's communications refer specifically to holding the line at Yorktown.

54. Davis to Lee, June 1, 1862, *O.R.*, XI, pt. 3, 568–69; Davis to Johnson and Sheffey, Jan. 18, 1865, *ibid.*, XLVI, pt. 2, 1092; Foote, *Civil War*, I, 465.

55. Johnston to Lee, Apr. 29, 1862, *O.R.*, XI,

pt. 3, 477; Lee to Johnston, May 1, 1862, *ibid.*, 485; Lee to Davis, June 5, 1862, *Wartime Papers*, 183–84; Griess, "Mahan," 236–37, 291–93, 307–8, 310; Hagerman, "From Jomini to Dennis Hart Mahan," 197–220; Hagerman, "The Professionalization of George B. McClellan," 114–15.

56. Jackson to Lee, June 6, 1862 (and endorsements by Lee and Davis), *O.R.*, XII, pt. 3, 906–7; Lee to Davis, June 10, 1862, *Wartime Papers*, 188; Lee to Jackson, June 11, 1862, *O.R.*, XI, pt. 3, 589.

57. Lee to Davis, June 10, 1862, *Wartime Papers*, 188; General Orders No. 75, Department of Northern Virginia, June 24, 1862, *ibid.*, 199; Lee to Cooper, Mar. 6, 1863, *ibid.*, 211; Foote, *The Civil War*, I, 498.

58. Richard Taylor, *Destruction and Reconstruction*, ed. Charles P. Roland, (Waltham, Mass., 1968), 80; McClellan to Stanton, May 8, 1862, *O.R.*, XI, pt. 3, 151; Freeman, *Lee*, II, 232.

59. McClellan to Stanton, June 2, 1862, *O.R.*, XI, pt. 1, 749.

60. McClellan to Lincoln, Apr. 7, 1862, *O.R.*, XI, pt. 1, 11–12; McClellan to Stanton, May 30, June 25 (two communications), 1862, *ibid.*, pt. 3, 201, pt. 1, 51, pt. 3, 254; McClellan to Banks, Apr. 1, 1862, *ibid.*, V, 59–60; McClellan to L. Thomas, Apr. 6, 1862, *ibid.*, XI, pt. 3, 74.

61. McClellan to Stanton, June 26, 28, 1862, *O.R.*, XI, pt. 3, 260, pt. 1, 61.

62. Lincoln to W. H. Seward, June 28, 1862, to Union Governors, July 3, 1862, to Halleck, July 4, 1862, Basler, *Collected Works*, V, 291–92, 304, 305; Foote, *The Civil War*, I, 530.

63. Taylor, *Destruction and Reconstruction*, 80.

64. W. Taylor, *Four Years With General Lee*, XI; Freeman, *Lee*, II, 233–35.

65. David Lawrence Valuska, "The Staff Organization of the Army of the Potomac Under General McClellan," unpublished master's thesis, Louisiana State University, 1966, *passim*, and especially appendix I, pp. 170–72.

66. Taylor, *Destruction and Reconstruction*, 83.

67. Clifford Dowdey, *Bugles Blow No More* (Boston, 1937), 179, 185–86; Hassler, *McClellan*, 150.

68. Freeman, *Lee*, II, 199.

69. Henry, *The Story of the Confederacy*, 161; J. Willard Brown, *The Signal Corps USA in The War of the Rebellion* (Boston, 1896), 317–18; Foote, *The Civil War*, I, 513.

70. Foote, *The Civil War*, I, 480.

71. Lee to Cooper, Mar. 6, 1863, *Wartime Papers*, 221.

72. F. J. Porter to S. Williams, July 7, 1862, *O.R.*, XI, pt. 2, 225–26; Hagerman, "The Professionalization of George B. McClellan," 128–29.

73. Goff, *Confederate Supply*, 54–58.

74. Grant to E. B. Washburne, June 1, 1862, *Papers of Grant*, V, 136.

8 ☆ LEE AND BRAGG ON THE OFFENSIVE

Braxton Bragg

I**N CAUSING THE EVACUATION** of Corinth, Halleck attained an objective he had pursued for months—breaking the Memphis and Charleston railway. Former Confederate War Secretary Walker had termed it "the vertebrae of the Confederacy." The next Union objective loomed not so obvious, for, other than the Mississippi River, federal armies no longer had available any of the water routes which previously served them so well. Thus Halleck, in choosing new objectives, changed his line of operations.[1]

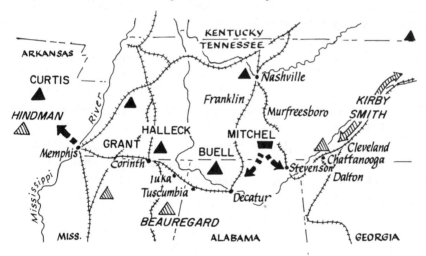

Situation after Fall of Corinth

Halleck's new plan, to "send all forces not required to hold the Memphis and Charleston Railroad to the relief of Curtis in Arkansas and to East Tennessee," "greatly delighted" President Lincoln. An advance due south along a destroyed railroad would have been very slow in any case, but after "consultation with medical officers," Halleck became convined that "to follow the enemy into the swamps of Mississippi" would prostrate his army, rendering it "disabled by disease." Thus, Halleck rejected an overland pursuit, a course his friend Sherman also regarded as "absurd." Instead, Halleck kept all of his troops in healthful locations and dedicated himself to improving the logistics of his army by restoring the railroads. Reliance on railroads increased the need to "clean out the guerrilla parties in West Tennessee and North Mississippi" who were "giving much annoyance in burning bridges, houses, and cotton."[2]

As a part of this program Halleck opened communications with Memphis, recently occupied by his river forces. He felt that a "corps of observation" could contain the main rebel army, for he was sure "Beauregard has not transportation to supply his army any considerable distance from his line of railroad." He hoped to accomplish the completion of the conquest of the Mississippi and the capture of the rebel post of Vicksburg by using the navy's "two flotillas," one moving from New Orleans, the other from Memphis.[3]

In assuming the offensive in two theatres, he returned troops to Curtis, the victor of Pea Ridge, who now received orders to try to consolidate his position in northern Arkansas. Since Johnston and Beauregard had sent Van Dorn and the bulk of the Confederate trans-Mississippi forces east of the river, Curtis should have had an easy time. But an increased number of Confederate troops under the vigorous Confederate Major General Thomas C. Hindman, a "jaunty little fellow" with "curls, rose-colored kid gloves, and rattan cane," dramatically changed the situation. Hindman, a politician and Mexican War veteran, rose to command in Arkansas after fighting well at Shiloh. Aided by the new conscription act, as well as the volunteering it engendered, "this audacious wonderman had raised an army of twenty thousand in his district after all available men had, presumably, been shipped east of the Mississippi for the Corinth campaign." Against this revitalized Confederate command, Curtis needed reinforcements to hold what he had won.[4]

Because of the lack of rail or river transportation from Missouri into Arkansas, this area did not offer, however, a fruitful line for major Union operations. Halleck's principal offensive movement would be on the other side of his department, where Buell would take advantage of the initiative of a subordinate to carry out another lightning advance. While the majority of Buell's forces had been involved in the Shiloh-Corinth campaign, Brigadier General Ormsby M. Mitchel, commanding south of Nashville, had moved south and seized the Memphis and Charleston Railroad at Huntsville and extended his control from near Chattanooga westward to Florence and Tuscumbia. Cutting this vital railway before Halleck, Mitchel's small force, barely 8,000 men, successfully dominated this region and supplied itself both by living off the country and by using a combination of rail and wagon haulage from Nashville to Athens. Though military operations thoroughly disrupted the railroads from Nashville to Decatur and Stevenson, Mitchel captured, virtually intact, the Memphis and Charleston lines from Tuscumbia to Stevenson. The energetic Union commander outnumbered his opponents and kept them busy by his constant menaces. These included his effort to capture Chattanooga by sending a band of twenty volunteers to break the railroad between Atlanta and Chattanooga. The daring raiders were detected, and, after an exciting locomotive chase, captured by the rebels before they could seriously harm the railroad.

To Halleck this stretch of railroad constituted an equivalent to the line of the Tennessee River which had lain open before him after the fall of Fort Donelson. On the day after Corinth fell, Halleck explained to Buell that "the first thing now to be done is to open the railroad to Decatur." Soon afterwards he emphasized: "Time with us is now everything. Not a moment must be lost in opening communication with Mitchel." Because the bulk of his army was still involved in pushing Beauregard "far enough south," Halleck explained, "to relieve our railroads from danger," he could immediately send only one of Buell's divisions to repair the bridges toward Decatur. Then Halleck, exasperated when he learned the division was doing nothing, found "the engineer regiment being kept on picket duty," and remonstrated, "This is all wrong." He explained to Buell: The whole force should work "with all possible energy to open our communications with Mitchel" so that they could meet the enemy at Chattanooga "with superior numbers."[5]

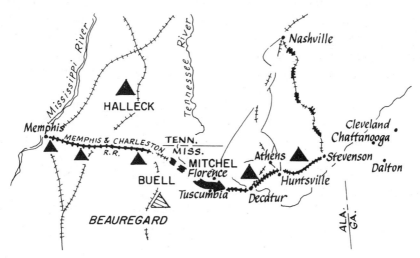

Halleck Moves to Open Communications

Despite delays Buell, ready to advance with four divisions by June 10, would take over 30,000 men to reinforce Mitchel, who already controlled an additional 8,000 men in Nashville and Middle Tennessee. Mitchel's southern opponent, the capable and experienced former regular officer, Edmund Kirby Smith, had been defending a line from Cumberland Gap to Chattanooga, his army of less than 10,000 men being "almost broken down by constantly moving from one end to the other of the line" to meet the recurring Union threats. Now he would face not only the combined forces of Buell and Mitchel, over 45,000 men, but George W. Morgan's 10,000 Union troops at Cumberland Gap.[6]

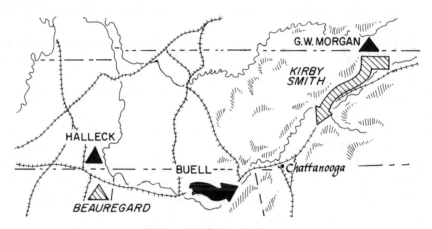

Planned Union Advance

Although his intelligence was inexact and he incorrectly thought a portion of Beauregard's army was reinforcing Kirby Smith, Halleck was certainly justified in giving Buell ambitious objectives. He ordered Buell to adopt the captured line of communications as his "line of operations" and move "with all possible dispatch" on "Chattanooga and Cleveland or Dalton." By moving on Chattanooga, Buell could "prevent a junction between Smith and Beauregard" and be "on the direct line to Atlanta." Halleck envisioned another rapid advance, again dividing the enemy's forces, which would turn the East Tennessee position and open a route of advance to Atlanta. So, in less than two weeks after the fall of Corinth, the optimistic Halleck reported to the secretary of war: Buell will "probably reach Decatur tomorrow night. If the enemy should have evacuated East Tennessee and Cumberland Gap, as reported, Buell will probably move on to Atlanta."[7]

Though they would soon lose Cumberland Gap, the Confederates had not evacuated East Tennessee. Still they faced a grave menace in both theatres. Their counterattack at Shiloh had not stopped the federal offensive. In Virginia, the rebels had halted McClellan's advance but not pushed him back very far. So in the East as well as in the West the Confederates needed more energetic and imaginative counteroffensives to stabilize their fronts and to recover lost and logistically vital areas of their territory.

☆   ☆

A heavy rain fell upon the Peninsula of Virginia July 2, 1862, as McClellan pulled his army away from Malvern Hill and continued his retreat to Harrison's Landing on the James River. Because Lee's army was, of course, in no condition to do much follow-up campaigning, the Federals proceeded essentially unmolested. Despite the discouraging news from Virginia, the North celebrated Independence Day with more than usual enthusiasm, buoyed somewhat by the news that they had captured the Confederate gunboat *Teaser* as it attempted to go down the James River and launch an observation balloon made of old silk frocks.

Celebrations notwithstanding, Lincoln meanwhile had planned decisive steps to improve the northern command structure. On July 11, 1862, he named Halleck to the vacant position of general in chief of all U.S. land forces. Lincoln had just made a quick trip to West Point, where Winfield Scott lived in retirement, and where Dennis Hart Mahan still taught. Recommended by General Scott and Professor Mahan, the appointment constituted a logical recognition of Halleck's successful western operations and of his obvious competence as a military strategist and administrator.[8]

By this time the War Board had become less of a formal entity. Hitchcock never emerged as a satisfactory chief of staff and frequently had requested to be relieved. "I am induced from considerations personal to myself," he had written as early as April 28, "to request leave to withdraw from the public service." On May 13 the infirm general plaintively had penned: "I have slight fevers every day, am subject to headaches, have lost all appetite, and at times am so weak as scarcely to be able to reach my room from the lower story of my hotel. I am sure, that if I remain here I shall be utterly prostrated." Stanton urged him to take a leave to Morristown, New Jersey, "for a change of atmosphere," which he did, but he wrote from there on May 26 that he was not "feeling strengthened to the point of making another experiment at Washington."

Hitchcock clearly had perceived his function to be one of operations and strategy formulation, and he had grown frustrated that his superiors did not take his advice. In a long letter to Winfield Scott, on May 28, 1862, Hitchcock made no mention of his ill health but implied rather clearly that he quit because he was irked. He went to New York for the summer and fall of 1862, where he resumed his general correspondence and religious writings, but he was retained in commission and he continued to receive copies of many letters exchanged among Lincoln and the high-level generals.[9]

Having come under critical fire from certain politicians, especially the radical Republicans, the War Board now adopted a lower profile. Though it ceased holding formal meetings as such and stopped recording exact transcriptions of its deliberations, it did continue in existence, in a formal sense, at least through mid-July, 1862, and informally thereafter. Stanton may not have been the least bit disappointed: he had said at the first War Board meeting that he *wanted* it to be an informal organization. He had established it primarily to help himself learn how the army functioned. After learning this, he did not need the collective meetings any longer. He had instituted a primitive form of general staff, and perhaps he dimly realized it, but he never truly saw the general staff as a necessary and permanent organ. Now at last a suitable occupant had been found for the position of general in chief.[10]

On the more immediately important operational level, Lincoln entertained great hopes for John Pope, commander of the newly created Army of Virginia, a force that resulted from the merger of Fremont's Mountain Department, Banks's Department of the Shenandoah, McDowell's Department of the Rappahannock, and Samuel D. Sturgis's Military District of Washington. As Pope energetically took up his new command, McClellan remained inert on the James River.

General in Chief Halleck first needed to decide whether to give McClellan the reinforcements which he had requested as necessary to resume the offensive, or to return his army to the northern Virginia theatre. Halleck promptly visited McClellan's headquarters. In taking with him Quartermaster General Meigs, Halleck informally continued War Board involvement in questions of strategy and in the integration of strategy and logistics.

Halleck found McClellan unwilling to attempt an advance without a reinforcement of 20,000 men. He also learned that McClellan was convinced that the enemy had "not less than 200,000" men, an estimate with which "most of his officers agreed."[11]

Doubtless Halleck and Meigs were puzzled as to why McClellan could not advance against 200,000 with his present 90,000 but believed an advance possible if his force were increased to 110,000. Upon their return to Washington, Meigs quickly prepared for the general in chief a careful analysis, estimating Confederate strength at 105,000 men, slightly above its actual number. Since the quartermaster general thought such an estimate could have been prepared by any "intelligent educated man," other estimates of enemy strength, Meigs thought, must, if made at all, have been "done by incompetent or unfaithful hands."[12]

The debunking of McClellan's estimate of rebel strength cast doubt on his credibility in other respects and confirmed suspicions that he would never take the offensive. And unless he did, his turning movement would become merely an exterior line of operation in which Lee, situated between the armies of Pope and McClellan, could concentrate against either. Already beginning to lose his "faith in McClellan's judgment," Halleck now believed that McClellan did "not understand strategy and should never plan a campaign."[13]

Halleck abhorred exterior lines and he would find that Lincoln fully shared his conviction. At this time, to the question as to why "the North with her great armies" so often faced the South in battle "with inferiority of numbers," the President explained, "The enemy hold the interior, and we the exterior lines." In other ways, too, Lincoln and Halleck would agree, for Lincoln had acquired an excellent feel for all aspects of military operations. He fully grasped the logistics of field armies and the significance of intrenchments and had learned to attach great importance to any chance "to get in the enemies' rear" or to "intercept the enemies' retreat."[14]

The military sophistication which the President had acquired in less than a year and a half extended to a clear appreciation of the degree to which the rebels had defeated McClellan at the Seven Days' Battles. Understanding that "the moral effect was the worst" aspect of those battles, he thought: It is probable that, "in men and material, the enemy suffered more than we, in that series of conflicts; while it is certain that he is less able to bear it." In addition, he wrote: I see the psychological "importance to us, for its bearing upon Europe, that we should achieve military success; and the same is true for us at home as well as abroad. Yet," comparing western triumphs with the popular fixation on the East, "it seems unreasonable that a series of successes extending through half-a-year, and clearing more than a hundred thousand square miles of country, should help us so little, while a half-defeat" at the Seven Days' Battles "should hurt us so much" in morale.[15]

As to the general in chief's specific recommendation to move McClellan's army north, the President was certainly in accord. Lincoln had realized that "Jackson's game" in the Valley campaign was, he wrote, to "keep three or four times as many of our troops away from Richmond as his own force amounts to." During the Seven Days' Battles, Lincoln had written McClellan: "We protected Washington and the enemy concentrated on you; had we stripped Washington, he would have been upon us before the troops sent could have got to you. . . . It is the nature of the case." Lincoln certainly welcomed Halleck's recommendation to eliminate the case of exterior lines.[16]

The decision to move the Army of the Potomac rapidly to the vicinity of Washington created, no matter how quickly they executed the movement, a period in which Lee would have the initiative and be able to concentrate against Pope. But "if John Pope possessed a coat of arms, it would have been bombast rampant upon an expansive field of incompetence." The physically imposing Pope, about whom it was rumored that he had gained the attention and confidence of President Lincoln because of his own talent as a raconteur, had more legitimate claims to command. He had graduated from West Point and served in the Mexican War. His wartime achievements included the capture of the Confederate Mississippi River stronghold of New Madrid and the well-advertised command of the force which had briefly followed Beauregard south from Corinth. His success and self-advertisement obscured his incapacity for large unit command.[17]

The commander of the new Army of Virginia immediately provoked controversial reactions because of his blustering pronouncements. First he issued orders which proclaimed that in the Shenandoah Valley and throughout his army's area of operations he would hold the populace responsible for injury to railroads and attacks upon trains or straggling federal soldiers. In case of guerrilla damage, citizens would be responsible financially, and if they fired upon a federal soldier from any house, his men would raze the building. Any southern civilians detected in committing acts against the Union army would be shot without civil process. Then Pope issued a bombastic address to his troops calling for a spirited offensive attitude: "I have come to you from the West," he said, "where we have always seen the backs of our enemies; from an army whose business it has been to seek the adversary and to beat him when he was found; whose policy has been attack and not defense." He later claimed that War Secretary Stanton had dictated the proclamation to him and probably he had, for it fit the secretary's style and uncomplicated strategic ideas. At any rate, it earned for Pope the enmity of many subordinates, particularly McClellan partisans, one of whom commented that Pope "has now written himself down [as] what the military world has long known, an ass." And another McClellanite was quoted as saying publicly, "I don't care for John Pope a pinch of owl dung."[18]

As the stage was being set for a Confederate offensive in Virginia, the Confederates changed western commanders and restructured their departments. Recognizing the almost total lack of communication with the trans-Mississippi, they made the region a separate department and unwisely placed the mediocre Theophilous H. Holmes over the dynamic Hindman. Thus they divided the vast frontier department.

Beauregard, in ailing health, left the army and department headquarters at Tupelo and took medical leave to Bladon Springs, a famous watering place on the Tombigbee River. He left the irritable and quarrelsome but highly qualified Braxton Bragg in temporary command. Beauregard fully expected to return eventually, but Jefferson Davis relieved him. Dissatisfied with Beauregard's retreat from Corinth after what Beauregard had represented as a victory at Shiloh, the President took the opportunity to ease the colorful Creole out of the post Davis had never meant for him to hold. Later, Beauregard received the Department of South Carolina, Georgia, and Florida, where his engineering and field experience well qualified him for the coastal defense mission of the department. The President needed him there to replace Major General John C. Pemberton, whom South Carolina's Governor Francis Pickens had frequently demanded be replaced and whom he described as "confused and uncertain about everything." And so Bragg permanently inherited the western command.[19]

When Halleck went to Washington to become general in chief, the Union command east of the Mississippi reverted to two separate departments, Grant's and Buell's. Halleck had wanted to reinforce Arkansas in order to repel a Confederate counterattack and conserve the gains made there when his forces from Missouri finally had driven the rebels back into Arkansas and menaced Little Rock, the state capital. Because of the fall of Memphis, Halleck could supply his troops in Arkansas by using the White and Arkansas rivers. He had planned for Grant to stand on the defensive in Mississippi and expected the navy and the army at New Orleans to complete the conquest of the Mississippi, whose defenses he had so adroitly turned by his advances up the Tennessee and in Missouri.

In Arkansas, advancing against the forces conjured up by the vigorous Hindman, the capable Curtis encountered unexpected difficulties. He immediately lost contact with Van Dorn, who had crossed the Mississippi, following his orders to join Beauregard at Corinth. Explaining how Van Dorn's army disappeared from his front, Curtis emphasized: The enemy possessed "supplies, steamboats, and railroads to expedite their trip down the Arkansas. Of course they could run away from us." The lack of water and rail communications and logistical problems aggravated by guerrillas slowed Curtis's advance toward Little Rock, prompting him to explain: "I have spread out my force to hold my lines of communication, which have been cut off for ten days, and to keep down rebel bands."[20]

Finally General Curtis fell back, "being destitute of forage and so pressed by rebels as to make picket and forage duty entirely insufferable." Faced by an "animated" enemy and with his "stock almost starving," he reported: "I left so many to guard my long lines I am unable to keep back the rebels that gather in front and on my right flank." Thus, "where the enemy presses in my force," he added, this "renders foraging impossible." Concentrated to face his enemy, he could not disperse enough to live off the country. Finally he reached the Mississippi, "safe at Helena."[21]

Neither reinforcements nor supplies could reach him by the Arkansas or White rivers for, on the morning of July 15, the newly completed Confederate ironclad *Arkansas* fought three Union vessels. The ironclad and her crew suffered considerably, but she inflicted serious damage upon the federal vessels, too, and her presence momentarily changed the complexion of warfare on the Mississippi. With the two Union "fleets separated by the Vicksburg batteries," the *Arkansas* posed "a terror to the divided flotilla."[22]

The *Arkansas* also temporarily affected operations against Vicksburg, because she emphasized that the Navy could not take Vicksburg. This would have to be a task for the army, which was making an effort from its base at New Orleans. The clash between the Union and Confederate armies occurred at Baton Rouge on August 5. Though the Confederates failed to take the city, the Union forces soon evacuated it but reoccupied it the next month. Thereafter the Federals pushed the Confederates into defensive positions along the bluffs near Port Hudson, Louisiana. After this engagement, the Confederates tenaciously held only the segment of the Mississippi River between Port Hudson and Vicksburg. On August 6 the Confederates suffered the bitter loss of their ironclad, the *Arkansas*, which in twenty-three days had carved a career that became a legend in the river war. The loss ended all Confederate possession of any formidable warships on the Mississippi. The brief career of the *Arkansas*, the inconclusive land operations at Baton Rouge, and the strong

Confederate batteries emphasized that the Navy alone would not open the river. Only a powerful land advance could achieve this goal, a conclusion which was just dawning on the new Union general in chief.

Halleck would have no better luck with his major offensive of the summer, Buell's thrust eastward into a cotton-growing region where Mitchel's troops had already foraged heavily. Logistical difficulties would have hampered Halleck's concept of a quick advance to Chattanooga in any event, but the cautious Buell proved a poor choice to execute this essentially daring plan in which he had little faith.[23]

Dazzled, perhaps, by his series of brilliant successes, Halleck insisted on the effort. True, the necessary line of communication, the Memphis and Charleston Railroad, lay parallel to the enemy's front, but Halleck correctly believed that Beauregard's army could not venture far from the railroad because of a lack of field transportation and because Grant had him blocked at Corinth. Halleck felt that if Buell could move rapidly on Chattanooga, he could take the city and then would have an adequate line of communications. Occupation of Chattanooga and the adjacent railway junctions of Dalton and Cleveland would cut the rail communications between Beauregard and Kirby Smith. Buell's army would then occupy a central position and could, if necessary, concentrate against first one and then the other of the two Confederate forces.

In his optimism and desire to exploit fully his success, Halleck overlooked a major difficulty. That he thought the loss of Chattanooga would trap Kirby Smith suggests that Halleck had not studied the East Tennessee map as thoroughly as he should. Kirby Smith could receive supplies from or retreat to Virginia over the East Tennessee and Virginia Railroad. More significantly, Halleck overlooked the difficulty of getting the railroads running again. Not only were all of his roads cut off from the north, but they were divided

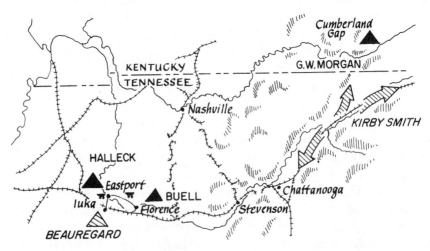

Union Logistical Situation — Confederate Advantage

into segments by broken bridges and destroyed sections. The problem of moving supplies to Florence illustrates the difficulties he faced. Eastport was the head of navigation on the Tennessee for most vessels because of shallow water above that city. The one steamer able to go above the Muscle Shoals plied back and forth between Eastport and Florence, but could not carry enough to supply that part of Buell's army at Florence. To supplement it, the quartermasters established a line of wagon transportation over the ten-mile route between Eastport and Iuka where a segment of the railroad was in working order east to Tuscumbia. But only "four half repaired locomotives" operated on that line of railroad and they could not carry enough to supply many men. When the river level fell and the steamer could no longer reach Florence, the advancing Federals established a wagon route between Eastport and Florence. Since no vessels could go up the river beyond Florence because of the Muscle Shoals, river transportation there depended on capturing or building the necessary vessels. These difficulties typically represent those met by Buell all along his supply routes to Chattanooga and illustrate the degree to which Halleck was misled in thinking he had a virtually intact line of communications. Halleck fell victim to optimism and inadequate information.[24]

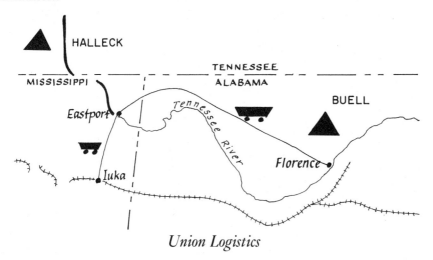

Union Logistics

These problems proved insuperable for a man of Buell's temperament. Not one to move fast enough to maintain the initiative in any case, Buell could not make the necessary improvisations. Though he told Halleck, I understand "what you have given me to do," Buell said, I expect "to accomplish it without unnecessary delay and in such a manner as neither to jeopardize my army nor its honor nor trifle with the lives of loyal citizens betrayed to the vengeance of the enemy by a promised protection and hurried abandonment." He therefore must be sure of "acting in force" with thorough and secure logistical preparation. Such deliberation was not what Halleck envisioned and was hardly in tune with the spirit or the needs of the campaign.[25]

By July 1 Buell had rail communications on the Memphis and Charleston, Nashville to Decatur, and Nashville to Stevenson routes, yet the gaps in each route made him hesitate. He felt unready for his final move while still deluged with guerrilla activity.

Though guerrillas had been menacing in West Tennessee, they had become a serious threat to Mitchel as soon as he had occupied North Alabama and Middle Tennessee. By May 10 he reported: "Guerrilla warfare has been inaugurated along my entire line, and we are attacked nightly at bridges and outposts." In early July the rebels launched two major raids against Buell's communications. Eight hundred of Colonel John Hunt Morgan's cavalry invaded his native Kentucky and on July 10 and 11 they captured depots at Glasgow and Lebanon. Rumors spread that the rebel raiders would soon attack Frankfort, Lexington, and Louisville, and even Cincinnati, Ohio. In a little over three weeks Morgan traversed 1,000 miles and took 1,200 prisoners.[26]

Simultaneously Brigadier General Nathan Bedford Forrest raided Middle Tennessee, "cut to pieces" a Union brigade at Murfreesboro, and captured almost a million dollars in supplies. He destroyed railway bridges and put the Nashville to Stevenson railway out of action for a week.[27]

This so disrupted Buell's communications that he felt "obliged to withdraw

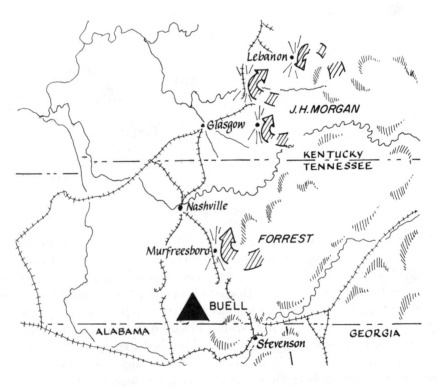

Confederate Raids

two more divisions from the main object to guard against the recurrence of such raids as are now going on in these two States." Concerned also about the political sensitivity of a border state, Halleck concurred, instructing Buell, "Do all in your power to put down the Morgan raid even if the Chattanooga expedition should be delayed."[28]

Thus began what would be a dominant theme in the west—guerrilla and raider paralysis of communications and enormous forces deployed to protect vulnerable railway lines. Raiders moved with ease through territory inhabited by their sympathizers and readily found weakly guarded and easily destroyed wooden bridges.

Buell's slow movement and then raid-induced halt loomed ominous for the Union. If the advance on Chattanooga should not go quickly and successfully, the Union would be surrendering the initiative to the rebels in the region between the Mississippi and the Appalachians. Here in April the Confederates had assembled a huge force for a counterattack at Pittsburg Landing. Halleck had brought about an equally imposing counterconcentration in time for the battle. He was still prepared for them if they should try again on the same line, for he had faith in the ability of Grant's force to hold West Tennessee while the Union repaired the railroads and consolidated its hold on that territory. Yet, if Buell did not move rapidly, Union armies would not threaten the Confederates east of the Mississippi at all; they would enjoy the liberty to choose another line of operations for a second attempt at a counteroffensive. The Confederate command almost certainly would avail themselves of the opportunity.

Bragg, before he could do anything else, first had to effect a considerable recuperation of his forces at Tupelo. He instituted a stringent series of policies. To stifle diminution by discharge, he once used an artillery battery to force reenlistment of a Tennessee volunteer regiment whose term had expired and wished to go home. Many men deserted but Bragg took drastic repressive measures: he had captured deserters shot while the army formed at attention to witness the punishment. Securing adequate subsistence remained a serious difficulty, aggravated by inadequate transportation. Bragg even encountered grave difficulty in delayed telegraphic exchanges with President Davis, and at last desperation forced him to rely upon the regular mails. But even with all these troubles, the army at Tupelo began to revive: health and general spirits picked up, the better water supply and more pleasant weather produced good effects, the troops secured new clothes and rested in comfortable quarters, and, most importantly, Bragg's organizational skills conferred new efficiency and engendered a readiness once again to take the field.[29]

Buell's advance on Chattanooga had caused great alarm in Richmond, and in late June the War Department dispatched reinforcements of troops in training to Kirby Smith. Since Davis and Lee had denuded the eastern seaboard of men to strengthen Virginia, Bragg's army provided the only source of significant reinforcements for East Tennessee. By June 30, as the Seven

Days' Battles raged, Bragg was sending a small division to Kirby Smith's aid and, to Secretary Randolph's appeal to "strike the moment an opportunity offers," Bragg promised that he would "start immediately to threaten and, if possible, attack."[30]

Confiding in his old commander, Beauregard, Bragg asserted that he could make no attack on Grant, because, he explained, "with the country between us reduced to a desert by two armies and a drouth of two months, neither of us could well advance in the absence of rail transportation." Relying on his "cordial and sincere relations" with Beauregard, Bragg sought "candid criticism" of his plan. By moving in Mississippi so "the impression is created that I am advancing," he explained, I will actually go "where our cavalry is paving the way for me in Middle Tennessee and Kentucky." "Before they can know my movement I shall be in front of Buell at Chattanooga, and by cutting his transportation may have him in a tight place." Thus his projected "rapid offensive" from East Tennessee, "following the consternation produced by" cavalry raids, was to be a turning movement, "gaining the enemy's rear, cutting off his supplies and dividing his forces so as to encounter them in detail!"[31]

With the Federals controlling the Memphis and Charleston railway, Bragg was on an exterior line; but he remedied this by his secrecy, his feint toward Grant, and, above all, by the excellent plan and organization of his movement by rail. He sent 35,000 men almost due south to Mobile, the garrison of Mobile "proceeding first, so as to reinforce General [Kirby] Smith at the earliest moment. As long as we are passing," he explained, "Mobile is safe, and at the close" of the movement "a sufficient force will be left there." Thus he speeded his operation by using the railroad as if it were a pipeline, already partly filled by the Mobile garrison. They accomplished in record time the 776-mile trip over six railroads, thanks to excellent preparations by Bragg's staff and the supplies provided along the route.[32]

Bragg's plan thus involved sending to Tennessee half of his original Mississippi army. In East Tennessee it would join with the forces of Major General Edmund Kirby Smith's Department of East Tennessee in an invasion of Kentucky, where Brigadier General Humphrey Marshall's small force from southwest Virginia would join the concentration. Moving rapidly and unexpectedly, Bragg eventually planned to threaten Buell's supply line by rail to Louisville and so turn the Union army out of its position and back to the Ohio River. If the Confederates surprised Buell, this strategic offensive could put Bragg in a position athwart Union communications where he could compel Buell to fight him, with the Confederates enjoying the advantage of the tactical defensive.

President Davis had been partly the architect of the earlier Shiloh campaign, ordering the troops concentrated from Mobile, New Orleans, and South Carolina. In spite of this involvement and an equal degree of participation in the planning and concentration for the Seven Days' campaign, the

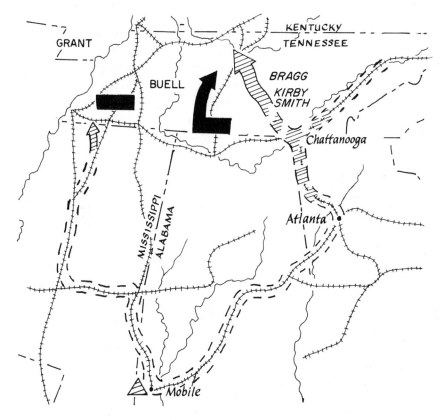

Planned Turning Movement

President played only a small role in Bragg's Kentucky campaign beyond
approving it and encouraging Bragg to assist Kirby Smith. Davis's limited
involvement was due to his and his secretary of war's absorption in the
operations in Virginia and the significant diminution of his headquarters' staff
by the assignment of Lee to the Army of Northern Virginia. This new
assignment naturally employed almost all of Lee's attention and energy, leaving him strictly an advisor with no time at all for the supervision of operations. This neglect of operations in the West produced an unfortunate effect,
because Bragg and Kirby Smith were independently inclined commanders
who failed to work together well. Bragg compounded the difficulty by leaving
two subordinate commanders in north Mississippi who did not prove very
effectual in cooperating with each other or with his campaign.

While July trickled away both sides enjoyed a lull before cataclysmic events
again erupted. On July 29 at Liverpool, England, a mysterious ship labeled
290 and named, after her launching, *Enrica*, went to sea ostensibly on a trial
run. Actually the Confederate cruiser *Alabama*, by late August she embarked
upon her devastatingly successful war against Union commerce. "I think she

was the most beautiful ship that ever touched the sea," her executive officer proudly stated. Her officers had previously staffed the fragile C.S.S. *Sumter*, a ship the South finally deemed impossible to maintain adequately and so disarmed and eventually sold at auction. The *Sumter* later became a blockade runner under the name *Gibraltar*. Comparatively, the proud *Alabama* offered luxury: built of the best available materials, copper-fastened, equipped with condensing apparatus and a cooling tank to supply fresh water at sea, with steam and sail she could attain speeds of thirteen knots. Ordinarily under sail with her hatches closed and smokestack lowered, she searched for prey while disguised as a merchant ship. No Confederate ensign would fly from her rigging until she had achieved deception. During her twenty-two months at sea, until the U.S.S. *Kearsarge* sank her off the coast of Cherbourg, France, the *Alabama* overhauled 294 vessels. Of these, she burned fifty-five American merchant ships, valued at over $4,500,000, and bonded ten others, valued at $562,000—the most outstanding record of any Confederate raider.[33]

During the doldrums of the midsummer, while Buell lay stalled by raids on his communications and Bragg began his secretive movement, Boston witnessed the sale at auction of numerous bells, which had been contributed by southern churches to be cast into cannon and which Butler had subsequently confiscated in New Orleans. The quiet was deceptive, however, for Halleck took his first drastic action as general in chief: he ordered the removal of McClellan's army from the Peninsula. Meanwhile Lee and Davis were maturing their strategy, and just as Bragg had done in the West, they planned in Virginia a strategic turning movement against the federal army under Pope.

The antecedents of this decision stretched as far back as the early part of Lee's service as chief of staff, when he had been concerned about preventing McDowell from cutting Confederate rail communications to the Shenandoah Valley and western Virginia. The supplies drawn from the Valley were so important that the President believed the loss of the Virginia Central Railroad and "communication with the valley at Staunton would be more injurious than the withdrawal from the Peninsula and the evacuation of Norfolk." The problems of feeding the city and the army, aggravated by the weakness of the Confederate commissary organization, meant a high priority for the "railroad and the country" north of Richmond where, from along the Rappahannock, Lee hoped to secure "corn and grain of all kinds."[34]

Since Lee had secured "the relief of Richmond from a state of siege" at the Seven Days' Battles, logistics thereafter became the dominant theme in his strategy. Though he had thought, in the Seven Days' Battles, that, had his plan not gone awry, "the Federal Army should have been destroyed," the primacy of logistics meant that he put aside what, if any, thoughts of annihilation he may have had. Supply needs made the protection of territory his paramount goal. To implement this objective, he could still use the strategy which he had already employed, one, he said, "of concentrating our forces to protect important points and baffle the principal efforts of the enemy."[35]

Yet this strategy did not suffice. At Fair Oaks and the Seven Days' Battles, this strategy had resulted in two essentially frontal attacks. President Davis agreed with Lee "as to the impropriety of exposing" their "brave and battle-thinned troops" to an enemy in a strong position. They required something more than concentration and they found it in the Seven Days' Battles plan. Lee explained this doctrine to Jackson, when he agreed with his subordinate that he was "right in not attacking them in their strong and chosen positions. They ought always to be turned as you propose," he agreed, "and thus force them on more favorable ground."[36]

Implicit in an earlier understanding among Davis, Lee, and Joe Johnston, these principles and objectives both permitted and urged offensive action. A policy to concentrate at Richmond and "fight the enemy before all his forces are united," Lee concurred, had been "the only one we can pursue." Lee also

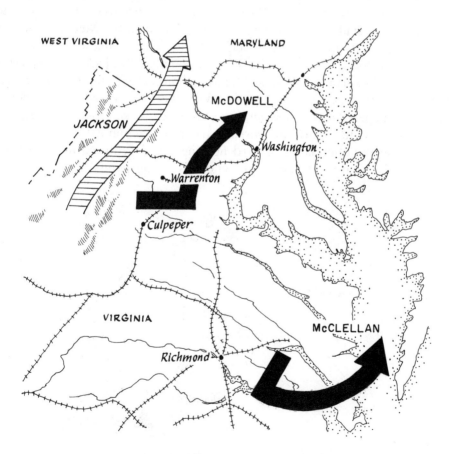

Planned Turning Movement

agreed with Johnston that, to keep McClellan from choosing "his mode of warfare," the South needed to "take the offensive, collect all the troops in the East and cross the Potomac with them." Even as McClellan was moving up the Peninsula, Davis expressed his accord with the two generals "as to the benefits of taking the offensive," an idea Lee revived after Fair Oaks when he again projected a crossing of the Potomac. If it were "possible to reinforce Jackson strongly," Lee thought, "it would change the character of the war," because the Confederates could then "cross Maryland into Pennsylvania," which "would call all the enemy from our southern coast & liberate those states."[37]

Such offensive ideas clearly forecast the concepts Lee matured by August. A reinforcement of Jackson constituted a concentration on a single line and his movement past the Federals into Pennsylvania would amount to a turning movement. In forcing the Union troops back, Jackson would be protecting logistically important regions and be relieving them even more by living on the enemy's country.

As Lee pondered his next move while remaining concerned about Mc-Clellan's inert army of 90,000, Pope started an advance toward Gordonsville on July 14. Lee had 80,000 men against Pope's 50,000, but McClellan hardly could be ignored. Lee took advantage of McClellan's quiescence and sent Jackson north toward Gordonsville with 12,000 men. On Jackson's request in early August Lee sent Ambrose P. Hill as a reinforcement, raising the strength of the expeditionary force to 24,000. With the Federals advancing slowly toward Culpeper, Jackson saw an opportunity to strike rapidly toward that place to destroy the first enemy corps to arrive. Lee reminded Jackson, It was "to save you the abundance of hard fighting that I ventured to suggest for your consideration not to attack the enemy's strong points, but to turn his

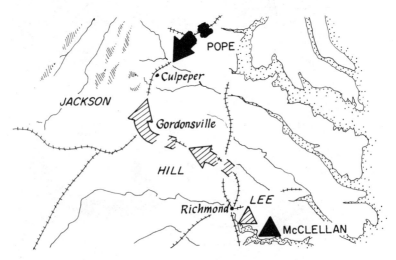

Union Advance and Confederate Response

position at Warrenton, &c., so as to draw him out of them. I would rather you have easy fighting and heavy victories." Jackson sought to operate from a central position and defeat Pope's corps one at a time as he had done at Cross Keys and Port Republic. Jackson's men moved too slowly, however, largely because he failed to keep his division commanders informed of his plans and their subsequent modifications.[38]

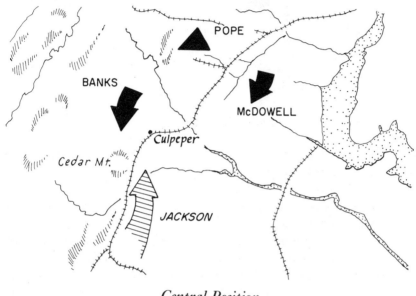

Central Position

Thus, at Cedar Mountain on August 9, Nathaniel P. Banks's federal corps struck the first blow against Jackson's two forward divisions. The Unionists thrust forward, inflicting grave casualties upon Jackson's force, until at last Hill came up and slashed a crushing counterattack into the northerner's east flank. Banks, making the mistake of attacking without reserves and sending no timely message for reinforcements, now faced the necessity of falling back. The ill-fought battle, mismanaged by both sides, cost Banks 2,353 casualties and Jackson 1,338. However, it revealed to the Confederates that Pope seemed to be in the process of launching a major offensive southward. Actually Pope, cautioned by Halleck, had orders to hold his position until the Army of the Potomac could unite with him.

Although he had already moved Burnside's corps to reinforce Pope, the general in chief did not "regard Pope and Burnside as safe" until McClellan's army joined them. "As things now are, with separate commands, there will," Halleck felt, "be no concert of action, and we daily risk being attacked and defeated in detail." Sure that the enemy was "massing his forces in front of generals Pope and Burnside, and that he expects to crush them and move forward to the Potomac," Halleck warned Pope, The rebels may "turn your right," and counseled him, Do not "expose yourself to any disaster." The

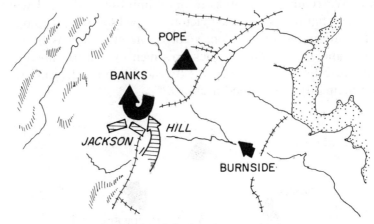

Battle of Cedar Mountain

strategic situation, together with reservations about Pope's ability as a commander, made Halleck "so uneasy" that he "could hardly sleep."[39]

Well might Halleck have been anxious, for, when Lee learned that McClellan was withdrawing his army to reinforce Pope, he had both the opportunity and the need to use his interior lines for his long-cherished offensive project. Concentrating most of his army on the Rappahannock, he sought to turn Pope's position. After a week of bafflement, he finally used Longstreet's corps to distract Pope, while he sent his other corps under Jackson to turn Pope's right. Jackson successfully passed to the west of the federal army and Lee was then on his way "north of the Rappahannock," where he could "consume provisions and forage now being used in supporting the enemy."[40]

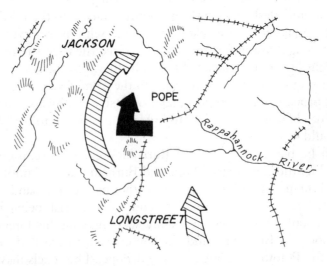

Confederate Turning Movement

☆ ☆

Meanwhile, to the west, Bragg's thrust into Tennessee and the subsequent invasion of Kentucky commenced. The plan called for Kirby Smith to move from Knoxville in early August against federal forces at Cumberland Gap under Brigadier General George W. Morgan. Bragg meanwhile delayed at Chattanooga awaiting more supply vehicles. Should Kirby Smith capture Cumberland Gap, Bragg intended to join him and united they would push into Middle Tennessee, hoping to turn Buell. Bragg had not initially intended to invade Kentucky; he simply wished to redeem Middle Tennessee, forcing Buell to retreat in order to regain his lines of communications.

Kirby Smith departed from Knoxville on August 14 with two divisions. Since Morgan's position at Cumberland Gap precluded a direct assault, Kirby Smith elected to try a turning movement. Unfortunately, he conducted it inefficiently, the men marched too far ahead of the wagons and for almost a week had to do without food save for meagre foragings gleanable from the rather mountainous countryside. They did gather apples and corn and captured some salt at Barboursville, which helped to make this limited diet more palatable. "I've just found out that CSA stands for 'Corn, Salt, and Apples,' " one soldier humorously complained.[41]

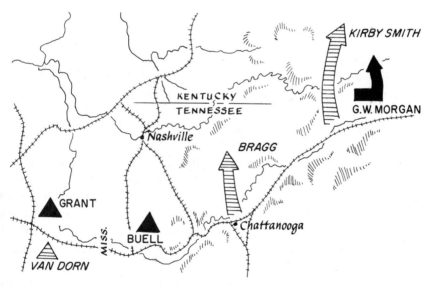

Opening of East Tennessee

As Kirby Smith finally turned the fortified position of Cumberland Gap and moved into Kentucky, Bragg crossed the Tennessee River and marched due north. Simultaneously Jackson's movement reached Pope's rear at Manassas where he captured the Union base, destroying what his army could not consume immediately or carry away. As soon as Pope grasped what was happening, he turned north along his devastated supply line. Lee's movement had thus accomplished its objective: it had drawn "the enemy from the Rappahannock frontier and caused him to concentrate his troops between Manassas and Centreville," giving "beef, flour, and forage" to the Confederates.[42]

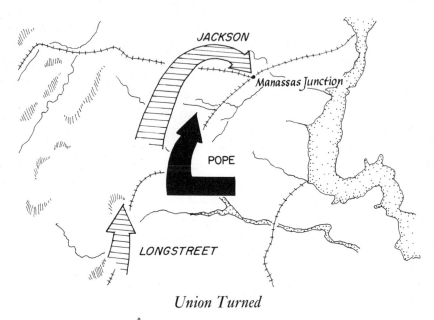

Union Turned

Another hope of Lee's would be dashed, however: "My desire," he had written, "has been to avoid a general engagement, being the weaker force, and by maneuvering, to relieve" the Rappahannock area of the enemy. But Lee had gotten Pope into such a predicament that, even had the Union general wished to ignore Jackson, he would have found it difficult. Jackson had destroyed Pope's depot and interdicted his communications, yet was himself on the Manassas Gap railway, able to draw supplies from the Valley. Pope could either retreat to Washington or attack Jackson to recover his supply line. But if Pope attacked, Lee's turning movement would change the Union army from the tactical defensive to the tactical offensive. Just as McClellan's turning movement to the Peninsula had forced the Confederates to attack, so also had Jackson's penetration of Pope's rear forced the Union army to assume the offensive.[43]

Even though Longstreet's corps was following Jackson's route, two days' march behind, Pope now had interior lines. Pope could exploit his position between Jackson and Longstreet to concentrate against Jackson. If this were done quickly, before Longstreet's corps arrived, the Federals could attack Jackson with a two-to-one numerical superiority. Thus the strategic offensive which had forced the enemy onto the tactical offensive had placed Jackson in what seemed to be a very risky situation. Yet clearly Lee did not so view it. Doubtless he had confidence that Jackson's great ability and the tactical skill of his now-veteran army would be a match for that bombastic "miscreant," Pope, who had never commanded in battle. Equally important was his confidence in the power of the defense, so recently demonstrated before Richmond.

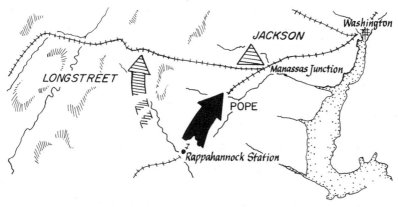

Union Offensive

What came to be called the Second Bull Run campaign opened on August 26, 1862, as Confederate cavalry under Fitzhugh Lee entered Manassas Junction and captured the rail point. Jackson's troops hurried to the area from their position below the Rappahannock, thus turning Pope's position. Now began a period of grave confusion for Pope, who even suffered the ignominy of losing his letterbooks to the southerners. Later Robert E. Lee wrote that at Second Bull Run Pope "did not appear to be aware of his situation."[44]

On August 27 Pope abandoned his position and sent troops toward Manassas and several other points. The next day Jackson concentrated north of the

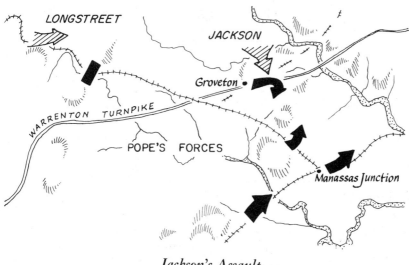

Jackson's Assault

Warrenton turnpike, just above Groveton, and waited. As Pope's troops approached, Jackson ordered an assault. Each side lost heavily in the bitter and stubborn struggle, until the Unionists withdrew during the night toward Manassas.

When Pope learned of the fight at Groveton, he mistakenly concluded that Jackson's forces were retreating, and so the Union general ordered his entire army to concentrate for a decisive assault. However, Jackson moved not in retreat but into an admirable defensive position behind an unfinished railroad bed. The grades and cuts provided ready-made intrenchments while the ties and rocks afforded cover. The Union attempt to launch a concentrated drive against Jackson proved piecemeal in execution. On August 29 Major General Fitz-John Porter failed to assault as ordered, and later Pope as well as others blamed his alleged disobedience and inexcusable delay for causing the ultimate failure. Meanwhile, as the indecisive skirmishing continued, Lee with Longstreet's corps moved briskly to effectuate a Confederate concentration.

During the night Longstreet's corps stretched out angularly in lines next to Jackson's. The Confederate army occupied a four-mile-long line shaped like an open V, facing the enemy to the east. Most significantly, an artillery battalion under a capable regular, Colonel Stephen D. Lee, nestled along a commanding ridge about a quarter of a mile long, near the apex. Their guns pointed northeast overlooking a field of fire embracing some two thousand yards. Only one question remained: would Pope be reckless enough to thrust his infantry into the waiting jaws?

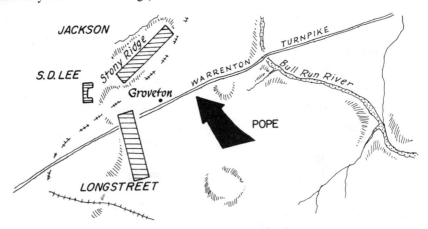

Confederate Tactical Defensive

The first federal bluecoats came into Confederate view by 7 A.M., August 30. Colonel Lee's guns opened fire, forcing the Unionists, even at that long distance, to move back. The federal long-range guns answered with a volley of their own, and then during the morning the same series repeated many times. At every appearance of Union infantry, Colonel Lee's well-commanded artillery harassed and drove them back.

Finally, at about 3 P.M., the Unionists advanced in heavy force against Jackson's left. Regiment after regiment of bluecoated soldiers moved toward Jackson's lines. The Confederates fought furiously, some quickly running out of ammunition. Three desperate charges successively came; all three fell back. At moments, southern soldiers scrambled out of their positions and stripped the dead and wounded enemy of cartridge boxes. Once some Federals got so close to Confederates whose ammunition had run low that the southerners resorted to throwing rocks at their advancing foe.

Jackson sent a desperate message to General Lee, requesting reinforcements. Lee immediately ordered Longstreet to send a division; but by the time Longstreet received the order, huge masses of federal troops began crossing the field of fire before Stephen D. Lee's artillery pieces. For thirty minutes Lee's guns belched incessantly. The massed batteries proved sufficient; the withering fire finally swept the blue waves from the field. The federal assault completely crumbled.

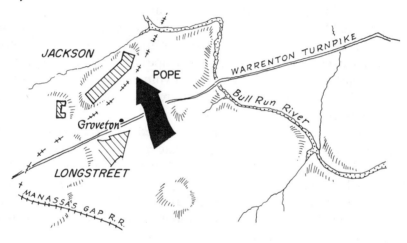

Longstreet Arrives on Flank

Robert E. Lee then counterattacked viciously, but, even though he had half of his army virtually at right angles to Pope's, failed to destroy Pope because the maneuverability and defensive power of Pope's troops enabled him promptly to cover his exposed flank and withdraw during the night. Pope's army was beaten but not routed. Against Lee's renewed attempt at a turning movement with Jackson's force, Pope easily maneuvered to cover his right flank and repulsed Jackson's superior force, which had been compelled to make a frontal attack against part of Pope's redeployed elements.

Unlike McClellan, Lee was naturally combative; though wishing to avoid battle and force Pope back by the threat to his communications, Lee remained alert for an advantageous opportunity to attack the enemy. In this sense, too, his campaign of Second Bull Run had been successful. Lee's casualties were favorable, 9,197 against 16,054 for Pope, because Jackson had been able to

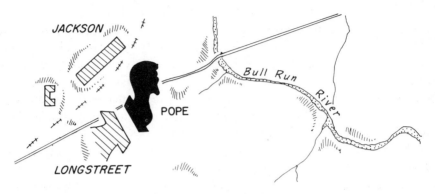

Pope's Maneuverability

withstand so long Pope's frontal assault, and the first of Lee's own attacks had been on a flank with artillery enfilading the federal troops attacking Jackson. As on the Peninsula and in the West, the movement to the rear to threaten something vital had given the army on the strategic offensive the opportunity to fight on the tactical defensive and so have an advantage. Though at the end it lay in an extremely perilous situation, Pope's army again demonstrated the mid-nineteenth-century army's virtual invulnerability to destruction in the open field. Yet the disastrous defeat discredited Pope, and the Union reassigned him to command in Minnesota.

As Halleck, barely in office a month, coped with the partly coordinated, partly fortuitous simultaneous Confederate advances, a new front erupted. The great Sioux Uprising had commenced in Minnesota on August 17, 1862, and would last until late September. The Sioux, alleging that they faced starvation on their reservations, murdered settlers near Acton, Minnesota, and thence committed various depredations. They ambushed federal soldiers at Redwood Ferry, but more troops moved in and successfully defended New Ulm and Fort Ridgely and finally defeated the Indians at Wood Lake on September 23. The uprising took perhaps 450 to 600 lives. The Federals captured more than 1,000 Indians and thirty-eight of them were put to death at Mankato, Minnesota, on December 26, closing a tragic interlude in the Civil War.

Though the Sioux War had the advantage of making the Minnesota command significant enough to render it a respectable shelf on which to place the inept but still popular Pope, it must have been the last straw for the overworked Halleck. With a staff of seven officers and sixteen enlisted men, he directed the armies of the United States. Between July 29 and September 12, he sent 421 telegrams. The originals of the telegrams received make a bound volume of 524 pages. Halleck also sent and received numerous letters. It is not surprising that during this period for four consecutive nights he "scarcely slept" and was "almost worn out."[45]

The news wires into both capitals, Richmond and Washington, hummed busily, for at the same time that the Second Battle of Bull Run raged, Confederates also pushed into Kentucky. On August 29 Kirby Smith's gray-clad forces crossed the last mountain range and saw spread out before them the beautiful, lush bluegrass region. Late that afternoon Kirby Smith's cavalry encountered Federals near Richmond, just south of Lexington, Kentucky.[46]

Then ensued probably the closest thing to a battle of annihilation in the entire war. The federal force, composed of hastily assembled raw recruits, exceeded 6,000 men. Kirby Smith brought up an attacking force, some 6,000 veteran infantry and 850 cavalry and launched an assault at dawn on the 30th. The hotly contested fight lasted all day, the Federals making stand after stand before successively being pushed back. The Confederate division commander, Brigadier General Patrick R. Cleburne, greatly distinguished himself as a combat leader. Though he had to be removed from the field late in the day, suffering from a painful wound in the cheek, his keen generalship had enabled his men thoroughly to vanquish the Federals. This, and his subsequent superb combat conduct, earned for the Ireland-born Cleburne promotion to major general, one of the only two such high commissions granted by the Confederacy to a foreign-born officer. The green federal outfit had been virtually destroyed. Those not killed or wounded ran away, but most were captured: 206 Federals died, 844 sustained wounds, and 4,303 became prisoners. The Confederates lost but 78 killed, 372 wounded, and one missing, while they captured all the enemy wagon trains and supplies, nine pieces of artillery, and 10,000 small arms. Kirby Smith then quickly secured the area between Richmond and Lexington. He remained in Lexington through September, establishing virtually complete control over central Kentucky. His cavalry periodically raided to the outskirts of Louisville and even to Covington, just across the Ohio River from Cincinnati.

Concern and excitement in the North mounted to a fever pitch. Cincinnati lay gripped in panic. Businesses suspended operations while impressed citizens busily built breastworks. Officials feared an uprising of local southern sympathizers. Major General Lew Wallace hurried in to take command of the city, where he proclaimed martial law.[47]

And in the East, on September 1, 1862, the last fighting of the Second Bull Run campaign occurred at Chantilly, or Ox Hill, Virginia. Lee, maintaining his offensive, sent Jackson's corps north around the Union right. He was blocked by skillfully maneuvered Federals and then in heavy rain engaged in severe fighting that lasted until evening, when the Unionists withdrew. Lee realized the futility of attacking Washington, but edged toward Leesburg and the crossings of the Potomac with an even more ambitious plan.

In Tennessee Bragg exultantly proclaimed that "the enemy is in full retreat, with consternation and demoralization devastating his ranks." While Kirby Smith had been marching to Kentucky, Bragg at Chattanooga had completed reorganizing his army. It now comprised two wings, the right under Leonidas Polk, the left under William J. Hardee, a total force of 27,816 men. After crossing the Tennessee River on August 28, he thrust off toward still a rather vague destination, largely dependent on what developed. The soldiers felt elated, their spirits high and their health good. At Chattanooga many of them had been visited by members of their families who had brought supplies, clothing, and home-cooked food. Simultaneous with the movements of Bragg and Kirby Smith, Lee launched a quite similar advance in the East.[48]

Success at Second Bull Run, leaving the enemy army "weakened and demoralized," enabled Lee to make a movement consistent with his purpose to make the "supplies of rich and productive districts . . . accessible," he said "to our army." He planned this extension of the campaign to carry out the original project to cross the Potomac, agreed upon in May by Davis, Lee, and Joe Johnston and again considered by Lee in June. As with the Second Bull Run campaign, they had designed this plan to cross the Potomac to enable a force weaker "in men and military equipments" to avoid the enemy's kind of war by forcing him back through a turning movement.[49]

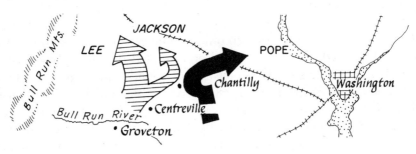

Situation after Second Bull Run

Lee could easily enter Maryland by turning the Union position at Washington and, he explained, "collect supplies to advantage in Maryland," thus being able to "supply ourselves with provisions and forage in the country in which we operate." Beyond supplying his army and permitting him to "annoy and harass the enemy," the movement would "detain the enemy upon the northern frontier until the approach of winter should render his advance into Virginia difficult, if not impracticable." He could remain in that flank position, confident that "as long as the army of the enemy are employed on this frontier," he need have "no fears for the safety of Richmond." With the onset of winter, he would have to leave Maryland for, having by then exhausted the forage and subsistence there, he would have to fall back to a railroad in order to supply animals and men through the winter. Though Lee did not seem to have forecast an offensive reaction by the enemy, a turning movement to occupy a flank position would give him the advantage of the tactical defensive. Even though he did anticipate that he might "enter Pennsylvania," unless it was "unadvisable upon political or other grounds," his primary objective seems to have been to supply his army and protect the harvest in Virginia by spending the fall in a logistically lucrative Maryland flank position.[50]

Lee's continuation north of the Potomac of his turning movement against Pope meant that he, Bragg, and Kirby Smith would be entering states with mixed sympathies but abundant supplies. In using a turning movement to force their opponents back, Bragg and Lee were using the same strategy employed by Union armies earlier in the year. But there was a significant difference. The earlier Union advances, solidly based on command of water routes of communications, had been penetrations; Bragg and Lee, without water or rail lines, were raiders. They could remain in Kentucky and Maryland during the fall when supplies were abundant, and only that long if the Union armies did not force them to fight rather than forage.

The inevitability of the eventual withdrawal of the raiding rebel armies did not allay the alarm of northern people and politicians. Though Union soldiers might take comfort from the Confederate raiders' logistical weakness, they should have been seriously concerned about an ominous development in the summer. The advances of both Curtis and Buell had been stopped by the combined activity of raiders and guerrillas. Without secure water communications in Arkansas or East Tennessee, Union commanders had found it necessary to use such large forces to guard their vulnerable communications that the strength of their advancing armies had been so diminished as to preclude further progress. Yet such expensive protection had not made their communications secure.

This powerful impact of guerrillas and raiders boded ill for any future Union advances which could not rely on water communications. But most Union leaders missed the significance of this ominous development because of the threat posed by the sudden reversal of fortunes brought about by turning movements by two major Confederate armies. Like the Union soldiers, the Confederate generals realized that lack of communications made their advances transitory, but they, too, saw the political impact which such spectacular operations must have.

Since Lee's movement into Maryland was a raid, he knew the political effect necessarily would be temporary. Though his advance and occupation might demonstrate the futility of trying to subdue the Confederacy, the inevitable withdrawal to Virginia would have the opposite effect, because the public would not understand the logistical impossibility of a raiding army's remaining indefinitely north of the Potomac. Though aware that he could aid Maryland in "throwing off the oppression" of U.S. rule, he realistically did "not anticipate," he said, "any general rising of the people in our behalf." The advance of Bragg and Kirby Smith in Kentucky and his temporary occupation of a part of Maryland did, however, make Lee think that it might be a propitious time for peace overtures, especially in view of the federal national elections that fall when he could expect still to be north of the Potomac. A "proposal of peace," reinforced by Lee's army ensconced in position north of the Potomac, "would enable the people of the United States to determine at their coming elections whether they will support those who favor a prolongation of the war, or those who wish to bring it to a termination."[51]

Lee promptly began his move to cross the Potomac, coinciding with Kirby Smith's arrival in the Bluegrass region of Kentucky and Bragg's march northward in Tennessee. These offensives would place a severe strain on the new Union command organization under General in Chief Halleck.

1. Walker to Benjamin, Feb. 17, 1862, *O.R.*, VII, 889.

2. Stanton to Halleck, June 11, 1862, *O.R.*, XVI, pt. 2, 8; Halleck to Stanton, June 9, 1862, *ibid.*, X, pt. 1, 671.

3. Halleck to Stanton, June 25, 12, 1862, *O.R.*, XVI, pt. 2, 62–63, 14; Halleck to Buell, June 17, 9, 1862, *ibid.*, 33, X, pt. 2, 280–81; W. T. Sherman to John Sherman, May 31, 1862, *Sherman Letters*, 154.

4. Jay Monaghan, *Civil War on the Western Border: 1854–1865* (Boston, Toronto, 1955), 255–56.

5. Halleck to Buell, May 31, June 4, 6, 1862, *O.R.*, X, pt. 2, 232–33, 629, 264–65; Halleck to John Pope, June 4, 1862.

6. E. Kirby Smith to S. Cooper, June 15, 1862, *O.R.*, XVI, pt. 2, 685.

7. Halleck to Buell, June 9, 11, 1862, *O.R.*, X, pt. 2, 281, XVI, pt. 2, 9; Halleck to Stanton, June 12, 1862, *ibid.*, XVI, pt. 2, 14.

8. Griess, "Mahan," 336.

9. Hitchcock to Stanton, Apr. 28, May 13, 26, 1862, Hitchcock to Scott, May 28, 1862, Hitchcock Papers, Library of Congress.

10. Upton, *Military Policy of the United States*, 291.

11. Halleck to Stanton, July 27, 1862, *O.R.*, XI, pt. 3, 337–38.

12. Meigs to Halleck, July 28, 1862, *O.R.*, XI, pt. 3, 340–41. See also: Halleck to McClellan, Aug. 6, 1862, *ibid.*, XII, pt. 2, 10–11. Meigs had relied on southern newspaper reports of Confederate strength. His estimate illustrates well what military intelligence terms "order of battle intelligence."

13. Halleck and Mrs. Halleck, July 5, 28, 1862, James Grant Wilson, "Types and Traditions of the Old Army. II. General Halleck—A Memoir," *Journal of the Military Service Institution of the United States*, xxxvi, 556, 557.

14. Lincoln to de Gasparin, Aug. 4, 1862, Basler, *Collected Works*, V, 355; Lincoln to Dix, June 30, 1862, *ibid.*, 194; Lincoln to McClellan, Apr. 9, May 24, 25, 1862, *ibid.*, 184–85, 232, 236. See also: Lincoln to Halleck, May 24, 1862, *ibid.*, 231; Lincoln to McDowell, May 30, 1862, *ibid.*, 252.

15. Lincoln to de Gasparin, Aug. 4, 1862, Basler, *Collected Works*, V, 355.

16. Lincoln to Fremont, June 15, 1862, Basler, *Collected Works*, V, 271; Lincoln to McClellan, June 28, 1862, *ibid.*, 289–91.

17. Williams, *Lincoln and the Radicals*, 141; Taylor, *Destruction and Reconstruction*, 88.

18. Pope to officers and soldiers of the Army of Virginia, July 14, 1862, *O.R.*, XII, pt. 3, 473–74; Jacob D. Cox, *Military Reminiscences of the Civil War*, 2 vols. (New York, 1900), I, 222–23; Warren W. Hassler, *Commanders of the Army of the Potomac* (Baton Rouge, 1962), 62; Foote, *The Civil War*, I, 648.

19. Francis Pickens to Jefferson Davis, June 12, 1862, in Rowland, *Jefferson Davis, Constitutionalist*, V, 275.

20. Curtis to Kelton, Apr. 28, 1862, *O.R.*, XIII, 367; Curtis to Ketchum, June 1, 1862, *ibid.*, 407.

21. Curtis to Ketchum, June 5, 21, 30, 1862, *O.R.*, *XIII*, 417, 441, 457; Curtis to Halleck, June 25, 1862, *ibid.*, 448; Halleck to Stanton, July 13, 1862, *ibid.*, 470.

22. Curtis to Halleck, Aug. 7, 1862, *O.R.*, XIII, 544.

23. Buell to Mitchel, Apr. 23, 1862, *O.R.*, X, pt. 2, 118; Buell to Military Commission, May 5, 1863, *ibid.*, XVI, pt. 1, 30; Halleck to Buell, June 11, 1862, *ibid.*, pt. 2, 10.

24. Halleck to Buell, June 16, 1862, *O.R.*, XVI, pt. 2, 27; statement of Buell before Military Commission, May 5, 1863, *ibid.*, pt. 1, 31; Darr to Fry, June 10, 1862, *ibid.*, pt. 2, 4; Fry to Nigh, June 16, 1862, *ibid.*, 31.

25. Buell to Halleck, July 11, 1862, *O.R.*, XVII, pt. 2, 122.

26. Mitchel to Stanton, May 10, 1862, *O.R.*, X, pt. 2, 180. See also: Mitchel to Stanton, May 4 (two communications), 6, 8, 12, 1862, *ibid.*, 161–63, 167, 174, 183; Mitchel to Buell, May 24, June 4, 1862, *ibid.*, 212, 257; G. W. Morgan to Stanton, May 11, 1862, *ibid.*, 181.

27. Buell to Halleck, July 13, 1862, *O.R.*, XVI, pt 2, 136.

28. Buell to Halleck, July 14, 1862, *O.R.*, XVI, pt. 2, 143; Halleck to Buell, July 14, 1862, *ibid.*, 143.

29. Horn, *Army of Tennessee*, 156–58; Connelly, *Army of the Heartland*, 196–204.

30. Randolph to Bragg, June 29, 1862, *O.R.*, XVII, pt. 2, 627; Bragg to Randolph, June 30, 1862, *ibid.*, 630. See also: Randolph to Leadbetter, June 30, 1862, *ibid.*, XI, pt 3, 626; Randolph to Bragg, June 30, 1862, *ibid.*, 627.

31. Bragg to Beauregard, July 22, 1862, *O.R.*, LII, pt. 2, 330–31; Bragg to Davis, July 21, 1862, *ibid.*, 330; Bragg to Cooper, July 23, 1862, *ibid.*, XVII, pt. 2, 656.

32. Bragg to Cooper, July 23, 1862, *O.R.*, XVII, pt. 2, 656.

33. Norman C. Delaney, *John McIntosh Kell of the Raider Alabama* (University, Ala., 1973), 129.

34. Lee to J. E. Johnston, Mar. 28, 1862, *Wartime Papers*, 139; Lee to J. E. B. Stuart, July 18, 1862, *O.R.*, XII, pt. 3, 916.

35. General Order No. 75, July 7, 1862, *Wartime Papers*, 21; Lee to Cooper, Mar. 6, 1863, *ibid.*, 221; Lee to Henry Clark, Aug. 8, 1862, *ibid.*, 249. Lee rarely used the word destroy. Though his vocabulary of objectives varied greatly, his favorite offensive action was to strike a "blow." A blow covered a great variety of actions including the "dispersion" of the enemy, or a "happy diversion of our favor." A blow that could have interrupted McClellan's use of the James River could "oblige him to break up his position and retire" or, if only partially successful, the blow could "anchor him in his present position." More explicit in meaning was to "drive" the enemy which, at this time, Lee used about half as often as striking a blow. "Attack" was also more specific than to strike a blow, and "destroy" and "crush" seemed to imply very significant results, but less than annihilation. On only one occasion did he envision an enemy force being annihilated, and this would result from getting in the rear of a small force. His phraseology varied from a movement to "annoy" or "harass" the enemy to action which would "bear down all opposition." To "suppress" an enemy he reserved for the "miscreant," John Pope. Defensive action included to "retard," "delay," "arrest," as well as "baffle." On one occasion he directed Jackson to "husband the strength of your command"; on another he ordered Jackson to "cache your troops" until "you strike your blow." For Lee's vocabulary of objectives from Mar. through Aug. 1862, see: *Wartime Papers*, 146, 151, 152, 155, 157, 160, 162, 168, 169, 188, 222, 232, 236, 238, 239–41, 248, 249, 251, 258, 270, 293; *O.R.*, V, 1103; XI, pt. 2, 956; XI, pt. 3, 523, 583, 584, 589, 647, 667, 673; XII, pt. 3, 856, 865, 883–84, 889, 891, 892, 906, 916–17, 925, 942.

36. Lee to Jackson, Aug. 4, 1862, *Wartime Papers*, 245.

37. J. E. Johnston to Lee, Apr. 22, 30, 1862, *O.R.*, XI, pt. 3, 456, 477; Lee to Johnston, May 1, 1862, *ibid.*, 485; Lee to Davis, June 5, 1862, *Wartime Papers*, 183–84.

38. Lee to Jackson, Aug. 7, 1862, *O.R.*, XII, pt. 3, 925–26.

39. Halleck to McClellan, Aug. 7, 9, 1862, *O.R.*, XI, pt. 3, 360, pt. 1, 85; Halleck to Pope, Aug. 7, 8, 1862, *ibid.*, XII, pt. 3, 543, 547; Halleck to Mrs. Halleck, Aug. 9, 1862, Wilson, "Halleck," 557.

40. Lee to Davis, Aug. 23, 1862, *Wartime Papers*, 262.

41. Horn, *Army of Tennessee*, 163–64; Connelly, *Army of the Heartland*, 205–12.

42. Lee to Davis, Aug. 30, 1862, *Wartime Papers*, 266–67.

43. Lee to Davis, *ibid.*, 267.

44. Earl Schenck Miers, *Robert E. Lee* (New York, 1970), 94.

45. Halleck to Mrs. Halleck, Sept. 2, 1862, Wilson, "Halleck," 558; Kenneth P. Williams, *Lincoln Finds a General*, 5 vols. (New York, 1949–58), II, 104. In contrast, the staff of von Moltke in the Franco-Prussian War numbered ninety-two.

46. Horn, *Army of Tennessee*, 164; Connelly, *Army of the Heartland*, 212–14.

47. Horn, *Army of Tennessee*, 164–65; Connelly, *Army of the Heartland*, 214–20.

48. Horn, *Army of Tennessee*, 165–66; Connelly, *Army of the Heartland*, 221–22.

49. Lee to Davis, Sept. 3, 1862, *Wartime Pa-*pers, 292–93; Lee to Cooper, Aug. 19, 1863, *ibid.*, 312–13.

50. Lee to Davis, Sept. 3, 4, 5, 1862, *Wartime Papers*, 292–96.

51. Lee to Davis, Sept. 3, 7, 8, 1862, *ibid.*, 292–93, 297, 301.

9 ☆ THE MARYLAND AND KENTUCKY RAIDS REPULSED

Don Carlos Buell

Lᴇᴇ's ᴀɴᴅ Bʀᴀɢɢ's separate raids put the new Union general in chief to an early test, an especially trying one because Halleck had come to Washington with genuine reluctance. He had done his "best to avoid it," because he had "studied out" and could "finish the campaign in the West" and felt he did not "understand" and could not "manage affairs in the East." His friend Sherman agreed that he "would prefer to finish" what he had "so well begun" in the West. Sherman nevertheless remained confident that Halleck would succeed and said, "Based on the absolute confidence I had conceived for your knowledge of national law and your comprehensive knowledge of things gathered, God only knows how." Grant, who had again characterized Halleck as "one of the greatest men of the age," took a more positive view of his chief's elevation. He wrote his friend and congressman, Elihu B. Washburne: Should Lincoln name Halleck as secretary of war or general in chief, a "better selection could not be made. He is a man of gigantic intellect and well studied in the profession of arms. He and I had several little spats but I like and respect him nevertheless."[1]

Reluctantly plunged into the tension between McClellan and the administration, Halleck reached Washington during what he regarded as a "time of great peril" with Lee's army between those of Pope and McClellan. The Battle of Second Bull Run climaxed a month of "terrible anxiety" in which he confided his fear of "the capture of Washington" to no one but Stanton, Quartermaster General Meigs, and a few of his staff. The slow pace of McClellan's movement further aggravated Halleck's fears. Though he resisted the idea of relieving McClellan, it exasperated Halleck that he could not "get General McClellan to do" what he wished. To increase the concentration around Washington, he ordered troops by rail from western Virginia, in addition to ordering up Burnside, who already had moved from North Carolina with an army augmented by reinforcements from the South Carolina coast.[2]

McClellan's arrival brought little immediate relief, for by then Pope was fighting at Bull Run. Anxiously Halleck warned Pope: "Look well for your right, and don't let the enemy turn it and get between you and the forts."

Pope's success in defeating Lee's effort to turn his right afforded small consolation, for Pope recommended withdrawing to the Washington intrenchments in order to avoid a "great disaster" to his army. Clearly demoralized, Pope planned "a vigorous defense of the intrenchments around Washington."[3]

After Pope's defeat, McClellan's presence proved a boon to the exhausted general in chief. With little sleep in four days, his chief of staff away, and only one regular staff officer available, Halleck finally wrote McClellan: "I beg of you to assist me in this crisis with your ability and experience. I am utterly tired out." After the fiasco of Pope's command, it followed naturally for Lincoln and Halleck to turn to this their most experienced general, one who commanded the full loyalty of the army, both leaders and rank and file. Both war secretary Stanton and treasury secretary Chase adamantly opposed McClellan's return but, though Lincoln did have doubts about McClellan, the President stood firm. Doubtless Lincoln experienced much inner torment; about this time he composed his remarkable "Meditation on the Divine" in which he mused about God's preference of sides in this war. "In great contests," Lincoln wrote, "each party claims to act in accordance with the will of God. Both *may* be, but one *must* be wrong."[4]

Assuredly both sides fervently prayed that God would smile upon *their* cause as Lee's men marched into northern territory singing "Maryland, My Maryland," and McClellan took confident and energetic control of his own and Pope's army. Yet Halleck had little respite, for he was evolving his relationship with Lincoln, a relationship complicated by Lincoln himself having been in truth the former general in chief. In spite of the War Board, Lincoln in the spring and early summer had been exercising minute control over operations in the East. Almost the entire administration also had been involved; in May McClellan's headquarters had been visited not just by Lincoln and Stanton but by the secretaries of state and navy as well as the attorney general and the senator-elect from Rhode Island. The secretary of the treasury, stationed with McDowell at Fredricksburg, had sent to Stanton a stream of reports on military operations.[5]

The President then sought to employ Halleck and give him full scope. Halleck wrote his wife: I have been treated "as well as I could wish. Indeed, they seem willing to give me more power than I desire on some points." Yet this proved to be a difficult task for Lincoln. With the post of general in chief so long vacant, he could hardly remember how to function with one. In referring to Stanton a proposal to send a small expedition to Texas, Lincoln remarked: "Perhaps General Halleck's opinion should . . . be asked." When the Second Bull Run campaign reached its crisis, Lincoln found it impossible not to revert to his old role. To an inquiry from McClellan in late August, the President responded: "I wish not to control. That I now leave to General Halleck, aided by your counsels." Yet in this tense time Lincoln could not restrain himself and, in the same message, gave McClellan the guidance he sought. Thereafter, Lincoln frequently entered into direct communication with eastern field commanders.[6]

But Lincoln's very active role always remained limited to Virginia. To an appeal for directions from the West, Lincoln responded: "For us here, to control him there on the ground would be a Babel of confusion which would be utterly ruinous." Halleck, in turn, took care not to interfere with arrangements the President had made in Virginia prior to his coming and declined an answer about Pope "without seeing the President, as General Pope is in command, by his orders, of the department."[7]

It also was too much for the Cabinet to stay out of military operations. Their intimate participation in the military events in the spring and the tradition of cabinet consultation in major decisions, including the recent precedent of cabinet detemination of Mexican War strategy under President Polk, dictated an involvement which took many forms. During the ensuing Antietam campaign, treasury secretary Chase recounted a meeting with the Kentucky politician and abolitionist Cassius Marcellus Clay. This major general; who had yet to see any service, told Chase "he had made up his mind to take [command of a] Department and the President and Stanton were willing he should take that beyond the Mississippi." They then called on Halleck with the proposition. The general in chief "received us kindly but was unwell," wrote Chase. "[He] showed no favor to the new Department project."[8]

The entrepreneurial spirit in military operations, so prominent early in the war, continued to infect the Cabinet. According to Chase, at the same meeting when he recommended a department for Clay, the Cabinet also discussed expeditions to "Petersburgh" and Charleston, South Carolina. Chase also proposed "a secret concerted attack on Richmond" with the help of the Navy for which Stanton would "furnish 10,000 men." Later Chase suggested the Charleston project to the secretary of the navy and the secretary of state. Believing that troops would be helpful in striking "overwhelming blows," the three secretaries determined to seek troops from the secretary of war. This expedition occupied the Cabinet for a month. After the Cabinet gave their approval to the Charleston expedition and another to open the Mississippi, Chase related: "The President seemed much pleased with both movements— but Halleck remained to be consulted. Would he oppose the President and Stanton? I thought not." Not surprisingly, Halleck wrote his wife how dissatisfied he was: "There are so many cooks. They destroy the broth."[9]

Definitely keeping a low profile as he worked in this environment, Halleck doubtless forfeited much of the control over the situation which Lincoln wished him to exercise. Lincoln later confided his disappointment to his private secretary, John Hay. "When it was proposed to station Halleck here in general command, he insisted, to use his language, on the appointment of a General-in-Chief who should be held responsible for results." The outcome proved a disappointment, the President continued, for "We then appointed him and all went well enough until after Pope's defeat, when he broke down—nerve and pluck all gone—and has ever since evaded all possible responsibility—little more since that than a first rate clerk."[10]

Yet it would have been difficult for Halleck to have done otherwise when Lincoln, instead of relying on briefings, visited the War Department telegraph office as often as four times a day to read the telegrams from the various army commanders. Second Bull Run, after which Halleck believed he had saved the capital by having brought McClellan's army from the Peninsula, coincided with Halleck's nights without rest and Lincoln's very direct involvement. It is difficult to tell exhaustion from a loss of nerve and pluck, something not necessarily likely when Halleck believed that his strategy had resulted in the averting of a worse disaster. More likely Halleck and Lincoln then became intimate collaborators and, as the President now had experience and competence in military affairs, Lincoln was bound to be the senior member of the partnership.

Halleck found changing from success to failure as disagreeable as moving from the virtually untrammeled command of his own huge department to become Lincoln's junior partner in chief command. Even worse for Halleck, he encountered a political-military environment in which politicians and newspapers attacked the administration for "rose-water statesmanship" and the army for "generals who are afraid to fight the enemy." Having entered a world with which Lincoln had been coping for more than a year, Halleck said: I wish "to go back to private life as soon as possible and never again to put my foot in Washington." While Lincoln came to believe that the general in chief had failed in leadership, Halleck felt that the political environment in which he and Lincoln had to work was impossible. The general, growing too wary and keeping too low a profile, over-reacted. Yet, though Lincoln and Halleck each endured disappointment, they made an effective team, one first tested by Lee's movement into Maryland.[11]

Because Lee planned to remain in Maryland through the fall, he needed at least a rudimentary line of communications to bring him ammunition, clothing, and such supplies as salt, coffee, and sugar. He intended to use a wagon route from Winchester, Virginia, through Harper's Ferry into Maryland. However, he found the Harper's Ferry position formidably garrisoned by a force of 12,000 men. Though detaching forces to take this position further dispersed his army, Lee apparently counted on McClellan's well-demonstrated caution and excessive deliberation of movement to protect him from interference. McClellan "is an able general, but a very cautious one," Lee evaluated. "His army is in a very demoralized and chaotic condition, and will not be prepared for offensive operations—or he will not think it so—for three or four weeks. Before that time I hope to be on the Susquehanna."[12]

But McClellan displayed his organizational gifts and quickly prepared the armies at Washington to combat what Halleck, immediately after Second Bull Run, had diagnosed as Lee's next move, to "cross the Potomac, and make a raid into Maryland or Pennsylvania." Having been prescient enough to make this judgment on the same day that Lee wrote Davis of his plan, Halleck soon began to be puzzled by Lee's purpose. Unable to perceive what benefits the raid could bring Lee, Halleck strongly suspected a feint to draw McClellan into Maryland so Lee could make a dash for Washington.[13]

Momentary alarm erupted from a "second-hand" report from Baltimore that the Confederate general, Braxton Bragg, was "advancing through the valley of the Shenandoah with 40,000 men—it is said for Pennsylvania." After some apprehension because of this not unusual overestimate of the Confederate transportation system, Lincoln grew very optimistic about the outcome of the campaign. Not only did he see Philadelphia not "in any danger," but he even explained lines of operations to the anxious governor of Pennsylvania. If half of McClellan's army moved to Harrisburg, "the enemy will turn upon," wrote Lincoln, "and beat the remaining half, and then reach Harrisburg before the part going there, and beat it too."[14]

More significant for Lincoln than the absence of any real threat from the raiders, the situation presented a golden opportunity for the concentrated forces under McClellan. In their flank position northwest of Washington, McClellan's men precluded an enemy advance northward, because Lee "dares not leave them in his rear." Perceiving Lee potentially in a serious predicament, Lincoln urged McClellan not to "let him get off without being hurt" and to "destroy the rebel army if possible." His belief in a chance for hurting the enemy rested on his hope that Lee would raid farther north and McClellan could get in his rear.[15]

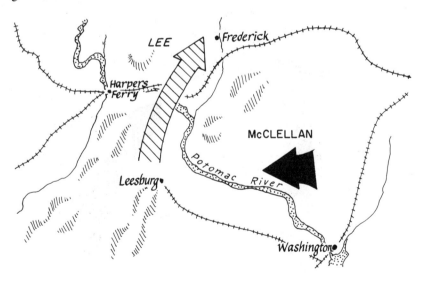

Flank Position

The President's confidence that the rebel raid offered a chance for a decisive stroke contrasted with the general in chief's suspicion that Lee must have something up his sleeve and planned a quick dash on Washington. The Pennsylvanians, who had sent their state's archives, bonds, and treasures to New York for safekeeping, did not share the complacency of both Lincoln and Halleck about any menace Lee might pose. In considerable anxiety, the Philadelphians asked for a general "who combines the sagacity of the statesman with the acuteness and skill of the soldier." When telling his alarmed fellow Pennsylvanians that the particular paragon they sought was unavailable, the unpanicked secretary of war could not resist telling them: "While confiding in his loyalty and courage, he would not, in my opinion, begin to fill the bill."[16]

Less concerned than Halleck that Lee planned to double back on Washington, McClellan moved his just-organized army with unaccustomed vigor, based in part on his capture, on September 13, of a copy of Lee's plans. The principal federal actor in the little drama that led to this fortuitous capture was Private John M. Bloss, Company F, Twenty-seventh Indiana, who approached Frederick, Maryland, with McClellan's advanced skirmishers. Resting in the grass, he spotted an envelope that wrapped a few cigars. He shared one with a comrade and then read the accompanying paper. "As I read,"

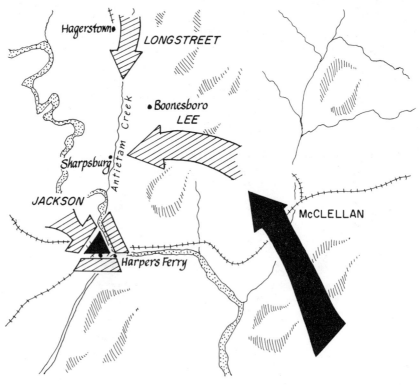

Confederate Concentration

Bloss reported in one of the war's great understatements, "each line became more interesting." He held a complete copy of Lee's Secret Order No. 191—the entire Confederate plan for the next four days. Within forty-five minutes of the initial find, the paper swished through the hands of all men in the chain of command upward to McClellan who "gave vent to demonstrations of joy." Orderlies and staff officers went "flying in all directions."[17]

Not aware of the tragedy, Lee first decided to withdraw across the Potomac because his dispersed army was unprepared. Then, when he learned of the fall of Harper's Ferry on September 15 and the ability of those forces now to concentrate, he decided to avail himself of the advantages of the tactical defensive to resist a Union attack on the north side of the river. This McClellan unleashed on September 17 in the Battle of Antietam—the bloodiest single day of the war. "No tongue can tell, no mind conceive, no pen portray the horrible sights I witnessed this morning," a Pennsylvania soldier noted. A Wisconsin man called the fearful battle "a great tumbling together of all heaven and earth." A Confederate Colonel termed it "artillery hell."[18]

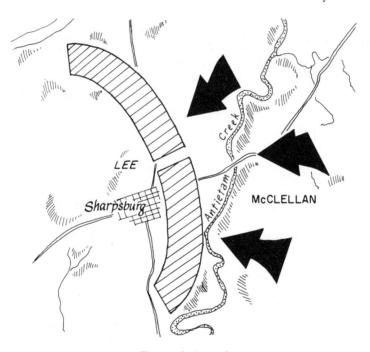

Frontal Assault

In a bloody day-long battle, the Confederates with difficulty fended off poorly coordinated frontal attacks by McClellan's far larger army. Graduating from West Point before Professor Mahan joined the faculty, Lee did not intrench his weak position. Serious numerical inferiority also contributed to the Confederate defenders suffering slightly heavier casualties than did McClellan's attacking force: 13,724 to 12,469; though including the 12,000 prisoners captured at Harper's Ferry, the total losses in the campaign stand about proportional to the numbers available on each side. Although Lee's army had been tactically successful in the defensive battle at Antietam, it was now immobile and in a precarious position where it could neither supply itself by foraging nor be supplied by rail. So Lee concluded his raid and withdrew into Virginia.

The withdrawal, the foreordained conclusion of any raid, proved that the Union had won the battle; thus the political benefits redounded to the Union. The first victory in the East in which the enemy had retreated provided Lincoln with the springboard for his preliminary emancipation proclamation and seriously dampened any Confederate prospects for diplomatic recognition by European powers. Even Lee's modest political expectations for a warm welcome by Marylanders had been disappointed. As the Confederates had entered Frederick, all stores closed, no flags flew, and an observer noted that "everything partook of a churchyard appearance." The whole episode in Frederick eventually got swept up into the body of American mythology. Poets bestowed fame on the near-centenarian Dame Barbara Fritchie, but in truth she did not live on the street through which Jackson's men marched, nor did she wave her U.S. flag at Confederates in defiance; she waved it to Union troops who entered the town after Jackson had passed. Reflecting the undercurrent of opposing sentiment, another elderly lady who lived in Frederick expressed her Confederate sympathies as the rebel column passed her doorstep when, with her hands raised and her eyes full of tears, she called down to them her heartfelt wish, "The Lord bless your dirty ragged souls!"[19]

The Confederates had woefully erred when they thought that the Marylanders wished to join their ranks. Doubtless the invader's underfed, dirty, and ragged condition sobered many potential sympathizers and created their negative responses. One Confederate veteran remembered long afterward that as far as he knew none of the rebels possessed any underclothing. And many marched shoeless on stone-bruised feet, looking like vagrant hoboes. "They were the dirtiest men I ever saw," one observer later recalled, "a most ragged, lean, and hungry set of wolves." Slowly their error in judgment dawned upon all of the previously optimistic southerners as it did upon the articulate private who wrote: "The large majority of the people were silent in regard to giving demonstrations of opinion; many because they were really hostile to us, and some because they knew that every one was narrowly watched by Spies, by the remnant of Yankee forces on parole in the town, and most of all by their own neighbors."[20]

Having left Maryland before the Union elections, Lee had failed in the political part of his campaign, but he adhered to his original military objective by remaining close to the south side of the Potomac. Here he found abundant forage and subsistence, still occupied a position on the flank of any Union advance into Virginia, and was well placed to cross again into Maryland to occupy the politically significant flank position he had originally chosen.

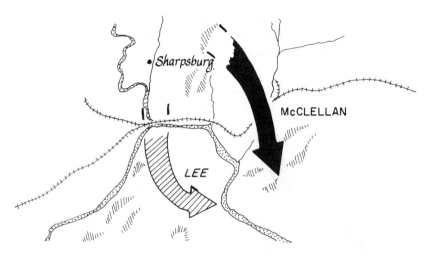

Withdrawal to Flank Position

☆   ☆

Meanwhile, in the West, Bragg moved northward as fast and steadily as he could, successfully bypassing Buell's army at Nashville. Combining a simultaneous advance by his Mississippi forces with his movement to concentrate with Kirby Smith and turn Buell, Bragg expected that his threat to Buell would draw forces from West Tennessee. He told Sterling Price in Mississippi: "The road is open for you into Western Tennessee." Realizing his part of the plan constituted a "bold move," Kirby Smith saw that, should he reach Kentucky, his position would be a "precarious one," unless Kentuckians rallied to the Confederate standard. Yet he believed the movement worthwhile for if he did "nothing more than get large quantities of supplies . . . and then fall back," he would clearly be "much better off" for having made the raid. But Kirby Smith hoped for the "brilliant results" of "permanently occupying Kentucky" and forcing "the abandonment of Middle Tennessee by the Federals."[21]

Bragg espoused objectives in Middle Tennessee even more vague than Kirby Smith had, for Bragg still kept West Tennessee as an objective. He expected to gain in either Middle or West Tennessee, for he thought that the advance of Price and Van Dorn would either prevent Buell's being reinforced or allow them to reoccupy West Tennessee. But Bragg confidently believed that he could either beat Buell's scattered forces or "by gaining his rear very much increase his demoralization and break him up." With the enemy's movements in doubt, Bragg initially had not decided whether to "strike Nashville, or perhaps, leaving that to the left, strike for Lexington and Cincinnati." Soon he decided to aim for Kentucky, counting on his turning movement to force Buell back to the Ohio. Anticipating that he would "thus have Buell pretty well disposed of," he expected "to free all Middle Tennessee of the enemy" and begin to rebuild the railroad. In essence Bragg seems to have relied on Buell's being so "demoralized, disheartened, and deceived" that he would abandon middle Tennessee.[22]

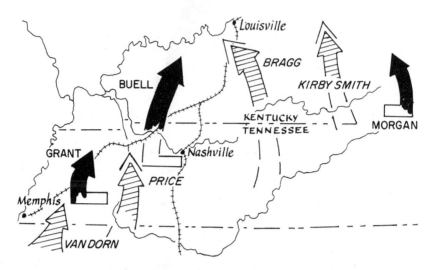

Planned Turning Relief of Tennessee

Bypassing Buell's position around Nashville, Bragg marched first toward Glasgow, a town about forty miles east of Bowling Green. Reaching there on September 13, he stopped for two days to rest, regroup and forage. Following President Davis's earlier orders to reassure the people of the invaded state, Bragg delivered himself of a flamboyant proclamation: "Kentuckians, I have entered your state with the Confederate Army of the West, and offer you an opportunity to free yourselves from the tyranny of a despotic ruler. We come not as conquerors or despoilers, but to restore to you the liberties of which you have been deprived by a cruel and relentless foe." He also promised to "enforce a rigid discipline and . . . protect all in their persons and property," but in this he went too far, carrying the sanctity of property rights to the extreme.[23]

One report stated that Bragg ordered a young Confederate soldier tried by court-martial and executed for taking a few apples from an orchard outside of Glasgow. There was more to the offense, as was the case in other instances, but Bragg's reputation for an overly harsh iron rule grew. Once he remarked to a subordinate officer: "I have no children. . . . I look upon the soldiers as my own, as my children." That officer repeated the remark to some soldiers who replied that Bragg "has a very large family and sometimes causes his boys to be shot."[24]

The Kentuckians, like the Marylanders, deeply disappointed Confederate hopes, showing little inclination to enlist. No doubt Bragg repulsed many persons with his harshness, but far more than the unhappy episode of Glasgow was to blame. "The people here have too many fat cattle and are too well off to fight," Bragg crossly remarked. The people of Kentucky embraced a curious mind-set: many of them followed Confederate exploits gleefully, cheered rebel prowess, and admired their accomplishments, but actually they harbored little expectation of ultimate Confederate success and had an even gloomier estimate about the well-being of Kentucky if it cast a pro-southern lot. And so the Kentuckians remained aloof and, for the most part, out of Bragg's ranks, though there were a number of Kentucky regiments in the Confederate army. This outcome proved even more exasperating than the failure in Maryland, because for the first time the Confederates possessed, thanks to recent captures, enough rifles to arm several thousand new troops. In fact, when Bragg later retreated from Kentucky, he possessed 15,000 more rifles than he had brought in. But in early September his hopes still soared high, for he had turned Buell out of Middle Tennessee and had directed Sterling Price to advance on Nashville. Bragg had left Price and Van Dorn in Mississippi, Price to watch Grant and Van Dorn to guard the Mississippi. With Price ordered to adance, Bragg now expected to reap some of the fruits of his brilliant maneuver.[25]

Though Bragg, at his great distance, did not understand the situation in Mississippi very well, he at least retained a vestige of unified command in the West. The Union lost its comparable unity when Halleck went to Washington. The new general in chief had put no one in his place as western generalissimo. His decision had been reluctant, but, to cope with the menace of political appointments, Halleck resolved to do away with his old, unified western department. "The friends of Governor Morton, of Ex-Governor Dennison, of Cassius M. Clay, and of Colonel Blair were pulling all kinds of political wires to cut up the West into departments for the benefit of each."

Halleck regarded this disparagement of professionalism and patronage approach to military appointments as an anathema. He hoped to head it off if "some of the generals out there would gain some brilliant victory, so as to cut off these pretensions of outsiders. But unfortunately nothing of the kind occurred." In the absence of the needed victory, he was asked, "Why keep in men who accomplish nothing? The only answer I can give is, why put in men who know nothing of military affairs. Under the circumstances I have been obliged to leave things as much as possible in status quo," a divided western command instead of the unity he had sought and obtained the previous March.

The radical attack on politically conservative generals and the widespread disparagement of the dig-in, no-win philosophy of West Point-educated officers remained fundamental to the strong demand for political generals. The discouraged Halleck found "hopeless" the task of keeping "separate military appointments and commands from politics," and attributed great "waste of

money and demoralization" and "terrible results" to "incompetent and cor-
rupt politicians in nearly all military offices high and low. . . . It is utterly
disheartening!" he stated. "Oh, the curse of political expediency!" Doubtless
Halleck exaggerated the effect, for, in fifteen years of army service, he had
absorbed fully the professional outlook. Nevertheless he accurately reflected
the point of view of the regulars and clearly perceived the political pressures
with which Lincoln had to deal.

The new general in chief sought to sustain "the military officers against
this political pressure," but he thought the radical critics likely to make their
point about the deficiencies of the professional soldiers and their strategy. He
stated: "Unless we have some success soon— I mean real substantial success—
the ultra radicals will force us to yield." Unlike the veteran politician Lincoln,
the too pessimistic soldier-businessman Halleck became demoralized by the
political environment. The military success, needed to protect the administration and the professional soldiers from the radicals, was also essential for
public morale and for insulating the administration from its vehement critics
on the left and right. But Halleck blamed the critics and attributed the lack
of success to partisanship in which "the rabid Abolitionists and Northern
Democrats of secession proclivities" had "done all in their power," he asserted, "to weaken and embarrass the administration and at the same time to
discourage and demoralize the Army. We are now reaping the fruits of their
accursed work."[26]

In Buell Halleck knew that he had a general vulnerable to the critics of the
professionals. Buell's "cautious vigor," which had earlier impressed Lincoln,
seemed all caution and no vigor as he had slowly advanced toward Chattanooga. But Buell now faced the most virulent form of a menace then plaguing
all the Union forces in the West. Buell reported: My "communications, 500
miles long, are swarming with an immense cavalry force of the enemy, regular
and irregular, which renders it almost impossible to keep them open." Twice
his railroads had been broken by the "formidable raids" of Forrest and Morgan, "causing great delay and embarrassment," he said, "so that we are barely
able to resist from day to day." Before Kirby Smith had advanced and prior
to the arrival of Bragg or his army, Buell had suspended his advance. With
his communications "constantly beset by a vastly superior cavalry force," his
"army could not be sustained in its present position, much less advanced,
until they were made secure."[27]

Buell stressed good communications, in part because he wanted his occupation of East Tennessee to be permanent. To enter East Tennessee but have
to withdraw for lack of supplies would be to "trifle with the lives of loyal
citizens," who would reveal themselves when a Union army entered but,
when it retreated, would thus be "betrayed to the vengeance of their enemies
by a promised protection and hurried abandonment." Buell's slow advance
had puzzled Halleck, "a problem," he admitted, "I am unable to solve." In
shifting his base to Nashville, Buell had already sought, without success, a

line of communications more secure against raiders. This change had only made him more vulnerable to the dual Confederate turning movement.[28]

Puzzling to Buell, the movements of Bragg and Kirby Smith posed an immediate problem for George W. Morgan, who commanded Union troops at Cumberland Gap and had earlier turned Kirby Smith out of that position. The situation was now reversed as Kirby Smith's superior force passed around him. But Morgan understood the situation and refused to budge from his fortified position at the Gap. Realizing that Kirby Smith was making a raid into Kentucky, he resolved "to await quietly here" he said, "until Smith is starved out and forced to fall back. . . . Smith cannot possibly remain three weeks in my rear." General Morgan could afford to wait, for he had five weeks of supplies on hand. To increase the Confederate general's difficulties, Morgan ordered the commander of a small cavalry force to fall back before Kirby Smith's advance and "to destroy all forage and drive before him all cattle along the route." Kirby Smith thus had to leave troops to besiege Morgan, but his logistical situation was better than Morgan thought. The fertile Bluegrass region of Kentucky would sustain the Confederates longer than the blockaded Morgan could last.[29]

Buell also knew that Kirby Smith was headed for Kentucky, but he did not know what Bragg was going to do. With Kirby Smith menacing his communications, he feared Bragg would veer west and seize a point on the railroad "and in four days have communication with his base" at Chattanooga. Particularly fearing that Bragg would take Nashville, Buell based his strategy on two objectives: that "Nashville can be held and Kentucky rescued."[30]

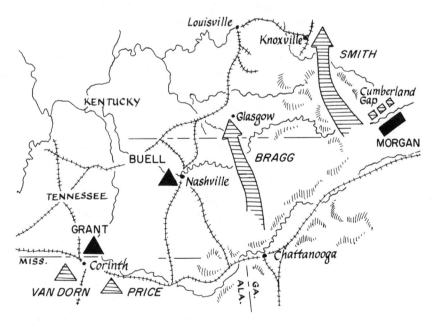

Dual Turning Movement

With its movements screened by the mountains and no communications to protect, Bragg's raiding army, though smaller than Buell's 50,000, held the initiative. But to convert his raid into a penetration and be able permanently to occupy any of Tennessee or Kentucky, both Bragg and his enemies knew that he "must destroy Buell's army or cast it off to the west a long distance" in order to control the line of the Louisville and Nashville Railroad and supply his army. Buell faced a dilemma: if he moved back to cover his communications and combat Kirby Smith, Bragg would swoop down on Nashville; if he protected Nashville, Bragg could move athwart the railroad to Louisville.[31]

But Bragg planned for Price, with 15,000 men, to move from north Mississippi directly northwest to Nashville. This would bring Price into conflict with Grant, whose mission during the summer had been to stand on the defensive. Guerrillas presented by far the major menace, for Grant, like Bragg, found "the country to be so dry that an attack" on Corinth was "hardly to be apprehended." Aware also that Bragg had left his front, he supposed that the enemy had sent "the mass of their disciplined troops to Richmond." Appropriately, Halleck had drawn down Grant's drought-immobilized forces to reinforce Buell and Curtis. But Grant still had a major task in combating "the system of guerrilla warfare now being prosecuted by some troops organized under authority of the so called Southern Confederacy, and others without such authority."[32]

Early Sherman had observed that "railroads are the weakest things in war; a single man with a match can destroy and cut off communications." The "constant interruption" of Grant's railroad service proved Sherman's prediction accurate: "bridges and water-tanks burned, trains fired into, track torn up" and "engines run off and badly damaged." This fate befell any "railroad running through a country where every house is a nest of secret, bitter enemies." Sherman characterized the situation as one in which, "though our armies pass across and through the land," he said, "the war closes in behind and leaves the same enemy behind." He added: It will be necessary to begin in "Kentucky and reconquer the country from there as we did from the Indians." Just as had Buell, Grant and his subordinates struggled against guerrillas and raiders and asked for more cavalry to suppress them.[33]

Grant's command was temporarily a strategic backwater from which Halleck could withdraw troops, though he intended that the fall campaign would "be opened there with energy" in October. This gave Grant and Sherman some leisure to devise a limited offensive. Sherman articulated their ideas well in projecting a move to cut the enemy's railroad at Granada. He hoped to "break up absolutely and effectually the railroad bridges, mills, and everything going to provide their armies" and, by making it "useless for a whole year," the enemy surely "must feel it."[34]

In such measures there would be operational as well as logistical advantages, for the railroad, to a degree, nullified federal control of and mobility along the Mississippi. With the railroad "in full operation they can keep pace with us up and down," Sherman wrote. Yet the significance of control of the river was logistical, because troops could land "at any point, and by a quick march break the railroad," he continued, "where we could make ourselves so busy that our descent would be dreaded the whole length of the river" by taking "negroes and other property."

The remedy for guerrilla warfare was, then, to avoid occupation of territory, "to leave the interior alone. Detachments inland can always be overcome or are at great hazard and they do not convert the people." The solution was to give the rebels a dose of their own medicine by raiding them. Sherman added a political dimension to this attack on the enemy's logistics. Since the southerners could not "be made to love us," he said, the raids would make them "fear us, and dread the passage of troops through their country." The rebels would thus "in time discover that war is not the remedy for the political evils of which they complained."[35]

Grant and Sherman did not have an opportunity to try their emerging strategy of exhaustion because Grant, "weak and threatened" by the enemy to the south, found an important rail junction "surrounded" for several days and another "threatened [with] a strong force of cavalry." In spite of this, Halleck, apprehensive of rebel reinforcements from Mississippi going to Bragg, directed Grant to "attack the enemy if you can reach him with advantage."[36]

The movement into Kentucky of their department commander with half of his army disorganized the Confederates. Leaving Price and Van Dorn as coequal commanders in Mississippi was a mistake, and Bragg finally realized he could not control them from Kentucky. He intended that they cooperate, but each had his own idea of what to do. They went their separate ways; Van Dorn bid farewell to Price thus: "However all this may turn out, I shall always be happy to be associated with you in this noble struggle, and I pray to God you may be victorious wherever you may go."[37]

Halleck's offensive directive set Grant in motion just as Price began Bragg's directed move north toward Nashville. Reaching Iuka and finding Grant's forces strong in the area, Price resolved to join Van Dorn in attacking Corinth. But Grant promptly took advantage of the division of the southerners to attack them before they could concentrate to attack him. Using his central position between the two armies, on September 19 he attacked Price at Iuka with the idea that "if he can be beaten there it will prevent either the design to go north or to unite forces and attack here."[38]

Grant employed a turning movement, dividing his army as had Lee at Second Bull Run. With General Ord in front with half the force, Grant sent the other half under Rosecrans to block the road south from Iuka. With this road occupied the rebels would find themselves in a serious predicament, for "no route would have been left them except East, with the difficult bottom of Bear Creek to cross, or Northeast, with the Tennessee River in their front, or to conquer their way out." Any of their attempts to avoid Rosecrans would "have brought General Ord with his force on the rear of the retreating column." Despite Rosecrans's failure to reach the road on time, the enemy assumed the tactical offensive, "took the initiative and became the attacking party."[39]

This attack enabled the enemy to hold the road open and escape. Each side had about 15,000 men, the attacking Confederates losing over 1,500 and Grant's defenders almost 800. The operation succeeded, said Grant, except "in not capturing the entire army or in destroying it, as I hoped to do." He also would not succeed in preventing Price and Van Dorn from uniting and carrying out an attack on Corinth, a movement which rendered his position "precarious."[40]

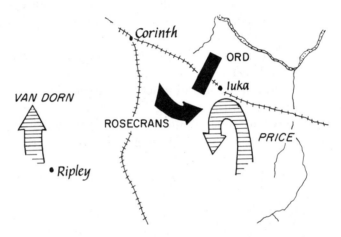

Grant Exploits Interior Lines with a Turning Movement

While Grant's energetic execution of Halleck's instructions protected Nashville from the southwest, Buell was trying to deal with the ambiguity presented by Bragg's apparent ability to drive either for Nashville or for Buell's communications. Buell prepared to cope with these threats by giving priority to Nashville. Like George W. Morgan at Cumberland Gap, he could hold out because he had accumulated vast quantities of supplies along his line of communications. He received a report stating: At Bowling Green alone "1,200,000 rations are here, except bread. We are out of bread, but can get flour, and are preparing to bake bread for the whole army." Further, he was preparing an alternate depot on the Ohio west of Louisville. If the Confederates cut his communications, Buell could undoubtedly outlast Bragg and force the Confederates to disperse their army in order to live on the country in Kentucky. This would reopen the federal supply line to Louisville. Thus Bragg had failed to demoralize Buell, who had not fled in panic to the Ohio River.[41]

But Buell could not adopt the strategy of starving Bragg off his communications and out of Kentucky. Conscious of the adverse "political effect of entirely abandoning" Nashville, he must have been equally conscious of the political effect of a passive defensive strategy. Once certain that Bragg had moved into Kentucky, he garrisoned Nashville and moved the bulk of his army toward Louisville. His political need to attack Bragg would likely be greater than any logistical need Bragg would have to attack him.[42]

As early as August 8 Halleck had been concerned enough about Buell to alert Grant to be prepared to send two divisions as reinforcements and had soon placed the new troops from Ohio and Indiana at Buell's disposal. The general in chief sent green troops to Buell's rear, to a newly organized department, the Ohio, headed by the capable engineer officer, Major General Horatio G. Wright. Wright's command comprised Kentucky, Ohio, Illinois, Indiana, and Michigan and it became the focal point of panic similar to that then felt in Pennsylvania. As the Confederates entered Kentucky and seemed headed for the Ohio River, a thousand "squirrel hunters," volunteers gathered from the Ohio Valley, commenced service near Cincinnati as home guards. Hardly more effective were the nearly 40,000 new troops, so "utterly raw" that they did not "know how to march or fire and can't be expected to do much in the way of fighting." These soldiers protected Louisville and Cincinnati, some of them having been unwisely risked in combat at Richmond, Kentucky, with disastrous consequences.[43]

With the great Ohio River cities protected in this improvised way and Nashville well fortified and garrisoned, Buell moved north toward Louisville

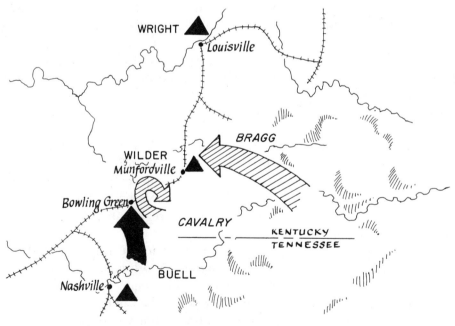

Fall of Munfordville

along the Louisville and Nashville Railroad. On September 14 his vanguard reached Bowling Green. Fifty miles to the north, at Munfordville, the Federals had a garrison of some 4,000 men. Buell planned to march quickly to Munfordville to unite with this force, but Confederate cavalry checked the federal advance out of Bowling Green, temporarily holding the blue column there. After one of Bragg's brigades on September 14 made an unwise, premature attack upon the Munfordville fort and had to fall back badly repulsed, Bragg ordered his whole army to converge on Munfordville the next day. The federal garrison was doomed.

A humorous episode ended the affair on September 17, rather than a bloody battle as occurred on that same day in Maryland. The garrison commander, Colonel John T. Wilder, an Indiana industrialist with no military experience whatsoever, adopted the unorthodox but sensible expedient of going with a flag of truce to Confederate Major General Simon Bolivar Buckner's headquarters and asking for advice about whether to surrender or fight. Shocked by this striking naiveté, Buckner could not bring himself to offer advice to his trusting enemy, but did grant Wilder's request that he be allowed to inspect the beleaguering forces and count the cannon arrayed against him. "I believe I'll surrender," Wilder concluded sadly.[44]

The whole Confederacy, and at that time even Bragg, now confidently expected that he would inflict a great and stinging defeat upon Buell. In his position on Buell's railroad, the Confederate general felt confident that the enemy would not attack him, "yet no other escape seems open to them," concluded Bragg. This was not the enemy's situation for, while the imperturbable Buell was preparing an alternate line of supply and retreat and was having bread baked, Bragg reported that his "greatest want has been breadstuffs" to feed his army. Bragg hesitated. He did not desire to engage Buell in a slugfest which, he correctly surmised, would most likely end in a costly stalemate anyway. Summing up his and Lee's doctrine of turning movements to recover territory, Bragg remarked to a subordinate, "This campaign must be won by marching, not fighting." But, having outmarched Buell, he was thwarted by Buell's deliberation and by his raiding army's lack of a supply line. Looking with longing at the "plentiful country" of the Bluegrass region, Bragg moved that way, leaving the "barren and destitute" country near Buell and, of necessity, relying on his Mississippi forces to complete the conquest of Middle Tennessee. He informed Van Dorn: "Nashville is defended by only a weak division; Bowling Green by only a regiment. Sweep them off and push up to the Ohio."[45]

Turning away from Buell, Bragg marched off to the Bluegrass and the Kentucky state capital, Frankfort. Marching north to Louisville, Buell amalgamated his army with the raw troops there and, under threat of removal from command, prepared to move against Bragg. The Confederate army was rationing well in the fertile regions of Kentucky, but without a supply line would have eventually been forced to retreat. Buell had successfully covered Nashville and the Louisville and Nashville Railroad.

As Buell made ready to advance from Louisville, Bragg took time out on October 2 to attend the inauguration of Kentucky's seccessionist governor, Richard Hawes, at Frankfort. Bragg received much criticism from bellicose southerners for thus spending such valuable moments, but the Confederacy attached great political importance to the technical and theoretical legitimacy of Kentucky as a state within the new nation. Furthermore, after appeals failed to induce Kentuckians to volunteer, Bragg wished to introduce conscription. For this he needed the legal sanction which the inauguration provided. Meanwhile, however, Buell was moving from Louisville, and Bragg lost his last hope of support from Price and Van Dorn in Mississippi.

Realizing that in Mississippi the Confederacy lacked unity of command, Secretary Randolph directed the senior officer, Van Dorn, to "assume forthwith the command of all the troops left in Mississippi including General Price's column. Concentrate them," he ordered, "without loss of time; . . . make proper disposition for the defense of the Mississippi River and also for an advance into Tennessee." The united forces of Van Dorn and Price then moved north to attack Corinth, strongly held by one of Grant's subordinates, the capable William S. Rosecrans. On October 3 and 4 the plucky Confederates approached Corinth from the northwest, which brought them against defenses originally erected the preceding spring by Beauregard to resist Halleck's advance. During the first morning, in the severe, though piecemeal, action, the Confederates penetrated the outer line of works, but found the recently built inner defenses too strong. Van Dorn fell back to regroup, but

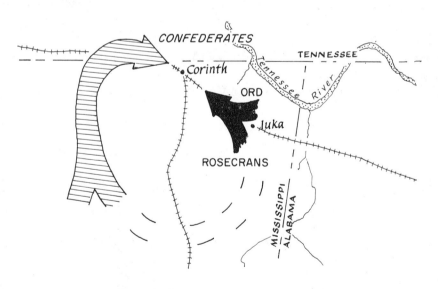

Grant's Communications Threatened

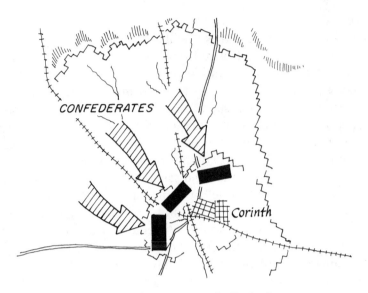

Confederates Attack Corinth

the contest nevertheless still remained in doubt by nightfall. The attacks renewed with vigor on the next day, assaults and counterassaults both quite costly. The brief but intense and bloody action concluded in early afternoon as the repulsed Confederates withdrew to Chewalla, ten miles northwest of Corinth. Of the approximately 20,000 men on each side the federal loss stood at 355 killed, 1,841 wounded, and 324 missing; the Confederates had 473 killed, 1,197 wounded, and 1,763 missing. Even while the unsuccessful attack was underway, Grant, from his headquarters at Jackson, again sought to take his enemy in the rear, not being able to "see how the Enemy are to escape without losing everything but their small arms." Too late to intervene during the battle, the force he sent did meet Van Dorn on his retreat westward and compelled the Confederate leader to take a circuitous route in order to find safety at Holly Springs, southwest of Corinth.[46]

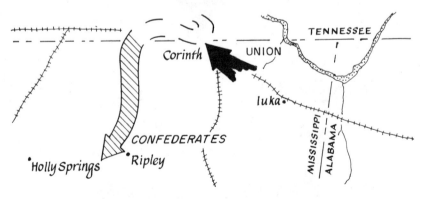

Confederate Withdrawal

Meanwhile the armies of Buell and Bragg moved toward a collision; it finally took place several days later, on October 8, 1862, near Perryville. Although it proved the major battle of the war on Kentucky soil, it produced inconclusive and, to some extent, even insignificant results. Buell had advanced on October 1 from Louisville with 60,000 men moving in four columns. Bragg's main force was located at Bardstown, thirty-five miles southeast, some 22,500 strong. Kirby Smith had 10,000 men dispersed in a wide area around Frankfort, Lexington, and Harrodsburg. On October 2 Bragg ordered Leonidas Polk to move his corps north to Frankfort to attack the enemy there in flank while Kirby Smith attacked the front. Bragg's plan for a bold Napoleonic concentration unfortunately was based upon faulty intelligence, but nevertheless could have achieved a brilliant partial success had Polk moved rapidly as ordered.

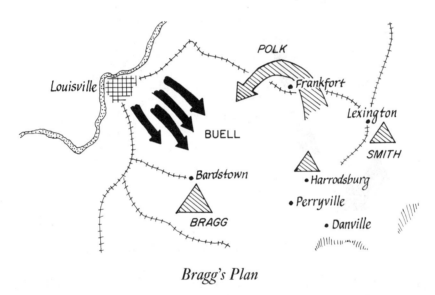

Bragg's Plan

On October 3 after hearing reports of his cavalry, Polk decided on his own initiative to retreat to Danville. Bragg long had felt Polk was unfit for field command and had wished to replace the bishop before now; but Polk's high rank and friendship with President Davis had forced Bragg to retain him. How correct Grady McWhiney was when he observed, "Older than Bragg, and closer to the President, Polk probably had been a bishop too long to be a successful subordinate." And as Bragg informed Davis, "With all his ability, energy, and zeal, General Polk, by education and habit, is unfitted for executing the orders of others. . . . He will convince himself his own views are better, and will follow them without reflecting on the consequences."[47]

Widely dispersed and all looking for water, the Federals approached Perryville on October 7. A severe drought for several weeks had dried up most of the streams and creeks. The opening clashes occurred as some of the

Federals encountered Hardee's men strongly emplaced on a ridge beyond Doctor's Creek, a tributary of Chaplin's Fork of the Salt River. A vigorous struggle for the nearby water pools ensued, continuing by the light of a full moon far into the night. The Confederates held. Buell realized during the night that a major engagement was shaping up and he ordered two additional corps to occupy the right and left of those Federals who had engaged. Skirmishing reopened at dawn on the Union left, the northern flank. But Buell preferred not to bring on the ultimate battle, if possible, until his other corps approached.

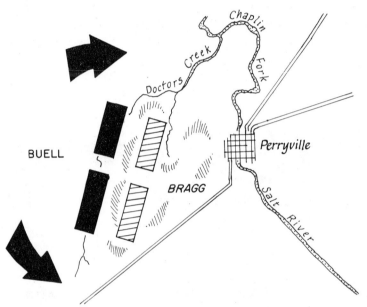

Reinforcement of Frontal Position

The battle developed quite disjointedly, for neither commander realized what he faced. Bragg persisted in believing that only a small enemy fragment stood at Perryville and he could easily and quickly dispatch it, while Buell erroneously believed he faced the whole Confederate force at Perryville, but he failed to launch a uniform attack. In fact, a queer atmospheric phenomenon prevented battle noises from being heard behind the lines and Buell did not realize the engagement's extent until late in the day.

About 1:00 p.m. the whole Confederate force moved forward in a general attack. In some of the war's most reckless and vicious hand-to-hand fighting, the Federals ebbed back under the steady pressure. In an outstanding example of the selfless bravery many Federals exhibited, a Yankee colonel commanding a battery of artillery continued single-handed to work one of the guns after nearly all of his officers and men had been killed. Finally, when the Confederate infantry closed in about him, instead of fleeing, he boldly drew his sword and stood at "parade rest." Impressed by the calm courage, the southern officer leading the assault ordered his men to hold fire and allowed the bluecoated officer to walk off the field. A reinforcing brigade moved too late to bolster the faltering Federals; the Confederates drove the brigade back and captured its commander. In fact, the circumstances of this capture well illustrate the battle's degree of confusion. The Union officer, searching for orders as to where he should place his brigade, rode up to Confederate General Polk, mistaking him for a Federal corps commander! "I have come to your assistance with my brigade," he proudly announced. Polk asked the name of his command and told the startled man, "There is some mistake about this. You are my prisoner."[48]

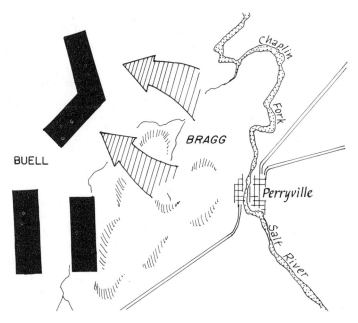

Confederate Advance

Near nightfall a similar and worse fate almost befell Polk; he nearly met the same end as had Zollicoffer so many months before at Fishing Creek. Polk saw a body of men he took to be Confederates firing obliquely into some newly arriving southern troops. "Dear me," he said to himself, "this is very sad and must be stopped." Finding no staff or aides nearby, Polk personally galloped up to the offenders and addressed a colonel in angry tones, inquiring what he meant by shooting at friendly troops and ordering him to cease at once. "I don't think there can be any mistake about it; I am sure they are enemy," the man replied, but in the enveloping darkness failed to note Polk's own uniform color. "Enemy!" Polk cried, "Why I have just left them myself. Cease firing, sir; what is your name, sir?" The man revealed that he was from an Indiana regiment. The astonished Polk envisioned no hope but to brazen it out and so answered his adversary's next question "and, pray sir, who are you?" with "I'll soon show you who I am, sir; cease firing, sir, at once." He then turned his horse to canter slowly down the Yankee line shouting in an authoritative voice to cease firing, until he reached a small woods, put the spurs to his steed, and galloped back to safety.[49]

The uncoordinated battle produced heavy casualties among the small proportion engaged: out of 36,940 in the fight 845 Federals were killed, 2,851 wounded, 515 captured or missing; and 510 Confederates were killed, 2,635 wounded, 251 missing, out of 16,000 who fought. The Federals had employed but nine brigades while another fifteen remained unoccupied although in supporting distance. Both sides had won a partial victory and many Confederate soldiers expected to fight again the next day, but Bragg chose to withdraw, back to East Tennessee. A little skirmishing on the roads the next day constituted mere anticlimax. Essentially unmolested in his retreat to East Tennessee, Bragg then based himself on the railroad at Murfreesboro. Ultimately, Perryville must be termed a Union victory, because the Confederates retreated, even though they won the tactical engagement. But it should be noted that the Confederate army had to retreat in any case, because, essentially a raiding force, it lacked rearward lines of communications.[50]

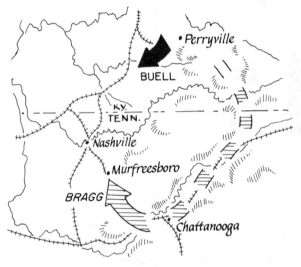

Bragg's Withdrawal

Bragg's retreat ended the Confederate late-summer ripostes to the Union spring offensive. The initial Confederate counterstrokes in the spring, at Shiloh and Fair Oaks and in the Seven Days' Battles, had been concentrations aimed at a Union army and had placed the Confederates on the tactical offensive in what amounted to essentially frontal attacks. For the second Confederate counteroffensive, both Bragg and Lee deliberately sought to avoid a conflict. Instead of concentrating and attacking as the Confederates had done at Shiloh, Fair Oaks, and in the Seven Days' Battles, they sought to recover lost territory by employing turning movements. Using his interior lines, Lee concentrated against Pope and turned him out of his position; but, though he failed to avoid battle, Lee was able to fight on the tactical defensive and suffer significantly fewer casualties. He was not so fortunate in his second turning movement for, with unusual celerity, McClellan caught Lee unprepared, forced battle on the unintrenched Confederate commander, and inflicted heavier casualties upon the defenders than those suffered by the attacking Union army. The capture of the garrison at Harper's Ferry did, however, more than square the casualty account for the campaign.

Bragg achieved more success in avoiding battle, though inadequate unity of command marred his complex campaign. Nevertheless, Bragg made a surprise change in the line of operations and the Confederates succeeded in concentrating in Kentucky troops from Mississippi, East Tennessee, and Marshall's small force from Virginia. Forced by a supply shortage from any position athwart Buell's communications, Bragg avoided a conflict early in the campaign. Despite being partially on the tactical offensive at Perryville, his army suffered moderately less than Buell's.

Since both Lee's and Bragg's movements into the border states were raids, each would have had to withdraw after the exhaustion of local subsistence and forage. Their defeats at Antietam and Perryville occasioned their withdrawals. Each movement succeeded in regaining some territory and delaying federal offensives until the fall season had almost ended. Much of the territory regained lay in Middle Tennessee, which Bragg was determined to hold.

As Bragg settled permanently onto his new line of operations in Middle Tennessee, the Confederacy separated the Mississippi portion of his old department, creating a separate entity. By intervening in the chaotic command situation left by Bragg in Mississippi, Davis and Randolph temporarily established a dual control in Mississippi even after they had directed Van Dorn to assume control in the district. At the same time that they brought about unity under Van Dorn, they organized what became a new department out of Mississippi and East Louisiana and gave its commander the mission of cooperating with the Louisiana forces west of the Mississippi in an effort to retake New Orleans. Major General John C. Pemberton, replaced by Beauregard at Charleston, came west to take over the new department. Van Dorn, leading his and Price's forces north, intended to carve a new department for himself out of West Tennessee. When he failed at Corinth, he retreated into Pemberton's department, finding himself "an isolated body in the field, relieved of command" by the creation of the new department under Pemberton.[51]

That Van Dorn and one of his subordinates, Mansfield Lovell, outranked Pemberton complicated the situation. Davis and Randolph solved this anomaly by promoting Pemberton to lieutenant general, passing over Lovell, who had surrendered New Orleans, and Van Dorn, just defeated at Corinth and possessed of a reputation for an unsavory private life. Van Dorn's career ended the following spring, when the irate husband of one of the general's alleged illicit lovers shot him. In the process of intervening to alleviate the disordered command situation left by Bragg in Mississippi, Davis and Randolph had created a new department reporting directly to them, leaving Bragg only with Middle Tennessee. Thus four separate commands now comprised Sidney Johnston's old department: Trans-Mississippi, Mississippi and East Louisiana, Middle Tennessee, and East Tennessee.

No Confederate command or other changes occurred in Virginia as Lee persisted in his original objective. Despite having to fall back into Virginia as a result of Antietam and being unable "to recross into Maryland," Lee succeeded in his plan by attaining its basic defensive objectives. Though he knew how "very difficult" it was "to operate untrammeled in an enemy's territory," he still wished "to recross the Potomac" farther up and again turn McClellan. Since this plan involved "an endeavor to defeat the enemy in battle" around Hagerstown, he did not attempt it, realizing that, with his weakened army, "the hazard would be great and a reverse disastrous."[52]

Having won the Battle of Antietam, McClellan exasperated his superiors by not pressing Lee. The Union general felt unable "to cross the river in pursuit of the retreating enemy" because, he said, "the means of transportation at my disposal was inadequate to furnish a single day's supply of subsistence in advance." His plan to deal with the Confederate forces by "pushing them out into the Shenandoah Valley as soon as practicable" was delayed by "instruction of the new troops" and by a lack of shoes, clothing, and draft animals for his field transportation.[53]

Lincoln and Halleck did not confine their disappointment solely to McClellan's failure to follow his defeated foe. A little over two weeks after Antietam, Grant achieved victory at Corinth, a success which followed close on the heels of his defeat of the enemy at Iuka. Two victories in quick succession made Halleck inquire, "Why not reinforce Rosecrans and pursue the enemy into Mississippi, supporting your army on the country?" Grant, however, believed "it idle to pursue farther without more preparation." The army could not "subsist itself on the country except in forage," and it was not ready because he had originally prepared the men "to follow but a few days and [they] are much worn out," he wrote Halleck. "Although partial success might result from further pursuit disaster would follow in the end. If you say so, however. . . ." Of course, Halleck did not say so and accepted the situation that logistical difficulties and fatigue prevented Grant from following an enemy who, in any case, had "fortifications to return to in case of need." Halleck thought Grant "a good general and brave in battle," but, culpably absent when the rebels attacked at Fort Donelson and Shiloh, "careless of his command."[54]

At the same time that Halleck was learning Grant's reasons for his immobility, Buell eked out a victory at Perryville. Again logistical problems prevented pursuit. It proved impossible for Buell to follow Bragg after Perryville. He explained: "The limited supply of forage which the country affords is consumed by the enemy as he passes. . . . The enemy has been driven into the heart of this desert and must go on, for he cannot exist in it. For the same reason we cannot pursue in it with any hope of overtaking him, for while he is moving back on his supplies and as he goes consuming what the country affords we must bring ours forward." For this reason, and because his old fears for the safety of Nashville revived, Buell proposed to move along the railroad and take his army to Nashville. Because of guerrilla activity and the dangers of more raids by Forrest and Morgan, he recommended that Kentucky be garrisoned by 30,000 men.[55]

The traditional image of victorious battles is that they have some significant outcome: if not the fall of a dynasty as after Hastings and Waterloo, at least the vigorous and deep advance which followed the fall of Fort Donelson. After Iuka and Corinth Grant moved not at all; Lee had only withdrawn over the Potomac after Antietam; and Buell did not succeed in occupying all of his old positions in Middle Tennessee. Each general pleaded logistical difficulties, pointing out his inability to supply his army if it moved rapidly after the retreating foe. After unplanned battles, the consequent lack of preliminary preparation for a forward movement, together with bad roads and, in Grant's case, wrecked railways, all worked to preclude any quick pursuit. Subsistence stockpiles must be accumulated in advance unless a thrust were made into territory relatively untouched by war as Lee and Bragg had done in entering two border states. Lincoln and Halleck were disappointed that four victories in less than a month had yielded them so little and that protracted preparations seemed needed in order to exploit the excellent campaigning weather of the fall.

But Buell had a railroad over which to advance and he wished to use it for his movement back to Middle Tennessee. Buell's plan, however, did not suit Halleck, if only because he feared that the circuitous route might give Bragg an opportunity to "make another raid into Kentucky." More important was Nashville's distance from Chattanooga. The President insisted: Buell's army "must enter East Tennessee this fall and it ought to move there while the roads are still passable." To the military reasons for a rapid advance were added the political, for, as Halleck explained: "Neither the Government nor the country can endure these repeated delays." Long dissatisfied with Buell, Lincoln and Halleck finally now replaced him with William S. Rosecrans, one of Grant's successful subordinates whom Halleck favored and of whose "energy and skill" Grant could not "speak too highly."

No Indian-fighting command was found for Buell. As Halleck, who regarded Buell as "slow but safe," had commented: "The Government seems determined to apply a guillotine to all unsuccessful generals. It seems rather hard to do this where the general is not in fault, but perhaps with us now, as in the French Revolution, some harsh measures are required." Even though he too had not advanced, Grant escaped the "guillotine." Such would not be the case with McClellan. Though Buell's removal was more prompt, Mc-

Clellan's would come only after a discussion about the proper strategy to pursue in the politically sensitive Washington-Virginia theatre.[56]

Logistics was not the only reason for McClellan's delay. Because Lee occupied a flank position, McClellan decided not to move directly on Richmond. Lee considered his position just south of the Potomac as logistically superior to Maryland for there, he said, is "plenty of beef and flour for our troops, hay for our horses, and some grain." He was also "gathering beeves, horses, and men" in the vicinity and "damaging the Baltimore and Ohio Railroad." Stragglers were returning and conscripts were being forwarded, enabling his army to have "an increase of over 20,000 men in eight days." His weaknesses consisted of a lack of pay for the men and a serious shortage of "clothes, shoes, and blankets. . . . The number of barefoot men is daily increasing," wrote Lee, "and it pains me to see them limping over the rocky roads."[57]

He planned, of course, to remain until the campaigning season ended "by threatening an advance into Maryland" or, if McClellan advanced against him, "to draw him into the valley," where Lee believed he could "operate to advantage, and at least have the benefit of the bountiful grain crops of this season." Initially he assumed that McClellan would "do little more this fall than to organize and instruct his new troops," preparatory to adopting his "most probable plan," an "advance south of the James River." Not until later did he realize that another Peninsula campaign was a political impossibility, for "the effect produced in the United States would be almost equivalent to a defeat." Federal activity on the North Carolina coast continued to worry him, especially the menace to the railway along the coast to Wilmington. Since the last link in the inner line from Danville, Virginia, to Greensboro, North Carolina, remained incomplete until May, 1864, were the line near the coast cut, "hopeless disaster might ensue." Among other motives, he was husbanding his army to conserve its "efficiency in future operations" along the coast in the winter.[58]

Lee's flank-position strategy proved effective, for McClellan believed it necessary to "fight the enemy near Winchester," because to cross lower down on the Potomac and pass to the east of him "would leave it in the power of the enemy to recross into Maryland," he explained, "and thus check our movements." With this analysis Lincoln and Halleck most emphatically disagreed, Halleck desiring that McClellan "cross lower down the Potomac."[59]

Inspired by the disagreement, Lincoln sent McClellan a closely reasoned letter, which, though "in no sense an order," was a clear and persuasive document. Referring to the subsistence problems of an advance, Lincoln reminded McClellan that he had called him "overcautious" because he assumed he could "not do what the enemy is constantly doing." Continuing this argument, the President reminded him of "one of the standard maxims of war, . . . 'to operate upon the enemy's communications as much as possible without exposing your own.' " McClellan, Lincoln said, acted "as if this applies against you, but cannot apply in your favor."

Before explaining the vulnerability of Lee's position, Lincoln pointed out that McClellan should not "dread his going into Pennsylvania." If he did, he would give up his communications and the Army of the Potomac would "have nothing to do but follow and ruin him." Lee, on the other hand, could easily be turned because the Union army, Lincoln explained, was "nearer Richmond by the route you can, and he must take." The President asked McClellan, "Why can you not reach there before him" when Lee's route would be the "arc of a circle" and McClellan's the chord? Logistics would be no problem on this march for, Lincoln continued, "the facility of supplying from the side away from the enemy is remarkable—as it were, by the different spokes extending from the hub towards the rim."

This situation enabled the Army of the Potomac to "menace the enemies' communications, which I would seize if he would permit," wrote Lincoln and, if Lee tried to outrun the Federals to Richmond, the President recommended to McClellan: "Press closely to him, fight him if a favorable opportunity should present, and, at least try to beat him to Richmond on the inside track."

Then Lincoln explained what had come to be and would remain his fundamental analysis of the problem posed in Virginia by the tactical power of the defense. It was best to fight the enemy far from Richmond, because, he said, "if we cannot beat him when he bears the wastage of coming to us, we never can when we bear the wastage of going to him." Lee, "in coming to us, tenders us an advantage which we should not waive," wrote Lincoln. Reminding McClellan of his own point about the importance of not trying to tackle the rebels in intrenchments, the President emphasized: Not only is beating Lee "easier near to us than far away," but "if we cannot beat the enemy where he now is, we never can, he being within the entrenchments of Richmond."

Thus did Lincoln in a letter to McClellan analyze the problem posed by the well-demonstrated primacy of the defensive. Unless there were to be a stalemate, with the Union army sitting in futility before the intrenchments of Richmond, something must be accomplished at a distance from those intrenchments. Lincoln did not subscribe to the thesis that Richmond, like Sebastopol, would fall if besieged. Nor did he have high expectations of what might be accomplished away from intrenchments. But he hoped that his army would fight if a "favorable opportunity" presented itself. Before Antietam he had hoped to "hurt" Lee and had urged McClellan to "destroy the rebel army if possible."[60]

Lincoln's was not a sanguine letter but neither was it pessimistic. Rather it exhibited a clear insight into the tactical realities revealed by Virginia operations and presented an excellent appraisal of the alternatives. Lincoln would not change this estimate for the remainder of the war, nor would the course of operations in Virginia give him any valid reason to do so.

Finally McClellan adopted Lincoln and Halleck's plan of turning Lee, but he was still not ready to move, his explanation about the condition of his horses eliciting from Lincoln this exasperated complaint: "I have just read your dispatch about sore-tongued and fatigued horses. Will you pardon me for asking what the horses of your army have done since the battle of Antietam that fatigues anything?" To McClellan's concern that "Bragg's army is probably now at liberty to unite itself with Lee's command," Halleck returned the testy reply: "I do not think that we need have any immediate fear of Bragg's army. You are within 20 miles of Lee's, while Bragg is distant about 400 miles." McClellan had exhausted Lincoln's patience, causing him to diagnose McClellan as having a disease, the "slows." Halleck had long been equally exasperated by his inability to "get General McClellan to move. He has now lain still *twenty days* since the battle of Antietam," he remarked, "and I cannot persuade him to advance an inch."[61]

Though McClellan began his movement at the end of October, he was removed in early November, immediately after the congressional elections. Lee remarked sadly to his wife, "I hate to see McClellan go. He and I had grown to understand each other so well."[62] Thus passed from the military scene one of the war's most controversial figures. Reappearing in 1864 as the Democratic presidential nominee, he would not again hold a military command.

Good management and good understanding of tactical realities were certainly McClellan's strengths. The success of his Peninsula strategy, however, was marred by his own delay at Yorktown and his retreat, during the Seven Days' Battles, to the James rather than merely shifting his base. His Peninsula performance, however, contrasts with his cool and assured conduct of the Antietam campaign and his general record prior to the Seven Days' Battles. Though his failure to confide early in Lincoln was doubtless a major factor, the administration's fickle treatment of their general added significantly to the tension between McClellan and his government which, in turn, contributed to McClellan's demoralization. Lincoln's inexperience as an administrator and lack, in Hitchcock, of a strong advisor helped to cause the administration's mistakes as did popular and radical dissatisfaction with slow progress in the crucial eastern theatre.

If Nathaniel P. Banks could accurately estimate enemy numbers, so, surely, could McClellan and his capable subordinates. It seems likely, therefore, that McClellan's exaggeration of the numbers of the rebels constituted in part a defense mechanism against his Washington critics. But it made him vulnerable to the equally able professionals, Halleck and Meigs. To a degree McClellan's performance depended on his perception of his approval and support in Washington. He did well when satisfied that he had Lincoln's approval and even better when called back after Pope's failure.

McClellan did have a bad case of the "slows," the disease being attributed to anything from untrained troops to real logistical problems. Joe Johnston thought its cause lay in his friend McClellan's cautious temperament, and another has suggested that he was psychologically defeated by an imagined southern superiority. Many other generals would suffer from an unwillingness to move until they were more or less completely ready. This can easily be either praised as a refusal to go off half-cocked or condemned as an unrealistic quest for perfection. The disease affected generals of undisputed competence, almost, for example, costing the very capable George H. Thomas his command in the last year of the war. The great or, at any rate, best generals of the war did not succumb to this disease. Lee would move with barefoot men when it seemed distinctly advantageous to do so and Grant would improvise and, to a degree, trust to luck in his 1863 Vicksburg campaign.

Yet McClellan does not look bad when compared with the Grant of Fort Donelson and Shiloh, absent from his army and surprised on both occasions; nor does McClellan compare unfavorably with the Lee who failed in western Virginia where McClellan succeeded, or the Lee of the bungled execution of the Seven Days' Battles. If the war had ended after Antietam, McClellan would seem far stronger. He cannot bear comparison, however, with Grant at Vicksburg or Lee at Chancellorsville, spectacular campaigns of mid-1863.[63]

In spite of McClellan's prolonged failure to follow up after Antietam, that victory was not barren. Lincoln turned it to good account politically.

1. Halleck to Sherman, July 16, 1862, *O.R.*, XVII, pt. 2, 100; Sherman to Halleck, July 16, 1862, *ibid.*, 100–101; Grant to Julia Grant, Apr. 30, 1862, to E. B. Washburne, July 22, 1862, *Papers of Grant*, V, 102, 225–26.

2. Halleck to Sherman, Aug. 25, 1862, *O.R.*, XVII, pt. 2, 186; Halleck to Mrs. Halleck, Aug. 9, Sept. 5, 1862, Wilson, "Halleck," 557, 558.

3. Halleck to Pope, Sept. 1, 1862, *O.R.*, XII, pt. 2, 82; Pope to Halleck, Sept. 1 (two communications), 1862, *ibid.*, 82–83.

4. Halleck to McClellan, Aug. 28, 31, Sept. 1, 1862, *O.R.*, XI, pt. 1, 97, 103, 104; Halleck to Mrs. Halleck, Sept. 2, 1862, Wilson, "Halleck," 558; Long, *Civil War, Day by Day*, 261.

5. William Sprague to Stanton, May 6, 1862, *O.R.*, XI, pt. 3, 146; W. H. Seward to Lincoln, May 14, 1862, *ibid.*, 170; McClellan to Stanton, May 15, 1862, *ibid.*, 174; S. P. Chase to Stanton, May 25, 1862, *ibid.*, XII, pt. 3, 229.

6. Halleck to Mrs. Halleck, Aug. 13, 1862, Wilson, "Halleck," 558; Lincoln to Stanton, Aug.

4, 1862, Basler, *Collected Works*, V, 357; Lincoln to McClellan, Aug. 29, 1862, *ibid.*, V, 399.

7. Lincoln to Boyle, Sept. 12, 1862, Basler, *Collected Works*, V, 416–17; Halleck to McClellan, Aug. 31, 1862, *O.R.*, XI, pt. 1, 102.

8. "Diary of Salmon P. Chase," *Annual Report of the American Historical Association for the Year 1902*, 2 vols. (Washington, 1902), II, 69, entry of Sept. 8, 1862.

9. "Chase Diary," 71, 78, 97, 103, entries of Sept. 9, 13, 27, 28, Oct. 16, 1862; *Diary of Gideon Welles*, ed. Howard K. Beale, 3 vols. (New York, 1960), I, 130; Halleck to Mrs. Halleck, Sept. 9, 1862, Wilson, "Halleck," 558.

10. Canby, *Lincoln and the Civil War*, 176.

11. Williams, *Lincoln and the Radicals*, 188; Halleck to Mrs. Halleck, Sept. 5, 1862, Wilson, "Halleck," 559.

12. Miers, *Lee*, 104.

13. Halleck to McClellan, Sept. 3, 1862, *O.R.*, XIX, pt. 2, 169; Halleck to McClellan, Sept. 7,

13, 14, 16, 19, 1862, *ibid.*, pt. 2, 201, 280, 281, 289, pt. 1, 41, pt. 2, 330; Halleck to Banks, Sept. 15, 1862, *ibid.*, pt. 2, 298.

14. Wool to Lincoln, Sept. 7, 1862, *O.R.*, XIX, pt. 2, 207; Lincoln to Buell and Wool, Sept. 7, 1862, Basler, *Collected Works*, V, 409; Lincoln to Webster, Sept. 9, 1862, *ibid.*, 412; Lincoln to Curtin, Sept. 12, 1862, *ibid.*, 417.

15. Lincoln to McClellan, Sept. 12, 15, 1862, Basler, *Collected Works*, V, 418, 426; Lincoln to Treat, Nov. 19, 1862, *ibid.*, 501–2.

16. Webster, Michael, and Forney, to Stanton, Sept. 10, 1862, *O.R.*, XIX, pt. 2, 251; Stanton to Webster, Michael, and Forney, Sept. 10, 1862, *ibid.*, 251.

17. Miers, *Lee*, 105.

18. Long, *Civil War, Day by Day*, 268; Herman Hattaway, *General Stephen D. Lee* (Jackson, Mississippi, 1976), 55.

19. Long, *Civil War, Day by Day*, 262; Henry, *Story of the Confederacy*, 183.

20. Miers, *Lee*, 104; Catton, *Terrible Swift Sword*, 449–50.

21. Bragg to Price, Aug. 2, 1862, *O.R.*, XVII, pt. 2, 662; Kirby Smith to Davis, Aug. 11, 1862, *ibid.*, XVI, pt. 2, 753; Kirby Smith to Bragg, Aug. 20, 24, 1862, *ibid.*, XVII, pt. 2, 766, 775.

22. Bragg to Kirby Smith, Aug. 12, 15, 1862, *O.R.*, XVI, pt. 2, 754, 759; Bragg to Price, Aug. 12, 27, 1862, *ibid.*, XVII, pt. 2, 677, 688; Bragg to Cooper, Aug. 28, 1862, *ibid.*, XVI, pt. 2, 785; Bragg to Polk, Sept. 11, 1862, *ibid.*, 811.

23. Horn, *Army of Tennessee*, 167; Connelly, *Army of the Heartland*, 223–26.

24. Horn, *Army of Tennessee*, 453n16; McWhiney, *Bragg*, I, 330.

25. Horn, *Army of Tennessee*, 167–68. In fact Bragg had taken 20,000 rifles into Kentucky to arm the anticipated recruits, and he came out with 35,000 rifles. See Connelly, *Army of the Heartland*, 273.

26. Halleck to John M. Schofield, Sept. 20, 1862, *O.R.*, XIII, 654.

27. Buell to Rosecrans, July 28, 1862, *O.R.*, XVI, pt. 2, 221; Buell to G. H. Thomas, July 23, 1862, *ibid.*, 202; Buell to Halleck, Aug. 6, 1862, *ibid.*, 266; Buell to G. H. Thomas, July 31, 1862, *ibid.*, XVI, pt. 2, 237–38; Buell to Halleck, Aug. 24, 29, 1862, *ibid.*, 406–7, 441–42.

28. Buell to Halleck, July 11, 1862, *O.R.*, XVI, pt. 2, 122; Halleck to McClellan, Aug. 7, 1862, *ibid.*, XI, pt. 3, 360.

29. G. W. Morgan to Buell, Aug. 16, 1862, *O.R.*, XVI, pt. 2, 352.

30. Buell to G. H. Thomas, Aug. 28, 1862, *O.R.*, XVI, pt. 2, 439; Buell to Halleck, Sept. 2, 1862, *ibid.*, 470–71. See also: Buell to Halleck, Aug. 16, 1862, *ibid.*, 344; Buell to Lincoln, Sept. 10, 1862, *ibid.*, 500; G. H. Thomas to Buell, Sept. 14, 1862, *ibid.*, 516.

31. Gilbert to Lincoln, Sept. 12, 1862, *O.R.*, XVI, pt. 2, 510.

32. Grant to Halleck, Aug. 9, 16, 1862, *Papers of Grant*, V, 296, 278; General Orders No. 60, Headquarters, District of West Tennessee, *ibid.*, 190.

33. Sherman to John Sherman, Dec. 24, 1861, Oct. 1, 1862, *Sherman Letters*, 136, 165–66; Sherman to Mrs. Sherman, Aug. 10, 1862, *The Home Letters of General Sherman*, ed. M. A. DeWolfe Howe (New York, 1909), 231; Sherman to Rawlins, July 8, 1862, *O.R.*, XVII, pt. 2, 84; McPherson to Halleck, Aug. 24, 1862, *ibid.*, 185; Grant to Halleck, Aug. 20, 1862, *Papers of Grant*, V, 313.

34. Halleck to Sherman, Aug. 25, 1862, *O.R.*, XVII, pt. 2, 186; Sherman to Grant, Aug. 13, 17, Oct. 4, *ibid.*, 166, 179, 259–62.

35. Sherman to Grant, Oct. 4, 1862, *O.R.*, XVII, pt. 2, 259–62.

36. Grant to Halleck, Sept. 1, 3, 1862, *Papers of Grant*, VI, 5, 12; Halleck to Grant, Sept. 11, 1862, *O.R.*, XVII, pt. 2, 214.

37. Van Dorn to Price, Sept. 8, 1862, *O.R.*, XVII, pt. 2, 696.

38. Grant to Halleck, Sept. 15, 1862, *Papers of Grant*, VI, 46.

39. Grant to Halleck, Oct. 22, 1862, *Papers of Grant*, 174–75.

40. Grant to Halleck, Oct. 1, 22, 1862, *Papers of Grant*, VI, 97, 175.

41. Rousseau to Fry, Sept. 13, 1862, *O.R.*, XVI, pt. 2, 513; Buell to Nelson, Sept. 22, 1862, *ibid.*, 533–34. See also: Buell to Anderson, Aug. 22, 1862, *ibid.*, 388; Buell to Bruce, Sept. 6, 1862, *ibid.*, 490; Fry to G. H. Thomas, Sept. 17, 1862, *ibid.*, 522; Buell to Gilbert, Sept. 19, 1862, *ibid.*, 527.

42. Buell to Halleck, Sept. 14, 1862, *O.R.*, XVI, pt. 2, 515.

43. Halleck to Buell, Aug. 8, 12, 1862, *O.R.*, XVI, pt. 2, 286, 314; Wright to Halleck, Aug. 29, 1862, *ibid.*, 448.

44. Horn, *Army of the Tennessee*, 168–69; Connelly, *Army of the Heartland*, 229–30.

45. Bragg to Cooper, Sept. 12, 17, 25, 1862, *O.R.*, XVI, pt. 2, 815, pt. 1, 968, pt. 2, 876; Bragg to Van Dorn, Sept. 25, 1862, *ibid.*, XVII, pt. 2, 713.

46. Grant to Halleck, Oct. 5, 1862, *Papers of Grant*, VI, 118.

47. McWhiney, *Bragg*, I, 275–76, 303–7.

48. Horn, *Army of Tennessee*, 454–55n50, n52; Connelly, *Army of the Heartland*, 255–65.

49. Horn, *Army of Tennessee*, 185.

50. Connelly, *Army of the Heartland*, 266–72.

51. Van Dorn to Randolph, October 12, 1862, *O.R.*, XVII, pt. 2, 727.

52. Lee to Loring, Sept. 25, 1862, *O.R.*, XIX, pt. 2, 625–26; Lee to Davis, Sept. 13, 1862, *Wartime Papers*, 306–7; Lee to Davis, Sept. 25, 1862, *O.R.*, XIX, pt. 2, 626–7.

53. McClellan to Halleck, Sept. 22, 27, 1862, *O.R.*, XIX, pt. 2, 342–43, pt. 1, 70–71; McClellan to L. Thomas, Aug. 4, 1863, *ibid.*, pt. 1, 79–80.

54. Halleck to Grant, Oct. 8, 1862, *O.R.*, XVII, pt. 1, 156; Grant to Halleck, Oct. 8, 1862 (two communications), *Papers of Grant*, VI, 133, 134; "Chase Diary," 52, entry of Aug. 1, 1862.

55. Buell to Halleck, Oct. 16, 17, 1862, *O.R.*, XVI, pt. 2, 619, 622.

56. Halleck to Rosecrans, Oct. 1, 1862, *O.R.*, XVII, pt. 2, 251; Grant to Halleck, Sept. 20, 1862, *ibid.*, pt. 1, 64; "Chase Diary," 52; Halleck to H. G. Wright, Aug. 25, 1862, *O.R.*, XVI, pt. 2, 421.

57. Lee to Davis, Sept. 23, 28, 1862, *O.R.*, XIX pt. 2, 622–23, 633; Lee to G. W. Smith, Oct. 9, 1862, *ibid.*, 658–59; Randolph to Lee, Oct. 8, 1862, *ibid.*, 656–57.

58. Lee to Randolph, Oct. 16, 25, Nov. 17, 1862, *O.R.*, XIX, pt. 2, 669, 681, *Wartime Papers*, 337–38; Lee to Davis, Oct. 22, Nov. 25, 1862, *O.R.*, XIX, pt. 2, 675, *Wartime Papers*, 345–46; Lee to G. W. Smith, Sept. 24, 1862, *O.R.*, XIX, pt. 2, 624–25.

59. McClellan to Halleck, Sept. 22, 27, Oct. 7, 1862, *O.R.*, XIX, pt. 2, 342–43, pt. 1, 70–71, pt. 1, 11–12; Halleck to McClellan, Sept. 26, 1862, *ibid.*, pt. 2, 360. See also: Halleck to McClellan, Oct. 6, 19, 1862, *ibid.*, pt. 1, 72, pt. 2, 442–43; Ingalls to Haupt, Oct. 12, 1862, *ibid.*, pt. 2, 414.

60. Lincoln to McClellan, Oct. 13, 1862, Basler, *Collected Works*, V, 460–62. The maxim quoted by Lincoln is from Jomini. See: Baron de Jomini, *The Art of War*, trans. G. H. Mendell and W. P. Craighill (Westport, Conn., 1971, a reprint of the 1862 edition), 80. Here Jomini is quoting from chapter 14 of his *Traité des grandes opérations militaire*. For so extensive a maneuver Jomini did not use the term "turning movement," treating it instead under the concept of base of operations. Lincoln's exposition here and the situation itself are perhaps more consistent with Jomini's base of operations approach than with the turning movement. See: *Art of War*, 77–84, 178–79, 188, 204–7.

61. Lincoln to McClellan, Oct. 25, 1862, Basler, *Collected Works*, V, 474; McClellan to Halleck, Oct. 25, 1862, *O.R.*, XIX, pt. 1, 84; Halleck to McClellan, Oct. 26, 1862, *ibid.*, 85; *Welles Diary*, 177; Halleck to Mrs. Halleck, Oct. 7, 1862, Wilson, "Halleck," 559.

62. Miers, *Lee*, 111.

63. Among some recent views of McClellan are, Hagerman, "The Professionalization of George B. McClellan"; Joseph L. Harsh, "On the McClellan-Go-Round," *Battles Lost and Won; Essays from Civil War History*, ed. John T. Hubbell (Westport, Conn., London, 1975), 55–72; Adams, *Our Masters the Rebels*, 90–97 and *passim*.

IO ☆ CONSOLIDATION AND ORGANIZATION

G. T. Beauregard

LINCOLN'S DECISION to announce a preliminary emancipation proclamation directly after the Union success that forced Lee to abandon the Maryland raid had complex roots. For more than any other reason Lincoln resorted to this political move in order to blunt some of the increasing radical Republican criticisms. Although at this point Lincoln still remained far short of seriously considering the use of black soldiers, that important military development grew logically out of freeing the slaves. Lincoln himself still remained indifferent toward total abolition and eventual integration. He preferred compensated emancipation, which in fact he urged Congress to approve, and colonization of the blacks outside the country. The previous August he had told a delegation of westerners, who offered two Negro regiments from Indiana, that he was not prepared to enlist Negroes as soldiers, but he did suggest using them as laborers. The editor of the New York *Tribune*, Horace Greeley, epitomized the more extreme pro-black position held by the radical Republicans with his stirring column, "The Prayer of Twenty Millions," questioning the President's policy on slavery. Lincoln had replied by writing, "I would save the Union. I would save it the shortest way under the Constitution. . . . If I could save the Union without freeing *any* slave I would do it, and if I could save it by freeing *all* the slaves I would do it; and if I could save it by freeing some and leaving others alone I would also do that."[1]

Lincoln earlier had endured difficulties with two generals' overstepping their authority and taking it upon themselves to announce emancipation. That had been the final straw which brought Fremont's downfall in Missouri. Ironically the very officer who immediately replaced Fremont, but only for one week, Major General David Hunter, later and in another theater repeated Fremont's action. Hunter proclaimed freedom for the slaves in the sea islands of South Carolina. Lincoln had ordered both decisions reversed. The time was not yet ripe.

But on August 25, 1862, the day before the Second Bull Run campaign began, with Lincoln's approval War Secretary Stanton authorized Major General Butler, in command of the southern department, to "receive into the service of the United States" Negro soldiers up to 5,000 in number and to train them as guards for plantations and settlements. The first regiment of free Negroes mustered into service at New Orleans on September 27. Earlier Hunter, in June, 1862, had organized a regiment of blacks that remained unofficially in existence until finally, after the first of the next year, it gained legal status as the First South Carolina Volunteers (African Descent). Hunter had responded humorously to an angry official inquiry as to whether or not he had formed a regiment of fugitive slaves. No indeed, Hunter replied, "No regiment of 'fugitive slaves' has been, or is being, organized in this department. There is, however, a fine regiment of loyal persons whose late masters are 'fugitive rebels.'" Doubtless this literary gem, circulating among the Washington social circuit and dispelling some of the public gloom over McClellan's failure on the Virginia Peninsula, was authored by Hunter's useful staff officer, the Ireland-born immigrant, Lieutenant Colonel Charles G. Halpine.[2]

One of the Civil War's more significant minor characters, Halpine, in addition to his staff work which even Halleck admired, published quite a lot of tension-releasing humor under the pseudonym "Private Miles O'Reilly" and otherwise proved a most effective propagandist in promoting public acceptance of using Negroes as soldiers. Halpine himself managed to miss out on achieving much historical fame in part by his poor luck. Before the Civil War, because of a meaningless feud, he lost an opportunity during the 1860 presidential campaign to become the first biographer of Abraham Lincoln. And perhaps as important as any reason, Halpine never got much publicity because he himself did not seek it; his biographer called him "a publicist, but not a self-publicist."[3]

Because widespread opposition to the use of Negroes as soldiers abounded among northern whites, Halpine faced quite a task overcoming it. And, to be sure, he himself was not an unprejudiced man: "The contrabands," he wrote, even while he enjoyed luxuries that the superabundance of cheaply hired black servants provided the army headquarters in South Carolina, "are numerous and ought all to be drowned." But his remarkable literary gifts proved effective in blunting opposition to blacks as soldiers by producing a popular song which almost everyone, except blacks, found marvelously funny: "Sambo's Right to be Kilt."

> Some tell us 'tis a burnin' shame
>   To make the naygers fight;
> And that the thrade of being' kilt
>   Belongs but to the white;
> But as for me, upon my sowl!
>   So liberal are we here,
> I'll let Sambo be murthered instead of myself,
>   On every day in the year.

And so on and on for many often-sung verses the words quite effectively persuaded numerous "whites to accept blacks as soldiers without in the least disturbing their fundamental prejudices against Negroes." Lincoln loved it, and told his secretary that it reminded him of what a church deacon said when a prostitute dropped five dollars into the collection plate: "No matter how she got it, the money was good and would do good." And do good "Sambo's Right To Be Kilt," for all its crude cruelty, did indeed. It became a hit among prejudiced whites everywhere, and especially among the New York Irish, who numbered among the bitterest foes of the Lincoln administration and who before had viciously opposed enlistment of black troops.[4]

What little resistance the song did not break down was dissipated by the Negroes' soldierly conduct. Before the war ended, 178,892 Negroes officially had served in the Union army, including some 7,000 noncommissioned officers and about 100 commissioned officers, virtually all at company-grade ranks, with less than a handful in field grades. Some of the black soldiers, 1,624, later transferred to the navy or to other branches of the public service. An indefinite number of other blacks unofficially served in the federal ranks, such as the occasional cooks.[5]

The Confederacy, of course, made military use of Negroes, too, as, for example, on October 10, 1862, when President Davis asked Virginia for a draft of 4,500 blacks to work on completion of the fortifications of Richmond. Obviously all the work in behalf of the southern war effort performed by blacks whites would otherwise have had to do, and so the Negroes—some quite willingly, and others under coercion—played significant roles. Throughout the Confederacy, for the war's duration, thousands of blacks dug field fortifications and threw up earthworks around cities and towns so that, as one scholar has so succinctly stated, "whites could fight more and dig less." In some instances military and local authorities impressed free blacks, paying them a private's wage of $11 per month.[6]

Despite a grave hesitancy on the part of high rebel leaders and scattered opposition, black troops even mustered into southern military ranks. Early in the war some of the Confederate states accepted Negroes into local units, and they drilled and paraded with white troops "at a time when," as Horace Greeley phrased it, "this would not have been tolerated in the armies of the Union." In the fall of 1861 several hundred Memphis Negroes had joined in a Confederate rally "brimful of patriotism, shouting for Jeff Davis and singing war songs." Davis himself remained opposed to enlistment of black troops until nearly the very end of the war, but he did revealingly once say that "should the alternative ever be presented of subjugation or of the employment of the slave as a soldier, there seems no reason to doubt what should be our decision." On March 13, 1865, the Confederate Congress belatedly passed an act authorizing the enrollment of 300,000 slaves in the army, with clear implication and general understanding that if the South attained its freedom, so also would these slave-soldiers. The blacks mustered, formed several companies, trained, drilled, and even paraded in some southern cities. But all this came too late and the war ended before the black units accompanied Confederate armies into combat.[7]

In the late summer and early fall of 1862 the tremendous success that the Union later enjoyed in recruitment and use of Negro troops remained only a dim promise of the future, and meanwhile the state-based system of raising forces resulted in a near-crisis situation. The South had no monopoly on states'-rights philosophy and suffered unexclusively from the difficulties of conservative attitudes and reactions engendered by it. Indeed, at the outset the North compared disadvantageously with the South, for the Confederate states at least shared cohesive common interests and goals. In the more complexly held-together and motivated North, states'-rights attitudes permeated the federal structure; as a consequence so also did they infuse the Union army organization.

When the war began, the administratively inferior condition of the federal government, as compared to that of the states, made it logical and expedient that the northern state governments carry out the details of mustering forces. The weakest element from the start in the federal administration had been War Secretary Cameron's ineptness. For that very reason Treasury Secretary Salmon P. Chase had assumed such a wide and flexible function, ranging far outside of the purview of the Treasury, and he had had much to do with the early appointments of high-ranking generals such as McDowell and McClellan. It had been Chase who drafted the orders for the enlargement of the regular army and for the creation on May 3, 1861, of the new federal volunteer army.

Federal officials early realized the importance of inducing short-term enlistees to remain in service, but that always proved difficult to accomplish. They tested a variety of expedients in the process of trying to prod militiamen to accept three-year terms; in some instances reluctant citizen-soldiers were "stripped of all clothing except underwear and kicked by all from the Colonel down" while others were "stripped of their arms, a white feather stuck over each ear and [they were] marched out . . . with the drums playing the Rogue's March. Crowds of people assembled to see them undergo the degrading penance." But however they did it, and in precious few instances did they do it very efficiently, the northern states continued in the responsibility of raising and maintaining the ranks of the troop units.[8]

This also conferred upon the state governments the privilege of selection of all officers from colonels to corporals and even to a degree in choosing generals, although the Lincoln government exercised considerable influence and regulation over general officer appointments. It not only provided a tremendous element of patronage for the state governors, it also ensured that the states retained, to a considerable extent, control of their units' destinies as well. "The greatest mistake made in our civil war," no less an authority than William T. Sherman later proclaimed, "was in the mode of recruitment and promotion." He continued, "When a regiment became reduced by the necessary wear and tear of service, instead of being filled up at the bottom, and the vacancies among the officers filled from the best non-commissioned officers and men, the habit was to raise new regiments, with new colonels, captains, and men, leaving the old and experienced battalions to dwindle away into mere skeleton organizations." Sherman offered sound reasons in favor of a different practice: "I believe that five hundred new men added to an old and experienced regiment were more valuable than a thousand men in the form of a new regiment, for the former by association with good, experienced captains, lieutenants, and non-commissioned officers, soon became veterans, whereas the latter were generally unavailable for a year."[9]

An episode involving War Secretary Stanton and then-Lieutenant Colonel James Harrison Wilson, otherwise a much more perspicacious soldier, illustrates that Stanton gradually came to realize the undesirable results of the states' dabbling in such matters. Wilson wrote a letter to a member of the Senate urging reorganization of, and new recruits to fill, the Second New York Cavalry, "although worn down to four troops," still "one of the best regiments in the service." Stanton angrily called Wilson in for an accounting and blasted: "By God, Sir, I am surprised! . . . If you had been one of those damned volunteers, I should have thought nothing of it, but, coming from you, Sir, a regular, who ought to know better, I am surprised, Sir, that you should write such a letter to any one except through the official channels." In spite of all its efforts the Union simply failed to reach its recruiting goals and organizational aspirations until 1863.[10]

A slight improvement in systematization of recruiting tided the Union over the winter of 1861–62, but the year of campaigning that followed—from the Seven Days' Battles through the spring of 1863—while the South proceeded to reap maximum benefit from its draft, marked the time of greatest Confederate and poorest Union efficiency.

General Upton characterized the situation at the time of the Seven Days' Battles as one in which the U.S. "government and the Confederates conducted war on contrary principles. The Government sought to save the Union by fighting as a Confederacy; the Confederates sought to destroy it by fighting as a nation." Referring to the state-based recruiting system, Upton explained that the "government recognized the states, appealed to them for troops, adhered to voluntary enlistments, gave the governors power to appoint all commissioned officers and encouraged them to organize new regiments." He scathingly contrasted the North's states'-rights approach with the enemy's ruthless centralization. He pointed out that the "Confederates abandoned State sovereignty, appealed directly to the people, took away from them the power to appoint commissioned officers, vested their appointment in the Confederate President, refused to organize war regiments, abandoned voluntary enlistments, and, adopting the republican principle that every citizen owes his country military service, called into the army every white man between ages of 18 and 35."[11]

During the first two years of the war the Union army diminished because of short-term enlistments, death, desertion, and sickness more rapidly than they could recruit men by the indirect means employed. When the ordinary methods failed, two alternatives remained: either to draft or to raise bounties to such an extent as to make them irresistibly tempting. The Union tried both, the draft initially in the form of a compulsory nine-month militia term. Those men drafted for this nine-month period could then volunteer instead for three years and receive a bonus of $100. The Militia Act of July 17, 1862, called for a draft of 300,000 men to serve nine months. On the surface it might appear that this signaled a federal supremacy and a diminution of states'-rights induced inefficiency and resistance, but such was not the case; the entire procedure still depended upon state administration. It far missed the mark in attaining numerical goals, and the partial benefits often came late. The returns came in from the several states so slowly that finally, on November 24, 1862, nearly three months after the expected completion of the draft, the War Department asked fourteen slack governors to report by telegraph immediately. The governor of Maryland replied that not all the counties had finished; the report from Massachusetts indicated that its draft had not been scheduled until December 8; and the Wisconsin governor stated, "We drafted 4,500. How many will come in and not be exempted it is impossible to tell." It proved later to be a mere 958. Other states also responded vaguely and sluggishly. The militia draft of 1862 had failed. It brought in an estimated 87,588—just over 25 percent of the goal—and of course many of them were short-term enlistees. The Union endured one more winter before resorting to a federal draft, because winter brought a time of somewhat diminished campaigning and, more importantly, a time when seasonal unemployment mounted, creating more volunteers from among a surplus labor population seeking steady employment until the following spring.[12]

With his successful administration and operation of conscription in the South, Confederate War Secretary Randolph succeeded in making his most significant contribution. Randolph further applied his keen mind to formulating a revision of the system that Congress incorporated into law with the September 27, 1862, second Conscription Act. It extended the upper age limits of men that the President could call in a draft from thirty-five to forty-five, a permission that Davis had requested from Congress in his August message to that body. But Randolph carefully calculated that age forty as a cut-off point should provide a sufficient number of men. He examined the 1850 census and from it estimated that this would give the Confederacy a total potential manpower pool of 863,500. With probably three-sevenths of this number exempted, there still would be 493,500 possible soldiers, and in fact that approximated the largest force the government had any hope of feeding, clothing, and arming. This figure, 5 percent of the Confederacy's total population, exceeded in proportion the number of men any European power had ever previously placed into the field. Davis accepted Randolph's views and limited the call to men under forty.

Randolph capably managed the conscription process, despite some difficulties and clashes with state officials. He agreed at one point during a dispute with the governor of Virginia to abide by the decision of Virginia's supreme court—a soothing diplomatic ploy. To the governor of Georgia he wrote, "I think we might as well drive out the common enemy before we make war on each other." Randolph settled all the severely ruffled feelings and the draft kept operating satisfactorily; he eventually lost his job because of quite another matter—his inability to work sufficiently well with Davis's collaborative system of strategy-making and management.[13]

After they performed effectively together in the summer of 1862, it thereafter became clear that Randolph and Davis "did not make a team." The President regarded Randolph as an indifferent administrator and Randolph, already dying of tuberculosis, most likely lacked the energy to do his part even in an adequately staffed headquarters. The "Rebel War Clerk," J. B. Jones, who kept a gossipy diary now prized by historians, wrote caustically of Randolph. However, we must be wary of Jones's assessment, as the clerk believed that Randolph's political advancement resulted from his distinguished ancestry. Jones not only felt that Randolph lacked initiative, but he also considered him inefficient. Brigadier General Wise, the hapless defender of Roanoke Island, who quite probably wished to become secretary of war, remarked that the country had no one in the office. "What is Randolph?" one of his subordinates querried. The general replied, "He is not Secretary of War; he is merely a *clerk*, an underling, and cannot hold up his head in his humiliating position."[14]

Relations between the President and the secretary of war grew increasingly cool and came to a climax in November, 1862. Randolph had begun to chafe under the desire for more discretionary power, perhaps the degree that had been accorded Lee. Without Davis's knowledge he sent an important order on October 27 to Lieutenant General Theophilus H. Holmes directing a major strategic alteration in the array of forces in the western and trans-Mississippi theatres. Davis informed Randolph that all future orders must go through the proper channel and that all matters of strategy as well as officer selection should be referred to the President before final action. Randolph tendered his resignation, which Davis accepted at once. Randolph left his office with considerable unfinished business that he easily could have dispatched, but he was not even willing to remain until a successor arrived.

Randolph later criticized Davis's lack of "system," his slowness, his lack of "time to discharge the duties of the office," and his inability to "discriminate between important and unimportant matters." Randolph also said: The President possesses "no practical knowledge of the workings of our military system in the field and frequently mars it by theories which he has had no opportunity to correct by personal observation and in which he will not permit amendment from the experience of others." Since Randolph felt that Davis meant well and understood "the abstract principles of military organization," he did not "apprehend disaster from his absorption of the office of Secretary of War."[15]

Thus Randolph reflected a popular notion that existed within the Confederacy. A southern general echoed the sentiment when he stated that "there is no Secretary of War," and that the War Department had been "razeed" down to a "second-class bureau of which the President himself is the chief." This overlooked that Davis, like Lincoln, felt he must keep in his hands all fundamental decisions about major troop movements and relied on his war secretary and, to a lesser degree, Adjutant and Inspector General Cooper as collaborators and advisors. Davis also conferred with principal field and area commanders when they visited Richmond and always had a flow of advice from Robert E. Lee, frequently by mail and occasionally in person. Every secretary of war influenced the President's ideas, as indeed Davis desired, to a greater or lesser degree depending primarily upon the personality and ability of the secretary; in the end Randolph stood at the bottom of the list, having had the least direct influence of them all.[16]

Nevertheless, he had contributed significantly to conscription, and he left another lasting legacy: Realizing the need for a better organization of the western armies, he worked with Davis in completing the fundamental departmental reorganization begun under Lee. Under Randolph, then, two major themes of Confederate war direction emerged: total practical mobilization of manpower and a workable and responsive approach to departmental organization, one which effectively reconciled local and national defense.

After Randolph's resignation, the President temporarily brought in Major General Gustavus W. Smith to keep the departmental machinery running. A West Pointer who primarily possessed technical and engineering interests, Smith had been employed momentarily as acting commander of the Army of Northern Virginia when Johnston had been wounded the previous May and before Robert E. Lee had been assigned to command. One Cabinet member revealed that Davis had three men in mind to replace Randolph: Joseph E. Johnston, Smith, and James A. Seddon. It would have been surprising had Davis selected Johnston since there had been friction in their personal relations. Smith might have had a chance for the place permanently had he not been so unpopular with both soldiers and civilians, as well as being a close friend of Johnston's and at the same time admitting little respect for Robert E. Lee. After Davis chose Seddon to be the new war secretary, Smith returned to military duty but soon resigned to become superintendent of an iron works in Georgia.

James Alexander Seddon, the Confederacy's fourth secretary of war, prominent Richmond lawyer and former U.S. and Confederate congressman, took office on November 21, 1862. Though his frail and sickly appearance made him look anything but warlike, he became the South's most effective war secretary. Save for Lee, he was Davis's most influential collaborator. Jones, the war clerk, thought that Seddon looked much better than his predecessor Randolph who, Jones said, "looked like a monkey." But the cadaverous Seddon surely cut a less-than-imposing figure. Rumors alleged that one could hear the rattle of his bones as he descended the stairways of his hotel. His complexion reflected a deathlike pallor and he wore his long, straggling hair under a skull cap which, together with his prominent nose, prompted many observers to think he looked like an old and sickly rabbi. Jones, with his characteristic overstatement, once wrote: "Mr. Secretary Seddon, who usually wears a sallow and cadaverous look, which, coupled with his emaciation, makes him resemble an exhumed corpse after a month's interment, looks today like a galvanized corpse which had been buried two months." But Seddon's looks were deceiving for, in spite of his frail frame, he exemplified industry and vigor. Despite tongue-in-cheek remarks like his promise to the northern invader about "hospitable graves . . . six feet to each . . . and a few inches more to their leader," poking fun at Lincoln's unusual height, he exercised considerable influence upon the South's military strategy.[17]

Like Randolph, Seddon had too many meetings that lasted too long. Though he found these conferences with Davis tedious and often unproductive, it was here that strategic decisions were fashioned, largely by Davis, Seddon, and Cooper. The keen mind of the intelligent secretary soon grasped the essentials of strategy and logistics. At home with day-to-day decisions about military operations, Seddon fulfilled many of the functions of a chief of staff. But his very effective and beneficial absorption in operations meant that logistics received inadequate attention. The weakness of the understaffed Confederate headquarters organization resulted in administrative vigor stretched too thin, and operations, daily pressing for decisions, pre-empted attention.

Seddon's propensities and ideas often placed him in sympathy with the western concentration bloc, an informal organization of great importance in the Confederacy. Unlike the relationships existing in a single office or among the individuals and groups within the Union War Department, this informal organization consisted of a network which spread across almost the entire Confederacy and embraced individuals with various previous associations and very diverse goals. This significant coalition began emerging during the fall of 1862. A powerful and complex group, it grew from a combination of four interrelated sub-blocs. The Abingdon-Columbia bloc, an intricate set of family relationships and the kin of General Joseph E. Johnston, comprised many powerful families which at one time flourished in the Abingdon, Virginia, vicinity and had gradually migrated either to South Carolina or to Kentucky.

Friendships, common strategic views, or particular antagonisms brought additional individuals into the other sub-blocs. Resentment against General Braxton Bragg, increasingly unpopular in command of the Army of Tennessee, bound together a second faction, one of the most militant of all informal groups within the Confederacy, the anti-Bragg bloc. Not all who disliked Bragg were members; subordinate generals within the Army of Tennessee, who formed a coalition late in 1862 to oust him, comprised the true anti-Bragg faction. A third group, the Kentucky sub-bloc, included a number of prominent Kentucky generals and politicians who maintained close relationships throughout the war. General Bragg's two alleged sins—questioning Kentucky's courage and failing, in his Kentucky raid, to recapture the state—bound them to the anti-Bragg bloc and to several other members of the various informal organizations. These people all shared the common and pervasive "Kentucky dream" to push the southern frontier to its natural geographic boundary, the Ohio River.

A fourth and even more widely ranging association revolved around the personality and ideas of General P. G. T. Beauregard. The Creole assiduously sought influence, keeping up a correspondence with many generals including his former subordinate, Bragg. William Porcher Miles of the House Military Affairs Committee and Louis T. Wigfall of the Senate Military Affairs Committee belonged to Beauregard's informal organization. Representative of the interrelationship of these groups was Texas Senator Wigfall's close personal association with Joseph E. Johnston. As Beauregard had commanded in the East as well as West and southeast, almost every officer in the Confederate army had served under him. One theme dominated his tireless correspondence: the need to use the railroad and the telegraph to apply on a national scale the Napoleonic strategy of an offensive concentration at the enemy's weak point. He became both the strategist and the publicist of the western concentration bloc, not only because of his extensive overlapping contacts but because he perceived the Tennessee and Kentucky area as the Union's weak point and he wished to direct a surpirse Confederate concentration against Rosecrans's army.

The combination of these four informal organizations formed the western concentration bloc. Its sub-blocs all agreed on one policy: reinforce the Tennessee and Kentucky line of operations. Through its various contacts, such as Senator Wigfall's attendance at law school with Secretary Seddon, it constantly lobbied for a strategy which would reinforce the Army of Tennessee with troops from Virginia. The western concentration bloc lasted for the war's duration and enjoyed a large voice in determining the military strategy belatedly adopted by the beleaguered Confederacy.[18]

In view of what social psychologists have learned about the informal organization as an institution within human society, this development should hardly surprise knowledgeable students. Indeed, it would have been striking if something similar to the western concentration bloc and its constituent informal organizations had not formed. As but recently born entities, the Confederate government and its army created new lines of authority. This new formal structure overlaid pre-existing networks of relationships that could not be erased immediately by the temporary authority of a newly established army. Extensive kinship networks, which predated the Confederate army's birth, survived far longer. Equally important, ties also survived from earlier organizations, such as the U.S. Army and the federal and state governments in which many Confederate leaders had served. The events of the Civil War hardly could erase residuals of such prior relationships as superior-subordinate, fellow officer, legislator, or uncle-nephew. Quite naturally when these informal structures developed, as they inevitably did, they followed pre-existing lines of relationship.[19]

Late in 1862 the western concentration bloc and its "uncrowned leader," Beauregard, evolved as an informal organization of significant potency in its conflict with the formal organization it overlapped. During its long existence, individual plans often varied, but reinforcement for the West remained the bloc's consistent refrain. Usually this involved a concentration in Tennessee for an offensive into Kentucky, whether or not it was specifically animated by Beauregard's concept that Rosecrans commanded the weakest Union army. Sometimes the friction between formal and informal organizations can be intense, such as that of the struggle of the western concentration bloc for greater recognition for their region. In the case of the Confederacy and its western concentration bloc, the conflict finally resolved at the end of the summer of 1863 when this diverse informal group fully won over the formal structure which adopted its strategic ideas.

Confederate strategy, always guided by President Davis, but inevitably also molded by the war secretaries and various generals whom Davis involved in the process, reached a fresh peak of maturity by the winter of 1862–63. Remaining consistent with his concern for safeguarding the resources and manpower of the Confederacy's entire geographic area, Davis evolved the implementing techniques from earlier fragmented experiments into a system of coherent regional commands and a simplified integration of strategic movements at the national level.

Neglecting logistics, Davis and his staff emerged as effective grand strategists. Except in the West, the Confederacy began with a fragmented array of miniature departments. By the spring of 1862 they were being consolidated rapidly, markedly enhancing unity of command. Progress was materially arrested in the summer when East Tennessee was separated from Bragg's western department, resulting in a lack of coordination between Bragg and Kirby Smith during their Kentucky operation. Equally detrimental to unity of command was Bragg's blunder in establishing the dual control of Price and Van Dorn in Mississippi. Decisive action from Richmond reorganized this structure and, before Secretary Randolph left office, Davis took the logical step of providing unity to the then-three western departments by establishing a single one at a higher level, the Department of the West, which embraced them all. On November 24 General Joseph E. Johnston accepted the assignment to command it. Johnston, too, proved an advocate of the ideas espoused by the western concentration bloc, because he willingly cast as secondary any efforts to conserve the Confederate hold upon the Mississippi River segment between Vicksburg and Port Hudson in order to bring the fullest force possible to bear for recovering and retaining Tennessee.

Since Davis knew that the Confederates could not "hope at all points to meet the enemy with a force equal to his own," he sought in the West, as elsewhere, to find "security in the concentration and rapid movement of troops." For this reason he ordered Johnston to coordinate Pemberton's Mississippi department with Bragg's in Middle Tennessee and Kirby Smith's in East Tennessee. Relieved of the burden of administration, Johnston had as his only mission strategic coordination. Davis found inspiration in the example of Bragg's successful summer troop movement by rail from Mississippi to Tennessee, and he intended Johnston "to operate in Napoleon's manner" by uniting "the forces in Mississippi and Tennessee in whichever might be first attacked." Gloomy about the difficulties of trying to coordinate two such distant departments, Johnston thought, like Randolph, that the Mississippi and trans-Mississippi armies should be the two to cooperate. However, the absence of rail communication in the trans-Mississippi area made that plan less realistic than the coordination of the Mississippi and Tennessee theatres, so dramatically bound together for Bragg's Kentucky campaign. Actually, reinforcing Mississippi was the difficult problem; reinforcing Tennessee was not. The distance from Charleston, South Carolina, to Chattanooga was only about two-thirds the distance from Jackson, Mississippi, to Chattanooga. Even Richmond lay closer to Chattanooga than Jackson and there were two departments en route, Western Virginia and East Tennessee, which meant that East Tennessee and Virginia would provide a full pipeline for conveying troops in either direction. Such a strategic union would be beneficial for the Virginia and Tennessee theatres, but it would leave Mississippi without a regional commander to provide prompt reinforcement. Tennessee and Mississippi were, therefore, linked, and movements between Tennessee and Virginia were in the hands of the War Department.[20]

As a western commander, Johnston became an advocate of reinforcement for the West. He regarded Middle Tennessee as the critical area—the most menaced and most important to defend. To Johnston the Mississippi River, more a barrier than an avenue for the Confederates, seemed far less important strategically. To Davis it was "clearly developed that the enemy has two principal objects in view, one to get possession of the Mississippi River and the other the capital of the Confederate States." This difference in strategic priorities between the President and the general would not be a problem until the spring. In the meantime, Johnston made his arrangements to move troops between Mississippi and Tennessee and, stressing to Davis and Seddon the weakness of Bragg's army, proved to be an effective advocate of the point of view of the western concentration bloc.[21]

Since the major source of western reinforcements was the Army of Northern Virginia, Lee became the bloc's natural adversary. The bloc wanted Davis to order some of the Virginia army's troops west; Lee opposed it. President Davis and Secretary Seddon stood in the middle between Lee and the westerners. The President and the secretary found the position a difficult one, because Lee was no ordinary department commander. Though he had ceased to discharge the duties of his formal position in charge of military operations, Lee retained a powerful informal position as Davis's advisor. Lee's status as the Confederacy's most successful army commander, combined with the President's great respect for Lee's judgment and Davis's feelings of close personal friendship, dictated that Lee's position ranked far above that of a mere department commander resisting the transfer of troops from his army.

In any lobbying effort with Davis, Lee, therefore, could match the aggregation of generals and politicians making up the western concentration bloc. Their margin of strength came from the quality of the military concept which Beauregard advanced. Use of the railroad for a surprise concentration was hardly a new idea. The Confederacy had used it at First Bull Run, Shiloh, and the Seven Days' Battles. Beauregard now advocated something different: he proposed a concentration for an offensive. He wanted to seize the initiative. The other distinctive feature of Beauregard's proposal was that the surprise offensive concentration against a weak enemy was to be national, though "not by abandoning all other points, however, but by a proper selection of the point of attack—the Yankees themselves," he wrote, "tell us where" by revealing their weakness. Beauregard stood upon sound ground in advocating so orthodox a concept as concentrating against weakness, a decision which Lee had made in the summer of 1862 when he attacked Pope rather than McClellan. Lee, as the most successful practioner of this strategy, would find it difficult to disagree with Beauregard's plea to view "the whole theatre of war as one subject of which all points were but integral parts." By the winter of 1862–63 Johnston's advocacy of the needs of Tennessee would confront Lee with the power of the western concentration bloc.[22]

President Davis thus made his strategic decisions in an environment in which the western concentration bloc persistently tried to bend them to conform to their regional predilections and to Beauregard's concept of an offensive concentration. At the same time the President had to contend with a situation in which the informal leader, Beauregard, did not command in the West and with the factionalism engendered in the western armies, particularly by the anti-Bragg bloc. In the East Davis was fortunate in having Lee, by his personality and success, establish his authority over the Army of Northern Virginia, which Beauregard had first commanded and then Joe

Johnston. Similarly, full harmony existed in strategic views between Davis and his favorite general and former chief of staff.

Whereas President Davis had personnel problems and strategic differences with his western command, Lincoln had comparable difficulties with his principal eastern army but enjoyed considerable harmony in the West. In appointing Halleck general in chief, Lincoln had placed in command a regular officer with genuine prestige in the army and substantial informal allegiance in his former western command. In thus bringing in an officer with both informal and formal claims to authority, the Union President significantly strengthened the long-ambiguous post of general in chief. The ease with which Buell's removal took place illustrates the strength and legitimacy of Halleck's and Lincoln's authority in the West. Though Buell had the loyalty of many and was liked by almost all of the senior officers of his army, all acquiesced in his removal and were loyal to Rosecrans.

The situation differed in the Army of the Potomac, where the removal of McClellan deprived that force of its creator and natural leader. Neither Halleck nor Lincoln enjoyed sufficient informal legitimacy fully to dominate that army and its senior generals. In fact the strategic ideas of Lincoln and army headquarters were always suspect among officers who resented the administration's treatment of McClellan and perceived any doctrine or strategy emanating from Washington as suspect, because they felt that it must be influenced by McClellan's opponents and by political radicals. Similarly, Lincoln found it difficult to pick a commander for that army who could secure the full allegiance of its senior officers, many of whom were still loyal to McClellan, his memory, and his strategy.[23]

If informal relationships handicapped its control of the Army of the Potomac, the Lincoln administration was especially fortunate in the informal structure of its Washington headquarters. This had been true to a striking degree even before Stanton organized the War Board. Totten, the chief engineer, for example, inquired at the outset if General Winfield Scott "would like to have Major Barnard attached to his personal staff as an Engineer Officer, attending daily at his office for instructions." Furthermore, and most significantly, Totten occasionally offered propositions on an informal basis, which could be considered, implemented, or filed and forgotten with a minimum of official fluster. Totten also helped Meigs to facilitate supply improvements, as in one instance when the engineer chief sent a personal recommendation to the quartermaster general in behalf of a horse supplier whom he knew. Totten later reflected: I was not " 'called out' for meddling with other people's business, but I was 'thought hard of' I am sure." In fact, he functioned very smoothly. Stanton himself bore witness to "the general diligence, ability, and fidelity manifested" not only by Totten and Meigs, but "by the Chiefs of the Several Bureaux of this Department," he reported.

"Whatever success may have attended its administration is, in a great measure, due to them and their subordinates."[24]

Indeed Stanton was a master manager. The various bureaus all worked in harmony, and then submitted detailed reports to him. Though he and his assistant secretaries managed very well in coordinating departmental activities, the brief formal existence of the War Board had helped in this immeasurably. In all the War Board activities as well as the ongoing functioning of the federal War Department, the striking degree of involvement of the assistant secretaries and especially the peripatetic field service performed by Thomas A. Scott and John Tucker stand out. Regardless of their titles, they functioned as sub-chiefs of staff, involved in personnel, intelligence, and supply matters constantly and even occasionally reporting on and evaluating operational matters as well. Noteworthy among the many functionaries that Stanton variously employed to provide input based upon personal investigations, observations, and evaluations in the field was Tom Scott. A most useful "Johnny on the Spot," Scott offered the important virtue of an uncanny ability to make hasty but rather accurate estimates of problems being encountered by forces, envision effective remedies, and make reasonable prescriptions.

To a somewhat lesser extent, the War Board had become involved in strategy determination. This was particularly true with Hitchcock's activities, as he always envisioned his primary and proper functions to be within that realm. The War Board arrived at one of the more crucial decisions in this respect when they concurred with Lincoln's apprehension that McClellan had not adequately planned for the security of Washington during the Peninsula campaign and had helped the President resolve to retain McDowell's corps.

But generally Stanton and his corps of assistants were seeking to facilitate logistics, not operations. Tucker, Scott, generals Lorenzo Thomas and Meigs, the journalist assistant war secretary Charles A. Dana, Stanton's military aide Edward Richard Sprigg Canby, and even such an unlikely individual as one lieutenant who officially served as Fremont's aide all worked as Stanton's special agents. They reported on things such as transportation, road construction and repair, cavalry horses, efficiency in filling requisitions, and a multitude of comparable activities. At times they rendered judgments on a higher level, as when Watson conveyed this observation: If Jefferson Davis "is a general, which I think he is, he will on some day, in less than ten days, concentrate all his forces suddenly and attack McDowell at Fredericksburg or between that point and Richmond." On another occasion Watson expressed this view: "The rule throughout this force is to do nothing that can be avoided, and nothing to-day that can be postponed until to-morrow [but] no harm is likely at this time to result from such state of things."[25]

The War Board had intermingled logistical and operational concerns. Particularly involved in operations were Quartermaster General Meigs and that capable general-purpose officer of the engineers, Brigadier General John G.

Barnard. When Halleck became general in chief, he succeeded to Hitchcock's mantle. Though the War Board ceased to exist formally, its legacy of inter-bureau cooperation remained so strong that the board continued to have a very significant, though informal, existence. Because of Hitchcock's role as chairman, Halleck inherited a measure of informal authority over the bureaus; due to bureau involvement in operational planning, these theoretically independent special staff sections concerned themselves with and responded more readily to operational requirements. Real staff coordination, in theory only reposing in the civilian secretary of war, therefore permeated a lower level—the professional soldiers.

Though meagre, Halleck's staff of twenty-three officers and men added immeasurably to an undermanned headquarters. Conversely, Halleck's inadequate staff gained significant augmentation by the informal additions from the personnel of the bureaus. Meigs, for example, had accompanied him on his visit to McClellan and had quickly prepared in his own office the creditable and accurate estimate of Lee's strength. Halleck's own staff, including his able chief, Brigadier General George W. Cullum, and his adjutant, Colonel John C. Kelton, later adjutant general of the army, integrated logistics, intelligence, and operations. Though the most intimate members of the informal headquarters staff were Meigs and Barnard, others were active, among them Colonel Edward D. Townsend, the acting adjutant general of the army. To a greater or lesser degree others, such as General Canby and the assistant secretaries, functioned as part of the informal headquarters staff.[26]

This staff effectively performed most of the duties of a modern general staff with Halleck as its de facto chief. It differed, however, in two important respects from the modern U.S. general staff. After his initial involvement with raising troops, Halleck ceased to be much concerned with the recruitment and formation of troops. Partly state and, after the introduction of the draft in 1863, more strongly federal, the provision of manpower for the Union armies rested largely in the hands of Stanton and state officials. The Union's informal general staff also differed from its modern American counterpart in the importance of the quartermaster general and the intermingling of operations, intelligence, and logistics, almost in a single unit. In the French staff model used in the U.S. Army today, these are discrete sections, G-3, G-2, and G-1.

The contemporaneous Prussian general staff closely approximated that of the Union. An outgrowth of the importance of the quartermaster in supplying and moving armies, the Prussian model groups in one section, the quartermaster or general staff, the same functions grouped under Halleck. This diagram illustrates how well the Prussian model actually applied to the Union situation. It depicts Halleck and Stanton both as chief of staff since each had direct access to the President. It also shows Halleck in charge of the general or quartermaster staff.[27]

This resulting informal structure possessed all of the modern organizational

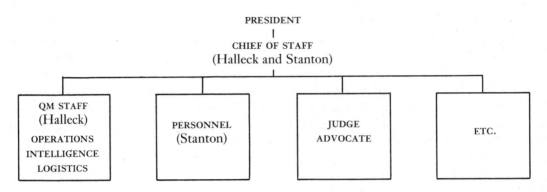

qualities which the Confederacy had briefly enjoyed during Lee's transitory service as Davis's chief of staff. In addition, it embraced a larger number of more experienced personnel than Lee had possessed, and its structure made it particularly effective in meeting the army's crucial logistical requirements. Davis's assignment of Lee to field command, wise as a temporary expedient, produced a serious and negative long-run impact because it doomed the Confederacy to nearly two years with a very inadequate headquarters staff.

☆   ☆

Halleck continually improved as an organizer, supplier, planner, and manager of war. Despite his new title, he never truly functioned as a commanding general in chief; he served as army chief of staff. He brought a leaven of greater concern for affairs in the West to the Washington command post; he always felt honestly that the war would be won or lost in the West and he steadfastly resisted withdrawal of troops from that region to bolster any eastern operations. He made his greatest contribution when he infused efficiency into the conduct of operations and prepared recommendations for strategic decisions and appointments to command. He struggled relentlessly to reform the system of promoting officers. "I have done everything in my power here to separate military appointments and commands from politics," he wrote, "but," overstating the situation, he lamented, "really the task is hopeless. . . . Oh, the curse of political expedience! It has almost ruined the Army, and if carried out will soon ruin the country." In truth, he proved rather effective in his effort: he requested and received the initiation of a board of officers to handle appointments and promotions, and he attacked the selection of officers on the basis of political influence by citing the case of a colonel who had been tried and convicted of gross midconduct and who then had not only avoided dismissal but had successfully maneuvered in Washington to secure a commission as brigadier general. Lincoln used the exposé not only as justification to allow the War Department more freedom in the appointment of officers but also as the impetus to initiate a new draft law. Halleck himself also contributed suggestions for new draft provisions, worked to make the existing law more stringent, and infused tougher regulations that shortened leaves of absence and reduced the amounts of baggage that armies regularly transported.[28]

In his successful career in the West, Halleck had as his primary task directing the movements of the many forces within his department and giving careful attention to logistics. He strove to see that each force promptly received needed supplies and promised reinforcements. He insisted that each subordinate commander shoulder responsibility for organization, discipline, training, and supply. Halleck ordered each soldier to carry one hundred rounds of ammunition and, if any inspection revealed a man short of his correct load, the man's captain would be arrested. Once when Halleck tasted some of the food typical of that which the men ate, he concluded that the large sick list resulted from unenlightened preparation and sanitation; he thereafter ordered company commanders and medical personnel to inspect each meal. He also assigned a competent West Pointer, Major Philip H. Sheridan, to quartermaster and commissary duties. Together they improved the mess conditions, saw to the construction or repair of needed roads, brought about better security and communication practices, regulated the supply of heavy artillery, and insisted upon the use of protective intrenchments. While one reporter reflected the naive impatience that hot-blooded, unsophisticated critics heaped upon Halleck, calling him an "irritated old maid, a silly school girl, a vacillating coquette," the general's methods produced the results he sought.[29]

As general in chief, Halleck still envisioned his function as managerial, but on a broader and higher plane. That his job might not have fit the specific profile which some persons thought it should matters quite little; the country's previous generals in chief had certainly never managed to lift out of the fog any clear image of their proper status. Though he may have wished to continue the strategic direction of armies as he had in the West, this could not be. He wrote his friend Sherman, I am "simply a military advisor to the Secretary of War and the President and must obey and carry out what they decide upon, whether I concur with their decisions or not. If I disagree with them in opinion, I say so, but when they decide it is my duty faithfully to carry out their decision." Pointing out that he was not the commander in chief, he stressed that the office was "not understood by the country. The responsibility and odium thrown upon it does not belong to it." Even if he disagreed with a selected policy, Halleck saw his duty as not to engage in any public criticism of a decision, lest, as he wrote, "I might embarrass the execution of a measure fully decided on. My mouth is closed except when officially called on to give such opinion. It is my duty to strengthen the hands of the President as Commander-in-Chief."[30]

Lincoln used Halleck politically as well. The President preferred to present a facade of impotence, implying to critics that he actually exercised little power and entrusted the serious military details to the military professionals. If Lincoln fired a general, Halleck signed the order. Naturally the fired general's supporters then blamed Halleck. If critics inquired about a military move, Lincoln would say, "I wish not to control. That I leave to General Halleck," or "You must call on General Halleck, who commands."[31]

But Halleck was by no means merely Lincoln's tool. The general freely suggested strategic principles and proposals and often succeeded in swaying Lincoln to his point of view. A believer in cabinet control, Secretary of the Navy Gideon Welles complained that Halleck, like the previous generals in chief, had "controlled and directed military movements and policy of the government, far more than the Cabinet." Welles lamented that the President relied "upon Halleck and apparently no one else in the War Department." Lincoln, Welles complained, "will not move or do except by the consent of the dull, stolid, inefficient and incompotent General-in-Chief."[32]

In spite of the clear compatibility between Lincoln and Halleck, other serious civilian-military tensions still vexed the Union. A major cause of these was the civilian exasperation with four apparently fruitless victories: after Antietam, Perryville, Iuka, and Corinth nothing had happened. Halleck found a military explanation as to why "these victories have not produced the usual results. In many instances," he suggested, "the defeated foe was not followed from the battlefield, and even where a pursuit was attempted, it almost invariably failed to effect the capture of the retreating army." History had taught the general in chief that "a victorious army is supposed to be in condition to pursue its defeated foe with advantage, and during such pursuit to do him serious if not fatal injury."

Finding part of the riddle's answer in logistics, he attributed it to too much rather than too little logistical support. He explained: "This defect has been attributed to our enormous baggage and supply trains and to a want of training in making marches. There is no doubt that the baggage trains of our armies have been excessively large"; the armies "can never move rapidly with such a mass of impedimenta." The reason for this was that "once accustomed to a certain amount of transportation, an army is unwilling to do without the luxuries" provided by the baggage train. "By the recent increase in the army ration, which was previously larger than in any other country, a considerable amount of transportation is employed in moving provisions and supplies which are not necessary for the subsistence of the soldiers." His limited experience in the field caused Halleck to overlook the more fundamental problems of operating from distant bases and in country already well foraged by friend or foe, and menaced by guerrillas and raids."[33]

The secretary of the navy, on the other hand, blamed fruitless battles on the education of the commanders, because "a defensive policy was the West Point policy . . . ," he wrote, adding further, "We had good engineers and accomplished officers, but no efficient, energetic commanding general [has] yet appeared from that institution." General Scott had set the tone with the defensive "error" and, with his anaconda plan, had been "unwilling to invade the seceding states" or "strike a blow."[34]

This widespread criticism of West Pointers, which a conservative member of Lincoln's Cabinet had adopted, had also penetrated the executive mansion. In a moment of discouragement, Lincoln attributed the tens of thousands of men on furlough to similar causes. "The army," he said, "like the nation, has become demoralized by the idea that the war is to be ended, the nation united, and peace restored, by *strategy*, and not by hard desperate fighting. Why, then, should not the soldiers have furloughs?"[35]

In writing his senator-brother, Sherman responded to the popular criticism of the generals, emphasizing: "Though our armies pass across and through the land, the war closes in behind and leaves the same enemy behind. We attempt to occupy places, and the people rise up and make the detachments prisoners." Then, identifying his brother with the critics, Sherman continued: "I know you all recognize in these facts simply that . . . McClellan is slow, Buell over-cautious, and Wright timid. This may be so, but the causes lie deeper," in the character of the war they were fighting.[36]

In defending himself against his critics, the recently dismissed Buell, stressing other factors, explained why he "did not immediately follow the enemy" after the Battle of Perryville, and sought "to answer the theories that have been advanced for the annihilation or capture of the entire rebel army under General Bragg." In response he pointed out that "there are few circumstances under which a disciplined and well managed army can be forced to a general battle against its will." In his situation wisdom dictated that he not try because, with many "raw and undisciplined" troops, he faced an enemy composed of "nearly all veteran troops," who "would have the advantage of the strong position which he selected." He could have fought, Buell wrote, but it would have exemplified the truism that "ignorance and error multiply battles far more than valor and generally with the penalty of disaster."

In Buell's case, furthermore, the enemy needed a battle. Since the Confederates were raiders, any permanent occupation would require seizing the supply line to Tennessee. "This subject could only be secured by giving battle to and destroying or driving from the field the army which was opposed to it. As to pursuing Bragg's retreating army," he emphasized that an army "can always retreat more rapidly than it can be pursued." Calling attention to the logistic variable overlooked by Halleck, he pointed out that the army following in the track of a retreating force "finds the country stipped of supplies; . . . it must carry everything along, with the hindrance of enormous trains, and the difficulties are increased with every day's march." With "strong positions reconnoitered in advance," the "retreating army [can prepare] a front of resistance more rapidly than the pursuer can prepare a front for attack."

Conceiving that the critics of West Point were advocating battles as ends in themselves, he stressed that "the object is not merely to give battle for the sake of fighting but to fight for victory." Judging this to be what the popular press sought, he urged that "the commander merits condemnation who, from ambition of popular clamor and without necessity or profit, has squandered the lives of his soldiers."[37]

Thus the fissure remained between many politicians and people and much of the press, on the one hand, and the professional soldiers on the other. The professionals had disappointed the public and were annoyed by and defensive about their political and newspaper critics. The public envisioned warfare in terms of battles; the generals viewed war in terms of campaigns. The President found himself caught in the middle between these contending views.

Lincoln had long since absorbed these military truisms and understood also the disadvantage imposed that fall by the Union system of recruiting. The President realized "one recruit into an old regiment is nearly or quite equal in value to two in a new one." Yet all of this did not adequately explain to him the fall inertia of the victorious Union armies. However, some hope remained for more fall offensives with the two new commanders, albeit West Pointers. Surely much could be expected of Rosecrans, the victor of Iuka and Corinth, and McClellan's replacement, Burnside, who had taken Roanoke Island.[38]

More pedestrian and easily overlooked, however, was the continuing of the federal onslaught against Confederate salt-securing capabilities, which had begun in earnest only during this fall; on October 23 Yankee soldiers destroyed the Goose Creek Salt Works near Manchester, Kentucky. A raid there earlier, in January, 1862, had resulted in the breakage of some kettles and pumps, but the Confederates easily had restored operations, and now the Unionists performed a much more thorough job.[39]

Elsewhere, too, the Federals attacked and exerted pressure upon the Confederacy's salt supply. Naval attacks frequently included raids upon the Gulf coast of Florida where by this time salt production had become quite important. "Salt works are as plentiful in Florida as blackbirds in a rice field," one northern newspaper had reported. They existed all along the Florida coast, but particularly on the Gulf side between Choctawatchee Bay and Tampa, especially centered around Saint Andrew's Bay and in Taylor County, usually at the heads of bays, from one to five miles inland from the open Gulf. Thus Union vessels needed to send a raiding party ashore and possibly had to move some distance overland in order to carry out the destructions. Saint Andrew's Bay proved to be a long-standing area of value to Confederate salt-making activities; although raids commenced occasionally during the fall of 1862, the last demolition did not come until February, 1865.[40]

It was not a simple matter to destroy a salt-making establishment; the kettles measured about an inch thick at the edge and from two to three inches thick in the bottom, thus rendering them exceedingly difficult to break up. Because some of the copper tubing used in the wells was about the same diameter as a twelve-pounder gun, the Federals typically destroyed them by filling them with twelve-pounder shells and railroad iron, none of which could be easily transported by a small raiding party.

These raids upon Confederate salterns also provided the first opportunity for a Negro unit to engage in combat. During a busy week, November 3-10, 1862, a black company conducted a highly successful marauding expedition, traversing the many rivers and bays of east Florida and Georgia between Saint Simon's Island and Fernandina. A reconnaissance in force, it had the combined purposes of salt destruction, foodstuff and supply raiding, the securing of whatever slaves they could liberate, and—perhaps most importantly—the initial testing of colored troops under fire. Aboard a captured steamboat and with occasional fire support from a small gunboat that ran in as close as she could, the Negro soldiers spread havoc along many miles of coastline. They drove away the Confederate pickets at point after point, killed nine enemy soldiers, took three prisoners, and destroyed nine saltworks as well as about $20,000 worth of horses, wagons, rice, corn, and other property, and they carried away 150 liberated slaves. Their commander wrote proudly that "the colored men fought with astonishing coolness and bravery." This first use of blacks as a military force against the Confederacy concluded as a splendid success.[41]

Not all the news about the salt supply during late 1862 was bad from the Confederate viewpoint, but most of it was. For example, southerners under Major General William Wing "Old Blizzards" Loring—who had been relegated to an out-of-the-way command in southwestern Virginia because his personality proved incompatible with that of Stonewall Jackson—conducted 5,000 men northward to the vicinity of Charleston in a raid that captured the Kanawha Valley salt wells and a large store of salt. They remained until the first of November and then withdrew in the face of an advancing federal army of 8,000 men. The gossipy war clerk, J. B. Jones, thought caustically, though of course unrealistically, about not making a determined effort to turn that raid into a penetration. "The President," Jones wrote in his diary, "may seem to be a good nation-maker in the eyes of distant statesmen, but he does not seem to be a good salt-maker for this nation. The works he has just relinquished to the enemy manufactures 7,000 bushels of salt per day—two million and a half a year—an ample supply for the entire population of the Confederacy. . . . A Caesar, a Napoleon, a Pitt, and a Washington, all great nation-makers, would have deemed this work worthy of their attention."[42]

Meanwhile, having replaced two major commanders and largely recovered from the late-summer Confederate raids, the Union was slowly readying its fall offensives, in spite of the need to incorporate into the armies the wave of several hundred thousand new volunteers called for in the summer. The plans for the fall campaign constituted an amalgam of the ideas of Lincoln and the new general in chief. Halleck now had his first real opportunity to propose initiatives, for the strategy of his first months as general in chief had been entirely defensive. To the concentration of Virginia and Maryland forces to oppose Lee he had added troops from the Atlantic coast and he had moved three divisions from Grant to aid Buell against Bragg. New troops had been hurried into service and rushed to these two focal points. Though he looked forward to the fall, all Halleck anticipated accomplishing in September was, he said, "to hold our positions and prepare for an onward movement."[43]

Halleck's record of achievement in the West led Sherman to expect a vigorous fall offensive, for, as he wrote Grant in early October: "You know how impetuous he is when he starts and I expect to hear, by every boat, of regiments by the dozen pouring on Richmond whilst McClellan holds Lee in check. Same for Buell. We down here will for the time being be lost sight of; but as soon as the Southern Army turns their faces South then look out for squalls." Though Sherman erred about the strategy employed against Lee, he correctly appreciated Halleck's concern for the Mississippi. When Halleck realized that the navy could not complete the opening of the river, he immediately planned "a land expedition . . . against Vicksburg as soon as troops can be spared for that purpose." The Confederate offensives forced deferment of this movement, but "as soon as the new troops are organized in the West," wrote the general in chief, I intend that "the fall campaign will be opened there with energy."[44]

Lincoln's strategic priorities differed from Halleck's, for, Stanton explained, the President regarded "an advance on East Tennessee as only second in importance to Richmond." More significant to the President than that Unionist region itself was the East Tennessee and Virginia Railroad. "To take and hold the Railroad at, or East of Cleveland in East Tennessee, I think fully as important as taking and holding Richmond," Lincoln wrote, a high priority indeed, for he believed that taking Richmond would "substantially end the war." The strategic importance of that railroad had impressed Lincoln early and this conviction intensified because of the belief that Beauregard had reinforced Lee for the Seven Days' Battles. Army headquarters planned a powerful raid from northwestern Virginia to cut this railroad in Virginia, but it failed "owing to the impossibility of supplying a force" there in the late fall.[45]

Initially no energetic fall campaign commenced against any of these objectives. All major forces stalled due to inadequate logistical preparation, and all were digesting their large infusions of green troops, many of whom served in new regiments under inexperienced officers. The dissatisfaction with and removal of Buell and McClellan also delayed any immediate advance. Meanwhile Halleck directed the flow of new troops, changing the direction of those in the West from Buell to Grant. Pursuing this same emphasis, he also shifted troops to Grant from the Department of the Ohio, which guarded Kentucky and part of Buell's line of communications. Since he still had some allegiance to his old trans-Mississippi command, Halleck initially agreed with Lincoln on the need to complete the conquest of Arkansas. Soon, however, he was shifting his emphasis, giving full primacy to the Mississippi campaign. "The great object," he said, "is now to take and hold the Mississippi."[46]

Though Halleck was clearly trying to give priority to the Mississippi, Grant had resources only slightly more ample than Rosecrans, and both of their armies were inferior to the immense forces concentrated in the Virginia theatre. Recognizing the significance of the Mississippi, Lincoln only gradually came to give it primacy in his strategy for the fall campaign. His first move in that direction came when he responded enthusiastically to a plan of Major General John A. McClernand, a strongly Unionist southern Illinois Democratic politician who had fought under Grant at forts Henry and Donelson and at Shiloh. McClernand conceived the idea of recruiting a special expedition of midwestern troops to open the Mississippi.

Turned down by Halleck, McClernand approached Lincoln, who found irresistible McClernand's inspired political-military entrepreneurship and, unlike Halleck, had confidence in McClernand's military capacity. Halleck gladly cooperated in raising the troops for the down-river expedition but forwarded all of them to Memphis within Grant's department. Though McClernand's orders specified that his force was to be under the jurisdiction of the general in chief, Halleck objected to McClernand's role and certainly found the extra-departmental operation an example of the President's inability to keep out of the details of military operations. As Halleck said of Lincoln, "His fingers itch to be into everything going on."[47]

Lincoln's other personal strategic plan involved a campaign in Texas. This project appealed to antislavery sentiment in New England because such an expedition was regarded as a prelude to settlement of the state by free labor from New England and also because it constituted a potential source of fibre for cotton-starved textile mills. The Union organized the expedition in a manner similar to McClernand's: the troops were to be raised in the interested region, New England, and led by an experienced political general, well identified with the concerned area. The President appointed Nathaniel P. Banks, governor of Massachusetts on the eve of the war, to raise the troops and, enjoying Lincoln's confidence in his military capacity, lead them to Texas by means of a water-borne campaign.[48]

These two ingenious examples of military-political entrepreneurship gained praise in the press. The *New York Times* entitled its editorial: "A New Era— Banks and McClernand." The editorial regarded "the organization of the movements led by Gens. McClernand and Banks, as among the most philosophic, practical and hopeful enterprises of the war." The conspicuous breaking of the professional-leadership monopoly doubtless gave some solace to many persons who thought political conviction, common sense, and enthusiasm better credentials for command than a West Point engineering background.[49]

In early November Lincoln changed the destination of Banks's expedition to the lower Mississippi. This diversion to a strategically more significant objective likely resulted because of the administration's losses in the fall elections, especially in the Midwest. Concern for losing the allegiance of this area influenced the President to direct the expedition to an objective of primary concern to that politically endangered region. Halleck favored the augmentation of the concentration on the great river, though the problem of exterior lines gave him difficulty in writing his instructions for Banks.

In drafting these orders, the general in chief could now say: "The President regards the opening of the Mississippi River as the first and most important of our military and naval operations, and it is hoped that you will not lose a moment in accomplishing it." Though on an exterior line, Halleck explained to Banks: The simultaneous "operations of General Rosecrans in East Tennessee, of General Grant in Northern Mississippi, and of General Steele in Arkansas will give full employment to the enemy's forces in the West, and thus prevent them from concentrating against you." Apparently optimistic about the possibility of early success, Halleck outlined the potential subsequent operations of taking Mobile, Alabama, and advancing up the Red River in Louisiana. The latter movement would have the added benefit of providing a base for a movement on Texas.[50]

Early November arrived before the fall offensive began, with Burnside leading in Virginia, Rosecrans in Tennessee, and Grant in Mississippi. To aid Grant, Halleck summoned assistance from Curtis in the trans-Mississippi, eventually detaching a significant portion of Curtis's troops and adding them to Grant's command. By giving control of the Mississippi operation to Grant, Halleck solved part of the problem of the divided command in the West, but he left Curtis out of the action, "to stand on the bank and present arms" as the expedition to open the river passed. To strengthen the movement, Halleck sought troops from throughout the West, including a post in Wyoming, part of the 700 men in Nebraska, and some of Pope's Indian fighters from Minnesota. He had already planned to reinforce New Orleans with new troops and, to assist operations in Virginia, he had arranged for a cooperating movement on southeastern Virginia and the North Carolina coast.[51]

Compared with Confederate leadership, Halleck had a particularly difficult coordinating task in the West, for Union organization had retrogressed just as the Confederates were making progress in theirs. Since the fall of 1861 the Confederates had markedly simplified and improved their departmental structure. Despite the unity of command under Sidney Johnston, they had created several miniature departments, more than a dozen altogether, with many directed exclusively toward coast defense. By the end of the fall of 1862 four major regional commands existed. Originally part of three departments, the trans-Mississippi was now united under the feeble direction of Lieutenant General Theophilus H. Holmes. In the winter the Confederacy would shelve him and replace him with the able Edmund Kirby Smith. Isolated by the lack of rail communication with the East, the trans-Mississippi had its separate logistical arrangements and would fight its own war, unable to give to or receive reinforcements from the eastern Confederacy.

The South's ranking field officers, Joseph E. Johnston in the West, Beauregard in South Carolina, Georgia, and Florida, and Lee in Virginia and North Carolina, controlled the three major eastern commands. The reorganization omitted from this structure the Department of Western Virginia, largely dedicated to the protection of western Virginia from raids against the saltworks and the East Tennessee and Virginia Railroad. The mountainous and infertile terrain, without adequate river or rail communications, precluded more serious military operations in western Virginia. Except in Beauregard's department, railroads joined coastal forces with those in the interior, thus permitting mutual reinforcement. Developed as a result of the lessons of the first year of the war, this organization both vastly increased the potential for strategic maneuver and diminished the command burden on the Richmond headquarters. This excellent departmental structure responded to real strategic needs, and, in part, compensated for Davis's failure to replace Lee as commanding general. The difficulty of finding someone suitable made it easier to decide to rely on what advice Lee had time to provide and the infrequent conferences which Davis could arrange.

The Union organization was more complex. They divided the coastline among four departments: the Gulf under Banks; the South, embracing the South Carolina, Georgia, and west Florida coasts, commanded by the marginal David Hunter; North Carolina under one of Professor Mahan's star pupils, John G. Foster; and Virginia, where the Norfolk and Peninsula area was competently administered by John A. Dix, an elderly politician with considerable regular army service in his youth. The major defect in the Union structure lay in the West, where three separate departments opposed Johnston's Department of the West. Kept separate by Halleck's fear of political interference if reorganized, the Department of the Ohio, ably commanded by Horatio G. Wright, confronted East Tennessee; Rosecrans's Department of the Cumberland faced Middle Tennessee; and Grant's Department of the Tennessee fronted north Mississippi. Although well connected with the others by rail and water, S. R. Curtis's Department of the Missouri was separate. But Curtis employed the good Union communications to operate on the Mississippi as well as to confront the Confederates in the trans-Mississippi, and Halleck did solve one problem by placing Curtis's forces on the Mississippi under Grant's orders.

This excessively divided structure put a heavy burden on the general in chief, but, with his informally expanded headquarters, his command organization proved equal to the demands. But he had an additional burden. Whereas Davis was trying to penetrate Union plans so as to be ready to meet the principal threat, Halleck had to coordinate a number of separate offensives. Local circumstances in each theatre severely conditioned the timing of each offensive. To try to synchronize them would be like moving a convoy which cannot depart until the last ship is ready. Halleck sought coordination but made little effort to secure perfect simultaneity.

Halleck's ungainly four-part western command, instead of the unified de-

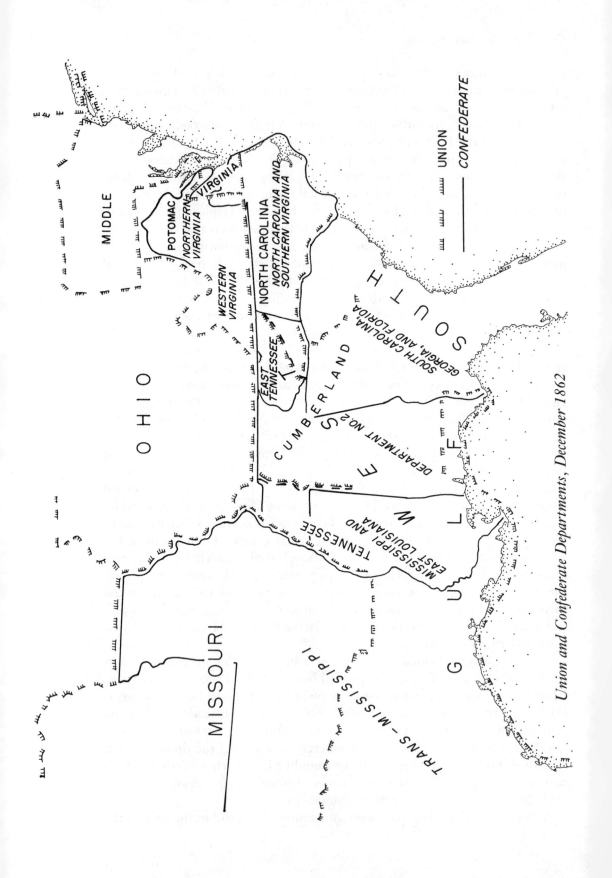

Union and Confederate Departments, December 1862

partment he had sought and had himself headed, well illustrated an important difference between Union and Confederate leadership. Fearful of disturbing arrangements lest he be forced into giving major posts to Cassius M. Clay and other politicians, Halleck was, in a sense, keeping the western command himself in order to avoid sacrificing military efficiency on the altar of political necessity. Lincoln, who was severely constrained to build support for the war, would have found it difficult not to recognize the important political interests whose representatives sought military appointments. Jefferson Davis behaved otherwise.

Davis had fewer political problems to which he paid relatively less attention and was far less trammelled in his military decisions and appointments. To an important degree the Confederate President exemplified the professional's ideal commander in chief for he took an essentially professional soldier's view of managing the war. Unlike the Union President, Davis almost ruthlessly suppressed political considerations in favor of purely military judgments. He even failed to explain fully to the public, almost as if military decisions did not need to be explained to the uninitiated. After his early appointment of politically available generals, he stringently applied to these appointees a military rather than a political test of fitness. Davis denied the important John B. Floyd command because he thought him an incompetent soldier. To the far more powerful Robert Toombs, he denied promotion to major general, ultimately prompting Toombs's resignation and withdrawal to Georgia, where he criticized the administration and denounced West Pointers.

Lincoln, of course, sought to forestall such situations and to make allies rather than enemies of such powerful politicians with military ambitions. Though he sought to persuade, Lincoln would not order Halleck to give Fremont a command and he followed professional advice in ultimately removing McClernand, for whom, however, he found another but innocuous command. Yet Lincoln kept many military politicians such as Banks and Butler in important commands and friendly to his cause and his administration. In commenting about the virtues of a masterful political and military juggling of appointments, he stated his goals well: "In a purely military point of view it may be that none of these things is indispensable, or perhaps, advantageous; but in another aspect, [the political], they would give great relief, while, at the worst, I think they could not injure the military service much."[52]

1. Long, *Civil War, Day by Day*, 254.

2. William Hanchett, *Irish Charles G. Halpine in Civil War America* (Syracuse, New York, 1970), 51.

3. *Ibid.*, 30, 34, 42.

4. *Ibid.*, 45, 70, 83, 84.

5. Dudley Taylor Cornish, *The Sable Arm: Negro Troops in the Union Army, 1861–1865* (New York, 1966), 214–28, 231, 254–58.

6. Thomas, *The Confederacy as a Revolutionary Experience*, 120.

7. Charles H. Wesley, "The Employment of Negroes as Soldiers in the Confederate Army," *Journal of Negro History* (July, 1919), 241–42, 245;

Davis to Senate and House of Representatives, Nov. 7, 1864, *O.R.*, IV, 111, 799.

8. Fred A. Shannon, *The Organization and Administration of the Union Army*, 2 vols. (Gloucester, Mass., 1965), I, 37.

9. Sherman, *Memoirs*, II, 387–88.

10. Wilson, *Under the Old Flag*, I, 537–39.

11. Upton, *Military Poilcy*, 275.

12. Shannon, *The Organization and Administration of the Union Army*, I, 273–90.

13. Rembert Patrick, *Jefferson Davis and His Cabinet* (Baton Rouge, 1944), 125.

14. Patrick, *Jefferson Davis and His Cabinet*, 127.

15. G. W. Randolph to T. J. Randolph, Jan. 20, 1863, Edgehill-Randolph Papers, University of Virginia, Charlottesville.

16. Patrick, *Jefferson Davis and His Cabinet*, 127.

17. *Ibid.*, 133.

18. Connelly and Jones, *The Politics of Command*, 53 and *passim*.

19. The position of Beauregard exemplifies both the role of ideas and of individuals in informal organizations. A group may be held together by allegiance to an individual or to an idea. In Beauregard's case, both his ideas and his personality provided a basis for unity in a typical situation of great complexity where "uncrowned leaders compete with crowned ones. Informal and often unaccountable groupings brought to life for various purposes press against one another" (Harvey C. Mansfield and Fritz Morstein Marx, "Informal Organization," ed. Fritz Morstein Marx, *Elements of Public Administration* [Englewood Cliffs, N.J. 1959], 286–87. See also: Beringer, *Historical Analysis*, 153–57).

20. Davis to Holmes, Dec. 21 (?), 1862, *O.R.*, LII, pt. 2, 397–99; Connelly and Jones, *Politics of Command*, 109.

21. Davis to Holmes, Dec. 21 (?), 1862, *O.R.*, LII, pt. 2, 397–99.

22. Beauregard to Villeré, May 26, 1862, *O.R.*, XIV, 955; Beauregard, "The First Battle of Bull Run," I, 223.

23. Amitai Etzioni distinguishes between leaders who have personal power which derives from their own characteristics and officers who derive their power from their office. Leaders who also have the power of office he terms formal leaders; those without are informal leaders. In these terms Beauregard was a formal leader during the period of his western command from Shiloh until his relief following the fall of Corinth. Thereafter he was an informal leader even though absent from the western army. Bragg's referring his plans to Beauregard was very tangible evidence of the absent Beauregard's personal power and informal leadership.

McClellan's situation was comparable, for he, too, passed from the formal leadership of command of the Army of the Potomac to informal leadership based on his personal power. Unlike Beauregard, McClellan did not seek to exercise that power. Nevertheless, McClellan's position as informal leader tended to make his successors in command mere officers.

As general in chief Halleck was a formal leader, possessing both office and personal power as far as the western armies were concerned. With the Army of the Potomac, however, he had only office, for his personal power was weaker than McClellan's. McClellan possessed a reputation from the U.S. Army equal to Halleck's, his personal power in the Army of the Potomac having been consolidated by his role as builder and commander. Halleck's personal power, ample in the West to remove Buell without difficulty, could not match McClellan's in the eastern army.

Lee almost immediately established personal power to become the formal leader of the Army of Northern Virginia, and Bragg might well have done likewise had his personal characteristics and his failure in Kentucky not alienated so many of his important subordinates.

The Presidents and their civilian secretaries of war enjoyed only the power of their formidable offices, though Davis's extensive military background gave him some personal power. Lincoln, on the other hand, derived benefit from Halleck's personal power; and from his fiction that Halleck controlled all military operations, the President doubtless also derived some authority with soldiers as well as protection from political critics. See: Amitai Etzioni, *A Comparative Analysis of Complex Organizations* (New York, 1961), 89–96.

24. Totten to Colonel Cullum, Apr. 20, 1861, to General Ripley and Governor Latham, July 13, 1861, to Colonel DeRussy, Aug. 27, 1861, to Meigs, Aug. 28, 1861, and to Barnard, June 2, 1863, all in Record Group 77, entry 146, Engineer Bureau Records, National Archives, Washington, D.C.; Stanton's Annual Report, 1863, Dec. 5, 1863, Stanton Papers, Library of Congress.

25. A myriad of letters exchanged between all the individuals mentioned exists, mostly preserved in the *Official Records*, to support the contentions made; the quotes are from Watson to McClellan, Apr. 25, 1862, *O.R.*, XII, pt. 3, 121;

and Watson to Stanton, June 26, 1862, *ibid.*, 261–62.

26. For evidence of the relations between Halleck and Townsend, see: E. D. Townsend, *Anecdotes of the Civil War in the United States* (New York, 1884), 88.

27. Adapted from Hittle, *The Military Staff*, 74.

28. Halleck to Schofield, Sept. 20, 1862, *O.R.*, XIII, 654; Ambrose, *Halleck*, 103–4.

29. Ambrose, *Halleck*, 47–48, 50–51.

30. Halleck to Sherman, Feb. 16, 1864, *O.R.*, XXXII, pt. 2, 407–8.

31. Ambrose, *Halleck*, 65.

32. *Welles Diary*, I, 527, 371, 320.

33. Report of the General in Chief, Nov. 25, 1862, *O.R.*, series 3, II, 877–78.

34. *Welles Diary*, I, 124–25.

35. Lincoln, memo on Furloughs, Nov. (?), 1862, Basler, *Collected Works*, V, 484.

36. W. T. Sherman to John Sherman, Oct. 1, 1862, *Sherman Letters*, 165–66.

37. Buell to military commission, Apr. 10, 1864, *O.R.*, XVI, pt. 1, 51–59.

38. Lincoln to Stanton, July 22, 1862, Basler, *Collected Works*, V, 338–39.

39. Lonn, *Salt as a Factor in the Confederacy*, 172, 182, 188, 293*n*59.

40. *Ibid.*, 288*n*27.

41. Cornish, *The Sable Arm*, 85–86; see also Lonn, *Salt as a Factor in the Confederacy*, 185–86, 293*n*59.

42. Lonn, *Salt as a Factor in the Confederacy*, 190–91.

43. Halleck to Sherman, Aug. 25, 1862, *O.R.*, XVII, pt. 2, 186.

44. Sherman to Grant, Oct. 4, 1862, *O.R.*, XVII, pt. 2, 261; Halleck to Sherman, Aug. 25,

1862, *ibid.*, 186; Halleck to Curtis, Aug. 7, 1862, *ibid.*, XIII, 544; Farragut to Halleck, June 28, 1862, *ibid.*, XV, 514–15; Halleck to Farragut, July 3, 1862, *ibid.*, 517; Halleck to Paine, Aug. 7, 1862, *ibid.*, 544.

45. Stanton to Mitchel, June 21, 1862, *O.R.*, XVI, pt. 2, 246; Lincoln to Halleck, June 30, 1862, Basler, *Collected Works*, V, 295; Lincoln to Seward, June 28, 1862, *ibid.*, 292; Wright to Halleck, Nov. 7, 1862, *O.R.*, XX, pt. 2, 24.

46. Halleck to Wright, Oct. 27, 20, Nov. 5, 10, 1862, *O.R.*, XVII, pt. 2, 298, XVI, pt. 2, 656, 10, XVII, pt. 2, 335; Wright to Halleck, Oct. 8, 1862, *ibid.*, XVI, pt. 2, 588–89; Halleck to Grant, Oct. 27, 30, Nov. 5, 10, 1862, *ibid.*, XVII, pt. 2, 298, 308, pt. 1, 467, 469; Halleck to Yates, Oct. 27, 30, 1862, *ibid.*, XVII, pt. 2, 298, 309; Halleck to Steele, Sept. 13, 1862, *ibid.*, XIII, 626; Halleck to Schofield, Sept. 16, 1862, *ibid.*, 641; Halleck to Curtis, Oct. 24, 1862, *ibid.*, 759; Curtis to Halleck, Oct. 25, 1862, *ibid.*, 761–63.

47. *Welles Diary*, I, 217; Ambrose, *Halleck*, 110.

48. *Welles Diary*, II, 26.

49. *New York Times*, Oct. 30, 1862, Ludwell H. Johnson, *Red River Campaign: Cotton and Politics in the Civil War* (Baltimore, 1958), 20–21.

50. Halleck to Banks, Nov. 9, 1862, *O.R.*, XV, 590–91.

51. Halleck to Curtis, Nov. 29, Dec. 9, 1862, *O.R.*, XXII, pt. 1, 794, 819–20; Curtis to Halleck, Dec. 9 (two communications), 1862, *ibid.*, 68, 820; Halleck to Grant, Dec. 7, 1862, *ibid.*, XVII, pt. 1, 473; Curtis to Sherman, Dec. 18, 1862, *ibid.*, pt. 2, 434; Dix to Halleck, Dec. 6, 1862, *ibid.*, XVIII, 473.

52. Lincoln to Stanton, Mar. 7, Dec. 18, 1863, Basler, *Collected Works*, VI, 127, VII, 78.

II ☆ UNION OFFENSIVES IN CONCERT

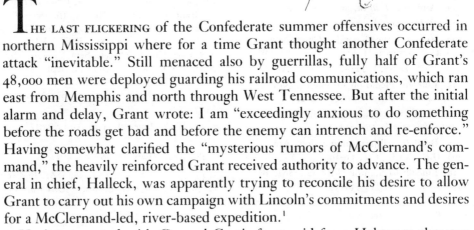

William S. Rosecrans

THE LAST FLICKERING of the Confederate summer offensives occurred in northern Mississippi where for a time Grant thought another Confederate attack "inevitable." Still menaced also by guerrillas, fully half of Grant's 48,000 men were deployed guarding his railroad communications, which ran east from Memphis and north through West Tennessee. But after the initial alarm and delay, Grant wrote: I am "exceedingly anxious to do something before the roads get bad and before the enemy can intrench and re-enforce." Having somewhat clarified the "mysterious rumors of McClernand's command," the heavily reinforced Grant received authority to advance. The general in chief, Halleck, was apparently trying to reconcile his desire to allow Grant to carry out his own campaign with Lincoln's commitments and desires for a McClernand-led, river-based expedition.[1]

Having arranged with General Curtis for a raid from Helena to threaten Grenada, Grant forced the enemy back to Grenada without fighting. This enabled him to "have the railroad completed to Grenada and a supply of provisions thrown in there. From that point Jackson, Mississippi, could be reached without the use of the road," Grant explained, and "Jackson once in our possession would soon insure the capitulation of Vicksburg." Grant's advance, Halleck said, "may change our plans in regard to Vicksburg. You will move your troops as you deem best to accomplish the great object in view." Thus Grant's advance put the regulars in charge and Grant would make his own plans, though any campaign was, to a degree, mortgaged to the original McClernand scheme.[2]

Approving the strategy of a water-borne turning movement, Halleck was delighted at the chance to pre-empt McClernand by having Grant entrust the expedition to Sherman. Grant then changed from his early preference for an overland advance, and harmony was assured when he decided to add a river approach under Sherman to his own well-launched overland thrust. But "so much newspaper spread eagle talk about the down-river move" eliminated any hope of surprise, and the plan Grant adopted became a simple advance on exterior lines with the enemy well aware of the necessary line of advance for each force.[3]

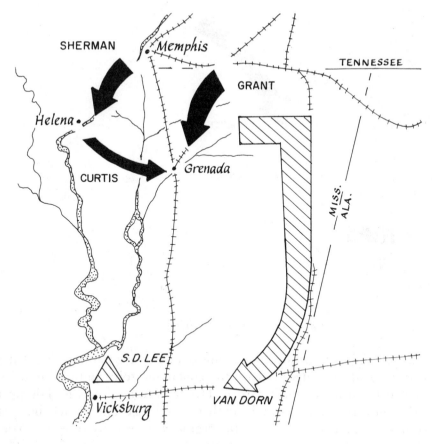

Grant's Plan

Unrelated to events on the Mississippi, a battle erupted on December 7 at Prairie Grove in far northwestern Arkansas. As two federal armies were advancing, 11,000 Confederates under the energetic Thomas C. Hindman attacked the 7,000 men of Brigadier General James Blunt on Illinois Creek about twelve miles southwest of Fayetteville. During the action the other Union army, 3,500 men under Brigadier General Francis J. Herron, joined Blunt.

Herron's men had covered 125 miles in a forced march of five days. Hindman had already driven in Blunt's pickets when he learned of Herron's approach. The Confederate leader decided to leave a containing force before Blunt's position and move the main rebel body to turn the federal position to the east, get between the two enemy armies, and defeat them in detail—first Herron and then Blunt. Bitter winter weather, freezing temperatures, first rain and then snow hampered the operations. The Confederate cavalry leading the way hit Herron's advanced units and drove them back, but then suddenly Hindman wavered. Instead of continuing to attack Herron's tired

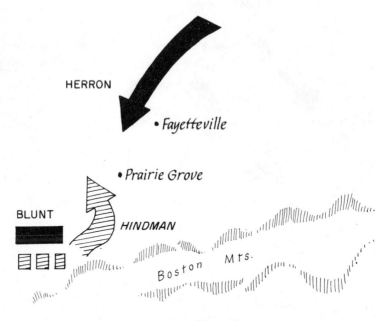

Interior Position

army as he originally planned, he assumed a defensive position. Eight miles away Blunt had been deceived by the containing force until he heard the fighting to his rear at Prairie Grove. Herron advanced against Hindman's position, but was repulsed. Hindman then ordered a counterattack, but abandoned it when he found that an entire regiment of recently recruited Arkansans had deserted. Herron then made two more unsuccessful assaults. About 11 A.M. Blunt began moving to Herron's relief. Early in the afternoon he arrived on the Confederates' left flank and opened an enfilade fire. The Federals made some progress at rolling up the rebel flank, but then were driven back by cavalry.

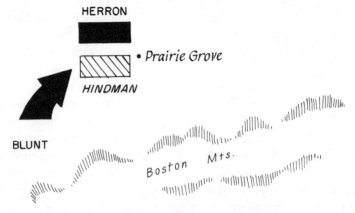

Blunt's Attack Prior to Confederate Withdrawal

The Confederates held their precarious positions until dark and withdrew during the night. One federal officer censured the whole operation as "a series of blunders" from which the Union force "narrowly escaped disaster where it should have met with complete success." The Federals lost 1,251 men while the Confederates sustained 1,317 casualties in this drawn battle, which resulted in continuing federal control of northwest Arkansas.[4]

The almost unnoticed Battle of Prairie Grove hardly made more impression on the public than did Grant's unspectacular movements in northern Mississippi. Popular attention fixed on Virginia, where Burnside had superseded McClellan. His plan approved by Lincoln and Halleck, Burnside proceeded to make, for the first time, a straightforward fighting advance directly on Richmond. On November 16, 1862, the Army of the Potomac's headquarters moved from Warrenton to Catlett's Station as Burnside shifted his force toward Fredericksburg. A part of Lee's army closely watched his every activity and followed his movement. On the 19th after marching from the main Confederate base at Culpeper, Longstreet's corps occupied the heights above Fredericksburg. Burnside was not moving to reach Richmond before Lee, but he did demonstrate the accuracy of the Lincoln-Halleck analysis—such a move would threaten Lee's communications and cause him to fall back.

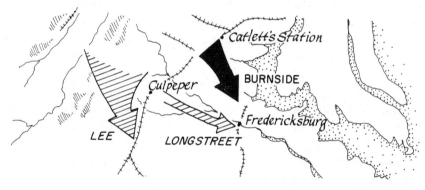

Movement to Fredericksburg

"Burnside is a brick." Or so many persons proudly proclaimed as they repeated the most often-spoken assessment of the new Army of the Potomac commander. Thirty-eight-year-old Ambrose E. Burnside impressed people with his vigorous campaigning, his victories in North Carolina, and with his imposing appearance, "a large man physically, about six feet tall," commented Assistant War Secretary Charles A. Dana. One of Burnside's division commanders, the recently promoted Major General Jacob D. Cox, who knew Burnside well, keenly delineated his "flashing eyes, his beard trimmed to the 'Burnside cut' with the mustache running into the side whiskers whilst the square and clean-shaven chin and jaws . . . gave a tone of decision and force to his features, [and] made up a picture that at once arrested the eye." Burnside exuded a "good-humored cordiality toward everybody," Cox continued, and exhibited a "seeming carelessness about his uniform," which in truth "was really a calculated affair" to add dash and popular appeal to his image. He cocked his hat at a rakish angle, buckled his pistol belt loosely so the weapon hung low on his hip, and he wore knee-high boots and elbow-length buckskin gloves.[5]

He might look the part, but inside Burnside simply did not measure up to his new assignment. He himself realized with trepidation that perhaps Lincoln should have named somebody else to command the army and actually tried to avoid the appointment. "His bearing under fire was good . . . and his personal courage beyond question," declared Cox; but "he shrank from responsibility with sincere modesty, because he questioned his own capacity to deal with affairs of great magnitude." Burnside also put forth an impressive but overblown intellectual facade: "when [Burnside] first talked to you, you would think he had a great deal more intelligence than he really possessed," Dana reported. "You had to know him some time before you really took his measure." In the days that followed, both Burnside's inadequacies and his duties plagued his mind. Driving hard, he overworked himself, slept very little, and became physically ill as a result. He proved the weakest of all the federal opponents that Robert E. Lee faced.[6]

At the end of October when McClellan and then Burnside began their move east of the Blue Ridge, Lee sought to continue his flank-position strategy by leaving Jackson in the Shenandoah Valley on "the supposition that by operating upon the flank and rear of the enemy," Jackson might prevent his progress southward and thus "retard & baffle" the enemy's plans. He also wished to protect that region itself, for "it would be grievous for the Valley & its supplies to fall into the hands of the enemy unnecessarily." Though he yearned "to strike a successful blow" to leave the enemy force "diminished and disheartened," Lee stuck with his Fabian strategy of avoiding combat.[7]

Jackson's flank position in the Valley continued the application of what had been the essential ingredient in Lee's strategy since midsummer. Lee summed it up thus: "The enemy apparently is so strong in numbers that I think it preferable to attempt to baffle his designs by maneuvering, rather than to resist his advance by main force. To accomplish the latter without too great risk and loss, would require more than double our present numbers." But Jackson's flank position failed to deter Burnside, and the menace of the Union movement eventually compelled Lee to call Jackson's corps also to Fredericksburg to challenge the Federal advance.

Even so, Lee continued preparations to make possible resistance by other means. His plan called for "the railroad from Fredericksburg to Aquia Creek to be entirely destroyed; the bridges, culverts, &c., to be broken; the cross ties piled and fired, with the rails piled on top, so as to prevent their future use." He also proposed "to break up the road from Fredericksburg back to Hanover Junction in the same way, and the Orange and Alexandria road from the Rappahannock to Gordonsville." Faced with this, Burnside either would have to wait for the railroad to be rebuilt or be encumbered by having "to move with a large wagon train." Yet Lee was reluctant to fall back so far along these lines, for the regions held substantial sources of supplies and he thus wished to "prevent their occupation by the enemy." Lee reported: If Burnside moves south of Fredericksburg, it will "cut us off from the supplies we are now drawing from the valley of the Rappahannock. I think it important to keep him at a distance as long as possible."[8]

But Burnside was not yet below Fredericksburg and, to facilitate this, Halleck began reinforcing Dix at Fort Monroe and alerting the forces on the Baltimore and Ohio and along the upper Potomac to be prepared to advance. By December 6, when Burnside reported, I have "nearly enough supplies to warrant us in beginning to move," Halleck knew that Grant was advancing and had sent an emphatic message to Rosecrans to move or be relieved. Aware that Dix and Foster had a simultaneous advance ready and Burnside's reinforcements were already in motion, the general in chief ordered his last eastern forces forward. Warning the commanders in western Virginia and along the Baltimore and Ohio to be alert for guerrilla raids, he directed that "the remainder of the available troops in that part of Western Virginia should be thrown forward, so as to threaten the valley of the Shenandoah and cover Harper's Ferry." Almost as an afterthought, he sought reinforcements from

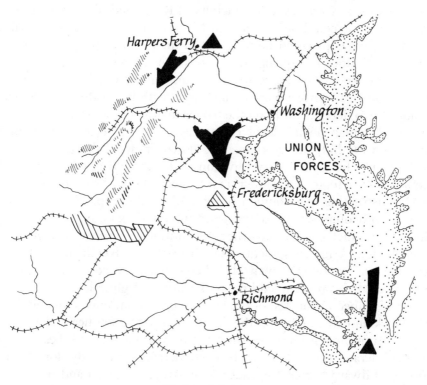

Union Advance

the most western part of this department. Against this campaign the Confederates were making similar but less elaborate preparations.[9]

The menace of Burnside's advance impelled President Davis to bring four brigades and a battalion from western Virginia to strengthen Lee and also caused Lee to look to the coast both as a source of reinforcements and as an area possibly threatened by Union winter operations. Since the enemy could not "attack all points at one time, . . . troops could be concentrated upon that where an assault could be made." This principle was to be applied across departmental lines, for Wilmington, North Carolina, could be aided by Beauregard's South Carolina department, from which troops could be drawn in "an emergency, and recalled to their position when no longer required."[10]

Lee was thus applying what had been the Confederacy's consistent policy since the fall of Fort Donelson. Faced with a major Union offensive, Lee hoped that he might secure reinforcements from the West and South. In early September, not knowing that Bragg was advancing northward through Tennessee, Lee wrote: I hope that Bragg's army can "be advantageously employed in opposing the overwhelming numbers which it seems to be the intention of the enemy now to concentrate in Virginia." In December, faced with Burnside's advance, he applied the general principle to suppose that "should there be a lull of war" in the South and West, "it might be advantageous to leave a sufficient covering force to conceal the movements, and draw an active force, when the exigency arrives, to the vicinity of Richmond. Provisions and forage in the meantime could be collected in Richmond. When the crisis shall have passed, these troops could be returned to their departments with reinforcements." But, since the spring, the seaboard had been relatively denuded of Confederate troops and there would be no "lull of war," for the West was facing a double advance almost simultaneous with Burnside's in Virginia. Lee would have to depend solely on the troops in Virginia and North Carolina.[11]

Burnside's plan finally devolved into essentially a frontal attack on Lee's position on the hill, Marye's Heights, above Fredericksburg. The principal assault would be made by the division under the old regular, Edwin Vose Sumner. On a foggy December 11 the men of the Army of the Potomac began constructing five pontoon bridges across the Rappahannock. Confederate sharpshooters several times drove the builders away, but federal guns joined in the duel and the construction continued. With two bridges finished by noon, four Union regiments then crossed the river in boats and drove away the Confederate riflemen. The Federals laid three other bridges and a blue-coated division occupied Fredericksburg by nightfall.

On December 12 the rest of the federal forces continued crossing the Rappahannock and spread out on the flat ground to the southeast of Fredericksburg, as Burnside obviously prepared to launch a major assault head-on against the Confederates the next day. The Confederates were ready, for, during the morning, Edward Porter Alexander, Longstreet's engineer and artillery chief, had reported: "We cover that ground now so well that we will comb it as with a fine-tooth comb. A chicken could not live on the field when we open on it!" As the fog cover lifted from the plain, the battle opened at mid-morning and the federal troops drove forward toward the hills. Apparently believing he faced only one Confederate wing, Burnside attacked the entire enemy army in a frontal assault. After the futile, wild, fantastic, and direct

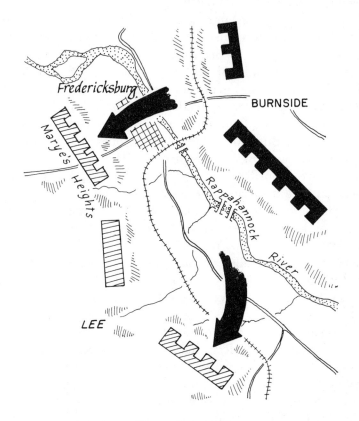

Frontal Assault

slam, one federal general said: "It was a great slaughter pen . . . they might as well have tried to take Hell." After Sumner's exhausted and battered division wore themselves out, Burnside sent in Hooker's division. Obviously disgusted with the impossible assignment, Hooker at last "finding that I had lost as many men as my orders required me to lose," suspended the attack. Robert E. Lee supposedly remarked, "I wish these people would go away and leave us alone," but the ineptitude of the Union attack prompted his fellow Confederate general, Joe Johnston, enviously to remark: "What luck some people have. Nobody will come to attack me in such a place."[12]

This Union attack failed just as had Pope's similarly rash assault at Second Bull Run. The cost was heavy, 12,653 Federals to 5,309 Confederates. In the poignant words of one outstanding historian of the Confederacy, Robert S.

Henry, "The town became a vast burying-ground—the yards, the gardens, the roadsides and open spaces, wherever trenches could be dug in the hard-frozen ground and bodies be thrust into them to be covered with the frozen clods. An empty ice-house was filled to the roof with bodies, to remain there through the rest of the war and finally, as unidentified dead, to be buried in the National Cemetery at Fredericksburg."

The Battle of Fredericksburg occasioned Lee's now-classic remark to Longstreet: "It is well that war is so terrible—we should grow too fond of it." At Fredericksburg, thanks to Burnside's frontal attack, Lee's use of "main force" for a defensive stand had thus worked out very favorably. True, Lee had let Burnside escape, and many southerners impatiently agreed with the London *Times* editorialist who contended that it had been within Lee's power to crush Burnside "horse, foot, and dragoons." Lee feebly replied in public that he had expected Burnside to attack again, but privately observed to Jeb Stuart: "No one knows how *brittle* an army is."[13]

Burnside in fact did order a renewal of the assaults, but his more prudent officers persuaded him to change his mind and not to attempt the asinine. Lee, meanwhile, also quite prudently chose not to counterattack, for although the Army of the Potomac lay beaten, it still was a mighty host, numerically superior, and well protected by massive artillery emplacements on the heights across the river. On December 15 the humiliated federal army completed its unmolested withdrawal to the north bank of the Potomac. For the Union, however, this did not end the Virginia campaign.

Just as the Battle of Fredericksburg closed, Dix reported from Fort Monroe that his demonstration had begun and Halleck urged Foster in North Carolina: "If you should be unable to made any considerable advances into the interior, it is to be hoped, nevertheless, that you will keep a large force of the enemy by your demonstrations." Though the expedition into the Shenandoah Valley was to get under way, Halleck was disappointed that the department commander did not think it prudent to supply additional forces for that move. The exasperated Halleck did not order them but warned: No forces "not absolutely necessary for defense, should be kept idle. It is complained that too many are injudiciously kept from the field, where we must encounter the enemy." With his other operations developing, Halleck urged Burnside to resume his offensive.[14]

The only theatre without forward movement was Rosecrans's in Middle Tennessee. When he had assumed command at the end of October, Bragg and Kirby Smith were then still moving south and the Army of the Cumberland was still in Kentucky. The new commander, having come from Mississippi, took some time to size up the situation. Initially Bragg's withdrawal from Kentucky aroused apprehension that he might "leave only a small force in East Tennessee and throw his main army into Mississippi against General

Grant." Grant agreed with Halleck and Rosecrans who warned him: "Beware of Bragg; it is nearly time for a few car-loads of his troops to arrive." The Confederates had done this once before when Van Dorn had left Arkansas after his defeat at Pea Ridge, leaving Curtis's pursuit stymied by guerrillas, lack of supplies, and no means of transportation except bad roads. The Confederates, Curtis had reported, "had supplies, steamboats, and railroads to expedite their trip down the Arkansas. Of course they could run away from us." The Union command realized that Bragg could do the same thing by moving quickly and leaving Rosecrans facing crippled railways and a country denuded of supplies and swarming with guerrillas. But Bragg, himself, was then in Richmond conferring on strategy and western reorganization. Since Middle Tennessee had far too much importance to the Confederates for them to risk giving it up without a struggle, the fears of the federal command proved groundless.[15]

Having moved to Nashville, Rosecrans prepared to follow Halleck's instructions "to take and hold East Tennessee, cutting the line of railroad at Chattanooga, Cleveland, or Athens, so as to destroy the connection of the valley of Virginia with Georgia and the other Southern states." Halleck wished that a considerable part of this might "be accomplished before the roads become impassable from the winter rains." Since Morgan had already made another raid, capturing Lexington, Kentucky, Rosecrans and Wright strengthened the protection of their railroads while Rosecrans waited for the road to be repaired and to begin the delivery of supplies. Meanwhile he had settled on a strategy of fighting the Confederates as near Nashville as possible, planning to "crush them in a decisive battle." But he remained immobile as Burnside and Grant advanced.[16]

Though Grant's campaign was under way and Grant himself was almost halfway between Corinth and Vicksburg, a cloud overhung the campaign. This cloud was McClernand's charter to command the down-river portion of the advance. Feeling that the "enterprise would be much safer" in Sherman's hands, Grant, in the absence of McClernand, had given it to Sherman. McClernand was still in Illinois and, in case Halleck did not understand about McClernand, Grant explained: It would be "particularly unfortunate to have either McClernand or Wallace sent to me. The latter I could manage if he had less rank, but the former is unmanageable and incompetent." Doubtless Halleck already knew this for, during the advance to Corinth, he had kept McClernand in charge of the reserves, safely out of harm's way. In fact, Halleck sent no orders to McClernand because, though he had read about the appointment in the newspapers, he had not been officially informed.[17]

Halleck obstructed the McClernand appointment because he was exasperated, he said, with "how difficult it is to resist political wire-pulling in military appointments. Every Governor, Senator and Member of Congress has his pet generals to be provided with separate and independent commands." Writing to his friend Schofield, Halleck explained: "I am sick and tired of this political military life. The number of enemies I have made because I would not yield my own convictions of right is already legion. If they would only follow the example of their ancestors, enter a herd of swine, run down some steep bank and drown themselves in the sea, there would be some hope of saving the country."[18]

When Halleck finally received orders to appoint McClernand, the orders arrived too late and Sherman was commanding the down-river expedition. McClernand, rightly suspecting sabotage, explained to Secretary Stanton: "Either through the intention of the General-in-Chief or a strange occurrence of accidents, the authority of the President and yourself, as evidenced by your acts, has been set at naught, and I have been deprived of the command that had been committed to me." Actually, McClernand was well out of it for the expedition was doomed.[19]

Rosecrans still delayed, placing his own good reasons ahead of the general in chief's anxiety. With many soldiers "barefoot, without blankets, without tents, without good arms, and cavalry without horses," Rosecrans had to wait for more than food and fodder. Planning a battle and a pursuit across the Tennessee River, he reasoned that wisdom indicated he should delay even into December for supplies before the battle, for "after all," he said, I will be "obliged to halt somewhere, to wait for indispensable supplies for which we have been waiting." Halleck explained that apprehensions about Britain's attitude created an additional reason for haste. Unperturbed, Rosecrans waited until he was ready. Convinced that the "true objective is now the enemy's force," Rosecrans said, I plan "to strike him a blow near us, which will virtually end the game."[20]

These ambitious objectives did not substitute for an advance in concert with the other armies. The situation in Virginia also precluded a movement by Burnside. His subordinate generals had completely lost confidence in him and the army was rife with dissension. For a while Halleck maintained pressure on Burnside to attack again, if only because the situation in the theatre was so favorable. Halleck knew that the western Virginia expedition to the Shenandoah Valley had started and the movements of Dix and Foster were bearing fruit. Foster reported that he had "fought four engagements . . . and whipped the enemy handsomely each time." He burned a railroad bridge and "tore up several miles of track of the Wilmington and Weldon Railroad." Dix and Foster thought enemy troops had moved from the Rappahannock to oppose them and Halleck told Burnside that his idleness permitted the enemy to use his interior lines and that "troops that fought at Fredericksburg [were] now in North Carolina." Even if no serious advance could take place on the Rappahannock, it would, Halleck stressed to Burnside, at least "be necessary that you occupy and press the enemy, so as to prevent large detachments" to southeastern Virginia and North Carolina.[21]

In spite of this pressure on him for support, Burnside had the effrontery to tell Lincoln: "It seems to be the universal opinion that the movements of the army have not been planned with a view to co-operation and mutual assistance." Expressing his belief that the Union should dismiss Stanton and Halleck and that he should "retire to private life," Burnside did not fully understand that his real problem resulted from the hostility of his senior officers to him and his plans for an advance. The conviction of many officers and rank and file that politicians had ordered the army into the suicidal Fredericksburg attack further depressed the morale of the Army of the Potomac. Radical rhetoric and the activities of the Committee on the Conduct of the War had convinced them that the strategy of the enthusiastic head-on attack had been imposed on the army. Many repined for McClellan.[22]

☆   ☆

Bogged down in dissension, Burnside remained immobile at Fredericksburg, while the two western offensives reached their climax. The first was Grant's, in which the separate parts each suffered different, though comparable, fates. Grant's flexible plan called for simultaneous movements with either Sherman's force working to distract and permitting Grant to advance or with Grant's army holding the enemy so Sherman "could operate in flank or on the rear." Sherman's advance would also give Grant access to water communications if they could link up.[23]

Grant never managed to commence his thrust. On December 11, Forrest, with 2,500 cavalrymen, left Columbia, Tennessee, for a raid upon Grant's communications. The effect of Forrest's raid was overshadowed by one more devastating to Grant's plans: on December 20 Earl Van Dorn's cavalry moved rapidly from Grenada, Mississippi, and pounced on Grant's huge supply depot at Holly Springs. As noted by Bruce Catton, "a jubilant Southern reporter saw panicky Yankees in flight 'clothed very similarly to Joseph when the lady Potiphar attempted to detain him,' and wrote breathlessly of 'tents burning, torches flaming, Confederates shouting, guns popping, sabres clanking, abolitionists begging for mercy, 'rebels' shouting exultingly, women *en dishabile* clapping their hands frantic with joy, crying 'Kill them! Kill them!' " The gleeful marauders took 1,500 prisoners and destroyed, for want of means to carry them away, more than one-and-one-half-million dollars worth of supplies. Van Dorn had captured the entire town and everything and everybody in it. Along with the military garrison and its commander, he even took as prisoner a much-flustered Mrs. U. S. Grant! The courteous Confederates quickly allowed her safely through the lines.[24]

Thus before Sherman was well started, Grant explained: "Raids made upon the railroad to my rear by Forrest northward from Jackson, and by Van Dorn northward from the Tallahatchie, have cut me off from supplies, so that farther advance by this route is perfectly impracticable." He added: Even with "everything for the subsistence of man or beast appropriated for the use of our army" and the men on half rations, "the country does not afford supplies for troops, and but a limited supply of forage."[25]

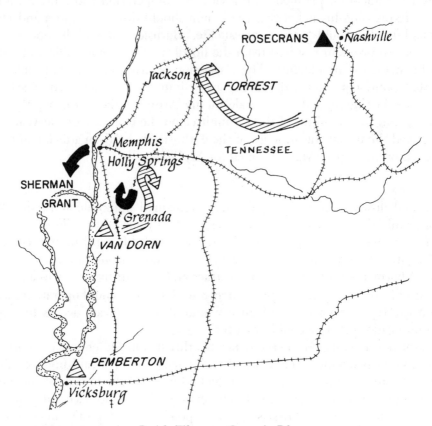

Raids Thwart Grant's Plans

But Sherman had already moved downriver with an expedition of 33,000 men on 60 transports, accompanied by seven gunboats, and was facing defenses under the nominal direction of Lieutenant General John C. Pemberton. In command of dispersed forces, Pemberton did not arrive in Vicksburg personally until after the battle had begun. Within the city, an engineer officer of limited imagination but sound ability, Major General Martin L. Smith, exercised command of troops and guns for immediate defense, and the youthful veteran of battles in the east, Brigadier General Stephen D. Lee, had some 2,700 men for mobile defense just outside the city. When Pemberton learned of Sherman's approach and Grant's halt, he began moving reinforcements to Vicksburg and eventually concentrated 12,000 troops there. However, the bulk of them, as well as a division dispatched by Jefferson Davis from Bragg's army in Tennessee, did not arrive until after the decisive action.

Sherman admitted that northern "preparations were extremely hasty," as "this was the nature of the plan," but actually he and Grant hurried in order to begin before McClernand arrived. The armada steamed down the Mississippi and then twelve miles up the Yazoo River. The men debarked on an area about six miles square, the Yazoo on the north, an old bed of the Mississippi on the west, a long, narrow lake on the south, and Chickasaw Bayou on the east. Terrain, more than planning, brought two Union brigades into assault positions at the bayou, where the able Confederate leader, Stephen D. Lee, had set a trap.

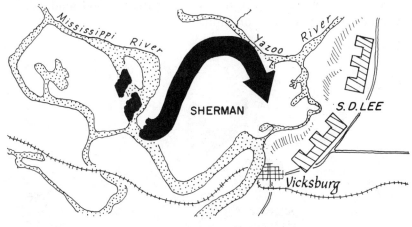

Union Landing

As Grant was retreating and Pemberton was using his railroad and central position to reconcentrate his troops at Vicksburg, Sherman wrote Grant's chief of staff: I "cannot describe with what painful suspense I listened for the sound of your guns in the distance while we lay in the swamp of the Yazoo. Observing the heavy re-enforcements pouring into Vicksburg, and not hearing you, I was forced at last to conclude that necessity had compelled you to fall back to Holly Springs." But Sherman felt it necessary to push ahead even without support from Grant.[26]

A morass of mud and water slowed the Federals and compelled the funneling of men over a log bridge. Sherman's force was organized into four divisions, the principal attack to be made by the one under Brigadier General George W. Morgan. "Tell Morgan to give the signal for the assault," Sherman rashly commanded; "we will lose 5,000 men before we take Vicksburg, and may as well lose them here as anywhere else." Gazing at the forbidding terrain that lay before the enemy's powerful emplacements, one of Morgan's brigade commanders incredulously asked, "General, do I understand that you are about to order an assault?" "Yes, form your brigade!" Morgan responded. "My poor brigade!" the man cried, but then saluted and said resolutely, "Your order will be obeyed, General."

The attackers reached within 150 yards of the intrenched Confederate main line, a concave and very strong position easily reinforceable at any point by using a road that ran along the rear. "All formations were broken," Morgan recalled. "The assaulting forces were jammed together and, with a yell of desperate determination, they rushed to the assault and were mowed down by a storm of shells, grape and canister, and minie-balls which swept our front like a hurricane of fire." Losses reached almost nine to one: 1,776 Union and 207 Confederate. "It was awful," one Union regimental commander commented, "a repetition of Balaklava, although mine was infantry and Earl Cardigan's force was cavalry." Sherman planned another assault; but dense fog settled and, a torrential rain instilling fear that a flood might drown the entire command, he withdrew on January 2, 1863.[27]

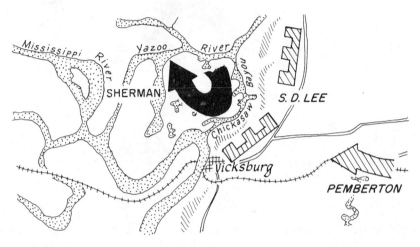

Union Withdrawal

☆   ☆

   While Grant and Sherman came to grief, Burnside tarried on the Potomac, and Dix and Foster demonstrated against the southern coast, Rosecrans at last advanced. Despite his commendable prudence, William Starke "Old Rosy" Rosecrans, now forty-three years old, previously had shown himself a combative commander. As a boy he had developed studious inclinations and read avidly, theology becoming a lifelong interest. He graduated from West Point in 1842, fifth in the class. For the next ten years he performed unexceptional engineering tasks, had no part in the Mexican War, and resigned in 1854. Undistinguished in civilian pursuits, by the war's outbreak in 1861 he headed an unsuccessful kerosene refinery in Cincinnati. Although starting the war as an aide to McClellan, he quickly gained combat command opportunities and performed well. Western Virginia, Corinth, Iuka, every action brought him favorable notice and a steady rise in rank. He was promoted to major general on September 17, 1862, and was a natural choice for Buell's replacement as commander of the Army of the Cumberland, a post he assumed on October 27. Handsome, red-faced, and excitable, and known to be aggressive, he was loved by his soldiers, and, though a Democrat, he was acceptable to the radicals.

Convivial and likable, Rosecrans merited the enthusiasm of his admirers. The troops particularly liked the way he inspected regiments. When he spotted a soldier with worn-out shoes or a ragged coat, he would tell him: "Go to your captain and demand what you need! Go to him every day until you get it! Bore him for it! Bore him in his quarters! Bore him at meal time! Bore him in bed! Don't let him rest." He gleefully explained that in this way demands for relief would flow upward through regiment, brigade, division, and corps until they reached army headquarters, and, he exclaimed, "I'll see then if you don't get what you want!"[28]

The men knew that Rosecrans worked exceedingly long and hard. Stories circulated that he often labored far into the night, always until two, usually four o'clock, and occasionally with no sleep at all. When aides dozed in their chairs, he tweaked their ears, patted their heads paternally, and sent them to bed. Interestingly, he preferred young and inexperienced men on his staff, "sandy fellows," he called them, "quick and sharp," with no fixed habits of thought or action which needed breaking. From troop commanders he demanded precision and high standards of conduct. He demanded and received authority to muster officers out of service if guilty of pillage, drunkenness, or misbehavior before the enemy. By every measure Rosecrans seemed a good man to conduct operations against the Confederates under Bragg.

Braxton Bragg, his ablest biographer Grady McWhiney succinctly observed, "represented an unusual combination of potentially dangerous eccentricities and high ability." Bragg possessed a weak body; hampered by illness all his life, his various sicknesses grew more intense and vexing whenever his responsibilities increased, and seemed related to the degree of his despondence or frustration, probably in part from psychosomia. His frailties characterized him as much as his ambition, worry, dissatisfaction, and contentiousness. "Too ambitious to be satisfied with himself or with others," McWhiney continues, Bragg "sought perfection, and was disappointed when he failed to find it or achieve it."[29]

Bragg had performed well as an administrator and an effective disciplinarian, but he lacked essential qualities of judiciousness, the ability to work well with people he disliked, and sufficient insight to learn from his mistakes; in the end his passion for discipline became as much a hindrance as it did an asset, undermining the confidence that he might otherwise have enjoyed from a crucial number of supporters. Ability to elicit exemplary obedience had always been his longest suit. During the Mexican War it won him wide respect from professional soldiers. One general testified that "all the officers who knew Bragg . . . thought he was perhaps the best disciplinarian in the United States Army." But in the Mexican War his reputation as a martinet began to emerge. One comment in the report of an investigation of an attempt against his life indicated: No reason could be ascertained for the dastardly effort "except that some of his men think he is too severe." Years later, one Civil War private wrote: "Breathe softly the name . . . Bragg, it has more terror than the [enemy] army." This same private later alleged: "We . . . did not . . . so much love our country as we feared Bragg." But Bragg was not bloodthirsty nor unreasonable: many more soldiers loved than hated him; he drove himself even harder than he did his troops, and he remained always genuinely devoted to their welfare. Still, his tactlessness offended and elicited enmity from many independently inclined southerners, and he became the victim of an inaccurate and bad press. The famous diarist Mary Boykin Chesnut noted that he had ordered the execution of a soldier for shooting a chicken, but she failed to include that, since one of the shots had missed the chicken and killed a man, the soldier actually had been tried and executed for murder. Likewise, although many officers eventually grew disgusted, distrustful, or somehow disenchanted with Bragg, many more of them remained his fervent supporters. Most importantly, Bragg retained a measure of the confidence and friendship of Jefferson Davis.[30]

Bragg had earned Davis's admiration and support despite their not having admired one another before the Civil War. Stationed in remote and quiescent Florida in mid-1861, Bragg had whipped his forces into formidable fighting units and then magnanimously offered to trade four of his well-trained regiments for four newly organized ones so he could repeat the seasoning process. This impressed Davis immensely. Commanders characteristically held tenaciously to all troops they possessed, and rarely indeed did a man willingly suggest an exchange of trained soldiers for raw recruits. Davis justly marked Bragg for higher responsibilities and later spoke of him as "the only General in command of an Army who had shown himself equal to the management of Volunteers and at the same time commanded their love and respect." Bragg further cemented Davis's high opinion of him when, immediately after the debacle at forts Henry and Donelson, Bragg sent some of his own troops to Sidney Johnston as reinforcements without awaiting word from the War Department. Bragg thereafter became a confidant of Davis, and Davis considered his opinions when he formulated strategy. Yet Bragg remained friendly with Beauregard, whom Davis distrusted as a field commander.[31]

But, if Davis stood resolutely behind his western general, many men held ambivalent attitudes toward Bragg and quite a few blamed him personally for the failure in Kentucky. It is not at all true, however, that Bragg had completely lost the confidence of his army. Only two of the twenty generals directly under his command in Kentucky openly expressed dissatisfaction with him as a superior. Thirteen generals and numerous colonels delivered firm expressions of support.[32]

In early December Davis personally visited Bragg's headquarters at Murfreesboro, Tennessee. After three days of careful conferences interspersed with extravagant parties and a review of Polk's corps which Davis pronounced "the best appointed troops he had seen—well appointed and well clad," Davis went on to Johnston's headquarters at Chattanooga and ordered that Bragg send 10,000 men to reinforce Pemberton's continuing defense of Vicksburg.

Clearly Davis felt that Bragg could perform good service even with reduced numbers and could spare some troops to defend the Mississippi against the well-advertised and very menacing federal advance then in progress. The troops, Stevenson's large division, arrived too late to assist in the repulse of Sherman.

The recently named Army of Tennessee occupied a semicircular and widely separated position southeast of Nashville so that it could gather supplies, watch the enemy, and concentrate readily wherever appropriate. Bragg effected some reorganizations, especially in his cavalry, recognizing the uncommonly good performance of Colonel Joseph Wheeler in the Kentucky retreat. The horsemen under their courageous twenty-six-year-old leader fought at least twenty-six engagements over a five-day period, fending off the federal pursuit. Bragg now elevated Wheeler to brigadier general, thus placing under the comparatively young man both the cantankerous and unpredictably independent Nathan Bedford Forrest and the strong-willed individualist John Hunt Morgan. While either subordination might have elicited grave difficulties, both Forrest and Morgan accepted the situation and continued their energetic efforts.[33]

Although there was some respite for socializing, and Morgan married a local belle, Bragg's cavalrymen served quite vigorously while the Confederates encamped along the Murfreesboro line. Forrest launched one of the raids so instrumental in cancelling Grant's overland advance. On December 11 he started from Columbia, Tennessee, and by the 15th crossed the Tennessee River at Clifton. On the 17th his men attacked and captured Lexington, taking 150 prisoners, 300 Sharp's rifles, a supply of ammunition, and two three-inch Rodman guns, which Stanley Horn called "the pride of Forrest's artillery for the rest of the war." He retreated and crossed the river on January 3, 1863, having in little more than two weeks killed or captured 2,500 enemy troops, taken 10 guns, and 10,000 rifles, and 1,000,000 cartridges. Further, he had wrecked the Mobile and Ohio Railroad, torn up many miles of track, and burned fifty trestle bridges.[34]

Meanwhile, Morgan also conducted a spectacular raid. Departing Alexandria, near Carthage, Tennessee, on December 21, he launched a Christmas-season foray into Kentucky against federal supply lines. He pushed near Louisville, destroyed a bridge at Muldraugh's Hill near Lincoln's birthplace, and fought an action at Bacon Creek before successfully returning to Tennessee by January 1. He estimated that his men destroyed over two million dollars worth of property, including the Louisville and Nashville Railroad from Munfordville to within eighteen miles of Louisville. Losing only 90 men, he captured nearly 2,000 prisoners. But, crucially, the raid failed to dislodge any Federals from their occupation of Nashville. Not only had Rosecrans accumulated enough supplies to last a month, but the Cumberland River had risen, thereby allowing a million rations to be sent to Nashville by water. So the well-prepared Rosecrans did not have to delay his advance.

And, most importantly, these raids by Forrest and Morgan resulted in depriving Bragg of more than half of his cavalry during the campaign that ensued in late December.[35]

The Federals engaged in some raiding of their own, preliminary to their offensive against Bragg's army. Arranged ahead of time between Rosecrans and Wright, the raid was to coincide with the advance of Rosecrans's Army of the Cumberland. On December 26, 1862, a small cavalry force under Brigadier General Samuel P. Carter, destined to be the only American officer to achieve the ranks of major general in the army and rear admiral in the navy, departed Manchester, Kentucky, for the upper Tennessee Valley. In a raid that lasted until January 5, Carter's men destroyed railroad bridges and fought various skirmishes, especially a hard contest on December 28 at Perkins's Mill or Elk Fort. But just as with Morgan's raid against the North, this raid against southern supply lines failed to affect significantly the battle which erupted along Stones River, save to deny the army commander use of some otherwise valuable cavalry.[36]

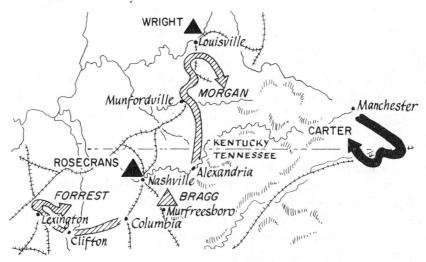

Raids on Communications

Rosecrans knew of Forrest's and Morgan's absences on their raids and also heard about the departing Confederate division bound for Mississippi. And so, having accumulated adequate supplies, "Old Rosy" advanced in late December directly upon Bragg's forces to "crush them in a decisive battle." The move commenced on December 26, continually harassed by the Confederate cavalry under Wheeler which had immediately sent word to Bragg so that the southern forces might concentrate. Further, Wheeler promised Bragg to hold the bluecoats for at least four days. He managed precisely that, and on the fifth day, December 31, 1862, the battle commenced.

"The field of battle offered no peculiar advantages for defense," Bragg's subordinate Hardee later noted. The general area, open farm country, provided no natural barriers. In spots where trees did grow, they stood in thick patches that offered concealment to the attacker and hampered Confederate cavalry and artillery movements. Even Rosecrans had expected that Bragg would choose to receive an assault at Stewart's Creek, some miles north of Murfreesboro, where the stream's steep banks afforded innate defensive advantages; but Bragg selected a field just two miles from town, near the Stones River. Bragg wished to hold the town because it was his supply depot and the surrounding country fed his army. This ill-suited stand so close to the unpredictable river in a heavy rainy period could have caused great awkwardness for the Confederates should the water overflow the banks; and it rained nearly every day between December 27 and January 4. Most serious of all, Bragg failed to have the army intrench. Bragg, in fact, never liked intrenchments and consistently deprecated their importance.[37]

While Rosecrans advanced along three roads, Wheeler led several cavalry regiments, amounting to some 2,500 men, on a daring raid. Despite his braggadocio and such flamboyant comments as announcing to his staff that a raid was impending with "The War Child Rides Tonight," Wheeler was diligent and active. As so well described by Robert S. Henry, "Starting on the night of December twenty-ninth, he made the entire circuit of Rosecrans' army, captured more than a thousand prisoners, destroyed all or parts of four wagon trains, with great quantity of supplies, and created such shortage of subsistence in the Union army during the three days' battle to come that men were reduced to eating the meat of the horses killed on the field." While Wheeler concluded his depredations upon one enemy corps's sumptuously

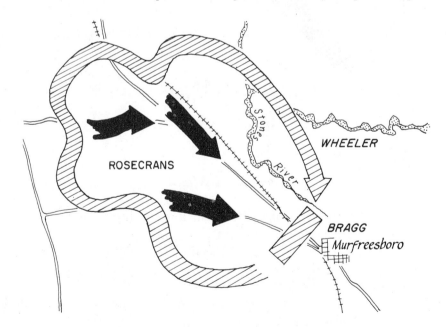

Union Advance and Wheeler's Raid

loaded 300-wagon supply train, the two armies spent their time getting into position.[38]

Through skirmishing and artillery fire, both adversaries tried to ascertain locations of opposing lines. That night, an eerie prelude to battle occurred. Just before tattoo the military bands of each army began to play their favorite tunes. The music carried clearly on the cold, still air and each could hear the other's playing. "Yankee Doodle" and "Hail, Columbia" drifted into everyone's ears, answered by "Dixie" and "The Bonnie Blue Flag." The exchange continued for a time and then one band struck up a tune known and loved by all soldiers, regardless of allegiance, "Home Sweet Home." Suddenly all the bands on both sides joined in its playing, while thousands of voices, most betraying homesickness, joined in with the words.[39]

Both commanders planned to attack the other's right, but Bragg's assault commenced first, and so at dawn on December 31, 1862, the Battle of Stones River or Murfreesboro opened. The temporarily superior Confederate con-

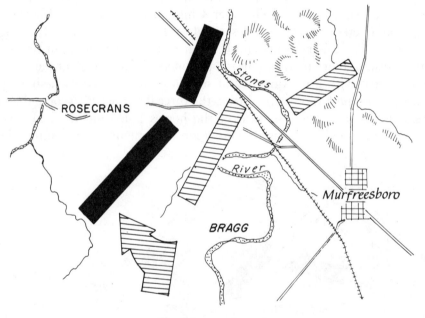

Confederate Attack

centration drove back the flank of Rosecrans's army through a ninety-degree angle. Some federal privates fleeing in panic through the cedar trees cried out, "We are sold again! We are sold again!" as many of them incredibly believed that Buell had "sold out" to Bragg at Perryville, and that now a similar deal existed between Bragg and Rosecrans. But the Confederate drive gradually lost momentum. In part this resulted because the division under Major General Benjamin F. Cheatham, despite Bragg's orders, moved sluggishly. Most of Bragg's critics either denied this fact or ignored it, but

Cheatham's delay cost the southerners time and casualties. Quite probably he was drunk. A private later claimed that during the battle many officers were so drunk that they could not even distinguish between Confederate and federal units.[40]

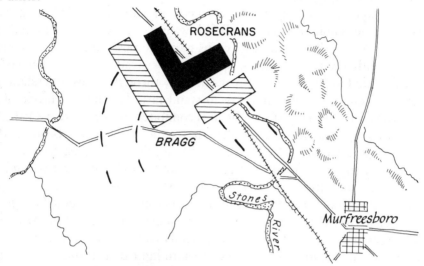

Positions When Rosecrans Stopped Bragg's Attack

Once Rosecrans realized that he had been forced onto the tactical defensive, he handled himself and his troops quite well. Shoring flagging lines, offering encouragement and showing high spirits, he rode hard from unit to unit, "a dead cigar clenched in his teeth, black hat jammed down on his head, his overcoat all streaked with blood—a shell had taken off the head of his chief of staff, riding beside him, and the general had been splattered." The historian Bruce Catton poignantly described the day when one admiring enlisted man looked at Rosecrans and observed that "he looked more like a third-rate wagon master than a great general, as he is."[41]

Bragg's sympathizers assert that had President Davis left with the army at Murfreesboro the division dispatched to Mississippi, the southerners would have crushed Rosecrans's force; but this relies on the doubtful assumption that Bragg would have held the division in reserve until the perfect moment and then hurled against the enemy's weakest point. Bragg's other faulty decisions belie the likelihood that he would have done better with more troops. His tactical plan lacked necessary subtlety and flexibility. Of Bragg's defective plan, his biographer succinctly observed: "Unless the Union army collapsed at the first onslaught, it would be pushed back into a tighter and stronger defensive position as the battle continued, while the Confederate forces would gradually lose momentum, become disorganized, and grow weaker. Like a snowball, the Federals would pick up strength from the debris of battle if they retreated in good order. But the Confederates would inevitably unwind like a ball of string as they advanced." The power of the defense and the maneuverability of the armies allowed Rosecrans to defend effectively his peculiar position, though he clearly lost the battle.[42]

The fray was actually two in one, two distinct engagements separated by a day of inaction. Bragg telegraphed Richmond: "The enemy has yielded his strong position" and, Bragg almost correctly presumed, he "is falling back. We occupy the whole field and shall follow him. . . . God has granted us a happy New Year." But while Rosecrans gave the possibility serious consideration, he either was too obtuse, optimistic, or steadfast to see that he had been defeated. He refused to retreat. In fact, through a misunderstanding, Rosecrans elected after the first day to stand fast. He rode with one of his corps commanders during the night to reconnoiter for a new rearward position. As they approached a creek that they expected to move beyond, they observed a number of mounted men with torches riding back and forth. Rosecrans hastily presumed: "They have got entirely in our rear and are forming a line of battle by torchlight," thus shutting off the route of federal retreat. So Rosecrans rode back to his headquarters and instructed his generals to "prepare to fight or die." Not until the next morning did the Unionists discover that the moving torches the generals had seen were being used by federal cavalrymen camped along the creek to light their campfires. On January 1, 1863, each commander anxiously waited to see what the other might do. Bragg, apparently with no plans to continue the attack, kept expecting that Rosecrans would retire; but the Federals remained immobile.[43]

On the morning of January 2 Bragg tried a brief exploratory artillery bombardment at the center. Then the armies watched each other for several more hours. Finally, late in the day, Bragg launched a segmented assault on the northeast side of Stones River. Neither side lost nor won any ground at all, though the casualties mounted; and the stalemate seemed to convince Bragg that he, rather than Rosecrans, had lost the battle. Bragg elected to retreat, deluded perhaps by Rosecrans's bringing in empty railway trains that night with troops on hand at the station to cheer, thus simulating the arrival of Union reinforcements. "Just as at Perryville," observed the biographer McWhiney, "Bragg seemed to change under stress from a bold and aggressive attacker to a hesitant and cautious retreater." A Confederate in the ranks wrote of the indecisive battle: "I am sick and tired of this war, and, I can see no prospects of having peace for a long time to come, I don't think it ever will be stopped by fighting, the Yankees cant whip us and we can never whip them, and I see no prospect of peace unless the Yankees themselves rebell and throw down their arms, and refuse to fight any longer."[44]

The armies remained unshaken by the immense losses in this hard-fought battle. The casualties stood at 12,906 Federals and 11,739 Confederates, 31 percent of the northern army, 33 percent of the southern. Each had made an earnest effort to annihilate the other by overwhelming the flanks, but with no better success than Burnside achieved in his frontal attack at Fredericksburg. In view of the more ample federal manpower resources, additional battles, with losses essentially even, would have given the Union an advantage, since attrition is a form of annihilation. However, the Confederates retreated. Even though Bragg withdrew, he did not go far—twenty miles southeast along the railroad. Rosecrans did not follow, being as depleted by his bloody victory as Bragg by defeat. Bragg, however, still hoped to make the campaign a success, but through the now-well-developed Confederate strategy of raids against communications.

Successful in stopping Buell's advance in August, 1862, the first raids, conducted by Forrest and Morgan, had been ordered by Kirby Smith, doubtless influenced by his military background that had included cavalry service on the frontier. Kirby Smith had seen the possibility of crippling the enemy's rail communications when he had told Morgan that he might "do great good by burning their line of transportation." He had had as his objective, in which he was quite successful, to "delay General Buell's movement and give General Bragg time to move on Middle Tennessee." Having fully grasped the significance of these raids, in December Bragg had sent half of his superior cavalry force to attack the enemy's "depots and lines of communications."[45]

Another former frontier cavalryman, Joseph E. Johnston, the new commander of the Department of the West, shared Bragg's appreciation of the strategic possibilities presented by this highly significant use of cavalry. Johnston thought Forrest's strike against the West Tennessee railroads might "delay General Grant," but Bragg became more enthusiastic and more perceptive when he saw that Forrest's raids might "force the enemy to retire from the Mississippi." Coupled with the raid of Van Dorn, Forrest's fulfilled Bragg's expectations. A former artilleryman who had tried hard to avoid frontier service, Bragg nevertheless clearly realized the strategic possibilities of the raid, even overestimating its power. Although hard pressed by interruption of his communications, Rosecrans did not stand in danger of being forced to evacuate Nashville, even though a Confederate said, "Gen Bragg feels confident of it. Thinks it certain, because the enemy can not subsist there."[46]

The federal armies started the war "at a distinct disadvantage to the Confederates in Cavalry." The U.S. Army had little mounted tradition, in part because Congress had not been anxious to fund such an expensive branch of the service. More important, when the war began, Winfield Scott was convinced that the Union did not need cavalry, in part because the wooded terrain of the South would limit its effectiveness and because he probably realized that mounted troops could have no role on a battlefield dominated by rifle-armed infantry. The Union War Department followed Scott's views and Secretary of War Cameron frequently wrote "Accept no cavalry" on state offers of cavalry units. Though the government soon yielded and accepted more, the numbers did not grow rapidly because of continued military opposition and a lack of cavalry equipment.[47]

The volunteers' enthusiasm for fighting on horseback met no such official opposition in the Confederacy. "Confederate Cavalry, like Topsy, just grew, expanding to considerable size under pressure of popular interest not especially by virtue of Governmental policy." The southerners overcame shortage of equipment by improvisation, one unit being armed with hatchets and shotguns rather than sabres and pistols. Confederate cavalry also enjoyed an early qualitative advantage over that of the Union. Better horsemanship among southern recruits facilitated training and promoted a higher degree of Confederate riding proficiency earlier in the war.[48]

In spite of the lack of an official policy with respect to the proportion of cavalry in the army, the military climate was favorable. President Davis had served with the dragoons on the frontier, and the mounted service contributed three of its veterans to high rebel command—Albert Sidney Johnston, Robert E. Lee, and Joseph E. Johnston, the highest-ranking field commanders in the Confederate army.[49]

The cavalry was proportionately well represented elsewhere in the Confederate army, for, of the fifty-six officers of regular mounted regiments in the Civil War, thirty served with the South. They also brought with them the foundations of the doctrines of dismounted combat and raiding communications which would prove so effective in the Civil War. The U.S. Army had already developed a strong tradition of mounted men fighting on foot and the warfare against the Indians in the 1850s had made the cavalry "adept at partisan warfare."[50]

The outcome at Stones River, however, had significance for the North. One observer thought: "The unexpected victory sent a wave of feeling through the North that lifted Rosecrans into high popular favor and bade fair to make him our foremost military leader." Rosecrans immediately became popular in Washington, and Stanton told him: "There is nothing you can ask within my power to grant to yourself and your heroic command that will not be cheerfully given." Because of the victory, Stanton wrote, "the country is filled with admiration of the gallantry and heroic achievement of yourself and the officers and troops under your command." Especial satisfaction must have come to Lincoln and others because of a rebel newspaper clipping sent to the President by General Dix. Commenting that Bragg, like Beauregard at Shiloh, first reported a victory, the anti-Davis *Richmond Examiner* editorialized, "So far the news has come in what may be called the classical style of the Southwest. When the Southern army fights a battle, we first hear that it has gained one of the most stupendous victories on record; that regiments . . . have exhibited an irresistible and superhuman valor unknown in history this side of Sparta and Rome. As for the generals, they usually get all their clothes shot off and replace them with a suit of glory. The enemy, of course, is simply annihilated. Next day more dispatches come, still very good, but not quite as good as the first. The telegrams of the third day are invariably such as to make a mist, a muddle, and a fog of the whole affair."[51]

Lincoln enjoyed, too, the congratulatory resolutions from the Indiana and Ohio legislatures and the thanks that Congress tendered Rosecrans. Following the defeat at Fredericksburg and the late-December failure at Vicksburg, Rosecrans's victory, however bloody and barren of results, amounted to a godsend for an administration attacked right and left for its incompetence and the vain attempts of its generals to deliver any results. Later Lincoln admitted to Rosecrans: "I can never forget, whilst I remember anything, that about the end of last year, and beginning of this, you gave us a hard earned victory which, had there been a defeat instead, the nation could scarcely have lived over. Neither can I forget the check you so opportunely gave to a dangerous sentiment" of defeatism "which was spreading in the north."[52]

Though of a strongly improvised character, Halleck's effort to bring about a coordinated offensive had succeeded remarkably well. Of the major forces ordered to advance, only Banks failed to move. He did not reach New Orleans until December 14 and concentrated on "organizing and drilling" his command, all "new troops, most of them never having handled a musket until their arrival" at New Orleans. The simultaneous advances had basically succeeded in preventing Confederate troop movements to major theatres, with the exception of the reinforcement of Lee by troops from western Virginia, a shift that would probably not have occurred had it been possible to supply the programmed advance through western Virginia. The only other movement had favored the Union because the division dispatched to Mississippi from Tennessee left before Stones River and arrived after Sherman's defeat.[53]

Besides Stones River, one other bright spot showed in the Union operations for the season. After defeat at Chickasaw Bluff, McClernand had arrived and superseded Sherman in command of the river force. Leaving their position before Vicksburg, McClernand and Sherman decided to attack an isolated Confederate post in Arkansas. On January 10, 1863, these federal forces neared Arkansas Post, or Fort Hindman, about fifty miles up the Arkansas River from its junction with the Mississippi. Late that morning McClernand commenced investing the fort and drove in upon the outer earthworks. The next day, aided by Union gunboats, the federal troops captured the place after a three-and-one-half-hour contest. The northern losses amounted to 1,061, out of 29,000 effectives, and 13 gunboats; the Confederates lost 109 killed and wounded, but almost all the rest of their 5,000, some 4,791, were captured. Nevertheless, the operation, while successful, failed to affect materially the Vicksburg campaign. The Union forces then moved to Milliken's Bend, near Vicksburg.

While the armies settled in for the winter season of rain and mud, Grant began trying various schemes to turn Vicksburg via new water communications. These hapless operations fared little better than earlier naval actions and seemed to indicate perhaps an impregnability based on the difficult terrain. Earlier, in December, 1862, a Confederate mine had sunk the federal ironclad *Cairo*. Then followed Sherman's fateful assault at Chickasaw Bayou.

The unusually high water of the winter of 1862–63, made military operations still more difficult; but, since Grant believed that idle troops grow soft and low in morale, he industriously engaged them in a series of labors. And Grant's troops typically did remain active and cheerful. One Illinois soldier wrote that his regiment was healthy and happy, and added, humorously, that as soon as the canals were finished here, "we are going round and cut a canal across the upper part of Florida, thereby cutting that invaluable state off from the 'Confed' and give the alligators a deed for it."[54]

In attempting, against Sherman's advice, to find water communications to Vicksburg's rear, Grant was reacting to the defeat of his own advance in December and, by implication, to the defeat of Buell by raiders in the summer. Grant was thus responding to the cavalry raid which was emerging as the critical dimension of the Union military problem.

With virtually unlimited war aims, the Union could not, in view of the pertinacity of their opponents and the Confederacy's intensive and effective military effort, expect to win by any single victory or by the acquisition of any block territory, even one of as great economic and political importance as Tennessee—despite Joe Johnston's extravagant characterization of that strategically important state as "the shield of the South." Victory, on the other hand, could come to the Confederates if they could hold out and wear down the Union's will to win.[55]

The Union thus had to face squarely the difficulty of conquering such a vast country, filled with a hostile population, while opposed by large, well-organized, well-led, and modern military forces. The first problem was that of communications. Roads would not do; only water or rails could support the necessarily large armies of invasion in their efforts to penetrate the enormous area of the Confederate West. The defending Confederate armies could take positions which blocked the essential lines of communications of the projected Union penetrations, and these lines were necessarily the lines of operations of the advancing armies. The defender's blocking position, as that of the Confederates at Chickasaw Bluffs, placed the advancing army in the disadvantageous position of having to attack an enemy in a position chosen by the defender because it exploited to the utmost all of the advantages of the defense. The attacker had as an alternative to seek to force the defender to retreat by turning his flank or threatening his communications, though, as Robert E. Lee showed in Virginia and Maryland and Bragg in Kentucky, both sides could use the turning movement. Further, the rebels could raid enemy territory. Though this would not add any territory to the Confederacy, it would disrupt a Union offensive.

Because of the necessary reliance on relatively uncommon rail or water routes of advance, blocking a penetration was far easier than closing a country to a raiding expedition. As Buell's and Grant's abortive advances had shown, the communications of a penetration were vulnerable to incursions by a defender. Whereas water communications offered relative security against raids, the Union armies now stood, except for those on the Mississippi, at the end of their heretofore ample western water communications. In order to penetrate the interior of Mississippi, Alabama, or Georgia, they would have to rely on railroads.

Communications

The defending Confederates could retreat, tearing up the railroad in the process. As the attackers advanced, laboriously rebuilding the trackage, they would gradually extend behind them a lengthening and vulnerable line of communications. But raiders could destroy the laboriously reconstructed tracks and bridges, involving days or even weeks to repair again. Though more difficult to accomplish, the destruction of a major depot, as Grant's at Holly Springs, could cripple the advancing army even more.

Conditions in the East were similar. Though transportation was easier, the problem of moving on a predictable line or objective was greater. This had created dissension in Burnside's headquarters and had led to a minor crisis in the Washington headquarters. To resolve the problem of Burnside's advance Lincoln told Halleck: Go with Burnside "to the ground, examine it as far as practicable, confer with the officers, getting their judgment, . . . in a word gather all the elements for forming a judgment of your own; and then tell Gen. Burnside that you *do* approve, or that you do *not* approve his plan. Your military skill is useless to me, if you will not do this."[56]

General Halleck gave emphasis to his refusal to work this way by resigning as general in chief. He said, The "very important difference in opinion in regard to my relations toward generals commanding armies in the field" means that "I cannot perform the duties of my present office satisfactorily to the President and to myself." Except when setting objectives or directing the transfer of troops, Halleck's policy called for giving only guidance. As he expressed it: "I have always, whenever it was possible, avoided giving positive instructions to generals commanding departments, leaving them the exercise of their own judgment while giving them my opinion and advice."[57]

Halleck derived this policy from army practice, his business experience, and what history told him of the unfortunate effects of too restrictive direction by Louis XIV of France and the Austrian Aulic Council. The more fundamental truth he had explained to the President the previous summer when asked to come to Washington. "If I were to go to Washington," he told Lincoln, "I could advise but one thing: to place all the forces in North Carolina, Virginia, and Washington under one head and hold that head responsible for the result." With his resignation, he was telling Lincoln the same thing: If you don't have confidence in the commander, replace him; if you do, don't try to tell him how to do his job.[58]

Lincoln withdrew his letter and Halleck withdrew his resignation. Doubtless Halleck made his point and Lincoln, the previously inexperienced administrator, learned something of value about how organizations work, even though he continued to confer and correspond directly with commanders of the Army of the Potomac. Correspondence with other theatres he left to Halleck as had been his custom.

On January 19, 1863, Burnside made an effort to turn Lee's position. As he moved up the Rappahannock, rains set in, and, as Burnside admitted, "from that moment we felt that the winter campaign had ended." His men dragged guns and pontoons into position through mud and roads that the officers and men found "shocking." The advance bogged in a hopeless mass of mud and slime; the Army of the Potomac literally stalled, unable to do anything. Ammunition trains and supply wagons mired, horses and mules dropped dead, the whole army lost its spirit. Artillery pieces literally sank into the mud and, unless buoyed up, sank until only the muzzles showed. Of the wreckage a reporter observed: "One might fancy that some new geologic cataclysm had overtaken the world and that he saw around him the elemental wrecks left by another Deluge." The soggy, hungry force, deprived of its supplies because wagons could not move, soon realized the question no longer was how to go on, but how to get back. After several days of humiliating and pain-wracked labor, it returned to its camps opposite Fredericksburg and established winter quarters.[59]

Now, wisely, Lincoln relieved Burnside and replaced him with Major General Joseph Hooker. This, however, did not solve the problem of the

Virginia theatre. Nor was the finding of a solution delegated to the commander. The solution, or doctrine for the theatre, was evolved in headquarters, completed before Burnside's removal, and became the subject of the
kind of general direction and advice which Halleck regarded as appropriate.
The roots of the doctrine ran back to the period before the Battle of
Fredericksburg.

Burnside's was the first real advance on Richmond from its northern side.
Its difficulties, accentuated by the stalemate at Fredericksburg, provoked
much discussion in Washington and in the Army of the Potomac. In that
discussion the problem of the power of the defense and logistical concerns
dominated; the varying proposals all addressed the same questions and, with
one exception, found the same answers.

After conferring with Burnside, Lincoln said the criteria for any plan demanded that the "crossing of the river be as nearly free from risk as possible"
and that the "enemy be prevented from falling back, accumulating strength
as he goes, into his intrenchments at Richmond." To accomplish these goals,
Lincoln had proposed the concurrent use of two water routes, the Rappahannock and the Pamunkey, to bring two separate 25,000-man forces into Lee's
rear, coincident with Burnside's advance. Lincoln proposed: All three forces
will "move simultaneously, General B's force in its attempt to cross the river,
the Rappahannock force moving directly up to the South side of the river to

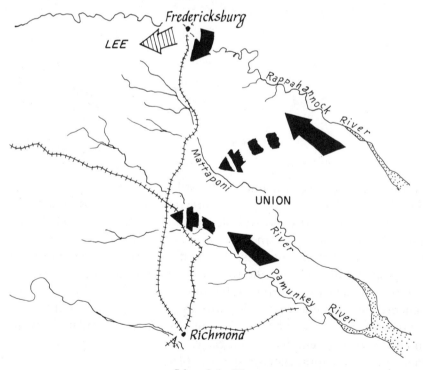

Lincoln's Plan

Railroad Communication.

his assistance, and ready, if found admissible, to deflect off to the turnpike bridge over the Mattapony [sic] in the direction of Richmond. The Pamunkey force to move as rapidly as possible up the North side of the Pamunkey, holding all the bridges, . . . and also, if possible, press higher up the streams and destroy the railroad bridges. Then, if Gen B. succeeds in driving the enemy from Fredericksburg, he the enemy no longer has the road to Richmond, but we have it and can march into the city. Or possibly, having forced the enemy from his line we would move upon and destroy his army."[60]

Two other proposals contained essentially similar elements, though they both laid even more emphasis on logistics and the turning movements aimed at Petersburg. To appreciate these other plans, it is necessary to understand the problem presented by Richmond's elaborate communications system. The

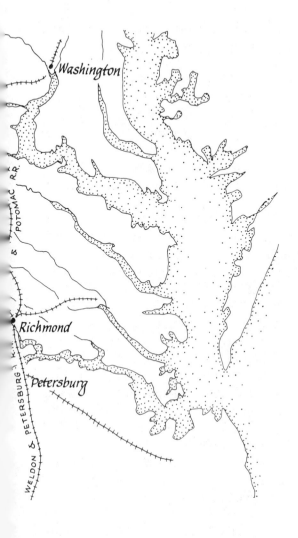

Confederate capital and the army defending it had many regions from which to draw supplies. One, north of the city, included the Shenandoah Valley. This northern area was reached by a railroad complex which ran north from Richmond—the Richmond, Fredericksburg and Potomac and the Virginia Central, which went through Charlottesville to the Valley. At Charlottesville the Virginia Central connected with the East Tennessee and Virginia Railroad, which ran to Lynchburg before going to the southwest. This route thus also provided an alternate route to Lynchburg as well as access to the second supply area, Southwest Virginia. The East Tennessee and Virginia connected, through Chattanooga, with Atlanta and the southwestern and Gulf states.

The Southside Railroad and the James River and Kanawha Canal provided a more direct route to Lynchburg. The Southside also intersected the Richmond and Danville, which, with the Weldon Railroad, provided additional rail connections to the third area, the southeast and the remainder of the South as far as the Mississippi River. Since both the Weldon and the Richmond and Danville intersected the Southside, Lynchburg had a second access to the lower South independent of Richmond, and Lynchburg was connected with Richmond not only by the Southside but by the canal along the James River and via the East Tennessee and Virginia to Charlottesville and the Virginia Central. Thus Richmond could communicate with all of its supply areas, including the lower South, by the canal and by any of the four railroads, radiating north, west, and south. This transportation network had to be fundamental to any plan to take Richmond.

Other proposals made in the fall approximated Lincoln's in that they hoped that "every preparation for crossing the river just below Fredericksburg" would "persuade the enemy, if possible, that" the Union army was "determined to advance on that line." At that moment 50,000 men on the south side of the James planned to "seize all the routes by which Richmond communicates with the South, and control the navigation of the canal. . . . The rebels would necessarily fall back from the Rappahannock, and thus expose their only remaining route of communication with the Confederacy, that by Gordonsville—Virginia Central Railroad. The magazines and arsenals and foundries of Richmond would be destroyed and the rebel army would speedily be without supplies of any kind. The plan [had] the advantage of bringing the Navy into cooperation." This proposed campaign against Richmond, like the others which heavily stressed logistics, had for its basis the realization that "however much railroads may multiply [the] means of defense, they are nevertheless of very little use to an army when invading the country of an enterprising enemy," because "he will tear up the track," and when federal troops "repair it every foot must be protected or he will make raids upon it and destroy it."[61]

One plan avoided dependence on vulnerable railways by advocating the building of roads to supply a direct movement on Richmond by linking the attacking army with the Virginia waterways. Another proposed using the Peninsula route, saying: It would not only avoid the logistical problem but the one presented by a direct advance at Fredericksburg in which the enemy is able "to post himself strongly and defy us. The whole strength of our army may not be sufficient to drive him away, and even were he driven away, at great sacrifice of blood on our part, the result would not be decisive. The losses to him in his strong positions would be comparatively slight, while ours would be enormous."

Use of the James River, argued Peninsula advocates, would permit the army to "be brought to points within 20 miles of Richmond without the risk of an engagement." Staying close to the river would greatly simplify logistics because the army could "get rid of all baggage, provisions, and infantry ammunition wagons, and the only vehicles [would] be the artillery and its ammunition wagons and ambulances." Like all the other proposals, this would cut "the railroads running South from Richmond" and "proceed to the investment or attack upon Richmond, according to the circumstances. Whether the investment of Richmond [would lead] to the destruction of the enemy army or not, it certainly [would] lead to the capture of the rebel capital."[62]

Only one of the plans provided for interdicting all of Richmond's communications. General John G. Barnard hypothesized that the force south of the James could get so close to the river as to cut all of the railways to the south and even, quite optimistically, be able to control the canal on the north bank. Another, more realistic proposal only assumed cutting the Weldon railway and recommended a raid to cut the enemy's "only remaining other southern channel, and only southwestern one, by an expedition 50 miles off, at Burke's Station."[63]

The Peninsula strategy, to which Lincoln promised to give "more deliberate consideration, with the aid of military men," presented "the old questions of preference between the line of the Peninsula, and the line we are now upon," he said. "The difficulties . . . pertaining to the Fredericksburg line are obvious and palpable. But now, as heretofore, if you go to James River, a large part of the army must remain on or near the Frederickburg line, to protect Washington. It is the old difficulty." Considering Lincoln and Halleck's well-known antipathy to operating on exterior lines, there could be no doubt of the outcome of the more deliberate consideration of the Peninsula plan. Further, the President and the headquarters staff had come to realize that the task of taking Richmond was perhaps too formidable and was certainly not the most promising line of operations.[64]

Even before the defeat at Fredericksburg and the essential failure of the fall campaign, Lincoln had come to realize fully the ascendancy of the defense and the relative indecisiveness of military operations. In late November he explained: "I certainly have been dissatisfied with the slowness of Buell and McClellan; but before I relieved them I had great fears I should not find successors to them, who would do better; and I am sorry to add, that I have seen little since to relieve those fears." Pointing out that this situation really inhered in the constraints of logistics and the strength of the defensive, he indicated: "I do not clearly see the prospect of any more rapid movements. I fear we shall at last find out that the difficulty is in our case rather than in particular generals."[65]

The special case of operations in Virginia was far more intractable than the general one. Concentration on the Mississippi involved not just the abandonment of offensive operations in Arkansas, but a shift from eastern departments also. Some of the troops in Wright's Department of the Ohio were sent to Grant, but headquarters was contemplating a more significant move. Recognizing the importance of the Mississippi and the indecisive character of

Virginia operations, Halleck had hoped that the Army of the Potomac could advance and "occupy the rebel army south of the Rappahannock." Explained Halleck, "This would have enabled us to detach sufficient forces to place the opening of the Mississippi beyond a doubt." Failure to push Lee's army that far "from the vicinity of Washington and the upper Potomac" meant that Lincoln and Halleck could then spare no troops from Virginia for the Mississippi campaign.[66]

An objective for Burnside to "occupy the rebel army south of the Rappahannock" recognized the remoteness of the likelihood of a decision in Virginia. The Mississippi case promised more results than the Virginia one, whether or not the control of the river was more important than the capture of Richmond. These priorities also acknowledged the impracticability of successfully beleaguering the Confederate capital. Gloomy that the support of the armies was consuming "the natural and monetary resources of the country," Quartermaster General Meigs doubted that he could provide for the army, concentrated and immobilized as it would be before Richmond. He told Burnside: The enemy would "cut your lines of supply and communication. In a desolated country, it will be almost impossible to support your army during a siege." Ironically, Meigs's logistical reasons for wishing to avoid one were identical to those of Lee in wishing not to be besieged. Neither any longer gave much credence to the idea that Richmond must fall as had Sebastopol and both feared that, deprived of the opportunity to move and draw resources from the countryside, the large armies could not be provisioned.[67]

Any failure to break all, or substantially all, of Richmond's communications would result in a siege. Destroying communications on the South only would leave the Virginia Central and the canal tapping the Shenandoah Valley and, via the East Tennessee and Virginia, Atlanta and the entire lower South. Whether this would have sufficed to sustain the city and the army is questionable, but two years later Richmond did hold out, during the winter of 1864–65, with only one link to the lower South and the Valley so devastated it could contribute relatively little.

None of the plans had presented a really plausible means of interdicting Richmond's communications. The consequences of such a failure were particularly evident to Halleck, an engineer who had published writings on fortifications. He recognized that field, rather than permanent, fortifications had largely defended Sebastopol; and he knew how long it had held out against a host of experienced, professional forces. Halleck and Lincoln had no realistic hope that they could conquer Richmond sooner, and probably little that they could capture it at all. Halleck also knew that defensive fortifications so economized on men that one man well intrenched equaled six in the attack. Such a favorable ratio for the defenders of fortifications in a siege would enable the rebels actually to reduce their forces in the Richmond vicinity.[68]

If, as the operations in 1862 indicated, the Unionists could not defeat the enemy in the field, clearly, as Lincoln had pointed out early in the fall, they could not beat him "within the entrenchments of Richmond." Lincoln and Halleck adopted the obvious solution: avoid a siege. The general in chief explained the alternative, which the President endorsed: abandon Richmond as an objective and adopt as the "first object" of a Virginia campaign "the defeat or scattering of Lee's army, which threatened Washington and the line of the Upper Potomac." Amplifying the headquarters doctrine, Halleck ordered the Army of the Potomac "to turn the enemy's works, or to threaten their wings or communications; in other words," he explained, "keep the enemy occupied till a favorable opportunity to strike a decisive blow." He also directed the employment of other measures against Lee's army: Use "cavalry and light artillery upon his communications, and attempt to cut off his supplies and engage him at an advantage."[69]

The ideas Halleck expressed harmonized with and, in truth, merely extended those expressed by Lincoln in September and October. Lincoln said: I "confidently believed last September that we could end the war by allowing the enemy to go to Harrisburg and Philadelphia, only that we could not keep down mutiny, and utter demoralization among the Pennsylvanians." Just as he had tried to trap Jackson with Fremont's and McDowell's forces the previous May, so also had Lincoln yearned for the chance to allow Lee to go too far and block his retreat. In October he had urged McClellan to threaten Lee's communications and either beat him to Richmond or fight him if he could create a favorable occasion. Halleck's instructions repeated all of these elements, including the stress on attacking the Confederate general's communications.[70]

The new aim of beating Lee's army in the field had political overtones also. Lincoln had learned that the public perceived the war in terms of battles and thus gave more credence to a "half-defeat" at the Seven Days' Battles than to the conquest of 100,000 square miles of territory in the West. A victory over Lee's army would have particular political significance because Lee's army had "threatened Washington and the line of the Upper Potomac," and, in addition, a victory over Lee near the nation's capital would be particularly satisfying and valuable for national morale. Nor did the Union really have much to lose in the event of failure, for a siege would surely depress public morale. Prolonged, it could bring a sense of futility that could do more harm than failure in battle.

A siege would also aggravate one of Lincoln's major problems, the radical and popular dissatisfaction with the West Point generals. Fully appreciating military realities and clearly comprehending the war as the soldiers understood it, Lincoln saw that the "strategy" which had disillusioned him in November amounted to an effort to cope with such intractable realities as logistics and the enemy's defensive power. Lincoln's own attempts to find a plan to solve the Fredericksburg deadlock had differed little from those of the regular officers with an engineering background. Yet Lincoln well perceived

and appreciated the radical and popular dissatisfaction with the war as conducted by the regulars. But, having mastered their special expertise, Lincoln
discerned, as the public did not, the significant reality in their professionalism. Caught between these two fires, Lincoln knew that a siege of Richmond
was out of the question. It might well amount to more than the regulars and
the administration could sustain politically.

The failure of December's well-coordinated simultaneous advances had
cost much in popular morale, though Rosecrans's bloody success at Stones
River had relieved the pattern of failure and given the northern public a
general whom they could hail as victorious. But Rosecrans's victory had
resulted in no significant advance and Grant's efforts had produced none
along the Mississippi, the primary Union objective against which they sought
to concentrate their most powerful forces. Lincoln and Halleck could hardly
have been more sanguine than the gloomy public; for all could see that Rosecrans had advanced hardly at all and that the enemy was skillfully applying a
formula for victory. Though the Confederates had been unable to concentrate
against any one of the advancing Union armies, powerful rebel armies blocked
each major route of advance and, aided by the defensive supremacy of rifle-
armed infantry, had, without concentrating, nullified Union numerical
superiority.

Perhaps more discouraging was the insecurity of the land communications
of the Union armies in the West. Because of guerrillas these armies could
barely keep open their communications in spite of deploying enormous numbers of troops for their protection. But the forces guarding railways proved
unable to resist the raids of the enemy cavalry. Enjoying virtual parity in
numbers with Union cavalry and displaying superiority in tactical skill, Confederate cavalry had smashed Grant's base at Holly Springs as Forrest and
Morgan moved almost at will against the railroads supplying Grant and Rosecrans. Union leaders pondered whether they could ever advance as long as
their fragile land communications faced two such formidable threats, guerrillas and cavalry raiders.

On the other hand Confederate rail communications in Virginia seemed
invulnerable. Richmond had so many rail lines that no plan of campaign could
interdict enough of them to ensure the fall of the capital. This had led Lincoln
and Halleck to proscribe any effort to besiege the rebel capital, and, instead,
to direct the Army of the Potomac to aim at the limited and quite unpromising
objective of trying to hurt Lee's strong and brilliantly led army.

This objective was easier to define than obtain, but Quartermaster General
Meigs undertook the task of explaining to Burnside how to apply the new
headquarters doctrine against Lee's army. Pointing out that the country's
"confidence and hope are dying," Meigs said: Though forcing a retirement
"of the rebel army from your front . . . would prolong the contest and be a
misfortune, even this would give some hope and heart to the country. But

what is needed is a great and overwhelming defeat and destruction of that army. Such a victory would be of incalculable value."

To Burnside the quartermaster general made clear how they might fill this very tall order, saying: No such battles as Fredericksburg, even if successful, will do, for "no battle fought with your back to the North or to the sea can give you such a victory." As had McClellan to Lincoln nearly a year before, Meigs pointed out: "This enemy has shown the skill in retreat, and when he finds the day going against him he will retreat—will save the bulk of his army and compel a siege of Richmond, during which, as when McClellan invested it, he will gather up his forces for another struggle."

And Meigs continued: A decisive victory will come, "if by a march as Napoleon made at Jena, as Lee made in his campaign against Pope, you throw your whole army upon his communications, interpose between him and Richmond or even take a position southwest of the bulk of his army, and he fights, if you are successful, he has no retreat. His army would be dispersed, and the greater portion of it would throw down its arms. The artillery and baggage camps would fall into your hands. The gain of the position would give you the strategic victory."

Explaining how Burnside might carry out this classic turning movement, Meigs recommended that Burnside move "up the Rappahannock, cross the river, aim for a point on the railroad between the rebels and Richmond, and send forward cavalry and light troops to break up the railroad and intercept retreat." Then, intercepting Lee's retreat, the army would "march to the sound of battle, concentrate upon any field, and compel a general engagement." Although good advice, Burnside would find the operation extraordinarily difficult to execute. The war would see many turning movements but the only one in which an entire army actually succeeded in getting into the rear of the enemy Grant directed against a far less competent opponent than Lee. Thus did Meigs explain the Lincoln-Halleck doctrine for Virginia operations, one which he bequeathed to Burnside's successor.[71]

1. Grant to Halleck, Oct. 17, 23, 29, Nov. 2, 10, 12, 24, 1862, *Papers of Grant*, VI, 155, 178–79, 210, 243, 288, 299–300, 345–346; Grant to Sherman, Nov. 3, 10, 14, 1862, *ibid.*, 254, 290–92, 310–12; Grant to Hamilton, Nov. 1, 1862, *ibid.*, 237; Hillyer to Sherman, Oct. 29, 1862, *O.R.*, XVII, pt. 2, 302–3; Halleck to Grant, Nov. 3, 10, 11, 23, 24, 25, Dec. 5, 1862, *ibid.*, pt. 1, 467–69, 471, 473; Halleck to Curtis, Nov. 3, Dec. 2, 4, 1862, *ibid.*, XIII, 778, XVII, pt. 2, 376, 382; Curtis to Halleck, Dec. 4, 1862, *ibid.*, XVII, pt. 2, 382.

2. Steele to Curtis, Nov. 27, 1862, *O.R.*, XVII, pt. 1, 529; Curtis to Halleck, Dec. 4, 1862, *ibid.*, pt. 2, 383–84; Halleck to Grant, Dec. 7, 1862, *ibid.*, pt. 1, 473; Grant to Steele, Dec. 8, 1862, *Papers of Grant*, VI, 408.

3. Halleck to Grant, Nov. 15, 1862, *O.R.*, XVII, pt. 1, 470; Grant to Halleck, Oct. 26, Dec. 5, 1862, *Papers of Grant*, VI, 199–201, 390; Grant to Steele, Dec 8, 1862, *ibid.*, 408; Curtis to Gorman, Dec. 23, 1862, *O.R.*, XXII, pt. 1, 859.

4. Schofield to Curtis, Jan. 1, 1863, *O.R.*, XXII, pt. 2, 6.

5. Hassler, *Commanders of the Army of the Potomac*, 97–98.

6. *Ibid.*, 99, 101.

7. Lee to Jackson, Nov. 9, 12, 14, 1862, *Wartime Papers*, 330, 333–34, 335–36; Lee to Randolph, Nov. 7, 1862, *ibid.*, 328. See also: Lee to Jackson, Nov. 25, 1862, *O.R.*, XXI, 1031–32.

8. Lee to Randolph, Nov. 10, 14, 1862, *Wartime Papers*, 332, *O.R.*, XIX, pt. 2, 717–18; Lee to Davis, Nov. 25, 1862, *Wartime Papers*, 345–46; Lee to Cooper, Nov. 18, 1862, *O.R.*, XXI, 1018; Lee to G. W. Smith, Dec. 6, 1862, *ibid.*, 1052.

9. Foster to Halleck, Dec. 1, 12, 1862, *O.R.*, XVIII, 469, 476; Halleck to Dix, Nov. 29, 1862, *ibid.*, 466; Halleck to Morell, Dec. 3, 1862, *ibid.*, XXI, 824; Halleck to Kelley, Dec. 3, 1862, *ibid.*, 825; Halleck to Wool, Dec. 4, 1862, *ibid.*, 829; Halleck to Burnside, Dec. 6, 1862, *ibid.*, 831; Halleck to Cox and Kelley, Dec. 9, 1862, *ibid.*, 843; Halleck to Wright, Dec. 12, 1862, *ibid.*, 848; Slocum to Halleck, Dec. 4, 1862, *ibid.*, 828; Burnside to Halleck, Dec. 6, 1862, *ibid.*, 105; Halleck to Rosecrans, Dec. 4, 1862, *ibid.*, XX, pt. 2, 118.

10. Lee to G. W. Smith, Dec. 12, 1862, *O.R.*, XXI, 1060.

11. Lee to Davis, Sept. 3, Dec. 6, 1862, *Wartime Papers*, 292–93, 353.

12. Long, *Civil War, Day by Day*, 296; Bruce Catton, *Never Call Retreat* (Garden City, 1965), 20; Miers, *Lee*, 120; Johnston to Wigfall, Dec. 15, 1862, Mrs. D. Giraud Wright, *A Southern Girl in '61* (New York, 1905), 106.

13. Miers, Lee, 120, 123; Henry, *Story of the Confederacy*, 213.

14. Halleck to Foster, Dec. 14, 1862, *O.R.*, XVIII, 481; Halleck to Wright, Dec. 14, 1862, *ibid.*, XXI, 849; Wright to Halleck, Dec. 13, 1862, *ibid.*, 854; Dix to Halleck, Dec. 13, 1862, *ibid.*, XVIII, 479.

15. Halleck to Rosecrans, Oct. 24, 1862, *O.R.*, XVI, pt. 2, 640–41; Grant to Halleck, Oct. 23, 1862, *ibid.*, XVII, pt. 2, 290; Rosecrans to Grant, Oct. 23, 1862, *ibid.*, 291; Curtis to Kelton, Apr. 28, 1862, *ibid.*, XIII, 367.

16. Halleck to Rosecrans, Oct. 24, 1862, *O.R.*, XVI, pt. 2, 640–41; Rosecrans to Halleck, Nov. 11, 17, Dec. 4, 10, 1862, *ibid.*, XX, pt. 2, 35–36, 59, 118, 150.

17. Grant to Halleck, Dec. 9, 14, 1862, *O.R.*,

XVII, pt. 1, 475, LII, pt. 2, 313–14; Halleck to Curtis, Dec. 12, 1862, *ibid.*, XVII, pt. 2, 402.

18. Halleck to Schofield, Nov. 28, 1862, *O.R.*, XXII, pt. 1, 793.

19. McClernand to Stanton, Jan. 3, 1863, *O.R.*, XVII, pt. 2, 528–30.

20. Rosecrans to Halleck, Dec. 4, 10, 1862, *O.R.*, XX, pt. 2, 118, 150; Halleck to Rosecrans, Nov. 27, Dec. 4, 5, 1862, *ibid.*, 102, 117–18, 123–24; Stanton to Rosecrans, Nov. 18, 1862, *ibid.*, 64; Rosecrans to Totten, Nov. 22, 1862, *ibid.*, 83.

21. Foster to Halleck, Dec. 23, 1862, *O.R.*, XVII, 489; Halleck to Dix, Dec. 24, 1862, *ibid.*, 490; Dix to Halleck, Dec. 29, 1862, *ibid.*, 496; Halleck to Burnside, Dec. 17, 23, 24, 26, 30, 1862, *ibid.*, XXI, 861, 876, XVIII, 491, XXI, 886, 899.

22. Burnside to Lincoln, Jan. 1, 1863, *O.R.*, XXI, 941.

23. Sherman to Gorman, Dec. 3, 1862, *O.R.*, XVII, pt. 2, 409; Sherman to Rawlins, Dec. 18, 1862, *ibid.*, 426; Grant to Sherman, Dec. 14, 1862, *ibid.*, 412. See also: W. T. Sherman to John Sherman, Dec. 14, 20, 1862, *Sherman Letters*, 174–75, 176–77.

24. Catton, *Never Call Retreat*, 34–35.

25. Grant to Commanding Officer, Expedition Down Mississippi, Dec. 23, 1862, *O.R.*, XVII, pt. 2, 463; Grant to Kelton, Dec. 25, 1862, *ibid.*, pt. 1, 478; Grant to McPherson, Dec. 26, 1862, *ibid.*, pt. 2, 488.

26. Sherman to Rawlins, Jan. 4, 1863, *O.R.*, XVII, pt. 1, 612.

27. D. Alexander Brown, "Battle At Chickasaw Bluffs," *Civil War Times—Illustrated* (July, 1970), 9, 45–46; Herman Hattaway, "Confederate Myth Making: Top Command and the Chickasaw Bayou Campaign," *Journal of Mississippi History* (Nov., 1970), 311–26.

28. Catton, *Never Call Retreat*, 37.

29. McWhiney, *Bragg*, I, 27–28.

30. *Ibid.*, 97, 98, 218, 259.

31. *Ibid.*, 190, 192, 199.

32. *Ibid.*, 330–31.

33. Horn, *Army of Tennessee*, 189, 193–95: Thomas Lawrence Connelly, *Autumn of Glory* (Baton Rouge, 1971), 13–29.

34. Horn, *Army of Tennessee*, 194; Connelly, *Autumn of Glory*, 13, 25–27.

35. Rosecrans to Halleck, Jan. 3, 1863, *O.R.*, XX, pt. 1, 185; Wright to Tuttle, Dec. 31, 1862, *ibid.*, pt. 2, 286.

36. Rosecrans to Wright, Dec. 9, 15, 1862, *O.R.*, XX, pt. 2, 150, 186; Wright to Halleck, Dec. 18, 1862, *ibid.*, 197–98.

37. Horn, *Army of Tennessee*, 196–97; McWhiney, *Bragg*, 195, 347–48; Connelly, *Autumn of Glory*, 44–67.

38. Catton, *Never Call Retreat*, 35–36; Henry, *Story of the Confederacy*, 222.

39. Horn, *Army of Tennessee*, 199.

40. *Ibid.*, 199, 201; McWhiney, *Bragg*, 353–54*n36*; Connelly, *Autumn of Glory*, 49, 62.

41. Catton, *Never Call Retreat*, 44.

42. McWhiney, *Bragg*, 353–54, 363–64.

43. Horn, *Army of Tennessee*, 205–6; Connelly, *Autumn of Glory*, 61–62.

44. McWhiney, *Bragg*, 372; Long, *Civil War, Day by Day*, 307.

45. Kirby Smith to Morgan, July 5, 1862, *O.R.*, XVI, pt. 2, 722; Kirby Smith to Cooper, July 19, 1862, *ibid.*, 729; Joseph H. Parks, *General Edmund Kirby Smith C.S.A.* (Baton Rouge, 1954), 197, 208; McWhiney, *Bragg*, 340.

46. Quoted in McWhiney, *Bragg*, 340, 341*n11*.

47. Thomas F. Thiele, "The Evolution of Cavalry in the American Civil War; 1861–1863," Ph.D. dissertation, University of Michigan, 1951, 5, 30–37; Stephen Z. Starr, *The Union Cavalry in the Civil War* (Baton Rouge, 1979), I, 48–49, 59, 65–67, 69.

48. Thiele, "Evolution of Cavalry," 25; Starr, *The Union Cavalry in the Civil War*, I, 109.

49. Thiele, "Evolution of Cavalry," 116–20; Starr, *The Union Cavalry in the Civil War*, I, 58.

50. Thiele, "Evolution of Cavalry," 24–26, 549.

51. William M. Lamers, *Edge of Glory, A Biography of General William S. Rosecrans, U.S.A.* (New York, 1961), 245; Stanton to Rosecrans, Jan. 5, 7, 1863, *O.R.*, XX, pt. 2, 299–300, 306; Dix to Lincoln, Jan. 7, 1863, *ibid.*, 308.

52. Lincoln to Rosecrans, Aug. 31, 1863, Basler, *Collected Works*, VI, 424–25.

53. Banks to Halleck, Dec. 18, 24, 1862, Jan. 7, 1863, *O.R.*, XV, 613, 618–19, 200–201.

54. Catton, *Never Call Retreat*, 87.

55. Horn, *Army of Tennessee*, 193.

56. Lincoln to Halleck, Jan. 1, 1863, Basler, *Collected Works*, VI, 31.

57. Halleck to Stanton, Jan. 1, 1863, *O.R.*, XXI, 940–41; Halleck to Wright, Nov. 18, 1862, *ibid.*, XX, pt. 2, 67.

58. Halleck to Lincoln, July 10, 1862, *O.R.*, XVI, pt. 2, 117.

59. Long, *Civil War, Day by Day*, 313; Foote, *The Civil War*, II, 128.

60. Lincoln to Halleck, Nov. 27, 1862, Basler, *Collected Works*, V, 514–15.

61. Barnard to Kelton, Nov. 28, 1862, *O.R.*, XXI, 807–8; Alexander to Barnard, Nov. 27, 1862, *ibid.*, 1117–21; Gibbon to ? (found among Burnside's papers), Nov. 30, 1862, *ibid.*, 812–13.

62. Alexander to Barnard, Nov. 27, 1862, *O.R.*, XXI, 1117–21; Franklin and Smith to Lincoln, Dec. 20, 1862, *ibid.*, 868–70.

63. Barnard to Kelton, Nov. 28, 1862, *O.R.*, XXI, 807–8; Gibbon to ? , Nov. 30, 1862, *ibid.*, 813.

64. Lincoln to Franklin and Smith, Dec. 22, 1862, Basler, *Collected Works*, VI, 15.

65. Lincoln to Schurz, Nov. 24, 1862, Basler, *Collected Works*, V, 509–11.

66. Halleck to Rosecrans, Jan. 30, 1863, *O.R.*, XXIII, pt. 2, 23.

67. Meigs to Burnside, Dec. 30, 1862, *O.R.*, XXI, 916–18. See also: Meigs to Burnside, Jan. 12, 1863, *ibid.*, 965–67.

68. Halleck, *Elements of Military Art and Science*, 1862 edition, 71–87, 374, 439–441.

69. Halleck to Burnside, Jan. 7, 1862, *O.R.*, XXI, 953–954; Lincoln to Burnside, Jan. 8, 1863, Basler, *Collected Works*, VI, 46.

70. Lincoln to Treat, Nov. 19, 1862, Basler, *Collected Works*, V, 501–2.

71. Meigs to Burnside, Dec. 30, 1862, *O.R.*, XXI, 916–18.

12 ☆ WINTER LULL, PLANS, AND MANEUVERS

Nathan B. Forrest

As the last weeks of 1862 slipped by, momentary inactivity prevailed in the East, while elsewhere Bragg and Rosecrans approached Stones River and Grant's first Vicksburg campaign reached its somewhat ignominious denouement. Farther west some minor skirmishing erupted at Bayou Bonfouca and at Petite Anse Island, Louisiana, and a more important series of lesser actions occurred in Mathews County, Virginia, along the Chesapeake Bay, resulting in destruction of twelve southern saltworks and a number of vessels.

As the fall campaign thus ended both Presidents turned to planning and rhetoric. Lincoln aimed at soothing proslavery Unionist Kentuckians by sending a message that he "would rather die than take back a word of the Proclamation of Freedom," his preliminary emancipation proclamation, while again he urged support for *gradual* abolishment of slavery and plans for compensating owners. On December 1, 1862, he delivered his State of the Union message, reporting satisfactory foreign relations, favorable developments in commerce, and a sound fiscal situation. Meanwhile, Davis declared Major General Benjamin F. Butler a felon, an outlaw, a common enemy of mankind; if captured, Davis asserted, he should not be considered a military prisoner, but should be hanged immediately. Bruce Catton well described the situation that existed in Louisiana under "Beast" Butler where "mere lieutenants of infantry lived in huge town houses, 'where they use the plate, drink the wine cellars dry, and in various ways spoil the Egyptians.' Most of them were looting and plundering without restraint, believing that General Butler expected it of them."[1]

Upon returning to Richmond from an investigative trip west, Davis struck a more positive note when he told a serenading crowd, The Confederacy offers the last hope "for the perpetuation of that system of government which our forefathers founded—the asylum of the oppressed and the home of true representative liberty." Davis even had come to conceive of northerners as a quite distinct people from southerners. "There is indeed a difference," he proclaimed; "let no man hug the delusion that there can be a renewed association between them. Our enemies are a traditionless and homeless race. From the time of Cromwell to the present moment they have been disturbers of the peace of the world. Gathered together by Cromwell from the bogs and fens of the north of Ireland and England, they commenced by disturbing the peace of their own country; they disturbed Holland, to which they fled; and they disturbed England on their return. They persecuted Catholics in England, and they hung Quakers and witches in America." He continued: "Every crime which could characterize the course of demons has marked the course of the invader." In part he was responding to Lincoln's final Emancipation Proclamation which the President issued, as he had forewarned, on January 1, 1863.[2]

Not all of President Davis's problems sprang from the threat of emancipation or the wickedness of General Butler. In the early spring the Confederate capital underwent a "bread riot" when a mob crowded around a wagon demanding bread. By this time some instances of genuine want had developed in the Confederate capital as well as in other cities of the beleaguered South. The mob soon began an angry plundering of whatever met their momentary fancy as they roamed the town and broke indiscriminately into various shops. President Davis personally came out to see them, made an address from a wagon near the Capitol, and threw them the money he had in his pocket. Militia and police then carefully dispersed the crowd.

The war grew somewhat less spectacular as winter ushered in a period of stalemate. In Virginia, as in Tennessee, the opposing armies lay inactive in winter quarters, while Grant in Mississippi ineffectually pursued various schemes to find a water route by which to turn Vicksburg. Because Grant still had the relatively secure Mississippi River for his principal line of communications and also possessed substantial numerical superiority, he did not yet feel the full impact which the problems of guarding communications and territory would pose in penetrating the vast and, as yet, untouched areas of the South.

At New Orleans, General Banks enjoyed similar opportunities because he too could base his operations on the Mississippi and on adjacent rivers and bayous. But he was dilatory in attempting to carry on his mission of advancing northward up the river to meet Grant, thus opening the river to Union navigation and completely separating the Confederacy.

Yet the principal difficulty in any campaign against Vicksburg remained logistical. Grant had a simple objective: to reach the railroad between Vicksburg and Jackson and so cut off the town's supplies, either to force its evacuation or compel the garrison to take the offensive to reopen its communications. A winter operation south along the railroad would be impossible on account of the mud. Grant thus found himself limited during these cold months to the Mississippi River. Even in the spring, an overland movement would be slow because of the necessity of rebuilding the railroad and vulnerable because the rebels could again destroy the railroad as they had in December.[3]

Therefore Grant abandoned the eighty-seven-mile railroad north of Jackson, Tennessee, and improved the rail line from Memphis to Corinth, eliminating his dependence on that segment broken earlier by Forrest. At the same time, he redeployed nearly a division of troops theretofore used for road guards. Grant never considered using land communications even when advised by Sherman to do so in the spring when the ground had dried. Grant scarcely thought of permitting his crucial move against Vicksburg to depend again on the flimsy, vulnerable railways which had already defeated him once.[4]

River communications solved the logistical problem well but presented Grant with an apparently insuperable tactical problem. The water route led him to fortified bluffs which seemingly he could not turn. The Union now faced the problem of how to turn this position when elsewhere, on both sides of the river, lay nothing but swamp, flooded terrain, and overgrown bayous.

Though he initially saw some promise in a bypass canal and took delight on hearing that "the President attaches much importance to this," Grant concentrated all of his attention on turning the enemy's right. He stuck with this plan even though he had developed on Lake Providence a more promising water route on the west side of the river. Lake Providence might "prove a good thing for us yet in some operation," thought Grant, but it would not help in getting within "striking distance of the enemy's lines of communication." Another element in the communications equation was introduced when the Union ram *Queen of the West* ran past the Vicksburg batteries. She proceeded to wreak havoc in the Confederate-held river segment, destroying much pork, hogs, salt, molasses, sugar, flour, and cotton, and taking a number of prisoners, including several ladies. She then pushed on all the way down to the Red River. But even this spectacular success did not alter Grant's concentration on Vicksburg's north side, and, throughout January, February, and early March 1863, he proceeded to establish communications through the Yazoo River and Steele's Bayou. If he succeeded in reaching the high ground in the rear of Vicksburg, the "enemy would," he wrote, "be compelled to come out and give us an open field fight, or submit to having all his communications cut and be left to starve out."[5]

Essentially Grant wished to send a fleet of gunboats and transports through the complex system of lakes, passes, and bayous interconnecting the Mississippi, Yazoo, and Tallahatchie rivers. His troops cut the levee at Yazoo Pass and the boats passed into Moon Lake and on into the bayous. The Confederates had felled trees as obstacles, but the Federals easily cleared these away. Just above Greenwood on the Tallahatchie, however, stood Fort Pemberton and it proved impassable. There the Confederates had closed the channel by sinking the famous steamer *Star of the West* squarely in the middle of the passage. During the brief firefight when the flotilla attempted to force past the blockship and little fort, the Confederates under Major General William Wing "Old Blizzards" Loring rained fire under the general's personal direction. Pacing the parapet of cotton bales, he called excitedly: "Give them blizzards, boys! Give them blizzards!"[6]

These water-borne expeditions also brought the wrath of other southern resisters upon the Unionists' heads. The boats inevitably brushed against numerous low-hanging branches and vines, from which there fell showers of rats, mice, beetles, snakes, lizards, and all manner of swamp vermin. Men had to stand on deck with brooms to sweep the creatures away. An occasional coon or wildcat shaken from the trees caused much more trouble; as one northern soldier wrote, they were "prejuduced against us and refused to be comforted on board, though I am sorry to say we found more Union feeling among the bugs."[7]

In mid-March another effort, the Steele's Bayou or Deer Creek expedition, almost brought a Union disaster. Eleven vessels pushed through heavily obstructed waterways, but the Confederates almost succeeded in bottling up and destroying the fleet. Sherman undertook a night march, daring and eerie, through swamp waters, the troop's only light provided by candles stuck in their rifle barrels, to arrive in the nick of time to drive away the attacking southerners and save the ships.

"The eyes and hopes of the whole country," wrote Halleck, "are now directed to your army. In my opinion, the opening of the Mississippi River will be to us of more advantage than the capture of forty Richmonds. We shall omit nothing which we can do to assist you." Aware of this and the fact that he had spent the winter months in vain, Grant began to ruminate upon a different approach. The activity on the lower Mississippi of the Union's most brilliant and determined naval leader helped him. On the night of March 14 Admiral Farragut led his Union squadron up the Mississippi River past the Port Hudson, Louisiana, batteries. Several ships sustained severe damage, two had to drop back, and a third ran aground and eventually caught fire and exploded. The guns proved very accurate, but two ships succeeded in getting through. Knowing of Farragut's exploit and that his ships now lay in the river between Vicksburg and Port Hudson, Grant realized that he could use his Lake Providence route and, as he told Banks, "by the use of your transports, I could send you all the force you would require." With this aid, Banks could take Port Hudson and approach Vicksburg from its vulnerable south side. In spite of this new idea, Grant kept his attention fixed on the enemy's right, for, if his Steele's Bayou plan finally failed, he still thought: "There is nothing left for me but to collect all my strength and attack Haynes' Bluff. This will necessarily be attended with much loss, but I think it can be done." He had, he said, still "really made but little calculation upon reaching Vicksburg by any other route than Haynes' Bluff."[8]

Grant's standing in northern public opinion flagged as attempt after attempt, it seemed, came to naught. Albert D. Richardson, a war correspondent with the New York *Tribune*, noted that "the people of the East, knowing about as much of the geography of the region of Grant's meanderings as they did of Japan, were utterly bewildered by the fragmentary and mixed-up newspaper telegrams about Lake Providence, Moon Lake, Steele's Bayou, Williams' Cut-off, the Yazoo, the Yallabusha, the Tallahatchie. . . . They only knew that months dragged wearily by . . . that the soldiers were reported dying from disease. . . . The country was heartsick for victory." Indeed, low spirits generally permeated the North. "Our poppycorn generals kill men as Herod killed the innocents," a Massachusetts private declared, and a Wisconsin major called this winter "the Valley Forge of the War."[9]

As Grant later said, the difficulties with the northern routes "may have been providential in driving us ultimately to a line of operations" which had "proven eminently successful." Having finally realized "that Vicksburg could only be turned from the south side," Grant felt "satisfied that one army corps, with the aid of two gunboats, can take and hold Grand Gulf," he wrote, "until such time as I might be able to get my whole army there and make provision for supplying them." He based this decision on his conviction "that an attack on Haynes' Bluff would be attended with immense sacrifice of life, if not with defeat. This, then, closes out the last hope of turning the enemy by the right." The earlier success in running the *Queen of the West* past Vicksburg made him realize that he did not have to depend on Banks or Farragut for transportation below, nor were his forces there necessarily limited to one corps or devoted solely to aiding Banks against Port Hudson. He could, as he had with the ram, "run the blockade with steamers sufficient to land troops" wherever he pleased on the east bank. His whole army could then be moved and supplied along the Lake Providence water route and a wagon road being built there.[10]

Developed from the concept of using the route west of the river to send a part of his army to aid Banks, Grant's ideas evolved until he decided to collect all of his "forces and turn the enemy's left," using his own naval resources to recross the river below Vicksburg and reach the high ground in the rear of the city. To this idea Grant added his original one of joining Banks. He was induced by Halleck who had asked, If Banks cannot "co-operate with you on Vicksburg, cannot you get troops down to help him on Port Hudson. . . ? I know you can judge of these matters there much better than I can here; but as the President, who seems to be rather impatient about matters on the Mississippi, has several times asked me these questions, I repeat them to you." Grant therefore decided: "Instead of operating up the Big Black toward Jackson and the bridge in the rear of Vicksburg, the main force shall proceed against Port Hudson." Grant made no resistance to this return to his original plan, for he realized that the suggestion of the President and the general in chief intended him to exploit an interior position between Vicksburg and Port Hudson to concentrate with Banks against the weaker enemy army, at Port Hudson, and, having defeated that force and established water communications with New Orleans, to bring the combined commands of Grant and

Banks against the rear of Vicksburg. In this way it would be possible to "attack these places separately with the combined forces."[11]

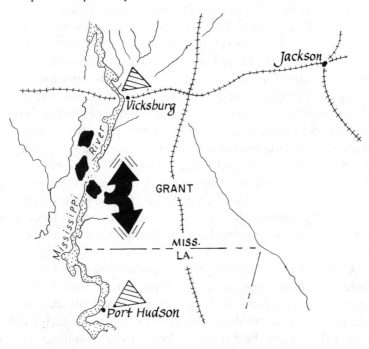

Planned Interior Lines

Halleck's message betrayed some lack of enthusiasm, engendered no doubt by his knowledge that Banks, "as the ranking general in the Southwest," was "authorized to assume control of any military forces from the Upper Mississippi which came within his command" and should "exercise superior authority as far north" as he went with his army. Halleck obviously had real misgivings about placing Grant and the Vicksburg campaign under Banks.[12]

Banks had begun his lower Mississippi command with an echo of his old Texas mission and the small expedition to that state had resulted in "disaster at Galveston" for several ships and 260 men. This unsuccessful diversion had not, Halleck said, been "contemplated or provided for in General Banks's instructions." This minor operation provided the motif for Banks's future conduct. Instead of going up the Mississippi to cooperate with Grant by attacking Port Hudson Banks headed up the Red River to "cut off many of their supplies," and, soon after, sent out four excursions in different directions in Louisiana. Undismayed by Halleck's enjoinder, "Nothing but absolute necessity will excuse any further delay" on your part, Banks persevered with his Louisiana raids, pausing only long enough for a "demonstration" on Port Hudson to help Farragut pass the batteries. Soon Banks resumed his diffuse operations which had been "interrupted by the naval and land expeditions to Port Hudson."[13]

The defeat of Banks's ill-fated force in Texas constituted an episode in a wide-ranging naval struggle. Using improvised gunboats, the Confederates had attacked the Union-held city of Galveston and its defending flotilla. After four hours of hotly contested fighting, the city surrendered. The Confederates captured one northern vessel, the *Harriet Lane*, her top officers all killed, while the *Westfield*'s crew blew her up in order to prevent capture. Other federal vessels scurried away and the blockade was thus momentarily disrupted. Admiral Farragut angrily wrote to a fellow sailor that this was "not only the most unfortunate thing that has ever happened to the Navy, but the most shameful and pusillanimous." But, meanwhile, off Charleston the Federals captured a blockade runner and its important dispatches fell into northern hands. Such actions occurred along all the coasts. Sometimes the Federals managed to hit the southern seacoasts and even get a distance up rivers; sometimes they captured or destroyed vessels, but on occasion they lost some of their own ships. One of the most momentous northern loses occurred on December 30, 1862, when the U.S.S. *Monitor* sank in a storm off Cape Hatteras.[14]

But the Union blockade became progressively more effective, steadily making Confederate importations more difficult and hazardous. Confederate raiding of Union commerce hurt the United States merchant marine but did not impede the flow of ocean trade in neutral ships, some of which had been U.S. ships which had changed their registry. Most effective in harassing commerce under the Union flag was the C.S.S. *Alabama*. On January 7, 1863, this vessel engaged in its only successful action against a warship and one of the war's rare ship-to-ship duels when it sank the U.S.S. *Hatteras* off Galveston, Texas. *Hatteras*, on blockade duty, had investigated a strange and unidentified vessel to find that it was the *Alabama* who vanquished the *Hatteras* with her superior guns. In sheer good luck for the Confederates, the engagement lasted but a short time; a longer duel would certainly have been precarious for the unarmored raider. "Fortune favors the brave, sir," declared the Union commander who had been picked up and afforded a stateroom by his enemy. "We take advantage of all fortune's favors," replied the *Alabama*'s executive officer.[15]

Also in January, Banks launched the first of several efforts to take the Confederate-held salt mine at Avery Island, Louisiana, but initially he met with little success. He sent to Vermilion Bay a steamer and two gunboats, one of which anchored within two miles of the saltworks. The other could get only to within five miles. That night the wind shifted, drove the water out, and both gunboats lay on a mud bank, stranded for more than two weeks. In Florida, the Union encountered better success against southern salt supplies when, on January 9, near St. Joseph's, boat crews from the U.S.S. *Ethan Allen* went ashore and destroyed the works there.

The blockade and minor coastal operations continued as Grant gradually evolved his new approach to Vicksburg and Rosecrans attempted to build up his cavalry in order to protect his vulnerable communications. Meanwhile, the Army of the Potomac had a new commander, the controversial Joseph Hooker, popular with radical politicians but not well liked either by many of his fellow soldiers or by his general in chief. Lincoln, who had more faith in Hooker, knew that the general had schemed to secure the command.

Red-faced, white-haired, and blue-eyed, Hooker blatantly suggested Americanism in his appearance and air; but he had recently made public statements that sounded decidedly un-American: specifically he suggested that Lincoln and the administration were imbeciles and nothing would proceed properly until the Union installed a military dictator. Otherwise, this *"beau-ideal* of a soldier in all physical qualities," as one observer described him, had shown considerable ability—both in battle and in self-promotion. Perhaps his occasionally too-loose and unguarded tongue resulted from constant heavy alcoholic drink, to which Lincoln's secretary attributed Hooker's consistently flushed skin tone. Twenty-ninth in the fifty-man West Point class of 1837, he resigned with the rank of captain after sixteen years of service. He worked as a farmer for five years and in the late 1850s became superintendent of military roads in Oregon. At the opening of the war Hooker managed to become a brigadier general of volunteers but obtained no command. An unemployed observer at First Bull Run, he soon thereafter secured an interview with Lincoln in which he grandly asserted: "It is no vanity in me to say I am a damned sight better general than you had on that field." While it might well have prompted others to write him off as a braggart, this optimism and self-confidence impressed the President. Hooker's brash bravado and thinly veiled self-seeking tendencies, more than any conviction, doubtless prompted the dictatorship remark.[16]

Knowing Hooker well, Lincoln, upon his appointment, sent him a meticulous letter containing this remarkable statement: "There are some things in regard to which, I am not quite satisfied with you. I believe you to be a brave and skillful soldier, which, of course, I like. I also believe you do not mix politics with your profession, in which you are right. You have confidence in yourself, which is a valuable, if not an indispensable quality. You are ambitious, which, within reasonable bounds, does good rather than harm. But I think that during Gen. Burnside's command of the Army, you have taken counsel of your ambition, and thwarted him as much as you could, in which you did a great wrong to the country, and to a most meritorious and honorable brother officer. I have heard, in such way as to believe it, of your recently saying that both the Army and the Government needed a Dictator. Of course it was not *for* this, but in spite of it, that I have given you the command. Only those generals who gain successes, can set up dictators. What I now ask of you is military success, and I will risk the dictatorship."[17]

Hooker also received from the President a general charge: to seek "military success" but "beware of rashness. Beware of rashness, but with energy and sleepless vigilance go forward and give us victories." Lincoln in a sense was echoing his earlier instructions to Burnside to "be cautious," and, though victories were needed, he may well have meant for Hooker, as he had told Burnside, not to "understand that the government, or the country, is driving you" to seek these victories rashly.[18]

Halleck issued more explicit instructions in that he sent to Hooker a copy of his last orders to Burnside which made clear that the "first object was, not Richmond, but the defeat or scattering of Lee's army." To accomplish this objective Halleck intended for the army "to turn the enemy's works, or to threaten their wings or communications; in other words, to keep the enemy occupied till a favorable opportunity offered to strike a decisive blow." Keeping the enemy occupied had another significance for, Halleck wrote, "the great object" was "to occupy the enemy, to prevent his making large detachments or distant raids, and to injure him all you can with the least injury to yourself." In spite of strong words about "the defeat or scattering of Lee's army," Halleck tempered his instructions with realism, only telling Hooker, "Act against the enemy when circumstances will permit." Winter mud and forage shortages meant, however, no real movement until the spring.[19]

Ironically, Lincoln and Halleck sought the same thing as Lee, to keep away from the intrenchments of Richmond. Being dependent for supplies on the Valley and the area north of Richmond, Lee was as much opposed to a siege as Lincoln and Halleck. The Union high command failed to grasp this weakness in Lee's situation. Lincoln and Halleck probably did not understand that a predominately agricultural country could have difficulty feeding an army based at the focus of an extensive railway network, supplemented by a canal.

Thus with reluctance Lincoln had adopted this pessimistic evaluation of military realities on the Virginia front. The experiences of McClellan and Burnside confirmed the judgment recommended by his headquarters staff. This group included Meigs and Barnard, engineer officers who had excelled at West Point and studied under Professor Mahan, and its chief, Halleck, also an engineer. Halleck believed that the Union could not hope to capture Richmond very quickly, and probably could not capture it at all.

From this estimate of the situation Lincoln and Halleck firmly concluded that they should not try to besiege Richmond. Such an operation would simply confer all of the advantages on the rebels. The best Union strategy in Virginia was, therefore, to keep away from Richmond and orient their operations on Lee's army rather than on the counterproductive objective of the rebel capital. This unconventional assessment, soundly based in both military history and engineering, did not promise success in Virginia because a well-led, veteran army constituted a most unpromising objective. As the alternative offered no hope, headquarters decided to count on their greater numbers and wait for the audacious Lee to make a mistake.

Secondly, Lincoln and Halleck concluded not to undertake major operations from southeast of Richmond, in spite of the vast superiority of the communications there and the opportunity which the rivers offered for turning the enemy's defensive positions. Not only was this line of operations interdicted for striking at Lee's army, it was equally prohibited in the event of a siege. The Army of the Potomac must carry out any siege from the north side of the city for the same reason that the southeast line of operations was forbidden. In spite of the far more secure and more efficient water communications offered by a base on the York or James rivers, the advantages of operations from that direction were more than nullified, because such a line would place the Union armies in the same exterior lines situation in which Halleck had found them on becoming general in chief. Notwithstanding the facilities for the rapid movement of troops by water between Washington and the York or James, the rebels would have the central position and could at least threaten the North's politically sensitive capital either directly or by turning its defenders and carrying out a raid into Maryland. Obviously if the rebels reduced the troops defending their capital to a very low level, they could suddenly concentrate the bulk of their forces on the northern Virginia line of operations. To avoid a repetition of Second Bull Run or a crossing of the Potomac, Union armies would have to remain on the defensive near Washington, a very unsatisfactory situation politically and militarily.

This sound strategic analysis inevitably created tensions with the field commanders due to its inherent negativism and pessimism, and because field commanders necessarily had to view their mission in positive if not always optimistic terms. The imposed strategy asked them to make Lee's formidable army their objective, something they regarded as a most unpromising assignment. It asked them to abandon the conventional and clearly attainable objective: a siege of the enemy's capital. Furthermore, it immeasurably complicated their logistics. Finally, the required line of operations did not offer any tactical benefits, if only because it converted the rivers into obstacles and deprived Union forces of most of the benefits of Union seapower. Operating on the Peninsula instead presented obvious advantages, and the field commanders knew that the powerfully fortified federal capital was invulnerable to any force the rebels could bring against it while facing the Army of the Potomac on the Peninsula. They perceived the basic truth that lay beneath the jokester's reference to the outer fortifications, so lengthened and strengthened that by now "they ought to be called fiftyfications." They viewed the needless, continuing overconcern for Washington as another instance of political considerations dictating military strategy.

When this strategy was placed in the emotional context of the Peninsula campaign, of the loyalties which the army's generals still had to their informal leader, McClellan, and of the withdrawal of the army from the Peninsula, Lincoln and Halleck found it impossible to have a meeting of the minds with many of the old leaders of the Army of the Potomac. Equally, Halleck and Lincoln could not easily forget the experience of Second Bull Run. Differences in the perspective from Washington and the field and divergent, even emotional, views of the people and events of the recent past as well as varying appreciations of the political impact of a threat to Washington all made an agreement on the strategy and on the line of operations seem hopeless.[20]

This evaluation of prospects in Virginia really meant that Lincoln was relying on Scott's anaconda plan. The main Union effort centered in Grant on the Mississippi, just as Scott had recommended. But the working of the anaconda plan would be slow in its operation. In the East the Union could perhaps hurt Lee's army now that Lincoln, with the appointment of Hooker, had superseded the dilatory McClellan and egregious Burnside by a confident new general, one not loyal to the memory of McClellan.

Quite popular with men in the ranks, Joseph Hooker genuinely deserved their adulation. He ordered that the issuance of tasty rations include fresh vegetables and soft bread, supervised a thorough cleanup of unsanitary camps, instituted liberal furlough policies, and induced paymasters to come up with the soldiers' six months of back pay. "Ah! the furloughs and vegetables he gave!" one infantryman warmly reminisced many years later. "How he did understand the road to the soldier's heart!" Flagging morale began to soar once again and health conditions vastly improved, causing overlong sick lists to shrink measurably. He also extended the use of divisional patches, identifying badges that had first been used in 1862 by the late Major General Philip Kearny, which encouraged higher unit pride and sense of identity. Thus, "Apollo-like," as one Wisconsin major called him, Hooker, by his care for his men, his unquestioned intelligence, and his marvelous good looks, had with the rank and file some of the old charisma which McClellan had possessed in such abundance.[21]

Still, he had his critics, and some of what they said contained at least elements of truth. The harshest judgment of all came from a cavalry officer, Charles F. Adams, Jr., son of the U.S. ambassador to England. In his typical New England puritanical fashion, young Adams termed Hooker "a noisy, low-toned intriguer" under whose influence the army headquarters became "a place to which no self-respecting man liked to go, and no decent woman would go. It was a combination of barroom and brothel." Poor Hooker even wound up having his name become a synonym for prostitute, many persons later believing he prodigiously patronized whorehouses. In truth he had attempted to corral prostitutes into one area and to police them better. The red-light district in Washington, bordered by Pennsylvania, Constitution, Twelfth, and Fifteenth streets, came to be called "Hooker's Division."[22]

The press had bestowed a swashbuckling sobriquet, "Fighting Joe," upon Hooker during the Peninsula campaign while he commanded a division. He disliked the nickname, however, because in truth it did not fit him precisely and, he lamented, "People will think I am a highwayman or a bandit." Quick-acting, sometimes too quick and therefore rash, frank and outspoken and quite nervous, he nevertheless normally possessed courtesy, polish, grace, dignity, and generosity, and he showed great courage under fire. But he had some erratic qualities. He espoused fatalistic beliefs. The exhilarating lure of battle intoxicated him. Unquestionably a fine commander, he had great potential; his volatile temperament alone prevented his being a match for so even-tempered and consistent an opponent as Robert E. Lee.[23]

With more than a year and a half of assorted high command experience behind him, Lee had fully matured his strategic ideas by the winter of 1862–63. He basically used a defensive posture, seeking, as he said, "to baffle the advance of the enemy." He employed orthodox means to concentrate against the main threat, for, "as the enemy cannot attack all points at one time," the Confederate "troops could be concentrated upon that where an assault should be made." He wished to apply this conventional strategy, characteristic of Napoleon and of Lee's own Seven Days' Battles and Second Bull Run campaigns, to the Confederacy as a whole by using the railroad and the telegraph for a tremendous expansion of the zone of maneuver. Since the enemy, he wrote, finds it impossible "to have a large operating army at every assailable point in our territory as it is for us to keep one to defend it," Lee believed: "We must move our troops from point to point as required & by close observation and accurate information the true point of attack can generally be ascertained." Preferably Lee would move troops to the threatened theatre from an area where a "lull of the war" prevailed, but he might also have to "risk some points in order to have a sufficient force concentrated," he said, "with the hope of dealing a successful blow when opportunity favors."[24]

In Lee's view the climate helped facilitate such a concentration. Both the Union and the Confederacy would conduct their operations in the deep South during the cold months when the weather and logistical difficulties would prevent them in Virginia and Tennessee. In the summer, they would confine their campaigning to the temperate regions, for, Lee naively believed, the hot climate of the lower South would preclude taking the field there. Lee anxiously hoped that the Confederates might shift troops so as to avail themselves of these complementary seasons, taking full advantage of them and at least forestalling Union efforts to do likewise.[25]

Should he eventually concentrate to resist a federal advance, Lee then planned to "retard and baffle" the Union offensive by placing "every obstacle in the way of his advance" and by "operating against the communications of the enemy." Lee would thus "baffle his designs by maneuvering rather than to resist by main force." Not totally rejecting the possibility of major battle with the enemy, he remained alert for opportunities, so, he wrote, I can "get him separated that I can strike him to advantage." Realistically, however, he assessed the outcome of a successful battle as likely to render an enemy "diminished and disheartened" but hardly annihilated.[26]

As the Union fall offensives petered out in early January, Lee saw as his primary task the application of these strategic principles to the conduct of operations in his own area of specific responsibility, Virginia and North Carolina. Though he understood that Foster's December "movements in North Carolina were intended more as a feint to withdraw troops from this point, when Genl Burnside could move at once upon Richmond," Lee believed it necessary to strengthen southeastern Virginia and North Carolina. The realization that "hopeless disaster" would result if the Union cut the railway to Wilmington and South Carolina contributed to this decision as did the initial movement in February of Burnside's Ninth Corps to the Norfolk area. Eventually Lee decided to send Longstreet and two divisions into the more hospitable climate south of Richmond where supplies were more plentiful. Though Lee had earlier apprehended that the Army of the Potomac might again invade the Peninsula, he was convinced from reading northern newspapers that such a move would be politically impossible, being "equivalent to a defeat" for the enemy. The Union's "best plan" was, he thought, to move a small force up the James River and "thus cause us to fall back, & to move his army now on the Rappahannock across the river." Thus Lee decided to hold the substantial force under Longstreet "in reserve, to be thrown on any point attacked or where a blow can be struck." By moving Longstreet's corps south of the James River, Lee was applying the principle of making "troops available in any quarter where they may be needed, after the emergency passes in one place to transfer them to any other point that may be threatened."[27]

Another and perennially important factor contributed to Lee's desire to move so many soldiers to southeastern Virginia. Though his victory at Fredericksburg had enabled him to retain control of the "forage & provisions" of "the Rappahannock Valley," his inability to supply his army there made Longstreet's movement an imperative decision. Before this took place Lee fretted that he might have "to yield to a greater force than that under the command of Genl Hooker"—the "scarcity of food" for "men & animals." Lee could draw scant comfort, nor his men much sustaining drive, from Commissary General Northrup's macabrely optimistic observation that if some of the Confederates had to go without meat they should remember that European peasants rarely ate meat and that peasants in Hindustan never had any. Since in any case Lee had to disperse his army to seek food, Longstreet's movement made even more sense, especially as Lee expected Longstreet to collect enough provisions to forward some to the army on the Rappahannock. Poor Lucius Northrup, unable to supply sumptuously even his own commissary office, sat with his chest wrapped with newspapers in place of unobtainable flannel and directed what meagre provender he could to Lee. But the beef cattle that came from Richmond arrived so thin that Lee decided he must wait until spring to try and fatten them sufficiently for slaughter.[28]

Protecting Lee's logistic base, the region north of Richmond and its railroads to the fertile Shenandoah Valley, made it vitally important to keep the enemy away from Richmond. But Lee's strategy had a more far-reaching and sophisticated aim. A successful defense that yielded no territory meant victory. Such "systematic success" would so discourage the northern population as to produce a "revolution among their people," which would make them turn against the war.[29]

In aiming to avoid battle yet baffle the enemy, Lee had as his model the flank position of the fall of 1862. After Antietam Lee believed that his position west of Washington had long prevented McClellan's advance toward Richmond and provided supplies for his army from an untapped area, while permitting almost the whole of central Virginia to be in his hands and gleaned by Confederate commissaries and quartermasters. For 1863 he aspired to concentrate his forces from south of the James, to move before Hooker was ready, and to "operate to draw him out," to turn him by moving into the Valley and reoccupying a well-supplied flank position, preferably north of the Potomac.[30]

Unlike Bragg, Lee did not place primary reliance on raids; Union land lines of communication were too short. Yet he did not neglect them and had effective assistance from the brilliant raider, John S. Mosby, who, with a small band, constantly threatened Union communications in northern Virginia. Known as "the Gray Ghost," the diminutive, 125-pound Mosby fired the popular imagination. On a quiet March night at Fairfax County Court House, Virginia, twenty-nine men under Mosby stealthily captured Union Brigadier General E. H. Stoughton, ignominiously in bed, plus thirty-two other prisoners, fifty-eight horses, and arms and equipment. Mosby turned down the covers, lifted the tail of the sleeping Stoughton's nightshirt, and gave him a swat on the buttocks. "General," he inquired, "did you ever hear of Mosby?" "Yes," Stoughton replied, excited and only half awake, "have you caught him?" "He has caught you!" replied Mosby.[31]

Lee initiated a less spectacular major raid on April 21. Confederates under Brigadier General William E. Jones commenced a raid on the Baltimore & Ohio Railroad in West Virginia; it lasted until May 21, resulting in considerable minor fighting and much alarm in the North. Not all went consistently in favor of the Confederates, however. In March a little battle erupted as federal cavalry crossed the Rappahannock seeking to damage the Confederates around Culpeper. In the hard-fought though small contest, the Federals lost 78 while the Confederates suffered 133 casualties, including young John Pelham, "the gallant Pelham," a favorite of Robert E. Lee's and a rising soldier beloved for his dash, good looks, and heroic conduct, especially at Fredericksburg. Legend holds that upon his death three girls in nearby towns put on mourning.

As Lee planned for the main spring campaign in Virginia, he was genuinely mystified as to the enemy's intentions. He betrayed his anxious impatience as he wrote late in February to his wife, "I owe Mr. F. J. Hooker no thanks for keeping me here in this state of expectancy. He ought to have made up his mind long ago what to do." Not only did Lee not know whether there would be an advance toward Richmond from the southeast, from the Rappahannock, or both, but the movement in March of Burnside's Ninth Corps to the west also confused him. Lee feared that the enemy was making a surprise concentration by deceiving the Confederates, having already "reinforced other points for offensive operations," and so would act on the defensive in the east while "re-enforcing their armies west with a view to offensive operations."[32]

This insight of Lee's compared precisely to the argument the western concentration bloc was making. Joe Johnston, commanding the Department of the West, had been constantly explaining that Bragg's too-weak army needed strengthening, especially because it guarded what he considered the Confederacy's most vital region, Tennessee. The lobbying efforts of the westerners were pervasive; even Lee's senior subordinate, the capable and ambitious James Longstreet, belonged to the informal organization of the western concentration bloc. He now advocated detaching his corps from Lee's army, away from the Rappahannock, for "operating elsewhere." In March Lee had consulted with the President, and they hoped that projected raids from Southwest Virginia into Kentucky would force Rosecrans to detach troops to cover his rear. Davis, however, remained unconvinced that these raids would suffice, believing that the "indicated" movement was for "Longstreet to re-enforce Bragg."[33]

The serious disaffection of many of Bragg's principal subordinates added to Davis's other anxieties about the situation in Tennessee: the anti-Bragg bloc was seeking to oust their commander. As Grant later noted, "Bragg was the most contentious of men, and there was a story in Mexico that he put everyone in arrest under him and then put himself in arrest." To his quarrelsomeness and natural acerbity was added acrimony following the retreat after the Battle of Stones River. Combined with this failure, Bragg's harsh discipline made him even more unpopular with the rank and file. One day near his Tullahoma headquarters he encountered a man from whom he requested information about the roads. The typical informal dress of the Army of Tennessee made it impossible for Bragg to tell if the man was a soldier, so he inquired if he belonged to Bragg's army. Not recognizing the general, the man shot back, "Bragg's army? Bragg's got no army. He shot half of them himself, up in Kentucky, and the other half got killed at Murfreesboro."[34]

Feeling himself subjected to a "deluge of abuse" by press and public, Bragg asked his corps commanders whether they supported his withdrawal. His opponents took advantage of this opportunity to seek a new commander, two of them feeling that "in the presence of the enemy" Bragg "lost his head." The President sent Joe Johnston to investigate, but Johnston, impressed with Bragg's good discipline and excellent management of his logistics, reported that Bragg should be retained. Johnston remained with Bragg's army until early May.[35]

In the meantime most of the war news came from activities upon the seas. On January 27 federal vessels led by the monitor-type U.S.S. *Montauk* attacked Fort McAllister, a tremendous earthwork on the Ogeechee River just south of Savannah, Georgia. The squadron bombarded for several hours before withdrawing in frustration. Again coast defenses showed their invulnerability to the Navy unless supported by land forces. The Confederates scored a victory on January 30 when the Union gunboat *Isaac Smith*, reconnoitering in the Stono River near Charleston, after Confederate batteries fired upon it ran aground and fell captive. Emboldened by this episode, on the last day of January 1863 two southern gunboats, concealed by a haze, slipped out of Charleston Harbor and assaulted the federal blockaders. They inflicted severe damage upon two ships and somewhat lesser injury to a number of other vessels before withdrawing unhurt. The Confederacy gleefully announced to foreign powers a lifting of the blockade, but the affair actually amounted only to a temporary interruption.

Federal naval forces opened February with a renewed attack upon Fort McAllister, but again failed. On the next day at Wale's Head, North Carolina, some Yankees destroyed a saltworks. Meanwhile in Arkansas federal forces drove the Confederates out of Batesville; and in Virginia Hooker reorganized his growing army, 135,000 men, into seven infantry corps and one corps of cavalry. Naval activity by individual ships continued, with U.S.S. *Conestoga* capturing two southern steamers on the White River, Arkansas, but C.S.S. *Florida* capturing and later destroying the clipper ship *Jacob Bell*, carrying more than $2,000,000 worth of cargo, in the West Indies.

On February 13, the same evening that Mrs. Lincoln entertained the famous midget "General" Tom Thumb and his diminutive bride at the White House, the Union gunboat *Indianola* with two barges capitalized upon darkness along the Mississippi and slipped past the Vicksburg batteries. But this did not strengthen Grant's water transportation below Vicksburg, for the next day the *Queen of the West* fell into Confederate hands after running aground while engaging batteries along the Red River.

The newly arrived *Indianola* stood steadfastly at the Red River mouth while Confederate riverboats tried to best her. Up the Mississippi, Confederate guerrillas attacked the *Hercules* and the Unionists in retaliation burned Hopefield, Arkansas. Two federal expeditions operated for four days each from Murfreesboro to Liberty, Tennessee, and from Memphis against guerrillas harassing the Union armies' rearward lines. Another federal anti-guerrilla expedition cleared a corridor from Lexington to Clifton, Tennessee. Finally, on February 24, the Confederates managed to do something about the menacing *Indianola*. Four southern ships, including the captured and repaired *Queen of the West*, attacked and fought at close quarters; eventually one rammed *Indianola*. After sinking part way, she surrendered. The loss proved momentarily a serious blow to Union river operations below Vicksburg, upon which would depend Grant's strategy against that city.

Pitifully demonstrating the limitations of guerrillas—the inability to seize and use rather than to destroy—on February 26 near Woodburn, Tennessee, Confederate guerrillas halted, captured, and burned a well-equipped 240-mule federal freight train. Later that night, in Mississippi, what resembled a huge ironclad boat floated past Vicksburg. Alarmed to an extreme, Confederates aboard the *Indianola* blew her up to prevent the Union from recapturing the formidable vessel. Alas, one of the destroyers lamented, "with the exception of the wine and liquor stores of *Indianola*, nothing was saved." Adding insult to injury, the ironclad hulk turned out to be merely an old coal barge rigged by the Federals with an $8.61 wooden superstructure to resemble an ironclad and launched as a joke. To the east, February ended with another Union success when the monitor *Montauk* chugged up the Ogeechee River south of Savannah, escorting other vessels, and destroyed C.S.S. *Nashville*.

Ruminating upon the vigorous Confederate winter guerrilla activity, Lincoln wrote to Rosecrans in Tennessee, "In no other way does the enemy give us so much trouble, at so little expense to himself, as by the raids of rapidly moving small bodies of troops (largely, if not wholly, mounted) harassing, and discouraging loyal residents, supplying themselves with provisions, clothing, horses, and the like, surprising and capturing small detachments of our forces, and breaking our communications." Rosecrans hardly needed this explanation of his problem from Lincoln. John Hunt Morgan, the dashing rebel raider, had captured Lexington, Kentucky, just before Rosecrans had assumed command and Morgan had made another Kentucky raid in December, breaking the Louisville and Nashville railway line, capturing almost 2,000 prisoners, and destroying two-million dollars worth of property. Simultaneously Forrest had raided Grant's communications in West Tennessee. "That Devil Forrest," as the Yankees sometimes called him, seemed nearly invulnerable; altogether he had twenty-nine horses shot out from under him during the war and once he even welcomed a few enemy bullets piercing his skin in order to "drain his boils."[36]

To defend against these raids, Rosecrans slowly accumulated with his army a huge stockpile of supplies. This was effective, for, in December, 1862, when Morgan had broken Rosecrans's communications north of Nashville, the Union army had been able to continue the Stones River campaign because of its large reserve of supplies in Nashville, and the winter rise in the Cumberland River enabled the Union to replenish these by steamer.

Though Morgan and Forrest made no more such spectatcular and damaging raids, Rosecrans faced a formidable mounted force assembled by Joe Johnston. Grasping the significance of Grant's December defeat by the destruction of his communications, Johnston concentrated with Bragg's army virtually all of the cavalry of his vast department. This huge force, 15,000 strong, prepared to strike again at Grant's communications, aid Bragg in battle, raid Rosecrans's communications, and dominate the regions adjacent to Bragg's force so that his men might rely on these areas for provisions.

Driving out Rosecrans's foragers, the Confederates supplied themselves and compelled Rosecrans to rely on the railroad for much of his forage as well as subsistence.

Naturally Rosecrans sought an increase in his mounted troops so as "to have cavalry enough to destroy the enemy's cavalry, and, this done," he wrote, "I can occupy this whole country with my forces and procure forage enough for this army." He made constant calls for more mounted troops for "preventing rebel enterprises," he explained, "on our communications, and [to] exclude him from using its forage and conscripting its men." So often did he ask that Halleck lectured him on "the enormous expense to the government" of his telegrams.[37]

Though the Union augmented Rosecrans's cavalry, it never matched Johnston's interdepartmental concentration with Bragg, and Rosecrans was never able to control a country "swarming with the meanest, bitterest kind of enemies." During the twelve months ending July 1, 1863, the trains ran the full distance from Louisville only seven months and twelve days. Every "bridge was destroyed and rebuilt, sometimes three and four times each." The only way to eradicate these guerrillas was "the use of a fine-tooth comb of immense size moving southward."[38]

The impact of rebel raids and guerrillas caused a tremendous dispersion of federal forces. Although the Union moved on the offensive with its main armies, it stood on the defensive in protecting its communications and its conquered territory. In January, 1863, against 13,000 Confederates who menaced north Mississippi and West Tennessee, the Union deployed 51,000 troops in a cordon to cover railroads and the routes of advance of potential raiders. Fifty-six thousand men were guarding Kentucky, West Virginia, and the line of the Baltimore & Ohio against the potential threat of 15,000 Confederates. Including the garrison of Washington and troops deployed by both sides in Missouri and Arkansas, 190,000 Union soldiers, over a third of those in the field, were defending territory and communications against 43,000 Confederates, about one-sixth of all those available. As captured territory increased and communications lengthened, this condition would be aggravated. Aware of this, the Confederates dedicated a part of their superior cavalry to raids which harassed communications and disturbed political conditions. The disposition of Grant's troops in the early spring of 1863 illustrates the effectiveness of the raiding strategy. His force before Vicksburg numbered 36,000 men; that of his rear-area commander, Stephen A. Hurlbut, headquartered at Memphis, numbered 62,000.[39]

Lincoln became alarmed by this development and the immense garrisons required and believed the situation would grow worse, for "as the rebellion grows weaker, it will run more & more into guerrillaism." Success of the anaconda strategy in diminishing the enemy main forces would not remedy this condition, for Lincoln thought that raids would "increase just in proportion as his larger armies will weaken and wane."[40]

The President moved rapidly to adopt one solution to this problem, if only because it was an extension and logical consequence of his Emancipation Proclamation, at the end of which he announced that those blacks freed by the proclamation would "be received into the armed service of the United States to garrison forts, positions, stations, and other places." Continued but unjustified skepticism as to whether blacks could be adequate soldiers did not include their manning rear-area fortified points or guarding railways, thus "leaving the white forces now necessary at those places, to be employed elsewhere." In this way Lincoln planned to ease manpower difficulties by tapping this new source of soldiers, "the great *available* and as yet *unavailed* of, force for the restoration of the Union."[41]

Arming southern Negroes most effectively harmonized with the basic anaconda strategy because Lincoln saw that it worked "doubly, weakening the enemy and strengthening" the Union because it took "so much labor from the insurgent cause," and supplied "the places which otherwise must be filled with so many white men." But Lincoln believed the program undermined the enemy in another way—psychologically. He thought that "the bare sight of fifty thousand armed and drilled black soldiers on the banks of the Mississippi would end the rebellion at once." He did not believe that the rebellion could survive if such a military force could "take shape, and grow, and thrive, in the South." As the recruiting went forward during the spring and summer of 1863, Lincoln, by then envisioning one hundred thousand Negro troops, believed: They are a "resource which, if vigorously applied now, will soon end the contest."[42]

Though the blacks as soldiers did not disappoint Lincoln, the President did prove too optimistic as to the decisive military and psychological impact of this significant measure. But he had a more immediate and purely operational solution to the problem of raids—the Union would not strengthen garrisons but "organize proper forces, and make counter-raids." And Lincoln continued to explain, "We should not capture so much of supplies from them, as they do from us; but it would trouble them more to repair railroads and bridges than it does us." An extension to the West of the plan against Lee to use "cavalry and light artillery upon his communications, and attempt to cut off his supplies," this headquarters view was pithily elaborated by Quartermaster General Meigs. Counter-raids were "the less costly mode" of protecting Rosecrans's communications, because they would employ enemy mounted troops in protecting their own communications and "one thousand cavalry behind an army will give full occupation to 10,000 in pursuit." Union raiders in the enemy's territory should "live upon the country, cut his communications," and make a rule "never to pass a bridge without burning it, a telegraph wire without cutting it, a horse without stealing or shooting it, a guerrilla without capturing him, or a negro without explaining the President's proclamation to him." In addition to protecting the Union force's own communications and harming those of the enemy, the counter-raids could have the effect of "sickening the people of a war which made their homes unsafe."[43]

While Meigs was explaining the virtues of the counter-raids, Rosecrans had an elaborately prepared raid under way, led by the ill-fated Colonel Abel D. Streight. Streight had marched up the Tennessee River by mid-April, initially covered by a corresponding movement by one of Grant's detachments near the river—his mission: "to cut the Georgia Railroad," which would be a signal for the advance of the federal army. The "rebels must be driven into Georgia." The Union hoped for good results from Streight's daring thrust, as his party included two companies of North Alabama Unionists, derisively known as "homemade Yankees," whom he anticipated would be extremely useful guides. But only about one-half the expedition had transportation at the outset, nine hundred hastily requisitioned quartermaster mules. They expected the rest to secure animals by commandeering them from rebel sympathizers along the way. Inadequately mounted and energetically pursued by the brilliant Forrest, Streight's force was overtaken on May 3 before it had done much damage. The end came humorously. The two forces formed battle lines in country so rough that they could only see portions of each other's units. Though Forrest had only 600 men—outnumbered 2½ to 1—he sent over a flag of truce and a note demanding immediate surrender "to stop the further and useless effusion of blood." Streight accepted a parley, and during the talks two of Forrest's artillery pieces moved continually past the Union commander's view, then, concealed by a rise in the ground, they crossed back to move past still again. "Name of God!" Streight cried at last. "How many guns have you got? There's fifteen I've counted already." Forrest looked around casually and replied, "I reckon that's all that has kept up." Streight surrendered his 1,466 men. All such efforts as Streight's miscarried, and Bragg's railroad was not broken once.[44]

The failure of Streight's raid, together with the continuing need to strengthen his cavalry and accumulate supplies, delayed Rosecrans beyond the early May date on which he had thought "fair weather and dry roads would permit campaigning." He would coordinate his movements with those of Burnside, the new commander of the Department of the Ohio, who had just arrived with reinforcements, his Ninth Corps from Virginia. Though a corresponding advance by Burnside would be very valuable to Rosecrans, Burnside could make no movement to East Tennessee because the logistical "difficulties of getting a Union army into that region, and of keeping it there" were so immense. "Start by whatever route they may, their lines of supply are broken before they get half way. A small force sufficient to beat the enemy now there" would be of no value, Lincoln explained, because the enemy would use its railroads to "re-inforce to meet them, until we should have to give back, or accumulate so large a force, as to be very difficult to supply, and as to ruin us entirely if a great disaster should befall it." Thus simultaneous advances by Rosecrans and Burnside would enable Burnside's relatively small army to succeed, because no reinforcements would be sent either way and Rosecrans's forward movement, aided by Burnside, would open railroad communications for Burnside in East Tennessee.[45]

The President and the general in chief clearly recognized the relation between the two departments, and their desire for an advance in Tennessee was second only to the paramount importance assigned to the Mississippi. Telling Rosecrans, in January, I know "that a part of Bragg's forces have been sent to Port Hudson and Vicksburg, and I have been urged to send part of your army down the Mississippi," Halleck revealed the priority assigned to Middle Tennessee when he indicated that he would withdraw no troops, even for Grant. Washington perceived the West as the decisive theatre, with only Missouri and Arkansas ranking below Virginia in its claim on Union resources.[46]

The Union spring offensive began early in 1863, in part because on Grant's front there had been no winter cessation. The commencement of the long-deferred naval attack on Charleston signaled the beginning of concerted action. This attack was one of the more spectacular of the constant Union raids and menaces along the Atlantic seaboard. The Confederates took them very seriously, because they threatened the north-south railway artery along the coast and the important ports of Wilmington and Charleston. Against these Union initiatives the Confederates frequently concentrated and reconcentrated their Atlantic forces by rail. Union troops also periodically carried out similar movements by water. The potential for command friction was great on the Union side because, as on the western rivers, the army and the navy worked by the traditional method of cooperation rather than the modern one of unified command. Though not as cordial and harmonious as that existing between Grant and David D. Porter in the west, cooperation was effective between the army and the navy on the coast.

Curiously, in 1863, the greatest friction occurred between army leaders, when part of John G. Foster's North Carolina forces joined David Hunter at Charleston. The tremendous acrimony contributed to Hunter's later recall. Sometimes changes improved command relations, as when General Henry M. Naglee wrote his superior officer: "I am most happy to advise you that I have been transferred," and added: "It may be equally agreeable and satisfactory to you, as it certainly is to myself, to be assured that the separation will be a permanent one." His superior officer entered into the spirit of the exchange when he wrote to Naglee: I "cordially reciprocate" the sentiments of "happiness you express in your announcement of a permanent separation." He assured Naglee: "I do not believe any one of your previous commanding officers was made more happy at parting than I was."[47]

After disagreements about Hunter's incorporation into his corps of Foster's reinforcement were stifled, the army was ready in late February for the attack on Charleston. Though the plan had originated with the navy and been opposed by Halleck, the fleet had not prepared in time. According to Lincoln the naval commander, Admiral Du Pont, who in "his constant call for more ships, more ironclads, was like McClellan calling for more regiments," caused the delay. Originally intended as a winter operation with ships and men to go to Banks at its conclusion, the project, because of its early April beginning, heralded the spring campaign. Halleck directed Rosecrans: "Give the enemy in your front plenty of occupation," and told Hooker to strike a "blow" because action would "take place both south and west, which may attract the enemy's attention particularly to those points."[48]

Though the removal of the Ninth Corps had weakened Hooker, the timing favored an offensive because of the Confederate preoccupation with the Virginia and North Carolina coast. In a sense the constant federal menaces there in fall and early winter had paid dividends to the Union, because Longstreet had left Lee and, with substantial forces, was moving on the offensive in southeastern Virginia; and, in North Carolina, the weakened Foster found himself beleaguered by another Confederate attack.

On April 7 nine federal ironclads under Samuel F. Du Pont steamed into Charleston Harbor and attacked Fort Sumter in the afternoon. Both Sumter and Fort Moultrie returned the fire. The Confederates threw 2,209 shells, compared with 154 from the ironclads. The fleet finally withdrew, battered by the forts and endangered by obstructions and torpedoes. The rebels disabled five Union vessels, causing Du Pont finally to conclude correctly he could not take Charleston by naval force alone, and, in the absence of any naval success, the land forces remained uncommitted. The navy's effort did not even have any effect as a diversion because Hooker was still not ready for an advance. Nevertheless, while Longstreet continued his siege of Suffolk, the situation remained favorable for the Army of the Potomac.

At the time that the ironclads failed against Charleston, Lincoln was conferring with Hooker as to the plan of campaign. The President took this opportunity to reiterate the doctrine worked out at headquarters in the winter. We have, Lincoln wrote, "*no* eligible route for us into Richmond; and consequently a question of preference between the Rappahannock route, and the James River route is a contest about nothing." Since it was futile to attempt to take the rebel capital, what was to be the mission of the Army of the Potomac? Lincoln explained: "Hence our prime object is the enemies' army in front of us," and against him Hooker had one definite advantage. "Our communications are shorter and safer than are those of the enemy. For this reason, we can, with equal powers fret him more than he can us. . . . While he remains intact, I do not think we should take the disadvantage of attacking him in his entrenchments; but we should continually harass and menace him, so that he shall have no leisure in sending away detachments. If he weakens himself, then pitch into him."[49]

Meanwhile, the Confederate high command was feeling the impact of the Union concentration in the West and Burnside's failure in the East. To bolster his official appeals for more troops, Joe Johnston used his friendship with Senator Wigfall, chairman of the Senate Military Affairs Committee. Johnston wrote to this leader in the western concentration bloc urging that "several divisions from Virginia ought to reinforce Bragg."[50]

Then in early April Pemberton misinterpreted some Mississippi River transport movements, making him believe that Grant was sending a sizable force to Rosecrans. Soon this inaccurate intelligence prompted Pemberton and Johnston to activate their reinforcement plan and send eight thousand men from Mississippi to Tennessee. This, in turn, caused alarm in Washington and induced Halleck to order Burnside to support Rosecrans. But Pemberton's report strengthened the impression of a federal concentration in Tennessee, an impression initiated by the transfer of Burnside and his Ninth Corps to Kentucky. Confederate War Secretary Seddon promptly requested that troops to strengthen Bragg be taken from Lee's army.

On the same day that the secretary made this request, Lee expressed his own similar suspicions when he said: I believe that the enemy has a "general plan to deceive us while reinforcing their western armies." Asking for "two or three brigades" from Longstreet's southeastern Virginia force, Seddon planned to add to these another from southwestern Virginia to make "an encouraging re-enforcement to the Army of the West" under Bragg. Since Burnside's corps, which had gone to Kentucky, had been in southeastern Virginia, the Union dispatch of forces, the secretary argued, "should be met there by a withdrawal of at least a part of our defensive reserves here." Nevertheless, Seddon was unwilling to order these brigades without Lee's "counsel and approval."[51]

This success by the western concentration bloc elicited an uncharacteristically drastic response from Lee. He repudiated his principle that, since the "enemy cannot attack all points at one time," the Confederates should make their "troops available in any quarter where they may be needed," and later "transfer them to any other point that may be threatened." Instead of concentrating, he advocated a broad front advance. If troops had been moved from Mississippi, Pemberton should "take the aggressive & call them back," and forces from southwestern Virginia should conduct "judicious operations" in Kentucky; but the "readiest method of relieving pressure" on the west would not be reinforcements, but for Lee's "army to cross into Maryland" if bad roads and lack of provisions did not make this impossible. He admitted that he had "thought it probable that the enemy may have determined to confine for the present the operations of the Army of the Potomac & of his army south of James River, to the defensive, while with a portion of his troops from the east he should operate in Kentucky or elsewhere in the west." Then, applying his principle of complementary seasons, Lee pointed out: The enemy would be able, when "the season shall suspend operations on the Mississippi, to return with an increased force to the east. There is, however, nothing as yet to indicate this determination except the transfer of Burnside's corps to Kentucky." He now felt sure that there was no western concentration.[52]

Despite Lee's emphatic objections, the War Department persisted. It not only renewed the request but enlarged it into a plan to add a total of twelve to fifteen thousand men to Bragg's army. Lee's second response was more temperate and grounded on different considerations. Without the men now sought from him, he said, I would "be unable to obtain the supplies we hoped to draw from the eastern portion of the department, which as far as I am able to judge, are essential." Referring to his own well-matured plan for re-enacting the previous year's crossing of the Potomac, Lee pointed out: As soon as I have "secured all the subsistence which could be obtained," with a "vigorous advance" the "Valley could be swept . . . and the army opposite me be thrown north of the Potomac." This projected operation would also have revealed the degree to which Hooker had been depleted, whether the enemy was really concentrating in the West, and, if done by the first of May, would catch "Hooker's army weakened by the expiration of the term of service of many of his regiments, and before new recruits can be received." Finally, Lee pointed out that it was not time to use complementary seasons to defend Tennessee, that Johnston should "concentrate the troops of his own department," and "the troops in the vicinity of Charleston, Savannah, Mobile, & Vicksburg will not be called in requisition at those places" after May.[53]

Though alluding to his recent strategic theory that, if Hooker's army were "thrown north of the Potomac," he believed "greater relief would in this way be afforded to the armies in Middle Tennessee and the Carolina coast," Lee was not really enunciating a new principle of strategy. He had not suddenly repudiated Napoleon and his own successful past operations. Lee had had as his motto "concentrate and crush," not disperse and attack. His new theories were rationalizations. Like his emphatic reaction, these were subconsciously designed to forestall the diminution of his army and prevent the derangement of his own plans for the spring campaign. His stout resistance also resulted in part from a realization that he now faced a strong military-political combination which even embraced Longstreet, his senior corps commander. Lee knew about some of the efforts of the western concentration bloc to secure reinforcements from his army and his vigorous reaction was doubtless based on his feeling that he must not only resist the reduction of his army but combat the bloc and conserve his influence with the President. Of course Lee himself perceived that "upon every proposition to remove troops from any section the apprehensions of the community exaggerate rumors, and create expectations of an immediate attack. The responsibility of the office charged with its defense tends to produce the same result." Yet Lee embellished his resistance with a novel strategic theory at variance with his own and Davis's usual practice, one which if advocated by any other commander would surely have elicited from the President a lecture on the principles of strategy.[54]

Because the intelligence that Grant was not reinforcing Rosecrans reached the President and the secretary about the same time as Lee's second set of objections to sending Virginia troops west, they dropped the project; and, as Lee had suggested and Davis and Seddon had already contemplated, they decided to rely solely on troops sent to Bragg from Beauregard's Department, the three states farthest southeast. With summer approaching and his recent success in repelling the naval attack on Charleston, Beauregard clearly had troops to spare.[55]

Though Lee retained all of his brigades, he could not move quite yet, he explained, "owing to the condition of our horses and the scarcity of forage and provisions." Because of this and the uncertainty of the enemy's intentions, Lee decided to retain Longstreet south of the James, Lee hoping to defend the Rappahannock without him or withdrawing, he said, "if we cannot resist alone."[56]

Yet Lee remained optimistic, saying, "If we can baffle them in their various designs this year & our people are true to our cause . . . , I think our success will be certain." Hoping during the year to establish his "supplies on a firm basis," he stated: "On every other point, if successful this year, next fall will be a great change in public opinion at the North. The Republicans will be destroyed & I think the friends of peace will become so strong as that the next administration will go in on that basis. We have only therefore to resist manfully." The key to victory, then, was continued application of his effective defensive policy of the previous year.[57]

Lee's political analysis was correct. The Lincoln administration badly needed a victory in Virginia and resolved to take the offensive, no matter how unpromising the military prospects. This, together with Lee's weakness on the Rappahannock, led Lincoln to cancel the withdrawal of troops and ironclads from Charleston for reinforcing Banks on the Mississippi. Instead of sending them to New Orleans, he ordered them to make a "demonstration" at Charleston to support Hooker's movement. Public opinion thus overmatched Lincoln's realism about Virginia operations and the overall Union blueprint for maximum concentration in the West. "The press had wrought the public mind to high expectation by predicting certain success" for Fighting Joe Hooker. One elated radical journal extravagantly believed that, "with Rosecrans in the West and Hooker in the East, there is not treason enough in the North, rebellion in the South, or imbecility or cross purposes sufficient in the Cabinet, to prevent the War from being brought to an early and satisfactory conclusion." By threatening Charleston Lincoln thus diverted forces from the West to help Hooker.[58]

Hooker's plan against Lee followed the headquarters recommendations of Halleck and Meigs. Halleck had encouraged the army to use "cavalry and light artillery upon [Lee's] communications, and attempt to cut off his supplies and engage him at an advantage." Agreeing, Meigs had advocated turning Lee on the west to "get on a point on the railroad between the rebels and Richmond." Hooker stated: I am "apprehensive" that Lee will "retire from before me the moment I should succeed in crossing the river," but with my cavalry already "established on the line of retreat between him and Richmond, they will be able to hold him and check his retreat until I can fall on his rear." His plan, which involved crossing the Rappahannock through "turning his position" to his right, was a bold one and planned at a propitious time. Nearly a third of Lee's army was absent, most of it participating in Longstreet's attack on Suffolk, an attack incidentally so menacing that Halleck sent 10,000 reinforcements. In view of Hooker's impending advance, Halleck was able to draw these troops from the Washington defenses. Hooker, not therefore weakened at all, had a two-to-one numerical superiority over Lee. Not every augury was favorable, however. Professional soldiers did not share the radical press's admiration of Hooker. At the time Hooker was preparing to advance, Sherman wrote: "I know Hooker well and tremble to think of his handling 100,000 men in the presence of Lee. I don't know or think Lee will attack Hooker in position because he will doubt if it will pay, but let Hooker once advance or move laterally and I fear for the result." Lee could hardly have been unaware of this professional estimate of his opponent.[59]

The spring offensive deceptively appeared quite coordinated when Hooker crossed the Rappahannock and one day thereafter Grant crossed the Mississippi. The Confederates were well engaged at Suffolk, and even Banks's indefatigable activities in the wrong direction against the wrong forces were chronologically harmonized with both movements. Rosecrans and Burnside also hoped to move together at that time. Actually less real concert existed than in the previous fall.[60]

After his effort to have a general advance in tune with the naval attack against Charleston, Halleck played a minimal role. He did plan to have a detachment from the Fort Monroe command menace Richmond and he again provided concerted action between the Virginia and North Carolina commands. With so many forces already in contact, Halleck's main task would have been to coordinate the advances of Hooker and Rosecrans. This he did not attempt, presumably because Rosecrans had his own timetable, dependent on strengthening his cavalry and accumulating his supplies. The effect of this lack of full concert permitted the Confederates again to shift significant numbers of troops from Tennessee to Mississippi. In addition, the Navy did not so threaten Charleston as to deter the transfer of sizable Confederate reinforcements from Beauregard's to Johnston's command.[61]

Though Grant's efforts had been unremitting, the timing of his advance, like Rosecrans's, depended on the completion of a considerable logistical preparation. For establishing a line of communications past Vicksburg on the west bank, the Union had to improve the thirty-seven-mile road, to dig a canal to make the waterway provide "good water communications" for the "barges and tugs," and to provide additional boats as an "aid in carrying subsistence" and "for ferrying any intermediate bayous." Favoring an advance down the railroad, Sherman was skeptical of the canal, "crooked, narrow and full of trees," which, he said, has "plenty of water now, but in two months will dry up." The road was worse, he added, "pure alluvium and three hours' rain will make it a quagmire over which a wagon could no more pass than in the channel of the Mississippi." He doubted the capacity of the system "for a military channel, capable of supporting an army large enough to operate against Jackson."[62]

Hoping possibly to take Vicksburg by "the starvation of the garrison," Grant gave the enemy's logistics almost as much attention as his own. He realized that naval control of the river south of Vicksburg had cut off Confederate supplies from west of the Mississippi; hence, he set out by raids to "destroy the resources of the enemy" east of the river. One operation burned 200,000 bushels of corn and brought back several hundred liberated Negroes. Grant issued directions: "Destroy corn, wheat crops, and everything that can be made use of by the enemy in prolonging the war. Mules and horses can be taken to supply all our wants, and, where it does not cause too much delay, agricultural implements may be destroyed. In other words, cripple the rebellion in every way, without insulting women and children or taking their clothing, jewelry, &c." One of Sherman's efficient regiments gained the overstated reputation of being able to "catch, scrape, and skin a hog without a soldier leaving the ranks."[63]

Grant's raids against the enemy's logistic base also contributed to his "desire to distract attention" from his forthcoming movement. A raid on the Mississippi north of Vicksburg helped this as did Streight's, sent by Rosecrans along the Tennessee. Another and more successful effort began on April 17 when troops under the capable Colonel Benjamin H. Grierson commenced their stunning raid from La Grange, Tennessee. An improbable cavalry leader, Grierson previously had been a professional bandmaster and had disliked and distrusted all horses since in childhood he received from a pony a kick which smashed one of his cheekbones, split his forehead, and left him scarred for life. Halleck insisted that he looked "active and wiry enough to make a good cavalryman," and the assessment proved correct; Grierson developed into a first-rate commander of horse soldiers. He also became somewhat of a federal poor-man's version of the Confederacy's eccentric Jeb Stuart: where Stuart kept a banjo player on his staff, Grierson kept a jew's-harp in his pocket, and where Stuart gaily chatted with press correspondents and liked to ride daringly all around enemy armies, Grierson enjoyed stealing away from his troops to unwind by playing the pianos in plantation houses along the way.

Grierson's 1,700 men eventually slashed, virtually unmolested, through Mississippi and finally connected with Banks's forces at Baton Rouge, Louisiana. As the Confederacy had moved most of its cavalry from Mississippi to aid Bragg in Tennessee, the dashing Grierson could complete his destructive raid with little interference. In addition to its intended effect in distracting the Confederates, it raised northern and depressed Confederate morale. A Confederate expedition into Missouri from Arkansas had little impact on Grant's campaign. By the end of April the rebel raiders had attacked Cape Girardeau and skirmished near Jackson, Missouri.

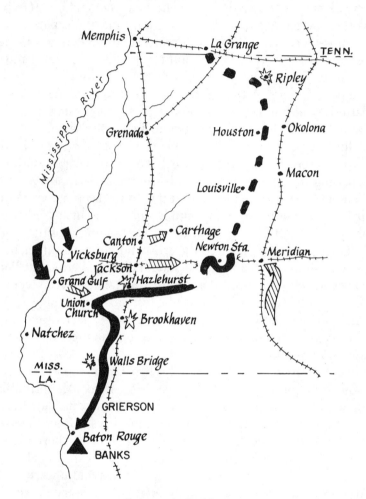

Grierson's Raid

The entirely inadvertent consequence of the movement north from Vicksburg of the empty vessels which had been used to concentrate Grant's army came too early to help Grant's advance. When reported, these ship movements convinced Pemberton and Joe Johnston that "Grant's army may join that of Rosecrans" and activated the whole Confederate system for reinforcing Tennessee from Mississippi. In mid-April Johnston had ordered the Mobile garrison to move north and Pemberton started 8,000 men for Mobile, all destined for Bragg's army. The alarm was perceived, however, as a false one and the troops had returned before Grant moved.[64]

Essential to Grant's plan was the presence of the Union fleet in the river south of Vicksburg. The fleet, which had been so effectively cooperating with the western armies since before the fall of Fort Henry, enthusiastically undertook the task of running the batteries. Without a unified command, the two services successfully relied on voluntary cooperation. Rarely have two men worked better together than did Grant and the capable and energetic naval commander, Acting Rear Admiral David D. Porter. On April 16, on the river near Vicksburg, as flares and tar barrels burst into flames along the bluffs, a little before midnight Porter's fleet of twelve vessels commenced their run past the city. Although hit often by fire from the powerful Confederate batteries, all but one of the vessels got through safely and soon concentrated near Hard Times on the west side of the Mississippi.

With his preparations nearly complete, Grant planned to leave Sherman temporarily before Vicksburg and take his other two corps south via road and canal, crossing the river at Grand Gulf. Sherman disapproved of the scheme even though Grant had told Halleck: I intend to "keep my army together and see to it I am not cut off from my supplies or beaten in any other way than in fair fight." Although Grant's plan called for holding a bridgehead and reinforcing Banks, Sherman believed the army did not have sufficient strength to strike at Vicksburg at all and that it should direct all efforts at Port Hudson. Grant's friend felt convinced that Grant was taking a risky course because, he said, the public "clamor is so great he fears to seem to give up Vicksburg." Sherman believed that Grant, fearing criticism for lack of energy or unwillingness to fight, "trembles at the approaching thunders of popular criticism and must risk anything.[65]

Sherman's apprehensions increased when Grant reported: "The water in the bayous is falling very rapidly . . . so that it is very doubtful that they can be made use of for the purposes of navigation." Since he had already resolved to move without the completion of the waterways, Grant determined to go anyway, directing "special attention to the matter of shortening the line of land transportation from above Vicksburg to the steamers below." He began his expedition to Grand Gulf with an improvised and uncertain supply line, "a narrow boggy road," because he thought "it necessary to take the risk, for fear the enemy may get before him." If concern that further delay would bring a "thunder of popular criticism" motivated him to act early, Grant did "not anticipate any trouble, however, if a landing" could be effected at Grand Gulf and, with his usual optimism, continued to have no "doubt of success in the entire cleaning out of the enemy from the banks of the river."[66]

In expressing his care, Grant said: "No risk should be taken in following the enemy until our forces are concentrated"; thus Grant hedged the confidence he always felt before an operation. He cautioned the incompetent

McClernand, who would land first at Grand Gulf, that "troops first there should intrench themselves for safety." On April 27, just before the operation commenced, Grant asked Sherman for a "heavy demonstration" against Vicksburg. The effect "would be good as far as the enemy are concerned," but, said Grant, I am "loth to order it because . . . our own people at home would characterize it as a repulse." Grant left the decision to Sherman, advising him; If you do it, protect yourself from criticism by publishing the "order beforehand, stating that a reconnaissance in force was to be made for the purpose of calling off the enemy's attention from our movements south of Vicksburg, and not with any expectation of attacking."[67]

Sherman was bitter that the newspapers "must be consulted," he said, "before I can make a simulated attack," but he carried it out, humorously dispatching his troops with orders that "every man look as numerous as possible" and warning his wife: "Prepare yourself for another blast against Sherman blundering and being repulsed at Haines whilst McClernand charges gallantly ashore at Grand Gulf, etc." Sherman's hostility to the political general and the press treatment of him McClernand cordially reciprocated; he had written Lincoln after the capture of Arkansas Post: "My success here is gall and wormwood to the clique of West Pointers who have been persecuting me for months."[68]

The knowledge that Stanton, through Assistant Secretary Dana, was watching them surely aggravated Sherman and Grant's apprehensions about popular pressure and criticism. In addition, Halleck had an aide with them, though likely his orders instructed him to watch McClernand. And meanwhile Adjutant General Thomas arrived on a mission to recruit black troops. Sherman observed: "We have Thomas and Dana both here from Washington, no doubt impressing on Grant the necessity of achieving something brilliant. It is the same old Bull Run mania." In a rare display of sarcasm, Grant assured Halleck: You will "receive favorable reports of the condition and feeling of this army from every impartial judge and from all who have been sent from Washington to look after its welfare."[69]

His observations and insights of Grant during the next few months inspired Dana to write a penetrating portrait of the western chieftain: "Grant was an uncommon fellow—the most modest, the most disinterested, and the most honest man I ever knew, with a temper that nothing could disturb, and a judgment that was judicial in its comprehensiveness and wisdom. Not a great man, except morally, not an original or brilliant man, but sincere, thoughtful, deep, and gifted with courage that never faltered. When the time came to risk all, he went in like a simple-hearted, unaffected, unpretending hero, whom no ill omens could deject and no triumph unduly exalt. A social, friendly man, too, fond of a pleasant joke and also ready with one; but liking above all a long chat of an evening, and ready to sit up with you all night. . . . Not a man of sentimentality, not demonstrative in friendship, but always holding to his friends; and just, even to the enemies he hated."[70]

At about this time criticisms of Grant's alcoholic drinking raged anew. Lincoln responded to one such assailant with, "If I knew what brand of whiskey he drinks I would send a barrel or so to some other generals." In truth, Grant did drink to excess on rare occasions, but his self-appointed keepers took good care of him and it did not cause him serious problems during the Civil War. In part, perhaps, he himself nurtured the hard-drinking image to impress his troops, though he never appeared before any of them except when cold sober. He did carefully cultivate and manage what his subordinates saw and thought of him. Most interestingly, one of his staff officers received the impression that he was "half a dozen men condensed into one."[71]

The presence of Assistant Secretary Dana at Grant's headquarters did indicate, however, that Grant did not yet enjoy the full confidence of the President. But Grant had planned well, showing that he had learned from cavalry breaking his land communications in December. He had limited all of his subsequent efforts against Vicksburg to moves based on the Mississippi and so he also based his late April turning movement primarily on the river. Learning the same lesson, cavalry veteran Joseph E. Johnston, the Confederate western commander, had concentrated his cavalry in Middle Tennessee, effectively defeating Rosecrans's plans to advance.

But, unaware of the effectiveness of this strategy, Johnston and the western concentration bloc so pressed for reinforcements for Bragg that Davis and Seddon sought men from Lee's army. Planning to turn Hooker as he had Pope, Lee reacted so strongly against the suggestion that he send troops to Bragg that he repudiated his own Napoleonic strategy of concentration by rail. Though he successfully rebuffed the requests for reinforcements, Lee was not ready for Hooker's advance because Longstreet, southeast of Richmond, was too far away to aid Lee promptly.

Hooker and Grant would, fortuitously, advance simultaneously, each planning to turn their opponents on the west. But their objectives were different. Grant aimed at Vicksburg and control of the Mississippi while Hooker sought to injure Lee's army.

1. Catton, *Never Call Retreat*, 70–71.

2. Long, *Civil War, Day by Day*, 308–9; Foote, *The Civil War*, II, 14.

3. Sherman to Rawlins, Apr. 8, 1863, *O.R.*, XXIV, pt. 3, 179–80.

4. Grant to Halleck, Jan 9, 14, 15, 1863, *O.R.*, XVII, pt. 2, 549, 560, 564; Grant to McClernand, Jan. 11, 13, 1863, *ibid.*, 553–54, 559; Grant to Hurlbut, Mar. 4, 1863, *ibid.*, XXIV, pt. 3, 83; Sherman to Rawlins, Apr. 8, 1863,

ibid., 179–80; Special Orders No. 15, Jan. 15, 1863, *ibid.*, XVII, pt. 2, 565.

5. Grant to Halleck, Jan. 14, 18, 20, Feb. 3, Mar. 7, 17, 1863, *O.R.*, XVII, pt. 2, 560, 573, XXIV, pt. 1, 8–9, 14, 19, 20; Grant to McPherson, Mar. 16, 1863, *ibid.*, pt. 3, 112; Halleck to Grant, Jan. 25, 1863, *ibid.*, pt. 1, 10.

6. Henry, *Story of the Confederacy*, 229.

7. Foote, *The Civil War*, II, 208.

8. Grant to Sherman, Mar. 22, 1863, *O.R.*,

XXIV, pt. 3, 127; Grant to Banks, Mar. 22, 1863, *ibid.*, 125–26; Grant to Porter, Mar. 23, 1863, *ibid.*, 132–33; Grant to Quinby, Mar. 23, 1863, *ibid.*, 134–35; Halleck to Grant, Mar. 20, 1863, *ibid.*, pt. 1, 22.

9. Richard Wheeler, *The Siege of Vicksburg* (New York, 1978), 28; Foote, *The Civil War*, II, 116.

10. Grant to Ellet, Mar. 24, 1863, *O.R.*, XXIV, pt. 3, 136; Grant to Farragut, Mar. 23 (two communications), 26, 1863, *ibid.*, 131, 147–48; Grant to Porter, Mar. 29, Apr. 2, 1863, *ibid.*, 152, 168; Grant to Kelton, July 6, 1863, *ibid.*, pt. 1, 44, 46; Crandall to Grant, Mar. 24, 1863, *ibid.*, pt. 3, 136–37.

11. Grant to Halleck, Apr. 2, 1863, *O.R.*, XXIV, pt. 1, 24; Dana to Stanton, Apr. 15, 1863, *ibid.*, 73; Halleck to Grant, May 11, 1863, *ibid.*, 36.

12. Halleck to Buell, Nov. 9, 1862, *O.R.*, XV, 590.

13. Banks to Halleck, Jan. 7, 24, Feb. 12, Mar. 21, 1863, *O.R.*, XV, 200–201, 661, 240–41, 251–56; Banks to Grant, Mar. 13, 1863, *ibid.*, XXIV, pt. 3, 104; Halleck to Banks, Feb. 2, 1863, *ibid.*, XV, 671; Halleck's Report, Nov. 15, 1863, *ibid.*, XXVI, pt. 1, 4.

14. Catton, *Never Call Retreat*, 78.

15. Delaney, *Kell*, 143–44.

16. Hassler, *Commanders of the Army of the Potomac*, 126–28.

17. Lincoln to Hooker, Jan. 26, 1863, Basler, *Collected Works*, VI, 78–79.

18. Lincoln to Hooker, *ibid.*; Lincoln to Burnside, Jan. 8, 1863, *ibid.*, 46.

19. Halleck to Burnside, Jan. 7, 1863, *O.R.*, XXI, 953–54; Halleck to Hooker, Jan. 31, 1863, *ibid.*, XXV, pt. 2, 12.

20. This seems the only explanation which fits all of the facts available. Conscious and unconscious partisans of what might be called the Peninsular school have interpreted Lincoln as interfering with field commanders who knew better how to direct the war in Virginia and have generalized this to cover Lincoln's conduct of operations in all theatres. They, as have others, discounted Halleck as a clerk and a pedant. As a general interpretation this fails if only because of Lincoln's very limited and declining involvement with army operations in other regions. It also ignores the general soundness of the strategy pursued elsewhere and the excellent analysis of the Virginia situation by Halleck, obviously a very competent engineer, military historian, and strategist. Lincoln's interference was hardly based on civilian ignorance when it relied on Halleck, the staff, and Lincoln's own very obvious mastery of military realities.

Conscious and unconscious opponents of the Peninsular school have stressed McClellan's weakness in execution, concluding that his strategy was faulty. Lincoln's emphasis upon the enemy army as an objective seemed orthodox and modern, whereas a preoccupation with territory and a place, the enemy capital, seemed to reflect that the field commanders had a less sophisticated understanding than did Lincoln, the generals' ideas even smacking of an archaic, pre-Napoleonic conception. Many of the exponents of this point of view wrote after World War II, when military operations seemed decisive and armies vulnerable, whereas writers in the Peninsula school, such as James G. Randall, were influenced by World War I and its exhibition of the apparent futility of the doctrine of attacking the enemy army.

Like the Peninsular school, the proponents of Lincoln also have difficulty generalizing their interpretation to the other theatres of the war. Nowhere else did Lincoln advocate the enemy army as an objective. His objectives in other theatres were not armies, but such goals as the East Tennessee Railroad and the Mississippi. The thesis here proposed has the opposite difficulty in that, having a generalized explanation for all operations outside of Virginia, it must also include the special case of Virginia, where Lincoln and Halleck were apparently inconsistent with the strategy advocated elsewhere when they preached attack on Lee's army, a strategy which they did not prescribe for other theatres. Lincoln's emerging feeling that lack of success was not due to the generals but to the "case," i.e., the military realities, and his subsequent reactions to the operations of Hooker and Meade indicated that Lincoln shared the generals' skepticism about the annihilation or even the disastrous defeat of an enemy army. What Lincoln meant seems, then, to be that action against Lee in the field was preferable to the futility of a siege against a well-fortified enemy in a city whose communications could not be interdicted. Of course, he hoped for a blunder by Lee, which would provide an opportunity to hurt the rebel army.

Thus strategy in Virginia was dictated by special circumstances, largely military but also political because of the proximity of Washington. The Richmond communications network had much to do with this, but geography contributed significantly. Rivers running to the southeast, which made a direct advance difficult, also made the Peninsula an ideal line of operations. The Shenandoah Valley, a major Confederate asset as it led into the Union rear, made a natural corridor for a turning movement; as a Union route of advance, it was almost useless, for it led away from the rear of the Confederate army. Finally, Virginia was special because of Robert E. Lee's unequaled operational skill and the morale and efficiency which he imparted to the Army of Northern Virginia. Lee and his army, admirably fitted, could resist harm and exploit the advantages of their theatre of operations.

Yet in their Virginia strategy Lincoln and Halleck also exhibited that they shared the generals' pessimism about battles and ability to hurt an enemy army. That they did not expect much from their Virginia strategy is indicated by their sending the Ninth Corps to the West in the spring of 1863 and their uncertainty as to whether troops sent west in the fall of that year would be returned for the 1864 campaign. If they had expected to achieve success against Lee, they would have retained the Ninth Corps under Hooker instead of sending it to facilitate Rosecrans's advance. Thus Lincoln's hopes for victory seemed to have centered in the West, in the tightening blockade, and, later, in a liberal reconstruction policy and in arming blacks.

21. Catton, *Never Call Retreat*, 94–98.

22. Foote, *The Civil War*, II, 232–34.

23. Hassler, *Commanders of the Army of the Potomac*, 129.

24. Lee to G. W. Smith, Nov. 28, Dec. 12, 1862, Jan. 4, 1863, *O.R.*, XXI, 1038, 1060, *Wartime Papers*, 384; Lee to G. W. C. Lee, Nov. 10, 1862, *ibid.*, 313; Lee to Davis, Dec. 6, 1862, *ibid.*, 353.

25. Lee to Davis, Oct. 22, 1862, Apr. 27, 1863, *O.R.*, XIX, pt. 2, 675, XXV, pt. 2, 752; Lee to Seddon, Apr. 9, May 10, 1863, *Wartime Papers* 430, 482; Lee to Cooper, Apr. 16, 1863, *ibid.*, 434.

26. Lee to Jackson, Nov. 9, 1862, *Wartime Papers*, 330; Lee to Davis, Nov. 25, 1862, *ibid.*, 345; Lee to Randolph, Nov. 10, 1862, *ibid.*, 332; Lee to G. W. C. Lee, Nov. 10, 1862, *ibid.*, 333; Lee to Seddon, Jan. 10, 1863, *ibid.*, 388–89.

27. Lee to Davis, Oct. 22, Nov. 25, 1862, Jan. 19, 1863, *O.R.*, XIX, pt. 2, 675, *Wartime Papers*, 345, 391; Lee to Longstreet, Mar. 16, 21, 1863, *O.R.*, XVIII, 922, *Wartime Papers*, 416; Lee to Randolph, Oct. 25, 1862, *O.R.*, XIX, pt.

2, 681; Lee to G. W. C. Lee, *Wartime Papers*, 382.

28. Lee to Seddon, Dec. 16, 1862, *Wartime Papers*, 364; Lee to G. W. C. Lee, Jan. 5, 1863, *ibid.*, 385; Lee to Davis, Apr. 2, 1863, *O.R.*, XXV, pt. 2, 700; Catton, *Never Call Retreat*, 491n5.

29. Lee to Longstreet, Mar. 27, 1863, *Wartime Papers*, 417; Lee to G. W. C. Lee, Feb. 28, 1863, *ibid.*, 411.

30. Lee to Longstreet, Apr. 2, 1863, *O.R.*, XVIII, 954; Lee to Davis, Apr. 2, 1863, *ibid.*, XXV, pt. 2, 700.

31. Foote, *The Civil War*, II, 244–45.

32. Lee to Mrs. Lee, Feb. 23, 1863, *Wartime Papers*, 408; Lee to G. W. C. Lee, Feb. 28, 1863, *ibid.*, 411; Lee to Davis, Mar. 19, Apr. 2, 1863, *O.R.*, XXV, pt. 2, 675, 700; Lee to Pendleton, Mar. 21, 1863, *ibid.*, 681; Lee to Longstreet, Apr. 2, 1863, *ibid.*, XVIII, 954.

33. Horn, *Army of Tennessee*, 193; Longstreet to Wigfall, Feb. 4, May 13, 1863, Louis T. Wigfall Papers, Library of Congress; Longstreet to Lee, Mar. 19, Apr. 3, 1863, *O.R.*, XVIII, 926–27, 959; Davis's endorsement, Lee to Cooper, Mar. 28, 1863, *ibid.*, XXV, pt. 2, 689: Connelly, *Autumn of Glory*, 93–111.

34. New York *Herald*, July 24, 1878; Foote, *The Civil War*, II, 170.

35. Memoirs of Major General Henry Heth, 140, Alderman Library, University of Virginia, Charlottesville.

36. Lincoln to Rosecrans, Feb. 17, 1863, Basler, *Collected Works*, VI, 108; Robert S. Henry, *"First With the Most" Forrest* (New York, 1944), 17.

37. Rosecrans to Halleck, Jan. 26, Feb. 12, 1863, *O.R.*, XXIII, pt. 2, 14, 31; Halleck to Rosecrans, Apr. 20, 1863, *ibid.*, 255–56; Lamers, *Rosecrans*, 248.

38. Lincoln to Rosecrans, Feb. 17, 1863, Basler, *Collected Works*, VI, 108; Halleck to Burnside, Jan. 7, 1863, *O.R.*, XXI, 953–54; Granger to Rosecrans, Mar. 24, 1863, *ibid.*, 168; Lamers, *Rosecrans*, 248.

39. William R. Livermore, *The Story of the Civil War*, 2 vols. (New York, 1913), I, 94, note 1 and map IV; Vincent J. Esposito, chief editor, *The West Point Atlas of American Wars*, 2 vols. (New York, 1959), I, map 102b.

40. Lincoln to Stanton and Halleck, July 27, 1863, Basler, *Collected Works*, VI, 352; Lincoln to Rosecrans, Feb. 17, 1863, *ibid.*, 108.

41. Emancipation Proclamation, Jan. 1, 1863,

Basler, *Collected Works*, VI, 30; Lincoln to Dix, Jan. 14, 1863, *ibid.*, 56; Lincoln to Andrew Johnson, Mar. 26, 1863, *ibid.*, 149. For Lincoln learning of the role of blacks as soldiers in the Revolution, see: Benjamin Quarles, *Lincoln and the Negro* (New York, 1962), 155.

42. Lincoln to Grant, Aug. 9, 1863, Basler, *Collected Works*, VI, 374; Annual Message to Congress, Dec. 8, 1863, *ibid.*, VII, 50; Lincoln to Andrew Johnson, Mar. 26, 1863, *ibid.*, 149–50; Lincoln to Hunter, Apr. 1, 1863, *ibid.*, 158; Lincoln to Grant, Aug. 9, 1863, *ibid.*, 374.

43. Lincoln to Rosecrans, Feb. 17, 1863, Basler, *Collected Works*, VI, 108; Meigs to Rosecrans, May 1, 1863, *O.R.*, XXXIII, pt. 2, 302–3.

44. Rosecrans to Halleck, Apr. 12, 1863, *O.R.*, XXIII, pt. 2, 232; Henry, *"First With the Most" Forrest*, 152–57.

45. Lamers, *Rosecrans*, 257; Lincoln to Fleming, Aug. 9, 1863, Basler, *Collected Works*, VI, 373.

46. Halleck to Rosecrans, Jan. 30, 1863, *O.R.*, XXIII, pt. 2, 23.

47. Erasmus D. Keyes, *Fifty Years' Observation of Men and Events* (New York, 1884), 478–79.

48. *Welles Diary*, I, 259; Halleck to Banks, Apr. 18, May 11, 1863, *O.R.*, XV, 702, 725–26; Halleck to Hooker, Mar. 27, 1863, *ibid.*, XXV, pt. 2, 158; Halleck to Rosecrans, Mar. 25, 1863, *ibid.*, XXIII, pt. 2, 171.

49. Lincoln Memorandum on Joseph Hooker's Plan of Campaign Against Richmond, Apr. 6–10, 1863, Basler, *Collected Works*, VI, 164.

50. Johnston to Wigfall, Mar. 4, 1863, Wigfall Papers, Library of Congress.

51. Lee to Longstreet, Apr. 6, 1863, *O.R.*, XVIII, 467; Seddon to Lee, Apr. 6, 1863, *ibid.*, XXV, pt. 2, 709.

52. Lee to G. W. Smith, Dec. 12, 1862, *O.R.*, XXI, 1060; Lee to Longstreet, Mar. 16, 1863, *ibid.*, XVIII, 922; Lee to Seddon, Apr. 9, 1863, *Wartime Papers*, 430.

53. Cooper to Lee, Apr. 14, 1863, *O.R.*, XXV, pt. 2, 720; Lee to Cooper, Apr. 16, 1863, *Wartime Papers*, 433–34; Lee to Davis, Apr. 16, 1863, *ibid.*, 435.

54. Longstreet to Lee, Mar. 19, 1863, *O.R.*, XVIII, 926; Lee to Seddon, Feb. 15, 1863, *ibid.*, XXV, pt. 2, 624.

Lee's elaboration of this strategic theory may well have been evidence of cognitive dissonance. This is a psychological condition caused by conflict between a person's desires or behavior, on one hand, and his perceptions or available information, on the other. It may also be caused by a realization that rejected alternatives also have significant merit. Either situation engenders a psychological need to diminish such dissonance, just as hunger creates a need to reduce physical discomfort. One of the ways to reduce dissonance is by changing perceptions of reality in order to reconcile the dissonance between them.

In Lee's case dissonance was created by the conflict between his realization that the western armies needed strengthening and his concern for the situation of his own army. He knew that troops were needed in Tennessee; but he also knew they were needed in Virginia, for he was desperate for supplies and apprehensive about being pushed back out of his important supply area north of Richmond. This dissonance was aggravated by his confidence in the ability of his fine army to deal with its opponent and by his plan to turn Hooker's army back to the Potomac—provided that his army was not weakened by loss of troops to other commanders.

Lee successfully reduced this post-decision dissonance by exaggerating the virtues of the accepted alternative. Not only did he overstress the applicability of his theory of complementary seasons, he developed a new theory that all Confederate armies should do as he and Bragg had done and as he planned to do again—take the offensive presumably and force their opponents back by threatening their communications. Since the western armies still had the same strength with which they had turned Buell back to the Ohio, their strategy would not require sending additional troops to Bragg. Lee could thus reason that the available troops were indeed quite equitably distributed, especially in view of the impending warm weather cessation of operations in the deep South. This theory not only justified retention of all his forces in Virginia, but also was consistent with his own plans for the spring campaign. Thus dissonance was reduced, as he unconsciously substituted this theory for the conventional and proven practice of using the railroad to concentrate forces at the threatened point.

In May, 1863, Lee again opposed long distance troop movements but, after Gettysburg, Lee reverted to his advocacy of concentration by rail and abandoned his new strategic theory. That theory had served its purpose, reducing the dissonance caused by the spring's conflict between two desirable strategic alternatives. It was not used in September, 1863, when Lee was again asked for forces to strengthen Bragg. It was apparently not needed because there was little discomfort (dissonance) created by knowledge of the good points of the rejected alternative—that is, Lee had little apprehension about Meade's pushing him back out of his supply area and, probably, little confidence in his own ability to accomplish much by turning Meade back. He doubtless recognized that the wiley and cautious Meade would be difficult to catch at a disadvantage but would be circumspect about an offensive with an army weakened by detachments. Lee ran less risk, had less emotional investment, and hence less dissonance in September than he had had in the spring. He felt less need to keep all of his forces in Virginia; the need in the West appeared more pressing after the defeats in Mississippi and Tennessee. This he could easily accede to Davis's desire to apply the conventional strategy and reinforce the west with troops sent by rail from Virginia. For a brief exposition of cognitive dissonance and an historical example, see Beringer, *Historical Analysis*, 137–52.

55. Lee to Cooper, Apr. 16, 1863, *Wartime Papers*, 434; Lee to Davis, Apr. 16, 27, 1863, *ibid.*, 435; *O.R.*, XXV, pt. 2, 752.

56. Lee to Davis, Apr. 16, 1863, *Wartime Papers*, 435; Lee to Longstreet, Mar. 21, 1863, *ibid.*, 416.

57. Lee to his wife, Apr. 19, 1863, *Wartime Papers*, 438; Seddon to Whiting, Apr. 7, 1863, *O.R.*, XVIII, 971; Seddon to Longstreet, Apr. 8, 11, 18, 1863, *ibid.*, 972, 979, 998; Seddon to Beauregard, Apr. 22, 1863, *ibid.*, 1012; Cooper to Beauregard, Apr. 30, 1863, *ibid.*, 1031; Cooper to D. H. Hill, Apr. 30, 1863, *ibid.*, 1032; Cooper to Longstreet, Apr. 30, 1863, *ibid.*, 1032; Beauregard to Seddon, Apr. 22, 1863, *ibid.*, 1013; Longstreet to Cooper, Apr. 30, 1863, *ibid.*, 1032; Lee to Cooper, Feb. 13, 1863, *ibid.*, XXV, pt. 2, 620; Lee to Davis Mar. 19, 1863, *ibid.*, 675.

58. Lincoln to Hunter and Du Pont, Apr. 14, 1863, Basler, *Collected Works*, VI, 173–74; *Welles Diary*, I, 294; *Spirit of the Times*, Jan. 31, 1863, Lamers, *Rosecrans*, 251–52.

59. Halleck to Burnside, Jan. 7, 1863, *O.R.*, XXI, 953–54; Meigs to Burnside, Dec. 30, 1862, *ibid.*, 916–18; Hooker to Lincoln, Apr. 11, 1863, *ibid.*, XXV, pt. 2, 199–200; Sherman to Mrs. Sherman, Apr. 17, 1863, *Home Letters*, 249.

60. Rosecrans to Halleck, Apr. 12, 1863, *O.R.*, XXIII, pt. 2, 232; Rosecrans to Thomas, Apr. 26, 1863, *ibid.*, 278; Burnside to Halleck, Apr. 29, 1863, *ibid.*, 292; Halleck to Burnside, Apr.

27, May 13, 1863, *ibid.*, 284, 327; Halleck to Burnside and Rosecrans, May 18, 1863, *ibid.*, 337.

61. Halleck to Dix, Apr. 17, May 2, 1863, *O.R.*, XXV, pt. 2, 255–26, XVIII, 682; Halleck to Keyes, Apr. 7, 1863, *ibid.*, XVIII, 586; Foster to Dix, Apr. 25, 1863, *ibid.*, 655; Dix to Foster, Apr. 29, 1863, *ibid.*, 668; Hunter to Lincoln, May 22, 1863, *ibid.*, XIV, 455–56.

62. Grant to Porter, Apr. 2, 1863, *O.R.*, XXIV, pt. 3, 168; Sherman to Grant, Apr. 8, 1863, *ibid.*, 179–80; Sherman to Mrs. Sherman, Apr. 17, 1863, *Home Letters*, 249–50; W. T. Sherman to John Sherman, Apr. 26, 1863, *Sherman Letters*, 201–2.

63. Grant to Kelton, Apr. 12, 1863, *O.R.*, XXIV, pt. 1, 28; Grant to Hurlbut, May 5, 1863, *ibid.*, pt. 3, 275; Dana to Stanton, Apr. 10, 1863, *ibid.*, pt. 1, 71; Sherman to Steele, Apr. 17, 1863, *ibid.*, pt. 3, 201–2. See also: Halleck to Hurlbut, May 13, 1863, *ibid*, pt. 3, 308–9.

64. Grant to Halleck, Apr. 4, 1863, *O.R.*, XXIV, pt. 1, 25; Grant to Hurlbut, May 5, 1863, *ibid.*, pt. 3, 274–75; Hurlbut to Grant, Apr. 13, 14, 1863, *ibid.*, 191, 193; Dana to Stanton, Apr. 15, 1863, *ibid.*, pt. 1, 73; Sherman to Rawlins, Apr. 19, 1863, *ibid.*, pt. 3, 208–9; J. E. Johnston to Buckner, Apr. 11, 1863, *ibid.*, XXIII, pt. 2, 752.

65. Sherman to Mrs. Sherman, Apr. 17, 1863, *Home Letters*, 249–50. See also: Sherman to Mrs. Sherman, Apr. 23, 1863, *ibid.*, 255–56.

66. Grant to Halleck, March 27, Apr. 19, 1863, *O.R.*, XXIV pt. 1, 23, 30; Grant to Sherman, Apr. 24, 1863, *ibid.*, pt. 3, 231; Grant to Sullivan, May 3, 1863, *ibid.*, pt. 3, 268; Dana to Stanton, Apr. 23, 1863, *ibid.*, pt. 1, 74; Sherman to Mrs. Sherman, Apr. 29, 1863, *Home Letters*, 256–58.

67. Grant to McClernand, Apr. 18, 1863, *O.R.*, XXIV, pt. 3, 205; Grant to Sherman, Apr. 27, 1863, *ibid.*, 240.

68. Sherman to Mrs. Sherman, Apr. 29, 1863, *Home Letters*, 256–58; McClernand to Lincoln, Jan. 16, 1863, *O.R.*, XVII, pt. 2, 566; Foote, *The Civil War*, II, 332.

69. Sherman to Mrs. Sherman, Apr. 23, 1863, *Home Letters*, 254–56; Grant to Halleck, Apr. 12, 1863, *O.R.*, XXIV, pt. 1, 29; Parsons to Halleck, Dec. 27, 1862, *ibid.*, XVII, pt. 2, 496.

70. Wheeler, *The Siege of Vicksburg*, 100–101.

71. Foote, *The Civil War*, II, 218.

13 ☆ THE SYMPHONY OF VICKSBURG, TULLAHOMA, AND GETTYSBURG

Thomas J. (Stonewall) Jackson

THOUGH AWARE of the propaganda significance of Vicksburg, Confederate generals were not impressed with its military or logistical import. The high commanders, especially those in the Army of Northern Virginia, discounted Vicksburg. Lee valued the city primarily because it interdicted federal commerce on the Mississippi River. Longstreet felt that they would lose little if it fell; "We would be no worse cut off from the West than we are now," he reasoned, and, "as to the Yankees using the river for trade, it cannot be done as long as we have the banks." The attitude in the western armies toward Vicksburg did not differ much. Joseph E. Johnston regarded Middle Tennessee as strategically more important, while Beauregard was almost unbelievably blasé. As early as June, 1862, he regarded "its fate as sealed." He had then felt that his retreat from Corinth had resulted in "the loss of all the Mississippi Valley," as well as the loss of any possibility of maintaining the flow of supplies from the area west of the river.[1]

Believing, then, that Vicksburg was simply one of many points at which the Confederates could harass Union commerce on the river, Confederate generals viewed the campaign on the river as secondary to other theatres. This attitude markedly contrasted with that of Lincoln and Halleck who directed the main federal effort on the river, an effort commanded by Grant with Sherman as his principal subordinate, together the two ablest Union commanders. Against this formidable pair the Confederacy pitted a general who proved most inadequate, John Clifford Pemberton.

Born in Philadelphia, Pemberton numbered among the small group of northern natives who achieved high Confederate rank. Because he eventually failed to hold Vicksburg, southerners typically forever afterwards considered him a pariah. Even one officer, kindly disposed toward his efforts, referred to him as a "poor jerk." Pemberton represents the classic Confederate example of the Peter Principle—he rose to his level of incompetence, even above it, receiving promotion after promotion not because his service warranted it but because, only fortuitously, he twice acquired commands calling for a higher rank. He was, in truth, honest and dedicated beyond question, though his northern birth forever remained a cloud above his head, engendering suspicion. His personality provided an additional impetus to those who disliked him. "Wanting in polish," Alfred Roman believed, he "was too positive and domineering in manner to suit the sensitive and polite people among whom he had been thrown."[2]

In South Carolina Pemberton declared martial law at an infelicitous moment; the people there never liked him. Furthermore, his brother officers grew jealous over his rapid rise in rank. Then, later, in command of the Department of Mississippi and Eastern Louisiana, he initially would confront operational conditions much like those he had faced in South Carolina. Both focused on fortifications and on batteries to resist a naval attack. His experience well prepared him to deal with these problems, but this very experience and the emphasis on fortifications made it difficult for him to deal with Grant's successful turning movement. Pemberton had had virtually no experience leading an army in the field.[3]

Having completed his fragile and uncertain logistical arrangements, Grant moved with McClernand's and McPherson's corps and reached the riverbank opposite Grand Gulf. On April 29 Admiral Porter's gunboats pounded enemy gun emplacements and attempted to clear the way for Grant's army to cross. But, after six hours, "finding the position too strong," Grant moved to "turn his position." During the night his leading force marched southward from Grand Gulf along the Louisiana shore to a new landing opposite Bruinsburg. Under cover of darkness the fleet followed the army and prepared to take it across. North of Vicksburg Sherman's men demonstrated against Hayne's and Drumgould's bluffs near Snyder's Mill to draw attention from the main attack. Then, outnumbering his enemy by more than two to one, Grant crossed the Mississippi, pushed away the Confederates covering Grand Gulf, forced its evacuation, and ordered Sherman's corps to join him. Grant promptly decided to "follow the enemy" and not stop until he had taken Vicksburg. Pleased with his easy success, Grant wrote: "Management I think has saved us an immense loss of life and gained all the results of a hard fight." Vicksburg had been turned. "All the campaigns, labors, hardships, and exposures, from the month of December previous to this time, that had been made and endured, were for the accomplishment of this one object."[4]

Grant's only moments of personal deprivation during the campaign occurred in the week before he captured Port Gibson, Mississippi, on May 1, the same day that the Battle of Chancellorsville commenced. Grant shortly afterwards made contact with Admiral Porter's fleet. After seven days on a borrowed horse, with "no change of underclothing, no meal except such as [he] could pick up sometimes at other headquarters, and no tent to cover [him]," he availed himself of the admiral's facilities. He took a hot bath, changed into underwear borrowed from one of the naval officers, ate a hearty meal and prepared a full report to Halleck. "Our victory has been most complete," he wrote, "and the enemy thoroughly demoralized."[5]

Grant's army continued to move across the river at Bruinsburg. One corps pushed rapidly inland toward Port Gibson, about thirty miles south of Vicksburg. A small, outflanked Confederate force at Grand Gulf hurried toward Port Gibson to intercept the federal corps. Hopelessly outnumbered but aided by a terrain rife with steep, sharp ridges and gullies covered with thick vines and snaring undergrowth, the southerners fought a plucky though vain defense.

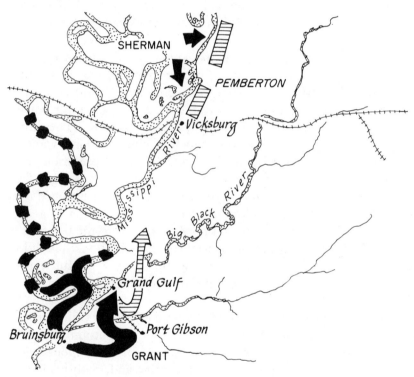

Grant Turns Vicksburg

Aside from following up success and not giving "the enemy time to reenforce and fortify," Grant had as his strongest reason for this decision his discovery that "the country will supply all the forage required for anything like an active campaign, and the necessary fresh beef." To take advantage of the abundant supplies in the area the army could not remain at Grand Gulf; it had to keep in motion in order to live off the country that the enemy otherwise would control. Later Grant explained his actions by saying: "A dispatch from General Banks showed him to be off in Louisiana not to return to Baton Rouge until May 10. I could not lose the time." "Information that General Joe Johnston was on his way to Jackson and that reinforcements were arriving there constantly" strengthened Grant's decision. The best justification was success: my rapid movement has "given us with comparative ease," he explained "what would have cost serious battles by delay."[6]

In spite of the emphatic directives of the general in chief, Grant received no help from Banks. After making one expedition "to destroy the saltworks" and contemplating an expedition to Mobile, Alabama, the Massachusetts politician concentrated his efforts on an advance up the Red River, even though Halleck had instructed him to "give but little [attention] to the occupation of territory" and "to concentrate his forces so as to strike an important blow." Though Banks did agree to accept aid from Grant in an attack on Port Hudson, he had planned to be ready on May 25 instead of April 25 as Grant intended.[7]

Ignoring Banks, Grant planned to exploit the condition of the enemy, whom he assessed as "badly beaten, greatly demoralized, and exhausted of ammunition. The road to Vicksburg is open. All we want now," he added, "are men, ammunition, and hard bread." We can "subsist our horses on the country, and obtain considerable supplies for our troops." The difficulty, of course, was provisioning the troops, much of whose rations would "have to be drawn from Millican's Bend. This is a long and precarious route," he continued, "but I have every confidence in succeeding in doing it." Organizing the effort delayed Grant for more than a week, as he arranged to run past the Vicksburg batteries an additional 400,000 rations of "hard bread, coffee, sugar, and salt." Ammunition could not be exposed to the batteries and had to come by wagon along with additional subsistence stores. He did not "calculate upon the possibility of supplying the army with full rations from Grand Gulf. I know," said Grant, "that will be impossible without additional roads."[8]

Rosecrans, commanding relatively the weakest of the Union armies, made no contribution, not moving forward, in spite of outnumbering Bragg in infantry by 50 percent. Although Rosecrans resorted to mounting infantry on mules, he continued quite inferior in cavalry and, with his long exposed line of railroad communications, remained unwilling to advance until his supply situation became more secure. Halleck, far from the scene, grew impatient with Rosecrans and tried to prod him into action by sending word that the first field commander who won a decisive victory would be made a major general in the regular Army. This merely insulted Rosecrans, who replied: "I feel degraded to see such auctioneering of honor. Have we a general who would fight for his own personal benefit when he would not fight for honor and the country?" To Halleck's satisfaction, if not to that of the more impatient civilian politicians, Rosecrans made his point.[9]

In the East, however, the Army of the Potomac was on the move just as Grant enjoyed his success in crossing the river. But there it was the Confederacy that enjoyed the marked superiority in generalship. Adequate as the leader of a corps, Fighting Joe Hooker also exemplified the Peter Principle when he assumed leadership of the Army of the Potomac; he would prove himself quite unequal to its demands. Headquarters in Washington devised a plan like Grant's for him: a turning movement against the enemy's left. But even Hooker's great numerical superiority and good plan could not counterbalance his deficiencies, for he had to contend with Lee, the Confederacy's best general.

First sending his cavalry to raid Lee's communications, Hooker prepared to cross the Rappahannock. The major part of Hooker's army crossed the Rappahannock at Kelly's and United States fords, plunging into the Wilderness clear of the left flank of Lee's army. On the thirtieth, a confident Hooker told his men: "The operations of the last three days have determined that our enemy must ingloriously fly, or come out from behind their defenses and give us battle on our ground, where certain destruction awaits him."

In Virginia, Hooker had picked an opportune time to attack, while a major part of Lee's army was foraging in southeastern Virginia. This foraging, so well described by Shelby Foote, resulted in "long trains of wagons, piled high with goods. . . , soon were grinding westward amid a din of cracking whips, ungreased axles, and teamster curses." Thus, with his men finally somewhat better provided for, Lee managed to ignore debilities caused by his own recent ill health. Just weeks before, his worried doctors had compelled him to undergo a complete physical examination. A throat infection had settled in his chest, causing him pains, limiting his sleep, and rendering him quite testy when awake. He grew so irritable and impatient that he provoked his staff

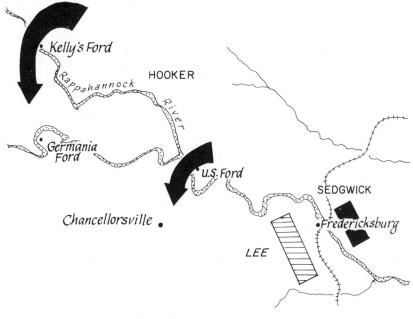

Hooker's Turning Movement

into irreverently nicknaming him "the Tycoon." He reported to his wife: The doctors are "tapping me all over like an old steam boiler before condemning it." But his resolution and will, coupled with Hooker's impending challenge, resulted in the subsiding of his symptoms. He was ready. As Bruce Catton so correctly assessed, what Hooker planned "would have worked, against most generals. Against Lee it failed so completely that its basic excellence is too easily overlooked." In truth Hooker was not terribly unjustified in his expansive prediction: "My plans are perfect, and when I start to carry them out, may God have mercy on Bobby Lee; for I shall have none."[10]

Employing his two-to-one numerical superiority, Hooker had crossed 70,000 of his men over the Rappahannock in a movement which turned the Confederate army. Lee, instead of falling back to the North Anna, the next river line, made a determined, skillful, and successful, but costly, effort to hold steady. First Lee moved the bulk of his force from Fredericksburg to block the Army of the Potomac's exits from the difficult Wilderness area.

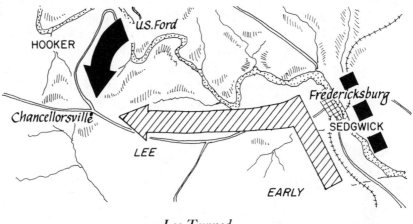

Lee Turned

In the complex three-day battle of Chancellorsville that ensued, Lee succeeded in turning Hooker's turning movement and then attacking the federal force in its flank. Had Hooker been as imperturbable and optimistic as Rosecrans had been at Murfreesboro, the Union army could have remained south of the river and claimed a victory, because it had advanced. On May 2 the Confederates, who had failed to push all the way to the river, themselves stood in a precarious position inviting counterattack. But Hooker frittered away his chance to redeem himself.

May 2 had been a costly day for the southerners regardless of anything that the Federals might still do: Stonewall Jackson sustained a wound that proved fatal. Hit by three bullets, two that shattered his left arm and one that pierced his upraised right hand, Jackson had to undergo an amputation during the

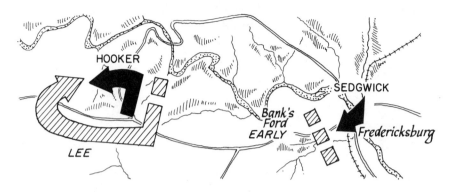

Hooker Turned

night. At first hopes soared for his speedy recovery, but six days later he suddenly took a turn for the worse. Developing pneumonia, he grew feverish. The fever, and the drugs the doctors administered, caused him to be delirious. Most often thereafter on his lips were the names of his hardest-hitting troop commander, Ambrose P. Hill, and his commissary officer, Wells Hawks. To Shelby Foote goes credit for the perceptive insight that "even in delirium he strove to preserve a balance between tactics and logistics." Jackson died on May 10. His last words would become institutionalized in southern folklore and used as a euphemism for death by at least two generations: "Let us cross over the river, and rest under the shade of the trees."[11]

At various times in the gloomy scrub timber on the disjointed battlefield, Confederate soldiers frequently fired upon their own men. Jackson proved only the most priceless of the many sacrifices rendered by the South at Chancellorsville; the engagement also took a high and dear toll of other useful officers—the number of generals lost was particularly crushing. The gradual depletion of resources for adequate replacement of lost lower-echelon commanders now became critical.

At daybreak on May 3, Stuart, temporarily leading Jackson's corps, seized a low hill named Hazel Grove, from which site his artillery fired on Chancellorsville. The rest of the Confederate line attacked the ever-constricting federal semicircle. Suddenly a shell struck a column of the Chancellor House, Hooker's headquarters, and falling debris temporarily disabled Hooker. Major General Darius Couch directed a withdrawal of the army toward United States Ford.

Lee's army occupied Chancellorsville about 10 A.M. They prepared to launch a new assault but never commenced it. On the night of May 2 Hooker had ordered John Sedgwick to drive Jubal Early's defenders from Fredericksburg and to attack Lee from the rear. Sedgwick assaulted Marye's Heights but failed twice. Other movements proved equally unsuccessful as a sub-battle, called Second Fredericksburg, unfolded. Eventually, however, the weakened

Confederate line gave way and Sedgwick's men surged forward. The way to
Chancellorsville lay open as Early retired southerly.

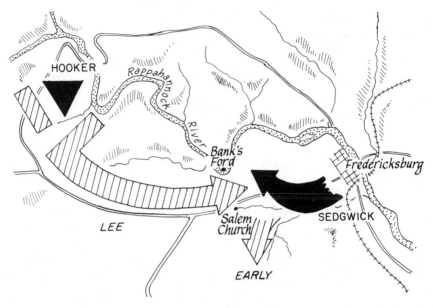

Sedgwick's Attack

Lee then turned a portion of his line around to confront Sedgwick at Salem
Church. A sharp battle broke out there in the late afternoon and lasted until
dark. Lee successfully halted Sedgwick's advance.

On the next day the Confederates counterattacked but failed to cut Sedgwick off from Bank's Ford over the Rappanhannock. Sedgwick fell back to
the ford and during the night crossed the river on pontoons. Lee then began
to concentrate all of his force against Hooker's men, now well dug in north of
Chancellorsville with their backs to United States Ford. Though his forces
still south of the river outnumbered all of Lee's, Hooker decided to withdraw.
Lee never had to make his attack against Hooker's strong position.

Though Hooker's decision may have been influenced by his injury, it was
not the only example of the Union commander's lack of aggressiveness during
the long battle. Hooker's nerve failed. As he said of himself: "For once I lost
confidence in Hooker."

His loss of nerve may have been due to a psychological acknowledgement
of the military supremacy of supposedly aristocratic southerners. That so
many of their opponents were from Virginia, the state which "seemed to
most truly represent the Cavalier ideal," intensified this inferiority complex.
This condition was aggravated by fighting Lee, who so well personified the
superiority of their aristocratic opponents. Hooker's "awe of Lee" may have
contributed to his failure to try to complete his initially successful turning

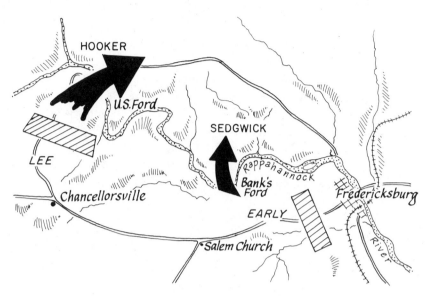

Union Withdrawal

movement. He may have had difficulty believing that he could win against Lee, Virginians, and southerners.[12]

Initially some news correspondents and other observers had more difficulty in determining who had won what in the Battle of Chancellorsville. An Episcopalian clergyman in New York, vexed by the unreconciled reports and rumors, noted in his diary: "It would seem that Hooker has beaten Lee, and that Lee has beaten Hooker; that we have taken Fredericksburg, and that the rebels have taken it also; that we have 4,500 prisoners, and the rebels 5,400; that Hooker has cut off Lee's retreat, and Lee has cut off Sedgwick's retreat, and Sedgwick had cut off everybody's retreat generally, but has retreated himself although his retreat was cut off. . . . In short, all is utter confusion. Everything seems to be everywhere, and everybody all over, and there is no getting at any truth." But after the movements were clarified, it was evident that Lee's battle had been a masterpiece of skill and audacity. Sometimes over-extravagantly termed Lee's greatest battle, to be followed two months later by his worst, Chancellorsville did become a textbook campaign, forever afterwards studied by fascinated military students. It also produced instantaneous jubilation within the Confederate ranks. When Lee rode forward to inspect the burning house which had served as Union army headquarters, the grayclad soldiers tendered him the wildest demonstration of their lives. An admiring staff officer later wrote: "As I looked upon him in the complete fruition of the success which his genius, courage, and confidence in his army had won, I thought that it must have been from such a scene that men in ancient times rose to the dignity of gods."[13]

Hooker's retreat across the river clearly indicated that he had been defeated. Lee had held the river line, but at frightful cost. The Federals with some 133,868 men at Chancellorsville and Fredericksburg lost 1,606 killed, 9,762 wounded, and 5,919 missing for a total of 17,278 casualties between April 27 and May 11; but the Confederates with effectives estimated at 60,000 lost 1,665 killed, 9,081 wounded, and 2,018 missing for a total of 12,764—a higher casualty percentage rate by far than the Federals suffered: 21 percent of the Confederates to 15 percent of the Federals. In previous centuries, merely to have maneuvered so as to be able to attack at right angles to Hooker's flank might have brought immediate Union retreat; or an attack, with such an advantageous position, would have meant catastrophic casualties for the Union force. At the Battle of Leuthen in 1757 the attackers, in not nearly so favorable a situation, suffered only 23 percent as many casualties as the defeated defenders. At Chancellorsville, Lee's army, in contrast, suffered 75 percent as many casualties as Hooker's. The power of the defense and of maneuver possessed by Civil War armies forced Lee to incur proportionately heavier casualties, in spite of his skillful and successful turning movement which permitted a model flank attack. What could Lee do next? Fortunately for Lee, Hooker withdrew on May 6, saving Lee still heavier casualties and the likely failure of resorting at last to a direct attack in an effort to push the Federals back over the Rappahannock. Lee's principal anxiety then became the need to restore quickly the railroads broken by the federal cavalry raid, "else," he said, "we shall have to abandon this country."[14]

Anxious to have "sufficient strength to operate advantageously," Lee immediately sought from the South Carolina coast enough men for his envisioned summer campaign of a turning movement to force Hooker back to or beyond the Potomac. Believing that no "serious effort could be made against Charleston this summer" and that any Confederate troops kept there would "perish of disease," he felt sure that his movement would also draw off Union forces on the coast to defend Washington.[15]

But Grant's success in turning the Vicksburg position and reaching the east bank below Vicksburg caused quite appropriate alarm in Richmond. Secretary Seddon immediately diverted from South Carolina to Mississippi 5,000 reinforcements intended for Bragg. Soon afterwards the secretary ordered Johnston, commanding the Department of the West, to leave Bragg's headquarters, take 3,000 men, and go to Mississippi to take charge there in person. Seddon then renewed his efforts to secure reinforcements from Lee of one division to go, not to Bragg in Tennessee, but all the way to Johnston and Pemberton in Mississippi. Lee again responded emphatically, saying that it was "a question between Virginia and the Mississippi," strong words from the war chief who had won at Chancellorsville while Longstreet and two divisions were away on another mission. But Lee held stronger ground when he pointed out: "The distance and the uncertainty of the employment of the troops are unfavorable." The President, already lukewarm about the proposal, reacted with: "The answer of General Lee was such as I should have anticipated, and in which I concur."[16]

Lee's realistic assessment of Confederate operations on the Mississippi reinforced his skepticism about such a long-distance move. He perceived that these operations were not to conserve the purely theoretical link with the trans-Mississippi but to prevent the Union from using the river "as a highway of commerce." He also remained optimistic in his belief that the "climate in June [would] force the enemy to retire" from his position near Vicksburg. Lee's own plan of operations depended, he said, not just on maintaining his existing strength, but on more men, for, he added, "unless we can obtain reinforcements we may be obliged to withdraw into the defenses around Richmond," a prospect he dreaded if only because it would deprive him of so much of the supply area upon which he depended.[17]

Convinced by Lee that the South should not send reinforcements from Virginia to Mississippi, the President and the secretary turned to Bragg's army, the one they had previously tried to strengthen, because they had been convinced that it was most in need. When requests for more men reached Bragg, he promptly responded by sending them in significant numbers. Even without troops from Virginia, Johnston began receiving a very respectable addition to his Mississippi command.

The Union hopes for a successful conclusion to the Vicksburg campaign depended in part upon Rosecrans's remaining sufficiently strong and doing at least enough to ensure effective limits upon reinforcements sent by Bragg to Pemberton. Halleck and Lincoln's strategy of concentration on the Mississippi had involved standing on the defensive in Missouri and Arkansas and transferring troops from Virginia if Union forces could push Lee far enough south of the Rappahannock to give full security to Washington and the upper Potomac. They did not assign such low priority to the Middle Tennessee area. Relatively few troops transferred from that theatre to Mississippi and all of them came from Horatio G. Wright's rear-area Department of the Ohio. On March 15 General Wright reported his belief: "If the present pleasant weather continues a short time, the condition of the roads and rivers will render an invasion of Kentucky by the rebels possible" and, indeed, likely. Reacting strongly, Lincoln and Halleck superseded the apparently inert and pessimistic Wright and replaced him with the usually aggressive Burnside.[18]

His setback at Fredricksburg had not discouraged Burnside; he had suffered adversity before. He had left the army in the 1850s and put his savings into a breechloading rifle he had invented. His venture failed, reducing him to selling his sword and uniforms for money to live on until his friend McClellan gave him a job in which he succeeded. He also had made a remarkable recovery from a severe personal disappointment: during his wedding ceremony, when his fiancée was asked the final question, she responded with an emphatic "no." With the same buoyancy with which he had surmounted these setbacks, Burnside rose above his defeat at Fredricksburg and his relief in January and went westward with enthusiasm to assume his new and important command. Significantly, headquarters assigned two divisions of his Ninth Corps to go with him. In addition to this reinforcement for the Middle and East Tennessee regions, simultaneous instructions to the Department of the Missouri, though stressing infantry for Grant, directed that Curtis send "all disposable cavalry" to Rosecrans, an order again reiterated the following month.[19]

The Union and Confederate armies used essentially the same method of control of forces available for transfer to a threatened point or for concentration. Each high command necessarily had to rely heavily on the local commanders for an estimate of their needs, not only for reinforcements to meet perceived threats or to overcome expected resistance but also for their ability to part with troops to strengthen another department. Halleck succinctly explained the responsibility of the local commander to Major General Samuel R. Curtis, who oversaw the Department of the Missouri. After telling Curtis that his mission was to retain in Missouri only "forces sufficient to hold a few important points" against "guerrillas and small detached forces," he ordered Curtis to send "all available troops" to Grant. How many troops were "all available"? Halleck explained: "That question is left to your judgment and discretion, under the responsibiilty which any officer incurs when directed to send all available troops upon a specified point." Halleck himself had received just such a request during the Seven Days' Battles the previous June. Then commanding the West, Halleck had received from the President "imperative" directions to send 25,000 men to McClellan, conditioned, however, by the need to adhere to his mission to hold his "ground and not interfere with the movement against Chattanooga and East Tennessee." Halleck's estimate that the dispatch of 25,000 men would compel the abandonment of Buell's Chattanooga expedition ended the request for this reinforcement. Just as, of necessity, Lincoln and Stanton at that time had to rely on Halleck's determination as to whether the dispatch of the reinforcements was consistent with his mission, so later Halleck, as general in chief, relied on Curtis's judgment as to what was necessary "to hold a few important points" and what force was, therefore, "available" for Grant and Rosecrans.[20]

The absence of a western commander to coordinate the departments of the Ohio and Cumberland placed an even greater strain on the judgment of local commanders. Nevertheless they cooperated cordially and developed a common plan for defense and offense. Against another raid, Rosecrans planned that, with large accumulations of supplies stored in places "strongly fortified," he would be independent of his communications. Since Wright had fortified the major towns in Kentucky, Rosecrans's strategy for meeting the enemy resembled that which Lincoln desired for the Antietam campaign, to "let them go to Kentucky, and . . . close the door against their return."[21]

Concerned about reinforcing Grant against the Confederate concentration building up under Johnston, at the end of May Halleck ordered the Ninth

Corps from Burnside to Grant. This cancelled Rosecrans's and Burnside's plan for simultaneous advances, which was almost ready. But Lincoln and Halleck were dissatisfied with the lack of an offensive in Middle Tennessee. Having exhausted by his long delay the credit built up by his victory at Stones River, Rosecrans, on June 2, received from the general in chief the warning: "If you can do nothing yourself, a portion of your troops must be sent to Grant's relief." Rosecrans planned "to hold the rebel army in Middle Tennessee" by avoiding an advance for fear that the Confederates might be willing to sacrifice Middle Tennessee to save Vicksburg. Rosecrans knew that Bragg's army already had been weakened by sending troops to Mississippi. An advance in Tennessee might drive them back to Chattanooga, "a position from whence they could send heavier detachments south." The Confederates could better reinforce Mississippi from Chattanooga, because they could more easily resist "our progress," Rosecrans explained, "over obstructed roads and destroyed railroads, which we would be obliged to repair, thus committing ourselves to labors and contingencies without effective help to General Grant or our own interests."[22]

In presenting the paradox that his inactivity might well be the best means of holding the largest number of Confederate troops in Tennessee, Rosecrans revived the fear felt in the fall that Bragg might disappear from his front and return to Mississippi. The Union commander in Tennessee thus pointed out an important limitation of the Lincoln-Halleck theory of simultaneous advances. The enemy might simply run away, leaving behind a thoroughly foraged country and destroyed communications which, by preventing an immediate Union advance, would effectively defend the abandoned front. In seeking the opinion of his generals, Rosecrans found that Major General George H. Thomas agreed. He commented: The enemy could "fall back" while "keeping up a sufficient show of force to hold us in check, draw us away from our base, attack and destroy our communications, or threaten them so strongly as to greatly weaken our main force, and then send reenforcements of artillery and infantry to Johnston" in Mississippi. The aggressive Philip H. Sheridan also agreed, saying: I do "not think an advance by our army at present likely to prevent additional re-enforcements being sent against General Grant by the enemy in our front," and added, I do not "think an immediate advance by our army advisable. It will be difficult, at the present time, to pursue Bragg to the Tennessee River, and subsist our men and animals, and keep open our communications."[23]

The critical variable, as Thomas and Sheridan emphasized, was the communications of the advancing army, a problem which had halted Buell in the summer and stopped Grant twice. As the enemy retreated over his own communications and his well-foraged country, the pursuers were "weakened," another adviser pointed out, "in proportion as we advance from our base of supplies." In addition, as Thomas explained, "the enemy with his large cavalry force could constantly threaten and render insecure, if not entirely destroy," the advancing forces' "extended line of communications." Agreeing with this assessment of the advantage which logistical realities conferred on the defender, Grant was similarly apprehensive, as he had been in the fall, saying: Bragg's "army can fall back to Bristol or Chattanooga at a moment's notice, which places, it is thought, he can hold, and spare 25,000 troops" for use in Mississippi.[24]

In unknowing agreement with Rosecrans and his generals and concerned for the Confederate Army of Tennessee should it "be compelled to abandon Middle Tennessee," Joe Johnston had reported: "The question of subsistence will make it difficult to put this army in a good position." In the mountainous and unproductive country to the rear of its present position Bragg would find it "difficult to feed this army; the cavalry (amounting to nearly 15,000) could not be kept together in East Tennessee or Georgia." The best course would be "to move into Northern Mississippi and West Tennessee, where the army could probably find provisions for several months." For this reason Johnston preferred, in the event of a retreat, to abandon the Middle Tennessee-North Georgia line and "send the whole army into West Tennessee to co-operate with that of Mississippi."

The Confederate department commander did not concern himself about Rosecrans's penetrating Georgia, for "the difficulty of subsisting an army in it would, fortunately, be felt by the enemy too." Johnston thought a campaign into Georgia out of the question, because the federal army "could not depend on the long line of railroad between Nashville and Atlanta." The latter city would be protected by logistical difficulties, the long, vulnerable railway, and a country so barren that Johnston said, I even doubt "if forage for a reasonable baggage train can be found in that district," an estimate also made by Rosecrans, who believed that "starvation" would befall Bragg in northern Georgia if he could drive him there. Agreeing with Johnston's strategic assessment, Bragg, after Union forces had driven him from Middle Tennessee, told Johnston, then in Mississippi: "This country can be risked," defended only by the "cavalry and from two to four brigades of infantry. Concentrate all else by the most rapid means" and "strike at once."[25]

In giving their general the opinions requested, Rosecrans's federal officers also perceived the problem of an advance in political terms, for, as one general expressed it, "Battles must be fought for political or military reasons." They realized the political significance of military events, recognizing that "the battle of Stones River saved the Northwest from falling under the domination of the peace or coward's party." One officer recalled: "Our army on the Rappahannock has always been beaten and seemingly neither we nor the country have much to hope for from their efforts." With nothing to hope for from the east, the "outcome at Vicksburg" must "necessarily have a guiding influence on the movements of this army." This dictated caution for diplomatic reasons because, as one general expressed it, "with Hooker already defeated, Grant defeated or forced to raise the siege of Vicksburg, and ourselves even repulsed, I can see no hope except the recognition of the independence of the Confederacy by foreign powers, and also by ourselves." With this concern for public opinion, the generals thought that they should not risk Rosecrans's army but instead "this great army, centrally situated," should "be held intact, and ready for any emergency, til after the fate of Vicksburg is decided."[26]

Insofar as Rosecrans was influenced by political considerations he adhered to the view of his generals, though he should have followed the advice of his chief of staff, Brigadier General James A. Garfield. More perceptive about the political situation and astute in assessing the impact of inaction on public opinion, this future President of the United States believed that "the turbulent aspect of politics of the loyal States renders a decisive blow against the enemy at this time of the highest importance to the success of the Government at the polls and in the enforcement of the conscription act," which Congress finally enacted early in March.[27]

Rosecrans's generals also considered the problem presented by Bragg's strong position. In another battle like Stones River "a victory would probably only once more prove the valor of the army," which could "only gain a victory at the sacrifice of much life without having obtained any decided advantage." Clearly understanding the power of the defense, enhanced by "topography or artificial obstructions," the Union generals saw no point in seeking "a mere victory," another "barren victory . . . unproductive of the grand results which make success valuable and compensate for the loss of life necessary to attain it; in short, those results which justify the fighting of battles." As one general observed: "There is no apparent advantage to be gained by simply driving Bragg from our front, extending and weakening our own line" of vulnerable communications. Of course, he continued, Bragg might not fight and simply "fall back slowly, watching us closely, ready to take advantage of accidents, obstructing our advance and attacking our lines of communications." Whether Bragg retreated with or without a fight, they would still be subject to the tyranny of logistics for, another general believed, "should we drive him back, say 40 miles, it is extremely doubtful, . . . whether we could keep our communications open with the limited supply of cavalry we have, as compared with theirs."[28]

With the professional military leadership under fire for a dig-in, afraid-to-fight policy, the generals, inevitably, responded to newspaper and political critics. Public "impatience and interference" should not be a reason to advance, even though an army "may not be gaining ground as rapidly as might be expected by politicians and other novices in the art of war." "We certainly cannot," one man wrote, "fight the enemy for the mere purpose of whipping him. . . . To whip him would gratify our just pride and delight the country, but what have we gained. . . ? The time has passed when the fate of armies must be staked because the newspapers have no excitement and do not sell well. I think our people have now comprehended that a battle is a very grave thing."[29]

Since the army should not fight another futile Stones River frontal battle even to please the critics, a "true line of attack" should be adopted, which, one general explained, was "to engage the attention of the enemy, and to march with the mass of our force upon his communications near Tullahoma. This movement, by compelling the enemy to fight us on our own battle-field, and by throwing him off his line of retreat, promises the destruction of his army, if successful." Difficult of execution, the turning movement to get the whole army in the enemy's rear had been attempted but had never been successfully applied during the war. Grant at Iuka had come close and Lee, at Second Bull Run, had inadvertently garnered some of the benefits. More successful had been movements like those of McClellan on the Peninsula, Lee's to Antietam, and Bragg's in Kentucky. These had simply aimed at turning the enemy to drive him back. Rosecrans would attempt it to avoid another frontal battle, break the deadlock in Middle Tennessee, and, as he had earlier hoped, be able to "crush them by a decisive battle" and "virtually end the game." Napoleon had thrice reached the enemy's rear; Rosecrans was going to make a well-prepared and brilliantly conceived and executed attempt against Bragg, seeking thus "by skillful maneuvering, to compel him to fight against his will, and, consequently, at a disadvantage."[30]

Such a move would also be risky, for, "as they say in the West, 'It is betting our bottom dollar,' " one general remarked. Turning Bragg would be hazardous: in so doing Rosecrans's army would leave itself without reliable communications. With inferior cavalry and concentrated to fight in a country already stripped by the enemy, the Union army might have to attack or retreat, even if they succeeded in getting astride Bragg's railway.[31]

A similar analysis had been made by the Confederates when Joe Johnston noted: Bragg's army is vulnerable for "the position of our troops is disadvantageous because for subsistence it is compelled to take ground west of the direct route from Murfreesboro to Chattanooga. It can, therefore, be turned by our right." Johnston added: If Rosecrans "made the attempt with his whole army, we might exchange bases with him very advantageously." By this Johnston apparently meant that Bragg's army would still be in touch with the Duck River Valley and have the Nashville and Decatur railroad to its right and rear. Rosecrans's back would face the Tennessee River and Chattanooga, obviously a serious predicament. Rosecrans would be risking too much to make such a move against Johnston.[32]

Aware of how time-consuming these were but believing "the most fatal errors of this war have begun in an impatient desire" by people who "would not take time to get ready," Rosecrans also felt that "the next fatal mistake" was "to be afraid to move when all the means were provided." Rosecrans would not prove himself afraid to move when ready, but he had a very exacting definition of being ready. His preliminary arrangements, stockpiling supplies and augmenting his cavalry, had been extemely elaborate. His biographer believes "that Rosecrans overemphasized these considerations." The cause of the "slows," as Lincoln termed the disease, consisted of too much preparation. Grant's willingness to move to Grand Gulf with a supply line of only a single road and an uncertain canal, a step which even Sherman regarded as unwise and hazardous, clearly indicates that the slows did not affect him.[33]

Grant's ability to move into almost virgin country vastly simplified the logistics of his advance. Instead of having to move over the track of a large retreating army into an area where the enemy had long subsisted, Grant was lucky to be campaigning with the growing season well along in a fertile region of Mississippi where planters had reduced the cultivation of cotton in favor of food crops. In addition to the usual fodder for the animals, the countryside abounded in human food, "corn, hogs, cattle, sheep, and poultry."[34]

The Mississippi farms thus relieved Grant's long and inadequate road communications, enabling him to "disregard his base and depend upon the country for meat and even for bread." This was fortunate, for Grant's line of wagon communications west of the river was tenuous indeed. In early spring, roads gradually emerged from the "drowned lands adjacent to the Mississippi," and, as Shelby Foote aptly observed, "so far they were little more than trails of slime through the surrounding ooze, not quite firm enough for wagons nor quite wet enough for boats." Grant's uncertain communications inhibited him very little because throughout the campaign he "continuously underestimated the force of the enemy both in men and artillery." About the beginning of the third week in May "ammunition and subsistence" reached Grant in sufficient quantities, enabling him to advance. He then planned to "send the wagons back for more to follow" and communicate with Grand Gulf "no more except it becomes necessary to send a train with heavy escort."[35]

Grant's good fortune and good planning in his supply arrangements extended rearward all the way to his base in the North. As he had abandoned the railroad running north through West Tennessee, all of his communications north of Vicksburg lay on the Mississippi River. By using this relatively secure route, he foiled one of the main Confederate plans to defeat him. Like Grant, the enemy command had learned a lesson the previous December when Van Dorn and Forrest had broken Grant's communications. The Confederate western commander, Joe Johnston, had then placed his main reliance for defeating Grant on cavalry raids against Union communications. Johnston intended his big cavalry concentration in Middle Tennessee, the same force which was delaying Rosecrans's advance, also to stop Grant by striking at the vulnerable West Tennessee rail communications. But Grant had abandoned these and was depending entirely on the relatively secure river.

In addition to forestalling his opponent's plans, Grant was to be aided by the failure of Pemberton, his immediate opponent, then experiencing his first command of a field army in combat. Initially Pemberton explained: I perceive that Grant's new position "threatens Jackson, and, if successful, cuts Vicksburg off from the east"; and he understood that Grant's turning movement would force him to assume the tactical offensive. To stop Grant he realized that his forces, scattered from Port Hudson to north of Vicksburg, must be "concentrated for defense of Vicksburg and Jackson." Yet Pemberton almost immediately lost his nerve, ordered the garrison back to Port Hudson, and fell back on the familiar strategy of protecting fortified points. He decided to ignore Grant's army and its threat to his communications and erect as the keystone of his strategy the passive concept that Vicksburg was the "vital point, indispensable to be held. Nothing can be done which might jeopardize it." A telegram from Davis helped in his decision for it reminded him: The holding of "both Vicksburg and Port Hudson is necessary to a connection with the Trans-Mississippi."[36]

In the middle of the second week in May, as Grant's resupplied army began its advance, Sherman clearly saw that "the enemy must come out and fight us soon," he wrote his wife, "or we will be in the rear." However, the delay to organize his supplies had complicated the situation: Joe Johnston, in Jackson assembling an army, already possessed 6,000 men, and Pemberton was making a partial concentration to the west, near Vicksburg, the new focus of his strategy. This situation of a divided enemy presented Grant with the opportunity of "threatening both and striking at either," whichever was most convenient. On the 12th an engagement erupted at Raymond, about fifteen miles from the Mississippi capital, as a Confederate brigade struck Grant's vanguard division. The contest lasted for several hours and then the numerically superior Federals commenced driving the southerners back toward Jackson. Both sides suffered about 500 casualties.[37]

This development, and encountering Confederate skirmishers along Fourteen-Mile Creek, prompted Grant to deal with the concentration at Jackson first. Not slow to avail himself of his interior position between enemy fragments, Grant used McClernand's corps as a covering force to hold Pemberton at bay while Sherman's and McPherson's corps concentrated against Johnston at Jackson. McClernand's role was hardly even necessary, for the demoralized and indecisive Pemberton was thinking defensively rather than in the spirit of Johnston's order to move on Grant's rear. Outnumbered almost five to one, Johnston began on the 14th to withdraw from Jackson northward, leaving only two brigades to try delaying the Federals. Very one-sided and brief fighting followed, and in the afternoon Grant's men occupied the capital.

Grant's turning movement now reached completion; he stood astride the railroad and had cut Vicksburg's communications.

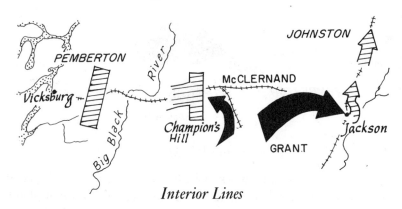

Interior Lines

   Turning then toward Vicksburg and Pemberton, Grant needed to guard his rear against Johnston's increasing army. Relying on logistical means for this, Grant ordered "immediately the effectual destruction of the river railroad bridge and the road as far east as practicable, as well as north and south" of Jackson. Grant could then concentrate first two and then three corps against Pemberton and push toward Vicksburg. He desired to get close to Vicksburg, if only to re-establish his communications with the river. Without these, he would have a hard time keeping his army concentrated because of its need to spread and move in order to subsist or, alternately, to augment its field transportation to draw supplies from the country. Pemberton, with his food and forage reserves in Vicksburg, would have no such need and could have placed Grant in a difficult supply situation if he could have held Grant east of the Big Black River. This Pemberton attempted to do on the 16th with a major engagement at Champion's Hill.[38]
   After managing to resist a serious threat in which Grant almost turned his left, Pemberton decided to withdraw. In this costly battle, federal effectives numbered about 29,000 with 410 killed, 1,844 wounded, and 187 missing, for a total of 2,441 casualties; Confederate effectives probably numbered somewhere under 20,000, and of them there were 381 killed, 1,800 wounded, and 1,670 missing, a total of 3,851 casualties. One federal brigade commander placed the battle among "the most obstinate and murderous conflicts of the war." "I cannot think of this bloody hill without sadness and pride," federal Brigadier General Alvin P. Hovey said to an Illinois soldier, roaming the field after the fighting had ended. "There they lay," he said, "the blue and the gray intermingled; the same rich, young American blood flowing out in little rivulets of crimson; each thinking he was in the right." Pemberton now decided to fall back to Vicksburg, though he fought a small holding action the next day at the Big Black River bridge. On May 18 the siege of Vicksburg

began. Three days later, at Port Hudson, Louisiana, Banks's men at last began their siege, also.[39]

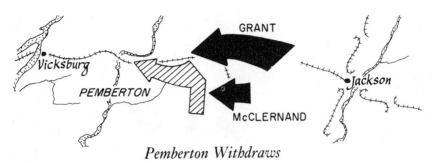

Pemberton Withdraws

Though his activity finally worked in harmony with Grant's, Banks had continued to display his talent for ignoring instructions and completely misunderstanding the situation. It almost seemed that perhaps Banks paid more attention to his personal appearance than to cooperation with his fellow generals. His looks rather impressed Admiral Porter: "Rather theatrical in his style of dress . . . he wore yellow gauntlets high upon his wrist, looking as clean as if they had just come from the glove-maker; his hat was picturesque, his long boots and spurs were faultless." Without telegraph communication with either Halleck or Grant, deep in central Louisiana Banks had pursued his own objectives. He called on Grant to "send a force to the Red River" so they could conquer "the whole country west of the Mississippi." Finally concluding that he could not fully exploit the "decisive advantages" he had gained on the Red River, on May 12 Banks, with reluctance, acknowledged: I do "not know that anything is left me but to direct my forces against Port Hudson," a courageous act on his part as he feared this involved "the probable loss of New Orleans."[40]

Halleck was able to "learn from the newspapers" Banks's position and grew frantic at this "eccentric" and "divergent" line of operations. In early May, while the general in chief had stressed that the Mississippi, "the all important object of the campaign," was "worth . . . forty Richmonds," Grant had urged Banks: "Join me or send all the force you can spare to cooperate in the great struggle for opening the Mississippi." Learning that Banks had at last reached Port Hudson, Grant declined Banks's request for reinforcement and, echoing Halleck's constant admonition, stressed that "concentration is essential to the success of the general campaign in the west; but Vicksburg is the vital point." Grant wished to capture that vital point before something occurred to make his position hazardous.[41]

Grant also knew that Pemberton would be tenacious in a conventional siege. He had known Pemberton since the Mexican War. "I remember," Grant later revealingly related, "when an order was issued that none of the junior officers should be allowed horses during the marches. Mexico is not an easy country to march in. Young officers not accustomed to it soon got footsore . . .[So finally] a verbal permit was [given], and nearly all of them remounted. Pemberton alone said, no, he would walk, as the [written] order was still extant not to ride—and he did walk, though suffering intensely. . . . This I thought of all the time he was in Vicksburg and I outside of it; and I knew he would hold on to the last."[42]

Hoping also that a prompt attack might catch the enemy unprepared and so avoid a drawn-out siege, Grant quickly tried two assaults. In the first, on May 19, about a thousand federal casualties resulted, a testament to the defensive strength of the Confederate position. A very large assault occurred on the 22nd with one brief breakthrough momentarily at a redoubt defending a railroad cut, but counterattacks closed the breach. Losses mounted heavily: of 45,000 Federals engaged, 502 were killed, 2,550 wounded, and 147 missing, for a total of 3,199 casualties; the Confederates lost fewer than 500 men. Grant tried no more attacks, but felt confident about the prospects of the siege.

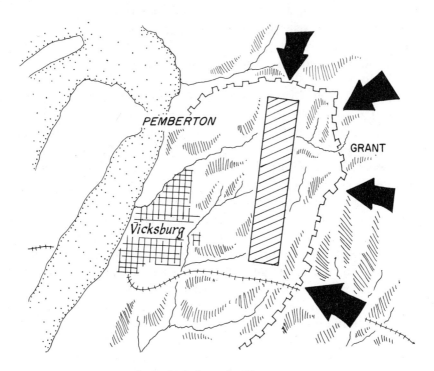

Assault before the Siege

"The enemy are undoubtedly in our grasp," he wrote on May 24. "The fall of Vicksburg and the capture of most of the garrison can only be a question of time. I hear a great deal of the enemy bringing a large force from the east to effect a raising of the siege. They may attempt something of the kind, but I do not see how they can do it." Grant already had defeated any advance by his systematic attention to Johnston's future logistical requirements. "The railroad," he explained, "is effectually destroyed at Jackson, so that it will take thirty days to repair it. This will leave a march of over 50 miles over which the enemy will have to subsist any army, and bring their ordnance stores and teams. My position is so strong that I could hold out for several days against a vastly superior force." With Johnston concentrated to fight but dependent on wagon transportation in a country already foraged by the Union army, Grant did "not see how the enemy could possibly maintain a long attack under these circumstances," because Johnston could no longer supply his army in combat.[43]

Nevertheless Grant prudently decided to employ some forces in vigilant watch of the crossings along the Big Black River. For that task he decided to relegate troops under the pesky political general, McClernand, whose favor in Grant's estimation had declined still further when McClernand botched one of the assaults upon Vicksburg, incorrectly announcing a breakthrough and calling for reinforcements. A few weeks later Grant at last would relieve and banish him. Dana humorously related the incident that ensued after Grant's direction to guard the river crossings: "McClernand scowled as he read the order. 'I'll be God-damned if I'll do it. I'm tired of being dictated to. I won't stand it any longer. And you can go back and tell General Grant.' Colonel Wilson promptly took exception to McClernand's disrespect for his commanding general, . . . McClernand cooled off, decided to obey the order, and said, 'I was simply expressing my intense vehemence on the subject matter, sir, and I beg your pardon.' Wilson reported the affair to Grant, who found McClernand's apology amusing. The next time Grant heard one of his aides explode with profanity, he said, 'He's not swearing—he's just expressing his intense vehemence on the subject matter.' "[44]

As Grant had earlier struggled with the problem of finding water communications for turning the Vicksburg defenses, Halleck, believing it to be "the most important operation of the war," had sent him the few available additional troops. In January a brigade had moved from Wright's Department of the Ohio and in March the general in chief had extracted eleven regiments and the marine brigade from Curtis's Department of the Missouri. Nevertheless, on May 31 Grant's confidence began to wilt and he reported: "Johnston is collecting a large force to attack me and rescue the garrison of Vicksburg." Johnston's army was swelling as troops arrived from Bragg. When Halleck received Grant's appeal, "I must be re-enforced," he responded immediately. Ordering additional forces from Missouri, Halleck applied the pipeline concept when he directed the new commander, Schofield, to "send those nearest and replace them from the interior." Schofield answered promptly, sending a full division, even though, he reported, "this leaves me very weak, but I will risk it, in view of the vast importance of Grant's success." Under Halleck's orders, the Ninth Corps, two divisions, also left from the Department of the Ohio, now commanded by Burnside. These reinforcements, as well as the three divisions and four regiments from his anti-guerrilla forces, enabled

Grant "to make the investment most complete" and left "a large reserve to watch the movements of Johnston." Grant's much strengthened army, together with the logistical obstacles placed in the way of Johnston's advance, completely defeated Confederate relief efforts.[45]

Meanwhile, Lincoln clung briefly to the hope that, though Hooker had failed at Chancellorsville, his cavalry raid had effected "some important breakings of the enemies' communications." The President was also interested in continuing offensive operations to exploit this and to "supersede the bad moral effect" of the defeat at Chancellorsville, but he did not want "anything done in desperation or rashness." Soon concluding, however, that the army would gain nothing by another attempt to cross the Rappahannock, Lincoln became content for Hooker to "keep the enemy at bay, and out of other mischief, by menaces and cavalry raids."[46]

Lee, of course, planned to move north, but supply difficulties and apprehensions about the Union forces on the coast had delayed his move "to anticipate an expected blow from the enemy." Despite his defensive successes at Fredericksburg and Chancellorsville, he felt reluctant to remain on the defensive along the Rappahannock. The victory at Chancellorsville had been costly and the battle, fought with his back against his valuable supply region and the railroad to the fertile Shenandoah Valley, had occurred in a place to which it was most undesirable to retreat. Unaware that Hooker had no new offensive planned, Lee was concerned about another turning movement which he thought he would have to receive "at a disadvantage, or to retreat." He believed Hooker would "endeavor to turn the left of my present position," he said, and "hold me in check, while an effort is made by the forces collected on the York River . . . to gain possession of Richmond." Were he stronger himself, Lee believed he "could prevent either and force him back" and so "frustrate their plans in part if not in whole."[47]

With the crop season well advanced Lee could alleviate some of his supply problems by advancing into areas not foraged by either army. With this significant logistical inducement added to the desire to avoid the "catastrophe" of being forced back into the intrenchments of Richmond and total dependence on railroads for supply, Lee began a move northwest to turn Hooker from his Rappahannock position. Still concerned about the enemy forces on the coasts, Lee proposed to march north "cautiously, watching the result, and not get beyond recall," he wrote, "until I find it safe."[48]

In addition to finding greener logistical pastures, Lee hoped to repeat his Antietam campaign by "relieving the Valley of the presence of the enemy & drawing his army north of the Potomac." Such a move, he believed, would have drawn federal troops away from the coasts of Virginia and North Carolina and, if he could again occupy a strong flank position in enemy territory, "their plan of the present campaign" would have been "broken up, and before new arrangements could have been made for its resumption, the summer would have ended."[49]

If successful, the campaign would have baffled Union designs in the east for the entire campaigning season and would have forwarded political objectives by helping "to repress the war feeling in the Federal States." Lee urged the President to try to prevent any public manifestations of hostility to the idea of peace negotiations, because, in the North, such hostility might "weaken the hands of the advocates of a pacific policy." Believing that peace negotiations would more likely begin if northerners thought they might bring reunion, Lee urged that the Confederacy not reject any sort of peace feeler for "when peace is proposed to us," he said, "it will be time enough to discuss its terms." With such a negotiation in progress, Lee told Davis: "The war would no longer be supported" in the North "and that after all is what we are interested in bringing about."[50]

Even though he knew that the Confederates must "husband" their strength, Lee could have been under no illusion that he could bring off such a protracted campaign without a battle. Knowing that Confederate manpower resources were "constantly diminishing," he certainly would have preferred to fight another Fredericksburg. His movement would facilitate this because, unlike his position on the Rappahannock, he would not be committed to fighting in a particular place, as he must in Virginia in order to cover his vital railroad and supply region. If he raided enemy territory, it would be politically if not strategically imperative for the Union army to take the offensive, giving the Confederates the advantage of the tactical defensive when, as Lee expressed it, "they meet us."[51]

Lee could thus stand on the defensive and, because he would be far from his own critical areas, could select a position strictly on its merits for the tactical defensive. Yet he realized that if he turned the enemy army, it might well be "drawn out in a position to be assailed," and he could hardly foreclose this opportunity in advance. After all, since the inept Hooker had exposed himself when he held the initiative, he might well again make his army quite vulnerable by committing a serious blunder when responding to Lee's initiative.[52]

And so, joined by Longstreet and his men from southeastern Virginia, Lee began to move his army north and west toward the Valley. Some Confederate elements encountered resistance from 6,000 Federals on June 14 and 15 in a battle of Second Winchester and at Stephenson's Depot, four miles to the north. After a short but sharp fight, the overwhelmed Federals tried to escape toward Harper's Ferry, but 3,358 able-bodied and 700 sick Yankees fell prisoner. The Confederates also seized 23 guns, 300 loaded wagons, over 300 horses, and large quantities of commissary and quartermaster stores. Confederate Major General Edward Johnson provided a humorous capstone. Formally nicknamed "Old Allegheny," but sometimes called "Old Clubby" by his soldiers because he preferred to direct their combat maneuvers with a heavy walking stick instead of a sword, he asserted happily that he had taken thirty prisoners himself "with his opera glass" before his private chase ended when he fell off his horse and into Opequon Creek.[53]

Earlier in June, as he first discerned signs of Lee's movement, Hooker said, If the enemy sends "a heavy column of infantry on the proposed raid, he can leave nothing behind to interpose any serious obstacle to my rapid advance on Richmond." This display of Hooker's obsession with Richmond caused Lincoln again to reiterate the headquarters doctrine of the futility of attacking that city. Lincoln strongly advised Hooker not to "go South of the Rappahannock, upon Lee's moving north of it." Buttressing his admonition with his typical humor, he warned Hooker not to get caught "like an ox jumped half over a fence," unable "to gore one way or kick the other. If you had Richmond invested to-day," he said, "you would not be able to take it in twenty days; meanwhile, your communications, and with them, your army would be ruined. I think Lee's Army, and not Richmond, is your true objective point."[54]

Except for Hooker's effort to turn Lee at Chancellorsville, the headquarters strategy had been to accept the stalemate in Virginia while concentrating in the West. Lincoln and Halleck both had charged Hooker to keep Lee occupied; in Lincoln's words, to "fret him and fret him." Since Lee was "as prudent as able," Halleck did not believe Lee would risk an attack on Hooker's army. More likely the Confederates would make a northward turning movement, one "exceedingly hazardous" for Lee, providing the Army of the Potomac had an "energetic commander" rather than Hooker, an implied suggestion which for the moment Lincoln resisted implementing.[55]

Lee's movement presented the long-awaited federal opportunity. Lincoln wrote Hooker: "I believe you are aware that since you took command of the army I have not believed that you had any chance to effect anything until now." With Lee moving toward Harper's Ferry, Lincoln believed the enemy would be vulnerable, giving back the opportunity of the Antietam campaign, which McClellan lost. Hooker understood and he proposed to attack Lee's rear units, intrenched near Fredericksburg. To this, Lincoln promptly objected, pointing out that Lee's detachment "would fight in entrenchments," and, he told Hooker, "have you at a disadvantage, and so, man for man, worst you at that point, while his main force would in some way be getting an advantage of you Northward."[56]

Lincoln and Halleck counseled Hooker in alternation. Halleck explained: The best way to exploit the situation is "to fight his movable column first instead of first attacking his intrenchments, with your own forces separated by the Rappahannock." As Lee advances, Lincoln suggested, "follow on his flank, and on the inside track, shortening your lines, whilst he lengthens his." Then, the general in chief advised, when Lee left "part of his forces in Fredericksburg, while with the head of his column, he moves . . . toward the Potomac," there would be an opportunity "to cut him in two, and fight his divided forces." The President, deploring that Hooker's late plan looked "defensive merely," echoed Halleck's earlier point that if the head of Lee's column were near the Potomac and the tail near Fredericksburg, "the animal must be very slim somewhere. Could you not break him?" he asked.[57]

Though the public in the northeast panicked at Lee's advance and Lincoln did call out 100,000 militia, the President nevertheless remained calm, reassuring his wife, I do "not think the raid into Pennsylvania amounts to anything at all." Rather than a menace, Lincoln perceived Lee's raid, like the previous advance to Antietam, as an opportunity to strike the enemy when vulnerable and far from his base, "the best opportunity," he said, "we have had since the war began." Lee, himself, had broken the stalemate in the East.[58]

At last underway, with his army well past Hooker's flank and lead units in Pennsylvania, Lee apparently began to feel real hope for the success of his movement. Though provisions were not plentiful, his animals now received enough grass, and the winter supply difficulties ended. Some units made such remarkable progress in their marches over the good roads that they enjoyed "breakfast in Virginia, whiskey in Maryland, and supper in Pennsylvania." Lee delighted in moving the whole army away from its cramped position behind the Rappahannock and hoped, by his advance, to eliminate the danger of a federal thrust in southeastern Virginia or North Carolina. As late as the middle of June, Lee had feared that the need to cover Richmond would make it "useless to attempt" his long-cherished maneuver; but with the encouragement of the secretary of war, he was at last well launched. Seddon instructed Lee: Take "some risk to promote the grand results that may be attained by your successful operations." After an anxious season of fending

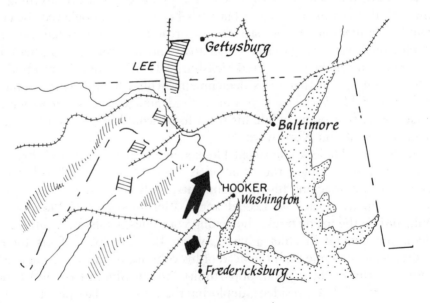

Lee Advances

off efforts to send a part of his army west, Lee found it exhilarating indeed to be on the march with almost all of his army together, headed north with Hooker's plan already baffled.[59]

With his lead corps gathering supplies in Pennsylvania, Lee wrote its commander: "Should we be able to detain Genl Hooker's army from following you, you would be able to accomplish as much unmolested as the whole army could perform with Hooker in its front." Despite a surprising dearth of forage, Lee had enough salt and flour for his army and estimated that, if necessary, his raiding army could retain its flank position throughout the summer. To facilitate this, he sought to take advantage of "the well known anxiety of the Northern Government for the safety of its capital." He suggested to the President: "If an army could be organized under the command of Genl Beauregard, and pushed forward to Culpeper Court House threatening Washington from that direction, it would not only effect a diversion most favorable for this army, but would I think, relieve us of any apprehension of an attack upon Richmond during our absence." Lee felt so confident his army would remain north of the Potomac for an extended time that he even suggested that Beauregard's department "be extended over North Carolina and Virginia."[60]

As Lee's army pushed into Pennsylvania, the Union high command concentrated every available man in an attempt to implement their strategy of using this opportunity to strike a meaningful blow. President Lincoln himself "examined into all the details" of the process "to satisfy himself that every man who could be spared from other places" had been sent to strengthen the army which would hit Lee. Even an armored train, "proof against musketry" and "against 12-pounder solid shot," was put into the field. Lincoln, however, restricted to the East this effort to "squeeze out" every man available. Unlike a year earlier during the battles before Richmond, he requested no troops from the West. The western concentration remained inviolable.[61]

In addition to the seasoned troops sent to the Army of the Potomac, forces of militia and untrained men assembled in Pennsylvania to guard against cavalry raids, to impede and contain Lee's advance, and to respond to the panicky public and officials. These forces effectively helped in crippling Lee's logistics by keeping "the rebels from seizing stock, flour, &c., to feed themselves." Headquarters did not confine its endeavors, however, simply to concentrating against Lee. It sought to take advantage of the opportunity presented by the Confederate concentrations in Pennsylvania and at Vicksburg by inaugurating raids against rebel railroads which would at last be relatively unprotected. Raiders from West Virginia cut the East Tennessee and Virginia Railroad, and in North Carolina General Foster struck with his cavalry against the critical railroads connecting Richmond with Wilmington and the lower south.[62]

In addition Lincoln and Halleck sought to weaken Lee by menacing his rear in its most sensitive spot, Richmond, and the railroads running north from that city. Reinforced by infantry from North Carolina, General Dix's already strengthened command at Fort Monroe sent out two forces, one to threaten Richmond and the other to cut the railroads. If nothing else, Dix could "at least find occupation for a large force of the enemy." Meanwhile, the Navy demonstrated up the James River. These expeditions had limited effect, however; Dix did briefly break the railroad north of Richmond.[63]

As Lee expanded the concept of his operation to include a role for Beauregard, he began to magnify the significance of his advance, believing that it "might even hope to compel the recall of some of the enemy's troops from the West." Probably his reading of the northern newspapers contributed to his enthusiasm and, as he focused his attention on his own army, he lost his appreciation of the realities of the total Confederate strategic situation. He overlooked that Burnside in Kentucky menaced Buckner's command in East Tennessee and he forgot that the President had told him that the already beleaguered Bragg had "bravely and patriotically detached strong re-enforcements to General Johnston—so much," said Davis, "that I have to warn him of his own necessities." Neglecting these realities and believing a report that Burnside had withdrawn from Kentucky, Lee thought that Burnside's supposed move should "enable Genls Buckner & Bragg to accomplish something in Ohio."[64]

Just as the previous September he had suggested that Bragg reinforce his crossing of the Potomac, Lee now wished General Beauregard to help "this army in its operations." Blending his old advocacy of concentration with his new idea of all forces on the offensive, he urged an invasion of Kentucky by Buckner from East Tennessee and Sam Jones from southwestern Virginia. Since the Confederacy's "true policy" in relation to the enemy was, Lee said, "so to employ our own forces as to give occupation to his at points of our selection," the armies of Buckner and Jones, if they were too weak to invade Kentucky, "should go where they can be of immediate service." They could be used, he continued, "to reinforce Genl Johnston or Genl Bragg, to constitute a part of the proposed army of Genl Beauregard at Culpeper Court House, or they might accomplish good results by going into northwestern Virginia. It should never be forgotten that our concentration at any point compels that of the enemy, and his numbers being limited, tends to relieve other threatened localities."[65]

Lee's almost euphoric suggestions about these extensive and diverse moves reached the President just as the rapid and well-conceived advance of Rosecrans's thoroughly prepared army had driven the weakened Bragg from Middle Tennessee.

If Rosecrans, like Buell and McClellan, suffered from the slows, he certainly threw off its symptoms when on June 23 he finally began to move. "Being determined to render useless their entrenchments and, if possible, secure their line of retreat by turning their right," Rosecrans aimed at reaching Bragg's rear and so "getting possession of his communications and forcing the enemy to a very disastrous battle." But as in most such ambitious turning

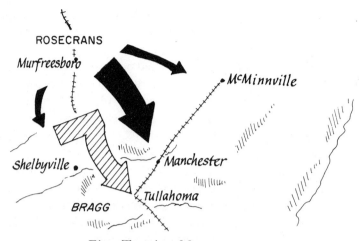

First Turning Movement

movements, Rosecrans failed to reach Bragg's rear. The march itself was slowed by "one of the most extraordinary rains ever known in Tennessee at that period of the year over a soil that became almost a quicksand." No believer in Joe Johnston's idea of exchanging bases with Rosecrans, Bragg fell back hurriedly.[66]

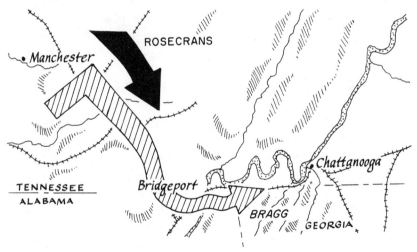

Second Turning Movement

Thus, with two successive movements, Rosecrans bloodlessly succeeded in turning Bragg entirely out of Middle Tennessee, an advance of eighty miles at a cost of only 560 casualties. Pursuit by the cavalry ended when the roads, "worn well-nigh impracticable from rain and travel," forced a halt. In country already well foraged by Bragg's army, the Union troops had to await the arrival of more supplies and the repair of the railroad before resuming their advance. Particularly important was the ripening of the corn crop in the region of operations, for this area had but "few fertile spots" and these had "been gleaned and scraped by the rebels with a powerful cavalry force since last winter."[67]

In his Tullahoma campaign Rosecrans had entirely freed Middle Tennessee of the enemy. Nevertheless he received no adulation as he had after his victory at Stones River. Miffed, he reflected the soldiers' belief that politicians only valued bloody battles when he wrote the secretary of war that he hoped that "the War Department may not overlook so great an event because it is not written in letters of blood."[68]

The optimism which led Lee to expand the scope of his campaign and urge Beauregard's coming to Virginia clashed with the gloomy realities perceived in the Confederate capital. Oppressed by the discouraging news of the Tullahoma campaign and the depressing situation at Vicksburg, the "President was embarrassed to understand" the proposal about Beauregard, for it was the "first intimation" that he had had "that such a plan was even in contemplation." So far was Lee from the outlook prevalent in Richmond that, on the eve of Gettysburg, General Cooper, explaining difficulties with Dix's expeditions in Virginia, asked whether Lee could "spare a portion" of his force.[69]

Excitement and uncertainty afflicted many areas in the North, too. As Lee's men neared Harrisburg, Pennsylvania, one reporter described the scene as one of "perfect panic." Alarmed and excited people loaded with baggage packed the crowded trains. "Every woman in the place seemed anxious to leave," the reporter noted, perhaps fearing rape. Meanwhile, busy workers frantically prepared books, papers, paintings, and valuables at the state capitol for evacuation.[70]

With Lee's army so far north Hooker's unimpressive responses exhausted the confidence of Lincoln. His credit had already long since run out with a number of newspaper editors. One of these had disgustedly written early in June, "Under the leadership of 'Fighting Joe Hooker' the glorious Army of the Potomac is becoming more slow in its movements, more unwieldly, less confident of itself, more of a football to the enemy, and less an honor to the country than any army we have yet raised." On June 24 Hooker promised to send a corps or two across the Potomac to make Washington secure and then to strike on Lee's probable line of retreat. But then he asked for instructions, admitting, "I don't know whether I am standing on my head or feet."[71]

On June 27, to Halleck's pleasure, Lincoln relieved Hooker and replaced him with the general in chief's choice, Major General George Gordon Meade. A corps commander in the Army of the Potomac, Meade, now in his late forties, was tall and spare but stooped, though graceful and soldierly. His slightly curling dark-brown hair was streaked heavily with gray and he was balding. Sometimes prone to self-pity and self-deprecation, he "was quite touchy and concerned with getting his just rewards and positions," and this propelled him occasionally into awkward situations. Furthermore, his hair-trigger temper and penchant to speak in the heat of a moment in a quite offensive and abrasive manner brought him a revealing nickname: his troops called him "a damned old goggle-eyed snapping turtle." The spectacles that myopia caused him to wear also brought him the nickname "Old Four Eyes." But this solid, honest, and somewhat gifted though not brilliant officer ought to have been called "Old Reliable." Nineteenth in the 1836 West Point class of fifty-six cadets, he had experienced combat during the Mexican War and from the outset of the Civil War had served competently as a brigade, division, and then corps commander. He possessed three highly noteworthy capabilities: "He was a master of logistics"; he could tell, even if awakened suddenly at any hour, merely from the sound of firing what troops were engaged; and "he had an extraordinary eye for topography." Altogether he made a dull but very capable army commander.[72]

Lee rated Meade as more able than Hooker but thought that the change of command, coming at a critical moment, signaled some difficulty in transition. Thus Lee's blinding exhilaration continued and doubtless constituted a factor in his conduct of the battle into which he blundered at Gettysburg. Initial numerical superiority and offensive tactical success on the first day led him into an ill-fated and unrealistic attempt to crush part of the Union army.

Following the loss of so valued and trusted a subordinate as Jackson, Lee had concluded that he had no single individual worthy to replace the fallen corps leader. For this reason he had reorganized his army into three, rather than two, bodies, one each under Longstreet, Richard Ewell, and Ambrose P. Hill. These three corps converged at the little town of Gettysburg for not much more military necessity than the hope that the Confederates could alleviate their shortage of shoes by plundering the shoe factory there. The first fighting opened on July 1 west of the town, and by midafternoon Ewell's corps had captured the place. Bruce Catton's description of Ewell is too classic to improve upon: "Bald, eccentric, oddly bird-like, with a nose like a hawk's beak jutting out between the bulging eyes of an affronted owl. He wore a wooden leg, carried crutches, and rode in a buggy because the Yankees had shot a leg off of him at Groveton, nine months earlier, but he was full of bounce and energy all the same." Still, Ewell also was a man of excessive prudence, and he lacked the insight and initiative of a Stonewall Jackson. Too, Ewell may have had severe mental problems. Legends persist that he sometimes hallucinated that he *was* a bird. For hours at a time he would sit in his tent softly chirping and, at mealtimes, he would accept only sunflower seeds or grains of wheat. For whatever reasons, Ewell failed to push on after seizing Gettysburg and to accomplish the rest of Lee's instruction, which the commander had qualified with the proviso "if practicable," and secure the high grounds southward. Meade also decided to concentrate at Gettysburg, even though he had already laid out a defensive line some distance east and south of the town.[73]

Lee, however, was able to concentrate more quickly than Meade and during the night his whole army assembled in and around Gettysburg, strung

out in a line along Seminary Ridge. Meade's men proceeded to occupy most
of the inverted fishhook terrain just to the east of Lee's position. Meade's fifty-
one brigades of infantry and seven of cavalry stretched along a formidable
three-mile line, an average of 27,000 men to the mile, or better than fifteen to
the yard. Lee's thirty-four brigades of infantry and one of cavalry occupied a
five-mile semicircle for an average of 10,000 men to the mile, or fewer than
six per yard. In artillery, Meade's 354 guns outnumbered Lee's 272, or 118
Federal guns to the mile as compared to 54 Confederate.

Ewell and Jubal Early talked Lee out of his best plan of attack at this point,
a hit upon Cemetery Hill. Lee tentatively decided to turn the Union position
as early as possible the next morning with Longstreet's corps slamming into
the federal left, then turning and rolling northward along Cemetery Hill.
Ewell had orders to make a diversionary attack.

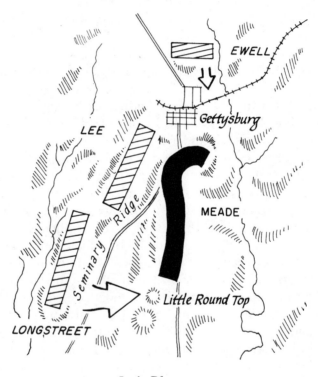

Lee's Plan

On July 2 Longstreet got his men up to the battle area in the quickest time
possible, but circumstances forced him to delay the actual assault. The head
of his column approached the area at about 7 A.M. but the tail lagged three
and a half hours behind. Unenthusiastic about the attack, Longstreet consumed so much time in properly assembling and aligning the corps that the
assault did not commence until 4 P.M. During all the time that passed, Meade
continued to move in troops to bring about a more and more complete con-

centration; by 6 P.M. he had achieved numerical superiority and had his left well covered.

As Longstreet began his attack, he was told that few or no Federals remained on Little Round Top. That had been momentarily true, but federal Brigadier General Gouverneur K. Warren, the Army of the Potomac's chief engineer, had seized the initiative and forced a defensive deployment in the nick of time. Some of Longstreet's men did reach the summit of Little Round Top and a vicious regimental attack ensued, but the Federals managed to hold this most strategic bit of ground. The attack fizzled with the nightfall. Bruce Catton assessed this day's fighting as having no pattern, "except for the undesigned pattern that can always be traced after the event . . . unpremeditated as a chain of lightning, searing and scarring both armies." As Warren put it, the fight "was no display of scientific maneuver, and should never be judged like some I think vainly try to judge a battle as they would a game of chess." Again, in one of Catton's most artful sentences, "It was a test of what men can nerve themselves to attempt and what they can compel themselves to endure, and at shattering cost it proved that the possibilities in both directions are limitless."[74]

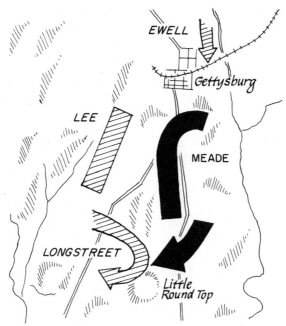

Longstreet Repulsed

During the night Lee decided to assail the federal center the next day with 15,000 infantry, mostly from Longstreet's corps but some from Hill's, the charge to be under one of Longstreet's division commanders, Major General George E. Pickett. One of the more unfortunate characters in American military history, Pickett had graduated last in the West Point class of 1846—

a class that also had included George B. McClellan and Thomas J. "Stonewall" Jackson. Pickett had enjoyed one exquisite taste of glory: During the Mexican War he had been the first American to scale the ramparts at Chapultepec. During the Civil War he had rendered solid service, but thus far his opportunities all had been quite unspectacular; now at last came a leading role and he grasped it eagerly. One British observer described him as a "desperate-looking character." Pickett mounted a sleek black horse, wore a small blue cap, buff gauntlets, and matching blue cuffs on a well-tailored uniform. He carried an elegant riding crop and wore brightly polished boots adorned with gold spurs. "Of middle height, slender, graceful of carriage— 'dapper and alert,' a familiar witness termed him, while another spoke of his 'marvelous pulchritude'—he sported a curly chin-beard and a mustache that drooped beyond the corners of his mouth and then turned upward at the ends. To add to the swashbuckling effect, his dark-brown hair hung shoulder-length in ringlets which he annointed with perfume."[75]

A terrific artillery bombardment upon the federal center preceded the charge. The Unionists were most "impressed by the noise, if not the effect, of the barrage." One colonel "compared its roar to 'that from the falls of Niagara.' " A sergeant "thought the cannonade 'the most terrible the new world has ever seen, and the most prolonged . . . terribly grand and sublime.' " And a lieutenant "noted that the earth shook as if in fright, and he likened the noise to 'one loud thunder clap.' "[76]

Such a bombardment might have had effect a half century earlier when defending soldiers had to stand in order to repel with their bayonets a possible cavalry charge. But by 1863 the long range of the infantry's rifles kept the cavalry at a safe distance, enabling the federal troops simply to lie safely in their positions, only a few men being hit by the scant number of shots that fell precisely upon them.

"What do you think of it?" Lee's artillery chief asked one of the infantry commanders. "Is it as hard to get there as it looks?" The man replied, "The trouble is not in going there, I was there with my brigade yesterday. There is a place where you can get breath and re-form. The trouble is to stay there after you get there, for the whole Yankee army is there in a bunch." The Yankee's guns replied to the Confederate fire and for a time there followed a combined Union and Confederate exchange that was "unearthly. Reportedly, it could be heard more than 150 miles away." At last, when the federal artillery chief, Brigadier General Henry J. Hunt, had his gunners pull back to safety, the Confederates wrongly concluded that they had disabled the enemy guns. Thus when the Confederates did charge, they faced an unexpected and murderous federal artillery barrage. Against attackers who must stand and expose themselves in order to advance, the field guns remained fearfully effective. Particularly deadly at close range was canister in which were fired a number of small balls with each shot. General Hunt always claimed, perhaps only a little extravagantly, that had his superiors allowed him, he could have stopped Pickett's charge with his guns alone. The episode fully exhibited the high value of artillery on the defense as contrasted with its relative ineffectiveness on the offensive. Its differential role only accentuated the primacy of the defense and increased the futility of frontal attacks against organized resistance.[77]

In the first part of the charge the Confederates were hit by long-range artillery, then by rifle fire which continued in salvos, and by Napoleons firing canister. Only about 5,000 of the assaulters managed even to get to Cemetery Ridge, not enough to breach the lines. Thus Pickett's charge fell back, vanquished. Pickett lost all three of his subordinate brigadiers, and of his thirteen colonels eight were killed and the other five were wounded. Indeed, of his thirty-five officers above the rank of captain only one came back unhurt. The enemy captured thirty of the thirty-eight regimental flags carried within musket range of a stone wall near the Gettysburg cemetery. That cemetery, incidentally, contained a sign whose message the sanguinary battle transformed into an unsurpassed irony: "All persons found using firearms in these grounds will be prosecuted with the utmost rigor of the law."[78]

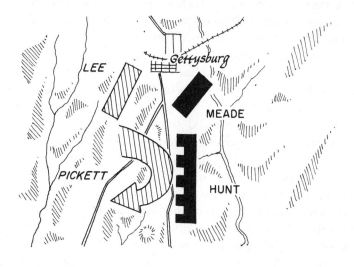

Pickett's Charge

In the battle the Federals had lost 212 killed and wounded out of each 1,000 engaged; the Confederates lost 301 per 1,000. The casualties were staggering: the Federals with over 85,000 men engaged sustained a total of 23,049 casualties; the Confederates' strength had been near 65,000 and their losses amounted to 28,063.

This heavy toll befell the Confederacy at the same time that the Vicksburg siege concluded with the city's capitulation on July 4. Pemberton had originally grasped the situation correctly, after his initial dazzling by the main distracting Union movements, and had wisely ordered a concentration of all of his forces, including Gardner's at Port Hudson, to drive back Grant's penetrating army. This orthodox effort to preserve his communications, directed by the general orders from his commander, Johnston, provided the only possible way to save Vicksburg. But Pemberton, having spent his career as a general officer dealing only with fortified positions, had never before fought in the field and almost immediately lost his nerve.

Becoming what the French call *fatigué*, demoralized and without the power of decision, he took refuge in the familiar—fortifications—and grasped at President Davis's emphasis on the importance of Vicksburg. As Grant approached Jackson, Johnston had ordered Pemberton to attack Grant's rear; but the indecisive Pemberton did not carry out the order nor did he follow Johnston's later instructions to save his army and join him by marching northeast. He remained in paralyzed inactivity. With modesty and humor Grant afterwards gave much credit to Pemberton by characterizing him as his "best friend." But Pemberton's help would have availed the Union little without Grant's energy and perceptiveness in exploiting the enemy's weakness by turning against Pemberton and Vicksburg rather than first joining Banks in concentrating against Port Hudson.[79]

After the siege commenced, Johnston received some additional troops from Tennessee and South Carolina; but the Union reinforced Grant much more heavily and there was virtually no likelihood that Johnston could raise the siege. Grant thus enjoyed to the fullest the tactical advantage of the defensive which his strategic offensive and successful penetration had brought him. Having interrupted Pemberton's communications, Grant, still on an interior line between Pemberton and Johnston, was on the defensive in intrenchments against the trapped Pemberton, with a covering force in the field on the defensive against an advance by Johnston. Communications along the Mississippi, protected by gunboats, remained completely secure and Grant had only to wait on the defensive until Pemberton, trapped against the river obstacle, surrendered when he exhausted his supplies.

From boats on the river and from troops in the encircling lines, the Vicksburg populace and defenders suffered onslaughts against nerve and will. One officer living within the besieged city declared by June 2 "that if the affair went on much longer 'a building will have to be arranged for the accommodation of maniacs,' because the constant tension was driving people out of their minds." Union gunboats lobbed huge mortar shells that made impact holes seventeen feet deep.[80]

On the field, the situation was described by Confederate Corporal Ephraim Anderson: "The enemy continued to prosecute the siege vigorously. From night to night and from day to day a series of works was presented. Secure and strong lines of fortifications appeared. Redoubts, manned by well-practiced sharpshooters, . . . parapets blazing with artillery crowned every knoll and practicable elevation. . . , and oblique lines of entrenchments, finally running into parallels, enabled the untiring foe to work his way slowly but steadily forward." Another Confederate soldier recalled that "fighting by hand grenades was all that was possible at such close quarters. As the Federals had the hand grenades and we had none, we obtained our supply by using such of theirs as failed to explode, or by catching them as they came over the parapet and hurling them back."[81]

"Vague and false rumors daily circulated within our lines," Anderson continued. "It soon became evident that there was not an abundant supply of rations . . . one day, . . . among the provisions sent up . . . the only supply in the way of bread was made of peas. . . . This 'pea bread' . . . was made of . . . 'cow peas,' which is, rather, a small bean, cultivated quite extensively as provender for animals. There was a good supply of this pea . . . and the idea grew . . . that, if reduced to the form of meal, it would make an admirable substitute for bread. . . . But the nature of it was such that it never got done, and the longer it was cooked the harder it became on the outside, . . . but, at the same time, it grew relatively softer on the inside, and, upon breaking it, you were sure to find raw pea meal in the center." And while the city trembled from the bombardments, the people therein gradually reduced their daily meals to one-half and then to one-quarter rations. One citizen who happened to have a good vegetable garden in his backyard complained that he could get no sleep, not because of the Union shelling but because he had to stay up every night guarding against hungry soldiers stealing all that he was growing. The Confederate engineer officer, Samuel Lockett, reported that the men ate "mule meat and rats and young shoots of cane." Dora Miller, one of the entrapped civilians, recalled that during the final days of the siege her servant found rats "hanging dressed in the market." Willie Tunnard, a Confederate enlisted man, wrote that rat flesh, when fried, had a flavor "fully equal to that of squirrels." One Missouri soldier stoutly held that "if you did not known it you could hardly tell the difference, when cooked," between mule meat and beef.[82]

At last, when Pemberton and all save two of his officers decided that they must surrender, even Brigadier General Stephen D. Lee, one of the two who voted against capitulation at that time, admitted: I "did not consider more than one-half of my men able to undergo the fatigues of the field." The federal losses amounted to 4,910 for the siege, while the Confederates had suffered casualties amounting to 2,872 killed, wounded, and missing, before then losing the whole army and all its equipage. The captives numbered 2,166 officers, 27,230 enlisted men, and 115 civilian employees; all of these were paroled except one officer and 708 men who elected to go north as prisoners rather than to await exchange and then have to fight again. The rebels also yielded 172 cannon, large amounts of every ammunition type, and some

60,000 shoulder weapons, many of such superior quality that some Union regiments exchanged their own for those that they found stacked by their vanquished enemy.[83]

The Confederacy could do little to salvage the situation at Vicksburg as the city and its defending army were completely lost; but Lee's army still stood before Meade's in Pennsylvania. Far from being demoralized and cowered by the repulse of Pickett's charge, many of the rebel soldiers merely had been enraged by what they had seen happen to their fellows and now stood eager for revenge. They wanted nothing better than for the Yankees to assault so they could treat the bluecoats in the same manner that they had been treated. "We'll fight them, sir, till hell freezes over," one of the men so inclined proclaimed, "and, then, sir, we will fight them on the ice."[84]

Having "failed to drive the enemy from his position," Lee waited a day, but Meade declined to counterattack. With the southern army concentrated, Lee found it difficult to forage for supplies, and Pennsylvania militia units in the vicinity aggravated the situation. Thus, "much hindered in collecting necessary supplies for the army by numerous bodies of local and other troops," Lee elected to withdraw across the mountains. On July 4, 1863, the Confederates commenced moving toward Hagerstown.

Since a Union force in their rear had destroyed the bridge, the Confederates could draw no provisions from south of the Potomac, thus rendering their situation more serious. Further, the gray army's room for maneuver had been curtailed by a sudden rise in the Potomac, making the waterway unfordable. With no ready means for crossing the river, Lee noted: I will "have to accept battle if the enemy offers it whether I wish it or not."

Digging in at a "strong position" north of the river with a "good supply of ammunition," Lee did not worry about this obstacle to his retreat. Tactically

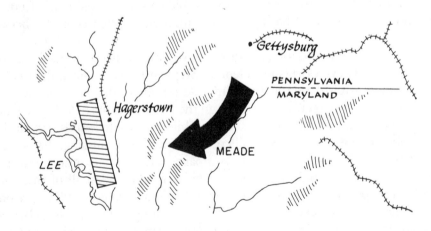

Lee's Flank Position

Lee had at last secured the strong flank position he had sought; Meade could not ignore him but would be compelled to attack in front if he attacked at all. However, the logistical difficulties of the position nullified its tactical and strategic advantages. The "chief difficulty" in Lee's situation was his inability "to procure subsistence." In addition to the river's cutting off wagon transportation, Lee found that their stock of flour was "affected by the high waters, which interfere with the working of the mills." Even when the river went down, it and Lee's tactically strong position still, he wrote, "circumscribed our limits for procuring subsistence for men & animals, which with the uncertain stage of the river, rendered it too hazardous for us to continue on the north side."[85]

Thus supply problems, not a precarious position, forced Lee finally to abandon his toehold in the north. As an afterthought he also recognized his inability to maneuver and the enemy's power "of accumulating troops" from Washington which further "gave him enormous odds." One of Jackson's old quartermaster officers, Major John Harman, procured the transportation facilities that allowed Lee's army to cross the river. The major directed the improvising of pontoons by tearing down abandoned houses for their timbers and floating the finished products down to the spot where they were linked and floored. "A good bridge," declared Lee, although one staff officer more critically assessed it as a "crazy affair." So Lee returned to Virginia to the same position from which during 1862 he had stymied McClellan for more than a month. But Meade, unintimidated by Lee's flank position, promptly crossed the Potomac below Lee and forced the Confederate army back farther until Lee had to leave the Valley. Finally the Confederate army took a position south of the Rappahannock, well above Fredericksburg on the Orange and Alexandria Railroad. By late July Lee found himself in essentially the same position where he had begun the campaign.

Though Lee believed that he had attained a "general success" in that the Union's plan of campaign had been "broken up," he recognized that he had failed to "detain" the enemy north of the river long enough to foil their plans for the entire year. As it was, he expected soon to "have them all back."[86]

Had he won at Gettysburg, Lee could have kept the Union Army north of the Potomac for a much longer time; instead he had to return to Virginia "rather sooner" than he had "originally contemplated." Nevertheless, Lee gave the campaign, if not the combat at Gettysburg, a favorable evaluation, believing that, though his army "did not win a battle, it conquered a success." Realizing "the army did all it could," he understood that he had "required of it impossibilities." Yet he thought that critics of the battle overlooked the success of the campaign and that his army "should not be censured for the unreasonable expectations of the public," nor for not having "fulfilled the anticipations of the thoughtless and unreasonable." The President, who agreed that the campaign had not been a failure, likewise disparaged the "criticisms of the ignorant," who looked at the battle rather than the campaign. In retrospect Davis believed that "the wisdom of the strategy was justified by the result."[87]

Though the public may have entertained unreasonable expectations, Lee's own subordinates criticized his departure from fighting only defensive battles, his consistent policy since the Seven Days' Battles. Longstreet, who believed that a defensive battle had been the agreed strategy, condemned the attack at Gettysburg and one of Lee's able cavalry leaders, Wade Hampton, echoed this view in thinking that the "Penn trip" amounted to a "complete failure." Stressing the tactical only, Hampton said: "The position of the Yankees there was the strongest I ever saw & it was in vain to attack it." When he referred to the campaign's strategy of turning the enemy and forcing him to assume the tactical offensive, General Hampton explained: I "thought the advantage we would have in Penn was that we would not be compelled to look for strategic points," as they had when defending on the Rappahannock, "but only critical ones, so that we might choose our own points at which to fight. But we let Meade choose his position & we then attacked."[88]

Jefferson Davis, who agreed that "the battle of Gettysburg was unfortunate," later defended Lee's attack, saying: "Had General Lee been able to compel the enemy to attack him in position, I think we should have had complete victory." The President pointed out, however, that Meade would not have done this in any case, as evidenced by his refusal to counter-assault after the battle. If Lee had turned Meade out of his Gettysburg position, Davis believed that Meade would have fallen back to his previously selected defensive position where "his ability to wait and the impossibility under such circumstances for General Lee to supply his army for any length of time" meant that, to precipitate any battle, Lee would have had to attack. Militarily Davis's point is certainly accurate, for Lee's raiding army had not interrupted Meade's communications; and its own lack of supply lines meant that it could not long remain concentrated in one place. Davis, however, overlooked that Meade would have been under irresistible political pressure to attack any Confederate army in Pennsylvania.[89]

Davis also pointed out that the Gettysburg campaign "impaired the confidence of the southern people so far as to give the malcontents a power to represent the government as neglecting for Virginia the safety of the more southern states." Not understanding Lee's strategy and not waiting for the Battle of Gettysburg to criticize Lee's campaign, Beauregard, the leader of the malcontent western concentration bloc, wrote Johnston asking: "Of what earthly use is this 'raid' of Lee's army into Maryland, in violation of all the principles of war? Is it going to end the struggle, take Washington, or save the Mississippi Valley?"[90]

Beauregard was quite correct technically in terming Lee's movement into Pennsylvania a raid rather than a penetration, because Lee always had lacked any line of supply. The Shenandoah Valley provided the Confederates with as fine an avenue for threatening the enemy's rear as the Virginia rivers afforded the Union armies; but it lacked the lines of communication south-ward to permit it to be the route of penetration similar to that enjoyed by the North.

Certainly Lee blundered in attacking at Gettysburg, but his decisions, at least during the first two days, easily engender sympathy. He had concentrated his army more rapidly than Meade and had caught the outnumbered Federals unprepared. Lee's plan to turn them on the second day was a good one, reminiscent of Second Bull Run and surely characteristic of Lee. The third day's doomed attempt to retrieve the failure of the second, like the last attack of the Seven Days' Battles, at Malvern Hill, was a serious mistake, but hardly characteristic of Lee before or after Gettysburg. As the year's campaign evolved, he successfully baffled Meade's fall efforts without another big battle. The strategic impact of the Battle of Gettysburg was, therefore, fairly limited. Principally, it cost the Confederacy an immense number of killed and wounded, far greater in proportion to Lee's resources than the battle losses suffered by the Union. As President Davis later wrote, stressing the casualties: "Theirs could be repaired, ours could not."

In July, 1863, Confederate losses in morale and position had been as severe as those in manpower. The loss of the Mississippi depressed southerners almost as much as it elated the North and Rosecrans's unspectacular success had brought his army within striking distance of Chattanooga and a key rail artery between Virginia and Georgia. Though the careful Meade had attained only a defensive success on northern soil, his victory, followed by Lee's retreat, appealed to the popular imagination and so contributed much besides attrition. The events of the early summer stood in stark contrast to the failures of the previous December. Then Halleck's carefully coordinated offensive had accomplished virtually nothing. Even Rosecrans's victory at Stones River had advanced his army barely half as far as his bloodless Tullahoma maneuver. But, largely fortuitously, the campaigns of the spring and early summer had good coordination and received much aid from Pemberton's bungling and Lee's mistake in persistently attacking Meade.

However, Union success was also earned by Union skill. Grant succeeded because his superb campaign had embodied all of the elements that had made for Napoleon's victories—distraction, a penetration to threaten communications and turn the enemy, and the use of interior lines. Grant simply and masterfully had outgenerated his opponents and, after he had settled down to a siege, they could do nothing about it. The symphonic application of simultaneous pressures provided the capstone: Lee's Pennsylvania campaign demanded that the Confederacy not use eastern reserves to attempt to lift the Vicksburg siege; Bragg, weakened to aid Johnston, was driven from Middle Tennessee by Rosecrans's brilliant Tullahoma campaign; and Johnston's fragment was too small to operate effectively against the heavily reinforced Grant. Each Union commander thus performed nearly perfectly and, with high ability and, often, brilliance, made the most of the mistakes of his opponents.

The Union high command had played its role by sustaining and formidably reinforcing Grant, successfully pressing Rosecrans to make use of his opportunity, and wisely, on the eve of battle, giving the command to the steady and capable Meade.[91]

☆ ☆ ☆

1. Lee to Seddon, May 10, 1863, *Wartime Papers*, 482; James Longstreet to L. T. Wigfall, May 13, 1863, Wigfall Papers, Library of Congress; Beauregard to Lovell, June 10, 1862, *O.R.*, XV, 752.

2. Hattaway, *Lee*, 207; Horn, *Army of Tennessee*, 211.

3. Horn, *Army of Tennessee*, 211–12; Connelly, *Autumn of Glory*, 38–41.

4. Grant to Sherman, Apr. 29, 1863, *O.R.*, XXIV, pt. 3, 246; Grant to Kelton, July 6, 1863, *ibid.*, pt. 1, 48; Grant to Halleck, May 3, 1863, *ibid.*, pt. 1, 32; Grant to Julia Grant, May 3, 1863, *Papers of Grant*, VIII, 155; Long, *Civil War, Day by Day*, 343, 344.

5. Foote, *The Civil War*, II, 350.

6. Grant to Halleck, May 3, 20, 24 (two communications), 1863, *O.R.*, XXIV, pt. 1, 32, 36, 37; Grant to Sherman, May 9, 1863, *ibid.*, pt. 3, 285–86.

7. Banks to Grant, Apr. 10, 30, May 6, 1863, *O.R.*, XXIV, pt. 3, 182, 247–48, 276; Banks to Halleck, Apr. 10, 23, 1863, *ibid.*, XV, 294–95, 298–99; Grant to Banks, Mar. 23, Apr. 14, 1863, *ibid.*, XXIV, pt. 3, 126, 192; Halleck to Banks, Apr. 9, 1863, *ibid.*, XV, 700.

8. Grant to Sherman, May 3, 9, 1863, *O.R.*, XXIV, pt. 3, 268–69, 285–86; Grant to Halleck, May 3, 1863, *ibid.*, pt. 1, 32; Dana to Stanton, May 9, 1863, *ibid.*, pt. 1, 83.

9. Rosecrans to Halleck, Mar. 6, 1863, *O.R.*, XXIII, pt. 2, 111.

10. Foote, *The Civil War*, II, 248, 258, 262; Catton, *Never Call Retreat*, 145.

11. Foote, *The Civil War*, II, 319.

12. Adams, *Our Masters the Rebels*, 101, 105, 142, 144. Adams implicitly assumes that the Army of the Potomac had the power "of destroying the Army of Northern Virginia." But such an unrealistic assumption is not necessary for there to have been a significant impact of the ideal held by many northerners that the aristocratic South "would naturally have a better disciplined and more effective army than the democratic North." This, together with the belief that the South had begun military prepara-

tions sooner, caused an "overestimation of enemy strength and ability, leading to the failure of nerve and the loss of opportunities."

Adams believes that this perception of the South particularly affected the Army of the Potomac, that McClellan's influence was fundamental in establishing in that army a conviction of southern superiority, and that his army, feeling "inferior long after he was gone," would thereafter "fight to survive, not to win." This attitude affected all generals, including Burnside and Hooker. It may, however, sometimes be difficult to distinguish pessimism engendered by a conviction of southern superiority from that caused by a perception of the superiority of the defensive. These attitudes reinforce one another, especially when soldiers believed that civilians wished them to fight meaningless frontal battles like Fredericksburg rather than operate from the Peninsula. In quoting Jacob D. Cox on McClellan's legacy, Adams well exhibits both of these influences at work on the Army of the Potomac. Cox wrote: "The general who indoctrinates his army with the belief that it is required by its government to do the impossible, may preserve his popularity with the troops and be received with cheers as he rides down the line, but he has put any great military success far beyond his reach."

The subject of the psychology of soldiers and commanders has received two important recent treatments in Norman Dixon, *On the Psychology of Military Incompetence*, and John Keegan, *The Face of Battle*. A psychological analysis of the Army of the Potomac and its commanders would require using the insights of these authors as well as Adams's, the work of Morris Janowitz and other military sociologists, and older studies such as that of Ardant du Picq.

Many civilians and soldiers during the war thought there was something wrong with the Army of the Potomac; they saw in it a spirit which distinguished it from other armies. Certainly its position near the capital and its creation by the politically controversial McClellan gave it a special place. The generals in the army argued that they had a more difficult problem than western armies, because they had to fight

Lee and Jackson rather than Bragg and Pemberton.

Though Halleck and Lincoln recognized special problems with the Potomac generals, they still saw the difficulty of the task facing the Army of the Potomac as a part of the general problem of the tactical power of the defense, the constraints of logistics, and the difficulty of coping with guerrillas and raiders. Halleck and Grant did agree in singling out one major extrinsic reason for the slow movements of all armies: long delays and indecisive campaigns were caused by too elaborate preparations and too much logistical impedimenta, a condition which has afflicted the U.S. Army ever since. We agree that essentially military factors amply suffice to explain the indecisive character of operations in Virginia and elsewhere, though we discount neither incompetence nor psychological factors and believe Michael Adams may have made a valuable contribution to our understanding of the psychology of some Union commanders (Adams, *Our Masters the Rebels*, 88, 90, 96, 98, 101, 103, 127, 130, 133, 142, 147, 148, 156, 172). For McClellan's influence see also: Cox, *Military Reminiscence of the Civil War*, I, 367–71.

13. Foote, *The Civil War*, II, 306, 315.

14. Lee to Seddon, May 6, 1863, *Wartime Papers*, 456.

15. Lee to Davis, Apr. 27, May 7, 1863, *O.R.*, XXV, pt. 2, 752, 782–83; Lee to D. H. Hill, May 12, 1863, *ibid.*, XVIII, 1057.

16. Lee to Davis, May 10, 1863, and Davis's endorsement, *O.R.*, XXV, pt. 2, 790.

17. Lee to Seddon, May 10, 1863, *Wartime Papers*, 482.

18. Wright to Halleck, Mar. 15, 1863, *O.R.*, XXIII, pt. 2, 142.

19. Rosecrans to Halleck, Mar. 10, 1863, *O.R.*, XXIII, pt. 2, 127; Halleck to Sumner, Mar. 17, 1863, *ibid.*, XXII, pt. 2, 158; Halleck to Curtis, Apr. 15, 1863, *ibid.*, 217; Foote, *The Civil War*, II, 24.

20. Halleck to Curtis, Feb. 17, 1863, *O.R.*, XXII, pt. 2, 113; Stanton to Halleck, June 28, 1862, *ibid.*, XVI, pt. 2, 69–70; Halleck to Stanton, June 30, 1862, *ibid.*, 74–75.

21. Rosecrans to Halleck, Mar. 10, 1863, *O.R.*, XXIII, pt. 2, 127; Rosecrans to Wright, Mar. 11, 1863, *ibid.*, 132.

22. Rosecrans to Halleck, June 2, 1863, *O.R.*, XXIV, pt. 3, 376.

23. Thomas to Rosecrans, June 9, 1863, *O.R.*, XXIII, pt. 2, 413–15; Sheridan to Goddard, June 9, 1863, *ibid.*, 411.

24. Van Cleve to Goddard, June 9, 1863, *O.R.*, XXIII, pt. 2, 415; Thomas to Rosecrans, June 9, 1863, *ibid.*, 413–15; Grant to Halleck, June 14, 1863, *ibid.*, XXIV, pt. 1, 42.

25. Johnston to Polk, Mar. 3, 1863, *O.R.*, XXIII, pt. 2, 660; Johnston to Cooper, Apr. 6, 1863, *ibid.*, 741; Johnston to Davis, Apr. 10, 1863, *ibid.*, 745; Bragg to Johnston, July 17, 1863, *ibid.*, LII, pt. 2, 508; Rosecrans to Halleck, Feb. 12, 1863, *ibid.*, XXIII, pt. 2, 59.

26. Stanley to Goddard, June 9, 1863, *O.R.*, XXIII, pt. 2, 412–13; R. B. Mitchell to Goddard, June 10, 1863, *ibid.*, 417–18; Granger to Rosecrans, June 9, 1863, *ibid.*, 404–5.

27. Garfield to Rosecrans, June 12, 1863, *O.R.*, XXIII, pt. 2, 423.

28. Crittenden to Goddard, June 9, 1863, *O.R.*, XXIII, pt. 2, 403; Wood to Goddard, June 9, 1863, *ibid.*, 406; Thomas to Rosecrans, June 9, 1863, *ibid.*, 413–15; Negley to Goddard, June 9, 1863, *ibid.*, 407; Palmer to Goddard, June 9, 1863, *ibid.*, 408; Wood to Garfield, June 17, 1863, *ibid.*, 433–434.

29. Granger to Rosecrans, June 9, 1863, *O.R.*, XXIII, pt. 2, 405; Stanley to Goddard, June 9, 1863, *ibid.*, 412–13.

30. Stanley to Goddard, June 9, 1863, *O.R.*, XXIII, pt. 2, 413; Wood to Garfield, June 17, 1863, *ibid.*, 433–34.

31. Stanley to Goddard, June 9, 1863, *O.R.*, XXIII, pt. 2, 413.

32. Johnston to Cooper, Apr. 6, 1863, *O.R.*, XXIII, pt. 2, 741.

33. Rosecrans to Halleck, Feb. 12, 1863, *O.R.*, XXIII, pt. 2, 59; Lamers, *Rosecrans*, 257.

34. Sherman to Mrs. Sherman, May 9, 1863, *Home Letters*, 259–60.

35. Grant to Halleck, May 11, 12, 1863, *O.R.*, XXIV, pt. 1, 35; Dana to Stanton, May 9, 14, 1863, *ibid.*, 83, 85; Foote, *The Civil War*, II, 323. Grant was planning to rely on the system of guarded convoys, traditionally used in Europe when there was fear of a raid on a supply line. Before the railroad, winter campaigns were almost impossible in the absence of unfrozen waterways and difficult then because of the scarcity of fodder. In a fertile southern region Grant could easily campaign in the traditional, pre-industrial way as early as May.

36. Archer Jones, "The Vicksburg Campaign," *Journal of Mississippi History* (Feb. 1967), 18–23.

37. Sherman to Mrs. Sherman, May 9, 1863, *Home Letters*, 259–60; Dana to Stanton, May 9, 1863, *O.R.*, XXIV, pt. 1, 83.

38. Grant to Sherman, May 14, 1863, *O.R.*, XXIV, pt. 3, 312.

39. Foote, *The Civil War*, II, 375.

40. Foote, *The Civil War*, II, 393–94; Banks to Halleck, Apr. 23, May 12 (two communications), 1863, *O.R.*, XV, 298–99, 314–15, 316–17; Banks to Grant, Apr. 30, 1863, *ibid.*, XXIV, pt. 3, 247–48.

41. Halleck to Banks, May 11, 19, 23, 1863, *O.R.*, XV, 726, XXVI, pt. 1, 494–95, 500–501; Grant to Banks, May 10, 31, 1863, *ibid.*, XV, 315–16, XXVI, pt. 1, 525.

42. Wheeler, *Siege of Vicksburg*, 27.

43. Grant to Halleck, May 24, 1863, *O.R.*, XXIV, pt. 1, 37.

44. Wheeler, *Siege of Vicksburg*, 188.

45. Halleck to Grant, Apr. 9, 1863, *O.R.*, XXIV, pt. 1, 27; Halleck to Wright, Jan. 8, 10, 1863, *ibid.*, XVII, pt. 2, 545, 550–51; Halleck to Curtis, Feb. 17, 1863, *ibid.*, XXII, pt. 2, 113; Curtis to Halleck, Mar. 24, 1863, *ibid.*, 176; Grant to Halleck, May 31, 1863, *ibid.*, XXIV, pt. 1, 40; Grant to Kelton, July 6, 1863, *ibid.*, 57; Halleck to Schofield, June 2, 1863, *ibid.*, XXII, pt. 2, 306; Schofield to Halleck, June 3, 1863, *ibid.*, 308; Halleck to Burnside, June 3, 1863, *ibid.*, XXIV, pt. 3, 383.

46. Lincoln to Hooker, May 7, 14, 1863, Basler, *Collected Works*, VI, 201, 217–18; Hooker to Lincoln, May 13, 1863, *O.R.*, XXV, pt. 2, 473; Stanton to Burnside, May 7, 1863, *ibid.*, 437–38. See also: Halleck to Stanton, May 18, 1863, *ibid.*, 505.

47. Lee to Davis, May 30, 1863, *Wartime Papers*, 496; Lee to Seddon, May 30, 1863, *ibid.*, 498; Lee to his wife, May 31, 1863, *ibid.*, 499.

48. Archer Jones, "The Gettysburg Decision Reassessed," *Virginia Magazine of History and Biography* (Jan. 1968), 64–66; Northrup to Lee, July 23, 1863, *O.R.*, LI, pt. 2, 738; Lee to Davis, June 2, 1863, *ibid.*, XXV, pt. 2, 848; Lee to Seddon, June 13, 1863, *ibid.*, XXVII, pt. 3, 886; Lee to Seddon, June 8, 1863, *Wartime Papers*, 505, Lee to Davis, June 15, 1863, *ibid.*, 515.

49. Lee to his wife, July 15, 1863, *Wartime Papers*, 551; Lee to Davis, July 12, 1863, *ibid.*, 548.

50. Lee to Davis, June 10, 25, 1863, *Wartime Papers*, 508–9, 530–31.

51. Lee to Davis, June 10, 1863, *ibid.*, 508;

Lee to his wife, July 15, 1863, *ibid.*, 551. See also: Lee to J. E. B. Stuart, June 2, 1863, *O.R.*, XXV, pt. 2, 850.

52. Lee to Seddon, June 8, 1863, *Wartime Papers*, 505.

53. Foote, *The Civil War*, 440.

54. Henry, *Story of the Confederacy*, 272; Hooker to Lincoln, June 10, 1863, *O.R.*, XXVII, pt. 2, 34; Lincoln to Hooker, June 5, 10, 1863, Basler, *Collected Works*, VI, 249, 257. See also: Halleck to Hooker, June 5, 1863, *O.R.*, XXVII, pt. 1, 31–32.

55. Lincoln to Hooker, June 10, 1863, Basler, *Collected Works*, VI, 257; Halleck to Stanton, May 18, 1863, *O.R.*, XXV, pt. 2, 505.

56. Lincoln to Hooker, June 5, 16, 1863, Basler, *Collected Works*, VI, 249–50, 281.

57. Lincoln to Hooker, June 10, 14, 16, 1863, Basler, *Collected Works*, VI, 257, 273, 280–81; Halleck to Hooker, June 5, 1863, *O.R.*, XXVII, pt. 1, 31.

58. Lincoln to Mary Todd Lincoln, June 16, 1863, Basler, *Collected Works*, VI, 283; Lincoln to Parker, June 30, 1863, *ibid.*, 311.

59. Foote, *The Civil War*, II, 443; Lee to Davis, May 11, June 15, 19, 1863, *Wartime Papers*, 484, 515, 521; Lee to Seddon, June 13, 1863, *O.R.*, XXVII, pt. 3, 886; Seddon to Lee, June 10, 1863, *ibid.*, 882. See also: Cooper to D. H. Hill, June 10, 1863, *ibid.*, 880.

60. Lee to Ewell, June 19, 1863, *Wartime Papers*, 521; Lee to Davis, June 23, 25, 1863, *ibid.*, 527–28, 530–31. See also: Lee to Davis, May 7, 1863, *O.R.*, XXV, pt. 2, 782–83.

61. Halleck to Meade, July 28, 1863, *O.R.*, XXVII, pt. 1, 104; Halleck to Schenck, July 9, 1863, *ibid.*, pt. 3, 623; J. R. Meigs to Meade, July 8, 1863, *ibid.*, 607.

62. Couch to Halleck, July 8, 1863, *O.R.*, XXVII, pt. 3, 611; Halleck to Kelley, June 25, July 4, 1863, *ibid.*, 330, 528; Halleck to Foster, June 8, July 5, 1863, *ibid.*, 36–37, 553.

63. Halleck to Dix, June 14, 18, July 1, 3, 4, 1863, *O.R.*, XXVII, pt. 3, 111, 206, pt. 2, 818, July 1, 3, 1863, pt. 3, 625; Dix to Halleck, June 29, July 11, 1863, *ibid.*, pt. 3, 412, 655; Halleck to Potter, June 22, 1863, *ibid.*, 265; Meigs to Ingalls, July 10, 1863, *ibid.*, 631; Welles to S. P. Lee, July 6, 1863, *ibid.*, 582–83.

64. Lee to Davis, June 23, 25, 1863, *Wartime Papers*, 528, 531; Davis to Lee, May 26, 1863, *O.R.*, LI, pt. 2, 717.

65. Lee to Davis, June 25, (two letters), 1863, *Wartime Papers*, 531, 532–33.

66. Rosecran's Report, July 24, 1863, *O.R.*, XXIII, pt. 1, 404, 408.

67. *Ibid.*; Rosecrans to Halleck, July 25, 1863, *ibid.*, pt. 2, 555.

68. Rosecrans to Stanton, July 7, 1863, *O.R.*, XXIII, pt. 2, 518.

69. Cooper to Lee, June 29, 1863, *O.R.*, XXVII, pt. 1, 75–76.

70. Long, *Civil War, Day by Day*, 367.

71. Foote, *The Civil War*, II, 447; Long, *Civil War, Day by Day*, 370–71.

72. Hassler, *Commanders of the Army of the Potomac*, 159–63.

73. Catton, *Never Call Retreat*, 163.

74. *Ibid.*, 186.

75. Foote, *The Civil War*, II, 532.

76. Edward G. Longacre, *The Man Behind the Guns: A Biography of General Henry J. Hunt, Commander of Artillery, Army of the Potomac* (South Brunswick, N.J., and New York, 1977), 173 and *passim*.

77. Foote, *The Civil War*, II, 541; Longacre, *The Man Behind the Guns*, 173.

78. Henry, *Story of the Confederacy*, 281.

79. *Meade's Headquarters 1863–1865, Letters of Colonel Theodore Lyman From the Wilderness to Appomattox*, ed. George R. Agassiz (New York, 1922), 102.

80. Catton, *Never Call Retreat*, 204–5.

81. Wheeler, *The Siege of Vicksburg*, 201–2, 229; Foote, *The Civil War*, II, 410.

82. Wheeler, *Siege of Vicksburg*, 201–2, 229.

83. Hattaway, *Lee*, 97.

84. Foote, *The Civil War*, II, 577.

85. Lee to Davis, July 7, 8, 10, 12, 1863, *Wartime Papers*, 541, 543–44, 545, 548; Lee to his wife, July 12, 15, 1863, *ibid.*, 547, 551.

86. Lee to Davis, July 12, 31, 1863, *Wartime Papers*, 548, 565; Lee to Margaret Stuart, July 26, 1863, *ibid.*, 561; Foote, *The Civil War*, II, 592.

87. Lee to his wife, July 15, 26, 1863, *Wartime Papers*, 551, 560; Lee to Margaret Stuart, July 26, 1863, *ibid.*, 561; Lee to Davis, July 31, 1863, *ibid.*, 565; Davis to Lee, Aug. 11, 1863, *O.R.*, XXIX, 639; Jefferson Davis, *The Rise and Fall of the Confederate Government*, 2 vols. (New York, London, 1958), II, 447.

88. Wade Hampton to J. E. Johnston, July 30, 1863, R. M. Hughes Papers, made available by Mrs. R. M. Hughes, Jr., and Mr. R. M. Hughes III, of Norfolk, Virginia.

89. Davis, *Rise and Fall of the Confederate Government*, II, 447–48.

90. *Ibid.*, 448; Beauregard to Johnston, July 1, 1863, *O.R.*, XXVIII, pt. 2, 173–74.

91. Davis, *Rise and Fall of the Confederate Government*, II, 447. Knowledgeable contemporaries made a realistic assessment of Lee's Gettysburg campaign. Individuals as different as Lincoln and Beauregard realized Lee was conducting a raid, not a penetration, which threatened northern cities. Lincoln perceived it as a Union opportunity and Lee and Davis soberly evaluated it in the light of its objective, to disrupt an expected Union offensive and to help supply Lee's army. Less knowledgeable contemporaries and subsequent writers have often endowed the campaign and, particularly, the battle with far greater significance.

The tremendous attention which the battle itself has received implies the notion that a Confederate victory would have led to some decisive result. These possibilities are worth probing. First, the most cataclysmic consequences would have been annihilation of the Union army. Another outcome might have been that the loss of a big battle on its own soil would have induced the Union to sue for peace.

In attempting to envision the effect of a Confederate victory at Gettysburg fairly, the first place to look for parallel examples ought to be the outcome of Lee's victories at the Seven Days' Battles, Second Manassas, Fredericksburg, and Chancellorsville. In no case did he annihilate the enemy, even though each of the opposing generals in those engagements had less tactical skill than Meade. In every instance little happened other than the enemy's falling back a few miles. One might also consider that perhaps a defeat at Gettysburg could have badly demoralized and disorganized the Union army; but in such an unlikely event Lincoln still had the option of recalling McClellan who possessed the proven ability to remedy such a situation. It is, of course, far more likely that Lincoln and Halleck would have called on Grant.

Few other Civil War battles yield even remotely any different analogy. Even Chattanooga (November, 1863), where the Confederate troops fled in demoralization, produced results little different from Lee's victories. Always the defeated army found safety in retreat. Save for a few instances—Richmond, Kentucky, or Nashville—none of them at all similar to the situation at Gettysburg and in no way arguably parallel, always the defeated Civil War army could find safety in retreat and still thereafter offer resistance.

If one scrutinizes the famous victories in Europe during the era of the musket and the bayonet, few yield any different possible results than those already explored. Of them all, Blenheim might be selected as the proper analogy, especially as the French center was broken. The French loss of two-thirds of their army opposed to only a 20 percent loss for the Anglo-Imperial forces certainly provides as great a tactical victory as one could expect. A comparable win at Gettysburg would have left Meade with barely 35,000 men to oppose perhaps 60,000 Confederates. The problem in making this analogy into a decisive battle is that, like the outcome of Blenheim, the enemy retreats, secures reinforcements from other armies, and the original situation is restored in a different place. One must recall that Blenheim was the first, not the last, battle in the War of the Spanish Succession.

From a military point of view, then, it is impossible to project any effect from a Confederate victory than that Meade, or his successor, would have fallen back to a strong position and would have been reinforced. Lee then would have been presented with the problem of winning all over again. The Union army in a strong defensive emplacement would have placed Lee in the position of either having to attack at a distinct disadvantage or attempting to maneuver the federal general out of position. In all probability, in view of the tenuous nature of Lee's supply and his original defensive purpose in entering Pennsylvania, he would have eventually fallen back to Virginia, though perhaps at his own more leisurely pace. Thus the case for Gettysburg's decisiveness must rest not upon military but upon political considerations.

The assumption of political significance probably depends upon the presumption of a Confederate success comparable to Blenheim. A Confederate victory comparable only to Second Manassas or the Seven Days' Battles, followed by the Army of the Potomac's standing in a strong position east of Gettysburg, does not suggest that any political consequences would have followed.

Let us assume the maximum: that following a hypothetical Union disaster at Gettysburg, resulting in perhaps the loss of two-thirds of Meade's army, the Federals had abandoned Washington and Baltimore in order to concentrate an immense force to defend Philadelphia. Would the outcome have been a northern perception that the war was lost and a public demand for ending the war on terms of Confederate independence? The loss of Washington in the War of 1812 and of both New York and Philadelphia in the American Revolution did not produce peace overtures to the British. Indeed, a good case can be made that there was more unity in support of the war by 1863 than existed when Washington and Philadelphia fell in earlier wars. And the American reaction to the loss of their capital in earlier wars was not unique. The losses of Vienna in 1805 and 1809 were mere incidents of campaigns whose decisive phases came later. Frederick's loss of Berlin to a Russian raiding party affected the outcome of the Seven Years' War not at all. The siege of Paris in 1870–71, following overwhelming military catastrophes, produced an intensification of French military efforts.

Of course, the administration would not have abandoned Washington and Baltimore even if McClellan had concentrated the main army before Philadelphia. Easily supplied, as well as evacuated, by water, Washington and Baltimore would have remained garrisoned and difficult to capture except by a major force. It would have been almost impossible for Lee to exploit the weakness of their garrisons unless he again risked dividing his army, as he did when he took Harper's Ferry during the Antietam campaign. In the midst of hostile Pennsylvania and facing a rapidly reinforcing enemy, Lee would have found it hard to maintain his position much less secure political benefits from winning a Blenheim at Gettysburg.

The significance of battles tends to be proportionate to the political stakes involved. If the cession of a province is the objective, a defeat, signalizing bleak military prospects, may cause the losing side to begin negotiations. If a fundamental shift in the balance of power is perceived as the issue, battles do not end wars. If national existence is at stake, neither Brandywine nor Long Island in the Revolution nor Shiloh, Vicksburg, and Gettysburg caused an end to war. It seems unlikely, therefore, that a defeat at Gettysburg, however, catastrophic, would have brought an end to the Civil War; for the Confederacy was aiming, if not at Union national existence, then at least at a fundamental change in the balance of power in North America. The Confederacy had goals too ambitious for them to be won by a Blenheim in Pennsylvania.

Perhaps, then, Lee and Davis's evaluation of the campaign as a success is more appropriate than terming it a Confederate high-water mark. Their estimate harmonizes both with the original objectives and with the opportunities actually available. Lee's advance into Pennsylvania did dominate military operations on the Virginia front for three months and, for at least two of these months, gave him new sources of supplies. These three months came in the middle of the campaigning season of 1863.

A defeat in battle and heavy casualties marred the campaign itself. But casualties could be expected as the result of the anticipated Union spring offensive. That the battle took place in Pennsylvania meant that the Confederates lost no territory, that they conserved the vital logistical area in Virginia, and that they were relieved temporarily of the burden of supporting their army. The Gettysburg campaign was a defeat for the Confederacy only if a victory in the battle could be expected to produce consequences quite unlike those of other Civil War victories. Only by a criterion that required the campaign to influence events on the Mississippi can Lee's invasion of Pennsylvania be termed correctly a failure; it delayed the fall of Vicksburg not at all.

Like the Battle of Gettysburg, the significance of the fall of Vicksburg lies primarily in the heavy casualties sustained by the Confederates. Pemberton surrendered nearly 30,000 men. True, the North secured control of the entire Mississippi River, for four days after Vicksburg surrendered, so also did Port Hudson, Louisiana, the last southern stronghold on the waterway; then Pemberton's bungling and Grant's energy and skill had turned a campaign with a logistical objective, opening the Mississippi to Union navigation and closing it to Confederate transit, into a successful campaign of annihilation. Like Floyd, Pemberton had given Grant and the navy a major victory of annihilation, losing one of the three major armies of the Confederacy precisely on the day after Lee had lost 28,000 men at Gettysburg. It was well for the Union that Pemberton had cooperated so effectively by losing his army, for, except for psychological and domestic political advantages, the conquest of the Mississippi proved almost a white elephant.

The loss of transit between East and West hurt Confederate supply not at all, for the two parts of the Confederacy effectively had long been separated logistically. Furthermore, contrary to the assumption commonly made, the Confederacy's main logistical need in moving supplies across the Mississippi was from east to west. The West did, however, possess food and livestock. "During the early stages of the war the Richmond bureaus had been anxious to secure wool, leather, and beef on the hoof from

this section and had enjoyed a limited success for a time." Otherwise, as early as 1861 Quartermaster General Abraham C. Myers had informed his Texas subordinates "that they would have to fend for themselves or trade with Mexico for supplies." In 1862 the loss of Memphis and New Orleans had "made communication with Texas little more than a theory." More critical for Confederate supply was the loss of New Orleans, because it "provided a base for the extension of Union control northward up the Mississippi Valley, enabling Union forces virtually to eliminate the movement of cattle, horses, sugar, wool and molasses east across the river and the movement of arms and equipment westward." For this reason the loss, a year later, of Vicksburg and Port Hudson "was not a vital blow in terms of supply management, for the two sections of the Confederacy had long since ceased to rely on each other" (Goff, *Confederate Supply*, 29, 133, 58, 59, 250).

The strategic consequences of the loss of communication between the two halves of the Confederacy were hardly more significant than the logistical. Though in November and December, 1862, Davis and Randolph unsuccessfully sought reinforcements from Arkansas, no Confederate troops had made any strategic movement from west to east of the river in more than a year, not since Van Dorn had joined Beauregard soon after Shiloh. Lacking trunkline railways in their portion of the transMississippi, the Confederates had to depend on the intermittently navigable rivers in Arkansas. This unreliable transportation system had limited movements between east and west of that rapid and temporary kind which had characterized Confederate operations east of the river. In mid-1862, with Union control of the Mississippi as far south as Vicksburg, the Confederates had lost even this limited capability, because the federal Navy controlled the mouths of the White and Arkansas rivers. With the loss of these river routes, the Confederates operated on exterior lines when compared with the opposing Union armies, who enjoyed the navigation of the Ohio, Missouri, and most of the Mississippi and had railroads in Missouri and a trunk-line between St. Louis and Louisville, Kentucky. Yet, after the fall of Vicksburg, these very deficiencies in the Confederate transportation network handicapped Union operations, because, to supply their armies, they had to rely on the Mississippi and its intermittently navigable tributaries.

That the Confederate trans-Mississippi was not a strategic or logistical unit with the area east of the river had been realized by Beauregard as early as the spring of 1862 when he had rather complacently accepted the loss of control of the Mississippi. This strategic situation had also been recognized when the region had been separated from Department Number Two and erected into a separate department. Subsequent enthusiasm in late 1862 for combining its forces with those in Mississippi, an enthusiasm shared by Davis as well as Johnston and Secretary of War Randolph, had been based on an erroneous idea that there were enormous and redundant forces in Arkansas.

To the Confederacy, the loss of the Mississippi was purely a loss of prestige and a psychological defeat: their country was cut in half. Not only then had the Union not gained much in securing the complement of the Confederate loss, because that loss was nearly zero, but in a sense it had acquired a real albatross—more territory to be guarded. Instead of Confederate troops guarding Vicksburg, there were now Union troops on duty there. They had to defend the long frontier between Memphis and Baton Rouge against raiders and individual snipers who would fire on passing steamboats. Though the river was perfectly secure for the passage of convoyed military supplies, normal traffic was subject to harassment and must be defended, if only because of the traditional importance of Mississippi River commerce and the prestige of having opened the river. After the fall of Vicksburg at least 15,000 men were employed in defending the nonmilitary commerce of the river and interdicting Confederate communications (Grant to Halleck, Sept. 30, 1863, *O.R.*, XXX, pt. 3, 944).

This commerce did not, however, revive to a volume even approaching its prewar level. In the fiscal year 1860, 333 American ships carrying 180,765 tons sailed from the mouth of the Mississippi. But during 1864, only 179 ships with 55,039 tons of cargo cleared the Crescent City. Though exports from New Orleans originated from many other sources than down-river traffic from the North, certainly much of the 70 percent reduction in tonnage must have resulted from the reduction in down-river trade from points north of Memphis. The North's commercial gains from the opening of the river were, then, not nearly as important as had been hoped nor as important as the traditional significance of the river would have indicated (U.S. Congress, Senate Executive Document, *Commerce and Navigation, 1860*, 36th Cong., 1st Sess., 1861. Serial No. 1087, 556; and U.S. Congress, Senate Executive Document, *Commerce and Naviga-*

tion, 1864, 38th Cong., 2nd Sess., 1865. Serial No. 1231, 448).

Several factors affected the diminished influence of the river on northern business. The close proximity of war activities to essential river towns such as Cincinnati and St. Louis lessened their worth as freight centers. Searching for alternative routes, the northwesterners increasingly shipped overland to Chicago and eastward via northern waterways (Emerson D. Fite, *Social and Industrial Conditions in the North During the Civil War* [New York, 1910], 48). Rail transportation appeared more and more attractive, not the least reason being the increasingly critical shortage of adequate crews and trained boatmen. And, quite importantly, despite Union naval patrols, southern guerrilla bands threatened the safety of shipments southward after Vicksburg's capitulation. Thus it became increasingly difficult to charter commercial vessels.

As to what the South lost, by far the heaviest deprivation was the army, together with its 172 cannon, about 60,000 muskets, and a significant amount of ammunition. But trade and supplies, limited long before Vicksburg fell, continued unabated. As late as April, 1864, Confederate leaders discussed the possibility of re-establishing a force on the river. Powerful Confederate forces still operated within striking distance, and guerrilla bands constantly harassed the Union positions. While southern forces might approach the river at their peril, they nevertheless obstinately made crossings. In February, 1864, War Secretary Seddon authorized military escort and protection for trading operations at selected points on the river. And in May, 1864, Union Brigadier General Mason Brayman, a troop commander stationed on the river, complained bitterly of the rife illicit traffic in contraband goods, carried on, he asserted, by many southerners who previously had taken loyalty oaths. Thus, the northerners never completely blocked the transfer of supplies across the great river (*O.R.*, XXXII, pt. 3, 856–58, pt. 2, 801, pt. 1, 508–9).

Except for the capture of the defending army, neither the South lost nor the Union gained very much strategically or logistically from the Union's capture of Vicksburg. The principal effect was psychological. In losing the river the South lost heavily in terms of morale. The North gained much. During 1862 the cry of "On to Vicksburg" had been as common in the midwestern states as the "On to Richmond" slogan had been in the east. The Lincoln administration thus gained a victory important for morale and "the

South was robbed of its greatest trump in domestic affairs—control of the mouth" of the Mississippi (Sylvanus Cadwallader, *Three Years With Grant as Recalled by War Correspondent Sylvanus Cadwallader*, ed. Benjamin P. Thomas [New York, 1956], 59; Thomas L. Connelly, "Vicksburg: Strategic Point or Propaganda Device?" *Military Affairs* [Apr., 1970], 49–53).

I4 ☆ TO CHATTANOOGA

James Longstreet

THE THREE MAJOR SUCCESSES which rewarded Grant, Meade, and Rosecrans did not signal a relaxation of a sustained Union offensive. Despite the summer heat, a long-planned effort against Charleston's defenses, primarily by the army, began early in July just as Sherman was pushing Johnston eastward to Jackson, the Mississippi capital, and Rosecrans, too, was again urged forward "to give the finishing blow to the rebellion," while Meade closely followed Lee into Virginia.[1]

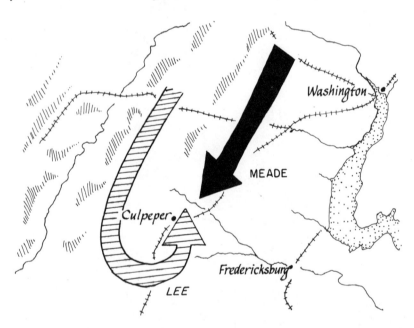

Lee's Withdrawal

But notwithstanding Lincoln's hopes for the exploitation of the victory at Gettysburg, Virginia became a quiet theatre. To be sure, Halleck desired that Meade give Lee another "severe pounding" and then launch raids along the coast. Lincoln was even more optimistic, almost emphatic, in his aspiration to take advantage of what he termed "the best opportunity we have had since the war began." With Lee's back against the suddenly unfordable Potomac, Lincoln hoped "to prevent his crossing and destroy him." Lincoln felt that, if the Battle of Gettysburg could be followed "by the literal or substantial destruction of Lee's army, the rebellion will be over."[2]

Meade proceeded cautiously, for he believed Lee did "not intend to cross the river," but, he said, "his bridges being destroyed, he has been compelled to make a stand, and will of course make a desperate one." But while Meade did expect to have ample time to attack Lee, he also anticipated finding him "in a strong position well covered with artillery." Meade had no "desire to imitate his example at Gettysburg, and assault a position where the chances were so greatly against success." Meade did find Lee at Williamsport in a strong position with his back to the river. After an almost unanimous vote of Meade's generals against an immediate attack, he ordered reconnoitering and, while this proceeded, Lee slipped away.

Lee's escape made the President frantic, because he believed that Lee had been within Meade's "easy grasp" and to have "closed upon him would," he stated, "in connection with our other late successes, have ended the war." With the Confederates' back to the river, Lincoln expected that Lee's army could have been destroyed and that "such destruction was perfectly easy." The President believed that victory was "certain" and confided to his secretary: "We had them in our grasp. We had only to stretch forth our hands and they were ours."[3]

The culmination of nine months of strategic thought and planning, which had been going on since the earlier opportunity of the Antietam campaign, doubtless stirred the President's unrealistic thought that the destruction of Lee's army would be easy. "We had," Lincoln explained, "gone through all the labor of tilling & planting an enormous crop & when it was ripe we did not harvest it." In his exasperation with "this weakness, this indifference" of the "Potomac generals" the President grandiosely thought: "If I had gone up there, I could have whipped them myself."[4]

Just as the immense significance of the strategic results blinded Lincoln to Meade's tactical difficulties, so too did the enormous tactical strength of Lee's position obscure for Meade the potentially decisive strategic outcome of a victory, however unlikely it might be. Though Meade conceded that "perhaps the President was right," he did not truly think so, especially after inspecting Lee's evacuated works. McClellan's success at Malvern Hill supported Meade's view, just as Lincoln's strategic hopes found reinforcement in the fate of the Confederate armies when they were pressed to the rivers at Fort Donelson and Vicksburg. Because of the large size of the strategic stakes, Meade should have promptly made an effort in a gamble against the long tactical odds; yet it is easy to sympathize with the reluctance of Meade and his generals who had just again observed the power of the defense when they had so successfully repelled Pickett's frontal assault at Gettysburg.[5]

In his disappointment at Lee's escape, Lincoln overlooked the real success which had rewarded his strategy. He had as his goal to concentrate in the West, keep away from a deadlock in Richmond's trenches, and wait for Lee to make a mistake. At Gettysburg, Lee made that mistake, a very big one, losing 28,000 men in a three-day, largely frontal battle. In proportion to the total Union and Confederate forces in the field, Lee's losses nearly doubled those of Meade. Whereas Lee and Davis regarded the Gettysburg campaign as a success, this evaluation was based on the assumption that it had thwarted a major Union offensive. With no such offensive in contemplation, Lincoln and Halleck correctly saw it as playing into the hands of their strategy and should have felt more satisfaction at the result. Meade took up a position along the Rappahannock on General Pope's line of operations of the previous summer and Lee settled into a position opposite him.

Events at Charleston rather starkly contrasted with these quiescent Virginia maneuvers, as Union forces launched a new attack, with Morris Island the initial objective. This attack was based on the concept of the army's capturing fortified points in order to open for the Navy the way into the harbor. Bruce Catton, in some of his most artful prose, wrote: "Nobody in the Civil War would have paid the least attention to Morris Island except for two facts: the main ship channel to Charleston ran parallel to its length a mile offshore, and the northern tip of the island was less than a mile from Fort Sumter. Because these things were so, Morris Island in 1863 became the deadliest sandpit on earth. It was dug up by spades and by high explosive, almost sunk by sheer weight of metal and human misery, fought for with a maximum of courage and technical capacity and a minimum of strategic understanding; a place of no real consequence, lying at the end of one of those insane chains of war-time logic in which men step from one undeniable truth to another and so come at last to a land of crippling nonsense."[6]

A new federal commander, a capable engineer officer, Brigadier General Quincy A. Gillmore, lead the operation. On July 10, 1863, Yankee troops landed on the south end of Morris Island in an attempt to take Fort or Battery Wagner, one of the harbor's main defenses. On the next day they assaulted and gained the parapet, but then had to withdraw under heavy fire. This episode, incidentally, drew special attention because of the role played in it by black troops. The earlier deployment of Negroes against saltworks in Florida did not receive much publicity. Among the leading regiments in the Battery Wagner attack was the Fifty-fourth Massachusetts, blacks who felt determined and even obligated to prove the valor and fighting capabilities of their race. Although unable to take the fort, they displayed a grim and vicious tenacity, staying on the walls until the Confederates literally shot them to pieces. The white colonel and his black orderly sergeant died side by side on the parapet. "As brave a colonel as ever lived," one Confederate defender conceded, and the men are "as fine-looking a set as I ever saw—large, strong, muscular fellows."[7]

The Federals wished to sieze Charleston for several reasons: one, symbolic, to secure the spot where the war had begun; another, and much more important, Charleston, along with Wilmington, North Carolina, provided the Confederates with ports from which they rather effectively maintained regular shipping through the sieve-like federal blockade. Between 1861 and 1865, 87 percent of all steamers and 81 percent of all sailing vessels attempting to enter or exit these two ports avoided capture.

After the failure of the assaults on July 10 and July 18, the Federals resorted to a somewhat more conventional siege operation, highlighted by three major artillery bombardments of unprecedented magnitude. The first lasted for seventeen days and nights, August 17 to September 2, 1863. Union artillery hurled 938 shots. As Bruce Catton put it, "Each day the garrison grew weaker and the Northern siege lines came closer, each day the fort looked less and less like a fort and more like an uneven mound of earth, and it went on week after week, . . . the bombardment growing worse each day, as if the whole war had turned into a struggle for possession of this poor sand hill." Lincoln, incidentally, apparently reflecting a nonchalant mood, spent the second day of the bombardment testing the new breech-loading Spencer rifle, firing a few shots in Treasury Park.[8]

Sumter's walls crumbled, but the rubble and sand formed an even more effective shield against further fire. The second bombardment of 627 shots lasted forty-one days, from October 26 to December 6, 1863. The Federals managed finally to force the Confederates to evacuate Battery Wagner and Morris Island, but the rebel force, under Beauregard, tenaciously held both Fort Sumter and Charleston. President Davis heartily applauded Beauregard's determination. Still a third bombardment occurred many months later, lasting for sixty days, from July 7 to September 8, 1864; but despite the heaviest possible artillery fire and the reduction of the fort to a mere pile of rubble the Confederate garrison of only 300 men held tenaciously. Every sunset they pluckily fired a defiant salute to their flag and each night repaired the worst damage caused by the day's shelling. Supply lines between the city and the fort remained open to the end.

When federal troops initially attacked at Charleston, the Confederate War Department promptly ordered troops to move from Wilmington, via the coastal pipeline, to reinforce the garrison under Beauregard. Virginia would send replacements for the men sent from Wilmington. Though these additional troops failed to prevent a partial Union success at Charleston, their availability via the pipeline from Virginia testified to the consistently employed Confederate economy of force which had earlier enabled Beauregard to send troops west where they became a part of Johnston's army.[9]

Against Grant's powerfully reinforced army, Johnston had not taken the offensive. Handicapped by railroads broken by Grant and a lack of field transportation, Johnston had declined to make a frontal attack against Grant's covering force commanded by Sherman. Johnston's failure caused President Davis to lose confidence in him. To a degree Johnston was a scapegoat for Davis's disappointment in a summer when Confederate defeat occurred on every front. Johnston's situation with his relieving army compared to that of Meade when he elected not to assail Lee at Williamsport—the almost certain tactical failure of a frontal attack balanced against a long-shot, immense strategic gain. Davis responded, like Lincoln, with great frustration and disappointment. In Johnston's case, friction had already occurred over rank between the touchy general and the President. Worn down by two years of intense labor, President Davis reacted vociferously against Johnston. Johnston's friend and western concentration bloc leader, Senator Wigfall, wrote: The President is denouncing Johnston "in the most violent manner . . . & attributing the fall of Vicksburg to him & to him alone, regretting that he had been sent to the West & accusing himself of weakness in yielding to outside influence etc. His utter want of capacity he had always known etc. Has it ever occurred to you that Davis' mind is becoming unsettled? No sane man would act as he is doing. I fear that his bad health & bad temper are undermining his reason & that the foundation is already sapped." During the summer the President and the general engaged in a correspondence full of recrimination, but, although one was considered, no court of inquiry convened and Johnston remained in command in Mississippi.[10]

In spite of Pemberton's major contribution to the disaster, the President did not blame him. But as no satisfactory assignment could be found for the unpopular lieutenant general, Pemberton finally resigned his commission. The loyal, Pennsylvania-born Confederate then selflessly accepted a commission as a lieutenant colonel in the artillery, where he served very capably until the war's end.

Johnston's assignment to conduct the relief operation at Vicksburg in effect eliminated the Department of the West. This left four separate departments in that region. East of the Mississippi were those of Johnston in Mississippi, Bragg in Middle Tennessee, and the quasi-independent Department of East Tennessee, to which Simon Bolivar Buckner had just been assigned. After surrendering Fort Donelson, the capable Buckner had been exchanged and served first as a division commander at the Battle of Perryville and then as commander at Mobile. Like most other Kentuckians with a genuine commitment to the Confederacy, Buckner belonged to the western concentration bloc. His relations with Bragg had been exacerbated when, in a step to secure greater unity of command, the War Department gave Bragg operational control of his department.

West of the Mississippi the removal of Lieutenant General Theophilus H. Holmes strengthened the Confederates. Called "Granny Holmes" by his men, the ineffectual and physically debilitated Holmes was suspected of having "softening of the brain" and was criticized as "weak, vacillating, and totally devoid of energy." The same critic believed that the fifty-nine-year-old Holmes's "entire administration revolved around the axis of a simple love for some wealthy Arkansas widow." Even so, Holmes was not easy on his subordinates and some of his men overheard him "cuss and roar" as he would "bawl out" his staff. After service in the trans-Mississippi as a district commander, Holmes received a largely administrative assignment in charge of reserve forces in North Carolina. Here he could do little harm and could make a contribution commensurate with his modest talents. The capable Edmund Kirby Smith, a veteran of First Bull Run and Bragg's Kentucky campaign, succeeded Holmes in command of the huge trans-Mississippi department.[11]

The Union administration in the West was far more fragmented than the Confederate for there the Union had five separate departments: Burnside in Kentucky with the mission of advancing into East Tennessee and protecting Kentucky and the Louisville and Nashville railroad from raids; Rosecrans in Middle Tennessee with the objective of taking Chattanooga and cutting the direct rail connection between Atlanta and Richmond; Banks on the lower Mississippi attempting to complete the conquest of the river at Port Hudson and then, presumably, continuing toward his original goal, Texas; the capable John M. Schofield, who had succeeded Curtis, trying to defend Missouri and, if he could get his troops back from Grant, invade Arkansas; and Grant, with the Army of the Tennessee, now in West Tennessee and along the Mississippi, having accomplished their aim, to open the river.

The Union general in chief turned his attention toward this complex of interrelated theatres in early July. Though the West badly needed a more unified command, Halleck maintained the organization which he had left undisturbed from the first for fear of presenting openings for the appointment of political generals. The general in chief did expect, however, to keep his strategy free of political influence, because, as he wrote his protégé, Schofield, "So long as we can attain success, the interference of politicians in military matters can be resisted, but on the first disaster they press upon us like a pack of hungry wolves."[12]

As Rosecrans prepared for another forward movement, Halleck acted on intelligence that Bragg was seeking help from Buckner as a reason to urge Burnside to advance into East Tennessee. But Burnside seemed immovable, apparently "tied fast to Cincinnati," and Rosecrans's preparations would, as usual, be slow, requiring "a great deal of care, labor, watchfulness, and combined effort, to insure the successful advance through the mountains on Chattanooga." Still the general in chief's attention focused on the Mississippi as the primary theatre. The river was still a center of activity, because Grant was engaged with Johnston and Banks was so apprehensive about his communications with New Orleans that, on the eve of Gillmore's Charleston offensive, Halleck entertained the thought of sending reinforcements from Charleston to Banks.[13]

After the fall of Vicksburg, Halleck based his concept for western campaigns on the use of the Mississippi River as "the base of future operations east and west." In this way the Union armies could exploit their interior position between the two halves of the severed Confederates, concentrating against first one and then the other. This did not, however, answer the "important question" of where to strike first. Halleck did ask Grant for his views, but Halleck clearly desired a concentration against the weaker half of the Confederacy, his old departmental area of the trans-Mississippi. He thought he saw large dividends from a campaign in Louisiana and Arkansas if the Union could control Little Rock and the line of the Arkansas River. The "large forces . . . comparatively neutralized in Missouri" by threatened raids from Arkansas could then be free to join Grant's army in "its operations at the South." This strategy also offered political advantages for, "if the organized rebel forces could be driven from Arkansas and Louisiana, these States would immediately be restored to the Union. Texas would follow almost of its own accord." Successful reconstruction of these states would have the added advantage of supplying political supporters for the Lincoln administration's policies against their radical opponents.[14]

A report of a Confederate raid into Missouri precipitated Union action in the West. Holmes, as commander of the district of Arkansas, initiated an unsuccessful July 4 assault on the fortified Union position of Helena. In this frenzied sideshow, something of an aberration on the same day that Vicksburg surrendered and the day after Pickett's charge, men fought fruitlessly in a parching heat that eventually induced many of them to risk their lives just to get sips of water from the canteens of the dead.

Soon after that assault, Schofield reported that another of Kirby Smith's subordinates, Major General Sterling Price, was leading a powerful raid toward Missouri. More able than Holmes, the portly Price, a well-respected former governor of Missouri, had fought in the Mexican War. In spite of involvement with defeats at Pea Ridge, Iuka, Corinth, and Helena, "Old Pap" Price enjoyed popularity with his men and respect from his opponents. To the report of Price's movement, Halleck responded immediately and emphatically. He directed Grant to reinforce Arkansas and ordered both commands to advance against Price by marching along the White River to "move on his rear, so as to cut off his retreat," thus compelling Price's 12,000 men to "disperse or surrender." In this way a major summer campaign began which would not capture Price but would lead, in September, to the fall of Little Rock when Union forces, drawn from Missouri, from Helena, and from Grant's army, would unite before Arkansas's capital and quickly prove able to turn Price's position and occupy the city.[15]

By the time this campaign had begun, Halleck had a clear conception of the overall summer strategy for the West. To Grant's suggestion for a move-

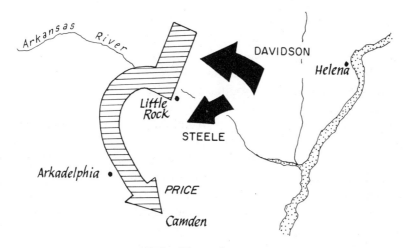

Price Turned

ment against Mobile, Alabama, Halleck responded that it would be "best to clean up a little." He believed Grant should drive Johnston back, assist Banks "in cleaning out Western Louisiana," and defeat Price and occupy the line of the Arkansas River. "When these things are accomplished," wrote Halleck, "there will be a large available force to operate either on Mobile or Texas." Thus he turned down Grant's very promising suggestion for a seaborne attack on Mobile which would have kept up the pressure on the weakened armies of Johnston and Bragg. Instead, he returned to his long-deferred project of using the Arkansas and White rivers as lines of operation and supply in order to conquer Arkansas and relieve Missouri from the threat of raids. Yet his strategy was sound in principle: Drive the weaker trans-Mississippi half of the Confederacy from the war and then concentrate all forces against the stronger half. But this strategy almost suspended offensive operations against the stronger half of the Confederacy.[16]

Halleck understood this and planned to strengthen the forces in Tennessee by returning Burnside's Ninth Corps to him or by using it to reinforce Rosecrans. The general in chief seemed resigned to surrendering the initiative east of the Mississippi when he realized that "if Johnston should unite with Bragg, we may be obliged," he explained, "to send Rosecrans more troops than the Ninth Corps," or "Johnston may be so reinforced as to require all" of Grant's forces to resist him. "In other words, wherever the enemy concentrates we must concentrate to oppose him."[17]

In rejecting the Mobile campaign, the general in chief saw no way to keep any pressure on Johnston's army in central Mississippi. Like Grant, Halleck understood the difficulty in attempting a summer march eastward across Mississippi in the face of drought, heat, and destroyed railroads. Only a campaign from Mobile northward along the Alabama River would have been feasible logistically and able fully to occupy Johnston's army in resisting so menacing a threat to southern communications and supplies.

Secretary of the Navy Gideon Welles, who was very hostile to Halleck, often characterized him as "heavy, sluggish, not prepared to express an opinion." Though Welles often viewed him inaccurately, there was some truth, in the summer of 1863, in Welles's failure "to see, hear, or obtain evidence of power, or will, or talent, or originality on the part of General Halleck. He has suggested nothing, decided nothing, done nothing, but scold and smoke and scratch his elbows." Rather than holding the initiative and vigorously exploiting victories, the general in chief seemed driven by events and at least partially paralyzed by the many difficulties he faced. To a degree any feeling of urgency for a more active campaign may have been tempered by the prevalent view that troops could not stand active operations in the southern summer. Even in the more temperate Virginia theatre, he cautioned Meade, "during this extreme heat, troops and animals should be moved as little as possible."[18]

Though both Banks and Grant preferred a campaign against Mobile after the completion of preliminary operations, Halleck preferred Texas. A directive from the President to mount an immediate expedition to Texas cut short the debate about where later to concentrate. Though Lincoln found Mobile "tempting," he wished to return to the original plan to open Texas cotton cultivation to free labor. French intervention in Mexico also convinced the President and secretary of state that they should plant the flag in Texas in order to forestall any possible French interest in that adjacent Confederate state. Banks therefore received a reinforcement of a corps of 13,000 men from Grant. Instead of the Red River route, Banks chose to go by sea, spending the fall, at first unsuccessfully, in making landings on the Texas coast. He failed, however, to occupy a significant amount of territory.[19]

On July 3, with the fall of Vicksburg clearly imminent, Grant and Sherman had begun to implement their next move. Telling Sherman that he wanted "Johnston broken up as effectually as possible, and [railroads] destroyed," Grant expressly directed Sherman, "Drive Johnston from the Mississippi Central Railroad; destroy bridges as far as Grenada with your cavalry, and do the enemy all the harm possible." Leaving it to Sherman to select Canton or Jackson as the "most effective place to strike," Grant envisioned that he would need to "attack Johnston" in order to reach the railroads. If, however, an unforeseen emergency developed, Sherman's move would not be a protracted expedition and his forces could soon return.[20]

At the same time, Sherman was explaining to Grant his ideas for executing their plan for action against Johnston. Though anxious to avoid marching because he feared "the dust, heat, and drought quite as much as the enemy," Sherman outlined his slightly more ambitious plan of advancing "on Jackson and, if necessary, Meridian, destroying, of course, the railroad and doing all manner of harm." Promptly approving Sherman's plan, Grant told him: "I want you to drive Johnston out in your own way, and inflict on the enemy all the punishment you can."[21]

Grant's efforts to provide complete security for the federal position on the east bank of the Mississippi also included an expedition northeastward against a Confederate force at work fortifying Yazoo City. In order "to break them up," the Union commander had to "drive the enemy from that place," to "gather the heavy guns the rebels have there, and to capture, if possible, the steamers the enemy have in the Yazoo River."[22]

Though Sherman did drive Johnston across the Pearl River, the overnight evacuation of Jackson by that elusive Confederate general "succeeded in carrying off most of his material and men," thus preventing Sherman from carrying out Grant's wish that Johnston receive a "good thrashing" and lose "artillery, transportation, and munitions of war." Yet the brief siege of Jackson and Sherman's outflanking intrenchments, which forced Johnston's withdrawal, did permit the accomplishment of Grant and Sherman's objectives for the campaign. These goals extended far beyond merely forcing Johnston's retreat. To have been able to "break up Johnston's army," even though it retained artillery and transportation, had permitted Sherman "to destroy the rolling stock and everything valuable for carrying on war."[23]

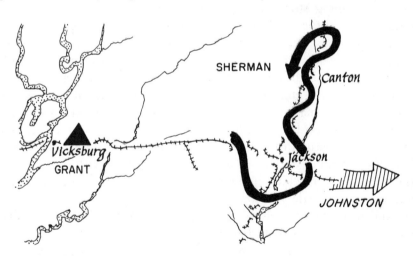

Evacuation of Jackson

Although directed to return to Vicksburg once he had accomplished this objective, Sherman with his destructive thoroughness made the task take several days. Regiments marched along the railroad tracks with his directions: "Turn over the track" with the "men forming line and seizing ties on one side and bearing it over, then making fires of the ties and placing the rails thereon, after which the line will form, march along, turn over and burn another section." They intended the fire not only to destroy the ties but to cause the rails "to be bent by the heat," early versions of the later-famous "Sherman neckties." Sherman also allowed some of the men to divert occasionally to nearby plantations for looting and destruction. In one bizarre episode a cavalryman carried away a grandfather's clock, intending only to take it apart to "get a pair of the little wheels out of it for spur rowels." The soldiers burned several houses, leaving nothing but their blackened chimneys, called thereafter "Sherman monuments," or perhaps more aptly, "Sherman tombstones."[24]

Johnston retreated eastward unpursued because Sherman had decided that a march toward Meridian would "be foreign," he said, "to our present enterprise." Grant, disappointed that Johnston had lost so little artillery and transportation, suggested adding pursuit to the plan after all and asked whether following Johnston would not "have the effect to make him abandon much of his train, and many of his men to desert." Sherman, however, stuck with Grant's earlier injunction to him, Do not "wear your men out," and, exercising the discretion given him, decided that the weather was "too hot and the country too destitute of water" to attempt to follow Johnston toward Meridian and Selma. "That," Sherman thought, "must be deferred to October."[25]

Grant had instructed Sherman: Since "the object of the expedition" is "to break up Johnston's army and divert it from our rear, and, if possible, to destroy the rolling stock and everything valuable for carrying on war, or placing it beyond the reach of the rebel army, you may return to Vicksburg as soon as this object is accomplished." Beginning his retreat, Sherman pointed with pride to the army's accomplishments: "The railroad has been broken up for 40 miles north, including the costly bridge above Canton and the extensive machine shops, cars, etc., in Canton, with fully 12 miles of track burned and destroyed. In like manner it has been destroyed for 60 miles south . . . and Jackson cannot again become a place for the assemblage of men and material with which to threaten the Mississippi River." Sherman had also broken the railroad for ten miles to the east of Jackson. Together with a ten-mile stretch to the west of town which he had broken in May, this destruction of communications had made Jackson no longer "a place for the enemy to collect stores and men from which to" base an attack on the Mississippi. His expedition had truly "fulfilled all that could have been reasonably expected."[26]

By evacuating Jackson, Grant and Sherman were implementing the ideas on which they had agreed the previous fall. Their fundamental concept had been to "hold to the river absolutely and leave the interior alone," except "by a quick march break the railroad, where," Sherman said, "we could make ourselves so busy that our descent would be dreaded the whole length of the river." Sherman, typically, then added a political dimension to the attack on the enemy's logistical infrastructure when he pointed out that "the loss of negroes and other property" would convince the enemy "that war is not the remedy for the political evils of which they complained."[27]

"The heat and dust being suffocating," Grant directed Sherman: "Take your own time returning" to Vicksburg. Meanwhile Grant used his remaining forces to inflict punishment on the Confederates wherever he found them. His expedition "to Yazoo City to break up that place" had succeeded; he captured the town "with considerable stores, five or six pieces of artillery, and several hundred prisoners," as well as one gunboat and all the public stores. After sending "a brigade to Natchez, to collect a large number of Texas cattle . . . destined for Johnston's army," Grant exultantly announced to the general in chief that, not only had he "captured numbers of prisoners and 5,000 head of Texas cattle," but his expedition had gone into Louisiana and "captured more prisoners" and "a number of trains loaded with ammunition. Over 2,000,000 rounds of musket ammunition were brought back to Natchez with the teams captured, and 268,000 rounds, besides artillery ammunition, destroyed."[28]

Grant liked this sort of operation, capturing cattle and ammunition, for it both weakened the Confederates and strengthened the Federals. Just as opening the Mississippi had hurt Confederate morale and communications as well as facilitated Union military and commercial navigation, capturing Confederate cattle and munitions for his own use was "like arming the negroes," because it would "act as a two-edged sword, cutting both ways." This approach, simultaneously aiding the Union and hurting the Confederacy, lay behind Grant's parole of the prisoners at Vicksburg. He thought it better than "unconditional surrender" because it left available Union "transports and troops for immediate use" rather than leaving them tied up guarding and shipping thousands of prisoners who would instead have to be fed and transported by the Confederates.[29]

After many months with Vicksburg as his objective, Grant now had "but little idea" of what was "next to be done with" the "western forces." He waited, expressing "hope to have instructions from Washington," continued his operations against Confederate bases and supplies near the river, and projected operations across the Mississippi in case he received no orders.[30]

Grant's success had, of course, made him the premier Union general and he soon received Halleck's "general views" on western military operations for his consideration. Grant's enhanced status was also acknowledged when the President himself wrote a critique of Grant's campaign. Lincoln wrote to him, "When you first reached the vicinity of Vicksburg, I thought that you should do what you finally did—march the troops across the neck, run the batteries with the transports, and thus go below." Rather than saying that he understood the situation as well as Grant, the President's message read: "When you got below, and took Port Gibson, Grand Gulf, and vicinity, I thought you should go down the river and join General Banks; and when you turned northward East of the Big Black, I feared you had made a mistake. I now wish to make the personal acknowledgement that you were right, and I was wrong."

From the beginning Grant had served under Halleck and Grant acknowledged his "many obligations" to Halleck for, Grant said, "the interest you have ever taken in my welfare and that of the army I have the honor to command." But no evidence exists that Halleck rated Grant any higher than his other western generals, Sherman, Thomas, or Schofield. That Vicksburg changed Halleck's estimate is indicated by the accurate, obviously sincere, yet almost extravagant compliment he paid Grant after reading his report: "In boldness of plan, rapidity of execution, and brilliancy of results, these operations will compare most favorably with those of Napoleon about Ulm."[31]

Grant had already responded to Halleck with his plan for an advance on Mobile. Grant now reasoned that Johnston's forces were "so broken that no danger need be apprehended from them for the next thirty days." The expedition should go by water, no advance toward it being possible from Vicksburg at that season of the year because the country through which an army would have to pass was "poor and water scarce." Though ready to help this expedition, Grant apparently thought that Banks should make the main attempt because the sea route was outside of Grant's own department and there was much sickness in his command "from long and excessive marching and labor." But Grant's newly won prestige did not suffice to enable his recommendation to prevail against Halleck's wish to slice away the trans-Mississippi, Lincoln's desire for renewing the Texas expedition, and Secretary of State Seward's apprehensions about the French intervention in Mexico.[32]

Grant soon received Halleck's directives to send back the Ninth Corps and to stress the trans-Mississippi by reinforcing Banks and the troops advancing against Little Rock. Nevertheless Grant continued to cherish his proposed campaign against Mobile for which he had his usual logistical objective, including the "break up" of the railroads in Alabama. Yet the objective was more ambitious, as Sherman hoped to meet Rosecrans's army "about Atlanta" in October so as to "occupy the line from Mobile to Selma, &c., to Huntsville and Chattanooga." Grant kept his Mobile idea alive when he visited New Orleans to confer with Banks and to lay groundwork for a future Alabama expedition. But fate intervened and forced a change; on September 4 in New Orleans Grant was injured in a fall from a horse and was bedridden for several weeks. He suffered three broken ribs, paralysis of one side, and a mind-befogging concussion. Even after their intense effects subsided they residually caused him great pain and trouble. Later in the fall he recovered just in time to take charge at Chattanooga, when he assumed command of the new Military Division of the Mississippi, embracing the armies at Chattanooga and Knoxville as well as his own in Mississippi.[33]

As Grant reinforced other armies and pursued his minor operations aimed at damaging the enemy's logistics, the Army of the Potomac was even more inert. In spite of his belief in the power of the defense, Meade thought he could "cope with" Lee "provided he is not found in a very strong position." Meade favored an immediate advance, believing that the enemy's "power over his people in bringing out men" would enable the Confederates to reinforce Lee's army more rapidly than the new Union draft could strengthen the Army of the Potomac. He was told, however: "Keep up a threatening attitude, but do not advance." Lincoln had decided on this acceptance of a renewal of the Virginia stalemate, having written Halleck: Meade seems to think "the government here is demanding of him to bring on a general engagement with Lee as soon as possible. I am claiming no such thing of him. In fact my judgment is against it." Lincoln's judgment seemed an overreaction to Meade's earlier failure to attack, for the President believed: If Meade "could not safely engage Lee at Williamsport, it seems absurd to suppose he can safely engage him now, when he has scarcely more than two-thirds of the force he had at Williamsport."[34]

The situation had thus returned to that after Chancellorsville, when nothing was expected of Hooker and the Virginia theatre had a low priority compared with the West. Halleck promptly withdrew 4,000 men from Meade to reinforce Gillmore's success at Charleston even though he knew that Meade must provide troops to meet an unexpected development, draft riots in New York. Though the Union originally scheduled less than 2,000 men for this duty, by mid-August they had sent 10,000 troops away for temporary duty. On July 13 riots had broken out in New York and elsewhere around the country, precipitated by the beginning of the enforcement of the newly enacted draft law.

On March 3, 1863, Lincoln had signed the long-overdue "Act for enrolling and calling out the National forces," the first effective federal draft law. It made liable to call, with certain exceptions, male citizens between the ages of twenty and forty-five. Men drafted had to serve for only three years and were entitled to the same bounties and pay advances received by volunteers. The total bounties eventually amounted to over three hundred million dollars—as much as the pay of the entire Union army and five times the cost of its ordnance. Exemptions extended to the mentally or physically unfit, a number of high federal and state officials, the sole surviving son of a family, or the only son of parents relying upon him for financial support. The act also called for the drafting of married men only if the eligible unmarried men in a given district were taken first. Beyond that, an unwilling draftee could either furnish a substitute or buy a commutation which went toward paying the bounties. Initially these latter cost $300, but the price rose and by August, 1864, it peaked at $900. For each state the law established draft districts which coincided with the congressional districts. Furthermore it divided the territories into draft districts. Eventually these subdivisions fell under the purview of the Washington-headquartered provost marshal general, James B. Fry.

Graduated from West Point in 1847, Fry spent a few years before the Civil War in command of a light artillery battery but otherwise he devoted his entire career to staff and administrative service. Though his views of what truly happened at Shiloh made him the target of Grant and Sherman's disapproving criticism, Grant nevertheless magnanimously recommended him as "the officer best fitted" to direct the new bureau. Despite vexing difficulties, inevitably caused by the controversial nature of the draft and a quite illconceived system, Fry performed his duties in an outstanding manner.

The draft bureau's greatest difficulties resulted from the extreme unpopularity of jobs in the administrative structure, especially after it became common knowledge that many of its workers suffered physical abuse from the irate populace. For this reason many bureau employees who justly should have been dismissed for incompetence retained their positions. Some of their lapses of efficiency produced amusing results. In September, 1863, they drafted a woman: the enrolling officer had copied her name, thinking it a man's, off the sign over the store which she and her husband operated. On another occasion the bureau drafted a 65-year-old crippled man who lay sick in bed when enrolled. He died a few days afterwards. Sometimes enrollers listed persons who were dead, too old, too young, in jail, already in the service, missing arms or legs, blind, or lame.

An assistant provost marshal general administered each district and supervised the enrolling officers. These latter individuals went door to door and performed the actual enrolling. On numerous occasions they encountered violent resistance and sometimes even were shot at while attempting to carry out their duties! By the war's end, thirty-eight of the officers had been murdered, another sixty wounded, and twelve others had suffered heavy losses in personal property damage fomented by rioters.

Public displays of disrespect for the draft occurred in every state. Many citizens resisted it by moving frequently from one district to another, hoping to make it difficult or impossible for the enrollers to locate them. Some persons blatantly encouraged evasion, but on September 15, 1863, Lincoln suspended the writ of habeas corpus for such individuals and also, incidentally, at the same time for those persons engaged in spying, aiding the enemy, or guilty of desertion.

The procedures followed to select a draft seemed fair enough, at least after the completion of the enrollments, and, save for several specific and violent exceptions, people finally accepted the results with resigned good humor. All the eligible names were placed on cards or paper slips of uniform size and the required number drawn out of a mixing container. Generally a blindfolded, prominent private citizen, specially selected for the occasion, did the drawing, although in Utica, New York, in order to avoid any chance of the man's somehow peeping, a blindfolded *blind* man did the drawing.

Many draftees seized the opportunity to run away during the ten-day period granted them before they had to report. Canada became the most popular refuge for draft-evaders, and eventually several thousand of them congregated about such places as Niagara Falls and Toronto. In November,

1864, at Niagara Falls they held a "convention" and composed a petition asking for clemency if they should return. The administration did not grant this request during the war nor did it prosecute the men afterwards.

The more pathetic methods of avoiding service included self-mutilation—especially the removal of teeth so that one could not properly bite the cartridge envelope when loading a firearm. Sometimes medical treatments were designed to feign an exempting ailment, such as an artfully induced hernia or the application of mercury to the rectum in order to give the appearance of hemorrhoids. Some evaders resorted to just plain faking, like pretending epilepsy or deafness. Occasionally these schemes backfired: One member of the Ohio State Legislature had all of his teeth removed after being told he had been drafted, only to learn that his neighbor had played a joke on him and he had not been drafted at all. In another instance, a clever surgeon tricked a "deaf" draftee into betraying his lie: While checking the man's knee the doctor said in a low whisper, "That's enough to exempt any man."

"That's what I wanted to hear," shouted the happy draftee. "What's wrong with my knee?"

"Nothing," replied the doctor, feigning surprise that he had been heard, "I was talking about your ears."

Many of the resisters, not yet U.S. citizens, deeply resented that they should be liable to a draft at all, though they typically had accepted state citizenship and voting rights granted by liberal local laws designed to encourage immigration. Foreigners eventually constituted between 20 and 25 percent of the Union army. Further, foreigners as well as numerous other persons bitterly felt that the draft fell heavier upon the poor, while persons who could afford it might hire a substitute or pay the commutation fee. In fact, however, statistics indicate that the war was *not* just a "poor man's fight," but that a representative cross-section of the entire nation served.

By 1864 the Union had finally curtailed the controversial commutation system and permitted its use only by religious objectors. Ironically, *they* typically felt morally bound also not to pay the fee, and usually they accepted the draft and served in noncombatant duties. During the first year of operation, the draft generated fifteen million dollars from persons buying their way out. Of 292,221 names drawn in the first draft, only 9,881 actually served; the remainder found an escape. Assuredly these last included a motley variety within their number; one observer asserted: "I, who know, say they were as arrant a gang of cowards, thieves, murderers, and black legs as were ever gathered inside the walls of Newgate or Sing Sing."

Like the Confederacy's draft, the Union conscription system was designed primarily to stimulate volunteering, and in this it succeeded very well. A draftee was not popular in the Union army: he was looked down upon because he had not given his services willingly. Ninety-four percent of the total who served in the Union forces volunteered; the draft produced 162,535 men or about 6 percent. Of these 46,347 gave personal service while 116,188 fur-

nished substitutes. An additional 86,724 men paid for commutation, which
generated a total revenue of $26,366,316.78. Four enrollments occurred: July,
1863, and March, July, and December, 1864. The total federal strength
officially reached 2,778,304, but that number included many thousands of
persons who enlisted more than once, and various men whose terms amounted
to only a few days. Probably around 2,000,000 individuals served the Union
in uniform. The Confederates had perhaps 750,000 separate personnel, so the
blue outnumbered the gray by about three to one in men who actually served
at one time or another.

But the promise offered by the Union draft law remained unfulfilled for
many months after its initial passage. In addition to the bureaucratic difficulty
of beginning its operation, the first draft calls also precipitated riots in Indiana, Ohio, and Wisconsin. Many northerners openly opposed the war effort
and encouraged resistance to the draft. Some opponents of the war organized,
one of these organizations being the Knights of the Golden Circle. This
subversive group agitated for the molding of a new country to be made up of
the southern states, Central America, northern South America, and the Car-
ibbean Islands. On one occasion they resorted to violence when, in Hunting-
ton, Indiana, some of their members forced their way into an arms depot and
siezed guns and ammunition.

Such activities made state and federal authorities nervous and provided a
reason for keeping relatively large numbers of troops in states far from the
rebel armies. The immediate impact upon the Army of the Potomac in the
summer of 1863 came from resistance to the draft in New York City. Spectacular and sordid riots began there on July 13. The city seethed with unrest,
intensified by the open expressions of draft disapproval by the state's governor, Horatio Seymour, and politicians not in wholehearted support of the
war who aggravated the situation with their inflammatory rhetoric.

As the drawing of the first lots began, a mob materialized consisting mostly
of foreign laborers; it eventually stormed the draft headquarters and then
rampaged. "A macabre episode," Lincoln's recent and able biographer Stephen B. Oates well described it. "A three-day orgy of violence which sickened
Lincoln to read about," it resulted in "breaking into saloons, looting jewelry
stores, ganging up on policemen, and even attacking the mayor's house. Then
in an explosion of racial fury, rioting whites stormed into New York's Negro
area, where they set an orphanage afire, hanged Negroes from lampposts and
incinerated them, clubbed and whipped others to death, and assassinated
policemen and white citizens who interferred. At last federal troops helped
restore order in New York but not before five hundred or more people had
died. 'Great God!' cried the *Christian Recorder*. 'What is this nation coming
to?' "[35]

The draft riots reinforced a pessimistic tone at the Washington headquarters; when optimism, even exuberance, should have prevailed, manpower difficulties made the general in chief pessimistic. Banks supported his request for reinforcements by pointing out that he was losing twenty-two regiments by the discharge of men who had enlisted for two years or for nine months. Halleck responded gloomily; discharges in Banks's command were typical. He wrote: These losses, totaling 75,000 to 80,000 men and afflicting the entire army, came "just at a time to prevent us from profiting from our recent victories." The draft did not sufficiently replace this reduction in force (exceeding Confederate losses at Vicksburg, Gettysburg, and Port Hudson together). The general in chief had weakened the Army of the Potomac, though he feared that this might "open the North to another raid" by Lee. Throughout the summer in Washington the conviction grew that the Confederates would strengthen Lee so he could carry out another raid and Halleck was even "strongly urged to bring reinforcements from Mississippi to protect Maryland and Pennsylvania from a threatened attack" by Lee, supported by troops from Bragg.[36]

Apprehensive at Meade's supposed peril, the general in chief felt overcommitted as he prosecuted an offensive toward Texas, another in Arkansas, and a third on the South Carolina coast. Though he had predicted that Johnston would join Bragg, he felt complacent about this possibility because Grant had reported that Johnston's army was "much demoralized and deserted by the hundreds. I do not believe," Grant said, "he can get back to Mobile or Chattanooga with an effective force of 15,000 men." Halleck had tried to distract Johnston by directing Grant: "Keep up the impression in your army that Mobile will be the next point of attack." He gained a more secure feeling when Grant reported, incorrectly, that Johnston had taken his army to Mobile, because "movements in Banks's department evidently indicate to them an early attack on that city."[37]

In spite of his defensive stance in Tennessee and Mississippi, Halleck remained anxious for an advance in Tennessee, "promptly and rapidly," to continue to take advantage of the weakening of Bragg's army in order to strengthen Johnston's for its effort to relieve Vicksburg. But both Burnside and Rosecrans were "hesitating to advance till" they could be reinforced. Both generals faced serious logistical problems, for Rosecrans still had to protect his railroad and forage for his army against an enemy superior in cavalry, and, for his advance, Burnside had no rail line of communication at all. Lincoln understood Burnside's difficulties and knew that the enemy could use its railroad to bring in reinforcements to meet any advance by Burnside. The President realized that a large invading army entering upper eastern Tennessee would have to plan to live on the enemy's country, and that this would make its supplies absolutely dependent on the success of the campaign. The lack of rail or water communications would, Lincoln said prophetically, "ruin us entirely if a great disaster should befall" Burnside's army. Lincoln also grew discouraged about the effectiveness of Rosecrans's supply efforts, asking the general: "Can the thing be done at all? . . . Do you not consume supplies as fast as you can get them forward?"[38]

Nevertheless, in late July Halleck ordered Burnside and Rosecrans forward. He instructed Rosecrans "to drive Bragg from Eastern Tennessee before he can be reinforced by Johnston." When Rosecrans still did not advance, Halleck sent "peremptory" orders, with directions to report his movements daily. Since he was almost ready, Rosecrans soon began his march, with Burnside starting simultaneously from Kentucky into upper East Tennessee. Rosecrans had as his goal to advance to the Tennessee River below Chattanooga, planning to cross the river and "flank the enemy's position at Chattanooga and even at Dalton, if not south." But the advance came far too late to exploit any involvement of Johnston with Grant near Vicksburg. As Halleck explained to Rosecrans: "Grant's movements at present have no connection with yours." Meanwhile the Confederates attempted again to seize the initiative.[39]

Union strategy in the summer of 1863 presented the Confederates with an unequaled opportunity to carry out the strategy long advocated by Beauregard and the western concentration bloc. Beauregard had written: "We must take the offensive . . . not by abandoning all other points, but by a proper selection of the point of attack—the Yankees themselves tell us where." With the Union armies inactive in Virginia and Mississippi, the Confederates need not abandon anything, and Rosecrans's army, between these two theatres, seemed the logical place to concentrate for an offensive. From his position at Charleston, a strategic backwater, Beauregard easily came to see "the whole theatre of war as one subject of which all points were but integral parts." The previous spring he had identified Middle Tennessee as the "most favorable strategic point for the offensive" and had proposed concentrating troops there from South Carolina, Mississippi, and Virginia. He had envisioned the defeat of Grant by a gigantic turning movement. After first defeating Rosecrans, Bragg's reinforced army could advance into West Tennessee and "cut off Grant's communications with the North," forcing Grant to retreat or to assume the tactical offensive and "fight his way through a victorious army equal to his own in strength, on its own selected battlefield." Furthermore Beauregard's estimate of the situation in Virginia resembled that of Lincoln and Halleck. He believed that Lee had sufficient strength easily to spare some troops for use elsewhere, and Beauregard advocated a surprise western concentration and offensive.[40]

In the summer of 1863 Beauregard continued lobbying for his offensive plan, delighted to find that Bragg held an "identical" view. Longstreet, a confidant of Senator Wigfall and long an advocate of sending his corps to Bragg's army, renewed his formal and informal efforts for carrying out ideas like Beauregard's. President Davis's friend, Lieutenant General Leonidas

Polk, wrote that the plan for a western concentration represented the views of "the most intelligent circles" at Bragg's headquarters. Wigfall's friendship with Secretary Seddon and his leadership of the western bloc meant that he certainly lobbied for an offensive to "concentrate and crush," as did many of the other members of the various informal organizations making up that group.[41]

The proposal for a Middle Tennessee concentration thus reached Davis and Seddon in many forms. They found the idea quite congenial to their strategic thinking, as they had several times instigated rapid troop movements by rail for defensive purposes. Now they had no trouble making the transition to an offensive application. But the Confederacy did not choose to concentrate in Middle Tennessee until the advances of Rosecrans and Burnside precipitated the decision. Then Bragg called Buckner's force from East Tennessee, and the War Department sought reinforcements from Johnston, who sent half of his infantry to Bragg. As he faced yet another crisis, the President turned to Lee.

Despite the view of Davis and Lee, many persons perceived the campaign and Battle of Gettysburg as a defeat, and by now the newspapers carried considerable criticism of Lee. Though this slightly undermined Lee's prestige, it did not diminish Davis's need for the "counsel" of his "dear friend." The President alluded to the time when Lee first had been "required in the field after the Battle of Fair Oaks." Davis wrote, I "deprived myself of the support you gave me here" in Richmond as general commanding. Especially did he require Lee's "advice during the recent period of disaster" in the summer of 1863. When, at the end of August, the President called him to Richmond for advice on the western situation and for almost two weeks of conferences on "military questions of a general character," Lee presented his counsel in a somewhat different tone. Knowing that Meade was weak after sending detachments to South Carolina made it difficult for him to plead that the Army of Northern Virginia could spare no forces for the West. An argument that he should take the offensive to take advantage of Meade's weakness seemed less than convincing in view of Bragg's increasingly difficult position. In spite of their optimistic view of the Gettysburg campaign, both Davis and Lee obviously were influenced by the public's perception and Lee grew far less able to resist the even more powerful pressure generated by the western concentration bloc. As Rosecrans crossed the Tennessee and Knoxville fell to Burnside, President Davis decided to send Longstreet with two divisions to Bragg.[42]

Spending so much time in Richmond also gave Lee an opportunity thoroughly to familiarize himself with the entire Confederate strategic situation. As a result he abandoned his temporary role of the past spring when he, like every other parochial-minded department commander, could spare no troops for other theatres. His advice again harmonized with his and Davis's more typical strategic thought, a reliance on the railroads to concentrate against the most menacing Union advance. But Lee's better judgment was tainted with reluctance, because he wanted instead to advance to take advantage of the diminution of Meade's army.[43]

In one respect Davis made the decision to reinforce from Virginia too late, for Burnside had already cut the East Tennessee and Virginia rail line. Longstreet's troops had to follow a roundabout route: Instead of traveling 500 miles directly to Chattanooga, the reinforcements took a circuitous path through North and South Carolina and Georgia, a distance stretching nearly 1,000 miles over ten different rickety railroads. Despite enormous difficulties, the first of Longstreet's men reached Bragg in ten days, and half the force arrived in eleven. "Never before were so many troops moved over such worn-out railways," a Confederate staff officer extravagantly stated. "Never before," he went on, "were such crazy cars—passenger, baggage, mail, coal, box, platform, all and every sort of wobbling on the jumping strap-iron—used for hauling good soldiers. But we got there nevertheless." That amounted to a slight overstatement: they did not all get there in time for the battle, but nearly two-thirds of them did arrive.[44]

The Confederates achieved complete surprise. Though in early September Rosecrans reported, accurately but with exaggeration, that Johnston had joined Bragg, Washington discounted this. President Lincoln read the report "with a quiet smile. He said he did not believe the story of Johnston's junction. Johnston was watching Mobile. Rosecrans was a little excited." On September 11, after Longstreet's men had been rolling southward for two days, Halleck told Rosecrans: "It is reported here by deserters that a part of Bragg's army is reinforcing Lee. It is important that the truth of this should be ascertained as early as possible."[45]

Rosecrans received better intelligence than Halleck for the deserters had deceived their interrogators. Desertion from Confederate ranks played a significant role throughout the entire war. One student computed the total number at 103,400—a stunning manpower leak—but this included untold numbers of men who actually were carefully coached infiltrators with a mission to deceive the enemy with false information. One of Rosecrans's staff officers later wrote, quite perceptively, that "the Confederate deserter was an institution which has received too little consideration. . . . He was ubiquitous, willing, and altogether inscrutable. Whether he told the truth or a lie, he was always equally sure to deceive. He was sometimes a real deserter and sometimes a mock deserter. In either case he was sure to be loaded."[46]

Complacent about Johnston and anxious that Lee might be reinforced, Washington headquarters was also distracted by rebel raiders. That summer John Hunt Morgan made his most spectacular, if least productive, raid. On July 8 Morgan reached the Ohio River just west of Louisville and after some brief skirmishing crossed into Indiana. Only militia and a small gunboat opposed the passage. A tremendous chase ensued. Eighteen days later, at Salineville, Ohio, quite near the Ohio-Pennsylvania line, after causing much apprehension, Morgan and his 364 tired and tattered men surrendered. They had, however, very effectively distracted Burnside from the advance into Tennessee which Burnside's urgent orders had directed him to make.

On August 20 some 450 Confederate and Missouri guerrillas under William Clarke Quantrill moved toward the unsuspecting antislavery and pro-Union Kansas town of Lawrence. The next day, the 21st, Quantrill's "bushwhackers" sacked the town, burning one and one-half million dollars' worth of property and killing about 150 men and boys; they spared only women and small children. The raid had complex roots: It began as a part of the ongoing "Kansas War" that had begun originally to decide whether that state should be slave or free; it grew from a desire for retaliation for the Federal's earlier wanton raid on Osceola, Missouri; and it matured because Quantrill personally bore a grudge against Lawrence. As incomparably described by Shelby Foote, Quantrill was "three weeks past his twenty-sixth birthday, wearing a gaudy, low-cut guerilla shirt, gray trousers stuffed into cavalry boots, a gold-corded black slouch hat, and four revolvers in his belt." This hot-blooded fanatic expected no quarter from his despised enemies and intended to give none. "With the exception of a single adult male civilian—the hated Jayhawk chieftain Senator James H. Lane, who was to be taken back to Missouri alive, if possible, for a semi-public hanging," Quantrill issued orders that "called for the killing of 'every man big enough to carry a gun.' " Though he did not capture Lane, Quantrill was quite thorough. "The town is a complete ruin," one eye-witness wrote. "The whole of the business part, and all good private residences are burned down. Everything of value was taken along by the fiends . . . I cannot describe the horrors."[47]

And elsewhere, far to the east, during late August, John S. Mosby and his Confederate raiders operated less spectacularly but very effectively in Virginia north of Meade's Rappahannock line. This increased Meade's concern for his very long stretch of railroad communications, which ran close to the northern Virginia stamping ground of Mosby's rangers.

Mosby's successes reflected the natural talent he possessed as a guerrilla chieftain. He had started the war as a first lieutenant but had resigned his commission in protest to the Confederate practice of allowing men to elect their own company officers. He served for more than a year thereafter as an uncommissioned, volunteer scout under J. E. B. Stuart. Mosby received another commission as first lieutenant early in 1863 and then promotions, to captain and two weeks later to major, in March of that year. His tiny physical frame and slouching stoop belied his muscular suppleness, vigor, and capability for great and sustained activity. His eyes, which did not glance but pierced, gave him added control, perhaps hypnotic, over his men. He personally shunned booty taken from the enemy, "as if it were tainted," a biographer noted, but allowed the men rewards of loot in proportion to how hard they fought in "hand-to-hand tussles." He demanded total abstinence from alcoholic drink.

Jealous and disdaining soldiers in the regular service, thinking that Mosby's men led an easy life, dubbed them "spoiled darlings," "feather-bed soldiers," and "carpet knights"; but in truth the rangers lived a hard, Spartan existence, almost always in the field even during winter. The unit never had a roll call, and rarely ever mustered in full at any single place—though it often hovered around Salem, Virginia, midway between the Bull Run and Blue Ridge mountains. The town met their various needs and they in turn provided protection from Yankees. It was said that residents could shout or wave a handkerchief from any window and know that one or more of the rangers caught the signal. Mosby knew his men all by name and sight, and new recruits joined only with personal endorsement from the seasoned members.

Mosby lived up to Stuart's enjoinder to "let Mosby's Regulars," as Stuart preferred they be called, "be a name of pride with friends and respectful trepidation with enemies." R. E. Lee's first official mention of Mosby noted that the guerrilla had "covered himself with honors," and Lee once exclaimed, "Hurrah for Mosby! I wish I had a hundred like him." On two occasions Mosby captured stores from the Federals that included fresh lemons, some of which perhaps, before his death, made their way to lemon-sucking Stonewall Jackson. The source of Jackson's lemons has puzzled some meticulous students. Seldom did a day pass in 1863 and 1864 that northern Virginians did not admiringly discuss Mosby's activities over their dinner table or around their fireplace.[48]

Meanwhile, in the West, chafing at momentary inactivity and disgusted with recent outcomes there, a Confederate Army chaplain wrote to Davis expressing his feelings, an attitude shared by many persons. "Every disaster that has befallen us in the West has grown out of the fact that weak and inefficient men had been kept in power," he lamented, and "I beseech of you to relieve us of these drones and pigmies."[49]

That chaplain, and the other western Confederates, soon had more to think about for at last on August 16 Rosecrans's Army of the Cumberland began another thrust. Rosecrans had delayed for six weeks, despite Halleck's expressed desire for an uninterrupted advance, while railroad repairs proceeded, supplies accumulated, and corn ripened. Rosecrans deemed all this quite necessary since he again would move his whole army around Bragg's in a raid to turn its Chattanooga position by threatening Confederate communications. Again the federal army would be out of touch with its own communications, depending, as in the Tullahoma advance in June, on what the army could carry with it, on its living off the country, and on what could be brought up by wagon by a circuitous route, through rugged country over bad roads. In his turning movement Rosecrans faced a far more difficult supply situation than had Grant in his similar move the preceding May.

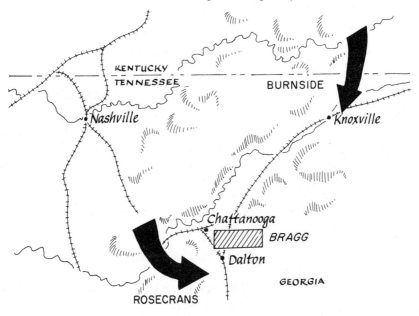

Rosecrans's Plan

Again distracting Bragg, this time by moving one corps toward Chattanooga and bombarding the city, Rosecrans succeeded in moving his other three corps over the unfordable Tennessee River and around Bragg's west flank, so threatening communications that the Confederate army abandoned

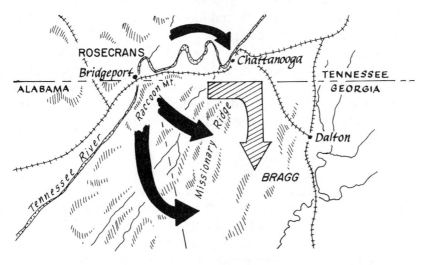

Turning Movement

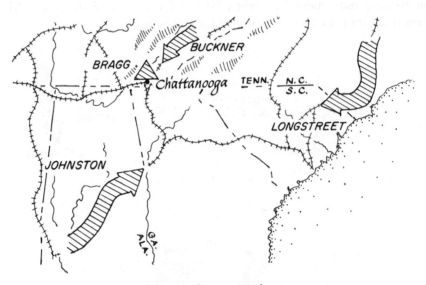

Confederate Concentration

Chattanooga and fell back to protect the railroad in north Georgia. The overconfident Rosecrans, lacking information from his inadequate cavalry, concluded that Bragg was withdrawing to Atlanta.

The Confederate retreat was a military necessity, but not nearly so precipitate as Rosecrans concluded. To the contrary, Bragg was strong and would soon become stronger. Far from retreating to Atlanta, the southerners masterfully employed their railways to assemble rapidly the most far-flung concentration since Shiloh. Rosecrans's complacency matched that of the Washington headquarters as he headstrongly rushed forward as if he had defeated the enemy army in battle and had it on the run. Nothing could have been further from the case. Bragg gave an uncharacteristically superior performance as he helped to further the notion of a demoralized withdrawal: scores of sham rebel deserters entered the Union lines to spread false stories of depressed Confederate morale because of the Chattanooga loss. All the while, the concentration continued as Buckner moved to join them, brigades from Johnston arrived, and Longstreet's men made a holiday frolic of their long train ride from Virginia.

While Rosecrans's army blundered on into Georgia in a widely dispersed marching order, the Confederates abandoned East Tennessee and concentrated its forces with Bragg's. Rosecrans faced a national concentration which had been carried out with considerable secrecy. Commanding the Federals' smallest major offensive army, Rosecrans thus fought a major battle outnumbered, a rare experience for a Union commander.

Except for a continuing apprehension that the Confederacy would reinforce Lee for a new advance and concern that the offensive against Little Rock might be in danger, optimism and confidence still reigned in the Washington headquarters. On September 3 Burnside had announced the occupation of Knoxville and on the 9th Rosecrans had reported: "Chattanooga is ours without a struggle and East Tennessee is free. Our move on the enemy's flank and rear progresses." Headquarters appreciated the significance of Rosecrans's second successful turning movement, for Lincoln's secretary reported: "We are quietly jolly over the magnificent news from all round the board. Rosecrans won a great and bloodless victory at Chattanooga." He credited the President with the good management, saying, "The old man sits here and wields like a back woods Jupiter the bolts of war and the machinery of government with a hand equally steady and equally firm." The discussion at headquarters revolved around whether the next advances of Rosecrans and Burnside should be "into Georgia and Alabama or into the Valley of Virginia and North Carolina."[50]

A report from Rosecrans on September 12 caused the first alarm in Washington. His right flank was very vulnerable to turning if Bragg fell back and then moved toward the Tennessee River by the better roads available to him. "It is desirable," Rosecrans wrote, "to have that avenue shut up. Can you not send a force from the Army of the Tennessee to do it?" Halleck instantly responded to this clear danger, informing Grant on September 13 that all of Grant's "available forces should be sent to Memphis, thence to Corinth and Tuscumbia, to cooperate with Rosecrans, should the rebels attempt that movement." Though the general in chief had recently worried about the "most important" movement on Little Rock, one which "must not fail," he now believed the Little Rock force "sufficiently strong" and ordered Hurlbut, Grant's district commander at Memphis: Send "all your available forces" east to aid Rosecrans. Burnside also received orders to join Rosecrans to enable him to hold Chattanooga, thus freeing Rosecrans to move west to cover his own right.[51]

On September 14 the War Department acquired intelligence that enemy troops were moving south through North Carolina; by the next day the Federals were almost certain that Longstreet had gone to reinforce Bragg. In a sense Halleck had anticipated this, though not for the right reasons. Writing Meade, Halleck stated: I believe "the enemy probably saw that if you and Rosecrans could hold your present position till Grant and Banks cleaned out the States west of the Mississippi, the fate of the rebellion would be sealed. . . . All the information I could gather until within the last few days indicated that you would be attacked." Now that the attack loomed not against Meade but toward Rosecrans, Halleck had little to do, for he had already ordered to Rosecrans ample reinforcements from Grant and Burnside.[52]

But none of these troops could reach Rosecrans in time. Bragg's army outnumbered Rosecrans's 70,000 to 60,000, the Confederate force having been nearly doubled by reinforcements, but Rosecrans enjoyed the advantage of the tactical defensive. Having turned the Confederates, the Federals had successfully executed a strategic offensive to threaten their opponent's communications. The Confederates would have to assume the tactical offensive to recover what they had lost. But Rosecrans had so dispersed his men they were vulnerable to just such an attack.

Suddenly realizing his danger, Rosecrans, like Lee before Antietam, succeeded in concentrating his army, which had scattered quite widely in order to pass through the mountains. Rosecrans faced a more formidable threat than he realized, for the Confederates planned not just to drive him back to secure their communications, but to employ their superior numbers to carry out their long-discussed major offensive against this weakest of the principal Union lines of operations.

After five days, September 9–13, of maneuvers and frustrating attempts to precipitate a favorable battle, Bragg finally began to gain the upper hand. He learned on the 11th that Longstreet's corps, released from duty on the Rapidan, was rushing to him by rail. On the 16th Bragg began his grand move, aiming to sweep through the front of Major General Thomas L. Crittenden's corps, pour northward, and interpose the Confederate army between Rosecrans's force and Chattanooga. Then Bragg intended to lunge southward, driving the vanquished Federals into McLemore's Cove, there to destory them. During the night preceding the battle, September 18, the two armies shifted for position. The area just west of Chickamauga Creek, so named by the Indians and meaning "River of Death," was densely wooded; neither side knew exactly where the units of the other stood.

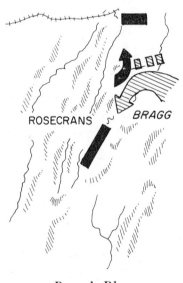

Bragg's Plan

On the morning of the 19th, federal Major General George H. Thomas ordered a division to reconnoiter toward the creek. They encountered Forrest's dismounted cavalry, drove them back, and the battle was on. The nearest Confederate infantry began to help, and the essentially frontal fighting lasted all day, with neither side gaining any decided advantage. Veritable dogfights erupted along the front; each side fed in divisions, brigades, or regiments as one or the other seemed to be gaining an advantage. On the Confederate left, troops under John B. Hood made the most progress, thrusting the foe back for a mile, then only to be thwarted when Hood and his staff rode into an unusual battlefield hazard—a nest of yellow jackets. The horses became so unmanageable and the officers so concerned over the insects, that they could not function, and the charge diminished.[53]

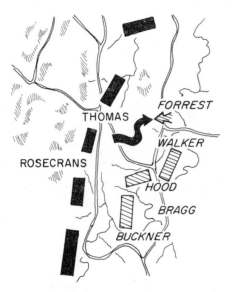

First Encounter

Then during the night the two forces rearranged their positions, well concentrated and facing each other. Most importantly, Longstreet arrived with half of his men. A brush with fate almost resulted in Longstreet's capture. Not met by any guide as they detrained at Catoosa Station, he and two staff officers soon rode into the federal lines. When no sentries challenged them, they realized the mistake and bluffed it coolly. Then Longstreet said, "Let us ride down a little way to find a better crossing." They just barely made it to the darkened safety of nearby trees.[54]

Rosecrans's army repeatedly countered Bragg's efforts to overlap its north flank and, during the fighting of the second day, the 20th, the Confederates had to resort to frontal assaults. Bragg issued orders for them to occur successively, north to south. He actually intended the main attack to occur near the northern flank, with a strong secondary attack by Longstreet down near the southern flank; but it turned out that Longstreet's men achieved a spectacular breakthrough.

The storming rebels swarmed through a gap in the Union line created by

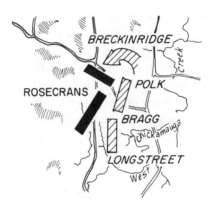

Attempted Flanking Movement

a mix-up in Union realignment orders. Rosecrans and his otherwise invaluable subordinate, Thomas, at this moment worked together poorly. The units became badly intermingled, and Rosecrans forgot the precise alignment. Upon receiving a request that one division close up a gap on the right flank of another, Rosecrans failed to recall that the Federals had still another division between the two in question. He sent an order to the unit on the extreme right to close on the flank of the specified unit to the left. The division commander so ordered, Brigadier General Thomas J. Wood, recently had been humiliated for failing to obey orders with sufficient haste. Perversely, Wood now merely asked for the obviously unwise order to be given him in writing. That done, Wood moved out of the very spot that Longstreet's troops slashed into. Alas for the Confederates, Bragg had failed to provide any general reserve and could not completely exploit and follow up Longstreet's success. Even so, the Federals suffered mightily and were pushed farther and farther into a more and more precarious position.

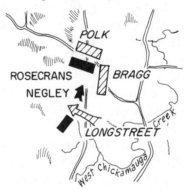

Longstreet's Breakthrough

As the well-travelled observer from Washington, Charles Dana, put it, "I saw our lines break and melt away like leaves before the wind." Stanley Horn phrased it, "The rush of Longstreet's exultant men was irresistible. They pounded through the Federal line with a power that swept everything before it." After the federal right completely crumbled, Yankees on the left began a retreat also. The jubilant Confederates swept forward, and here occurred a famous and humorous incident often recalled in later years. Major General Benjamin F. Cheatham cried, "Forward, boys, and give 'em hell!" The excited clergyman, Bishop/General Polk, approved of the idea but felt constrained to guard his tongue and so cried out to his men: "Give 'em what General Cheatham says, boys!" The fleeing Federals did not stop until they got to Rossville on the outskirts of Chattanooga, leaving behind 8,000 men who fell captive, 15,000 small arms, 51 pieces of artillery, and all manner of supplies, animals, and vehicles. Only the magnificent efforts of George H. Thomas saved the blue army from even worse disaster.[55]

"Slow Trott" Thomas, as his contemporaries called him, or "Old Pap" Thomas, as many of his soldiers soon came to know him, earned a new nickname in this battle: "the Rock of Chickamauga." A Virginian by birth, Thomas had married a northern girl and had renounced loyalty to his native state. With a splendid physical figure, he stood six feet tall and weighed 200 pounds; always neat in dress and appearance, he was extremely conscious also of how his troops looked, often remarking that the fate of a battle might depend upon the condition of a belt buckle. He also carefully looked after his troops' welfare, and they in turn loved him as soldiers loved few other generals of the Civil War, especially on the Union side. At Chickamauga he formed a defensive perimeter behind which most of Rosecrans's fleeing army eventually found safety.[56]

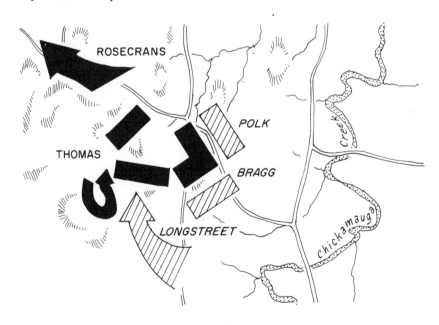

Thomas Holds Lines

Rosecrans and his other high-ranking subordinates, Crittenden and Alexander McCook, fled to Chattanooga, thinking the rebels were destroying their entire army. But Thomas remained on the field, turning two brigades to block Longstreet and employing a reserved brigade to protect the new flank. In splendid battlefield initiative, the reserve commander eventually abandoned his flank protection duty and moved to join Thomas, whose two brigades by then were quite precariously engaged. As nightfall finally came, they still held the lines. Ambrose Bierce, later famous as a short-story writer and journalist, remembered well the blissful moment when the fighting ended at last: "Away to our left and rear some of Bragg's men set up the 'rebel yell.' It was taken up successively and passed round to our front, along our right and in behind us again until it seemed almost to have got to the point whence it started. It was the ugliest sound that any mortal ever heard—even a mortal exhausted and unnerved by two days of hard fighting, without sleep, without rest, without food, and without hope. There was, however, a space somewhere at the back of us across which that horrible yell did not prolong itself—and through that we finally retired in profound silence and dejection, unmolested."[57]

As reports which began to reach Bragg indicated the magnitude of the federal retreat, he began to suspect overstatement. His sharp inquiry gave rise to another delightful story that has sometimes been overused to illustrate Bragg's unwillingness to fight. "Do you know what a retreat looks like?" he asked. The soldier, nettled by such insinuating doubt, answered, "I ought to know, General, I've been with you during your whole campaign."[58]

The tactical success of the Confederates at Chickamauga meant that their relative losses amounted to less than the tactical offensive would indicate, 18,450 for the Confederacy and 16,170 for the Union. But, again, the defensive power of the Civil War army had demonstrated not just the power to resist attack, but the capability to maneuver and thus survive a major breakthrough in the line. Writing of this battle, Lincoln well summed up the difference between victory and defeat, even in such a serious tactical defeat as Chickamauga: "The result is that we are worsted, if at all, only in the fact that we, after the main fighting was over, yielded the ground, thus leaving considerable of our artillery and wounded to fall into the enemies' hands, for which we got nothing in return." In evaluating battles in terms of attrition, Lincoln must have been heartened by escaped prisoners reporting "rebel soldiers as saying that a few more such battles will kill them all off." Accounts from enemy territory, though exaggerating, said that Bragg's "victory has crippled him."[59]

The Union should have been well prepared for this emergency, having ordered troops to Rosecrans a week earlier, even before they learned of Longstreet's reinforcement. But Halleck's plans to reinforce Rosecrans had gone awry: Hurlbut did not receive his telegram of September 13 until September 22; Grant did not receive his of the same date until September 25! Later messages Hurlbut received sooner, but that inert political general reacted slowly and, by September 21, all he had accomplished was to order six regiments "to be ready to move." Burnside did not move at all, even though urged by a telegraph message from the President himself. Finally, in response to a telegram from Burnside describing his success in driving some rebels northeast into Virginia, the President wrote to him: Your telegram made "me doubt whether I am awake or dreaming. I have been struggling for ten days, first through General Halleck, and then directly, to get you to go to assist General Rosecrans in an extremity, and you have repeatedly declared you would do it, and yet you steadily move the contrary way." It looked as if troops ordered from Minnesota might reach Rosecrans before those ordered from Tennessee and Mississippi.[60]

Against this discouraging background in the early hours of September 24 the President, General Halleck, and the secretaries of state and treasury met in the office of the secretary of war, who opened the meeting by asking how many reinforcements Burnside could add to Rosecrans's forces and in what time.

Halleck replied twenty thousand men in ten days, if uninterrupted. The President then said, "before the ten days Burnside will put in enough to hold the place (Chattanooga)."

Stanton to Halleck—How many in eight days?

Halleck—12,000.

The President—After Burnside begins to arrive, the pinch will be over.

Stanton—Unless the enemy, anticipating reinforcements, attacks promptly.—(To Halleck)—When will Sherman's (army) reach Rosecrans?

Halleck—In about ten days, if already moved from Vicksburg. His route will be to Memphis, thence to Corinth and Decatur, and a march of a hundred or a hundred and fifty miles on the north side of the Tennessee River. Boats have already gone down from Cairo, and every available man ordered forward, say from twenty to twenty-five thousand.

Stanton—Are any more available elsewhere?

Halleck—A few in Kentucky; I don't know how many. All were ordered to Burnside.

Stanton—I propose then to send 30,000 from the Army of the Potomac. There is no reason to expect that General Meade will attack Lee, although greatly superior in force; and his great numbers where they are, are useless. In five days 30,000 could be put with Rosecrans.

The President—I will bet that if the order is given tonight, the troops could not be got to Washington in five days.

Stanton—On such a subject I don't feel inclined to bet; but the matter has been carefully investigated, and it is certain that 30,000 bales of cotton could be sent in that time by taking possession of the railroads and excluding all other business, and I do not see why 30,000 men cannot be sent as well. But if 30,000 cannot be sent, let 20,000 go.[61]

Much discussion followed with "the President and Halleck being evidently disinclined to weaken Meade's force" now that he presumably had a chance to strike at the enfeebled Lee. Meade's army had just been strengthened by the return of the troops sent to New York to enforce the draft. The President's original enunciation of his theory of simultaneous advances had posited: take advantage of the enemy's use of their interior lines by standing on the defensive where they have concentrated and advancing upon the forces weakened by concentration. In accord with this Halleck had earlier instructed Meade to make preparations at least to "threaten Lee, and, if possible, cut off a slice of his army."

But Meade had been discouraging about what he could do against Lee, believing that he could expect no "greater success then requiring him to fall still farther back." Nevertheless Meade had just been in Washington to confer with the President about transferring men from his army. He had "satisfied" the President that it was not desirable to reduce his force and had returned to the Army of the Potomac with a plan for an immediate advance. For these reasons the President and General Halleck hesitated to weaken Meade, yet at the same time they did not have much hope about what he could accomplish. Thus the President and the general in chief yielded to the urgings of Stanton and the secretaries of state and treasury. A force of two corps, commanded by Fighting Joe Hooker, received orders the next day. The distance via the Baltimore & Ohio Railroad was 1,200 miles, 200 miles farther than Longstreet's route. Because of the superior condition of northern railroads, the first troops reached the Tennessee River in seven days, the last men arriving in eleven and one-half days. Longstreet's first troops had taken ten days, his last sixteen. More significant than the difference in speed was that 25,000 men had been sent, a force about double that of Longstreet. In effect the North thus possessed interior lines between the East and West. The longer distance which northern trains had to travel was shorter in time because of the superiority of northern railways. Only surprise had made possible the successful Confederate concentration for Chickamauga.[62]

But immense forces sent to reinforce Chattanooga were, in a sense, redundant, for Rosecrans had dug in well and Bragg had no intention of attacking him. Further, the Union could not send these troops actually into Chattanooga, because they could not supply them there. Burnside remained in upper East Tennessee where he could, with difficulty, live off the country. Hooker stayed well away, along a railroad to the west. Sherman's arrival was delayed because his route along the Memphis and Charleston rail line and the

Tennessee River proved slow. Originally chosen in order to cover Rosecrans's right, the route was a poor one, Sherman's men ending up having to march most of the way. This, too, was almost immaterial; by now Rosecrans's army was starving.

Bragg's position interrupted rail and water communications to Chattanooga, forcing Rosecrans's huge army to depend on a poor wagon road through hilly and denuded country. Sixty miles in length, this route reached the extreme limit of the radius of wagon transportation, and the road was strewn with dead animals. Over this route came bread and supplies. Cattle driven in over the mountains, for lack of fodder on the way, arrived so emaciated that, according to Grant, "the troops were in the habit of saying, with faint facetiousness, that they were living on 'half rations of hard bread and *beef dried on the hoof*.' " With only half rations for the men, the Union had nothing for the animals, which were dying rapidly, "nearly ten thousand of which had already starved, and not enough were left to draw a single piece of artillery or even the ambulances to convey the sick."[63]

But meanwhile Confederate strength around Chattanooga decreased; a major part of Bragg's army, Longstreet's corps, went to Knoxville to re-establish the Confederate line of operations previously abandoned in favor of maximum concentration for Chickamauga. Though this Confederate deployment aroused apprehensions for Burnside's safety and for the security of the occupation of the East Tennessee area, now liberated at last, the Federals sent no troops to aid him as long as Chattanooga remained invested. While the federal government thus focused attention upon the Chattanooga problem, the Confederacy pondered how best to exploit the Chickamauga victory and thus military action momentarily diminished.

Farther to the West, activity also subsided somewhat after a southern morale-raising gunboat triumph on September 8 at Sabine Pass, Texas, which turned back a substantial expedition sent by General Banks. The hero of the hour, Confederate Lieutenant Richard Dowling, received many tributes but none more lavish nor descriptive than that delivered by a captured federal officer: "You and your forty-three men, in your miserable little mud fort in the rushes, have captured two gunboats, a goodly number of prisoners, many stands of small arms and plenty of good ammunition—and all that you have done with six pop-guns. . . . And that is not the worst of your boyish tricks. You have sent three Yankee gunboats, 6000 troops and a general out to sea in the dark." But two days later the Confederates had to face the spirit-crushing evacuation of Little Rock, the capital of Arkansas. Halleck's combined movement had succeeded at last. Trying to arouse the trans-Mississippi citizenry, the department commander, E. Kirby Smith, issued a coloful but ineffective proclamation: "Your homes are in peril. Vigorous efforts on your part can alone save portions of your State from invasion. You should contest the advance of the enemy, thicket, gully, and stream; harass his rear and cut off his supplies."[64]

In Tennessee, September ended with the commencement of a two-and-one-half-week cavalry raid under Major General Joseph Wheeler against the communications of Rosecrans's Army of the Cumberland. Bragg was trying his favorite strategy, cavalry raids, in an effort to force the enemy back by breaking the rail lines that supplied the wagon road.

The stalemate at Chattanooga and the steady debilitation of the army finally caused Rosecrans's removal. This usually careful but confident general seemed paralyzed by his predicament. His last report, "our future is not bright," epitomized his inability to deal with the situation. Lincoln reasoned that Rosecrans had become "confused and stunned like a duck hit on the head" ever since the Battle of Chickamauga. On October 16 orders from Washington created a new Military Division of the Mississippi, combining the departments of the Ohio, the Cumberland, and the Tennessee, and placed Major General Ulysses S. Grant in command. The same order, by Grant's choice, replaced Rosecrans with his capable subordinate, George H. Thomas. Sherman succeeded Grant in command of the Army of the Tennessee.[65]

Grant's first mission, to open a better line for supplies, suited him, a congenial task for Grant who had based his Vicksburg campaign on a successful solution to the logistical aspects of turning the Confederate position. Arriving at Chattanooga on October 23, he promptly adopted a plan developed by the Army's chief engineer, the very capable Brigadier General William F. "Baldy" Smith. This plan involved driving the enemy back and opening a much shorter river and road route from the railhead. Accomplished by surprise and a sharp clash with some Confederate troops, the opening of the route was complete by the end of October. This "cracker line," as

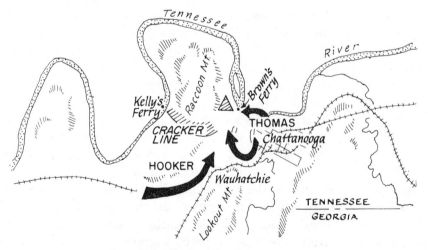

Opening the Cracker Line

lighthearted troops soon dubbed it, enabled the federal bases in Alabama to supply the city much more efficiently than via the long, rugged, and difficult mountain trail north of the Tennessee River. Within only a few days a full complement of supplies began getting through. Bragg's siege gradually loosened and, after a week, it ceased to be a siege at all.

While Grant's supply lines continued effectively provisioning Chattanooga, both Lincoln and Davis took time away from apprehensive attention to events in the West to formulate rhetoric that proved beneficial in maintaining civilian morale. Lincoln received and accepted an invitation to make a "few appropriate remarks at the dedication" of the new National Cemetery at Gettysburg scheduled for November 19. Davis, visiting bombarded Charleston, hailed a group of distinguished citizens, military units, and the general public, and even while the federal artillery pieces roared in the background, spoke with determination. While Charleston "was now singled out as a particular point of hatred to the Yankees," he said, he "did not believe Charleston would ever be taken." If it should be, he urged that the "whole be left one mass of rubbish."[66]

But as the Charleston bombardment persisted unrelentingly and unprofitably, and minor engagements continued in Virginia—especially Mosby's raids in northern Virginia lasting throughout November—the most ominous unfolding of events remained in Tennessee. Grant had as his objective now to concentrate his forces and fully relieve Chattanooga by making the "enemy fall back to a respectful distance." Since the immediate problem had been logistical, he could afford to be patient after he had implemented the plan for shortening the wagon supply route.[67]

Grant felt extreme apprehension for his left flank, fearing that, if Bragg should move between himself and Burnside, "it would greatly disturb us," he said, and "lead to the abandonment of much territory temporarily and to great loss of public property." Because of "a lack of provisions and forage" his army could not prevent such a movement, its still "delapidated and dying beasts" unable even to move the artillery. Nevertheless, it would put him in the rear of any enemy that moved around his flank and he thought that "the rebel force making such a movement would be totally annihilated." Still Grant was not sanguine enough of the enemy's annihilation to wish for them to make the movement and so, to protect himself, he ordered Sherman to "drop everything" and hurry forward. Grant meanwhile attempted to provide immediate protection for his left rear by giving "instructions to collect all provision and forage which the enemy would have to depend on for his subsistence" should Longstreet or Bragg attempt thus to turn his position.[68]

After moving from Vicksburg to Memphis, Sherman's corps trudged eastward on a tedious march along the railroad and the Tennessee River. Longstreet's movement against Burnside made haste essential for by November 16 the Confederates neared Knoxville. An engagement erupted at Campbell's Station, where Longstreet tried, but failed, to cut Burnside's supply line.

Burnside then withdrew into the city, and Longstreet commenced a siege. Grant proceeded as quickly as possible to make plans to "force the enemy back" and "place a force between Longstreet and Bragg that must inevitably make the former take to the mountain passes by every available road to get back to his supplies."[69]

By November 21, with Sherman nearing, Grant prepared for action. He desired that Sherman get far enough to reach the Confederates' right before recrossing the Tennessee River and striking at the north end of Missionary Ridge. At the same time, he wanted Thomas to hit the ridge's center and Hooker to move from Lookout Valley to Chattanooga Valley and strike the Confederate left. Hooker, however, encountered a delaying action, but the Confederate command did not correctly assess the situation and on the 22nd detached a corps under Simon Buckner to reinforce Longstreet.

On November 23 the three-day Battle of Chattanooga commenced. Thomas's Army of the Cumberland moved toward Orchard Knob, a Confederate outpost about one and one-half miles in front of Bragg's main position on Missionary Ridge. The knob fell to the Federals with but few casualties being sustained.

On the next day, the 24th, occurred the dramatic and misnamed "Battle Above the Clouds." Three federal divisions crossed Lookout Creek and began the hard climb up the heights. Again, in dispirited fighting, losses were slight

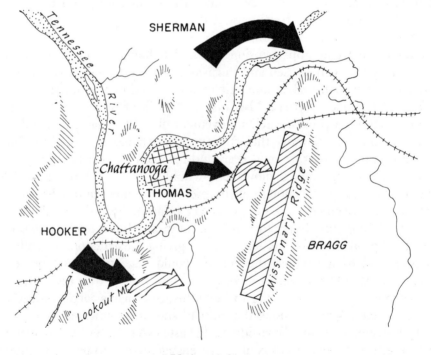

Union Advance

but the Federals succeeded. This attack cleared the final pathway for the main federal thrust.

The decisive action took place the next day, the 25th. This Battle of Missionary Ridge was the war's most notable example of a frontal assault succeeding against intrenched defenders holding high ground. It resulted from confusion, luck, and lackluster Confederate effort. Grant ordered Sherman to turn the enemy position by moving against Tunnel Hill and the north end of the ridge. Hooker would move from Lookout Mountain to cut off retreat routes while Thomas hit the center when Sherman reached the ridge.

Sherman attacked soon after sunrise but accomplished little. Heavy fighting continued into mid-afternoon. Hooker, too, encountered difficulty in effecting his movement. That left only Thomas in front of the enemy's position. Thomas's men swarmed into the enemy on the lower slopes and, overwhelming the defenders, continued, against their discouraged foe, an unplanned assault. The troops scaled the two-hundred to four-hundred feet of rock- and brush-encrusted incline, slashed into the Confederate line, and broke it in several places. Bragg's demoralized and beaten army could do no more than stagger back toward Chickamauga Creek. During the night Bragg managed to get his army below the creek and into a new assembly area where they found safety.

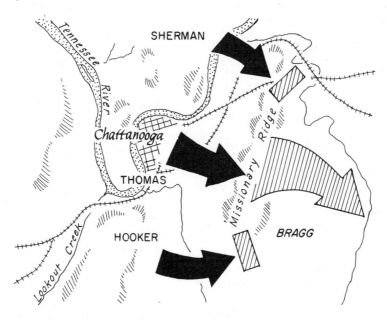

Frontal Assault

But the Federals now had avenged the Confederacy's Chickamauga achievement, rendered Chattanooga quite secure from recapture, and partially opened the road to further invasion of Georgia. The casualties amounted to relatively small numbers for a major battle: the Federals lost 5,824 while the Confederates lost 6,667, many of them prisoners who fell into northern hands after the demoralized flight before Thomas's frontal assault.

The tremendous achievement of the campaign and Battle of Chickamauga had raised Confederate hopes and prospects; now these had been dashed. The campaign had wrought many changes. Bragg would resign, good for the Confederacy if a suitable successor could be found. The North had attained unity of command in the West when Grant had attained the prestige to rise to the position, once occupied by Halleck, of western commander. Simultaneous with Chattanooga, an indecisive campaign in Virginia ushered in the muddy winter, a period of inactivity in the field and of active planning and significant command changes at the various headquarters.

1. Stanton to Rosecrans, July 7, 1863, *O.R.*, XXIII, pt. 2, 518.

2. Halleck to Foster, July 5, 1863, *O.R.*, XXVII, 533; Lincoln to Parker, June 30, 1863, Basler, *Collected Works*, VI, 311; Lincoln to Halleck, July 6, 7, 1863, *ibid.*, VI, 318, 319.

3. Meade to Mrs. Meade, July 10, 1863, George Meade, *The Life and Letters of George Gordon Meade*, 2 vols. (New York, 1913) II, 133–34; Meade to Halleck, July 8, 1863, *O.R.*, XXVII, pt. 1, 84; Halleck to Meade, July 28, 1863, *ibid.*, 104–5; Lincoln to Meade, July 14, 1863 (unsent), Basler, *Collected Works*, VI, 327–28; Lincoln to Howard, July 21, 1863, *ibid.*, VI, 341; *Lincoln and the Civil War*, 67.

4. *Lincoln and the Civil War*, 67, 69; *Welles Diary*, I, 439.

5. Meade to Halleck, July 31, 1863, *O.R.*, XXVII, pt. 1, 109.

6. Catton, *Never Call Retreat*, 217.

7. *Ibid.*, 220.

8. *Ibid.*, 222.

9. Cooper to Whiting, July 10, 1863, *O.R.*, XXVIII, 187.

10. Gilbert E. Govan and James W. Livingood, *A Different Valor: The Story of General Joseph E. Johnston, C.S.A.* (Indianapolis, New York, 1956), 225–26.

11. Albert Castel, "Theophilus Holmes—Pallbearer of the Confederacy," *Civil War Times—Illustrated* (July 1977), 11–17.

12. Halleck to Schofield, July 7, 1863, *O.R.*, XXII, pt. 2, 355.

13. Halleck to Burnside, July 4, 6, 1863, *O.R.*, XXIII, pt. 2, 514, 517; Halleck to Rosecrans, July 13, 1863, *ibid.*, 531; Rosecrans to Halleck,

July 11, 1863, *ibid.*, 529; Halleck to Gillmore, July 5, 1863, *ibid.*, XXVIII, 14.

14. Halleck to Grant, July 11, 1863, *O.R.*, XXIV, pt. 3, 497–98; *Lincoln and the Civil War*, 73, note by Tyler Dennett.

15. Halleck to Grant and Prentiss, July 15, 1863, *O.R.*, XXIV, 513.

16. Halleck to Banks, July 24, August 10, 1863, *O.R.*, XXVI, pt. 1, 652–53, 673; Halleck to Grant, July 22, 1863, *ibid.*, XXIV, pt. 3, 542.

17. Halleck to Grant, July 11, 1863, *O.R.*, XXIV, pt. 3, 497–98.

18. *Welles Diary*, I, 373 (The phrase "scratch his elbows" was a later addition by Welles.); Halleck to Meade, Aug. 7, 1863, *O.R.*, XXIX, pt. 2, 13.

19. Lincoln to Stanton, July 29, 1863, Basler, *Collected Works*, VI, 354–55; Lincoln to Grant, Aug. 9, 1863, *ibid.*, 374.

20. Grant to Sherman, July 3 (two communications), July 4, 1863, *O.R.*, XXIV, pt. 3, 460, 461, 473; Grant to Banks, July 4, 11, 1863, *ibid.*, XXIV, pt. 3, 470, 500.

21. Sherman to Osterhaus, July 4, 1863, *O.R.*, XXIV, pt. 3, 475; Grant to Sherman, July 4, 1863, *ibid.*, 473.

22. Grant to Sherman, July 11, 1863, *O.R.*, XXIV, pt. 3, 501; Rawlins to Herron, July 11, 1863, *ibid.*, 500; Grant to Banks, July 11, 1863, *ibid.*, 500. See also Grant to Sherman, July 13, 1863, *ibid.*, 508, and Grant to Herron, July 14, 1863, *ibid.*, 509.

23. Sherman to Porter, July 14, 1863, *O.R.*, XXIV, pt. 3, 531; Grant to Sherman, July 11, 13, 18, 1863, *ibid.*, 501, 507, 528; Grant to Hurlbut, July 21, 1863, *ibid.*, 539.

24. General Orders No. 15, Thirteenth Army Corps, July 18, 1863, *O.R.*, XXIV, pt. 3, 529; Sherman to Ord, July 15, 1863, *ibid.*, 515; Foote, *The Civil War*, II, 622.

25. Sherman to Ord, July 17, 1863, *O.R.*, XXIV, pt. 3, 522; Grant to Sherman, July 17, 1863, *O.R.*, XXIV, pt. 3, 522. Compare with Grant to Sherman, July 13, 1863, *ibid.*, 507, and see Sherman to Ord, July 18, 1863, *ibid.*, 528; Grant to Sherman, July 17 (two communications), 18, 20, 1863, *ibid.*, 522, 528, 536; Sherman to Ord, July 17, 1863, *ibid.*, 522.

26. Grant to Sherman, July 13, 1863, *O.R.*, XXIV, pt. 3, 507–8; Orders No. 60, Headquarters Army in the Field (Sherman), July 19, 1863, *ibid.*, 533–34; Sherman to Porter, July 19, 1863, *ibid.*, 531.

27. Sherman to Grant, October 4, 1862, *O.R.*, XVII, pt. 2, 260–61.

28. Grant to Sherman, July 13, 20, 1863, *O.R.*, XXIV, pt. 3, 508, 536; Grant to Schofield, July 15, 1863, *ibid.*, 516; Grant to Halleck, July 15, 18, 24, 1863, *ibid.*, 529–30, 547.

29. Grant to Banks, July 4, 11, 1863, *O.R.*, XXIV, pt. 3, 470, 499.

30. Grant to Banks, July 10, 1863, *O.R.*, XXIV, pt. 3, 492–93; Grant to Banks, July 11, 1863, *ibid.*, 499–500; Grant to Schofield, July 15, 1863, *ibid.*, 516–17.

31. Halleck to Grant, July 11, Aug. 1, 1863, *O.R.*, XXIV, pt. 3, 497–98, pt. 4, 63; Grant to Halleck, Aug. 11, 1863, *ibid.*, pt. 3, 587–88; Lincoln to Grant, July 13, 1863, Basler, *Collected Works*, VI, 326.

32. Grant to Hurlbut, July 21, 1863, *O.R.*, XXIV, pt. 3, 539–40; Grant to Halleck, July 18, 24, 1863, 529–30, 546–47.

33. Sherman to Rawlins, Sept. 22, 1863, *O.R.*, XXX, pt. 3, 773; Sherman to Rawlins, Sept. 21, Oct. 14, 1863, *O.R.*, XXX, pt. 3, 758, pt. 4, 356; Grant to Halleck, Aug. 1, 11, 23, 1863, *ibid.*, XXIV, pt. 3, 569, 587–88, XXX, pt. 3, 129.

34. Halleck to Meade, July 30, 1863, *O.R.*, XXVII, pt. 1, 108, Lincoln to Halleck, July 29, 1863, Basler, *Collected Works*, VI, 354.

35. Frank L. Klement, *The Copperheads in the Middle West* (Chicago, 1960), 26–27; Long, *Civil War, Day by Day*, 325, 384–6; Eugene Converse Murdock, *Patriotism Limited, 1862–1865* (Kent, Ohio, 1967), *passim;* Fletcher Pratt, *Stanton: Lincoln's Secretary of War* (New York, 1963), 310–12, 356; James G. Randall, *Constitutional Problems Under Lincoln* (New York, 1926), 244, 264–68; Stephen B. Oates, *With Malice Toward None:*

The Life of Abraham Lincoln (New York, 1977), 357; Eugene Converse Murdock, *One Million Men—The Civil War Draft in the North* (Madison, Wisc., 1971), 130–31.

36. Banks to Halleck, July 23, 1863, *O.R.*, XXVI, pt. 1, 651; Halleck to Banks, July 26, Sept. 8, 1863, *ibid.*, 653–54, 719–20; Halleck to Gillmore, July 28, 1863, *ibid.*, XXVIII, pt. 2, 29; Halleck to Rosecrans, Aug. 20, Sept. 11, 1863, *ibid.*, XXX, pt. 3, 83, 530; Halleck to Grant, Sept. 17, 1863, *ibid.*, 694.

37. Grant to Halleck, July 24, Aug. 30, 1863, *O.R.*, XXIV, pt. 3, 546–47, XXX, pt. 3, 224; Halleck to Grant, Aug. 3, 1863, *ibid.*, XXIV, pt. 3, 571.

38. Halleck to Burnside, July 6, 1863, *O.R.*, XXIII, pt. 2, 517; Halleck to Gillmore, July 28, 1863, *ibid.*, XXVIII, pt. 2, 28; Lincoln to Fleming and Morrow, Aug. 9, 1863, Basler, *Collected Works*, VI, 373; Lincoln to Rosecrans, Aug. 10, 1863, *ibid.*, VI, 377–78.

39. Halleck to Rosecrans, July 24, 25, Aug. 4, 5, 25, 1863, *O.R.*, XXIII, pt. 2, 552, 554–55, 592, XXX, pt. 3, 162; Halleck to Burnside, July 24, 1863, *ibid.*, XXIII, pt. 2, 553; Rosecrans to Halleck, Aug. 30, 1863, 30–33, 242.

40. Beauregard to C. J. Villeré, May 25, 1863, *O.R.*, XIV, 955; Beauregard, "The First Battle of Bull Run," 223; Beauregard to J. E. Johnston, May 15, 1863, Alfred Roman, *The Military Operations of General Beauregard*, 2 vols. (New York, 1883), II, 84–85.

41. Connelly and Jones, *Politics of Command*, 122–33.

42. Davis to Lee, July 28, Aug. 2, 11, 24, 1863, *O.R.*, LI, pt. 2, 741–42, 749–50, XXIX, pt. 2, 639–40, LI, pt. 2, 759.

43. See, for example: Lee to Davis, Sept. 29, Oct. 1, 1863, *O.R.*, XXIX, pt. 2, 756, 766.

44. Turner, *Victory Rode the Rails*, 283–85; Foote, *The Civil War*, II, 709.

45. *Lincoln and the Civil War*, 86–87; Halleck to Rosecrans, Sept. 11, 1863, *O.R.*, XXX, pt. 3, 530.

46. Horn, *Army of Tennessee*, 248, 462n20.

47. Foote, *The Civil War*, II, 704; Long, *Civil War, Day by Day*, 399.

48. Virgil Carrington Jones, *Ranger Mosby* (Chapel Hill, N.C., 1944), 13–14, 19, 75, 78, 105–6, 108–9, 159–60.

49. Long, *Civil War, Day by Day*, 397.

50. Halleck to Grant, Sept. 9, 1863, *O.R.*, XXX, pt. 3, 474–75; Rosecrans, to Halleck, Sept. 9, 1863, *ibid.*, 479; Halleck to Burnside, Sept.

11, 1863, *ibid.*, 55; *Lincoln and the Civil War*, 90–91.

51. Rosecrans to Halleck, Sept. 12, 1863, *O.R.*, XXX, pt. 3, 561; Halleck to Grant or Sherman, Sept. 13, 1863, *ibid.*, 592; Halleck to Grant, Sept. 9, 1863, *ibid.*, 474–75; Halleck to Hurlbut, Sept. 13, 1863, *ibid.*, 592; Halleck to Burnside, Sept. 13, 1863, *ibid.*, 617.

52. Halleck to Meade, Sept. 15, 1863, *O.R.*, XXIX, pt. 2, 187.

53. Horn, *Army of Tennessee*, 462*n33*: Connelly, *Autumn of Glory*, 193–207.

54. Henry, *Story of the Confederacy*, 311; Horn, *Army of Tennessee*, 264, 269, 270, 462–63*n37*: Connelly, *Autumn of Glory*, 207–8.

55. Henry, *Story of the Confederacy*, 311; Horn, *Army of Tennessee*, 264, 269, 270, 464*n57*: Connelly, *Autumn of Glory*, 209–27.

56. Martin Blumenson and James L. Stokesbury, *Masters of the Art of Command* (Boston, 1975), 155–62.

57. Curt Johnson and Mark McLaughlin, *Civil War Battles* (New York, 1977), 104.

58. Horn, *Army of Tennessee*, 277; Connelly, *Autumn of Glory*, 228–34.

59. Lincoln to Mrs. Lincoln, Sept. 24, 1863, Basler, *Collected Works*, VI, 478; Meigs to Stanton, Oct. 3, 1863, *O.R.*, XXX, pt. 4, 57; Hurlbut to Rawlins, Oct. 2, 1863, *ibid.*, 29.

60. Hurlbut to Halleck, Sept. 21, 1863, *O.R.*, XXX, pt. 3, 759; Lincoln to Burnside, Sept. 25, 1863, Basler, *Collected Works*, VI, 480–81. The letter was not sent.

61. David Donald, ed., *Inside Lincoln's Cabinet: The Civil War Diaries of Salmon P. Chase* (New York, London, Toronto, 1954), 201–3.

62. *Inside Lincoln's Cabinet*, 203; Halleck to Meade, Sept. 15, 1863, *O.R.*, XXIX, pt. 2, 186; Meade to Halleck, Sept. 15, 1863, *ibid.*, 188; Meade to Mrs. Meade, Sept. 24, 1863, *Life and Letters*, II, 150–151; Turner, *Victory Rode the Rails*, 285, 286, 290, 293.

63. Grant, *Personal Memoirs*, 311–12.

64. Catton, *Never Call Retreat*, 234; Long, *Civil War, Day by Day*, 415.

65. Rosecrans to Halleck, Oct. 16, 1863, *O.R.*, XXX, pt. 4, 415; *Lincoln and the Civil War*, 106.

66. Long, *Civil War, Day by Day*, 429.

67. Grant to Halleck, Nov. 12, 1863, *O.R.*, XXXI, pt. 3, 122.

68. Grant to Halleck, Oct. 26, Nov. 2, 1863, *O.R.*, XXXI, pt. 1, 738–39, pt. 3, 15; Grant to Sherman, Oct. 24, 1863, *ibid.*, pt. 1, 713; Dana to Stanton, Nov. 19, 1863, *ibid.*, pt. 2, 61.

69. Grant to Sherman, Nov. 11, 1863, *O.R.*, XXXI, pt. 3, 119; Grant to Burnside, Nov. 14, 1863, *ibid.*, 145.

15 ☆ A WINTER OF PLANNING

George G. Meade

WHILE GRANT CARRIED the significant Chattanooga campaign to a successful conclusion, to the east the perennial problem of the Virginia stalemate went through another appraisal with a new participant, George G. Meade. The new commander of the Army of the Potomac typified Civil War regular army generals. Secretary of the Navy Welles saw Meade as "not great" and characterized him as "rather a 'smooth bore' than a rifle," but Welles knew that the other officers regarded Meade well. A West Pointer and an engineer officer appointed a brigadier general early in the war, Meade appreciated General Scott's anaconda strategy. Meade believed that "the blockade and the heavy expenditures required to maintain their large armies," already wearing down the rebels, showed, he remarked, "the sagacity of our policy of keeping them hemmed in by land and sea." He viewed the war as one "of dollars and cents—that is of resources . . . in which the North, being the biggest cat and having the longest tail, ought to have the endurance to maintain the contest" longer.[1]

Like most other generals in the Army of the Potomac, he remained loyal to McClellan but perceived his faults, recognizing that he "errs on the side of prudence and caution, and that a little rashness on his part would improve his generalship." Meade's strategic ideas and his loyalty to the builder of the army left him with an enduring belief that the Peninsula "was the true and only practicable approach to Richmond." This led him to denounce the "blind infatuation of the authorities at Washington" which prevented a return to that line of operations. A McClellan partisan in 1862, he denounced "the stupidity of the authorities" and, Meade added, the "willful blindness of our rulers" in altering McClellan's plans. He equally criticized Secretary Stanton's initial enunciation that warfare was a matter of enthusiasm rather than military science. To Meade, the secretary appeared "by his cry 'Fight, fight—be whipped if you must, but fight on,' as very much of the bull-in-a-china-shop order, and not creditable to his judgment." Like many other commanders Meade thought civilians saw battles as ends in themselves but "a good general fights at the right time and place, and if he does not, he is pretty sure to be whipped and stay whipped."[2]

But Meade described himself as "among the *fire-eaters*." He felt that, even if Union forces were compelled to take the wrong line of operations and could not turn the enemy, he favored "making an attempt to whip them, . . . even though," he remarked, frontal fights being inherently indecisive, "we should not be either able or desirous of following up our victory." He had "tired of this playing war without risks. We must encounter risks," he explained, "if we fight, and we cannot carry on war without fighting. That was McClellan's vice. He was always waiting to have everything just as he wanted it before he would attack." A general who could diagnose the cause of the "slows" could presumably avoid showing any symptoms of the disease. He believed that "with anything like equal advantages" the army could "whip" Lee's. He even had confidence in the possibility of successful frontal assaults.[3]

But Meade's initiation to army command came at Gettysburg, where he saw Lee wait for a day after the battle, "expecting," Meade wrote, "that, flushed with success, I would attack them when they would play their old game of shooting us behind breastworks—a game we played this time to their entire satisfaction." Meade declined to attack Lee, "in consequence," he explained, "of the bad example he had set me in ruining himself attacking a strong position." Besides this inhibition of his earlier aggressiveness, Meade remained hostile to "interference by politicians with military men," exemplifying the old breach between the political leadership and the professional soldiers. He realized his immediate apprehension, that the politicians would require him "to attack a position too strong," when critized for his failure to attack at Williamsport. In writing his wife he stated: This criticism was "exactly what I expected; unless I did impracticable things, fault would be found with me."[4]

Meade's stereotype of the politicians also prevented him from understanding the headquarters doctrine for dealing with Lee. He emphasized: "The Government insists on my pursuing and destroying Lee. The former I can do, but the latter will depend on him as much as on me, for if he keeps away I can't destroy." I see myself pushed, he commented, "to attempting to pursue and destroy an army nearly equal to my own, falling back on its resources and reinforcements and increasing its *morale* daily. This has been the history of all my predecessors." With this perception he could not understand why, at the end of July, headquarters had ordered him not to attempt to advance, even though he knew that Lincoln did not think he would have any opportunity to harm Lee.[5]

Different objectives for the Army of the Potomac caused this gap in understanding. Meade perceived its objective as Richmond. Completely at odds with every element of the headquarters doctrine, he declared, "Richmond need not and should not be attacked at all; . . . the proper mode to reduce it is to take possession of the great lines of railroad leading to it from the South and Southwest, cut these and stop any supplies going there, and their army will be compelled to evacuate it and meet us on ground we select ourselves."

With this view he naturally remained quite critical of a line of operations leading directly from Washington, and he added his belief in logistical insufficiency of any route other than the Peninsula. He particularly disparaged the line of operations leading southwestward from Washington. He saw the Orange and Alexandria Railroad as "insufficient by one third to carry the daily supplies" of the army. The distance to the enemy stretched 150 miles, requiring large forces to guard it. When he took up this line in July, 1863, he pointedly told Halleck he planned "to test the question which has been raised of the capacity of the Orange and Alexandria Railroad to supply the army and the practicality of such a long line of communications."[6]

The gap between Meade and his superiors intensified further because he far better grasped Lee's logistical situation. Meade knew that in 1862 in the Antietam campaign Lee crossed into Maryland to procure "food and clothing," as well as to require the Union forces "to chase them around, until," he wrote his wife, "we find them in some strong position, when they will give us battle." In Lee's retreat from Gettysburg, Meade felt pleased to have kept Lee out of the Shenandoah Valley flank position, where he thought Lee "would have stayed, as he did last year, employing his army in gathering the bountiful crops of that region, and sending them to his depots at Staunton and Gordonsville for use in the winter." The general then asked whether he should occupy the Valley. Failing to understand Meade's objective to undermine Lee's logistics, Halleck tersely replied: "I see no advantage in the reoccupation of the Shenandoah Valley. Lee's army is the objective point."[7]

But Meade failed to understand the depth of Lee's logistical problems, for, like Halleck and Lincoln, he thought Lee planned to fall back to Richmond. He believed Lee's "policy" was "to draw us as far as possible from the Potomac," he explained, "and then to attack our rear, cut off if possible our lines of communication and supply, and compel us, in order to keep these open, so to weaken our force in front as to prevent our attacking them, and enabling them, if they can collect sufficient force, to attack us."[8]

Meade's attitude of distrust toward his civilian superiors exemplified the suspicion felt by many professional soldiers. The situation was aggravated in the politically sensitive Army of the Potomac, because radical politicians disparaged McClellan and the soldiers remained loyal to his memory. This army failed to respond to Halleck's leadership. Not only did McClellan still retain his informal leadership with many of the generals, but the conviction that politicians dominated Halleck undermined Halleck's prestige as a successful commander and a highly respected regular. Meade believed the general in chief was "under Washington influence," though, "as a soldier," he "ought to know better."[9]

On the other hand Meade exemplified much that the politicians objected to in the professional soldiers. In his order congratulating the Army of the Potomac on its victory at Gettysburg Meade emphasized: We must "drive from our soil every vestige of the presence of the invader." Lincoln "did not like the phrase" because the references to "invader" and "our soil" displayed, the President said, "a dreadful reminiscence of McClellan. The same spirit moved McC to claim a great victory because Pa. & M. were safe. The hearts of 10 million people sunk within them when McClellan raised that shout last fall. Will our generals never get that idea out of their heads? The whole country is our soil."[10]

Though Meade, like McClellan, wholeheartedly supported the restoration of the Union, the use of such a phrase suggested, at the very least, a likewarmness which caused many political leaders to believe that decisive victories eluded the generals because they did not really want them. Meade also aroused suspicion as one more dig-in, defensive-minded West Pointer. As Lincoln's secretary remarked of the Army of the Potomac's new commander: "I doubt him. He is an engineer."[11]

Victories by West Pointers still had not dispelled civilian skepticism of the professional's doctrine of the supremacy of the defensive. Even someone as knowledgeable as a general of civilian background who had lost a leg at Gettysburg believed that "Grant and Rosecrans have won their great successes by disregarding the warnings and the maxims of the books and plunging ahead." Lincoln's brilliant secretary well understood and strongly disagreed with the regulars' faith in the power of the defense. He recounted with pleasure the incident of "a Western brigade plunging over an open field under the direct fire of an earthwork, crossing a slough, cutting through an abattis, and storming the work successfully, thus performing four impossibilities. Battles are won and campaigns frequently decided by the accomplishment of what seems impossible or absurd."[12]

Misunderstandings thus exacerbated the distrust between civilians and soldiers. Generals believed they were still evaluated by "partisan feeling" and their operations "were judged, not by their own merits" but by party or factional criteria. John Gibbon, able regular and a corps commander at Gettysburg, felt that those who disagreed with McClellan's views or his Democratic affiliation condemned his movement to the Peninsula. At a large dinner party in the winter of 1863–64 he explained: Many people "did not seem to fancy my assertion that *all* competent military commanders followed generally the same military principles, irrespective of their personal or political opinion's for this classification included McClellan and he had 'demonstrated himself incompetent!' " Gibbon's experience with judgments of operational matters subordinated to partisan views found confirmation at the close of the banquet when one of the guests congratulated him "for being such a *staunch friend of McClellan*," because of his assertion of the universality of the principles of war.[13]

Lincoln fully appreciated, and himself shared to some degree, the civilian suspicion of the generals in McClellan's old army. Though the President thoroughly grasped tactical realities, he believed the Potomac commanders overestimated them. Nevertheless, he had grounded his doctrine for Virginia operations upon a realization of the power of intrenched defenders. The departure of Longstreet in September, 1863, to aid Bragg precipitated a test of Lincoln's doctrine. It also provided an opportunity for Meade to understand it, and the results made Lincoln, if not Halleck, comprehend even more acutely the defensive power of a field army as perceived by Meade on the basis of his combat experience.

In mid-September, after Meade was persuaded that Longstreet had gone West, he began to probe Lee's position with cavalry, trying to ascertain the degree of weakness of Lee's army. The President thought Meade should "move upon Lee in the manner of general attack, leaving to developments whether he will make it a real attack," because Lincoln felt this "would develop Lee's real condition and purposes better than cavalry alone." Apprehensive that Lee could turn his left by crossing the Rappahannock at Fredericksburg, Meade wanted more positive instructions. Having already crossed the Rappahannock, Meade saw that he had a good chance of crossing the Rapidan, turning Lee's right, and forcing him to fall back fifteen or twenty miles. He expected Lee to contest the crossing with sharp fighting. Meade now accurately comprehended that Lee's policy was "to check and retard" his "advance as long and wherever he can."[14]

Although Meade still preferred to advance on Richmond via McClellan's Peninsula route, he knew headquarters had interdicted this "as it uncovers Washington." Still not grasping that Lincoln and Halleck had no interest in a siege of Richmond, Meade could see no point in simply turning Lee back a few miles for, he explained "I could not follow him to the fortifications of Richmond with the small army I have." Meade questioned his superiors: What are "the advantages to be gained and the course to be pursued in the event of success" in a battle to maneuver Lee back a short distance? Success would result in the lengthening of his communications and an increase in the number of men required to hold them. Meade thus summarized his view of the Virginia stalemate: "In fine, I can get a battle out of Lee under very disadvantageous circumstances, which may render his inferior force my superior, and which is not likely to result in any very decided advantage, even in case I should be victorious."[15]

Possibly Meade believed offensive victories were impossible, because he was a prisoner of the McClellan-induced culture of southern superiority. In view, however, of Meade's earlier combativeness and his perceptive diagnosis of the cause of McClellan's "slows," a mature understanding of military realities seems the most likely explanation for his operational outlook.[16]

Meade's request for directions produced an immediate reaction from the general in chief. Disclaiming any "idea of playing the part of an Austrian ruler" who overcontrolled generals in the field, Halleck, as usual, confined himself to a statement of objectives. Disparaging Richmond as a point of "very great military importance," Halleck reiterated the headquarters doctrine: The "objective point" is "Lee's army, and the object to be attained is to do as much harm as possible with as little injury as possible to yourself. If Lee holds a position too strong to be attacked, and he cannot be turned by maneuvering, then his outposts and detachments can be attacked, his communications threatened by raids, or his supplies of the adjacent country collected for the support of our army."[17]

The President responded more explicitly and emphatically. "To avoid misunderstanding," Lincoln wrote, "let me say that to attempt to fight the enemy slowly back into his intrenchments at Richmond, and there to capture him, is an idea I have been trying to repudiate for quite a year. My judgment is so clear against it, that I would scarcely allow the attempt to be made, if the general in command should desire to make it." Strengthening his point about the futility of driving the rebels back to the fortifications of Richmond, Lincoln stressed: "If our army can not fall upon the enemy and hurt him where he is, it is plain to me that it can gain nothing by attempting to follow him over a succession of intrenched lines into a fortified city."[18]

The President's strong reaction showed more than his realization that Meade's estimate of the situation indicated a bankruptcy of the strategy of hurting Lee's army in Virginia. Lincoln also realized the alarming implication for his whole strategy of simultaneous advances. By simultaneous advances Lincoln had assumed that Union forces could take advantage of any Confederate concentration. Rather than moving its troops to match that of the enemy, the Union army would go on the defensive against the rebels, where they massed their forces while taking the offensive against those Confederates necessarily weakened to provide the concentration elsewhere. But Meade insisted that the power of the defense was too strong even for this strategy.[19] Lincoln examined the implications:

And yet the case presents matter for very serious consideration in another aspect. These two armies confront each other across a small river, substantially midway between the two Capitals, each defending its own Capital, and menacing the other. General Meade estimates the enemies' infantry in front of him at not less than forty thousand. Suppose we add fifty percent to this, for cavalry, artillery, and extra-duty men stretching as far as Richmond, making the whole force of the enemy sixty thousand. General Meade, as shown by the returns, has with him, and between him and Washington, of the same classes of well men, over ninety thousand. Neither can bring the whole of men into a battle; but each can bring as large a percentage in as the other. For a battle, then, General Meade has three men to General Lee's two. Yet, it having been determined that choosing ground, and standing in the defensive, gives so great advantage that the three can not safely attack the two, the three are left simply standing on the defensive also. If the enemies' sixty thousand are sufficient to keep our ninety thousand away from Richmond, why, by the same rule, may not forty thousand of ours keep their sixty thousand away from Washington, leaving fifty thousand to put to some other use? Having practically come to the mere defensive, it seems to be no economy at all to employ twice as many men for that object as are needed. With no object, certainly, to misle[a]d myself, I can perceive no fault in this statement, unless we admit we are not the equal of the enemy man for man.[20]

This reasoning resulted in the call of Meade to Washington, where he successfully defended his army against reduction and Lincoln and Halleck approved his plan to advance against Lee. But apprehensions about the consequences of the Battle of Chickamauga reinforced the discouragement about the Virginia theatre and doubts about the whole concept of simultaneous advances. After initial disagreement, Lincoln and Halleck had yielded to Stanton and others and dispatched to Rosecrans substantial reinforcements from the Army of the Potomac. This decrease in the Army of the Potomac temporarily removed the pressure for Meade to advance against the Army of Northern Virginia.

Learning that Meade had also lost troops, Lee returned to the idea of taking the initiative. Earlier he had planned to advance, and, during the previous August, had exhibited a quite belligerent attitude toward Meade's army. He had then wished to "attack Meade," being restrained in part by "the fear of killing our artillery horses," he explained. "They are much reduced, & I fear the hot weather & scarce forage keep them so." Convinced of the enemy's weakness, Lee had wanted "to bring General Meade out" by again turning him and then attempting "to crush his army while in its present condition," depleted by detachments and discharge of veterans. Significantly reduced in strength by the loss of Longstreet, he abandoned this objective, only to revive it after he learned that Meade's army had been diminished to aid Rosecrans. Lee then prepared "a move upon General Meade to prevent his further reinforcing General Rosecrans." For this operation Lee returned to his traditional objective, "to strike a blow at the enemy" by "throwing him further back towards Washington." On October 9 Lee began to move west and then north around Meade's flank. Two days later the vigilant Meade, apprised of Lee's movement, began to retreat.[21]

Meade well understood Lee's purpose and, as a result of his earlier correspondence and conference with Lincoln and Halleck, comprehended the headquarters doctrine that Lee's army, not Richmond, was the objective. As one of Meade's staff officers expressed it: "Our object is Uncle Lee's army (one might properly say our only object), we have to watch and follow his movements, so as, 1st, to catch him if possible in a good corner; or, 2nd, to prevent his catching us in a bad corner; also 3rd, to cover Washington and Maryland, which, for us, is more important than for him to come to Richmond." Although pessimistic enough to wish for the Peninsula line of operations, Meade intended to hurt Lee in the maneuvers of the fall of 1863. But as he coped with the "fancy antics" of "Uncle Lee's" turning movement, Meade could not shake off his belief that the newspapers' and the politicians' conception of war would dominate Union strategy. The papers were saying,

" 'The fine autumn weather is slipping away.' Certainly; and shall we add, as a corollary, 'Therefore let another Fredericksburg be fought!'"[22]

But Meade's caution extended beyond avoiding another Fredericksburg, and he watched carefully as the operation progressed, for he did not want the Confederates to catch him as they had Pope in the campaign of Second Bull Run, yet he also sought an opportunity to strike Lee, explaining to the general in chief: I suppose Lee will "turn me again, probably by the right, . . . in which case I shall either fall on him or retire nearer Washington, according as his movements indicate the probability of his being able to concentrate more rapidly than I can."[23]

Meade was wise to be cautious; Lee indeed aimed at another Second Bull Run, hoping to reach the enemy's rear. But Washington did not fully share Meade's respect for Lee. Lee's turning movement had come at a time when army headquarters was becoming convinced that Lee had sent more reinforcements to Bragg. Though Lincoln was comprehending of and sympathetic with Meade's pessimism about an offensive, Halleck, much less so, strongly believed there was something amiss with the Army of the Potomac. "That army fights well when attacked, but all its generals have been unwilling to attack, even very inferior numbers. It certainly is a very strange phenomenon," wrote Halleck. In ignoring the offensives of Burnside and Hooker, Halleck displayed an exasperation with Meade and an even greater frustration than Lincoln's with the Virginia stalemate. As Meade fell back before a supposedly weakened Lee, Halleck, though he ordered troops from New York and alerted more elsewhere, told Meade he thought Lee was "bullying" him and, in the words of the often irascible Meade, inflicted on him so many "truisms" that Meade asked to be "spared" more.[24]

Lee had not sent more reinforcements to Bragg and, if he had bullied Meade, he had not done so sufficiently to avoid having a lead division blunder into a trap on October 14 and suffer heavy casualties at Bristoe Station. When the two armies completed their rapid march to the vicinity of Washington, Meade, though ahead of Lee and well concentrated, had not discerned in Lee's dispositions any flaw which he could exploit. Since the Union had no intention of further reinforcing Rosecrans, Lee's basic objective in the campaign had been meaningless. Meade's rapid retreat had defeated Lee's goal of reaching his rear and, finding Meade near Washington, Lee did "not deem it advisable to attack him in his entrenchments, or to force him further back by turning his present position, as he could quickly reach the fortifications around Washington and Alexandria." In mid-October his present position offered no logistical advantages. Lee wrote Davis: I will have to move westward "for subsistence for the army, this region being entirely destitute, and the enemy having made the railroad useless to us by the complete destruction of the Rappahannock bridge. Such a movement would take us too far from other points where the army might be needed and the want of clothing, shoes, blankets, and overcoats would entail great suffering upon our men." Recognizing, he continued, "no benefit in remaining where we are," Lee retreated, and destroyed the railroad, hoping to "prevent another advance of the enemy in this direction this season."[25]

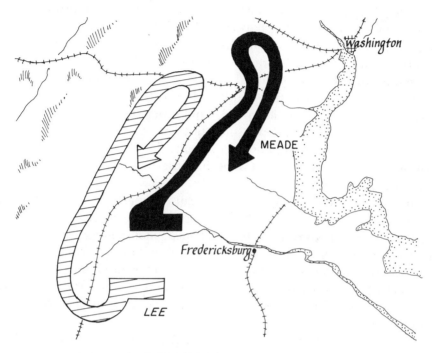

Lee's Turning Movement Fails

In his withdrawal Lee had so effectively destroyed the railroad that Meade thought the campaign was "virtually over for the present season" and that this indicated purely defensive purposes on Lee's part and his intention "to detach troops to the southwest, based on the presumed delay" in any advance by Meade caused by the destruction of the railroad. Meade's superiors felt almost certain that Lee had already sent reinforcements west. Meade's estimate of the situation precipitated a conference in Washington and the President agreed with him "that there was not much to be gained by any farther advance; but General Halleck was very urgent that something should be done, but what that something was he did not define." With the President fully convinced of the further depletion of Lee's army, Meade began an offensive, made possible by the speed with which the Union could repair the railroad. Meade planned to aim at Lee's army, but headquarters also prepared for the contingency that Lee might simply fall "back to the defenses of Richmond."[26]

While Meade planned his late fall offensive against Lee, Grant completed his victory at Chattanooga. Having made Bragg "take a respectful distance" from the Tennessee River, Grant now sought to "push Bragg," and he directed, "Cut off a good portion of his rear troops and trains. His men have manifested a strong desire to desert for some time past, and we will now give them a chance." Grant sought in pursuing Bragg to "bring him to battle again, if possible." Sherman, in agreement, said: "If we catch Bragg before he joins Longstreet we will make short work of him." But the Union troops soon found the Confederates so "strongly posted on the hills" that it looked as if it would be "hard to dislodge them." Except to "turn the enemy's position" and so force him back, Grant concluded that he did not, after all, "care about the pursuit being continued farther south." He had the railroad between Bragg and Longstreet "effectually destroyed," and ordered the demolition, at Dalton, of the Confederate rail depot south of Chattanooga and of "all materials that might be used in the support of any army," if "it were practicable to do so without a battle." Otherwise Grant did little about Bragg's army after his victory at Chattanooga.[27]

Grant thought Bragg's defeat likely to cause Longstreet to retreat toward Georgia; nevertheless, he dispatched reinforcements under Sherman to break Longstreet's siege of Knoxville. He even hoped, should Longstreet not retreat and, "knowing Sherman's promptness and ability," that Sherman might "destroy," capture, or "crush" Longstreet's army. Though Grant's vague hopes for dramatic results did not materialize, Union forces did compel Longstreet to withdraw after an unsuccessful attack on Burnside's intrenched positions before Knoxville.[28]

In spite of the Union's at last opening railway communications from Nashville to Chattanooga, the successes at Chattanooga and Knoxville did not yet fully solve the problems of the forces in East Tennessee. Because one railroad could provide for no more than sixty to seventy thousand men, Union quartermasters found it difficult to meet the needs of the big army at Chattanooga much less Burnside's men and animals in East Tennessee. This army badly needed subsistence and fodder from the Chattanooga railhead; it was attempting, without complete success, to provide for itself by living off the East Tennessee countryside and on supplies brought by wagon transportation from Kentucky over exhausted country, bad roads, and mountainous terrain. Burnside's soldiers in this way managed to subsist themselves but were running short of clothing and shoes. Their horses and mules were dying for lack of forage.

The Union's logistical situation in Tennessee closely resembled that of Lee in Virginia, except that, whereas they both shared the problem of bad railroads, a shortage of commissary and quartermaster supplies at the source aggravated Lee's condition. Every winter taxed Lee because his immobilized army had only limited opportunities for foraging and was thus compelled to depend heavily on the unreliable bureaus in Richmond.

While Grant and Sherman had been engaged in solving the problems of the armies at Chattanooga and Knoxville, they continued to think of the offensive against the enemy's logistics which they had planned during the summer. Sherman had earlier written: "The easiest way to relieve pressure on Rosecrans would be for the Texas expedition to be directed on Mobile and all our available forces . . . moving on Meridian and Selma, uniting . . . with the New Orleans forces. . . . This would force Joe Johnston to make very heavy detachments from Bragg." Grant, too, had thought that "at least a demonstration" toward Mobile "would either result in the abandonment of that city or force the enemy to weaken Bragg's army to hold it."[29]

Their new assignments widened Grant and Sherman's perspective and they both saw new opportunities to weaken the Confederate forces. Sherman considered his position "at the shoulder of the Tennessee" as a "fine point from which to pierce Alabama" and to strike at "Meridian and Selma. It would paralyze all Mississippi." Merely assembling Union troops at that place would, he felt, threaten the rebels and "consume large quantities of corn, hogs, and cattle, that are now regularly collected and sent round to Bragg." Grant, likewise, envisioned new raids, seeing East Tennessee as a base for "a cavalry raid on the enemy's line of communication," the railroads south of Chattanooga or east of Atlanta. He also fretted about the raids into West Tennessee of the Confederate cavalrymen Forrest and Chalmers. Grant applied his characteristic two-edged sword when he ordered General Hurlbut: "Collect mules and horses in West Tennessee and Northern Mississippi to supply all required in your command. From North Mississippi collect all serviceable animals and beef-cattle you can reach. . . . That country ought to be put in such condition it will not support Chalmers' command any longer." To Sherman he gave similar instructions: "Troops should collect all the forage and supplies they can and mules and horses from the country. What we do not get the rebels will." He, too, thought of raiding Mississippi and Alabama and sought cavalry from Arkansas for the purpose.[30]

While he had earlier marched eastward Sherman well summed up: "I find plenty of corn, cattle, hogs, &c., on this route, but I don't think there will be much left after my army passes. I never saw such greedy rascals after chickens and fresh meat." He then went on to make a facetious proposal to accomplish many of his and Grant's offensive and defensive objectives: "I don't know but it would be a good plan to march my army back and forth from Florence and Stevenson to make a belt of devastation between the enemy and our country."[31]

Believing that the "victory here [at Chattanooga] has been complete," Grant characteristically had turned his attention to a winter campaign even before Knoxville was relieved. It is hardly surprising that Grant, having had his always-overriding concern for logistics reinforced by saving a situation rendered critical because of communications, would immediately return to his old policy of striking a crippling blow at Confederate war resources. He hoped to concentrate the troops of his enlarged command for "an offensive against Mobile and the interior of Alabama." Pointing out that the mountainous country of north Georgia provided little subsistence or forage for an invading army, that the roads were bad and the winter weather an impediment, and that, at Chattanooga, the "supplies and means of transportation would not admit of a very early campaign, if the season did," he yet wanted "to avoid keeping so large a force idle for months." Since the same roads that held him back would "be so bad that the enemy cannot move a large army into Tennessee," he wrote, a "comparatively small force will be able to hold the present line, and thereby relieve the railroads and enable them to accumulate supplies by the time the roads become passable."

The men thus released from Tennessee could embark on boats "at Nashville, as if to return to West Tennessee and Vicksburg," but land at New Orleans "before the enemy [could] get wind" of the move. Grant proposed then to reach Mobile, "secure that place, or its investment, by the last of January. Should the enemy make an obstinate resistance at Mobile," he added, "I would fortify outside and leave a garrison sufficient to hold the garrison of the town, and with the balance of the army make a campaign into the interior of Alabama and possibly Georgia." He could, he thought, "secure the entire states of Alabama and Mississippi and part of Georgia, or force Lee to abandon Virginia and North Carolina," for "without his force the enemy have not got army enough to resist" the 35,000 men he thought he could have for the operation. The Alabama capital, Montgomery, and the Confederate arsenal of Selma would be captured or destroyed.[32]

Though he ultimately received permission for this offensive, other matters were, General Halleck explained, more pressing. Rebels were "advancing upon Little Rock" and "seriously threatening West Tennessee and the Mississippi River" as well as Port Hudson. General Banks also needed more assistance. So, after completing the "expulsion of the enemy from East Tennessee," troops not needed by Banks nor for "cleaning out West Tennessee and the Mississippi" could take part in the Mobile enterprise. The general in chief explained: Though Banks's operations in Texas "perhaps presented less advantages than a movement on Mobile and the Alabama River," it was "necessary as a matter of political or state policy, connected with our foreign relations, and especially with France and Mexico, that our troops should occupy and hold at least a portion of Texas." Thus Halleck stressed, as he had the previous summer, that he considered it better to concentrate all "efforts for the present to the entire breaking up of the rebel forces west of the Mississippi River, rather than to divide them by also operating against Mobile and Alabama." If successful, headquarters could then reconcentrate the forces for operations east of the river. A campaign in the trans-Mississippi or against Mobile would, however, have to be subordinated to clean-up operations in East and West Tennessee.[33]

☆   ☆

While Grant was recommending that he entirely alter his line of operations, Meade, who also would have preferred a comparable change, completed his plans for an advance upon Lee. Meade had explored the possibilities of various turning movements. He rejected a wide displacement to the west of Lee because it would involve a "march of 60 miles," he declared, "entire abandonment of my communications," and would "expose the army in case of disaster to having its retreat cut off." After having Lincoln reject a proposal for a wide march toward the east, because it involved adopting the Fredericksburg line of operations, Meade settled on a movement toward Lee's immediate right and rear.[34]

In attaining his first objective, the crossing of the Rappahannock, Meade captured most of two Confederate brigades holding a bridgehead north of the river. He then planned a surprise crossing of the Rapidan to the east of Lee, expecting to get between Lee's two corps and attack them separately.

Concentrating all of his forces for the turning movement, Meade did not distract Lee, relying rather on the speed of his well-prepared advance. But the bumbling commander of his lead corps crossed the river slowly and then took the wrong road. A one-day march consumed two days and Lee, alerted to the danger, moved his rear corps forward and covered his right flank by facing his whole army eastward and digging in. Instead of turning Lee, Meade's army confronted Confederate troops in a line of intrenchments seven miles long, on a good site behind Mine Run.

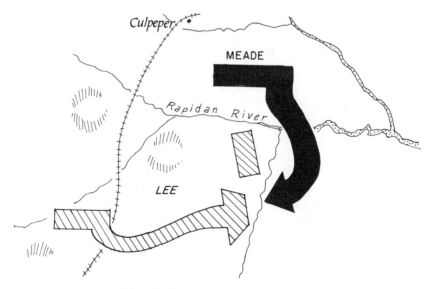

Meade's Turning Movement Fails

Unwilling so easily to abandon his effort, Meade resolved to attack in November aiming at what he thought was a weak point in the intrenchments. Many soldiers prepared by writing their names and addresses on slips of paper so that they could be identified if killed. Some morbidly added the words, "killed in action, November 30, 1863." The attack did not take place.

The rebels had further strengthened their works; they contained no weak point after all. Meade, promptly approving his corps commander's recommendation not to assault, decided to abandon his campaign. Lee then sought a second Chancellorsville by turning Meade's abortive turning movement. But when on December 2 Confederate troops slipped into the Union rear, they found the Union's position vacant and Meade's columns moving north across the Rapidan. Both armies then went into winter quarters.[35]

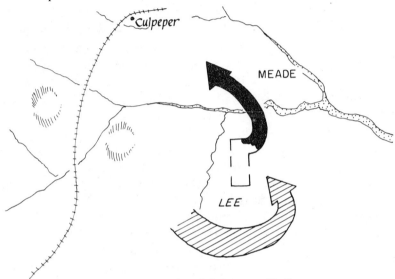

Lee's Turning Movement Fails

Disappointed in his expectation of a "great and decisive battle," Meade was further depressed by his anticipation that headquarters would relieve him of command for his failure to carry out his planned assault at Mine Run. His conviction that politicians saw war in terms of such attacks was in part based on his belief that they had ordered Burnside's futile and costly frontal attack at Fredericksburg. Thus Meade knew he courted "certain personal ruin," because politicians would insist that he "be relieved from the Army of the Potomac." His hostility to his conception of civilian strategy led him sarcastically to write: "It will be said I did wrong in deciding this question by reasoning, and that I ought to have tried, and then a failure would have been evidence of my good judgment; but I trust I have too much reputation as a general to be obliged to encounter certain defeat, in order to prove that victory was not possible."[36]

Meade not only thought that he had been wise in not adding "disaster to failure" but also felt that he would lose his command by refusing "knowingly and willfully" to have "thousands of brave men slaughtered for nothing." To his surprise the President did not relieve him. Nevertheless, Meade remained convinced that politicians and newspapers controlled Union strategy and that they believed it " 'would be better to strew the road to Richmond with the dead bodies of our soldiers than that there should nothing be done!' " Among the critics of the professional soldiers, Meade's reputation suffered further because some of them discerned a resemblance between his operations and those of McClellan. Meade's movement "was regarded as 'fishy' because it was the same as that adopted by McClellan, who having been declared 'a failure' as commander, the man who did anything as he did, was either 'incompetent' or open to the charge of 'disloyalty.' "[37]

☆ ☆

As Meade and Lee went into winter quarters, Grant struggled with the problems of East Tennessee. When Grant assumed command, Halleck had explained to him the importance of delivering "the loyal inhabitants of East Tennessee from the hands of the rebels" and "the restoration of East Tennessee to the Union" as well as the significance of securing Union access to the valuable agriculture products available there. These considerations, together with breaking the East Tennessee and Virginia railroad, cutting off the supply of "iron and other military materials from the vicinity of Chattanooga," and threatening "manufactures at Rome, Atlanta, &c.," had motivated the dual advances of Burnside into East Tennessee and Rosecrans to Chattanooga. The area had adversely impressed Sherman, for, he reminded Grant, "East Tennessee is my horror. That any military man should send a force into East Tennessee puzzles me."[38]

The assumption that Longstreet would retreat into Virginia proved incorrect, when that Confederate general remained for the winter and subsisted his substantial force northeast of Knoxville. Grant felt secure, however, because he had prevented the Confederates from using the East Tennessee and Virginia railroad to supply an advance on Knoxville by directing Union troops to destroy the railroad to the northeast.[39]

But the question of Longstreet's army refused to remain dormant. Grant wondered, in view of the excellent rail connections between East Tennessee and eastern Virginia, whether Lee would not exploit the East Tennessee flank position and "reinforce Longstreet about Bristol and return to Knoxville." Halleck asked if Grant proposed "to pursue Longstreet into Virginia. That line of operations," he said, "is a good one if the army can be supplied on it." Though Grant replied that the resources of the country would not support an advance into Virginia, Halleck's southern newspapers reported that Longstreet was raiding in Kentucky and he emphasized "the holding of Tennessee and the prevention of the enemy from getting supplies there." Since "Meade's operations have failed to produce any results," Halleck observed, "Lee may send by rail reinforcements to Longstreet without our knowing it." The southern papers were wrong, but Grant remained concerned.[40]

Though Grant had in East Tennessee "as much force as could be subsisted for the present," he hoped to destroy more of the railroad to prevent the rebels' coming in the spring and, perhaps, fighting there "the last great battle of the war." This he wished to avoid for he did not want to fight in East Tennessee, preferring "to select my own campaign in the spring," he said, "instead of having the enemy dictate it to me." Nevertheless, he intended to collect stores there "for the subsistence of a large army."[41]

Though Halleck persistently pressed Grant to see that Longstreet was "driven out" of East Tennessee, Grant, after several efforts, concluded that he could not manage it. After conferences with Burnside's successor, the reliable John G. Foster, Grant found that "scanty clothing and short rations," together with "very few animals in East Tennessee in condition to move artillery or other stores," made an advance almost impossible. Foster reported that "many animals are dying daily" and that he was "entirely destitute of bread, coffee and sugar." Grant could not help Foster because Thomas's army at Chattanooga consumed everything available and his "animals were dying of starvation too." Thomas had pointed out: "It takes all the means we have to supply the troops here. The railroad is entirely unequal to the emergency. . . . My only hope is that we can stand it longer than the enemy."[42]

Inability to furnish provisions for an army adequate to the task prevented any campaign against Longstreet. Even if I advanced "against Longstreet in overwhelming force," Grant wrote, "he will simply fall back toward Virginia until he can be reinforced or take up an impregnable position." This fundamental condition of Civil War warfare meant that unless Grant and Foster could cripple Longstreet in some way, there was no point in pushing him back. Unless seriously hurt, Longstreet could "return with impunity" when the army which had pushed him back had to withdraw, because he would have destroyed the railroad, the only supply line. In any case, Longstreet was doing no harm in Tennessee and, by staying there, Grant explained, he "makes more secure other parts of our possessions."[43]

As Grant began to cope with the problem of Longstreet's menacing position in East Tennessee, the Confederates were making significant command changes. The defeat at Chattanooga had precipitated Bragg's resignation. Indeed Bragg's usefulness as a field commander had been demolished earlier, in the Murfreesboro campaign and its aftermath. Too many soldiers hated him by that time. Graphically illustrative, one soldier, upon learning incorrectly that Mrs. Bragg had died, wrote: "I assure you, had it of been him instead of her, there would have been rejoicing in the Southern Army as far as privates are concerned. No one man, that ever lived, I don't believe ever had as much hatred expressed against him, as Bragg." The general eventually even lost confidence in himself. On the last day of November, 1863, he received approval from Richmond to relinquish his command.[44]

President Davis wanted Lee for the critical and ill-starred western position, but to move Lee there would only create the problem of finding another suitable commander for Virginia. Since the ablest lieutenant general in the

West, William J. Hardee, declined permanent appointment, the choice fell between the two seasoned and available full generals, Beauregard and Johnston. Both possessed qualifications and received recommendations, though Davis lacked confidence in either. As the lesser of two evils, Davis chose Johnston, who turned over his Mississippi department to the fighting ecclesiastic, Leonidas Polk. Recommended by Lee and Hardee, Beauregard would probably have been a better choice, for his old army had much loyalty to him and he now consistently kept the President well informed of his plans.

In another blunder, this one political, Davis appointed the unpopular and recently defeated Bragg to Lee's old post in Richmond. Yet militarily he made a shrewd choice for it employed Bragg's field experience, his excellent strategic sense, and his acknowledged administrative capacity. In providing this much-needed strength at headquarters, Davis wisely, though belatedly, repaired his 1862 mistake of leaving vacant this position. Thus Davis, as he tyically did, subordinated political to military considerations. But in appointing Bragg rather than a more popular general, the President drew another check against his fast-dwindling balance of political capital. Lincoln would never have made such a costly choice nor would he have conceived that his political assets would have permitted it.

President Davis limited western changes to personnel, but in the North the creation under Grant of the Military Division of the Mississippi constituted a major advance in Union departmental arrangement. The Union's western armies had been burdened for well over a year with an excessively decentralized structure. The grouping under Grant resembled the one which the Confederates instituted in the fall of 1862. As in Joseph E. Johnston's Department of the West, Grant exercised only operational control, with his subordinate departments continuing to report directly to Washington for administrative matters. But Grant's new military division, created during the siege of Chattanooga, was too oriented toward that objective, and Schofield's Missouri department and Banks's in Louisiana had not been included. The War Department could very properly have made these a part of the Division of the Mississippi for, unlike the Confederate situation, excellent communications provided by the Mississippi River and the railroads in Missouri linked the Union trans-Mississippi area to the east.

With forces around the periphery of the Confederacy, the Union had a more difficult task of organization than did the Confederates, excepting, of course, for their problem of lack of communication with their trans-Mississippi region. Within the Confederate eastern area, the departmental structure frequently changed to reflect the alterations in the strategic situation. Though reorganizations sometimes lagged behind the military changes which prompted them and the boundaries chosen were not always the best, the system of redrawing departmental lines served the Confederacy well, providing a desirable means of responding to altered military realities. After the fall of Chattanooga and Knoxville, Davis completely united the forces of Tennessee and East Tennessee, leaving in the western region only the two commands of Johnston in north Georgia and Polk in Mississippi and Alabama. In view of the scarcity of capable army generals, Davis displayed wisdom in leaving these armies separate, rather than appointing a third officer to coordinate their activities.

Though the superior Union headquarters staff had been able to cope with the greater decentralization inherent in the Union structure, the vigor of central control seemed to diminish in the fall and winter of 1863–64. Banks, for example, freely planned his own campaigns, and Halleck informed Gillmore: You are "at liberty to undertake such operations in your department as you may deem best." The task of constantly planning and coordinating offensives on many fronts demanded more sustained activity than the defense; for the most part the Confederate defensive system required response only, and that in accord with well-practiced, pre-existing plans to move reserves by rail.[45]

Quality of command performance sometimes declined because the war exacted such a toll on many of the participants, especially those in the war departments, where there was never a lull. Just as the constant strain and unremitting labor drained Jefferson Davis's emotinal, intellectual, and physical energies, so the two years of constant and vigorous activity wore down the younger and healthier Halleck. Along with the weakening of his energy to maintain control of all operations, Halleck also lost some of his determination to dominate the situation at headquarters. He seemed to Lincoln to have "shrunk from responsibility whenever it was possible." Halleck truly welcomed the emergence of Grant as general in chief.[46]

Lincoln, on the other hand, well conserved all of his energies and devoted them to politics and only the most basic questions of policy and strategy. Aided by a strong Cabinet and by Halleck and the headquarters staff, he could, and wisely did, delegate all detail and all but the most fundamental decisions. Unlike other participants, Lincoln managed to sustain most of his vigor throughout the war.

The placing of Bragg in charge of military operations not only strengthened the Confederate headquarters organization but completed the restoration of harmony in Confederate strategy making. As a long-time disciple of Beauregard, Bragg brought the ideas of the western concentration bloc into the formal structure of the Davis administration. The President could have brought in the bloc, and at the same time made political capital of it, by choosing Beauregard instead of Bragg; but the President distrusted the ability of the flamboyant Creole and was suspicious of his widespread political connections. Davis could work with Bragg but not with Beauregard.

Bragg's position in Richmond gave him contact with Lee and this led to a relationship of collaboration. In the winter and spring of 1863 Lee had been at odds with the western concentration bloc as he had warded off their efforts to obtain from his army reinforcements for the West. In addition to reacting as any other department commander would, Lee believed, incorrectly, that Richmond was the primary Union objective and, for this reason, the President should not weaken his army. In Lee's anxiety to retain all his troops, he had advanced some strategic theories completely at variance with those he had always espoused and practiced. Thus he argued that troops moving by rail would always arrive "too late" and, therefore, he favored maintaining the existing force distribution. By midsummer of 1863, he had abandoned his advocacy of strategic principles so much at variance with his own and the President's. By the time Longstreet went to reinforce Bragg, Lee had fully mastered the western situation and grasped its problems and importance. His advice now harmonized once more with his principle and practice of using the railroad for concentration to meet the enemy's offensives.

With Bragg in Richmond and Lee again advocating ideas in harmony with the strategic views of the western concentration bloc, Confederate planning stressed the problem of the West. Beauregard's role grew necessarily smaller, now that his ideas were so firmly established in Richmond. Alarmed that the federal movement of troops from Virginia to Tennessee showed that Halleck was "just finding out what can be done with sudden and rapid concentration of troops," Beauregard was depressed by the Confederates' situation because they had "no more troops to concentrate." Although at one point he advocated a surprise move of Longstreet's forces to join "Lee's, to crush Meade before the return of the latter's three corps sent to defeat Bragg," Beauregard limited his proposals to counter-concentration in the West. Richmond followed this line of thought also and it finally resulted in a recommendation for a daring offensive into Middle Tennessee.[47]

A variety of suggestions had been offered for consideration, including one of many by Longstreet, which proposed mounting his entire corps for a gigantic raid into Kentucky. Finally, in early March, Bragg urged on Johnston and Longstreet the offensive at last decided on in Richmond. The plan blended the ideas of Lee and the western concentration bloc, but Lee's approach predominated. Rather than advocating an attack against Union weakness, it was based on Lee's stated belief: The "enemy's great effort will be in the west and we must concentrate our strength there to meet him." Nor did the campaign respond to the bloc's faith in reconquering territory, for Lee explained: "We are not in condition, and never have been, in my opinion, to invade the enemy's country with a prospect of permanent benefit." But characteristically, Lee continued: The proper strategy against the enemy is to "alarm and embarrass him to some extent and thus prevent his undertaking anything of magnitude against us." He wished to prepare for the enemy's expected western offensive and, as he had tried to do in Virginia the previous spring, "take the initiative and fall upon them unexpectedly." In this way the Confederates "might derange their plans and embarrass them the whole summer."[48]

Typical of Lee, the proposal included a turning movement, but one which long had been Bragg's "favorite." In phrases like those of Lee, Bragg explained: It is "not deemed advisable to attempt the capture of the enemy's fortified position by direct attack, but to draw him out and then, if practicable, force him to battle in the open field. To accomplish this object we should so move as to concentrate our means between the scattered forces of the enemy, and failing to draw him out for battle, to move upon his lines of communications." The turning movement was a replica of the Kentucky campaign against Buell, except that Johnston and Longstreet would unite between Chattanooga and Knoxville. After their junction they would march toward Nashville and either capture the city or move in its rear, which would "isolate that position and compel a retrograde movement of the enemy's main force."[49]

In its advance the army would, according to Lee, "be recruited by men from Tennessee and Kentucky." Sounding much like Beauregard, Lee had confidence that "a victory gained there would open the country . . . to the Ohio." As in Beauregard's thinking, this plan called for a surprise concentration with troops from South Carolina and Mississippi joining Johnston and Longstreet for the advance.[50]

The executors of the proposed offensive raised insuperable objections. The advance of both armies would, of course, be a raid and the Tennessee country they must cross had "been exhausted by the enemy, and did not abound" in supplies even when occupied by the Confederates. A raid into the enemy's rear, if the Confederates could carry it out, would mean that a victory would be "indispensable as the only way of avoiding the other alternative of utter destruction or loss" of the army. Longstreet displayed as much pessimism as did Johnston, realizing that it would really be their forces which would be turned; if the Federals stood pat and fortified in their rear, the Confederates, without a supply line, would, he wrote, "be obliged to disperse in the mountains and many of us perish or surrender to the enemy without a fight."[51]

Though too ambitious to be practical from either a logistical or strategic standpoint, the offensive was, in a sense, the apogee of Confederate strategic planning. It even included one of Bragg and Johnston's favorites, "a heavy column of cavalry . . . to operate on the enemy's line of communication and distract his attention." It blended well Lee's concept of a spoiling attack through a turning movement and Beauregard's very broadly based surprise concentration by rail. Bragg's nostalgia for his Kentucky invasion and Lee's ignorance of the western logistical situation led them both to recommend a march, not through a fertile area like the Shenandoah Valley but through country where Grant, with even his ample resources, was having difficulty subsisting his forces. A sense of desperation, perhaps, led them to advocate a campaign which was too daring and one which Johnston properly rejected.[52]

As all of the principal Confederate leaders and factions were working on conventional ways of defeating the coming Union offensive, Union leaders were approaching the war from a different perspective and were employing somewhat different operational concepts. Lincoln believed that the proper view of the war had become one of wearing down the enemy. He concurred with the general's emphasis on the need for more cavalry, for, he thought, "as the rebellion grows weaker, it will run more and more into guerrillaism." The fall of Knoxville and Chattanooga convinced Lincoln that, with the cutting of the East Tennessee and Virginia railroad, the Union was making significant progress. Writing Rosecrans, when he was astride the railroad at Chattanooga, the President said: You have the enemy "by the throat and he must break your hold, or perish." Lincoln had believed that Rosecrans needed only a tenacious defensive at Chattanooga, for, using another simile, he now thought: "The rebellion can only eke out a short and feeble existence, as an animal sometimes may with a thorn in its vitals." Lincoln saw that controlling the Mississippi and then breaking the direct rail link between Richmond and the southwest crippled the Confederacy both militarily and economically. His policy of raising black troops had succeeded and he urged each field commander to press black recruiting for his own army, thus using this "powerful instrument of weakening the enemy and increasing his own force." By December the President noted that there were 100,000 Negroes in service, thus, he wrote, "giving the double advantage of taking so much labor from the insurgent cause, and supplying the places which otherwise must be filled with so many white men. So far as tested, it is difficult to say they are not as good soldiers as any."[53]

To his attack on the enemy's logistics, Lincoln increasingly added a political dimension as opportunities for reconstruction expanded in the trans-Mississippi. General Rosecrans had asked the President: Would it not be desirable "to offer a general amnesty to all officers and soldiers in the Rebellion? It would give us," he added, "moral strength and weaken them very much." The President immediately responded that he did "intend doing something like" Rosecrans's suggestion, "whenever the case shall appear ripe enough to have it accepted in the true understanding, rather than as a confession of weakness and fear."[54]

The victory at Chattanooga made the situation ripe enough and Lincoln's December, 1863, message to Congress provided the platform for announcing his Proclamation of Amnesty and Reconstruction. In this he attempted to establish loyal governments. If a number of voters, equal to 10 percent of the vote cast in 1860, should take an oath of allegiance and form a government, the United States would recognize and support it. Thus Lincoln tried to mobilize the support of the many southerners whom he thought were "ready to swing back to their old bearings."[55]

The Confederates did seem to want to negotiate for, on the same day that Lee retreated from Gettysburg, the Confederate gunboat *Torpedo* carried Vice President Alexander H. Stephens down the James River on an unsuccessful mission to Hampton Roads. He had wished to speak about prisoner exchange and also possible terms to end the war, but the Federals refused. Lincoln was not seeking negotiation. He wished to build up loyal governments, arm southern Negroes, and, by combining military and economic pressure with the olive branch of amnesty, defeat the rebels by political and psychological means.

To the limited military measures of Scott's anaconda plan Grant was adding an important and distinctive extension, one in which Sherman would discover significant political implications. During the winter following his victory at Chattanooga, Grant had the leisure to work out his operations for the coming year. Though the war had been successful in the West, Grant had to address the same problem, the strength of the defense, which had so long challenged and baffled Lincoln and Halleck in Virginia.

In addition to the problem of strong positions and the difficulty and cost of attacking the opponents' intrenchments, Grant needed to consider the ability of the enemy general to retreat. The attacker could not "overtake him unless it should be his desire to give battle." With competent adversaries such as Longstreet and Johnston and with no navigable rivers against which to trap them, Grant's army would have difficulty doing anything to the rebels except pushing or turning them back. Sherman even expressed skepticism about the function of a battle when he later expressed: I have no "regret that the enemy spared me a battle."[56]

With a foe like Johnston or Longstreet, who could "simply fall back . . . until he could be reinforced or take up an impregnable position," the ever-critical problem of supply became decisive. Sherman colorfully phrased the situation: It was "these cursed wagons and mules that bother us. If soldiers and mules could flourish without eating, 'I myself would be a soldier.' It is not 'villainous saltpeter' that makes one's life so hard, but grub and mules." These necessities, food and forage, required railroad transportation because the armies of the Military Division of the Mississippi had already reached the limits of the region in which the Union could supply them by water.[57]

Advancing by rail went slowly because of the necessity of rebuilding the railroad which the retreating army had inevitably destroyed. Wagon transportation was limited in radius and that radius usually contracted, as had happened on the route from Kentucky to East Tennessee, when the teams had eaten the forage available along their route. An army could live off the country only if it could keep in motion, a difficult task when faced by a strong enemy force which constantly took up nearly impregnable positions. The question of logistics had been paramount throughout all of Grant's operations in Mississippi and Tennessee.

These insuperable problems led Grant finally to abandon his ideas of driving Longstreet out. Instead, Grant decided to try to block that line of operations by more complete railway destruction and to reach the only worthwhile objective in that direction, the saltworks in Virginia, by a risky cavalry raid. In directing this raid, he pointed out that "the destruction of important bridges between Bristol and Saltville and of the salt-works there" would compensate for great risks.[58]

Along with the railroad, the southwestern Virginia saltworks had long been an objective of Union raids. Grant's choice of the salterns fortuitously coincided with a most vigorous northern effort generally to deprive the South of salt. Commencing spectacularly on December 10, 1863, the Federals launched a devastating raid into Florida. There, on the West Arm of Saint Andrew's Bay, the South was producing 400 bushels of salt daily. The Confederate government had built a works and a surrounding village of twenty-seven buildings covering three-fourths of a square mile. Many hundred ox and mule teams constantly labored in hauling salt to a depot in Montgomery. The marauders inflicted a loss amounting to half a million dollars. After burning all the buildings, the Federals captured the field piece which had defended the place and which also had occasionally harassed the blockading fleet. They then pushed down the bay and destroyed no less than 198 private salt-making establishments. Elsewhere, too, the universal pressure eroded southern salt resources. On Christmas Day at Bear Inlet, North Carolina, the Union troops destroyed several saltworks. By the close of 1863 the total loss in salt and salt manufacturers amounted to well over $6,000,000. In dry measure, the Confederacy probably lost 5,196 bushels of salt per day. It seems amazing, then, that the South continued as well as it did with salt-making. Often, somehow Phoenix-like, demolished saltworks rose from their ashes and ruin. The *New York Herald* noted on January 5, 1864, that "Saltworks are as plentiful in Florida as blackbirds in a rice field." The frenzied destructive effort continued, even into late February, 1864.[59]

But Grant had more to concern him than depriving the southern war economy of salt. He was seeking an aproach to overcome the defensive power which Confederate armies displayed in the field. Besides this and coping with the logistical requirements of his own troops, Grant also had to defend Union territorial acquisitions. His own concerns and those of his superiors included not only East and West Tennessee, Arkansas, and Louisiana, but the navigation of the Mississippi and the protection of sites such as Vicksburg and Port Hudson. Disliking to "be content with guarding territory already taken from the enemy," Grant felt "regret" that defensive missions had to tie up so many combatants. All concerned seemed to agree that "the policy of holding numerous points with large garrisons for the purpose of protecting the country from rebel raids is not wise." It was "not worth its cost," because such a policy "scatters a command along a thin weak line."[60]

Though the Union employed counter-raids, it could find no method to keep raiders out and Sherman concluded to let a raider "rampage at pleasure in West Tennessee until the people are sick and tired of him." This military approach fitted Sherman's ideas for reconstructing the rebels, as he "would not coax them" back into the Union nor "even meet them half way, but make them so sick of war that generations would pass before they again appeal to it."[61]

The exception to Sherman's laissez-faire policy with respect to raiders was the Mississippi. "To secure the safety of the navigation of the Mississippi River I would slay millions," Sherman wrote. "On this point I am not only insane, but mad." To resolve this quesiton he proposed counter-raids and retaliation. The Union could find no satisfactory way to hold conquered territory, and the raids of the Confederate cavalry general, Forrest, continued to agitate Grant even well into 1864.[62]

Raids did not constitute the only difficulty for the defense. A major Confederate counteroffensive, such as Chickamauga, always posed a real threat. Such an enemy maneuver was quite menacing because the Confederates possessed excellent telegraphic and rail communications between their various lines of operations and had shown, as at Shiloh and Chickamauga, their ability to use their interior lines of operation for offensive as well as defensive purposes.

During the period after the fall of Vicksburg, the Confederates were not nearly as active in this way as the Union leaders imagined. In addition to actual Confederate troop movements which worried them, the Union commanders were, at one time or another, apprehensive that the Confederates had reinforced their armies in Middle Tennessee, East Tennessee, near Vicksburg, and at Mobile, and that Bragg had sent troops to Lee.[63]

The power of the initiative conferred upon the enemy by their interior lines perturbed Grant as it long had Lincoln and Halleck. Grant said: I want "to be able to select my own campaign in the spring instead of having the enemy dictate it for me." Though the general in chief warned Grant that the South was working on a new railroad to "open a continuous interior line from Richmond to the southwest," Halleck enthusiastically endorsed Grant's desire to gain the initiative, saying: "If you can carry into effect your idea of forcing the enemy to fight you in the next campaign on ground of your own selection, it will be a great gain. In most of our operations heretofore the rebels have had an advantage in this respect."[64]

Having tried for many months to cope with these various problems, Grant naturally evolved what became an interrelated group of solutions. Finding a way to overcome the Confederacy's strategic advantage of effective employment of its interior lines comprised one of the principal elements of the well-integrated strategic approach which Grant and his associates developed after his elevation to the consolidated western command. In November and December Grant "discussed the question of future operations with W. F. Smith, Rawlins," Sherman, and others and made plans which provided a key to Grant's thinking. These campaigns themselves, rather than explicitly formulated ideas, exhibit Grant's answer to the question of how he could successfully further prosecute the war.[65]

Grant based his plans on what has been called the strategy of exhaustion. This strategy differs from attrition in that it does not aim to decimate, much less destroy, the manpower of the enemy's armed forces, but rather seeks to destroy their logistical support. If the armies fail to receive food and clothing, forage, shoes, harnesses for the horses and mules, and necessary weapons and ammunition, they cease to be effective. Even if they sustain no combat losses, armies need additional men as replacements for losses incurred through desertion, discharge, and death or disability from natural causes. If this supply of new men can be cut off, this, like interdicting supplies, would contribute to "exhausting" the enemy's forces rendering them less and less potent. The Vicksburg campaign, like the Union blockade, aimed at exhaustion, and Halleck had stated that the advance on Chattanooga and Knoxville had the same goal. It was a natural strategy for Grant, a former quartermaster, and was the objective of his Jackson campaign and of his projected move against Mobile.

Grant evidently agreed with the Union consensus as to the difficulty, even impossibility, of destroying an opposing army in the field. All Union generals regarded the frontal fight as indecisive, and Hooker, Rosecrans, and Meade had all been thwarted in their efforts to attack the Confederates in the rear. The three commanders had tried turning movements, which might have been decisive had they reached the opposing forces' rear; of the efforts, only Rosecrans's had succeeded in turning the foe out of his position. Grant alone, during the war, had succeeded in carrying out this classic maneuver to a degree sufficient to effect annihilation. But the circumstances were clearly special. Both Floyd and Pemberton had readily allowed themselves to be trapped against rivers, making their capitulations virtual certainties.

And by now both Floyd and Pemberton held no command and even Bragg had relinquished his duties in the field. It was hardly realistic to expect from the Confederate generals in the field in 1864 the kind of helpful performance provided in 1862 and 1863 by Floyd and Pemberton. Annihilation held too little promise if an acceptable alternative existed.

Sherman formulated the advantage of the defense when he hoped that the Confederates might concentrate in East Tennessee. "If we could draw all of Lee's army into East Tennessee," Sherman wrote, "they would be bound to go ahead or fall back. The mountains on either flank will restrict their line to the railroad and the army which is on the defensive has the advantage." With the terrain precluding a turning movement, the Confederates would have to attack in front, something Sherman obviously desired.[66]

Grant quite clearly understood the means for dealing with enemy armies: destroy their sources of supply and undermine their logistics until they withered away or became so feeble that they could be destroyed or brushed aside. The two strategies, annihilation and exhaustion, produced the same final result. How could a country on the offensive implement the strategy of exhaustion? Except against an island nation like Japan or the United Kingdom, a blockade clearly would not suffice. The conquest of territory, and the consequent denial to the Confederacy of the manpower, food, and mineral and industrial production of the occupied regions, seemed the only viable course open to the Union. Also politically and economically expedient, this approach would permit reconstruction of the occupied areas and allow them to contribute their resources to the Union war effort.

This would lead to the dictation of peace terms only if the adversary did not then resort to widespread guerrilla warfare. Avoiding the main occupying forces, guerrillas would concentrate against small garrisons and, like all defenders, retreat in the face of superior forces. They would find their most promising objectives in the vulnerable supply lines and other logistical installations of their adversary. In this sense this kind of warfare is a form of the strategy of exhaustion, one applied on the defensive as the Confederates had already done with their raids and guerrilla activities in the rear of the Union armies. Whether the defeated power would resort to this form of warfare would partially depend, on the one hand, on the level of their morale and the degree of allegiance to their cause and, on the other, on the acceptability of the peace terms offered by the victorious power.

But in its implementation the strategy of exhaustion, by conquering territory, did not entirely avoid the difficulty faced by the strategy of annihilation in overcoming the traditional supremacy of the defense, augmented by improved firearms, better organization, and greater maneuverability; in seeking to occupy an adversary's country an invader must also face a defending force. The course of the war through 1863 had demonstrated the difficulty of pushing back or maneuvering an army out of a given area. Though seizing key enemy areas presented far fewer obstacles than annihilation, the force on the offensive would still have to cope with the defender's army and thus have to overcome many of the difficulties inherent in the strategy of annihilation.

The more land the Union acquired, the more men it had to detail to guard it. The farther Union forces advanced, the longer and more insecure became their communications through occupied but still hostile country. The Union had, in the winter of 1863–64, still a long way to go. It had advanced through only one genuinely Confederate state, Tennessee, and the eastern third of that state supported the Union. The distance through Alabama or Georgia to the Florida border was twice the distance across Tennessee from the Kentucky to the Alabama and Georgia borders. In more than two years of campaigning, the Union forces had advanced through only one-third of the West. Ahead lay the hardest two-thirds because they had at last run out of water communications and must henceforth rely exclusively on the very vulnerable railroads. Further, they had now reached the gates of the lower South, the first states to secede, in which they could expect to find fewer sympathizers and more hostility. Halleck's concentration against the trans-Mississippi had captured some important points, but the rebellion was still very much alive in those Confederate states.

The defense of Union territory against raids and the possibility of reconquest absorbed immense numbers of troops. Even on June 1, 1863, approaching the height of the Vicksburg campaign, Grant had 60,000 men of his command before Vicksburg while 40,000 remained under the control of Hurlbut at Memphis to resist guerrillas and the threat of raids by 6,000 Confederates in northern Mississippi. At this same time, when both Rosecrans in Middle Tennessee and Hooker in Virginia were ostensibly engaged with the enemy, the area in the rear of their armies, from Washington, D.C., through Maryland, West Virginia, Ohio, and Kentucky, contained 112,000 men, a force equal to Hooker's Army of the Potomac and much larger than Rosecrans's Army of the Cumberland. In addition to coping with guerrillas, this huge defensive force faced only 22,000 Confederates. On the seacoast, the Union, using its naval superiority, could threaten raids and, by capturing ports or breaking railroads, interrupt Confederate communications with its vital overseas or domestic sources of supply. Yet, because the Confederates employed their railroads along the coast as a filled pipeline to move reinforcements to any threatened point, they had, in the Carolinas, Georgia, and Florida, only 33,000 men deployed to resist 31,000 federal troops already on the coast, plus any which might be moved there. The accounts on defending territory hardly favored the Union.[67]

Grant well knew the vulnerability of communications. In December, 1862, he had the experience of being extended "like a Peninsula into an enemies country with a large Army depending for their daily bread upon keeping open a line of railroad running one hundred & ninety miles through an enemy's country, or at least through territory occupied by a people terribly embittered and hostile to us." Soon after writing this the destruction of his depot at Holly Springs and Forrest's interruption of his railroad farther north at Jackson, Tennessee, stopped his overland advance to Vicksburg in December, 1862. This problem of the importance and security of communications was as old as warfare itself. In 480 B.C. the Persian King, Xerxes, had been compelled to withdraw a large part of his invading force from Greece because the defeat of his fleet at the Battle of Salamis deprived him of secure water communications with his base in Asia Minor, and only water communications had the capacity to supply his large army.[68]

Grant, of course, more vividly and realistically appreciated his own difficulties than he did those of his adversaries, which, in his ignorance of their problems, he tended to discount. If the Union could push southern armies back, the defending forces would eventually shrink in some proportion to the diminution of the country from which they drew their recruits and supplies. Further, soldiers recruited in regions which passed under Union occupation tended to desert to go home to look after their families. On the other hand, and somewhat more rapidly, the strength of the advancing Union armies would diminish as their communication lines grew longer and the hostile area which they must garrison and guard against raiders expanded. As Grant succinctly summarized it: "As the enemy falls back he increases in strength by gathering in railroad garrisons whilst I am weakened by leaving behind protection for my avenues of supply."[69]

If the federal armies decreased in size at a rate greater than the Confederates, the advancing forces would eventually be little larger than those of the defenders and thus the North would have to halt its advance. This very prospect worried Grant and Sherman, and they were skeptical of their ability to defend their railroad communications at all if they had to extend them much more. The problem seemed immense in the fall of the third year of the war. The precedent of the long and, for the British, unsuccessful war of the American Revolution discouraged them still more.

Apparently the Union had two strategies, neither of which would work. Annihilation would fail because the mid-nineteenth-century army was virtually invulnerable. Exhaustion by territorial acquisition might well fail, even if they could successfully protect their rail lines of communications, because of the progressively larger number of troops required to garrison conquests and guard the communications from raiders and guerrillas.

But Grant evolved a solution to the problem: for the implementation of the strategy of exhaustion he would rely heavily on raids himself rather than on the further occupation of the enemy's country, because they avoided both the liabilities which might well defeat penetrations. They required no communications, because the advance was temporary, and the raiding forces, usually in motion, could live off the country. Furthermore, since the Union would not have to hold the region permanently, it would need no additional troops as garrisons. As a bonus, Confederate resistance might well help the Union protect its conquests because Confederate forces otherwise dedicated to menacing Union-held territory might be diverted to resist Union forces.[70]

Lincoln and the headquarters staff had advocated counter-raids for more than a year, and Grierson's successful venture, as well as Streight's disaster, had been instances thereof. But Grant did not base his strategy of exhaustion by raids, rather than occupation through penetration, on a reliance on the usual hit-and-run cavalry operation. Infantry, which would not have to flee so soon, would carry out the projected raids. Infantry armies would, with their engineers and large numbers of troops, have the skill and manpower to do more thoroughly the job of destruction of war resources. Furthermore, living off the country, they would eat up agricultural resources.

Early in his independent command in Mississippi, Grant had wished to wreck rebel railroads and had agreed with the policy that otherwise to "leave the interior alone" seemed the best course. Consistently Grant had defined the war in logistical terms. His successful Vicksburg campaign had solved a problem in logistics—how to turn the Confederate position, using efficient and secure water communications. Vicksburg and the control of the Mississippi itself had been components in the execution of the anaconda strategy. But again free to choose his own goals, he had selected Jackson, Mississippi, its railroads, and everything "of value for the enemy to carry on war with." In order to reach Jackson and destroy the railroad Grant had ordered that Johnston's army be "broken up" and pushed across the Pearl River.[71]

The Mobile campaign, which he proposed in July, had the same logistical objective, Confederate communications, supplies, and arsenals in the Mobile, Selma, and Montgomery areas of Alabama and, possibly, in the adjacent area of Georgia, the important rail and manufacturing center of Atlanta. This vital southern area again became the goal of the major offensive which Grant planned. As he had taken the line of the Mississippi, he now proposed to secure the line "from Chattanooga to Mobile, Montgomery and Atlanta being the important intermediate points." He advocated simultaneous advances from Mobile toward Montgomery and from Chattanooga toward Atlanta. The destruction of the communications along that line would interdict the movement of Confederate supplies and troops. The raiding armies would consume food and forage along the line and destroy so many other things of value which the South needed to carry on war that the Confederate western forces would be seriously hurt, if not disabled.[72]

Sherman explained the concept after he had "a long conversation with General Grant." Sherman and Grant did "not believe in holding possession of any part of the interior. This requires a vast force, which is rendered harmless to the enemy by its scattered parts"; thus "a large army is wasted in detachments." Grant's plans, therefore, embraced a line, not an area. His projected advances from Mobile and the Tennessee were in their purpose more in the nature of raids than efforts to acquire more of the Confederacy. He was, in a sense, going to apply to the opposition that disconcerting raiding strategy which they were using against him, while occupying no new region which he or his superiors would have to defend. Carrying the war to the enemy would also cover existing conquests.[73]

As Grant's proposed offensive envisioned a combined attack against both Mobile and the Confederates in North Georgia, the Union armies would operate on exterior lines. Grant, acutely aware of this, knew that the rebels had often exploited the telegraph, the railroad, and interior lines. Originally Grant had planned to defend on the Tennessee and concentrate the bulk of his troops on the Mobile line. As modified, both forces would advance. Between them the Confederates occupied positions along a telegraph line and railroad running from Chattanooga to Mobile. Union forces would be without telegraphic, much less railroad, communications. Mobile and the Tennessee were, Grant realized, "objectionable as starting points to be all under one

command, from the fact that the time it will take to communicate from one
to the other will be so great; but Sherman or McPherson, one of whom would
be entrusted with the distant command, are officers of such experience and
reliability that all objection on this score, except that of enabling the two
armies to act as a unit," would be removed. Extraordinarily able men in
command would thus make up for the lack of a telegraph. To the exterior line
problem, the inability to act as a unit, "the same objection will exist—probably not to so great an extent, however—if a movement is made in more than
one column. This will have to be with an army of the size we will be compelled to use," said Grant. With forces of such magnitude, the Union would
find it impossible to concentrate or supply them on one line, and inevitably
require two lines of advance into Georgia and Alabama.[74]

In any event, the Union could not possibly avoid this situation of multiple
exterior lines of operation. Grant had other ideas for dealing with this problem. Two of these were old ones. He had already disabled the Confederate
line of operations toward Vicksburg when Sherman had taken Jackson and
demolished the railroads. Grant planned to remove the menace of a southern
offensive into his rear through East Tennessee by a similar measure to have
the railroad "entirely destroyed" to "secure East Tennessee from another
invasion by the enemy." He could thus protect himself from some Confederate offensives and have released troops available for use on other lines of
operation.[75]

On these other lines he planned to practice the distraction of the enemy,
which had so effectively aided his movement south of Vicksburg. Although
the South had interior lines for more rapid defensive or offensive action, they
needed to know where to concentrate. If Grant could organize threatening
and confusing movements everywhere, his men would be well advanced before
the rebels could tell which offensive to resist with their defensive reserves.
The key to the solution of this problem lay in using Union naval superiority
to permit the movement from Mobile, landing before the Confederates could
"get wind of" the plan. The surprise Union concentration could expect to
make rapid advance for, Grant thought, "the enemy have not got army enough
to resist the army I can take."[76]

The problem of logistics was not so elegantly solved. By starting from two
bases and having a large accumulation of supplies "on the Tennessee River,
so as to be independent of the railroads . . . for a considerable length of time,"
Grant relied primarily on having his armies live off the country and by having
them move "with less than half the transportation they have been heretofore
accustomed to. . . . It will be impossible," he added, "to subsist a large wagon
train, and besides they will impede the progress of armies marching over the
narrow and mountainous roads of the South." The Mobile force would be in
a particularly favorable position because, by avoiding the long overland march
from Vicksburg, it would reach vital Confederate areas immediately. In addition, it was well situated for foraging because it could expect to advance

rapidly over virgin territory where no troops had previously fought or been quartered.[77]

But Grant, in his most fundamental insight about the liability of exterior lines, recognized that his own armies were just as invulnerable as Longstreet's. With generals such as Sherman and McPherson, "officers of such experience and realiability," Grant realized that the superiority of the defense would work as effectively for him as it would for the enemy and that it was as difficult for the Confederates to harm Sherman or McPherson as it had been for him to hurt Longstreet. Of course, the advances would occur simultaneously so that if the Confederates, by concentrating, threw one force on the defensive, the other force would be free to pursue its advance. Here, without realizing it, he adhered to Lincoln's strategy of simultaneous advances.

Grant's operation on exterior lines embodied much of the essence of the turning movement, for all forces threatened the Confederacy's vital communications links. It was immaterial whether the advancing troops were conducting a raid or a penetration, for powerful infantry forces would be menacing vital railroads and essential shops and factories. They could achieve surprise by their sudden descent on Mobile, exploiting Grant's old "friend," Union naval superiority. This strategy was, of course, analogous to a turning movement with less than the whole army, such as Lee's at Second Bull Run and Grant's at Iuka. Those moves had necessarily given the enemy a central position, which had enabled him to concentrate against the turning force. Pope had attacked Jackson not only to recover his communications but to take advantage of his central position between Lee's two corps. So also to exploit any interior position, the Confederates would have to take the offensive. The troops landing at Mobile would be quite comparable to Jackson's corps in Pope's rear, except that they would be more vulnerable because the army on the Tennessee would be out of supporting distance.

Actually the Confederates would be at liberty to concentrate against either force; if the rebel concentration should prove too powerful to resist, these Union raiders on an exterior line still would be secure. Without the necessary intent to conquer and hold the territory into which they marched or the need to hold a particular line of communications or follow any settled line of operations, they could retreat in any direction. Just as cavalry, such as Grierson's, started from one point only to return to friendly territory at another, so too could these infantry raiders do so on an exterior line.

Pursuers necessarily move more slowly than those fleeing, because the latter cross rivers and then destroy bridges and boats. Further, they also substantially retard the progress of those following through the use of rear-guard actions which require the pursuers' advance guard to deploy from column of march to line of battle, and so delay both the advance guard and all troops behind. Since raiders were expected to retire when they had completed their work of destruction, they would lose no prestige first by being forced to do so. Retirement would not indicate the failure of a mission unless the raiding army had to retreat prematurely, before completing any destruction.

Finally, Grant placed faith in his numerical predominance. Because his army possessed an overall superiority of two to one, one of the offensive forces was bound to get through and that was all he needed to implement the strategy of exhaustion. The havoc which even one raiding army with a large number of infantry and engineers could wreak would likely cripple Confederate war resources significantly. In addition, by raiding, or converting a penetration into a raid, Grant had solved the problem which had so concerned Union leadership in the spring of 1863. He, Halleck, and especially Rosecrans had been concerned about the situation that would have been created by Bragg's simply leaving Tennessee with the bulk of his force, something Bragg and Johnston actually considered. If this had happened, Rosecrans would have been unable to advance immediately, because he first would have had to complete the time-consuming tasks of reconstructing the railroad and accumulating supplies. Grant proposed to solve this problem for the future by converting a penetration into a raid. The Union army could then advance rapidly by the expedient of giving up its communications and living off the country, something made possible by the rapid movement through enemy country which would occur if the Confederates abandoned a line of operations.

Grant's evolution of a carefully integrated, if almost entirely implicit, plan of campaign gave added significance to his command of the large Military Division of the Mississippi. The Union had a better command situation in Virginia also because the capable Meade at last had grasped the headquarters doctrine of aiming at Lee's army rather than Richmond. The Confederates, too, had strengthened their command by substituting Johnston for Bragg and by using Bragg to augment their weak headquarters staff. Both sides would take other measures to prepare for the spring campaign, and the most significant of these would be the elevation of Grant to the post of general in chief.

1. *Welles Diary*, I, 349; Meade to Mrs. Meade, Nov. 24, 1861, *Life and Letters*, I, 230–31.

2. Meade to Mrs. Meade, Feb. 23, June 18, Sept. 3, Oct. 12, Nov. 22, 1862, *Life and Letters*, I, 247, 276, 307, 319, 330.

3. Meade to Mrs. Meade, Jan. 2, 18, Mar. 17, Apr. 20, 1863, *Life and Letters*, I, 344–45, 348, 360, 368.

4. Meade to Mrs. Meade, July 5, 10, 14, 1863, *Life and Letters*, II, 125, 134; Meade to W. F. Smith, July 5, 1863, *O.R.*, XXVII, pt. 3, 539.

5. Meade to Mrs. Meade, July 16, 18, Aug. 3, 6, 1863, *Life and Letters*, II, 135, 136, 141.

6. Meade to Mrs. Meade, Nov. 13, 22, 1862, *Life and Letters*, I, 326, 330; Meade to Halleck, July 28, 1863, *O.R.*, XXVII, pt. 1, 103–4.

7. Meade to Mrs. Meade, Sept. 13, 1862, July 26, 1863, *Life and Letters*, I, 310, II, 137; Meade to Halleck, July 26, 1863, *O.R.*, XXVII, pt. 1, 101; Halleck to Meade, July 27, 1863, *ibid.*, 101.

8. Meade to Mrs. Meade, Nov. 23, 1862, July 26, 1863, *Life and Letters*, I, 331, II, 137.

9. Meade to Mrs. Meade, Nov. 13, 22, 1862, *ibid.*, I, 326, 330.

10. General orders No. 68, July 4, 1863, quoted in Basler, *Collected Works*, VI, 318; Lincoln to Halleck, July 6, 1863, *ibid.*, 318; *Lincoln and the Civil War*, 67.

11. *Lincoln and the Civil War*, 66.

12. *Ibid.*, 102–3.

13. John Gibbon, *Personal Recollections of the Civil War* (New York, London, 1928), 206–7.

14. Lincoln to Halleck, Sept. 15, 1863, Basler, *Collected Works*, VI, 450; Meade to Halleck, Sept. 16, 18, 1863, *O.R.*, XXIX, pt. 2, 196, 201–2.

15. Meade to Mrs. Meade, Sept. 13, 1863, *Life and Letters*, II, 148–49; Meade to Halleck, Sept. 18, 1863, *O.R.*, XXIX, pt. 2, 202.

16. Michael Adams believes that Meade's conduct was conditioned by the belief in southern superiority (Adams, *Our Masters the Rebels*, 147–48).

17. Halleck to Meade, Sept. 19, 1863, *O.R.*, XXIX, pt. 2, 206–7.

18. Lincoln to Halleck, Sept. 19, 1863, Basler, *Collected Works*, VI, 466–68.

19. The proportions governing this are as follows: If Meade's and Lee's armies are assumed to be equal and Meade's were strengthened by one-third, Meade would outnumber Lee four to three. If Lee's army were reduced by one-third, Meade would outnumber Lee by three to two. If reducing Lee's army had added one-third to Bragg's, Bragg would outnumber Rosecrans by only four to three, making the Confederate concentration more advantageous for Meade than for Bragg.

20. Lincoln to Halleck, Sept. 19, 1863, Basler, *Collected Works*, VI, 466–68.

21. Lee to Davis, Aug. 22, 24, 1863, *O.R.*, XXIX, pt. 2, 661, *Wartime Papers*, 594; Lee to Longstreet, Aug. 31, 1863, *ibid.*, 594; Lee to Polk, Oct. 26, 1863, *ibid.*, 614; Lee to Imboden, Oct. 9, 1863, *ibid.*, 607; Lee to Seddon, Oct. 11, 1863, *ibid.*, 607.

22. *Meade's Headquarters*, 29, 31–32, 61.

23. Meade to Halleck, Oct. 15, 1863, *O.R.*, XXIX, pt. 2, 326.

24. Lee to Davis, Oct. 17, 1863, *Wartime Papers*, 608–9; Halleck to Meade, Oct. 7, 15, 18, 1863, *O.R.*, XXIX, pt. 2, 262, 328, 346; Halleck to Foster, Oct. 10, 1863, *ibid.*, 277; Meade to Halleck, Oct. 18, 1863, *ibid.*, 346.

25. Lee to Davis, Oct. 17, 1863, *Wartime Papers*, 608–9.

26. Meade to Halleck, Oct. 20, 21, 1863, *O.R.*, XXIX, pt. 2, 359, 361; Halleck to Foster, Oct. 10, 1863, *ibid.*, 277; Lincoln to Halleck, Oct. 24, 1863, Basler, *Collected Works*, VI, 534; Meade to Mrs. Meade, Oct. 23, 1863, *Life and Letters*, II, 154.

27. Grant to Sherman, Nov. 25, 27, 1863, *O.R.*, XXXI, pt. 2, 46, 46–47; Rawlins to Sherman, Nov. 26, 1863, *ibid.*, 46; Sherman to Hurlbut, Nov. 26, 1863, *ibid.*, pt. 3, 255; Grant to Hooker, Nov. 28, 1863, *ibid.*, pt. 2, 48.

28. Grant to John G. Foster, Nov. 28, 1863, *O.R.*, XXXI, pt. 3, 166; Grant to Halleck, Nov. 29, 1863, *ibid.*, 270; Grant to Burnside, Nov. 29, 1863, *ibid.*, 273.

29. Sherman to Rawlins, Sept. 22, 1863, *O.R.*, XXX, pt. 3, 773; Grant to Kelton, Sept. 25, 1863, *ibid.*, 841; also Sherman to Hurlbut, Sept. 25, 1863, *ibid.*, 844–45; Grant to Halleck, Sept. 30, 1863, *ibid.*, 944; Sherman to Rawlins, Oct. 14, 1863, *ibid.*, pt. 4, 355; Sherman to McPherson, Oct. 24, Nov. 9, 1863, *ibid.*, XXXI, pt. 1, 720, pt. 3, 102.

30. Sherman to Hurlbut, Oct. 23, 1863, *O.R.*, XXXI, pt. 1, 710; Sherman to Adjutant General, Nov. 8, 1863, *ibid.*, pt. 3, 90; Sherman to Halleck, Nov. 16, 18, 1863, *ibid.*, 185, 168; Sherman to Haines, Nov. 23, 1863, *ibid.*, 237; Sherman to McPherson, Nov. 9, 1863, *ibid.*, 189; Grant to Halleck, Nov. 6, 12, 1863, *ibid.*, 122; Grant to Burnside, Nov. 6, 1863, *ibid.*, 67; Grant to Hurlbut, Nov. 9, 1863, *ibid.*, 103; Grant to Sherman, Nov. 13, 1863, *ibid.*, 140.

31. Sherman to Crook, Nov. 6, 1863, *O.R.*, XXXI, pt. 3, 69–70.

32. Grant to Granger, Nov. 29, 1863, *O.R.*, XXXI, pt. 2, 49; Dana to Stanton, Nov. 29, 1863, *ibid.*, 71–72; Grant to Halleck, Dec. 7, 1863, *ibid.*, pt. 3, 349–50.

33. Dana to Grant, Jan. 10, 1864, *O.R.*, XXXII, pt. 2, 58; Halleck to Grant, Dec. 11, 17, 1863, Jan. 8, 1864, *ibid.*, XXXI, pt. 3, 376, 454, XXXII, pt. 2, 40–42.

34. Meade to Halleck, Nov. 2, 20, 1863, *O.R.*, XXIX, pt. 2, 409, 474; Halleck to Meade, Nov. 3, 1863, *ibid.*, 412.

35. Foote, *The Civil War*, II, 876.

36. Meade to Mrs. Meade, Nov. 25, Dec. 2, 1863, *Life and Letters*, II, 156–58.

37. Meade to Mrs. Meade, Dec. 2, 1863, *ibid.*, 158; *Meade's Headquarters*, 61; Gibbon, *Personal Recollections*, 207.

38. Halleck to Grant, Oct. 20, 1863, *O.R.*, XXXI, pt. 1, 667–69; Sherman to Grant, Dec. 1, 1863, *ibid.*, pt. 3, 297.

39. Grant to Foster, Dec. 2, 6, 1863, *O.R.*, XXXI, pt. 3, 310–11, 345; Grant to Halleck, Dec. 2, 1863, *ibid.*, 312.

40. Grant to Halleck, Dec. 8, 1863, *O.R.*, I, XXXI, pt. 3, 356–57; Halleck to Grant, Dec. 8, 13, 1863, *ibid.*, 357, 396.

41. Grant to Halleck, Dec. 17, 1863, *O.R.*, I, XXXI, pt. 3, 429–30; Grant to Foster, Dec. 17, 1863, *ibid.*, 433; Sherman to Banks, Jan. 16, 1864, *ibid.*, XXXIV, pt. 2, 431.

42. Halleck to Grant, Dec. 23, 1863, *O.R.*, XXXI, pt. 3, 472; Grant to Halleck, Feb. 12, 1864, *ibid.*, XXXII, pt. 2, 474–75; Foster to Grant, Jan. 12, 1864, *ibid.*, 71; Thomas to Grant, Feb. 8, 1864, *ibid.*, 352.

43. Grant to Halleck. Feb. 12, 1864, *O.R.*, XXXII, pt. 2, 374–75.

44. McWhiney, *Bragg*, 374–75, 377; Long, *Civil War, Day by Day*, 441, 447.

45. Halleck to Gillmore, Dec. 21, 1863, *O.R.*, XXVIII, pt. 2, 134.

46. Canby, *Lincoln and the Civil War*, 167.

47. Beauregard to Whiting, Dec. 25, 1863, *O.R.*, XXVIII, pt. 2, 580; Connelly and Jones, *Politics of Command*, 141–42.

48. Lee to Longstreet, Mar. 8, 1864, *O.R.*, XXXII, pt. 3, 494–95; Lee to Davis, Feb. 3, 1864, *Wartime Letters*, 666–67.

49. Bragg to Johnston, Mar. 7, 12, 1864, *O.R.*, XXXII, pt. 3, 592, 614–15.

50. Lee to Longstreet, Mar. 8, 1864, *O.R.*, XXXII, pt. 3, 595; Bragg to Johnston, Mar. 12, 1864, *ibid.*, 615.

51. John B. Sale, Memorandum, Mar. 19, 1864, *O.R.*, LII, pt. 2, 642–43; Longstreet to Johnston, Mar. 5, 1864, *ibid.*, 634.

52. Bragg to Johnston, Mar. 12, 1864, *O.R.*, XXXII, pt. 3, 614.

53. Lincoln to Stanton and Halleck, July 27, 1863, Basler, *Collected Works*, VI, 352; Lincoln to Rosecrans, Oct. 12, 1863, *ibid.*, 510; Lincoln to Halleck, Sept. 21, 1863, *ibid.*, 471; Lincoln, Message to Congress, Dec. 8, 1863, *ibid.*, VII, 50–51; Stanton to Foster, July 20, 1863, *O.R.*, XXVII, pt. 3, 732.

54. Rosecrans to Lincoln, Oct. 3, 1863, Basler, *Collected Works*, VI, 498; Lincoln to Rosecrans, Oct. 4, 1863, *ibid.*, 498.

55. Canby, *Lincoln and the Civil War*, 77.

56. Grant to Kelton, Dec. 23, 1863, *O.R.*, XXXI, pt. 2, 36; Grant to Halleck, Feb. 12, 1864, *ibid.*, XXXII, pt. 2, 374; Grant to Schofield, Feb. 26, 1864, *ibid.*, 472; Grant to W. S. Smith, Feb. 29, 1864, *ibid.*, 500; Sherman to Halleck, Feb. 29, 1864, *ibid.*, 498. During this period after Vicksburg, in Grant's vocabulary of action against the enemy, the words "drive," "push," and "fall back" predominate. "Battle," "blow," and "whipped" are mentioned as well as giving the enemy "a good thrashing." The results of the action would leave the country "cleaned," the enemy "broken," "demoralized and deserting," or even about to "perish" from "general discouragement." There are instances of "victory," a "crippled" enemy, and "damage" which was "crushing."

On one occasion, when he anticipated that the enemy might attempt the turning movement actually proposed for Johnston and Longstreet, Grant, like the two Confederate generals, expected that, being in their rear, they would be "totally annihilated," thus suffering "disaster." On another such occasion he hoped to "destroy," "capture," or "crush" the enemy force. Except for this hope of something decisive through cutting the enemy's line of retreat, the various words and phrases, including " to break up" an enemy army or to make it "take a respectful distance," seem to mean much the same thing: to drive the enemy back or out of a particular region. Grant's associates used essentially the same nomenclature, though Sherman wanted on one occasion to "whale" the enemy and on another to avoid a "stern chase."

The references are all from the *Official Records* and may be found, not in the order cited, in XXIV, pt. 3, 501, 507, 529, 539, 546, 547, 550, 588; XXX, pt. 4, 403; XXXI, pt. 2, 46, 49, 93; XXXI, pt. 3, 15, 122, 181, 266, 270, 273, 298, 311, 339, 386, 388, 431, 473, 479; XXXII, pt. 2, 100, 143, 193, 198, 337, 374, 375, 402; XXXII, pt. 3, 441. Other references to objectives may be found in XXIV, pt. 3, 516, 517, 522, 528; XXX, pt. 3, 944; XXXI, pt. 2, 48; XXXI, pt. 3, 345; XXXII, pt. 2, 99, 100, 193, 194, 199, 463.

57. Sherman to Porter, Oct. 25, 1863, *O.R.*, I, XXXI, pt. 1, 738.

58. Grant to Schofield, Feb. 16, 1864, *O.R.*, I, XXXII, pt. 2, 402.

59. Long, *Civil War, Day by Day*, 444, 449, 469; Lonn, *Salt as a Factor in the Confederacy*, 177, 179–80, 198–99, 288.

60. Halleck to Grant, Dec. 11, 1863, *O.R.*, XXXI, pt. 3, 376; Grant to Hurlbut, Nov. 9, 1863, *ibid.*, 103; Grant to W. S. Smith, Dec. 17, 1863, *ibid.*, 431; Grant to Thomas, Dec. 20, 1863, *ibid.*, 455; Grant to Halleck, Sept. 30, Dec. 14, 18, 20, 23, 1863, Jan. 15, 1864, *ibid.*, XXX, pt. 3, 944, XXXI, pt. 3, 403, 436, 454,

473, XXXII, pt. 2, 99–100; Sherman to Grant, Dec. 19, 29, 1863, *ibid.*, XXXI, pt. 3, 445, 527; Sherman to Halleck, Nov. 16, Dec. 29, 1863, *ibid.*, 167–68, 497–98; Halleck to Sherman, Nov. 17, 1863, *ibid.*, XXXI, pt. 3, 178; Sherman to Hurlbut, Nov. 18, 1863, *ibid.*, 187.

61. Sherman to Grant, Dec. 19, 1863, *O.R.*, XXXI, pt. 3, 445; Sherman to Porter, Dec. 21, 1863, *ibid.*, 461; Sherman to Halleck, Sept. 17, 1863, *ibid.*, 698.

62. Sherman to Logan, Dec. 21, 1863, *O.R.*, XXXI, pt. 3, 459; Grant to Sherman, Apr. 8, 15, 17, 21, 1864, *ibid.*, XXXII, pt. 3, 288, 366, 385, 437–38.

63. Halleck to Grant, July 22, Sept. 29, 1863, *O.R.*, XXIV, pt. 3, 542, XXX, pt. 3, 923; Schofield to Grant, Feb. 26, 1864, *ibid.*, XXXII, pt. 2, 472; Burnside to Halleck, Aug. 25, 1863, *ibid.*, XXX, pt. 3, 169; Halleck to Burnside, Oct. 24, 1863, *ibid.*, XXXI, pt. 1, 718; Grant to Thomas, Feb. 6, 1864, *ibid.*, XXXII, pt. 2, 337; Grant to Sherman, July 14, 1863, *ibid.*, XXIV, pt. 3, 509; Sherman to Banks, Jan. 16, 1864, *ibid.*, XXXII, pt. 2, 114–15; Grant to Halleck, July 24, 1863, Jan. 16, Feb. 4, 6, 27, 1864, *ibid.*, XXIV, pt. 3, 546, XXXII, pt. 2, 109, 323, 334, 481; Halleck to Rosecrans, Aug. 20, Sept. 11, 1863, *ibid.*, XXX, pt. 3, 83, 530.

64. Grant to Halleck, Dec. 17, 1863, *O.R.*, XXXI, pt. 3, 430; Grant to Schofield, Feb. 11, 1864, *ibid.*, XXXII, pt. 2, 367; Halleck to Grant, Dec. 26, 1863, Jan. 8, 1864, *ibid.*, XXXI, pt. 3, 497, XXXII, pt. 2, 41–42.

65. Wilson, *Under the Old Flag*, I, 315, 321–22; Sherman to Logan, Dec. 21, 1863, *O.R.*, XXXI, pt. 3, 459; Grant to Halleck, Dec. 20, 1863, *ibid.*, 454.

66. Grant to Halleck, Feb. 12, 1864, *O.R.*, XXXII, pt. 2, 475; Sherman to Grant, Jan. 19, 1864, *ibid.*, 147.

67. *The West Point Atlas of American Wars*, I, Map 92.

68. Grant to Mary Grant, Dec. 16, 1862, *Papers of Grant*, VII, 44.

69. Grant to Hudson, Nov. 15, 1862, *Papers of Grant*, VI, 320.

70. In the vocabulary of the 1960s, Grant was trying to develop a workable plan for counterinsurgency. Annihilation was, in many respects, comparable to the "search and destroy" strategy used in Vietnam.

71. Sherman to Grant, Oct. 4, 1862, *O.R.*, XVII, pt. 2, 260–61; Grant to Sherman, July 18, 1863, *ibid.*, XXIV, pt. 3, 528.

72. Grant to Halleck, Jan. 15, 1864, *O.R.*, XXXII, pt. 2, 100–101.

73. Sherman to Halleck, Dec. 26, 1863, *O.R.*, XXXI, pt. 3, 498. Before the eighteenth century most western European governments and armies lacked the organization and funding to have supply lines, difficult in any case because of primitive communications. This condition compelled them to keep moving in search of supplies and, often, booty as a substitute for or source of pay. All armies were essentially raiders. Often soldiers foraged the country directly for booty as well as subsistence. This practice caused many desertions. In the Thirty Years' War a commander reported of the strength of his force that "there would be no serious gaps in their numbers if only the stragglers, plunderers, and robbers, whose irresponsibility there is . . . no means of checking, would come back to their colors." It also caused serious economic loss in the waste of supplies and unauthorized appropriation of loot by the soldiers. It was a political as well as military and economic liability in that it aroused the profound hostility of civilians toward any army among them and toward the authority it represented.

In modern times this logistical system and the concomitant strategy made the Thirty Years' War notorious. Gustavus Adolphus, the leading soldier of the war, though careful of the territory of his allies, "plundered," according to C. V. Wedgwood, "as no man had plundered before in that conflict, because he plundered systematically to destroy the resources of his enemies." This strategy ultimately resulted in a complete tyranny of logistics in which "the provision of food in a starving country was the guiding consideration of warfare. . . . Fighting was uncoordinated and spasmodic, the headquarters staff being unable to move the mass of troops easily or with purpose." For example, a lack of food in a "lean, wasted and spoiled" country largely defeated an important Swedish invasion of Bohemia. Without a better logistic organization, the Swedes were unable to cope with the so-devastated country (all quotations from C. V. Wedgwood, *The Thirty Years War* [London, 1938], 443, 330, 434–35, 444).

In the eighteenth century, stronger, more efficient, and more affluent governments could adequately pay and ration their armies, although much came by requisition from occupied territory. Though nonmilitary influences contributed to this change, the military reason sufficed. The new logistical system gave the armies greater ability to orient their operations on the enemy's force rather than on their own supply needs, conserved the occupied district's resources for the benefit of the conquering prince, reduced desertion by working through quartermasters, and thus also significantly diminished civilian hostility toward the occupying enemy, another advantage for the conqueror. Pre–eighteenth-century armies with an inadequate logistical organization had, of necessity, relied heavily on the terror caused by their presence to obtain the political objectives of the war. Armies with supply lines, though chained to these ever since, had more liberty of military action and could more easily permanently occupy a country because they had not so much aroused the hostility of the civilians.

Grant's policy of raids may, then, be seen as a reversion to older methods of warfare made necessary, in part, by the pre-existing hostility of civilians in an essentially national war. There were political penalties in this course. The southern tradition of Sherman's devastation illustrates the obstacle to political unity raised by a resort to an earlier system, discarded in part because of its political liabilities.

But, not wishing to aim at the enemy army, Grant could revert to the older logistical system and make a virtue of it by destroying railroads and resources that supported the war effort. For older logistical methods see: Martin van Creveld, *Supplying War: Logistics from Wallenstein to Patton* (Cambridge, London, New York, Melbourne, 1977), 6–17.

Grant's strategy may also be viewed as contemporaneous in that it imitated the Confederates' in relying on raids against communications. It may also be seen as modern in that the aim of Grant's raids was identical with one of the principal objectives of strategic bombing in World War II. This parallel is particularly apt in that the really successful part of the strategic bombing of Germany in World War II was the attack against the German railroads; the parallel is not complete in that terrorizing civilians was not one of Grant's direct goals, though Sherman's addition of a political objective made the impact on civilian morale a significant by-product.

Grant's strategy was total in the sense that a strategy of exhaustion aimed at civilian resources rather than directly at armies. As noted above, totality in this sense is not a new idea, Jenghiz Khan being one of its most notable practitioners. In totality of support of the war, the North and South made adequate efforts. The South maintained a little over 3 percent of its population under arms, the North, a trifle less. In view of their per capita output and the state of development of their financial systems, the Civil War combatants made respectable showings, comparable to eighteenth-century Britain, Holland, and Prussia and to Revolutionary France. Compared with the 10 percent under arms in twentieth-century wars, 3 percent seems small; but neither Union nor Confederate financial systems nor their economic productivity made possible such a sustained effort. The Union objective in the war, the extinction of the Confederacy, was, of course, total.

74. Grant to Halleck, Jan. 15, 1864, *O.R.*, XXXII, pt. 2, 101.

75. Grant to Schofield, Feb. 26, 1864, *O.R.*, XXXII, pt. 2, 472.

76. Dana to Stanton, Nov. 29, 1863, *O.R.*, XXXI, pt. 2, 72; Grant to Halleck, Dec. 7, 1863, *ibid.*, pt. 3, 350.

77. Grant to Halleck, Jan. 15, 1864, *O.R.*, XXXII, pt. 2, 100; Grant to Thomas, Feb. 9, 1864, *ibid.*, 354–55.

16 ☆ GRANT IN COMMAND

Ulysses S. Grant

THE YEAR 1864, one of quite desperate fighting, opened with an apparent inconsistency: both presidents halted the carrying out of certain death sentences. Lincoln commuted the punishment of a deserter "because," he said, "I am trying to evade the butchering business lately." Davis, likewise, suspended the scheduled execution of an errant Virginia private.[1]

Otherwise during the year's early months the Presidents engaged in a more serious business, tightening the conscription systems. On February 1 Lincoln ordered the drafting of a half million men by March 10 to serve either for three years or for the remaining duration of the war. On February 17 Davis received congressional sanction to suspend habeas corpus until August 2 in order to meet resistance to the southern conscription law and to counter other disloyal activities. On that day the Confederate Congress also passed a law retaining "for the war" all men between the ages of eighteen and forty-five, inclusive, if already in service. The Union, rather than using such compulsion, relied on re-enlistment of volunteers, spurred by a thirty-day furlough which substantially reduced all northern armies during the winter of 1863–64. The southern lawmakers also lowered the age limit for draftees to seventeen and raised it to fifty, thus creating a class of reserves which, together with exempts, the South could use for local defense. These reserves released veteran units to strengthen the main armies while the boys, middle-aged men, and those in essential occupations could resist Union raiders and help protect the seacoast.[2]

Good leadership ranked equally with adequate manpower. By this point in the war both sides had completed most of the elevations of men to ranks higher than brigadier general. A total of 229 men eventually gained a senior-level generalcy. Of these the Confederacy ultimately named eight full generals, seventeen lieutenant generals, and seventy-two major generals; by the war's end, the North had elevated one man to lieutenant general, nine men to major generals in the regular army, and 122 men to major generals of volunteers.

Sound and discernible military reasons typically prompted a general's elevation in rank, but both Presidents occasionally granted promotions for broader considerations. Lincoln, who remained quite responsive to political, ethnic, and other factors, surpassed Davis in this respect. The particular case of Alexander Schimmelfennig stands out. Lincoln and Stanton once conversed over the selection of new brigadiers and Lincoln finally said:

> "Well, Mr. Secretary, I concur in pretty much all you say. The only point I make is, that there has got to be something done that will be unquestionably in the interest of the Dutch, and to that end I want Schemmelfinnig appointed."
>
> The Secretary replied: "Mr. President, perhaps this Schemmel-what's-his-name is not as highly recommended as some other German officer."
>
> "No matter about that," said Lincoln, "his name will make up for any difference there might be, and I'll take the risk of his coming out all right." Then, with a laugh, he repeated, dwelling upon each syllable of the name, and accenting the last one, "Schem-mel-fin-*nig* must be appointed."

Some legitimate reason did underlie a promotion for Schimmelfennig because he was cited for valorous conduct at Second Bull Run. But alas, poor Schimmelfennig did not live up to his valorous promise. A wound he received in the arm during the early skirmishing before Gettysburg knocked him off his horse. He ran to a nearby farm and spent the next several days hiding out—one source says in a woodshed and another a pigsty. Afterwards, unable to face serving further in his command, he sought and received a transfer to South Carolina, where he soon fell victim to malaria. He did recover to preside over the capitulation of Charleston but then contracted tuberculosis, from which he died on September 5, 1865.[3]

The average age of the higher-ranking, active-duty Civil War general, through retirement, resignation, casualties, and the addition of new men, changed downward as the war progressed. By the end of the war's first full year, seventy-five northern and forty-eight southern generals had attained a rank above brigadier. Their average ages were 43.6 and 44.8 years, respectively. At the war's end, ninety-four Union and seventy-six Confederate officers with major generalcies or higher ranks still remained in service. The average age, after the four years of war, had decreased to 42.5 years for both armies.

Five states of the Confederacy (Virginia, North and South Carolina, Georgia, and Tennessee) contributed two-thirds of the southern generals elevated above brigadier. The remaining six states, comprising the Gulf Coast area, could boast of only five higher generals. To the north, the states of Ohio, New York, Pennsylvania, and New Jersey accounted for sixty-two (47 percent) of the senior Union generals. Twenty-eight more (21 percent) were spread out among the six northeastern states. States in the midwest contributed only five upper-ranking generals to the Union cause. But this uneven distribution by states in truth rather accurately reflected the population distribution; only a few slight variations appear. Also, like the population as a whole, most Civil War generals (78 percent) were born in rural areas or small towns with under 3,000 residents. There is no apparent correlation as to whether a man received a Civil War generalship due to the occupation his father pursued; but interestingly, about a quarter of the generals on either side who gained promotion above brigadier came from families with professional ties.

Regardless of social class, which varied considerably on both sides, few Civil War generals who lacked formal education gained promotion. Eighty percent of the total had graduated from college. More than one-half of those above brigadier had graduated from West Point. Of the twenty-five highest-ranking southern generals, only Nathan Bedford Forrest was not a college graduate. On the Union side, out of the top twenty generals only Edwin V. Sumner and John Wool did not have a college degree, and they were respected senior officers of the regular army.

Promotion to the highest grades of general proved almost impossible for men without any military experience prior to the Civil War. Of the top twenty Confederates, only two were new to the military profession, Forrest and Wade Hampton, both of whom had attained considerable economic success and status before the war. All of the top twenty Union generals had become well-qualified military men before hostilities began.

Of the generals who had attended West Point, the Union officers as a whole boasted a much higher academic standing; almost 40 percent of the North's West Point generals finished in the top quarter of their class, whereas only 25 percent of the South's West Pointers ranked that high. And conversely, 23 percent of the South's generals ranked in the bottom quarter of their class, while only 6 percent of the North's West Pointers ranked that low in scholarship. The top assignments, however, did not go to the low achievers: only three of the Confederacy's poorer students (Hood, Longstreet, and Holmes) attained rank beyond major general, and none of the top northern generals had finished in the bottom 25 percent of a West Point class.

Though some historians call the Mexican War a "rehearsal for conflict," statistical investigation reveals that Mexican War service by itself offered little of value in propelling a man upward in general grade rank. Mexican War service *and* a West Point education were most effective aids to promotion, but only in combination. Individuals who lacked either variable did discernibly less well in attaining high Civil War rank. The pattern grows more pronounced among the top generals in both armies. Seventeen of the top twenty-five Confederate generals and eleven of the twenty top Union generals possessed both qualifications.

In 1860 only one-half of the men who became Civil War generals were then in active military service. The others, the civilians who became general officers, can be divided into three categories: those with no military experience other than militia duty, those who had resigned from the U.S. Army at some previous time, and those with some other type of military service. None of the three categories stands out as having produced more generals than did the others; they are almost equally divided. The move upward from major general in the Confederacy, however, quite typically was limited only to former regular army officers. At least half of the civilians who became generals had taken an active part in politics before the Civil War, and men with political experience tended to begin the war with higher ranks. But interestingly and significantly, the very highest ranks attained by civilians went to politicians who also had Mexican War experience.

Promotion to the various upper grades of general did not always result from logical progression through regular advancement. To be sure, all of the Confederate lieutenant generals had previously held the rank of major general, but several of the major generals never had held the rank of brigadier. Even more haphazardness marked some of the rank skippping by Union generals, because it was possible for a man to hold four ranks simultaneously: substantive and brevet ranks in the regular army and substantive and brevet ranks in the volunteer army. The North had soon awarded so many brevet generalcies that the positions became meaningless and Congress eventually passed a law denying to holders of brevet ranks any exercise of authority as such.

The year 1862 saw the most rapid expansion of the list of senior generals for both sides: during that time new appointments to major generalcies and above numbered thirty-eight for the Confederates and eighty for the Federals. The same year the Confederacy promoted its first lieutenant generals and named Bragg a full general, the last man to attain that rank in the South's regular army. Within the group that the Union elevated Lincoln ultimately found the men he most needed: Grant, Sherman, Meade, Sheridan, and Thomas. Fewer, though some crucial, key adjustments came in 1863 and 1864; for the most part attrition necessitated elevations in these latter years.

Civil War generals had little job security. In addition to dangerous working conditions that resulted in numerous fatalities, political misfortune or combat ineffectiveness might result in loss of command. Nevertheless few generals were actually dismissed unwillingly from service; they were allowed either to languish in staff assignments or at remote locations or they resigned. The attrition rate for all Confederate general officers amounted to nearly 30 percent, while the Federals lost almost 36 percent of their generals during the war's course. The South suffered 18 percent of its generals either killed in action or dying from wounds, while only 8 percent of the Union generals experienced similar fates. The position of Confederate brigadier carried more danger than the other generalcies: 20 percent of them died in combat. Relatively few of the Confederate generals resigned, 4.5 percent, while 19 percent of the Union generals voluntarily yielded their commissions.

Despite resignations, retirements, and deaths, the number of generals in grade grew as the war wore on. These increases came gradually, with the exception of the high incidence of appointments during 1862. Of the 583 northerners who gained substantive generalcies, 374 remained in grade at war's end. The Confederate President named 425 individuals to one of the South's four grades of general; 299 remained in grade at the return of peace.[4]

Though both sides largely devoted the winter of 1863–64 to personnel changes, planning, and preparations, they did engage in some desultory activity. On February 17 the Confederate submarine C. S. S. *H. L. Hunley* claimed its only prize. Destroying itself also in the process, just off the Atlantic coast near Charleston it pushed a torpedo against the side of the U. S. S. *Housatonic*. The sinking of this Union warship sent shock waves of consternation through the blockading fleet. But the South had ready no more submarines, only this experimental and only "semi-submersible," cigar-shaped vessel. The *Hunley* proved too unreliable, especially in her vexing inability to rise after having submerged. Some thirty-three men had died during her earlier tests and now she took another six-man crew, as well as herself, to a watery grave. The time for this revolutionary idea in sea warfare simply had not yet sufficiently ripened.

Almost simultaneously, elsewhere, occurred the major battle of the war in Florida, Olustee or Ocean Pond. Under orders from Union Major General Quincy A. Gillmore, Brigadier General Truman F. Seymour advanced into Florida to "cut off a rich source of the enemy's supplies," to recruit black troops, and "to inaugurate measures for the speedy restoration of Florida to her allegiance, in accordance with instructions from the President." Some 5,500 federal troops moved toward Lake City, Florida, and on February 20 seized the occasion to attack approximately 5,000 Confederates mustered nearby. The southerners, under Irish-born Brigadier General Joseph Finegan, fighting well from behind strong fieldworks, eventually forced an enemy retreat and launched a half-hearted cavalry pursuit. After the bluecoats fell back to Jacksonville, the grayclads repaired the damaged railroads. Federal casualties amounted to 203 killed, 1,152 wounded, and 506 missing, the Confederates losing 93 killed and 841 wounded.[5]

While Finegan was winning his defensive battle in Florida, there arrived near Americus, Georgia, the first federal prisoners of war to be held in Camp Sumter, later known as Andersonville Prison. And on February 28 a federal cavalry force of about 3,500 men under Judson Kilpatrick left bivouac on the Rapidan with the hope of penetrating Richmond and liberating the federal prisoners incarcerated there. Kilpatrick, a flamboyant man called everything ranging from "Kill-Cavalry" to "a hell of a damned fool," thought that cavalry could "fight anywhere except at sea." He believed that spectacular successes could help fulfill his later political ambitions of eventually becoming President of the United States. His undersized body, lantern jaw, stringy blonde side whiskers, and bandy legs that imposed a rolling quality to his gait induced one staff officer to say that "it was hard to look at Kilpatrick without laughing," but he managed to manifest enough professional air to impress the federal high command who authorized his bizarre scheme. Perhaps, though it cannot be certain, he stretched his sanctioned activities with sub rosa machinations designed to make his raid all that he would need for enduring prominence. With Kilpatrick was young Colonel Ulrich Dahlgren, son of the famous admiral and innovator of naval ordnance, John A. Dahlgren. The lad would soon attain notoriety.[6]

The March 1 raid on Richmond failed and, further, Dahlgren and his 500 men, when within two miles of the city, became separated from the main body. The next day Fitzhugh Lee, Robert E. Lee's nephew and a Confederate cavalry leader, prepared an ambush at Mantapike Hill. Dahlgren fell into the trap, one hundred or more of his men fell captive, and he himself was killed. Later, official and unofficial allegations asserted that papers had been found on Dahlgren which revealed him to have been involved in a scheme to assassinate President Davis. The episode spurred much vindictive feeling and exhibited a morbid evidence of Confederate success when an enterprising Richmond merchant acquired Dahlgren's artificial leg and displayed it in his store window.

But Sherman led one of the most significant raids of the winter, that to Meridian, Mississippi. This campaign combined almost all of the elements in Grant's new strategy of raids. Resembling a large-scale test of the concept and a dress rehearsal for the spring campaign in the West, the offensive grew out of a desire to support with infantry the long-planned cavalry raid into Mississippi which Major General W. Sooy Smith would conduct from Memphis. Smith hoped to "destroy railroads, bridges, corn not wanted, and strike quick and well every enemy that should offer opposition." By the middle of January, 1864, Grant, apparently familiar with the idea before Sherman went to the Mississippi, had approved a plan for Sherman to advance from Vicksburg with an army of 20,000 men, largely infantry.[7]

Coordinating with Smith's advance from the north, Sherman, Grant explained to Halleck, would "move out to Meridian with his spare force (the cavalry going from Corinth) and destroy the [rail]roads east and south of there so effectually the enemy will not attempt to rebuild them during the rebellion. He will then return unless the opportunity of going into Mobile with the force he has is perfectly plain." The expedition would hurt Confederate logistics for, said Grant, "the destruction which Sherman will do to the [rail]roads around Meridian will be of material importance to us in preventing the enemy from drawing supplies from Mississippi and in clearing that section of all large bodies of rebel troops." Sherman's advance, like his July, 1863, march to Jackson, was to be a raid. After destroying the railroads and logistical installations around Meridian, he planned to return to Vicksburg.[8]

Grant realized that the railroads would permit the Confederates to concentrate against Sherman troops from Mobile, north Georgia, and even the Georgia and Carolina coasts. To help counter this he planned from Chattanooga "to threaten an advance and try to detain the force now in Thomas' front." Grant expressed his confidence in the defensive power of competently led armies when he said that "Sherman will be instructed, while left with large discretionary powers, to take no extra hazard of losing his army or of getting it crippled too much for efficient service in the spring."[9]

In preparing his campaign, Sherman asked Banks to threaten Mobile by having "boats maneuvering" in the Gulf near Mobile to "keep up the delusion and prevent the enemy drawing from Mobile a force to strengthen" Bishop Polk's Confederates covering Meridian. "A feint kept up there for a week might be most useful," Sherman wrote, "for if we destroy Meridian and its railroad connection," which "is the only link that unites Mississippi to Alabama and Georgia," then "Mobile would have no communication to the interior save by the Alabama River, and would to that extent be weakened . . . I will surely succeed," he added, "if General Polk is not too heavily reinforced from Mobile and Atlanta."[10]

Grant arranged another distraction to forestall the possibility of Confederate reinforcements for Polk through Atlanta. Along the Tennessee, in addition to those forces commanded by Thomas, those farther west under Major General John A. Logan were also to be active. Grant instructed Thomas: "To co-operate with" Sherman's "movement you want to keep up appearances of preparation of an advance from Chattanooga; it may be necessary, even, to move a column as far as LaFayette. The time for this advance, however, would not be before the 30th" of January, "or when you might learn the enemy were falling back." Logan too was directed "to keep up a threatened advance on Rome, with a view of retaining on this front as large a force of the enemy as possible."[11]

When ready to advance, Sherman moved in coordination with W. Sooy Smith's cavalry, which, advancing from Memphis to Meridian, would be "superior to that of Forrest." Smith would have to face only mounted men because the Confederate infantry under Polk must deal with Sherman's army advancing from Vicksburg. Though Sherman planned to "use all caution," he felt "no doubt" of success "unless Johnston has caught wind of our movement," he said, "and brought an additional force from Georgia which I do not believe." Though support for his two-pronged advance derived from the dual diversions of Thomas and Logan on the Tennessee and by the Navy's distracting movements before Mobile, Sherman provided yet one more move to confuse the enemy. He sent gunboats and infantry up the Yazoo "to reconnoiter and divert attention." This "would make a diversion" and "confuse the enemy" still more.[12]

With some pride, Grant's chief of staff could report a well-coordinated movement: "General W. S. Smith was to have moved from Memphis . . . with a large force of cavalry, General Sherman at the same time from Vicksburg eastward a formidable force of all arms, and General Logan has already thrown a pontoon bridge across the Tennessee. . . . The forces at Chattanooga are not inactive. From all these expeditions and threatening movements it is hoped much will be accomplished, and especially in forcing the enemy back from within striking distance of our communications."[13]

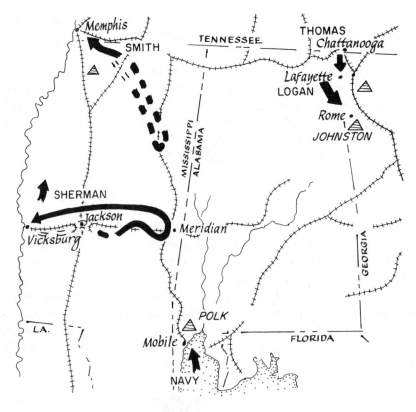

Sherman's Planned Raid

The Meridian campaign thus contained most of the elements of Grant's solution to Union military problems. Sherman's superiority over Polk, which enabled him to capture Meridian without a battle, demonstrated that the Union had selected a weak line for its offensive. Though he had not conducted a seaborne offensive, Sherman had used seapower effectively in the naval demonstration against Mobile. The objective was logistical, enemy transportation and supplies, and, by neutralizing Confederate communications in Mississippi, Grant and Sherman hoped to make the occupied territory of West Tennessee and the navigation of the Mississippi more secure, resulting also in definitely disabling the interior lines of communications for any major enemy counteroffensive either north or west from Mississippi. The "destruction of the railroad east and west, north and south of Meridian, will close the door of rapid travel and conveyance of stores from Mississippi and the Confederacy east," which would, Sherman explained, "make us all less liable to the incursions of the enemy toward the Mississippi River."[14]

On February 3 Sherman's raiding army, 21,000 strong, began its rapid advance. Living off the country, finding "corn and meat" en route, they solved the supply problem and deprived the enemy of those resources. They made the existing territory more secure, but acquired no new land which would require defense. The confused Confederates did order reinforcements from Johnston's army in north Georgia, but, before they arrived, Sherman had reached his objective. On February 14 his troops entered Meridian and, as Sherman put it, "for five days 10,000 men worked hard and with a will in that work of destruction. . . . Meridian, with its depots, store-houses, arsenals, hospitals, offices, hotels and cantonments no longer exists." Further, the Federals destroyed about 115 miles of railroad, 61 bridges, and 20 locomotives. Sherman then returned to Vicksburg.[15]

The operation on exterior lines seemed successful. Grant believed that the Confederates thought that Sherman had as his objective Mobile and had reinforced it with troops sent from North Carolina and from Charleston. He also believed that troops had started south from Johnston's army at Dalton, but "General Thomas' movement, intended to keep force from leaving Johnston, has had the effect to bring back one division which had already started south."[16]

Nevertheless, Sherman's situation, apparently exposed to a Confederate concentration from three points of the compass, caused "much anxiety" in Washington. Grant, however, confident of the power of the defense, felt no alarm, for "with a man like Sherman to command, he is in no great danger" from a superior concentration. As a raider, Sherman was doubly safe because of his choice of lines of retreat. Grant felt certain that Sherman would "find an outlet. If in no other way," he wrote, "he will fall back on Pascagoula, and ship from there under protection of Farragut's fleet."[17]

Sherman, then, was as safe from the rebels as Longstreet when near Knoxville had been from Grant. Until the close of the campaign, Grant remained unsure of Sherman's line of retreat, directing the continuation of distracting movements until the Union knew he had "struck a safe lodgment somewhere." Sherman's intrinsic security together with effective distraction demonstrated the possibility, with superior numbers, careful planning, and effective coordination, of defeating an alert enemy who possessed interior lines. A successful and very destructive raid resulted.[18]

General Sooy Smith, however, moved so sluggishly that he failed to coop-

erate and, on February 22, he met ignominious defeat at the hands of Bedford
Forrest near Okolona, Mississippi. Nevertheless, Sherman's campaign achieved
all of its logistical objectives. "A full hundred miles of railroad" lay destroyed,
he "lived off the country and made a swath of desolation 50 miles broad across
the State of Mississippi," and brought in 500 prisoners and "about 10 miles
of negroes." He had expected to "be tempted to swing around to Mobile" but
pushed on neither there nor to Selma, for "without other concurrent operations it would have been unwise."[19]

The Meridian campaign yielded the only fruit of Grant's prodigious planning for significant winter campaigns. He had wished to start his long-
deferred Mobile project immediately after the battle of Chattanooga,
proposing it to Halleck on November 29; and, when he again submitted
it on December 7, he asked Halleck to reply by telegraph. Hearing nothing
from Halleck except concern about East and West Tennessee, the Mississippi,
and the trans-Mississippi, Grant sent a representative to Washington.[20]

Meanwhile, Grant had been trying to expand his influence in order to
secure better coordination of Union forces. Though he controlled a vast theatre, he could not afford to ignore others, for, as Longstreet's arrival from
Virginia to fight at Chickamauga dramatically illustrated, the Confederates
succeeded very well in integrating their efforts. Therefore, Grant sought by
both formal and informal means to extend his influence over all major theatres
of operations.[21]

His principal means was to try to place either Sherman or his new associate, Brigadier General William F. "Baldy" Smith, in command of the Army
of the Potomac. Because of Grant's experience working with Smith at Chattanooga and Smith's congenial strategic views, Smith, like Sherman, would
likely carry out a coordinated campaign. In this way Grant hoped to circumvent what he perceived as the failure of Washington to provide central control. Smith, a veteran of the Army of the Potomac, had held a high command
there until removed because he could not get along with Burnside. Though
this background might well make Smith a more congenial commander for the
eastern army than Sherman, a vexing difficulty persisted in that Smith, only
a brigadier general, would need to be promoted, with a date of rank going
back to the time of an earlier, abortive nomination to major general.

To bring about Smith's appointment, Grant initially relied on Charles A.
Dana, formerly with Horace Greeley's *New York Tribune* and now assistant
secretary of war and attached to Grant's headquarters. Grant earlier had met
Dana when Secretary Stanton had sent Dana to Grant's headquarters in
March, 1863, ostensibly to report on "the condition of the pay service in the
Western armies." Actually Dana had been part of Stanton's informal organi-
zation. The secretary had sent Dana "to report daily to him the military
proceedings, and to give such information as would enable Mr. Lincoln and

himself to settle their minds as to Grant, about whom at that time there were many doubts, and against whom some complaint." Dana had been on "friendly terms with all the generals" and got along well with Grant. They met again, because Dana, having been sent in August "to observe and report the movements" of Rosecrans, was at Chattanooga when Grant arrived in October. Grant first employed Dana to write the secretary of war on behalf of his Mobile plan, and then in mid-December he asked Dana "to go to Washington to represent more fully his views and wishes with regard to the winter campaign" and to lobby for Sherman or "Baldy" Smith as commander of the Army of the Potomac.[22]

Dana promptly went to Washington and by December 21 could tell Grant of "detailed conversations with the President, the Secretary of War, and General Halleck" and report that they felt that from the Army of the Potomac "nothing is to be hoped under its present commander," Meade. Smith seemed to be viewed favorably and Dana felt optimistic that the President would appoint him. Secretary Stanton was enthusiastic about the Mobile expedition, because "Bragg's army [will] become prisoners of war without our having trouble of providing for them," he said; but the campaign would have to wait because of "the anxiety which seems to exist respecting East Tennessee." Though Halleck understood that Grant could not supply in Tennessee "an army large enough to make Longstreet's dislodgement certain," Mobile would have to wait until it was "settled" with the President and the secretary that Longstreet "must be left in that region." On January 10 Dana reported that Grant would be allowed to undertake the Mobile expedition even if he did not expel Longstreet, provided Grant thought it safe simply to leave an army to observe him.[23]

By this time Grant had apparently abandoned both his Mobile plan and one for pushing back the Confederates in North Georgia. He had dissipated so many men in reinforcing East and West Tennessee and had lost so many in re-enlistment furloughs that he could not assemble an adequate force. Without informing Washington, he decided on Sherman's Meridian expedition as the only operation he could carry out that winter. He retained his hopes for Smith's promotion to a "higher command" as late as January 13, but Halleck deferred, if not dashed, these aspirations when he told Grant that no major general vacancies existed, "because by some error more than the number authorized were made last summer, and some major-generals now in service must be dropped."[24]

When Grant, his staff, Smith, and sometimes Sherman and Dana had been discussing future campaigns for the West and scheming to place their man in command of the army of the Potomac, logically they also worked out a strategy for that force. Coordination between the armies of the East and West implied some specific campaign for Meade to harmonize and cooperate with those being considered for the West. The plan was not revealed until Halleck, in a January 8, 1864, letter which explained the military situation in other theatres, solicited Grant's views without revealing that they eagerly awaited them and would treat his ideas with respect. Grant promptly responded, writing one letter explaining his proposals for the spring advance from Mobile and Chattanooga and another outlining eastern operations.[25]

The plan was pure Grant. It prescribed a raid against the enemy's railroads and logistic infrastructure. He suggested that operations should "commence at once by removing the war to a more southern climate, instead of months of inactivity in winter quarters." To accomplish this he proposed that a force of 60,000 men start from southeastern Virginia, advance to the rail junction of Weldon, ruin the railroads, and then move south along the railroad to Raleigh, completing the destruction of the outer of the two Confederate north-south rail lines. From Raleigh "the most interior lines of railway left to the enemy, in fact the only one they would then have, would be so threatened as to force him to use a large part of his army in guarding it. This would

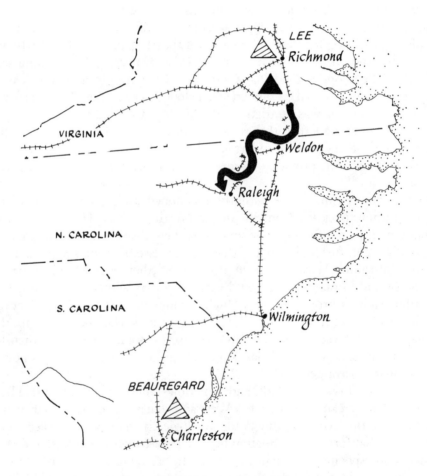

"The Plan Was Pure Grant"

virtually force an evacuation of Virginia and indirectly of East Tennessee." This major success would be made possible by seizing the initiative, drawing "the enemy from campaigns of their own choosing, and for which they are prepared," and by a surprise seaborne attack on a weak line or, as Grant expressed it, drawing them "to new lines of operations never expected to become necessary."

Explaining his strategy of exhaustion, Grant gave a very full account of the logistical objectives of the campaign and of the advantages of his policy of raiding but not occupying enemy territory. Though the forces at Raleigh would draw supplies from the nearby port of New Bern until they had captured Wilmington, they would be in "new fields, where they could partially live upon the country and would reduce the stores of the enemy. It would cause thousands of North Carolina troops to desert and return to their homes. It would give us," Grant explained, "possession of many negroes who are now indirectly aiding the rebellion" and "effectually blockade Wilmington, the port now of more value to the enemy than all the balance of their sea coast."[26]

This campaign obviously resembled his initial proposal for Mobile and it was also a large-scale replica of the Meridian plan. As before, Grant placed reliance on the fleet and intended that the army live off the country. In addition, the raiding army, on an interior line between Beauregard at Charleston and Lee in Virginia, could cut Lee's supplies.

In emphasizing that the "final decision" would "probably depend, under the President," upon Grant, Halleck forecast Grant's impending appointment as general in chief. Nevertheless Halleck reflected hostility toward Grant's proposed course of action, reacting to it entirely in the context of operations in Virginia. To Halleck, Grant was merely reviving old, rejected ideas, another variant of the Peninsula enterprise. Insofar as he understood it as something different, "Old Brains" saw it as another coastal operation, and he had always opposed "all the isolated expeditions on the sea and Gulf coast," believing that "the troops so employed would do more good if concentrated on some important line of military operations. We have given too much attention to cutting the toe nails of our enemy instead of grasping his throat," declared Halleck. He failed to comprehend that in aiming at the North Carolina railroads and the port of Wilmington, Grant proposed to grasp the Confederacy's throat, its logistical throat.

In an uncharacteristically disorganized response, Halleck laid out the Virginia operational doctrine which headquarters had thrashed out and settled more than a year earlier. Citing Napoleon in support of the thesis, Halleck stressed: "The overthrow of Lee's army" was "the object of operations" in Virginia, because "we cannot take Richmond . . . till we destroy or disperse that army." This meant that there could be "but little progress" in the Virginia theatre "till that army was broken or destroyed." To do this, he explained, we should attack between Washington and "Richmond, on our shortest line of supplies, and in such a position that we can combine our whole force."

Missing the point of Grant's strategy, Halleck reiterated his and Lincoln's old concern: "If we operate by North Carolina or the Peninsula, we must act with a divided army on exterior lines, while Lee, with a short interior line, can concentrate his entire force on either fragment." Halleck felt certain which fragment Lee would choose. To provide an adequate force for North Carolina would so weaken Meade that Lee could "make another invasion of Maryland and Pennsylvania," which, together with "the political importance of Washington," would mean that "popular sentiment will compel the Government to bring back the army in North Carolina to defend Washington, Baltimore, Harrisburg, and Philadelphia."

Obsessed with the stalemate in Virginia and the futility of a siege of Richmond, the general in chief failed to see Grant's suggestion in any other light. Undoubtedly Halleck would have understood had he known that, as late as April of 1864, Lee wrote: "With our present supplies on hand the interruption of the trains on the southern roads would cause the abandonment of Virginia." Unable to emancipate himself from conventional concerns about the South's army, its power on the defensive, and the acquisition of territory, Halleck could not grasp the vulnerability of rebel logistics and that Grant's raiding strategy offered a solution to the problem of the strength of the defense in Virginia by avoiding, rather than attacking, the Confederates. On the other hand, Halleck stood on firm ground when he pointed out that the Union did not have available during that winter of re-enlistment furloughs the 60,000 men Grant specified. Meade's effective force numbered only 70,000. If Grant could have read Lee's mail, learning of his logistic vulnerability and how starkly the lack of fodder for their weakened animals immobilized the Confederates, he would have seen that the North would not need a force as large as 60,000 men.[27]

It is unlikely that these letters were the only exchange of strategic ideas, for headquarters had called one of Grant's staff officers with whom he was intimate, Brigadier General James Harrison Wilson, to Washington to head the Cavalry Bureau. In Washington, Grant's informal group kept in touch. Wilson lived in the same boardinghouse with his close friend, Assistant Secretary Dana, where also boarded Congressman Elihu B. Washburne, whom Grant knew well, having resided in Washburne's district. Grant's chief of staff, John A. Rawlins, had been politically active in that same district. Rawlins himself visited Washington during the winter and doubtless called on his friends Washburne, Wilson, and Dana as well as the War Department. None other than the influential Washburne would introduce the bill to create the rank of lieutenant general, an idea which he had broached as early as December 9.[28]

Grant had solicited advice from General George H. Thomas about Grant's North Carolina project and, in lobbying for it, had secured the aid of Foster,

Burnside's successor in East Tennessee. It would have been surprising indeed if Grant, with an excellent informal organization with good contacts in both Congress and the War Department, had not had his views advanced by others and obtained from them some intimations of how Washington was receiving his plans. Nevertheless, not until the latter part of February, on the eve of Grant's promotion, did he receive Halleck's emphatic brief against his ideas, possibly his first knowledge of the adverse reaction to his suggestions for an eastern campaign.[29]

On February 1 the House of Representatives passed a bill reviving the rank of lieutenant general. Though the Confederacy had established the rank in the fall of 1862, the Union had not, partly in deference to the memory and prestige of the revered George Washington. The debate on the bill clearly indicated that Congress had Grant in mind. The assumption of the nearly sacred rank of lieutenant general would make Grant the senior officer of the army and automatically place him over Halleck, the general in chief. On February 24 the bill passed the Senate. Lincoln, having investigated Grant and finding that he harbored no political ambitions, was only too glad to comply with the wishes of Congress. Halleck facilitated matters by resigning and was then appointed chief of staff, the post he had in reality held all along.

On March 8 Grant came to Washington to receive his commission as lieutenant general. Due to a misunderstanding, nobody met Grant's train and so he proceeded unescorted to Willard's Hotel, where he registered and went to the dining room for dinner. Almost immediately everyone there recognized him. People stood up or stretched and turned to see their new military saviour. "Three cheers for Lieutenant General Grant!" some man yelled. Others joined in the boisterous exclamation and pounded on tables until Grant, highly embarrassed, stood up, fumbled with his napkin, and bowed. Then he sat down and tried to go on eating, but soon a Pennsylvania congressman arrived, snatched him up, introduced him all around, and took him in tow to the White House.[30]

There, a weekly reception was in progress. Soon surrounded by a sea of suffocating well-wishers, Grant was hoisted upon a crimson sofa so everybody could get a good look at him—"The only real mob I ever saw in the White House," one reporter recalled. In wild disorder, women had their laces torn and crinolines crushed and they, too, climbed on tables and chairs, in part to escape more damage and in part also to see the general. "Rowdy and unseemly," Gideon Welles termed it, and Grant escaped "flushed, heated and perspiring with the unwanted exertion."[31]

Grant's elusive personality piqued and puzzled people. Richard Henry Dana, Jr., felt he "had no gait, no station, no manner." He had "rather the look of a man who did, or once did, take a little too much to drink," and save for the hard look in his clear blue eyes he resembled a half-pay character who had nothing better to do than hang around the entrance to Willard's, cigar in mouth. To be sure, he had a certain aura of resolution, but Dana shook his head disapprovingly: "To see him talking and smoking in the lower entry of Willard's, in that crowd, in such linen, the general in chief of our armies on whom the destiny of empire seems to hang!" To complete this enigmatic portrait, another later observed that Grant "was a man in whom the men had confidence, but they did not love." Others might ride by troops and consistently raise a ripple of applause, but Grant never did. One woman who saw him frequently in Washington perceptively noted that, even in a crowd, Grant always seemed to be alone. Friendly and approachable, still he had "a peculiar aloofness," some mysterious atmosphere surrounded him; "he walked through a crowd as though solitary."[32]

On March 9, in stark contrast to the preliminaries, Grant returned to the White House to take part in a simple ceremony in which Lincoln conferred the third star. Grant then spent a day in conference with the President, Halleck, and Stanton before visiting Meade's headquarters. Grant and Meade proved most compatible; Baldy Smith accompanied Grant to see Meade, but Grant now had no motive to elevate him to command of the Army of the Potomac. The lieutenant general now possessed the maximum control over Union armies that a soldier could achieve.[33]

When Grant assumed command of all of the armies of the United States, he not only already had developed, and tested in the Meridian expedition, a complete strategic offensive system, but a specific plan for 1864. The only question that remained was what to do in the East. His North Carolina campaign he had intended for the winter, to be carried out simultaneously with a movement on his part in the West. As it would have been equally efficacious in the spring and so thoroughly typified Grant's strategic thinking, it remained on his mind when he came east and entered into his discussions.[34]

He abandoned his proposed undertaking promptly, though probably reluctantly, and adopted a new plan, "fixed upon almost immediately," apparently as a result of his day of conferences in Washington and with Meade. Any North Carolina operation varied so from the settled headquarters doctrine for Virginia operations that Grant had no choice. Further, Grant did not find that kind of campaign feasible politically. He found anything so apparently indirect, so like afraid-to-fight West Point generalship, incompatible with popular and political demands for a direct approach. He could not run the risk that a raid by Lee would cause public opinion to dictate his movements; he could not adopt a strategy reminiscent of McClellan's when that general was likely to be running for President against Lincoln. But most of all he believed the campaign in Virginia had come to have a "chivalric significance." Lee's army, "the foremost army of the Confederacy under the Confederacy's foremost leader," had assumed in the country, especially in Washington and the East, a significance which made it impossible for Lieutenant General Grant, the North's foremost general, to "decline a trial with Lee." The new lieutenant general must fight Lee directly in terms the country could understand.[35]

Grant had been, and doubtless still was, anxious to avoid commanding in Virginia. Though he recognized that the Army of the Potomac would not welcome him, an outsider, he explained the more substantial reasons for his reluctance when he wrote from Vicksburg in August, 1863: "Here I know the officers and men and what each Gen. is capable of as a separate commander. There I would have to learn. Here I know the geography of the country and its resources. There it would be a new study."[36]

If Grant had any difficulty understanding that nonmilitary factors required him to be with the Army of the Potomac, his friends and advisors did not. When he visited Ohio at the end of December, Sherman said to Grant: I realize "the intense interest felt for us. Our army is on all lips, and were you to come to Ohio, you would hardly be allowed to eat a meal from the intense curiosity to see you and hear you." Sherman then warned his friend that, since he had a "position of more power than Halleck or the President," he must, for the sake of the country, protect his reputation and power. "For the sake of future generations risk nothing," he stressed, and added, "Let us risk, and when you strike, let it be as at Chattanooga." As "Washington's legitimate successor" the lieutenant general must conserve his prestige and let others suffer defeat. Believing Grant should continue to campaign in the West, the decisive theatre, Sherman urged Grant: "Come out West. Here lies the seat of the coming empire, and from the West, when our task is done, we will make short work of Charleston and Richmond and the impoverished coast of the Atlantic."[37]

Though Sherman's advice was wise, Rawlins, aided by his background in Illinois politics, realized "that Congress must have created and the President must have bestowed the rank of lieutenant general upon Grant the better to clothe him with power for a trial of prowess and leadership with Lee." Rawlins, supported in his argument by Grant's friend, Congressman Washburne, and by Assistant Secretary Dana, also felt that the "National Capital" was "still beleagured by a formidable and unbroken army of the enemy. Unless this army of foes is defeated and broken, and our Capital relieved of its fierce frowns," he stressed, "we cannot hope that the recognition of the rebel government will be much longer postponed by European governments." Though their judgment about chances for Confederate recognition was wrong, they accurately assessed the domestic political significance of the Virginia theatre.[38]

Thus Grant not only had to modify his eastern strategy but found himself drawn into a contest with Lee, the most experienced, successful, and capable practitioner of theatre army operations on either side. Yet Grant had attained his original goal: the movements of the eastern armies would definitely coordinate with those in the West where Grant possessed, in Sherman, an able commander who well understood the plans for the spring campaign. But this hardly attained the outcome for which Grant had hoped. The purpose of having Smith in Virginia was to insure that the Army of the Potomac acted aggressively enough to prevent Lee's sending forces from his army to interfere with the main offensive in the West. Instead of directing the double advances from Chattanooga and Mobile, Grant found himself in Virginia with the holding operation.

Nevertheless, the Union gained one benefit from the way things had worked out. As lieutenant general, Grant could strengthen his Mobile operation. Instead of using only troops from the Military Division of the Mississippi, he would reduce Banks's department to the lowest possible level, which, with reinforcements from Missouri, would give Banks "a force of over 30,000 effective men with which to move against Mobile." His "demonstration, to be followed by an attack," was to "be cooperative with movements elsewhere." This constituted one of four principal advances intended to begin simultaneously on a signal from Grant and specifically directed to cooperate with that of Sherman from Chattanooga.[39]

As Grant earlier had explained to Halleck, he needed two lines of operations because of the large number of men to be used. Though on an exterior line, the attempt to seize Mobile and march inland would not only function as a turning movement, threatening the vital areas of Montgomery and Selma and drawing there forces which might oppose Sherman, but, said Sherman, would "in a measure solve the most difficult part of my problem—provisions." Union forces would accomplish this by providing, along the Alabama River, an alternate line of communications for Sherman's army when it was far from his original base, Chattanooga. Initially Sherman's advance would have to be a penetration, because he wished to take the important rail and manufacturing center of Atlanta. Such an objective would necessarily immobilize Sherman's force and make it dependent on communications. Sherman assuredly would welcome any line of communications supplementary to the fragile railroad from Louisville to Nashville to Chattanooga and on to Atlanta. In addition it was important that he not begin his raid too soon because of the perennial exterior lines problem. He needed initially to orient his operations on Johnston's army, because he had as one of his "chief objects" to "prevent Joe Johnston from detaching against Grant" until Grant had secured a position "below Richmond." The joining of these two armies at Atlanta would, moreover, have broken every east-west railway and have completed the objective, "to dissever the Confederacy."

Banks, rather than Sherman or McPherson, would command the Mobile column. Grant apparently felt that the strength and vigor of Sherman's advance from Chattanooga would render Banks secure against a Confederate concentration. Grant instructed Sherman: "You I propose to move against Johnston's army, to break it up and to get into the interior of the enemy's country as far as you can, inflicting all the damage you can against their war resources." The campaign plan, modeled on Sherman's raids to Jackson in

July, 1863, and to Meridian in February, 1864, did not provide that any Union troops commence a raid until after the fall of Atlanta. Then Sherman would move as a raiding force toward water communications on the coast at Savannah or Mobile.[40]

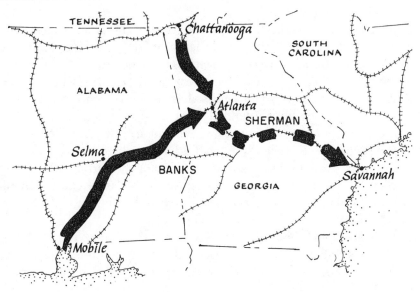

Grant's Plan

The order for the long-contemplated movement of Banks on Mobile constituted one of the few significant initial benefits which Grant derived from his appointment as lieutenant general, though Halleck would very likely have ordered it in any case. Grant already had control of all western operations, except those of Banks, and enjoyed great influence with the headquarters staff and Lincoln; in addition, Grant's small informal group was strategically placed. As the most successful of Halleck's former subordinates and favored generals, he had a strong position with the general in chief. His congressional patron, Washburne, wielded a great deal of influence, being a candidate for speaker of the House of Representatives. Grant's prestige as a winner and his close contact with Assistant Secretary Dana gave him the ability to shape Stanton's and Lincoln's decisions. His informal authority had enabled him to nominate his own man for commander of the Army of the Potomac. The authority that Grant gained over Banks's movements, however, proved a purely illusory gain, for Banks never reached Mobile. He went off instead on the disastrous Red River Campaign.

The Red River Campaign was the culmination of the scheme to try to drive the trans-Mississippi from the war before the Union concentrated against the area east of the river. Halleck had pursued this plan on military grounds, but it fit Lincoln's political strategy in that the President wanted to see "a free-state reorganization of Louisiana in the shortest possible time." Banks, himself, expressed interest in the campaign because he could capture enormous quantities of cotton, immensely valuable for the cotton-starved mills of his home state, Massachusetts.[41]

Sherman also favored the campaign for some of the same strategic reasons which motivated his Meridian raid, declaring it "only justified on the ground of rapid execution and to result in setting free the troops hitherto held to defend points." Upon his return from Meridian, Sherman visited New Orleans to confer with Banks about the Red River movement. "General Banks seemed to be all ready, but intended to delay his departure a few days, to assist in the inauguration of a civil government in Louisiana." Sherman observed the preparations, including "scaffolding for the fireworks and benches for the audience." Banks urged him to remain, for the particularly impressive ceremonies "would include the performance of the 'anvil chorus' by all the bands in his army and during the performance the church bells were to be rung, and cannons were to be fired by electricity."[42]

Sherman declined, though, believing such ceremonies "out of place at a time when it seemed to me," he explained, "every minute were due to the war." Such a dilatory approach should have made him even more concerned, however, for he was contributing 10,000 men to the campaign with the understanding that it should be a thirty-day raid. With the plan envisioning a quick advance and a quick retreat like his Meridian campaign, he expected to have his men back on the upper Tennessee by April 15. If Sherman had been conducting the operation, it doubtless would have worked this way and Banks's forces would have returned just barely in time for the move against Mobile.[43]

But Banks did not even start until March 12. Ponderously pushing up and along the Red River into the heart of Louisiana, his advance units on March 14 easily captured Fort DeRussy near Simsport, while other federal troops pushed toward Alexandria. On March 16 the Unionists occupied Alexandria, experiencing little difficulty. But after these initial successes, Banks became more timid; fearing attack, he delayed and then only gingerly pushed ahead, with his supply wagons and related personnel and equipment moving in front of his infantry.

The federal commander had little sound reason for his fears, since he had about 28,000 men compared to only about 14,000 Confederate defenders under President Davis's former brother-in-law, the capable Richard Taylor. For several days small and scattered skirmishes sporadically erupted, but on April 8 Taylor elected to make a stand at Sabine Crossroads, near Mansfield. Here, Taylor had decided, should be the place to fight a decisive battle to prevent Banks from reaching Shreveport. Predictably, the defensive site proved beneficial to the Confederates.

Banks's men, strung out in a long file, moved on a road quite far inland from the river. Low water also hindered the accompanying gunboats as they tried to attain supporting distance. After several small engagements, late in the afternoon Taylor struck. In the full-scale but disjointed and frenzied fighting that followed, Confederate troops forced Banks's men back briskly and they lost several guns. Soon outflanked on both sides, they panicked and fell back, although only to Pleasant Grove where a stout defense held until the southern assault petered out. During the night Banks retired to Pleasant Hill and formed a better defensive line. The Federals lost 2,235 men, most of them captured, in this battle that marked Banks's farthest thrust into Louisiana; but the Confederates suffered very high casualties, too, perhaps as many as 1,000 men.

The next day, Taylor assaulted Banks at Pleasant Hill. Increasing in intensity as the day wore on, the attacks sporadically gained some ground, pushing the federal defenders back into their reserve lines; but the power of the defense again showed its characteristic strength. Yet Banks's men suffered heavily because he handled them ineptly, but they achieved a tactical victory, losing 1,369 to the Confederates' 1,626 casualties. Banks decided at this moment to abandon his effort and on the next day began to retreat.

Taylor wished to pursue and force another fight, but Kirby Smith, the department commander who arrived personally on the scene, refused to order the needed additional troops to Taylor. The Confederates did follow as far as Alexandria, and there it appeared another battle might develop.

Low water in the Red River delayed Banks's ships from passing through. Always a critical factor in western rivers, the depth of the water over rapids had fallen to three feet and the navy's ironclads drew seven feet. Grant ordered the already delayed Banks to halt his retreat and protect the fleet. Lieutenant Colonel Joseph Bailey, an engineer and ex-lumberman from Wisconsin, solved the navy's problem. Three thousand men and 300 wagons set

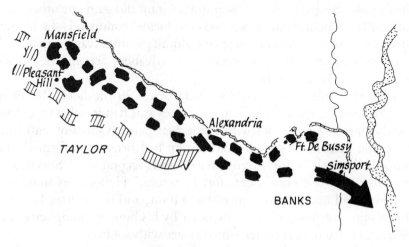

Banks's Red River Campaign

to work building jetties to narrow the channel, thus enabling each heavy ironclad under a full head of steam to shoot the rapids. Almost comically, as the ungainly armored vessels careened downstream, sputtering and throwing smoke and steam and spray, all hands whooped and shouted, while army bands stood and played on the riverbanks to cheer the venture along.

Banks finally returned to New Orleans, long after he should have been at Mobile. It was then too late to carry out the original Mobile Plan.

Even before the fleet had been rescued, the reports of Banks's management of the campaign did not compliment him. The naval commander, the very capable Admiral David Porter, wrote Sherman that it was "a crying sin to put the lives of thousands in the hands of such men. You know my opinion of political generals." Sherman would not get his 10,000 men back in time for the spring campaign. Porter sympathized: "I imagine your disappointment at having your well-laid plans interferred with and having part of your command mixed up in an affair the management of which would be discreditable to a boy nine years of age."[44]

Later, when asked by the Committee on the Conduct of the War what he had intended the operation to accomplish, Porter replied, "I never understood." He elsewhere stated that "the whole affair was a cotton speculation." Banks allegedly had brought speculators with him, and one steamer was loaded down with ice and champagne and with bagging and ropes for the baling of cotton. To the delight of those persons who disdainfully disapproved of the government's program that allowed and even encouraged cotton trade with the enemy, most of the bales that traders managed to get to Alexandria, where they hoped to effect an exchange, were seized by Colonel Bailey and used in building his dams.[45]

Banks's fluke campaign notwithstanding, Grant did gain one other tangible and immediate benefit from his accession to formal command—he obtained a more exact synchronization of the spring simultaneous advances than Halleck had ever secured or really attempted. Four advances actually began within two or three days of each other.

But with the lieutenant general's headquarters in the field, the situation initially changed almost as little in appearances as it had in substance. Lincoln remained commander in chief with Halleck at hand as chief of staff, issuing orders to the field armies, orders which he had originated formally rather than informally with Grant. Grant's friend and "second self," Sherman, considered this the best arrangement, for, he wrote, "Halleck has more reserve booklearning and knowledge of men than Grant, and is therefore better qualified for his present post; whereas the latter by his honesty, simplicity, candor and reliance on friends, is better suited to act with soldiers."[46]

Sherman elaborated his own plans, intending to "knock," or "whip Joe Johnston or drive him back" and "do as much damage to the resources of the enemy as possible." He originally intended to push Johnston across the Chat-tahoochee, opening a route to connect his right with Banks, and to send a cavalry raid "to break up the [rail]roads between Montgomery and Georgia." Grant provided supplies at Pensacola so it could be a refuge for this cavalry force. Sherman would cover his rear in East Tennessee by destroying "a considerable section of the railroad" toward Virginia, "bending and twisting the rails or carrying them to Knoxville." He wished to delay this, however, "till the last movment" so as not to "reveal" the "plans not to operate up toward Virginia."[47]

Grant also arranged for more substantial forms of distraction of the enemy, with Sherman ordering the forces at Vicksburg and Memphis "to keep the enemy busy" and "to seem most active; to hold there all the enemy possible." Sherman agreed with Major General C. C. Washburn, the "sober and ener-getic" new commander at Memphis, when that general wrote him: Confed-erate raids in West Tennessee—most notably the capture on April 12 of Fort Pillow on the Mississippi—were intended "to disturb your equanimity." Sherman, therefore, determined not to "let Forrest draw off" his "mind from the concentration" against Johnston. To accomplish the reverse he had, to coincide with his own advance, ordered out cavalry from Memphis with "a good force of infantry of about 4,000 men as a solid column, against which Forrest could make no impression by his bold dashes." Sherman did not intend these efforts to distract the Confederates in Mississippi in order to protect the communications of his main army so much as to defend occupied territory and divert rebel forces from his front. Though apprehensive about his supply situation, Sherman secured his communications by accumulating a large reserve at Chattanooga, by advancing with the minimum amount of transportation, and by living off the country to the maximum degree possible.[48]

By April Grant clearly saw that Banks would provide no help. Halleck believed that Banks's operations amounted to "about what should have been expected from a general so utterly destitute of military education and military capacity." Agreeing, Grant "had been satisfied for the last nine months that to keep General Banks in command was to neutralize a large force and to support it most expensively." Grant reluctantly concluded that he could not carry out the Mobile operation and that he did not see that anything could "be done this spring with troops west of the Mississippi except on that side." The problem of the Massachusetts political general seemed insuperable. The President would agree to Banks's removal only "very reluctantly as it would give offense to many of his friends, and would probably be opposed by a portion of the cabinet. Moreover, what could be done with Banks? He has many political friends who would probably demand for him a command equal to the one he now has." The problem of paralysis in the trans-Mississippi provoked much exasperated thought, including Grant's of Halleck, himself, taking command in that region. Finally Banks's incapacity was nullified when the Union combined his Department of the Gulf with Arkansas in the newly created Military Division of the West Mississippi under E. R. S. Canby, Stanton's former military aide. Canby controlled all operations and ordered Banks not to leave his headquarters in New Orleans.[49]

But for the failure of Banks to reach Mobile, Grant would have again included every element of his strategy in his final plan for the West. Though he intended the forces not to acquire or defend new territory, the "objective" was logistical, the enemy's "war resources," and the problem of supplies was largely to be solved by living at the enemy's expense. Without maximum exploitation of the countryside, Sherman's big army could not have survived on the supplies provided by a single-track railroad. Grant ordered the troops to defend already captured territory and to distract the enemy by raids from Memphis and Vicksburg as well as by the two principal advances from Chattanooga and Mobile. The destruction of the railroad beyond Knoxville protected the East Tennessee line. Sea power was to have been used to strike a weak enemy line, and Banks's simultaneous attack on Mobile, a "main feature" of the plan, would also have exploited the inescapable circumstances of exterior lines to threaten the enemy's vital agricultural and industrial resources in Alabama.[50]

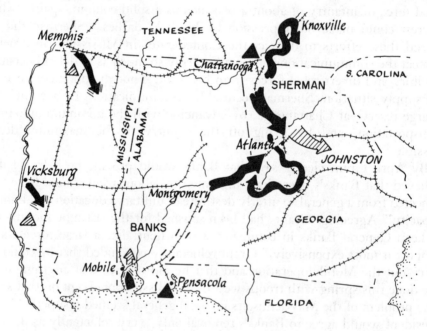

Grant's Western Strategy

A consciousness of the need to offset the Confederates' advantage of interior lines tied together the principal eastern and western advances. Whether Sherman's army would whip, knock, break up, or simply push Johnston's army, the preliminary objective was the same. Sherman explained to Grant that, while his two smaller armies, McPherson's Army of the Tennessee and Scho-field's Army of the Ohio, would work to outflank the enemy, his biggest army, the Army of the Cumberland under Thomas, would "move straight on Johnston wherever he may be, fighting him cautiously, persistently, and to the best advantage." Sherman would make these moves, always keeping "in mind that Johnston is at all times to be kept so busy," he wrote Grant, "that he cannot, in any event, send any part of his command against you or Banks."[51]

In Virginia, Grant envisioned a comparable mission for Meade's force, having instructed Meade: "Lee's army will be your objective point. Wherever Lee goes, there you will go also." The Federals needed to keep both Lee's army and Johnston's army closely engaged, in order to prevent the enemy's use of its interior lines to reproduce the triumph of Chickamauga. The Union leaders continued to overestimate what the Confederates had done with their interior lines. Grant's chief of staff, Rawlins, still believed, for example, that the rebels had sent troops "from Corinth in 1862 to defeat McClellan" at the Seven Days' Battles.[52]

As they planned the impractical March offensive in Tennessee, the leaders in Richmond displayed a significant degree of optimism. Lee did not really participate in this hopefulness because for him the winter of 1863–64 degen-erated into one of having to prove his patience as well as tenacity. One of his biographers asserts that "the gentleness in Lee grew" during this winter. He became "a gray and simple soldier, riding among his troops and smiling kindly as his eyes fell upon the tattered uniforms and familiar faces." More and more, Lee handled all complaints by giving in to individual requests, if at all possible, in order, as he so often said, to " 'suage him, Colonel, 'suage him."[53]

The soldiers in Lee's army also developed a certain stoic attitude. One Alabama man wrote his wife of weather "as cold as the world's charity," and counted thirty-one men in his brigade without "a sign of a shoe on their feet." Across the river one day the Yankees watched the doubtlessly cold baptism of a southern soldier and joined in the singing of hymns. But humor and confidence remained, as everyone laughed at a story about the angels who flew down to conduct Stonewall Jackson into heaven and learned that by a rapid flank march he already had cut his way in.[54]

In November, worried about logistics, Lee feared, needlessly, that he might have to withdraw from the Rapidan, leaving "the richest portion of the State of Virginia at the mercy of the enemy." The Mine Run campaign disap-pointed him and not merely because of the loss of 3,000 men when Meade captured his Rappahannock bridgehead. He wrote of the incident: Meade's movement to the Mine Run intrenchments "led me to believe that he would attack, and I desired to have the advantage that such an attempt on his part would afford." In the fall Lee had worried more about the western situation than his own, but realized the two theatres were inseparable because, he explained, "the enemy may penetrate Georgia and get possession of our depots of provisions and important manufacturers." Upon the defense of that region against Grant and Sherman depends "the safety of the points now held by us on the Atlantic," he added, "and they are in as great danger from his successful advance as by the attacks to which they are at present directly subjected." For this reason Lee had suggested that, "if a portion of Meade's army is sent west, a part of this could be withdrawn."[55]

He did not underestimate the enemy whose "custom . . . when he wished to attack one point is to threaten a distant one." Lee explained: The enemy did this because "he may suppose that our armies, being connected by shorter lines than his, can concentrate more rapidly." Grant, Lee believed, was a master of deception. "He deceived Pemberton when he turned him" at Vicksburg, and in the recent Meridian raid "Sherman threw dust in Polk's eyes." Lee saw the essentials of the war much as did Grant, and the importance and the vulnerability of the West convinced him that "the first efforts of the enemy will be directed against Genl Johnston or Genl Longstreet, most probably the former." Grant's western affiliation also helped to convince Lee that the North regarded the West as its main objective. When northern newspapers reported that Grant would command in Virginia, so sure was Lee that Richmond would not be attacked that he declared: The report was "a stratagem to attract our attention here, while he was left unmolested to deal us a blow from the West."[56]

As Lee worried about the sophistication of the enemy's strategy, Grant did likewise. Notwithstanding his confident belief that both Lee and Johnston would be kept closely engaged, Grant grew concerned by a rumor that Johnston was reinforcing Lee. Thus Grant explained to Sherman his apprehension: "If the two main attacks, yours and the one from here, should promise great success, the enemy may, in a fit of desperation, abandon one part of their line of defense and throw their whole strength upon a single army, believing that a defeat with one victory to sustain them is better than a defeat all along their line." Furthermore, perhaps recalling the inertia of Rosecrans and Meade after the victories at Stones River and Gettysburg, Grant stressed that the enemy would also be "hoping, too, at the same time, that the army meeting with no resistance will rest perfectly satisfied with their laurels, having penetrated to a given point south, thereby enabling them to throw their forces first upon one and then on the other."

Thus Grant described the problem of the enemy's disappearing from the front. The menace of Bragg's abandoning the Middle Tennessee line of operations during the siege of Vicksburg had concerned Grant, Halleck, and, particularly, Rosecrans. The logistical problems of rebuilding broken railroads made a rapid pursuit so difficult as to render this a workable strategy for a desperate enemy. "With the majority of military commanders," Grant thought, "they might do this." As a remedy, he prescribed converting the advance from a penetration into a raid. To the veteran raider, Sherman,

Grant stressed; "You have had too much experience in traveling light and subsisting upon the country to be caught by any such ruse. I hope my experience has not been wasted. My directions, then, would be, if the enemy in your front show signs of joining Lee, follow him up to the full extent of your ability. I will prevent the concentration of Lee upon your front if it is in the power of this army to do it."[57]

Grant expected "to fight Lee . . . if he will stand," and Rawlins anticipated a "terrible battle" before Lee's men reached Richmond. Grant believed "in the ability of his army to cope successfully with that of Lee," a normal outlook for one as naturally sanguine as Grant. He had behind him two years of success and now commanded a far larger field army. Certainly his formidable preparations engendered optimism, for even one of Meade's skeptical staff officers believed in the possibility of an "overwhelming victory." He persisted in this even though he warned "there was no proper ground for it." Victories like that were only "read in books, but they do not happen often, particularly with such armies to oppose as those of the Rebels." He was not the only one to cherish such a hope for Congressman Washburne was on hand at the opening of the campaign "to behold Grant swallow Lee at a mouthful." Yet Grant was certainly as realistic as Meade's staff officer who did "not, for a moment look for the 'annihilation,' the 'hiving,' or the 'total route' of Lee. Such things exist only in the *New York Herald*."[58]

Actually Grant considered abandoning his communications and turning the left of the Army of Northern Virginia. To do so would have cut Lee's line of retreat to the west and south. This turning movement to the west, the decisive direction, would have enabled Grant to invest "Richmond as he had invested Vicksburg and starve out Lee." Grant remarked: By "throwing myself between Lee and his communications" and "if I had been as fortunate as I was when I threw my army between Pemberton and Joe Johnston, the war would have been over a year sooner." But moving "from the Rapidan to Lynchburg" with only "twelve days rations" and facing a Confederate army with rail connections eastward to Richmond and the lower South, the Union army would have been in a very precarious situation. It would not have possessed a supply line and, face to face with an enemy army, could not live off the country. Grant would have to take the offensive against the Army of Northern Virginia and push it back to Richmond so he could break all of Lee's supply lines and re-establish those of the Army of the Potomac. Since this was very risky and difficult, he, like Meade earlier, rejected the plan. Grant "did not dare this risk"; "if I had failed," he stated, "it would have been very serious for the country." Grant's natural confidence had not deserted him, however. He explained what deterred him: "I was new to the army, did not have it in hand and did not know what I could do with the generals or the men."[59]

Faced with Lee's skillfully led veteran army, Grant had no course open but to turn Lee on the east where Grant could base himself on the series of

Virginia rivers. This would force Lee back, but likely accomplish nothing more beyond the principal mission of so engaging Lee's army that he could not send reinforcements to Johnston. What could Grant do to win the chivalric trial of champions with Lee, which the public of his country expected?

Beyond immobilizing Lee's army, Grant aimed to take Richmond. As Rawlins expressed it: Any battle would "decide the fate of Richmond," the "desired end" of the campaign being "victory and Richmond," for, "Richmond ours, all will be well. Nothing after the defeat of Lee and the capture of Richmond by our armies can successfully make head against our onward sweep through the remaining states in rebellion." Just as Sherman had "the heart of Georgia" as "his ultimate aim," Grant had the Confederate capital as his objective, a goal more political and psychological than logistical and one which he hoped to achieve with a sophisticated and multipart plan.[60]

In view of Richmond's elaborate communications network, Halleck, Meigs, and the other engineer officers at headquarters had decided that its capture could not be accomplished. But Lincoln's confidence emancipated Grant, and he had the freedom to plan his own campaign, untrammeled by literal adherence to the headquarters doctrine of not aiming at Richmond. The course of action he adopted resembled that contemplated by Halleck in the previous fall. The initial part of Grant's scheme was reminiscent of his first advance against Vicksburg in that it proposed a surprise, waterborne turning movement aimed to capture the city, while Lee's army was occupied with Meade's to the north. Major General Benjamin F. Butler would move by water up the James to City Point, only ten miles from Petersburg and twenty from Richmond. Unlike Meade's force, "Lee's army being the object point," Butler's army should aim at Richmond. Grant told Butler: The Confederate capital is "to be your objective point," and, "if you cannot carry the city, at least detain as large a force there as possible."[61]

One of Grant's staff officers regarded Butler as "sharp, shrewd, able, without conscience or modesty—overbearing. A bad man to have against you in a criminal case." His ability also impressed Grant, Rawlins noting that "in Sherman, Meade and Butler, General Grant has three generals, all in important commands, whom he can trust." In making his estimate of Butler, Grant ignored the views of Halleck who believed that it seemed "but little better than murder to give important commands to such men as Banks, Butler, [and] McClernand." Upon this misplaced confidence in Butler rested Grant's hope for a quick victory and his expectation that Lee would not fight north of Richmond. The project for a movement by Butler was not new, for Major General John G. Foster, who had thought such a move could take Petersburg, had brought it up; Grant merely changed the objective to Richmond. Foster's plan, in turn, had much similarity to the one John G. Barnard proposed to Halleck in the fall of 1862.[62]

Grant strengthened Butler's Army of the James by bringing Major General Quincy A. Gillmore and a major part of his force from the Department of the

South. Moving secretly at night by water, Butler's advance, simultaneous with Grant's, would place him unexpectedly in the Confederate rear. Butler's army, though on an exterior line, would be safe because he would have water communications protected by ironclads and be "close to the south bank of the James River." After having taken City Point, Butler was directed: "Fortify, or rather intrench, and concentrate all your forces for the field there as rapidly as you can." Most likely Butler would not need the security of these initial intrenchments, however, for Grant hoped that the Army of the James would reach Richmond. Grant explained to Butler: When you reach Richmond, "invest all the South side of the river and fortify yourself there." Thus Grant relied on the defensive strength of Butler's troops and the use of sea power. Butler's staff well understood their mission: "Fasten" our "teeth on Lee's line of supplies & he must leave his positions to come beat us off." Lee would thus be caught between Meade and Butler's intrenched army and might well have to abandon Richmond and retreat westward.[63]

Though hoping for much from Butler's ability and his significantly augmented force, Grant had many other parts to his plan to work out, including complexities corresponding to the difficulty of taking such a communications hub as Richmond. The Weldon Railroad linked that city with the lower South as did the Richmond and Danville Railroad. Even if the Federals could interrupt both of these railroads south of the city, Richmond would still enjoy rail communication with the lower South as well as with the Shenandoah Valley and the southwestern part of Virginia all the way into East Tennessee. The Southside Railway, which ran from Petersburg to Lynchburg, provided a connection between Lynchburg and the Richmond and Danville road. Through Lynchburg passed the East Tennessee and Virginia Railroad, which also went north to join the Virginia Central at Charlottesville. Since the Virginia Central connected the Valley with Richmond, the Confederate capital enjoyed a complete, if circuitous, railway connection with North Carolina. Nor did this route rely entirely on a single track railroad, for Lynchburg could be reached from Richmond by the James River and Kanawha Canal, which ran beside the James on its north side.

For the Weldon Railroad Grant relied on Butler's movement, directing him, in addition, to "inflict a blow on the enemy's resources" while attacking communications and distracting the enemy. Two raids by the forces in West Virginia, whose main duty had been to protect the Baltimore & Ohio Railroad, would provide the other principal means of achieving in Virginia the goals of distraction and destruction of war resources. These two raids would keep "the present line covered" and, at the same time, "occupy the attention of a large force, and thereby hold them from re-enforcing elsewhere." Grant meant for the raids to "destroy the East Tennessee and Virginia Railroad" and to attack rebel resources in the area by wrecking an ironworks and doing "anything else that can be accomplished in the way of destroying what may be made useful by the enemy in prolonging the war." Grant thus sought wherever possible to pursue the strategy of exhaustion, while at the same time aiming at Richmond's communications and seeking to distract southern forces which might oppose his two main efforts. He relied on raids from West Virginia due to the primitive communications of that region, which almost precluded penetrations.[64]

Except for having an objective more political and psychological than logistical, Grant had embodied within his Virginia campaign all of the elements of the strategy which he had evolved while in the West. Though the defense of the territory of Maryland and Pennsylvania against another raid by Lee required more strength than he would have liked, he turned this to his advantage by prescribing a distracting advance into the Valley by Franz Sigel's force defending the Baltimore and Ohio Railroad. In addition Sigel's activity could well supplement the raids. Grant's confidence grew as his plans matured and every sign indicated that both Butler and the western raids would be ready to move on time and in full force.[65]

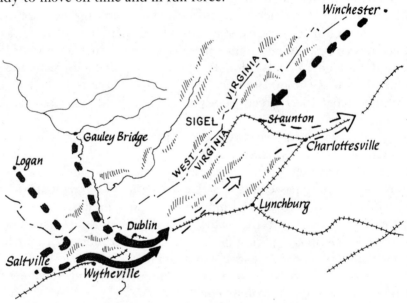

Grant's Plan for Western Virginia

As he became increasingly confident of an easy approach, Grant was again tempted to turn Lee on the west to prevent his escape in that direction and try a campaign of annihilation. If Grant could have been "certain" that Butler could have his "left resting on the James above the city," he would have moved around Lee's left flank, joined Butler west of the city, and reestablished his communications while severing all of Lee's. Thus, with Lee's army cut off from the south and the west, Grant would have an excellent chance of repeating with Lee and Richmond what he had achieved at Vicksburg, for Lee's line of retreat to the north or east would provide a far less promising route of escape than that which Pemberton had had available. But the movement depended on Butler's success. If Butler failed, Grant could not then unite his forces and would lack communications as he faced Lee, who would still have rail connections to Richmond and the South. This same situation he had initially rejected as too risky. Thus, Grant decided to stick with the more cautious course of turning Lee on the east.[66]

Though Lee could retreat westward toward Lynchburg, Grant assumed that he would not abandon Richmond immediately. "Should Lee fall back within his fortifications, either before or after giving battle," Grant planned to "form a junction with Butler and the two forces . . . draw supplies from the James River," and, "once established on the James River," Grant could abandon the supply line from Washington. For the contingency that he and Butler would invest Richmond from the east and south, Grant provided for a siege train.[67]

Any siege of Richmond should not be unduly prolonged, however, because Meade's advance would have cut the railroads to the north and Butler's movement would have cut the road to Weldon. Thus, Lee could not possibly have more than one railroad left open and that ran on the south side of the James, perilously close to Butler's northward-facing flank of Grant's by-then united army. Even if Lee could hold off those Union forces and keep the railroad and the canal open, Grant had hopes that the expeditions from West Virginia could "cut the main lines of the road connecting Richmond with all the South and Southwest," thus forcing an evacuation of Richmond and a retreat westward by Lee's army. Though, typically, Grant had no carefully drawn plan as to how all this would work, he had confidence in his numerical superiority, in the competence of Meade and Butler, and in Sherman's ability to prevent Lee from receiving reinforcements from the armies in the southwest.[68]

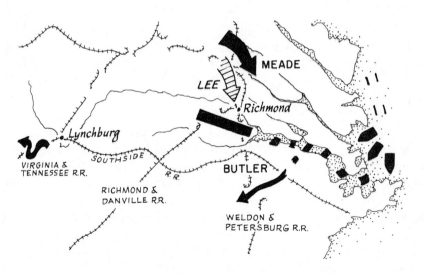

Grant's Planned Offensive

Under Grant's leadership the Union armies were again ready for simultaneous advances, movements which were to be even better synchronized than those guided by Halleck in December, 1862. But Grant's objectives differed. Though he directed the Virginia armies in an effort to take Richmond, his basic goal was for Sherman to take the rail hub of Atlanta and then embark on a raid to break the remaining railways connecting the upper and lower South. The strategy of raids had already received a final and successful test in Sherman's February raid to Meridian. Though Grant's new approach to the strategy of exhaustion made Sherman's movements the most significant of the campaign, the public would give undue attention to the Virginia theatre, where Grant faced Lee.

For coping with Grant, Lee had no elaborate plans even though he saw 1864 as the critical year for the Confederacy because of the northern presidential election. He had as his objective to "resist manfully" until the South had sapped the North's will-to-win. If that strategy succeeded, the polls would reflect it in the 1864 election—in the repudiation of Lincoln and the Republicans and by the election of a President and Congress dedicated to peace. The Union conquest of the Mississippi in 1863 had struck a severe blow to the strategy of wearing down the enemy by denying him military success. Nevertheless, the strategy could work in 1864. If Union arms failed to achieve a significant victory, perhaps northern morale would fail and the advocates of peace would win the fall elections.

But Lee became pessimistic, seeing that the Confederates had "to conform to their plans . . . and concentrate wherever they are going to attack us." Oppressed by the condition of his men and animals, he expressed gloom when he said, "The great obstacle everywhere is scarcity of supplies. That is the controlling element to which everything has to yield."[69]

Lee saw the war in the same terms as Grant. Though Lee well understood the Union general and grasped the importance Grant attached to winning in the West, Lee did not divine his enemy's strategy. He foresaw traditional responses to federal offensives but could hardly comprehend that Grant had spent a winter developing a campaign which would exploit Confederate logistical vulnerability and, in part, circumvent its railway-age Napoleonic defensive strategy.

To combat the Union spring offensive, the Confederacy did complete the total mobilization of its manpower. It retained on duty all whose terms of service would expire in 1864, abolished substitution, and sought to inaugurate "a system of delicate gleaning from the population of the country, involving the most laborious, patient, cautious, and intelligent reinvestigation into the relation of every man to the public defense." Nevertheless the new and more stringent conscription measures failed to produce many new men. More effective was the extension of the draft age to create a reserve force, a national approach to the plan, begun in 1863, of local defense forces raised by state conscription. All men aged seventeen and those between forty-six and fifty were brought into these reserve forces, which could be mobilized if needed in the last year of the war the Confederacy raised fifty thousand reserves, and, though "their equipment gave the appearance that they had ransacked a museum," they provided a very significant reinforcement.[70]

The plan for reserves placed each state's force under seasoned generals, who, if uneven in quality, proved fully equal to these responsibilities. Among them were Theophilus Holmes and Brigadier General James Lawson Kemper, incapacitated for field duty by his wound at Gettysburg. With Grant concentrating most of Gillmore's troops in Virginia, these reserves permitted the Confederates to strip the entire Atlantic Coast to support the armies in Virginia. Soon after Grant began his advance, the War Department ordered "every organized brigade in the Department of South Carolina and Georgia" to Virginia. From Florida even Brigadier General Joseph Finegan, the victor of Olustee or Ocean Pond, was ordered to Virginia, finishing the war commanding his brigade against Grant's concentration there.[71]

Of course Lee would, as usual, have preferred to forestall the North, wishing to seize any opportunity to strike a blow which would "embarrass, if not entirely thwart the enemy in concentrating his different armies, and compel him to conform his movements" to Lee's own. Lee's principal hope rested on the impractical proposal to enter Tennessee. He could plan no such effort himself until late in the spring, because, as usual, his animals had suffered too much from lack of forage to enable him to move until they were revived by the spring grass. Otherwise, during the winter he supported a lesser objective, increasing the security of the always-menaced North Carolina flank. He did have confidence in the railway pipeline system of defense, because when the enemy concentrated a force against one point, "he must withdraw it from some other point, whence," he explained, "our forces must also move to meet it." Nevertheless, for this offensive against federal bases in North Carolina, he could, in the winter, "spare troops for the purpose." They were still so engaged when the campaign opened in Virginia in May.[72]

1. Long, *Civil War, Day by Day*, 453.

2. *Ibid.*, 459, 465; Moore, *Conscription and Conflict*, 308.

3. James B. Fry, in *Reminiscences of Abraham Lincoln, by Distinguished Men of His Time*, ed. Allen Thorndike Rice (New York, 1888), 391–92; Francis B. Heitman, *Biographical Register and Dictionary of the United States Army, 1789–1903*, 2 vols. (Washington, 1903), I, 864.

4. Most of the foregoing is based upon the promising quantitative work of a student at the University of Missouri-Kansas City, Richard A. Vollmer. He is completing an M.A. thesis which carefully probes promotion of Civil War officers. We owe him a large debt. Archer Jones also has written an unpublished manuscript, "A Note on the Promotion of Confederate Generals"; also useful is Arthur P. Wade, "Roads to the Top—An Analysis of General Officer Selection in the United States Army, 1789–1898," *Military Affairs* (Dec., 1976), 157–63. Lastly, all Civil War students stand in obligation to the important labor of love done by Ezra J. Warner, *Generals in Gray* (1959) and *Generals in Blue*

(1964), (Baton Rouge, Louisiana State University Press).

5. Halleck to the Joint Committee on the conduct of the war, Apr. 5, 1864, *O.R.*, XXXV, pt. 1, 292; Gillmore to Halleck, Jan. 15, 1864, *ibid.*, 278.

6. Foote, *The Civil War*, II, 572–73; Emory M. Thomas, "The Kilpatrick-Dahlgren Raid," *Civil War Times Illustrated* (Feb., 1978), 4–5, 8, 48.

7. Sherman to Rawlins, Mar. 7, 1864, *O.R.*, XXXII, pt. 1, 174; Sherman to Grant, Jan. 6, 1864, *ibid.*, pt. 2, 36; Sherman to McPherson, Jan. 10, 1864, *ibid.*, 61–62; Sherman to Grant and Halleck, Jan. 12, 1864, *ibid.*, 75; Grant to Sherman, Jan. 15, 1864, *ibid.*, 105.

8. Grant to Halleck, Jan. 15, 1864, *O.R.*, XXXII, pt. 2, 100–101.

9. *Ibid.*

10. Sherman to Banks, Jan. 16, 1864, *O.R.*, XXXII, pt. 2, 114–15.

11. Grant to Thomas, Jan. 19, 1864, *O.R.*, XXXII, pt. 2, 143; Grant to Logan, Jan. 24, 1864, *ibid.*, 198.

12. Sherman to Grant, Jan. 24, 1864, *O.R.*, XXXII, pt. 2, 201; Sherman to Porter, Jan. 19, 1864, *ibid.*, 147.

13. Rawlins to Dodge, Jan. 30, 1864, *O.R.*, XXXII, pt. 2, 265.

14. Sherman to Banks, Jan. 16, 1864, *O.R.*, XXXII, pt. 2, 114.

15. Sherman to Tuttle, Feb. 6, 1864, *O.R.*, XXXII, pt. 2, 340; Long, *Civil War, Day by Day*, 460, 464.

16. Grant to Halleck, Feb. 4, 27, 1864, *O.R.*, XXXII, pt. 2, 323, 481.

17. Halleck to Grant, Feb. 27, 1864, *O.R.*, XXXII, pt. 2, 481; Grant to Halleck, Feb. 27, 1864, *ibid.*, 481; Grant to W. S. Smith, Feb. 29, 1864; *ibid.*, 500.

18. Grant to W. S. Smith, Feb. 29, 1864, *O.R.*, XXXII, pt. 2, 500.

19. Sherman to Halleck, Feb. 29, Jan. 29, 1864, *O.R.*, XXXII, pt. 2, 498–99, 259.

20. Dana to Halleck, Nov. 27, 1863, *O.R.*, XXXI, pt. 2, 71–72; Grant to Halleck, Dec. 7, 1863, *ibid.*, pt. 3, 349–50; Dana to Stanton, Dec. 12, 1863, *ibid.*, pt. 2, 73.

21. Grant's associate, Horace Porter, says that it was "plain that General Grant would never be free to make his selection of officers, and organize his forces as he desired, until he should be made general in chief. Elihu B. Washburne, the member of Congress from the Galena district in Illinois, General Grant's old home, soon introduced a bill creating the grade of lieutenant-general, and it was passed by both houses of Congress, with the implied understanding that General Grant was to fill the position." Though there is no evidence that Grant inspired Washburne, the exasperation which Porter indicates may well have been felt by Grant (General Horace Porter, *Campaigning With Grant*, ed. Wayne C. Temple [Bloomington, Ind., 1961], 17).

22. Dana, *Recollections of the Civil War*, 20–21, 29, 104; Dana to Stanton, Dec. 12, 1863, *O.R.*, XXXI, pt. 2, 73; Wilson, *Under the Old Flag*, I, 317.

23. Dana to Grant, Dec. 21, 1863, *O.R.*, XXXI, pt. 3, 457–58; Dana to Grant, Jan. 10, 1864, *ibid.*, XXXII, pt. 2, 58; Wilson, *Under the Old Flag*, I, 317.

24. Grant to Halleck, Dec. 14, 23, 1863, Jan. 13, 15, 1864, *O.R.*, XXXI, pt. 3, 403, 473, XXXII, pt. 2, 79–80, 99–101; Grant to Sherman, Jan. 15, 1864, *ibid.*, XXXII, pt. 2, 105; Grant to Thomas, Jan. 19, 1864, *ibid.*, 142–43; Halleck to Sherman, Jan. 15, 1864, *ibid.*, 106; Halleck to Grant, Jan. 13, 1864, *ibid.*, 80.

25. Wilson, *Under the Old Flag*, I, 317, 321–22; Stanton to Burnside, Jan. 29, 1864, *O.R.*, XXXIII, 443; Halleck to Grant, Jan. 8, 1864, *ibid.*, XXXII, pt. 2, 40–42; Grant to Halleck, Jan. 15, 1864, *ibid.*, 99–101.

26. Grant to Halleck, Jan. 19, 1864, *O.R.*, XXXIII, pt. 1, 394–95.

27. Halleck to Grant, Feb. 17, 1864, *O.R.*, XXXII, pt. 2, 411–13; Lee to Bragg, Apr. 7, 1864, *Wartime Papers*, 693.

28. Wilson, *Under the Old Flag*, I, 315–17, 325, 342–43, 345–46; Bruce Catton, *Grant Takes Command* (Boston, 1968), 103.

29. Grant to Thomas, Jan. 19, 1864, *O.R.*, XXXII, pt. 2, 142–43; Thomas to Grant, Jan. 30, 1864, *ibid.*, 264; Foster to Halleck, Feb. 24, 26, 1864, *ibid.*, XXXI, pt. 1, 286, XXXIII, 602–4; Sherman to Grant, Jan. 19, 1864, *ibid.*, XXXII, pt. 2, 147. Foster was very receptive, having proposed a comparable plan when he commanded on the coast (Foster to Halleck, Oct. 8, 1863, *ibid.*, XXIX, pt. 2, 267).

30. Catton, *Never Call Retreat*, 298.

31. *Ibid.*

32. *Ibid.*, 298–99.

33. Catton, *Grant Takes Command*, 125–31.

34. Foster to Halleck, Feb. 24, 1864, *O.R.*,

XXXI, pt. 1, 286; Halleck to Grant, Mar. 24, 1864, *ibid.*, XXXIII, 721. Halleck obviously refers to the map in *O.R.*, Atlas, Plate 135A. This map, Halleck said to Grant, was "before us the other day." The only day Grant and Halleck could have been together, except the preceding, was one during Grant's first visit to Washington. The map has all possible lines of operation sketched on it, including one from New Bern, North Carolina, to Raleigh, North Carolina, and East Tennessee to Richmond. Also included are lines from Chattanooga to Atlanta and between Atlanta and Mobile and Atlanta and Savannah, and, interestingly, one from the head of the York River to Richmond. For other indications that an advance by the Army of the Potomac, accompanied by Grant, was to be primary and had been settled early, see Rawlins to Mrs. Rawlins, Mar. 22, 23, 25, 1864, James Harrison Wilson, *The Life of John A. Rawlins* (New York, 1916), 403, 403–4, 404–5. For evidence that it was not settled prior to Grant's arrival in Washington, see Halleck to B. F. Butler, Mar. 6, 1864, *O.R.*, XXXIII, 649; Special Orders No. 110, War Department, Mar. 8, 1864, *ibid.*, 657.

35. Grant to Burnside, Apr. 5, 1864, *O.R.*, XXXIII, 807. Grant was responding to a suggestion from Burnside that his corps be used to advance into North Carolina to cut the railroads. Grant responded to Burnside rather testily, indicating perhaps that this was a sore subject with him; Cyrus B. Comstock Diary, Library of Congress, entry of July 15, 1864; James Harrison Wilson and Charles A. Dana, *The Life of Ulysses S. Grant* (New York, 1868), 168–69.

36. Grant to Dana, Aug. 5, 1863, Williams, *Lincoln Finds a General*, V, 100–101. See also: Grant to E. B. Washburne, Aug. 30, 1863, James Grant Wilson, *General Grant's Letters to a Friend* (New York and Boston, 1897), 27–28.

37. Sherman to Grant, Dec. 29, 1863, Mar. 10, 1864, *O.R.*, XXXI, pt. 3, 527–28, XXXII, pt. 3, 50.

38. Wilson, *Life of Rawlins*, 190–92; Rawlins to Mrs. Rawlins, Mar. 28, 1864, *ibid.*, 407; Adams, *Our Masters the Rebels*, 155–59. For a somewhat comparable view, see: Reed, *Combined Operations*, 324–29.

39. Grant to Banks, Mar. 31, 1864, *O.R.*, XXXIV, pt. 1, 11. See also: Grant to Halleck, Mar. 25, 1864, *ibid.*, XXXIV, pt. 2, 721; Grant to Banks, Mar. 15, 1864, *ibid.*, 610–11.

40. Sherman to Mrs. Sherman, June 30, 1864, *Home Letters*, 300; Sherman to Grant, Apr. 10, 1864, *O.R.*, XXXII, pt. 3, 314; Foster to Halleck, Feb. 21, 1864, *ibid.*, XXXII, pt. 1, 47; Grant to Meade, Apr. 9, 1864, *ibid.*, XXXIII, 828; Grant to Sherman, Apr. 4, 1864, *ibid.*, XXXII, pt. 3, 245–46; *ibid.*, Atlas, Plate 135A. Grant's almost identical instructions to Sherman for the Jackson expedition were "to break up Johnston's army and divert it from our rear, and, if possible, to destroy the rolling stock and everything valuable for carrying on war" (Grant to Sherman, July 13, 1863, *ibid.*, XXIV, pt. 3, 507).

41. Johnson, *Red River Campaign*, 46.

42. Sherman to Steele, Mar. 4, 1864, *O.R.*, XXXIV, pt. 2, 497; Sherman, *Memoirs*, I, 397.

43. Sherman, *Memoirs*, I, 397.

44. D. D. Porter to Sherman, Apr. 14, 16, 1864, *O.R.*, XXXIV, pt. 3, 153, 169.

45. Catton, *Never Call Retreat*, 337–42.

46. Sherman to John Sherman, Dec. 12, 1863, Sherman Letters, 220; Sherman to Mrs. Sherman, Mar. 12, 1864, *Home Letters*, 286–87.

47. Sherman to Halleck, Apr. 2, 1864, *O.R.*, XXXII, pt. 3, 221–22; Sherman to Grant, Apr. 10, 1864, *ibid.*, 312–14; Sherman to Schofield, Mar. 18, Apr. 20, 24, 1864, *ibid.*, 87–88, 475, 426; Grant to Sherman, Apr. 7, 8, 1864, *ibid.*, 280, 288; M. C. Meigs to Grant, Apr. 8, 1864, *ibid.*, 300. See also: Sherman to Grant, Mar. 24, Apr. 2, 24, 1864, *ibid.*, 178, 221, 465–66; Grant to Sherman, Mar. 31, 1864, *ibid.*, 213; Sherman to Schofield, Apr. 1, 1864, *ibid.*, 213.

48. Sherman to McPherson, Apr. 6, 8, 11, 19, 24, 1864, *O.R.*, XXXII, pt. 3, 273, 294, 326, 414, 479; Grant to Sherman, Apr. 15, 1864, *ibid.*, 366; Washburn to Sherman, Apr. 24, 1864, *ibid.*, 484; Sherman to Washburn, Apr. 28, 1864, *ibid.*, 527; McPherson to Hurlbut, Apr. 19, 1864, *ibid.*, 415–16; McPherson to Slocum, Apr. 19, 1864, *ibid.*, 416; Rochester to McPherson, Apr. 21, 1864, *ibid.*, 439; Sherman to Hurlbut, Apr. 9, 1864, *ibid.*, 310; Sherman to Grant, Apr. 2, 10, 22, 24, 1864, *ibid.*, 221, 313–14, 443, 466; Sherman to Rawlins, Apr. 4, 19, 1864, *ibid.*, 247–48, 310–11; Sherman to Halleck, Apr. 2, 24, 1864, *ibid.*, 222, 469; Sherman to Meigs, Apr. 9, 1864, *ibid.*, 311; Meigs to Sherman, Apr. 20, 1864, *ibid.*, 434; Sherman to Thomas, Apr. 11, 19, 1864, *ibid.*, 323, 413; Sherman to Schofield, Apr. 24, 1864, *ibid.*, 475.

49. Grant to Halleck, Apr. 22, 29, 1864, *O.R.*, XXXIV, pt. 3, 252–53, 331; Halleck to Grant, Apr. 29, 1864, *ibid.*, 332; Halleck to Sherman, Apr. 29, 1864, *ibid.*, 333.

50. W. T. Sherman to J. Sherman, June 9, 1864, *Sherman Letters*, 235–36.

51. Sherman to Grant, Apr. 10, 1864, *O.R.*, XXXII, pt. 3, 313–14. Clearly neither Grant nor Sherman envisioned destroying or annihilating Johnston's army. They expected battles, of course, but hardly conceived that they would eliminate Johnston's army. They expected Sherman to use his numerical superiority to drive Johnston back by turning him. Thus, in this same letter, Sherman said: "Should Johnston fall back behind the Chattahoochee I would feign to the right, but pass to the left, and act on Atlanta, or its eastern communications, according to developed facts." Compared with the instruction "to break up Johnston's army," essentially identical to that for the successful Jackson expedition, Sherman's language contained actually more combative words than Grant's.

Since they had discussed this campaign at length before Grant's final return to the east, there is no doubt that they were in full agreement. Since they knew that, in Johnston, they had a wily opponent, they could not have entertained any hopes for blunders, such as those of Floyd and Pemberton which would have permitted them to trap and capture Johnston's army. Halleck's advance against Beauregard accurately forecast what to anticipate. They expected a great deal from Banks's big army pushing from Mobile.

52. Grant to Meade, Apr. 9, 1864, *O.R.*, XXXIII, 828; Rawlins to Mrs. Rawlins, July 21, 1864, James Harrison Wilson Papers, Library of Congress.

53. Miers, *Lee*, 161–62.

54. *Ibid.*, 162.

55. Lee to Seddon, Nov. 12, 1863, *Wartime Papers*, 623; Lee to Cooper, Dec. 3, 1863, *ibid.*, 631; Lee to Davis, Dec. 3, 1863, *ibid.*, 641–42; Lee to Davis, Feb. 18, 1864, *ibid.*, 674.

56. Lee, endorsement on Whiting's letter, Jan. 11, 1864, *O.R.*, XXIX, 910; Lee to Davis, Mar. 25, 1864, *Wartime Letters*, 682–83; Lee to Longstreet, Mar. 28, 1864, *ibid.*, 684–85.

57. Grant to Sherman, Apr. 19, 1864, *O.R.*, XXXII, pt. 3, 409.

58. Rawlins to Mrs. Rawlins, Mar. 25, Apr. 20, Mar. 22, 1864, Wilson, *Life of Rawlins*, 405, 420, 403; Grant to Butler, Apr. 18, 1864, *O.R.*, XXXIII, 904–5; *Meade's Headquarters*, 99, 124, 318. See also: Rawlins to Mrs. Rawlins, May 9, 1864, James Harrison Wilson Papers, Library of Congress. Though it has often been assumed that Grant aimed at the destruction of Lee's army, it is most unlikely that Grant had any such idea. If Grant had initially intended to seek decisive action with Lee's army, he would not have allocated so many men to Butler's army nor have left uncommitted the reserve of 30,000 men at Washington. Thus an effort to use Meade's army to destroy Lee's was contrary to his original plan for the East and quite out of character with his previous operations. That Grant and Meade got along well suggests also that Grant shared some of Meade's well-known belief in the power of defense. Grant realized that the public expected him to defeat Lee in battle and this Grant tried to do, but without any such extravagant expectation as destroying Lee's army in the field.

59. New York *Herald*, July 24, 1878, 4.

60. Rawlins to Mrs. Rawlins, Mar. 22, 25, Apr. 6, 1864, Wilson, *Life of Rawlins*, 403, 405, 412–13.

61. Halleck to Foster, Oct. 10, 1863, *O.R.*, XXIX, pt. 2, 277; Grant to Butler, Apr. 2, 18, 1864, *ibid.*, XXXIII, 795, 904–5.

62. Comstock Diary, entry of Apr. 1, 1864; Rawlins to Mrs. Rawlins, Apr. 23, 1864, Wilson, *Life of Rawlins*, 423; Halleck to Sherman, Apr. 29, 1864, *O.R.*, XXXIV, pt. 3, 33. Grant's confidence in Butler is reflected in his instructions to him which are quite like those to Sherman and unlike those to Franz Sigel, in whom he lacked confidence. He declined to lay out Butler's campaign for him, though he did provide him with two competent field commanders, W. F. Smith and Q. A. Gillmore (see: Grant to Butler, Apr. 2, 16, 18, 1864, *O.R.*, XXXIII, 794–95, 885–86, 905–6; Grant to Sigel, Mar. 29, 1864, *ibid.*, 765–66; Babcock to W. F. Smith, Apr. 29, 1864, *ibid.*, 1019).

63. Foster to Halleck, Feb. 24, 26, 1864, *O.R.*, XXXI, pt. 1, 286, XXXIII, 604; Grant to Halleck, Feb. 12, 1864, *O.R.*, XXXII, pt. 2, 374–75. Barnard to Kelton, Nov. 28, 1862, *ibid.*, XXI, 807–8; Grant to Butler, Apr. 2, 16, 28, 1864, *O.R.*, XXXIII, 1009, 795, 886; *Lincoln and the Civil War*, 172. There is no reason to believe that Grant copied this plan from anyone. It obviously was the common property of the headquarters staff and the Army of the Potomac. Its compatibility with Grant's ideas is also obvious as is its similarity to the strategy for the West with Butler playing the role of Banks.

64. Barnard to Kelton, Nov. 28, 1862, *O.R.*, XXI, 807; Grant to Sigel, Apr. 15, 1864, *ibid.*, XXXIII, 874; Grant to Butler, Apr. 2, 16, 1864, *ibid.*, 795, 885; Grant to Sigel, Mar. 29, Apr.

15, 1864, *ibid.*, 765–66, 874; Grant to Ord, Mar. 29, 1864, *ibid.*, XXXIII, 758.

65. For signs of apprehension about a possible raid by Lee, see: Grant to Meade, Apr. 9, 1864, *O.R.*, XXXIII, 828; Grant to Sigel, Apr. 15, 1864, *ibid.*, 874; Grant to Halleck, Apr. 29, 1864, *ibid.*, XXXIII, 992.

66. Grant to Butler, Apr. 18, 1864, *O.R.*, XXXIII, 904–5; Grant to Meade, Apr. 9, 1864, *ibid.*, 838; Meade to Grant, Apr. 17, 1864, *ibid.*, 889–90; Grant to Halleck, Apr. 29, 1864, *ibid.*, 1017.

67. Grant to Halleck, Apr. 29, 1864, *O.R.*, XXXIII, 1017–18; Grant to Meade, Apr. 17, 1864, *ibid.*, 889.

68. Grant to Meade, Apr. 9, 1864, *O.R.*, XXXIII, 282; Rawlins to Mrs. Rawlins, Mar. 28, 1864, Wilson, *Life of Rawlins*, 407.

69. Lee to Longstreet, Mar. 28, 1864, *Wartime Papers*, 685.

70. Moore, *Conscription and Conflict*, 239–40, 305, 308–10, 315–19, 333–34, 356.

71. Davis to Lee, May 12, 1864, *O.R.*, LI, pt. 2, 922.

72. Lee to Davis, Mar. 25, 1864, *Wartime Papers*, 684; Lee to Longstreet, Mar. 28, 1864, *ibid.*, 685; Lee to Davis, Jan. 2, 1864, *ibid.*, 646; Lee, endorsement on Whiting's letter, Jan. 11. 1864, *O.R.*, XXIX, 910.

17 ☆ THE FINAL SIMULTANEOUS ADVANCES

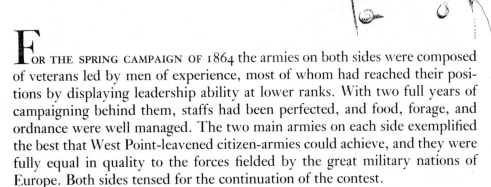

Richard S. Ewell

Fᴏʀ ᴛʜᴇ sᴘʀɪɴɢ ᴄᴀᴍᴘᴀɪɢɴ ᴏꜰ 1864 the armies on both sides were composed of veterans led by men of experience, most of whom had reached their positions by displaying leadership ability at lower ranks. With two full years of campaigning behind them, staffs had been perfected, and food, forage, and ordnance were well managed. The two main armies on each side exemplified the best that West Point-leavened citizen-armies could achieve, and they were fully equal in quality to the forces fielded by the great military nations of Europe. Both sides tensed for the continuation of the contest.

Except for the debilitation of his animals due to lack of forage, Lee was ready. He had changed his army but slightly, again keeping it in three corps. Longstreet's force had rejoined in April after it became clear that a major federal offensive indeed would take place in Virginia. Ecstatic to be back on their home soil, Longstreet's men had demonstrated emotionally when Lee reviewed them on parade. They broke into cheers and echoed with one of the most exuberant rebel yells of all time; one man who was there still remembered, forty years later, that "the effect was as of a military sacrament." Lee was well served by the experienced and extremely capable Longstreet. The talented A. P. Hill also led a corps reasonably well for a year, as had the less able, one-legged Richard S. Ewell; but poor health handicapped the performance of both of these men. The brilliant and dashing J. E. B. Stuart continued to lead Lee's cavalry.[1]

Meade, also, had reorganized his army into three large corps under the best generals. The first, every bit as able as Longstreet, Winfield Scott Hancock, who would be the Democratic military-hero nominee for President sixteen years later, Grant called the "most conspicious figure of all general officers who did not exercise a separate command." Tall, handsome, and imposing in appearance, "Hancock the Superb" invariably inspired confidence and his men "always felt that their commander was looking after them." The second, a lieutenant with Grant in the Mexican War, John Sedgwick, had earned the respect of the men in the Army of the Potomac and nearly matched Hancock's performance in maneuvering his troops. The third leader, Gouverneur

K. Warren, capable earlier when leading a division, now experienced difficulty due to deficiency in delegating responsibility.[2]

In addition to Meade's army, Grant had moved into Virginia a separate corps, the Ninth, led by Burnside. Though better suited to a subordinate role than chief command, the experienced but often inept Burnside would perform barely adequately in the management of his large force. With the addition of Burnside, the Federals opposing Lee on the Rapidan outnumbered him by about 120,000 to 65,000.

Lee was prepared to dispute the route to Richmond, an area valuable both for the supply of his army and because through it ran the railroad to the fertile Shenandoah Valley. Most enlisted men on each side expected a bloody and closely contested campaign. After the limited operations and essential planning which characterized the winter doldrums, they seemed at moments to relish their conclusion, which came abruptly with the opening of May, 1864. The Army of the Potomac crossed the Rapidan and on May 5 commenced the Battle of the Wilderness. "A beautiful spring day on which all this bloody work is being done," wrote one Confederate private.[3]

Initiative rested with the Federals. Instead of having difficult relations with headquarters in Washington, Meade worked harmoniously with Grant, who accompanied and guided the Army of the Potomac. Lee faced a cold, calculating, and relentless foe in the two-dozen-a-day cigar-smoking and calmly whittling Grant. Perhaps more importantly Lincoln gave Grant great latitude in conducting his campaign. The lieutenant general had more flexibility than his predecessors, the President extending to him the kind of trust bestowed only on McClellan in the first days of his command. Lincoln now could tolerate and even chuckle about a general whom someone facetiously described as "a man who could be silent in several languages." For a few days scant news reached the capital. One anxious congressman asked Lincoln what was happening. "Well, I can't tell much about it," the President replied. "You see, Grant has gone into the wilderness, crawled in, drawn up the ladder, and pulled in the hole after him, and I guess we'll have to wait till he comes out before we know just what he's up to."[4]

Grant espoused a keener optimism than did the rank and file. Hopeful of the effect of the advance of Butler's powerful army and skeptical that Lee would resist their own formidable federal army outside of the fortifications of Richmond, Grant and Meade intended "to turn the right flank of the enemy." Grant felt that forty-eight hours would "demonstrate whether the enemy intends giving battle this side of Richmond." He and Meade eagerly desired to reach the easy supply route of the James River and begin, if it proved necessary, the siege of Richmond. Grant directed Meade, who believed that Lee was "simply making a demonstration to gain time" and would not "give battle": Avoid letting the Confederates secure the initiative, and, if any "opportunity presents itself for pitching into a part of Lee's army," do so promptly.[5]

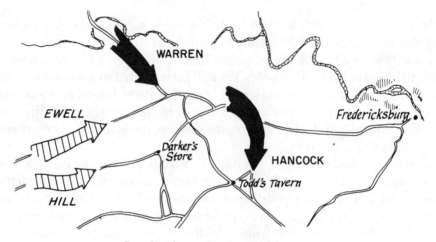

Crook Aborts Staunton Maneuver

After crossing the Rapidan on May 4, the Army of the Potomac had to wait in the Wilderness for its supply train. The Federals detected some enemy activity along the road from Orange Court House, where Lee had placed Ewell's corps. Both armies seemed unaware of their proximity to each other, but, as always, Lee's cavalry scouts enabled him to make satisfactory responses. Early on May 5 the Federals struck Ewell, incorrectly thinking his corps was only a smaller fragment, and the fight escalated. In the dense, undergrown labyrinth that made up the Wilderness, one Union officer "noted that this was like no fight he had ever heard of." While two lines of rival infantry usually met in a quite brief exchange at close range, one or the other quickly giving way, "here there was no giving way whatever. The men simply lay on the ground or knelt behind logs and stumps and kept on firing, and the very intensity of their fire pinned both sides in position—the only chance for safety was to crouch low or lie flat; if a man stood up either to advance or to run away he was almost certain to be shot." The woods caught fire and "the crackle of flames mingled with the wild yelling and cursing of men and the swinging, whacking crash of rifle fire, and the dense forest seemed to trap the roar of battle"; thus, Bruce Catton described the battle where "wounded men were seen to load and cap their muskets so that they could shoot themselves if the fire reached them."[6]

Catton concluded that "in this forest it was almost as bad to win as to lose. Either way, a battle line was certain to get thrown into hopeless disorder. Along five miles of fighting front there was hardly one brigadier who could really control his own line, because there was hardly one brigadier who could put his hand on more than a fraction of his own command. The lines had been jumbled as they had never been jumbled before."[7]

The Union attack drove Ewell's lead division under Major General Edward Johnson backward until Ewell was able to support it. Unable to fall back slowly and with vision impaired by the heavy thicket, the Virginians who bore the brunt of the onslaught broke and fled rearward. For a moment the Union seemed to hold the advantage but a successful counterattack by the just arrived Georgians under Brigadier General John B. Gordon caused both Union flanks to be overlapped while pressing a frontal assault.

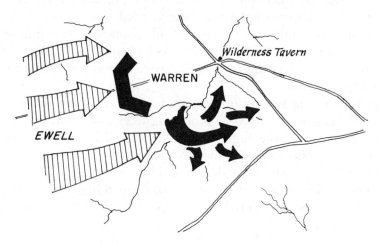

The Confederates Overwhelm the Union Flank

Two additional blue divisions on the Union left tried in vain to find the flank they had been told to support and were driven eastward in confusion, some of their numbers actually running into Confederate lines as they lost direction in the heavy undergrowth. Having counterattacked and restored his position, Ewell halted and dug in because Lee wished to avoid a general engagement until Longstreet's corps, far to the southwest, could join Ewell's and Hill's.

Meanwhile A. P. Hill advanced on the Orange Plank Road to a position

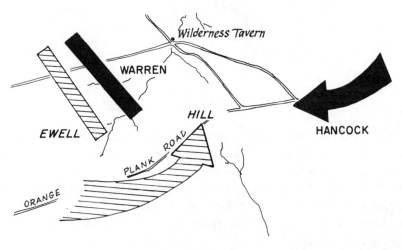

Warren's Redeployment and Hill's Threat of Interior Position

which threatened to insert him between Warren and Hancock, whose corps
Meade had ordered to march northwest to close on Warren. Lee was present
at Hill's headquarters. In an event that could have changed the course of the
war, a platoon of Union skirmishers emerged, rifles at ready, from a stand of
pines just as Lee had dismounted to confer with Hill and Stuart. Apparently
startled by the confrontation with these Confederate generals, the federal
soldiers faded back into the woods instead of opening fire and advancing
against Lee and two of his key generals. As a result, Lee, fearful that Union
troops would similarly stumble into the space between Hill and Ewell, extended Hill's left flank.[8]

Hancock arrived at two o'clock leading his four divisions. Though Meade
had ordered Hancock to attack before Longstreet could join Lee, Hancock,
learning that he faced the aggressive Hill, delayed his attack to improvise
crude log breastworks along the road in his rear. At 3:30 Hancock advanced
on the Confederates, who were dug in amid the tangled mass of Wilderness
foliage. Twenty-five thousand Union troops seemed likely to overwhelm the
scant 7,500 Confederates entrenched before them. In the withering blind

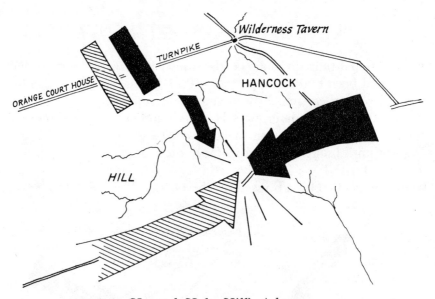

Hancock Halts Hill's Advance

firing that followed, the standing and advancing blue infantry was thrust four
times toward gray defenders. Finally, in a see-saw exchange of ground, both
sides stalled as night fell.

Grant's plan for the morning of May 6 included engaging Ewell to prevent
reinforcement of Hill's interior flank while Hancock and Burnside drove a
wedge between the Confederate positions, probably confronting the then
advancing Longstreet as well.

Lee, too, planned to take the offensive as his scattered forces came together.

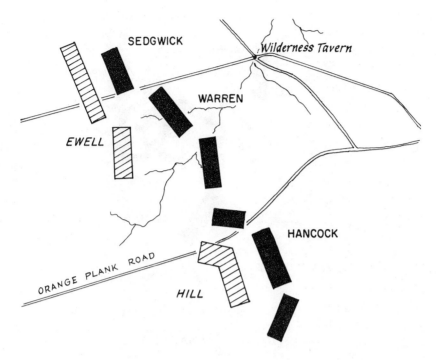

Positions at Dusk May 5

He wished Longstreet to approach Hill's rear, while Hill slipped northward to close the gap with Ewell. At the same time Longstreet and a part of Hill's force would turn Hancock's left flank.

As the fighting resumed at 5 A.M. on the 6th, Burnside wandered, disoriented, trying to find the gap he was to fill. Hill's line was crumbling as Longstreet's troops arrived and pushed forward, stalling Hancock's advance. By ten o'clock the Confederate line was recovered. Longstreet then began his turning movement with a force directed by his staff officer, Sorrel, and succeeded in collapsing Hancock's position. But the inspiring Hancock rallied his men and successfully stood behind the breastworks he had prepared the day before. Meanwhile Burnside had at last found the enemy, but Hill readily repulsed his attack.

Toward sunset Gordon's Confederate brigade swept the federal right flank and proceeded rapidly and successfully until sunset. But he received no support and failed to generate a full-scale attack. During the night new lines were drawn, firmly anchored, and well dug in.

Lee was pleased with the day's fighting as, with the help of the terrain, he had definitely halted Grant's turning movement. The next day the two armies remained in their positions, both digging. Neither commander could see a weak spot in the confusing tangle of the Wilderness.

Though Lee had done more than demonstrate and delay, the bloody and inconclusive two-day struggle in the Wilderness did not dampen Grant's

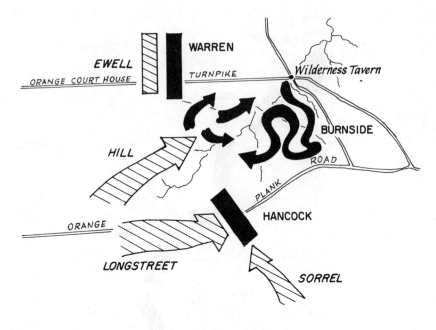

Burnside Repulsed

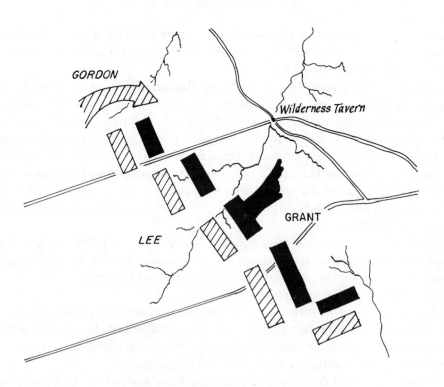

Gordon's Sweep and Stalemate

optimism, which gained further reinforcement from his learning that forces from West Virginia had "cut the Tennessee railroad and destroyed a depot of supplies at Dublin." More important, Butler had advanced on time, landed his army at Bermuda Hundred, and encountered "no opposition thus far. Apparently a complete surprise." Furthermore, Butler's cavalry was moving to break the Petersburg and Weldon railroad. The energetic Butler seemed to be pursuing faithfully the objectives "indicated in conference with the lieutenant-general" and was clearly "carrying out that plan."[9]

Although Meade met disappointment in his hope that "a vigorous attack" would "overthrow the enemy," Grant said: I feel that the results of the Battle of the Wilderness "were decidedly in our favor." The Union would have obtained even more significant rewards, Grant felt, had the extensive use of field fortifications by the Confederates not made them almost invulnerable to assault. The need to protect the Army of the Potomac's immense supply train from a raid prevented the Union from inflicting any "heavy blow on Lee's army." Nevertheless, the tactical operations appeared favorable, for, though Grant estimated his losses at 12,000, he reported to Halleck: Those "of the enemy must exceed ours." In fact the Federals suffered 17,666 casualties, while the Confederates lost about 7,500 men.[10]

Grant clearly saw, however, that his plans were working. He felt certain he was holding all corps of Lee's army in front of him, while Confederate communications west and south of Richmond were being cut by cavalry from West Virginia and by Butler's army, which, achieving surprise, was on schedule. As Grant again attempted to slip past Lee's eastern flank, advancing toward Spotsylvania Court House, he expected "to form a junction with General Butler as early as possible." That Grant immediately attempted another turning movement raised morale, in spite of heavy casualties suffered in the Wilderness. Representative of the federal army's response, one soldier later gravely asserted that "the most thrilling moment of the whole war" came when his column turned south at the Chancellorsville crossroads and the man realized that they were advancing instead of retreating. Unlike the results of the battles of Burnside and Hooker, Grant's tactical failure did not signal retreat. Even if public opinion had not required him to persevere, Grant understood that his duty to keep Lee from reinforcing Johnston would have necessitated an unabated offensive in Virginia.[11]

But Grant's own plans for the Virginia campaign implied an immediate renewal of the effort to turn Lee. The failure of the first attempt lacked significance, because Grant intended to base his army on the Virginia rivers, permitting successive movements to pass around Lee's eastern flank. The enlisted men called these maneuvers "the jug-handle movement."[12]

Grant's comprehensive plans included far more than the interaction of the armies on the Rapidan. Telling Halleck, "My exact route to the James River I have not yet definitely marked out," Grant intended, if Butler succeeded, to reinforce him from the 30,000 men in reserve at Washington. Grant even momentarily revived the idea of the westward turning movement. He considered taking advantage of a possible weakness of Lee's western flank which, if combined with a signal success on Butler's part, would have enabled Grant to move Meade's army west to Gordonsville and then south, in order to trap Lee's army. In any case, the siege train was ordered to Butler, and the men instructed to serve Butler as infantry until needed for the siege. This optimism apparently spread through the troops, the rumor being that "Butler has taken Petersburg."[13]

At this point, Grant launched a raid with his strong cavalry corps. He expected to dominate the Confederate cavalry and, as in a similar raid in the Chancellorsville campaign, to break Lee's railroads. The soldiers could cross eastern Virginia and join Butler's army near Richmond. The results of the raid proved negligible even though, to impart vitality to his superior cavalry, Grant had brought from the West a young infantry officer, Philip H. Sheridan.

Short and cocky in appearance, Sheridan possessed a demeanor that fit his aggressive nature. He had been suspended from West Point for "boisterous" behavior—chasing a fellow cadet with a bayonet. Bruce Catton called him "a tough little man . . . bandy-legged and wiry, with a black bullet head and a hard eye, wearing by custom a mud-spotted uniform, flourishing in one fist a black hat which, when he put it on, seemed to be at least two sizes too small for him." Somewhat consciously flamboyant, Sheridan rode his rounds on a great, black horse at a pounding gallop in a way that caused someone to comment that he "rolled and bounced upon the back of his steed much as an old salt does when walking up the aisle of a church after a four years' cruise at sea."[14]

Another Halleck protégé, like Sherman and Thomas, Sheridan had found favor with Grant. Halleck liked Sheridan because of his good service against the Indians on the Pacific coast and had first appointed him a quartermaster and then to his staff, from which Halleck later secured him the command of a cavalry regiment. Moving up rapidly, Sheridan performed well with an infantry division and had impressed Grant at the Battle of Chattanooga. Confident, capable, and always energetic, he seemed to Grant just the man to infuse vigor and efficiency into the powerful cavalry of the Army of the Potomac. But, unfamiliar with mounted troops, Sheridan turned in a lackluster initial performance. Nevertheless he grew rapidly into the job. Meanwhile, Sherman was advancing with an equally fine army.

Except for the lack of a cavalry leader with potential that equalled Sheridan's, Sherman was as well served as Meade. Heading the Military Division of the Mississippi, Sherman had an army group, with its largest unit the Army of the Cumberland. The solid and capable but slow-moving "Rock of

Chickamauga," George H. Thomas, commanded that army of fully 60,000 men.

Next in size was Grant's old Army of the Tennessee, led by the brilliant young James B. McPherson. An engineer officer, first in his 1853 West Point class, McPherson had been sent by Halleck to serve as Grant's engineer officer at Fort Donelson. His great ability had soon caused his shift to troop duty, where he proved so able he rivaled Sherman in Grant's esteem.

The smallest unit, Burnside's old Army of the Ohio, was now under John M. Schofield, who had succeeded John G. Foster during the late winter. After briefly replacing Burnside, the competent Foster found that his bad leg made him unfit for the strenuous field duty required in East Tennessee. Headquarters then sent him to the Department of the South, stretching along the south Atlantic coast, replacing Gillmore, who had gone with most of his troops to serve under Butler on the James. The young Schofield had transferred from command in Missouri where, against his will, he had become involved in the crossfires of the divisive radical-against-conservative politics of Missouri. His departure made available a department for Rosecrans, one pleasing to his partisans and very suitable because both factions in Missouri found him acceptable. Another Halleck protégé, Schofield later would become general in chief of the army. Experienced in departmental command, he lacked much background with an army in the field. He would learn, however, under an able tutor, the brilliant and experienced William T. Sherman.

Tall and slender, the red-haired Sherman presented an attractive appearance which reinforced the charm of his conversation. He was a polished, brilliant man, having been raised as the ward of a prominent lawyer and politician, Thomas Ewing. Sherman's widowed mother could not raise the eleven children with whom she was left, and so the Roman Catholic Ewing family took him in. His parents originally named him only Tecumseh after the Indian chief and called him Cump. He acquired his Christian name when the Ewing's priest baptized him on St. William's Day. As a child Sherman hated his red hair, an object of derision from other youths, causing him to resort to dye, which turned his hair an odd shade of green. Fortunately he outgrew his childhood troubles; when a cadet at West Point he was popular and was regarded as bright, but he was always prepared for any lark. Besides being a great storyteller, Sherman made the best hash at the academy and, at the risk of expulsion, he sometimes went with friends to Benny Haven's nearby tavern to eat oysters and drink beer.

Sherman's foster sister, Ellen, wrote to him all through his West Point years and they eventually fell in love. He once penned a note to her informing her that he had taken up art: "I have great love for painting, and find that I am so fascinated that it amounts to pain to lay down the brush." They married in 1850 and, like so many young officers, rather than face the bleak isolation of married life on the frontier and frequent separations, he chose to leave the army. He tried banking in San Francisco and New York City; but although hardworking and quite honest, he failed in this career, losing all his real estate and other investments as well as a result of the panic of 1857. "I am doomed to be a vagabond," he wrote Ellen; "I look upon myself as a dead cock in the pit, not worthy of future notice."

Nevertheless 1859 brought him a new opportunity—he became the first superintendent of a new military college in Louisiana, the future Louisiana State University. There he learned much about the southern people but never came to accept their views on secession. After that state seceded, he went to St. Louis, Missouri, and took employment as president of a street railway company. He was offered an appointment as assistant secretary of war but declined, wishing the Lincoln administration "all success in its almost impossible task of governing this distracted and anarchical people."

Thus began to develop his hard attitude. In 1863 he wrote to his brother, Senator John Sherman of Ohio: "It is about time the North understood the truth, that the entire South, man, woman, and child is against us." But, as he had indicated in 1862 to Grant, if "we cannot change the hearts of the people of the South, . . . we can make war so terrible that they will realize" its folly, "however brave and gallant and devoted to their country" they may be. In 1863, to a southern woman who complained about his soldiers' stealing, he answered, "Madam, . . . war is cruelty . . . the crueler it is, the sooner it will be over." Now, during the Atlanta campaign, to his wife he explained: "To realize what war is, one should follow our tracks."

Sherman suffered strained relations with the press. He often told correspondents bluntly that they published too much information that gave aid to the enemy, and he once jailed a reporter who disregarded his restrictions. But not all of the media men reciprocated Sherman's feeling. A Boston editor, after reading one of Sherman's public defenses of Grant, exclaimed, "How his wrath swells and grows. He writes as well as he fights." Indeed Sherman did turn pithy phrases. Widely read, broad in his interests, he possessed a mind ever active.

He deserved his high esteem with both the public and the military. His subordinates and the rank and file respected him and were fiercely loyal to him. A veteran of First Bull Run and Shiloh, Sherman well grasped the realities of combat and, from his later campaigns, had ample experience directing troop movements. All this, however, exacted a heavy toll upon his physical person. Ellen visited him late in 1863 and reported to her father, "He looks more wrinkled than most men of sixty." Sherman was then not forty-three. "I never saw him but I thought of Lazarus," wrote one observer, noting Sherman's nervous, fidgety manner, sunken temples, and scraggly beard. Another witness recalled that he was a chain-smoker and that he puffed through each cigar "as if it was a duty to be finished in the shortest possible time."

Ironically, he was almost two years older than Grant and once had been Grant's military superior; but he humbly sensed a greater genius in Grant and now gladly served as his right hand. Thus Sherman approached his most important command with the maturity of three years of hard and active campaigning, had learned much from his mistakes, and had thought a great deal about the best tactics as well as the solutions to problems of logistics and strategy.[15]

Sherman's opponent, Joseph E. Johnston, had headed the Confederate forces at First Bull Run, but his battle experience lacked the intimacy of Sherman's, first gained at a subordinate level. Since the Battle of Fair Oaks, Johnston had participated in no combat and, except for his relief operations near Vicksburg, no further field service. He would not enjoy the full confidence of his more combat-seasoned corps commanders. Of medium height, bald with a graying goatee, Johnston had an attractive appearance and the demeanor, it was said, of a gamecock. Warm in manner, he elicited the affection of those around him. Like Lee, he was unpretentious. The dining arrangements for Johnston and his staff impressed visitors as Spartan: visiting during Johnston's Vicksburg relief operation, the British Lieutenant Colonel Fremantle of the Coldstream Guards noted that the staff's "only cooking utensils consisted of an old coffee-pot and frying pan—both very inferior articles. There was only one fork (one prong deficient) between himself and staff and," wrote Fremantle, "this was handed to me, ceremoniously as the 'guest.' " Colonel Fremantle observed that Johnston's "officers evidently stand in great awe of him." This awe was not based on ceremony for, when riding the railroad, Johnston would help "wood up" the engine, working "with so much energy as to cause his 'Seven Pines' wound to give him pain." Thus, Johnston possessed a magnetism which evoked intense loyalty and which imparted itself to the rank and file of the Army of Tennessee. To succeed the hated Bragg would have been an advantage in any case, but Johnston communicated to his men his care for them and remained ever popular with the army.[16]

In addition to Joe Wheeler, his able young cavalry leader, Johnston enjoyed the services of the best corps commander in the West, the veteran William J. Hardee. The equal of Longstreet or Hancock, Hardee had served in the western army, where Sidney Johnston had employed him as his principal subordinate.

A newcomer from Virginia, John B. Hood, headed Joe Johnston's other corps. This young adopted son of Texas had graduated from West Point in 1853 and had begun the war leading a regiment in Virginia. Brave and aggressive, the capable Hood had risen to major general, being twice wounded severely. After promotion to lieutenant general in February, 1864, he was assigned to one of Johnston's two corps. Very able at the brigade and division level, in his new position Hood now stood at, if not a trifle beyond, the level at which he could perform adequately. Another promotion, which he later received, would prove to be another excellent example, like the elevation of Pemberton, of the operation of the Peter Principle: promotions until he reached the level at which he was incompetent.

Besides the advantage of greater experience, Sherman enjoyed numerical superiority over Johnston—with almost 100,000 men he outnumbered Johnston at least two to one. But the strength of the foe's position offset this advantage: the Confederates occupied a craggy site so naturally formidable and so well fortified by skill and care that Sherman picturesquely called it "the terrible door of death."[17]

Once well intrenched in the mountainous territory of north Georgia, the southern portion of the Appalachian Mountains, to turn Johnston's position Sherman planned to "throw McPherson rapidly on his communications" while, with his other two armies, he planned to "occupy Johnston's whole attention" by "attacking at the same time cautiously in front." McPherson had as his mission to reach the enemy rear at Resaca and "there break the railroad and leave Johnston out of rations." Sherman worried about "the possibility of Johnston turning on McPherson" and crushing his small army, widely separated from the two other Union armies. To avoid this eventuality, Sherman instructed McPherson to be careful. "After breaking the road," Sherman directed McPherson "to retire to the mouth of the Snake Creek

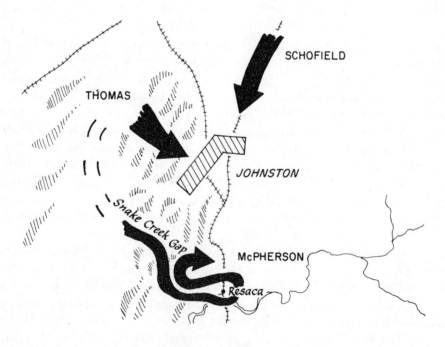

Sherman's Plan

Gap, and be ready to work on Johnston's flank in case he retreats south." In retreating into the rugged Snake Creek Gap, McPherson would be safe against Johnston, "covered against him by the very mountains he chose to cover himself."[18]

Sherman was thus exercising extreme caution in dividing his forces in the face of the enemy's well-led veterans. The Union general still underestimated the power of the defense. A month later he was wiser, writing: "I regard each of my three armies as able to hold in check any attempt of the enemy to mass and overwhelm a part until the others come up." Hindsight made Sherman realize that he had missed a great victory. McPherson, with "twenty-three thousand of the best men in the army," would have been able to place "his whole forces astride the railroad above Resaca, and there have easily withstood the attack of all of Johnston's army, with the knowledge that Thomas and Schofield were at his heels." McPherson's position would have been comparable to Jackson's in the Second Bull Run campaign except that McPherson would have blocked Johnston's retreat south. Sherman did not believe Johnston would "have ventured to attack him in position, but would have retreated eastward." The result, Sherman thought, would have been the capture of "half his army and all his artillery and wagons at the beginning of the campaign."[19]

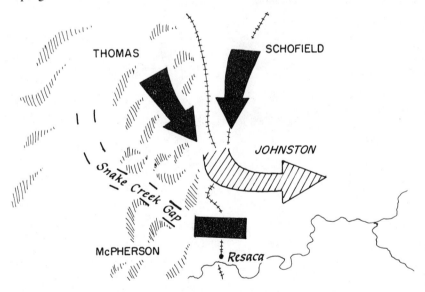

Sherman's Missed Opportunity

While Grant was engaged in the Wilderness, Sherman began his move. Johnston's dispositions made him vulnerable at Resaca, the town being guarded only by one brigade. On May 9 McPherson reached Resaca. But the town remained in Confederate hands and McPherson withdrew according to plan. Still, the menace to his rear impelled Johnston to begin a withdrawal to cover

Resaca, forestalling Sherman's desire to follow McPherson with all his forces to reach Johnston's rear "and interpose between him and Georgia."[20]

In Richmond, the Confederates had already taken a measure to counter Sherman's offensive. At the first inkling of Sherman's advance, they had ordered troops from Alabama and Mississippi, with General Polk instructed to leave his department and command them himself. Polk marched with alacrity, for he had thought "favorably of moving on Sherman's flank." Polk did not reach Sherman's flank but he did reach Resaca in time to cover Johnston's retreat. Further, Polk brought 14,000 men, so many that he was criticized in Richmond for excessively weakening Mississippi and Alabama. Thus, the Confederates did concentrate against Sherman, something they could not have done had Banks's failure not eliminated the campaign's "main feature, a simultaneous attack" on Mobile.[21]

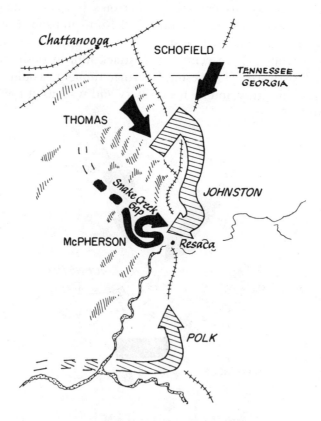

Confederate Response to Union Threat

While Sherman and Johnston directed their armies south to face each other at Resaca, Grant was having no more success in Virginia trying to reach Lee's communications near Spotsylvania Court House, an important strategic site only because roads passed through it to Chancellorsville, Wilderness Tavern, and Fredericksburg. The Army of the Potomac lost two precious hours during its night march on May 7 because of an incident between two of their own cavalry regiments. The veteran Third Pennsylvania Cavalry halted beside a fresh regiment which had just reached the front. The battle-hardened Pennsylvanians, enviously eyeing the fresh horses of the newcomers, suddenly and spontaneously abandoned their battle-weary horses and took those of the green troopers. The exchange of horses was not accomplished without an hour's fistfight between the men of the two regiments which blocked the road and caused the two-hour delay. Though the enlisted men initiated the exchange of horses, the next morning the officers of the Third Pennsylvania looked their men over and remarked, sagely: "The horses look remarkably well after the night's march," and the first sergeant innocently said, "Yes sir."[22]

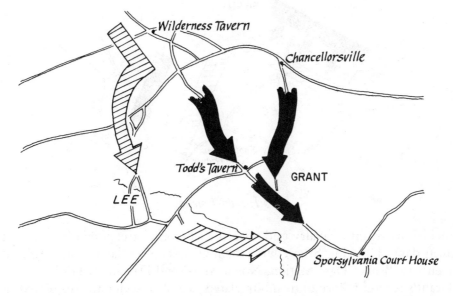

Grant's Turning Attempt

As the huge Union army marched eastward, Lee received reports of the movements and sent troops to block the way. Confederate cavalry slowed the advance by cutting down trees and by harassing the soldiers in column. Lee's men succeeded in beating Grant's army to Spotsylvania Court House and formed a battle line about three miles away. The Federals assaulted.

The general attack failed, though various fights erupted at Todd's Tavern, Corbin's Bridge, Alsop's Farm, and Laurel Hill, creating a somewhat fluid situation. During the next night both sides formed new lines. Lee did his best with the weakened command which fate forced upon him: substitutes now led two of his three corps since Longstreet was still out wounded and Ambrose P. Hill had fallen sick.

The next day, May 9, brought no heavy fighting, but the widespread skirmishes continued. One of Grant's most beloved subordinates, John Sedgwick, tried to instill confidence in his men when he saw his artillery men attempting to duck sharpshooters' bullets. They shouldn't worry, he assured, the sharpshooters were so far away "they couldn't hit an elephant at this distance." "The General!" someone then cried. A bullet had struck just under Sedgwick's left eye and killed him instantly. Grant, when told, seemed stunned. "Twice he asked, 'Is he really dead?' Later he told his staff that to lose Sedgwick was worse than to lose a whole division of troops."[23]

After constant readjustment by both sides, by May 9 Lee had his army firmly intrenched in an irregular position somewhat resembling a horseshoe. Grant issued orders for a federal advance the next day. Meanwhile Sheridan

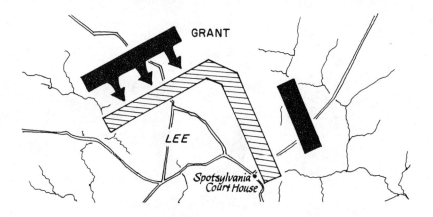

Lee's Intrenchments

launched his gigantic cavalry raid toward Richmond, stretching over the next sixteen days. Drawing Stuart with them at first, Sheridan's men fought at Davenport, Beaver Dam Station, North Anna, and Davenport Ford.

Grant's second failure to turn him elated Lee. Not seeing the disjointed, if bloody, encounters in the Wilderness and Spotsylvania as major battles, Lee perceived only that he had outmaneuvered his powerful and well-led foe. On May 9 Lee reported to the President that he had "succeeded so far in keeping on the front and flank of that army, and impeding its progress, without a general engagement, which" he promised, "I will not bring on unless a favorable opportunity offers, or as a last resort. Every attack made upon us has been repelled and considerable damage done to the enemy. With the blessing of God, I trust we shall be able to prevent Gen. Grant from reaching Richmond." Lee's confidence was only tempered by a fear "that the army of General Grant would be reinforced by forty thousand men from the West."[24]

Grant had thus twice tasted disappointment in his expectation of passing around either of Lee's flanks, as he found the enemy "in very strong force," displaying, he said, "a strong determination to interpose between us and

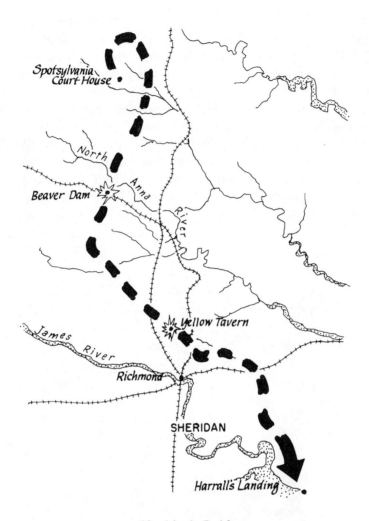

Sheridan's Raid

Richmond to the last." Frustrated before Lee, Grant lost his optimism about Butler, too, when there was "no indication of any portion of Lee's army being detached for the defense of Richmond." It was understandable that Lee was not detaching troops to protect Richmond, for, although on May 9 Butler had thrust his whole army out against the Richmond-Petersburg lines of communications south of the James, Butler suddenly grew confused, flustered, and queasy. Butler ordered everyone back into their original lines the next morning. Snatching defeat from the jaws of victory, he simply could not bring himself to achieve a big goal. He blamed his subordinates and, amidst much carping, he sat and his army did little.[25]

Butler's reports did not clearly describe what was happening, but they distinctly indicated that he did not really understand the situation. Grant learned from Butler that he was "intrenching for fear of accident to the Army of the Potomac." Expecting to complete this in three days, Butler reported that his lines would be so extensive as to require an exceedingly large garrison, leaving only a very weak "movable column." He also asked for 10,000 reinforcements from the reserve, pointing out that they could be spared if Grant had "been in any degree successful"; but, he wrote, "if the Army of the Potomac is unsuccessful, then we want them here for the safety of the country," presumably because they would be out of harm's way behind his strong intrenchments. All Butler accomplished and all he apparently planned to accomplish was to make a "demonstration" against "the railroad between Petersburg and Richmond" and, he added, we "have succeeded in destroying a portion of it so as to break the connection." That this modest achievement had come about only by "pretty severe fighting" did not reassure Grant, nor

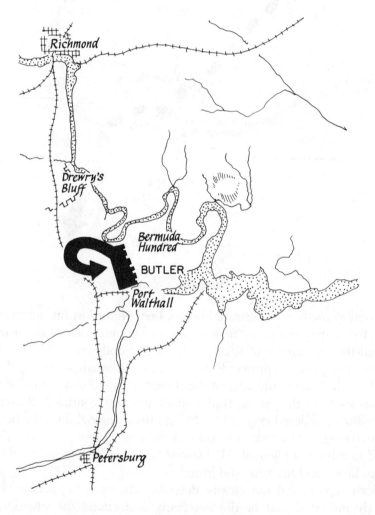

Butler's Intrenchments

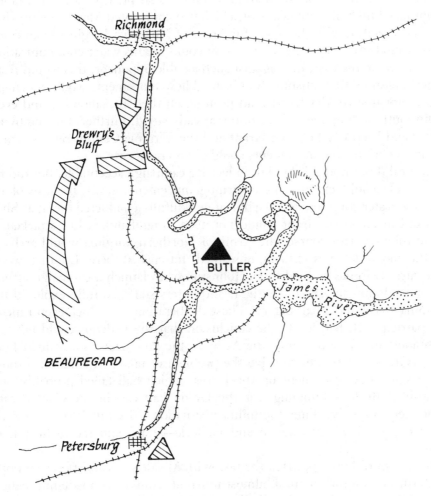

Confederate Reinforcements

did the knowledge that General Beauregard was "in command in person." This bleak outlook later gained reinforcement by Butler's report that he had intrenched in "a position which, with proper supplies," he explained "we can hold out against the whole of Lee's army." Butler guaranteed: "General Grant will not be troubled with any further reinforcements to Lee from Beauregard's forces."[26]

Lincoln's secretary well summed up Butler and similar generals when he remarked: Butler's conduct is "marked by the two faults which seem inseparable from civilian generals (expecting those who have a natural aptitude for military affairs, which B has not): too great rashness & too great timidity in constant alteration. His ignorance of war leads him constantly to require impossibilities from his subordinates and to fear impossibilities from the enemy."[27]

Since his plans to take Richmond by Butler's surprise advance had failed, Grant faced the same predicament which had confronted Meade the previous fall—how to deal with the powerful Army of Northern Virginia in an essentially frontal situation. Of course, Grant could use his water communications to turn Lee on the east, but, against such an able opponent, this would result in nothing more than pushing him back. These movements would inevitably lead Grant first to McClellan's old position on the Chickahominy and eventually south of the James where Butler already stood. Further, turning by the east would keep Lee between Grant and the Virginia Central railway. Such a sequence of turning movements could cut no railways.

Grant did not find this kind of indecisive campaign acceptable, nor did the public. He could execute these turning movements easily because of the available water communications; but, if he skillfully conducted them, as Sherman did in Georgia, Grant would not need to fight unless Lee attacked. If Grant followed this course, the Army of Northern Virginia would arrive at the Richmond defenses virtually unscathed. Intrenched there, Lee then would have surplus forces to send to aid Johnston or to launch a campaign against the upper Potomac. Of course the headquarters staff had fully explored this dilemma a year and a half before. These deliberations, in which even Lincoln had participated, had led to the conclusion that the Federals could not take Richmond and, as a recourse, the Army of the Potomac should aim at Lee's army. Grant had sought to solve the problem of taking Richmond through Butler's surprise movement up the James, which had failed probably only because of Butler's bungling, for the Union had caught the Confederates completely unready. Thus the military situation led Grant also toward the solution prescribed by Lincoln and Halleck—attack and try to hurt Lee's army.

But Grant did not approach the task with Meade's pessimistic, even hopeless, attitude. Grant's natural, almost inherent, confidence made him believe he could succeed where others had not. He had failed previously during the war only in his first advance against Vicksburg and he had brilliantly redeemed that. Yet his persistence in turning Vicksburg to avoid another frontal assault at Chickasaw Bluffs indicates that he realized how desperate an expedient was a frontal attack. But he had no choice, because Lee and his army proved too skillful for Meade's army to hit in flank or rear. Yet he still had hope, suggested by the recent complete success of the unintended frontal attack at Chattanooga. In addition, if Grant had any incentive to imitate Meade's post-Gettysburg passivity, the need to keep Lee from turning him on the west persisted as a strong motive for a close embrace of his opponent, as did the necessity of preventing Lee from detaching reinforcements for Johnston.

Grant had one more significant motive for attacking Lee's army. He needed to control the Virginia Central Railroad which tapped the fertile Shenandoah Valley and the farming and mineral regions of southwestern Virginia. When, as he had planned, Grant ultimately moved south of the James, he would not thereby cut all of Richmond's southern communications even had he taken Petersburg. The railroad to Danville would still be open and the link would be completed, which it was on May 22, between Danville and Greensboro, North Carolina, giving Richmond another contact with the South. This road, like the canal and the Virginia Central, also provided a connection to Lynchburg. Union underestimation of Confederate logistic difficulties included the assumption that, for a successful siege, the North needed to cut the canal and all of Richmond's rail links. This meant that, if the Union wanted to cut the critical Virginia Central, it had to drive Lee straight back toward Richmond.[28]

Grant's May 5 and 6 attacks during the confused fighting in the Wilderness had been incidents of trying to turn Lee's position when in doubt as to whether Lee was delaying or making a stand. Now Grant was going to attack frontally, rather than turn, Lee's army. The situation presented some hopeful aspects, for Grant remembered Bragg's extensive intrenchments at Chattanooga and noted that Lee lacked Bragg's advantage of commanding heights and a long period of occupation. With Lee's army so much smaller than his, Grant remained convinced that recent southern losses had been devastating and his estimates made him "satisfied the enemy are very shaky, and are only kept up to the mark by the greatest exertions on the part of their officers." Apparently Grant, recalling how Bragg's demoralized men had finally fled before Thomas's frontal assault at Chattanooga, hoped that Lee's shaky men might do the same.[29]

Existing tactical conditions, however, hardly favored the attack. One of Meade's staff officers described the scene: The "typical 'great white plain,' with long lines advancing and maneuvering, led on by generals in cocked hats and by bands of music, exist not for us." In the wooded country I have "scarcely seen a Rebel save killed, wounded, or prisoners! I remember how even line officers, who were in the Battle of Chancellorsville, said: 'Why, we never saw any Rebels where we were; only smoke and bushes, and lots of our men tumbling about." Maneuvering the army proved very difficult on narrow roads, "ill known and intricate over bogs and rivers"; so difficult was it that there was no "marshal of France that could do it with his army."

But the "great feature" of the tactical situation was, he said,

the extraordinary use made of earthworks. When we arrive on the ground, it takes of course a considerable time to put troops in position for attack, in a wooded country; then skirmishers must be thrown forward and an examination made for the point of attack, and to see if there be any impassable obstacles, such as streams or swamps. Meantime what does the enemy? Hastily forming a line of battle, they then collect rails from fences, stones, logs and all other materials and pile them along the line; bayonets with a few picks and shovels, in the hands of men who work for their lives, soon suffice to cover this frame with earth and sods; and within one hour, there is a shelter against bullets, high enough to cover a man kneeling, and extending often for a mile or two. When our line advances, there is the line of the enemy, nothing showing but the bayonets, and the battle-flags stuck on the top of the work. It is a rule that, when the rebels halt, the first day gives them a good rifle-pit; the second, a regular infantry parapet with artillery in position; and the third a parapet with an abatis in front and entrenched batteries behind. Sometimes they put this three days' work into the first twenty-four hours.[30]

No wonder Grant stated in a new and pessimistic estimate of his situation, "We can maintain ourselves at least, and in the end beat Lee's army," even though it might be "necessary to fight it out on this line if it takes all summer."[31]

Indeed, the Battle of Yellow Tavern on May 11 seemed to indicate that perhaps the Union might well need all summer or more. Though Stuart, the famed "Cavalier of Dixie," fell mortally wounded, the helter-skelter cavalry encounter gave the Confederates the required time to make more formidable additions to Richmond's strength. They successfully forced back Philip Sheridan's Union cavalry toward the James River with little accomplished.

The struggle with Lee put Grant at another disadvantage. Though initially Meade "had maneuvered the army, . . . gradually, and from the nature of things, Grant had taken control." Commanding an unfamiliar force through an ungainly dual-headquarters system, Grant faced a general who had a good deal more operational experience than he and one who had commanded the same army for amost two years. In addition, Grant would face Lee in a situation analogous to siege warfare, in which the Union general's background as a quartermaster would be of considerably less value than Lee's as an engineer and as an expert in topograhy. Moreover, the Confederate general and his subordinates were more familiar with the terrain than the Union leadership, which had to rely on very inaccurate maps.[32]

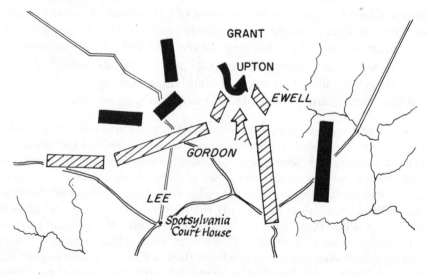

The "Mule Shoe"

On May 10 the general assaults at Spotsylvania began in raging fury. Although some Federals reached the enemy parapets, twice they assaulted and twice they were thrown back. At the salient, called the "Mule Shoe," in the center of the Confederate line, Emory Upton's division breached Ewell's line, but John B. Gordon's troops came up and partially plugged the momentary gap. During the night Upton had to withdraw.

There followed a day's breathing spell, but chilling rains that continued through the next night prevented the troops from garnering much rest. Grant decided to unleash a full assault upon the "mule shoe" salient at dawn the next day. The necessary maneuvers occurred in unbelievably difficult conditions. One Union division, as Bruce Catton said, "oozed along down a slanting field," and its commander at last told his staff officers in some desperation: "For heaven's sake, at least face us in the right direction, so that we shall not march away from the enemy and have to go round the world and come up in their rear." In truth, had they been able to do it fast enough, they would have preferred hitting the Confederates' rear; as it was, they had to assail an impossible front.[33]

It proved one of the most terrible fights of the whole war. In Bruce Catton's words, "Never before on earth had so many muskets been fired so fast on so narrow a front and at such close range. . . . A whole grove of trees behind the Rebel line was killed by shots that flew too high, and the logs of the breastworks were splintered and, a Confederate officer said expressively, 'whipped into basket-stuff.' Bodies of dead and wounded men were hit over and over again until they simply fell apart and became unrecognizable remnants." A man in the Iron Brigade exclaimed: It was "the most terrible twenty-four hours of our service in the war." Catton described it as "a close-range

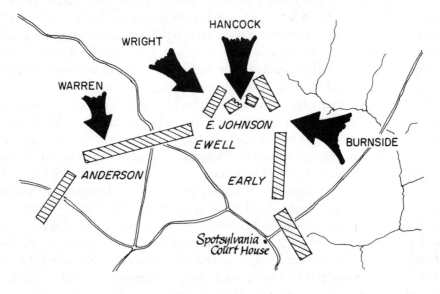

"Bloody Angle"

struggle in the mud that began before dawn and lasted until nearly midnight, the worst of it centering about a little angle in a trench," forever afterward called "the *bloody* angle." Lee's line broke under the furious onslaught, and an entire infantry division fell captive, along with twenty guns. But the Federals actually won "no more than a pen-full of prisoners and a quarter section of splintered groves and pastures, crisscrossed by rifle pits where dead bodies had been trampled out of sight in the mud. Next day the fighting went on as if nothing had happened." The rebels had mended their line again and the two armies stood very nearly where they had when it all began.[34]

Committed and involved at Spotsylvania, Grant ordered from Washington the reserves which he had held back to reinforce either Meade's or Butler's armies. At one point he had felt triumph almost within his grasp because an attack "would have proven entirely successful if it had commenced one hour earlier." A report of an initial success of May 12, when Hancock's attack captured three generals, thirty to forty guns, and over two thousand prisoners, also encouraged him. With high hopes for a breakthrough, Grant ordered: "Push the enemy with all your might. . . . We must not fail." Meade issued instructions "to move on the enemy regardless of consequences," adding the directive, "Don't hesitate to attack with the bayonet."[35]

The ensuing three-day attempt to break through the Confederate defenses had failed, because the intrenchments were too strong and the tactical skill and the counterattacks of the very maneuverable Confederate formations too formidable. The result of these efforts, in Meade's view, awarded to the Union army "the prestige of success, which is everything." The losses, said Meade, had been "frightful; I do not like to estimate them," though the Confederate losses were "fully as great."[36]

In heavy rain, which made the roads almost impassable, Grant spent the next week looking for a weak spot and seeking, unsuccessfully, first to "get by the right flank of the enemy for the next fight" and then attempting, again without good results, a surprise attack against Lee's left flank. Some minor engagements occurred every day, but nothing decisive developed except that the Union army did slightly move to the southeast.[37]

As this was taking place, Butler's campaign reached its ignominious end. On the 15th Butler planned an attack but delayed arranging his defensive lines. At Drewry's Bluff his men strung telegraph wire on stumps, one of the first uses of wire entanglements in Virginia. The next day, May 16, Beauregard attacked Butler's force. The Creole tried to turn Butler's right, seeking to drive him from his base for ultimate destruction, a daring venture indeed since Butler's force outnumbered the Confederates. Some heavy fighting ensued, but Beauregard failed in his ambitious objective. But, with the help of Butler's ineptness, the Confederates achieved a valuable success at the Battle of Drewry's Bluff, or Fort Darling as the engagement is also called. On May 17 the federal army pulled back timidly into a peninsula formed by the rivers and allowed Beauregard to close them in with entrenchments. Although he had missed another opportunity, Butler believed he had narrowly escaped disaster. Later General Barnard inspected Butler's position, pinned between the James River on the north, the Appomattox on the south, and Beauregard's men in front. Barnard characterized the position: "like a bottle with Butler corked up inside of it." This felicitous simile appealed to Grant, who used it in his report.[38]

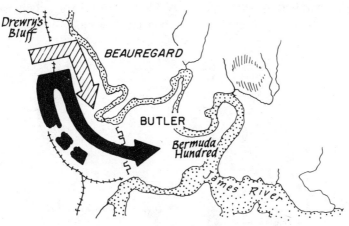

Butler in a Bottle

Meanwhile, in Georgia, Sherman faced Johnston's recently strengthened force. Rather than attacking, Sherman turned, a comparatively easy task

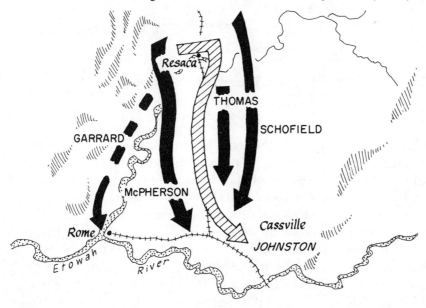

Johnston Turned

because Johnston's front paralleled his railroad communications. This, Johnston explained, "enabled him to press me back by fortifying the moment he halted. He had made an assault upon his superior forces too hazardous." On May 16 Johnston retreated again, falling back to Cassville. Here he found the opportunity for which he had been waiting. He planned to fall upon Schofield's small army of 13,000 men with two of the three corps of his army of 60,000. But mistaken apprehensions by Hood caused the rebels to abandon the attack and the army then retreated to Allatoona Pass.[39]

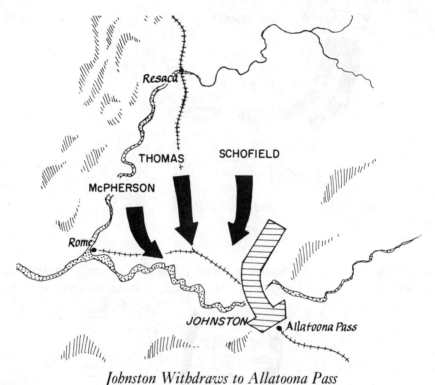

Johnston Withdraws to Allatoona Pass

☆   ☆

While Sherman successfully turned Johnston almost forty miles back from his Resaca position, Grant, by May 18, abandoned the experiment of trying to fight a battle with Lee around Spotsylvania. In fact, the experience of these ten days of intermittent battle caused Grant to halt attacks against Lee's position and seek by additional turning movements to catch him in a mistake and, by probing only, to find an authentic weak spot. Grant had realized, Meade felt, that "Virginia and Lee's army is not Tennessee and Bragg's army," for, in their last effort they had "found the enemy so strongly entrenched that even Grant thought it useless to knock our heads against a brick wall," explained Meade, "and directed a suspension of the attack."[40]

Grant then began on the night of May 20–21 a dual-purpose turning movement, reminiscent of Sherman's first maneuver with McPherson to Snake Creek Gap. But, unlike Sherman early in his campaign, Grant held no apprehensions about the enemy's concentrating against his detached force. Taking advantage of Hancock's high competence and the intrinsic invulnerability of large Civil War infantry units, Grant ordered Hancock's corps "southeast with all his force and," he said, "as much cavalry as can be given to him, to get as far toward Richmond on the line of the Fredericksburg railroad as he can make, fighting the enemy in whatever force he may find him. If the enemy makes a general move to meet this they will be followed by the other three corps of the army, and attacked if possible before time is given to entrench."[41]

Also similar in concept to Lee's Second Bull Run campaign, Grant's objective was to threaten his enemy's communications with a part of his force, just as Jackson had threatened Pope's. If Lee were lured, as had been Pope, into attacking the threatened force, Grant could come upon his rear and assault him where he was unprotected by intrenchments. If the effort failed to pro-

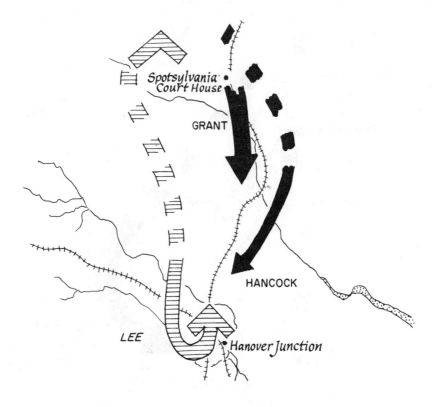

Lee Outmaneuvers Grant's Turning Movement

duce a battle under favorable circumstances, Grant would still at least have maneuvered Lee out of his strongly intrenched Spotsylvania position.

But instead of attacking Hancock, Lee moved his men south and, when Grant's whole army arrived on the North Anna, it found Lee with his troops well intrenched in another V-shaped position. Lee had been almost equally frustrated by the tactics employed by the enemy, whose position at Spotsylvania he perceived as "strongly entrenched, and," he wrote, "we cannot attack it with any prospect of success without great loss of men." He wished to turn Grant, but, he reported, I found "neither the strength of our army nor the condition of our animals will admit, of any extensive movement with a view to draw the enemy from his position." He did not underestimate the determination of his opponent for he realized: "The importance of this campaign to the administration of Mr. Lincoln and to General Grant leaves no doubt that every effort and every sacrifice will be made to secure its success." Though he wanted to "strike him," he said, "whenever the opportunity presents itself," he regarded Hancock's corps as too well covered and did not attack. Having to retreat disappointed him because he "preferred contesting

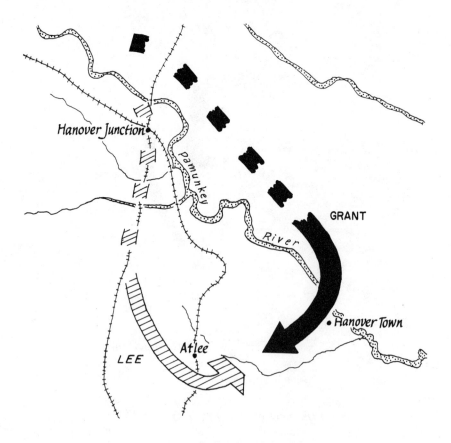

Another Turning Movement Fails

the enemy's approach inch by inch," but his "solicitude for Richmond" and his fear that the enemy might get past him to the capital dictated his withdrawal.[42]

Though Lee's men protected the Virginia Central south of Hanover Junction, Grant, with his army across the railroads north and west of that point, took advantage of the opportunity to "leave a gap in the roads north of Richmond so big that to get a single track they [would] have to import rails from elsewhere." This modest gap was all he accomplished in the Battle of the North Anna, May 23–26, for Grant did not intend again to attack the Confederate army when Lee was ready for him. Pleased with his railway destruction and already having decided to rely on raids to interdict Richmond's communications to the north, Grant promptly moved his force around Lee's eastern flank and by May 29 reached the vicinity of Richmond near the scene of the beginning of the 1862 Seven Days' Battles.[43]

In so quickly abandoning a good position for carrying out additional destruction of the Virginia Central, Grant remained conscious that he had yet to "win" a battle. Neither the Battle of the Wilderness nor the Battle of Spotsylvania precipitated any Confederate retreat, the classic indicator of victory. If Lee truly had lost as heavily as Grant believed, then Grant had indeed won major victories. But an enemy on the verge of collapse from 50 percent casualties was not something the newspapers could report with either color or conviction, nor people readily appreciate. In any case, the public expected more.

As Grant pondered his next move, Sherman on May 22 was prepared, with "wagons loaded and ready for a twenty days expedition," to thrust his whole

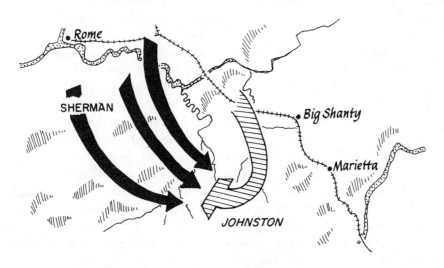

Sherman's Turning Movement Fails

army around Johnston's left flank, aiming at Marietta or even for the Chatta-hoochee. But he found himself unable to reach Johnston's rear when he discovered on May 26 the Confederates across his path at Dallas and New Hope Church. Again a stalemate resulted as he faced the rebels behind "hasty but strong parapets of timber and earth." He, too, intrenched. "If we can induce the enemy to attack us," he wrote, "it is to our advantage." Beyond probes and occasional assaults, Johnston would not oblige him. Sherman called it "a big Indian war," where in wooden country the enterprising rebels used spades and axes so fast that they could build new works as rapidly as they were dislodged from old ones. Always protected by barricades, and so concealed by branches and underbrush, "we cannot see them until we receive a sudden and deadly fire," he explained. So Sherman sidled his army to the left to cover and get closer to the railroad.[44]

Meanwhile, news from Halleck confirming Butler's failure and warning Grant, "Do not rely on him," aggravated Grant's problem of getting south of the James and past Lee's army. Grant hoped that Butler had not failed com-pletely but at last reluctantly concluded: The 33,000-man "force under Gen-eral Butler is not detaining 10,000 men in Richmond and is not even keeping the roads south of the city cut." Thus Grant, while still on the North Anna, ordered all men from Butler's force to join him "except enough to keep a foothold at City Point." Halleck promptly sent to Butler generals Meigs and Barnard of the headquarters staff to decide on "how many troops could be spared and on the means of water transportation." Anticipating that he would soon again be moving around Lee's eastern flank, Grant directed that the troops from Butler's army should move to his prospective new base, most probably West Point, at the head of the York River and at the head of the railroad through White House which had supplied McClellan on the Penin-sula in 1862.[45]

Grant's mention of a base on the Peninsula provoked an immediate reaction from Halleck, because Grant's mention of a base so close to McClellan's of two years before caused considerable alarm. After interdicting the Peninsula and a North Carolina expedition, Grant and Meade seemed headed for a siege of Richmond from the Peninsula. Having achieved initial victories greeted with national thanksgiving, Grant now indicated that he would end up ex-actly where McClellan, the likely 1864 Democratic presidential candidate, had been two years before, a position that Lincoln and Halleck had regarded as so futile and so dangerous to Washington that they had recalled McClellan.

As Grant's message clearly forecast a siege, Halleck promptly reminded him of the objectives which long ago had caused headquarters to reject pre-cisely that. "Demonstrations on that place," Halleck wrote, "exhaust us more than they injure the rebels, for it will require 2 men outside to keep 1 in Richmond. I once thought that this could be more than compensated for by destroying their lines of supply, but experience has proved that they can repair them just about as fast as we can destroy them." Again he reiterated that Lee's "army, not Richmond, is the true objective point of the campaign."

Besides worrying about the unfavorable terrain and the Chickahominy River, Halleck apparently remembered Jackson's Shenandoah Valley campaign and that of Second Bull Run and therefore feared that, if Lee's army remained intact, the Union forces would soon lose what they "may have gained in West Virginia or around Richmond." He not only shared Grant's disappointment in Butler, but, objecting to exterior lines, wished that "everything was away from the south side of the James and with you." He wrote Grant: "It would be much better. I do not like these divided commands, with the enemy intervening. I would rather use them together under your own eye."[46]

With the relatively small forces needed to hold the intrenchments of Richmond, a position on an exterior line would invite a Confederate concentration against Washington or the upper Potomac. To avoid this, federal forces would have to operate from the north. Halleck promptly sent Grant a brief favoring this. After pointing out that a position on the east would leave to Richmond "the James River Canal, and one or more of the railroads south of that river," Halleck argued: "Even if your cavalry should cut these communications, they will soon be reopened." As an alternative, he urged Grant: Besiege the city from the northwest with one flank resting on the James where "you will hold the canal, and can, with your cavalry, control the railroad lines south of the James River." Halleck simply ignored the inconsistency of the cavalry's being able to interdict the railroads in his plan but not in others. He suggested that Grant's line of communications be due north, along the Richmond, Fredricksburg and Potomac Railroad. The siege from the northwest would take place "over favorable ground" and toward the side of the city "most favorable for an attack, as the Tredegar Iron Works, the arsenal, the waterworks, and all the flouring mills lie on the northwest side of the city, and exposed to a bombardment from that direction." Except to say that Grant's flanks would be "pretty safe," the chief of staff did not allude to another obvious advantage—in a northwest position Grant's army would be closer to the Shenandoah Valley than Lee's.[47]

Since, in spite of his arguments, Halleck apparently did not think it likely that Grant would follow his advice, the chief of staff sent him General Barnard of the headquarters staff. An expert on the Chickahominy, Barnard, said Halleck, had "great military ability," and was a man whose "mind is clear and judgment excellent."[48]

A siege also created a problem with public opinion, one which Grant understood, for he was not unaware of the "chivalric significance" of his contest with Lee. Yet by the time he received Halleck's signal, Grant realized that a very ticklish question had been passed from Lincoln to him. Stanton had hailed as "superb victories" Grant's unavailing struggle at Spotsylvania, together with his unavoidable but bloody conflict in the Wilderness. After "great success and complete victory," Grant was perceived as "pursuing" Lee. These titanic struggles, with their horrible casualties, seemed like preludes to the imminent "capture or destruction of the rebel forces."[49]

Although heavy, Grant's casualties in the first three weeks were not large in view of his involvement in two major and prolonged battles. He had lost about one-third of his army, a loss comparable to that of Rosecrans and Bragg at Stones River or Lee at Gettysburg, all incurred in only three days. Nevertheless, the absolute numbers, nearly 40,000 men, had made quite a ghastly impression on public opinion. The victories so far had yielded no dramatic result. If these victories and these casualties were going to be a prelude, not to the destruction or capture of the enemy army but to a siege, they would seem to have been futile and wasteful. Thus, Grant and Lincoln faced the problem of maintaining public morale and will to win, when expensive victories thus far had produced no results and could produce none comparable to Vicksburg or Chattanooga. Meade questioned "whether the people [would] ever realize this."[50]

To make the civilians comprehend, they would have to be told that, on the always politically sensitive Virginia front, the lieutenant general had not won a great victory but had lost thousands of men in an unsuccessful experiment; that even Grant could not attain "victories" against unblundering opponents; that to conceive of war in terms of battles was to misunderstand; and that the North could not win by a dramatic success but only by the tedious process of undermining the enemy's logistics. Even if the public were thus successfully re-educated, the danger still existed that they might conclude their champion had failed and that Lee and the rebels were supreme, and so give up the struggle for the Union.

Rather than making the northerners realize the failure of past operations and that battles were merely incidents of movements against communications, the safer approach was to sustain morale by showing that the victories had been productive, thus justifying the heavy casualties of the Wilderness and Spotsylvania. Though he may have been weakening in his conviction that Confederate losses were as great as his own, Grant took this as a basis for his justification. In part at least, and perhaps entirely, an authentic belief on his part, Grant's thesis used the battles and the Confederate losses to explain the failure of the Confederates to assume the offensive. If Hancock's corps of his own army had already lost half of its original strength, in what condition was Lee's force even if it had not lost quite as many men as Grant's? Thus Grant promptly replied to Halleck, explaining: "Lee's army is really whipped. The prisoners we now take show it, and the action of his army shows it unmistakably. A battle with them outside of their entrenchments cannot be had."[51]

Nevertheless, Grant told Halleck: "Our success over Lee's army is already assured." Simultaneously, Charles A. Dana, again at Grant's headquarters, relayed the same interpretation to Stanton: "One of the most important results of the campaign thus far is the entire change which has taken place in the feelings of the armies. Rebels have lost all confidence and are morally defeated. This army has learned to believe that it is sure of victory. Even our officers," Dana went on to explain, "have ceased to regard Lee as an invincible military genius. On the part of the rebels this change is evidenced, not only by their not attacking, even when circumstances seem to invite it, but by the unanimous statements of prisoners taken from them."[52]

This was not new with Grant for a similar idea had antedated the campaign. Sherman, too, saw that "Grant's battles in Virginia" were "fearful but necessary. Immense slaughter is necessary to prove that our Northern armies can and will fight," he added. To "impress the Virginians with the knowledge that the Yankees can and will fight them fair and square" would be "immense moral power," he continued, and this "moral result must precede all mere advantages of strategic movements, and this is what Grant is doing." These fearful battles were not necessary in the West, because, Sherman wrote, "Out here the enemy knows we . . . fight like the devil; therefore he maneuvers for advantage of ground."[53]

Assistant Secretary Dana continued to elaborate the thesis and, stressing the difficulties and realities of the military situation, said: "General Grant means to fight here if there is a fair chance, but he will not run his head against heavy works." Later, the former journalist explained to Stanton: Grant had hoped that, before reaching Richmond, he would have a chance to defeat Lee's army by "fair fighting," but "the expectation has been foiled by Lee's success in avoiding battle upon equal terms" and always taking refuge behind his breastworks.[54]

Thus Grant shrewdly turned against Lee the Confederate general's prestige in the North and Lee's successful offensive maneuvers against earlier commanders of the Army of the Potomac. Lee's failure to take the offensive was evidence of the beneficial effects of the initial battles of the campaign. These battles had reduced the formidable Confederate army, which had twice invaded the North, merely to cringing behind breastworks, unwilling to fight fairly, and unable to prevent the siege of its capital. After the war, Grant summed this up well in his attrition thesis: "Lee had to fight as much as I did, . . . every blow I struck weakened him, and when at last he was forced into Richmond it was a far different army from that which menaced Washington and invaded Maryland and Pennsylvania. It was no longer an invading army. The Wilderness campaign was necessary to the destruction of the Southern Confederacy."[55]

Toward the end of the operations around Spotsylvania, Grant had begun to look for other means of interdicting the railroads, especially as his western

Raiders Break Railway

raiders had broken the Virginia and Tennessee west of Lynchburg. In view of this success, Grant wondered whether the West Virginia force of Sigel could not "go up the Shenandoah Valley to Staunton[.] The enemy," Grant said, "is evidently drawing supplies largely from that source, and if Sigel can destroy the road there, it will be of vast importance."[56]

After the limited railroad destruction on the North Anna and after the pattern of the campaign had more clearly emerged, Grant began to push raids against Richmond's communications. While he moved from the North Anna, he kept one cavalry division busy working on the railroads between Richmond and Hanover Court House. By this time, however, a Union defeat had given Grant an opportunity to launch against the Richmond communications something more substantial than a cavalry raid.[57]

Major General Franz Sigel had indeed advanced up the Valley toward Staunton. Like Butler, the equally energetic and quite as incompetent Sigel had advanced at the same time as had Grant, overcoming considerable obstacles, including one twenty-five-mile stretch of road which was "one continued canal of mud 3 and 4 feet deep, with pointed rocks at the bottom." To compound difficulties, most of Sigel's staff officers, like himself, were German and could not intelligibly convey orders in English. Not only that, his men had little respect for him "and his crowd of foreign adventurers," owing particularly to an early May fiasco of a sham battle Sigel prescribed for training purposes. With elaborate, colored diagrams showing all the elements of his command, Sigel still could not control his units nor quite remember where they were; he forgot to call back one unit which continued skirmishing far into the night. "It was the funniest farce ever witnessed anywhere," lamented one of his subordinates. And now Sigel approached battle against troops under the capable Confederate Major General John C. Breckinridge while his own forces were spread over many miles along the Valley. "The verdict is clear," concludes Jack Davis, an historian of the engagement, "Franz Sigel was not just an incompetent; he was a fool."[58]

Sigel's 6,500 men in two divisions, one infantry and one cavalry, clashed with Breckinridge's 5,150, two brigades of infantry and one of cavalry augmented by a wide array of other units including Mosby's rangers and the cadet battalion from the Virginia Military Institute. The Institute contingent numbered 264 with their artillery section of two pieces, a fifer and two drummers, and seven field and staff officers. "I would be glad to have your assistance at once," Breckinridge had dramatically written them; "the air was rent with wild cheering at the thought that our hour was come at last," voiced one cadet.[59]

Justly called the "West Point of the Confederacy," V.M.I. had provided graduates who fought the enemy on every front, infused much of the little drill and discipline within the southern armies, and gave the Confederacy seventeen of her sons who became general officers. The cadets had brushed close to combat several times previously; Stonewall Jackson had called them out often, but still they had seen no action until now. The veterans derided the youngsters and sang nursery rhymes to taunt them. Many soldiers opined that the boys would not fight, they would break and run under fire. The night before they went into action their popular professor of tactics was asked to pray. He spoke "of home, of father, of mother, of country, of victory and defeat, of life, of death, of eternity." Breckinridge promised that he would not use them unless absolutely necessary, but the boys surmised: "If they are going to pray over us, maybe they think we are going to get into a fight after all."[60]

The cadets moved forward "in beautiful order as tho' going to dress parade," thought one of Breckinridge's staffers; and one little girl in New Market mistook their natty uniforms and unique flag and cried out, "The French have come! the French have come!" The battle's first contact came accidentally when a federal lieutenant marched up to a Confederate unit, thinking it merely dust-covered friends, and the fight was on. Despite Sigel's and his subordinates' blundering, it proved a hotly contested battle and Breckinridge found he needed every unit he could get, including the cadets. From early in the morning, May 15, Breckinridge continually attacked, and by eleven o'clock forced Sigel back about 800 yards. A gap appeared in the Confederate line. "Put the boys in . . . ," said Breckinridge gravely, "and may God forgive me for the order."[61]

The going was tough for everyone, but the cadets' advance was "a sublime sight," thought a Confederate officer. They were, he said, "as brave and chivalrous a command as ever fired a gun," and another man declared: It "surpassed anything that I witnessed during the war." As the boys advanced, a combination of circumstances forced a federal battery to their front to abandon an artillery piece and the cadets took it, a magnificent prize, the finest trophy for which they could have reasonably wished. A legend grew, commencing almost at once, that the boys had taken a whole battery in hand-to-hand combat and they alone had "won" the battle. The truth was glorious enough. No one unit won the battle, but Davis convincingly argues that "it could not have been won without any one of them." Breckinridge, too, gained fame from the affair. Destined to become Confederate secretary of war early in 1865, because of the victory he was able to join Lee with the bulk of his forces at a crucial time during the campaign north of Richmond. The truly giddy optimists even mused, "Had a new Stonewall been born" in the form of the hard-drinking Kentuckian?[62]

No more than 4,100 of the Confederates had actually participated in the battle, and of that number at least 531 became casualties, just above 13 percent. But Sigel paid dearly. Under continued attack, by 4 P.M. he ordered a general retreat and then precipitately fell back in disorder to Strasburg, abandoning much equipment. Four days later he was relieved. He had lost 96 dead on the field, 255 missing, in all 841 federal casualties counting the 520 wounded that returned with him. The Confederates captured a total of five guns, with ammunition chests, and some 170 horses plus a treasure trove of additional accoutrements. "Some of the men have made their fortunes on

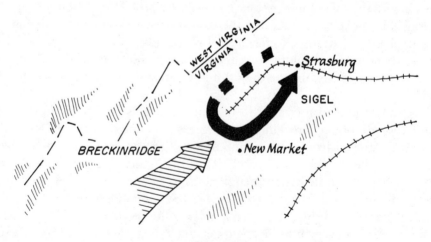

Sigel's Defeat

the field nearby," one Confederate wrote home telling about the gleaning. Five cadets had been killed outright, five more died later, and another forty-seven were wounded, their casualties amounting to just under 23 percent of those engaged. "Well done, Virginians! Well done, men!" Breckinridge told the boys. He was proud of them, more than he could say.[63]

One of Sigel's subordinates quipped: "We are doing a good business in this department. Averell is tearing up the Virginia and Tennessee Railroad while Sigel is tearing down the Valley turnpike," a jibe that became popular throughout the Union. The proud "I fights mit Sigel" turned into a new and sour song, "I fights no more mit Sigel," sung by the disillusioned retreating soldiers. When details of the battle and retreat began to circulate more widely, a new quip was coined, "Who runs mit Sigel?" Grant was furious when Halleck wrote him about Sigel: "Instead of advancing on Staunton he is already in full retreat on Strasburg. If you expect anything from him you will be mistaken. He will do nothing but run. He never did anything else."[64]

Lacking Butler's imposing political base, Sigel was immediately superseded by the experienced but not very talented regular officer, Major General David Hunter, who was at hand and without a command. Taking advantage of the withdrawal from the Valley and the shifting to Richmond of the bulk of the Confederate forces which had beaten Sigel, Hunter moved promptly to carry out Grant's instructions. The substitution of Hunter for Sigel gave Grant real hope that the West Virginia forces might accomplish something in the Valley. Hunter, with his four divisions, was instructed to advance to Charlottesville and Lynchburg, "living on the country," and that the railroads and canal should be destroyed "beyond possibility of repair for weeks." Since the other raid from West Virginia had succeeded in reaching the East Tennessee and Virginia Railroad and the raiders were by then moving east, it looked as if Grant's original plan might work. All forces might meet to destroy the railroads in the Valley and the western part of the state.[65]

Because of the uncertainty of what Hunter could accomplish and the need for doing a thorough and long-lasting job on the railroads, Grant sent two-thirds of the cavalry of the Army of the Potomac, commanded by Sheridan himself, "to effectually break up the railroad connection between Richmond and the Shenandoah Valley and Lynchburg." Grant directed that over fifty miles of track be wrecked and insisted that "every rail of the road destroyed should be so bent or twisted as to make it impossible to repair the road without supplying new rails." In addition to functioning as a "diversion" in support of Hunter's raid, Sheridan was instructed to unite with Hunter and both forces return to the Army of the Potomac. As this cavalry raid was beginning and "to aid the expedition under General Hunter, it is necessary," said Grant, "that we should detain all the army now with Lee until the former gets well on his way to Lynchburg. To do this effectually it will be better to keep the enemy out of the entrenchments of Richmond than to have them go back there." Largely for this reason Grant briefly deferred the long-projected movement to cut Richmond's communications to the south by besieging the city from the south side of the James River.[66]

Since Confederate cavalry turned back Sheridan's force June 11–12, 1864, at Trevilian Station, the success of Grant's plans depended upon Hunter's raid. Though Grant did not make clear whether Hunter should move toward

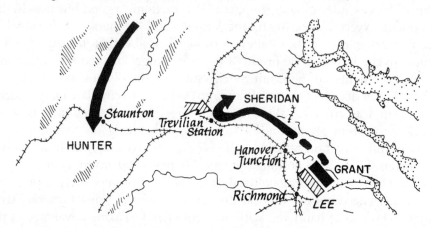

Another Attempt to Secure the Valley

Lynchburg or Charlottesville, his assigned objective was clear, "the destruction of the Virginia Central Railroad," with the additional injunction to "lose no opportunity to destroy the canal." Moving toward Lynchburg, Hunter captured Staunton after meeting the enemy, "killing William E. Jones, their commanding general, and totally routing them after a battle of ten hours duration." Having captured 1,500 prisoners and united his force with the other raiders, Hunter promised: We will "move south immediately to perform our work."[67]

As Grant prepared for his next move, Sherman faced Johnston's army. In less than three weeks Sherman had turned the enemy back nearly sixty miles. He found the "weather fine and the grass luxuriant," which, together with the rapid repair of the railroad, meant his supply situation was excellent. Without the impulsion of public opinion directed at Grant, Sherman could pause to "replenish and fit up" and "get ready for the Chattahoochee," the river just north of Atlanta, which he planned to reach by a most ambitious turning movement. He wrote: My fear was not of Johnston but of Forrest's cavalry "swinging over against my communications." Appealing for troops to guard his communications, he remarked: "Back us up with troops in the rear, so that I will not be forced to drop detachments as road guard, and I have an army that will make a deep hole in the Confederacy." He had already made something of a hole, for he had destroyed ironworks and flour mills and the fall of Rome, Georgia, had yielded "a good deal of provisions and plunder, fine ironworks and machinery." Lest he seem too leisurely, for the second time he reminded Halleck to notify Grant that he was conscious of one of his main tasks, to "hold all of Johnston's army too busy to send anything against him."[68]

Grant deferred his long-planned move south of the James until the raids under Hunter and Sheridan had well started. He made one more effort to attack Lee and blundered on June 1–3 at Cold Harbor where, thinking he had discovered a weak spot, he found a powerful and well-intrenched enemy. Maneuvers in which Grant hoped to catch Lee at a disadvantage preceded the battle. Discovering Butler bottled up and heeding Halleck's injunction, "Do not rely on him," Grant ordered a major part of Butler's force to join him north of the river, the number having been determined during the Meigs-Barnard visit. The advance of this contingent, commanded by Grant's old associate, Baldy Smith, coordinated with Grant's movement which turned Lee out of the North Anna position. Landing at White House as Grant completed his move from the North Anna, Smith's corps would be separated from the Army of the Potomac as it marched to join the left of that force. Grant saw that Lee might seek either to cut Smith off "or, by a dash, to crush him and get back before we are aware of it," he said. As in the case of Hancock's isolated corps in the move from Spotsylvania, Grant perceived an opportunity in Smith's exposed position. Thus Grant said, "Nothing would suit me better than such a move," which would place Confederates between Smith and his army where, with the defensive power of Smith's infantry corps and the ability of the cavalry to detect the move, he could have a battle in the open.[69]

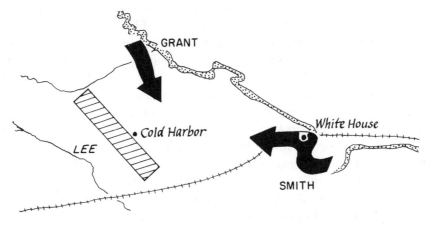

Lee Remains Intrenched

Disappointed in the refusal of the Confederates to move against Smith, Grant ended up resisting a counterattack by Lee's army, both sides being in long-intrenched lines ending near Cold Harbor in the southeast. With Hunter's raid in progress and Sheridan's in contemplation, Grant pondered what to do with the Army of the Potomac before Hunter's move had advanced enough for Meade and his men to move south of the James. He decided on another series of disastrous frontal assaults. At Cold Harbor, as the order for attack reached the federal troopers, Colonel Horace Porter noted with dismay that the men simply sat "calmly writing their names and home addresses on slips of paper and pinning them on the back of their coats, so that their dead bodies might be recognized and their fates made known to their families at home." Not so much without hope as resigned to desperate fighting, the men, as they had at Mine Run, thus devised the first American "dog tags," later worn by all U.S. soldiers.[70]

The weather had been hot and it seemed hotter amidst the barren landscape of Cold Harbor. One federal officer expressed the thoughts of many participants when he wondered how the place had received its name in the first place: no harbor lay within miles and nothing was cold about it save the attitudes of the armies toward each other. Rather like a bake oven than a cold harbor, the Yankee officer thought; and as he surveyed the roads ankle deep in powdery dust that hung in low, choking clouds when columns marched by, he concluded that no rational man ever would want to come there. A veteran years later remarked that he had never heard any old soldier say he wished to revisit Cold Harbor.[71]

Like any great battle, though, it produced its share of good stories. One of the best concerned Corporal Mike Scannell of the Nineteenth Massachusetts. After one of many color-bearers had fallen victim to Confederate fire, Scannell's regimental commander asked him to take the flag. No thanks, "too many corporals have already been killed carrying colors," the soldier replied. "I'll make you a sergeant on the spot," promised his somewhat disconcerted colonel. "That's business," answered the corporal. "I'll carry the colors." One man later related that running forward he suddenly saw every one of his fellow soldiers drop to the ground, and he thought someone had passed an order for all of them to lie down, so he did likewise. In truth all of the others had been shot and were dead. A similar experience befell another Yankee, who all at once noticed that he was alone and concluded that he had fallen behind. He rushed forward to catch up and discovered himself in another company. Every other soldier in his own line had been shot down.[72]

The assaulting troops never caught sight of their enemy. They saw only a line of flashing fire and surging smoke, and all they heard was unbroken musketry fire that seemed "like one continual crash of thunder." They charged valiantly and without hope across an open field, later to be told by a Confederate officer during a burial truce: "It seemed almost like murder to fire upon you." Bruce Catton correctly termed Cold Harbor "a wild chain of doomed charges, most of which were smashed in five or ten minutes and none of which lasted more than half an hour."[73]

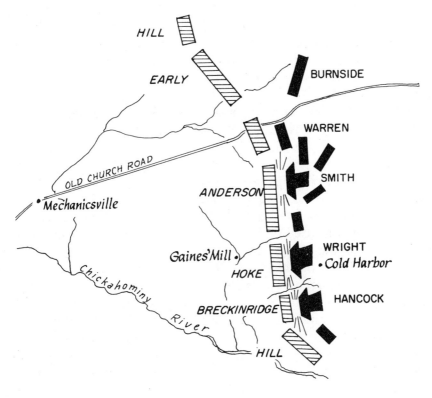

Frontal Assault

Many factors influenced Grant's ill-fated decision to launch the attack against Confederate intrenchments at Cold Harbor, where the first two days of fighting cost the Union 5,000 men and on the third day 7,000 men fell in a single hour. Since Spotsylvania, though Grant had been careful not to "run his head against heavy works," he felt Lee's line stretched out "as thin and weak as possible." He discussed "the matter thoroughly" and received support from his most influential staff officer, a young engineer and former West Point faculty member, Lieutenant Colonel Cyrus B. Comstock. Unlike Rawlins, whose influence was in eclipse, Comstock advocated battle, and had the reputation of constantly preaching a policy toward Lee's army of "smash 'em up." Remembering that "he had succeeded in breaking the enemy's line at Chattanooga, Spotsylvania and other places under circumstances which were not more favorable," Grant decided to attack, the promise of and need for a victory being so great.[74]

A successful gamble on an attack upon Lee could have brought the large rewards "of driving him into Richmond, capturing the city perhaps without a siege and putting the Confederate government into flight." Instead of waiting for the slow process of Sherman's application of the strategy of exhaustion, by attacking at Cold Harbor Grant thus had a chance of hastening the war's conclusion. He may have absorbed some of the apprehensions of his friend and former banker, Sherman, who feared Union financial collapse unless victory came soon. Though Grant discounted them, he was not unaffected by "constant rumors that, if the war continued much longer, European powers would recognize the Confederacy, and perhaps give it material assistance."

Even if unsuccessful, an attack would respond to the need "to keep the enemy so engaged . . . that he [could] detach no troops to interfere with the operations of Hunter." Also, having just engaged in his correspondence to Halleck about campaigning on McClellan's old ground, Grant was acutely conscious of the imperative political need for a victory.

A long siege that did not result from a successful battle would provoke criticism as an example of the no-win, West Point, dig-in strategy. More important, all eyes focused on the lieutenant general, and advances not preceded by victories did not capture the public's imagination nor raise its morale. Neither the logistics of successful marches nor effective screening and deception for these marches made good newspaper copy. Because Richmond enjoyed so many alternate lines for its supply, a long siege appeared very likely in any case. If this siege could seem to result from a successful battle, the public could better sustain the frustrations of that protracted operation, for "many of the people in the north were becoming discouraged at the prolongation of the contest. If the army were transferred south of the James without fighting a battle on the north side, people would be impatient at the prospect of an apparently indefinite continuation of operations."[75]

Civil War operations had shown that it was often possible to push back unintrenched defending troops, and this might well have occurred at Cold Harbor had Grant not delayed the attack so long that the Confederates had ample time to intrench. Though Grant assumed that he could avoid heavy losses by promptly stopping the attack as he had once done at Spotsylvania, the front was so broad and the Confederate defenses so strong that the 7,000 casualties were sustained before he could halt the attack. On this day, June 3, the Confederates lost about 1,500 men. It is likely that, with better reconnaissance and more thorough staff work, the Federals would not have made the attack at all. This kind of staff performance, which also resulted in Baldy Smith's being twice directed to the wrong destination, had existed since the crossing of the Rapidan. With two staffs operating, Grant's and Meade's, each tended to rely on the other and, as a consequence, proper reconnaissance and adequately detailed elaboration of directives often were not carried out at all.

Grant's campaign against Lee had started out to employ Butler's surprise advance to enable him to capture Richmond. Butler's failure confronted Grant with the choice of using successive turning movements to force Lee back to Richmond or to change his plan and try for a major victory over Lee. This victory, for which the northern public yearned, eluded him at Spotsylvania and forced him again to change his plan and resort to turning Lee back until Grant blundered into a bloody failure when he attacked at Cold Harbor. Preparing for the inevitable siege, Grant waited as raiders sought to break some of Richmond's rail communications.

Butler's failure and Grant's heavy casualties and lack of success in his subsequent attacks on Lee deprived the Union public of any tangible evidence of success. These failures, accompanied by heavy casualties, depressed popular morale, dampened their enthusiasm for battles, and damaged Grant's reputation in spite of his efforts to represent his costly battles as the cause of Lee's purely defensive stance.

But in its essentials Grant's plan was working, for, in spite of no movement against Mobile, Sherman was making steady, if undramatic, progress toward Atlanta, the rail and supply center which was his first objective. Sherman's advance, however, was difficult for, like Lee, Johnston dug in elaborately and his men were rarely seen outside of their long lines of intrenchments north of Marietta. During seemingly endless skirmishing, picket-line sniping, and general volleying, for a time the Army of the Cumberland expended 200,000 rounds of small-arms ammunition daily. Some of the more ardent subordinate generals thought that the federal troops were losing their fighting spirit, being intimidated by the enemy intrenchments. Schofield saw it otherwise: "The American soldier fights," he asserted, "very much as he has been accustomed to work his farm or run his sawmill; he wants to see a fair prospect that it is going to pay." Momentarily for the Union cause, with the two main advances appearing to have become sluggish, queasy apprehensions grew that perhaps indeed it was not going to pay.[76]

1. Catton, *Never Call Retreat*, 315.

2. Grant, *Memoirs*, 534, 582.

3. Long, *Civil War, Day by Day*, 492.

4. Foote, *Civil War*, II, 218; Miers, *Lee*, 171.

5. Grant to Burnside, May 2, 1864, *O.R.*, XXXVI, pt. 2, 337; Grant to Halleck, May 4, 1864, *ibid.*, 370; Meade to Grant, May 5, 1864 (two communications), *ibid.*, 403, 404; Hunt to Abbot, May 4, 1864, *ibid.*, 373; Rowley to Meade, May 5, 1864, *ibid.*, 405; Grant to Meade, May 5, 1864, *ibid.*, 403.

6. Bruce Catton, *A Stillness at Appomattox* (Garden City, 1953), 83.

7. *Ibid.*, 83.

8. Foote, *The Civil War*, III, 156.

9. Meade, Circular, May 5, 1864, *O.R.*, XXXVI, pt. 2, 405; Butler to Grant, May 5, 6, 1864, *ibid.*, 430, 471; Porter, *Campaigning with*

Grant, 46, 78; Catton, *A Stillness at Appomattox*, 67.

10. Meade to Hancock, May 6, 1864, *O.R.*, XXXVI, pt. 2, 445; Grant to Halleck, May 7, 8, 1864, *ibid.*, 526, 480.

11. Catton, *A Stillness at Appomattox*, 402n27.

12. *Ibid.*, 406n1.

13. Grant to Halleck, May 6, 8, 9, 1864, *O.R.*, XXXVI, pt. 2, 437, 526, 561; Grant to Meade, May 9, 1864, *ibid.*, 562; Dana to Stanton, May 9, 1864, *ibid.*, pt. 1, 65; Stanton to Butler, May 9, 1864, *ibid.*, pt. 2, 587; Halleck to Augur, May 9, 1864, *ibid.*, 586; Halleck to Butler, May 12, 1864, *ibid.*, 688; Marsena R. Patrick Journal, Library of Congress, entries of May 10 and 11, 1864.

14. Catton, *A Stillness at Appomattox*, 45.

15. Richard Wheeler, ed. *We Knew William Tecumseh Sherman* (New York, 1977), 1–2, 4,

6–8, 10–12, 21, 44–45, 69; Foote, *The Civil War*, II, 62.

16. Henry, *Story of the Confederacy*, 262.

17. Catton, *Never Call Retreat*, 321.

18. Sherman to Grant, May 4, 1864, *O.R.*, XXXVIII, pt. 4, 25; Sherman to Halleck, May 5, 9, 1864, *ibid.*, 34, 88; Sherman to Webster, May 9, 1864, *ibid.*, 89; Sherman to Schofield, May 7, 8, 1864, *ibid.*, 65, 84.

19. Sherman to Schofield, June 30, 1864, *O.R.*, XXXVIII, pt. 4, 644; Sherman, *Memoirs*, II, 34.

20. Sherman to Halleck, May 10, 1864, *O.R.*, XXXVIII, pt. 4, 111.

21. West to S. D. Lee, May 1, 1864, *O.R.*, XXXVIII, pt. 4, 655; Bragg to Polk, May 23, 1864, *ibid.*, 737; W. T. Sherman to J. Sherman, June 9, 1864, *Sherman Letters*, 235–36.

22. Catton, *A Stillness at Appomattox*, 95.

23. *Ibid.*, 109.

24. Lee to Davis, May 9, 1964, *Lee's Dispatches*, eds. Douglas Southall Freeman and Grady McWhiney (New York, 1957), 176.

25. Grant to Halleck, May 10, 11, 1864, *O.R.*, XXXVI, pt. 2, 595, 627–28.

26. Butler to Stanton, May 7 (two communications), 1864, *O.R.*, XXXVI, pt. 2, 517; Porter, *Campaigning with Grant*, 91; Stanton to Grant, May 10, 1864, *O.R.*, XXXVI, pt. 2, 595; Butler to Stanton, May 9, 1864, *ibid.*, 10–11. See, however: Meade, General Orders, May 10, 1864, *ibid.*, 598.

27. *Lincoln and the Civil War*, 195.

28. Barnard to Kelton, Nov. 28, 1862, *O.R.*, XXI, 807–8; Gibbon to unknown recipient, Nov. 30, 1862, *ibid.*, 813. For use of this circuitous route, see: Lee to Davis, May 14, 1864, *Lee's Dispatches*, 178.

29. Grant to Halleck, May 11, 1864, *O.R.*, XXXVI, pt. 2, 627–28.

30. *Meade's Headquarters*, 99–101, 141–42.

31. Grant to Halleck, May 10, 11, 1864, *O.R.*, XXXVI, pt. 2, 595, 627–28.

32. Meade to Mrs. Meade, May 19, 1864, *Life and Letters*, II, 197.

33. Catton, *A Stillness at Appomattox*, 121.

34. Catton, *Never Call Retreat*, 360–61; Catton, *A Stillness at Appomattox*, 125–28.

35. Grant to Halleck, May 12, 1864, *O.R.*, XXXVI, pt. 2, 652; W. S. Hancock to A. A. Humphreys, May 12, 1864, *ibid.*, 657; Hancock to S. Williams, May 12, 1864, *ibid.*, 657; Hancock to Meade, May 12, 1864, *ibid.*, 657; Grant

to Burnside, May 12, 1864, *ibid.*, 671; G. K. Warren to Cutler, May 12, 1864, *ibid.*, 671; Humphreys to Warren, May 12, 1864, *ibid.*, 663.

36. Meade to Mrs. Meade, May 13, 1864, *Life and Letters*, II, 195.

37. Warren to Humphreys, May 13, 1864, Grant's endorsement, *O.R.*, XXXVI, pt. 2, 715.

38. Howard P. Nash, Jr., *Stormy Petrel: The Life and Times of General Benjamin F. Butler, 1818–1893* (Rutherford, Madison, Teaneck, N.J., 1969), 197.

39. Johnston to Davis, May 21, 1864, *O.R.*, XXXVIII, pt. 4, 736.

40. Grant to Burnside, May 18, 1864, *O.R.*, XXXVI, pt. 2, 880; Dana to Stanton, May 18, 1864, *ibid.*, pt. 1, 73; Meade to Mrs. Meade, June 5, May 19, 1864, *Life and Letters*, II, 201, 197.

41. Grant to Meade, May 18, 1864, *O.R.*, XXXVI, pt. 2, 864–65.

42. Lee to Davis, May 18, 1864, *Lee's Dispatches*, 183–85; Lee to Davis, May 22, 1864, *Wartime Papers*, 746.

43. Grant to Halleck, May 26, 1864, *O.R.*, XXXVI, pt. 3, 207; Grant to Halleck, May 20, 25, 1864, *ibid.*, XXXVI, pt. 3, 3–4, XXXVII, pt. 1, 536; Dana to Stanton, May 30, 1864, *ibid.*, XXXVI, pt. 1, 82.

44. Sherman to Halleck, May 20, 21, 28, 29, 1864, *O.R.*, XXXVIII, pt. 4, 260, 274, 331, 343; Catton, *Never Call Retreat*, 325.

45. Halleck to Grant, May 17, 1864, *O.R.*, XXXVI, pt. 2, 841; Grant to Halleck, May 21, 22, 1864, *ibid.*, XXXVI, pt. 3, 43, 77.

46. Halleck to Grant, May 23, 24, 1864, *O.R.*, XXXVI, pt. 3, 114, 145. See also: Comstock Diary, entry of July 15, 1864.

47. Halleck to Grant, May 23, 27, 1864, *O.R.*, XXXVI, pt. 3, 114, 245–46.

48. Halleck to Grant, May 31, 1864, *O.R.*, XXXVI, pt. 3, 375–76.

49. Grant to Halleck, May 16, 1864, *O.R.*, XXXVI, pt. 2, 809–10; Halleck to Grant, May 16, 1864, *ibid.*, 811; Stanton to Butler, May 9, 1864 (two communications,), *ibid.*, 587; Stanton to Parker, May 13, 1864, *ibid.*, 694.

50. Meade to Mrs. Meade, June 5, 1864, *Life and Letters*, II, 201.

51. Grant to Halleck, May 26, 1864, *O.R.*, XXXVI, pt. 3, 206–7.

52. Dana to Stanton, May 26, 1864, *O.R.*, XXXVI, pt. 1, 79, 82, 89.

53. Sherman to Stanton, May 23, 1864, *O.R.*, XXXVIII, pt. 4, 294; Sherman to Mrs. Sherman, May 20, 1864, *Home Letters*, 291. Sherman's letters were written before those of Grant and could hardly have been inspired by Grant in any case. Clearly this concept antedated the campaign, though it hardly was a major consideration in the initial planning. The idea had its roots in the special image of the Army of the Potomac. Derived probably from its year under McClellan, the reputation the Army of the Potomac had acquired in Washington was that of a slow, defensive-minded army which never attacked. This image persisted in spite of its offensive battles at Antietam, Fredricksburg, and Chancellorsville. The outcome of these battles reinforced its reputation for failure and may have caused the impression that it was somehow psychologically defeated by Lee. Though the leaders of the army did not, of course, share this view, it undoubtedly influenced headquarters' and Grant's action.

54. Dana to Stanton, May 30, June 4, 1864, *O.R.*, XXXVI, pt. 1, 82, 89.

55. New York *Herald*, July 24, 1878, 4. See also: Grant, *Memoirs*, 452–54.

56. Grant to Halleck, May 17, 1864, *O.R.*, XXXVII, pt. 1, 475.

57. Humphreys to Burnside, June 2, 1864, *O.R.*, XXXVI, pt. 3, 503.

58. Sigel to Grant, Apr. 12, 1864, *O.R.*, XXXIII, 844; William C. Davis, *The Battle of New Market* (Garden City, 1975), 13, 42, 112, 131.

59. Davis, *New Market*, 47, 50.

60. *Ibid.*, 47, 78–79, 93.

61. *Ibid.*, 122.

62. *Ibid.*, 137, 140, 144, 181, 223–24n14.

63. *Ibid.*, 146–47, 160.

64. *Ibid.*, 166–68; Halleck to Grant, May 17, 1864, *O.R.*, XXXVI, pt. 2, 840.

65. Grant to Halleck, May 25, 1864, *O.R.*, XXXVII, pt. 1, 536; Halleck to Grant, May 21, June 4, 1864, *ibid.*, XXXVII, pt. 1, 507, XXXVI, pt. 3, 569.

66. Grant to Meade, June 3, 1864, *ibid.*, 526; Meade to Grant, June 3, 1864, Grant's endorsement, *ibid.*, pt. 3, 527; Dana to Staunton, June 4, 5, 1864, *ibid.*, pt. 1, 89, 90; Grant to Meade, June 19, 1864, *ibid.*, pt. 3, 779.

67. Grant to Hunter, June 6, 1864, *O.R.*, XXXVII, pt. 1, 598; Hunter to Adjutant-General, June 8, 1864, *ibid.*, 606; Butler to Grant, June 7, 1864, *ibid.*, XXXVI, pt. 3, 691; Grant to Halleck, June 11, 1864, *ibid.*, XXXVII, pt. 1, 624.

68. Sherman to Webster, May 19, 1864, *O.R.*, XXXVIII, pt. 4, 248; Sherman to Halleck, May 19, 1864, *ibid.*, 248; Sherman to governors of Indiana, Illinois, Iowa, and Wisconsin, May 23, 1864, *ibid.*, 295; Sherman to Halleck, May 5, 20, 1864, *ibid.*, 34, 260.

69. Halleck to Grant, May 17, 1864, *O.R.*, XXXVI, pt. 2, 841; Grant to Halleck, May 23, 1864, *ibid.*, pt. 3, 77; Grant to Meade, May 30, 1864, *ibid.*, pt. 3, 323; Grant to Smith, May 30, 1864, *ibid.*, 371.

70. Miers, *Lee*, 173.

71. Catton, *A Stillness at Appomattox*, 149.

72. *Ibid.*, 161.

73. *Ibid.*, 163.

74. Dana to Stanton, May 30, 1864, *O.R.*, XXXVI, pt. 1, 82; Porter, *Campaigning with Grant*, 172; Wilson, *Under the Old Flag*, I, 44–48. Wilson's interpretation of Comstock's influence is not reflected in Comstock's diary.

75. Dana to Stanton, June 1, 1864, *O.R.*, XXXVI, pt. 1, 85; Porter, *Campaigning with Grant*, 172–73. In mentioning popular discouragement and impatience, Porter does not completely deal with the impact of public opinion on Grant's action. Grant's "personal and official" friend, Sherman, believed him very responsive to it. During the Vicksburg campaign Sherman felt Grant's strategy was dictated by a concern for the opinion of the public whose "clamor is so great he fears to seem to give up the attack on Vicksburg." Grant, Sherman said, "trembles at the approaching thunders of popular criticism and must risk anything." Popular desire for victories in the field must have been a significant pressure on Grant throughout his campaign against Lee (Sherman to John Sherman, Dec. 30, 1863, *Sherman Letters*, 220; Sherman to Mrs. Sherman, Apr. 17, 1863, *Home Letters*, 250. See also: Comstock Diary, entry of July 10, 1864; Grant to Mary Grant, Dec. 15, 1862, *Papers of Grant*, VII, 44; Grant to Jesse Root Grant, Apr. 21, 1863, *ibid.*, VIII, 109–10).

76. Catton, *Never Call Retreat*, 326.

18 ☆ THE FALL OF ATLANTA

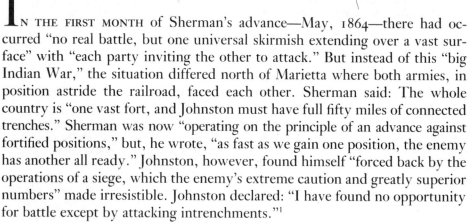

John B. Hood

I n the first month of Sherman's advance—May, 1864—there had occurred "no real battle, but one universal skirmish extending over a vast surface" with "each party inviting the other to attack." But instead of this "big Indian War," the situation differed north of Marietta where both armies, in position astride the railroad, faced each other. Sherman said: The whole country is "one vast fort, and Johnston must have full fifty miles of connected trenches." Sherman was now "operating on the principle of an advance against fortified positions," but, he wrote, "as fast as we gain one position, the enemy has another all ready." Johnston, however, found himself "forced back by the operations of a siege, which the enemy's extreme caution and greatly superior numbers" made irresistible. Johnston declared: "I have found no opportunity for battle except by attacking intrenchments."[1]

The lines changed position, but slowly and with little consequence as each refortified. In spite of having 100,000 men to Johnston's 60,000, Sherman found it difficult to overlap his enemy because the fortifications enabled Johnston to hold his lines with only one-third of his force, leaving the rest free for contingency use. Sherman even believed, incorrectly, that Johnston had "militia from the extreme south to man his extensive lines," leaving "him his three corps for maneuvers." As former lawyer Sherman continued "to study the case of the intrenched stalemate," he promised to "proceed with due caution and try to make no mistake." Of course, he sought, in vain, to "induce the enemy to attack" and took care not to "run head on to his fortifications." His immobility throughout the first three weeks of June probably would have been unavoidable in any case. It rained almost incessantly.[2]

Without the pressure of an impatient public, which Grant faced, Sherman could afford to be deliberate; in fact, the secretary of war wrote him: "Do not imagine that we are impatient of your progress; instead of considering it slow, we regard it as rapid, brilliant, and successful beyond our expectations. Take your time, and do your work in your own way." Compared with Rosecrans's long delays, Sherman's timetable seemed quick indeed. But he progressed more slowly than Grant, partly because he did not hurry, thus enabling him to suffer casualties only slightly greater than Johnston's and proportionately much less, while Grant's and Lee's armies both suffered the same percentage of casualties. The repair of the railroad that Johnston destroyed frequently delayed Sherman: whereas Grant had rivers on his left flank for communications, as he advanced Sherman had "only one source of supply. Grant had several in succession."[3]

Sherman worked patiently against Johnston's fortified positions, waiting for dry weather and the repair of his railroad. Simply by pressing Johnston he was carrying out part of his mission. "One of my chief objects being to give full employment to Johnston," he wrote, "it makes but little difference where he is, so long as he is not on his way to Virginia." He was "to prevent Joe Johnston from detaching against Grant till he got below Richmond." He assured the secretary of war: "General Grant may rest easy that Joe Johnston will not trouble him, if I can help it by labor or thought."[4]

He wrote Grant that the army was well, except the cavalry which had one commander "over-cautious" and the other "lazy." McPherson and Schofield had done nicely, but, he explained, "my chief source of trouble is with the Army of the Cumberland, which is dreadfully slow. A fresh furrow in a plowed field will stop the whole column, and all begin to intrench." Part of the trouble emanated from the commander, Thomas, who, like his army, was "habituated to be on the defensive." Even Thomas's overly sedentary lifestyle offended Sherman, who "came out without tents and ordered all to do likewise, yet Thomas," he remarked, "has a headquarters camp on the style of Halleck at Corinth; every aide and orderly with a wall-tent, and a baggage train big enough for a division."[5]

As Sherman and Grant carefully prepared for their next moves, their main armies did not occasion immediate concern in Richmond; David Hunter's victory in the Shenandoah Valley, however, caused serious alarm in Richmond. With Breckinridge withdrawn to reinforce Lee, the Confederate forces in the Valley had been weak even before their defeat enfeebled them. Lee as well as Davis saw clearly that the enemy could do "great evil" in the Valley. They perceived Hunter's move as part of a Union "plan which was to destroy all communications with Richmond, as well from the west as from the south, and thus compel the evacuation of the capital." To recover that vital area would require one of Lee's three corps. He and the President decided "to hazard the defense of Richmond" and send the one commanded by the colorful veteran, Lieutenant General Jubal A. Early. Lee's conviction that the Army of the Potomac was "very much shaken" and anxious to avoid battle made the decision easier. The assault at Cold Harbor only reinforced this impression and convinced General Bragg, who remarked: "Grant has been so much crippled by his constant repulses . . . that I apprehend but little damage from him now." Thus Early's corps, sent from Richmond, reached Lynchburg before Hunter.[6]

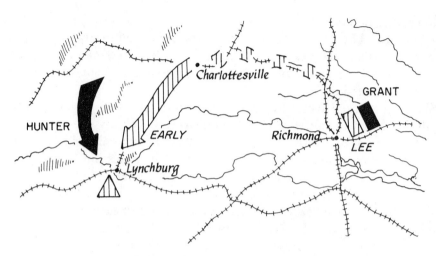

Lee Reinforces Using Interior Lines

Later, while moving toward Petersburg, Grant learned of this Confederate use of interior-line redeployment by railroad. This, of course, Grant had anticipated, but he felt no concern for Hunter. The Confederates could not surprise Hunter because his particularly strong cavalry element provided excellent reconnaissance capabilities. Knowing Hunter's force was strong in infantry as well as cavalry, Grant did not worry even though it was "too late to get word to General Hunter" of Lee's movement of troops westward. Grant noted: Hunter is "likely to get word through his large cavalry force. Such a force as he has should never be surprised or find difficulty in making their way to a place of safety if attacked by a superior force. The only apprehension I have for Hunter is that he may get out of ammunition."[7]

Grant also relied on that special characteristic of raiding armies which gave them an extra measure of protection, the ability to retreat in any direction. As with Sherman's Meridian expedition, similar to Hunter's in concept and related in purpose, Grant felt confident that the raid could nullify the enemy's interior-lines advantage. Nevertheless, as with the Meridian expedition, he sought "another diversion . . . for the protection of" Hunter and made this a part of the mission of yet another raid, that of two cavalry divisions sent to break the railroads running southwest and west from Richmond. Even knowledge that Confederate forces superior to Hunter's blocked the Valley in his rear did not perturb Grant. He instructed Hunter, who was in the vicinity of Lynchburg, "to save his army in the way he thinks best, either by getting back into his own department or by joining" the Army of the Potomac. Grant only wished that it were safe for Hunter to join Meade's army "by taking a wide sweep south," destroying the railroads to the south, and the one between Lynchburg and Petersburg, en route.[8]

The intervention of a superior Confederate force kept Hunter out of Lynchburg and limited his destruction of railroads. Nevertheless, having retreated into West Virginia, he could optimistically report that his raid had "been extremely successful, inflicting great injury upon the enemy and victorious in every engagement." He continued: "Running short of ammunition, and finding it impossible to collect supplies while in the presence of an enemy believed to be superior to our force in numbers and constantly receiving re-enforcements from Richmond and other points, I deemed it best to withdraw."[9]

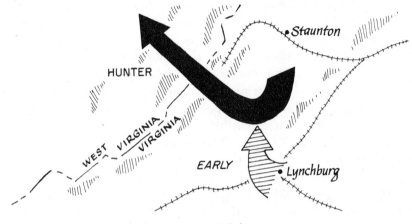

Hunter Withdraws

As Grant awaited the results of these raids, he replied to Halleck's earlier brief on behalf of a siege of Richmond from the northwest. Expressing anxiety about raiders and his long-established preference for water communications, Grant objected, saying: The Fredericksburg railroad "would give us a long vulnerable line of road to protect, exhausting much of our strength in guarding it." In responding to Halleck's earlier exposition of the established strategy of defeating Lee's army in the field rather than besieging Richmond, Grant explained the policy he had pursued since he had become aware that Butler would fail: "My idea from the start has been to beat Lee's army, if possible, north of Richmond, then, after destroying his lines of communication north of the James River, to transfer the army to the south side and besiege Lee in Richmond, or follow him south if he should retreat."

This plan had not been a complete success, for, Grant explained, "without greater sacrifice of human life than I am willing to make, all cannot be accomplished that I had designed outside of the city." Cold Harbor had convinced him that he would have to proceed immediately to a siege, though not from the Peninsula but from south of the James. Even so, his hope for a more significant success and the need for a victory before beginning the siege rendered him determined, in spite of Cold Harbor, to continue his post-Spotsylvania strategy of trying to "take advantage of any favorable circumstance that may present itself" for an attack on Lee's army.[10]

Grant felt that Lee had "recklessly laid himself open to ruin" in the way he handled his army at Chancellorsville in 1863 and hoped that Lee, if he fought north of Richmond, would provide the Union army with a comparable opportunity. But Grant had been disappointed. Lee displayed no reckless daring and gave Grant no such opening. And so, Grant told Halleck: "The enemy deems it of the first importance to run no risks with the armies they now have." Unable to achieve anything significant against the Confederates, Grant explained: "They act purely on the defensive, behind breastworks, or feebly on the offensive immediately in front of them, and where in case of repulse they can instantly retire behind them." Candidly summing up the real results of the pre-siege phase of the campaign, Grant indicated that he felt he definitely possessed the initiative, because the Confederates' constant resort to digging in showed they could "protect themselves only by strong intrenchments, while," he said, "our army is not only confident of protecting itself without intrenchments, but . . . can beat and drive the enemy wherever and whenever he can be found without this protection."[11]

Other commanders in Virginia, McClellan, Pope, Hooker, and Meade, had encountered great difficulty in maintaining the initiative against Lee. In spite of Grant's success in making steady progress toward Richmond, his efforts, too, had largely produced negative results. The communications north of Richmond still remained essentially intact and, after Grant's move from the North Anna, the pattern of the campaign that had emerged showed that "the rebs keep taking up strong positions and intrenching themselves. This compels us," Meade explained before Cold Harbor, "to move around their flank, after trying to find some weak point to attack. This operation has occurred four times, namely crossing the Rapidan, at old Wilderness, at Spotsylvania Court House, and recently at North Anna. We shall have to do it once more before we get them into their defenses at Richmond, and then will begin the tedious process of a quasi-siege, like that at Sebastopol; this will last as long, unless we can get hold of their railroads and cut off their supplies, when they must come out and fight."[12]

Grant did not delay after Cold Harbor, he explained to Halleck, primarily to have one more opportunity to catch Lee in a mistake. He delayed to permit the cavalry to "be sent west to destroy the Virginia Central Railroad. . . . When this is effected," he added, "I will move the army to the south side of the James River," where "I can cut off all sources of supply to the enemy, except what is furnished by the canal. If Hunter succeeds in reaching Lynchburg that will be lost to him also. Should Hunter not succeed I will still make the effort to destroy the canal by sending cavalry up the south side of the river with a pontoon train to cross wherever they can."[13]

Thus Grant planned a deep turning movement, finally getting in Lee's rear and placing his army where Butler's should have been at the end of the first week of May. With the Virginia Central cut by cavalry and by Grant's destruction when on the North Anna, Richmond must fall, deprived of all communications except possibly the quite inadequate canal. Long ago Lincoln

and Halleck had concluded that this could not be done. Whether Grant
agreed or not, it remained his only course, for he had certainly given a full
and fair trial to the headquarters strategy.

A little over a week after Cold Harbor, Grant had finished preparations to
march on Petersburg. Raids under Sheridan and Hunter started well, and the
movement began only after necessary delays to complete coordination with
Butler and finish the removal of rails to White House "so that the enemy
cannot use the iron for the purpose of relaying other roads." Starting south
on June 12, Grant, covered by a second line of intrenchments built in the rear
of the front line, secretly withdrew from Lee's front. With pontoons and
ferries, ordered the previous month, the march went smoothly, Lee being
completely deceived as to the scope of the turning movement.

Good screening by the one available cavalry division and excellent logistical
arrangements made Grant's biggest turning movement flawless until the two
leading corps reached Petersburg on June 15. Here the operation stalled
because of poor execution by two corps under Smith and Hancock. The

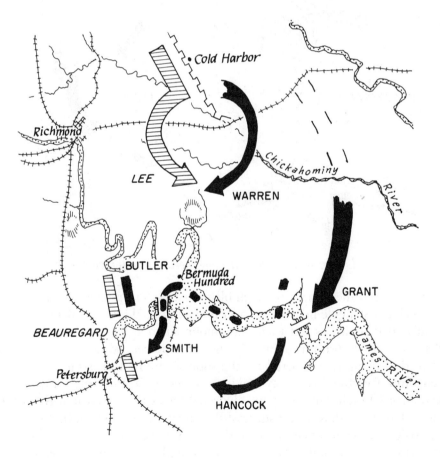

Union Movements toward Petersburg

usually energetic Smith, a veteran of the battles of Fredericksburg and Cold Harbor, overcautiously approached Beauregard's formidable but quite weakly manned fortifications. The usually superb Hancock did not well support Smith's circumspect advance because Hancock had not received adequate orders. Against the frantic efforts of the skillful Beauregard, this feeble and bumbling offensive failed to take Petersburg. More Union troops arrived but reinforcements from Lee to Beauregard offset them and, after further unsuccessful Union assaults on June 16, 17, and 18, both sides dug in. They had made no break in any of the Confederate railways south of Richmond.[14]

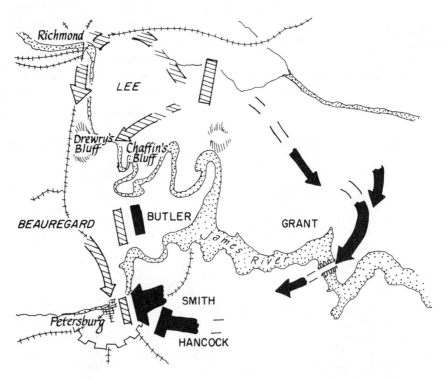

Union Delays Permit Confederate Reinforcement

Thus ended the campaign which blemished Grant's reputation. In six weeks of incessant struggle he had lost over 60,000 men. The Confederates had not tabulated their losses but they had amounted to at least 30,000. It is likely that each army lost approximately the same percentage of its forces. Thus, instead of being remembered for the sophistication of his strategy and as an economizer of lives by always taking the enemy in the rear, Grant became known as a butcher of men who advocated the head-on collision. Rather than viewed as the architect of a successful strategy of exhaustion, because of this campaign Grant has been perceived by many evaluators as a practitioner of the strategy of annihilation, victorious, if at all, only after paying a hideous human toll.

Yet Grant did not prefer this type of campaign. He probably wished to unite Burnside's corps with the two corps from Butler's Army of the James and send the whole force, nearly 60,000 men, into North Carolina under the command of Baldy Smith. While Meade then pressed Lee as he had done at Mine Run the previous fall, Smith could have been destroying Confederate communications in North Carolina, cutting the Confederacy off from its imports through Wilmington and going far toward driving North Carolina from the war. Unless Beauregard had displayed far more competence than Smith, and Lee had been willing and able to spare very large reinforcements for North Carolina, Lee's army would soon have run short of supplies because, concentrated and closely pressed by Meade, it could have done little or no foraging. With such a threat in Lee's rear, Grant need not have worried that troops from Virginia would move as far as to strengthen Johnston in Georgia.

Yet even if a strategy of such obliquity and subtlety had been acceptable to Lincoln and intelligible to public opinion, it would have failed if Butler had insisted on the command, and his monumental operational incompetence would surely have defeated the North Carolina invasion. Thus politics conditioned, and to a large extent dictated, Grant's eastern campaign of 1864. Incompetents, whose important political constituencies made their removal impossible, commanded two of the three armies in the theatre. Furthermore, both Lincoln and Grant knew that the public envisioned a contest between the two champions and national morale needed field victories over armies. The character of Grant's campaign had indeed been fundamentally conditioned by political factors.[15]

The plan Grant actually adopted, if implemented and completed, would have satisfied the populace, because it would have taken Richmond, or begun its siege, very early in the campaign. Perhaps Grant made his gravest mistake when he misjudged Butler. Impressed by the Massachusetts politician's energy and his accurate perception of the role his army could play, Grant failed to realize that Butler, devoid of any operational experience, could not implement the concept he shared with Grant. European military history contains ample precedents for remedying the incompetence of generals appointed for political reasons or because of social prestige: the French paired an inept general with an experienced and proven commander; the Germans used the chief of staff; and the British employed a second in command. Grant blundered in declining to try any of these.[16]

If someone had capably managed Butler's big army, it certainly could have taken Petersburg, perhaps have reached the south side of the James, and possibly even have taken Richmond—all before the battles at Spotsylvania. To counter such a threat successfully, Lee would have had to detach very nearly a corps, leaving his army too weak to avoid being quickly and easily turned, thus ensuring a speedy retreat to the vicinity of Richmond and a siege with most railroads closed to him.

Realizing that Butler had failed, Grant had to improvise a new campaign plan. To cut the railroads north of Richmond, he had to advance directly on the city, for turning Lee by his eastern flank would have left the railroads intact. But Grant felt he could not accomplish his goal if he left both the Virginia Central Railroad and the canal open to Lynchburg. Thus he had a strong motive to push Lee back directly on Richmond in order to complete, north of the city, the necessary railway destruction before moving to the south of Richmond. Political concerns, combined with the importance of breaking the Virginia Central, induced him to attack Lee's army in position at Spotsylvania. That failing, he began turning Lee from his positions, all the while seeking a weak spot for a successful attack and a battlefield victory.[17]

Both sides believed that the campaign had hurt the enemy more than it had hurt themselves. The effect of attrition had been about even, with Lee losing nearly the same percentage of his smaller army as did Grant of his larger force. Many of Lee's replacements, long-organized units from the southern coasts, probably caused the quality of his force to be better sustained than Meade's. Some Union replacement units, "wholly untrained in the manual of arms," had to be held in depots for two days to learn these rudiments. The battles had a more severe impact on the morale of Meade's army because they took the offensive against an intrenched enemy. One of Grant's staff officers noted: "Troops do not fight as well as when we started. Best officers and best men gone—losses enormous." In early July he reported Hancock as saying, "With 12 brigades he has lost 25 brigade commanders and his men are not half as good as when he started. Meade is doubtful if our men can be relied on as yet."[18]

Thus attrition had seriously affected both armies. Overall, Grant was optimistic, believing that every day of the war the enemy lost "at least a regiment, without any population to draw from to replace it, exclusive of losses in battle." But the North's resources were not as well mobilized, General Halleck reporting: "We are now not receiving one-half as many as we are discharging. Volunteering has virtually ceased" and the draft was not having much effect. Overreacting, Halleck saw Union "armies melting away to a frightful rate," and feared that, without more draftees, the Union armies would "go to the wall." Sherman most emphatically agreed with Halleck, because half of his army was entitled to discharge by October. All the enemy needs to do, wrote Sherman, is "simply hold on here" and "defeat us by the superior method they have of recruitment."[19]

The campaign from the Wilderness to Petersburg justified the pessimists. The advocates of the Peninsula route forever afterwards could say that Grant had only succeeded in reaching essentially the same location that McClellan attained two years before and had taken longer while sustaining far more casualties. Those persons skeptical of attempting a direct attack on the enemy's army felt vindicated, Baldy Smith characterizing the campaign as "a succession of useless slaughters." As the army began "the tedious process of a quasi-siege, like that at Sebastopol," Meade felt vindicated. The power displayed by the tactical defensive showed his "sound judgment, both at Williamsport and Mine Run. In every instance that we have attacked the enemy in an intrenched position," he continued, "we have failed, except in the case of Hancock's attack at Spotsylvania, which was a surprise discreditable to the enemy." Converted fully at Gettysburg to a belief in the power of the defense, Meade expected little else. "Although this army has not accomplished all that ignorant people anticipated, it has," he wrote, "done more than could reasonably be counted on." Success "consisted only in compelling the enemy to draw in towards Richmond; our failure," he explained, "has been that we have not been able to overcome, destroy, or bag his army." As a result "both sides suffered great losses," he continued, "probably proportionate to our original strength, and it is highly probable that both sides have repaired their losses by reinforcements."[20]

Though Grant's strategy of attacks against Lee's army had been dictated in part by public opinion, national morale was depressed by the large casualties caused by so many battles in such a short span of time. One observer felt that these were "the darkest of many dark days through which passed the friends and lovers of the Federal Union," and another discerned "very great discouragement over the North, great reluctance to recruiting," and a "strong disposition for peace." In addition Grant had not produced any clear-cut military success of the kind the public could appreciate; there had been no Battle of Cannae nor even any precipitate rebel retreat after any of Grant's battles.[21]

Less than a success politically, Grant's campaign vindicated the headquarters belief in the futility of a siege, a doctrine borne out by Grant's inability to cut enough of Richmond's extensive communication network. Halleck spoke extremely critically of Grant's "fatal mistake in putting himself south of the James River." Thus, Halleck asserted, "He cannot now reach Richmond without taking Petersburg, which is strongly fortified." The chief of staff perceived Grant in a position comparable to McClellan's in the summer of 1862, on an exterior line. Halleck believed that Lee could take advantage of the economy of force provided by the fortification of Richmond and "at any time detach 30,000 or 40,000 men" without Grant's being aware of it. The chief of staff had wanted a siege from the north side, a position which would have covered Washington and the Potomac. When one of Grant's staff officers "asked him what he supposed we could do with a siege of Richmond on [the] north side," Halleck responded "by asking what we could do by a siege on [the] S. side." The headquarters doctrine had received full confirmation—the only thing worse than a siege was a siege on exterior line.[22]

Grant's failure to take Richmond further showed the wisdom of the Lincoln-Halleck policy of concentrating in the West and not seeking to take the enemy capital. Since Grant advocated this too, the ultimate success of Sherman's campaign justified Grant's strategy also, because Grant had as the original mission for the Army of the Potomac the immobilization of Lee so that he could not again send reinforcements to the West. But, by mid-June, 1864, despite Lincoln's sharing Grant's hopes about taking Petersburg and telegraphing Grant, saying, "I begin to see it. You will succeed. God bless you all," the Union advance in truth had stalled, heralding the start of the lowest ebb in the northern populace's will to win. The necessary siege of Petersburg, coupled with a long and tedious campaign between Sherman and Johnston in Georgia, began to suggest that victory was perhaps either impossible or too costly to be worthwhile.[23]

Gradually Sherman moved enough forces northeastward toward the railroad to compel Johnston to shift and counter them. This Johnston did on June 4 in a rainstorm, moving his army away from New Hope to an already-prepared position along Lost, Pine, and Bush mountains. Once more Johnston managed to move in time to block Sherman, leaving only the option of frontal assault upon strong defensive emplacements. Again small-scale fighting took place and Sherman eschewed making that rash and costly mistake.

Sherman and Johnston Sidle Eastward

Though continually delayed by the fortified lines persistently erected by the Confederates and by the need to restore railroad service, Sherman progressed slowly but surely. His communications in his rear remained secure, however, in part because General Washburn at Memphis was performing his duty of distracting Forrest and thus preventing raids on Sherman's communications. In early June Washburn dispatched a major cavalry expedition into Mississippi under Brigadier General Samuel D. Sturgis. Various preliminary skirmishes occurred as Sturgis's men searched for Forrest's, but on June 10 the Federals found the rebels near Brice's Crossroads, south of Corinth, Mississippi. The fight that followed, culminating in Sturgis's total rout, proved one of Forrest's great moments. Forrest captured most of the enemy artillery,

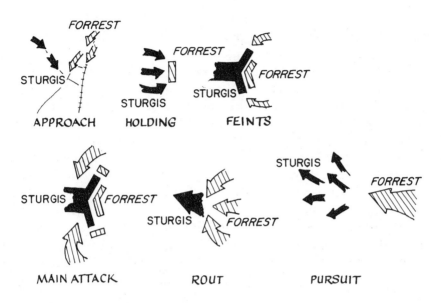

Sequence of Events in Sturgis's Defeat

176 wagons, quantities of supplies, and more than 1,500 prisoners. The encounter ranks as a classic of its kind. Of Sturgis's 8,000 men, 2,240 became casualties while Forrest, with 3,500 men, lost but 492. But despite this accomplishment, the episode had nevertheless induced Forrest to abandon his plans for a raid on Sherman's communications. Sherman had wanted just such moves as Sturgis's when he directed "great and constant activity" for "diverting the enemy's attention so far as possible from the operations in Georgia."[24]

Not all Confederate raiders operated on the defensive, however. On June 8 John Hunt Morgan, on his last raid—for he would be killed on September 4—captured Mount Sterling, Kentucky. He not only snared a federal garrison, but some of his men also robbed the local bank of $18,000. Far across the globe, at Cherbourg, France, another kind of rebel raider, the C.S.S. *Alabama*, pulled into port badly in need of refitting. Before she could secure the repairs and get away, U.S.S. *Kearsarge* arrived to blockade the ship. There was little to do but to fight, and this occurred on June 19. The clash proved to be the greatest ship-to-ship encounter of the war upon the open seas, and it cost the *Alabama* her life as she went to the bottom after a desperate battle.

On the same day that Grant's army began crossing the James River, June 14, Sherman's men in Georgia slashed forward in skirmish lines against Johnston's well-placed works. During the indecisive fighting near Pine Mountain, in truth little more than an overgrown hill, a federal artillery shell struck and instantly killed Confederate Lieutenant General Leonidas Polk. But the lines held. Indeed this episode amounted to little more in the first place than Sherman's spiteful and frustrated insistence that his men lob some artillery shells in the direction of the Confederate officers he had spied with his field glasses. He already knew the futility of assaults. Legends grew that Sherman himself had sighted the gun and purposely killed Polk; in truth, he did not even know until later who had been there upon the hilltop.

On June 16, further exhibiting the broad scope of the war, the Confederacy authorized Lieutenant Bennett H. Young to organize raiders in Canada for a dash into New England. Also, this mid-June, Grant's initial unsuccessful assaults upon Petersburg had cost 8,150 killed or wounded Federals in four days.

The summer, therefore, commenced with the two major federal offensives stagnated: Grant and Lee dug in before Petersburg facing fortifications just as, in Georgia, Sherman's Federals again discovered that Johnston had moved to still another new and impregnable line. On June 22 Grant attempted to drive against the Weldon and Petersburg Railroad, but Lee's wary men halted and pushed back the surging Yankees. So three days later Meade's Federals commenced a more bizarre operation: their engineers began digging a tunnel toward the Confederate lines in order eventually to blow apart the southern earthworks.

Begun at first almost as a concession to the mining engineer, Lieutenant Colonel Henry Pleasants, and a group of coal miners he had assembled from Schuylkill County, Pennsylvania, the idea evolved into a major project, strongly backed by General Burnside. "That God-damned fort is the only thing between us and Petersburg, and I have an idea we can blow it up," Pleasants had said. He organized the men into three shifts and they dug around the clock. Blacksmiths in the Ninth Corps artillery units remodeled the available picks better to suit mining work. They secured needed timbers, first by tearing down a nearby railroad bridge and thereafter by operating an abandoned sawmill several miles to the rear. They improvised handbarrows from cracker boxes, reinforced with iron hoops taken from pork barrels, and nailed on handles. All the dirt taken out of the tunnel they concealed in a ravine under freshly cut bushes. And after much insensitive response from various high officers to requests for instruments to determine locations within the tunnel, Burnside wired a friend in Washington to send down a theodolite.[25]

Meanwhile, in Georgia, except on one occasion, Sherman carefully avoided assaulting the Confederate breastworks. At Kennesaw Mountain, June 27, hoping that the Confederates were so spread out as to make their center vulnerable, he attacked knowing that, even if he failed, the effort would be worthwhile because "it would show the enemy," he explained, "that we would attack breastworks and that they must keep them well manned." The venture failed, costing 1,999 men compared to a Confederate loss of 442.

Sherman had many other and quite valid reasons for his inept attack at Kennesaw Mountain. The wet ground still precluded a movement by the whole army. One wing of his army had extended so far from the railroad that

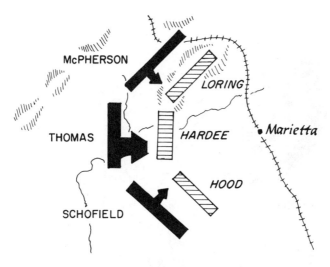

Failure of Frontal Assault

wagons could supply it no longer. He also hoped that Johnston had over-extended his line, thus rendering him vulnerable to a frontal assault. If he had "broken Johnston's center," he could have "pushed his army back in confusion, and with great loss." In addition Sherman had a reason for making even an unsuccessful attack: "The enemy as well as my own army had settled down into the belief that flanking alone was my game." He not only wished to convince Johnston of the necessity of manning his fortifications strongly, but he wanted to make his own force more aggressive. Sherman had observed: "The moment the enemy was found behind anything like a parapet, why everybody would deploy, throw up counterworks and take it easy, leaving it to the 'old man' to turn the position."[26]

Only at Kennesaw Mountain did Sherman attack. Johnston always deployed and intrenched his army too well for the careful Sherman to find a weak point. The Confederate performance impressed the Union generals, and Sherman himself remarked: "No officer or soldier who ever served under me will question the generalship of Joseph E. Johnston. His retreats were timely, and he left nothing behind." Sherman also considered Johnston predictable, for he "was a sensible man and only did sensible things." For the rest of the campaign, both armies consistently and rapidly intrenched and threw up breastworks whenever they stopped long enough. Federal troopers admiringly remarked that "the Rebels must carry their breastworks with them"; the Confederates in turn had a saying that "Sherman's men march with a rifle in one hand and a spade in the other.[27]

Sherman persevered, hoping to "find a soft place." With Johnston's back to the railroad it was, Sherman wrote, "difficult to turn his position without abandoning our railroad," but General Thomas thought this "decidedly better than butting against breastworks twelve feet thick." Sherman then planned

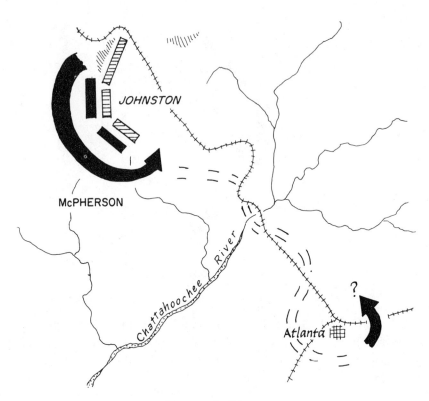

Sherman's Plan

to move McPherson's army from the left on the railroad to the extreme right and to "cut loose from the railroad with ten days' supplies in wagons." This would have forced Johnston to retreat or, Sherman explained, "come out of his intrenchments and attack General Thomas, which is what I want, for General Thomas is well intrenched." But General Schofield, thinking about Johnston's third alternative, asked: Could not "Johnston, in anticipation of your present movement, . . . bring up to Marietta two or three weeks' supplies, close the gorge of his lines in [the] rear of Marietta, and meet you there in a strongly intrenched position with a greater amount of supplies than you can carry?"[28]

Buell had defeated Bragg's turning movement during the Kentucky campaign in this way. Bragg's raiding army reached Buell's rear, but, with a large reserve of supplies, Buell could wait, forcing Bragg either to attack or to move away and live off the country. Sherman, certain that he had "contemplated every move on the chessboard of war," had the answer in the new raiding strategy which he could now apply. He told Schofield: I do not believe that Johnston would "be willing to have me interpose between him and the rest of the Confederacy. I am not bound to attack him in his position after getting below him." Were this to happen and Johnston waited, relying on his greater accumulation of supplies, Sherman would begin his raid. He could, he said, then cross "the Chattahoochee and destroy all his railroads before he can prevent it."[29]

Sherman could attempt this "desperate game" because he had well fortified his communications and Grant had just released him from his obligation to keep Johnston fully occupied. Engaged in besieging Richmond and Petersburg, Grant had reached the point where he did not worry about reinforcements from Johnston to Lee. Grant had Halleck tell Sherman: "The movements of your army may be made entirely independent of any desire to retain Johnston's forces where they are. He does not think Lee will bring any additional troops to Richmond, on account of the difficulty of feeding them." But Sherman did not need this liberty because, when the Union army turned him, Johnston fell back to cover his communications. Since Sherman had promptly reached the Chattahoochee, within sight of Atlanta, his raid would not begin until after Atlanta fell.[30]

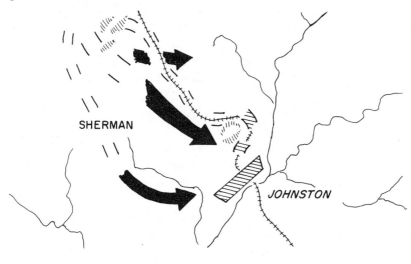

Johnston Falls Back

☆   ☆

As he was settling into intrenchments before Petersburg, Grant learned from Halleck that Rosecrans and Curtis, the commanders in Missouri and Kansas, were "continually calling for more troops," wanting "20,000 men to oppose 2,000 guerrillas." Commenting that these generals would make "the same call if they were stationed to Maine," Grant had already determined to move an army corps of 20,000 men from Canby's Division of the West Mississippi to Virginia. He thus decided on a fundamental, if not major, strategic redisposition, moving troops to Virginia and obliging Canby to cancel a campaign to aid Sherman by at last advancing on Mobile. He was not motivated by frivolity but by the power of intrenched defenders and the consequent "tedious" nature of the siege of Richmond. He explained to Halleck: "In consequence of the very extended lines we must have, a much larger force will be necessary than would be required in ordinary sieges against the same force that now opposes us. With my present force I feel perfectly safe against Lee's army, and, acting defensively, would feel safe against Lee and Johnston combined; but we must act offensively." In moving these troops from the trans-Mississippi, he clearly enunciated one aspect of his strategy for the year, to concentrate in Georgia and Virginia and conduct no offensive west of the Mississippi "until the rebellion east of it" was "entirely subdued." Grant's reinforcement from the West would be timely, for the lieutenant general was about to discover the disadvantages of a siege on exterior lines.[31]

Absorbed with his movement against Petersburg and pleased with Hunter's success, Grant remained unaware that Hunter's precipitate retreat from Lynchburg signified that Lee had sent a full army corps to restore the situation in the Valley. Rather than having concern for the Valley and Hunter's hasty westward withdrawal, Grant, who thought Hunter had double his 12,000 men, wanted the general to start "to Charlottesville to destroy the road there effectively. If he could get on the canal," Grant wrote, "it would be a great help." Responding to Halleck's warnings that Hunter was far away and the generals along the Baltimore and Ohio were incompetent, Grant allowed Halleck to assemble ships at Fort Monroe so he could, if necessary, bring reinforcements rapidly to Washington. Nevertheless, he remained optimistic that the absent Hunter would prevail. "It is important to our success here" at Petersburg, he wrote Halleck, "that another raid should be made up the Shenandoah Valley, and stores and communications broken." He still anticipated an advance to Charlottesville and the raiders' ability to "utterly destroy the railroad and canal."[32]

As Grant was thinking about applying his strategy of exhaustion by raids, Lieutenant General Jubal A. Early had not only recovered the entire Valley but, as instructed, had crossed into Maryland. Early proved quite dogged and efficient in his latest role; his pusillanimity at Gettysburg was a singular aberration. As Bruce Catton unforgettably described him: He was " 'Old Jube' to his troops, a sardonic man twisted by arthritis, caustic and provoking and profane, always riding in a queer hunched-over manner, 'solemn as a country coroner going to his first inquest': respected by all but liked by hardly anybody. He had not patience with any human shortcoming." His melodramatic raid upon Washington began when he moved north in the Shenandoah Valley with 10,000 infantry and 4,000 cavalry and, with little opposition, reached Winchester on July 2. By the 5th he began crossing the Potomac at Shepherdstown into Maryland. Seriously jolted by the alarming news of a threat upon the capital itself, the War Department sent frantic calls for 24,000 militia from New York and Pennsylvania. Early's men captured Hagerstown on July 6 and one of his subordinate commanders collected $20,000 from the populace in retribution for federal Major General David Hunter's Shenandoah depredations of June.[33]

Besides feeding his corps and controlling for Lee's army the coming harvest in the Valley, Early was menacing the politically sensitive capital. To Lincoln, Early's movement across the Potomac again presented the opportunity to get in the rear of a raiding force. But the Washington area lacked adequate resources, as Halleck most emphatically explained to Grant: "If you propose to cut off this raid and not merely to secure our depots we must have more forces here." Lincoln wrote, I believe "with decent management we [can] destroy any enemy who crossed the Potomac," and ordered Grant: Bring reinforcements "with you personally, and make a vigorous effort to destroy the enemies' force in this vicinity. I think there is really a fair chance to do this if the movement is prompt." Grant did not respond to Lincoln's order: he felt optimistic about Hunter and the forces available and he did not wish to damage his prestige by going to Washington without a victory at Petersburg. As one of his staff officers remarked, he did "not wish to go till he goes from Richmond." Grant himself made a comparable point to Lincoln, for, on public opinion, "it would have a bad effect for me to leave here," he explained.[34]

Grant was concerned about the quality of the commanders facing Early, especially when Grant learned that the enemy was approaching a force commanded by the consistently defeated General Sigel. Grant asked that Sigel be relieved, "at least until present troubles are over. I do not feel certain at any time that he will not, after abandoning stores, artillery, and trains, make a successful retreat to some safe place."[35]

As Early approached Washington, a number of skirmishes erupted over a broad area, at Antietam Bridge, at Frederick, and at Sandy Hook, Maryland, and a rather stubborn fight ensued on July 9 at Monocacy, Maryland, just southeast of Frederick. Here the blocking federal force consisted mostly of inexperienced, untrained, and short-term men who broke after suffering nearly 2,000 casualties to the Confederates' loss of only around 700 men. Lincoln announced calmly, though: "They cannot fly to either place [Baltimore or Washington]. Let us be vigilant but keep cool."[36]

Wahington was, however, in peril. Not only was Hunter far away, but he had "proven himself far more incompetent than even Sigel." Further, the Union possessed no unity of command for "General Halleck will not give orders except as he receives them," wrote Dana; "the President will give none." With only "raw militia, invalids, convalescents from the hospitals, a few dismounted and disorganized cavalry sent up from James River" to defend it, Washington needed more than an effective command. Worrying about the defense of Washington and the "immense depot of stores" there, Halleck asked Grant: "What can we do with such forces in the field against a column of 20,000 veterans?"[37]

Early's men invaded the Washington suburbs on July 11 but were com-

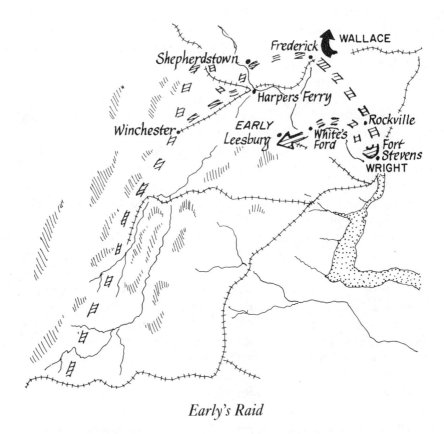

Early's Raid

pelled to withdraw the next day and to hurry in frustration back toward the
Potomac. To defend the capital, the militia of the District of Columbia mustered, the invalids organized, the office personnel turned out under arms; but
the real security was not provided by this motley and raw conglomerate:
about noon on the eleventh two divisions of the Sixth Corps arrived from
City Point. Led by the capable Horatio G. Wright, the veterans had come on
the ships gathered for this contingency. As Early's troops threatened Washington's fortifications, President and Mrs. Lincoln both visited one of the
defenses, Fort Stevens, where they witnessed an attack, Lincoln seeming
more curious than worried. On the next day the President again visited the
fort and came under enemy fire. Several persons urged Lincoln to take cover,
but he yielded only when a young captain, Oliver Wendell Holmes, Jr., who
thereby gained an enduring niche in American folklore, shouted, "Get down,
you fool!"[38]

    After the city's escape from capture, Grant immediately renewed his hopes
for a successful raid by his own forces. Remaining optimistic, he expected a
pursuit by the heterogenous force under Wright, stronger after being reinforced by the Nineteenth Corps from Canby. Grant said: Early "should have
on his heels veterans, militiamen, men on horseback, and everything that can

be got to follow and eat out Virginia clear and clean as far as they go, so that crows flying over it for the balance of the season will have to carry their provender with them." As Early's powerful corps did not withdraw very far, Grant's desire to "make all the Valley south of the Baltimore and Ohio Road a desert as high up as possible" would have to wait for more than two months. Lincoln, with different hopes, was downcast by the ineffective counteroffensive by Wright's motley force. With much sarcasm, the President remarked: "Wright telegraphs that he thinks the enemy are all across the Potomac but that he has halted & sent out an infantry reconnoissance [sic] for fear he might come across the rebels & catch some of them."[39]

Wishing to remove the Nineteenth Corps and Wright's Sixth Corps so that he could use them in the impending operations around Richmond, Grant then began to think defensively. He thus proposed to make Washington, Baltimore, and Harper's Ferry into basic training camps and to fortify Baltimore, even though he did not believe Early would make another raid into Maryland. Early would, Grant thought, "attempt to go through Western Virginia to Ohio, possibly taking Pittsburg [sic] by the way." But Halleck sought to impress on Grant that he was not merely dealing with raiders but now stood in an exterior-lines situation. "So long as you were operating between Washington and the enemy," wrote Halleck, "your army covered Maryland and Pennsylvania and I sent you all the troops from here and the North which could take the field or guard your depots and prisoners of war." Halleck argued that the capital needed more forces because, without adequate cavalry, he could not detect another Confederate advance in time to bring reinforcements even by the rapid water transportation available. He continued: With Grant's army south of the James and Lee's between it and Washington, Lee could thus "make a pretty large detachment unknown to us for a week or ten days and send it against Washington." He then asked: "Will it be safe to have this risk repeated? Is not Washington too important in a political as well as a military point of view to run any serious risk at all?"[40]

Thus, as Halleck had feared, the Confederates had again exploited their interior lines and their ability to turn Union forces by using the Valley route. The result had been, Davis observed, that "to save their capital" Union "troops en route to Grant were diverted to Washington, and other troops were drawn from Grant to the same place, and the enemy soon had a large force on the upper Potomac." This Union force necessitated retaining Early's corps in the Valley in order to protect that area and cover the route to Lynchburg. There were again two main lines of operations in Virginia.[41]

While Grant coped with Early's raid, Sherman delayed while he prepared to make another move. After reaching the Chattahoochee, Sherman explained to Halleck: "I am now far ahead of my railroad and telegraph, and want them to catch up and may be here some days." He could temporarily outrun his rail communications, because, as earlier, he lived partially off the country, "leaving it bare as a desert." Nevertheless, he said, I find "the task of feeding this vast host is a more difficult one than to fight." His various arrangements to protect his railroad had worked well, for, though it had been broken twice, his men had repaired it quickly. He felt pleased with the success of his plans for the diversion of the enemy in Mississippi, seeing the defeat of Sturgis as productive for "he kept Forrest away." It delighted him that Canby, Banks's new superior, was sending two additional raids into Mississippi as well as promising Sherman's often-requested move of even a small force against Mobile. Though no longer the major diversion originally planned, the capture of Mobile still remained fundamental to Grant's western plan because Sherman expected eventually to rely on a "base of supplies" on "the south coast."[42]

In fact, in reaching the outskirts of Atlanta, Sherman had already "fulfilled the first part of the grand plan." Grant stood below Richmond and no longer worried about Johnston's reinforcing Lee, unless Atlanta fell. In that event, he wrote Halleck, I expect the enemy to "bring most of Johnston's army here with the expectation of driving us out, and then unite against Sherman. They will fail if they attempt this programme. My greatest fear is of their sending troops to Johnston first." Writing Sherman after Early's raid that the enemy might send 25,000 against him, he explained that Early's raid had failed and, as the troops were not needed to defend Richmond, they would thus "be an element of weakness to eat up their supplies." To protect against a repetition of the Chickamauga reinforcement, Grant advised Sherman to disable the line of operations from Virginia by "destroying the railroads as far to the east and south" as possible, collect supplies, and select a position he could "hold until help could be had." And Grant promised, I will make "a desperate effort to get a position here which will hold the enemy without the necessity of so many men. If successful, I can detach from here for other enterprises, looking as much to your assistance as anything else."[43]

Sherman did as advised about destroying the railroads but declined to assume the defensive. Instead, he turned Johnston's eastern flank. Confident of his army, he said: I do "not fear Johnston with re-enforcements of 20,000 if he will take the offensive." He did recognize the danger of his long line of communications "and the superiority of the enemy's cavalry in numbers and audacity." Nevertheless he launched his own raids to break Atlanta's rail communications. One, originating in Tennessee, succeeded but another, by his own cavalry, turned out "to be a humbug." He assessed his cavalry as timid, for "when twenty-five of the enemy are seen anywhere, they are considered in force."[44]

Sherman, now ready to advance, would face a new enemy commander, John B. Hood. President Davis had decided to relieve General Joseph E. Johnston because, as in the past, Johnston, by not revealing his plans, again aroused the suspicion that in truth he had no plans. This had happened when he commanded in Mississippi after the fall of Vicksburg. President Davis had

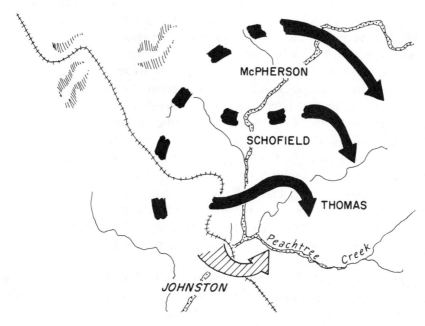

Johnston Turned to Peachtree Creek

then complained to Lee, "I can only learn from him of such vague purposes as were unfolded when he held his army before Richmond." As before, Johnston simply continued his supposedly skillful delaying action. To halt Sherman, the former cavalryman reverted to his plans of the previous year and proposed breaking the enemy's communications with cavalry raids. He wrote Bragg: "We have not cavalry enough. Can you not send such an expedition from East Tennessee or Mississippi?"[45]

General Bragg's response was discouraging, for the Confederacy had no cavalry in East Tennessee and the formidable Forrest in Mississippi was in "proportion to the enemy confronting him much weaker than General Johnston." Upset because Polk had brought to aid Johnston many more men than anticipated, Davis and Bragg were very apprehensive about the safety of Mississippi. They were sure that the commander of Alabama and Mississippi needed all of his forces to protect "the stored and growing supplies" there and also to protect Selma with its valuable arms factories.[46]

Criticisms of Johnston's generalship by Hood and Hardee aggravated Davis's dissatisfaction with Johnston's failure to halt Sherman's advance. Bragg's disappointment that Johnston had not tried his March offensive and Bragg's hostilities toward his old enemies in the Army of Tennessee may have helped him reach a conclusion that the force needed new leadership. Polk's death had eliminated one of his old enemies. He felt that if the President placed Hood in command, the army could take the offensive, especially if Davis also replaced Hardee, another old critic. With Hood in command and Hardee and the other old generals removed, Bragg believed the new leadership would carry out a "new policy" which would make Bragg's old army "invincible."[47]

Davis believed that he had concentrated a major force with Johnston. "Charleston, Savannah, Mobile, Mississippi, and North Alabama were stripped to give him a force which would insure success so speedily that the troops could return to these places in time to prevent disaster." The President, believing Atlanta should have been "best defended by holding some of the strong positions north of it," would have relieved Johnston earlier had he believed the general planned to retreat to Atlanta. But Johnston's considerable skill and his force, though powerful, had not been equal to the task of stopping the more powerful Union army under its capable commander, Sherman.[48]

Though Davis, valuing Hardee, did not accept Bragg's thesis in full, he shared the belief that Johnston possessed sufficient strength and had in fact received too many reinforcements from Mississippi. Even if Johnston should not seek a battle to try to halt Sherman's remorseless advance, the President certainly believed that he could reveal his plans. After a personal visit by Bragg produced no satisfaction, the President wired Johnston: "I wish to hear from you as to present situation, and your plan of operations so specifically as will enable me to anticipate events." Johnston ambiguously replied: "As the enemy has double our number, we must be on the defensive. My plan of operations must, therefore, depend upon that of the enemy. It is mainly to watch for an opportunity to fight to advantage. We are trying to put Atlanta in condition to be held for a day or two by the Georgia militia, that army movements may be freer and wider." To this the adjutant and inspector general replied on July 17: "As you have failed to arrest the advance of the enemy to the vicinity of Atlanta, far in the interior of Georgia, and express no confidence that you can defeat or repel him, you are hereby relieved from the command of the Army and Department of Tennessee, which you will immediately turn over to General Hood." That Hood gained the appointment caused Hardee so much dissatisfaction he asked for a transfer, but at this time Davis refused.[49]

Both Hood and Hardee had worked for Johnston's removal, but Hood's informal links carried more weight. Bragg had supported Hood and opposed his old critic Hardee. Johnston, who had befriended Bragg earlier, had not received any support from him, and certainly none from the disappointed Davis who still blamed him for the loss of Vicksburg. Johnston's removal marked a breaking point in the campaign.

Sherman wrote his wife: "I am glad I beat Johnston, for he had the most exalted reputation with our old army as a strategist." Johnston has retained this reputation ever since, largely founded on his supposed mastery of Fabian strategy in conducting a masterful defense against Sherman.

What then of Johnston's supposed mastery? His admirers, impressed with his secrecy, attribute it to flexibility, but "secrecy was not necessarily evidence of a great strategic mind at work . . . a disturbing looseness to Johnston's planning belies a crafty general employing Fabian strategy to draw Sherman deep within Georgia for destruction." T. L. Connelly concludes that Johnston's "standing was based more upon what he allegedly could have done if he had been given the opportunity than by any real achievement." Johnston never knew what to do and he never developed any specific plan of response. Even "after retreating across the Etowah, Johnston continued to insist that he desired to fight Sherman," but he did not get above the haziness. "If he planned to retreat deliberately across the Chattahoochee, he had misled the government," Connelly correctly observes, but "probably Johnston did not intend to mislead the government." The fact remains "that Johnston had a relatively limited capacity as an overall planner, and in effect had not decided." Johnston, even after five months of campaigning, was "ill pre-pared," knowing but "little of the terrain," and thus erroneously equated his situation with that of Lee's in Virginia. His "narrow administrative scope" also seriously limited his effectiveness. And, save for the government's disas-trous decision to replace him with so rash a man as Hood, it was just as well that he was removed. His replacement by Hood, who failed so dramatically, thus helped to conserve Johnston's reputation, one bolstered by his own personal magnetism. In addition he found many supporters because his feud with Davis made the President's enemies his friends.[50]

Johnston's successor, John Bell Hood, was a mere thirty-three-years old. His leadership offered the promise of more aggressive but perhaps less crafty action than Johnston's. "All lion, none of the fox," Robert E. Lee had said of Hood. Mary Chesnut referred to a "fierce light," she thought, "the light of battle" in Hood's eyes. Born in Kentucky, Hood had served six years in Texas, in effect moved his home of record, and considered that state his home. A West Pointer, he enjoyed the most spectacular step-by-step rise in rank of any Civil War officer; he began as a first lieutenant and distinguished himself on at least a dozen fields, reaping rewards of promotion after promo-tion. He attained general grade status on March 3, 1862, then sequentially as brigade and division commander he showed himself a man of considerable ability, efficiency, doggedness, and charisma. At Gettysburg he sustained a severe wound that permanently disabled his left arm, but he could not bear to be apart from his troops when two months later they departed to enter combat with Longstreet's corps at Chickamauga. In that battle Hood suffered a leg wound that necessitated amputation on the field. Still he persisted on active duty, although his walk at best was a hobble aided by a crutch and he could sit a horse only by being strapped into the saddle. And now, raised to full general, to date from July 18, 1864, Hood immediately changed the army's policy. Most federal officers believed that they could trounce the Confederates in the head-on clashes they expected Hood to initiate, and thus they, too, echoed the cheers given by the large faction of men in the Confed-erate Army elated by the change.

On the death of Polk, Davis promoted Lieutenant General Alexander P.

Stewart, one of Polk's division leaders, to corps command. A West Pointer, Stewart had early left the regular army to become a professor of mathematics and physics in Tennessee colleges. As he had served with distinction in all of the battles of the Army of Tennessee, he was a natural choice to succeed Polk. To replace Hood, Davis chose Lieutenant General Stephen D. Lee, then on departmental duty in Mississippi. Promotion to lieutenant general had come at age thirty to this talented and experienced West Pointer, the youngest man on either side to gain so high a Civil War rank. Moving from the artillery in Virginia, he served as a brigadier during the Vicksburg campaigns and thereafter had become a major general commanding all cavalry in Mississippi until he took over the department when Polk joined Johnston. With the ever-reliable, though disaffected, Hardee completing the trio of corps commanders, Hood would be well served.

Hood assumed his new responsibilities with instructions from Secretary Seddon to "be wary no less than bold" and to try "to cut the communications of the enemy." Like Johnston, Hood asked for raids by Forrest; but when these were denied, he, unlike Johnston, attempted to do the work himself by promptly sending his own cavalry under his dynamic twenty-seven-year-old cavalry leader, Joseph Wheeler. The indefatigable, ever active, and thrice-wounded Wheeler would lead the bulk of the army's cavalry north against Sherman's long and tenuous railroad communications.[51]

On July 19, the day after Hood's promotion, Sherman made "a bold push for Atlanta." The next day, catching Sherman's forces on the move, Hood attacked Thomas on the north but, after "close and severe" fighting, the Federals beat off the rebels in the Battle of Peachtree Creek. Sherman then immediately moved Schofield and McPherson around to the east side of the

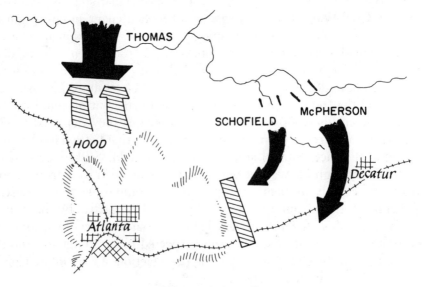

Frontal Assault

city in order to reach and break up the railroad which ran east to Augusta and Charleston. Two days later Hood displayed what he had learned from serving under Lee when he used Hardee's corps to turn Sherman's left in the Battle of Atlanta. Sherman thus described it: "The enemy appeared suddenly out of the dense woods in heavy masses on our extreme left . . . and for some hours our left flank was completely enveloped." The fighting that resulted was continuous until night with heavy loss on both sides; but the attack was beaten off and Sherman's army enveloped two sides of Atlanta. In spite of Hood's near success, Sherman wrote his wife: "I am glad when the enemy attacks, for the advantage then is with us."[52]

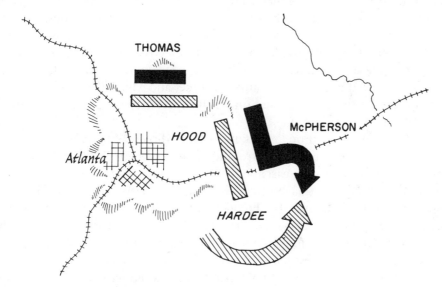

Hardee Turns McPherson

In the Battle of Peachtree Creek the 20,000 Federals engaged suffered 1,779 casualties to Hood's 4,796. In the Battle of Atlanta the 30,000 Federals lost 3,722 while Hood lost perhaps as many as 10,000 casualties among his 40,000 engaged. Hood could not afford such casualties and abandoned his attacks. Though Hood's turning movement at the Battle of Atlanta was well conceived, Sherman's forces again exhibited the agility of veteran armies and the difficulty involved in hurting them.

General McPherson lost his life in the engagement. In replacing him Sherman "made no mistake" when he chose the able, one-armed veteran of Gettysburg, O. O. Howard, "a Christian, elegant gentlemen, and conscientious soldier." Howard University is named after this versatile officer who, after the war, headed the Freedman's Bureau and closed his military career on the frontier in a memorable pursuit of Chief Joseph of the Nez Perce. The selection of Howard to command the Army of the Tennessee so miffed Fighting Joe Hooker that, to Sherman's great relief, he asked to be relieved.[53]

In Georgia, on July 28, the last of Hood's rash onslaughts against Sherman's forces took place. From early afternoon until dark two Confederate corps slammed hopelessly into the Union lines. The Federals lost just under 600 men to perhaps as many as 5,000 southern casualties. At last the Confederates abandoned the assaults and pulled back into Atlanta's fortifications to withstand the siege. Almost all the Confederate soldiers performed their duty stoically, though a very few finally had enough and broke to the rear. One such episode of battle fatigue gives rise to the story: "What are you running for?" shouted one Georgia officer to a fleeing soldier. Without breaking the pace the soldier shouted back, "Bekase I kaint fly!"[54]

Operations reached a stalemate. Hood, losing about 15,000 men compared to about 6,000 for Sherman, had failed to make any impression on the hasty field fortifications erected by Sherman's big, well-led army of veteran troops. Hood's attacking might possibly have been effective in pushing an army of equal size back a few miles; but only at the Seven Days' Battles had such assaults succeeded in repelling a superior force, and McClellan's army did not have in those battles the relative numerical superiority of Sherman's. Now it was only a matter of time.

Never having planned on "attacking Atlanta direct," Sherman had always intended "to make a circuit, destroying all its railroads." After thoroughly breaking the railroad to the east, he then sought to cut Atlanta's last rail link, that to Macon. To do this he moved around the city's west flank in early August but was again met by Hood and, as usual, each side intrenched. Sherman then had his heavy artillery "hammer away" at the city while, he said, "I think of the next move." He did not want a "further prolongation" of the line, preferring "to cast loose" from his base and "make a desolating circle around Atlanta." While deciding what to do, he convinced Hood he was

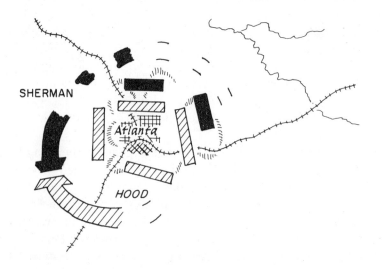

Atlanta Campaign Stalemated

extending his lines south to force him "to give up Atlanta or fight at great disadvantages." But in August, rather than prolonging his line or "making a wide circuit in this hot weather," Sherman tried cavalry raids against the Macon railroad. These availed him little, no more than the raid of Wheeler's Confederate cavalry on his communications helped Hood. Wheeler now was in East Tennessee, which Sherman regarded as "a good place for him to break down his horses, and a poor place to steal new ones."[55]

Before Sherman began the now-necessary casting loose from his base to move around Atlanta, he and Grant wanted alternative places ready on the coast, in Florida, at Savannah, Georgia, or Mobile. Sherman's delay was not matched elsewhere as General Washburn in Memphis continued effectively to carry out his duty distracting the Confederates in Mississippi. To do this he had a capable leader, Major General Andrew J. Smith, who had returned with his division from Banks's ill-fated Red River expedition. First ordered to move by water against Mobile, Smith was redirected by Sherman to move against Forrest to avenge Sturgis's defeat.

In late June, Andrew J. Smith had departed from Memphis with 14,000 troops and on July 5 had turned southward from LaGrange, Tennessee. To oppose them the Confederates could assemble only 7,000 troops, mostly from Forrest's cavalry command, under Lieutenant General Stephen D. Lee, who had not then joined the army in Georgia. Despite efforts by Lee to gather any additional troops, he was unable to effect a larger concentration against the Union raid.

Smith moved into Mississippi in close formation. A small skirmish erupted above Ripley on July 7, but then the Federals proceeded unopposed through

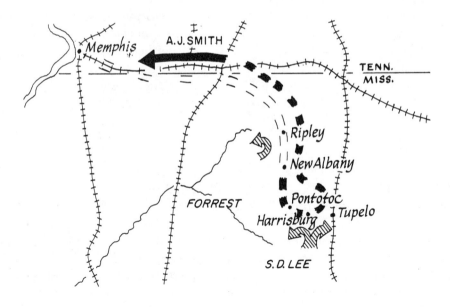

Smith's Raid

New Albany to a position just north of Pontotoc by July 10. After several days of attempting to push farther southward, Smith abandoned his efforts and marched suddenly toward Tupelo. Lee and Forrest determined to attack Smith on the morning of the 14th. The Confederates assaulted on schedule, but in an uncoordinated and piecemeal fashion. Lee's men charged and, after moving back and forth for nearly three hours, finally retired into defensive lines. The Federals, except for pushing one brigade slightly forward, made no countermovements. During the night the northerners burned what remained of Harrisburg, unwittingly providing the Confederate artillerymen with good, silhouetted targets. The southerners also tried a small night attack, but accomplished little. Nevertheless, Smith yielded the strategic victory to the Confederates, electing then to retreat all the way back to Memphis. The battle satisfied neither side, for the Confederates had failed to achieve a hoped-for destruction of Smith's force and at the same time had been kept occupied and away from Johnston's aid; but the Federals were denied any chance to wreak devastating havoc in Mississippi's grain-growing region. Now Forrest again had freedom to roam with his cavalry.

But the Confederates never did manage to do any effective damage to Sherman's supply lines. The task was too big for the available cavalry forces. Hood really needed Wheeler with his army, and the constant federal raids into Mississippi so effectively distracted Davis that he long kept Forrest committed to protecting the South's vulnerable logistic base in that state. Two years before, raids against communications had become one of the major prescriptions for the defeat of Union advances in the West. The erosion of cavalry superiority together with the menace of the raids in Mississippi deprived the Confederates of their hitherto powerful defensive measure.

The task of destruction of Sherman's communications was difficult in any case, because an elaborate system of blockhouses, one at every bridge, protected the rail lines, and at every railway station between the federal army and Nashville the North had posted garrisons of infantry. Since they could employ trains to concentrate quickly an effective fighting force at any point, any raiding party had to work fast and retreat rapidly. The speed and ease with which Sherman's men repaired the occasional damage dazzled the southerners. With remarkable efficiency, Sherman's repair crews could get disabled trains rolling again so rapidly that a legend grew among the Confederates that Sherman carried duplicates of all the bridges. In truth, his wagons did carry ample supplies of cross-ties, bridge timbers, and rails. The Federals enjoyed such an embarrassment of riches that rather than waste time with wrecked rolling stock of any kind, they simply tumbled the locomotive and cars off the track to make room for the next train. Exaggerated rumors held that somewhere below Chattanooga so much wreckage lay beside a long embankment that a man could walk five miles on the debris without setting foot on the ground. On one occasion repair crews worked with such speed and skill that they replaced a 90-foot-high, 900-foot-long bridge spanning the Chattahoochee in four-and-one-half days. And they did not even need the spare parts they usually carried: all the timbers they used were living trees when the job began. One tall tale further illustrates though overstates: A Confederate soldier happily told another he had heard that "General Wheeler had blown up the tunnel near Dalton, and that the Yanks would have to retreat because they could get no more rations." To which the other replied, "Oh, hell! Don't you know that old Sherman carries a duplicate tunnel along with him?"[56]

In Virginia Halleck's pessimism about threats to Washington proved prophetic when, on July 24, Jubal Early's corps scored a morale-raising victory over a federal force in the Valley in the Second Battle of Kernstown. The Federals stood firm for a time, but finally retreated in some confusion with Early in slow pursuit. Early's men wrecked miles of railroad and fought numerous skirmishes against momentarily hapless Federals. The Confederates even prepared once more to cross the Potomac.

Meanwhile Grant readied a major effort against the Confederates at Petersburg. Having failed in an effort to extend his flank and break the railroad going south to Weldon, North Carolina, and only temporarily broken Richmond's railroads by cavalry raids, he planned an operation directly against Lee's position. As Grant had surveyed the problem of the siege, he had seen two alternatives—"by a bold and decisive attack to break through the enemy's center" or a turning movement, in which "the whole Army of the Potomac, with ten days' rations," would "march around Petersburg and come in above." Meade recommended the former, explaining: "The movement on the enemy's right flank as suggested is liable to the objection of separating your forces with the enemy between the two parts," and "having to abandon the communications of this army." The old difficulty of turning an enemy by a raid would, Meade felt, be insuperable, because his army would be in the rear of Lee's which would have rail communications north of Richmond and more supplies stockpiled than the Army of the Potomac's ten days' rations. In that case it would be the Union army which was turned and must attack to extricate itself. Meade saw "the danger after crossing the Appomattox that the enemy may be found strongly posted behind Swift Run, requiring further flank movements, more time, further separation from a base, and more hazard in reopening communications, our experience since crossing the Rapidan having proved the facility with which the enemy can interpose to check an onward movement." Grant accepted Meade's recommendation, and waited for an opportunity to break the line of Lee's fortifications.[57]

While studying the problem of the siege, Grant had been most reluctant to be distracted from his Petersburg operations by events in the Valley and around Washington, unless Wright's and Hunter's forces could break the Virginia Central Railroad to the Valley. In stressing raids to break Richmond's rail communications, Grant at one point projected raids south toward Weldon and westward to Danville. At the same time, unable to count on Wright and Hunter, he planned a combined cavalry and infantry movement above the James to break the railroads north of the city. But Grant was not relying exclusively upon raids against Richmond's communications and had had minute examinations made of the enemy's lines about Petersburg, looking for a point at which to make a breakthrough. No real weak points being discovered, Grant decided, in spite of Meade's reservations, to rely upon the mine being laid under rebel lines by the men of Burnside's corps.[58]

As Grant ordered the raiders to the railroads north of Richmond, he saw that the expedition might "cause such a weakening of the enemy at Petersburg as to make an attack there possible, in which case," he told Meade, "you would want to spring Burnside's mine." His raid on the railroads failed but, he reported, finding that it drew all the enemy "forces from Petersburg except three divisions, I determined to attack and try to carry the latter place," using Burnside's mine.[59]

During July digging had gone forward under the Confederate lines. Within three weeks after the digging had commenced, the shaft ran twenty feet underground and extended more than 500 feet forward until it was squarely beneath the Confederate redoubt. The miners then dug a seventy-five-foot shaft running across the tunnel's end, thus making it form a "T", with the shaft, the shank, and the crossbar running along beneath the rebel works. They filled it with four tons of powder placed in various well-selected spots and connected together with spliced fuses. With Confederate attention drawn toward the operation north of Richmond, Union forces exploded the mine on July 30.

At first the blast was delayed, the fuse having gone out. A brave sergeant, Harry Reese, the mine boss, crawled in to find the trouble. He and a lieutenant, Jacob Douty, who went in later to check on Reese and to bring the necessary materials, respliced and relit the fuse. And at 4:45 A.M. it happened. "It seemed to occur in slow motion," as described by Bruce Catton, "first a long, deep rumble, like summer thunder rolling along a faraway horizon, then a swaying and swelling the ground up ahead, with the solid earth rising to form a rounded hill, everything seeming very gradual and leisurely. Then the rounded hill broke apart, and a prodigious spout of flame and black smoke went up toward the sky, and the air was full of enormous clods of earth as big as houses, of brass cannon and detached artillery wheels, of wrecked caissons and fluttering tents and weirdly tumbling human bodies; and there was a crash 'like the noise of great thunders,' followed by other, lesser explosions."[60]

"A fort and several hundred yards of earth work with men and cannon was literally hurled a hundred feet in the air," wrote a southern soldier as he recalled viewing what he termed "probably the most terrific explosion ever known in this country." The painfully dug 586-foot-long tunnel had allowed the Unionists to blast a crater 170 feet long, sixty to eighty feet wide, and thirty feet deep. Possibly 278 Confederates were killed.[61]

A furious charge followed but the secessionists rallied and fought furiously to close the gap. The black northern units originally scheduled and trained to make the leading assaults were superseded by less-ready white troops at the last minute and this proved a costly command blunder. Further, the Union had gathered an inadequate mass for the total effort but, ironically, channeled too many men though too narrow a gap, thereby blunting the thrust and losing precious time. By early afternoon the bluecoats subsided. The North had lost 4,000 men to 1,500 southerners. Grant summed it up to Halleck: It was "the saddest affair I have witnessed in the war," and added, "Such an opportunity for carrying fortifications I have never seen and do not expect again to have." And so this second major frontal assault upon Petersburg therefore ended, again in failure.[62]

Thus Grant made his only frontal assault of the siege, one into which he was lured by the hope that the effect of the mine would make a breakthrough possible. Compared with Cold Harbor and earlier battles, this attack did not produce heavy casualties. But casualties were a sensitive matter, especially as the presidential election was drawing near. Lincoln made this clear when he read a message Grant sent to Sherman in which he expressed concern about Early's men reinforcing the Confederates in Georgia. Grant had written that he would make a "desperate effort" to hold Lee with fewer men. Lincoln had noticed this and telegraphed: I hope "the effort shall not be desperate in the sense of great loss of life." Lincoln was, in fact, resigned to the prolonged siege of Richmond, something he had foreseen. He did not urge Grant to assault but rather enjoined him to "hold on with a bull-dog gripe, and chew & choke, as much as possible."[63]

The Confederates meanwhile managed another token invasion of Pennsylvania. Fragments of Early's cavalry rode into Chambersburg. They demanded $500,000 in currency or $100,000 in gold in further reparation for Hunter's Shenandoah depredations; and when the people could not raise the sum, they burned the town. They then raided from town to town, with a federal force in hot pursuit, and escaped back into West Virginia by August 3. Other harassing operations also continued in the Valley.

Realizing at last the importance of this line of operations, Grant kept two corps based near Washington and, after giving Halleck temporary command during the Chambersburg raid, created under Sheridan a unified command, the Middle Division, embracing northern Virginia, Washington, West Virginia, Maryland, and Pennsylvania. Though belatedly hoping that Sheridan could "put himself south of the enemy and follow him to the death," Grant still looked to his original objective, "a complete smash-up of the enemy's roads about Gordonsville and Charlottesville." Grant considered this of immediate importance because the enemy was "gathering in their crops in the Valley counties, and sending them to Richmond by canal and railroad." All agreed, for Halleck wrote: "I concur with General Sheridan, and think that much greater damage can be done to the enemy by destroying his crops and communications north of the James than on the south."[64]

Though Grant assembled nearly 50,000 men on the Valley line of operations, his basic objective remained that of exhausting the enemy's resources for the support of his armies. Sheridan's instructions reflected this: "Give the enemy no rest, and if it is possible to follow to the Virginia Central road, follow that far. Do all the damage to railroads and crops you can. Carry off stock of all descriptions, and negroes, so as to prevent further planting. If the war is to last another year we want the Shenandoah Valley to remain a barren waste." But since Sheridan's army was believed to be only slightly larger than Early's, Grant instructed Sheridan to take care and not "attack fortifications." To Sheridan, Grant wrote: "I would not have you make an attack with the advantage against you, but would prefer just the course you seem to be pursuing—that is, pressing closely upon the enemy, and when he moves, follow him up, being ready at all times to pounce upon him if he detaches any considerable force" to Richmond.[65]

Sheridan's stalemated position in the north end of the Valley became for Grant as important a part of the campaign as the deadlock at Petersburg. He was anxious to keep his intrenched opponent from further reinforcing Early and was even hopeful of compelling Lee "to recall a large portion of Early's force." If Grant could make this happen, Sheridan was to "strike suddenly and hard." In mid-August Grant again planned a raid by Hancock's corps against the railroads north of Richmond. In addition to facilitating a cavalry raid against the Virginia Central Railroad, Grant directed that Hancock's infantry "consume or destroy all the forage and provisions" found. Grant told Hancock not to worry about communications: "With the force at your command you will always be able to get back to that point or some other on the James River. . . . You can always be supplied by steamers." Grant also hoped that this raid against "a sensitive point with the enemy" would produce the desired results.[66]

But the plan was complex; if Hancock's move induced the enemy again to strip the Petersburg defenses, Grant planned to move a corps south to work on destroying the Weldon railway "til recalled, or forced away by the enemy's operations." This is precisely what happened. Hancock failed, but he opened the way for General Warren's corps not just to destroy but to dig in astride the railway. This threat to Richmond's southern communications had, Grant rationalized, produced a very desirable effect, even if not the intended one. "I am not so particular about holding the Weldon road permanently," he wrote, "as I am to destroy it effectually, and to force the enemy to attack us with the advantages on our side." The Confederates did attack and Grant reinforced by bringing Hancock all the way from north of the James.[67]

As a result of this Battle of the Weldon Railroad, beginning on August 18, Union troops did dig in on the railway and, in spite of heavy casualties and strong counterattacks, permanently blocked this railway, so important for supplying Richmond and Lee's army. On August 25 a reinforced Confederate corps slashed into federal infantry, surprised while at work destroying the rails south of Petersburg. The Union troops were badly defeated, one combat-fatigued division fleeing in panic. Since the beginning of the campaign, its three brigades had lost nine brigade commanders and forty regimental commanders. The southerners drove back the Union forces who lost 2,372 men compared with 720 for the Confederates. The Weldon Railroad continued in use with wagons hauling supplies around the break. By other routes, also, supplies continued to reach the Confederate capital and its defenders.[68]

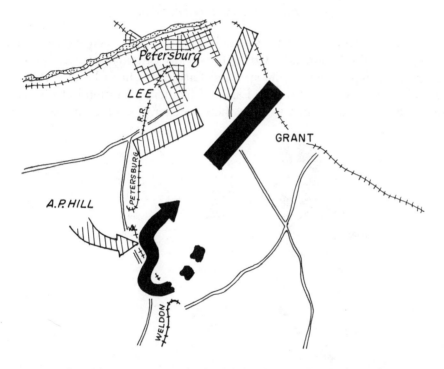

Conclusion of Struggle Which Broke Weldon Railroad

Grant felt little disappointment, having expected "no great results" from the movement other than to "demonstrate to the enemy that he has now the minimum garrison possible to hold his present lines with, and that to hold his roads he must re-enforce" from Early's army in the Valley.[69]

Hancock's raid and the Battle of the Weldon Railroad did not affect the situation in the Valley nor provide Sheridan with an opportunity to attack. The Confederates broke the deadlock. Made overconfident by Sheridan's caution, Early moved forward with less than 19,000 men. He met Sheridan's 48,000 men, also advancing. On September 19 the two forces collided. After a struggle in which Union cavalry overlapped his flank, Early fell back,

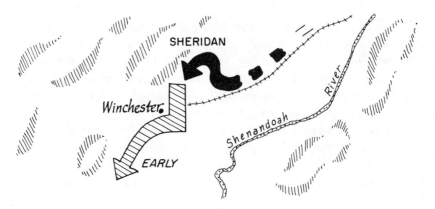

Early Flanked by Sheridan

abandoning Winchester. Proportionately his losses had been severe, 4,600 to only 5,000 on the Union side. Characteristically Sheridan pressed his advantage and, on September 22, he attacked Early at Fisher's Hill, twelve miles south of Winchester. Distracting Early with a demonstration in front, Sheridan again used his cavalry to turn the Confederates. Once more Early re-

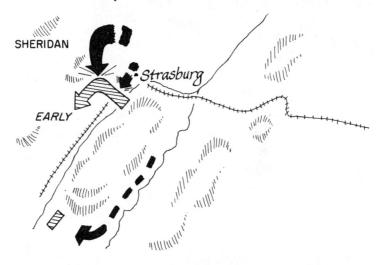

Sheridan Flanks Early

treated and, though he lost few men, fell back far up the Valley. Sheridan followed, destroying crops and barns and driving off livestock.

Sheridan himself reported his success rather matter-of-factly: "I have destroyed over 2,000 barns filled with wheat, hay and farming implements; over 70 mills, filled with flour and wheat; have driven in front of the army over 4,000 head of stock, and have killed and issued to the troops not less than 3,000 sheep. . . . The people here are getting sick of the war." One historian called it an "alliance of famine" in which "mills, barns, hay, wheat, straw were given to flames, . . . and even the county almshouse came in for its share of pillaging." But a federal officer explained: "Should complaints come in from the citizens . . . tell them they have furnished too many meals to guerrillas to expect much sympathy." Guerrilla activity had been continuous in the Valley as it had in northern Virginia. Sheridan reported: "Since I came into the Valley, from Harper's Ferry up to Harrisonburg, every train, every small party, every straggler has been bushwhacked."[70]

The successful operation had made Sheridan a confirmed believer in the strategy of exhaustion. He wrote Grant: "I believe concentration at vital points, and the destruction of subsistence resources to be everything." Sheridan's victory at Fisher's Hill elated Grant, who now, foreseeing the destruction of the enemy's crops and railroads, told Sheridan: "Keep on, and your work will cause the fall of Richmond." With Early in retreat Grant requested: "If you can possibly subsist your army to the front for a few days more, do it, and make a great effort to destroy the roads about Charlottesville and the canal wherever your cavalry can reach it." But Sheridan found the transportation difficulties too great to move to Charlottesville and said: "The best policy will be to let the burning of the crops of the Valley be the end of this campaign, and let some of this army go somewhere else."[71]

Fortunately for Grant and Sheridan the forces had not departed before the reinforced Early counterattacked in mid-October. Finding Sheridan near Winchester, the indomitable Confederate leader carried out a fine turning movement against an army without a general. Sheridan was away in Washington, conferring about the disposition of his troops, which he now thought he no longer needed against Early. The rebel turning movement succeeded brilliantly, one entire Union corps fleeing the battlefield in hopeless panic.

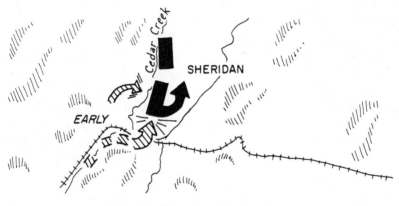

Early's Turning Movement

The reliable Horatio Wright rallied the remaining two corps, delayed the enemy, and covered the disheartened Union retreat. At this point Sheridan made his theatrical appearance, riding up from Winchester, waving his hat, and rallying his troops as he came. Red-faced, and his horse all flecked with foam, he charged into his dispirited men, who had greeted his appearance

with cheers, and shouted: "God *damn* you, don't cheer me! There's lots of
fight in you men yet! Come up, God damn you! Come up!" The re-forming
Union forces counterattacked, catching many Confederate troops looting the
plentiful Union supplies, and once more defeated the skillful Early. The
campaign in the Valley ended; with the region now denuded of supplies, the
major forces of both sides evacuated.[72]

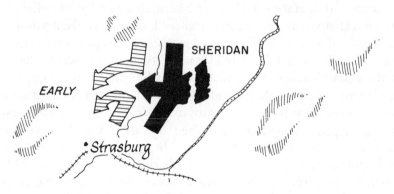

Sheridan's Counterattack

☆   ☆

When this dramatic Valley campaign was about to begin, Union forces at
last had attacked Mobile, one of the Confederacy's final two open ports. The
naval effort to close the port had the assistance of only 4,000 men from the
Army. Lack of troops limited the Army to this auxiliary role and precluded
any effort to take the town or advance inland toward Hood's rear. Canby had
committed his forces that remained, after sending almost 20,000 men to Virginia, to assisting A. J. Smith's offensive against Forrest and as a reserve
should Kirby Smith succeed in crossing Richard Taylor's 9,000 men to the
east side of the Mississippi. The vigilant river patrol of the federal Navy and
the near mutiny of the troops ordered to cross delayed the Confederate effort
until, in a mix-up of orders, it was abandoned. Only General Taylor, without
his men, reached the east bank where he assumed command. But Kirby
Smith's attempt did have the effect of diverting Union forces and precluding
a really menacing Union movement by sea into Alabama. Again the trans-
Mississippi had absorbed Union attention and aided the defense of the eastern
Confederacy.[73]

The Union Mobile expedition was commanded by the Union's greatest
sailor, David G. Farragut, who had behind him more than a half century of
uninterrupted naval service. Two old brickwork forts, Morgan on the western
tip of Mobile point and Gaines opposite on Dauphin Island, protected Mobile. Together they commanded the 2,000-yard-wide channel at the bay's
entrance. During the war the Confederates had strengthened the defenses by
adding some powerful rifled pieces, increased the garrisons, erected Fort

Powell to the northwest of Dauphin Island to guard the pass to Mississippi Sound, and heavily mined all but a 500-yard safe passage through the main channel. During the Civil War, mines, highly refined by the able and inventive Brigadier General Gabriel J. Rains, were called "torpedoes." Rains devised the system at Mobile whereby enemy vessels trying to cross the bay had either to get through the minefield or pass directly under the guns of Fort Gaines.

Farragut's force seized the harbor on August 5, and on the 22nd reduced Fort Morgan. It did so in a naval battle during which the courageous and determined Farragut gained immortal fame by shouting, "Damn the torpedoes! Full speed ahead!" Though "Damn the torpedoes" has an incredibly reckless sound, Farragut's subordinate, Captain Thornton A. Jenkins, observed, after the admiral committed his ships to action, Farragut did "the only safe thing possible to do." An attempt to turn back under enemy fire would have been far worse. The rebels sent out a powerful ironclad ram vessel to try to stop the invaders' ships. "The heavier vessels seemed to contend with each other for the glory of sinking the daring rebel ram, by running themselves up on her decks," wrote one Yankee commander. Two big screw sloops, first the *Monongahela* and then the *Lackawanna*, slammed into the southern ironclad but each suffered more damage than it inflicted. The damaged *Lackawanna* continued its efforts but got into the way and almost hit Farragut's flagship. "Can you say 'For God's sake' by signal?" Farragut exasperatedly barked to a nearby officer. Assured so, he directed, "Then say to the *Lackawanna*, 'For God's sake, get out of the way and anchor!' "

The Union vessels concentrated their fire upon the Confederate flagship *Tennessee*, and three hot hours of fighting finally proved decisive. "Hanging on to us like a dog," the *Tennessee*'s pilot proclaimed, as one Union monitor maintained a position just fifty yards astern. "Firing the two 11-inch guns in her forward turret like pocket-pistols," she wrecked the *Tennessee*. Impotent and "lying like a log in the water," she capitulated and this doomed the two forts. They surrendered after further stubborn but brief resistance.

Though the Confederates now had lost their sea outlet, Mobile persevered until the end. Snug behind inner forts and the torpedo barrier, the city proved impervious to naval assault. The Confederate garrison remained until April 12, 1865, when it retreated into Mississippi. Farragut had accomplished a spectacular achievement, nonetheless, by destroying Mobile's usefulness for blockade runners. Union casualties numbered 319, with 145 killed, and one ship sunk, the *Tecumseh*, the greatest single ship disaster in the U.S. Navy until World War II. The rebel fleet lost 12 killed, 20 wounded, and 280 captured, including an admiral and a captain. But, otherwise, the distraction, thus achieved for Sherman's benefit, mattered little because the Union could spare only a small land force to aid Farragut. There were not nearly enough troops for an advance up the Alabama River. The few available tried, but without success, running up the final cost of the Union operations at Mobile to 1,417 casualties. As Grant lamented, "I had tried for more than two years to have an expedition sent against Mobile when its possession by us would have been of great advantage. It finally cost [many] lives to take it when its possession was of no importance."[74]

In another episode during August the Confederates turned the tables on Union western forces. On August 21 Forrest raided the city of Memphis, almost capturing Major General Cadwallader C. Washburn himself. When Washburn's predecessor, General Stephen Hurlbut, learned of the raid and that Washburn had barely avoided capture by escaping through a window wearing only his night shirt, he commented: "They removed me from command because I couldn'tkeep Forrest out of West Tennessee, and now Washburn can't keep him out of his own bedroom." But Washburn's energetic, if unsuccessful, efforts to defeat Forrest fulfilled the purpose of distracting Forrest away from Sherman's hundreds of miles of vulnerable railroad communications. From the federal viewpoint it was better for Forrest to be chasing Washburn out of his bedroom than to be raiding Sherman's communications.[75]

In Virginia the Confederate ranger, Lieutenant Colonel John S. Mosby, continued raiding Union communications. More guerrillas than raiders, Mosby's small band immobilized large Union forces. They continued achieving good results through 1864, although some of the Confederate high command lost its appreciation for guerrilla activity. Earlier praised by Seddon and Lee, the partisans eventually accumulated bitter critics who swayed others to conclude, as did Lee, that they concentrated too much on sutler's wagons, terrorized citizens, and would not fight when needed to augment conventional operations. Too many persons misunderstood remarks like that of Baron von Massow, a Prussian lieutenant who served briefly with Mosby, who once declared, "Ah, this is not fighting; it's horse stealing." Years later Mosby wrote to a lifelong friend, "The North has always given our command more credit for the damage done than the South has. . . . I can say, like Hannibal, that my history has been written by my enemies. The best testimony in our favor are the dispatches of Grant, Sheridan, and Halleck."[76]

Even at sea Confederate raiders still enjoyed success. Thirty-five miles off the eastern shore of Maryland the C.S.S. *Florida* seized four prizes. On August 6 the C.S.S. *Tallahassee* left Wilmington, North Carolina, now the South's last seaport, and made a three-week cruise during which she garnered more than thirty prizes.

All of these raids, including Early's to Washington, produced minor consequences compared with Sherman's around to the south of Atlanta. On August 28 Sherman rapidly moved his three armies southward toward the railroad. Taken unaware, Hood sent Hardee's corps south to hold the railroad. Hardee met Howard's Army of the Tennessee intrenched at Jonesboro and Hood directed Hardee to have "the men go at the enemy with bayonets fixed, determined to drive everything they may come against." But Hardee's attack failed and Sherman's other two armies, north on the railroad, separated

Hardee from Hood and the army's other two corps in Atlanta. His communications cut, on September 1 Hood evacuated Atlanta, joining Hardee to the south on the railroad to Macon. Occupying the city on September 2, Sherman gleefully telegraphed Washington: "Atlanta is ours, and fairly won." He followed Hood a short distance, but, finding the enemy "in another of his well-chosen and hastily constructed lines," decided "not to push much farther on this raid."[77]

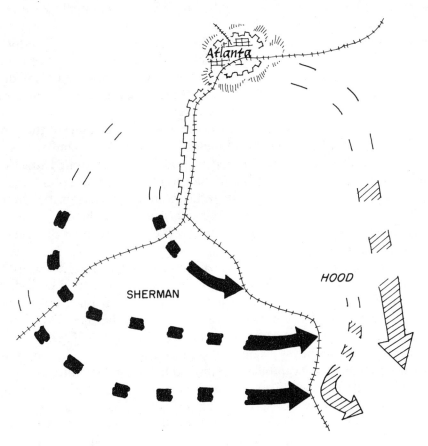

Hood's Communications Cut

With the fall of Atlanta, Grant's strategy secured its first triumph. A major city as well as a railway hub and supply depot, Atlanta had both logistical and symbolic significance. The existence elsewhere of another east-west railway link did, however, limit Atlanta's importance. This still-unbroken line ran through Macon, some 100 miles south of Atlanta. Although Union forces had closed the port of Mobile, the major manufacturing centers of Selma and Augusta remained untouched and still enjoyed uninterrupted rail connections. The fall of Atlanta had hurt Confederate logistics badly but not fatally. A major operational achievement, the capture of Atlanta produced only limited strategic results. Federal forces had taken the city despite the failure of a major feature of Grant's plans, for the belated occupation of Mobile Bay had very little impact upon the Confederate concentration against Sherman. Banks's failure on the Red River had truly defeated Grant's intent to have a powerful army in Johnston's rear.

Grant's own operations in Virginia enjoyed even less success than Sherman's. His army in the enemy's rear had taken the field on time and in full strength, but Butler's inept handling had nullified its potentially great effect. Like Sherman, Grant had managed to keep all of his opponents' forces committed to his front. No repeat of Chickamauga occurred, Grant's efforts to defeat Lee in battle failed, and he became deadlocked in a siege. His exterior position south and east of Richmond exposed Washington to a Confederate concentration, a situation of which Lee and Davis dramatically availed themselves in Early's raid to the outskirts of Washington.

In a sense Grant's campaign realized the worst expectations of the professional soldiers. Butler, the political general, bungled badly and with disastrous effect, and efforts to hurt Lee's army with essentially frontal attacks met the bloody repulse which Professor Mahan and the experience of the war had taught them to expect. In addition, the siege operations against Richmond and Petersburg were not only just as inconclusive as Lincoln and Halleck had expected but Early's raids confirmed their apprehensions about the danger of operating on exterior lines.

With only one of Richmond's railroads cut, Grant's strategic success was limited to Sheridan's September devastation in the Valley. His lack of a tactical victory against Lee's army indicated political failure. Public disappointment with Grant's campaign became a factor at the end of May when a small group of disaffected radicals nominated Fremont for President. Soon afterward, the Republicans renominated Lincoln without serious opposition. He ran as a Union party candidate committed to saving the Union by winning the war. But the Democrats delayed their convention, carefully watching the rising peace sentiment in the country. To Grant's costly and apparently fruitless victories was added the embarrassment of Early's raid. Many people clearly perceived what they regarded as the incompetence of the Lincoln administration, and powerful radicals in his own party began planning a late-September convention to find another nominee to lead the party. At the end of August the Democratic convention wrote a peace platform, but nominated McClellan who expressed a firm, personal commitment to continuing the war. Nevertheless, many observers foresaw a Democratic victory in the fall. It looked as if Lee's strategy, to "resist manfully" until the North tired of the war, was working.

On September 2 three important newspaper editors, including the famous Horace Greeley, wrote letters to northern governors promoting the shelving of Lincoln. Then, at that critical moment, Atlanta fell and this visible military success changed the political climate. Subsequently, with this new climate, reinforced by Sheridan's victories over Early, Fremont withdrew from the race and the peace plank in the Democratic platform became a greater liability to McClellan.

Sherman's operational success had thus become a political one as well. It also laid the foundation for a strategic move which fundamentally extended the means of accomplishing the strategy of exhaustion which the anaconda plan had as its objective. With the recent furtherance of this strategy brought about by the closing of Mobile, raids would expand the scope and means of executing it. As conceived by Grant and Sherman, these raids would be carried out not by cavalry but by a balanced army of infantry, cavalry, and artillery. Sherman had as his next task to conduct this raid, but a dramatic Confederate campaign accompanied its execution, a campaign which would test all of the elements in Grant's strategy and exhibit fully the strength and versatility of Grant's strategic concepts.

Sherman took his first step in preparing his raid by the distinctive way he dealt with Atlanta. On September 7 he ordered its total evacuation by the citizenry. Hood protested vehemently, but Sherman replied, "You cannot qualify war in harsher terms than I will. War is cruelty, and you cannot refine it. . . . You might as well appeal against the thunderstorm as against these terrible hardships of war. They are inevitable." Those persons who preferred could go south, Hood's men assisting them as best they could; the rest had to go north. Between September 11 and September 20 they left, some 446 families totaling about 1,600 people. Thus Atlanta not only fell, it disappeared, though later to rise phoenix-like from its ashes, for, when Sherman finally left, he burned it. But these preparations and the repose he allowed his army presented Hood with an opportunity to seize the initiative.[78]

1. Sherman to Halleck, June 2, 4, 23, 1864, *O.R.*, XXXVIII, pt. 4, 385, 401, 572–73; Johnston to Davis, July 8, 1864, *ibid.*, pt. 5, 869; W. T. Sherman to J. Sherman, June 9, 1864, *Sherman Letters*, 236.

2. Polk to Johnston, June 13, 1864, *O.R.*, XXXVIII, pt. 4, 773; Sherman to Stanton, June 16, 1864, *ibid.*, 492; Sherman to Halleck, May 30, June 5, 8, 11, 1864, *ibid.*, 351, 408, 433, 454–55.

3. Stanton to Sherman, Aug. 6, 1864, *O.R.*, XXXVIII, pt. 5, 390; Sherman to Mrs. Sherman, June 30, 1864, *Home Letters*, 300. Johnston's casualties ran much higher than might have been expected in view of his cautious defensive policy. In part, the necessity for both armies to "feel" for the enemy caused this. This inevitably involved much skirmishing and small-unit fighting, implying significant casualties. The Atlanta campaign well illustrates this process at work. In May, 1864, the Confederates, under the cautious Joseph E. Johnston, lost 9,187 killed and wounded and an unknown number of prisoners. These huge losses were incurred without any battle at all and occurred while pursuing a most circumspect and strictly defensive policy involving not only elaborate use of intrenchments but fortified picket lines as well. These losses largely resulted from keeping in touch with the enemy in order to know his location, strength, and the direction in which he was moving.

Although on the offensive, Sherman, whose strategy and tactics were equally circumspect, lost only a few more, 10,528 killed and wounded and 1,240 missing. Though only maneuvering to threaten and to seek a tactical advantage, both sides lost as many men as if they had fought a major battle and the Confederates lost 87 percent as many men as the Federals. Assuming Johnston's missing were in the same ratio as Sherman's, he lost over 18 percent of his army in less than a month, whereas Sherman lost less than 11 percent.

Any explanation of the tactical defenders' casualties must take into account that there will be an almost equal constant added to each side because of the costly kind of reconnaissance involved in "feeling" for the dispersed enemy. In addition, a defense was rarely a pure defense. At Cold Harbor and Kennesaw Mountain, where the intrenched defenders enjoyed total success, the attackers lost almost five times as many men as the defenders. More usual was the situation where the attackers enjoyed a partial success, which made necessary a counterattack in order to preserve the integrity of the kind of linear defense then used. Because of the losses incurred in these local defeats and on the offensive in the counterattacks, the defensive was rarely so pure that the five-to-one loss ratio characteristic of the defense of intrenchments was mixed only with the nearly one-to-one constant for the reconnaissance. At the Battle of Fredericksburg, where the Confederates enjoyed a superior defensive position and had no casualties from reconnaissance, the ratio of casualties was less than five-to-two because of Confederate losses incurred in a successful Union attack and in the counterattacks needed to restore the line.

4. Sherman to Halleck, June 11, 1864, *O.R.*, XXXVIII, pt. 4, 455; Sherman to Stanton, June 15, 1864, *ibid.*, 480; Sherman to Mrs. Sherman, June 30, 1864, *Home Letters*, 300.

5. Sherman to Grant, June 18, 1864, *O.R.*, XXXVIII, pt. 4, 507.

6. Lee to Davis, May 23, June 6, 11, 1864, *Wartime Papers*, 747, 767, 774–75; Bragg to Davis, June 7, 1864, *O.R.*, XXXVIII, pt. 4, 762; Davis to H. V. Johnson, Sept. 18, 1864, *ibid.*, XLII, pt. 2, 1258–59.

7. McEntee to Sharpe, June 28, 1864, *O.R.*, XXXVII, pt. 1, 684; Grant to Halleck, June 17, 1864, *ibid.*, 644–45.

8. Halleck to Grant, June 19, 22, 1864, *O.R.*, XXXVII, pt. 1, 650–51, 660; Meade to Grant, June 19, 21, 1864, *ibid.*, XXXVII, pt. 1, 651, XXXVI, pt. 3, 786–87; Grant to Meade, June 19, 21 (two communications), 1864, *ibid.*, XXXVI, pt. 3, 779; XXXVII, pt. 1, 657.

9. Hunter to Adjutant-General, June 28, 1864, *O.R.*, XXXVII, pt. 1, 683–84.

10. Grant to Halleck, June 5, 1864, *O.R.*, XXXVI, pt. 3, 598–99.

11. Dana, *Recollections of the Civil War*, 215; Grant to Halleck, June 5, 1864, *O.R.*, XXXVI, pt. 3, 598–99.

12. Meade to Mrs. Meade, June 1, 1864, *Life and Letters*, II, 200.

13. Grant to Halleck, June 5, 1864, *O.R.*, XXXVI, pt. 3, 598–99.

14. Dana to Stanton, June 7, 8, 11, 1864, *O.R.*, XXXVI, pt. 1, 91, 92–93, 95; Grant to Butler, June 6, 1864, *ibid.*, XXXVII, pt. 1, 598–99; Grant to Abercrombie, June 7, 1864, *ibid.*, XXXVI, pt. 3, 690; Grant to Meade, June 8, 1864, *ibid.*, XXXVI, pt. 3, 695.

15. Adams, *Our Masters the Rebels*, 155–59.

16. Babcock to W. F. Smith, Apr. 29, 1864, *O.R.*, XXXIII, 1019; Meigs and Barnard to Halleck, May 24, 1864, *ibid.*, XXXVI, pt. 3, 177–78.

17. Grant's motives and the real intent of his operations from Spotsylvania on are not as clear as our exposition makes them. It is not likely that, whatever they were, they were as explicit in Grant's own thinking as in the foregoing. This interpretation of the campaign from Spotsylvania to Petersburg seems the best one to reconcile Grant's behavior with his earlier and his subsequent operations and it is consistent with the few documentary evidences available. Since the campaign failed to take Richmond in 1864 or to defeat Lee's army in a significant way, Grant's memoirs offer little help, because, like most memoirs, they do not chronicle failure.

18. Abercrombie to Williams, June 8, 1864, *O.R.*, XXXVIII, pt. 3, 730; Comstock Diary, June 22, July 2, 1864; Richard J. Sommers, *Richmond Redeemed: The Siege of Petersburg* (Garden City, N.Y., 1981), 234.

19. Grant to Sherman, Aug. 9, 1864, *O.R.*, XXXVIII, pt. 5, 334; Sherman to Halleck, Aug. 20, 1864, *ibid.*, 609; Halleck to Grant, June 27, July 10, 1864, *ibid.*, XXXIV, pt. 4, 568, XXXVII, pt. 2, 385.

20. Comstock Diary, July 17, 1864; Meade to Mrs. Meade, June 1, 5, 6, 24, 1864, *Life and Letters*, II, 200, 201, 206.

21. Adams, *Our Masters the Rebels*, 159–60.

22. Halleck to Sherman, July 16, 1864, *O.R.*, XXXVIII, pt. 5, 150–51; Comstock Diary, July 15, 1864.

23. Lincoln to Grant, June 15, 1864, Basler, *Collected Works*, VII, 393.

24. Webster to Washburn, June 16, 1864, *O.R.*, XXXIX, pt. 2, 124–25.

25. Catton, *A Stillness at Appomattox*, 220.

26. Sherman to Thomas, June 24, 1864, *O.R.*, XXXVIII, pt. 4, 582; Sherman to Grant, July 12, 1864, *ibid.*, pt. 5, 123; Sherman to Halleck, July 9, 1864, *ibid.*, 91.

27. Horn, *Army of Tennessee*, 327, 331; Sherman to Corse, Oct. 7, 1864, *O.R.*, XXXIX, pt. 3, 135; Connelly, *Autumn of Glory*, 358–60.

28. Sherman to Webster, June 28, 1864, *O.R.*, XXXVIII, pt. 4, 629; Thomas to Sherman, June 27, 1864, *ibid.*, 612; Sherman to Halleck, July 1, 1864, *ibid.*, pt. 5, 3; Schofield to Sherman, June 30, 1864, *ibid.*, pt. 4, 643.

29. Sherman to Schofield, June 30 (two communications), 1864, *O.R.*, XXXVIII, pt. 4, 644.

30. Sherman to Schofield, June 30, 1864, *O.R.*, XXXVIII, pt. 4, 644; Sherman to Halleck, July 1, 1864, *ibid.*, pt. 5, 3; Halleck to Sherman, June 28, 1864, *ibid.*, pt. 4, 629.

31. Halleck to Grant, June 22, 1864, *O.R.*, XXXIV, pt. 4, 504, Grant to Halleck, June 23, 24, 1864, *ibid.*, 514–15, 527; Canby to Farragut, July 1, 1864, *ibid.*, XLI, pt. 2, 3; Canby to Washburn, June 28, July 2, 1864, *ibid.*, XXXIV, pt. 4, 579, XLI, pt. 2, 21–22.

32. Grant to Halleck, June 28, July 6 (two communications), 1864, *O.R.*, XXXVII, pt. 1, 383, pt. 2, 79, 80; Halleck to Grant, July 3, 5, 1864, *ibid.*, pt. 2, 15, 59; Comstock Diary, July 15, 1864.

33. Catton, *Never Call Retreat*, 388.

34. Halleck to Grant, July 8, 1864, *O.R.*, XXXVII, pt. 2, 120; Grant to Lincoln, July 10, 1864, *ibid.*, 156; Lincoln to Grant, July 10, 1864, Basler, *Collected Works*, VII, 437; Comstock Diary, July 10, 1864; *Lincoln and the Civil War*, 206.

35. Grant to Halleck, July 7, 1864, *O.R.*, XL, pt. 3, 59.

36. Lincoln to Swann and others, July 10, 1864, Basler, *Collected Works*, VII, 437–38.

37. Dana to Grant, July 12, 1864, *O.R.*, XXXVII, pt. 2, 223; Halleck to Grant, July 10, 1864, *ibid.*, 157.

38. This is probably what Holmes said. For a full discussion, see John H. Cramer, *Lincoln Under Enemy Fire* (Baton Rouge, 1948), 101–24.

39. Grant to Halleck, July 14, 15, 1864, *O.R.*, XXXVII, pt. 2, 300, 329; *Lincoln and the Civil War*, 210.

40. Grant to Halleck, July 15, 17, 20, 1864, *O.R.*, XXXVII, pt. 2, 328–29, 361, 400; Halleck to Grant, July 19, 1864, *ibid.*, 384–85.

41. Davis to H. V. Johnson, Sept. 18, 1864, *O.R.*, XLII, pt. 2, 1259.

42. Sherman to Halleck, July 5, 1864, *O.R.*, XXXVIII, pt. 5, 50; Sherman to Grant, July 12, 1864, *ibid.*, 123; Sherman to Mrs. Sherman, July 9, 1864, *Home Letters*, 300–301.

43. Sherman to Grant, July 12, 1864, *O.R.*, XXXVIII, pt. 5, 123; Grant to Halleck, July 15, 1864, *ibid.*, 143–44; Grant to Sherman, July 16, 1864, *ibid.*, 149.

44. Sherman to Halleck, July 16, 1864, *O.R.*, XXXVIII, pt. 5, 150.

45. Davis to Lee, July 21, 1863, *O.R.*, XXVII, pt. 3, 1031; Johnston to Bragg, June 26, 1864, *ibid.*, XXXVIII, pt. 4, 792.

46. Bragg to Johnston, June 27, 1864, *O.R.*, XXXVII, pt. 4, 797; Bragg to Davis, June 29, 1864, *ibid.*, 805; Davis to Johnston, July 7, 11, 1864, *ibid.*, pt. 5, 867, 875–76.

47. Bragg to Davis, June 4, July 27, 1864, *O.R.*, XXXVIII, pt. 4, 762, LII, pt. 2, 713.

48. Davis to H. V. Johnston, Sept. 18, 1864, *O.R.*, XLII, pt. 2, 1258–59.

49. Davis to Johnston, July 16, 1864, *O.R.*, XXXVIII, pt. 5, 882; Johnston to Davis, July 16, 1864, *ibid.*, 882; Cooper to Johnston, July 17, 1864, *ibid.*, 885; Davis to Hood, *ibid.*, 946.

50. Sherman to Mrs. Sherman, July 29, 1864, *Home Letters*, 303–4; Connelly, *Autumn of Glory*, 102–3, 286–88, 365–67, 369–72.

51. Seddon to Hood, July 17, 1864, *O.R.*, XXXVIII, pt. 5, 885; Hood to Davis, Aug. 9, 1864, *ibid.*, 951.

52. Sherman to Halleck, July 21, 23, 1864, *O.R.*, XXXVIII, pt. 5, 211, 234–35; Sherman to Mrs. Sherman, Aug. 2, 1864, *Home Letters*, 306.

53. Sherman to Halleck, Sept. 4, 1864, *O.R.*, XXXVIII, pt. 5, 793.

54. Bell I. Wiley, "The Common Soldier of the Civil War," *Civil War Times—Illustrated* (July, 1973), 26.

55. Sherman to Halleck, July 6, Aug. 17, 18, 1864, *O.R.*, XXXVIII, pt. 5, 66, 547, 570; Sherman to Thomas, Aug. 10, 1864, *ibid.*, 447–48; Sherman to Schofield, Aug. 10 (two communications), 1864, *ibid.*, 450, 451; Sherman to Grant, Aug. 10, 1864, *ibid.*, 447; Hood to Davis, Aug. 9, 1864, *ibid.*, 951.

56. Horn, *Army of Tennessee*, 472–73n67; Connelly, *Autumn of Glory*, 326–90ff.

57. Grant to Meade, June 28, July 3, 1864, *O.R.*, XL, pt. 2, 477–78, 599; Meade to Grant, June 28, 1864, *ibid.*, 619–20.

58. Grant to Meade, July 5, 8, 14, 24, 26, *O.R.*, XL, pt. 3, 5, 72–73, 224, 424, 458; (two-

communications), Grant to Halleck, June 27, July 9, 14, 16, 22, 23, *ibid.*, pt. 2, 462, pt. 3, 92, 223, 224, 276, 385, 408–9; Meade to Grant, July 24, 26, 1864, *ibid.*, pt. 3, 425, 458.

59. Grant to Meade, July 25, 1864, *O.R.*, XL, pt. 3, 438; Grant to Halleck, July 30, 1864, *ibid.*, pt. 1, 17.

60. Catton, *A Stillness at Appomattox*, 242.

61. Long, *Civil War, Day by Day*, 548.

62. Catton, *A Stillness at Appomattox*, 252.

63. Lincoln to Grant, July 17, Aug. 17, 1864, Basler, *Collected Works*, VII, 444, 499.

64. Grant to Halleck, July 24, Aug. 1, 1864, *O.R.*, XXXVII, pt. 2, 426, 558; Halleck to Grant, Aug. 3, 1864, *ibid.*, 582–83.

65. Grant to Sheridan, Aug. 14, 26, Sept. 9, 1864, *O.R.*, XLIII, pt. 1, 791, 917, pt. 2, 57.

66. Grant to Halleck, Aug. 12, 14, 1864, *O.R.*, XLIII, pt. 1, 775, XLII, pt. 2, 167; Grant to Sheridan, Aug. 17, 20, 1864, *ibid.*, XLIII, pt. 1, 822, 856; Grant to Meade, Aug. 19, 20, 1864, *ibid.*, XLII, pt. 2, 293, 327; Grant to Hancock, Aug. 13, 1864, *ibid.*, 148.

67. Grant to Meade, Aug. 17, 19, 20, 1864, *O.R.*, XLII, pt. 2, 245, 295, 327; Grant to Halleck, Aug. 16, 1864, *ibid.*, 210; Meade to Grant, Aug. 17, 22, 1864, *ibid.*, 245, 327.

68. Meade to Grant, Aug. 26, 1864, *O.R.*, XLII, pt. 2, 517; Hancock to Meade, Aug. 26, 1864, *ibid.*, 524.

69. Grant to Sherman, Aug. 18, 1864, *O.R.*, XXXVIII, pt. 5, 569.

70. Catton, *Never Call Retreat*, 392; Jones, *Ranger Mosby*, 236–37; Sheridan to Grant, Oct. 7, 1864, *O.R.*, XLIII, pt. 2, 308.

71. Grant to Sheridan, Sept. 23, 26, 1864, *O.R.*, XLIII, pt. 2, 152, 177; Sheridan to Grant, Oct. 1, 12, 1864, *ibid.*, 249, 346.

72. Catton, *Never Call Retreat*, 393.

73. Canby to Farragut, July 18, 26, 1864, *O.R.*, XLI, pt. 2, 228–29, 399; Canby to Halleck, July 22, Aug. 22, 29, 31, 1864, *ibid.*, 325, 798, 915, 950; Canby to Washburn, July 27, 1864, *ibid.*, 419–20; S. D. Lee to J. G. Walker, July 6, 1864, *ibid.*, 994; S. D. Lee to Kirby Smith or Walker, July 16, 1864, *ibid.*, 1030; Bragg to Kirby Smith, July 22, 1864, *ibid.*, 1030; Kirby Smith to Bragg, Aug. 3, 1864, *ibid.*, 1037; Robert L. Kerby, *Kirby Smith's Confederacy* (New York, London, 1972), 328–29.

74. Johnson and McLaughlin, *Civil War Battles*, 127–34.

75. Henry, *First With the Most Forrest*, 338.

76. Jones, *Ranger Mosby*, 152, 173–75, 326n57.

77. Sherman to Halleck, Aug. 13 (two communications), 17, Sept. 3, 1864, *O.R.*, XXXVIII, pt. 5, 482, 547, 777; Grant to Sherman, Aug. 14, 18, 1864, *ibid.*, 488, 569; Stroup to Hardee, Aug. 31, 1864, *ibid.*, 1007.

78. Wheeler, *We Knew Sherman*, 69.

19 ☆ THE DEFEAT OF THE CONFEDERACY

William T. Sherman

GENERAL HOOD made the first move after the fall of Atlanta, but he first took time for brief recriminations. In blaming his subordinates for Atlanta's loss he took as his model his mentor, Bragg. In truth, the brilliant and experienced Sherman had outgeneraled Hood; Hood, however, chose to believe otherwise, explaining: "According to all human calculations we should have saved Atlanta had the officers and men done what was expected of them." The loss of life in the last battle "was so small that it is evident that our effort was not a vigorous one." The 1,485 killed, "a very small number," he felt, indicated a "disgraceful effort."[1]

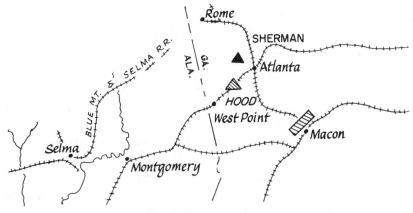

Situation before Hood's Move

If Hood emulated Bragg in blaming subordinates, he immediately showed that he at least had learned the essence of Lee's manner in maneuvering an army. To President Davis, Hood proposed: I will "place our army upon the communications of the enemy, drawing our supplies from the West Point and Montgomery Railroad. Looking to this, I shall at once proceed to strongly fortify Macon." His concept was a good one, for in Alabama lay a railroad which could supply a perfect route by which to turn and force back Sherman's army at Atlanta. This would secure for Hood an even better route than the Virginia railroads and the Shenandoah Valley had provided for Lee.[2]

Hood's projected turning movement could also lead him to his other line of communications, a return to a flank position neglected by Johnston in his retreat from Resaca to Kingston and then Marietta. About twenty miles east of Kingston lay Rome. About forty miles southwest of Rome began the railroad from Blue Mountain to Selma, still under construction northwest toward Rome, where it would have connected with Chattanooga and Atlanta. Selma itself had rail and water connections with southern Alabama and Mississippi. Johnston could have based his army on the Blue Mountain railroad. Had Johnston done this, it would have put him on the flank of any advance by Sherman toward Atlanta, thus threatening Yankee communications or forcing Sherman to move toward Rome and follow Johnston as he retreated toward Selma. Though an important industrial city with a big Confederate armaments complex and situated in a rich agricultural region of Alabama, Selma lacked the strategic and logistical significance of Atlanta and was far more difficult to reach because of the rail gap. Unless he finished the railway, Sherman would have had to rely on wagon transportation for forty miles through country where he could not feed his draft animals because the passage of his and Johnston's armies would have denuded the area. The retreat toward Rome and the Blue Mountain railroad would not have been, for Johnston, a new or innovative maneuver, for it was well known in military history as the "flank position." A flank position is essentially identical to a turning movement. They differ in that the flank position is assumed during a retreat, a turning movement by an advance to create the threatening situation.[3]

The evidence indicates that Sherman did not think of nor prepare for this move on Johnston's part. Sherman did have a remedy, however: If he had not divided his army he could have ignored Johnston and begun earlier his raid to the sea. For Hood to return to north Georgia by a turning movement required less nerve than for Johnston to have uncovered Atlanta by retiring toward Rome and Alabama. Atlanta had already fallen. Hood also received some very distinguished advice, for President Davis visited his army. Davis had at last ordered Forrest onto Sherman's communications and, when he visited Hood, together they agreed on the bold move of extending Hood's turning movement into north Georgia. Hood would thus draw his supplies from Lieutenant General Richard Taylor's adjacent Department of Alabama, Mississippi, and East Louisiana.

To coordinate supplies and operations which might embrace these two departments, the President combined them into the Military Division of the West. Essentially redundant in Virginia, General Beauregard was assigned to the new command, one with a scope that matched his skill and experience. Though Beauregard set to work with his customary energy, he enjoyed only minimal control over Hood's movements, because that general was already committed to a campaign which Beauregard endorsed and which the President himself had previously approved. In addition, Hood, regarding himself as essentially independent, limited himself to being pleased to receive "advice from a general so eminent as Beauregard." Untrammelled by Beauregard, the President, by transferring Hardee to the command of the Department of South Carolina, Georgia, and Florida, also relieved Hood of Hardee's unwanted presence.[4]

The bold move devised by Hood and Davis promised important results. They expected that Hood would take up a strong stance on Sherman's communications, thus, Davis later wrote, forcing "Sherman to move to attack us in position." But risks abounded, too, all noted prophetically by Hood's predecessor. Carefully observing the situation, the unemployed Johnston observed: Hood's "movement has uncovered the route (thro' Macon) by which the army of Virginia is supplied, and the shops at which ammunition is prepared and arms repaired for the Army of Tennessee. If Sherman understands that either Charleston, Savannah, Pensacola or Mobile is as good a point for him as Chattanooga, he will not regard Hood's move." Davis and Hood understood this, too, and, should Sherman ignore Hood and march for the coast, they believed militia could delay Sherman enough for Hood to overtake him. Sherman would then have been in the predicament of facing an enemy army supplied by rail, without any supply line of his own.[5]

Hood moved north on October 1 and soon reached Sherman's railroad. Almost immediately he interrupted the line at Big Shanty and Kennesaw Water Tank, Georgia. On October 3 Sherman, leaving one corps to garrison Atlanta, marched north to protect his communications from Hood's turning movement. But Hood moved rapidly and erratically, eluding Sherman and breaking the railroad, though he failed in his assaults against most of Sherman's fortified points.

In one of these, a fight of some proportions developed at Allatoona Pass, Georgia. A Confederate division under Major General Samuel G. French assailed some 2,000 Federals holding a railroad pass defended by a makeshift fort. Sherman had sent a message the day before which read: "Hold fast. We are coming." French got word that a huge federal force was on its way and so, as the plucky Federals under Brigadier General John Corse did indeed hold brilliantly during the day of assault, French elected to withdraw, though in fact reinforcements from Sherman were not moving in mass to the vicinity. This incident inspired the evangelist P. P. Bliss to write the hymn, "Hold the Fort, For We Are Coming."

With Hood's turning movement well launched, Davis revealed in a speech at Columbia, South Carolina, how grandiose his vision had become. Speaking reassuringly of Hood, Davis said, "His eye is now fixed upon a point far beyond that where he was assailed by the enemy. . . . And if but a half, nay, one-fourth, of the men to whom the service has a right, will give him their strength, I see no chance for Sherman to escape from a defeat or a disgraceful retreat." Then on October 5, at Augusta, Davis told a cheering crowd, "Never before was I so confident that energy, harmony and determination would rid the country of its enemy and give to the women of the land that peace their good deeds have so well deserved." Though the Federals had finally invaded Georgia, he continued, "we must beat Sherman, we must march into Tennessee . . . we must push the enemy back to the banks of the Ohio."[6]

Hood's successful move resembled Lee's Antietam or Gettysburg raids, Bragg's Kentucky campaign, or, on a larger scale, Rosecrans's movements around Bragg. As in these earlier parallel maneuvers, Hood had left his railway and, living off the country, was proceeding to threaten his enemy's vital rear. As expected, Sherman, who had already strengthened the fortified points on his communications back to Chattanooga, began to fall back with the bulk of his army to cover his communications.

The comparison with these earlier threatening raids is inexact in two significant ways. In marching toward Rome, not far from the Blue Mountain railroad to Selma, Hood could re-establish his communications and could remain in that vicinity indefinitely. His campaign could thus become a penetration like McClellan's on the Peninsula and Grant's below Vicksburg. Hood

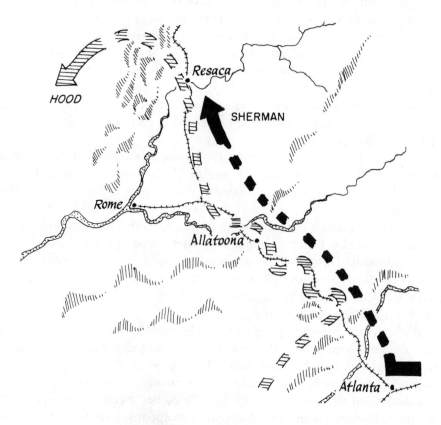

Hood Turns Sherman

was, of course, also returning to occupy the flank position, which Johnston had neglected in his retreat. In another important respect this movement differs from similar ones during the war: Hood's theatre of operations was so large that he could choose not to fight. Since the tactical defensive, though very powerful, had turned out to involve a very high percentage of casualties, it would have been well for the Confederates and their depleted manpower to avoid a battle, even on the typically advantageous tactical defensive. This Hood did. He completely avoided Sherman's army, while first attacking the railroad almost up to Chattanooga and then falling back into Alabama, where he continued his threat to Sherman's railroads. Near Resaca the two armies had approached each other, but Hood, distrusting the morale of his army, declined to await an attack by Sherman and proceeded west into Alabama. Even though Hood had at one time separated his three corps rather widely in their mission of railway destruction and Sherman had detachments stationed throughout the area, Hood easily avoided Sherman.

Before Hood's initiative enticed him back to north Georgia, Sherman realized his vulnerability as long as he remained quiescent in Atlanta; as he told a friend, "I've got my wedge pretty deep, and must look out that I don't get my fingers pinched." His next move was not clearly indicated because Banks had made no campaign in Alabama and Canby's small force had only entered the harbor of Mobile, the city and the route to the interior of Alabama still remaining in rebel hands. Without control of Mobile and this route, Grant and Sherman could not carry out their original intentions.[7]

When the "campaign commenced, nothing else was in contemplation but that Sherman, after capturing Atlanta, should connect with Canby at Mobile." Such a move would have again severed the Confederacy and cut off the eastern portion from the resources of Alabama and Mississippi. But Grant had directed the Nineteenth Corps from Louisiana to Virginia and most of Canby's remaining forces were guarding the Mississippi to prevent Kirby Smith from sending reinforcements east of the river. Realizing this, Grant wanted to change the line of operations and wished for some of "Canby's troops to act upon Savannah" while Sherman moved east to Augusta. Soon after the fall of Atlanta he telegraphed Sherman, "I should like to hear from you on this matter."[8]

Sherman had already written Halleck in August: "If I should ever be cut off from my base, look out for me about St. Marks, Florida, or Savannah, Georgia." Nevertheless, since he had focused all of his thoughts on Mobile, he was at first reluctant to consider changing his objective. Sherman did not think in terms of territorial acquisition, realizing his army could not "afford to operate farther dependent on the railroad," and he even advised Canby: Do not "bother with the city of Mobile, which will simply absorb a garrison for you." But he felt apprehensive because the enemy still held Savannah, his place to link with the fleet. However, Grant encouraged him, indicating plans to capture Wilmington as well as Savannah. The lieutenant general wrote: I

realize "the difficulties of supplying your army, except when you are constantly moving beyond where you are"; but he expected him to keep moving
because he could confuse the enemy by moving "so as to threaten Macon and
Augusta equally."[9]

By September 20 Sherman had reoriented his thinking and stood ready to
march across Georgia to Savannah. As he explained: "Where a million people
live my army won't starve." Grant's new plan pleased Sherman, for it contained so many elements of their mutual strategy: the use of sea power to
surprise a weak enemy line while taking another in the rear; reliance on the
variable objectives of a raiding force to confuse and so avoid the enemy's
force; solving Union logistical problems by living off and exhausting the
enemy's resources; and, of course, a march which would "absolutely sever
the Southern Confederacy." Added to all of this, taking Wilmington thus
produced the effect of "cutting off all foreign trade" to the enemy. Feeling
exuberant, Sherman concluded his letter to Grant: "If you can whip Lee and
I can march to the Atlantic, I think Uncle Abe will give us twenty days' leave
of absence to see the young folks."[10]

The Confederate offensive announced by Davis interrupted the plans Grant
and Sherman had nearly matured. The publicity of Davis's speeches made
Sherman believe that "the taking of Atlanta broke upon Jeff. Davis so suddenly as to disturb the equilibrium of his usually well-balanced temper, so
that . . . he let out some thoughts which otherwise he would have kept to
himself." So the raid to the coast was postponed by Hood's bold march
against Sherman's communications. As Sherman moved to cope with Hood,
he would have been "tempted" to dash for the sea had the Union already
occupied Savannah. Then, by the beginning of October when he realized
Hood was headed for Alabama and the Blue Mountain railway, Sherman had
decided it was feasible to move even without the possession of Savannah.[11]

Upon the outcome of Sherman's delayed raid to the coast rested the prospects for Grant's fall strategy. Though in September Sheridan had succeeded
supremely well against Early, the siege of Petersburg dragged on, and Grant
realized that the fall of Richmond would take months. Grant planned to take
the port of Wilmington and move to control "the South side or Lynchburg
and Petersburg road; then, if possible, to keep the Danville road cut." If
Sheridan could break the canal and the railroads north of the city, Richmond's
complex communications might be cut. Before he was ready for his movement against the railway, Grant tried to surprise Richmond. At the end of
September he had Butler strengthen his forces north of the James at the same
time that he directed Meade to create the impression that he was concentrating on the south end of the line. "The object of this movement," Grant
explained, "is to surprise and capture Richmond, if possible." If Butler failed,
he would attract enough troops north of the James to give Meade a chance
against Petersburg. "The prize sought," wrote Grant, "is either Richmond or

Petersburg." Grant intended the timing of the operation "to prevent the enemy from sending reinforcements to Early" to retrieve the double defeats of Winchester and Fisher's Hill on September 19 and 22.[12]

On September 29 a two-pronged federal drive commenced, one north of the James against the Richmond defenses, followed by the one against Petersburg. The Confederates lost Fort Harrison to the north and, though they vigorously counterattacked the next day, could not retake it. Nevertheless, the southerners constructed new outer works between the fort's line and Richmond. This was the last of the major federal attempts upon the city from north of the James. To the south, at Peebles' farm, a momentary breach occurred but counterattacks closed it. Still, the siege lines effectively stretched even longer and the Confederate defenders could do nothing save spread their forces thinner and thinner. But the Southside Railroad was intact and the Confederates still received supplies over the Weldon Railroad by using wagons to go around the gap. Rail and canal connections to Lynchburg still remained untouched.

Though Sherman's capture of Atlanta and Sheridan's devastation of the Valley constituted major military achievements, they had to compete in the headlines with spectacular if not substantial Confederate activities. On October 19, the same day as Sheridan's significant triumph over Early at Winchester, "war came to Vermont." Confederate Lieutenant Bennett H. Young with some twenty-five followers stormed into the little town of St. Albans, fifteen miles below the Canadian border. With the hope of burning and looting several towns, Young's men proceeded to rob three banks; but then the citizens turned out to fight. After a half-hour struggle the Confederates fled. The citizens pursued them to the Canadian border and arrested Young and twelve others, recovering about one-third of the stolen money. The rest of Young's party got away, but abandoned any further marauding attempts.[13]

In Missouri, Major General Sterling Price began a raid from Arkansas which, for a time at least, did prove an effective diversion. J. Henry Behan, an obscure captain stationed in Meridian, Mississippi, had proposed the raid to Davis on July 23. The primary goal: take St. Louis and cross the Mississippi River, invading Illinois and beyond. If that proved impossible, the secondary goal would be to recover Missouri for the South, a goal that well suited Price, a former legislator, lawyer, farmer, congressman, and governor of that state. In either event the Confederates intended the operation to attract a significant degree of federal attention.[14]

Price gathered a motley force of 12,000 men, only one-third of them with firearms but augmented by fourteen pieces of artillery. They entered Missouri on September 19, advancing on a broad front. Concentrating at Frederickstown on September 25, they fought a bloody six-hour fight at Pilot

Knob for Fort Davidson. Greatly outnumbered, the federal garrison under Sherman's brother-in-law, Brigadier General Thomas Ewing, evacuated but blew up most of the fort and supplies.

While Ewing delayed, one of Sherman's federal corps of 6,000 men under the able Major General A. J. Smith was diverted from its progress toward Nashville and sent to assist in Missouri. As Price neared St. Louis, the timely arrival of Smith's command precluded an attack on the city. Price then wheeled to the west, adopting the secondary plan, and proceeded along the south bank of the Missouri River, destroying sections of railroad.

With Ewing's men and another force of some 7,000 under Brigadier General Alfred Pleasonton in pursuit, Price's men occupied Hermann on October 5, bypassed the capital, Jefferson City, on the 7th, but took Boonville on the 9th, and captured Glasgow on the 15th along with its garrison of over 400 Federals. On the same day other units in Price's command, after stampeding some 700 Federals, captured Sedalia.

Thousands of state militia mobilized, but Price continued westward, skirmishing daily, and easily swept aside all the organized resistance he faced. Meanwhile Pleasonton's 7,000 men pursued Price's rear, while A. J. Smith's corps, augmented by Missouri militia, moved toward Price's flank. And in Kansas, a few thousand militia mustered under James G. Blunt, one of the victors of Prairie Grove. This force met Price at Waverly, made a stand, but was gradually pushed aside. Actions flared at Lexington on October 19, Little Blue River on the 20th, and on the 22nd at Independence and Big Blue (Bryam's Ford).

But now the federal defense ahead of Price to the west united under the command of the veteran Major General Samuel R. Curtis, who elected to stand fast just south of Brush Creek near the Kansas-Missouri border. Price now had Federals to his front and rear. Despite his open route of retreat to the south, he chose to exploit his central position between the Federals, hoping to attack them both in successive operations. He would first defeat Curtis and then turn and destroy the now-united forces under Pleasonton and Smith.

In the Battle of Westport, October 23, 1864, Price's force fruitlessly assaulted Curtis's defensive lines. The Confederates charged valiantly, fought vainly for some four hours, and failed. This marked the end of Price's disappointing raid. He had failed to attract anywhere near the number of hoped-for Missouri recruits, and, while causing a great deal of local uproar, some disruption of federal supply lines, and Smith's diversion, he did not gain any great material advantage for the Confederacy. In the battle each side lost about 1,500 men.

After his repulse at Westport, Price retreated sixty-one miles in two days, halting to fight on October 25 a costly rear-guard action at Mine Creek near the Marais des Cygnes River in Kansas. Price then continued his withdrawal, fighting further delaying actions. With only 6,000 survivors, he made an

arduous detour through the Indian Territory to avoid Fort Smith and finally
re-entered southern lines at Laynesport, Arkansas, on December 2. He had
marched 1,424 miles, fought forty-three battles or skirmishes, and lost half of
his command. His return marked the end of organized Confederate military
operations in the whole trans-Mississippi region, although guerrilla operations
persisted unabated and General Kirby Smith continued to command a nomi-
nally large force and territory.

Price's Raid

☆   ☆

As Price was raiding Missouri and Sherman, in north Georgia, was watching Hood over in north Alabama, the plans for Sherman's raid to the sea were
nearing completion. The objectives of this long-planned climax to the western
campaign fitted well with the Union administration's anaconda strategy. Hal-

leck wrote Sherman: "Deprived of the grain, iron, and coal of Northern Georgia, Alabama, and Mississippi, and the harbor of Wilmington closed as effectively as Mobile, Savannah, and Charleston now are, they can hardly hold out in strong force for another year. Your mode of conducting war is just the thing we want. We have tried the kid glove policy long enough." An authority on the laws of war, Halleck explained that Sherman's removal of civilians from Atlanta was "justified by the laws and usages of war," as would be the depredations planned for his march. Since the population was hostile, they should be so treated. Halleck also saw a political advantage in abandoning the kid-glove policy, after trying "three years of conciliation and kindness without any reciprocation." By implication, Sherman might produce a better result from an application of the "severe rules of war."[15]

But there were apprehensions in Washington. Hood's possible moves worried Grant and at one point he did not believe that Hood would follow Sherman's raid to the sea, but, Grant wrote, he will "probably strike for Nashville, thinking by going north he could inflict greater damage upon us than we could upon the rebels by going south." When Sherman moved to the sea, Grant expected him to face little opposition, only being "bushwhacked by all the old men, little boys, and such railroad guards as are still left at home." Having suffered from Early's raid the previous summer, Grant realized the political consequences of any move on Nashville by Hood. Lincoln, on the other hand, doubted the whole concept, being "*anxious* if not fearful," that "a misstep by General Sherman might be fatal to his army." In replying, Grant had changed his mind and now thought that Hood would follow Sherman, who, he believed, would have only 30,000 men, a force smaller than Hood's. Nevertheless Grant emphatically reminded Secretary Stanton of the basic invulnerability of armies and the advantage of elusiveness enjoyed by raiders. "Such an army as Sherman has (and with such a commander) is hard to corner or capture." But the unpredictability of Hood's future actions had made the Union high command uncertain and indecisive.[16]

Sherman, meanwhile, anxiously waited to "move through Georgia, smashing things to the sea." Exasperated that Hood's turning movement had forced him back, he did not wish to "remain now on the defensive." Sherman emphasized the futility of occupying territory when he wrote Grant: "Until we can repopulate Georgia, it is useless to occupy it." The raiding strategy would provide an antidote for the old problem of the departure of Hood's army from Sherman's front. Instead of a slow advance, reconstructing damaged railways, Sherman's raiding army could move briskly, making enemy resources their objective. By going onto Sherman's communications, Hood had vacated Sherman's front and the Union general was now ready to take advantage of this.[17]

Having overcome opposition in Washington, Grant authorized Sherman to raid, going "to either the Savannah River or any of the navigable streams emptying into the Atlantic or Gulf." The lieutenant general gave Sherman his objective: "You will, no doubt, clean the country where you go of railroad tracks and supplies. I would also move every wagon, horse, mule, and hoof of stock, as well as the negroes"; and, not neglecting Lincoln's policy of exploiting this military resource, Grant urged: "As far as arms can be supplied, either from surplus or capture, I would put arms in the hands of negro men. Give them such organization as you can."[18]

Expecting Sherman to choose the Atlantic coast, Grant anticipated that Sherman would break "such an extent of roads that the enemy will be effectually cut in two for several months." He also foresaw that Sherman would eventually occupy Augusta, Georgia, take up a position there, and supply himself from the coast at Savannah. Augusta was a better and easier place to occupy than Atlanta, because it cut "the same line of road that Atlanta does, with the advantage of water communication with the Atlantic" via the Savannah River. "This also has the advantage of cutting the southern line of railroads" from Macon to Savannah or Augusta "as well as the central through Augusta and Atlanta." Thus Grant envisioned a raid by Sherman, followed by the establishment of a new position at Augusta with short and secure water communications. This position would permanently dissever the Confederacy, ensuring the continued disruption of their transportation network.[19]

But Hood also had planned a new move. Assuming that Sherman had dispersed his forces, some in Middle Tennessee and some in north Georgia, Hood planned to cross the Tennessee River and march into Middle Tennessee. Although President Davis understood that, with Sherman's army divided, it would be possible to defeat the Union forces in Middle Tennessee and "advance to the Ohio River," he did not really endorse Hood's new campaign. The passive observer of Hood's enterprises, Johnston, saw that "if Sherman understands his game, he can now cut off Lee's supplies" by marching to an alternate base on the coast. "Sherman in his extreme caution may not venture upon such a course. Should he do so, he'll win."[20]

Hood's whole operation was vague in details and too optimistic. His thinking that Sherman did not know his whereabouts provoked from Beauregard the remark: "You must have a low estimate of the judgment of your wily adversary." Not discounting the possibility that Sherman could march south from Atlanta, Hood believed, "It will be the best thing that could happen for our general good." Nevertheless, Beauregard instructed that, if Sherman did do so, the railroad "should be taken up in his front, or if time does not permit this it should be destroyed." Though delayed several weeks by a lack of supplies, Hood's advance toward Nashville was to be no raid. As he progressed he reported: There are "plenty of mills in our possession," and he foresaw "no difficulty about supplies." As he continued forward, he found he could easily repair the railroad and directed that it be put into service in his rear. Since there were "certain supplies necessary to this army which cannot be obtained from the surrounding country," Hood said, he would otherwise need to rely on wagon transportation, "at all times slow and limited." He insisted, therefore, on the restoration of rail service immediately, because, he added, "the permanent occupation of this country absolutely requires that this road be repaired."[21]

Ambiguities as to the future actions of both Hood's and Sherman's armies caused uncertainty and apprehension in the opposing commands. But Hood's possible movements gave Sherman more concern than Hood expressed about Sherman's. So before Sherman could begin marching to the sea, he felt the need, he said, to "follow Hood till he is beyond reach of mischief and then resume the offensive." Though he could not decide whether or not Hood would follow him, Sherman wrote: I am sure that "he and Beauregard will concoct more mischief."

George H. Thomas, the Rock of Chickamauga, had already been assigned the role of defending Tennessee, for which he would have "ample force" with the supplemental troops ordered by Grant and sent back by Sherman. To cope with the serious possibility of Beauregard's sending Hood into Tennessee, Sherman also prescribed a movement from Mobile "vigorously up the Alabama River" as well as distracting feints by troops on the Mississippi and the Tennessee. He hoped that "these cooperating movements" would "completely bewilder Beauregard," and he would "burst with French despair."[22]

In addition to these raids, Sherman made other preparations for any possible response by Hood's army. Sherman instructed Thomas "to push south from Decatur and the head of the Tennessee for Columbus, Mississippi, and Selma, not absolutely to reach these points, but to divert or pursue according to the state of facts. If, however, Hood turns on you," Sherman warned, "fight him cautiously, taking advantage of your fortifications and the natural obstructions of the country." Grant then intervened, "regretting" that he had not arranged the strategy earlier. Concerned also about the threat presented by Hood's army, Grant prescribed his usual strategy and explained: "The best way to drive him back, in my opinion, is that being pursued and recommended by Sherman." He ordered Halleck to arrange a "column of 10,000 men" which should "move from Vicksburg to Meridian and Selma" to "operate on Beauregard's communications as to greatly relieve Sherman and Thomas." Grant's intervention thus injected into the campaign the last of the elements of his strategy, a raid into the enemy's rear to distract, threaten, and destroy resources. A small raid into Mississippi and Alabama would thus help Sherman's big raid to the sea.[23]

As Sherman made ready for his march to the coast, Grant made further plans for two possible Confederate ventures in the West. If Hood "actually attempted an invasion of Tennessee" or if Forrest's raiders were "approaching the Ohio River," Grant intended to concentrate all troops from Missouri with Thomas in Tennessee. If, however, Hood followed Sherman, Thomas would send no "pursuing column" after Hood. Instead, with Tennessee secure from invasion and Price's raid repulsed, Grant would transfer troops from the West to Virginia. With these reinforcements he could then carry out plans to attack

Wilmington and land forces on the Georgia coast to cooperate with Sherman. In addition, if Hood's army were thus removed from the West, Grant contemplated leaving Sherman largely unaided to cope with Hood, using the western reinforcements to strengthen "the armies operating against Richmond" enough to extend his lines to cut the railroads to Danville and Lynchburg.[24]

Sherman found excitement, not in the prospect of a well-planned defense of Tennessee but in the opportunity to "push straight down into the heart of Georgia, smashing things generally." Though Hood's army, his principal opposition, would be behind him, he had to worry about delay, for he would be living off the country. Writing Halleck, Sherman explained: "I must have alternatives, else, being confined to one route, the enemy might so oppose that delay and want would trouble me, but having alternatives, I can take so eccentric a course that no general can guess my objective. Therefore, have lookouts at Morris Island, South Carolina, Ossahaw Sound, Georgia, Pensacola and Mobile bays. I will turn up somewhere." Sherman perceived this offensive as "far better than defending a long line of railroad" or coping with Hood by having "to chase him all over creation" and "trusting to some happy accident to bring him to bay and to battle."[25]

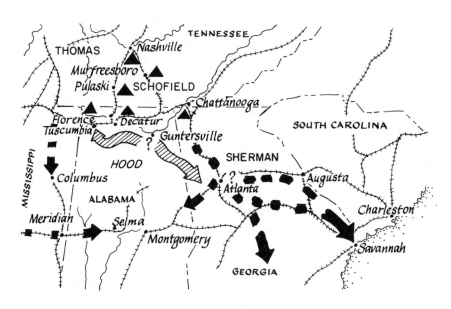

Projected Movements of Hood's and Sherman's Campaigns

As usual, Sherman introduced a political element into his strategy: "This movement is not purely military or strategic, but will illustrate the vulnerability of the South. They don't know what war means, but when the rich planters of the Oconee and Savannah see their fences and corn and hogs and sheep vanish before their eyes they will have something more than a mean opinion of the 'Yanks.' " There was yet a more sophisticated effect which Sherman expected. He proposed "to demonstrate the vulnerability of the South and make its inhabitants feel that war and individual ruin are synonymous terms." More important, he believed that his march would psychologically demolish the South, and, he wrote, it would be "fatal to the possibility of a Southern independence; they may stand the fall of Richmond, but not of all Georgia." His raid would thus destroy the enemy's morale and will to continue the struggle, for, "if the North can march an army right through the South, it is proof positive that the North can prevail in this contest."[26]

Before "going into the very bowels of the Confederacy," where he proposed "to leave a trail that [would] be recognized fifty years hence," Sherman issued detailed regulations. Soldiers, he ordered, would "forage liberally on the country during the march," but "must not enter the dwellings of the inhabitants, or commit any trespass, but during a halt or a camp they may be permitted to gather turnips, potatoes, and other vegetables, and to drive in stock in sight of their camps." To corps commanders alone was "intrusted the power to destroy mills, houses, cotton-gins, &c." In so doing he ordered them to follow this principle: "In districts and neighborhoods where the army is unmolested no destruction of such property should be permitted; but should guerrillas or bushwhackers molest our march, or should the inhabitants burn bridges, obstruct roads, or otherwise manifest local hostility, then, army commanders should order and enforce a devastation more or less relentless according to the measure of such hostility." The rule differed for the needs of the army. In addition to food, the soldiers could take "horses, mules, wagons, &c" for the needs of cavalry, artillery, quartermasters and commissaries, but "leave each family a reasonable portion for their maintenance." The army also planned to gather able-bodied Negroes along the way. Such careful rules reflected the laws of war, but Sherman probably did not expect his men to adhere strictly to them once the march began.[27]

Sherman departed Atlanta on November 12 with 62,000 men and moved between Macon and Augusta, confusing his enemy about his objective. He avoided both cities, aiming to destroy the railroads as he marched virtually unopposed to Savannah. Tennessee was protected by the ample forces at Thomas's disposal and, to support him, Grant decided to modify his own plans for the armies before Richmond, explaining: "I would not if I could just now do anything to force the enemy out of Richmond or Petersburg. It would liberate too much of a force to oppose Sherman with." But he prepared for the offensive, should Sherman's movement "cause General Lee to detach largely from the force defending Richmond to meet him." By directing Meade to prepare to move with twelve days' rations, Grant clearly planned, if a substantial force left Richmond, for Meade to follow with a raiding army. Thus, in refraining from an offensive, Grant followed Rosecrans's strategy of the spring of 1863; but, in being prepared to follow quickly as a raider, Grant had solved the problem of pursuit which had baffled Rosecrans and his generals. Grant's preparations were unneeded, however, for Lee remained in the Richmond-Petersburg lines while Sherman marched to the sea.[28]

Once under way, at long last, while the marchers sang, joked, and laughed, Sherman had a striking realization of his immense responsibility: "Success would be accepted as a matter of course, whereas, should we fail, this march would be adjudged the wild adventure of a crazy fool." But his men pushed on with little difficulty and ten days after leaving Atlanta reached Milledgeville, then Georgia's capital. Here the Yankees set up a mock legislature, the soldiers voting, after spirited debate, to repeal Georgia's ordinance of secession. Then, liquor injecting its influence, the "legislators" vandalized the capitol and state library. They threw the books not taken as souvenirs out the windows into the mud, where passing horses and men trampled them underfoot.[29]

Meanwhile, Hood completed preparations to advance into Tennessee. His army, proceeding into northern Alabama and nearing the Tennessee River, had picked up supplies and was at last ready to march north. One corps crossed the river on the night of October 29, but Hood delayed crossing the whole army while waiting for Forrest's cavalry. Forrest arrived several vexing days late for the expected rendezvous, but when he came he had with him an exonerating treasure. He had captured the riverboat *Mazeppa* with a load which included nine thousand pairs of shoes. But even this did not contain sufficient shoes for all the men in Hood's army, and the rest fashioned moccasins out of fresh beef hides, tied on with the hairy side turned in.

Hood's scheme offered chance for some success if he moved fast enough and executed his plans effectively. The federal forces in Tennessee were not united, being scattered instead all over the middle part of the state and vulnerable to defeat in detail. Until Thomas managed by early December to mass his available 55,000 men in and near Nashville, the principal concentrated federal force in the vicinity numbered only 32,000 under the scholarly and underrated John M. Schofield near Columbia, Tennessee. Hood possessed at the outset about 30,000 infantry and 8,000 cavalry.

In spite of his long delay, poised on the Tennessee, Hood achieved surprise. The enemy did not believe he would advance in "such weather" with "the present condition of the roads," even though Thomas warned Schofield that Hood could turn his right flank. But, aware of Hood's advance, Schofield withdrew to Columbia.[30]

High hopes and keen attention focused upon Hood's tattered army, while Davis offered encouragement and reassurance to the people. In a message to the Congress, the President correctly observed that "there are no vital points on the preservation of which the continued existence of the Confederacy depends." On November 21, 1864, the same day that Lincoln penned his famous Bixby letter, the eloquent consolation to a widow who supposedly

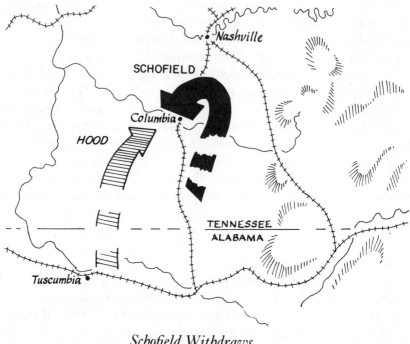

Schofield Withdraws

had yielded five sons, "so costly a sacrifice upon the altar of Freedom" (two of them in truth had deserted and another had been honorably discharged), the Confederate Army of Tennessee advanced.[31]

Now with three corps, one each under the capable Major General Benjamin F. Cheatham, and Lieutenant Generals Stephen D. Lee and Alexander P. Stewart, the southerners managed to move with remarkable speed, considering the unfavorable weather and the poor condition of the roads. A cold rain soon turned into snow and sleet. Where the ground did not freeze, it became a quagmire. Hood's men made contact with Schofield's forces at Columbia on November 27.

The two armies drew up in line of battle and lay opposite each other throughout the day. They fired artillery barrages and exchanged small-arms fire, but neither side tried any charges. Schofield chose not to fight Hood south of Columbia, for he expected Hood to attempt to turn his position, and thus Schofield during the night moved his entire command north of the river to prepared positions. On the north side Schofield felt secure, reporting: "I think I can now stop Hood's advance by any line near this, and meet in time any distant movement to turn my position." Schofield's conclusion that he could resist Hood at Columbia gained support from erroneous reports from his cavalry that Forrest had crossed the Duck River well to the east. Schofield had reason to rely on his cavalry, for it had received a new commander, the able and energetic James H. Wilson, sent from Virginia where he had served under Sheridan.[32]

The two armies continued to skirmish and fire at each other with artillery as Hood determined to divide his forces. Leaving Lee with two divisions at Columbia, hoping to fool Schofield into thinking the whole Confederate force still remained in position, Hood with the rest of the army tried a turning movement to reach the federal rear near Spring Hill. Cheatham's and Stewart's corps and Edward Johnson's division of Lee's corps commenced the movement on the night of November 28. But things began sluggishly. Hood determined to cross the Duck River on pontoon bridges about three miles above Columbia, yet his infantry did not even begin to cross until daybreak on the 29th. Still Lee managed to deceive Schofield completely. The Confederates in Columbia made such a ruckus that the Unionists believed the whole Confederate army remained in their front.

Schofield held his entire army opposite Columbia until near noon on November 29, when he began to withdraw gradually to the north. So the Federals continued to play into Hood's hands, moving slowly and filling the road with crawling wagons. By 3:00 P.M., Hood had moved his lead troops to a spot overlooking the pike from Columbia to Spring Hill and Franklin. He knew that Lee was busy drawing Schofield's attention to the rear. Hood and his generals gained sight of the enemy's wagons; and Hood, according to his memoirs, ordered Cheatham and Cleburne immediately to "take possession of and hold that pike at or near Spring Hill." Hood later said he also meant that the Confederates should attack the nearby bluecoats and destroy them.

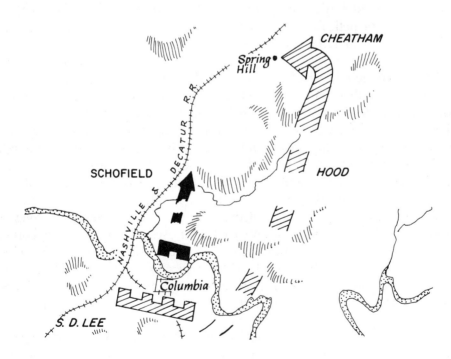

Hood's Maneuver

Supposedly he sent a courier with an order to Cheatham, after the latter had gotten into the Federals' path, to attack at once. But "through some misunderstanding or physical exhaustion or too much whiskey going the rounds," or some hitch, the order was not executed and probably not even delivered.[33]

Meanwhile, earlier in the day, Lee not only fired at Schofield's men across the Duck River, he also attempted to force a pontoon crossing. The Federals resisted Lee's advance until about 2:30 A.M., then left his front, and Lee pursued as rapidly as he dared during the darkness. By 9:00 A.M. he had moved his advance columns into Spring Hill, about ten miles from Columbia. But Hood had not attacked, and Schofield's men had slipped safely past in the night toward Franklin. Hood's turning movement had failed even though during the march Schofield's lines had strung out over five miles. The northerners had required all night to get under way, and daybreak drew near before the last wagon even left Spring Hill. This "Spring Hill Affair" became perhaps the most controversial of the nonfighting events of the entire war.

Schofield's men marched easily into Franklin, about twenty-five miles above Columbia and twelve above Spring Hill. Immediately they began intrenching in a strong hillside defensive position. The Army of Tennessee followed in pursuit, Stewart's corps in the lead, Cheatham's next, and Lee's to the rear. The advance guard made contact with the Federals about three miles south of Franklin and at approximately 3:30 P.M. began to establish a battle line. Lines of intrenchments, which touched the river bank both above and below the main area of settlement, surrounded the city of Franklin, located in a bend of the Harpeth River. Schofield had fortified these lines and now occupied them with all 32,000 of his men.

Hood, very eager for action, decided not to wait until Lee moved up with his corps, though Lee had almost all of the army's artillery because of the action at Columbia. Nor did Hood again turn Schofield; instead he resolved to make a frontal assault. Though late in the day, Hood thought that he should launch an attack right away. Probably the frustration at Spring Hill caused him to act rashly; he began hurling his men against the federal lines in piecemeal, uncoordinated, and fruitless attempts to break through. Lee reached the scene about 4:00 P.M. and Hood ordered him with one division to augment the attack. The fight continued late into the night, the Confederates making some headway against portions of the well-fortified lines; but the strong position favored the Federals. Despite frightful losses, Hood never called off the attacks. The Confederates hurled violent charges as late as 9:00 P.M. Yet Hood did not commit Lee's other two divisions at all, though he did finally get some of the artillery moved up and he ordered the guns to fire a hundred rounds each into the federal works early the next morning, when the troops would then charge again.

Meanwhile, Schofield evacuated Franklin. Sufficient units remained on the battlefield to exchange skirmish fire with the Confederates until about 3:00 A.M., but then the last of the bluecoats moved out toward the safety of

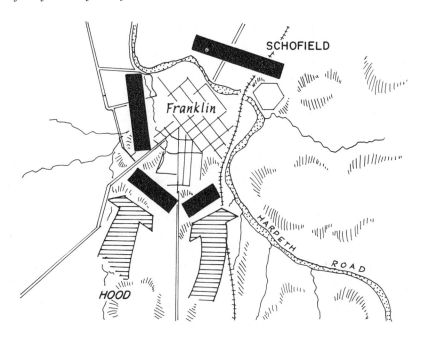

Hood's Frontal Assault

Nashville, twenty-five miles northward. Hood's army had suffered nearly three times the number of casualties as had the enemy's and could not pursue because of exhaustion and disorganization. The Federals had lost 2,326 men to the Confederates' loss of 6,252, including five generals killed, one captured, and six more wounded. The battle amounted to a staggering southern disaster.

On the next day, December 1, once more the Army of Tennessee began marching toward Nashville. The lead corps reached the environs of the city at about 2:00 P.M. on the 2nd, where they were confronted by Thomas's whole army. And while Hood was making this dramatic but costly progress toward Nashville, Sherman was moving toward Savannah.

Sherman's march from Atlanta most appropriately alarmed the Confederate high command, even though they long continued to underestimate his force by one half. Covering Macon, Georgia, Howell Cobb, the prominent politician and able soldier, wrote President Davis: "Sherman's move upon this place is formidable, and the most dangerous of the war. His policy is universal destruction." Surprised because he thought Sherman was near Chattanooga, Beauregard reacted emphatically to the enemy's destructive progress. His command, like Sherman's Military Division of the Mississippi, existed only for strategic coordination, administration and logistics remained with the subordinate departments. Nevertheless, Beauregard promptly ordered Richard Taylor to leave Alabama and take command in Georgia, a part of Hood's department. Richmond endorsed this prompt response. Realizing that no force could resist Sherman, Beauregard instructed Taylor to "cut and block up all dirt roads in advance of him; remove or destroy supplies of all kinds in his front." Illustrating his instructions with Roman history, he telegraphed Taylor: "Adopt Fabian system. Don't run risk of losing your active forces and guns available for the field to hold any one place or position, but harass at all points. Hannibal held the heart of Italy sixteen years, and then was defeated."[34]

Beauregard himself followed Taylor to Georgia; but this was not the only measure taken to secure unity of command. Before Beauregard arrived, Hardee's South Carolina command had been extended over Georgia south of the Chattahoochee. To gain greater coordination, the War Department gave General Bragg, then commanding in North Carolina, authority over Hardee until Beauregard arrived in Georgia and his Military Division of the West was extended to include Hardee's department. Never had the Confederate departmental structure displayed greater flexibility, though all in vain. The forces deployed were too minute compared to Sherman's veteran army of 62,000 men.[35]

The only hope to prevent Sherman from reaching the Atlantic coast from whence "he might then re-enforce Grant" was for Hood to "take the offensive at the earliest practicable moment and deal the enemy rapid and vigorous blows, striking him while thus dispersed, and by this means distract Sherman's advance into Georgia." Though Beauregard had left to Hood the decision whether to advance or follow Sherman, Beauregard really believed it impractical for Hood to follow. The railways were dilapidated and the 275-mile march was impeded by wet roads and high creeks, "almost impassable to artillery and wagon trains." Pursuing Sherman would be hard and, to take Hood's whole army would, Beauregard believed, open to Thomas's forces "the richest position of the State of Alabama and would have made nearly certain the capture of Montgomery, Selma, and Mobile.[36]

President Davis, seriously doubting the efficacy of Hood's offensive, wrote Beauregard: "Until Hood reaches the country proper of the enemy he can scarcely change the plans for Sherman's or Grant's campaigns. They would, I think, regard the occupation of Tennessee and Kentucky of minor importance." After conferring with Robert E. Lee about the possibility of sending troops from Richmond, the President rejected that alternative. Davis scarcely offered a solution to the problem by proposing to bring in Forrest and his cavalry "to impede the march of Sherman's army and prevent it from foraging on the country." Beauregard had a similar but more drastic remedy. He appealed to the people of Georgia: "Obstruct and destroy all roads in Sherman's front, flank, and rear, and his army will soon starve in your midst!"[37]

Sherman moved too rapidly and deceptively for any such measure to work. His adversaries prepared for him at Augusta, but he avoided that city. The Confederates suspended their law limiting reserve forces to service in their states, but still they could field only a weak and motley force against Sherman. General Hardee had over 14,000 effectives present for duty, but Sherman rightly called them a "mongrel mass" for most were unfit for real field service, being largely composed of artillerymen, ill-trained reserves mostly beyond military age, and fragmentary and depleted units. Even so, the numbers were so small compared to Sherman's that on one occasion Beauregard vetoed the adoption of "the flanking position recommended by the President in his telegram of the 20th instant," saying: "It could not be carried into effect, with our small force." While temporarily in command, Bragg well summed up the situation: "I must candidly express my belief that no practicable combinations of my available men can avert disaster." Sherman agreed, characterizing the Confederate defensive efforts as "puerile."[38]

As Sherman approached Savannah, Thomas, at Nashville with 55,000 men, prepared for Hood. One reason for Hood's success against Schofield and Thomas was the belief held by the Union generals that their troops were quite inferior to Hood's in number and quality. In truth, however, Schofield with over thirty thousand veterans had been at least in a class with Hood's force of less than forty thousand. Further, the morale of the Confederate army was sagging, a process accelerated by the defeat and heavy losses at Franklin. Nevertheless, Thomas felt unsure of many of his men, having "lost nearly 15,000 men, discharged by expiration of service," and gained "12,000 of perfectly raw troops." His inferiority in cavalry caused pessimism, especially since the almost-mythical Forrest commanded the enemy cavalry. Thomas did expect one major reinforcement, the corps of the redoubtable Andrew Jackson Smith, en route from Missouri where it had gone to cope with Price's raid.[39]

In spite of his victory, Schofield had evacuated Franklin because "a worse position for an inferior force could hardly be found." With Hood on his heels he joined Thomas at Nashville just as A. J. Smith was arriving. Thomas had already mobilized everyone—"Quartermaster's men, Veteran Reserves, fellows convalescent, and darkeys under arms and busy on earth-works." Thomas then telegraphed Halleck: "After General Schofield's fight of yesterday, feeling convinced that the enemy very far outnumbered him in infantry and cavalry, I determined to retire to the fortifications around Nashville, until General Wilson can get his cavalry equipped. He had now but one-fourth the number of the enemy, and consequently is no match for him."[40]

This telegram produced an immediate and very strong reaction in Washington. The next morning Secretary Stanton telegraphed Grant: "The President feels solicitous about the disposition of General Thomas to lay in fortifications for an indefinite period 'until Wilson gets equipments.' This looks like McClellan and Rosecrans strategy of do nothing and let the rebels raid the country. The President wishes you to consider the matter." Grant reacted immediately. Wanting to avoid having to "abandon the line of the Tennessee" and hoping "to annihilate Hood's army," Grant told Thomas:

"Arm and put in the trenches your quartermaster employés citizens, &c."
This would enable Thomas with his whole army to turn Hood. Grant explained: "With your citizen employés armed you can move out of Nashville
with all your army and force the enemy to retire or fight upon ground of your
own choosing." Almost immediately Grant grew impatient and directed
Thomas: "Attack Hood at once, and wait no longer for a remount of your
cavalry. There is great danger of delay resulting in a campaign back to the
Ohio River." When Thomas still did not move, Grant planned to replace him
with Schofield.[41]

Grant's drastic reaction to Thomas's failure to make an immediate attack
was certainly motivated in part by Lincoln's concern about a Confederate
army on the outskirts of Nashville, a city not menaced for more than two
years. Hood's movement came as a rude shock. He had advanced from the
Tennessee to Nashville with startling rapidity—in less than two weeks, quite
a contrast to the time it had taken Union forces to move from Nashville to
Chattanooga.

The President expressed his concern about the enemy's position at Nashville before Sherman reached the coast, a movement about which Lincoln had
reservations. The outcome of Sherman's campaign was still doubtful. So
Grant became vulnerable to criticism, because the effectiveness of his strategy
since the fall of Atlanta had yet to be proven. And Grant, no more than
Lincoln, wanted "the mortifying spectacle . . . of a rebel army moving for the
Ohio River" just as Congress was convening. Even if this embarrassing situation did not develop, the President worried that Hood would hold Thomas
at Nashville and detach part of the Confederate forces to operate "against
other important points." Reports also reached headquarters that a rebel force
might invade eastern Kentucky under the leadership of the popular Kentuckian, John C. Breckinridge.[42]

Grant's primary concern was that Hood would turn the Nashville position,
in spite of Thomas's report that "iron-clads and gun-boats are so disposed as
to prevent Hood from crossing the river." In urging Thomas to attack, Grant
said: Avoid "a foot race to see which, you or Hood, can beat to the Ohio."
Grant was worrying about more than a repeat of Bragg's Kentucky campaign.
Hood had already advanced a distance of two hundred miles.[43]

Though Grant decided against relieving Thomas, the general's inactivity
continued to cause concern. The secretary of war thought: Thomas is "unwilling to attack because it is hazardous, as if all war was anything but
hazardous. If he waits for Wilson to get ready, Gabriel will be blowing his
last horn." Thomas had promised to "attack Hood at once," but a "terrible
storm of freezing rain" delayed him for six days. This did not curb Grant's
impatience, for, he continued, I "fear either Hood or Breckinridge will get to
the Ohio River." But, also, with Hood far from his base, Grant saw "one of
the finest opportunities ever presented of destroying one of the three armies
of the enemy. If destroyed," he said, "he can never replace it." The lieutenant

general explained: "Let there be no further delay. Hood cannot stand even a drawn battle so far from his supplies of ordnance stores. If he retreats and you follow, he must lose his material and much of his army."[44]

Thomas waited. For two weeks the armies methodically went about strengthening their emplacements. Hood also hoped Thomas would attack, wisely judging his own forces not strong enough to charge the federal fortifications. The two armies remained in a temporary stalemate, while Thomas, badgered by Grant, awaited suitable weather. The armies fired occasional discharges of artillery at each other; but during the first half of December the southern troops manning icy breastworks suffered mostly from the elements and from lack of adequate supplies, while the more secure and well-situated northerners conserved their strength. Hood foolishly had sent most of Forrest's cavalry to Murfreesboro on an independent operation against a federal garrison of 8,000 men. Thus the bluecoats could attack the Confederates while the southerners lacked their "eyes" and their most effective flank protection.

On December 13 the ice began to melt, making it possible to "move without skates." Federal morale stood high, for General Thomas was "judicious and brave" and the troops felt "great confidence in him." On the evening of December 14 Thomas finished preparations to make his move.[45]

A dense fog hovered during the early morning of December 15, concealing the northern troops. Thomas's battle plan called for a strong attack upon the Confederate left, a skirmish advance in the center, the mass of the soldiers withdrawing from the center to join the cavalry for an envelopment of the Confederate left flank, and a feint against the right. In this almost perfectly coordinated maneuver, reminiscent of Frederick the Great, the only serious flaw was that Thomas did not use his artillery particularly well. The weather also dulled the shock effect of the plan because, when the ice melted, it produced mud, which slowed maneuvers.

Hood at first was deceived as to the direction of Thomas's main attack. The feints met success, and soon the principal force hurled heavy blows against the Confederate left with telling effect. By 1:00 P.M. Hood began shifting troops from the less-threatened center to the precarious left. Even with this added strength, the left could not hold, and just before dark the lines in that sector crumbled. The Federals turned the flank and began driving men back along the Granny White Pike, pushing them southward for about two miles before halting at nightfall.

Thomas was pleased. With the Confederate flank crushed, he believed that his men easily could finish the job in the morning. But the Confederates did not merely rest during the night; they knew renewed attacks would come and they worked at further preparing their new lines—now only about half as long as the day before.

The Unionists opened their attack on December 16, beginning at 9:00 A.M. with a two-hour artillery bombardment. Then they moved forward in several waves. Assault after assault receded, repulsed by the intrenched defenders. But on the extreme left the Federals hammered away with advantageously positioned artillery, and by 3:30 P.M. the bluecoats pinned down the southerners on the left so that temporarily they could not fire back. A massed division then charged suddenly over the Confederate intrenchments. The lines, thus pierced, gave way and broke apart at many points.

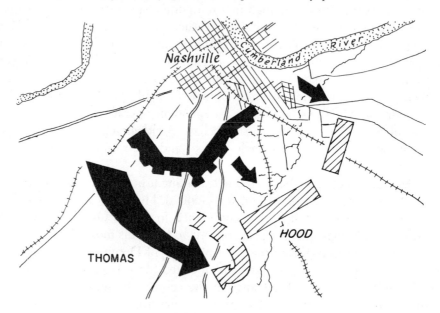

Thomas's Feints and Flank Movement

Stephen D. Lee shifted some of the men from his corps and halted the enemy. The Federals began slipping around toward Lee's rear but Lee held sufficiently long to prevent a rout. The Confederates pulled back in some disorder, but offered enough stiff resistance to induce prudence in their pursuers. After numerous holding actions, the Confederates eventually effected disengagement in spite of a vigorous pursuit by Wilson's well-led cavalry.

Thomas had suffered 3,061 casualties, while Hood lost 1,500 killed and wounded and another 4,500 men captured. For a two-day battle of such magnitude, the casualties ran remarkably low, but the fighting marked the last major battle in the West. The dream of a southern advance into the North thus faded forever.

After the first day of the battle Grant had urged Thomas: "Push the enemy now, and give him no rest until he is entirely destroyed." A vigorous pursuit would "break up Hood's army and render it useless for future operations." Though the pursuers, as usual, could not overtake the retreating army, the hurried retreat caused Hood further losses through straggling and desertion, the breaking down of horses, wagons, and artillery, and further damage to the army's already disastrously low morale. The men had lost confidence in

Hood and the only lift their morale received was a rumor that their "Uncle Joe" Johnston would resume command. As they marched south they sang, to the tune of the "Yellow Rose of Texas," a song they named the "Gallant Hood of Texas."

> So now I'm marching southward;
> My heart is full of woe.
> I'm going back to Georgia
> To see my Uncle Joe.
> You may talk about your Beauregard
> and sing of General Lee
> But the gallant Hood of Texas
> Played hell in Tennessee.[46]

Two weeks after the battle, Hood's enfeebled Army of Tennessee managed to encamp safely at Tupelo, Mississippi. Hood's campaign had failed to draw Sherman from his march through Georgia. Had Thomas not attacked, Hood would then have had to winter in Middle Tennessee, if his tenuous supply line had permitted even that. His already demoralized army would, in any case, have been sadly weakened by desertion and exposure. Confederate quartermasters could not nearly match their Union counterparts in providing for winter campaigning. Indeed it is difficult to see what, if anything, positive Hood could have accomplished on this mission. Davis wisely counseled against it, and Beauregard may well have given his assent reluctantly to a headstrong general, already appointed with plans approved by the President, whom he found it impossible to control.

Hood's invasion of Tennessee nullified one of the Confederacy's great advantages, the long lines of Union communications. In pushing North, Hood's enemy became stronger as Thomas collected the garrisons along the railroad. True, many of the garrison regiments were green and commanded by generals who had failed in the past, but they could fight effectively in fortifications. In addition, at Nashville, the trenches were manned in part by 7,000 quartermaster employees formed into a unit for the purpose.

Thus Hood completed the destruction of his army. He had begun it in the Atlanta campaign when his attacks seriously reduced its numbers and morale. At Franklin he took another major step toward its depletion when he made a futile frontal attack against Schofield's dug-in position. When Hood faced Thomas at Nashville, he had neither the numbers nor the morale to resist the rather old-fashioned battle conducted by Thomas. Reminiscent of the Stones River attacks, Thomas twice succeeded in bending and turning Hood's flanks. Thomas would have preferred to wait until his cavalry was stronger and delay had further weakened Hood. But Grant's somewhat unreasonable anxiety, partly motivated by concern for public opinion, forced an earlier battle, Thomas triumphing brilliantly in spite of his misgivings. With the help of the weather and the low morale of Hood's army, Thomas came close to fighting the battle of annihilation which had for so long existed in the minds of the public, politicians, and journalists. Together with Sherman's achievement in reaching the sea, the victory at Nashville added markedly to an admirable Christmas season enjoyed by the northern public and leaders.

On December 10 Sherman gained the Atlantic coast near Savannah. News of his raid had reached Washington only through southern newspapers which the northern command for this reason read with more than the usual interest. Lincoln, especially, was relieved when Sherman at last arrived at the coast safely and reported: "The weather has been fine, and supplies were abundant. Our march was most agreeable, and we were not at all molested by guerrillas." He told of complete success: "We have not lost a wagon on the trip, but have gathered a large supply of negroes, mules, horses, &c. . . . We have utterly destroyed over 200 miles of rails, and consumed stores and provisions that were essential to Lee's and Hood's armies." The only criticism of Sherman was that so few Negroes had come with him and Halleck told him, "You did not carry them out in your great raid."[47]

Sherman immediately acted to communicate with the fleet and, on December 13, Fort McAllister, defending the Ogeechee River below Savannah, fell to the Federals. Savannah was doomed. The Confederates evacuated the city on December 20, the 10,000 garrison troops escaping on an ingenious pontoon bridge made of thirty rice flats, but leaving behind their heavy guns and large amounts of cotton. Sherman pushed in unmolested and telegraphed Lincoln his famous message: "I beg to present you, as a Christmas gift, the city of Savannah, with 150 heavy guns and plenty of ammunition, and also about 25,000 bales of cotton." Sherman occupied the city for four weeks, letting his men rest while he accumulated supplies for his next move.[48]

In assessing the march to the sea, one of the Yankee troopers recalled: "We had a gay old campaign." And remembered: We "destroyed all we could not eat, stole their niggers, burned their cotton & gins, spilled their sorghum, burned & twisted their R. Roads and raised Hell generally." One Confederate officer estimated the number of runaway slaves at 10,000. Hundreds of these died along the way of hunger, disease, or exposure. This southerner also noted that "the whole region stunk with putrefying carcasses" of cattle, hogs, mules, and horses killed by the Federals, "and earth and air were filled with innumerable turkey buzzards battening upon their thickly strewn death feasts." Sherman himself estimated that his army did $100,000,000 worth of damage. Of this, he noted, about one-fifth "inured to our advantage," while "the remainder is simple waste and destruction."[49]

Sherman took pride in his railway demolition which "was performed better than usual" because he had "an engineer regiment provided with claws to twist the bars after being heated." When Sherman had passed, the Confederates assessed the damage. On the railroad from Atlanta to Augusta, thirty-eight miles of track were broken. Fifteen miles would require new rails; on twenty-three miles they could straighten the bent rails. On the route from Macon to Augusta inspection found "about 100 miles seriously injured." The middle of February was the earliest date by which they might be repaired.

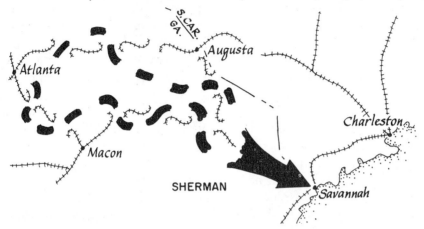

Sherman's March and Railroad Destruction

And Sherman had accomplished another of his goals. He wrote Halleck: "We are not only fighting hostile armies, but a hostile people, and must make old and young, rich and poor, feel the hard hand of war, as well as their organized armies. I know that this recent movement of mine through Georgia has had a wonderful effect in this respect. Thousands who had been deceived by their lying papers into the belief that we were being whipped all the time, realized the truth." President Davis succinctly summed up the nonmaterial impact of this significant march: "Sherman's campaign has produced [a] bad effect on our people. Success against his future operations is needed to reanimate public confidence."[50]

Sherman's march produced a devastating effect on southern logistics. Confederate supply already had received a serious blow just before the 1864 campaign began. The Chickamauga-Chattanooga campaign had "lost one of the main railroad supply lines from Georgia to Virginia" and gave up "much of the niter and nearly all of the copper production" of the Confederacy. For the 1864 campaign the Confederate armies possessed a sufficient supply of adequate shoes and clothing, though barely so. The total amount of food and fodder was also adequate but "the cotton states had surpluses while Virginia was in short supply." This meant dependence on the railroad for interregional shipments. Despite rapidly deteriorating rolling stock and rails, the railroads in 1864 equalled the task but were "stretched to their utmost capacity; if rail transportation were disrupted, the war effort would grind to a halt." Sherman's raid succeeded in "knocking the Confederate war effort to pieces." By concentrating on the destruction of the railroads he conducted "the most lethal onslaught possible." Though most powderworks survived his raid, "Sherman thoroughly smashed the Macon-Savannah Railroad and thus permanently severed Lee from his south Georgia subsistence and from the ordnance production of Columbus and Macon."[51]

As Sherman paused to accumulate supplies and receive instructions for his next move, the Confederates sought means for coping with him and repairing the damage to the Army of Tennessee. Beauregard quickly relinquished control of Hardee's department to go to the western part of his vast division. Having belatedly learned of Hood's defeat, he received permission to replace him with General Taylor. Hood simplified matters by resigning. Reaching the army in north Mississippi, Beauregard found its morale so low that he granted furloughs, something he had initially opposed. Beauregard was then enjoined to send reinforcements to Hardee, but he reported: "The disorganization and demoralization of the Army of Tennessee" is so great that, over the bad roads and railroads, "no reenforcements can be sent to General Hardee from this army." In spite of this and his and Taylor's protests that Selma and the "rich Valley of the Alabama River" would be exposed, the President insisted. Polk's old Mississippi corps could remain with Taylor, but the two original corps must move to Georgia. Reluctantly Beauregard dispatched on January 20 two corps, only 15,000 men present, and prepared to follow them in command. He would be leading only sad remnants of the army he had concentrated before Shiloh.[52]

Despite his victory at Nashville, Thomas's superiors believed him "slow in mind and in action." They could not expect a winter raid from him. Grant, therefore, planned to use Thomas's available troops elsewhere and ordered two divisions to Baltimore, "to be thrown where they may be wanted on arrival." When Grant understood that Beauregard was sending the bulk of Hood's army to resist Sherman, Grant clearly saw the shape of the winter campaign. He planned for the force from Thomas, already moving east, to support Sherman; others of Thomas's troops he would send to Canby to move, at last, on Mobile and raid up the Alabama River toward Montgomery and Selma, where "the rebels have a very large amount of supplies. . . . If these can be captured and the railroads destroyed," he wrote, "their Western armies cannot get ammunition and ordnance stores."[53]

But the shape of the winter campaign would depend primarily on the use made of Sherman's army. With the fall of Savannah, Sherman could write Grant: This "completes the first part of our game, and fulfills a great part of your instructions." Grant had already written Sherman that he now wanted "to get control of the only two through routes from east to west" by taking Savannah and a point farther north. After briefly entertaining the idea of moving Sherman's army to Virginia to "close out Lee," Grant adhered to his strategy of exhaustion in his use of Sherman's "spare army." Instead of taking a position at Augusta Sherman should march to Virginia, another raid which would "disorganize the South, and prevent the organization of new armies from their broken fragments." As for Lee, Grant, with some levity, explained: "My own opinion is that Lee is averse to going out of Virginia, and if the cause of the South is lost he wants Richmond to be the last place surrendered. If he has such views it may be well to indulge him until everything else is in our hands." In accommodating the enemy's desire to retain Richmond, Grant followed the basic Lincoln-Halleck strategy of concentration in the West, even though his old western army now operated in the southeast. More important, he adhered to his own strategy of exhaustion by directing Sherman to attack the enemy's logistics rather than using his army to take Richmond.[54]

Having already expressed the desire to resume the "journey to Raleigh," Sherman felt ready, explaining: "I feel no doubt as to our future plans; I have thought them over so long and well that they appear as clear as daylight." He wrote: I wish Grant "would run down and see us; it would have a good effect, and would show to both armies that they are acting on a common plan." But Grant and Sherman could not confer, relying instead on mail carried by steamers. With 60,000 men "full of experience and full of ardor," Sherman readied himself to follow Grant's instructions to "break up the railroads in South and North Carolina, and join the armies operating against Richmond." He would, he explained, employ his usual strategy: I will "make a good ready and then move rapidly to my objective, avoiding a battle at points where I would be encumbered by wounded, but striking boldly and quickly when my objective is reached."[55]

"I left Augusta untouched on purpose," Sherman remarked, "because the enemy will be in doubt as to my objective point after crossing the Savannah River, whether it be Augusta or Charleston, and will naturally divide his forces." As in his march from Atlanta, Sherman then planned to move between them, breaking the railroad, taking Columbia, and then striking for North Carolina, communicating with the fleet at Wilmington before he advanced on Raleigh or Weldon. He preferred Wilmington, "a live place," to taking the politically significant city of Charleston, "dead and unimportant when its railroad communications are broken." His objective was clear. He wrote Grant: "I feel confident that I can break up the whole railroad system of South Carolina and North Carolina, and be on the Roanoke, either at Raleigh or Weldon by the time spring fairly opens."[56]

This move would force Lee "to come out of Richmond or acknowledge himself beaten." The prospect of Lee moving "would not alarm me," Sherman wrote Grant, for "if you feel confident that you can whip Lee outside of his intrenchments, I feel equally confident that I can handle him in open country." Sherman expected Lee to "throw himself rapidly between me and Grant," he reported. But, realizing that to exploit his interior lines Lee would have to be on the offensive, Sherman explained: "I would force him to attack me at a disadvantage, always under the supposition that Grant would be on his heels; and if the worst came to the worst I could fight my way" to the coast. Thus again did Sherman and Grant plan to take the enemy in the rear and employ the power of the defense to cope with the problem of exterior lines, relying, in an emergency, on the ability of a raiding army to reach the coast and the fleet.[57]

Because this was to be a winter march, Sherman delayed in order to accumulate supplies. While waiting to fill his wagons before he would "be off again on another raid," Sherman received many letters of congratulations. "One from General Hitchcock and one from Professor Mahan" gave him the greatest pride. "Such men do not flatter and are judges of what they write." Proud of his accomplishments, he was a little embarrassed on New Year's Day to be "toasted, etc., with allusions to Hannibal, Caesar, etc.," he wrote, "but in reply I turned all into a good joke by saying that Hannibal and Caesar were small potatoes as they had never read the *New York Herald*, or had a photograph taken."[58]

As Sherman paused, a significant campaign was taking place on the North Carolina coast, while in Virginia the siege of Petersburg had continued with but few major incidents. In late September, Grant, in his attempt to take Richmond by surprise, had extended his flank farther beyond the Weldon Railroad and at the end of October had made a major but unsuccessful effort to cut the Southside Railroad. Except for this, his siege had been relatively uneventful, and he had concentrated on trying to hold the maximum number of Confederate troops in the vicinity of Richmond for the benefit of Sherman and to assist Sheridan in his campaign against Early in the Valley. But Grant fixed his eye on the North Carolina coast, where he had originally projected a major campaign for early 1864. Grant anxiously had wanted to close Wilmington, the last Confederate port and through which came the final critical supplies of shoes for the southern Army.

The expedition was delayed until the Navy removed the menace by powerful Confederate ironclad, the C.S.S. *Albemarle*. A small launch accomplished this at the end of October when she managed to reach the *Albemarle* at her anchorage and sink her by placing a torpedo along side. A combined navy and army force could now close the port of Wilmington by capturing Fort Fisher, which guarded the river up to the city. It pleased Grant that his capable collaborator from the Mississippi, Admiral David D. Porter, commanded the naval forces. Porter had taken this post after returning from leading the flotilla which had accompanied Banks's ill-fated Red River campaign. Since North Carolina was in General Benjamin F. Butler's department, Grant selected one of the political general's capable subordinates to lead the expedition against the well-defended position, one so important that President Davis had sent his chief of staff, Braxton Bragg, to take charge of the department.

Grant was dismayed when Butler, who had failed so dismally in May, decided to exercise his prerogative as department commander and assume personal charge of the expedition. Though Grant had found that "as an administrative officer" Butler had "no superior," he commanded best where "no great battles are to be fought." To Grant's suggestion in July that Butler be given a western department far from the enemy, Halleck had replied that to send the quarrelsome radical general "to Kentucky would probably cause an insurrection in that State and an immediate call for large reenforcements. Moreover, he would probably greatly embarrass Sherman, if he did not attempt to supercede him, by using against him all his talent at political intrigue and his facilities for newspaper abuse." To place Missouri under Butler's control would have the same result, except that there "would be a free fight between him and Rosecrans," the Missouri commander, resulting in "local difficulties, and calls for reinforcements likely to follow. Inveterate as is Rosecrans's habit of continually calling for more troops, Butler differs only in demanding instead of calling."[59]

Since no other assignment had been found, Butler had remained in command in eastern Virginia and North Carolina. His decision to assume personal charge of the Wilmington expedition entailed an additional delay because Butler needed time to prepare for the novel plan he had adopted to help take Fort Fisher. The general prepared a ship filled with gunpowder which, if it could be "run up near the shore under the fort and exploded, it would create havoc and make the capture of the fort an easy matter." Skeptical of the powder-ship scheme, Grant, writing Sherman, said of the project: "While I hope for the best [I] do not believe a particle in" it. Halleck reacted more emphatically, saying "that Butler's torpedo ship would have about as much effect on the forts as if he should——at them."[60]

Grant had wanted the expedition to close Wilmington to start in early December, while the Confederates in North Carolina were preoccupied with Sherman. At the same time Grant directed a raid from the North Carolina coast inland to the railroad and a successful march of over 20,000 of Meade's infantry southward, destroying more of the Weldon railway. But Butler's delay did not cause his failure.[61]

In mid-December Butler and Porter arrived off Fort Fisher and sent in the powder ship. "At two o'clock in the morning the explosion took place—and produced no more effect on the fort, or anything else on land, than the bursting of a boiler anywhere on the Atlantic Ocean would have done." The fleet then bombarded the fort while Butler landed a part of his force which reached within 100 yards of the defenses. But suddenly Butler ordered a retreat, one so precipate that 600 men were left on the beach until the Navy rescued them. The expedition sailed back to Virginia, exasperating Admiral Porter who, writing his friend Sherman, said: The future fall of the city would "let people see the folly of employing such generals as Butler and Banks. I have tried them both, and God save me from further connection with such generals."[62]

One New York newspaper gloated over the failure of the colorful Butler, saying he "should have landed on the beach wearing those ostrich feathers which he wore in the streets of New York, brandishing his puissant horse-pistols, and fixing on Fort Fisher the terrors of his revolving orb." With the fall elections past, Grant could at last induce Lincoln to relieve the politically powerful Butler for "gross and culpable failure." Sherman delighted in hearing that Butler had gone home to the textile town of Lowell "where he should have stayed and confined his bellicose operations to the factory girls." Butler cordially reciprocated the hostility of the regulars and, in his farewell address to his troops, attacked Grant's spring campaign: "I have refused," he said, "to order the useless sacrifice of the lives of such soldiers, and I am relieved from your command. The wasted blood of my men does not stain my garments."[63]

When a new expedition returned to Fort Fisher in January, the urbane and competent Alfred H. Terry led the army forces. Terry had studied law at Yale and, while practicing in Connecticut, had been a member of the militia. By demonstrated ability he had risen to command of a corps in Butler's army. Grant did not misplace his confidence in Terry for, with smooth efficiency, on January 4 federal troops embarked at Bermuda Hundred. On the 12th the immense federal fleet of about 60 vessels and a large number of troop transports with 8,000 men arrived off Fort Fisher. Packing the greatest naval firepower in history to that time, on January 13 the fleet began bombarding. In the next three days it hurled some 20,000 projectiles. Then, put ashore without opposition, the troops moved to invest the fort. Two days later, Fort Fisher fell, just after Butler had testified to the radical-dominated Committee on the Conduct of the War that Fort Fisher could not be taken by assault.

In addition, Terry's effective work on land inflicted on the Confederates 2,500 casualties, including 2,000 prisoners, at a Union loss of less than 1,400. In addition Terry showed up the political general, Butler, because, as Sherman pointed out, "he had the same troops with which Butler failed to make the attempt." Relishing Terry's success as much as Butler's fiasco, Sherman also "rejoiced that Terry was not a West Pointer" because it disproved allegations that the West Pointers deliberately conspired to insure the defeat of generals who had not attended the Academy. With pleasure Halleck reported to Canby: Banks, dissatisfied with his limited command, was "still lounging around Congress and the White House, very bitter, I understand, on you and me. I think he and Butler are about played out."[64]

Meanwhile the winter weather precluded major operations in the Petersburg siege. Nevertheless, Grant had been tempted when Sherman reached the sea at Savannah. If Grant moved Sherman's 60,000 men to Virginia, he could "wipe out Lee," but Thomas's victory made him adhere to his original strategy of continuing to concentrate in the West and rely on raids to wreck the enemy's railroads. The winter weather and the two months required to bring Sherman's army to Virginia contributed to this decision, as did the difficulty of provisioning so many men in Virginia. On the move, Sherman's army was very easily supplied and Quartermaster General Meigs was elated to find an army which could "move more than twenty-five miles from a navigable river or railroad without perishing."[65]

Having ordered a part of Thomas's army to Baltimore, Grant again contemplated using it about Richmond and Petersburg but decided to direct Schofield's 20,000-man Army of the Ohio to North Carolina. He ordered Schofield to land on the coast and take Wilmington. With the capture of Fort Fisher, the situation of Wilmington paralleled that of Mobile—the harbor was closed to blockade runners, but, with the city still in Confederate hands, Union ships could make no use of the port. He then directed Schofield "to give General Sherman material aid, if needed in his march north," to "open a base of supplies for him on his line of march," and to move inland and open a railroad to Goldsborough.[66]

One reason for moving Schofield, Grant explained to Sherman, was that Thomas "indicated a sluggishness that satisfied me that he would never do to conduct one of your campaigns." More importantly Grant needed to be prepared for Lee's use of his interior line between Grant and Sherman. If Lee should leave Richmond, he would present "the only danger to the easy success" of Sherman's move north. If Lee met Sherman's raiding army, Sherman, without communications, could not halt but would have to take the offensive against Lee's army, "compelled to beat it, or find the sea coast." Grant therefore wanted Schofield to provide Sherman with railroad communications to the coast and be available to reinforce him. In addition to Schofield's army and Terry's force, Grant strengthened Sherman with all available troops in the Department of the South. Altogether Sherman would have at least 100,000 men to face the puny Confederate forces assembling in North Carolina, scarcely 40,000 if they could concentrate in time. Sherman then should be irresistible; but, in addition, Grant promised him: "Should you be brought to a halt anywhere, I can send two corps of 30,000 effective men to your support from the troops about Richmond."[67]

Schofield's landing on the North Carolina coast was reminiscent of Grant's plan of a year earlier to land an army of 60,000 there to break the railroads and drive North Carolina from the war. The other parts of his plan for early 1865 consistently followed his basic strategic concepts. Schofield would take Sherman's opponents in the rear, and, instead of concentrating against Lee, Grant directed the carrying out of many other raids. His strategy had taken a long time to reach fruition, because his and Sherman's conventional operations in Virginia and Georgia had absorbed the summer months. Now that they had defeated Hood, and Sherman had embarked on his second raid, Grant's strategy became fully effective.

Grant had long believed that, if the Union mounted forces in the West had effective leaders, "they could travel over that Western country with impunity." As Sherman marched northward, Grant sought to take advantage of Union cavalry superiority and directed Thomas to send a raid from East

Tennessee into South Carolina, "destroying the railroad and the military resources of the country." He stressed to Thomas: "This expedition goes to destroy and not to fight battles." The force did not start in time and was finally redirected to East Tennessee to be at hand for Lee's possible retreat in that direction, when the Union might need "a very considerable force in the section." He also ordered Thomas to send the vigorous A. J. Smith to Canby with 23,000 troops.[68]

With these powerful forces Grant directed Canby to raid from Mobile into the interior of Alabama, "subsisting off the country through which they are passing." Grant explained the objectives: "It is important to prevent, as far as possible, the planting of a crop this year and to destroy their railroads, machine-shops, &c. It is also important to get all the negro men we can before the enemy put them in the ranks." Canby's operation, dependent on concentrating dispersed forces, was slow starting. But Halleck told him to be prompt, warning him: "General Grant is very impatient at delays and too ponderous preparations. He says that nearly all our generals are too late in starting, and carry too much with them."[69]

Canby, as directed, had already been industrious in sending cavalry raids into Mississippi to interrupt Hood's communications before Nashville. He now planned three additional raids from the Mississippi in cooperation with his Mobile operation. In addition Grant took further advantage of the Union cavalry's ascendancy when he instructed Thomas to send a powerful expedition south to the same objective. Grant intended for this formidable mounted force, led by the energetic and capable James H. Wilson, to aid Canby's move north from Mobile by taking the defenders in the rear. Grant also directed Wilson to "destroy the enemy's line of communication and military resources," as well as "destroy or capture their forces brought into the field." Wilson's movement assumed greater importance when Grant realized that the enemy would concentrate to defend Mobile, making Wilson's advance "effective and easy, and," he explained, it "will tend in the end to secure all we want without a long march into the interior by our infantry forces." Relying almost exclusively on powerful raiding elements, Grant explained the principle to Canby: "An army the size of the one you will have can always get to some place where they can be supplied if they should fail to reach the point started for."[70]

Thus Grant had projected three major cavalry expeditions: from the Mississippi toward Selma, from the Tennessee toward Selma, and from East Tennessee into South Carolina. Two major infantry raids did, however, carry the main burden of the strategy of exhaustion—Canby's into Alabama with 40,000 men and Sherman's into South and North Carolina, reinforced to 100,000 men with 30,000 more in reserve. By landing Schofield in North Carolina and establishing rail communications with the coast, Sherman could convert his raid into a penetration so that he could maneuver against Lee without having either to attack or retreat to the coast to re-establish communications. Every area east of the Mississippi would either have already been raided or was included in the plan for the winter and spring.[71]

With the growing strength and efficiency of Union cavalry, Grant had provided a larger role for mounted forces. In giving orders to buy more horses, he explained his policy: "If we can keep the enemy's cavalry on the move we will soon wear them out, and be able to ride over their whole country comparatively unmolested." He did not overlook Virginia in the program, for, as soon as the weather permitted, Grant directed Sheridan to move from Winchester to Richmond, aiming to "destroy the railroad and canal in every direction, so as to be of no further use to the rebellion." He explained to Sheridan that his "additional raid—with one now about starting from East Tennessee under Stoneman numbering 4,000 to 5,000 cavalry; one from Vicksburg, numbering 7,000 or 8,000 cavalry; one from Eastport, Mississippi, 10,000 cavalry; Canby from Mobile Bay, with about 38,000 mixed troops— these three latter pushing for Tuscaloosa, Selma, and Montgomery; and Sherman with a large army eating out the vitals of South Carolina—is all that will be wanted to leave nothing for the rebellion to stand upon."[72]

Because he relied exclusively on the strategy of exhaustion, Grant's own role in this final campaign was limited to that of general in chief. The mission of the Army of the Potomac remained what he had intended for it—to hold Lee's forces in Virginia and assume the offensive only if Lee sufficiently weakened himself. Though Lee's army could not exist without supplies, Grant understood that the indirect nature of the strategy of exhaustion would mask its effectiveness from the public. He explained: "I shall necessarily have to take the odium of comparative inactivity, but if it results, as I expect it will, in the discomfiture of Lee's army, I shall be entirely satisfied."[73]

Sherman's army of 60,000 under his immediate command was the first raid to move, beginning its march north in the first week of January. The enemy did not know his initial objective, and he had helped intensify this confusion not just by the inherent ambiguity of whether he aimed at Augusta or Charleston but by directing the forces of the Department of the South to aid him by making diversions on the coast in order to create the impression he was aiming at Charleston. He again opposed Hardee, commanding a motley force numbering 30,000 on paper but with hardly 15,000 able to take the field. General Beauregard was in Alabama, "hurrying troops forward as rapidly as [the] bad condition of the roads [would] permit." The force he was hurrying to South Carolina was the Army of Tennessee. Instead of only two corps, Beauregard had three en route, since General Taylor had reported: I can "resist a raid without Stewart's corps and cannot fight a battle with it against an army." The reinforcement Beauregard brought, the once formidable army which had so long defended Tennessee and Georgia, now numbered only 10,800 infantry and artillery. Its morale remained low, Hardee receiving the following report from Augusta: "Nine hundred men from the West have arrived; one-half deserted."[74]

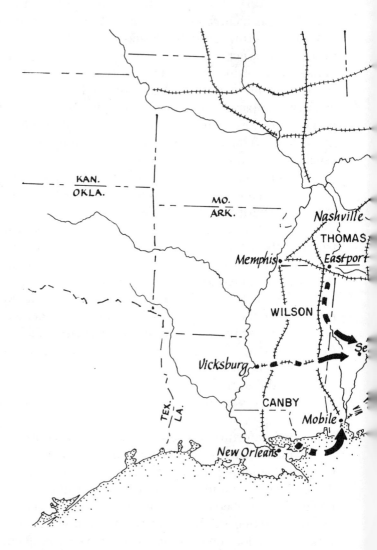

Upon his return from Mississippi Beauregard again assumed control of the Department of South Carolina, Georgia, and Florida, directing within his vast division three departments stretching from the Atlantic to the Mississippi. His assumption of immediate command of the forces opposing Sherman was reassuring to Hardee, who explained that if Beauregard would join him in person, "if only for one day," it would be a source of "great relief." But Beauregard could provide little more than the inspiration of his presence. He explained: "The enemy moving with a certain number of days' rations for all his troops, with the hope of establishing a new base at Charleston after its fall, has in reality no lines of communication which can be threatened or cut. His overpowering force enables him to move into the interior of the country like an ordinary moveable column." Beauregard soon learned that Sherman

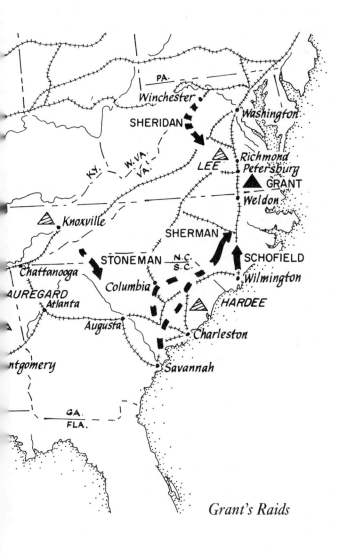

Grant's Raids

was not aiming at Charleston. He reported: "Our forces, about 20,000 effective infantry and artillery, more or less demoralized, occupy a circumference of about 240 miles from Charleston to Augusta. The enemy, well organized and disciplined, and flushed with success, . . . is concentrated upon one point (Columbia) of that circumference." Beauregard had already informed Lee that he could not concentrate in time.[75]

By his great numerical superiority, by moving rapidly, and, above all, by deceiving the enemy, Sherman avoided the armies of Beauregard and Hardee. Had they known his objective and been able to concentrate in his front, even with their meagre numbers they would have had a slight chance to stop his raid. If he had been brought to a halt and been unable to get past an enemy concentration, his lack of a supply line would have forced him to attack or move toward the coast and take advantage of Grant's "precaution to have supplies ready" wherever Sherman might "turn up." Rather than being stopped by his dispersed enemy, Sherman was slowed by the rainy winter weather, which, he reported, had already "nearly drowned some of [his] columns in the rice fields of the Savannah." The "foul weather and roads would have stopped travel to almost any other body of men." The impressed observers even included Johnston, who had believed that nobody could make a campaign over that land in winter. Now, more ruefully than grudgingly, he admitted that there truly had been no army like Sherman's since the days of Julius Caesar.[76]

While a futile peace conference went on between Confederate representatives and federal officials, including Lincoln, at Hampton Roads, Sherman's men pushed into the heart of South Carolina. Sherman spent one cold night sleeping on the floor of an abandoned country mansion. The fire burned low and he awakened uncomfortably cold. He arose and renewed the flames with an old, wooden mantel clock and a bedstead, "the only act of vandalism," he later asserted, "that I recall done by myself personally during the war." They reached Columbia, the capital, on February 17. Unique among the spectators observing Sherman's entry were numerous recently liberated Union prisoners of war. One of them, S. H. M. Byers, slipped up to Sherman and handed him a copy of a song he had composed, while incarcerated, called, "Sherman's March to the Sea." The song, later nationally famous and sung for three generations, pleased Sherman who thereupon elevated Byers to a position on his staff. About one-third of the city accidentally burned, and Sherman pushed on. On February 22 the Federals entered the city of Wilmington without opposition.[77]

Meanwhile, the Confederates had changed commanders. The fall of Atlanta, Sherman's march, and Hood's disastrous Tennessee campaign naturally discredited Davis's strategic management. Like any regime defeated in war, Davis's was losing the confidence of the people. The Confederate Congress established by law the position of general in chief and, as intended, Davis appointed Lee to that post. This involved no displacement of Bragg. The departure of Beauregard for his southwestern command had left no senior officer in charge in North Carolina. The importance of the port of Wilmington, together with a lack of confidence in the local commander, indicated a command change. Bragg was apparently available for the assignment because, though valuable, he had not made himself indispensable to Davis. Perhaps, too, the unsuccessful outcome of his recommendation of Hood to succeed Johnston had somewhat discredited his advice. He had not, of course, superseded Lee as the President's most valued collaborator, for Lee's influence had never been stronger.

Soon after Bragg's departure Davis revived his old idea of extending Lee's "command over the Southern Atlantic States" or even all the Confederacy east of the Mississippi. Davis knew that Lee did not believe he could continue to exercise an army command and at the same time command so large a region. Nevertheless when offered the post of general in chief, Lee accepted with, certainly, the realization that it was a political necessity for him to do so. The formal, or "nominal," changes altered the situation little for, as Davis wrote: "There had always been entire co-intelligency and accord between General Lee and myself." The only exception to this harmony between Lee and Davis had taken place in 1863 when the western concentration bloc had, with ultimate success, contested Lee's influence.[78]

At the same time the invaluable Seddon left the War Department, giving way to the popular John C. Breckinridge. Though a successful major general, the victor of New Market could do nothing to revive the Confederacy's failing manpower or to shore up its collapsing supply system.

In addition, a change in the command opposing Sherman took place almost immediately. Beauregard, whose health was known to be bad, had perhaps compromised his credibility by sending to President Davis one of his flights of strategic hyperbole proposing that 35,000 of Lee's men join him against Sherman to "crush him, then to concentrate all forces against Grant, and then to march on Washington to dictate peace." At the same time Hood's emphatic failures had improved Joe Johnston's reputation. So on February 23 Johnston superseded Beauregard, the Creole becoming second in command and thereby ending by implication the Military Division of the West. At almost the same time an anomaly in the Confederate departmental structure ended when Johnston assumed formal control over Bragg's meagre forces in North Carolina.[79]

The change thus restored the Johnston and Beauregard command team, the winning combination of the first Battle of Bull Run; but there would be no magic in the now-veteran pair. Johnston, ordered to "concentrate all available forces and drive back Sherman," replied that it was too late. Neverthe-

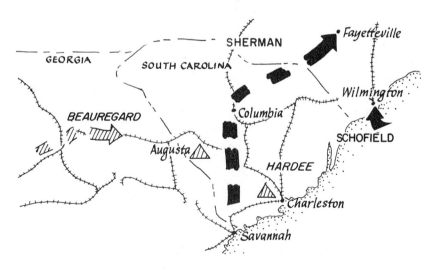

Sherman's Advance

less, he made a sincere effort; even Jefferson Davis admitted that the first part
of the order was "well executed" and, though driving back Sherman "was
more desirable than practical," Johnston deserved "credit due to a vigorous
effort."[80]

Now with a superabundance of seasoned general officers, but not enough
rank and file, Generals Johnston, Beauregard, and Bragg, Lieutenant Generals Hardee, Stephen D. Lee, Hampton, and others lacked the resources for
effective resistance to Sherman's powerful and skillfully conducted offensive.
They maneuvered as best they could and slapped feebly at Sherman's host.
In the ineffectual Battle of Kinston, North Carolina, March 8–10, Confederate numbers proved too meagre to sustain more than mere momentary drives.

But on March 9, in South Carolina, a small southern morale-raising episode
took place. Confederate cavalry under Wade Hampton and Joe Wheeler moved
in to attack and completely surprised federal cavalry encamped near Solemn
Grove and Monroe's Cross Roads. Brigadier General Judson Kilpatrick was
nearly captured in his bed but, fleeing without his trousers, managed to
escape and rally his men. The Federals then overcame the southern advantage
and defeated Hampton in a counterattack. The affair later became unofficially
dubbed "the Battle of Kilpatrick's Pants."

In North Carolina, on March 11, Sherman's men occupied Fayetteville.
They fought a small battle on the 16th at Averysborough and a rather desperate affair at Bentonville on March 18–21, where Johnston had concentrated
to attempt the defeat of Sherman before he united with Schofield. The Union
army fended off several strained Confederate assaults and finally the southerners prudently disengaged. The rebels lost over 2,600 men, many of them
captured, to the Yankees' 1,500 or more casualties. This was the last offensive
effort of any consequence as the bedraggled and badly out-numbered southern force lay impotent before Sherman's victorious armies.

Meanwhile Canby at last moved against Mobile. Having been much delayed by bad weather, including gales and fog, he aroused Grant's ire. The
lieutenant general, irritated that Canby had even asked to build a railroad,
was disappointed that he was so late that his raid could not be "co-operative
with Sherman's" march into the Carolinas. Grant reiterated his directions "to
push forward promptly and to live upon the country and destroy railroads
and machine shops, &c., not to build them." Now he again explained the
mission: "Take Mobile and hold it, and push your forces to the interior to
Montgomery and Selma. Destroy railroads, rollingstock, and everything useful for carrying on war, and when you have done this take such positions as
can be supplied by water." Emphasizing the superiority of secure water communications, he explained: "By this means alone you can occupy positions
from which the enemy's roads in the interior can be kept broken."[81]

The 10,000 defenders held out until April 8 when they evacuated the city.

But, as Grant had anticipated, the Union did not need Canby's advance. Union armies had reached Canby's goal from the Tennessee River by a raid, directed by Grant, which essentially took the enemy in the rear as they concentrated against the threat to Mobile.

Union Major General James H. Wilson, having conducted the Civil War's most effective pursuit after a battle following Hood's defeat at Nashville, had encamped his 13,480 cavalrymen in north Alabama for the severest part of the winter. Commencing on March 18 he led them on a slashing and devastating raid. Going into Selma, Alabama, and thence eastward into Georgia, where he eventually captured the fleeing Jefferson Davis, Wilson destroyed almost all of the South's remaining industrial capacity: ironworks, foundries, machine shops, rolling mills, collieries, factories, niter works, arsenals, a navy yard, a powder magazine, steamboats, locomotives and railroad cars, and untold quantities of quartermaster, commissary, and ordnance stores.

But Sherman's march was so successful it really obviated the operations of Canby and Wilson. On reaching Fayetteville in central North Carolina Sherman reported: "The utter demolition of the railroad system of South Carolina, and the utter destruction of the enemy's arsenals at Columbia, Cheraw, and Fayetteville are the principles of the movement. These points were regarded as unaccessible to us, and now no place in the Confederacy is safe against the Army of the West. Let Lee hold on to Richmond and we will destroy his country, and then of what use is Richmond?" Sherman's position in North Carolina well illustrated the achievements of the western armies. His Army of the Tennessee was about to make a junction in North Carolina with Schofield's Army of the Ohio. The distance between these forces and the rivers which had originally supplied them exhibited the efficacy of the Lincoln-Halleck policy of concentrating in the West and the Grant-Sherman strategy of raids. That the Union Department of the South became a part of Sherman's Military Division of the Mississippi most dramatically symbolized the effectiveness of these strategies.[82]

The march through the Carolinas produced a devastating effect on Confederate logistics. Sherman's "movements in South Carolina in January and February nailed the lid on Lee's coffin by cutting Lee off from his Deep South supply source." This Sherman realized when he wrote: My marches were "as much an attack on Lee's army as though I were operating within the sound of his artillery." Lee had continued to meet some of his needs by means of the railroad which ran east through Augusta, but Sherman cut this. "The evacuation of Charleston combined with the fall of Fort Fisher and Wilmington to cut off Lee's indispensable sources of foreign supply." Lee's troops had long been immobilized at Richmond, "marooned in a wasteland" of country denuded of resources and "dependent on railroad transportation for all its subsistence," just as Lee had feared. In spite of Sherman's march, Lee had miraculously been provisioned to the end, but it would not have continued long.[83]

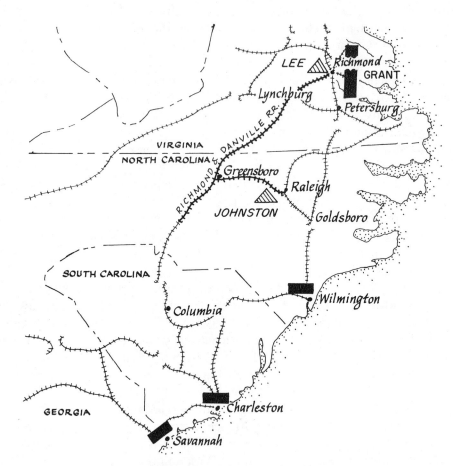

Lee's Last Line of Communications

As a result of Grant's raids against southern railroads, "dissolving armies wandered about the country while factories produced and the storehouses held supplies that could not be moved to the troops. Shortages had hamstrung the armies." Organized resistance in terms of major armies in the field came virtually to an end. The strategy of exhaustion through raids had succeeded.[84]

After his victory at Bentonville, Sherman paused at Goldsborough, waiting for the repair of the railroad from the coast. He had promised provisions to his "dirty, ragged, and saucy" army and was troubled because, without the railroad, they had run short. "As long as we move we can gather food and forage," he wrote, "but as soon as we stop trouble begins. I feel sadly disappointed the railroads are not done." Though he wrote, I believe that nothing has "tended more to break the pride of the South than my steady persistent progress," he was concerned that Joe Johnston "may travel back toward Georgia," and added, "I don't want to follow him again over that long road." He worried even more that the defeated enemy might scatter and then "band together as highwaymen and keep the country in a fever, begetting a guerrilla war." He worried about "guerrilla bands, a thing more to be feared than organized war."[85]

At the end of March Sherman visited Grant at his headquarters near Petersburg to plan their final movements. Sherman arrived in Virginia to meet Grant immediately after Lee had launched a desperate and inadequate attack upon Fort Stedman. He took the fort but lost momentum and could not exploit the fleeting advantage. Counterattacks forced the southerners out. Indeed the Federals so little believed that the episode represented any threat that they did not interrupt a parade which General Grant and President Lincoln were reviewing just behind the combat zone. A Virginia lieutenant, captured in the first wave of the assault, while being escorted to the rear caught a glimpse of the notables "seemingly not in the least concerned and as if nothing had happened." To be sure, nothing much had happened.[86]

This vain effort culminated what Lee's army had found to be their most difficult winter.

During the late fall and winter of 1864–65 the Confederate War Department had well maintained the strength of Lee's army even though Lee had sent a division of cavalry and more than a division of infantry south to strengthen Wilmington and resist Sherman. But the War Department could maintain Lee's strength only by sending him conscripts and soldiers taken from safer and better-fed assignments than the Army of Northern Virginia. In one significant respect these reluctant replacements were an element of weakness: they communicated their low morale to the veterans of an army heretofore characterized by its confidence and spirit.

The dramatic decline in Confederate morale which commenced with the fall of Atlanta was fully evident in Lee's army. Morale was especially depressed among soldiers from Georgia and the states menaced by Sherman, their letters from home fully conveying civilian gloom about the future.

The winter supply situation, much worse than usual in Lee's now concentrated, trench-bound army, further depressed the soldiers' spirits. In January a soldier wrote: "There are a good many of us who believe that this shooting match has been carried on long enough. A government that has run out of rations can't expect to do much more fighting, and to keep on in a reckless and wanton expenditure of human life. Our rations are all the way from a pint to a quart of cornmeal a day, and occasionally a piece of bacon large enough to grease your palate." In addition to poor morale the army suffered from physical weakness due to an inadequate diet. Both were reflected in desertions which took nearly eight percent of Lee's army between February 15 and March 18.[87]

As Lee's debilitated army failed in its desperate and hopeless attack at Fort Stedman, Grant was ready for his own initiative because Sheridan had completed his raid. During the first days of March Sheridan had made his cavalry raid from Winchester to Richmond. Easily brushing aside feeble opposition,

Sheridan advanced to Staunton where he turned east, defeating Early's minute force and capturing 1,200 prisoners. Occupying Charlottesville, he then
began his work of destroying railroad bridges and track between Staunton
and Richmond. In addition, one force went from Charlottesville almost as far
as Lynchburg, "destroying every bridge on the road and in many places miles
of track." His troopers also "proceeded along the canal . . . destroying every
lock and in many places the bank of the canal." The raid would seriously
affect Richmond's supplies, for Sheridan reported: "We have found great
abundance in this country for our men and animals; in fact, the canal has
been the great feeder of Richmond." By the middle of March Sheridan's men
had completed their work and reached the vicinity of Richmond, ready for a
new assignment.[88]

Grant was ready for Sheridan to start on another raid to cut the roads on
the south of Richmond. In addition, Grant, concerned about "Lee and Johnston attempting to unite," wrote, "I feel extremely desirous of not only cutting the lines of communication between them, but of having a large and
properly commanded cavalry force ready in case the attempt is made." Grant
ordered Sheridan out, supported by two infantry corps, to "reach the right
and rear of the enemy," not "to attack the enemy in his entrenched position
but to force him out if possible." If this attempt failed, he directed Sheridan
to carry out his raid against the two railroads to the south, "the only avenues
of supply to Lee's army," and either to return or "go into North Carolina and
join General Sherman."[89]

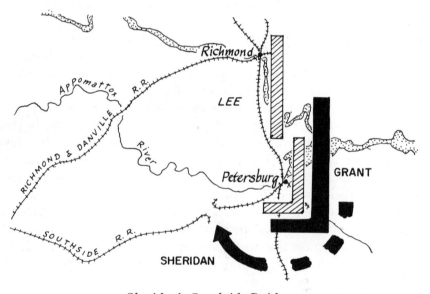

Sheridan's Southside Raid

In two days Sheridan and his two corps had made such good progress that
it looked as if they could "turn the enemy's right with the assistance of a corps

of infantry, entirely detached from the balance of the army." Sheridan succeeded in doing just this. Pushing to the enemy's rear, he met 19,000 Confederates under Pickett. Retreating until his 12,000 men were reinforced by the corps of 16,000 infantry, he attacked. Turning Pickett in the Battle of Five Forks on April 1, Sheridan broke the Southside Railroad and arrived at Lee's rear, with the Richmond and Danville Railroad at his mercy. Having already shifted his troops to his left, Grant could complete the turning movement the next day by driving through the intrenchments of the thinly manned extension of Lee's right flank thus reaching the rear of Petersburg.[90]

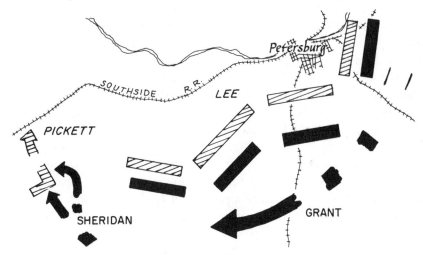

Sheridan Turns Pickett

Faced with the menace of this successful turning movement, Lee immediately ordered the long-contemplated evacuation of Richmond and Petersburg. But, though Grant had not reached his rear, Lee faced a serious problem in conducting his withdrawal; his line of retreat lay not directly to the rear but southwestward along the railroad to Danville. He would have to hurry to prevent Grant's forces from reaching the railroad before he did. But Lee began his movement with 200 guns and over 1,000 wagons, "heavy impedimenta for an army whose escape required speed."[91]

Lee did enjoy the advantage of retreating along his supply line. The commissary general had, miraculously, accumulated a reserve in Richmond which Lee wished sent along the railroad to meet his army at Amelia Court House. But when Lee reached Amelia, he found no supplies because his inadequate staff had not given the order in time. Being ahead of Grant, Lee, unwisely as it turned out, stopped his westward march for a day to search for food. Finding none in a countryside already thoroughly denuded by Confederate commissaries, he resumed his retreat, having given Grant a precious and probably essential day in his march to block Lee's retreat along the Richmond and Danville Railroad. The combination of Lee's delay and the fact that his line of retreat did not run directly to his rear enabled Grant's turning movement to succeed.

Lee's retreat with an army of starving men encumbered by a large baggage and artillery train drawn by debilitated and hungry animals no longer led toward his North Carolina base; Grant's pursuit not only followed directly in Lee's track but continued, as a turning movement, on a parallel route keeping between Lee and the North Carolina line.

Lee led a dispirited and dwindling army. The heavy losses in prisoners at Fort Stedman and Five Forks dramatically emphasized the dismal state of its morale even before defeat and a total failure of supply. According to one participant for many, if not most, soldiers "the Confederacy was considered as 'gone up,' and every man felt it his duty, as well as his privilege, to save himself. I do not mean to say that there was any insubordination whatever; but the whole left [right] of the army was so crushed by the defeats of the last few days, that it straggled along without strength, and almost without thought. So we moved in disorder, keeping no regular column, no regular pace . . . there were not many words spoken. An indescribable sadness weighed upon us."[92]

Grant's superior cavalry played a critical role. Sheridan harried the flank of Lee's army and delayed the retreat. On one occasion, at the Battle of Sayler's Creek, they got ahead of a portion of Lee's army, and, assuming the defensive, blocked the retreat, contributing significantly to taking six thousand prisoners.

Essential to this success was the defensive power of the cavalry when fighting dismounted and augmented by having most regiments armed with repeating rifles. These weapons possessed a much higher rate of fire than muzzle-loaders and enabled an unintrenched defender to fire from a prone position. In its retreat Lee's army was almost systematically "cut off by wide turning movements of the cavalry, who dismounted" and, using "the defensive power obtained by the effective fire of their dismounted men," forced further delay. Finally Grant had pushed so many men ahead of Lee at Appomattox Court House that Lee halted his retreat and surrendered.[93]

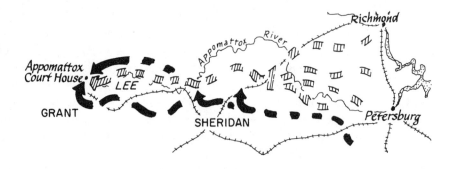

Evacuation and Continuous Turning Movement

The Appomattox campaign was Grant's third turning movement and capitulation of the war. He had made this one against not an inept opponent but against Lee himself. It had succeeded in part because of Lee's attempt to bring away his trains and his one-day delay in search of supplies. But more basically Grant's success rested on the exhaustion of Lee's army in physical well-being because of its prolonged and intensifying supply difficulties and its debilitation in morale due to its loss of faith in victory as it began the fifth spring campaign of a war that seemed already lost.

In constantly turning the enemy and thus in part also avoiding the obstructed track of the retreating enemy, Grant's last campaign epitomized the best tradition of Napoleonic operations and, at the same time, introduced an important innovation when he exploited the American doctrine of cavalry fighting dismounted. But the more impressive operations had been outside of Virginia where, by raids and the movement of troops by sea, Grant had rapidly accelerated the application of the strategy of exhaustion. And Sherman's brilliantly executed raids through Georgia and the Carolinas provided the centerpiece of the final campaign because of their political as well as military effect.

These raids had been facilitated by Hood's conversion of his turning movement into an advance on Nashville, thus giving the Union armies the advantage of the strategic defensive and, by his costly attack at Franklin, also conferring on them the opportunity to fight on the tactical defensive. By waiting before Nashville, Hood provided Thomas with the opportunity to attack the already demoralized Confederate army and the defeat and retreat completed the depletion of the Army of Tennessee in numbers and morale. Thus Hood helped the Union apply the strategy of annihilation to his army, and Grant, adhering to his basic strategy, then used his "spare army" not to try to annihilate Lee but to reinforce his application of the strategy of exhaustion.

After Lee evacuated Richmond, Davis had looked to Lee's joining Johnston in North Carolina to attack Sherman: "If successful, it was expected the reviving hope would bring reinforcements to the army, and Grant, being then far removed from his base supplies, and in the midst of a hostile population," might be driven back. Foreseeing the war entering a guerrilla stage, President Davis proclaimed: "We have now entered upon a new phase of the struggle. Relieved of the necessity of guarding particular points, our army will be free to move from point to point, to strike the enemy far from his base." He closed his proclamation: "Let us then, not despond, my countrymen, but, relying on God, meet the foe with fresh defiance and with unconquered and unconquerable hearts."[94]

The public did not respond. Furthermore there was no stronger negative reaction than that of the Confederacy's military leadership. After Lee's surrender, the President went to North Carolina, where he met Johnston and

Beauregard. These professional soldiers, not at all inclined to wage guerrilla warfare, argued emphatically the uselessness of continued resistance. Like almost all of the senior Confederate generals, they had relinquished secure berths in the U. S. Army for new careers with the Confederacy. Commanding its armies and departments fell quite within their life-long expectations and their concept of duty to their states. If they thought of it seriously, they would have perceived that leading guerrilla bands would fall outside of these ideals; and they would very likely have seen it as demeaning to their status.

After Johnston and Beauregard had impressed the President with the futility of further organized resistance, Davis ordered Johnston to surrender his forces to Sherman.

On April 14, the Good Friday that saw Lincoln's tragic assassination, the Federals raised the U.S. flag over Fort Sumter. General Robert Anderson, who had lowered the same flag four years earlier, seized the halyards and hoisted the federal banner once more above the fort that was the very symbol of the war. And two days later, in North Carolina, plans were set for the meeting between Johnston and Sherman.

Johnston found his interview with Sherman more pleasant than his last meeting with Davis. Johnston and Sherman had not known each other before the war but respected each other's generalship. Their meeting was harmonious for another reason—Sherman did not want Johnston's army to scatter and become guerrillas; Johnston, unwilling to become a guerrilla chieftain, anxiously awaited the opportunity to surrender. Years later Johnston's story of the surrender was related.

> Their first interview near Greensboro resulted in an engagement to meet for further discussion the following day. As they were parting, Johnston remarked: "By the way, Cumps, Breckinridge, our Secretary of War, is with me. He is a very able fellow, and a better lawyer than any of us. If there is no objection, I will fetch him along tomorrow."
>
> Bristling up, General Sherman exclaimed, "Secretary of War! No, no; we don't recognize any civil government among you fellows, Joe. No, I don't want any Secretary of War."
>
> "Well," said General Johnston, "he is also a major general in the Confederate army. Is there any objection to his presence in the capacity of major general?"
>
> "Oh!" quoth Sherman, in his characteristic way, "major general! Well, any major general you may bring, I shall be glad to meet. But recollect, Johnston, no Secretary of War. Do you understand?"
>
> The next day, General Johnston, accompanied by Major General Breckinridge and others, was at the rendezvous before Sherman.
>
> "You know how fond of his liquor Breckinridge was?" added General Johnston, as he went on with his story, "Well, nearly everything to drink had been absorbed. For several days, Breckinridge had found it difficult, if not impossible, to procure liquor, he showed the effect of his enforced abstinence. He was rather dull and heavy that morning. Somebody in Danville had given him a plug of very fine chewing tobacco, and he chewed vigorously while we were

awaiting Sherman's coming. After a while, Sherman arrived. He bustled in with a pair of saddlebags over his arm, and apologized for being late. He placed the saddlebags carefully upon a chair. Introductions followed, and for a while General Sherman made himself exceedingly agreeable. Finally, someone suggested that we had better take up the matter in hand.

"Yes," said Sherman; "but, gentlemen, it occurred to me that perhaps you were not overstocked with liquor, and I procured some medical stores on my way over. Will you join me before we begin work?"

General Johnston said he watched the expression of Breckinridge at this announcement, and it was beatific. Tossing his quid into the fire, he rinsed his mouth, and when the bottle and the glass were passed to him, he poured out a tremendous drink, which he swallowed with great satisfaction. With an air of content, he stroked his mustache and took a fresh chew of tobacco.

Then they settled down to business, and Breckinridge never shone more brilliantly than he did in the discussions which followed. He seemed to have at his tongue's end every rule and maxim of international and constitutional law, and of the laws of war,—international wars, civil wars, and wars of rebellion. In fact, he was so resourceful, cogent, persuasive, learned, that, at one stage of the proceedings, General Sherman, when confronted by the authority, but not convinced by the eloquence or learning of Breckinridge, pushed back his chair and exclaimed: "See here, gentlemen, who is doing this surrendering anyhow? If this thing goes on, you'll have me sending a letter of apology to Jeff Davis."

Afterward, when they were nearing the close of the conference, Sherman sat for some time absorbed in deep thought. Then he arose, went to the saddlebags, and fumbled for the bottle. Breckinridge saw the movement. Again he took his quid from his mouth and tossed it into the fireplace. His eye brightened, and he gave every evidence of intense interest in what Sherman seemed about to do.

The latter, preoccupied, perhaps unconscious of his action, poured out some liquor, shoved the bottle back into the saddlepocket, walked to the window, and stood there, looking out abstractedly, while he sipped his grog.

From pleasant hope and expectation the expression on Breckinridge's face changed successively to uncertainty, disgust, and deep depression. At last his hand sought the plug of tobacco, and, with an injured, sorrowful look he cut off another chew. Upon this he ruminated during the remainder of the interview, taking little part in what was said.

After silent reflections at the window, General Sherman bustled back, gathered up his papers, and said: "These terms are too generous, but I must hurry away before you make me sign a capitulation. I will submit them to the authorities at Washington, and let you hear how they are received." With that he bade the assembled officers adieu, took his saddlebags upon his arm, and went off as he had come.

General Johnston took occasion, as they left the house and were drawing on their gloves, to ask General Breckinridge how he had been impressed by Sherman.

"Sherman is a bright man, and a man of great force," replied Breckinridge, speaking with deliberation, "But," raising his voice and with a look of great intensity, "General Johnston, General Sherman is a hog. Yes, sir, a *HOG*. Did you see him take that drink by himself? . . . No Kentucky gentlemen would ever have taken away that bottle."[95]

☆   ☆   ☆

1. Hood to Davis, Sept. 6, 1864, *O.R.*, XXXVIII, pt. 5, 1023; Hood to Bragg, Sept. 3, 5, 1864, *ibid.*, 1016, 1021.

2. Hood to Davis, Sept. 6, 1864, *O.R.*, XXXVIII, pt. 5, 1023–24.

3. For a discussion of the applicability of the flank position to Johnston's situation, see: Matthew Forney Steele, *American Campaigns*, 2 vols. (Washington, 1943), I, 551–52.

4. Davis to Maury, Sept. 2, 1864, *O.R.*, XXXIX, pt. 2, 812; Connelly, *Autumn of Glory*, 472–80.

5. J. E. Johnston to B. R. Johnston, Oct. 6, 1864, Robert M. Hughes, "Some War Letters of General Joseph E. Johnston," *Journal of the Military Service Institution of the United States* (May-June, 1912), 319–28; Davis, *The Rise and Fall of the Confederate Government*, II, 567–68.

6. Long, *Civil War, Day by Day*, 579–80; Horn, *Army of Tennessee*, 375–77; Connelly, *Autumn of Glory*, 480–93.

7. Catton, *Never Call Retreat*, 398.

8. Grant to Halleck, Oct. 4, 1864, *O.R.*, XXXIX, pt. 3, 64; Grant to Sherman, Sept. 10, 1864, *ibid.*, pt. 2, 355; Canby to Sherman, Oct. 18, 1864, *O.R.*, XLI, pt. 4, 66; Canby to Halleck, Nov. 12, 1864, *ibid.*, 528–29.

9. Sherman to Halleck, Aug. 11, 1864, *O.R.*, XXXVIII, pt. 5, 482; Sherman to Grant, Sept. 10, 12, 1864, *ibid.*, XXXIX, pt. 2, 355–56, 364; Sherman to Canby, Sept. 10, 11, 1864, *ibid.*, 358, 362–63; Grant to Sherman, Sept. 10, 12, 1864, *ibid.*, 355, 364–65.

10. Sherman to Grant, Sept. 20, 1864, *O.R.*, XXXIX, pt. 2, 411–13; Sherman to Thomas, Oct. 1, 1864, *ibid.*, pt. 3, 13.

11. Sherman to Grant, Nov. 6, 1864, *O.R.*, XXXIX, pt. 3, 558; Sherman to Halleck, Sept. 25, 1864, *ibid.*, pt. 2, 464; Sherman to Grant, Sept. 28, Oct. 1, 1864, *ibid.*, pt. 2, 502, pt. 3, 3.

12. Grant to Sherman, Sept. 12, 1864, *O.R.*, XXXIX, pt. 2, 364; Grant to Sheridan, Sept. 26, 1864, *ibid.*, XLIII, pt. 2, 177; Grant to Meade, Sept. 27, 1864, *ibid.*, XLII, pt. 2, 1046; Grant to Butler, Sept. 27, 1864, *ibid.*, 1058–59; Grant to Lincoln, Sept. 29, 1864, *ibid.*, 1090; Grant to Halleck; Sept. 29, 1864, *ibid.*, 1091.

13. Long, *Civil War, Day by Day*, 585–86.

14. Kirby Smith to Davis, Nov. 16, 1864, *O.R.*, XLI, pt. 4, 1052–53.

15. Halleck to Sherman, Sept. 26, 28, 1864, *O.R.*, XXXIX, pt. 2, 480, 503.

16. Grant to Sherman, Oct. 11 (two communications), 12, 1864, *O.R.*, XXXIX, pt. 3, 202, 222; Stanton to Grant, Oct. 12, 1864, *ibid.*, 222; Grant to Stanton, Oct. 13, 1864, *ibid.*, 239; Lincoln to Sherman, Dec. 26, 1864, Basler, *Collected Works*, VIII, 181.

17. Sherman to Grant, Oct. 9, 11, 1864, *O.R.*, XXXIX, pt. 3, 162, 202.

18. Grant to Halleck, Oct. 4, 1864, *O.R.*, XXXIX, pt. 3, 64; Grant to Sherman, Oct. 12, 1864, *ibid.*

19. Grant to Rawlins, Oct. 29, 1864, *O.R.*, XLI, pt. 4, 305–6.

20. Davis to Hood, Nov. 7, 1864, *O.R.*, XXXIX, pt. 3, 896; Hood to Davis, Nov. 6, 1864, *ibid.*, 891; Hood to Seddon, Nov. 4, 9, 1864, *ibid.*, 888, 904; J. E. Johnston to B. R. Johnston, Nov. 8, 1864, Hughes, "Some War Letters of General Joseph E. Johnston," 319.

21. Hood to Davis, Nov. 6, 1864, *O.R.*, XXXIX, pt. 3, 891; Hood to Cobb, Nov. 11, 1864, *ibid.*, 911; Brent to Taylor, Oct. 23, 1864, *ibid.*, 844–45; Hood to Beauregard, Nov. 8, 25, 1864, *ibid.*, XXXIX, pt. 3, 900, XLX, pt. 1, 1245; Hood to Seddon, Nov. 28, Dec. 12, 1864, *ibid.*, XLV, pt. 1, 1254; pt. 2, 680; Hood to Maury, Dec. 6, 1864, *ibid.*, pt. 2, 656.

22. Sherman to Schofield, Oct. 17, 1864, *O.R.*, XXXIX, pt. 3, 335; Sherman to Halleck, Oct. 19, 1864, *ibid.*, 357–58; Sherman to Slocum, Oct. 16, 1864, *ibid.*, 305–6; Sherman to Grant, Oct. 10, 1864, *ibid.*, 174; Sherman to Thomas, Oct. 20, Nov. 2, 1864, *ibid.*, 377–78, 601; Sherman to Grant, Oct. 22, 1864, *ibid.*, 394–95; Sherman to Halleck, Nov. 3, 1864, *ibid.*, 613–14.

23. Sherman to Thomas, Oct. 20, Nov. 2, 1864, *O.R.*, XXXIX, pt. 3, 378, 601; Grant to Halleck, Nov. 6, 1864, *ibid.*, 657; Halleck to Grant, Nov. 6, 1864, *ibid.*, 657; Halleck to Grant, Nov. 4, 6, 1864, *ibid.*, XLI, pt. 4, 424, 448; Halleck to Canby, Nov. 7 (two communications), 1864, *ibid.*, 463–64.

24. Grant to Rawlins, Oct. 19, 1864, *O.R.*, XLI, pt. 4, 305–6; Grant to Sherman, Sept. 12, 1864, *ibid.*, XXXIX, pt. 2, 364–65; Grant to Halleck, Oct. 4, 13, Nov. 12, 1864, *ibid.*, pt. 3, 63–64, 239–40, 750; Grant to Halleck, Oct. 18, 1864, *ibid.*, XLIII, pt. 2, 402; Grant to Butler, Oct. 3, 1864, *ibid.*, XLII, pt. 3, 78; Halleck to Grant, Oct. 22, Nov. 5, 6, 1864, *ibid.*, XLI, pt. 4, 172, 438, 448; Halleck to Canby, Oct. 17, 1864, 25.

25. Sherman to Rosecrans, Oct. 29, 1864,

O.R., XXXIX, pt. 3, 493–94; Sherman to Halleck, Oct. 19, 24, 1864, *ibid.*, 357–58, 413; Sherman to Grant, Oct. 22, Nov. 6, 1864, *ibid.*, 395; 658–59.

26. Sherman to Halleck, Oct. 19, 1864, *O.R.*, XXXIX, pt. 3, 357–58; Sherman to Grant, Sept. 20, Nov. 6, 1864, *ibid.*, pt. 2, 411–12; pt. 3, 659–60.

27. Special Field Orders No. 120, Nov. 9, 1864, *O.R.*, XXXIX, pt. 3, 713–14. Though not as knowledgeable as Halleck in military law and history, Sherman was well aware of the historical precedents and the "well-established principles of war" governing his treatment of civilian property. The previous winter he had explained these, pointing out that they must govern because "the people of the South, having appealed to war, are barred from appealing for protection to our constitution." Their hostility and participation in guerrilla war also made their case different from the usual European case where, he added, "wars are between kings or rulers through hired armies, and not between peoples. These remain, as it were, neutral, and sell their produce to whatever army is in possession.

"Napoleon when at war with Prussia, Austria, and Russia bought forage and provisions of the inhabitants, and consequently had an interest to protect the farms and factories which ministered to his wants. In like manner the Allied Armies in France could buy of the French habitants whatever they needed, the produce of the soil or the manufactures of the country. Therefore, the general rule was and is that war is confined to the armies engaged, and should not visit the houses of families or private interests. But in other examples a different rule obtained the sanction of historical authority. I will only instance one, where in the reign of William and Mary the English army occupied Ireland, then in a state of revolt. The inhabitants were actually driven into foreign lands, and were dispossessed of their property and a new population introduced."

Sherman pointed out that, rather than a war of rulers, the war in which they were engaged was national, "essentially a war of races." Sherman's policy was not new on either side and Halleck had pointed out that the enemy had long followed this policy, "not only in Maryland and Pennsylvania, but also in Virginia and other rebel states." There was no requirement "to treat the so-called non-combatants and rebels better than they themselves treat each other." In the application of his policy, Sherman did not allow any certificates to be given. Normally, these were given by foraging armies and were payable by

the enemy government, in some cases being credited to the contribution levied. Not recognizing the Confederacy, the Union armies had given none in the South except to citizens who could prove their loyalty. These were payable by the United States. In eliminating them altogether, Sherman assumed all Georgians were hostile. Thus, as Sherman accurately realized, his policy had many precedents, including the warfare of the English against their Irish subjects (Sherman to Sawyer, Jan. 31, 1864, *Sherman Letters*, 223–24; Halleck to Sherman, Sept. 28, 1864, *O.R.*, XXXIX, pt. 2, 503).

28. Grant to Stanton, Nov. 13, 1864, *O.R.*, XLII, pt. 3, 612; Grant to Meade, Nov. 15, 1864, *ibid.*, 620. In the context of the operations in the Civil War up to the fall of 1864, this movement of the two armies away from one another looks peculiar and, perhaps, unconventional, as does the reliance on living off the country. Such movements have been fairly common in military history as, for example, in the war of the American Revolution when Greene and Cornwallis, after fighting each other at Guilford Court House, North Carolina, each marched away from the other, Cornwallis to Virginia and Greene to South Carolina. In a case in the Thirty Years' War quite comparable to that of Hood and Sherman, Wallenstein and Gustavus, after fighting an inconclusive battle, each marched away from the other and toward the other's base area. Wallenstein, unlike Gustavus, Sherman, and Hood, succeeded in drawing his opponent after him. In that war, armies customarily lived off the country and often practiced Grant and Sherman's raiding strategy of exhaustion.

29. Wheeler, *We Knew Sherman*, 82–83; Grant to Stanton, Nov. 13, 1864; *O.R.*, XLII, pt. 3, 612; Grant to Meade, Nov. 15, 1864, *ibid.*, 620.

30. Thomas to Halleck, Nov. 19, 1864, *O.R.*, XLV, pt. 1, 944; Thomas to Schofield, Nov. 19, 1864, *ibid.*, 944; Schofield to Thomas, Nov. 24, 1864, *ibid.*, 1016.

31. Long, *Civil War, Day by Day*, 593.

32. Schofield to Thomas, Nov. 28, 1864, *O.R.*, XLV, pt. 1, 1106.

33. Hattaway, *Lee*, 134.

34. Cobb to Davis, Nov. 17, 1864, *O.R.*, XLIV, 861; Beauregard to Cooper, Nov. 13, 1864, *ibid.*, XXXIX, pt. 3, 917; Beauregard to Taylor, Nov. 16, 17, 1864, *ibid.*, XLV, pt. 1, 1213, 1218.

35. Cooper to Hardee, Nov. 17, 1864, *O.R.*, XLIV, 864; Beauregard to Cooper, Nov. 19,

1864, *ibid.*, 866; Davis to Bragg, Nov. 22, 1864, *ibid.*, 891; Seddon to Bragg, Nov. 27, 1864, *ibid.*, 901; Cooper to Beauregard, Nov. 30, 1864, *ibid.*, 911.

36. Beauregard to Cooper, Nov. 16, 1864, *O.R.*, XLIV, 859; Brent to Hood, Nov. 17, 1864, *ibid.*, XLV, pt. 1, 1215; Beauregard to Hood, Nov. 18, 1864, *ibid.*, 1220; Beauregard to Davis, Dec. 6, 1864, *ibid.*, XLIV, 932.

37. Davis to Beauregard, Nov. 30, 1864, *O.R.*, XLIV, 910; Davis to Lee, Dec. 19, 1864, *ibid.*, 966; Lee to Davis, Dec. 19, 1864, *ibid.*, 966; Davis to Brown, Nov. 22, 1864, *ibid.*, 881; Beauregard to the People of Georgia, Nov. 18, 1864, *ibid.*, 867.

38. Abstract of Return, Department of South Carolina, Georgia, and Florida, Nov. 20, 1864, *O.R.*, XLIV, 874; Beauregard endorsement, Dec. 24, 1864, Chisolm to Hardee, Dec. 20, 1864, *ibid.*, 970; Bragg to Seddon, Nov. 27, 1864, *ibid.*, 901; Sherman to Grant, Dec. 16, 1864, *ibid.*, 728; Sherman to Halleck, Dec. 13, 1864, *ibid.*, 702.

39. Thomas to Grant, Nov. 25, 1864, *O.R.*, XLV, pt. 1, 1034.

40. Van Duzer to Eckert, Nov. 30, 1864, *O.R.*, XLV, pt. 1, 1168; Thomas to Halleck, Dec. 1, 1864, *ibid.*, pt. 2, 3.

41. Stanton to Grant, Dec. 2, 1864, *O.R.*, XLV, pt. 2, 15–16; Grant to Thomas, Dec. 2 (two communications), 6, 1864, *ibid.*, 17, 70.

42. Grant to Thomas, Dec. 11, 1864, *O.R.*, XLV, pt. 2, 143; Halleck to Thomas, Dec. 14, 1864, *ibid.*, 180.

43. Thomas to Halleck, Dec. 2, 1864, *O.R.*, XLV, pt. 2, 18; Grant to Thomas, Dec. 8, 1864, *ibid.*, 97.

44. Stanton to Grant, Dec. 7, 1864, *O.R.*, XLV, pt. 2, 84; Thomas to Grant, Dec. 6, 9, 1864, *ibid.*, 70, 114; Grant to Thomas, Dec. 8, 11, 1864, *ibid.*, 97, 143.

45. Van Duzer to Eckert, Dec. 13, 1864, *O.R.*, XLV, pt. 2, 171; Sherman to Grant, Dec. 16, 1864, *ibid.*, XLIV, 728.

46. Grant to Thomas, Dec. 15, 1864, *O.R.*, XLV, pt. 2, 195; Horn, *Army of Tennessee*, 418; Connelly, *Autumn of Glory*, 508–12.

47. Grant to Stanton, Dec. 13, 1864, *O.R.*, XLIV, 701; Halleck to Sherman, Dec. 30, 1864, *ibid.*, 836.

48. Sherman to Lincoln, Dec. 22, 1864, *O.R.*, XLIV, 783.

49. Catton, *Never Call Retreat*, 415–16.

50. Gilmer to Seddon, Jan. 3, 1865, *O.R.*,

XLIV, 1014–15; Davis to Taylor, Jan. 12, 1865, *ibid.*, XLV, pt. 2, 778; Sherman to Halleck, Dec. 24, 1864, *ibid.*, XLIV, 799.

51. Goff, *Confederate Supply*, 210–12, 217–18, 250.

52. Beauregard to Cooper, Dec. 28, 1864, *O.R.*, XLIV, 996; Beauregard to Davis, Jan. 13, 17, 1865, *ibid.*, XLV, pt. 2, 780–89; Davis to Taylor, Jan. 12, 1865, *ibid.*, 778–79; Beauregard to Davis, Jan. 13, 1865, *ibid.*, 780; Seddon to Beauregard, Jan. 15, 1865, *ibid.*, 785; Taylor to Davis, Jan. 15, 1865, *ibid.*, 785; Beauregard to Brent, Jan. 20, 1865, *ibid.*, 800.

53. Grant to Sherman, Jan. 21, 1865, *O.R.*, XLVII, pt. 2, 101; Sherman to Grant, Dec. 16, 1864, *ibid.*, XLIV, 728; Grant to Halleck, Dec. 30, 1864, Jan. 4, 18, 1865, *ibid.*, XLV, pt. 2, 420, 506, 609–10; Halleck to Grant, Dec. 30, 1864, *ibid.*, 420.

54. Sherman to Grant, Dec. 24, 1864, *O.R.*, XLIV, 797; Grant to Sherman, Dec. 3, 6, 18, 27, 1864, *ibid.*, 612, 636, 740–41, 820.

55. Sherman to Grant, Dec. 16, 24, 1864, *O.R.*, XLIV, 727, 797–98; Sherman to Halleck, Dec. 13, 31, 1864, *ibid.*, 701, 842; Grant to Sherman, Dec. 27, 1864, *ibid.*, 820.

56. Sherman to Grant, Dec. 24, 1864, *O.R.*, XLIV, 797–98; Sherman to Halleck, Dec. 24, 1864, *ibid.*, 798–800.

57. Sherman to Grant, Dec. 24, 1864, *O.R.*, XLIV, 797; Sherman to Halleck, Dec. 24, 1864, *ibid.*, 799.

58. Sherman to Mrs. Sherman, Jan. 2, 5, 1865, *Home Letters*, 323, 327.

59. Grant to Halleck, July 1, 1864, *O.R.*, XL, pt. 2, 558; Halleck to Grant, July 3, 1864, *ibid.*, 598.

60. Grant, *Memoirs*, 507; Grant to Sherman, Dec. 3, 1864, *O.R.*, XLIV, 611; Halleck to Sherman, Jan. 1, 1865, *ibid.*, XLVII, pt. 2, 3.

61. Grant to Meade, Nov. 30, Dec. 3, 5 (two communications), *O.R.*, XLII, pt. 3, 748, 784, 804, 806; Grant to Porter, Nov. 30, 1864, *ibid.*, 750; Grant to Butler, Dec. 4, 1864, *ibid.*, 799; Grant to Halleck, Dec. 7, 1864, *ibid.*, 842.

62. Grant, *Memoirs*, 508; Porter to Sherman, Dec. 29, 1864, *O.R.*, XLIV, 832.

63. Robert Holzman, *Stormy Ben Butler* (New York, 1954), 151; Grant, *Memoirs*, 509; Sherman to Porter, Jan. 17, 1865, *O.R.*, XLVII, pt. 2, 69; Grant to Sherman, Mar. 16, 1865, *ibid.*, 859; Butler to Soldiers of the Army of the James, Jan. 8, 1865, *ibid.*, XLVI, pt. 2, 71.

64. Sherman to Grant, Jan. 29, 1865, *O.R.*,

XLVII, pt. 2, 154; Halleck to Canby, Feb. 28, 1865, *ibid.*, XLVIII, pt. 1, 1002.

65. Grant to Sherman, Dec. 18, 27, 1864, *O.R.*, XLIV, 740, 820; Meigs to Sherman, Dec. 15, 1864, *ibid.*, 715–16.

66. Grant to Schofield, Jan. 31, 1865, *O.R.*, XLVII, pt. 2, 190.

67. Grant to Sherman, Dec. 27, 1864, Jan. 21, 1865, *O.R.*, XLIV, 820, XLVII, pt. 2, 101; Longstreet to Lee, Feb. 23, 1865, *ibid.*, XLVI, pt. 2, 1253; Lee to Davis, Feb. 23, 1865, *Wartime Papers*, 909–10.

68. Grant to Meade, Sept. 25, 1864, *O.R.*, XLII, pt. 2, 1008; Grant to Thomas, Jan. 31, Mar. 7, 1865, *ibid.*, XLIX, pt. 1, 616, 854; Halleck to Thomas, Jan. 26, 1865, *ibid.*, 584.

69. Grant to Halleck, Jan. 4, 1865, *O.R.*, XLVIII, pt. 1, 408; Halleck to Canby, Jan. 19, Feb. 28, 1865, *ibid.*, 580, 1002; Grant to Canby, Feb. 27, 1865, *ibid.*, XLIX, pt. 1, 781.

70. Grant to Thomas, Feb. 14, 22, 1865, *O.R.*, XLIX, pt.1, 708, 881; Canby to Thomas, Feb. 22, 1865, *ibid.*, 757; Grant to Canby, Feb. 9, 1865, *ibid.*, XLVIII, pt. 1, 786; Canby to Halleck, Nov. 19, 20, 25, Dec. 9, 16, 1864, *ibid.*, XLI, pt. 4, 609, 623, 673, 807, 869.

71. Grant to Sherman, Jan. 21, Feb. 1, Mar. 16, 22, 1865, *O.R.*, XLVII, pt. 2, 101, 193, 859, 949.

72. Grant to Halleck, Jan. 6, 1865, *O.R.*, XLVI, pt. 2, 53; Grant to Sheridan, Feb. 20, 25, 1865, *ibid.*, 605–6, 701; Grant to Meade, Feb. 20, 21, 1865, *ibid.*, 598, 609; Meade to Grant, Feb. 20 (two communications), 25, 1865, *ibid.*, 597, 598; Sheridan to Grant, Feb. 20, 25, 1865, *ibid.*, 605, 701.

73. Grant to Stanton, Feb. 4, 1865, *O.R.*, XLVI, pt. 2, 365.

74. Sherman to Foster, Jan. 19, 1865, *O.R.*, XLVII, pt. 2, 96–97; Beauregard to Cooper, Jan. 28, 1865, *ibid.*, 1050; Beauregard to Davis, Feb. 2, 1865, *ibid.*, 1078; Hardee to Cooper, Jan. 30, 1865, *ibid.*, 1061.

75. Hardee to Cooper, Jan. 28 1865, *O.R.*, XLVII, pt. 2, 1051; Davis to Beauregard, Feb. 4, 1865, *ibid.*, 1090; Brent, Notes of a Conference, Feb. 3, 1865, *ibid.*, 1085; Beauregard to Lee, Feb. 15, 16, 1865, *ibid.*, 1193, 1202; Chisolm to Beauregard, Feb. 10, 1865, *ibid.*, 1140.

76. Sherman to Grant, Jan. 19, Mar. 12, 1865, *O.R.*, XLVII, pt. 2, 156, 794; Grant to Sherman, Feb. 1, 1865, *ibid.*, 193; Catton, *Never Call Retreat*, 434.

77. Wheeler, *We Knew Sherman*, 95. For a convincing argument about the controversial burning of Columbia, see Marion Brunson Lucas, *Sherman and the Burning of Columbia* (College Station, London, 1976).

78. Davis to Bragg, Oct. 15, 1864, *O.R.*, XLII, pt. 3, 1149; Davis to Seddon, Nov. 10, 1864, *ibid.*, 1207; Davis to Lee, Jan. 18, 1865, *ibid.*, XLVI, pt. 2, 1091; Davis to Johnson and Sheffey, Jan. 18, 1865, *ibid.*, 1092; Davis, *Rise and Fall of the Confederate Government*, II, 631.

79. Lee to Breckinridge, Feb. 19, 21, 1865, *Wartime Papers*, 904, 906; Lee to Davis, Feb. 23, 1865, *ibid.*, 909; Breckinridge to Lee, Feb. 20, 1865, *O.R.*, XLVI, pt. 2, 1242; Beauregard to Davis, Feb. 21, 1865, *ibid.*, XLVII, pt. 2, 1238; Davis to Lee, Feb. 21, 1865, *ibid.*, 1237; General Orders No. 1, Feb. 25, 1865, *ibid.*, 1274; Anderson to Bragg, Mar. 6, 1865, *ibid.*, 1334.

80. Lee to Johnston, Feb. 22, 1865, *O.R.*, LXVII, pt. 2, 1247; Johnston to Lee, Feb. 22, 1865, *ibid.*, 1247; Davis, *Rise and Fall of the Confederate Government*, II, 632.

81. Canby to Halleck, Feb. 28, 1865, *O.R.*, XLIX, pt. 1, 789; Grant to Meigs, Mar. 9, 1865, *ibid.*,868; Grant to Canby, Mar. 9, 1865, *ibid.*, 875.

82. Sherman to Stanton, Mar. 12, 1865, *O.R.*, XLVII, pt. 2, 793.

83. Goff, *Confederate Supply*, 212–13, 217–18, 233–34, 250; Sherman to Halleck, Dec. 24, 1864, *O.R.*, XLIV, 799.

84. Goff, *Confederate Supply*, 240–41.

85. Sherman to Mrs. Sherman, Mar. 23, Apr. 9, 28, 1865, *Home Letters*, 335, 343, 350; Sherman to Grant, Mar. 23, 1865, *O.R.*, XLVII, pt. 2, 969.

86. Catton, *Never Call Retreat*, 438.

87. Freeman, *Lee*, III, 507, 515, 516, 522, 529, 532, 535, 541, 542.

88. Sheridan to Halleck, Mar. 2, 1865, *O.R.*, XLVI, pt. 2, 792; Sheridan to Grant, Mar. 10, 1865, *ibid.*, 918–19.

89. Grant to Sheridan, Mar. 21, 28, 1865, *O.R.*, XLVI, pt. 3, 67, 234.

90. Grant to Sheridan, Mar. 29, 30, 1865, *O.R.*, XLVI, pt. 2, 266, 325.

91. Freeman, *Lee*, IV, 58-59.

92. Freeman, *Lee's Lieutenants*, III, 688-90.

93. George T. Denison, *A History of Cavalry From the Earliest Times* (London, 1913), 392. The British, who studied the American Civil War, developed the concept of mounted infantry in part from this campaign. They used it with great success in the Megiddo campaign in Palestine in

1918, when British cavalry reached the Turkish rear, dismounted, and, using machine guns as well as rifles, blocked the retreat of the Turkish army. The similarities with the use of Sheridan's cavalry are striking.

It is sometimes said that Wilson's raid to Selma was the precursor of the blitzkrieg of World War II. A better case could be made for Megiddo and the campaign from Five Forks to Appomattox.

The aged Jomini, closely following the campaigns of the Civil War, characterized Grant's campaign as "brilliant" (H. de Jomini, *Précis de l'art de la guerre ou nouveau tableau analytic des*

principes et combinaisons de la stratégie, de la grande tactique, et la politique militaire, F. Lecomte, ed., 2 vols. [Paris, 1894], 11, 403).

94. Davis, *Rise and Fall of the Confederate Government*, II, 676–77. Long before, during the Mexican War, Davis had perceived the difficulties which an invading army would face in a hostile country. See: Davis to Robert J. Walker, Nov. 30, 1846, Robert J. Walker Papers, Z 659 F, Folder 1, Mississippi Department of Archives and History.

95. John S. Wise, *The End of an Era* (Boston, New York, 1899), 450–52.

20 ☆ SOLDIERS AND CIVILIANS

Robert E. Lee

With only a minute nucleus of regular officers both the North and the South had managed very well. Warfare often seems a contest to see who can outblunder whom; but, in spite of such tragedies as Burnside's attack at Fredericksburg and Pemberton's retreat into Vicksburg, both sides conducted the war competently and realistically. As might have been expected, in view of the common parentage of both armies, their respective leadership did not differ significantly in outlook and doctrine.[1]

Educated at West Point, the professional leaders had been conditioned by their engineering-oriented schooling, their Mexican War experience, and their reading of history. Their familiarity with Napoleonic campaigns had caused their belief in the attainability of decisive battle, but their realization of the tactical power of the defense convinced them that they could not gain such a result in a frontal fight. Knowing the value of intrenchments and field fortifications, they soon almost universally employed them. Their efficacy only reinforced what West Point and Mahan had already taught them and confirmed their conviction of the tactical supremacy of the defensive.

They had learned the turning movement, seen as the key to victory in battle, as much from Scott and Taylor in Mexico as from their study of Napoleon. For a battle to be decisive, the attacker must reach the enemy's rear with his entire army, forcing him to make a frontal attack to extricate himself and recover his communications. This difficult feat even Napoleon achieved only rarely. Grant achieved it three times, at Fort Donelson, Vicksburg, and Appomattox, though with the aid of inept or weakened opposition. Count Alfred von Schlieffen's later tongue-in-cheek observation could well apply to Grant's Fort Donelson and Vicksburg successes: in order to attain a Cannae, "a Hannibal is needed on the one side and a Terentius Varro on the other, both cooperating."[2]

These tactical realities caused most leaders on both sides to make territory their objective. Avoiding a futile pursuit of the strategy of annihilation, Union generals sought to conquer the Confederacy to deprive its armies of their source of supplies, weapons, and recruits. For the same reasons, Confederate generals anxiously desired to conserve their territory and its essential logistical resources. Though the southern people and politicians favorably received this strategy, one well adapted to the weaker party, a large segment of the North criticized the anaconda strategy of Union generals. Conditioned to understand war in terms of decisive battles and the tactics of frontal combat, the northern people and their political leaders grew impatient waiting for decisive victories which would end the rebellion quickly. Though Lincoln fully appreciated this point of view, he soon learned the military realities as his generals perceived them.

The Union strategy of territorial conquest began brilliantly in the West when Halleck secured nominal control over most of Missouri, conquered Middle and West Tennessee, and penetrated into north Mississippi and Alabama. At that point the advance halted because there the secure, efficient communications of the Tennessee River ended; and there the most basic Union problem of all emerged, logistics. The vast size of the Confederacy, its poor roads, and its somewhat limited production of food and fodder which an invader could appropriate would have made the implicit strategy of defeating the enemy by conquering territory very difficult in any case. In addition, the limited rail and water routes of invasion made obvious the Union lines of operation, enabling the Confederates easily to concentrate against them.

The problem presented by rebel guerrilla activity and early Confederate strength in cavalry bore an intimate relationship to Union logistical difficulties. Most important in the Tennessee theatre, raids by guerrillas and by substantial forces of regular cavalry could destroy the fragile railroads upon which the supply of invading armies depended. Though obsolete on the battlefield, cavalry, as brilliantly led by Forrest and Morgan, well displayed its potential for its other traditional role—attacking the enemy's logistics. Even an inferior mounted force is formidable in this role; and the near parity enjoyed by the Confederates early in the war permitted them temporarily but completely to stop Union advances in the West.

Along the secure water route of the Mississippi in late 1862 the necessity for keeping to this line of communications made Grant's line of operations so obvious that the Confederates could force him to approach them head on. A Union frontal attack failed at Chickasaw Bluffs, and Van Dorn's rebel cavalry raid at Holly Springs stymied an attempt to turn the Vicksburg position. Grant then directed all of his energy to efforts to turn this Confederate citadel along a water route.

In the East a similar situation prevailed. The lines of operations by rail in Virginia were also easily discernible, though the Confederates could turn the Union army on the west and the Union forces could turn the Confederates on the east. Lee used this advantage in 1862 and 1863, and McClellan and Grant, each in his own way, exploited the Union ability to turn the Confederates. Because of the short line of communications in Virginia, guerrillas and cavalry raiders mattered less in that congested theatre.

The relatively small size of the Virginia theatre meant that any Union advance must inevitably arrive at Richmond, the fortified obstacle and communications hub. Any movement, whether directly from Washington or by the Peninsula, must reach its unavoidable dénouement in a siege of Richmond, with some of the city's communications intact and the defenders behind breastworks. Of the two major efforts to take the rebel capital, McClellan's in 1862 and Grant's in 1864, the latter had the better chance of success. Grant's plan, by distracting Lee and forcing the Confederate army to remain far north of Richmond, would have permitted Butler's powerful movement up the James, for which the Confederates had not adequately prepared, to take the city or interdict much of its communications. Since McClellan's Peninsula campaign lacked any element of surprise, it probably could not have ended victoriously except by a long siege. Paradoxically, in view of the reputations of the generals, McClellan's campaign provoked two enemy attacks and proved much more advantageous for the Union in terms of attrition.

Because of the difficulty of taking Richmond by cutting its communications and because of the tactical advantages enjoyed by its intrenched defenders, the Union high command early abandoned the idea of a siege, and indeed any strategy of territorial conquest in Virginia, and gave priority to other theatres. Ironically, Lee had the same objective, avoiding being besieged in Richmond, though his motives differed. He distrusted the Confederacy's ability to supply a siege, considering the rickety southern railroads and the defective Confederate commissary organization.

When Union concentration in the West resulted in Grant's capture of Vicksburg and the opening of the prestigious Mississippi, many northerners felt the rebellion had been crushed. Not only had the Federals cut the Confederacy in half, but, in the surrender of Pemberton's army, the rebels had suffered what seemed a well-nigh crippling blow to their field forces. Yet, instead of capitulation, a counteroffensive took place at Chickamauga which surprised the complacent Union high command. Although the Union conquest of Vicksburg was important, it could not be decisive. Though more crushing than almost any of Napoleon's triumphs, it could not end the war on the Union's terms because the North had a total political goal, the extinction of the Confederacy. Total political victory required total military victory.

Military strategy is the dependent variable of tactical and logistical conditions. With the opening of the father of waters, the Union had used the last exploitable western river route of invasion from the north, leaving only the coast and its rivers and the railroad lines as routes for further federal advances. The limited carrying capacity of the railroads and, above all, their vulnerability to guerrillas and to cavalry raiders made them unpromising avenues. In addition, the whole strategy of exhaustion by territorial occupation began to seem quite dubious when the Union armies confronted the task of conquering and holding the large, populous, and thoroughly rebellious state of Georgia. The previous conquest of partially loyal Tennessee had taken them two years.

Faced with the tactical supremacy of the defense, the stalemate in the East, and the almost insuperable logistical obstacles in the West, the Union followed two divergent lines of thought, though both of them adhered to the basic concept of the strategy of exhaustion. Lincoln, the politician, sought to undermine the Confederacy by enticing its states back into the Union through a liberal reconstruction plan. Aiming particularly at Tennessee, Florida, Arkansas, and Louisiana, he hoped first to redeem these states and thus gradually to break down the Confederacy. Simultaneously he began to push a plan of recruiting southern blacks into the Union Army. Even if unsuitable for field service, these former slaves could surely perform the duties of occupation of conquered territory and protection of communications from raiders and guerrillas. Since the Union devoted almost a third of its army to these security duties, such service provided ample scope for less demanding employment of black soldiers. More important, no plan could better implement the strategy of exhaustion, because, as Lincoln said, every recruit drawn from rebel territory subtracted from the Confederacy's productive population and was worth two in the North as "it adds one to us, and takes one from the enemy."[3]

But soon the black troops evolved into effective fighting units, engaged in all forms of combat. "It is hard to realize," Dudley Cornish, the pioneer scholar on the subject, observed, "how revolutionary the experiment of permitting Negroes to bear arms was considered, how fraught with imagined dangers to the Union cause, how galling to white pride." The experiment proved a significant military success and not only because of the value of blacks in combat. By the war's end the Negroes constituted slightly more than 12 percent of the Union land forces.[4]

Lincoln's strategy was political and psychological in that he sought to draw states from the Confederacy by amnesty and a liberal reconstruction policy while demoralizing the enemy through wholesale employment against them of their former slaves enlisted as soldiers. In addition, his arming of southern blacks helped solve Union military manpower problems; but at the same time it was part of the strategy of exhaustion in that it deprived the rebel economy of productive laborers.

The thinking in Grant's headquarters was more purely military. Grant viewed the Gulf and Atlantic coasts as the remaining southern areas accessible by a water route of advance and wished to exploit the Alabama and Savannah rivers as lines of communications into the interior. But his strategy placed primary reliance on his significant innovation, raids. Though Lincoln and Quartermaster General Meigs early had urged counter raids by Union cavalry and Rosecrans had tried them, Grant expanded the concept to one of complete reliance on systematic raids by the armies of the Union. These forces would occupy no more territory; instead they would destroy the logistical base of the Confederate war machine. Grant's collaborator, Sherman, added to this concept by using such a military strategy to "demonstrate the vulnerability of the South" and produce a profound political impact by bringing the war home to all rebel states, thus exhibiting the inability of the Confederacy to protect its territorial integrity. And so, adventitiously, Grant's purely military strategy became the stick for the carrot of Lincoln's political strategy of generous reconstruction terms. Sherman's raids had, however, another, unintended, political effect in that after the war they remained particularly abhorrent to southerners, being an obstacle to reconciliation because, perhaps, they were a symbol of defeat.[5]

In concentrating in the West the Union high command had followed the most fundamental principle of offensive operations, concentrate against enemy weakness. Avoiding the unpromising Virginia theatre and the virtually unobtainable objective of Richmond, they utilized the superior line of communications provided by the Mississippi River. A corollary of the principle of concentrating against weakness is the maxim of reinforcing success. To this the Union also adhered when federal armies and fleets followed up on their achievements in taking New Orleans, opening the Tennessee and Cumberland, and capturing Corinth and a portion of the Memphis and Charleston Railroad.

Later, in adopting the strategy of exhaustion, Grant also pursued the path of least resistance. Avoiding the difficulties of holding territory, and protecting it and rail communications against raiders and guerrillas, he also evaded the harder task of trying to destroy defensively powerful and elusive enemy armies. Instead he concentrated against the Confederacy's weakness, the most fragile link in its inadequate logistic infrastructure, the precariously functioning southern railway system.

But the Union initially limited the application of Grant's strategy to his old theatre, the West. Lincoln and Halleck rejected it for the East, in part because they could not conceive of the recommended North Carolina raid as other than another scheme to take Richmond, a task they believed impossible. Absorbed by their own logistical and transportation problems, Lincoln and Halleck probably could not conceive that the Confederates had more severe difficulties than their own. Far removed from the field, they could not understand what appeared so obvious to the experienced Grant. Denied his plan to break the North Carolina railroads, Grant found himself forced into a contest with Lee, one in any case practically demanded by Union public opinion. The result, a siege which lasted until the end of the war, confirmed the wisdom of the Lincoln-Halleck strategy of avoiding Richmond and, interestingly, gave the lie to Lee's apprehensions about such a siege. In that crisis the Confederates managed, after all, to supply Lee's army and their capital.

In spite of the failure of Banks's major raiding column to participate in his campaign, Sherman succeeded in applying Grant's raiding strategy when he marched to Savannah. Though the raid had no dramatic and immediate impact on enemy logistics or will to continue the war, its effect, nevertheless, was felt throughout the Confederacy. Sherman had not intended one consequence of his campaign: the virtual destruction of the Confederate army opposed to him, brought about by Hood's frantic efforts to stop Sherman.

Johnston had failed to stop Sherman with his use of the power of the defense, and Hood had failed to save Atlanta with an offensive directed against Sherman's army. Davis and Hood then began a campaign which reflected Lee's method in Virginia, but employed the greater maneuver room afforded by the Georgia-Alabama theatre and relied on the line of communications and operations available on the railroad running northeast from Selma and Montgomery toward Rome, Georgia. Because of the greater space, Hood, unlike Lee, could avoid entanglement with the enemy army. When faced, near Rome in October, with a situation which could give rise to something like Antietam or Gettysburg, the Confederate general, with no mountains at his back, managed deliberately to avoid a battle, retreat into Alabama, and base himself on his alternate line of communications. Yet Hood still threatened Sherman's supplies to Atlanta and prevented his further advance.

The fall of Atlanta helped to remove a major obstacle to Lincoln's re-election and so, despite Hood's success, perhaps the end of the war was in sight. Nevertheless, it seemed as if the continuing Confederate ability to use its western geographical extent to avoid the attrition of battles would force Sherman back to his starting point and perhaps farther. It seems likely that, had Johnston earlier exploited that flank position, he could have planned to fall back on the same Selma-Montgomery line and thus perhaps have forestalled Atlanta's capitulation. If this had happened, the Union might have been faced with a stalemate, as the armies marched to and fro while Sherman's futilely tried to come to grips with Johnston's. Since Lee's fear that the Confederacy could not supply his army in Richmond had proven groundless, the modern condition of a World War I–type deadlock around Richmond and Petersburg would have been complemented by old-fashioned conditions of a stalemate induced by maneuver and countermaneuver in the West.

Grant's explicit adoption of the strategy of exhaustion through raids prevented this outcome when sought by Hood and would have had equal effect without Atlanta's fall had Johnston based himself in Alabama. Sherman could have begun his raid at any time; the raid was the antidote both for the flank position and the turning movement as well as for the enemy's adoption of a different line of operations.

Numerical superiority, coupled with the tactical supremacy of the defense, enabled Sherman to adopt exterior lines, leaving Hood between his army and Thomas's. To exploit this interior position, Hood had to assume the offensive, precipitating his doomed and disastrous march to Nashville.

The grand strategies of both sides were, then, quite symmetrical—the Union attempting exhaustion by territorial acquisition, the Confederacy defending against this. The Confederacy first attacked the Union's logistics by raids; Grant, adopting the same policy, expanded it and made it the cornerstone of his strategy. There are similar parallels in the management of military operations and the war effort.

Both Presidents proved able executives and excellent commanders in chief;

but Lincoln had a more difficult task, and not only because the Union bore the disadvantageous burden of acting on the offensive: lacking Davis's military knowledge and administrative experience, the Union President had much more to learn. Unlike Davis, Lincoln had to harmonize the widely different views and aims of the northern people and politicians and try to draw all factions into full support of the war. The influence which various viewpoints imposed upon strategy and the perception that military appointments were also political further complicated his job. Though the radicals vociferously coupled antislavery war aims with the appointment of generals and the advocacy of a particular strategy, their emphasis on the idea of a decisive battle and a popular fixation on the Virginia front further increased the complexity of Lincoln's military problems. They almost made antithetical Lincoln's work of building unity and following professional military advice.

Davis, on the other hand, lacked most of these problems because little controversy existed among that large majority of southerners whose loyalty belonged to the Confederacy. He took full advantage of this situation to promote general officers almost entirely on the basis of merit and to follow fully in his strategy the dictates of military rather than political considerations. The Confederate President doubtless took too few pains to interpret his decisions to his fellow countrymen, sometimes acting almost as if the public possessed no right to question his professional military judgment. His appointment in 1864 of Bragg as general commanding well illustrates a wise military decision but at the same time an egregious political blunder.

Lincoln skirted such costly choices. The northern President fortunately chose the vigorous and capable, though radical, Stanton as secretary of war. Partly by design and partly by accident Stanton fostered, through his War Board, a modern general staff organization. Lincoln again showed discernment when he chose the sagacious and indefatigable Halleck as general in chief. Halleck completed the effective Union command organization when he began exploiting the informal unity of the staff which Stanton had initiated. Like Davis, Lincoln retained control of strategy, but he worked through the knowledgeable Halleck, largely ignoring the naive strategic ideas of Stanton.

Lincoln and Halleck made a good team, one well supported by the excellent headquarters staff. Halleck and the staff effectively implemented Lincoln's plan of simultaneous advances, especially in the well-synchronized offensives of December, 1862. And from the Lincoln-Halleck team there emerged in the fall of 1862 the basic strategy of concentrating in the West and of avoiding, as futile, a Richmond siege. Instead of concentrating in the politically sensitive but militarily unpromising Virginia theatre, Lincoln and Halleck devoted as many resources as they dared to the West and the Mississippi River line of operations. Their strategy became even more effective in application because the Confederate high command did not clearly comprehend it. But the northerners did occasionally blunder. Rewarded with the fall of Vicksburg and the capture of Pemberton's army, Lincoln and Halleck displayed a complacency which proved a factor in the southern success in the Chickamauga campaign. A more serious mistake was the post-Vicksburg preoccupation with exploiting the North's central position and control of the Mississippi to concentrate on the politically significant conquest of the Confederate trans-Mississippi. This strategy contributed to Chickamauga and ended with Banks's fiasco on the Red River. They wasted the resources diverted to this trans-Mississippi effort. The immense geographical extent of the region made military successes and territorial conquests essentially illusory, as Price's late 1864 Missouri raid dramatically demonstrated. For a long time the trans-Mississippi constituted Lincoln and Halleck's strategic tar baby.

Not only a western outlook but Halleck's western generals dominated the Lincoln-Halleck strategy of the war. When the war concluded, Halleck generals commanded everywhere east of the Mississippi. Only Meade, in the shadow of both Grant and Sheridan, did not belong to Halleck's original command. The Union's first western generalissimo favored Grant, Thomas, Schofield, and Sherman. If Halleck seemed too self-effacing and insufficiently assertive as general in chief, his loyalty, like his competence, stood out as a major asset, and his unprepossessing and unmartial image helped make him a perfect conductor of criticism away from the President.

Upon achieving his victory at Chattanooga, Grant became the de facto general in chief. His informal clique, a small-scale analogue of the Confederacy's western concentration bloc, had strong links in Washington through Congressman Washburne and Assistant Secretary Dana. Too, in his mentor Halleck he enjoyed a powerful ally at headquarters. Sherman's old and strong friendship with Halleck reinforced this relationship. The prestige of Grant's victories completed the establishment of the informal authority which enabled him to determine the strategy for 1864 and to nominate his man to replace Meade. Except for the veto of his proposal for a North Carolina raid, his plans, which Lincoln approved, essentially continued the pattern the Union had followed since the fall of 1862—hold in Virginia and concentrate in the West.

Grant's elevation to formal authority as lieutenant general initially changed very little. The strategy remained the same and he served under Lincoln, who still retained at hand the headquarters staff. The change to formal power produced an unfortunate situation for Grant, for he, rather than Sherman or Baldy Smith, received the thankless job of coping with the Virginia stalemate and trying to secure the victories demanded by the public and needed for Lincoln's re-election.

Lincoln wisely left the conduct of operations in Virginia to Grant and, of course, adhered to the western strategy outlined by Grant prior to his appointment as lieutenant general. He did this in spite of Grant's failure to do more than besiege Richmond from the southeast. Probably, Lincoln and Halleck realized that, if Grant could do no better, they really had no choice but to accept the long-avoided siege on exterior lines. Though Lincoln and Halleck demonstrated a better strategic understanding than McClellan and Hooker, they had in the fall of 1863 blamed Meade for his failure to do more. Now they gave Grant their confidence and allowed him to approach the Virginia problem in his own way.

With Grant as general in chief, Lincoln, of course, remained commander in chief. The President kept in close touch with military events, supervising major decisions. He still integrated the political and the military, as when General Peter J. Osterhaus received a promotion on his "high merit, and somewhat on his nationality." Lincoln worked with Secretary Stanton and, with Grant absent from Washington, he inevitably continued his contact with Halleck. Halleck functioned as the "military head" in Washington "to keep things from getting into a snarl." In a sense the old formal organization grew into an informal one. The reverse was also true after Halleck literally became chief of staff. His formal authority now extended to the staff bureaus and he was the "common head to make the different bureaus act in concert."[6]

Though formally exercising the coordinating role of a modern chief of staff, Halleck actually functioned as the chief of staff to Lieutenant General Grant. Commanders in the field no longer received from Halleck the old stream of advice and instructions. Missing these, Sherman asked him for "a word now and then of advice and encouragement." Thus Sherman requested: "Write me a note occasionally and suggest anything that may occur to you, as I am really in a wilderness down here," and later wrote: "I value your opinion of matters of importance above those of any other, because I know you to be frank, honest, and learned in the great principles of history."[7]

In reply, Halleck explained: "I must be exceedingly cautious about making military suggestions not through General Grant. . . . I therefore make all suggestions to him and receive his orders. In my present position I cannot assume responsibility except in matters of mere administration or in way of advice." As heretofore, Halleck, the lawyer, took care to observe the limitations and proprieties of his office. He would not overstep the bounds of his position nor derogate it, as he had shown quite early by submitting his resignation when Lincoln asked him to select a plan of campaign for Burnside. But, though Halleck's command influence was much curtailed, his staff position changed little from that which he inherited on becoming general in chief in the summer of 1862. Stanton, through his concept of the War Board, had established the essential principle and Halleck ably carried it out.[8]

Grant performed well as general in chief because of his superb plan and its brilliant execution by Sherman. For the two months of May and June, 1864, Grant devoted his own energies to the contest with Lee. To some degree this contest temporarily dominated Grant's thinking, as his own prestige became involved. He even deviated briefly from his strategic plan when he ordered the Nineteenth Corps from the Gulf to reinforce Virginia, thus so weakening

Canby as to prevent him from sending an adequate force to Mobile in August. In a sense Grant momentarily adopted the public's ideas, wishing for and, to a degree, seeking a decisive victory over Lee.

But Lincoln and his generals had already realized, at least implicitly, that frontal battles had lost much, if not most, of their old efficacy for bringing about a major attrition of the enemy's strength. Armies continued to suffer heavy battle casualties, but the losses rarely diverged very much from comparable percentages of each of the forces engaged and, as in the Seven Days' Battles, might be proportionately heavier for the victor. The Seven Days' Battles themselves brought Lee and Davis to the same realization and, in henceforth relying on turning movements for counteroffensives, the Confederate leadership sought to turn to their advantage the tactical supremacy of the defense. Lincoln and his generals did also rather explicitly understand that only by the difficult feat of reaching the enemy's rear could they obtain decisive results. Grant had well exhibited this at Fort Donelson and Vicksburg.

Understanding the indecisiveness and, therefore, the relative insignificance of battles is simply another way of perceiving the primacy of the defense when well-articulated and relatively maneuverable units of rifle-armed infantry dominated the battlefield. In the absence of effective cavalry or of formations vulnerable because they could not quickly maneuver or face to cover their flanks, battles ceased to have their old importance and victors might well suffer proportionately or even absolutely higher casualties than the vanquished. Civil War generals implicitly realized this; civilians did not and often sought nonmilitary explanations, finding a scapegoat in unenthusiastic generals.[9]

Grant's decision to seek confrontation in a frontal fight made the campaign from the Wilderness to Petersburg a dress rehearsal for World War I. The same assaults upon intrenchments caused the same heavy casualties for attackers; and the defenders' counterattacks, to maintain the integrity of their continuous linear defenses, also resulted in similarly heavy casualties suffered later by the defenders in 1914–18. Nevertheless, as in World War I, the attackers usually lost more, and the total casualties on both sides were immense, because assaults occurred frequently and because the troops remained in close contact, exposed to losses from artillery fire, sniping, and skirmishing.

In World War I, just as in the Civil War, the side conducting the offensive often labored under the delusion that its attacks had only very narrowly missed a decisive success, a "breakthrough," and that the defenders' casualties were heavier and the defenders' morale and resources had reached the point of exhaustion. Soldiers and official histories have sought to justify what had been done and to maintain that what is now usually viewed as the futile and blundering slaughter of the western front from 1914 to 1918 was, in fact, purposeful and necessary.

Virginia in 1864 and the western front in World War I differed in that Grant himself and his proponents among historians have come to dominate the interpretation of the 1864 campaigns in a way that the generals of World War I and the official histories have utterly failed to do. The reputations of French Marshal Joffre and British Field Marshal Haig, who between them lost millions of men, have been greatly diminished by the historical estimate of the egregiousness of their repeated offensives, of their inability to appreciate this, and of their stubborn persistence in continuing to make the same blunder again and again.

Significantly, in the 1864 Virginia campaign Grant and Meade did not long continue to make the same mistake. Though after the war Grant, quite naturally, justified his attacks as necessary, at the time he and Meade realized their futility and stopped them. They knew that the enemy had not lost many more men than they had, and Meade perceived that great numerical superiority did not after all make successful attacks possible. Though they were confirming what most of the younger West Pointers had believed at the beginning of the war, during their brief experiment with dogged attacks, Grant and Meade gained an understanding that required western leaders in World War I almost the entire four years to learn. In a sense they acquired in a month the wisdom of Pétain.

Closer to the tactical situation and present on some of the battlefields, these Americans could learn much faster than their counterparts a half century later who, commanding army groups, worked far to the rear and saw their war solely through maps and reports. Unlike the generals of World War I, neither Grant nor Meade had begun his operation with any belief in the efficacy of the strategy of annihilation or with any conviction that his army could destroy Lee's. They had learned most of the realities of war before they faced the trench deadlock and had, in fact, only adopted attacks against intrenchments because of the failure of Butler's movement on the enemy's rear.

Thus these Civil War realists quite easily abandoned an experiment which had failed and in which both probably initially invested only limited confidence. In addition, the campaign in Virginia constituted only a part of Grant's plan for the war in 1864. He did not have to win there, for Sherman was making steady progress into Georgia and success in the West could be decisive.

Furthermore, the very failure of the offensives removed one of the major reasons for conducting them. The public political opinion which had demanded a contest with Lee and had hailed Grant's victories in the Wilderness and at Spotsylvania recoiled at the human cost. Though arguing that these battles played an indispensable role in driving Lee back to Richmond and making the siege possible, Grant in his interpretation also showed that the task had been accomplished and Union success required no more such battles. Insensibly, also, Grant's campaign thus made public and political opinion ready to view success in war not in terms of glorious victories but in terms of Sherman's unspectacular penetration of the heart of the enemy's country. The fall of Atlanta proved a timely evidence of success.

In Allied countries during World War I, politicians and the newspapers, largely closing ranks in a display of national unity, essentially remained supportive of the efforts of the military leaders. In the Union in 1864 politics-as-usual and a faultfinding and partisan press would have prevented the glossing over of continual failures or the unreserved acceptance of official interpretations if Grant and Meade had persisted in their attacks. Failure could not for long have been unanimously and uncritically received as success.

Finally, Grant and Meade had a most practical reason for abandoning costly attacks: they were running out of men. Even before Cold Harbor, Hancock's second corps had lost half of its original strength. Many of the replacements were not recruits to bring the veteran regiments up to strength; they were new units, many of which were cavalry without horses and redundant heavy artillery units serving as infantry. After Cold Harbor, the militia which the Union sent forward had only to serve one hundred days and were so green that they had to learn the manual of arms after they reached the Army of the Potomac. Whereas the effective conscription of the belligerents in World War I supplied the armies with every man civilian employment could spare, the defective Union draft could not provide the stream of suitable replacements which Grant and Meade would have needed had they, like the generals of World War I, wished to continue the policy of attacking their intrenched enemy.

Public opinion forced Grant into more of a frontal combat with Lee than he desired, the contest of champions sought by the public and their civilian leaders, when, near their capital, their lieutenant general faced the legendary Lee. The battles resulted in disillusionment, for the victories cost so many lives that they lost their glamour and, apparently, produced little effect in winning the war. When the public and its leaders no longer demanded battles and victories, they had at last, to a degree, learned what their generals had known all along.

The role of public opinion in the Union and in the Allied situation in World War I differed ironically. Much of the civilian-military tension in the Civil War revolved around a civilian demand for direct offensive action and a military insistence that the defense was too strong. The soldiers were correct. In World War I the Allied generals persisted, to the dismay of many civilian leaders, in piling up huge casualties in attacking the intrenched enemy. In this later war the many civilians correctly understood the situation, recognizing the futility of the attacks. In fact French rank and file even mutinied, saying they would defend but no longer attack.

If attention is focused on Lincoln's relation to his Virginia commanders, his conduct of the war seems an effort to dominate these operations. From his conflicts with McClellan through his coaching of Hooker and pushing of Meade, it is a story of the President's increasingly sophisticated effort to mold Virginia operations. If put in the perspective of all operations, these episodes become a special case of presidential concern for a politically vital theatre on which centered popular and congressional attention. Lincoln's intervention with Hooker and Meade consisted largely of an effort to impress on them the headquarters doctrine of the futility of a Richmond siege. Indeed a difficult task, it meant telling the generals that he hoped for little from them—that their mission was secondary. As Lincoln wrote Hooker, he did not believe he "had any chance to effect anything." The generals had great difficulty accepting this pessimistic, if realistic, estimate, and they never fully understood the headquarters' position that their only appropriate course consisted of trying to hurt Lee's army should Lee make a mistake. Aware of the popular clamor for a victory in Virginia and the radical demand for generals who would pitch into the enemy, the Army of the Potomac generals misunderstood Lincoln, thinking he wished battles like Fredericksburg, which they perceived as futile and politically inspired.

Meade and most generals believed that Grant's campaign from the Wilderness to Petersburg vindicated the soldiers in their argument with the civilians over the nature of war and the feasibility of decisive frontal battles. In spite of the record of such citizen soldiers as Forrest, the generals were also convinced that the abysmal military records of Banks and Butler proved their contention that high command should be left to the professionals. The regulars tended to overlook the political value of the continued service of such generals as Banks. Nor did the regulars grasp that Lincoln fully understood their conception of military operations and often correctly estimated the military costs of the political advantage gained through political generals in command.

Lincoln's military leadership, however, amounted to far more than his understanding the use of political generals, his role in developing what proved to be the realistic strategy for Virginia, his heeding Halleck's advice to concentrate in the West, and his deciding on a grand strategy. Lincoln's distinctiveness lay in his intelligence, which enabled him to learn the elements of the art of war of the mid-nineteenth century and grasp quickly the realistic and sophisticated ideas of the country's capable military leadership. This permitted him rapidly to overtake Davis in the area in which the Confederate President initially excelled.

Lincoln's administrative style contributed to his ability to master in a very short time what others had taken years to acquire. In spite of, or perhaps because of, his lack of administrative experience he did not immerse himself in details of day-to-day decision-making. His constant visits to the telegraph office to see how operations were proceeding constituted the act of an interested and informed observer, not those of the harried executive who must decide all. This style gave him the leisure not only to learn but also to think. He had ample opportunity to mature a strategy for Virginia, just as he deliberated on the best policy for emancipation. Largely leaving routine operations to Stanton, Halleck, and the staff, Lincoln concentrated upon fundamental military and political questions.

Lincoln, of course, cannot be well evaluated simply in terms of a military leader. Beyond fundamental political and economic questions such as banking and the tariff, politics and diplomacy were inextricably bound up with the conduct of the war. He succeeded well in blending with the war's conduct all of the connected ingredients. A consummate politician, Lincoln faced worthy opponents in the dedicated radical leadership; yet most of the time he harnessed their energy to move in the directions he desired and built national unity behind the war for the Union.

Lincoln's many attributes included an ability to draw the best from those around him, such as Stanton and Halleck; an excellent knowledge, gained during the conflict, of the art of war and how to use this knowledge to understand and guide the war effort; an administrative capacity that permitted him to delegate efficiently and to concentrate on fundamental problems; and a superior ability to integrate the military and political factors. His own grand strategic contributions exemplify the latter. The use of black troops simultaneously weakened the rebels, strengthened the Army, and pleased the radicals; his reconstruction policy sought both to entice states away from the Confederacy and to conciliate conservative opinion at home. Lincoln's military performance supports his acknowledged greatness.

Grant's strategy is usually associated with its executor, Sherman, and Grant with the 1864 campaign in Virginia. Of course Sherman, Grant's personal and official friend, had much to do with the development of the plan for 1864. But the strategy distinctly belonged to Grant and he applied it, when possible, in Virginia as well as in Sherman's operations and in his multiple raids of the winter of 1865. In addition to a clear grasp of the right course of action, Grant added his unobtrusive but firm dominance of his subordinates, his talent for delegation, and his good management. Grant's qualities always eluded the brilliant and verbal Sherman, who never could fathom wherein lay the essential genius of the reticent Grant. But Sherman undoubtedly would have agreed with one of Meade's staff officers, equally baffled by the enigma of the quiet and unprepossessing Grant: Colonel Lyman finally concluded that Grant "does everything with a specific reason; he is eminently a wise man." The same might well have been said of Lincoln.[10]

In the Confederacy, as in the Union, the President determined strategy. Unlike Lincoln, Jefferson Davis had no powerful and vocal radicals advocating their ideas and pushing favored generals. Though he had pressures for providing for the defense of every locality, these caused no distortion in Confederate policy, because almost every Confederate geographic area had importance as a source of recruits and supplies.[11]

Under Davis's leadership the Confederacy skillfully reconciled the defense of exposed territory against raids with powerful resistance on the main lines of operations. The fortunate location of southern railroads made possible a uniting of the major and minor theatres. Thus the Confederacy integrated the defense of the Atlantic seaboard with the defense of northern Virginia by converting the railway lines from Richmond to Savannah into a pipeline full of troops which they could concentrate at any threatened point. They applied a similar concept less systematically to the defense of the line from Richmond to Chattanooga, a mountainous and less vulnerable frontier. State militia forces, largely composed of men otherwise exempt from Confederate service, well supplemented their ability to reinforce rapidly. Thus the Confederates united powerful resistance on the main lines of advance with the defense of vital resource areas and railroad lines by using the railways to combine dispersion with concentration. They succeeded well in joining to the national effort the concern for local defense, which had compelled the states to create and maintain their own emergency forces. Composed of men from vital occupations, or otherwise exempt, and of those unfit or beyond the age for field service, these formations received a significant augmentation in 1864. The reserves provided at all times some form of protection, even when all regular troops were deployed elsewhere. Though they might do no more than man fortifications, they possessed psychological importance in that they maintained local morale and demonstrated to the enemy the presence of organized defensive forces.

The successful integration of almost every rail-connected point into a national system of strategic defense permitted an application on an unprecedented scale of the Napoleonic concept of concentration at the critical point. Both the civilian and military leadership of the Confederacy agreed on this, But they disagreed over whether they should apply this system and concept to an offensive. The partisans of the offensive, the western concentration bloc, wished to seize the initiative and bring about a surprise offensive convergence against a weak Union line. Beauregard expressed it in classical form; others, such as the Kentuckians, simply wanted to recover their state. The coincidence of relative Union weakness in Middle Tennessee enabled all factions to coalesce to form the bloc and unite behind Beauregard's application of the principle. In the winter and spring of 1863 this brought them into conflict with Lee, not because he did not understand nor had not used the principle to animate his strategy, but because Beauregard's proposal involved weakening Lee's army. In defending his own army against reduction, Lee was led, temporarily, to repudiate the principle. In the Chickamauga campaign the western concentration bloc partly succeeded. The long-advocated offensive came only as a counteroffensive, as at Shiloh, to retrieve a loss. Once the Confederates had assembled their troops in the West, their high command, including Lee, pushed for offensives in Tennessee long after they had lost the element of surprise and the Union counterconcentration had made such an operation unrealistic. The massing of troops in North Georgia may even have caused Davis and Lee to harbor unrealistic expectations in 1864 about what Johnston and Hood could achieve against Sherman.

But the Confederates used their railways for concentration at successive points so systematically and efficiently that in his strategy for 1864 Grant included key elements intended to prevent a further repetition of this fundamental rebel strategic theme. In order for this policy to succeed, Richmond must supply good direction and constantly restructure departmental lines to reflect the changing military situation. Beginning with an array of miniature departments, Davis soon enlarged them until, in the fall of 1862, he had evolved a system embracing four regional commands. Disrupted by the Vicksburg campaign, the western region was not restored until the fall of 1864 when Davis placed Beauregard in command of the Military Division of the West to which, when Sherman marched to the sea, Davis also subordinated South Carolina, Georgia, and Florida. Though more effective under Beauregard than Johnston, even this large division lacked the resources to combat Sherman's Military Division of the Mississippi. The Confederacy's departmental organization had been better structured than the Union's, in part because of Halleck's fear that alteration might provide openings for political generals. With the emergence of Grant after Vicksburg, a western regional command again became possible and the Union structure, on the whole, thenceforth equalled that of the Confederates.

The collaboration between Davis and Lee proved most fruitful for the Confederacy during Lee's brief term in 1862 as general commanding. Thereafter, though Lee remained a constant and wise advisor, his removal from Richmond not only limited his influence but on occasion deprived him of the information needed to give well-founded advice. Equally important, Lee's absorption in his own army for a time deprived him of the perspective needed to formulate balanced views. His primary role, then, amounted essentially to that of the brilliant, really unequalled, department and army commander. He grasped the part which his effective defense of his theatre could play in wearing down the enemy's will to win. A master of the Napoleonic method, Lee in his strategy remained, however, essentially defensive and so fought most of his battles. Yet his strategy often seemed offensive, for on four occasions he employed a turning movement to force the enemy back. Three of these, Second Bull Run, Antietam, and Gettysburg, resulted in battles, but his fundamental purpose remained to keep the enemy at bay and to cover his Virginia supply base. His campaigns compare well with those waged by the masters of the art of war in any age.[12]

Lee resembled Grant in his confidence and his prescience in perceiving the weakness and likely mistakes of his opponents. He possessed greater operational skill than Grant, but he had neither opportunity nor need to make Grant's innovation in strategy. Though more aggresive than most commanders, Lee exemplified in many ways the Civil War soldier in his emphasis upon logistics, grasp of lines of operation, appreciation of the power of the defense, and understanding of the essential role of the turning movement. In a war where soldiers had to be led rather than commanded, he had no superior in his ability to inspire his men. If Grant was the strategic innovator, Lee was the classic soldier.

Without Lee to play the part of Halleck, Davis had to be his own chief of staff. In part he well employed Randolph and Seddon in this role; but, until Bragg came to Richmond, Davis primarily carried the burden. He carried too much. Not only did he lack Lincoln's opportunity to reflect and plan, a task appropriated by Beauregard, but he was physically and emotionally exhausted by overwork.

Davis's improvisation of conducting his headquarters business for so long a time without a chief of staff cost the Confederacy heavily. Not only did headquarters lack sufficient staff but this weakness drew the secretary of war into the conduct of operations. Though this exploited his authority over the staff in order to provide, as in the North, good integration of logistics with operational concerns, the overcommitment of the secretary deprived Confederate supply management of the administrative vigor that characterized the North. That the Confederacy could supply Richmond during the siege from June, 1864, through March, 1865, shows that the southern system could be made to work. But the absorption in day-to-day operational concerns of both the President and the secretary helped delay adequate address to problems until they had become crises and contributed to the failure to apply more than partial and piecemeal solutions to railroad control.

In bringing Lee in as general commanding, Davis prescribed the correct formal structure by uniting the entire headquarters under his chief of staff. For momentarily good reasons he eliminated this position with disastrous long-run consequences. The Union, on the other hand, supplanted a faulty formal organization with an effective informal organization, one which approximated Davis's transitory formal structure.

The long interval without a chief of staff perhaps constituted Davis's major failing as commander in chief. He understood what a proper headquarters needed but neglected to supply it. Lincoln, with less understanding of the appropriate formal structure, possessed enough wisdom not to dispense long with a general in chief and not to trifle with an informal mechanism that worked well.

Davis's occasional politically insensitive behavior marks him as less skillful a politician than Lincoln, but the vigor and success of his leadership in the military sphere suggests no shortcomings. In its stress upon almost exclusively national forces, its early and ready adoption of conscription, and its ruthless integration of local defense into national strategy, Davis's leadership apparently exhibited real revolutionary zeal. The radical and centralized character of this approach seems at odds with the legitimist and states-rights origins of the secession movement.[13]

The roots of Davis's centralized approach lay, however, not in his political but in his military background. A fundamental departure for America, conscription, with the right to hire a substitute, was routine in France, the

country to which all American soldiers looked for guidance. Just as cogni-
zance of European systems made conscription seem normal to Davis and
Randolph, so also did a knowledge of European wars make obvious a policy
of exclusively national forces and a strategy based on the mobility of all
reserves. Davis's West Point and professional army background and outlook
gave him confidence in military prescriptions and a familiarity with European
ways.

In a sense Davis both epitomized and gave the lead to the Confederacy's
willingness to subordinate politics and civilian standards and traditions to
soldierly models and ideas. He sacrificed states' rights to wartime centralization and was instrumental in establishing what Grant called a "military des-
potism." State recruiting gave way to national conscription and Davis fully
integrated local defense into the operations of the principal theatres. Through
him the Army's needs supplanted political traditions, and the example of
European armies became an effective substitute for revolutionary zeal in carrying out a rebellion which stressed its constitutional legitimacy and dedication to states' rights. These methods made the Confederate war effort better
mobilized and more effectually directed than that of the Union where civilian
and states'-rights traditions more constantly impeded dedication to the Union.[14]

In August, 1864 Sherman lamented the comparative weakness of the Union's
manpower system. He wrote: "I think more than half this army is entitled to
discharge between this [month] and October, so that if Hood can simply hold
on here he will be enabled to defeat us by the superior method they have of
recruitment. In the South all men are soldiers, and they are not held for
limited terms, but for life if the war lasts that long." This vigorous manpower
policy, which Sherman so much admired, ultimately extended to the enlistment of slaves. Since such enlistment implied emancipation, the Confederacy, in the end, sacrificed even slavery to military necessity.[15]

Even if Lincoln, without Davis's background and outlook, could have envisioned this degree of centralization, he did not have the capability to implement it. He lacked the national unity of goal and initial political base to carry
it out. Davis, on the other hand, magnificently exploited his political resources to mobilize for war. In his large measure of success as a military
leader, Davis reflected all of the strengths of the U.S. Army, whose realism,
high competence, and ability to innovate its leaders so well displayed in their
conduct of the Civil War.

Although in operational skill Lee stands out above all other army commanders, the major military contribution to victory remains the strategy of
Grant. Not only effective in fulfilling its logistical and political objectives, in
the fall of Atlanta it provided the victory needed by the public, which predictably had eluded Grant in Virginia. The fall of Atlanta was, however, but
the beginning. By April, 1865, Grant's strategy of raids had deprived the
Confederate armies on the eastern seaboard of bases. With trunk-line railroads
thoroughly broken, the eastern armies would have found it virtually impos-

sible to maintain any line of operations; they would have had to become raiders with only limited prospects for resupply of essential ordnance and quartermaster stores. These eastern forces represented three of the five major Confederate departments: Northern Virginia; South Carolina, Georgia, and Florida; and Tennessee and Georgia. Only the armies in the trans-Mississippi and Alabama and Mississippi still possessed bases, and Wilson's Selma raid had seriously crippled that of the latter. Regardless of the fate of individual armies, Grant's systematic application of the strategy of exhaustion through raids had been truly successful in carrying out his objective to "leave nothing for the rebellion to stand upon."[16]

Yet the Union victory was not exclusively, nor perhaps even predominantly, military. Significantly, the war did not end in a guerrilla struggle. Even though that method of warfare had played a major role since early in the conflict, the South did not continue it past the surrender of Lee's depleted army at Appomattox. Such warfare would have been formidable indeed, for the organized forces of the Confederacy still numbered well over 100,000 men. With these well-armed and well-led veterans as guerrillas, the war then might well have been just beginning.

But all the main Confederate forces surrendered shortly after Lee's, commencing with Joe Johnston's prompt capitulation to Sherman in North Carolina. Symbol for the North, the defeat of Lee's army had a comparable importance for the South as well. But Sherman's raids also had a special significance as he demonstrated his ability to move at will throughout the Confederacy. Sherman had written that his movement to Savannah would disprove Jefferson Davis's "promises of protection. If we can march a well-appointed army right through his territory," he wrote, "it is a demonstration to the world, foreign and domestic, that we have a power which Davis cannot resist. This may not be war, but rather statesmanship, nevertheless it is overwhelming to my mind that there are thousands of people abroad and in the South who will reason thus: If the North can march an army right through the South, it is proof positive that the North can prevail in this contest."[17]

Sherman's raids were thus a powerful symbol and an important agent in creating a universal conviction of defeat and causing the destruction of the Confederacy's willingness to carry on the struggle. Significant also was Lincoln's decisive reelection in which he received 55 percent of the popular votes and won in the Electoral College 212 to 21. Lee had hoped to "resist manfully" until the enemy gave up, but now a minimum of four more years of war loomed ahead for the exhausted Confederacy. Certainly also the moderation of Lincoln's reconstruction policy and the tacit disappearance of the slavery issue constituted a major factor in the Confederacy's ready collapse.[18]

Further, Sherman's raids did not merely disrupt slavery but took away the work force needed whether the South was slave or free, Union or Confederate. A continuation of the struggle by means of guerrilla warfare would have been even more destructive to the organization of production as well as to slavery. And a guerrilla war in which the Union enlisted slaves in their counterinsurgent forces would have had revolutionary social consequences.[19]

To be sure, the Confederate military establishment would have found guerrilla warfare uncongenial to its view of war and its pretensions as commanders of the armies of a republic of acknowledged independence. More important, all Confederates probably would have found such warfare equally distasteful. Such a further struggle for independence would have been no less an admission of defeat for a nation which had commenced the war with all the trappings and status of sovereignty. The South had already lost complete territorial integrity and all of the panoply of a fully independent nation. Sherman correctly assessed the South as a whole when he wrote that he did not believe Davis would adopt guerrilla warfare because it was "derogatory to the high pretenses of his cause." A continued struggle was too much at variance with the way the Confederacy had begun and required far more nationalism than the South possessed.[20]

1. Norman F. Dixon in his *On the Psychology of Military Incompetence* points out the advantage the United States enjoyed in having its officer corps open to talent rather than recruiting it exclusively from one class. "The best generals on both sides in the American Civil War," he says, "could probably have beaten any comparable team from Europe, for the war made the profession of generalship a career open to talent and freed it from the rule of the authoritarians who flourish in rigid societies."

It is interesting to compare the performance of Civil War generals with the characteristics of incompetence which Dixon has compiled:

1. A serious wastage of human resources and failure to observe one of the first principles of war—economy of force.
2. A fundamental conservatism and clinging to outworn tradition.
3. A tendency to reject or ignore information.
4. A tendency to underestimate the enemy.
5. Indecisiveness.
6. An obstinate persistence in a given task.
7. A failure to exploit a situation.
8. A failure to make adequate reconnaissance.
9. A predilection for frontal assaults.
10. A belief in brute force.
11. A failure to make use of surprise.
12. An undue readiness to find scapegoats.
13. A suppression or distortion of news.
14. A belief in mystical forces.

Elsewhere Dixon notes some additional characteristics, prominent in the exemplary incompetence displayed by the British in the Crimean War and the early stages of the Boer War. Among these are: "an inability to profit from past experience"; "an apparent imperviousness by commanders to loss of life and human suffering amongst their rank and file, or (its converse) an irrational and incapacitating state of compassion"; and, finally, "procrastination."

These traits are conspicuous by their absence among most of the principal commanders in the Civil War, thus providing negative support for the thesis that the war was conducted competently. Procrastination, diagnosed by Lincoln as a disease, the slows, is present, of course. Equally conspicuous, however, is learning the power of the defense from experience and a resistance to what the military leaders perceived as a civilian insistence on the use of brute force and frontal assaults (Norman Dixon, *On the Psychology of Military Incompetence* [New York, 1976], 12, 67, 152–53. Italics were omitted.)

2. R. Ernest Dupuy and Trevor N. Dupuy, *Military Heritage of America* (New York, Toronto, and London, 1956), 189.

3. Lincoln to Stanton, Oct. 10, 1862, Basler, *Collected Works*, V, 456.

4. Cornish, *The Sable Arm*, 262, 266, 288.

5. Sherman to Thomas, Oct. 20, 1864, *O.R.*, XXXIX, pt. 3, 377–78.

Drawing most of his examples and inspiration from the Civil War, the American military writer, John Bigelow, distinguished three kinds of strategy. These were:

"1st. Strategy proper, or regular strategy, which aims at depriving the enemy of his supplies.

2nd. Tactical strategy, which aims at overmatching him on the field of battle.

3rd. Political strategy, which aims at embarrassing his government."

Bigelow noted that "political strategy is often an incident of regular strategy. The same fields and mills which feed an army may feed a noncombatant population. Hence, in destroying crops and agricultural implements and machinery, though the object be only to prevent the supplying of a hostile army, more or less hardship must of necessity be inflicted upon the people." Sherman's march from Atlanta to the sea is his illustration of combining regular and political strategy.

Regular and political strategy were related to tactical strategy through the turning movement. He wrote that "where the objective is the enemy's army, and it is too strongly posted to admit of attack, a movement against its communications, or some point of material importance to it, will cause it to abandon its position, and probably to take upon itself the burden of the tactical offensive. The most common use in fact of regular and political strategy is in such subordination to tactical strategy."

It is significant that Bigelow, writing in the tradition of the Civil War, should assign to regular strategy first place in his system and point out that tactical strategy had failed during the Civil War. Emphasizing that in 1864 Grant and Sherman had tried tactical strategy without success, it was only, Bigelow wrote, "by carrying their regular strategy to its legitimate conclusion that Grant and Sherman finally overcame their opponents" (John Bigelow, Jr., *The Principles of Strategy Illustrated Mainly from American Campaigns* [New York, London, 1891], 77, 122, 141).

6. Lincoln to Sherman, July 16, 1864, Basler, *Collected Works*, VII, 463; Halleck to Grant, May 2, 1864, *O.R.*, XXXVI, pt. 2, 328; Comstock Diary, July 15, 1864.

7. Sherman to Halleck, July 9, 1864, *O.R.*, XXXVIII, pt. 5, 91–92; Sherman to Halleck, Oct. 11, 1864, *ibid.*, XXIX, pt. 3, 203.

8. Halleck to Sherman, July 16, 1864, *O.R.*, XXXVIII, pt. 5, 150–51.

9. Some historians have found the explanation for the power of the defense and the indecisiveness of battles in generals dominated by misguided theories of war or intimidated by the enemy. No such exogenous causes are needed; the tactical conditions of the mid-nineteenth-century stage in the constant evolution of warfare render such explanations unnecessary though not irrelevant.

The reasons for the decline in the ability of armies to hurt one another very seriously in frontal battles such as at Blenheim are extremely complex, have not yet been fully developed, and are, in any case, far beyond the scope of this work. One reason may be found in the reduced effectiveness of cavalry against infantry armed with bayonets and, later, with rifles rather than muskets. More significant were the tremendous changes in the organization of infantry which vastly increased its ability to disperse and to deploy rapidly. These changes, which augmented its defensive power, also helped to make possible the decisive turning movements such as those of Ulm, Vicksburg, and the Franco-Prussian War. Robert S. Quinby, *The Background of Napoleonic Warfare* (New York, 1957) provides a good place to begin the study of these important changes. A brilliant, but inadequate and dated, interpretation may be found in J. Colin, *The Transformations of War*, trans. L. H. R. Pope-Hennessy (London, 1912), which might be supplemented by Archer Jones, "The Evolution of Warfare—an Interpretation," *Proceedings of the South Carolina Historical Association*, 1967, 5–12.

10. *Meade's Headquarters*, 358–59.

11. A very good recent general history of the Confederacy is Emory M. Thomas, *The Confederate Nation: 1861–1865* (New York, 1979). For material pertinent to our arguments see especially chapters 9 and 10.

12. For a comparison of Lee with other Confederate generals, see the Appendix on Mobilization and Combat Effectiveness.

13. For an intriguing treatise that supplements our assertions, although which in some respects runs counter to our arguments, see Paul D. Escott, *After Secession: Jefferson Davis and the Failure of Confederate Nationalism* (Baton Rouge, 1978), especially pp. 47–69, 88–94, 99–104, 113–29, 135–60, 168–84, 191, 196–97, 205–8.

14. Grant's report, July 22, 1865, *O.R.*, XXXIV, pt. 1, 10. For evidence that the Confederacy's superior military manpower system may have made possible considerably greater combat effectiveness, see the Appendix on Mobilization and Combat Effectiveness.

15. Sherman to Halleck, Aug. 20, 1864, *O.R.*, XXVIII, pt. 5, 609.

16. Grant to Sheridan, Feb. 20, 1865, *O.R.*, XLVI, pt. 2, 606.

17. Sherman to Grant, Nov. 6, 1864, *O.R.*, XXXIX, pt. 3, 658–61.

18. Ella Lonn, *Desertion during the Civil War* (New York, London, 1928), 27.

19. Raimondo Luraghi, *The Rise and Fall of the Plantation South* (New York, London, 1978), 106.

20. Sherman to Mrs. Sherman, July 26, 1864, *Home Letters*, 301.

An Introduction to the
Study of Military Operations

Oₙₑ OF THE BASIC DISTINCTIONS in the study of military operations is that between attack and defense. The party which perceives itself the weaker usually chooses the defense, the stronger form of combat. The superiority of the defense rests upon many factors. The defender can choose his ground, a hill, for example, exploiting the potential advantages offered by topography. He can improve on nature by the creation of artificial obstacles and fortifications. In addition, the defender has less stringent command and control requirements and, typically, would know the terrain better.

The strength of the defense manifests itself in two ways: in the power to resist a frontal assault and in the ability to retreat. But the defender enjoys all of the benefits of being on the defensive only if the enemy attacks in front, the direction from which the defender expects, and has prepared for, his opponent's approach. If the defender retreats, he loses his superiority in capability to resist frontal assaults but gains, in its stead, an advantage that usually belongs to the attacker, the initiative. The defender chooses the timing and direction of retreat and usually moves over friendly and familiar territory. The pursuers must contend with rear guards, who may either fight or create obstacles such as broken bridges. Further, the pursuers may be uncertain as to the specific route of retreat.

The actual combat of attackers against defenders is that branch of warfare called tactics. In ancient times tactics varied depending on the composition of the armies, i.e., whether composed of infantry and/or cavalry and whether armed with bows, spears, and/or swords. The tactics of the battle itself generally consisted of each army's rushing at the other and fighting it out frontally until one side retreated. Then a Greek general introduced the most basic of tactical concepts: strengthening one part of the line and pushing the attack where local superiority existed. One of the first recorded instances of this, the battle of Leuctra, occurred in 371 B.C., when the Theban general Epaminondas defeated the always formidable Spartan army thus:

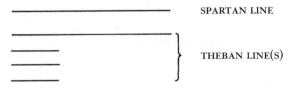

SPARTAN LINE

THEBAN LINE(S)

Horizontally the lines represent men side by side in rows, called ranks, facing forward, e.g., toward the enemy. Vertically the Theban lines represent men in depth from front to rear; men thus arrayed are said to be in files. This idea has endured and, as armies became more flexible, generals sought to concentrate, that is, to direct more men toward some particular area—the left in the diagram above—and attack where they thought the enemy weakest or where an attack was not expected. This presumed weak point might be in the center, on either flank, or anywhere in the enemy line.

In the flanking or enveloping movement, another basic concept in tactics, the attacker seeks to overlap the enemy's line thus:

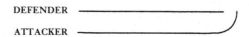

and attack the opposing troops from the side. Just as an individual fighter is more vulnerable and less able to defend his side, so also is an army, because a body of men arrayed to fight in one direction cannot as readily defend themselves when attacked from any other. The flanking movement may also seek to reach the rear of the enemy thus:

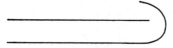

This would constitute an envelopment. Frederick the Great of Prussia favored the oblique attack, another form of the flanking movement. This involves placing the whole attacking army in a flanking position thus:

In any version of the flank attack, the attacking army attempts to "roll up" the defending army by successively attacking and defeating small parts of it. These small parts, on the edge of the battle array, are especially defenseless because they face in the wrong direction, exposing their vulnerable side.

Defense against the flanking or enveloping movement requires redeploying part or all of the defending army thus:

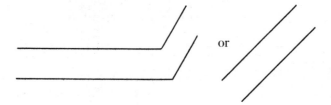

This kind of redeployment is difficult during an attack, especially if the attackers achieve surprise. Success in making a change of front would depend on having a very maneuverable, well-articulated army which responds readily to the orders of superior and subordinate commanders.

The other defense against a flanking movement is for the whole army to retreat. And this also requires the same attributes of maneuverability and good articulation. Failure to execute successfully a deployment to face the outflanking forces or to disengage and retreat promptly from the field of battle usually results in the defeat of the defending army with heavy casualties as the flank attack rolls up the defending line, killing, wounding, or capturing the successively overwhelmed defenders.

Quite obviously, the flank attack, like the concentration at one point in the front, seeks to obtain a local superiority of force and carry out a successful attack before being defeated at other places, weakened by the concentration for attack. Success depends on making the attack at an unexpected time and place. Distracting the enemy's attention away from the point of attack, often by a feint or demonstration elsewhere, i.e., a phony attack, facilitates this. Attacking the defenders when they are unprepared is even more effective than having numerical superiority at the point of assault.

Maximum benefit from this principle accrues when a part of the attacking army can move around the flank of the defending army and assault its rear:

The enveloping force would come unexpectedly on the rear of the defending army, which is facing toward its front.

It is very difficult to redeploy so as to fight both front and rear simultaneously, and retreat is much more difficult because the attacker may be blocking, in whole or in part, the escape route. Even with the presence of roads or, at any rate, a lack of natural obstacles, retreat toward the flank is dangerous because it exposes the withdrawing army's side and does not take it away from the enemy very quickly.

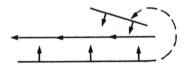

Though it is very difficult to accomplish, a very large portion, or even all, of an attacking army can move far to the rear of the enemy line.

DEFENDER	*rear*	
INITIAL POSITION	*front* *front*	
ATTACKER		
	rear	

ATTACKER	*rear*	
FINAL POSITION	*front* *rear*	
DEFENDER		
	front	

Called a turning movement, such a maneuver usually dictates that, at least for a time, the contending armies lose contact with each other.

A very wide and deep turning movement could aim, not at the enemy's army, but at its communications. In interrupting communications, the turning force places the defending force in a quandary most easily solved by a retreat of the whole army and, subsequently, an attack to drive the turning force from its communications. A spectacularly successful modern example of the turning movement took place during the Korean War. United Nations forces defended the Pusan area against almost the entire North Korean army.

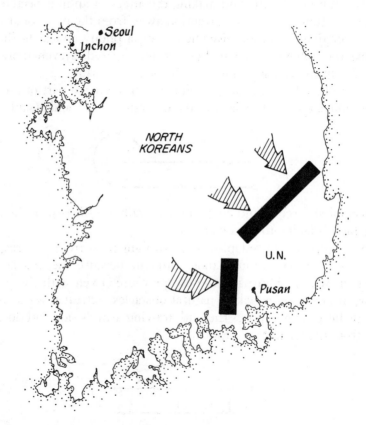

A wide, deep turning movement by sea landed a powerful United Nations force at Inchon, which force soon captured the South Korean capital at Seoul and broke the communications of the North Korean army. This loss of communications, when combined with a powerful U.N. offensive on the Pusan perimeter, forced the North Korean army into a pell-mell retreat into North Korea, one so hasty that its great losses in equipment and disorganization rendered it virtually incapable of a successful defense of North Korea.

Such a wide and deep turning movement, when carried out by the entire attacking army, is even more menacing because it may well enable the attackers entirely to block the retreat. When this happens, the defenders are con-

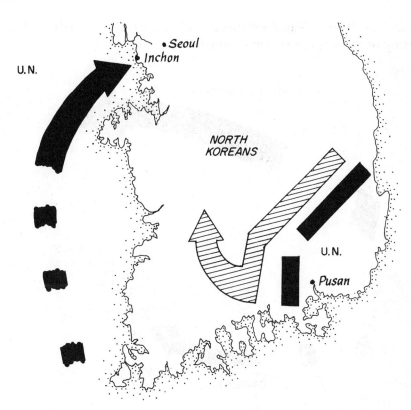

verted into attackers, thus conferring on the original attackers the advantage of fighting on the defensive. Though difficult to accomplish, the movement can bring about spectacular results, if successful. Napoleon demonstrated this in his Ulm campaign.

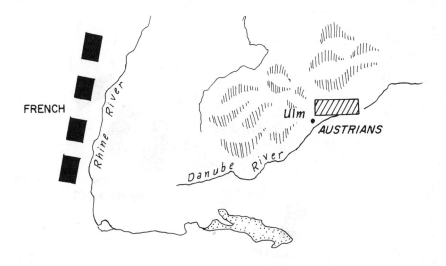

Crossing the Rhine, Napoleon moved only his cavalry directly on Ulm and the army of the inept Austrian commander, Mack.

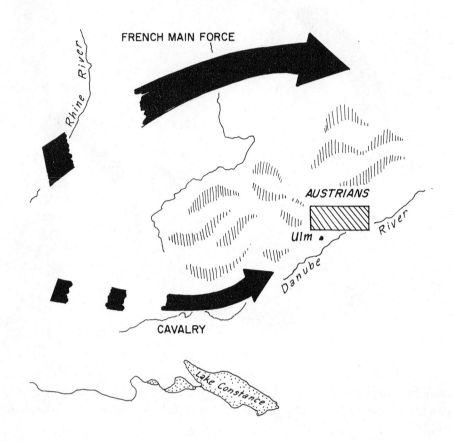

The other corps reached the rear of the Austrian army taking Mack by surprise.

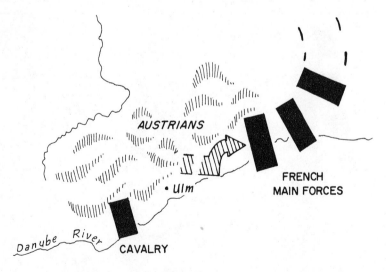

Its retreat blocked, the heavily outnumbered Austrian army surrendered when its break-out attack against the French failed. By blocking Mack's line of retreat, Napoleon forced the Austrian general to attack him, thus shifting to the defender all of the disadvantages of the offensive—heavier casualties and the likelihood of failure.

Campaigns such as this one by Napoleon exhibit that branch of the art of war called strategy. Strategy means the movement of armies to bring about battle under favorable conditions or the retreat of the enemy, and has the objective of producing tactical contact with the enemy at his weak spot. As in tactics, concentrating superior forces at the point of attack, attacking from a direction in which the defender is not prepared to resist, or, by a turning or comparable movement, shifting to the defender the burden and disadvantages of the offensive can accomplish this.

The dividing line between tactics and strategy is often not clear. For example, when an army has actual combat in view, its movements are sometimes called grand tactics. Similarly, the integration of several theatres of operation and of land and naval operations is sometimes called grand strategy. Field Marshal Lord Wavell, comparing military operations to the card game of bridge, perceptively likened strategy to the bidding and tactics to the play of the hands.

There have been numerous efforts to establish general principles for tactics and strategy. They all deal with both offense and defense, but, because the defense is the stronger, they stress the problem of overcoming the power of the defense. The U.S. Army currently recognizes nine of these principles:

The principle of the *objective* states that the nation and all units of the armed forces must have an objective, i.e., have an explicit notion of what they are trying to accomplish.

The principle of the *offensive* points out that defense alone cannot accomplish success in war. Victory ultimately depends on successful offensive operations.

The principle of *simplicity* emphasizes the difficulty of executing overly complicated plans and, for this reason, defender as well as attacker should keep plans as simple as possible.

The principle of *maneuver* affirms the absolutely essential role of mobility in military operations.

The principle of *unity of command* stresses the need for all forces to cooperate for the successful accomplishment of the objective.

The principle of *surprise* points out the value of doing the unexpected. Surprise confers two benefits: the psychological, where the unexpected disconcerts the enemy, rendering him prone to panic, hasty decisions, and other comparable behavior helpful to the attacker achieving surprise; and the cognitive, in the sense that a surprised enemy is one who is unprepared for the action and is thus more vulnerable.

The principle of *security* stresses the need to avoid being caught by surprise.

It does not prescribe an effort to be equally safe everywhere but does, by implication, emphasize the role of intelligence, the systematic effort to find out about the enemy and assess his capabilities. To know enemy intentions would be ideal, but, to avoid surprise, intelligence stresses knowing what the enemy could do so as to avoid surprise, should he carry out any one of his possible actions. The intelligence and security principle includes security against enemy intelligence. Of course, intelligence about the enemy forms the basis of offensive as well as of security measures.

The foregoing seven principles consist very largely of statements of the obvious or, at best, common sense. Nevertheless, military leaders often ignore them and action contrary to these principles has been the foundation of one of the more important military traditions, incompetent generalship leading to bungled battles and campaigns. The last two principles of operations do, in a sense, include the first seven and are complementary and even different statements of the same fundamental idea.

The principle of *economy of force* enjoins that no more force be used than is needed to accomplish the objective. Redundant forces in one place or at one task necessarily imply the possibility of inadequate forces elsewhere.

The principle of *mass* or *concentration*, the last of the nine, effectively embodies or interrelates most of the others. This principle, fundamental to both tactics and strategy, states that victory depends on superiority of force, obtainable only by concentrating a relatively larger percentage of forces at one point.

The most fundamental means of attaining the expected superiority at the point of concentration is, of course, to deceive the enemy as to the point of concentration. The German military writer Carl von Clausewitz summed it up well when he said: "We try to fall upon a point in the enemy's position; that is, a part of his Army (a Division, a Corps), with a great preponderance of force, whilst we keep the other parts in uncertainty, that is to say, occupy them." Uncertainty and occupation would prevent the enemy from perceiving the point of intended concentration.[1]

Scholars of the art of war have differed about how to select properly the point of concentration. In tactics, Clausewitz stressed "decisive points" and advocated as the objective "that part of the enemy's Army, which, in its destruction, will yield decisive advantages"; in strategy, he pointed to "the enemy's principal Army," or at least "a very important portion of the hostile forces." Others have emphasized increasing the probability of a successful attack more than Clausewitz did and, consequently, emphasized less the decisiveness of the point of attack. One theme suggested exploiting enemy weakness, pointing out the impossibility of the enemy being "in force everywhere; one of [the] corps is bound to get through, in which case they can all be united at the same point and take advantage of the gap made by the corps which will have penetrated his line." Distracting the enemy facilitates the search for a weak point, Clausewitz's principle of keeping the enemy army "occupied" and in "uncertainty." To thus distract the enemy Clausewitz advocated: We should "threaten him at all other parts of his position. . . . This will make him divide his forces and then we can take advantage of the geographical conditions to reunite our own at the critical point before he can unite his."²

During World War I the defense dramatically exhibited its supremacy and Allied generals apparently followed Clausewitz's injunction and pursued "decisive" objectives but failed at great cost because they lacked the needed "great superiority" at that point; B. H. Liddell Hart responded to this when he laid great stress on choosing "the line of least resistance—so long as it can lead you to any objective which would contribute to your underlying object." Surprise provides a reliable aid in the task and distraction seeks to accomplish this. Conversely, if the enemy had adequate warning, he could, if his mobility was adequate, accomplish a counter concentration in time to eliminate the attacker's superiority.³

Obviously the application of the principle of concentration embodies the other principles of war. Concentration usually implies a surprise offensive against an objective selected because of its vulnerability and importance. Concentration includes maneuver or mobility as well as unity of command to secure the cooperation of all forces involved. The plan has to be simple enough to be executed properly and in time and must include economy of force for, as Clausewitz pointed out, "If we are very weak, then we can spare very few troops to occupy the enemy at other points, that we may be as strong as possible at the decisive point." It must also incorporate security— be alert to prevent the enemy from doing to you what you are planning to do to him.⁴

The Swiss military writer Baron Henri Jomini developed a simple system of strategic analysis. This involved the use of the concept of lines of operations in order to understand the opportunities for strategic concentration. Jomini defined a line of operations as simply the axis of advance and retreat of an army or a major portion thereof. The formula has utility only when the enemy is employing more than one line of operation. But this situation will invariably occur in the grand strategy of integrating two or more theatres of operations, each of which will contain at least one line.

In Jomini's application of this idea, concentration takes place from one line to another. Jomini emphasized exploiting mobility for concentration. If communications were equal on both sides, then the side having lines of operation closer together could concentrate more quickly. This led Jomini to use a circle or an arc concept and speak of interior and exterior lines. Thus the lines of operations A, B, and C, representing one side in the operation, are interior (closer to one another) and lines X, Y, and Z are exterior. Armies on lines A, B, and C can therefore concentrate against an army on lines X, Y, and Z faster than any of those armies on exterior lines can concentrate in order to come to each other's aid. In this situation the armies on the interior lines,

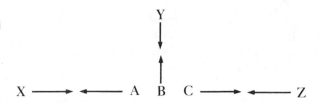

occupying a central position, can concentrate against one of the armies on the exterior lines even though the armies on the exterior lines are not surprised at all and begin their counter concentration the moment the enemy's concentration begins. The forces on interior lines are simply those which may concentrate more rapidly; they may, on occasion be geometrically exterior but, because they enjoy superior communications, be able to concentrate more rapidly.

The obvious advantage of interior lines, or the central position, diminishes as the area of operations grows smaller. At some point a strategically central position become a tactically enveloped position and the forces on the inside can no longer maneuver because the forces on the outside have become mutually supporting. Beginning with the tactical situation, Clausewitz, who had read Jomini's writings, made this point most succinctly:

> In tactics, we always seek to get around the enemy, that is to say, that portion of his force against which our principal attack is directed, partly because the convergent action of the combatant forces is more advantageous than the parallel, partly because it is the only method of cutting the enemy off from his line of retreat.
>
> If this, which relates to the enemy and his position tactically, is used, strategically, and applied to the enemy's theatre of War (therefore also to his subsistence lines), then the separate columns or Armies, which should envelop the enemy, will be in most cases so far apart from each other that they cannot take part in one and the same battle. The enemy will be in the middle, and may be able to turn with the mass of his forces against these Corps singly, and beat them in detail. Frederick II's campaigns furnish examples of this, more especially those of 1757 and 1758.[5]

Since Clausewitz picked two exceptionally good examples of the use of interior lines, it is worthwhile to explain the campaign of 1757 in order to illustrate fully the concept which will have great value in understanding the American Civil War.

In the campaign of 1757 Frederick faced a desperate situation, beset by the Austrians in the East and a Franco-Imperial army in the West. Small Prussian forces covered each of these large forces. Believing the Franco-Imperialists the most menacing, Frederick advanced rapidly westward to join his covering force.

Having concentrated his two forces, Frederick engaged and, at the battle of Rossbach, decisively defeated the Franco-Imperial army. Meanwhile, the Austrians had defeated his covering force which was retreating before their

superior army. Frederick now hurried eastward on his interior line of operations, marching 170 miles in twelve days while his western covering force
easily held in check the defeated Franco-Imperialists.

Joining his recently defeated covering force, Frederick now concentrated
against the Austrians whom he defeated at Leuthen, thus successfully ending
the campaign of 1757 by an energetic exploitation of his interior lines of
operations.

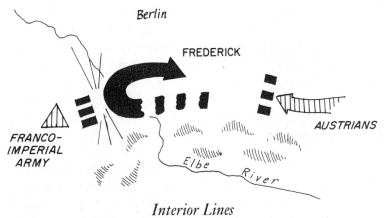

Interior Lines

From time to time scholarly and military critics have disputed the objective
of the concentration of a superior force at one point. Since the defeat of the
enemy army to the greatest degree possible is clearly the object in a battle,
this disagreement largely has to do with strategy and critics have defined it as
a choice between making the objective the destruction of the enemy armed
forces or the acquisition of enemy territory. In some cases the political objective determines the choice. In Frederick the Great's First Silesian War, for
example, he had as his objective the seizing of a province, which he accomplished at the outset of the war. His objective thereafter was defensive, to
hold that province, and his means of accomplishing this did not need to
include the difficult task of destroying the Austrian armies. Often, however,
if not almost always, the political object will not so easily determine the
means, i.e., the military objective.

There is an alternate strategy to one which aims directly at the enemy's
army. Instead the attacker adopts a logistical objective. If the nation on the
offensive could deprive the enemy's armed power of its logistical support, or
any essential element thereof, the enemy would have to disband his armies
and they, like the single army, would be as effectively defeated as if in
combat. The means of accomplishing this without the defeat of the armed
forces seem most obvious through sea power. Here, the navy's weapon, the
blockade, aims precisely at such an objective, and in the case of insular
countries, such as Japan and the United Kingdom, could accomplish the
objective of depriving the enemy's armies of their essential supplies and
equipment. There are, of course, parallel uses for air power.

Land war offers, as an analogy of the blockade, the occupation of some key portion of the enemy's country. For example, suppose the enemy country had a particularly fertile region, the source of much of the food which supported the civilian population and the armed forces. Occupation of this region could seriously handicap, if not cripple, the enemy's ability to carry on the war. In 1914 Germany inadvertently followed this strategy, for, in the Germans' unsuccessful effort to annihilate the French army by attacking it in flank and rear by advancing through Belgium, they advanced into a small part of northeastern France. Though defeated at the Marne and driven back, they still retained much of this region of France. Although small in comparison to the total land area of France, part of this region was highly industrialized, containing three-fourths of the blast furnaces in France. Except for imports of steel, the French economy and armaments industry would have been seriously weakened. Thus, without so intending, the Germans had pursued a strategy oriented toward depriving the French armies of their weapons and ammunition.

An early formulation of this concept of defeating the enemy armed forces by a logistically oriented strategy first came from the German military historian, Hans Delbruck. He called this the strategy of exhaustion, in contrast to the strategy of annihilation. By exhaustion, he did not mean attrition, for attrition is obviously a form of annihilation. Rather, he meant, in part, depriving the armies of their supplies, and proposed this as an alternative to the costly and difficult task of annihilation. The British soldier and historian, J. F. C. Fuller, adopted the name and somewhat narrowed the concept when he defined the strategy of exhaustion as based on the realization that "to deny to the enemy what may be called his 'vital area of operations'—that part of his country essential to the maintenance of his forces—became even more important than winning victories in the field, because it knocked the bottom out of the enemy's fighting power."[6]

The rationale for the strategy of exhaustion rests, of course, upon the dependence of armies upon supplies. Logistics, the third branch of the art of war, deals with the movement of troops and the support of military operations, including supplies, transport, replacements, etc. The strategy of exhaustion aims at disrupting an army's logistics, and the most critical logistical need of an army is, obviously, food for the men. Of almost equal importance before the twentieth century was forage for cavalry horses and the animals who pulled the artillery, wagons, and ambulances. The animals needed forage whether in camp or on the move. Ammunition supply caused less concern in the nineteenth than in the twentieth century because armies were not in continuous contact with one another and, in the Civil War, combatants largely used single-shot, muzzle-loading rifles and artillery, both of which had low rates of fire and of ammunition consumption.

All other logistical needs, except medical supplies, consisted essentially of providing substitutions for things worn out. Wagons, rifles, artillery, horses, uniforms, all needed periodic replacement. The most critical need was boots, especially for an army on the move. Armies travelled on foot and wore out boots rapidly. Barefoot armies move with difficulty in the summer and cold weather immobilizes them. The Duke of Marlborough's Blenheim campaign well illustrates the importance of the replacement of worn-out boots. Making a strategic march from the Netherlands to Bavaria, the Duke arranged to have his army met en route by a new supply of boots. After pausing to issue them and thus ensure the continued mobility of his force, Marlborough resumed the march which would lead him to his famous victory at Blenheim.

Other items of clothing and equipment also wear out or become casualties of combat. In addition, there is a commerce of people, as replacements join the army, and the sick, invalids, and those transferred or on furlough leave it. Thus an army resembles a city on the move but, unlike a city, it does not have a well-developed system of communications that evolved as it grew. Not engaged in manufacturing or commerce, it has less need for transportation facilities than has an ordinary city. These needs are, nevertheless, very substantial.

Armies require, therefore, efficacious means of transportation—which military practitioners call lines of communications—the most efficient being via water. In modern times railroads have provided another relatively effectual means of transportation and, because of their speed, have demonstrated their importance for carrying troops in strategic maneuver. Before the motor truck, even hard-surfaced roads did not help in supplying an army by road over great distances, because wagons drawn by horses, mules, or oxen were so inefficient. A team of horses, for example, could pull a large canal boat as easily as it could pull a mere wagon. In addition, the draft animals would require much forage which the teams would have to obtain along the wagon route. And if the wagons had to carry forage for the animals, their effectiveness would be further reduced and their radius of action from a point of water or rail communications would be severely limited.

Subsistence of the men and forage for the animals generated by far the largest volume of a nineteenth-century army's commerce. In an agricultural region, an army may obtain these things locally but only for a short time, as it soon exhausts the local supplies. An army may live off the country longer if it disperses itself over a wider territory, moves from place to place, or employs some combination of these two. It can, however, only furnish its food and fodder needs in this way if the enemy permits. An active enemy nearby will make it dangerous to disperse and thereby limit an army's movement and supply.

This logistical method, living off the country, lends itself to supplying marches when the enemy does not pose an immediate threat. As it passes through an agricultural country, friendly or unfriendly, an army has constantly available new sources of food and fodder. If an army can avoid the enemy's force, it can raid the opponent's territory, relying on the enemy farms for its immediate needs. It must, however, keep moving and must retreat if the enemy army forces it to remain too long in one place. Living off the country virtually disappeared in the twentieth century as the increased size of armies made them much more dependent on the improved means of communications also characteristics of this century.

All major campaigns exhibit the influence and interdependence of logistics, strategy, and tactics, the three branches of the art of war. Illustrative is a twentieth-century campaign, the World War II campaign of the breakout from the Normandy beachhead in the summer of 1944. The Anglo-American forces successfully landed, established their beachhead, and built up their strength by the end of July 1944. The Germans deployed significant forces against them and the armies made contact along a continuous and stabilized front. On the northeast the British, under Field Marshal Montgomery, attacked but could not break through the tactically very strong German defenses.

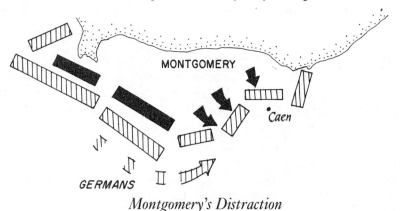

Montgomery's Distraction

This unsuccessful assault did, however, distract the Germans and cause them to concentrate some of their strongest units opposite the British. The United States forces then attacked on the weaker southwest part of the line and, with the aid of heavy air bombardment, tactically managed to pierce the German line and enable Patton's Third Army to pass through to execute turning movements, the basic strategy of the campaign. Though able to threaten the Germans so as to drive them out of France altogether, the turning movements failed either to catch them in their original position or to trap them against the Seine River where air bombing had destroyed the bridges.

In pursuing the Germans, the British made the main effort along the coast because of the need to capture the port of Antwerp in order to provide the armies with a shorter supply route. The British achieved their objective, but Patton's successful pursuit of the Germans stopped at the end of August near the German frontier because of a shortage of gasoline. Thus logistical considerations dictated that Antwerp be the objective, and another logistical factor, the inability to supply continually an advance by the whole Anglo-American

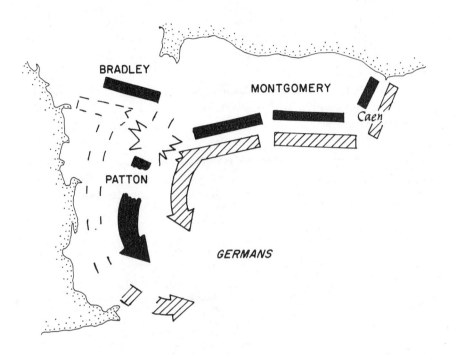

Tactical Success — Breakout

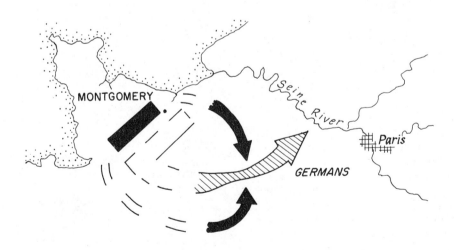

Turning Movement

force, compelled the discontinuance of a very promising pursuit of German forces. The tactical success of the breakthrough had made possible the advance by Patton's army and the execution of a strategic turning movement which caused the precipitate retreat of the Germans. Logistics then dominated the campaign.

Thus, all three branches of the art of war—logistics, strategy, and tactics—played crucial and interrelated roles in the Civil War, but more or less their relative importance was in that order. Tactically, Civil War armies indeed were able to hurt each other—sometimes a great deal—but mutually and indecisively. Poorly chosen tactics rendered higher casualty lists on both sides. The war was decided by the formulation and execution of superior strategy, psychological damage, and scale-tipping impact upon logistics.

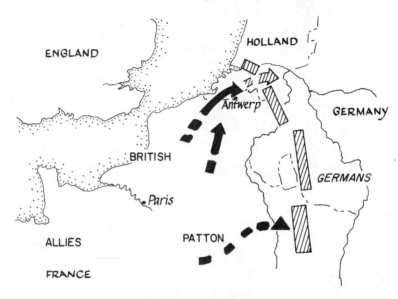

Logistic Considerations

☆   ☆   ☆

1. Carl von Clausewitz, *On War*, trans. J. J. Graham, 3 vols. (New York, 1966), III, 190.

2. *Ibid.*, III, 182, 192, 209; de Bourcet, quoted in B. H. Liddell Hart, *The Ghost of Napoleon* (New Haven, 1933), 57.

3. B. H. Liddell Hart, *Strategy*, revised edition (New York, 1954), 348.

4. Clausewitz, *On War*, III, 21.

5. *Ibid.*, 211–212.

6. Gordon A. Craig, "Delbruck, The Military Historian," *Makers of Modern Strategy*, ed.

Edward Meade Earle (New York, 1943), 272–73; J. F. C. Fuller, *The Second World War, 1939–1945* (New York, 1949), 35. This approach of dividing strategy according to two objectives much simplifies the subject, because, in addition to sea and air power, it also embraces guerrilla warfare, another form of the strategy of exhaustion. For a convenient summary of the schools of strategic thought, see J. C. Wylie, *Military Strategy: A General Theory of Power Control* (New Brunswick, N.J., 1967), 37–64.

Mobilization and Combat Effectiveness

IN HIS CLASSIC *Numbers & Losses in the Civil War in America: 1861–65*, Colonel T. L. Livermore stated: "Substantially the whole military population of the Confederate states was placed under arms in the war of the Rebellion." With a population, including slaves, amounting to only 40 percent of that possessed by the Union, the Confederate armies nevertheless numbered at least 55 percent of the strength of the Union forces. Though by one of Colonel Livermore's calculations Confederate forces equalled as much as 70 percent of the Union's, the lower percentage, based on returns from the field, seems more accurate.[1]

Earlier reliance on the draft and more ambitious initial mobilization plans account for the superior Confederate performance. The Confederates had a particularly difficult task, because the armed forces officially included only whites. Thus, drawing only upon a little over 60 percent of its population, the Confederacy, compared with the Union, had to employ more of the marginally fit and more who had lukewarm or even hostile feelings toward the war. Colonel Livermore believes that the Confederacy enlisted, for the equivalent of a three-year term, a force approximately equal to 87 percent of its white male population between the inclusive ages of eighteen and forty-five. Of course the armies in the field actually numbered far less than this proportion would indicate because of desertion, casualties, and other causes.[2]

For the years 1861 through 1863 Colonel Livermore offers relatively complete official data on all battles in which as many as 1,000 men on either side were hit by enemy projectiles or, very rarely, stabbed by a bayonet. Of these battles, twenty-six are combats in the field, the remainder being assaults on fortifications. In these twenty-six battles Confederate strength averaged 78 percent of Union strength, although during this period the Confederate armies averaged about 56 percent of the Union. Thus the Confederates brought a much higher percentage of their forces into battle. The effectiveness of Confederate strategy in exploiting interior lines may account for some of this disparity. More battles took place in which the Confederates accomplished a significant concentration than in which the Union made comparable movements. The Union need to guard supply lines from raiders and guerrillas offers a far more important explanation. At times these forces numbered 30 percent of Union armies east of the Mississippi. If 30 percent is deducted from the average Union strength, then Confederate forces amounted to 80 percent of the Federals, quite comparable to the 78 percent taken into battle.

The Union had two and one-half times the population of the Confederacy. That the Federals possessed battle strength scarcely 25 percent greater than the Confederates' indicates two important factors: the superior Confederate mobilization and the Union's need to guard its communications from guerrillas and from the very effective Confederate policy of cavalry raids.

Colonel Livermore's data also cast light on two other questions: one, the hypothesis that the Confederates had less efficiency on the offensive because of their failure to realize the effectiveness of the rifle; the other, Robert E. Lee, by his propensity for the offensive, cost the South more casualties than others of his rank in the Confederacy. As the following data will exhibit, neither of these hypotheses is true. The data demonstrate, however, the greater expense of the defensive in casualties than the use of breastworks and rifles would lead one to expect. The rigid linear system of defense used in battles probably explains this for it meant that breaks in lines had to be prevented or closed by counterattack regardless of the impact on the defenders' casualties.[3]

To evaluate relative combat efficiency we chose the twenty-six field engagements of 1861–63 because the data for them were complete. We determined the attacker by considering it to be the side which made the first tactical offensive move. Thus we classify Second Bull Run as a Union attack because, though the Confederates were on the strategic offensive, the Union forces made the first tactical offensive move. The winner was determined by who retreated, except for Williamsburg, where the retreat was planned regardless of the outcome of the battle.

The following twenty-six battles were used:

BATTLE	ATTACKER	WINNER
Bull Run	Union	Confederate
Wilson's Creek	Union	Confederate
Pea Ridge	Confederate	Union
Shiloh	Confederate	Union
Williamsburg	Union	Confederate
Fair Oaks	Confederate	Union
Seven Days' Battles	Confederate	Confederate
Cedar Mountain	Union	Confederate
Second Bull Run (Manassas & Chantilly)	Union	Confederate
Antietam	Union	Union
South Mountain	Union	Union
Corinth	Confederate	Union
Perryville	Union	Union
Chickasaw Bayou & Bluff	Union	Confederate
Fredericksburg	Union	Confederate
Prairie Grove	Confederate	Union
Stones River	Confederate	Union
Champion's Hill	Union	Union
Chancellorsville & Fredericksburg	Union	Confederate
Gettysburg	Confederate	Union
Chickamauga	Confederate	Confederate
Chattanooga	Union	Union
Mine Run	Union	Confederate
Fort Donelson	Confederate	Union
Arkansas Post	Union	Union
Richmond	Confederate	Confederate

The first test of efficiency was to array the battles in terms of the tactical offensive, thus:

	UNION	CONFEDERATES
Win	6	3
Lose	9	8

Applying an odds ratio[4] by cross multiplying (6 x 8 = 48; 3 x 9 = 27), the odds of a Union attack succeeding were 48 to 27, or about 2 to 1, as compared to the chances of a Confederate attack. The comparative odds on a winning Confederate attack or defense were, of course, the reverse: 1 to 2. This indicates greater Union effectiveness, but, in view of Union numerical superiority, says nothing about efficiency. In successful Union offensive battles their numbers were 1.63 of Confederate numbers; in losing attacks, 1.4. In winning Confederate attacks their numbers were 1.08 of Union numbers; in losing attacks .87.

Since losses might provide an insight into efficiency, the following table compares numbers engaged, casualties as a percentage of numbers engaged, and, as something of an absolute measure, casualties as a percentage of enemy casualties. We also divided casualties between killed and wounded and missing on the hypothesis that newly organized regiments might exhibit a higher number of missing.

		% K & W	% MSNG	% CAS	% ENEMY NOS	% ENEMY CAS	EFFIC INDEX	ENEMY EFFIC INDEX
Union Attacks	Won	10.1	.8	10.9	163.3	78.8	84	165
	Lost	8.8	3.6	12.4	140.4	166.9	68	124
	Total	9.3	2.6	11.9	147.7	122.4	74	137
Confederate Attacks	Won	22	1.4	23.4	108.2	105.7	132	239
	Lost	20.6	10.1	30.7	86.7	128.4	187	179
	Total	21.2	6.7	27.9	94.1	119.9	165	199
All Win Attacks		14.9	1	15.9	135.8	92.7	103	202
All Lose Attacks		13	6	19	114.9	142.1	111	150
All Attacks		13.7	4.1	17.8	121.8	120.9	108	167
Union Defend	Won	16.2	4.6	20.8	115.3	77.9	179	187
	Lost	14.3	9.7	24	92.4	94.6	239	132
	Total	15.6	6.3	21.9	106.3	83.4	199	165
Confederate Defend	Won	9.5	.9	10.4	71.2	59.9	124	68
	Lost	13.8	8.7	22.5	61.2	126.9	165	84
	Total	10.9	3.4	14.3	67.7	81.7	137	74
All Win Defend		12.7	2.6	15.3	87	70.4	150	111
All Lose Defend		14	9.2	23.2	73.6	107.9	202	103
All Defend		13.2	4.8	18	82.1	82.7	167	108
All Union Win		13.4	2.8	16.2	133.4	78.2	135	179
All Confederate Win		13.8	1	14.8	80.5	78	126	111
All Union Lose		10.2	5.2	15.4	124.2	128.2	111	126
All Confederate Lose		18	10	28	75	127.9	179	135
All Union		12.3	4	16.3	128.3	104.7	117	157
All Confederate		15	5	20	78	96	157	117

We also used T. L. Livermore's efficiency index. The index number reflects the number of killed and wounded per thousand men on the other side. A higher number indicates greater efficiency, i.e., greater success in hitting enemy targets.

A number of observations may be made from this table:

Losses on the attack have no relation to winning or losing, though the percentage of missing has. A hardly meaningful reduction in the number of killed and wounded in part offsets the higher percentage of missing.

Confederate attackers sustained over twice the casualties of Union attackers, whereas Union defenders suffered a significantly higher proportion of casualties than Confederate defenders. Yet the correspondence is not perfect, for Union offensive casualties are lower in proportion. If Union defensive casualties were to Confederate offensive casualties as Confederate defensive casualties were to Union offensive casualties, Union offensive casualties would have been higher; thus: 21.9 percent : 27.9 percent :: 14.3 percent : 18.2 percent. But in fact, Union offensive casualties were only 11.9 percent. These figures suggest that the Confederates made more intense and/or sustained offensive efforts.

Yet another measure, which takes account of absolute numbers, is the percentage of enemy casualties. This indicates that higher Union casualties fully offset higher Confederate offensive casualties. On the attack Union armies lost 122.4 percent of defender's casualties, essentially the same as Confederate armies on the attack, 119.9 percent of the defender's casualties.[5]

Since the defenders won seventeen of the twenty-six battles, the defense clearly predominated. The odds ratio did indicate that the Union forces had about twice the chance of conducting a successful defense. Again, this indicates greater Union effectiveness but, in view of their comparative numerical advantage, says nothing about their efficiency. In successful Union defenses they outnumbered the attackers 1.15 to 1. In their three losing defenses, Union forces were 92.4 percent of the attacker's strength. The comparable Confederate percentages were: winning defense 71.2 percent, losing defense 61.2 percent.

Neither Union killed and wounded nor missing seem related to whether they won or lost. With the Confederates, on the other hand, a significant difference stands out: total casualties for the losing defense amounted to double those of the winning defense. A 45 percent increase in killed and wounded and the large number of missing account for this difference. Unlike the Union forces in a winning defense, the Confederates in their successful defenses lost very few missing. It seems that, when the Confederates won, they did very well but, when they failed, they experienced disaster.

Union defensive casualties were much higher than Confederate defensive casualties. Higher Confederate casualties, and perhaps effort, on the attack explain this difference, though Union defensive casualties ran lower in proportion. If Union offensive casualties were to Confederate defensive casualties as Confederate offensive casualties were to Union defensive casualties, Union defensive casualties would have been higher; thus: 11.9 percent : 14.3 percent :: 27.9 percent : 33.5 percent. But Union defensive casualties were only 21.9 percent rather than the proportional 33.5 percent.

T. L. Livermore's efficiency index offers still another means of measuring combat efficiency. The comparative indices in which 1,000 attackers shot the following index numbers of defenders are:

	WIN	LOSE	AVERAGE
Union	84	68	74
Confederate	132	187	165
Average	103	111	108

These suggest that the Confederates performed more capably than the Union did, but displayed their best effectiveness when they lost, whereas Union troops performed best when they won. But, since the Union had more men, superior Confederate efficiency may be an illusion; the Confederates may simply have had more targets available. This system of measuring combat efficiency clearly has defects; something better is needed.

☆　　☆

Writing about fifteen years after Livermore, F. W. Lanchester elegantly solved with his square law the problem of determining combat efficiency. Lanchester assumed that the losses per unit of time on each side would be directly proportional to the numerical strength of the opposing force. Thus the superior force would inflict on the inferior casualties in proportion to its larger size. If, for example, the superior force had twice as many men as the inferior one, it would, in the first unit of time, inflict on the inferior twice the casualties inflicted on it by the inferior. In the next unit of time the superior force would be proportionately stronger than two to one and the relative casualties in the smaller force would be greater. If a force of 1,000 fought to a finish an opponent 500 strong, the force of 1,000 would be reduced to 866 men while the force of 500 would have been annihilated.[6]

From this reasonable assumption Lanchester derived the proposition that the fighting strength of units was proportional to the square of their numerical strength. This would be true only if the fighting value of one unit equalled that of the other and neither was enjoying the advantages of the defense. Thus his square law defined the fighting strength of a unit as proportional to "the square of its numerical strength multiplied by the fighting value of its individual units."

This makes it possible to solve for the fighting value of opposing units in any battle if we know their initial strength and their casualties. If the fighting value is equal, the number indicating fighting value is one. If one side is superior, its value will be greater than one; if it is inferior, the number will be less than one. The square law will have compensated for the differences in numbers on each side.

In the twenty-six selected battles, we determined the final strength of each side by subtracting the killed and wounded. In battles in which the Confederates attacked, their fighting value was .86; in the battles in which the Union attacked, theirs was .53. Both numbers reflect the disadvantage of the offensive but the difference is significant, even startling. According to Lanchester's square law the fighting value of Confederate armies far exceeded that of the Union.[7]

It is impossible to ignore the results of the application of this method, which has so much logical validity that it is still accepted and used in operations research on combat problems. The most likely explanation is not that one Reb could beat ten Yanks but that the Union system of forming new regiments did great harm to combat efficiency as did their practice of discharging veterans whose terms of service had expired. Though the Federals made every effort to use new regiments to guard communications until they were seasoned, they could not consistently apply this. Even if they could, it would not have been fully effective, for neither the rank and file nor their officers and noncommissioned officers, when they were at last committed, would have had the benefit of actual combat. If the Federals had consistently used the Confederate system of sending replacements to existing regiments and of never discharging veterans, they would have obviated both of these problems.

This hypothesis receives support when the missing are included for calculating the strengths at the close of the battle. Instead of a value of .86, the Confederates have a value of .92, and the Union force drops from .53 to .42. Green troops under inexperienced leaders were more likely to desert, become lost, or be taken prisoner. This significant tendency in the figures supports the hypothesis that the two systems of recruiting and retention accounted for the marked difference in fighting value. The results with Lanchester's equation support General Sherman's estimate that old troops had twice the value of new troops.

Much more work could be done in the application of Lanchester's simple method to these battles, especially as the results for different battles vary markedly. The actual composition of armies could also be examined. We have attempted here to urge additional research by those interested and to adduce the strong indication that the two systems of recruiting had a marked impact on military operations. If this hypothesis is true, it strongly disparages the Union's states'-rights way of fighting the war as well as endorses the centralized methods employed by the Confederates.

With the foregoing data and interpretation as a base, it is relatively easy to determine whether R. E. Lee was more or less combative and efficient than other Confederate generals.[8]

	% ENEMY NUMBERS	% CASUALTIES	% ENEMY CASUALTIES	LIVERMORE'S EFFICIENCY INDEX
Confederate Win Attack	113	25.8	88	170.3
Lee Win Attack	104.7	21.6	130	102.6
Confederate Lose Attack	85.4	28	132.3	167.2
Lee Lose Attack	90	37.4	121.8	235.6
Confederate Win Defend	85	5.7	63.8	61.7
Lee Win Defend	67.2	12.3	59.3	146.6
Confederate Lose Defend	57.2	21.7	139	143.6
Lee Lose Defend	67	23.5	115.4	192
All Confederate (w/o Lee)	80.7	21.8	115	141.2
All Lee	75.6	19.7	92	158.4

	CONFED BATTLES	LEE	% OF TOTAL	OTHERS	% OF TOTAL	% OF LEE'S	% OF OTHERS'
Battles	26	9	35	17	65		
All Attack	11	2	18	9	82	22	53
Win Attack	3	1	33	2	67	(50)	(22)
Lose Attack	8	1	12.5	7	87.5	(50)	(78)
All Defend	15	7	47	8	53	78	47
Win Defend	9	5	55.5	4	44.5	(71)	(50)
Lose Defend	6	2	33.3	4	66.7	(29)	(50)
All Win	12	6	50	6	50	67	35.3
All Lose	14	3	21.4	11	78.6	33	64.7

Using the square-law equation, Lee had a value of .7 on the offensive; .85 if missing are subtracted from the final strength. These compare with .86 and .92 for all Confederate attacks, including Lee's. Since Lee was on the offensive only twice, it would probably be unwise to attach much significance to the difference between Lee and all other Confederates. With Lee on the defensive Union values are .55 and .49. These compare with .53 and .42 for all Union attacks.

From the foregoing it is clear that the combat effectiveness of the Army of Northern Virginia did not differ significantly from other Confederate armies, assuming, of course, that the Army of the Potomac was representative of other Union armies. All of the data on Lee confirms that he was a representative Confederate general except that he won more and was on the tactical offensive less. Being more often on the defensive correlates both with winning and with his overall lower record of casualties.

The foregoing superficial quantitative analysis should raise more questions than it answers. It should also exhibit that those interested in Civil War tactics will find many opportunities to employ various quantitative approaches to provide more sophisticated understandings of different battles and of the tactics of the war. Certainly the hypothesis of Confederate combat superiority should be carefully tested against individual battles to ascertain whether it correlates with, among other factors, the length of service and degree of combat experience of the units engaged, with the amount of offensive and defensive combat by each side, and with the quantity and quality of field fortifications used.[9]

☆   ☆   ☆

1. Livermore, *Numbers & Losses in the Civil War in America*, 10, 47, 62.

2. *Ibid.*, 21–22, 51–63.

3. McWhiney, *Southerners and Other Americans*, 103–27; Connelly and Jones, *Politics of Command*, 33.

4. For a 2 x 2 contingency table of the form:

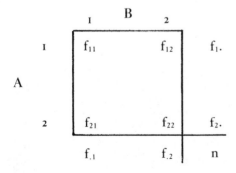

the odds (cross product) ratio is defined by $\alpha = f_{11}f_{22}/f_{21}f_{12}$. α has an interpretation. If we think of the column totals as being fixed, then f_{11}/f_{21} is the odds of being in the first row conditioned upon being in the first column, and f_{12}/f_{22} is the corresponding odds for the second column. The relative odds or odds ratio is:

$$(f_{11}/f_{21})/(f_{12}/f_{22}) = f_{11}f_{22}/f_{21}f_{12} = \alpha$$

Thus for the table:

	UNION	CONFEDERATE
Win	6	3
Lose	9	8

$\%$ is the odds of a Union attack winning and $\frac{3}{8}$ is the odds of a Confederate attack winning. The relative odds are $\frac{48}{27}$ or about two to one.

For this the authors are much indebted to Professors Doris Hertsgaard and Robert Gordon of the North Dakota State University Department of Mathematical Sciences.

5. If actions involving very large numbers of prisoners are omitted, these figures differ. Omitting Fort Donelson, Arkansas Post, and Richmond, Kentucky, these numbers are 130 percent and 112 percent.

6. F. W. Lanchester, *Aircraft in Warfare—The Dawn of the Fourth Arm* (London, 1916), 43–44; see also: 39–42, 45–66.

7. Two of the more important models of combat developed by the British engineer F. W. Lanchester are those which produced Lanchester's linear and square laws. Philip M. Morse and George E. Kimball describe these models in detail in their pioneer work *Methods of Operations Research* (New York, 1951). The linear law is derived from a model in which battles are assumed to consist of a large number of individual duels. The square law, on the other hand, is derived from a model in which it is assumed that the firepower of each side is more extended. Specifically, the assumption is made in the latter model that each participant in an engagement can fire at every (or almost every) opponent. This leads to the following differential equation·

$$dm/dn = n/mE,$$
where

m = number of combatants in one force (say the attacking force) at any instant of time

n = number of combatants in the other force (say the defending force) at the same instant

The parameter E, called the *exchange rate*, is the ratio between the average number of defending and the average number of attacking combatants

lost. The solution of the differential equation may be written:

$$E = \frac{n_o^2 - n^2}{m_o^2 m^2}$$

where m_o, n_o are initial numbers of combatants, m, n are numbers remaining at some later time. This equation is called *Lanchester's square law*.

The value of E is a measure of the superiority of one force over the other in terms of such factors as weapons, training, and tactical posture; and its value is independent of the numbers of combatants on each side. In the case of attackers versus defenders, E measures the superiority of the attackers' weapons and training over those of the defenders. Observe that if E were less than one, the defenders would be superior.

Values measuring Union and Confederate efficiency were obtained as follows: All of the battles examined were divided into two groups, those in which the Union was the attacker and those in which the Confederacy attacked. In each battle the initial (m_o, n_o) and final (m, n) strengths of each side were substituted into the square law equation to obtain a value of E. Values of E were then averaged separately for the two groups of battles. Values for individual battles varied widely.

The authors are much indebted to Professor R. R. Hare of the Department of Mathematical Sciences of North Dakota State University. He alerted us to the importance of Lanchester's work, discussed it at some length, and kindly performed the calculations for us.

8. The presence of the three battles with disproportionate numbers of prisoners affects these figures significantly. Without Fort Donelson, Arkansas Post, and Richmond, Kentucky, these comparisons would be:

	% ENEMY NUMBERS	% CASUALTIES	% ENEMY CASUALTIES	LIVERMORE'S EFFICIENCY INDEX
Confederate Win Attack	114	28	114	172
Lee Win Attack	104.7	21.6	130	102.6
Confederate Lose Attack	86.5	21.4	96.6	172.7
Lee Lose Attack	90	37.4	121.8	235.6
Confederate Win Defend	85	5.7	63.8	61.7
Lee Win Defend	67.2	12.3	59.3	146.6
Confederate Lose Defend	67	17	111.5	139
Lee Lose Defend	67	23.5	115.4	192
All Confederate	84.5	18	99.5	141
All Lee	75.6	19.7	92	158.4

9. For some historical applications of quantitative methods see: T. N. Dupuy, *Numbers, Predictions and War: Using History to Evaluate Combat Factors and Predict the Outcome of Battles* (Indianapolis, New York, 1979), 97–99, 156–58; Janice B. Fain, *The Lanchester Equations and Historical Warfare: An Analysis of Sixty World War II Land Engagements* (Arlington, Va., 1975); Daniel Willard, *Lanchester as a Force in History: An Analysis of Land Battles of the Years 1618–1905* (Research Analysis Corporation, McLean, Va., 1962); Herbert K. Weiss, "Combat Models and Historical Data: The U.S. Civil War," *Operations Research* (Sept.-Oct., 1966), 759–91.

☆ BIBLIOGRAPHY OF WORKS CITED ☆

Adams, George Worthington. *Doctors in Blue: The Medical History of the Union Army in the Civil War.* New York, 1961.

Adams, Michael C. C. *Our Masters the Rebels: A Speculation on Union Military Failure in the East, 1861–1865.* Cambridge, Mass.; London, England, 1978.

Alger, John I. *Antoine-Henri Jomini: A Bibliographical Survey.* West Point, N. Y., 1975.

———. "Thought, Theory and the Military Mind." Paper presented at the Northern Great Plains History Conference, Fargo, N.D., Oct. 27, 1978.

Ambrose, Stephen E. *Halleck: Lincoln's Chief of Staff.* Baton Rouge, La., 1962.

Anderson, Bern. *By Sea and By River: The Naval History of the Civil War.* New York, 1962.

Barnard, J. G. *The Peninsular Campaign and its Antecedents.* New York, 1864.

Bearss, Edwin C. *The Fall of Fort Henry.* Dover, Tenn., 1963.

———. *The Battle of Wilson's Creek.* Bozeman, Mont., 1975.

Beauregard, G. T. *A Commentary on the Campaign and Battle of Manassas. . . .* New York, 1891.

———. "The First Battle of Bull Run," *Battles and Leaders of the Civil War.* Edited by C. C. Buel and R. U. Johnson. 4 vols. New York, 1887–88.

———. *Principles and Maxims of the Art of War—Outpost Service; general instructions for battles; Reviews.* Charleston, 1863.

———. *With Beauregard in Mexico: The Mexican War Reminiscences of P. G. T. Beauregard.* Edited by T. Harry Williams. Baton Rouge, La., 1956.

Beringer, Richard E. *Historical Analysis: Contemporary Approaches to Clio's Craft.* New York, Santa Barbara, Chichester, Brisbane, Toronto, 1978.

Bigelow, John, Jr. *The Principles of Strategy Illustrated Mainly from American Campaigns.* New York, London, 1891.

Black, Robert C., III. *The Railroads of the Confederacy.* Chapel Hill, N.C., 1952.

Blumenson, Martin, and Stokesbury, James L. *Masters of the Art of Command.* Boston, Mass., 1975.

Boatner, Mark Mayo, III. *The Civil War Dictionary.* New York, 1959.

Brown, D. Alexander. "Battle at Chickasaw Bluffs." *Civil War Times—Illustrated* (July, 1970), 9, 45–46.

Brown, J. Willard. *The Signal Corps USA in The War of the Rebellion.* Boston, Mass., 1896.

Cadwallader, Sylvanus. *Three Years With Grant as Recalled by War Correspondent Sylvanus Cadwallader.* Edited by Benjamin P. Thomas. New York, 1956.

von Caemmerer, Rudolph. *The Development of Strategical Science in the Nineteenth Century.* Translated by Karl von Donat. London, 1905.

Canby, Courtlandt, editor. *Lincoln and the Civil War; A Profile and a History.* New York, 1960.

Castel, Albert. "Theophilus Holmes—Pallbearer of the Confederacy." *Civil War Times—Illustrated* (July, 1977), 11–17.

Catton, Bruce. *The Coming Fury.* Garden City, N. Y., 1961.

———. *Grant Takes Command.* Boston, Mass., 1968.

———. *Mr. Lincoln's Army.* Garden City, N. Y., 1962.

———. *Never Call Retreat*. Garden City, N. Y., 1965.

———. *A Stillness at Appomattox*. Garden City, N. Y., 1953.

———. *The Terrible Swift Sword*. Garden City, N. Y., 1963.

———. *U.S. Grant and the American Military Tradition*. New York, 1954.

Chambers, Lenoir. *Stonewall Jackson*. 2 vols. New York, 1959.

Chase, Salmon P. "Diary of Salmon P. Chase." *Annual Report of the American Historical Association for the Year 1902*. 2 vols. Washington, 1902.

———. *Inside Lincoln's Cabinet: The Civil War Diaries of Salmon P. Chase*. Edited by David Donald. New York, London, Toronto, 1954.

Chesnut, Mary Boykin. *A Diary from Dixie*. Edited by Ben Ames Williams. Boston, Mass., 1949.

von Clausewitz, Carl. *On War*. Translated by J. J. Graham. 3 vols. New York, 1966.

Colin, J. *The Transformations of War*. Translated by L. H. R. Pope-Hennessy. London, 1912.

Commissary General of Subsistence, Papers of the. Military History Research Collection, Carlisle Barracks, Pennsylvania.

Comstock, Cyrus B. Diary, Library of Congress, Washington, D.C.

Connelly, Thomas Lawrence. *Army of the Heartland*. Baton Rouge, La., 1967.

———. *Autumn of Glory*. Baton Rouge, La., 1971.

———. "Vicksburg: Strategic Point or Propaganda Device?" *Military Affairs* (April, 1970), 49–53.

Connelly, Thomas Lawrence, and Jones, Archer. *The Politics of Command: Factions and Ideas in Confederate Strategy*. Baton Rouge, La., 1973.

Cooling, Benjamin F. *Symbol, Sword, and Shield: Defending Washington During the Civil War*. Hamden, Conn., 1975.

Cornish, Dudley Taylor. *The Sable Arm: Negro Troops in the Union Army, 1861–1865*. New York, 1966.

Coulter, E. Merton. *The Confederate States of America, 1861–1865*. Baton Rouge, La., 1950.

Cox, Jacob D. *Military Reminiscences of the Civil War*. 2 vols. New York, 1900.

Craig, Gordon A. "Delbruck, The Military Historian." *Makers of Modern Strategy*. Edited by Edward Meade Earle. New York, 1943.

Craighill, William P. *The Army Officer's Pocket Companion; Principally Designed for Staff Officers in the Field*. New York, 1862.

Cramer, John H. *Lincoln Under Enemy Fire*. Baton Rouge, La., 1948.

Creasy, Sir Edward. *The Fifteen Decisive Battles of the World from Marathon to Waterloo*. London, 1851.

van Creveld, Martin. *Supplying War: Logistics from Wallenstein to Patton*. Cambridge, London, New York, Melbourne, 1977.

Cullum, George W. "Biographical Sketch of Major-Gen. Henry W. Halleck." Sir Sherston Baker, *Halleck's International Law*, 3rd edition. 2 vols. London, 1893.

Cunningham, Horace H. *Doctors in Gray: The Confederate Medical Service*. Baton Rouge, La., 1958.

Current, Richard N. "God and the Strongest Battalions," *Why The North Won the Civil War*. Edited by David Donald. London and New York, 1960.

Dana, Charles A. *Recollections of the Civil War*. New York, 1898.

Davis, Burke. *Our Incredible Civil War*. New York, 1960.

Davis, Jefferson. *Jefferson Davis, Constitutionalist*. Edited by Dunbar Rowland. 10 vols. Jackson, Mississippi, 1923.

———. *The Papers of Jefferson Davis*. Edited by Haskell Monroe and James T. McIntosh.   vols. Baton Rouge, La., 1971– .

———. *The Rise and Fall of the Confederate Government*. Edited by Bell I. Wiley. 2 vols. New York, London, 1958.

Davis, William C. *The Battle of New Market*. Garden City, N. Y., 1975.

———. *Duel Between the First Ironclads*. New York, 1975.

Delaney, Norman C. *John McIntosh Kell of the Raider Alabama*. University, Ala., 1973.

Denison, George T. *A History of Cavalry From the Earliest Times*. London, 1913.

Dixon, Norman. *On the Psychology of Military Incompetence*. New York, 1976.

Dowdey, Clifford. *Bugles Blow No More*. Boston, Mass., 1937.

Duncan, John. "A Historian in His Armchair; An Interview with Bell I. Wiley." *Civil War Times—Illustrated* (April, 1973), 240.

Dupuy, R. Ernest. *Men of West Point: The First 150 Years of the United States Military Academy*. New York, 1951.

Dupuy, R. Ernest, and Dupuy, Trevor N. *Military Heritage of America*. New York, Toronto, and London, 1956.

Dupuy, Trevor N. *Numbers, Predictions and War: Using History to Evaluate Combat Factors and Predict the Outcome of Battles*. Indianapolis, New York, 1979.

Eaton, Clement. *A History of the Southern Confederacy*. New York, 1954.

Elliott, Charles Winslow. *Winfield Scott: The Soldier and the Man*. New York, 1937.

Elting, John R. "Jomini: Disciple of Napoleon?" *Military Affairs* (Spring, 1964), 17–26.

Engineer Bureau Records, National Archives, Washington, D.C.

Escott, Paul D. *After Secession: Jefferson Davis and the Failure of Confederate Nationalism*. Baton Rouge, La., 1978.

Esposito, Vincent J., chief editor. *The West Point Atlas of American Wars*. 2 vols. New York, 1959.

Etzioni, Amitai. *A Comparative Analysis of Complex Organizations*. New York, 1961.

Fain, Janice B. *The Lanchester Equations and Historical Warfare: An Analysis of Sixty World War II Land Engagements*. Arlington, Va., 1975.

Fite, Emerson D. *Social and Industrial Conditions in the North During the Civil War*. New York, 1910.

Fogel, Robert William. *Railroads and American Economic Growth*. Baltimore, Md., 1964.

Foote, Shelby. *The Civil War: A Narrative*. 3 vols. New York, 1958–74.

Freeman, Douglas Southall. *Lee's Lieutenants*. 3 vols. New york, 1942–44.

———. *R. E. Lee*. 4 vols. New York & London, 1934–35.

Fuller, J. F. C. *The Second World War, 1939–1945*. New York, 1949.

Gibbon, John. *Personal Recollections of the Civil War*. New York, London, 1928.

Goff, Richard D. *Confederate Supply*. Durham, N.C., 1969.

Govan, Gilbert E., and Livingood, James W. *A Different Valor: The Story of General Joseph E. Johnston, C.S.A.* Indianapolis, New York, 1956.

Gow, June I. "Theory and Practice in Confederate Military Administration." *Military Affairs* (October, 1975), 118–23.

Grant, Ulysses S. *General Grant's Letters to a Friend.* Edited by James Grant Wilson. New York and Boston, 1897.

———. *The Papers of Ulysses S. Grant.* Edited by John Y. Simon. Carbondale and Edwardsville, Ill., 1967– .

———. *Personal Memoirs of U.S. Grant.* Edited by E. B. Long. Cleveland and New York, 1952.

Griess, Thomas F. "Dennis Hart Mahan: West Point Professor and Advocate of Professionalism, 1830–1871." Ph.D. dissertation, Duke University, 1969.

Guide to Federal Archives Relating to the Civil War. Washington, 1962.

Hagerman, Edward. "The Evolution of Trench Warfare in the American Civil War." Ph.D. dissertation, Duke University, 1965.

——— "From Jomini to Dennis Hart Mahan: The Evolution of Trench Warfare and the American Civil War." *Civil War History* (September, 1967), 197–220.

———. "The Professionalization of George B. McClellan and Early Civil War Command: An Institutional Perspective." *Civil War History* (June, 1975), 113–35.

———. "The Reorganization of Field Transportation and Field Supply in the Army of the Potomac, 1863: The Flying Column and Strategic Mobility." *Military Affairs* (December, 1980), 182-86.

———. "The Tactical Thought of R. E. Lee and the Origins of Trench Warfare in the American Civil War. 1861-62." *The Historian* (November, 1975), 21-38.

Halleck, H. Wager. *Bitumen: Its Varieties, Properties and Uses.* Washington, 1841.

———. *Collection of Mining Laws of Spain and Mexico.* San Francisco, Calif., 1859.

———. *Elements of Military Art and Science* or *Course of Instruction in Strategy, Fortifications, Tactics of Battles, etc., Embracing the Duties of Staff, Infantry, Cavalry, and Engineers.* New York, 1846.

———. *Elements of Military Art and Science.* New York, 1862.

———. *International Law or Rules Regulating the Intercourse of States in Peace and War.* New York and San Francisco, 1861.

Hanchett, William. *Irish Charles G. Halpine in Civil War America.* Syracuse, N. Y., 1970.

Harrison, Lowell H. "Conscription in the Confederacy." *Civil War Times—Illustrated* (July, 1970), 10–18.

Harsh, Joseph L. "Battlesword and Rapier: Clausewitz, Jomini, and the American Civil War." *Military Affairs*, XXXVIII (December, 1974), 133–38.

———. "On the McClellan-Go-Round," *Battles Lost and Won; Essays from Civil War History.* Edited by John T. Hubbell. Westport, Conn.; London, 1975.

Hartje, Robert. *Van Dorn: The Life and Times of a Confederate General.* Nashville, Tenn., 1967.

Hassler, Warren W., Jr. *Commanders of the Army of the Potomac.* Baton Rouge, La., 1962.

———. *George B. McClellan, Shield of the Union.* Baton Rouge, La., 1957.

Hattaway, Herman. "Confederate Myth Making: Top Command and the Chickasaw Bayou Campaign." *Journal of Mississippi History* (November, 1970), 311–26.

———. *General Stephen D. Lee.* Jackson, Miss., 1976.

Hattaway, Herman, and Jones, Archer. "Lincoln as Military Strategist." *Civil War History* (December, 1980), 293–303.

Hay, John. *Lincoln and the Civil War in the Diaries and Letters of John Hay.* Edited by Tyler Dennett. New York, 1939.

Heitman, Francis B. *Biographical Register and Dictionary of the United States Army, 1789–1903.* 2 vols. Washington, 1903.

Henry, Robert S. *"First With the Most" Forrest.* New York, 1944.

———. *The Story of the Confederacy.* Revised edition. New York, 1936.

Herald (New York), July 24, 1868.

Hesseltine, William B. *Ulysses S. Grant, Politician.* New York, 1935.

Heth, Henry, Major General. Memoirs. Alderman Library, University of Virginia, Charlottesville.

Hitchcock, Ethan Allen. *Fifty Years in Camp and Field: Diary of Major-General Ethan Allen Hitchcock, U.S.A.* Edited by W. A. Croffut. New York, 1909.

———. Papers. Library of Congress, Washington, D.C.

Hittle, J. D. *Jomini and His Summary of the Art of War.* Harrisburg, Pa., 1947.

———. *The Military Staff: Its History and Development.* Harrisburg, Pa., 1952.

Holzman, Robert. *Stormy Ben Butler.* New York, 1954.

Horn, Stanley F. *The Army of Tennessee.* Indianapolis, Ind., 1941.

Howard, Michael. *The Franco-Prussian War.* New York, 1961.

———. "Jomini and the Classical Tradition in Military Thought," *The Theory and Practice of War.* Edited by Michael Howard. Bloomington, London, 1965.

Hughes, Robert M. Papers. Made available by Mrs. R. M. Hughes, Jr., and Mr. R. M. Hughes, III, of Norfolk, Va.

———. "Some War Letters of General Joseph E. Johnston." *Journal of the Military Service Institution of the United States* (May-June, 1912), 319–28.

Jamieson, Perry D., "The Development of Civil War Tactics." Ph.D. dissertation, Wayne State University, 1979.

Johnson, Curt, and McLaughlin, Mark. *Civil War Battles.* New York, 1977.

Johnson, Ludwell H. *The Red River Campaign: Cotton and Politics in the Civil War.* Baltimore, Md., 1958.

Johnston, Angus J. *Virginia Railroads in the Civil War.* Chapel Hill, N.C., 1961.

Johnston, William Preston. "Albert Sidney Johnston at Shiloh," *Battles and Leaders of the Civil War.* Edited by C. C. Buel and R. U. Johnson. 4 vols. New York, 1887–88.

Jomini, H. *The Art of War.* Translated by G. H. Mendell and W. P. Craighill. Philadelphia, Pa., 1862.

———. *Précis de l'art de la querre ou nouveau tableau analytic des principes et combinaisons de la stratégie, de la grande tactique, et la politique militaire.* Edited by F. Lecomte. 2 vols. Paris, 1894.

Jones, Archer, *Confederate Strategy from Shiloh to Vicksburg.* Baton Rouge, La., 1961.

———. "The Evolution of Warfare—an Interpretation." *Proceedings of the South Carolina Historical Association* (1967), 5–12.

———. "The Gettysburg Decision Reassessed." *Virginia Magazine of History and Biography* (January, 1968), 64–66.

———. "Jomini and the Strategy of the American Civil War, A Reinterpretation." *Military Affairs* (December, 1970), 127–31.

———. "The Vicksburg Campaign." *Journal of Mississippi History* (February, 1967), 18–23.

Jones, Archer, jt. auth. see Connelly, Thomas L.

Jones, Archer, jt. auth. see Hattaway, Herman.

Jones, Virgil Carrington. *Ranger Mosby*. Chapel Hill, N.C., 1944.

Kamm, Samuel R. *The Civil War Career of Thomas A. Scott*. Philadelphia, Pa., 1940.

Keegan, John. *The Face of Battle*. New York, 1976.

Kerby, Robert L. *Kirby Smith's Confederacy*. New York, London, 1972.

Keyes, Erasmus D. *Fifty Years' Observation of Men and Events*. New York, 1884.

Klement, Frank L. *The Copperheads in the Middle West*. Chicago, Ill., 1960.

Lamers, William M. *Edge of Glory, A Biography of General William S. Rosecrans, U.S.A.* New York, 1961.

Lanchester, F. W. *Aircraft in Warfare—The Dawn of the Fouth Arm*. London, 1916.

Lanza, Conrad H. *Napoleon and Modern War*. Harrisburg, Pa., 1943.

Lee, Robert E. *Lee's Dispatches*. Edited by Douglas Southall Freeman and Grady McWhiney. New York, 1957.

————. *The Wartime Papers of R. E. Lee*. Edited by Clifford Dowdey and Louis H. Manarin. Boston, Mass., 1961.

Lewis, Emanuel Raymond. *Seacoast Fortifications of the United States: An Introductory History*. Washington, 1970.

Lewis, Lloyd. *Captain Sam Grant*. Boston, Mass., 1950.

Liddell Hart, B. H. *The Ghost of Napoleon*. New Haven, Conn., 1933.

————. *Strategy*. Revised edition. New York, 1954.

Lincoln, Abraham. *The Collected Works of Abraham Lincoln*. Edited by Roy P. Basler. 8 vols. New Brunswick, N. J., 1953.

Livermore, Thomas L. *Numbers and Losses in the Civil War in America, 1861–1865*. Boston & New York, 1901.

Livermore, William R. *The Story of the Civil War*. 2 vols. New York, 1913.

Long, A. L. *Memoirs of Robert E. Lee*. New York, 1886.

Long. E. B. *The Civil War, Day by Day: An Almanac, 1861–1865*. New York, 1971.

Longacre, Edward G. *The Man Behind the Guns: A Biography of General Henry J. Hunt, Commander of Artillery, Army of the Potomac*. South Brunswick, N. J., and New York, 1977.

Lonn, Ella. *Desertion during the Civil War*. New York, London, 1928.

————. *Salt as a Factor in the Confederacy*. University, Ala., 1965.

Lucas, Marion Brunson. *Sherman and the Burning of Columbia*. College Station, London, 1976.

Luraghi, Raimondo. *The Rise and Fall of the Plantation South*. New York, London, 1978.

Lyman, Theodore. *Meade's Headquarters, 1863–1865; Letters of Colonel Theodore Lyman From the Wilderness to Appomattox*. Edited by George R. Agassiz. New York, 1922.

MacDougall, P. L. *The Theory of War*. Second edition. London, 1858.

Mahon, John K. "Civil War Infantry Assault Tactics." *Military Affairs* (Summer, 1961), 57–67.

Mansfield, Harvey C., and Marx, Fritz Morstein. "Informal Organization," *Elements of Public Administration*. Edited by Fritz Morstein Marx. Englewood Cliffs, N. J., 1959.

Matloff, Maurice, editor. *American Military History*. Washington, 1969.

Maude, F. N. *The Evolution of Modern Strategy.* London, 1905.

———. "Strategy," *The Encyclopaedia Britannica.* XXV (London and New York, 1926), 991–94.

Mayer, George. *The Republican Party, 1854–1966.* Second Edition. New York, 1967.

McClellan, George B. *The Armies of Europe: comprising descriptions in detail of the military systems of England, France, Russia, Prussia, Austria, Sardinia, Adapting their Advantages to all arms of the United States Service: and embodying the Report of Observations in Europe during the Crimean War, as military commissioner from the United States government, in 1855–56.* Philadelphia, Pa., 1861.

———. *McClellan's Own Story.* New York, 1887.

McWhiney, Grady. *Braxton Bragg and Confederate Defeat.* New York, 1969.

———. *Southerners and Other Americans.* New York, 1973.

Meade, George. *The Life and Letters of George Gordon Meade.* 2 vols. New York, 1913.

Miers, Earl Schenck. *Robert E. Lee.* New York, 1970.

Minter, Winfred P. "Confederate Military Supply." *Social Science (June, 1959),* 163–71.

Monaghan, Jay. *Civil War on the Western Border: 1854–1865.* Boston, Toronto, 1955.

Moore, Albert B. *Conscription and Conflict in the Confederacy.* New York, 1924.

Moore, John G. "Mobility and Strategy in the Civil War." *Military Affairs* (Summer, 1960), 68–77.

Morrison, James L. "Educating the Civil War Generals: West Point, 1833–1861," *Military Affairs* (October, 1974), 108–11.

Morse, Philip M., and Kimball, George E. *Methods of Operations Research.* New York, 1951.

Murdock, Eugene Converse. *One Million Men—The Civil War Draft in the North.* Madison, Wis., 1971.

———. *Patriotism Limited, 1862–1865.* Kent, Ohio, 1967.

Nash, Howard P., Jr. *Stormy Petrel: The Life and Times of General Benjamin F. Butler, 1818–1893.* Rutherford, Madison, Teaneck, N.J., 1969.

Nevins, Allan. *The War for the Union.* 4 vols. New York, 1959–71.

Oates, Stephen, *With Malice Toward None: The Life of Abraham Lincoln.* New York, 1977.

Official Records of the Union and Confederate Navies in the War of the Rebellion. 30 vols. Washington, 1894–1922.

Parks, Joseph H. *General Edmund Kirby Smith, C.S.A.* Baton Rouge, La., 1954.

Patrick, Marsena R. Journal. Library of Congress, Washington, D.C.

Patrick, Rembert W., *Jefferson Davis and His Cabinet.* Baton Rouge, La., 1944.

Porter, General Horace. *Campaigning With Grant.* Edited by Wayne C. Temple. Bloomington, Ind., 1961.

Pratt, Fletcher. *Stanton: Lincoln's Secretary of War.* New York, 1963.

Pratt, Harry Edward. *Lincoln, 1809–1839.* Springfield, Ill., 1941.

Quarles, Benjamin. *Lincoln and the Negro.* New York, 1962.

Quinby, Robert S. *The Background of Napoleonic Warfare.* New York, 1957.

Ramsdell, Charles W. "General Robert E. Lee's Horse Supply, 1862–1865." *American Historical Review* XXXV (July, 1930), 758–77.

Randall, James G. *The Civil War and Reconstruction.* Boston, Mass., 1937.

————. *Constitutional Problems Under Lincoln.* New York, 1926.

Randolph, George Wythe. Edgehill-Randolph Papers. Alderman Library, University of Virginia, Charlottesville, Va.

Reed, Rowena. *Combined Operations in the Civil War.* Annapolis, Md., 1978.

Rhodes, Charles Dudley. "Montgomery C. Meigs," *The Dictionary of American Biography.* Edited by Dumas Malone and Allen Johnson. VI (New York, 1928–36), 508.

Rice, Allen Thorndike, editor. *Reminiscenses of Abraham Lincoln, by Distinguished Men of His Time.* New York, 1888.

Ringold, May S. *The Role of the State Legislatures in the Confederacy.* Athens, Ga., 1966.

Robertson, James I., Jr. "Stonewall in the Shenandoah: The Valley Campaign of 1862." *Civil War Times—Illustrated.* XI (May, 1972), entire special issue, 3–49.

Roman, Alfred. *The Military Operations of General Beauregard.* 2 vols. New York, 1883.

Rothstein, William G. *American Physicians in the 19th Century.* Baltimore, Md., 1972.

Russell, William H. *My Diary North and South.* Edited by Fletcher Pratt. Gloucester, Mass., 1969.

Scott, H. L. *Military Dictionary: Comprising Technical Definitions; Information on Raising and Keeping Troops, Actual Service, Including Makeshifts and Improved Materials; and Law, Government, Regulation and Administration Relating to Land Forces.* New York, 1861.

Shannon, Fred A. *The Organization and Administration of the Union Army.* 2 vols. Gloucester, Mass., 1965.

Sherman, William T. *The Home Letters of General Sherman.* Edited by M. A. DeWolfe Howe. New York, 1909.

————. *Personal Memoirs of General W. T. Sherman.* 2 vols. New York, 1890.

————. *Personal Memoirs of General W. T. Sherman.* 2 vols. New York, 1904.

————. *The Sherman Letters; Correspondence Between General and Senator Sherman, 1837 to 1891.* Edited by Rachel Sherman Thorndike. New York, 1894.

Smith, Charles H. *Bill Arp: From the Uncivil War to Date.* Atlanta, Ga., 1903.

Sommers, Richard J. *Richmond Redeemed: The Siege at Petersburg.* Garden City, N. Y., 1981.

Stanton, Edwin M. Papers, Library of Congress, Washington, D.C.

Starr, Stephen Z. *The Union Cavalry in the Civil War.* One vol. to date. Baton Rouge, La., 1979.

Steele, Matthew Forney. *American Campaigns.* 2 vols. Washington, D.C., 1943.

Stickles, Arndt M. *Simon Bolivar Buckner.* Chapel Hill, N.C., 1940.

Still, William N. *Iron Afloat: The Story of the Confederate Armorclads.* Nashville, Tenn., 1971.

Stohlman, Robert F., Jr. *The Powerless Position: The Commanding General of the Army of the United States, 1864–1903.* Manhattan, Kan., 1975.

Strahler, Arthur N. *The Earth Sciences.* Second edition. New York, Evanston, London, 1963, 1971.

————. *Introduction to Physical Geography.* Second edition. New York, London, Sydney, Toronto, 1965.

Taylor, George Rogers. *The Transportation Revolution, 1815–1860.* New York, 1951.

Taylor, Richard. *Destruction and Reconstruction.* Edited by Charles P. Roland. Waltham, Mass., 1968.

Taylor, Walter H. *Four Years with General Lee.* Edited with new introduction, index, and notes by James I. Robertson, Jr. New York, 1962.

Thiele, Thomas F. "The Evolution of Cavalry in the American Civil War, 1861–1863." Ph.D. dissertation, University of Michigan, 1951.

Thomas, Benjamin P. *Abraham Lincoln.* New York, 1952.

Thomas, Benjamin P., and Hyman, Harold M. *Stanton, The Life and Times of Lincoln's Secretary of War.* New York, 1962.

Thomas, Emory M. *The Confederacy as a Revolutionary Experience.* Englewood Cliffs, N.J., 1971.

———. *The Confederate Nation: 1861–1865.* New York, 1979.

———. "The Kilpatrick-Dahlgren Raid—Part 1." *Civil War Times—Illustrated.* XVI (February, 1978), 4–6, 8–9, 46–48.

Townsend, E. D. *Anecdotes of the Civil War in the United States.* New York, 1884.

Turner, George E. *Victory Rode the Rails.* Indianapolis, Ind., 1953.

U.S. Congress, Senate Executive Document, *Commerce and Navigation, 1860,* 36th Congress, 1st Session, 1861. Serial No. 1087.

U.S. Congress, Senate Executive Document, *Commerce and Navigation, 1864,* 38th Congress, 2nd Session, 1865. Serial No. 1231.

Upton, Emory. *The Military Policy of the United States from 1775.* Washington, 1907.

Urquhart, David. "Bragg's Advance and Retreat," *Battles and Leaders of the Civil War.* Edited by C. C. Buel and R. U. Johnson. 4 vols. New York, 1887–88.

Valuska, David Lawrence. "The Staff Organization of the Army of the Potomac Under General McClellan." Master's thesis, Louisiana State University, 1966.

Vandiver, Frank. *Ploughshares Into Swords: Josiah Gorgas and Confederate Ordnance.* Austin, Tex., 1952.

Visher, Stephen Sargent. *Climatic Atlas of the United States.* Cambridge, Mass., 1954.

Wade, Arthur P. "Roads to the Top—An Analysis of General Officer Selection in the United States Army, 1789–1898." *Military Affairs* (December, 1976), 157–63.

Walker, Robert J. Papers. Mississippi Department of Archives and History.

The War of the Rebellion: A Compilation of the Oficial Records of the Union and Confederate Armies. 128 vols. Washington, 1880–1901.

Warner, Ezra J. *Generals in Blue.* Baton Rouge, La., 1964.

———. *Generals in Gray.* Baton Rouge, La., 1959.

Wedgwood, C. V. *The Thirty Years War.* London, 1938.

Weigley, Russell F. *Quartermaster General of the Union Army.* New York, 1959.

Weiss, Herbert K. "Combat Models and Historical Data: The U.S. Civil War." *Operations Research* (September-October, 1966), 759–91.

Welles, Gideon. *Diary of Gideon Welles.* Edited by Howard K. Beale. 3 vols. New York, 1960.

Werlich, Robert. *"Beast" Butler.* Washington, 1962.

Wesley, Charles H. *The Collapse of the Confederacy.* New York, 1968.

———. "The Employment of Negroes as Soldiers in the Confederate Army." *Journal of Negro History.* IV (July, 1919), 239–53.

Wheeler, Richard. *The Siege of Vicksburg.* New York, 1978.

———, editor. *We Knew William Tecumseh Sherman.* New York, 1977.

Wigfall, Louis T. Papers. Library of Congress, Washington, D.C.

Wiley, Bell I. "The Common Soldier of the Civil War." *Civil War Times—Illustrated* XII (July, 1973), entire special issue, 1–64.

———. *Confederate Women.* Westport, Conn., 1975.

Willard, Daniel. *Lanchester as a Force in History: An Analysis of Land Battles of the Years 1618–1905.* Research Analysis Corporation, McLean, Va., 1962.

Williams, Joseph E., editor. *Prentice-Hall World Atlas.* Englewood Cliffs, N.J., 1960.

Williams, Kenneth P. *Lincoln Finds a General.* 5 vols. New York, 1949–58.

Wilson, James Grant. "Types and Traditions of the Old Army. II. General Halleck—A Memoir." *Journal of the Military Service Institution of the United States.* XXXVI.

Williams, T. Harry. *Americans at War.* Baton Rouge, La., 1960.

———. "The Attack upon West Point during the Civil War." *Mississippi Valley Historical Review* (March, 1939), 491–504.

———. *Beauregard, Napoleon in Gray.* Baton Rouge, La., 1955.

———. *Lincoln and his Generals.* New York, 1952.

———. *Lincoln and the Radicals.* Madison and Milwaukee, Wis., 1965.

———. "The Return of Jomini: Some Thoughts on Recent Civil War Writing." *Military Affairs.* XXXIX (December, 1975), 204–6.

Wilson, James Grant. "Types and Traditions of the Old Army. II. General Halleck—A Memoir." *Journal of the Military Service Institution of the United States.* XXXVI, 537–56, and XXXVII, 333–56.

Wilson, James Harrison. *The Life of John A. Rawlins.* New York, 1916.

———. Papers. Library of Congress, Washington, D.C.

———. *Under the Old Flag.* 2 vols. New York and London, 1912.

Wilson, James Harrison, and Dana, Charles A. *The Life of Ulysses S. Grant.* New York, 1868.

Wise, John S. *The End of an Era.* Boston, New York, 1899.

Wright, Mrs. D. Giraud. *A Southern Girl in '61.* New York, 1905.

Wyeth, John. *Life of Gen. Nathan Bedford Forrest.* New York, 1899.

Wylie, J. C. *Military Strategy: A General Theory of Power Control.* New Brunswick, N.J., 1967.

Yearns, Wilfred B. *The Confederate Congress.* Athens, Ga., 1960.

☆ NOTE ON THE AUTHORS ☆

HERMAN HATTAWAY is professor of history, University of Missouri-Kansas City, and lecturer in church history, Holyrood Seminary (Anglican Catholic Church). He received his B.A., M.A., and Ph.D. degrees from Louisiana State University in 1961, 1963, and 1969 respectively. Author of numerous articles on Civil War and military history, in 1976 he received the Jefferson Davis Award for best 1976 book on Confederate history: *General Stephen D. Lee* (University Press of Mississippi).

ARCHER JONES is professor of history, North Dakota State University, Fargo, North Dakota. He received his B.A. degree from Hampden-Sydney College in 1949 and his M.A. and Ph.D. degrees from the University of Virginia in 1953 and 1958. He has written about a dozen articles on Civil War history as well as *Politics of Command*, with T. L. Connelly (Louisiana State University Press, 1973), and *Confederate Strategy from Shiloh to Vicksburg* (Louisiana State University Press, 1961). In 1973 he received the Jefferson Davis Award.